Student Resource Handbook

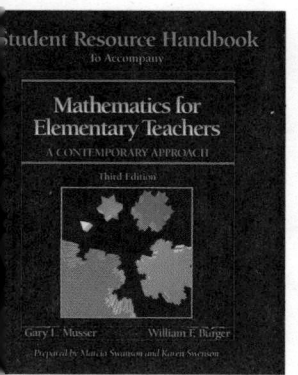

ISBN 0-02-418691-0

This handbook is designed to enhance student learning, as well as to begin to model effective classroom practices. Features include:

- **Directions in Education.** Specially written articles that provide insights into major issues of the day, including the Standards of the National Council of Teachers of Mathematics.
- **Warm-ups.** Short problem-solving activities.
- **Hands-On Activities.** Activities that help students develop inital understandings at the concrete level.
- **Mental Math.** Short activities to help develop better mental math skills.
- **Solutions.** Solutions to all items in this handbook to enhance self-study.
- **Exercises.** Additional practice for building skills in the concepts contained in this book.
- **Self-Test.** New ten-item tests in a variety of assessment formats designed to assess student knowledge of key ideas in this book.
- **Resource Articles.** Up-to-date references from journals for elementary teacher to help provide a connection to the classroom.

Problem-Solving Study Guide

ISBN 0-02-381304-0

This study guide has been expanded to include more strategy practice problems. The problem-solving strategies that are contained in this book are explored further in the following four main components:

- **Opening Problem.** An introductory problem to motivate the need for a strategy.
- **Solution/Discussion/Clues.** A worked-out solution of the opening problem together with a discussion of the strategy and some clues on when to select this strategy.
- **Practice Problems.** A second problem that uses the same strategy together with a worked-out solution and two practice problems.
- **Mixed Strategy Practice.** Four practice problems that can be solved using one (or more) of the strategies introduced to that point.

Student Hints and Solutions Manual

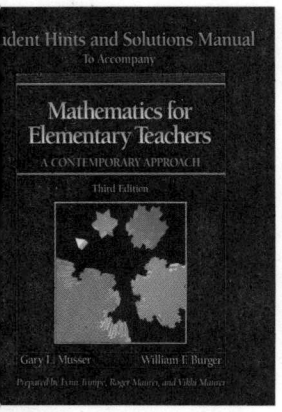

ISBN 0-02-421514-7

This manual, which is new to the third edition, is designed to help students improve their problem-solving abilities when working problems for which answers are provided in this book. The manual contains features:

- **Hints.** Hints are provided to give students a start on all Part A problems in this book.
- **Additional Hints.** For more challenging problems, a second hint is provided.
- **Complete Solutions to Part A Problems.** Carefully written out solutions are provided to model one correct solution.

Mathematics for Elementary Teachers

A CONTEMPORARY APPROACH

Third Edition

Gary L. Musser
William F. Burger

OREGON STATE UNIVERSITY

Macmillan College Publishing Company
New York

Maxwell Macmillan Canada
Toronto

Maxwell Macmillan International
New York   Oxford   Singapore   Sydney

The excerpts from school mathematics materials, called Student Page Snapshots, one in each chapter, and 16 color pages in the Connections to School Mathematics are reprinted from Macmillan/McGraw-Hill School Publishing Company, *Mathematics in Action,* Grades 5, 6, 7, and 8, (PE), New York, 1991. Reprinted with permission of Macmillan/McGraw-Hill School Publishing Company from *Mathematics in Action,* Pupil Edition, Grades 4–8, by Audrey Jackson, Martin L. Johnson; Steven J. Leinwand; Richard D. Lodholz; Gary L. Musser; and Walter Secada. Copyright © 1994 Macmillan/McGraw-Hill School Publishing Company.

Editor: Robert W. Pirtle
Production Supervisor: Elaine W. Wetterau
Production Manager: Nicholas Sklitsis
Cover Designer: Cathleen Norz
Cover photograph: Interactive Images, Inc.
Photo Researcher: Diana Gongora
Illustrations: Rolin Graphics Inc.

This book was set in 10/12 Souvenir by The Clarinda Company and was printed and bound by R. R. Donnelley & Sons. The cover was printed by Lehigh Press.

Macmillan College Publishing Company
866 Third Avenue, New York, New York 10022

Macmillan College Publishing Company is part
of the Maxwell Communication Group of Companies.

Maxwell Macmillan Canada, Inc.
1200 Eglinton Avenue East
Suite 200
Don Mills, Ontario M3C 3N1

Musser, Gary L.
    Mathematics for elementary teachers : a contemporary approach /
Gary L. Musser, William F. Burger.—3rd ed.
        p.   cm.
    Includes index.
    ISBN 0-02-385452-9
    1. Mathematics.   2. Mathematics—Study and teaching (Elementary)
I. Burger, William F.   II. Title.
[QA39.2.M855   1993]
510–dc20
                                                                    93-9196
                                                                        CIP

Printing: 1   2   3   4   5   Year: 4   5   6   7   8

Photograph Credits

Chapter 1, opposite page 1, *Portrait of George Pólya*, courtesy of Professor G. L. Alexanderson, Santa Clara University, Santa Clara, California, Department of Mathematics; page 38, *Karl Friedrich Gauss* and *Sophie Germain*, Giraudon/Art Resource, New York.

Chapter 2, page 40, *Codex Dresdensis*, plates 48 and 49, courtesy of Sachsische Landesbibliothek, Dresden, Germany; page 92, *Emmy Noether*, The Bryn Mawr College Archives, Bryn Mawr, Pennsylvania; page 93, *David Hilbert*, courtesy of Professor G. L. Alexanderson.

Chapter 3, page 138, *John von Neumann*, with compliments of Nicholas A. Vonneuman; *Julia Robinson*, courtesy of George M. Bergman, University of California, Berkeley.

Chapter 4, page 140, Figure 1, *Chinese Abacus*, Figure 3, *Napier's Rods*, and Figure 4, *Slide Rule*, Smithsonian Institution, Washington, D.C.; Figure 5, *Pascal's Adding Machine*, and page 141, Figure 6, *Leibniz's "Reckoning Machine,"* courtesy of the Science Museum Library, South Kensington, London, England; Figure 2, *Japanese Abacus*, and Figure 7, *Babbage's Difference Engine*, The Bettmann Archive, New York; Figure 8, Apple Macintosh LC-III, and Figure 9, *Apple Powerbook Laptop*, courtesy of Apple Computer, Inc., photographs by John Greenleigh; page 183, *Grace M. Hopper*, courtesy of the Official U.S. Navy Photo, photograph by James S. Davis; *John Kemeny*, courtesy of Dartmouth College Archives, Hanover, New Hampshire.

Chapter 5, page 186, *Pierre de Fermat*, Giraudon/Art Resource, New York; page 216, *Srinivasa Ramanujan*, Trinity College Library, Cambridge, England; *Constance Reid*, courtesy of Constance Reid.

Chapter 6, page 218, *Rhind Papyrus*, The British Museum, London, England; page 265, *Evelyn Granville*, American Mathematical Society, Providence, Rhode Island; Paul Erdös, courtesy of Professor G. L. Alexanderson.

Chapter 7, page 268, *The Parthenon*, courtesy of Peter Greenberg; page 322, *David Blackwell*, George M. Bergman, University of California, Berkeley; *Sonya Kovalevskaia*, The Mittag–Leffler Institute, Djursholm, Sweden.

Chapter 8, page 322, *Chinese Mathematical Text,* The Needham Research Institute, Cambridge, England; page 358, *Grace Chisholm Young*, courtesy of Sylvia Wiegand; *Martin Gardner*, courtesy of Martin Gardner.

Chapter 9, page 360, *Pythagoras*, courtesy of Brown Brothers, Sterling, Pennsylvania; page 424, *Paul Cohen*, courtesy of Paul Cohen; *Rózsa Péter*, courtesy of Bela Andrasfai.

Chapter 10, page 426, *"California Racket"–cartoon*, Stephen Conley; *"Dominating College Lacrosse"–cartoon*, Gary Visgaitis; *"College Senior Plans"–cartoon*, Elys A. McLean; and *"World Population"–cartoon*, Marty Baumann, USA TODAY; p. 474, *Leonhard Euler*, The Bettmann Archive, New York; *Mina Rees*, CUNY Graduate School and University Center, New York.

Chapter 11, page 476, *Blaise Pascal*, Giraudon/Art Resource, New York; page 524, *Olga Tausky–Todd*, California Institue of Technology Archives, Pasadena, California; *Stanislaw Ulam*, Los Alamos Scientific Laboratory, Los Alamos, California.

Chapter 12, page 526, *Pierre van Hiele* and *Dieke van Hiele–Geldof*, courtesy of Pierre van Hiele, Voorburg, The Netherlands; page 610, *Cathleen Morawetz*, courtesy of James Hamilton, *R. L. Moore*, University of Texas at Austin Center for American History.

Chapter 13, page 612, *Archimedes*, courtesy of the Science Museum Library, South Kensington, London, England; page 692, *Andrew Gleason*, courtesy of Andrew Gleason; *Maria Agnesi*, Library of Congress, Washington, D.C.

Chapter 14, page 694, *Euclid*, courtesy of Brown Brothers, Sterling, Pennsylvania; page 760, *Hypatia*, The Bettmann Archive, New York; *Benoit B. Mandelbrot*, courtesy of Benoit B. Mandelbrot, IBM, T. J. Watson Research Center.

Chapter 15, page 762, *Descartes*, Giraudon/Art Resource, New York; page 808, *Shiing-Shen Chern*, courtesy of Shiing-Shen Chern; *H. S. M. Coxeter*, courtesy of H. S. M. Coxeter, University of Toronto, Canada.

Chapter 16, pages 680 and 681, *Circle Limit III*, December 1959, woodcut by M. C. Escher, *Design Drawing for Intarsia Wood Panel with Fish*, 1940, M. C. Escher, and *Symmetry Drawing E 42*, 1941, M. C. Escher, M. C. Escher Foundation, Baarn, Holland, all rights reserved; page 876, *Edward Begle,* News and Publications Service, Stanford University, Stanford, California; page 876, *Jaime Escalante*, Tony Friedk.

A Special Dedication to Bill

My coauthor, colleague, and friend, Bill Burger, passed away March 23, 1991, at the young age of 46. Bill was a superb teacher, researcher, colleague, and a pillar of the community. A strong family man, he left his wife, Adrienne, and daughter, Mary, who were very, very dear to him.

I was fortunate to have collaborated with Bill for over 13 years. We had many discussions about students, mathematics, and pedagogy that I will treasure forever. Bill was a class act—integrity and quality were always foremost in his mind. I continue to profit from my many years of work with him. He is missed greatly by all of his students and colleagues, but especially by his family and me. Thanks, Bill, for our many great conversations and for your outstanding contribution to mathematics education.

Our department has established the William F. Burger Award, which is given to the graduate teaching assistants who have maintained the most outstanding teaching records. Anyone wishing to honor Bill can contribute to a fund established in his name to support this award by writing to the Chairperson, Department of Mathematics, Oregon State University, Corvallis, OR 97331-4605.

*To
Irene, Greg, Marge, G. L., and Mary*

Preface

To the Student

Welcome to a world of mathematical understanding that I hope you will find stimulating, rewarding, enlightening, and fun. I salute you for choosing teaching as a profession and hope that your experiences with this book will help prepare you to be the best possible teacher of mathematics that you can be. Over the years many of our students have remarked. "This is the first time that I've *understood* mathematics—I didn't know that math could be this interesting." This book incorporates the same clarity and spirit that have infused a new sense of confidence about mathematics in many students. But, don't get the impression that all of the ideas herein are simple, because they can be very challenging. You will have to work at it! However, new ideas are introduced at understandable levels. Then the abstractions that make mathematics such a powerful and useful subject evolve naturally. The following study features have been incorporated to help you improve your effectiveness in learning the material.

Study Features

1. *Focus Ons.* Each chapter begins with a brief historical/cultural introduction to the new material.
2. *Boldface Type.* Key terms appear in boldface.
3. *Italics.* Certain words are set in italics for emphasis.
4. *Full-color.* Color has been used in this edition to make the book more pleasing to study, but especially to clarify concepts.
5. *Examples.* Many examples are provided to illustrate major ideas.
6. *Boxes.* Main definitions and results are highlighted by boxes.
7. *Exercise/Problem Sets.* These section-end sets are organized into exercises (to help build your knowledge, skill, and understanding) and problems (to apply the material in new situations). Questions dealing with calculators are indicated with calculator icons. Answers for all Part A exercises and problems are provided at the end of the book before the index.
8. *Chapter Review.* Major ideas, vocabulary, and notation are presented to summarize the chapter material and to stimulate your recall of the major ideas.
9. *Chapter Test.* A comprehensive chapter test of knowledge, skill, understanding, and problem solving appears in each chapter.
10. *Student Resource Handbook.* This handbook, which may be made

available through your bookstore, is full of "hands-on" activities with activity cards, extra exercises in a friendly format, assessment questions, references to relevant readings in teachers' journals, and Directions in Education articles on current issues in math education.

11. *Problem-Solving Study Guide.* This study guide, which also can be made available through your bookstore, contains additional practice in applying the problem-solving strategies found in each chapter of this textbook. There are over 200 practice problems together with example problems to help you become more proficient in solving problems. This resource can also serve as a sourcebook of problems for you to use when you become a teacher.

One new feature of this third edition is the *People in Mathematics* vignettes at the end of each chapter. In addition to famous classical European mathematicians whose contributions were made before the twentieth century, many mathematicians from the twentieth century have been included to help paint a picture of mathematics as a subject that continues to grow. People are cited who represent a broad cross section of nationalities and genders, as well as various time periods. When you read these brief stories, you will be introduced to people who have contributed to mathematics and mathematics education in different ways. For example, in addition to famous mathematicians who have had substantial impact on the subject itself, included are researchers, teachers, writers, curriculum developers, and computer scientists who have contributed to and popularized mathematics. As an elementary teacher, you, too, will be making a contribution to mathematics education in your own way.

To the Instructor

This textbook represents the experience of a combined total of over 40 years of teaching prospective elementary teachers. Recommendations from (i) the Mathematical Association of America's Committee on the Mathematical Education of Teachers *A Call for Change: Recommendations on the Mathematics Preparation of Teachers;* (ii) the National Council of Teachers of Mathematics, *An Agenda for Action,* its *Curriculum and Evaluation Standards for School Mathematics,* and its *Professional Standards for Teaching Mathematics;* and (iii) the National Council of Supervisors of Mathematics' *Position Paper on Basic Mathematical Skills,* as well as major state-wide recommendations, have been incorporated whenever possible. In addition, I have received valuable advice from many of our colleagues around the country through questionnaires, reviews, focus groups, and personal communications. I have taken great care to respect this advice and to ensure that the content of the book has mathematical integrity and is accessible and helpful to the variety of students who will use it.

Content Features

Number Systems: This book is a presentation of the mathematics central to a comprehensive elementary and middle-school mathematics curriculum.

Insofar as possible, topics are covered sequentially to parallel their development in the school curriculum. For example, fractions and integers are each treated as extensions of whole numbers. Rational numbers are then developed briskly as extensions of both the fractions (by adjoining their opposites) and the integers (by adjoining their reciprocals). The mathematical structure of an ordered field continues to serve to unify this presentation. As students see new mathematical systems evolve, they see what new properties each system contributes and how each new structure differs from those studied previously. Also, diagrams displaying interrelationships between and among mathematical systems are used to help make similarities and differences more apparent.

Approach to Geometry: Geometry is organized from the point of view of the five-level van Hiele model of a child's development in geometry. The material progresses from visual first experiences to analytical descriptions of shapes to relationships among shapes to deductive reasoning in geometry. However, the formal study of axiomatics in geometry, the highest level in the van Hiele model, is not included. Chapter 12 includes work with dot paper, paper folding, and tracing paper to provide an informal introduction to the many terms and relationships associated with geometric figures. This introduction allows one to cover this chapter on geometry earlier in a course.

Deductive Thinking: The use of deduction is promoted throughout the book. The approach is gradual, with later chapters having more multistep problems. In particular, the last sections of Chapters 14, 15, and 16 offer a rich source of interesting theorems and problems.

Problem-Solving Approach: An extensive collection of problem-solving strategies is progressively developed; these strategies can be applied to a generous supply of problems in the exercise/problem sets. Exercises are designed to help students develop their knowledge, skill, and understanding of the material of each section, whereas problems require innovative thinking. The depth of problem-solving coverage can be varied by the number of strategies selected throughout the book and by the problems assigned. There are well over 100 new exercises and problems in this Third Edition. In addition, a unique supplement, the *Problem-Solving Study Guide,* provides students with additional development and practice on the strategies. Through its carefully structured sets of accessible, yet thought-provoking, problems, this study guide enables students to learn how to use the problem-solving strategies more effectively.

Computation: Chapter 4, *Whole-Number Computation—Mental, Electronic, and Written,* provides a comprehensive introduction to mental math, estimation, and the calculator; these three topics are also applied in the later chapters, including those on fractions, decimals, real numbers, percents, statistics, and probability. Mental math, estimation, and calculators are currently receiving much attention due to the recommendations of several professional groups. The techniques introduced here are in use in many of the current school text series. Work with fraction calculators is included. The T1-34 scientific calculator (about $20) can be used to simplify calculations involving fractions, statistics, and other number bases. The Math Explorer, which is used in many schools, is used to show its capability to do long division with remainder and calculate using fractions.

Computers: The Technology Section allows for the inclusion of BASIC or Logo in your course at any time. Where relevant, chapter-by-chapter programs and problems are provided for each language to point out how computers may be usefully employed for calculations, to solve problems, or to develop concepts. The Computer Exploration Software for Geometry subsection provides many problems where students can investigate geometric principles and formulate and test conjectures using any of the several exploration software packages. Finally, a section on graphics calculators has been added to give students experiences in this technology that is working its way down the mathematics curriculum.

Additional Topics: Since reviewers were split concerning where these topics should appear in the text, they are placed separate from the chapters to allow for maximum flexibility. Topic One, *Elementary Logic,* may be used anywhere in a course; Topic Two, *Relations,* requires the language of sets in Chapter 2; Topic Three, *Advanced Counting Techniques: Permutations and Combinations,* may be used to extend Chapter 11— *Probability;* Topic Four, *Clock Arithmetic—A Mathematical System,* uses the concepts of opposite and reciprocal, and hence may be most instructive after Chapter 6—*Fractions* and Chapter 8—*Integers* have been completed. This last section also contains an introduction to modular arithmetic.

Pedagogical Features: The general organization of the book was motivated by the "mathematics learning cube."

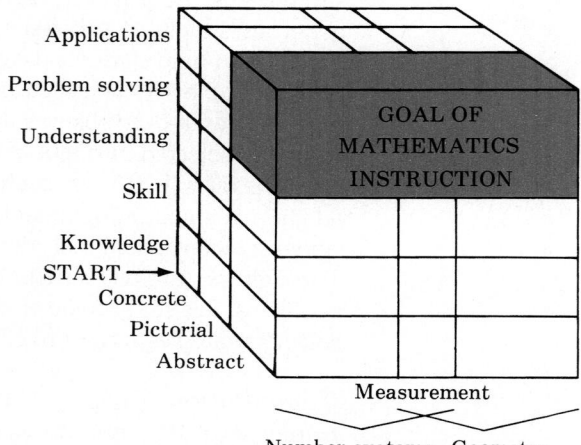

The three dimensions of the cube—cognitive levels, representational levels, and mathematical content—are integrated throughout the textual material as well as in the problem sets and chapter tests. Experience has shown that the use of this model helps students learn the material presented herein more easily. This model also provides them with a sound conceptual frame work to plan for their own mathematics instruction when they become teachers. The initial two pages of each chapter present a Focus On that provides an historical perspective on the material in the chapter. Mathematical Morsels appear at the end of each section to provide enrichment as well as a human touch. The *Writing/Discussing for Understanding* and the *Projects* sections at the end of each chapter allow students to pursue many mathematical ideas more deeply. The *People in Mathematics* vignettes provide some history as well as motivation to succeed. Finally, to provide students with a link to their future classrooms, a *Student Page Snapshot* from a school textbook appears in each chapter and a section at the end of the book, *Connections to School Mathematics,* displays the *NCTM Curriculum and Evaluation Standards* together with 16 school textbook pages to illustrate how the Standards can be implemented.

Course Options

The material in this book has been organized to allow for a wide variety of courses. At Oregon State University, all preservice elementary teachers are required to take 15 quarter-hours of mathematics. This book is used for the first 9 quarter-hours, a one-year sequence. Each week, students attend 3 one-hour lectures and a 1-hour lab in which materials from the *Student Resource Handbook* are covered. This book, together with the *Problem-Solving Study Guide,* is also used in a 3 quarter-hour junior level course in problem solving for elementary teachers. This course is devoted entirely to developing the students' facilities in applying Pólya's four-step process and the strategies introduced at the beginning of each chapter.

We recognize that mathematics program requirements vary from place to place. Hence we suggest courses of various lengths and emphases. Some possibilities are listed next.

Basic course: Chapters 1–7.

Basic courses with Computers: Chapters 1–7 and Programming in BASIC or Logo from the Technology Section.

Basic course with Logic: Topic 1, Chapters 1–7.

Basic course with Informal Geometry: Chapters 1–7, 12.

Basic course with Introduction to Geometry and Measurement: Chapters 1–7, 12, 13.

Course Through Real Numbers: Chapters 1–9.

Course Through Real Numbers with applications: Chapters 1–9, 10, and/or 11.

Course Through Real Numbers with Geometry: Chapters 1–9, 12, 13, 14 (Sections 1 and 2), 15 (Sections 1 and 2), 16 (Sections 1 and 2).

Course in Geometry: Chapters 12–16 (with or without Programming in Logo—Turtle Geometry and exploration software.)

The courses listed above are a few of the possible routes through the book. Of course, time permitting, each can be enriched by some additional problem solving or work with computers. Notice that Chapters 10 and 11 are independent of each other. Also, Chapters 14, 15, and 16 are independent of each other, except that Sections 14.1 and 14.2 are prerequisite for Sections 16.2 and 16.3. The final section in each of Chapters 14, 15, and 16 is intended to illustrate a particular approach to solving geometric problems. Together, they illustrate the power of an eclectic approach. Each of these three sections can be covered, omitted, or, perhaps, saved for a separate course on geometry for elementary teachers.

Supplements for Students

Student Resource Handbook: The Student Resource Handbook, which simulates many common manipulatives, provides a lab activity for each chapter. Two-dimensional manipulatives are contained in the handbook so that new materials do not have to be purchased. Even more important, students can do these activities independently outside of class if a lab setting is not available. In addition to the hands-on activities, the resource contains warm-ups, additional practice in a friendly format, a practice self-test, and a list of relevant articles from professional teaching journals for further reading; answers are provided to promote student independence. Finally, there are 17 two-page articles, "Directions in Education," that provide an important link to contemporary classroom practices. The handbook was prepared by Marcia Swanson, a former student in my courses for elementary teachers and now a principal for the Greater Albany Public Schools, and Karen Swenson, a former secondary teacher who is a professor of mathematics education at George Fox College.

Problem-Solving Study Guide: This guide is a collection of four-page units, one for each of the 21 problem-solving strategies in the text. The first page of each unit introduces the strategy through a demonstration problem; the second presents a solution to the demonstration problem plus a discussion and some clues on when to try the strategy. The third page contains one worked-out problem that uses the strategy plus two more problems for practice, and the fourth page has four problems that can be solved using strategies introduced up to that point. This study guide, which contains over 200 carefully arranged problems, was prepared by Don Miller, professor of mathematics at St. Cloud State University.

Student Hints and Solutions Manual: This manual is designed to help you improve your ability to solve problems. All of the problems in Part A of this book have hints (if you need them) to help you get started. The more difficult ones have an additional hint if you were unsuccessful in solving a problem using the hint. Finally, one correct written-out solution is included for each problem (although there may be other correct ways to solve the problem). This manual was prepared by Lynn Trimpe and Roger Maurer of Linn–Benton Community College and Vikki Maurer.

Compact Disk: A computer-driven compact disk is available to supplement this book. This disk contains a complete copy of the book with many dynamic, interactive activities to enhance learning. Also, there are many extra features including special calculators and computer software, convenient study aids, ways to efficiently review as you are studying new material, and a rich collection of resources and references to journal articles and children's literature centered around mathematics. This compact disk is a resource that you will be able to use over and over again when you are a student *and* when you become a teacher. The inside front cover of this book contains a more complete description of the compact disk as well as the other supplements. I thank Lew Hollerbach and his crew at *infon.* for their creative work on this compact disk.

Supplements for Instructors

Computerized Test Bank: For the Third Edition, this test bank contains true–false, multiple choice, and open-ended items. Many of the items were contributed by colleagues who used our first edition and, hence, have been class tested. Disks are available for Macintosh and MS-DOS computers; customized tests, complete with graphics, are easily prepared using either format. This test bank was prepared by Debra Pharo of Northwestern Michigan College, with the assistance of Tommy Bryan of Baylor University.

Instructor's Manual: This manual contains the following: (a) a chapter-by-chapter discussion of the text material, (b) exercise/problem suggestions for various sections, (c) overhead transparency masters, (d) student "expectations" (objectives) for each chapter, (e) answers for all Part B exercises and problems, and (f) answers for all the even-numbered problems in the *Problem-Solving Study Guide.*

Summary of Changes in the Third Edition

Based on broad-based and thorough external review of the second edition, many changes were made that make the book's coverage more complete. Yet it is even more flexible to use. The following changes are the most prominent.

- Chapters 1, 2, 3, 6, 12, 13, 14, and 16 have been reorganized into shorter sections. These changes make it easier to use the text for shorter courses by omitting some sections. In addition to splitting Chapter 1 into two sections, the development has been expanded to help ease students into the problem-solving process.
- Two new sections, *Functions,* in Chapter 2, and *Functions and Their Graphs,* in Chapter 9, have been added. Although not required, the use of graphics calculators is encouraged in graphing.
- The section *Writing/Discussing for Understanding* includes questions that require students to think more deeply about the topics in the chapter. *Projects* have also been included to provide more comprehensive assignments for out-of-class work.
- The brief list of the *NCTM Curriculum and Evaluation Standards* for grades K-5 and 6-8 was moved into the book from the *Instructor's Manual* to form part of the *Connections to School Mathematics,* which replaced the *Epilogue.* These *Standards* are brought to life by showing how they appear in a K-8 mathematics textbook series.
- Each chapter now contains three additional problems that can be solved using the strategy introduced in that chapter.
- More models, examples, and applied problems have been included.
- The constructive use of calculators has been increased.
- The Exercise/Problem sets have been revised substantially.
- A new innovative art program and four-color design will capture students' attention.

- People in Mathematics vignettes have been added at the end of each chapter. These stories not only honor many of the giants in mathematics throughout history, but also many people who have contributed to mathematics in many different ways. Hopefully, the accomplishments of these people will help students see how they, themselves, will be making a significant contribution through their own teaching.

Acknowledgments

I would like to thank several people for their assistance in the preparation of the three editions of this book. First I offer special thanks to our former students: Karen Swenson for her creative contributions to the problems sets; Dale Green, who helped with problem research; David Metz for his research and composition of the People in Mathematics vignettes, and Roger Maurer, who helped with the construction of the problem sets in the Topics sections; Kathleen Seagraves Higdon, who provided many thoughtful ideas and an excellent first draft of the section on Programming in BASIC; and Kris Warloe, who helped with the chapter-by-chapter computer problem sets. Next, my student, friend, and elementary teacher, Ron Bagwell, deserves special praise and thanks for his creative artwork in the Mathematical Morsels. Also I offer my appreciation to Naomi Munton, who typed the original manuscript; Tilda Runner, who assisted in the preparation of the manuscript and drew figures for preliminary editions; Donna Templeton, who typed the problem sets; Sue Borden for her assistance in preparing the computerized test bank; Julie Borden for her expert word processing and graphics; Lilian Brady, Tommy Bryan, Christie Gilliland, and Rosemary Troxel for their meticulous proofreading; and Christie Gilliland for checking answers and preparing the manuscript for many of the problem sets. I also thank my colleague, Mike Shaughnessy, for sharing the list of Suggestions from Successful Problem Solvers. Lynn Trimpe, my coauthor on another textbook, was a tremendous help in reorganizing the problem sets and in adding many applications and items in the Writing/Discussing for Understanding and Projects sections. I would like to single out my production supervisor, Elaine Wetterau, for my highest praise—she's one of the best in the business and very dear to my heart. Finally, I especially want to commend my executive editor extraordinaire, Bob Pirtle, for his innovation thinking and desire to go the extra mile.

We greatly appreciate the contributions that reviewers have made to our book. In particular, we thank the following people whose suggestions helped us prepare for the Second Edition.

Reviewers of Our First Edition and Portions of Our Second Edition

Peter Braunfeld, University of Illinois

Tom Briske, Georgia State University

Thomas Butts, University of Texas, Dallas

John Dossey, Illinois State University

Ruhama Even, Michigan State University

Iris B. Fetta, Clemson University

Majorie Fitting, San Jose State University

Susan Friel, Math/Science Education Network, University of North Carolina

John G. Harvey, University of Wisconsin–Madison

Alan Hoffer, University of California, Irvine

Joe Kennedy, Miami University

Robert S. Matulis, Millersville University

Joe K. Smith, Northern Kentucky
  University
J. Phillip Smith, Southern Connecticut
  State University
Judy Sowder, San Diego State
  University
Larry Sowder, San Diego State
  University

Lynn Trimpe, Linn–Benton
  Community College
Bruce Vogeli, Columbia University
Kenneth C. Washinger, Shippensburg
  University

Questionnaire Respondents for the Second Edition

Susan Baniak, Otterbein College
James Bierden, Rhode Island College
Peter Braunfeld, University of Illinois
Randall Charles, San Jose State
  University
Deann Christianson, University of the
  Pacific
Henry A. Culbreth, Southern Arkansas
  University–El Dorado
Gregory Davis, University of
  Wisconsin–Green Bay
Roger Engle, Clarion University
Julie Guelich, Normandale Community
  College
Brother Joseph Harris, C.S.C., St.
  Edward's University
Patricia Henry, Weber State College
Linda Hill, Idaho State University
Pat Jones, Methodist College
Susan Key, Meridien Community
  College
Mary Kilbridge, Augustana College
Judith Koenig, California State
  University, Dominquez Hills
Charles R. Luttrell, Frederick
  Community College
Carl Maneri, Wright State University
George F. Mead, McNeese State
  University

James A. Nickel, University of Texas,
  Permian Basin
Bill W. Oldham, Harding University
Debra Pharo, Northwestern Michigan
  College
Tom Richard, Bemidji State University
Bill Rudolph, Iowa State University
Lee K. Sanders, Miami University,
  Hamilton
Ann Savonen, Monroe County
  Community College
Karen Sharp, Mott Community
  College
Keith Shuert, Oakland Community
  College
Ron Smit, University of Portland
Raymond E. Spaulding, Radford
  University
Sister Carol Spiegel, BVM, Clarke
  College
Viji Sundar, California State
  University, Stanislaus
Karen Swenson, George Fox College
Barbara Walters, Ashland Community
  College
Joyce Wellington, Southeastern
  Community College
Stanley J. Zehm, Heritage College

Computer Test Bank Contributors for the Second Edition

Darrel Austin, Anderson University
Susan Baniak, Otterbein College
Deann Christianson, University of the
  Pacific
Gregory Davis, University of
  Wisconsin–Green Bay
Roger Engle, Clarion University
Mary Kilbridge, Augustana College
Carl Maneri, Wright State University

James A. Nickel, University of Texas,
  Permian Basin
Karen Sharp, Mott Community
  College
Sister Carol Spiegel, BVM, Clarke
  College
Barbara Walters, Ashland Community
  College

Reviewers of This Third Edition

Christine Browning, Western Michigan
  University
Tommy Bryan, Baylor University

Lucille Bullock, University of Texas
Ann Dinkheller, Xavier University;
John Dossey, Illinois State University

Sheryl Ettlich, Southern Oregon State College
Virginia Ellen Hanks, Western Kentucky University
Richard Kinson, University of South Alabama
John Koker, University of Wisconsin
Josephine Lane, Eastern Kentucky University

Mercedes McGowen, Harper College
Flora Alice Metz, Jackson State Community College
Barbara Moses, Bowling Green State University
James Riley, Western Michigan University

Questionnaire Respondents for the Third Edition

Mary Alter, University of Maryland
James Barnard, Western Oregon State College
Judy Bergman, University of Houston–Clearlake
Harold Brockman, Capital University
Judith Brower, North Idaho College
Harmon Brown, Harding University
Christine Browning, Western Michigan University
Joyce W. Bryant, St. Martin's College
Lynn Cleary, University of Maryland
Sister Marie Condon, Xavier University
Lynda Cones, Rend Lake College
Greg Crow, John Carroll University
Doris Edwards, Northern State College
Ann Farrell, Wright State University
Margaret Friar, Grand Valley State College
Judy Gibbs, West Virginia University
Anna Mae Greiner, Eisenhower Middle School
Virginia Hanks, Western Kentucky University
Dave Hansmire, College of the Mainland
Joseph Harris, St. Edward's University
John Harvey, University of Wisconsin
Ina Lee Herer, Tri-State University
Sandra Hsieh, Pasadena City College
Jo Johnson, Southwestern College
Patricia Johnson, Ohio State University
Mike Kilgallen, Lincoln Christian College
Josephine Lane, Eastern Kentucky University
Don Larsen, Buena Vista College
Louise Lataille, Westfield State College

Vernon Leitch, St. Cloud State University
Lawrence Levy, University of Wisconsin
Betty Long, Appalachian State University
Nancy Maushak, William Penn College
Edith Maxwell, West Georgia College
Kent Morris, Cameron University
Barbara Moses, Bowling Green State University
Gale Nash, Western State College of Colorado
Jerry Neft, University of Dayton
Susan Novelli, Kellogg Community College
Jan Odell, Richland College
Debra Pharo, Northwestern Michigan College
Robert Preller, Illinois Central College
Tom Richard, Bemidji State University
Jan Rizzuti, Central Washington University
Frances Rosamond, National University
Albert Roy, Bristol Community College
Joseph Shields, St. Mary's College, MN
Lawrence Shirley, Towson State University
Rick Simon, Idaho State University
James Smart, San Jose State University
Larry Sowder, San Diego State University
Ruthi Sturdevant, Lincoln University, MO
Ann Sweeney, College of St. Catherine, MN
Martha Van Cleave, Linfield College

Barbara Walters, Ashland Community
    College, KY
Jerry Wilkerson, Missouri Western
    State College
Delbert Williams, University of Mary
    Hardin–Baylor

Chris Wise, University of
    Southwestern Louisiana
Makia Zimmer, Bethany College

Special thanks are due to James Riley for contributing several interesting new problems to our extensive collection. I also want to give special thanks and acknowledgment to Marcia Swanson, Karen Swenson, Don Miller, Lynn Trimpe, Roger Maurer, and Vikki Maurer for their authorship of our written supplements, to Leesa I. McMahon and Heather Zimmers for their outstanding work in the preparation of our CD, to our students who have enthusiastically made many helpful suggestions to improve the book, and to the Oregon State University Department of Mathematics and higher administration for their strong support of mathematics education. Finally, comments from colleagues are encouraged and welcome. Please feel free to send suggestions to Gary Musser, Department of Mathematics, Oregon State University Corvallis, OR 97331, FAX: 503-737-0517, or e-mail address: musser @ math.orst.edu

G. L. M.

Brief Contents

Contents

Mathematics for Elementary Teachers

A CONTEMPORARY APPROACH

1

Introduction to Problem Solving

George Pólya

George Pólya: The Father of Modern Problem Solving

George Pólya was born in Hungary in 1887. After receiving his Ph.D. at the University of Budapest, where his dissertation involved questions in probability, he taught at the Swiss Federal Institute of Technology in Zurich. In 1940 he came to Brown University in the United States and then joined the faculty at Stanford University in 1942.

In his studies, he became interested in the process of discovery, or how mathematical results were derived. He felt that to understand a theory, one must know how it was discovered. Thus his teaching emphasized the process of discovery rather than simply the development of appropriate skills. To promote the problem-solving approach, he developed the following four steps:

1. Understand the problem.
2. Devise a plan.
3. Carry out the plan.
4. Look back.

This chapter provides an introduction to Pólya's four-step approach.

Pólya's accomplishments include over 250 mathematical papers and three books that promote his popular approach to problem solving. His famous book *How to Solve It*, which has been translated into 15 languages, introduced his four-step approach together with heuristics, or strategies, which are helpful in solving problems. Other important works of Pólya are *Mathematical Discovery*, Volumes I and II, and *Mathematics and Plausible Reasoning*, Volumes I and II.

Pólya, who died in 1985 at the age of 97, left mathematics with an important legacy of teaching for problem solving. In addition, he left the following "Ten Commandments for Teachers."

1. Be interested in your subject.
2. Know your subject.
3. Try to read the faces of your students; try to see their expectations and difficulties; put yourself in their place.
4. Realize that the best way to learn anything is to discover it by yourself.
5. Give your students not only information, but also know-how, mental attitudes, the habit of methodical work.
6. Let them learn guessing.
7. Let them learn proving.
8. Look out for such features of the problem at hand as may be useful in solving the problems to come—try to disclose the general pattern that lies behind the present concrete situation.
9. Do not give away your whole secret at once —let the students guess before you tell it— let them find out by themselves as much as is feasible.
10. Suggest it; do not force it down their throats.

PROBLEM-SOLVING STRATEGIES

1. *Guess and Test*
2. *Use a Variable*
3. *Draw a Picture*
4. *Look for a Pattern*
5. *Make a List*
6. *Solve a Simpler Problem*

Because problem solving is the main goal of mathematics, this chapter introduces the six strategies listed in the Problem-Solving Strategies box that are helpful in solving problems. Then, at the beginning of each chapter, an initial problem is posed that can be solved by using the strategy introduced in that chapter. As you move through this book, the Problem-Solving Strategies boxes at the beginning of each chapter expand, as should your ability to solve problems.

Initial Problem

Place the whole numbers 1 through 9 in the circles in the accompanying triangle so that the sum of the numbers on each side is 17.

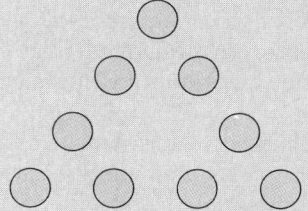

INTRODUCTION

Once, at an informal meeting, a social scientist asked of a mathematics professor, "What's the main goal of teaching mathematics?" The reply was, "Problem solving." In return, the mathematician asked, "What is the main goal of teaching the social sciences?" Once more the answer was "Problem solving." All successful engineers, scientists, social scientists, lawyers, accountants, doctors, business managers, and so on, have to be good problem solvers. Although the problems that people encounter may be very diverse, there are common elements and an underlying structure that can help to facilitate problem solving. Because of the universal importance of problem solving, the main professional group in mathematics education, the National Council of Teachers of Mathematics, recommended in its 1980 *An Agenda for Action* that "problem solving be the focus of school mathematics in the 1980s." The National Council of Teachers of Mathematics' 1989 *Curriculum and Evaluation Standards for School Mathematics* called for increased attention to the teaching of problem solving in K–8 mathematics. Areas of emphasis include word problems, applications, patterns and relationships, open-ended problems, and representing problem situations verbally, numerically, graphically, geometrically, or symbolically. This chapter introduces a problem-solving process together with six strategies that will aid you in solving problems.

1.1

THE PROBLEM-SOLVING PROCESS AND STRATEGIES

Pólya's Four Steps

In this book we often distinguish between "exercises" and "problems." Unfortunately, the distinction cannot be made precise. To solve an **exercise**, one applies a routine procedure to arrive at an answer. To solve a **problem**, one has to pause, reflect, and perhaps take some original step never taken before to arrive at a solution. This need for some sort of creative step on the solver's part, however minor, is what distinguishes a problem from an exercise. To a young child, finding $3 + 2$ might be a problem, whereas it is a fact for you. For a child in the early grades, the question "How do you divide 96 pencils equally among 16 children?" might pose a problem, but for you it suggests the routine exercise "find $96 \div 16$." These two examples illustrate how the distinction between an exercise and a problem can vary, since it depends on the state of mind of the person who is to solve it.

Doing exercises is a very valuable aid in learning mathematics. Exercises help you to learn concepts, properties, procedures, and so on, which you can then apply when solving problems. This chapter provides an introduction to the process of problem solving. The techniques that you learn in this chapter should help you to become a better problem solver and should show you how to help others develop their problem-solving skills.

A famous mathematician, George Pólya, devoted much of his teaching to helping students become better problem solvers. His major contribution is what has become known as the four-step process for solving problems.

Step 1: Understand the Problem

- Do you understand all the words?
- Can you restate the problem in your own words?
- Do you know what is given?
- Do you know what the goal is?
- Is there enough information?
- Is there extraneous information?
- Is this problem similar to another problem you have solved?

Step 2: Devise a Plan

Can one of the following strategies (heuristics) be used? (A **strategy** is defined as an artful means to an end.)

1. Guess and test.	**12.** Work backward.
2. Use a variable.	**13.** Use cases.
3. Draw a picture.	**14.** Solve an equation.
4. Look for a pattern.	**15.** Look for a formula.
5. Make a list.	**16.** Do a simulation.
6. Solve a simpler problem.	**17.** Use a model.
7. Draw a diagram.	**18.** Use dimensional analysis.
8. Use direct reasoning.	**19.** Identify subgoals.
9. Use indirect reasoning.	**20.** Use coordinates.
10. Use properties of numbers.	**21.** Use symmetry.
11. Solve an equivalent problem.	

The first six strategies are discussed in this chapter; the others are introduced in subsequent chapters.

Step 3: Carry Out the Plan

- Implement the strategy or strategies that you have chosen until the problem is solved or until a new course of action is suggested.
- Give yourself a reasonable amount of time in which to solve the problem. If you are not successful, seek hints from others or put the problem aside for a while. (You may have a flash of insight when you least expect it!)
- Do not be afraid of starting over. Often, a fresh start and a new strategy will lead to success.

Step 4: Look Back

- Is your solution correct? Does your answer satisfy the statement of the problem?
- Can you see an easier solution?
- Can you see how you can extend your solution to a more general case?

Usually, a problem is stated in words, either orally or written. Then, to solve the problem, one translates the words into an equivalent problem using mathematical symbols, solves this equivalent problem, and then interprets the answer. This process is summarized in Figure 1.1.

Learning to utilize Pólya's four steps and the diagram in Figure 1.1 are first steps in becoming a good problem solver. In particular, the "Devise a Plan" step is very important. In this chapter and throughout the book, you will learn the strategies listed under the "Devise a Plan" step, which will, in

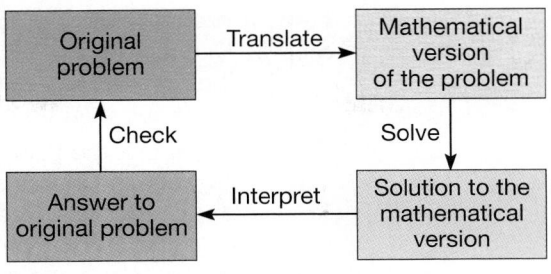

FIGURE 1.1

turn, help you decide how to proceed to solve problems. However, selecting an appropriate strategy is critical! As we worked with students who were successful problem solvers, we asked them to share "clues" that they observed in statements of problems that helped them select appropriate strategies. Their clues are listed after each corresponding strategy. Thus, in addition to learning *how* to use the various strategies herein, these clues can help you decide *when* to select an appropriate strategy or combination of strategies. Problem solving is as much an art as it is a science. Therefore, you will find that with experience you will develop a feeling for when to use one strategy over another by recognizing certain clues, perhaps subconsciously. Also, you will find that some problems may be solved in several ways using different strategies.

In summary, this initial material on problem solving is a foundation for your success in problem solving. Review this material on Pólya's four steps as well as the strategies and clues as you continue to develop your expertise in solving problems.

Problem-Solving Strategies

The remainder of this chapter is devoted to introducing several problem-solving strategies.

STRATEGY 1: GUESS AND TEST

Problem

Place the digits 1, 2, 3, 4, 5, 6 in the circles in Figure 1.2 so that the sum of the three numbers on each side of the triangle is 12.

We will solve the problem in three ways to illustrate three different approaches to the Guess and Test strategy. As its name suggests, to use the Guess and Test strategy, you guess at a solution and test to see if you are correct. If you are incorrect, you refine your guess and test again. This process is repeated until you obtain a solution.

Step 1: Understand the Problem
   Each number must be used exactly one time when arranging the numbers in the triangle. The sum of the three numbers on each side must be 12.

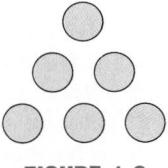

FIGURE 1.2

First Approach: Random Guess and Test

Step 2: Devise a Plan

Tear off six pieces of paper and mark the numbers 1 through 6 on them and then try combinations until one works.

Step 3: Carry Out the Plan

Arrange the pieces of paper in the shape of an equilateral triangle and check sums. Keep rearranging until three sums of 12 are found.

Second Approach: Systematic Guess and Test

Step 2: Devise a Plan

Rather than randomly moving the numbers around, begin by placing the smallest numbers—namely, 1, 2, 3—in the corners. If that does not work, try increasing the numbers to 1, 2, 4, and so on.

Step 3: Carry Out the Plan

With 1, 2, 3 in the corners, the side sums are too small; similarly with 1, 2, 4. Try 1, 2, 5 and 1, 2, 6. The side sums are still too small. Next try 2, 3, 4, then 2, 3, 5, and so on, until a solution is found. One also could begin with 4, 5, 6 in the corners, then try 3, 4, 5, and so on.

Third Approach: Inferential Guess and Test

Step 2: Devise a Plan

Start by assuming that 1 must be in a corner and explore the consequences.

Step 3: Carry Out the Plan

If 1 is placed in a corner, we must find two pairs out of the remaining five numbers whose sum is 11 (Figure 1.3). However, out of 2, 3, 4, 5, and 6 only $6 + 5 = 11$. Therefore, we conclude that 1 cannot be in a corner. If 2 is in a corner, there must be two pairs left that add to 10 (Figure 1.4). But only $6 + 4 = 10$. Therefore, 2 cannot be in a corner. Finally, suppose that 3 is in a corner. Then we must satisfy Figure 1.5. However, only $5 + 4 = 9$ of the remaining numbers. Thus, if there is a solution, 4, 5, and 6 will have to be in the corners (Figure 1.6). By placing 1 between 5 and 6, 2 between 4 and 6, and 3 between 4 and 5, we have a solution.

Step 4: Look Back

Notice how we have solved this problem in three different ways using Guess and Test. Random Guess and Test is often used to get started, but it is easy to lose track of the various trials. Systematic Guess and Test is better because you develop a scheme to ensure that you have tested all possibilities. Generally, Inferential Guess and Test is superior to both of the previous methods because it usually saves time and provides more information regarding possible solutions.

Additional Problems Where the Strategy "Guess and Test" Is Useful

1. In the following **cryptarithm**, that is, a collection of words where the letters represent numbers, *sun* and *fun* represent two three-digit

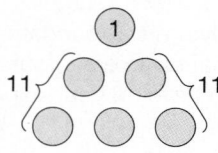

FIGURE 1.3

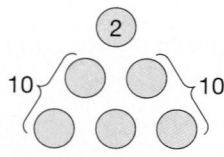

FIGURE 1.4

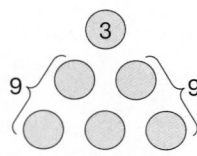

FIGURE 1.5

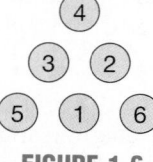

FIGURE 1.6

numbers, and *swim* is their four-digit sum. Using all of the digits 0, 1, 2, 3, 6, 7, and 9 in place of the letters where no letter represents two different digits, determine the value of each letter.

$$
\begin{array}{r}
sun \\
+fun \\
\hline
swim
\end{array}
$$

Step 1: Understand the Problem

Each of the letters in *sun*, *fun*, and *swim* must be re-placed with the numbers 0, 1, 2, 3, 6, 7, and 9, so that a cor-rect sum results after each letter is replaced with its associated digit. When the letter *n* is replaced by one of the digits, then $n + n$ must be *m* or $10 + m$, where the 1 in the 10 is carried to the tens column. Since $1 + 1 = 2$, $3 + 3 = 6$, and $6 + 6 = 12$, there are three possibilities for *n*, namely, 1, 3, or 6. Now we can try various combinations in an attempt to obtain the correct sum.

Step 2: Devise a Plan

Use inferential guess and test. There are three choices for *n*. Ob-serve that *sun* and *fun* are three-digit numbers and that *swim* is a four-digit number. Thus we have to carry when we add *s* and *f*. Therefore, the value for *s* in *swim* is 1. This limits the choices of *n* to 3 or 6.

Step 3: Carry Out the Plan

Since $s = 1$ and $s + f$ leads to a two-digit number, *f* must be 9. Thus there are two possibilities:

$$
\text{(a)} \quad
\begin{array}{r}
1\,u\,3 \\
+9\,u\,3 \\
\hline
1\,w\,i\,6
\end{array}
\qquad
\text{(b)} \quad
\begin{array}{r}
1\,u\,6 \\
+9\,u\,6 \\
\hline
1\,w\,i\,2
\end{array}
$$

In (a), if $u = 0$, 2, or 7, there is no value possible for *i* among the remaining digits.
In (b), if $u = 3$, then $u + u$ plus the carry from $6 + 6$ yields $i = 7$. This leaves $w = 0$ for a solution.

Step 4: Look Back

The reasoning used above shows that there is one and only one solution to this problem. When solving problems of this type, one could randomly substitute digits until a solution is found. However, Inferential Guess and Test simplifies the solution process by look-ing for unique aspects of the problem. Here the natural places to start are $n + n$, $u + u$, and the fact that $s + f$ yields a two-digit number.

2. Use four 4s and some of the symbols $+$, $\times$, $-$, $\div$, ( ) to give expres-sions for the whole numbers from 0 through 9: for example, $5 = (4 \times 4 + 4) \div 4$.

3. For each shape in Figure 1.7, make one straight cut so that each of the two pieces of the shape can be rearranged to form a square.

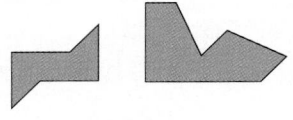

FIGURE 1.7

(Note: Answers for these problems are given after the Solution of the Initial Problem near the end of this chapter.)

Clues

The Guess and Test strategy may be appropriate when:

- There is a limited number of possible answers to test.
- You want to gain a better understanding of the problem.
- You have a good idea of what the answer is.
- You can systematically try possible answers.
- Your choices have been narrowed down by the use of other strategies.
- There is no other obvious strategy to try.

Review the preceding three problems to see how these clues may have helped you select the Guess and Test strategy to solve these problems.

STRATEGY 2: USE A VARIABLE

Observe how letters were used in place of numbers in the previous "sun + fun = swim" cryptarithm. Letters used in place of numbers in this way are called **variables** or **unknowns**. The Use a Variable strategy, which is one of the most useful problem-solving strategies, is used extensively in algebra and in mathematics that involves algebra.

Problem

What is the greatest number that evenly divides the sum of any three consecutive whole numbers?

By trying several examples, you might guess that three is the greatest such number. However, it is necessary to use a variable to account for all possible instances of three consecutive numbers.

Step 1: Understand the Problem

The whole numbers are 0, 1, 2, 3, . . . , so that consecutive whole numbers differ by 1. Thus an example of three consecutive whole numbers is the triple 3, 4, and 5. The sum of three consecutive whole numbers has a factor of 3 if 3 multiplied by another whole number produces the given sum. In the example of 3, 4, and 5, the sum is 12 and 3×4 equals 12. Thus $3 + 4 + 5$ has a factor of 3.

Step 2: Devise a Plan

Since we can use a variable, say x, to represent any whole number, we can represent every triple of consecutive whole numbers as follows: $x, x + 1, x + 2$. Now we can proceed to see if the sum has a factor of 3.

Step 3: Carry Out the Plan

The sum of x, $x + 1$, and $x + 2$ is

$$x + (x + 1) + (x + 2) = 3x + 3 = 3(x + 1).$$

Thus $x + (x + 1) + (x + 2)$ is three times the whole number $x + 1$. Therefore, we have shown that the sum of any three consecutive whole numbers has a factor of 3. The case where $x = 0$ shows that 3 is the *greatest* such number.

Step 4: Look Back

Is it also true that the sum of any five consecutive whole numbers has a factor of 5? Or, more generally, will the sum of any n consecutive whole numbers have a factor of n? Can you think of any other generalizations?

Additional Problems Where the Strategy "Use a Variable" Is Useful

1. Show that the sum of any five consecutive odd whole numbers has a factor of 5.

Step 1: Understand the Problem

First, since any even number has a factor of 2, it can be expressed as $2m$, where m is a whole number. Since each odd number is one more than the preceding even number, any odd number can be written in the form $2m + 1$, where m is a whole number. Also, consecutive odd numbers differ by two.

Step 2: Devise a Plan

To get information about the sum of *any* five consecutive odd numbers, a variable can be used. The next step is to represent the five numbers and add them to see if 5 is a factor of the sum.

Step 3: Carry Out the Plan

If $2m + 1$ is our first odd number, the next four are $2m + 3$, $2m + 5$, $2m + 7$, and $2m + 9$. Their sum is $(2m + 1) + (2m + 3) + (2m + 5) + (2m + 7) + (2m + 9) = 10m + 25$. Since $10m + 25 = 5(2m + 5)$, this sum has a factor of 5.

Step 4: Look Back

Here are some similar statements that can be investigated:

(i) The sum of any four consecutive odd numbers has a factor of 4.

(ii) The sum of any seven consecutive odd numbers has a factor of 7.

(iii) The sum of any five consecutive even numbers has a factor of 5.

Test some of these. Then state a couple of generalizations.

2. A dog's weight is 10 kilograms plus half its weight. How much does the dog weigh?

3. The measure of the largest angle of a triangle is nine times the measure of the smallest angle. The measure of the third angle is equal to the difference of the largest and the smallest. What are the measures of the angles? (Recall that the sum of the measures of the angles in a triangle is 180°.)

Clues

The Use a Variable strategy may be appropriate when:

- A phrase similar to "for any number" is present or implied.
- A problem suggests an equation.
- A proof or a general solution is required.
- A problem contains phrases such as "consecutive," "even," or "odd" whole numbers.
- There is a large number of cases.
- There is an unknown quantity related to known quantities.
- There is an infinite number of numbers involved.
- You are trying to develop a general formula.

Review the preceding three problems to see how these clues may have helped you select the Use a Variable strategy to solve these problems.

STRATEGY 3: DRAW A PICTURE

Often problems involve physical situations. In these situations, drawing a picture can help you better understand the problem so that you can formulate a plan to solve the problem. As you proceed to solve the following "pizza" problem, see if you can visualize the solution *without* looking at any pictures first. Then work through the given solution using pictures to see how helpful they can be.

Problem

Can you cut a pizza into 11 pieces with four straight cuts?

Step 1: Understand the Problem
Do the pieces have to be the same size and shape?

Step 2: Devise a Plan
An obvious beginning would be to draw a picture showing how a pizza is usually cut and count the pieces. If we do not get 11, we have to try something else (Figure 1.8). Unfortunately, we get only eight pieces this way.

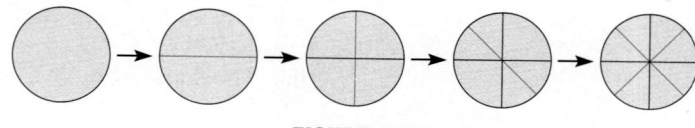

FIGURE 1.8

Step 3: Carry Out the Plan
See Figure 1.9.

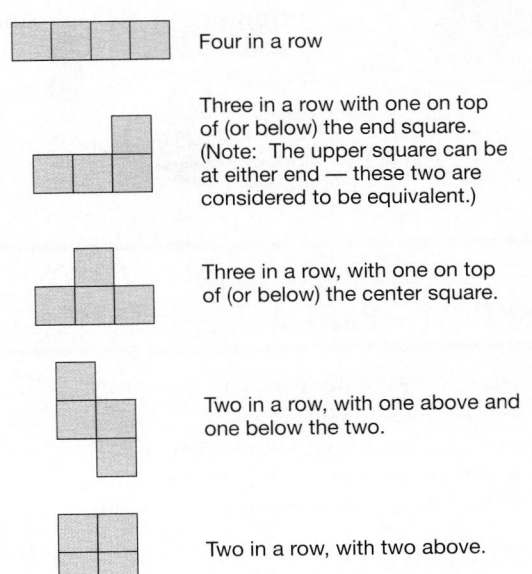

FIGURE 1.9

Step 4: Look Back

Were you concerned about cutting equal pieces when you started? That is normal. In the context of cutting a pizza, the focus is usually on trying to cut equal pieces rather than the number of pieces. Suppose that circular cuts were allowed? Does it matter if the pizza is circular or square? How many pieces can you get with five straight cuts? *n* straight cuts?

Additional Problems Where the Strategy "Draw a Picture" Is Useful

1. A **tetromino** is a shape made up of four squares where the squares must be joined along an entire side (Figure 1.10). How many different tetromino shapes are possible?

Step 1: Understand the Problem

The solution of this problem is easier if we make a set of pictures of all possible arrangements of four squares of the same size.

Step 2: Devise a Plan

Let's start with the longest and narrowest configuration and work toward the most compact.

Step 3: Carry Out the Plan

Not a tetromino

A tetromino

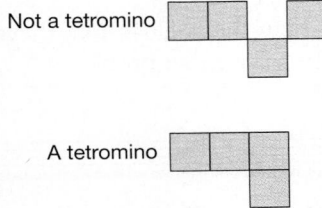

FIGURE 1.10

Four in a row

Three in a row with one on top of (or below) the end square. (Note: The upper square can be at either end — these two are considered to be equivalent.)

Three in a row, with one on top of (or below) the center square.

Two in a row, with one above and one below the two.

Two in a row, with two above.

Step 4: Look Back

Many similar problems can be posed using fewer or more squares. The problems become much more complex as the number of squares increases. Also, new problems can be posed using patterns of equilateral triangles.

2. If you have a chain saw with a bar 18 inches long, determine if a 16-foot log, 8 inches in diameter, can be cut into 4-foot pieces by making only two cuts.

3. It takes 64 cubes to fill a cubical box that has no top. How many cubes are *not* touching a side or the bottom?

Clues

The Draw a Picture strategy may be appropriate when:

- A physical situation is involved.
- Geometric figures or measurements are involved.
- You want to gain a better understanding of the problem.
- A visual representation of the problem is possible.

Review the preceding three problems to see how these clues may have helped you select the Draw a Picture strategy to solve these problems.

MATHEMATICAL MORSEL

There is a story about Sir Isaac Newton, coinventor of the calculus, who, as a youngster, was sent out to cut a hole in the barn door for the cats to go in and out. With great pride he admitted to cutting two holes, a larger one for the cat and a smaller one for the kittens.

PROBLEM SET 1.1—PART A

1. If the diagonals of a square are drawn in, how many triangles of all sizes are formed?

2. The distance around a standard tennis court is 228 feet. If the length of the court is 6 feet more than twice the width, find the dimensions of the tennis court.

3. A multiple of 11 I be,
   not odd, but even, you see.
   My digits, a pair,
   when multiplied there,
   make a cube and a square
   out of me.

   Who am I?

4. Show how 9 can be expressed as the sum of two consecutive numbers. Then decide if *every* odd number can be expressed as the sum of two consecutive numbers. Explain your reasoning.

5. Using the symbols $+$, $-$, $\times$, and $\div$, fill in the three blanks below to make a true equation. (A symbol may be used more than once.)

$$6 \underline{\quad} 6 \underline{\quad} 6 \underline{\quad} 6 = 13$$

6. In the following figure (called an **arithmogon**), the number that appears in a square is the sum of the numbers in the circles on each side of it. Determine what numbers belong in the circles.

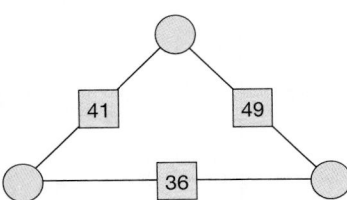

7. Talia walks to school at point B from her house at point A, a distance of six blocks. For variety she likes to try different routes each day. How many different paths can she take if she always moves closer to B? One route is shown.

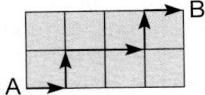

8. Jill goes to get some water. She has a 5-liter pail and a 3-liter pail and is supposed to bring exactly 1 liter back. How can she do this?

9. Place 10 stools along four walls of a room so that each of the four walls has the same number of stools.

10. Susan has 10 pockets and 44 dollar bills. She wants to arrange the money so that there is a different number of dollars in each pocket. Can she do it? Explain.

11. Arrange the numbers 1, 2, . . . , 9 in the accompanying triangle so that each side sums to 23.

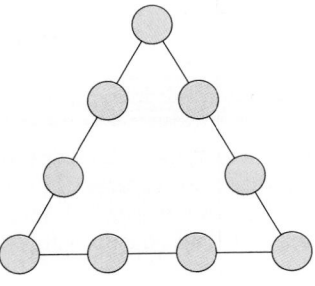

12. Place the digits 1 through 9 so that you can count from 1 to 9 by following the arrows in the diagram.

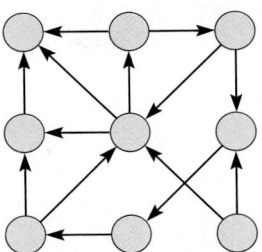

13. There are eight consecutive odd numbers which when multiplied together yield 34,459,425. What are they?

14. Scott and Greg were asked to add two whole numbers. Instead, Scott subtracted the two numbers and got 10, and Greg multiplied them and got 651. What was the correct sum?

15. Five friends were sitting on one side of a table. Gary sat next to Bill. Mike sat next to Tom. Howard sat in the third seat from Bill. Gary sat in the third seat from Mike. Who sat on the other side of Tom?

16. Using the numbers 9, 8, 7, 6, 5, and 4 once each, find the following.

(a) The largest possible sum:

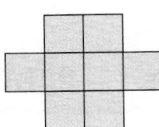

(b) The smallest possible (positive) difference:

17. Using the numbers 1 through 8, place them in the following eight squares so that no two consecutive numbers are in touching squares (touching includes entire sides or simply one point).

18. A **squared rectangle** is a rectangle whose interior can be divided into two or more squares. One example of a squared rectangle follows. The number written inside a square gives the length of a side of that square. Determine the dimensions of the unlabeled squares.

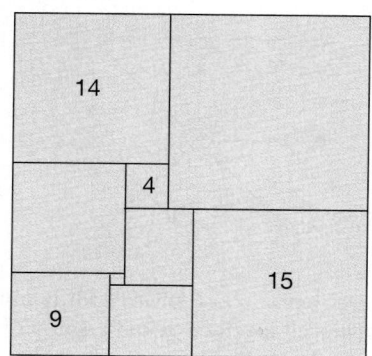

19. Seven years ago my son was one-third my age at that time. Seven years from now he will be one-half my age at that time. How old is my son?

20. A man's age at death was $\frac{1}{29}$ of the year of his birth. How old was he in 1949?

21. Solve this cryptarithm where each letter represents a digit and no digit represents two different letters.

$$
\begin{array}{r}
\text{USSR} \\
+ \ \text{USA} \\
\hline
\text{PEACE}
\end{array}
$$

22. Suppose that classified employees went on strike for 22 working days. One of the employees, Kathy, made $9.74 per hour before the strike. Under the old contract, she worked 240 six-hour days per year. If the new contract is for the same number of days per year, what increase in her hourly wage must Kathy receive to make up for the wages she lost during the strike in one year?

23. Three nickels, one penny, and one dime are placed as shown. You may move only one coin at a time, to an adjacent empty square. Move the coins so that the penny and the dime have exchanged places and the lower middle square is empty. Try to find the minimum number of such moves.

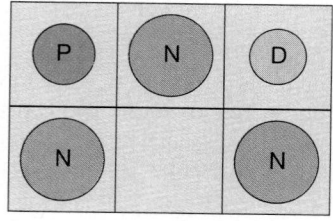

24. Using a 5-minute and an 8-minute hourglass timer, how can you measure 6 minutes?

25. On a balance scale, two spools and one thimble balance eight buttons. Also, one spool balances one thimble and one button. How many buttons will balance one spool?

26. Place the numbers 1 through 8 in the circles on the vertices of the following cube so that the difference of any two connecting circles is greater than 1.

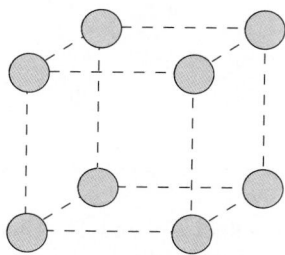

27. Think of a number. Add 10. Multiply by 4. Add 200. Divide by 4. Subtract your original number. Your result should be 60. Why?

28. The digits 1 through 9 can be used in decreasing order, with + and − signs, to produce 100 as shown: $98 - 76 + 54 + 3 + 21 = 100$. Find two other such combinations that will produce 100.

29. Three people on the first floor of a building wish to take the elevator up to the top floor. The maximum weight that the elevator can carry is 300 pounds. Also, one of the three people must be in the elevator to operate it. If the people weigh 130, 160, and 210 pounds, how can they get to the top floor?

30. The Indian mathematician Ramanujan observed that the taxi number, 1729, was very interesting because it was the smallest counting number that could be expressed as the sum of cubes in two different ways. Find a, b, c, and d such that $a^3 + b^3 = 1729$ and $c^3 + d^3 = 1729$.

PROBLEM SET 1.1—PART B

1. Carol bought some items at a variety store. All the items were the same price, and she bought as many items as the price of each item in cents. (For example, if the items cost 10 cents, she would have bought 10 of them.) Her bill was $2.25. How many items did Carol buy?

2. You can make one square with four toothpicks. Show how you can make two squares with seven toothpicks (breaking toothpicks not allowed), three squares with 10 toothpicks, and five squares with 12 toothpicks.

3. A textbook is opened and the product of the page numbers of the two facing pages is 6162. What are the numbers of the pages?

4. Place numbers 1 through 19 into the 19 circles so that any three numbers in a line through the center will give the same sum.

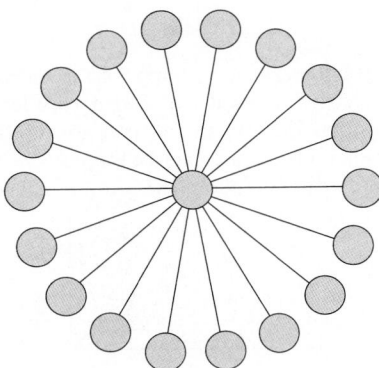

5. Using three of the symbols +, −, ×, and ÷ *once* each, fill in the following three blanks to make a true equation. (Parentheses are allowed.)

$$6 \underline{\qquad} 6 \underline{\qquad} 6 \underline{\qquad} 6 = 66$$

6. In the following arithmagon the number that appears in a square is the product of the numbers in the circles on each side of it. Determine what numbers belong in the circles.

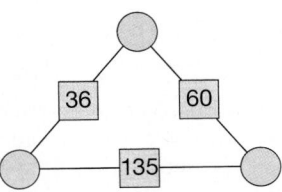

7. A water main for a street is being laid using a particular kind of pipe that comes in either 18-foot sections or 20-foot sections. The designer has determined that the water main would require 14 fewer sections of 20-foot pipe than if 18-foot sections were used. Find the total length of the water main.

8. Find the largest eight-digit number made up of the digits 1, 1, 2, 2, 3, 3, 4, and 4 such that the 1s are separated by one digit, the 2s by two digits, the 3s by three digits, and the 4s by four digits.

9. Mike said that when he opened his book, the product of the page numbers of the two facing pages was 7007. Without performing any calculations, prove that he was wrong.

10. A magician had his subject hide an odd number of coins in one hand and an *even* number of coins in another. He then told the subject to multiply the number of coins in the right hand by 2 and in the left hand by 3, and announce the sum of these two numbers. The magician immediately said which hand had the odd number of coins. How did he do it?

11. A hiker traveled at an average rate of 2 kilometers per hour (km/h) going up to a lookout and traveled at an average rate of 5 km/h coming back down. If the entire trip (not counting a lunch stop at the lookout) took approximately 3 hours and 15 minutes, what is the total distance the hiker walked? Round your answer to the nearest tenth of a kilometer.

12. The Smiths were about to start on an 18,000-mile automobile trip. They had their tires checked and found that each was good for only 12,000 miles. What is the smallest number of spares that they will need to take along with them to make the trip without having to buy a new tire?

13. Given: Six arrows arranged as follows:

Goal: By inverting two *adjacent* arrows at a time, rearrange to the following:

Can you find a minimum number of moves?

14. Fill in the circles using the numbers 1 through 9 once each and have the sum along each of the five rows total 17.

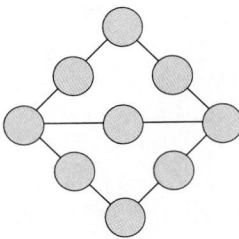

15. Two friends shopping together encounter a special "3 for 2" shoe sale in which if two pairs of shoes are purchased at the regular price, a third pair (of lower or equal value) is free. Neither friend wants three pairs of shoes, but Pat would like to buy a $56 and a $39 pair while Chris is interested in a $45 pair. If they buy the shoes together to take advantage of the sale, what is the fairest share for each to pay?

16. Find digits A, B, C, and D that solve the following cryptarithm.

$$\begin{array}{r} ABCD \\ \times \quad 4 \\ \hline DCBA \end{array}$$

17. Using a 5-minute and an 8-minute hourglass timer, how can you measure 1 minute?

18. A **squared square** is a square whose interior can be subdivided into two or more squares. One example of a squared square follows. The number written inside a square gives the length of a side of that square. Determine the dimensions of the unlabeled squares.

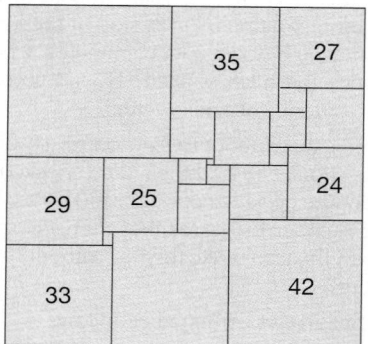

19. If possible, find an odd number that can be expressed as the sum of four consecutive counting numbers. If impossible, explain why.

20. Think of a number. Multiply by 5. Add 8. Multiply by 4. Add 9. Multiply by 5. Subtract 105. Divide by 100. Subtract 1. How does your result compare with your original number? Explain.

21. In the square array on the left below, the corner numbers were given and the boldface numbers were found by adding the adjacent corner numbers. Following the same rules, find the corner numbers for the other square array.

```
  6  19  13        —  10  —
  8      14       15      11
  2   3   1        —  16  —
```

22. Together, a baseball and a football weigh 1.25 pounds, the baseball and a soccer ball weigh 1.35 pounds, and the football and soccer ball weigh 1.9 pounds. How much does each of the balls weigh?

23. Five women participated in a 10-kilometer (10 K) Volks-walk, but started at different times. At a certain time in the walk the following descriptions were true.

1. Rose was at the halfway point (5 K).
2. Kelly was 2 K ahead of Cathy.
3. Janet was 3 K ahead of Ann.
4. Rose was 1 K behind Cathy.
5. Ann was 3.5 K behind Kelly.

(a) Determine the order of the women at that point in time. That is, who was nearest the finish line, who was second closest, and so on?

(b) How far from the finish line was Janet at that time?

24. A square can be divided into four identical smaller copies of itself as follows.

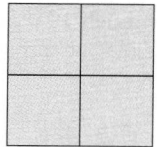

Any subdivision of a shape into identically shaped smaller copies of itself is called a **reptile** dissection. Each of the following shapes can also be divided into four smaller, identical copies of themselves. Show how this can be done in each case.

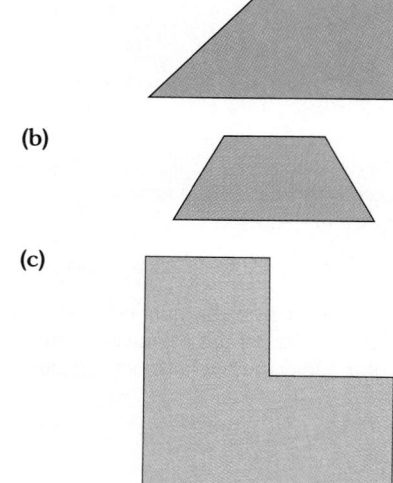

(a)

(b)

(c)

25. The floor of a square room is covered with square tiles. Walking diagonally across the room from corner to corner, Susan counted a total of 33 tiles on the two diagonals. What is the total number of tiles covering the floor of the room?

26. Pick any two consecutive numbers. Add them. Then add 9 to the sum. Divide by 2. Subtract the smaller of the original numbers from the answer. What did you get? Repeat it with two other consecutive numbers. Make a conjecture (educated guess) about the answer and prove it.

27. An **additive magic square** has the same sum in each row, column, and diagonal. Find the error in this magic square and correct it.

```
47  56  34  22  83   7
24  67  44  26  13  75
29  52   3  99  18  48
17  49  89   4  53  37
97   6   3  11  74  28
35  19  46  87   8  54
```

28. José discovered what he thought was a method for? generating a **Pythagorean triple**, that is, three whole numbers a, b, c such that $a^2 + b^2 = c^2$. Here are his rules: Take any odd number (say, 11). Square it (121). Subtract 1 and divide by 2 (60). Add 1 (61). (Note: $11^2 + 60^2 = 121 + 3600 = 3721 = 61^2$.) Try another example. Prove that José's method always works by using a variable.

29. Solve the following cryptarithm where D = 5.

$$\begin{array}{r} \text{DONALD} \\ +\text{GERALD} \\ \hline \text{ROBERT} \end{array}$$

30. How many guests were present at a dinner if every two guests shared a bowl of rice, every three guests shared a bowl of broth, every four guests shared a bowl of fowl, and 65 bowls were used altogether?

31. Using the triangle in Problem 11 of Part A, determine if you can make similar triangles using the digits 1, 2, . . . , 9, where the side sums are 18, 19, 20, 21, and 22.

1.2

THREE ADDITIONAL STRATEGIES

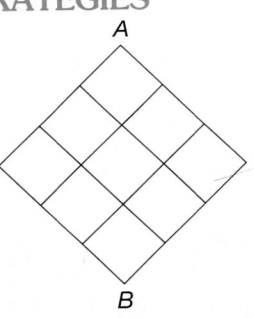

FIGURE 1.11

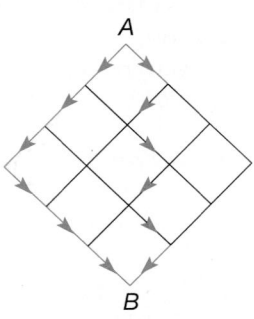

FIGURE 1.12

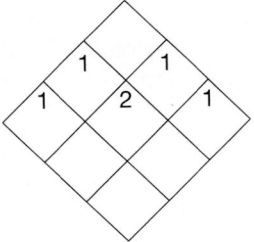

FIGURE 1.13

STRATEGY 4: LOOK FOR A PATTERN

When using the Look for a Pattern strategy, one usually lists several specific instances of a problem and then looks to see if a pattern emerges that suggests a solution to the entire problem. For example, consider the sums produced by adding consecutive odd numbers starting with 1: 1, $1 + 3 = 4 (= 2 \times 2)$, $1 + 3 + 5 = 9 (= 3 \times 3)$, $1 + 3 + 5 + 7 = 16$ $(= 4 \times 4)$, $1 + 3 + 5 + 7 + 9 = 25 (= 5 \times 5)$, and so on. Based on the pattern generated by these five examples, one might expect that such a sum is always going to be a perfect square.

Problem

How many different downward paths are there from A to B in the grid in Figure 1.11? A path must travel on the lines.

Step 1: Understand the Problem

What do we mean by different and downward? Figure 1.12 illustrates two paths. Notice that each such path will be 6 units long. Different means that they are not exactly the same; that is, some part or parts are different.

Step 2: Devise a Plan

Let's look at each point of intersection in the grid and see how many different ways we can get to each point. Then perhaps we will notice a pattern (Figure 1.13). For example, there is only one way to reach each of the points on the two outside edges; there are two ways to reach the middle point in the row of pointslabeled 1, 2, 1; and so on. Observe that the point labeled 2 inFigure 1.13 can be found by adding the two 1s above it.

Step 3: Carry Out the Plan

To see how many paths there are to any point, observe that you need only *add* the number of paths required to arrive at the point or points immediately above. To reach a point beneath the pair 1 and 2, the paths to 1 and 2 are extended downward resulting in $1 + 2 = 3$ paths to that point. The resulting number pattern is

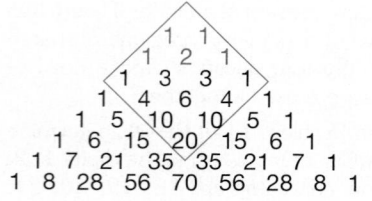

FIGURE 1.14

shown in Figure 1.14. Notice, for example, that $4 + 6 = 10$ and $20 + 15 = 35$. (This pattern is part of what is called **Pascal's triangle**. It is used again in Chapter 11.) The surrounded portion of this pattern applies to the given problem; thus the answer to the problem is 20.

Step 4: Look Back

Can you see how to solve a similar problem involving a larger square array, say a 4×4 grid? How about a 10×10 grid? How about a rectangular grid?

A pattern of numbers arranged in a particular order is called a number **sequence**, and the individual numbers in the sequence are called **terms** of the sequence. The **counting numbers**, 1, 2, 3, 4, . . . , give rise to many sequences. (An **ellipsis**, the three periods after the 4, means "and so on.") Several sequences of counting numbers follow.

Sequence	Name
2, 4, 6, 8, . . .	The **even** (counting) **numbers**
1, 3, 5, 7, . . .	The **odd** (counting) **numbers**
1, 4, 9, 16, . . .	The **square** (counting) **numbers**
1, 3, 3^2, 3^3, . . .	The **powers** of three
1, 1, 2, 3, 5, 8, . . .	The **Fibonacci sequence** (after the two 1s, each term is the sum of the two preceding terms)

Inductive reasoning is a type of reasoning used to draw conclusions or make predictions about a large collection of objects or numbers, based on a small representative subcollection. For example, inductive reasoning may be used to find the ones digit of the 400th term of the sequence 8, 12, 16, 20, 24, ... By continuing this sequence for a few more terms, 8, 12, 16, 20, 24, 28, 32, 36, 40, 44, 48, 52, 56, 60, . . . , one can observe that the ones digit of every fifth term starting with the term 24 is a four. Thus, the ones digit of the 400th term must be a four.

Additional Problems Where the Strategy "Look for a Pattern" Is Useful

1. Find the ones digit in 3^{99}.

Step 1: Understand the Problem

The number 3^{99} is the product of 99 threes. Using the exponent key on one type of scientific calculator yields the result $\boxed{1.71792506 5^{47}}$. This shows the first digit, but not the ones (last) digit, since the 47 indicates that there are 47 places to the right of the decimal. (See the discussion on scientific notation in Chapter 4 for further explanation.) Therefore, we will need to use another method.

Step 2: Devise a Plan

Consider 3^1, 3^2, 3^3, 3^4, 3^5, 3^6, 3^7, 3^8. Perhaps the ones digits of these numbers form a pattern that can be used to predict the ones digit on 3^{99}.

Step 3: Carry Out the Plan

$3^1 = \mathbf{3}$, $3^2 = \mathbf{9}$, $3^3 = 27$, $3^4 = 81$, $3^5 = 243$, $3^6 = 729$, $3^7 = 2187$, $3^8 = 6561$. The ones digits form the sequence 3, 9, 7, 1, 3, 9, 7, 1. Whenever the exponent of the 3 has a factor of 4, the ones digit is a 1. Since 100 has a factor of 4, 3^{100} must have a ones digit of 1. Therefore, the ones digit of 3^{99} must be 7, since 3^{99} precedes 3^{100} and 7 precedes 1 in the sequence 3, 9, 7, 1.

Step 4: Look Back

Ones digits of other numbers involving exponents might be found in a similar fashion. Check this for several of the numbers from 4 to 9.

2. Which whole numbers, from 1 to 50, have an odd number of factors? For example, 15 has 1, 3, 5, and 15 as factors, hence has an even number of factors: four.

3. In the next diagram, the left "H"-shaped array is called the 32-H and the right array is the 58-H.

0	1	2	3	4	5	6	7	8	9
10	11	12	13	14	15	16	17	18	19
20	㉑	22	㉓	24	25	26	27	28	29
30	㉛	㉜	㉝	34	35	36	37	38	39
40	㊶	42	㊸	44	45	46	㊼	48	㊾
50	51	52	53	54	55	56	㊷	㊸	㊹
60	61	62	63	64	65	66	㊸	68	㊹
70	71	72	73	74	75	76	77	78	79
80	81	82	83	84	85	86	87	88	89
90	91	92	93	94	95	96	97	98	99

(circled: 21, 23, 31, 32, 33, 41, 43, 47, 49, 57, 58, 59, 67, 69)

(a) Find the sums of the numbers in the 32-H. Do the same for the 58-H and the 74-H. What do you observe?

(b) Find an H whose sum is 497.

(c) Can you predict the sum in any H if you know the middle number? Explain.

Clues

The Look for a Pattern strategy may be appropriate when:

- A list of data is given.
- A sequence of numbers is involved.
- Listing special cases helps you deal with complex problems.
- You are asked to make a prediction or generalization.
- Information can be expressed and viewed in an organized manner, such as in a table.

Review the preceding three problems to see how these clues may have helped you select the Look for a Pattern strategy to solve these problems.

STRATEGY 5: MAKE A LIST

The Make a List strategy is often combined with the Look for a Pattern strategy to suggest a solution to a problem. For example, here is a list of all the squares of the numbers 1 to 20 with their ones digits in boldface.

1,   **4**,   **9**,   1**6**,   2**5**,   3**6**,   4**9**,   6**4**,   8**1**,   10**0**,
12**1**,   14**4**,   16**9**,   19**6**,   22**5**,   25**6**,   28**9**,   32**4**,   36**1**,   40**0**

The pattern in this list can be used to see that the ones digits of squares must be one of 0, 1, 4, 5, 6, or 9. This list suggests that a perfect square can never end in a 2, 3, 7, or 8.

Problem

The number 10 can be expressed as the sum of four odd numbers in three ways: (i) 10 = 7 + 1 + 1 + 1, (ii) 10 = 5 + 3 + 1 + 1, and (iii) 10 = 3 + 3 + 3 + 1. In how many ways can 20 be expressed as the sum of eight odd numbers?

Step 1: Understand the Problem

Recall that the odd numbers are the numbers 1, 3, 5, 7, 9, 11, 13, 15, 17, 19, ... Using the fact that 10 can be expressed as the sum of four odd numbers, we can form various combinations of those sums to obtain eight odd numbers whose sum is 20. But does this account for all possibilities?

Step 2: Devise a Plan

Instead, let's make a list starting with the largest possible odd number in the sum and work our way down to the smallest.

Step 3: Carry Out the Plan

$$20 = 13 + 1 + 1 + 1 + 1 + 1 + 1 + 1$$
$$20 = 11 + 3 + 1 + 1 + 1 + 1 + 1 + 1$$
$$20 = 9 + 5 + 1 + 1 + 1 + 1 + 1 + 1$$
$$20 = 9 + 3 + 3 + 1 + 1 + 1 + 1 + 1$$
$$20 = 7 + 7 + 1 + 1 + 1 + 1 + 1 + 1$$
$$20 = 7 + 5 + 3 + 1 + 1 + 1 + 1 + 1$$
$$20 = 7 + 3 + 3 + 3 + 1 + 1 + 1 + 1$$
$$20 = 5 + 5 + 5 + 1 + 1 + 1 + 1 + 1$$
$$20 = 5 + 5 + 3 + 3 + 1 + 1 + 1 + 1$$
$$20 = 5 + 3 + 3 + 3 + 3 + 1 + 1 + 1$$
$$20 = 3 + 3 + 3 + 3 + 3 + 3 + 1 + 1$$

Step 4: Look Back

Could you have used the three sums to 10 to help find these 11 sums to 20? Can you think of similar problems to solve? For example, an easier one would be to express 8 as the sum of four odd numbers, and a more difficult one would be to express 40 as the sum of 16 odd numbers. We could also consider sums of even numbers, expressing 20 as the sum of six even numbers.

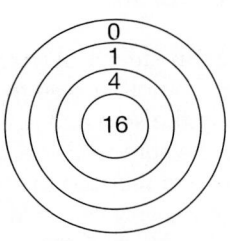

FIGURE 1.15

Additional Problems Where the Strategy "Make a List" Is Useful

1. In a dart game, three darts are thrown. All hit the target (Figure 1.15). What scores are possible?

Step 1: Understand the Problem

Assume that all three darts hit the board. Since there are four different numbers on the board, namely, 0, 1, 4, and 16, three of these numbers, with repetitions allowed, must be hit.

Step 2: Devise a Plan

We should make a systematic list by beginning with the smallest (or largest) possible sum. In this way we will be more likely to find all sums.

Step 3: Carry Out the Plan

$$0 + 0 + 0 = 0, \quad 0 + 0 + 1 = 1, \quad 0 + 1 + 1 = 2,$$
$$1 + 1 + 1 = 3, \quad 0 + 0 + 4 = 4, \quad 0 + 1 + 4 = 5,$$
$$1 + 1 + 4 = 6, \quad 0 + 4 + 4 = 8, \quad 1 + 4 + 4 = 9,$$
$$4 + 4 + 4 = 12, \quad \cdots, \quad 16 + 16 + 16 = 48$$

Step 4: Look Back

Several similar problems could be posed by changing the numbers on the dartboard, the number of rings, or the number of darts. Also, using geometric probability, one could ask how to design and label such a game to make it a fair skill game. That is, what points should be assigned to the various regions to reward one fairly for hitting that region?

2. How many squares, of all sizes, are there on an 8 × 8 checkerboard? (See Figure 1.16; the sides of the squares are on the lines.)

3. It takes 1230 digits to number the pages of a book. How many pages does the book contain?

FIGURE 1.16

Clues

The Make a List strategy may be appropriate when:

- Information can easily be organized and presented.
- Data can easily be generated.
- Listing the results obtained by using Guess and Test.
- Asked "in how many ways" something can be done.
- Trying to learn about a collection of numbers generated by a rule or formula.

Review the preceding three problems to see how these clues may have helped you select the Make a List strategy to solve these problems.

The problem-solving strategy illustrated next could have been employed in conjunction with the Make a List strategy in the preceding problem.

STRATEGY 6: SOLVE A SIMPLER PROBLEM

Observe that each of the sums of odd numbers in step 3 of the problem in strategy 5 involved the use of several "ones." Another way to solve this problem is to decide how many "ones" can be in the sum and then find what other odd numbers are required to complete the sum to 20 as a sum of eight odd numbers. In this way the problem has been reduced to a series of simpler problems. For example, if there are 7 ones, only one odd number can be added to the 7 to obtain 20, namely 13. Next, if there are 6 ones, then two odd numbers, other than 1, must be added to obtain 14; the only possibilities are 11 and 3, 9 and 5, and 7 and 7. The following table lists all other such arrangements.

(1) Number of Ones	(2) Amount Needed to Obtain 20	(3) How Many Summands Are Needed for the Number in Column (2)? [8 Minus the Number in Column (1)]	(4) Solutions
7	13	1	$13 + 1 + 1 + 1 + 1 + 1 + 1 + 1$
6	14	2	$11 + 3 + 1 + 1 + 1 + 1 + 1 + 1$
			$9 + 5 + 1 + 1 + 1 + 1 + 1 + 1$
			$7 + 7 + 1 + 1 + 1 + 1 + 1 + 1$
5	15	3	$9 + 3 + 3 + 1 + 1 + 1 + 1 + 1$
			$7 + 5 + 3 + 1 + 1 + 1 + 1 + 1$
			$5 + 5 + 5 + 1 + 1 + 1 + 1 + 1$
4	16	4	$7 + 3 + 3 + 3 + 1 + 1 + 1 + 1$
			$5 + 5 + 3 + 3 + 1 + 1 + 1 + 1$
3	17	5	$5 + 3 + 3 + 3 + 3 + 1 + 1 + 1$
2	18	6	$3 + 3 + 3 + 3 + 3 + 3 + 1 + 1$

Additional Problems Where the Strategy "Solve a Simpler Problem" Is Useful

1. Find the sum $\dfrac{1}{2} + \dfrac{1}{2^2} + \dfrac{1}{2^3} + \cdots + \dfrac{1}{2^{10}}$.

Step 1: Understand the Problem

This problem can be solved directly by getting a common denominator, here 2^{10}, and finding the sum of the numerators.

Step 2: Devise a Plan

Instead of doing a direct calculation, let's combine some previous strategies. Namely, make a list of the first few sums and look for a pattern.

Step 3: Carry Out the Plan

$$\frac{1}{2}, \quad \frac{1}{2} + \frac{1}{4} = \frac{3}{4}, \quad \frac{1}{2} + \frac{1}{4} + \frac{1}{8} = \frac{7}{8} \quad \frac{1}{2} + \frac{1}{4} + \frac{1}{8} + \frac{1}{16} = \frac{15}{16}$$

The pattern of sums, $\dfrac{1}{2}, \dfrac{3}{4}, \dfrac{7}{8}, \dfrac{15}{16}$, suggests that the sum of the ten fractions is $\dfrac{2^{10} - 1}{2^{10}}$, or $\dfrac{1023}{1024}$.

Step 4: Look Back

This method of combining the strategy of Solve a Simpler Problem with Make a List and Look for a Pattern is very useful. For example, what is the sum $\dfrac{1}{2} + \dfrac{1}{2^2} + \cdots + \dfrac{1}{2^{100}}$? Because of the large denominators, you wouldn't want to add these fractions directly.

2. Following the arrows in Figure 1.17, how many paths are there from *A* to *B*?

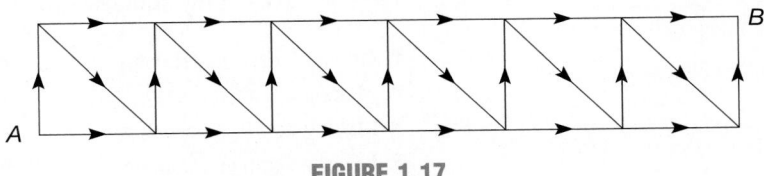

FIGURE 1.17

3. There are 20 people at a party. If each person shakes hands with each other person, how many handshakes will there be?

Clues

The Solve a Simpler Problem strategy may be appropriate when:

• The problem involves complicated computations.
• The problem involves very large or very small numbers.
• A direct solution is too complex.
• You want to gain a better understanding of the problem.
• The problem involves a large array or diagram.

Review the preceding three problems to see how these clues may have helped you select the Solve a Simpler Problem strategy to solve these problems.

RECAPITULATION

When presenting the problems in this chapter, we took great care in organizing the solutions using Pólya's four-step approach. However, it is not necessary to label and display each of the four steps every time you work a problem. On the other hand, it is good to get into the habit of recalling the four steps as you plan and as you work through a problem. In this chapter we have introduced several useful problem-solving strategies. In each of the following chapters, a new problem-solving strategy is introduced. These strategies will be especially helpful when you are making a plan. As you are planning to solve a problem, think of the strategies as a collection of tools. Then an important part of solving a problem can be viewed as selecting an appropriate tool or strategy.

STUDENT PAGE SNAPSHOT

✓ UNDERSTAND
✓ PLAN
✓ TRY
✓ CHECK
✓ EXTEND

PROBLEM SOLVING

Strategies Review

Here are some of the strategies you have used to solve problems.

- Guess, Test, and Revise
- Making a Table
- Making an Organized List
- Using a Simpler Problem

- Looking for a Pattern
- Drawing a Diagram
- Working Backward
- Solving a Simpler Problem

Solve the problem. Tell which strategy you used.

1. Keith's hobby is bird-watching. He saw 80 birds in three days. The number he saw on the second day was 5 fewer than the number he saw on the first day. The number he saw on the third day was 15 more than the number he saw on the second day. How many birds did Keith see each day?

2. Jake, Marie, Pedro, and Amy enjoy bird-watching while cross-country skiing. Jake skied 1.5 kilometers. Pedro skied $\frac{1}{3}$ the distance that Marie did. Amy skied 1 less kilometer than Pedro. Jake skied twice the distance that Amy did. What distance did Marie ski?

3. Mr. Katz has $5 in $1 bills and $25 in $5 bills. He is going to give his son an amount of money to spend at the zoo using 3 bills. How many amounts are possible?

4. Gabriella is making an eagle needlepoint wall hanging that is $17\frac{1}{2}$ inches by $17\frac{1}{2}$ inches. She is making a blue border that is 2 inches wide at the top, bottom, and sides. What is the area of the border?

5. Tony plans to go bird-watching every 5 days and sky-watching every 3 days. If he starts by bird-watching on a Saturday and sky-watching on the next day, on what day of the week will he do both things on the same day?

We end this chapter with a list of suggestions that students who have successfully completed a course on problem solving felt were helpful tips. Reread this list periodically as you progress through the book.

SUGGESTIONS FROM SUCCESSFUL PROBLEM SOLVERS

- Accept the challenge of solving a problem.
- Rewrite the problem in your own words.
- Take time to explore, reflect, think, ...
- Talk to yourself. Ask yourself lots of questions.
- If appropriate, try the problem using simple numbers.
- Many problems require an incubation period. If you get frustrated, do not hesitate to take a break—your subconscious may take over. But do return to try again.
- Look at the problem in a variety of ways.
- Run through your list of strategies to see if one (or more) can help you get a start.
- Many problems can be solved in a variety of ways—you only need to find one solution to be successful.
- Do not be afraid to change your approach, strategy, and so on.
- Organization can be helpful in problem solving. Use the Pólya four-step approach with a variety of strategies.
- Experience in problem solving is very valuable. *Work lots of problems*; your confidence will grow.
- If you are not making much progress, do not hesitate to go back to make sure that you really understand the problem. This review process may happen two or three times in a problem since understanding usually grows as you work toward a solution.
- There is nothing like a breakthrough, a small *aha!*, as you solve your problems.
- Always, always look back. Try to see precisely what was the key step in your solution.
- Make up and solve problems of your own.
- Write up your solutions neatly and clearly enough so that you will be able to understand your solution if you reread it in 10 years.
- Develop good problem-solving helper skills when assisting others in solving problems. Do not give out solutions; instead, provide meaningful hints.
- By helping and giving hints to others, you will find that you will develop many new insights.
- Enjoy yourself! Solving a problem is a positive experience.

MATHEMATICAL MORSEL

Sophie Germain was born in Paris in 1776, the daughter of a silk merchant. At the age of 13, she found a book on the history of mathematics in her father's library. She became enthralled with the study of mathematics. Even though her parents disapproved of this pursuit, nothing daunted her—she studied at night wrapped in a blanket, because they had taken her clothing away from her to keep her from getting up. They also took away her heat and light. This only hardened her resolve until her father finally gave in and she, at last, was allowed to study to become a mathematician.

PROBLEM SET 1.2—PART A

Use any of the six problem-solving strategies introduced thus far to solve the following.

1. (a) Complete this table and look for a pattern.

Sum	Answer
1	1
1 + 3	4
1 + 3 + 5	
1 + 3 + 5 + 7	
1 + 3 + 5 + 7 + 9	

(b) How many odd whole numbers would have to be added to get a sum of 81? Check your guess by adding them.

(c) How many odd whole numbers would have to be added to get a sum of 169? Check your guess by adding them.

(d) How many odd whole numbers would have to be added to get a sum of 529? (You do not need to check.)

2. Find the missing term in each pattern.

(a) 256   128   64   _____   16   8

(b) 1 $\dfrac{1}{3}$ $\dfrac{1}{9}$ _____ $\dfrac{1}{81}$

(c) 7   9   12   16   _____

(d) 127,863   12,789   _____   135   18

3. Sketch a figure that is next in each sequence.

(a)

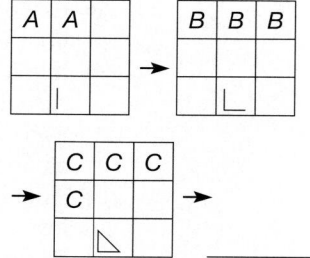

(b)

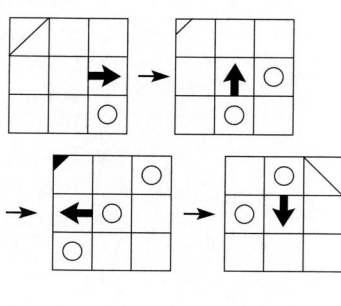

4. Consider the following differences. Use your calculator to verify that the statements are true.

$$6^2 - 5^2 = 11$$
$$56^2 - 45^2 = 1111$$
$$556^2 - 445^2 = 111{,}111$$

(a) Predict the next line in the sequence of differences. Use your calculator to check your answer.

(b) What do you think the eighth line will be?

5. Look for a pattern in the first two number grids below. Then use the pattern you observed to fill in the missing numbers of the third grid.

21	7	3
3	1	3
7	7	1

72	36	2
8	4	2
9	9	1

60	6	
		5
2		

6. The **triangular numbers** are the whole numbers that represent triangular arrays of dots. The first five triangular numbers are shown.

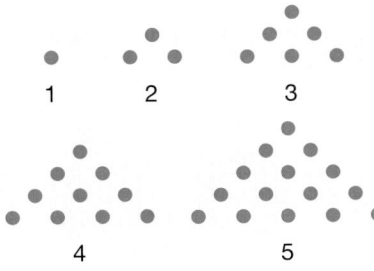

1   2   3

4   5

(a) Complete the following table and look for a pattern.

Number	Number of Dots (Triangular Numbers)
1	1
2	3
3	
4	
5	
6	

(b) Make a sketch to represent the seventh triangular number.

(c) How many dots will be in the tenth triangular number?

(d) Is there a triangular number that has 91 dots in its shape? If so, which one?

(e) Is there a triangular number that has 150 dots in its shape? If so, which one?

(f) Write a formula for the number of dots in the nth triangular number.

(g) When the famous mathematician Carl Friedrich Gauss was in fourth grade, his teacher challenged him to add the first one hundred counting numbers. Find this sum.

$$1 + 2 + 3 + \cdots + 100$$

7. As mentioned in this section, the square numbers are the counting numbers 1, 4, 9, 16, 25, 36, ... Each square number can be represented by a square array of dots as shown in the following figure, where the second square number has four dots, and so on. The first four square numbers are shown.

(a) Find two triangular numbers (refer to Problem 6) whose sum equals the third square number.

(b) Find two triangular numbers whose sum equals the fifth square number.

(c) What two triangular numbers have a sum that equals the 10th square number? The 20th square number? The nth square number?

(d) Find a triangular number that is also a square number.

(e) Find five pairs of square numbers whose difference is a triangular number.

8. Linda pulled out one full page from the Sunday newspaper. If the left half was numbered A4 and the right half was numbered A15, how many pages were in the A section of the newspaper?

9. Determine which of the following numbers is larger.

$$1993 \times (1 + 2 + 3 + 4 + \cdots + 1994)$$
$$1994 \times (1 + 2 + 3 + 4 + \cdots + 1993)$$

10. You have five identical coins and a balance scale. One of these coins is counterfeit and either heavier or lighter than the other four. Explain how the counterfeit can be identified and whether it is lighter or heavier than the others with only three weighings on the balance scale. (HINT: Solve a simpler problem—Given just three coins, can you find the counterfeit in two weighings?)

11. Would you rather work for a month (30 days) and get paid 1 million dollars or be paid 1 cent the first day, 2 cents the second day, 4 cents the third day, 8 cents the fourth day, and so on? Explain.

12. Find the perimeters and then complete the table.

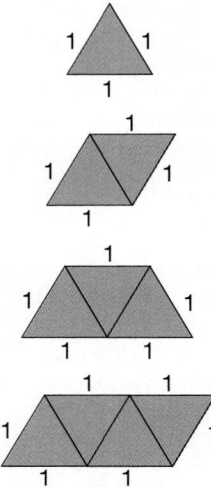

Number of Triangles	1	2	3	4	5	6	10		n
Perimeter							40		

13. Your rectangular garden, which has whole-number dimensions, has an area of 72 square feet. However, you have absentmindedly forgotten the actual dimensions. If you want to fence the garden, what possible lengths of fence might be needed?

14. If you place a 1 in front of the number 5, the new number is 3 times as large as the original number.
   (a) Find another number (not necessarily a one-digit number) such that when you place a 1 in front of it, the result is 3 times as large as the original number.
   (b) Find a number such that when you place a 1 in front of it, the result is 5 times as large as the original number. Can you find more than one such number?
   (c) Find a number such that when you place a 2 in front of it, the result is 6 times as large as the original number. Can you find more than one such number?
   (d) Find a number such that when you place a 3 in front of it, the result is 5 times as large as the original number. Can you find more than one such number?

15. New lockers are being installed in a school and will be numbered from 0001 to 1000. Stick-on digits will be used to number the lockers. A custodian must calculate the number of packages of numbers to order. How many 0s will be needed to complete the task? How many 9s?

16. The integers greater than 1 are arranged as shown.

	2	3	4	5
9	8	7	6	
	10	11	12	13
17	16	15	14	

·   ·   ·

   (a) In which column will 100 fall?
   (b) In which column will 1000 fall?
   (c) How about 1999?
   (d) How about 99,997?

17. How many equilateral triangles of all sizes are there in the $3 \times 3 \times 3$ equilateral triangle shown here?

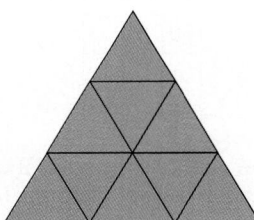

18. How many cubes are in the 100th collection of cubes in this sequence?

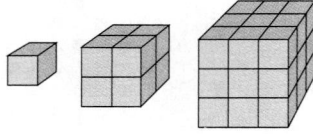

19. The Fibonacci sequence is 1, 1, 2, 3, 5, 8, 13, 21, . . . , where each successive number is the sum of the preceding two: for example, $13 = 5 + 8$, $21 = 8 + 13$, and so on. Observe the following pattern.

$$1^2 + 1^2 = 1 \times 2$$
$$1^2 + 1^2 + 2^2 = 2 \times 3$$
$$1^2 + 1^2 + 2^2 + 3^2 = 3 \times 5$$

Write out six more terms of the Fibonacci sequence and use the sequence to predict what $1^2 + 1^2 + 2^2 + 3^2 + \cdot \ \cdot \ \cdot + 144^2$ is without actually computing the sum. Then use your calculator to check your result.

20. Write out 16 terms of the Fibonacci sequence and observe the following pattern.

$$1 + 2 = 3$$
$$1 + 2 + 5 = 8$$
$$1 + 2 + 5 + 13 = 21$$

Use the pattern you observed to predict the sum

$$1 + 2 + 5 + 13 + \cdots + 610$$

without actually computing the sum. Then use your calculator to check your result.

21. Pascal's triangle is where each entry other than a 1 is obtained by adding the two entries in the row above it.

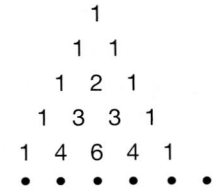

(a) Find the sums of the numbers on the diagonals in Pascal's triangle as are indicated in the following figure.

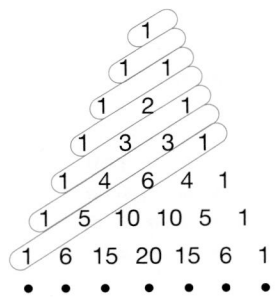

(b) Predict the sums along the next three diagonals in Pascal's triangle without actually adding the entries. Check your answers by adding entries on your calculator.

22. Answer the following questions about Pascal's triangle (see Problem 21).
(a) In the triangle shown below, one number, namely 3, and the six numbers immediately surrounding it, are encircled.

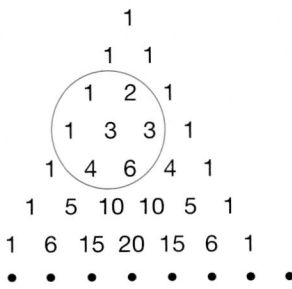

Find the sum of the encircled seven numbers.
(b) Extend Pascal's triangle by adding a few rows. Then draw several more circles anywhere in the triangle like the one shown in part (a). Explain how the sums obtained by adding the seven numbers inside the circle are related to one of the numbers outside the circle.

23. The pilot of a small plane must make a round trip between points A and B, which are 300 miles apart. The plane has an airspeed of 150 mph, and the pilot wants to make the trip in the minimum length of time. This morning there is a tailwind of 50 mph blowing from A to B and therefore a headwind of 50 mph from B to A. However, the weather forecast is for no wind tomorrow. Should the pilot make the trip today and take advantage of the tailwind in one direction or should the pilot wait until tomorrow assuming that there will be no wind at all? That is, on which day will travel time be shorter?

24. Consider the following sequence of shapes. The sequence starts with one square. Then at each step squares are attached around the outside of the figure, one square per exposed edge in the figure.

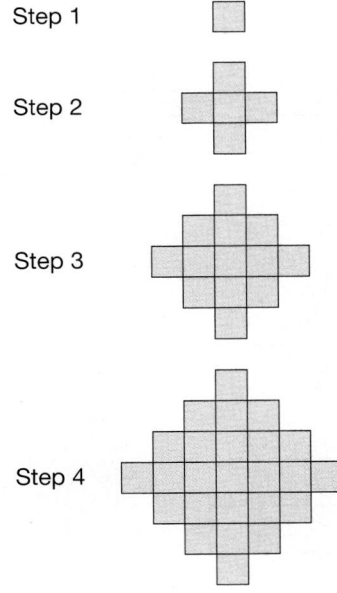

(a) Draw the next two figures in the sequence.
(b) Make a table listing the number of unit squares in the figure at each step. Look for a pattern in the number of unit squares. (HINT: Consider the number of squares attached at each step.)
(c) Based on the pattern you observed, predict the number of squares in the figure at step 7. Draw the figure to check your answer.

(d) How many squares would there be in the 10th figure? In the 20th figure? In the 50th figure?

25. In a dart game, only 4 points or 9 points can be scored on each dart. What is the largest score that it is *not* possible to obtain? (Assume that you have an unlimited number of darts.)

26. If the following four figures are referred to as stars, the first one is a three-pointed star and the second one is a six-pointed star. (NOTE: If this pattern of constructing a new equilateral triangle on each side of the existing equilateral triangle is continued indefinitely, the resulting figure is called the **Koch curve** or **Koch snowflake**.)

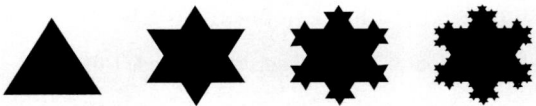

(a) How many points are there in the third star?
(b) How many points are there in the fourth star?

PROBLEM SET 1.2—PART B

1. Find the missing term in each pattern.
(a) 10   17   _____   37   50   65
(b) $1 \quad \dfrac{3}{2} \quad \text{_____} \quad \dfrac{7}{8} \quad \dfrac{9}{16}$
(c) 243   324   432   _____   768
(d) 234   _____   23,481   234,819   2,248,200

2. Sketch a figure that is next in each sequence.
(a)

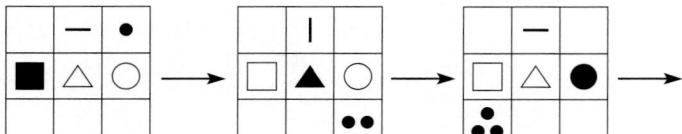

(b)

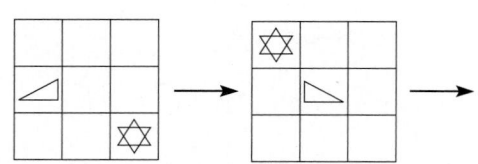

3. While only 19 years old, Carl Friedrich Gauss proved in 1796 that *every* positive integer is the sum of at the most three triangular numbers (see Problem 6 in Part A).
(a) Express each of the numbers 25 to 35 as a sum of no more than three triangular numbers.
(b) Express the numbers 74, 81, and 90 as sums of no more than three triangular numbers.

4. The **rectangular numbers** are whole numbers that are represented by certain rectangular arrays of dots. The first five rectangular numbers are shown.

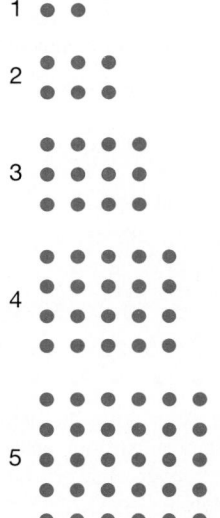

(a) Complete the following table and look for a pattern.

Number	Number of Dots (Rectangular Numbers)
1	2
2	6
3	
4	
5	
6	

(b) Make a sketch to represent the seventh rectangular number.

(c) How many dots will be in the tenth rectangular number?

(d) Is there a rectangular number that has 380 dots in its shape? If so, which one?

(e) Write a formula for the number of dots in the nth rectangular number.

(f) What is the connection between triangular numbers (see Problem 6 in Part A) and rectangular numbers?

5. The **pentagonal numbers** are whole numbers that are represented by pentagonal shapes. The first four pentagonal numbers are shown.

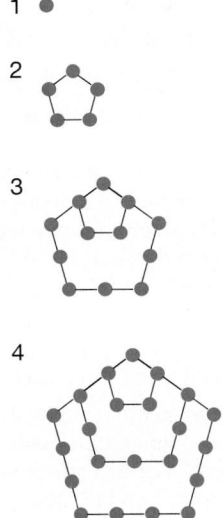

(a) Complete the following table and look for a pattern.

Number	Number of Dots (Pentagonal Numbers)
1	1
2	5
3	
4	
5	

(b) Make a sketch to represent the fifth pentagonal number.

(c) How many dots will be in the ninth pentagonal number?

(d) Is there a pentagonal number that has 200 dots in its shape? If so, which one?

(e) Write a formula for the number of dots in the nth pentagonal number.

6. Consider the following products. Use your calculator to verify that the statements are true.

$$1 \times (1) = 1^2$$
$$121 \times (1 + 2 + 1) = 22^2$$
$$12321 \times (1 + 2 + 3 + 2 + 1) = 333^2$$

Predict the next line in the sequence of products. Use your calculator to check your answer.

7. Consider the following process.

1. Choose a whole number.
2. Add the squares of the digits of the number to get a new number.
3. Repeat step 2 several times.

(a) Apply the procedure described to the numbers 12, 13, 19, 21, and 127.

(b) What pattern do you observe as you repeat the steps over and over?

(c) Check your answer for part (b) with a number of your choice.

8. What is the smallest number of whole-number gram weights needed to weigh any whole-number amount from 1 to 12 grams on a balance scale? How about from 1 to 37 grams? What is the most you can weigh using six weights in this way?

9. How many triangles are in the picture?

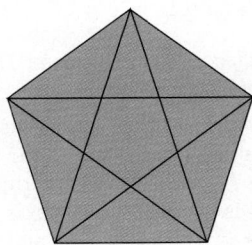

10. A **cevian** is a line segment that joins a vertex of a triangle and a point on the opposite side. How many triangles are formed if eight cevians are drawn from one vertex of a triangle?

11. (a) How many cubes of all sizes are in a $2 \times 2 \times 2$ cube composed of eight $1 \times 1 \times 1$ cubes?

(b) How many cubes of all sizes are in an $8 \times 8 \times 8$ cube composed of 512 $1 \times 1 \times 1$ cubes?

12. What is the smallest number that can be expressed as the sum of two squares in two different ways? (You may use one square twice.)

13. How many cubes are in the 10th collection of cubes in this sequence?

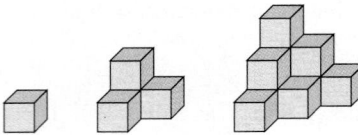

14. The 2×2 array of numbers $\begin{bmatrix} 4 & 5 \\ 5 & 6 \end{bmatrix}$ has a sum of 4×5, and the 3×3 array $\begin{bmatrix} 6 & 7 & 8 \\ 7 & 8 & 9 \\ 8 & 9 & 10 \end{bmatrix}$ has a sum of 9×8.

(a) What will be the sum of the similar 4×4 array starting with 7?

(b) What will be the sum of a similar 100×100 array starting with 100?

15. The Fibonacci sequence was defined to be the sequence $1, 1, 2, 3, 5, 8, 13, 21, \ldots$, where each successive number is the sum of the preceding two. Observe the following pattern.

$$1 + 1 = 3 - 1$$
$$1 + 1 + 2 = 5 - 1$$
$$1 + 1 + 2 + 3 = 8 - 1$$
$$1 + 1 + 2 + 3 + 5 = 13 - 1$$

Write out six more terms of the Fibonacci sequence and use the sequence to predict the answer to

$$1 + 1 + 2 + 3 + 5 + \cdots + 144$$

without actually computing the sum. Then use your calculator to check your result.

16. Write out 16 terms of the Fibonacci sequence.

(a) Notice that the fourth term in the sequence (called F_4) is odd: $F_4 = 3$. The sixth term in the sequence (called F_6) is even: $F_6 = 8$. Look for a pattern in the terms of the sequence and describe which terms are even and which are odd.

(b) Which of the following terms of the Fibonacci sequence are even and which are odd: F_{38}, F_{51}, F_{150}, F_{200}, F_{300}?

(c) Look for a pattern in the terms of the sequence and describe which terms are divisible by 3.

(d) Which of the following terms of the Fibonacci sequence are multiples of 3: F_{48}, F_{75}, F_{196}, F_{379}, F_{1000}?

17. Write out 16 terms of the Fibonacci sequence and observe the following pattern.

$$1 + 3 = 5 - 1$$
$$1 + 3 + 8 = 13 - 1$$
$$1 + 3 + 8 + 21 = 34 - 1$$

Use the pattern you observed to predict the answer to

$$1 + 3 + 8 + 21 + \cdots + 377$$

without actually computing the sum. Then use your calculator to check your result.

18. Answer the following for Pascal's triangle.

(a) In the following triangle, six numbers surrounding a central number, 4, are circled. Compare the products of alternate numbers moving around the circle; that is, compare $3 \cdot 1 \cdot 10$ and $6 \cdot 1 \cdot 5$.

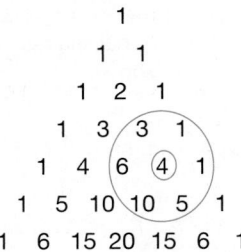

(b) Extend Pascal's triangle by adding a few rows. Then draw several more circles like the one shown in part (a) anywhere in the triangle. Find the products as described in part (a). What patterns do you see in the products?

19. A certain type of gutter comes in 6-foot, 8-foot, and 10-foot sections. How many different lengths of gutter can be formed using three sections of guttering?

20. Consider the sequence of shapes shown in the following figure. The sequence starts with one triangle. Then at each step, triangles are attached to the outside of the preceding figure, one triangle per exposed edge.

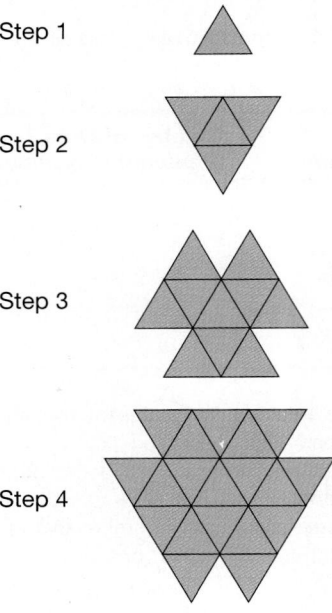

Step 1

Step 2

Step 3

Step 4

(a) Draw the next two figures in the sequence.

(b) Make a table listing the number of triangles in the figure at each step. Look for a pattern in the number of triangles. (HINT: Consider the number of triangles added at each step.)

(c) Based on the pattern you observed, predict the number of triangles in the figure at step 7. Draw the figure to check your answer.

(d) How many triangles would there be in the 10th figure? In the 20th figure? In the 50th figure?

21. The heights of five famous man-made structures are related as follows.

1. The height of the Statue of Liberty is 65 feet more than half the height of the Great Pyramid at Giza.
2. The height of the Eiffel Tower is 36 feet more than three times the height of Big Ben.
3. The Great Pyramid at Giza is 164 feet taller than Big Ben.
4. The Leaning Tower of Pisa is 137 feet shorter than Big Ben.
5. The total of all of the heights is nearly half a mile. In fact, the sum of the five heights is 2264 feet.

Find the height of each of the five structures.

22. (a) How many equilateral triangles of all sizes are in a $6 \times 6 \times 6$ equilateral triangle similar to the one in Problem 17 of Part A?

(b) How many would be in an $8 \times 8 \times 8$ equilateral triangle?

23. Prove or disprove: In any set of four consecutive Fibonacci numbers, the difference of the squares of the middle pair equals the product of the end pair.

24. Can an 8×8 checkerboard with two opposite corner squares removed be exactly covered (without cutting) by thirty-one 2×1 dominoes? Give details.

25. What fraction of the square region is shaded? Assume that the pattern of shading continues forever.

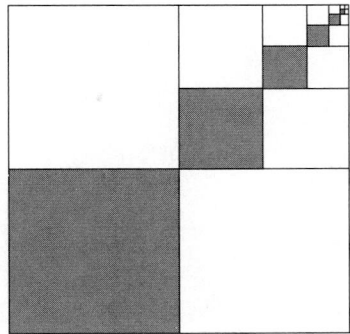

26. Refer to the following figures to answer the questions. (NOTE: If this pattern is continued indefinitely, the resulting figure is called the **Sierpinski triangle** or the **Sierpinski gasket**.)

(a) How many black triangles are there in the fourth figure?

(b) How many white triangles are there in the fourth figure?

(c) If the pattern is continued, how many black triangles are there in the nth figure?

(d) If the pattern is continued, how many white triangles are there in the nth figure?

SOLUTION OF INITIAL PROBLEM

Place the whole numbers 1 through 9 in the circles in the triangle so that the sum of the numbers on each side is 17.

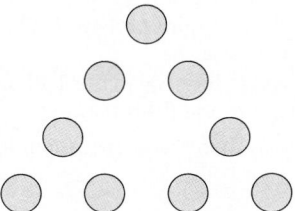

Strategy: Guess and Test

Having solved a simpler problem in this chapter, you might easily be able to conclude that 1, 2, and 3 must be in the corners. Then the remaining six numbers, 4, 5, 6, 7, 8, and 9, must produce three pairs of numbers whose sums are 12, 13, and 14. The only two possible solutions are as shown.

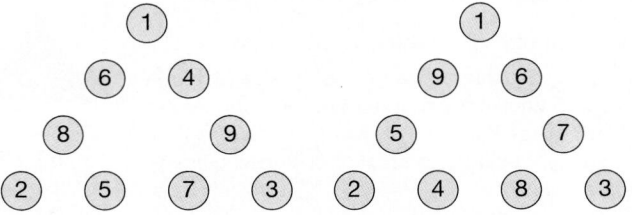

SOLUTIONS FOR ADDITIONAL PROBLEMS

Guess and Test 6

1. $s = 1, u = 3, n = 6, f = 9, w = 0, i = 7, m = 2$
2. $0 = (4 - 4) + (4 - 4)$
   $1 = (4 + 4) \div (4 + 4)$
   $2 = (4 \div 4) + (4 \div 4)$
   $3 = (4 + 4 + 4) \div 4$
   $4 = 4 + 4 \times (4 - 4)$
   $5 = (4 \times 4 + 4) \div 4$
   $6 = ((4 + 4) \div 4) + 4$
   $7 = 4 + 4 - (4 \div 4)$
   $8 = ((4 \times 4) \div 4) + 4$
   $9 = 4 + 4 + (4 \div 4)$
   There are many other possible answers.
3.

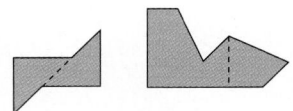

Use a Variable 9

1. $(2m + 1) + (2m + 3) + (2m + 5) + (2m + 7) + (2m + 9) = 10m + 25 = 5(2m + 5)$
2. 20 kilograms
3. 10°, 80°, 90°

Draw a Picture 11

1. 5
2. Yes; make one cut, then lay the logs side by side for the second cut.
3. 12

Look for a Pattern 18

1. 7
2. Square numbers
3. (a) 224; 406; 518   **(b)** 71
   (c) The sum is seven times the middle number.

Make a List 21

1. 48, 36, 33, 32, 24, 21, 20, 18, 17, 16, 12, 9, 8, 6, 5, 4, 3, 2, 1, 0
2. 204
3. 446

Solve a Simpler Problem 22

1. $\dfrac{1023}{1024}$
2. 377
3. 190

WRITING/DISCUSSING FOR UNDERSTANDING

1. Find a problem you want to spend time solving, making sure it *is* a problem for you, not an exercise. Then begin to solve the problem, writing down all of your steps and writing down your insights into the problem as they occur to you. Also, write down the things you say to yourself as you solve the problem. Focus on your approach to the problem, the strategies you use, and how you are feeling about your success with the problem. The goal here is for you to learn about your own problem-solving process, not necessarily to find the solution to the problem at this time.
2. Select six problems from this chapter's problem sets, one for each of the strategies. Identify the clue that led you to select the strategy you used and explain how the clue was useful.
3. Select three problems from this chapter's problem sets. Using the "Look Back" step, for each of the three problems construct two new problems that are extensions or minor modifications of the original problems.

4. Suppose that you were developing a two-week unit on problem solving to teach to sixth-grade students. How would you introduce the unit to motivate the students? What strategies would you include and in what order? What kinds of problems would you emphasize? What difficulties do you anticipate students would have, and how might you minimize those difficulties?

5. Explain how the following NCTM Standards contained in the Connections to School Mathematics section near the end of the book are reflected in this chapter.

- Use problem-solving approaches to investigate and understand mathematical content.
- Develop and apply a variety of strategies to solve problems, with emphasis on multistep and nonroutine problems.
- Verify and interpret results with respect to the original problem situation.
- Recognize and apply deductive and inductive reasoning.

PROJECTS

1. The Fibonacci sequence discussed in Section 1.2 shows up in some surprising places. The sequence has application in plant and animal growth patterns, musical scales, proportions in art and architecture, computer science, and other areas. Find out how the Fibonacci sequence is related to at least one of these areas and discuss your findings in writing. Be sure to include diagrams and/or pictures, where appropriate.

2. Examine an elementary school textbook series and describe its approach to problem solving.

CHAPTER REVIEW

Major Ideas

1. Problem solving should be one of your major goals when learning and teaching mathematics.

2. Pólya's four-step process is an excellent organizational tool to help promote successful problem solving. These four steps are
   (a) Understand the problem.
   (b) Devise a plan.
   (c) Carry out the plan.
   (d) Look back.

3. Problems, especially applied problems, involve several steps, as illustrated in the following diagram.

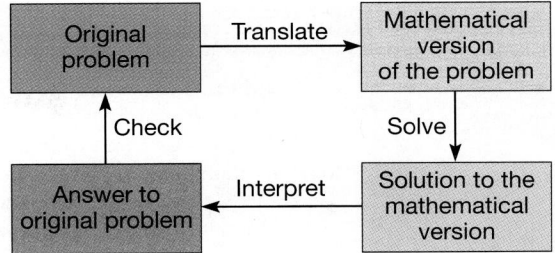

4. Problem-solving strategies are an important ingredient in successful problem-solving. You should always consider various possible strategies as you plan to solve any problem. The strategies introduced in this chapter were

(a) Guess and test.   **(b)** Use a variable.
(c) Draw a picture.   **(d)** Look for a pattern.
(e) Make a list.   **(f)** Solve a simpler problem.

The clues listed for each strategy help in deciding which strategy to use.

SECTION 1.1:   THE PROBLEM-SOLVING PROCESS AND STRATEGIES

Vocabulary/Notation

Ideas

Using the strategies Guess and Test 5, Use a Variable 8, and Draw a
  Picture 10 to solve problems

SECTION 1.2:   THREE ADDITIONAL STRATEGIES

Vocabulary/Notation

Ideas

Using the strategies Look for a Pattern 17, Make a List 20, and Solve
  a Simpler Problem 22 to solve problems

PEOPLE IN MATHEMATICS

Carl Friedrich Gauss (1777–1855), according to the historian E. T. Bell, "lives everywhere in mathematics." His contributions to geometry, number theory, and analysis were deep and wide-ranging. Yet he also made crucial contributions in applied mathematics. When the tiny planet Ceres was discovered in 1800, Gauss developed a technique for calculating its orbit, based on meager observations of its direction from earth at several known times. Gauss contributed to the modern theory of electricity and magnetism, and with the physicist W. E. Weber constructed one of the first practical electric telegraphs. In 1807 he became director of the astronomical observatory at Gottingen, where he served until his death. At age 18, Carl devised a method for constructing a 17-sided regular polygon, using only compass and straightedge. Remarkably, he then derived a general rule that predicted which regular polygons are likewise constructible.

Sophie Germain (1776–1831), as a teenager in Paris, discovered mathematics by reading books from her father's library. At age 18, Sophie wished to attend the prestigious Ecole Polytechnique in Paris, but women were not admitted. So she studied from classroom notes supplied by sympathetic male colleagues, and began submitting written work using the pen name Antoine LeBlanc. This work won her high praise, and eventually she was able to reveal her true identity. Sophie is noted for her theory of the vibration patterns of elastic plates, and for her proof of Fermat's last theorem in some special cases. Of Sophie Germain, Carl Gauss wrote, "When a woman, because of her sex, encounters infinitely more obstacles than men . . . yet overcomes these fetters and penetrates that which is most hidden, she doubtless has the most noble courage, extraordinary talent, and superior genius."

CHAPTER 1 TEST

1. Explain the difference between an "exercise" and a "problem."

2. List the four steps of Pólya's problem-solving process.

3. List the six problem-solving strategies you have learned in this chapter.

   For each of the following problems, read the problem carefully and solve it. Identify the strategy you used.

4. Can you rearrange the 16 numbers in this 4 × 4 array so that each row, each column, and each of the two diagonals total 10? How about a 2 × 2 array containing two 1s and two 2s? How about the corresponding 3 × 3 array?

1	1	1	1
2	2	2	2
3	3	3	3
4	4	4	4

5. In three years, Chad will be three times my *present* age. I will then be half as old as he. How old am I now?

6. There are six baseball teams in a tournament. The teams are lettered A through F. Each team plays each of the other teams twice. How many games are played altogether?

7. A fish is 30 inches long. The head is as long as the tail.

If the head was twice as long and the tail was its present length, the body would be 18 inches long. How long is each portion of the fish?

8. The Orchard brothers always plant their apple trees in square arrays, like those illustrated.

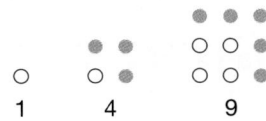

This year they planted 31 more apple trees in their square orchard than last year. If the orchard is still square, how many apple trees are there in the orchard this year?

2

Sets, Whole Numbers, and Numeration

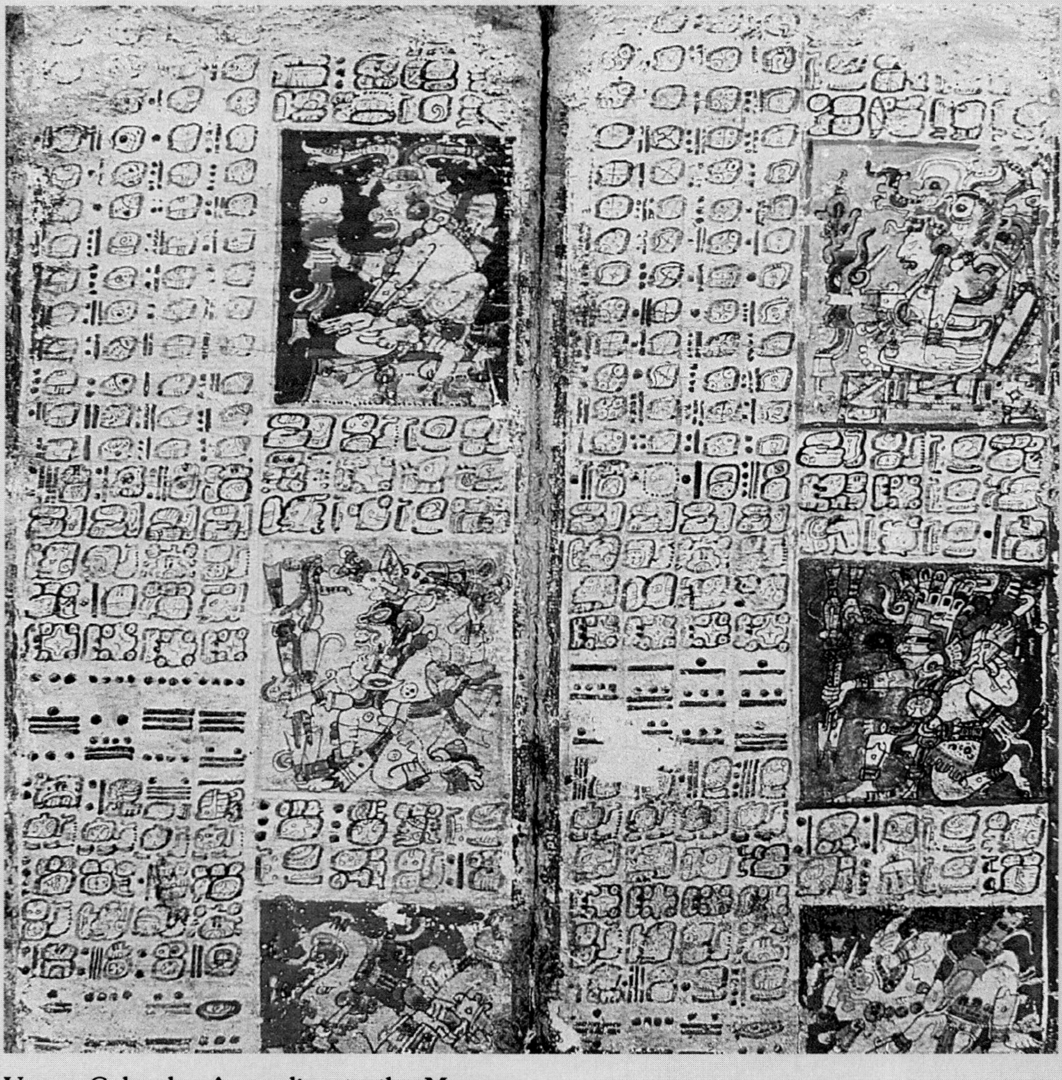

Venus Calendar According to the Mayans

The Mayan Numeration System

The Maya people lived mainly in southeastern Mexico, including the Yucatan Peninsula, and in much of northwestern Central America, including Guatemala and parts of Honduras and El Salvador. Earliest archaeological evidence of the Maya civilization dates to 9000 B.C., with the principal epochs of the Maya cultural development occurring between 2000 B.C. and A.D. 1700.

Knowledge of arithmetic and calendrical and astronomical matters was more highly developed by the ancient Maya than by any other New World peoples. Their numeration system was simple, yet sophisticated. Their system utilized three basic numerals: a dot, •, to represent one; a horizontal bar, —, to represent five; and a conch shell, ⬭, to represent zero. They used these three symbols, in combination, to represent the numbers 0 through 19 as illustrated.

0	1	2	3	4
5	6	7	8	9
10	11	12	13	14
15	16	17	18	19

For numbers greater than 19, they initially used a base 20 system. That is, they grouped in twenties and displayed their numerals vertically. Three Mayan numerals are shown together with their values in our system and the place values initially used by the Mayans on the right.

		•	8000 $(=20^3)$
	••	• •	400 $(=20^2)$
•	⬭	•••	20
⬭	•	—	1
20	806	10871	

The sun, and hence the solar calendar, was very important to the Maya. They calculated that a year consisted of 365.2420 days. (Present calculations measure our year as 365.2422 days long.) At some point, the Maya decided to incorporate their chronological count into their mathematical system. Since 360 had convenient factors and was close to 365 days in their year and 400 in their numeration system, they changed their place values from 1, 20, 20^2, 20^3, and so on, to 1, 20, $20 \cdot 18$ (= 360), $20^2 \cdot 18$ (= 7200), $20^3 \cdot 18$ (= 144,000), and so on. Interestingly, the Maya could record all the days of their history simply by using the place values through 144,000. The Maya were also able to use larger numbers. One Mayan hieroglyphic text recorded a number equivalent to 1,841,641,600. Finally, the Maya, famous for their hieroglyphic writing, also used the 20 ideograms pictured here, called head variants, to represent the numbers 0 to 19. The Mayan numeration system is studied in this chapter.

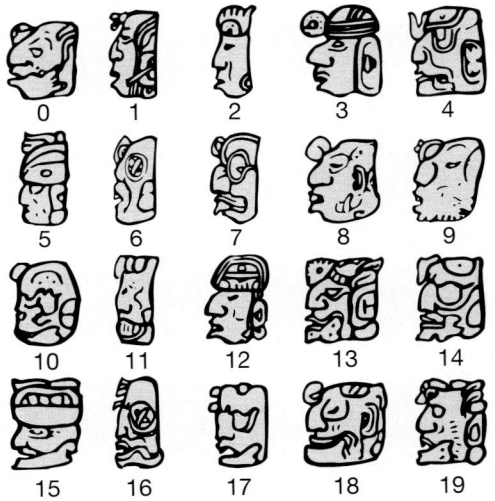

0   1   2   3   4
5   6   7   8   9
10 11 12 13 14
15 16 17 18 19

PROBLEM-SOLVING STRATEGIES

1. Guess and Test
2. Use a Variable
3. Draw a Picture
4. Look for a Pattern
5. Make a List
6. Solve a Simpler Problem
7. *Draw a Diagram*

STRATEGY 7: DRAW A DIAGRAM

Often there are problems where, although it is not necessary to draw an actual picture to represent the problem situation, a diagram that represents the essence of the problem is useful. For example, if we wish to determine the number of times two heads can turn up when we toss two coins, we could literally draw pictures of all possible arrangements of two coins turning up heads or tails. However, in practice, a simple tree diagram like the following one suffices.

Outcomes when two
coins are tossed

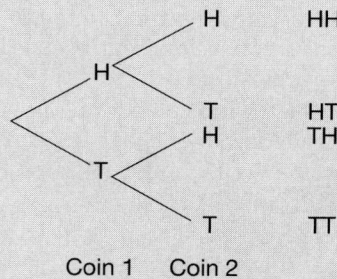

Coin 1   Coin 2

This diagram shows that there is one way to obtain two heads out of four possible outcomes. Another type of diagram is helpful in solving the next problem.

Initial Problem

A survey was taken of 150 college freshmen. Forty of them were majoring in mathematics, 30 of them were majoring in English, 20 were majoring in science, 7 had a double major of mathematics and English, and none had a double (or triple) major with science. How many students had majors other than mathematics, English, or science?

Clues

The Draw a Diagram strategy may be appropriate when:

• The problem involves sets, ratios, or probabilities.
• An actual picture can be drawn, but a diagram is more efficient.
• Representing relationships among quantities.

A solution of the Initial Problem above appears on page 88.

INTRODUCTION

Much of elementary school mathematics is devoted to the study of numbers. Children first learn to count using the **natural numbers** or **counting numbers** 1, 2, 3, . . . (the **ellipsis**, or three periods, means "and so on"). This chapter develops the ideas that lead to the concepts central to the system of **whole numbers** 0, 1, 2, 3, . . . (the counting numbers together with zero) and the symbols that are used to represent them. First, the notion of a one-to-one correspondence between two sets is shown to be the idea central to the formation of the concept of number. Then operations on sets are discussed. These operations form the foundation of addition, subtraction, multiplication, and division of whole numbers. Finally, the Hindu–Arabic numeration system, our system of symbols that represent numbers, is presented after its various attributes are introduced by considering other ancient numeration systems.

2.1

SETS AS A BASIS FOR WHOLE NUMBERS

Sets

A collection of objects is called a **set** and the objects are called **elements** or **members** of the set. Sets can be defined in three common ways: (1) a verbal description, (2) a listing of the members separated by commas, with braces ("{" and "}") used to enclose the list of elements, and (3) **set-builder notation**. For example, the verbal description "the set of all states in the United States that border the Pacific Ocean" can be represented in the other two ways as follows:

1. *Listing*: {Alaska, California, Hawaii, Oregon, Washington}.
2. *Set-builder*: $\{x \mid x$ is a U.S. state that borders the Pacific Ocean}. (This set-builder notation is read: "The set of all x such that x is a U.S. state that borders the Pacific Ocean.")

Sets are usually denoted by capital letters such as A, B, C, and so on. The symbols "$\in$" and "$\notin$" are used to indicate that an object is or is not an element of a set, respectively. For example, if S represents the set of all U.S. states bordering the Pacific, then Alaska $\in S$ and Michigan $\notin S$. The set without elements is called the **empty set** (or **null set**) and is denoted by { } or the symbol $\varnothing$. The set of all U.S. states bordering Antarctica is the empty set.

Two sets A and B are **equal**, written $A = B$, if and only if they have precisely the same elements. Thus $\{x \mid x$ is a state that borders Lake Michigan} = {Illinois, Indiana, Michigan, Wisconsin}. Notice that two sets, A and B, are equal if every element of A is in B, and vice versa. If A does not equal B, we write $A \neq B$.

There are two inherent rules regarding sets: (1) the same element is not listed more than once within a set, and (2) the order of the elements in a set is immaterial. Thus, by rule 1, the set $\{a, a, b\}$ would be written as $\{a, b\}$ and by rule 2, $\{a, b\} = \{b, a\}$, $\{x, y, z\} = \{y, z, x\}$, and so on.

The concept of a 1-1 correspondence, read "one-to-one correspondence," is needed to formalize the meaning of a whole number.

Definition

One-to-One Correspondence

A **1-1 correspondence** between two sets A and B is a pairing of the elements of A with the elements of B so that each element of A corresponds to exactly one element of B, and vice versa. If there is a 1-1 correspondence between sets A and B, we write $A \sim B$ and say that A and B are **equivalent** or **match**.

Figure 2.1 shows two 1-1 correspondences between two sets A and B.

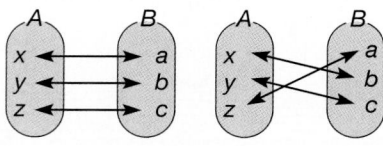

FIGURE 2.1

There are four other possible 1-1 correspondences between A and B. Notice that equal sets are always equivalent, since each element can be matched with itself, but that equivalent sets are not necessarily equal. For example, $\{1, 2\} \sim \{a, b\}$, but $\{1, 2\} \neq \{a, b\}$. The two sets $A = \{a, b\}$ and $B = \{a, b, c\}$ are not equivalent. However, they do satisfy the relationship defined next.

Definition

Subset of a Set: $A \subseteq B$

Set A is said to be a **subset** of B, written $A \subseteq B$, if and only if *every element of A is also an element of B.*

The set consisting of New Hampshire is a subset of the set of all New England states and $\{a, b, c\} \subseteq \{a, b, c, d, e, f\}$. Since every element in a set A is in A, $A \varnothing \subseteq A$ for all sets A. Also, $\{a, b, c\} \not\subseteq \{a, b, d\}$ because c is in the set $\{a, b, c\}$ but not in the set $\{a, b, d\}$. Using similar reasoning, you can argue that $\varnothing \subseteq A$ for any set A since it is impossible to find an element in $\varnothing$ that is not in A.

If $A \subseteq B$ and B has an element that is not in A, we write $A \subset B$ and say that A is a **proper subset** of B. Thus $\{a, b\} \subset \{a, b, c\}$, since $\{a, b\} \subseteq \{a, b, c\}$ and c is in the second set *but* not in the first.

Circles or other closed curves are used in **Venn diagrams** (named after the English logician John Venn) to illustrate relationships between sets. These circles are usually pictured within a rectangle, U, where the rectangle represents the **universal set** or **universe**, the set comprised of all elements being considered in a particular discussion. Figure 2.2 displays sets A and B inside a universal set U. Set A is comprised of everything inside circle A, and set B is comprised of everything inside circle B, including set A. Hence

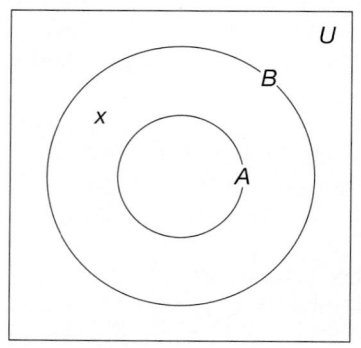

FIGURE 2.2

A is a *proper* subset of *B* since $x \in B$, but $x \notin A$. The idea of proper sub-set will be used later to help establish the meaning of the concept "less than" for whole numbers.

Operations on Sets

Two sets *A* and *B* that have no elements in common are called **disjoint sets**. The sets {*a, b, c*} and {*d, e, f*} are disjoint, whereas {*x, y*} and {*y, z*} are not disjoint, since *y* is an element in both sets. Two disjoint sets are pictured in Figure 2.3.

There are many ways to construct a new set from two or more sets. The following operations on sets will be very useful in clarifying our under-standing of whole numbers and their operations.

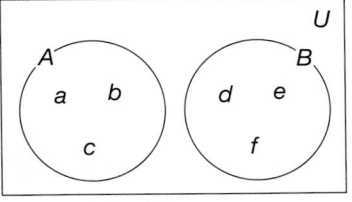

FIGURE 2.3

Definition

Union of Sets: *A* ∪ *B*

The **union** of two sets *A* and *B*, written **A ∪ B**, is the set which con-sists of all elements that belong either to *A* or to *B* (or to both).

Informally, $A \cup B$ is formed by putting all the elements of *A* and *B* to-gether. The next example illustrates this definition.

EXAMPLE 2.1   Find the union of the given pairs of sets.
(a) {*a, b*} ∪ {*c, d, e*}
(b) {1, 2, 3, 4, 5} ∪ ∅
(c) {*m, n, q*} ∪ {*m, n, p*}

Solution
(a) {*a, b*} ∪ {*c, d, e*} = {*a, b, c, d, e*}
(b) {1, 2, 3, 4, 5} ∪ ∅ = {1, 2, 3, 4, 5}
(c) {*m, n, q*} ∪ {*m, n, p*} = {*m, n, p, q*}   ■

NOTE: The small solid square (■) is used to mark the end of an example or mathematical argument.

Notice that although *m* is a member of both sets in Example 2.1(c), it is listed only once in the union of the two sets. The union of sets *A* and *B* is displayed in a Venn diagram by shading the portion of the diagram that rep-resents $A \cup B$ (Figure 2.4). The notion of set union is the basis for the ad-dition of whole numbers, but only when disjoint sets are used. Notice how the sets in Example 2.1(a) can be used to show that $2 + 3 = 5$.

Another useful set operation is the intersection of sets.

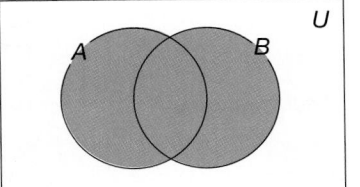

Shaded region is *A* ∪ *B*

FIGURE 2.4

Definition

Intersection of Sets: *A* ∩ *B*

The **intersection** of sets *A* and *B*, written **A ∩ B**, is the set of all ele-ments common to sets *A and B*.

Thus $A \cap B$ is the set of elements shared by A and B. Example 2.2 illustrates this definition.

EXAMPLE 2.2   Find the intersection of the given pairs of sets.
(a) $\{a, b, c\} \cap \{b, d, f\}$
(b) $\{a, b, c\} \cap \{a, b, c\}$
(c) $\{a, b\} \cap \{c, d\}$

Solution
(a) $\{a, b, c\} \cap \{b, d, f\} = \{b\}$ since b is the only element in both sets.
(b) $\{a, b, c\} \cap \{a, b, c\} = \{a, b, c\}$ since a, b, c are in both sets.
(c) $\{a, b\} \cap \{c, d\} = \varnothing$ since there are no elements common to the given two sets.   ■

Figure 2.5 displays $A \cap B$. Observe that two sets are disjoint if and only if their intersection is the empty set. Figure 2.3 shows a Venn diagram of two sets whose intersection is the empty set.

Often there are situations where, instead of considering elements of a set A, it is more productive to consider all elements in the universal set *other than* those in A. This set is defined next.

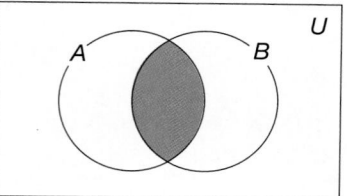

Shaded region is $A \cap B$.

FIGURE 2.5

> **Definition**
>
> ### Complement of a Set: $\overline{A}$
>
> The **complement** of a set A, written $\overline{A}$, is the set of all elements in the universe, U, that are *not* in A.

The set $\overline{A}$ is shaded in Figure 2.6.

EXAMPLE 2.3   Find the following sets.
(a) $\overline{A}$ where $U = \{a, b, c, d\}$ and $A = \{a\}$
(b) $\overline{B}$ where $U = \{1, 2, 3, . . .\}$ and $B = \{2, 4, 6, . . .\}$
(c) $\overline{A \cup B}$ and $\overline{A \cap B}$ where $U = \{1, 2, 3, 4, 5\}$, $A = \{1, 2, 3\}$, and $B = \{3, 4\}$

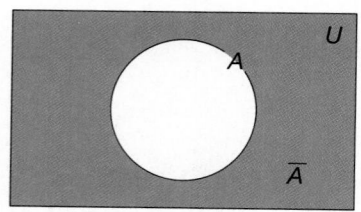

Shaded region is $\overline{A}$.

FIGURE 2.6

Solution
(a) $\overline{A} = \{b, c, d\}$
(b) $\overline{B} = \{1, 3, 5, . . .\}$
(c) $\overline{A \cup B} = \overline{\{4, 5\} \cup \{1, 2, 5\}} = \{1, 2, 4, 5\}$
(d) $\overline{A \cap B} = \overline{\{3\}} = \{1, 2, 4, 5\}$ ■

The next set operation forms the basis for subtraction.

> **Definition**
>
> ### Difference of Sets: $A - B$
>
> The **set difference** (or **relative complement**) of set B from set A, written $A - B$, is the set of all elements in A that are *not* in B.

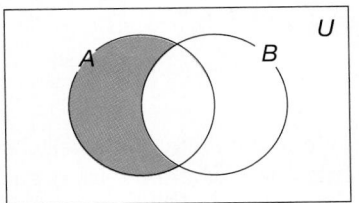

Shaded region is $A - B$.

FIGURE 2.7

In set-builder notation, $A - B = \{x \mid x \in A \text{ and } x \notin B\}$. Also, as can be seen in Figure 2.7, $A - B$ can be viewed as $A \cap \overline{B}$. Example 2.4 provides some examples of the difference of one set from another.

EXAMPLE 2.4   Find the difference of the given pairs of sets.
(a) $\{a, b, c\} - \{b, d\}$
(b) $\{a, b, c\} - \{e\}$
(c) $\{a, b, c, d\} - \{b, c, d\}$

Solution
(a) $\{a, b, c\} - \{b, d\} = \{a, c\}$
(b) $\{a, b, c\} - \{e\} = \{a, b, c\}$
(c) $\{a, b, c, d\} - \{b, c, d\} = \{a\}$ ■

In Example 2.4(c), the second set is a subset of the first. These sets can be used to show that $4 - 3 = 1$.

Another way of combining two sets to form a third set is called the Cartesian product. The Cartesian product, named after the French mathematician René Descartes, forms the basis of whole-number multiplication and is also useful in probability and geometry. To define the Cartesian product, we need to have the concept of ordered pair. An **ordered pair**, written (a, b), is a pair of elements where one of the elements is designated as first (a in this case) and the other is second (b here). The notion of an ordered pair differs from that of simply a set of two elements because of the preference in order. For example, $\{1, 2\} = \{2, 1\}$, *as sets*, because they have the same elements. But $(1, 2) \neq (2, 1)$, *as ordered pairs*, since the order of the elements is different. In fact, two ordered pairs (a, b) and (c, d) are equal if and only if $a = c$ and $b = d$.

Definition

Cartesian Product of Sets: $A \times B$

The **Cartesian product** of set A with set B, written $A \times B$ and read "A cross B," is the set of all ordered pairs (a, b), where $a \in A$ and $b \in B$.

In set-builder notation, $A \times B = \{(a, b) \mid a \in A \text{ and } b \in B\}$.

EXAMPLE 2.5   Find the Cartesian product of the given pairs of sets.
(a) $\{x, y, z\} \times \{m, n\}$ **(b)** $\{7\} \times \{a, b, c\}$

Solution
(a) $\{x, y, z\} \times \{m, n\} = \{(x, m), (x, n), (y, m), (y, n), (z, m), (z, n)\}$
(b) $\{7\} \times \{a, b, c\} = \{(7, a), (7, b), (7, c)\}$ ■

Notice that when finding a Cartesian product, all possible pairs are formed where the first element comes from the first set and the second element comes from the second set. Also observe that in part (a) of Example 2.5, there are three elements in the first set, two in the second, and six in their Cartesian product, and that $3 \times 2 = 6$. Similarly, in part (b), these sets can be used to find the whole-number product $1 \times 3 = 3$.

Finite and Infinite Sets

There are two broad categories of sets: finite and infinite. Informally, a set is **finite** if it is empty or can have its elements listed (where the list eventually ends), and a set is **infinite** if it goes on without end. A little more formally, a set is finite if (1) it is empty or (2) it can be put into a 1-1 correspondence with a set of the form $\{1, 2, 3, \ldots , n\}$, where n is a counting number. On the other hand, a set is infinite if it is *not* finite.

EXAMPLE 2.6   Determine if the following sets are finite or infinite.
(a) $\{a, b, c\}$ **(b)** $\{1, 2, 3, \ldots\}$ **(c)** $\{2, 4, 6, \ldots , 20\}$

Solution
(a) $\{a, b, c\}$ is finite since it can be matched with the set $\{1, 2, 3\}$.
(b) $\{1, 2, 3, \ldots\}$ is an infinite set.
(c) $\{2, 4, 6, \ldots , 20\}$ is a finite set since it can be matched with the set $\{1, 2, 3, \ldots , 10\}$. (Here, the ellipsis means to continue the pattern until the last element is reached.) ∎

An interesting property of *every* infinite set is that it can be matched with a proper subset of itself. For example, consider the following 1-1 correspondence:

$$A = \{1, 2, 3, 4, \ldots , n, \ldots\}$$
$$\updownarrow \ \updownarrow \ \updownarrow \ \updownarrow \qquad \updownarrow$$
$$B = \{2, 4, 6, 8, \ldots , 2n, \ldots\}$$

Note that $B \subset A$ and that each element in A is paired with exactly one element in B, and vice versa. Notice that matching n with $2n$ indicates that we never "run out" of elements from B to match with the elements from set A. Thus an alternative definition is that a set is infinite if it is equivaient to a proper subset of itself. In this case, a set is finite if it is not infinite.

MATHEMATICAL MORSEL

There are several theories concerning the rationale behind the shapes of the 10 digits in our Hindu–Arabic numeration system. One is that the number represented by each digit is given by the number of angles in the original digit. Count the "angles" in each digit below. (Here an "angle" is less than 180°.) Of course, zero is round, so it has no angles.

EXERCISE/PROBLEM SET 2.1—PART A

Exercises

1. Indicate the following sets by the listing method.
   (a) Whole numbers between 5 and 9
   (b) Even counting numbers less than 15
   (c) Even counting numbers less than 151
   (d) Whole numbers greater than 8
   (e) Odd whole numbers less than 100
   (f) Whole numbers less than 0

2. True or false?
   (a) $7 \in \{6, 7, 8, 9\}$
   (b) $\frac{2}{3} \in \{1, 2, 3\}$
   (c) $5 \notin \{2, 3, 4, 6\}$
   (d) $1 \notin \{0, 1, 2\}$
   (e) $\{1, 2, 3\} \subseteq \{1, 2, 3\}$
   (f) $\{4, 3\} \subset \{2, 3, 4\}$
   (g) $\{1, 2, 5\} \subset \{1, 2, 5\}$
   (h) $\varnothing \subseteq \{\ \}$
   (i) $\{2\} \nsubseteq \{1, 2\}$
   (j) $\{1, 2\} \nsubseteq \{2\}$

3. List all the subsets of $\{a, b, c\}$.

4. List the proper subsets of $\{\bigcirc, \triangle\}$.

5. Find four 1-1 correspondences between A and B other than the two given in Figure 2.1.

6. Draw a Venn diagram like the following one for each part. Then shade each Venn diagram to represent each of the sets indicated.

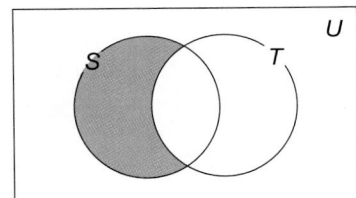

   (a) $\overline{S}$
   (b) $\overline{S} \cap T$
   (c) $\overline{S} \cup \overline{T}$

7. Draw Venn diagrams that represent sets A and B as described below.
   (a) $A \subset B$
   (b) $A \cap B = \varnothing$
   (c) $A \cap B \neq \varnothing$

8. Let $A = \{a, b, c\}$, $B = \{b, c\}$, and $C = \{e\}$. Find each of the following.
   (a) $A \cap B$
   (b) $B \cup C$
   (c) $A - B$

9. Let $W = \{$women who have won Nobel prizes$\}$, $A = \{$Americans who have won Nobel prizes$\}$, and $C = \{$winners of the Nobel prize in chemistry$\}$. Describe the elements of the following sets.
   (a) $W \cup A$
   (b) $W \cap A$
   (c) $A \cap C$

10. Given $A = \{0, 1, 2, 3, 4, 5\}$, $B = \{0, 2, 4, 6, 8, 10\}$, and $C = \{0, 4, 8\}$, find each of the following.
    (a) $A \cup B$
    (b) $B \cup C$
    (c) $A \cap B$
    (d) $B \cap C$
    (e) $B - C$
    (f) $(A \cup B) - C$

11. Let $M =$ the set of the months of the year
    $J = \{$January, June, July$\}$
    $S = \{$June, July, August$\}$
    $W = \{$December, January, February$\}$
    List the members of each of the following.
    (a) $J \cup S$
    (b) $J \cap W$
    (c) $S \cap W$
    (d) $J \cap (S \cup W)$
    (e) $M - (S \cup W)$
    (f) $J - S$

12. (a) If $x \in X \cap Y$, is $x \in X \cup Y$? Justify your answer.
    (b) If $x \in X \cup Y$, is $x \in X \cap Y$? Justify your answer.

13. A Venn diagram can be used to illustrate more than two sets. Shade the regions that represent each of the following sets.
    (a) $A \cap (B \cap C)$
    (b) $A - (B \cap C)$
    (c) $A \cup (B - C)$

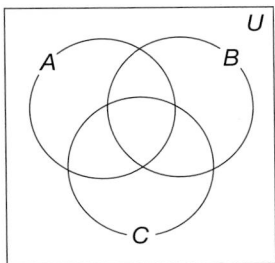

14. Represent the following shaded regions using the symbols A, B, C, $\cup$, $\cap$, and $-$.

    (a)

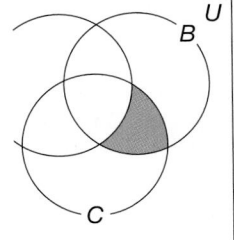

    (b)

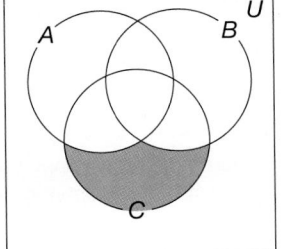

(c)

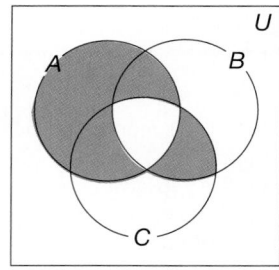

15. Let $A = \{3, 6, 9, 12, 15, 18, 21, 24, \ldots\}$ and $B = \{6, 12, 18, 24, \ldots\}$.
  (a) Is $B \subseteq A$?   **(b)** Find $A \cup B$.   **(c)** Find $A \cap B$.
  (d) In general, when $B \subseteq A$, what is true about $A \cup B$? About $A \cap B$?

16. In the drawing, C is the interior of the circle, T is the interior of the triangle, and R is the interior of the retangle. Copy the drawing on a sheet of paper and then shade in each of the following regions.

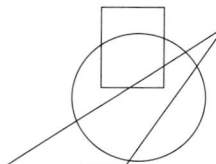

  (a) $C \cup T$ **(b)** $C \cap R$
  (c) $(C \cap T) \cup R$ **(d)** $(C \cup R) \cup T$
  (e) $(C \cap R) \cap T$ **(f)** $C \cap (R \cap T)$

17. Verify that $\overline{A \cup B} = \overline{A} \cap \overline{B}$ in two different ways as follows.
  (a) Let $U = \{1, 2, 3, 4, 5, 6\}$, $A = \{2, 3, 5\}$ and $B = \{1, 4\}$. List the elements of the sets $\overline{A \cup B}$ and $\overline{A} \cap \overline{B}$. Do the two sets have the same members?
  (b) Draw and shade a Venn diagram for each of the sets $\overline{A \cup B}$ and $\overline{A} \cap \overline{B}$. Do the two Venn diagrams look the same?
  NOTE: The equation $\overline{A \cup B} = \overline{A} \cap \overline{B}$ is one of two laws called **DeMorgan's laws.**

18. Find the following Cartesian products.
  (a) $\{a\} \times \{b, c\}$ **(b)** $\{5\} \times \{a, b, c\}$
  (c) $\{a, b\} \times \{1, 2, 3\}$ **(d)** $\{2, 3\} \times \{1, 4\}$
  (e) $\{a, b, c\} \times \{5\}$ **(f)** $\{1, 2, 3\} \times \{a, b\}$

19. Determine how many ordered pairs will be in the following sets.
  (a) $\{1, 2, 3, 4\} \times \{a, b\}$
  (b) $\{m, n, o\} \times \{1, 2, 3, 4\}$

20. If A has two members, how many members does B have when $A \times B$ has the following number of members?
  (a) 4   **(b)** 8   **(c)** 9   **(d)** 50   **(e)** 0   **(f)** 23
  If an answer is not possible, explain why.

21. The Cartesian product, $A \times B$, is given in each part below. Find A and B.
  (a) $\{(a, 2), (a, 4), (a, 6)\}$
  (b) $\{(a, b), (b, b), (b, a), (a, a)\}$

22. True or false?
  (a) $\{(4, 5), (6, 7)\} = \{(6, 7), (4, 5)\}$
  (b) $\{(a, b), (c, d)\} = \{(b, a), (c, d)\}$
  (c) $\{(4, 5), (7, 6)\} = \{(7, 6), (5, 4)\}$
  (d) $\{(a, c), (d, b)\} = \{a, c, d, b\}$
  (e) $\{(c, d), (a, b)\} = \{(c, a), (d, b)\}$

23. Determine which of the following sets are finite. For those sets that are finite, how many elements are in the set?
  (a) {ears on a typical elephant}
  (b) $\{1, 2, 3, \ldots, 99\}$
  (c) $\{0, 1, 2, 3, \ldots, 200\}$
  (d) Set of points belonging to a line segment
  (e) Set of points belonging to a circle

Problems

24. **(a)** If X has five elements and Y has three elements, what is the greatest number of elements possible in $X \cap Y$? In $X \cup Y$?
  (b) If X has x elements and Y has y elements with x greater than or equal to y, what is the greatest number of elements possible in $X \cap Y$? In $X \cup Y$?

25. How many different one-to-one correspondences are possible between $A = \{1, 2, 3, 4\}$ and $B = \{a, b, c, d\}$?

26. How many subsets does a set with the following number of members have?
  (a) 0   **(b)** 1   **(c)** 2   **(d)** 3   **(e)** 5   **(f)** n

27. If it is possible, give examples of the following. If it is not possible, explain why.
  (a) Two sets that are not equal but are equivalent
  (b) Two sets that are not equivalent but are equal

28. **(a)** When does $D \cap E = D$?
  (b) When does $D \cup E = D$?
  (c) When does $D \cap E = D \cup E$?

29. Carmen has eight skirts and seven blouses. Show how the concept of Cartesian product can be used to determine how many different outfits she has.

30. How many matches are there if 32 participants enter a single-elimination tennis tournament (one loss eliminates a participant)?

31. A poll of 100 registered voters designed to find out how voters kept up with current events revealed the following facts.

  65 watched the news on television.
  39 read the newspaper.
  39 listened to radio news.
  20 watched TV news and read the newspaper.
  27 watched TV news and listened to radio news.

9 read the newspaper and listened to radio news.
6 watched TV news, read the newspaper, and listened to radio news.

(a) How many of the 100 people surveyed kept up with current events by some means other than the three sources listed above?

(b) How many of the 100 people surveyed read the paper but did *not* watch TV news?

(c) How many of the 100 people surveyed used only one of the three sources listed to keep up with current events?

32. At a convention of 375 butchers (*B*), bakers (*A*), and candlestick makers (*C*), there were

50 who were both *B* and *A* but not *C*
70 who were *B* but neither *A* nor *C*
60 who were *A* but neither *B* nor *C*
40 who were both *A* and *C* but not *B*
50 who were both *B* and *C* but not *A*
80 who were *C* but neither *A* nor *B*

How many at the convention were *A*, *B*, and *C*?

33. Can you show a 1-1 correspondence between the points on base $\overline{AB}$ of the given triangle and the points on the two sides $\overline{AC}$ and $\overline{CB}$? Explain how or why you cannot.

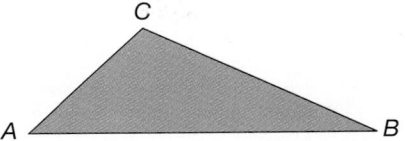

34. Can you show a 1-1 correspondence between the points on chord $\overline{AB}$ and the points on arc $\overparen{ACB}$? Explain how you can or why you cannot.

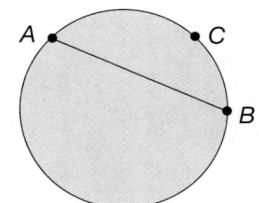

EXERCISE/PROBLEM SET 2.1—PART B

Exercises

1. Represent the following sets using set-builder notation.
(a) {0, 2, 4, . . . , 12}   **(b)** {1, 4, 9, 16, 25, . . .}
(c) {0, 1, 2}   **(d)** ∅

2. Which of the following sets are equal to {4, 5, 6}?
(a) {5, 6}
(b) {5, 4, 6}
(c) Whole numbers greater than 3
(d) Whole numbers less than 7
(e) Whole numbers greater than 3 or less than 7
(f) Whole numbers greater than 3 and less than 8
(g) {e, f, g}
(h) {4, 5, 6, 5}

3. Write a set that is equivalent to, but not equal to, the set {a, b, c, d, e, f}.

4. List all subsets of {○, △, □}. Which are proper subsets?

5. How many proper subsets does $R = \{r, s, t, u, v\}$ have?

6. Show three different 1-1 correspondences between {1, 2, 3, 4} and {x, y, z, w}.

7. Let $A = \{1, 2, 3, 4, 5\}$, $B = \{3, 4, 5\}$, and $C = \{4, 5, 6\}$. In the following, insert ∈, ⊂, ⊆, or ⊄ to make a true statement.
(a) 2 _____ A   **(b)** B _____ A
(c) C _____ B   **(d)** 6 _____ C
(e) A _____ A   **(f)** B ∩ C _____ A

8. Let $A = \{0, 10, 20, 30, . . .\}$ and $B = \{5, 15, 25, 35, . . .\}$. Decide which of the following are true and which are false. Explain your answers.
(a) A equals B.
(b) B is equivalent to A.
(c) A is a proper subset of B.
(d) B is equivalent to a proper subset of A.
(e) There is a proper subset of B that is equivalent to a proper subset of A.

9. Let $R = \{a, b, c\}$, $S = \{c, d, e, f\}$, $T = \{x, y, z\}$. List the elements of the following sets.
(a) $R \cup S$ **(b)** $R \cap S$ **(c)** $R \cup T$
(d) $R \cap T$ **(e)** $S \cup T$ **(f)** $S \cap T$

10. Find each of the following differences.
(a) {h, i, j, k} − {k}
(b) {○, △, /, □} − {△, □}
(c) {3, 10, 13} − { }
(d) {0, 1, 2, . . .} − {12, 13, 14, . . .}
(e) {people} − {married people}
(f) {two-wheeled vehicles} − {two-wheeled vehicles that are not bicycles}
(g) {0, 2, 4, 6, . . . , 20} − {12, 14, 16, 18, 20}
(h) {a, b, c, d} − { }

11. Draw a Venn diagram like the following for each part. Then shade each Venn diagram to represent each of the sets indicated.

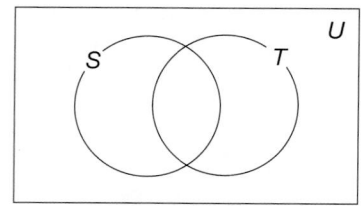

(a) $T - S$
(b) $(S - T) \cup (T - S)$
(c) $(S - T) \cap (T - S)$

12. If A is the set of all sophomores in a school and B is the set of students who belong to the orchestra, describe the following sets in words.
(a) $A \cup B$ (b) $A \cap B$ (c) $A - B$ (d) $B - A$

13. In each of the following cases, find $B - A$.
(a) $A \cap B = \varnothing$ (b) $A = B$ (c) $B \subseteq A$

14. Let $A = \{a, b, c, d, e\}$, $B = \{c, d, e, f, g\}$, and $C = \{a, e, f, h\}$. List the members of each set.
(a) $A \cup B$ (b) $A \cap B$
(c) $(A \cup B) \cap C$ (d) $A \cup (B \cap C)$

15. Let $A = \{50, 55, 60, 65, 70, 75, 80\}$
    $B = \{50, 60, 70, 80\}$
    $C = \{60, 70, 80\}$
    $D = \{55, 65\}$
List the members of each set.
(a) $A \cup (B \cap C)$
(b) $(A \cup B) \cap C$
(c) $(A \cap C) \cup (C \cap D)$
(d) $(A \cap C) \cap (C \cup D)$
(e) $(B - C) \cap A$
(f) $(A - D) \cap (B - C)$

16. A Venn diagram like the following one can be used to illustrate more than two sets. Shade regions that represent the sets indicated.

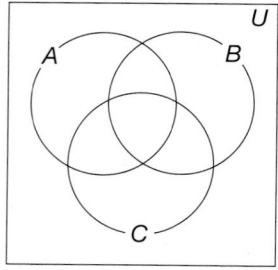

(a) $(A \cup B) \cap C$
(b) $\overline{A} \cap (\overline{B} \cap \overline{C})$
(c) $(A \cup B) - (B \cap C)$

17. Represent the following shaded regions using the symbols A, B, C, $\cup$, $\cap$, and $-$.

(a)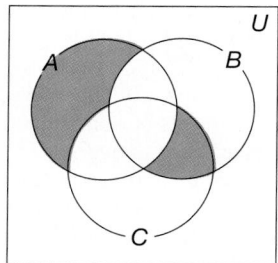

(b)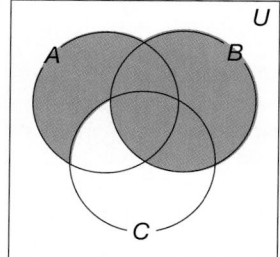

(c)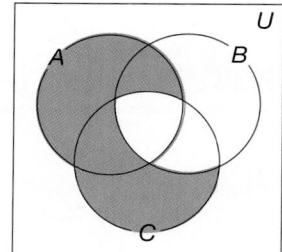

18. Use Venn diagrams to determine which, if any, of the following statements are true for all sets A, B, and C.
(a) $A \cup (B \cup C) = (A \cup B) \cup C$
(b) $A \cup (B \cap C) = (A \cup B) \cap C$
(c) $A \cap (B \cap C) = (A \cap B) \cap C$
(d) $A \cap (B \cup C) = (A \cap B) \cup C$

19. Verify that $\overline{A \cap B} = \overline{A} \cup \overline{B}$ in two different ways as follows.
(a) Let $U = \{2, 4, 6, 8, 10, 12, 14, 16\}$, $A = \{2, 4, 8, 16\}$, and $B = \{4, 8, 12, 16\}$. List the elements of the sets $\overline{A \cap B}$ and $\overline{A} \cup \overline{B}$. Do the two sets have the same members?
(b) Draw and shade a Venn diagram for each of the sets $\overline{A \cap B} = \overline{A} \cup \overline{B}$. Do the two Venn diagrams look the same?
NOTE: The equation $\overline{A \cap B} = \overline{A} \cup \overline{B}$ is one of the two laws called **DeMorgan's laws**.

20. Find the following Cartesian products.
(a) $\{a, b, c\} \times \{1\}$ (b) $\{1, 2\} \times \{p, q, r\}$
(c) $\{p, q, r\} \times \{1, 2\}$ (d) $\{a\} \times \{1\}$

21. Determine how many ordered pairs will be in $A \times B$ under the following conditions.
  (a) A has one member and B has four members.
  (b) A has two members and B has four members.
  (c) A has three members and B has seven members.

22. Find sets A and B so that $A \times B$ has the following number of members.
  (a) 1 **(b)** 2 **(c)** 3 **(d)** 4 **(e)** 5 **(f)** 6 **(g)** 7 **(h)** 0

23. The Cartesian product, $X \times Y$, is given in each part below. Find X and Y.
  (a) {$(b, c), (c, c)$}
  (b) {$(2, 1), (2, 2), (2, 3), (5, 1), (5, 2), (5, 3)$}

24. Show that the following sets are finite by giving the set of the form {1, 2, 3, . . . , n} that matches the given set.
  (a) {121, 122, 123, . . . , 139}
  (b) {1, 3, 5, . . . , 27}

25. Show that the following sets are infinite by matching each with a proper subset of itself.
  (a) {2, 4, 6, . . . , n, . . .}
  (b) {50, 51, 52, 53, . . . , n, . . .}

26. True or false?
  (a) The empty set is a subset of *every* set.
  (b) The set {105, 110, 115, 120, . . .} is an infinite set.
  (c) For all sets X and Y, either $X \subseteq Y$ or $Y \subseteq X$.
  (d) If A is an infinite set and $B \subseteq A$, then B also is an infinite set.
  (e) For all finite sets A and B, if $A \cap B = \varnothing$, then the number of elements in $A \cup B$ equals the number of elements in A plus the number of elements in B.

Problems

27. How many 1-1 correspondences are there between the following pairs of sets?
  (a) Two two-member sets
  (b) Two four-member sets
  (c) Two six-member sets
  (d) Two sets each having m members

28. Find sets (when possible) satisfying each of the following conditions.
  (a) Number of elements in A plus number of elements in B is greater than number of elements in $A \cup B$.
  (b) Number of elements in I plus number of elements in J is less than number of elements in $I \cup J$.
  (c) Number of elements in E plus number of elements in F equals number of elements in $E \cup F$.
  (d) Number of elements in G plus number of elements in K equals number of elements in $G \cap K$.

29. Your house can be painted in a choice of seven exterior colors and 15 interior colors. Assuming that you choose only one color for the exterior and one color for the interior, how many different ways of painting your house are there?

30. A university professor asked his class of 42 students when they studied for his class the previous weekend. Their responses were as follows.

  9 said they studied on Friday.
  18 said they studied on Saturday.
  30 said they studied on Sunday.
  3 said they studied on both Friday and Saturday.
  10 said they studied on both Saturday and Sunday.
  6 said they studied on both Friday and Sunday.
  2 said they studied on Friday, Saturday, and Sunday.

  Assuming that all 42 students responded and answered honestly, answer the following questions.
  (a) How many students studied on Sunday but not on either Friday or Saturday?
  (b) How many students did all of their studying on one day?
  (c) How many students did not study at all for this class last weekend?

31. At an automotive repair shop, 50 cars were inspected. Suppose that 23 cars needed new brakes, and 34 cars needed new exhaust systems.
  (a) What is the least number of cars that could have needed both?
  (b) What is the greatest number of cars that could have needed both?
  (c) What is the greatest number of cars that could have needed neither?

32. If 70% of all students take science, 75% take social science, 80% take mathematics, and 85% take English, at least what percent take all four?

33. (a) Show a 1-1 correspondence between the points on the given circle and the triangle in which it is inscribed. Explain your procedure.

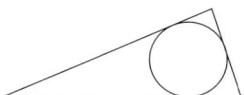

  (b) Show a 1-1 correspondence between the points on the given triangle and the circle that circumscribes it. Explain your procedure.

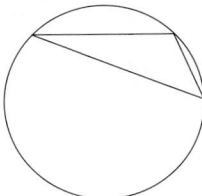

34. A schoolroom has 13 desks and 13 chairs. You want to arrange the desks and chairs so that each desk has a chair with it. How many such arrangements are there?

2.2

WHOLE NUMBERS AND NUMERATION

Numbers and Numerals

As mentioned earlier, the study of the set of whole numbers, $W = \{0, 1, 2, 3, 4, . . .\}$, is the foundation of elementary school mathematics. But what precisely do we mean by the whole number 3? A **number** is an idea, or an abstraction, that represents a quantity. The symbols that we see, write, or touch when representing numbers are called **numerals**. There are three common uses of numbers. The most common use of whole numbers is to describe how many elements are in a finite set. When used in this manner, the number is referred to as a **cardinal number**. A second use is concerned with order. For example, one may be second in line, or your team may be fourth in the standings. Numbers used in this way are called **ordinal numbers**. Finally, **identification numbers** are used to name such things as telephone numbers, bank account numbers, and social security numbers. In this case, the numbers are used in a numeral sense in that only the symbols, rather than their values, are important. Before discussing our system of numeration or symbolization, the concept of cardinal number will be considered.

What is the number 3? What do you think of when you see the sets in Figure 2.8? First, there are no common elements. One set is made up of

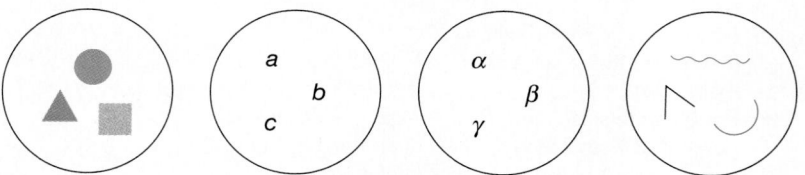

FIGURE 2.8

letters, one of shapes, one of Greek letters, and so on. Second, each set can be matched with every other set. Now imagine all the infinitely many sets that can be matched with these sets. Even though the sets will be made up of various elements, they will all share the common attribute that they are equivalent to the set $\{a, b, c\}$. The common *idea* that is associated with all of these equivalent sets is the number 3. That is, *the number three is the attribute common to all sets that match the set* $\{a, b, c\}$. Similarly, the whole number 2 is the common idea associated with all sets equivalent to the set $\{a, b\}$. All other nonzero whole numbers can be conceptualized in a similar manner. Zero is the idea, or number, one imagines when asked: "How many elements are in the empty set?"

Although the preceding discussion regarding the concept of a whole number may seem routine for you, there are many pitfalls for children who are learning the concept of numerousness for the first time. Chronologically, children first learn how to *say* the counting chant "one, two, three, ..." However, saying the chant and *understanding* the concept of number are not the same thing. Next, children must learn how to match the counting chant words they are saying with the objects they are counting.

For example, to count the objects in the set $\{\triangle, \bigcirc, \square\}$, a child must correctly assign the words "one, two, three" to the objects in a 1-1 fashion. Actually, children first learning to count objects fail this task in two ways: (1) they fail to assign a word to each object, hence their count is too small, or (2) they count one or more objects at least twice and end up with a number that is too large. To reach the final stage in understanding the concept of number, children must be able to observe several equivalent sets, as in Figure 2.8, and realize that when they count each set, they arrive at the same word. Thus this word is used to name the attribute common to all such sets.

The symbol **$n(A)$** is used to represent the **number of elements in a finite set** A. More precisely, (1) $n(A) = m$ if $A \sim \{1, 2, \ldots, m\}$, where m is a counting number, and (2) $n(\varnothing) = 0$. Thus

$n(\{a, b, c\}) = 3$ since $\{a, b, c\} \sim \{1, 2, 3\}$, and

$n(\{a, b, c, \ldots, z\}) = 26$

since $\{a, b, c, \ldots, z\} \sim \{1, 2, 3, \ldots, 26\}$,

and so on, for other finite sets.

Ordering Whole Numbers

Children may get their first introduction to ordering whole numbers through the counting chant "one, two, three, ..." For example, "two" is less than "five," since "two" comes before "five" in the counting chant.

A more meaningful way of comparing two whole numbers is to use 1-1 correspondences. We can say that 2 is less than 5, since any set with two elements matches a proper subset of any set with five elements (Figure 2.9). The general set formulation of "less than" follows.

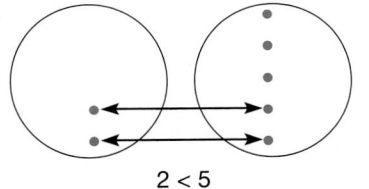

2 < 5

FIGURE 2.9

Definition

Ordering Whole Numbers

Let $a = n(A)$ and $b = n(B)$. Then $a < b$ (read "a **is less than** b") or $b > a$ (read "b **is greater than** a") if A is equivalent to a proper subset of B.

The "greater than" and "less than" signs can be combined with the equal sign to produce the following symbols: $a \leq b$ (a **is less than or equal to** b) and $b \geq a$ (b **is greater than or equal to** a).

A third common way of ordering whole numbers is through the use of the whole-number "line" (Figure 2.10). Actually, the **whole-number line** is a sequence of equally spaced marks where the numbers represented by the marks begin on the left with 0 and increase by one each time we move one mark to the right.

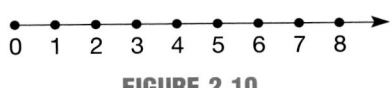

0 1 2 3 4 5 6 7 8

FIGURE 2.10

EXAMPLE 2.7   Determine the greater of the two numbers 3 and 8 in three different ways.

Solution

(a)   ***Counting Chant:*** One, two, *three,* four, five, six, seven, *eight.* Since "three" precedes "eight," eight is greater than three.

(b)   ***Set Method:*** Since a set with three elements can be matched with a proper subset of a set with eight elements, 3 < 8 and 8 > 3 [Figure 2.11(a)].

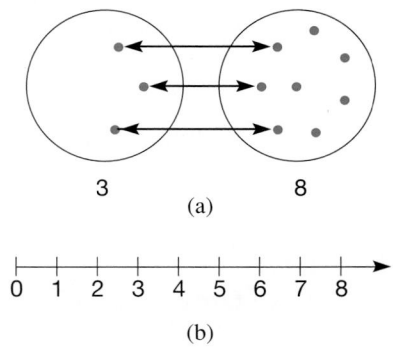

(a)

0 1 2 3 4 5 6 7 8

(b)

FIGURE 2.11

(c)   ***Whole-Number Line:*** Since 3 is to the left of 8 on the number line, 3 is less than 8 and 8 is greater than 3 [Figure 2.11(b)].   ■

Numeration Systems

To make numbers more useful, systems of symbols, or numerals, have been developed to represent numbers. In fact, throughout history, many different numeration systems have evolved. The following discussion reviews various ancient numeration systems with an eye toward identifying features of those systems that are incorporated in our present system, the Hindu–Arabic numeration system.

The Tally Numeration System

The **tally numeration system** is composed of single strokes, one for each object being counted (Figure 2.12).

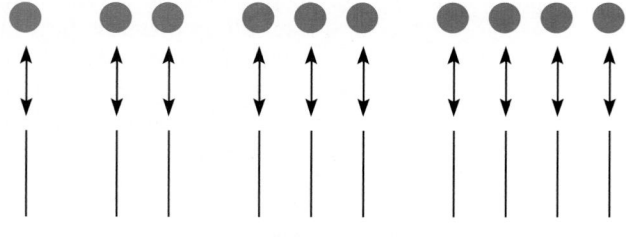

FIGURE 2.12

The next six such tally numerals are

An advantage of this system is its simplicity; however, two disadvantages are that (1) large numbers require many individual symbols, and (2) it is difficult to read the numerals for such numbers. For example, what number is represented by these tally marks?

The tally system was improved by the introduction of **grouping**. In this case, the fifth tally mark was placed across every four to make a group of five. Thus the last numeral above can be written as follows:

Grouping makes it easier to recognize the number being represented; in this case, there are 37 tally marks.

The Egyptian Numeration System

The **Egyptian numeration system**, which developed around 3400 B.C., involves grouping by ten. In addition, this system introduced new symbols for powers of ten (Figure 2.13).

Staff (one)	Heelbone (ten)	Scoll (hundred)	Lotus flower (thousand)	Pointing finger (ten thousand)	Fish (hundred thousand)	Astonished man (million)

FIGURE 2.13

Examples of some Egyptian numerals are shown in Figure 2.14. Notice how this system required far fewer symbols than the tally system once numbers greater than ten were represented. This system is also an **additive** system, since the values for the various individual numerals are added together.

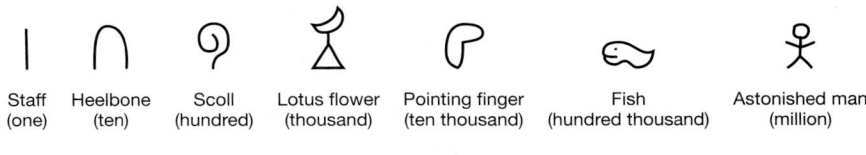

321   1034   1,120,013

FIGURE 2.14

Notice that the order in which the symbols are written is immaterial. A major disadvantage of this system is that computation is cumbersome. Figure 2.15 shows, in Egyptian numerals, the addition problem that we write as 764 + 598 = 1362. Here 51 individual Egyptian numerals are needed to express this addition problem, whereas our system requires only 10 numerals!

FIGURE 2.15

The Roman Numeration System

The **Roman numeration system**, which developed between 500 B.C. and A.D. 100, also uses grouping, additivity, and has many symbols. The basic Roman numerals are listed in Table 2.1.

TABLE 2.1

Roman Numeral	Value
I	1
V	5
X	10
L	50
C	100
D	500
M	1000

Roman numerals are made up of combinations of these basic numerals, as illustrated next.

CCLXXXI (equals 281)   MCVIII (equals 1108)

Notice that the values of these Roman numerals are found by adding the values of the various basic numerals. For example, MCVIII means $1000 + 100 + 5 + 1 + 1 + 1$, or 1108. Thus the Roman system is an additive system.

Two new attributes that were introduced by the Roman system were a subtractive principle and a multiplicative principle. Both of these principles allow the system to use fewer symbols to represent numbers. The **subtractive** principle permits simplifications using combinations of basic Roman numerals: IV (I to the left of V means five minus one) for 4 rather than using IIII, IX (ten minus one) for 9 instead of VIIII, XL for 40, XC for 90, CD for 400, and CM for 900 (Table 2.2). Thus, when reading from left to right, if the values of the symbols in any pair of symbols increase, group the pair together. The value of this pair, then, is the value of the larger numeral less the value of the smaller. To evaluate a complex Roman numeral, one looks to see if any of these subtractive pairs are present, groups them together mentally, and then adds values from left to right. For example,

in   MCMXLIV

think   M   CM   XL   IV,   which is $1000 + 900 + 40 + 4$.

Notice that without the subtractive principle, 14 individual Roman numerals would be required to represent 1944 instead of the seven numerals

TABLE 2.2

Roman Numeral	Value
IV	4
IX	9
XL	40
XC	90
CD	400
CM	900

used in MCMXLIV. Also, because of the subtractive principle, the Roman system is a **positional** system, since the position of a numeral can affect the value of the number being represented. For example, VI is six, whereas IV is four.

EXAMPLE 2.8   Express the following Roman numerals in our numeration system.
(a) MCCCXLIV   **(b)** MMCMXCIII   **(c)** CCXLIX

Solution
(a) *Think:* MCCC   XL   IV,   or $1300 + 40 + 4 = 1344$
(b) *Think:* MM   CM   XC   III,   or $2000 + 900 + 90 + 3 = 2993$
(c) *Think:* CC   XL   IX,   or $200 + 40 + 9 = 249$ ■

The Roman numeration system also utilized a horizontal bar above a numeral to represent 1000 times the number. For example, $\overline{V}$ meant 5 times 1000, or 5000; $\overline{XI}$ meant 11,000; and so on. Thus the Roman system was also a **multiplicative** system. Although expressing numbers using the Roman system requires fewer symbols than the Egyptian system, it still requires many more symbols than our current system and is cumbersome for doing arithmetic. In fact, the Romans used an abacus to perform calculations instead of paper/pencil methods as we do (see the Focus On for Chapter 3).

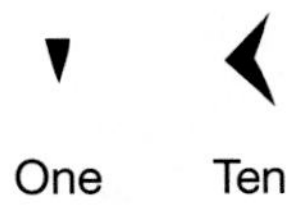

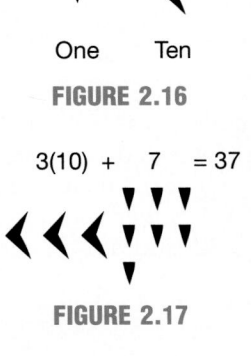

One   Ten

FIGURE 2.16

$3(10) + 7 = 37$

FIGURE 2.17

The Babylonian Numeration System

The **Babylonian numeration system**, which evolved between 3000 and 2000 B.C., used only two numerals, a one and a ten (Figure 2.16). For numbers up to fifty-nine, the system was simply an additive system. For example, 37 was written using three tens and seven ones (Figure 2.17). However, even though the Babylonian numeration system was developed about the same time as the simpler Egyptian system, the Babylonians used the sophisticated notion of **place value**, where symbols represent different values depending on the place in which they were written. This is another example of a positional system where the position of the individual numerals affects values. Figure 2.18 displays three Babylonian numerals that illustrate this place-value attribute, which was based on 60.

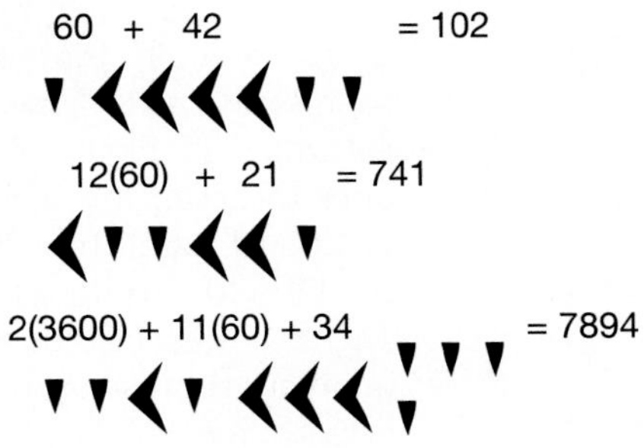

$60 + 42 = 102$

$12(60) + 21 = 741$

$2(3600) + 11(60) + 34 = 7894$

FIGURE 2.18

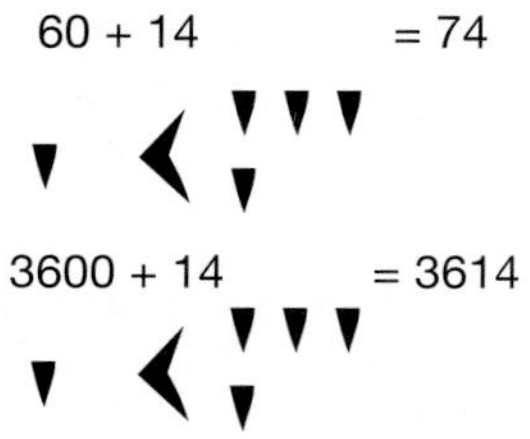

60 + 14   = 74

▼ ◀ ▼▼▼
     ▼

3600 + 14   = 3614

▼ ◀ ▼▼▼
     ▼

FIGURE 2.19

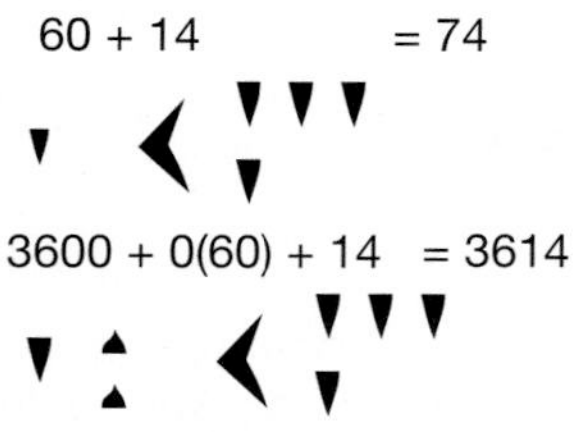

60 + 14   = 74

▼ ◀ ▼▼▼
     ▼

3600 + 0(60) + 14 = 3614

▼ ▲ ◀ ▼▼▼
  ▲   ▼

FIGURE 2.20

Unfortunately, in its earliest development, this system led to some confusion. For example, as illustrated in Figure 2.19, the numerals representing 74 $(= 1 \cdot 60 + 14)$ and 3614 $(= 1 \cdot 60 \cdot 60 + 0 \cdot 60 + 14)$ only differed in the spacing of symbols. Thus there was a chance for misinterpretation. From 300 B.C. on, a separate symbol made up of two small triangles arranged one above the other was used to serve as a **placeholder** to indicate a vacant place (Figure 2.20). This removed some of the ambiguity. However, two Babylonian tens written next to each other could still be interpreted as 20, or 610, or even 3660. Although their placeholder acts much like our zero, they did not recognize zero as a number.

EXAMPLE 2.9   Express the following Babylonian numerals in our numeration system.

(a) 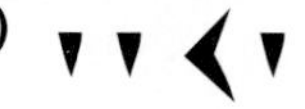 ▼▼ ◀ ▼   (b)  ▼ ▲ ▼   (c)  ◀◀ ▼ ◀ ▼▼▼
                                                          ▼▼

Solution

(a)  ▼▼ ◀ ▼

2(60) + 11 = 131

(b)  ▼ ▲ ▼
      ▲

3600 + 0(60) + 1 = 3601

(c)  ◀◀ ▼ ◀ ▼▼▼
              ▼▼

21(60) + 15 = 1275

The Mayan Numeration System

The **Mayan numeration system**, which developed between A.D. 300 and A.D. 900, was a vertical place value system, and it introduced a symbol for **zero**. The system used only three elementary numerals (Figure 2.21). Several Mayan numerals are shown in Figure 2.22 together with their respective values. The symbol for twenty in Figure 2.22 illustrates the use of

•   —   ◁⊕▷

one   five   zero

FIGURE 2.21

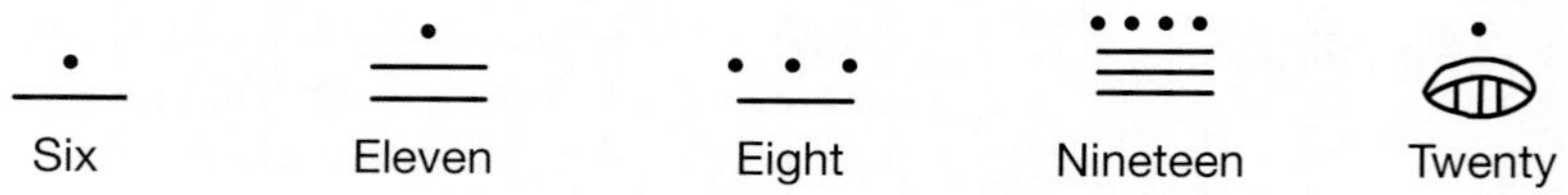

•	•	• • •	• • • •	•
—	═	—	═	◁⊕▷
			═	
Six	Eleven	Eight	Nineteen	Twenty

FIGURE 2.22

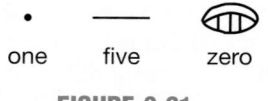

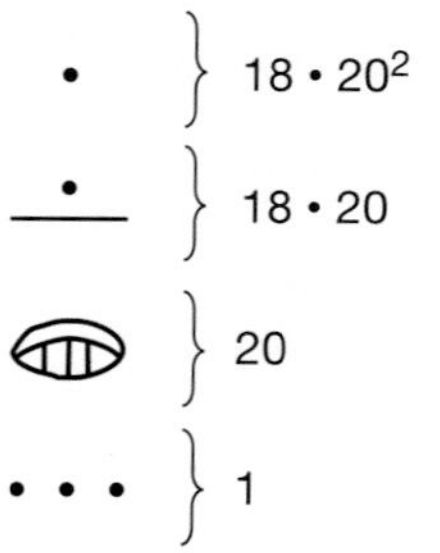

•   } 18 · 20²

—   } 18 · 20

◁⊕▷   } 20

• • •   } 1

FIGURE 2.23

place value in that the "dot" represents one "twenty" and the ◁⊕▷ represents zero "ones." The various place values for this system are illustrated in Figure 2.23. The bottom section represents the number of ones (3 here), the second section from the bottom represents the number of 20s (0 here), the third section from the bottom represents the number of 18 · 20s (6 here), and the top section represents the number of 18 · 20 · 20s (1 here). Reading from top to bottom, the value of the number represented is $1(18 \cdot 20 \cdot 20) + 6(18 \cdot 20) + 0(20) + 3(1)$, or 9363. (See the Focus On at the beginning of the chapter for additional insight into this system.)

Notice that in the Mayan numeration system, you must take great care in the way the numbers are spaced. For example, two horizontal bars could represent $5 + 5$ as ═ or $5 \cdot 20 + 5$ as ═, depending on how the two bars are spaced. Also notice that the place-value feature of this system is somewhat irregular. After the ones place comes the 20s place. Then comes the $18 \cdot 20$s place. Thereafter, though, the values of the places are increased by multiplying by 20 to obtain $18 \cdot 20^2$, $18 \cdot 20^3$, $18 \cdot 20^4$, and so on.

EXAMPLE 2.10   Express the following Mayan numerals in our numeration system.

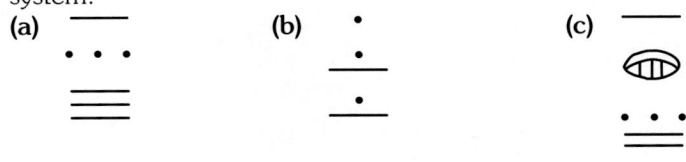

Solution

(a)
$$\left. \begin{array}{r} \text{———} \\ \bullet \ \bullet \ \bullet \\ \equiv \end{array} \right\} \begin{array}{l} 5 \cdot 20 \\ \\ + \ 18 \\ \hline 118 \end{array}$$

(b)
$$\left. \begin{array}{r} \bullet \\ \text{———} \\ \text{———} \\ \text{———} \end{array} \right\} \begin{array}{l} 1 \cdot 18 \cdot 20 \\ 6 \cdot 20 \\ + \quad\quad 6 \\ \hline \quad 486 \end{array}$$

(c)
$$\left. \begin{array}{r} \text{———} \\ \oval \\ \bullet \ \bullet \ \bullet \\ \equiv \end{array} \right\} \begin{array}{l} 5 \cdot 18 \cdot 20 \\ 0 \\ + \quad\quad 13 \\ \hline \quad 1813 \end{array}$$ ■

Table 2.3 summarizes the attributes of the number systems we have studied.

TABLE 2.3

System	Additive	Subtractive	Multiplicative	Positional	Place Valued	Has a Zero
Tally	Yes	No	No	No	No	No
Egyptian	Yes	No	No	No	No	No
Roman	Yes	Yes	Yes	Yes	No	No
Babylonian	Yes	No	Yes	Yes	Yes	No
Mayan	Yes	No	Yes	Yes	Yes	Yes

MATHEMATICAL MORSEL

When learning the names of two-digit numerals, some children suffer through a "reversals" stage, where they may write 21 for twelve or 13 for thirty-one. The following story from the December 5, 1990 *Grand Rapids* [Michigan] *Press* stresses the importance of eliminating reversals. "It was a case of mistaken identity. A transposed address that resulted in a bulldozer blunder. City orders had called for demolition on Tuesday of a boarded-up house at 451 Fuller Ave. S.E. But when the dust settled, 451 Fuller stood untouched. Down the street at 415 Fuller S.E., only a basement remained."

EXERCISE/PROBLEM SET 2.2—PART A

Exercises

1. In the following paragraph numbers are used in various ways. Specify whether each number is a cardinal number, an ordinal number, or an identification number.

Linda dialed *314-781-9804* to place an order with a popular mail-order company. When the sales representative answered, Linda told her that her customer number was *13905*. Linda then placed an order for *6* cotton tee shirts, stock number *7814,* from page *28* of the catalog. For an extra *$10* charge, Linda could have next-day delivery, but she chose the regular delivery system and was told her package would arrive November *20*.

2. Define each of the following numbers in a way similar to the way in which the number three was defined in this section. (HINT: You may decide "impossible.")
 (a) 7   **(b)** 1   **(c)** −3   **(d)** 0

3. Explain how to count the elements of the set

$$\{a, b, c, d, e, f\}$$

4. Which number is larger, 5 or 8? Which numeral is larger?

5. Determine the greater of the two numbers 4 and 9 in three different ways.

6. Use the definition of "less than" given in this section to explain why there are exactly five whole numbers that are less than 5.

7. Change to Egyptian numerals.
 (a) 9   **(b)** 23
 (c) 453   **(d)** 1231

8. Change to Roman numerals.
 (a) 76   **(b)** 49
 (c) 192   **(d)** 1741

9. Change to Babylonian numerals.
 (a) 47   **(b)** 76
 (c) 347   **(d)** 4192

10. Change to Mayan numerals.
 (a) 17   **(b)** 51
 (c) 275   **(d)** 401

11. Change to numerals we use.
 (a) ⟨▼▼   **(b)** ▼⟨▼⟨
 (c) ▼⟨▼⟨▼▼▼   **(d)** MCMXCI
 (e) CMLXXVI   **(f)** MMMCCXLV

(g) 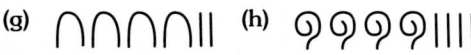 **(h)** ꝙꝙꝙꝙꝙ||||

(i) ♊♊♊∩ **(j)** ⠿

(k) ⠿ **(l)** ⠿

12. Perform each of the following numeral conversions.
 (a) Roman numeral DCCCXXIV to a Babylonian numeral

 (b) Mayan numeral $\frac{\bullet}{=}$ to a Roman numeral

 (c) Babylonian numeral  to a Mayan numeral

13. Imagine representing 246 in the Mayan, Babylonian, and Egyptian numeration systems.
 (a) In which system is the greatest number of symbols required?
 (b) In which system is the smallest number of symbols required?
 (c) Do your answers for parts (a) and (b) hold true for other numbers as well?

14. One system of numeration in Greece in about 300 B.C., called the Ionian system, was based on letters of the alphabet. The different symbols used for numbers less than 1000 are as follows.

$$\begin{array}{cccccccccccccc} \alpha & \beta & \gamma & \delta & \epsilon & \varsigma & \xi & \eta & \theta & \iota & \kappa & \lambda & \mu & \nu \\ 1 & 2 & 3 & 4 & 5 & 6 & 7 & 8 & 9 & 10 & 20 & 30 & 40 & 50 \end{array}$$

$$\begin{array}{ccccccccccc} \xi & o & \pi & \varrho & \rho & \sigma & \tau & \upsilon & \phi & \chi & \psi & \omega & \lambda \\ 60 & 70 & 80 & 90 & 100 & 200 & 300 & 400 & 500 & 600 & 700 & 800 & 900 \end{array}$$

To represent multiples of 1000 an accent mark was used. For example, $'\epsilon$ was used to represent 5000. The accent mark might be omitted if the size of the number being represented was clear without it.
 (a) Express the following Ionian numerals in our numeration system.
  (i) $\mu\beta$
  (ii) $\chi\kappa\epsilon$
  (iii) $'\gamma\phi\lambda\gamma$
  (iv) $'\pi'\theta\omega\alpha$
 (b) Express each of the following numerals in the Ionian numeration system.
  (i) 85
  (ii) 744
  (iii) 2153
  (iv) 21,534
 (c) Was the Ionian system a place-value system?

Problems

15. Some children have difficulty with reversals; that is, they confuse 13 and 31, 27 and 72, 59 and 95. What numerals would give Roman children similar difficulties? How about Egyptian children?

16. **(a)** How many Egyptian numerals are needed to represent the following problems?
  (i) $59 + 88$
  (ii) $150 - 99$
  (iii) $7897 + 934$
  (iv) $9698 - 5389$
 (b) State a general rule for determining the number of Egyptian numerals needed to represent an addition (or subtraction) problem written in our numeral system.

17. A newspaper advertisement introduced a new car as follows: IV Cams, XXXII Valves, CCLXXX Horsepower, coming December XXVI—the new 1993 Lincoln Mark VIII. Write the Roman numeral that represents the year of the advertisement.

EXERCISE/PROBLEM SET 2.2—PART B

Exercises

1. Write sentences that show the number 45 used in each of the following ways.
 (a) As a cardinal number
 (b) As an ordinal number
 (c) As an identification number

2. Decide whether the word in parentheses is being used in the "number sense" (as an idea) or in the "numeral sense" (as a symbol for an idea).

 (a) Camel is a five-letter word. (camel)
 (b) A camel is an animal with four legs. (camel)
 (c) Tim is an Anglo–Saxon name. (Tim)
 (d) Tim was an Anglo–Saxon. (Tim)

3. Explain why each of the following sets can or cannot be used to count the number of elements in {a, b, c, d}.
 (a) {4} **(b)** {0, 1, 2, 3} **(c)** {1, 2, 3, 4}

4. Place < or > in the blanks below to make each statement true. Indicate how you would verify your choice.
   (a) 3 _____ 7
   (b) 11 _____ 9
   (c) 21 _____ 12

5. Use the set method as illustrated in Figure 2.9 to explain why 7 > 3.

6. Some calculators can count. See if yours can by pressing $\boxed{1}\ \boxed{+}\ \boxed{=}\ \boxed{=}\ \boxed{=}\ \boxed{=}$. What does your calculator display? If, in fact, your calculator has the constant feature, it can be very handy. Have your calculator
   (a) count by 2s.
   (b) count by 4s.
   (c) count by 5s.
   (d) count by 11s.

7. What is the largest number that you can enter on your calculator
   (a) if you may use the same digit more than once?
   (b) if you must use a different digit in each place?

8. Change to Roman numerals.
   (a) 79
   (b) 3054

9. Change to Egyptian numerals.
   (a) 2431
   (b) 10,352

10. Change to Mayan numerals.
    (a) 926
    (b) 37,865

11. Change to Babylonian numerals.
    (a) 117
    (b) 3521

12. Express each of the following numerals in our numeration system.
    (a)
    (b)

    (c) MCCXLVII
    (d) ⟪ ⟨ ⟪ ▾▾

13. Complete the following chart expressing the given numbers in the other numeration system.

	Babylonian	Egyptian	Roman	Mayan
(a)				•⊕
(b)			CXLIV	
(c)		⌒⌒ΧΧ∩∩∩		
(d)	⟨▾▾ ▾▾▾			

14. After the credits for a film roll by, the Roman numeral MCMLXXXIX appears, which represents the year in which the film was made. Express the year in our numeration system.

Problems

15. The following Chinese numerals are part of one of the oldest numeration systems known.

一	1	十	10
二	2	百	100
三	3	千	1000
四	4		
五	5		
六	6		
七	7		
八	8		
九	9		

The numerals are written vertically. Some examples follow.

十二   represents 12

二十   represents 20

三百六十七   represents 367

(a) Express each of the following numerals in this Chinese numeration system: 80, 19, 52, 400, 603, 6031.
(b) Is this system a positional system? Is this system an additive system? A multiplicative system?

16. Two hundred persons are positioned in 10 rows, each containing 20 persons. From each of the 20 columns thus formed, the shortest is selected, and the tallest of these 20 (short) persons is tagged A. These persons now return to their initial places. Next, the tallest person in each row is selected and from these 10 (tall) persons the shortest is tagged B. Which of the two tagged persons is the taller (if they are different people)?

17. Braille numerals are formed using dots in a two-dot by three-dot Braille cell. Numerals are preceded by a backwards "L" dot symbol. The following shows the basic elements for Braille numerals and two examples.

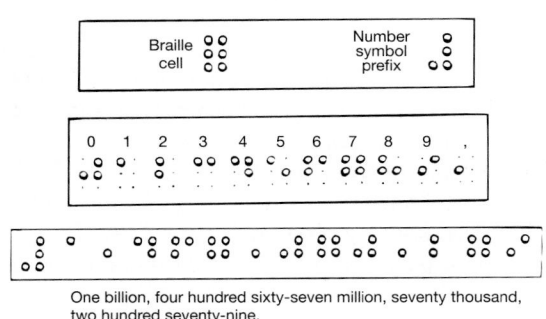

One billion, four hundred sixty-seven million, seventy thousand, two hundred seventy-nine.

Eight hundred four million, six hundred forty-seven thousand, seven hundred.

Express these Braille numerals in our numeration system.

(a)

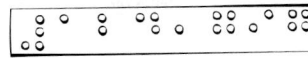

(b)

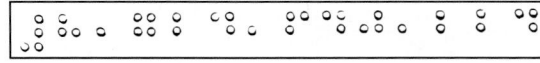

2.3

THE HINDU–ARABIC SYSTEM

The Hindu–Arabic Numeration System

The **Hindu–Arabic numeration system** that we use today was developed about A.D. 800. The following list features the basic numerals and various attributes of this system.

1. *Digits: 0, 1, 2, 3, 4, 5, 6, 7, 8, 9.* These 10 symbols, or **digits**, can be used in combination to represent all possible numbers.

2. *Grouping by tens* (*decimal system*). Grouping into sets of 10 is a basic principle of this system, probably because we have 10 "digits" on our two hands. (The word "digit" literally means finger or toe.) Ten ones are replaced by one ten, ten tens are replaced by one hundred, ten hundreds are replaced by one thousand, and so on. Figure 2.24 shows how grouping is helpful when representing a collection of objects. The number of objects grouped together is called the **base** of the system; thus our Hindu–Arabic system is a base ten system.

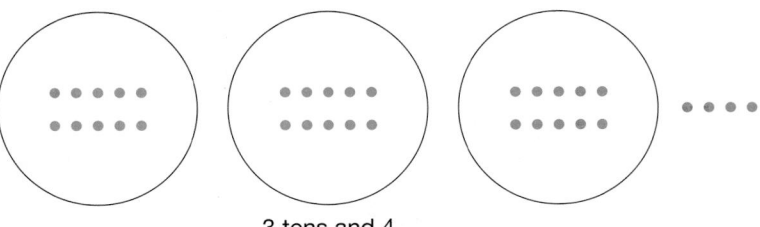

3 tens and 4

FIGURE 2.24

NOTE: Recall that an element is listed only once in a set. Although all the dots in Figure 2.24 look the same, they are assumed to be unique, individual elements here and in all such subsequent figures.

The following two models are often used to represent multidigit numbers.

(a) **Bundles of sticks** can be any kind of sticks banded together with rubber bands. Each 10 loose sticks are bound together with a rubber band to represent 10, then 10 bundles of 10 are bound together to represent 100, and so on (Figure 2.25).

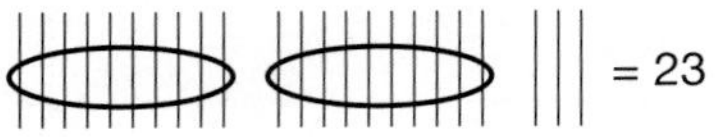

(b) **Base ten pieces** (also called **Dienes blocks**) consist of individual cubes, called "units," "longs," made up of ten units, "flats," made up of ten longs, or one hundred units, and so on (Figure 2.26). Inexpensive two-dimensional sets of base ten pieces can be made using grid paper cutouts.

= 23

FIGURE 2.25

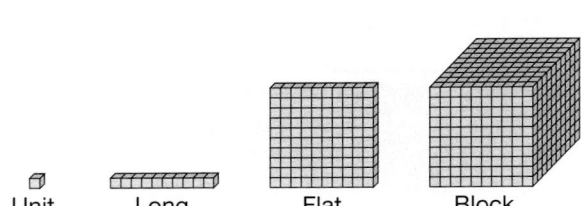

| Unit | Long | Flat | Block |

FIGURE 2.26

3. *Place value (hence positional).* Each of the various places in the numeral 6523, for example, has its own value.

thousand	hundred	ten	one
6	5	2	3

The 6 represents 6 thousands, the 5 represents 5 hundreds, the 2 represents 2 tens, and the 3 represents 3 ones due to the place-value attribute of the Hindu–Arabic system.

The following device is used to represent numbers written in place value. A **chip abacus** is a piece of paper or cardboard containing lines which form columns, and chips or markers are used to represent unit values. Conceptually, this model is more abstract than the previous models because markers represent different values, depending on the columns in which the markers appear (Figure 2.27).

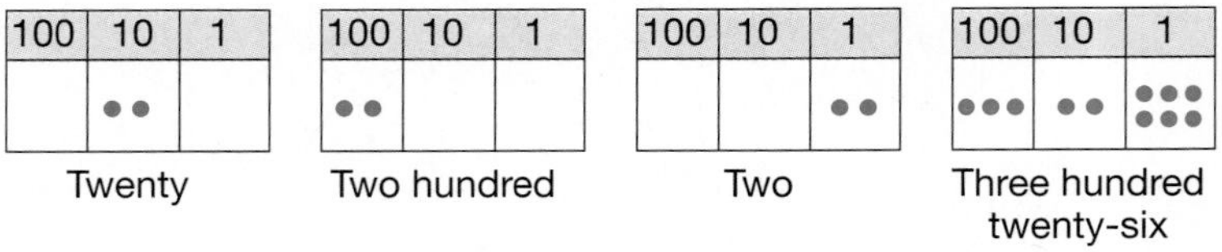

100	10	1		100	10	1		100	10	1		100	10	1
	••				••					••		•••	••	:::

| Twenty | Two hundred | Two | Three hundred twenty-six |

FIGURE 2.27

4. *Additive and multiplicative.* The value of a Hindu–Arabic numeral is found by *multiplying* each place value by its corresponding digit and then by *adding* all the resulting products.

Place values:	thousand	hundred	ten	one
Digits:	6	5	2	3
Numeral value:	$6 \times 1000 + 5 \times 100 + 2 \times 10 + 3 \times 1$			
Numeral:	6523			

Expressing a numeral as the sum of its digits times their respective place values is called the numeral's **expanded form** or **expanded notation**. The expanded form of 83,507 is

$$8 \times 10{,}000 + 3 \times 1000 + 5 \times 100 + 0 \times 10 + 7 \times 1.$$

Because $7 \times 1 = 7$, we can simply write 7 in place of 7×1 when expressing 83,507 in expanded form.

EXAMPLE 2.11 Express the following numbers in expanded form.
(a) 437   **(b)** 3001

Solution
(a) $437 = 4(100) + 3(10) + 7$
(b) $3001 = 3(1000) + 0(100) + 0(10) + 1$ or $3(1000) + 1$ ■

Notice that our numeration system requires fewer symbols to represent numbers than did earlier systems. Also, the Hindu–Arabic system is far superior when performing computations. The computational aspects of the Hindu–Arabic system will be studied in Chapter 3.

STUDENT PAGE SNAPSHOT

Decimal Place Value

A. Pluto is the planet farthest from the Sun. Its maximum distance from the Sun is 4,587,000,000 mi. Traveling this distance at a mile a second would take you about 146 years!

You can use this **place-value chart** to help you read and write numbers. It shows the names of the **periods,** or groups of three digits.

Trillions			Billions			Millions			Thousands			Ones		
H	T	O	H	T	O	H	T	O	H	T	O	H	T	O
		.				4	5	8	7	0	0	0	0	0

Standard form: 4,587,000,000

Short word name: 4 billion, 587 million

Read: four billion, five hundred eighty-seven million

1. What is the value of the digit 5 in this number?

Naming Hindu–Arabic Numerals

Associated with each Hindu–Arabic numeral is a word name. Some of the English names are listed below.

0	zero	10	ten
1	one	11	eleven
2	two	12	twelve
3	three	13	thirteen (three plus ten)
4	four	14	fourteen (four plus ten)
5	five	21	twenty-one (two tens plus one)
6	six	87	eighty-seven (eight tens plus seven)
7	seven	205	two hundred five (two hundreds plus five)
8	eight	1,374	one thousand three hundred seventy-four
9	nine	23,100	twenty-three thousand one hundred

Here are a few observations about the naming procedure.

1. The numbers 0, 1, . . . , 12 all have unique names.

2. The numbers 13, 14, . . . , 19 are the "teens," and are composed of a combination of earlier names, with the ones place named first. For example, "thirteen" is short for "three ten," which means "ten plus three," and so on.

3. The numbers 20, . . . , 99 are combinations of earlier names but *reversed* from the teens in that the tens place is named first. For example, 57 is "fifty-seven," which means "five tens plus seven," and so on. The method of naming the numbers from 20 to 90 is better than the way we name the teens, due to the left-to-right agreement with the way the numerals are written.

4. The numbers 100, . . . , 999 are combinations of hundreds and previous names. For example, 538 is read "five hundred thirty-eight," and so on.

5. In numerals containing more than three digits, groups of three digits are usually set off by commas. For example, the number

$$123,456,789,987,654,321$$

quadrillion   trillion   billion   million   thousand

is read "one hundred twenty-three quadrillion four hundred fifty-six trillion seven hundred eighty-nine billion nine hundred eighty-seven million six hundred fifty-four thousand three hundred twenty-one." (Internationally, the commas are omitted and single spaces are used instead. Also, in some countries, commas are used in place of decimal points.) Notice that the word "and" does not appear in any of these names; it is reserved to separate the decimal portion of a numeral from the whole-number portion.

Figure 2.28 graphically displays the three distinct ideas that children need to learn in order to understand the Hindu–Arabic numeration system.

Nondecimal Numeration Systems

Our Hindu–Arabic system is based on grouping by 10. To understand our system better and to experience some of the difficulties children have

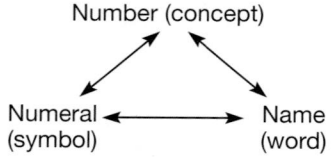

FIGURE 2.28

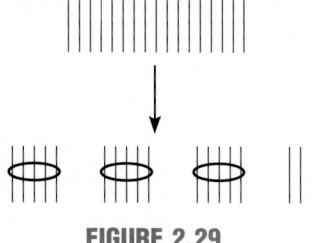

FIGURE 2.29

when learning our numeration system, it is instructive to study similar systems, but with different place values. For example, suppose that a Hindu–Arabic-like system utilized one hand (five digits) instead of two (ten digits). Then, grouping would be done in groups of five. If sticks were used, bundles would be made up of five each (Figure 2.29). Here seventeen objects are represented by three bundles of five each with two left over. This can be expressed by the equation $17_{ten} = 32_{five}$, which is read "seventeen base ten equals three two base five." (Be careful not to read 32_{five} as "thirty-two" because thirty-two means "three tens and two," not "three fives and two.") The subscript words "ten" and "five" indicate that the grouping was done in tens and fives, respectively. For simplicity, the subscript "ten" will be omitted, hence 37 will always mean 37_{ten}. (With this agreement, the numeral 24_{five} could also be written 24_5 since the subscript "5" means the usual base ten 5.) The 10 digits 0, 1, 2, . . . , 9 are used in base ten; however, only the five digits 0, 1, 2, 3, 4 are necessary in base five. A few examples of base five numerals are illustrated in Figure 2.30.

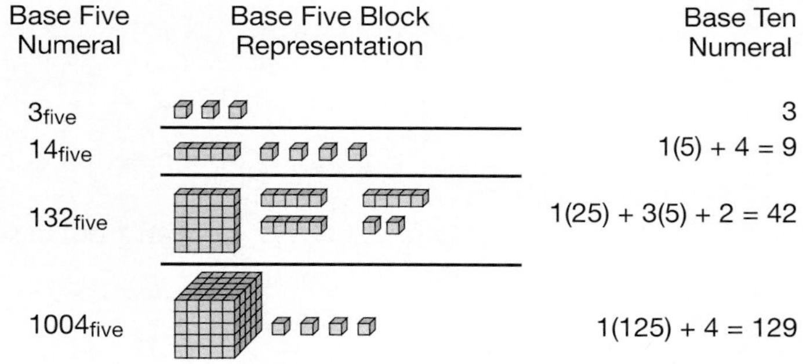

Base Five Numeral	Base Five Block Representation	Base Ten Numeral
3_{five}		3
14_{five}		$1(5) + 4 = 9$
132_{five}		$1(25) + 3(5) + 2 = 42$
1004_{five}		$1(125) + 4 = 129$

FIGURE 2.30

Counting using base five names differs from counting in base ten. The first ten base five numerals appear in Figure 2.31. Interesting junctures in counting come after a number has a 4 in its ones column. For example, what is the next number (written in base five) after 24_{five}? after 34_{five}? after 44_{five}? after 444_{five}?

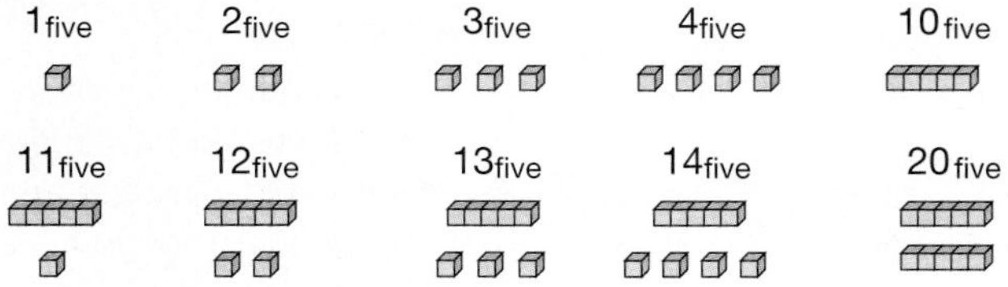

1_{five}	2_{five}	3_{five}	4_{five}	10_{five}
11_{five}	12_{five}	13_{five}	14_{five}	20_{five}

FIGURE 2.31

Figure 2.32 shows how to find the number after 24_{five} using multibase pieces.

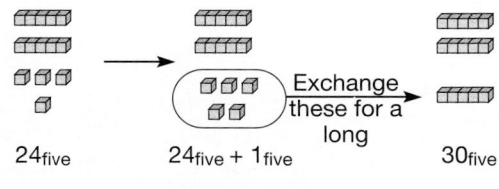

24_{five} $24_{five} + 1_{five}$ Exchange these for a long 30_{five}

FIGURE 2.32

Converting numerals from base five to base ten can be done using (1) multibase pieces, or (2) place values and expanded notation.

EXAMPLE 2.12   Express 123_{five} in base ten.

Solution
(a) *Using Base Five Pieces*: See Figure 2.33.

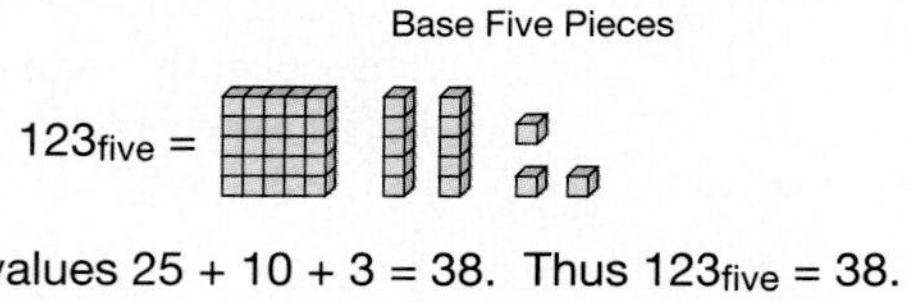

Base Five Pieces

$$123_{\text{five}} = $$

Base ten values $25 + 10 + 3 = 38$. Thus $123_{\text{five}} = 38$.

FIGURE 2.33

(b) *Using Place Value and Expanded Notation*

Place values
in base ten $\longrightarrow$

25	5	1

$123_{\text{five}} = $ 1 | 2 | 3 $= 1(25) + 2(5) + 3(1) = 38$ ■

Converting from base ten to base five also utilizes place value.

EXAMPLE 2.13   Convert from base ten to base five.
(a) 97   **(b)** 341

Solution
(a)

25	5	1
?	?	?

$97 = $ $\longleftarrow$ Base five place values
expressed using base ten numerals

Think: How many 25s in 97? There are three since $3 \cdot 25 = 75$ with 22 remaining. How many 5s in the remainder? There are four since $4 \cdot 5 = 20$. Finally, since $22 - 20 = 2$, there are two 1s.

$$97 = 3(25) + 4(5) + 2 = 342_{\text{five}}.$$

(b) A more systematic method can be used to convert 341 to its base five numeral. First, find the highest power of 5 that will divide into 341; that is, which is the greatest among 1, 5, 25, 125, 625, 3125, and so on, that will divide into 341? The answer in this case is 125. The rest of that procedure uses long division, each time dividing the remainder by the next smaller place value.

$$
\begin{array}{c}
2 \\
125\overline{)341} \\
\underline{250} \\
91
\end{array}
\quad
\begin{array}{c}
3 \\
25\overline{)91} \\
\underline{75} \\
16
\end{array}
\quad
\begin{array}{c}
3 \\
5\overline{)16} \\
\underline{15} \\
1
\end{array}
\quad 1
$$

Therefore, $341 = 2(125) + 3(25) + 3(5) + 1$, or 2331_{five}. More simply, $341 = 2331_{\text{five}}$, where 2, 3, and 3 are the quotients from left to right and 1 is the final remainder.   ■

When expressing place values in various bases, **exponents** can provide a convenient shorthand notation. The symbol a^m represents the product of m factors of a. Thus $5^3 = 5 \cdot 5 \cdot 5$, $7^2 = 7 \cdot 7$, $3^4 = 3 \cdot 3 \cdot 3 \cdot 3$, and so on. Using this exponential notation, the first several place values of base five, in reverse order, are $1, 5, 5^2, 5^3, 5^4$. Although we have studied only base ten and base five thus far, these same place-value ideas can be used with any base greater than one. For example, in base two the place values, listed in reverse order, are $1, 2, 2^2, 2^3, 2^4, \ldots$; in base three the place values are $1, 3, 3^2, 3^3, 3^4, \ldots$. The next two examples illustrate numbers expressed in bases other than five and their relationship to base ten.

EXAMPLE 2.14   Express the following numbers in base ten.
(a) 11011_{two}
(b) 1234_{eight}
(c) $1ET_{\text{twelve}}$ (NOTE: Base twelve has twelve basic numerals: 0 through 9, T for ten, and E for eleven.)

Solution

(a) $11011_{\text{two}} = $

2^4	2^3	2^2	2	1
1	1	0	1	1

$= 1(16) + 1(8) + 0(4) + 1(2) + 1(1) = 27$

(b) $1234_{\text{eight}} = $

8^3	8^2	8	1
1	2	3	4

$= 1(8^3) + 2(8^2) + 3(8) + 4(1) = 512 + 128 + 24 + 4 = 668$

(c) $1ET_{\text{twelve}} = $

12^2	12	1
1	E	T

$= 1(12^2) + E(12) + T(1) = 144 + 132 + 10 = 286$ ■

Converting from base ten to other bases is accomplished by using grouping just as we did in base five.

EXAMPLE 2.15   Convert from base ten to the given base.
(a) 53 to base two
(b) 1982 to base twelve

Solution

(a) $53 = $

2^5	2^4	2^3	2^2	2	1
?	?	?	?	?	?

Think: What is the largest power of 2 contained in 53?
Answer: $2^5 = 32$. Now we can find the remaining digits by dividing by decreasing powers of 2.

$$
\begin{array}{ccccc}
1 & 1 & 0 & 1 & 0 \quad 1\\
32\overline{)53} & 16\overline{)21} & 8\overline{)5} & 4\overline{)5} & 2\overline{)1}\\
\underline{32} & \underline{16} & \underline{0} & \underline{4} & \underline{0}\\
21 & 5 & 5 & 1 & 1
\end{array}
$$

Therefore, $53 = 110101_{\text{two}}$.

$12^3 (= 1728)$	$12^2 (= 144)$	$12^1 (= 12)$	1

(b) $1982 =$

?	?	?	?

$$\begin{array}{r} 1 \\ 1728\overline{)1982} \\ 1728 \\ \hline 254 \end{array} \qquad \begin{array}{r} 1 \\ 144\overline{)254} \\ 144 \\ \hline 110 \end{array} \qquad \begin{array}{r} 9 \\ 12\overline{)110} \\ 108 \\ \hline 2 \end{array} \qquad \begin{array}{r} 2 \\ 1\overline{)2} \\ 2 \\ \hline 0 \end{array}$$

Therefore, $1982 = 1192_{\text{twelve}}$.   ■

MATHEMATICAL MORSEL

Consider the three cards shown here. Choose any number from 1 to 7 and note which cards your number is on. Then add the numbers in the upper right-hand corner of the cards containing your number. What did you find? This "magic" can be justified mathematically using the binary (base two) numeration system.

EXERCISE/PROBLEM SET 2.3—PART A

Exercises

1. Write each of the following numbers in expanded notation.
   (a) 70   **(b)** 300   **(c)** 746
   (d) 984   **(e)** 60,006,060   **(f)** 840,001

2. Write each of the following expressions in standard place-value form.
   (a) $1(10^3) + 2(10^2) + 7(1)$
   (b) $5(10^5) + 3(10^2)$
   (c) $8(10^6) + 7(10^4) + 6(10^2) + 5(1)$
   (d) $2(10^9) + 3(10^4) + 3(10^3) + 4(10)$
   (e) $6(10^7) + 9(10^5)$

3. Write these numerals in words.
   (a) 2,000,000,000

   (b) 87,000,000,000,000
   (c) 52,672,405,123,139
   (d) 98,000,000,000,000,000

4. List three attributes of our Hindu–Arabic numeration system.

5. (a) Group this entire set of x's (by circling them) in base 3.

   x x x   x x x   x x x   x x x   x x x
   x x x   x x x   x x x   x x x   x x
   x x x   x x x   x x x   x x x   x x

   (b) Write the base three numeral for the number of x's in the set.

6. Write a base four numeral for the following set of base four pieces. (Make all possible trades first.)

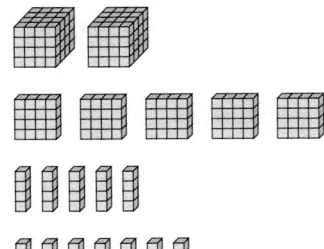

7. To express 651 with the smallest number of base eight pieces (blocks, flats, longs, and units), you need _____ blocks, _____ flats, _____ longs, and _____ units.

8. Represent each of the following numerals with multi-base pieces.
   (a) 134_{six} **(b)** 1011_{two} **(c)** 3211_{four}

9. Represent each of the following with bundling sticks and chips on a chip abacus.
   (a) 24   **(b)** 221_{four} **(c)** 167_{eight}

10. (a) Draw a sketch of 62 pennies and trade for nickels and quarters. Write the corresponding base five numeral.
   (b) Write the base five numeral for 93 and 2173.

11. Write each of the following base seven numerals in expanded notation.
   (a) 15_{seven} **(b)** 123_{seven} **(c)** 5046_{seven}

12. (a) Write out the base five numerals in order from 1 to 100_{five}.
   (b) Write out the base two numerals in order from 1 to 10000_{two}.
   (c) Write out the base three numerals in order from 1 to 1000_{three}.
   (d) In base six, write the next four numbers after 254_{six}.
   (e) What base four numeral follows 303_{four}?
   (f) What base nine numeral follows 888_{nine}?

13. Convert each base ten numeral into a numeral in the base requested.
   (a) 395 in base eight
   (b) 748 in base four
   (c) 54 in base two

14. The base twelve numeration system has the following twelve symbols: 0, 1, 2, 3, 4, 5, 6, 7, 8, 9, T, E. Change each of the following numerals to base ten numerals.

(a) 142_{twelve} **(b)** 234_{twelve} **(c)** 503_{twelve}
(d) $T9_{twelve}$ **(e)** $T0E_{twelve}$ **(f)** $ETET_{twelve}$

15. Write each of the following numbers in base six and base twelve.
   (a) 74   **(b)** 128   **(c)** 210   **(d)** 2438

16. Convert the following base five numerals into base nine numerals.
   (a) 12_{five} **(b)** 204_{five} **(c)** 1322_{five}

17. How many different symbols would be necessary for a base 23 system?

18. What is wrong with the numerals 85_{eight} and 24_{three}?

Problems

19. Mike used 2989 digits to number the pages of a book. How many pages does the book have?

20. The sum of the digits in a two-digit number is 12. If the digits are reversed, the new number is 18 greater than the original number. What is the number?

21. To determine a friend's birth date, ask him or her to perform the following calculations and tell you the result.

Multiply the number of the month in which you were born by 4 and add 13 to the result. Then multiply that answer by 25 and subtract 200. Add your birth date (day of month) to that answer and then multiply by 2. Subtract 40 from the result and then multiply by 50. Add the last two digits of your birth year to that answer and finally, subtract 10,500.
   (a) Try this sequence of operations with your own birthday. How does place value allow you to determine a birth date from the final answer? Try the sequence again with a different birth date.
   (b) Use expanded notation to explain why this technique always works.

22. What bases make these equations true?
   (a) $32 = 44$ _____   **(b)** $57_{eight} = 10$ _____
   (c) $31_{four} = 11$ _____   **(d)** $15_x = 30_y$

23. The set of even whole numbers is the set

$$\{0, 2, 4, 6, \ldots\}$$

What can be said about the ones digit of every even number in the following bases?
   (a) 10   **(b)** 4   **(c)** 2   **(d)** 5

24. Suppose that you want to find out my telephone number (it consists of seven digits) by asking me questions that I can only answer "yes" or "no." What method of interrogation leads to the correct answer after the smallest number of questions? (HINT: Use base two.)

EXERCISE/PROBLEM SET 2.3—PART B

Exercises

1. Write each expression in place-value form.
   (a) $3(1000) + 7(10) + 5$ (b) $7(10{,}000) + 6(100)$

2. State the place value of the digit 2 in each numeral.
   (a) 6234   (b) 5142   (c) 2168

3. Words and their roots often suggest numbers. Using this idea, complete the following chart. (HINT: Look for a pattern.)

Word	Latin Root	Meaning of Root	Power of 10
Billion	bi	2	9
Trillion	tri	3	(a)
Quadrillion	quater	(b)	15
(c)	quintus	5	18
Sextillion	sex	6	21
(d)	septem	7	(e)
Octillion	octo	8	27
Nonillion	novem	(f)	(g)
(h)	decem	10	33

In following with this idea, on the premodern calendar the names for September, October, November, and December suggest the numbers of the months. What was September's number on the premodern calendar? What was October's number? November's? If December was the last month of the premodern calendar year, how many months made up a year?

4. To express 69 with the fewest pieces of base three blocks, flats, longs, and units, you need _____ blocks, _____ flats, _____ longs, and _____ units.

5. Write each of the following base three numerals in expanded notation.
   (a) 22_{three} (b) 212_{three} (c) 12110_{three}

6. Write a base three numeral for the following set of base three pieces. (Make all possible trades first.)

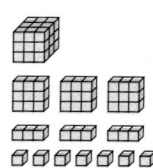

7. Represent each of the following with bundling sticks, multibase pieces, and chips on a chip abacus.
   (a) 38   (b) 52_{six} (c) 1032_{four}

8. Suppose that you have 10 "longs" in a set of multibase pieces in each of the following bases. Make all possible exchanges and write the numeral the pieces represent in that base.
   (a) Ten longs in base eight
   (b) Ten longs in base six
   (c) Ten longs in base three

9. (a) Write out the first twenty base four numerals.
   (b) How many base four numerals precede 2000_{four}?
   (c) Write out the base six numerals in order from 1 to 100_{six}.

10. (a) What is the largest six-digit base two number? What are the next three base two numbers that follow it? Give your answers in base two numeration.
    (b) What is the largest three-digit base four number? What are the five base four numbers that follow it? Give your answers in base four numeration.

11. True or false?
    (a) $7_{eight} = 7$ (b) $30_{four} = 30$
    (c) $8_{nine} = 8_{eleven}$ (d) $30_{five} = 30_{six}$

12. If all the letters of the alphabet were used as our single-digit numerals, what would be the name of our base system? If a represented zero, b represented one, and so on, what would be the base ten numeral for the "alphabet" numeral zz?

13. Find the base ten numerals for each of the following.
    (a) 342_{five} (b) $TE0_{twelve}$ (c) 101101_{two}

14. Convert each base ten numeral into its numeral in the base requested.
    (a) 142 in base twelve
    (b) 72 in base two
    (c) 231 in base eight

15. Convert these base two numerals into base eight numerals. Can you state a shortcut? [HINT: Look at part (d).]
    (a) 1001_{two} (b) 110110_{two} (c) 10101010_{two}
    (d) 101111_{two}

16. The hexadecimal numeration system, used in computer programming, is a base sixteen system which uses the symbols 0, 1, 2, 3, 4, 5, 6, 7, 8, 9, A, B, C, D, E, and F. Change each of the following hexadecimal numerals to base ten numerals.
    (a) $213_{sixteen}$ (b) $A4_{sixteen}$
    (c) $1C2B_{sixteen}$ (d) $420E_{sixteen}$

17. Write each of the following base ten numerals in base sixteen (hexadecimal) numerals.
    (a) 375   (b) 2941
    (c) 9520   (d) 24,274

Problems

18. Propose new names for the numbers 11, 12, 13, . . . , 19 so that the naming scheme is consistent with the numbers 20 and above.

19. A certain number has four digits, the sum of which is 10. If you exchange the first and last digits, the new number will be 2997 larger. If you exchange the middle two digits of the original number, your new number will be 90 larger. This last enlarged number plus the original number equals 2558. What is the original number?

20. What number is twice the product of its two digits?

21. Find the missing base.
  (a) $28 = 34$ _____   **(b)** $28 = 26$ _____
  (c) $23_{\text{twelve}} = 43$ _____

22. Under what conditions can this equation be true: $a_b = b_a$? Explain.

23. Write a 10-digit numeral such that the first digit tells the number of zeros in the numeral, the second digit tells the number of ones, the third digit tells the number of twos, and so on. For example, the numeral 9000000001 is not correct because there are not nine zeros and there is one 1.

24. As described in the Mathematical Morsel, the three cards shown here can be used to read minds. Have a person think of a number from 1 to 7 (say, 6) and tell you what card(s) it is on (cards *A* and *B*). You determine the person's number by adding the numbers in the upper right-hand corner ($4 + 2 = 6$).

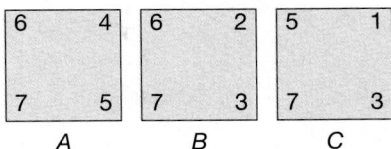

  (a) How does this work?
  (b) Prepare a set of four such magic cards for the numbers 1–15.

25. (a) Assuming that you can put weights only on one pan, show that the gram weights 1, 2, 4, 8, and 16 are sufficient to weigh each whole-gram weight up to 31 grams using a pan balance. (HINT: Base two.)
  (b) If weights can be used on either pan, what would be the fewest number of gram weights required to weigh 31 grams, and what would they weigh?

2.4

FUNCTIONS

The Concept of Function

The concept of function is central to mathematics. This section begins by listing several examples of functions. After the definition of function, several ways of representing functions are shown. In Chapter 9, graphs of important types of functions that model applications in society will be studied. The following are examples of functions.

1. Recall that a sequence is a list of numbers, called terms, arranged in order, where the first term is called the **initial term**. For example, the sequence of consecutive even counting numbers listed *in increasing order* is 2, 4, 6, 8, 10, ... Another way of showing this sequence is by using arrows:

$$1 \rightarrow 2, \ 2 \rightarrow 4, \ 3 \rightarrow 6, \ 4 \rightarrow 8, \ 5 \rightarrow 10, \ . \ . \ .$$

Here, the arrows assign to each counting number its double. Using a variable, this assignment can be represented as $n \rightarrow 2n$. Not only is this assignment an example of a function, a function is formed whenever each counting number is assigned to one and only element.

Some special sequences can be classified by the way their terms are found. In the sequence 2, 4, 6, 8, . . . , each term after the first can be found by adding 2 to the preceding term. This type of sequence, in which successive terms differ by the same number, is called an arithmetic sequence. Using variables, an **arithmetic sequence** has the form

$$a, a + d, a + 2d, \ldots$$

Here a is the initial term and d is the amount by which successive terms differ. The number d is called the **common difference** of the sequence.

In the sequence 1, 3, 9, 27, . . . , each term after the first can be found by multiplying the preceding term by 3. This is an example of a geometric sequence. By using variables, a **geometric sequence** has the form

$$a, ar, ar^2, ar^3, \ldots$$

The number r, by which each successive term is multiplied, is called the **common ratio** of the sequence. Table 2.4 displays the terms for general arithmetic and geometric sequences.

TABLE 2.4

Term	1	2	3	4	. . .	n	. . .
Arithmetic Sequence	a	$a + d$	$a + 2d$	$a + 3d$	. . .	$a + (n - 1)d$	. . .
Geometric Sequence	a	ar	ar^2	ar^3	. . .	ar^{n-1}	. . .

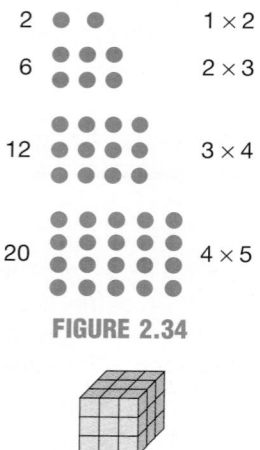

FIGURE 2.34

Using this table, the 400th term of the arithmetic sequence 8, 12, 16, . . . is found by observing that $a = 8$ and $d = 4$; thus the 400th term is $8 + (400 - 1)4 = 1604$. The 10th term of the geometric sequence 4, 8, 16, 32, . . . is found by observing that $a = 4$ and $r = 2$; thus the 10th term is $4 \cdot 2^{10-1} = 2048$.

2. Rectangular numbers are numbers that can be represented in arrays where the number of dots on the shorter side is one less than the number of dots on the longer side (Figure 2.34). The first six rectangular numbers are 2, 6, 12, 20, 30, and 42. The length of the shorter side of the nth array is n and the length of the longer side is $n + 1$. Thus the nth rectangular number is $n(n + 1)$, or $n^2 + n$.

3. Figure 2.35 displays a 3 by 3 by 3 cube that is composed of three layers of nine unit cubes for a total of 27 of the unit cubes. Table 2.5 shows several instances where a larger cube is formed from unit cubes. In general, if there are n unit cubes along any side of a larger cube, the larger cube is made up of n^3 unit cubes.

FIGURE 2.35

4. Amoebas regenerate themselves by splitting into two amoebas. Table 2.6 shows the relationship between the number of splits and the number of amoebas after that split, starting with one amoeba. Notice how the number of amoebas grows rapidly. The rapid growth described in this table is called **exponential growth**.

TABLE 2.5

Number of Unit Cubes on a Side	1	2	3	4	5	6	. . .
Number of Unit Cubes in the Larger Cube	1	8	27	64	125	216	. . .

TABLE 2.6

Number of Splits	Number of Amoebas
1	2
2	4
3	8
4	16
.	.
.	.
.	.
n	2^n

Although the preceding examples are different in some ways, underlying each of them is the concept of function.

Definition

Function

A **function** is a rule that assigns to each element of a first set an element of a second set in such a way that no element in the first set is assigned to two different elements in the second set.

The concept of a function is found throughout mathematics and society. Simple examples in society are (a) to each person is assigned his or her social security number, (b) to each item in a store is assigned a unique bar code number, and (c) to each house on a street is assigned a unique address.

A function, f, that assigns an element of set A to an element of set B is written $f: A \rightarrow B$. If $a \in A$, then the **function notation** for the element in B that is assigned to a is $f(a)$, read "f of a" (Figure 2.36). Consider how each of examples 1 to 4 above satisfies the definition of a function.

1. *Even numbers:* Assigned to each counting number n is its double, namely $2n$; that is, $f(n) = 2n$.
2. *Rectangular numbers:* If there are n dots in the shorter side, there are $n + 1$ dots in the longer side. Since the number of dots in the nth rectangular number is $n(n + 1)$, we can write $f(n) = n(n + 1)$. So $f(n) = n(n + 1)$ is the function that produces rectangular numbers.
3. *Cube:* Assigned to each number n is its cube, that is, $f(n) = n^3$.
4. *Amoebas:* Assigned to each number of splits, n, is the number of amoebas, 2^n. Thus $f(n) = 2^n$.

NOTE: We are not required to use an f to represent a function and an n as the variable in $f(n)$. For example, the rectangular number function may be written $r(x) = x(x + 1)$ or $R(t) = t(t + 1)$. The function for the cube could be written $C(r) = r^3$. That is, a function may be represented by any upper- or lowercase letter. However, the variable is usually represented by a lowercase letter.

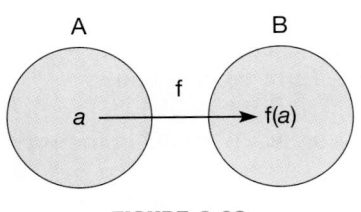

A   B

$a \longrightarrow f(a)$

f

FIGURE 2.36

EXAMPLE 2.16   Express the following relationships using function notation.
(a) The cost of a taxi ride given that the rate is $1.75 plus 75 cents per quarter mile
(b) The degree measure in Fahrenheit as a function of degrees Celsius, given that in Fahrenheit it is 32° more than 1.8 times the degrees measured in Celsius
(c) The amount of muscle weight, in terms of body weight, given that for each 5 pounds of body weight, there are about 2 pounds of muscle
(d) The value of a $1000 investment after t years at 7% interest, compounded annually, given that the amount will be 1.07^t times the initial principal

Solution
(a) $C(m) = 1.75 + 4m(0.75)$, where m is the number of miles traveled
(b) $F(c) = 1.8c + 32$, where c is degrees Celsius
(c) $M(b) = \frac{2}{5}b$, where b is the body weight
(d) $P(t) = 1000(1.07^t)$, where t is the number of years ∎

Representations of Functions

If f represents a function from set A to set B, set A is called the **domain** of f and set B is called the **codomain**. The doubling function, $f(n) = 2n$, can be defined to have the set of counting numbers as its domain and codomain. Notice that only the even numbers are used in the codomain in this function. The set of all elements in the codomain that the function pairs with an element of the domain is called the **range** of the function. The doubling function as described above has domain $\{1, 2, 3, \ldots\}$, codomain $\{1, 2, 3, \ldots\}$, and range $\{2, 4, 6, \ldots\}$ (Figure 2.37). Notice that the range must be a subset of the codomain. However, the codomain and range may be equal. For example, if $A = \{a, e, i, o, u\}$, $B = \{1, 2, 3, 4, 5\}$, and the function g assigns to each letter in A its alphabetical order among the five letters, then $g(a) = 1$, $g(e) = 2$, $g(i) = 3$, $g(o) = 4$, and $g(u) = 5$ (Figure 2.38). Here the range of g is B. The notation $g: A \rightarrow B$ is used to indicate the domain, A, and codomain, B, of the function g.

A function can assign more than one element from the domain to the same element in the codomain. For example, for sets A and B in the preceding paragraph, a letter could be assigned to 1 if it is in the first half of the alphabet and to 2 if it is in the second half. Thus a, e, and i would be assigned to 1 and o and u would be assigned to 2.

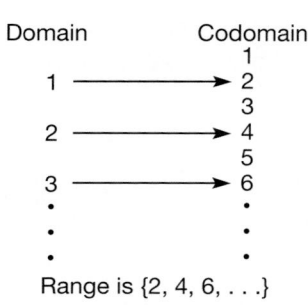

Range is $\{2, 4, 6, \ldots\}$

FIGURE 2.37

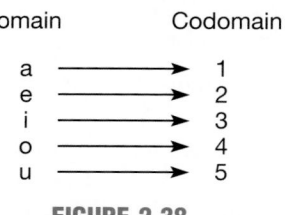

FIGURE 2.38

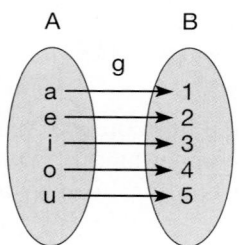

FIGURE 2.39

Functions As Arrow Diagrams

When sets A and B are finite sets with few elements, functions can be defined by using **arrow diagrams**. The arrow diagram associated with the function is shown in Figure 2.39. To be a function, exactly one arrow must leave each element in the domain and point to one element in the codomain. However, not all elements in the codomain have to be hit by an arrow. For example, in the function shown in Figure 2.38, if B is changed to $\{1, 2, 3, 4, 5, \ldots\}$, the numbers 6, 7, 8, . . . would not be hit by an arrow. Here the codomain of the function would be the set of counting numbers and the range would be the set $\{1, 2, 3, 4, 5\}$.

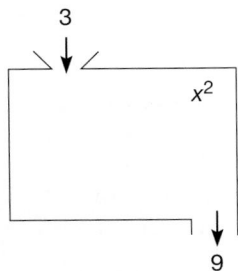

A	B
a	1
e	2
i	3
o	4
u	5

FIGURE 2.40

FIGURE 2.41

Functions As Tables

The function in Figure 2.38, where B is the set $\{1, 2, 3, 4, 5\}$, also can be defined using a table (Figure 2.40). Notice how when one defines a function in this manner, it is implied that the codomain and range are the same, namely set B.

Functions As Machines

A dynamic way of visualizing the concept of function is through the use of a machine. The "input" elements are the elements of the domain and the "output" elements are the elements of the range. The function machine in Figure 2.41 takes any number put into the machine, squares it, and then outputs the square. For example, if 3 is an input, its corresponding output is 9. In this case, 3 is an element of the domain and 9 is an element of the range.

Functions As Ordered Pairs

The function in Figure 2.39 also can be expressed as the set of ordered pairs $\{(a, 1), (e, 2), (i, 3), (o, 4), (u, 5)\}$. This method of defining a function by listing its ordered pairs is practical if there is a small finite number of pairs that define the function. Functions having an infinite domain can be defined using this ordered-pair approach by using set-builder notation. For example, the squaring function $f: A \rightarrow B$, where $A = B$ is the set of whole numbers and $f(n) = n^2$, is $\{(a, b) \mid b = a^2, a$ any whole number$\}$, that is, the set of all ordered pairs of whole numbers, (a, b), where $b = a^2$.

Functions As Graphs

The ordered pairs of a function can be represented as points on a two-dimensional coordinate system (graphing functions will be studied in depth in Section 9.3). Briefly, a horizontal line is usually used for elements in the domain of the function and a vertical line is used for the codomain. Then the ordered pair $(x, f(x))$ is plotted. Five of the ordered pairs associated with the squaring function, $f(x) = x^2$, where the domain of f is the set of whole numbers, are illustrated in Figure 2.42. Graphing is especially useful when a function consists of infinitely many ordered pairs.

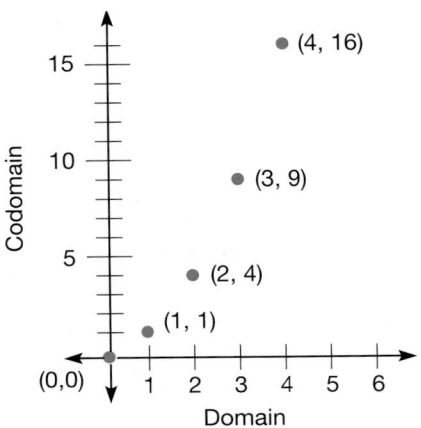

FIGURE 2.42

Functions As Formulas

In Chapter 13 we derive formulas for finding areas of certain plane figures. For example, the formula for finding the area of a circle is $A = \pi r^2$, where r is the radius of the circle. To reinforce the fact that the area of a circle, A, is a function of the radius, we sometimes write this formula as $A(r) = \pi r^2$. Usually, formulas are used to define a function whenever the domain has infinitely many elements. In the formula $A(r) = \pi r^2$, we have that the domain of the area function is any number used to measure lengths, not simply the whole numbers: $A(1) = \pi$, $A(2) = 4\pi$, $A(0.5) = (0.5)^2 \pi = 0.25\pi$, and so on.

Slide

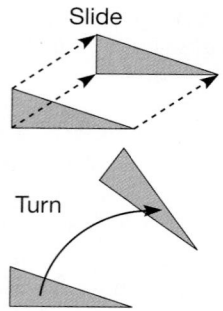

Turn

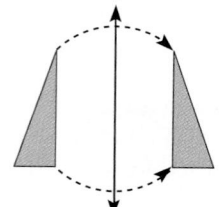

Flip

Functions As Geometric Transformations

Certain aspects of geometry can be studied more easily through the use of functions. For example, geometric shapes can be slid, turned, and flipped to produce other shapes (Figure 2.43). Such transformations can be viewed as functions that assign to each point in the plane a unique point in the plane. Geometric transformations of the plane are studied in Chapter 16.

EXAMPLE 2.17   Identify the domain, codomain, and range of the following functions.

(a) $a \to 1$ **(b)**
$\quad\ b \to 2$
$\qquad\quad 3$

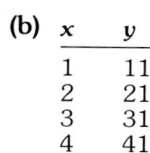

x	y
1	11
2	21
3	31
4	41

(c) $g: R \to S$, where $g(x) = x^2$, R and S are the counting numbers.

(d)

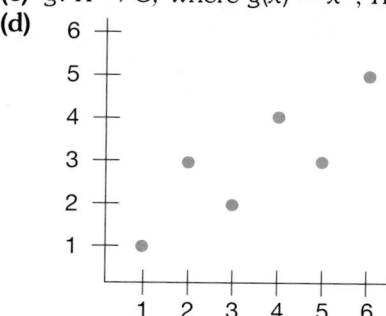

FIGURE 2.43

Solution
(a) Domain: $\{a, b\}$, codomain: $\{1, 2, 3\}$, range: $\{1, 2\}$
(b) Domain: $\{1, 2, 3, 4\}$, codomain: $\{11, 21, 32, 41\}$, range = codomain
(c) Domain: $\{1, 2, 3, 4, \ldots\}$, codomain = domain, range:

$$\{1, 4, 9, 16, \ldots\}$$

(d) Domain: $\{1, 2, 3, 4, 5, 6\}$, codomain = domain, range:

$$\{1, 2, 3, 4, 5\}$$

Computer spreadsheet applications are examples of one especially valuable use of the concept of function. A **spreadsheet** is composed of several columns, *A*, *B*, *C*, *D*, ... Usually, the first column(s) are for inputs and other columns are for the corresponding outputs. These outputs are determined by formulas. The spreadsheet in Table 2.7 shows the outputs based on inputs in columns *A* and *B*, where *C*, *D*, and *E* are defined as follows:

$$C = (A + B)/4, \quad D = (A - B)/2, \quad \text{and} \quad E = (A/B) + 1$$

TABLE 2.7

	A	*B*	*C*	*D*	*E*
1	24	12	9	6	3
2					
3					
4					
5					
6					
7					

Notice how this spreadsheet function requires values for both *A* and *B* to find outputs *C*, *D*, and *E*. In this case we say that *C* (as well as *D* and *E*) is a function of both *A and B*. This is an example of a **function of several variables**, namely, one that requires more than one input.

EXAMPLE 2.18   Determine the values of *C*, *D*, and *E* for the spreadsheet in Table 2.7 for *A* = 20 and *B* = 4.

Solution

$C = (A + B)/4$, so $C = (20 + 4)/4 = 6$
$D = (A - B)/2$, so $D = (20 - 4)/2 = 8$
$E = (A/B) + 1$, so $E = (20/4) + 1 = 6$ ∎

MATHEMATICAL MORSEL

"Yeah Houston . . . . .
you're not going to
believe this . . . . . .

Suppose that a large sheet of paper one-thousandth of an inch thick is torn in half and the two pieces are put on a pile. Then these two pieces are torn in half and put together to form a pile of four pieces. If this process is continued a total of 50 times, the last pile will be over 17 million miles high!

EXERCISE/PROBLEM SET 2.4—PART A

Exercises

1. Which of the following arrow diagrams represent functions? If one does not represent a function, explain why not.

(a)

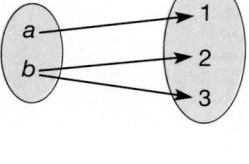

(b)

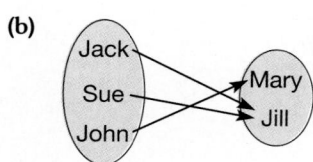

(c)

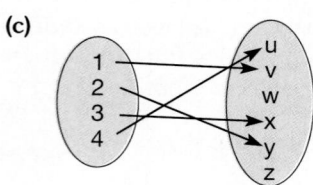

(d)

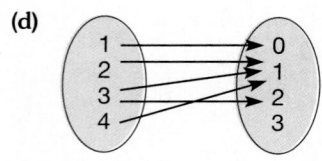

2. List the ordered pairs for these functions using the domain specified. Find the range for each function.
(a) $C(t) = 2t^3 - 3t$, with domain $\{0, 2, 4\}$
(b) $a(x) = x + 2$, with domain $\{1, 2, 9\}$
(c) $P(n) = \left(\dfrac{n+1}{n}\right)^n$, with domain $\{1, 2, 3\}$

3. Which of the following lists of ordered pairs could belong to a function? For those that cannot, explain why not.
(a) $(7, 4)$ $(6, 3)$ $(5, 2)$ $(4, 1)$
(b) (red, 3) (blue, 4) (green, 5) (yellow, 6) (black, 5)
(c) $(1, 1)$ $(1, 2)$ $(3, 4)$ $(4, 4)$
(d) $(1, 1)$ $(2, 1)$ $(3, 1)$ $(4, 1)$
(e) (a, b) (b, b) (d, e) (b, c) (d, f)

4. Using the function machines, find all possible missing whole-number inputs or outputs.
(a)

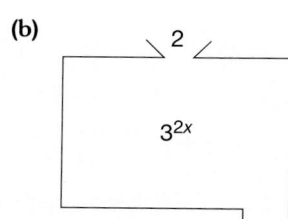

(b)

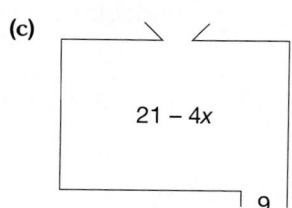

(c)

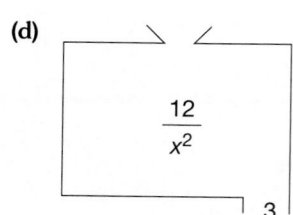

(d)

(d)
12 / x²
3

5. Which of the following assignments describe a function? If one does not, explain why not.
(a) Each U.S. citizen → his or her birthday
(b) Each vehicle registered in Michigan → its license plate
(c) Each college graduate → his or her degree
(d) Each shopper in a grocery store → number of items purchased

6. The functions below are expressed in one of the following forms: a formula, an arrow diagram, a table, or a set of ordered pairs. Express each function in each each of the other three forms.
(a) $f(x) = x^3 - x$ for $x \in \{0, 1, 4\}$
(b) $\{(1, 1), (4, 2), (9, 3)\}$
(c)

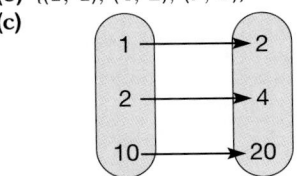

(d)

x	$f(x)$
5	55
6	66
7	77

7. Inputs into a function are not always single numbers or single elements of the domain. For example, a function can be defined to accept as input the length and width of a rectangle and to output its perimeter.

$$A(l, w) = 2l + 2w$$
$$\text{or } A: (l, w) \to 2l + 2w$$

For each function defined below, evaluate $f(2, 5)$, $f(3, 3)$, and $f(1, 4)$.
(a) $f(x, y) = x^2 + y^2$
(b) $f: (a, b) \to 3a + 1$
(c)

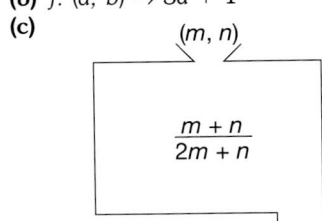

(d) $f: (x, y) \to x$ or y, whichever is larger

8. Determine if the following sequences are arithmetic sequences, geometric sequences, or neither. Determine the common difference (ratio) and 200th term for the arithmetic (geometric) sequences:

(a) 7, 12, 17, 22, 27, . . .
(b) 14, 28, 56, 112, . . .
(c) 4, 14, 24, 34, 44, . . .
(d) 1, 11, 111, 1111, . . .

9. How many numbers are in this collection?

1, 4, 7, 10, 13, . . . , 682

10. A 6% sales tax function applied to any price p can be described as follows: $f(p)$ is $0.06p$ rounded to the nearest cent, where half-cents are rounded up. For example, $0.06(1.25) = 0.075$, so $f(1.25) = 0.08$ since 0.075 is rounded up to 0.08. Use the 6% sales tax function to find the correct tax on the following amounts.
(a) $7.37   (b) $9.25   (c) $11.15
(d) $76.85

Problems

11. (a) The function $f(n) = \frac{9}{5}n + 32$ can be used to convert degrees Celsius to degrees Fahrenheit. Calculate $f(0)$, $f(100)$, $f(50)$, and $f(-40)$.
(b) The function $g(m) = \frac{5}{9}(m - 32)$ can be used to convert degrees Fahrenheit to degrees Celsius. Calculate $g(32)$, $g(212)$, $g(104)$, and $g(-40)$.
(c) Is there a temperature where the degrees Celsius equals the degrees Fahrenheit? If so, what is it?

12. Find the 458th number in the sequence

21, 29, 37, 45, . . .

13. A fitness club charges an initiation fee of $85 plus $35 per month.
(a) Write a formula for a function, $C(x)$, that gives the total cost for using the fitness club facilities after x months.
(b) Calculate $C(18)$ using the formula you wrote in part (a). Explain in words what you have found.
(c) When will the total amount spent by a club member first exceed $1000?

14. The second term of a certain geometric sequence is 1200 and the fifth term of the sequence is 150.
(a) Find the common ratio, r, for this geometric sequence.
(b) Write out the first six terms of the sequence.

15. Consider the following sequence of toothpick figures.

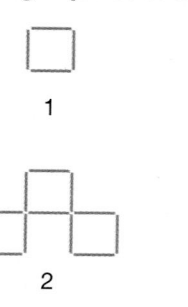

1

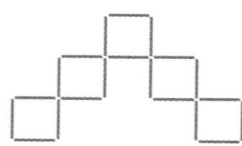

2

3

4

(a) Let $T(n)$ be the function representing the total number of toothpicks in the nth figure. Complete the following table, which gives one representation of the function T.

n	$T(n)$
1	4
2	
3	
4	
5	
6	
7	
8	

(b) What kind of sequence do the numbers in the second column form?

(c) Represent the function T in another way by writing a formula for $T(n)$.

(d) Find $T(20)$ and $T(150)$.

(e) What are the domain and range of the function T?

16. Consider the following sequence of toothpick figures.

1

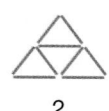

2

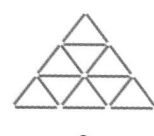

3

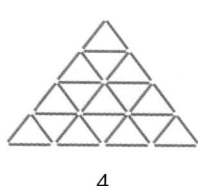

4

(a) Let $T(n)$ be the function representing the total number of toothpicks in the nth figure. Complete the following table, which gives one representation of the function T.

n	$T(n)$
1	3
2	
3	
4	
5	
6	
7	
8	

(b) Do the numbers in column 2 form a geometric or arithmetic sequence, or neither?

(c) Represent the function T in another way by writing a formula for $T(n)$.

(d) Find $T(15)$ and $T(100)$.

(e) What are the domain and range of the function T?

17. Suppose that $100 is earning interest at an annual rate of 5%.

(a) If the interest earned on the $100 is simple interest, the same amount of interest is earned each year. The interest is 5% of $100, or $5 per year. Complete a table like the one following to show the value of the account after n years.

Number of Years, n	Annual Interest Earned	Value of Account
0	0	100
1	5	105
2	5	110
3		
4		
5		
.		
.		
10		

(b) What kind of sequence, arithmetic or geometric, do the numbers in the third column form? What is the value of d or r? Write a function $A(n)$ that gives the value of the account after n years.

18. (a) If the interest earned on the $100 is compound interest and is compounded annually, the amount of interest earned at the end of a year is 5% of the current balance. After the first year the interest is calculated using the original $100 plus any accumulated interest. Complete a table like the one following to show the value of the account after n years.

Number of Years, n	Annual Interest Earned	Value of Account
0	0	100
1	0.05(100) = 5	105
2	0.05(105) = 5.25	110.25
3		
4		
5		
.		
.		
10		

(b) What kind of sequence, arithmetic or geometric, do the numbers in the third column form? What is the value of d or r? Write a function $A(n)$ that gives the value of the account after n years.

(c) Over a period of 10 years, how much more interest is earned when interest is compounded annually than when simple interest is earned?
(NOTE: Generally, banks do pay compound interest rather than simple interest.)

19. A clown was shot out of a cannon at ground level. Her height above the ground at any time t was given by the function $h(t) = -16t^2 + 64t$. Find her height when $t = 1, 2,$ and 3. How many seconds of flight will she have?

EXERCISE/PROBLEM SET 2.4—PART B

Exercises

1. Which of the following arrow diagrams represent functions? If one does not represent a function, explain why not.

(a)

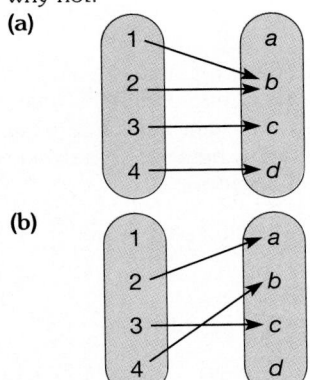

(b)

(c)

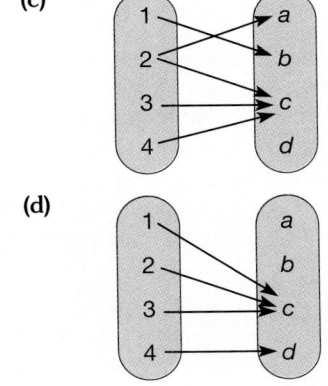

(d)

2. List the ordered pairs for these functions using the domains specified. Find the range for each function.

(a) $f(x) = 2x^2 + 4$, with domain: {0, 1, 2}
(b) $g(y) = (y + 2)^2$, with domain: {7, 2, 1}
(c) $h(t) = 2^t - 3$, with domain: {2, 3}

3. Which of the following lists of ordered pairs could belong to a function? For those that cannot, explain why not.

(a) (Bob, m)
(Sue, s)
(Joe, s)
(Jan, s)
(Sue, m)

(b) (dog, 3)
(horse, 7)
(cat, 4)
(mouse, 3)
(bird, 7)

(c) (a, x)
(c, y)
(x, a)
(y, y)
(b, z)

(d) (1, x)
(a, x)
(Joe, y)
(Bob, x)

(e) (1, 2)
(2, 3)
(2, 1)
(3, 3)
(3, 1)

4. Using the following function machines, find all possible missing whole-number inputs or outputs.

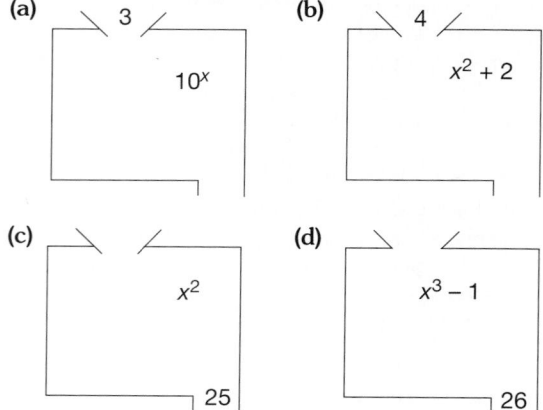

(a) 3 → 10^x
(b) 4 → $x^2 + 2$
(c) x^2 → 25
(d) $x^3 - 1$ → 26

5. Which of the following assignments describe a function? If one does not, explain why not.
(a) Each registered voter in California → his or her polling place
(b) Each city in the United States → its zip code
(c) Each type of plant → its genus
(d) Each pet owner in the United States → his or her pet

6. The functions shown next are expressed in one of the following forms: a formula, an arrow diagram, a table, or a set of ordered pairs. Express each function in each of the three other forms.
(a)

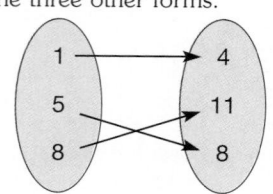

(b)

x	f(x)
3	$\frac{1}{3}$
4	$\frac{1}{4}$
1	1
$\frac{1}{2}$	2

(c) {(4, 12), (2, 6), (7, 21)}
(d) $f(x) = x^2 - 2x + 1$ for $x \in$ {2, 3, 4, 5}

7. Some functions expressed in terms of a formula use different formulas for different parts of the domain. Such a function is said to be defined piecewise. For example, suppose that f is a function with a domain of {1, 2, 3, . . .} and

$$f(x) = \begin{cases} 2x & \text{for } x \le 5 \\ x + 1 & \text{for } x > 5 \end{cases}$$

This notation means that if an element of the domain is 5 or less, the formula $2x$ is used. Otherwise, the formula $x + 1$ is used.
(a) Evaluate each of the following: $f(3)$, $f(10)$, $f(25)$, $f(5)$.
(b) Sketch an example of what a function machine might look like for f.

8. Oregon's 1991 state income tax rate for single persons can be expressed as follows, where i = taxable income.

Taxable Income (i)	Tax Rate (T_i)
$0.05i$	$i \le 2000$
$100 + 0.07(i - 2000)$	$2000 < i \le 5000$
$310 + 0.09(i - 5000)$	$i > 5000$

(a) Calculate $T(4000)$, $T(1795)$, $T(26,450)$, and $T(2000)$.
(b) Find the income tax on persons with taxable incomes of $49,570 and $3162.
(c) A single person's tax calculated by this formula was $1910.20. What was that person's taxable income?

9. The output of a function is not always a single number. It may be an ordered pair or a set of numbers. Several examples follow. Assume in each case that the domain is the set of natural numbers or ordered pairs of natural numbers, as appropriate.
(a) $f: n \rightarrow$ {all factors of n}
Find $f(7)$ and $f(12)$.
(b) $f(n) = (n + 1, n - 1)$
Find $f(3)$ and $f(20)$.
(c) $f: n \rightarrow$ {natural numbers greater than n}
Find $f(6)$ and $f(950)$.
(d) $f(n, m) =$ {natural numbers between n and m}
Find $f(2, 6)$ and $f(10, 11)$.

10. Determine if the following sequences are arithmetic sequences, geometric sequences, or neither. Determine the common difference (ratio) and 200th term for the arithmetic (geometric) sequences.
(a) 5, 50, 500, 5000, . . .
(b) 8, 16, 32, 64, . . .
(c) 12, 23, 34, 45, 56, . . .
(d) 1, 12, 123, 1234, . . .

Problems

11. Find the 731st number in this collection:

$$2, 9, 16, 23, 30, . . .$$

12. How many numbers are in this sequence?

$$16, 27, 38, 49, . . ., 1688$$

13. The volume of a cube whose sides have length s is given by the formula $V(s) = s^3$.
(a) Find the volume of cubes whose sides have length 3; 5; 11.
(b) Find the lengths of the sides of cubes whose volumes are 64; 216; 2744.

14. If the interest rate of a $1000 savings account is 5% and no additional money is deposited, the amount of money in the account at the end of t years is given by the function $a(t) = (1.05)^t \cdot 1000$.
(a) Calculate how much will be in the account after 2 years; 5 years; 10 years.
(b) What is the minimum number of years that it will take to more than double the account?

15. A rectangular parking area for a business will be enclosed by a fence. The fencing for the front of the lot, which faces the street, will cost $10 more per foot than the fencing for the other three sides. Use the dimensions shown to answer the following questions.

Street

Parking Area   85 ft

125 ft

(a) Write a formula for a function, $F(x)$, that gives the total cost of fencing for the lot if fencing for the three sides cost $x per foot.
(b) Calculate $F(11.50)$ using the formula you wrote in part (a). Explain in words what you have found.
(c) Suppose that no more than $9000 can be spent on this fence. What is the most expensive fencing that can be used?

16. The third term of a certain geometric sequence is 36 and the seventh term of the sequence is 2916.
(a) Find the common ratio, r, of the sequence.
(b) Write out the first seven terms of the sequence.

17. Consider the following sequence of toothpick figures.

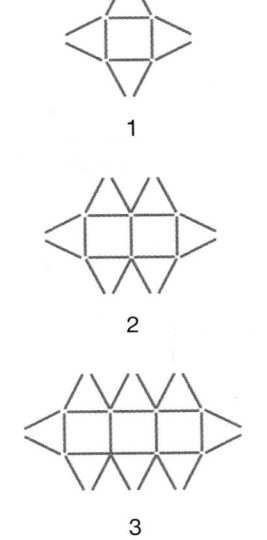

1

2

3

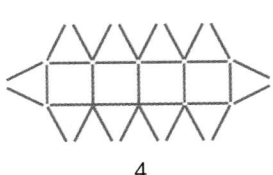

4

(a) Let $T(n)$ be the function representing the total number of toothpicks in the nth figure. Complete the following table, which gives one representation of the function T.

n	$T(n)$
1	12
2	
3	
4	
5	
6	
7	
8	

(b) What kind of sequence, arithmetic or geometric, do the numbers in the second column form? What is the value of d or r?

(c) Represent the function T in another way by writing a formula for $T(n)$.

(d) Find $T(25)$ and $T(200)$.

(e) What are the domain and range of the function T?

18. The population of Mexico in 1990 was approximately 88,300,000 and was increasing at a rate of about 2.5% per year.

(a) Complete a table like the one following to predict the population in subsequent years, assuming that the population continues to increase at the same rate.

(b) What kind of sequence, geometric or arithmetic, do the figures in the third column form? What is the value of r or d?

(c) Use the sequence you established to predict the population of Mexico in the year 2000 and in the year 2005. (NOTE: This means assuming that the growth rate remains the same, which may not be a valid assumption.)

(d) Write a function, $P(n)$, which will give the estimated population of Mexico n years after 1990.

19. The 114th term of an arithmetic sequence is 341 and its 175th term is 524. What is its 4th term?

Year	Increase in Population	Population of Mexico
1990	0	88,300,000
1991	0.025 × 88,300,000 = 2,207,500	90,507,500
1992	0.025 × 90,507,500 = 2,262,688	92,770,188
1993		
1994		
1995		

SOLUTION OF INITIAL PROBLEM

A survey was taken of 150 college freshmen. Forty of them were majoring in mathematics, 30 of them were majoring in English, 20 were majoring in science, 7 had a double major of mathematics and English, and none had a double (or triple) major with science. How many students had majors other than mathematics, English, or science?

Strategy: Draw a Diagram

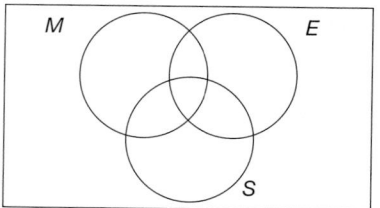

A Venn diagram with three circles, as shown above, is useful in this problem. There are to be 150 students within the rectangle, 40 in the mathematics circle, 30 in the English circle, 20 in the science circle, and 7 in the intersection of the mathematics and English circles but outside the science circle.

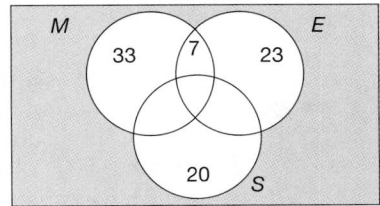

There are 33 + 7 + 23 + 20, or 83, students accounted for, so there must be 150 − 83, or 67 students outside the three circles. Those 67 students were the ones who did not major in mathematics, English, or science.

Additional Problems Where the Strategy "Draw a Diagram" Is Useful

1. A car may be purchased with the following options:
   Radio: AM/FM, AM/FM Cassette, AM/FM Cassette/CD
   Sunroof: Pop-up, Sliding
   Transmission: Standard, Automatic
   How many different cars can a customer select among these options?
2. One morning a taxi driver travels the following routes: North: 5 blocks; West: 3 blocks; North: 2 blocks; East: 5 blocks; and South: 2 blocks. How far is she from where she started?
3. For every 50 cars that arrive at a highway intersection, 25 turn right to go to Allentown, 10 go straight ahead to Boston, and the rest turn left to go to Canton. Half of the cars that arrive at Boston turn right to go to Denton and one of every five that arrive at Allentown turns left to go to Denton. If 10,000 cars arrive at Denton one day, how many cars arrived at Canton?

WRITING/DISCUSSING FOR UNDERSTANDING

1. Discuss the strengths and weaknesses of the numeration systems you studied in this chapter.
2. Invent your own "new" numeration system. Share it with another student to determine how to teach it effectively *without comparing it to any other system.*
3. Students often conceive of zero as representing "nothing." How might this conception of zero create difficulties for students as they progress in their study of mathematics?
4. Explain how the following NCTM Standards are reflected in this chapter.
   - Construct number meanings through real-world experiences and the use of physical materials.
   - Understand our numeration system by relating counting, grouping, and place-value concepts.

PROJECTS

1. Consult a book on the history of mathematics to find out more about the evolution of the Hindu–Arabic number symbols and numeration system. Write a summary of your findings.
2. Examine a set of elementary textbooks or sets of classroom materials to determine what physical representations (bundling sticks, multibase pieces, etc.) are commonly used. Explain how one can construct a set from readily available and inexpensive materials.

CHAPTER REVIEW

Major Ideas

1. Sets and ideas associated with sets form a convenient language to help clarify the concepts underlying many ideas in mathematics. Sets can be used to develop the concept of number.
2. Our system of numeration, the Hindu–Arabic system, is a decimal place-value system. This system replaced many other systems that have some of the same attributes but were not as efficient. The main attributes of this numeration system are:
   (a) Ten basic digits, including zero.
   (b) Grouping by tens.
   (c) Place value.
   (d) Additive and multiplicative.
3. Bases other than ten can be studied to gain additional insight into our decimal Hindu–Arabic system.

   Following is a list of key vocabulary, notation, and ideas for this chapter. Mentally review these items and, where appropriate, write down the meaning of each term. Then restudy the material that you are unsure of before proceeding to take the chapter test.

SECTION 2.1:   SETS AS A BASIS FOR WHOLE NUMBERS

Vocabulary/Notation

Counting numbers 43
Whole numbers 43
Set ({. .}) 43
Element ($\in$) 43
Is not an element of ($\notin$) 43
Member 43
Set-builder notation ({..|..}) 43
Empty set ($\varnothing$) or null set 43
Equal sets (=) 43
1-1 correspondence 44
Equivalent sets ($\sim$) 44
Matching sets 44
Subset ($\subseteq$) 44

Proper subset ($\subset$) 44
Venn diagram 44
Universal set (U) 44
Disjoint sets 45
Union ($\cup$) 45
Intersection ($\cap$) 45
Complement ($\overline{A}$) 45
Set difference ($-$) 45
Ordered pair 47
Cartesian product ($\times$) 47
Finite set 48
Infinite set 48
DeMorgan's laws 50, 52

Ideas

SECTION 2.2:   WHOLE NUMBERS AND NUMERATION

Vocabulary/Notation

Ideas

SECTION 2.3:   THE HINDU–ARABIC SYSTEM

Vocabulary/Notation

Ideas

SECTION 2.4: FUNCTIONS

Vocabulary/Notation

Ideas

PEOPLE IN MATHEMATICS

Emmy Noether (1882–1935) was born and educated in Germany and was graduated from the University of Erlangen, where her father Max Noether taught mathematics. There were few professional opportunities for a woman mathematician, so Emmy spent the next eight years doing research at home and teaching for her increasingly disabled father. Her work attracted the attention of the mathematicians Hilbert and Klein, who invited her to the University of Gottingen—at that time one of the world's leading centers of mathematics. Initially, Emmy's lectures were announced under Hilbert's name, because the university refused to admit a woman lecturer. Conditions improved, but in 18 years at Gottingen, she was routinely denied the promotions that would have come to a male mathematician of her ability. When the Nazis came to power in 1933, she was dismissed from her position. She emigrated to the United States and spent the last two years of her life at Bryn Mawr College. In 1983, the French mathematician Jean Dieudonne wrote that Emmy Noether "was by far the best woman mathematician of all time, and one of the greatest mathematicians of the twentieth century."

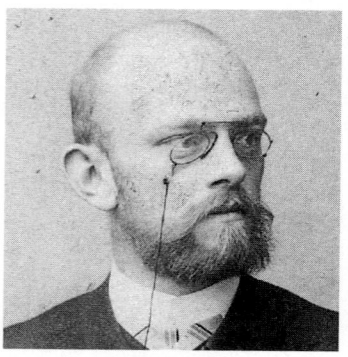

David Hilbert (1862–1943), professor of mathematics at the University of Gottingen, surveyed the spectrum of unsolved problems in 1900, and selected 23 for special attention. He felt these 23 were crucial for progress in mathematics in the coming century. Hilbert's vision was proved to be prophetic. Mathematicians took up the challenge, and a great deal of progress resulted from attempts to solve "Hilbert's problems." Hilbert himself made important contributions to the foundations of mathematics, and attempted to prove that mathematics was self-consistent. He became one of the most influential mathematicians of his time, yet he once remarked that when he read or heard new ideas in mathematics, they seemed "so difficult and practically impossible to understand," until he worked the ideas through for himself.

CHAPTER 2 TEST

Knowledge

1. True or false?
(a) If $A \sim B$, then $A = B$.
(b) If $A \subset B$, then $A \subseteq B$.
(c) $A \cap B \subseteq A \cup B$.
(d) $n(\{a, b\} \times \{x, y, z\}) = 6$.
(e) If $A \cap B = \varnothing$, then $n(A - B) < n(A)$.
(f) $\{2, 4, 6, \ldots, 2000000\} \sim \{4, 8, 12, \ldots\}$.
(g) The range of a function is a subset of the codomain of the function.
(h) $VI = IV$ in the Roman numeration system.
(i) $\div$ represents one hundred six in the Mayan numeration system.
(j) $123 = 321$ in the Hindu–Arabic numeration system.

Skill

2. For $A = \{a, b, c\}$, $B = \{b, c, d, e\}$, $C = \{d, e, f, g\}$, $D = \{e, f, g\}$, find each of the following.
(a) $A \cup B$
(b) $A \cap C$
(c) $A \cap B$
(d) $A \times D$
(e) $C - D$
(f) $(B \cap D) \cup (A \cap C)$

3. Write the equivalent Hindu–Arabic base ten numeral for each of the following numerals.
(a) ∩∩∩|| (Egyptian)
(b) CMXLIV (Roman)
(c) : (Mayan)
(d) ▏❮❮❮ !!! ▼▼▼

(e) 10101_{two}
(f) ET_{twelve}

4. Express the following in expanded form.
(a) 759
(b) 7002
(c) 1001001_{two}

Understanding

5. Use the Roman and Hindu–Arabic systems to explain the difference between a *positional* numeration system and a *place-value* numeration system.

6. Determine conditions, if any, on nonempty sets A and B so that the following equalities will be true.
(a) $A \cup B = B \cup A$
(b) $A \cap B = B \cap A$
(c) $A - B = B - A$
(d) $A \times B = B \times A$

7. If (a, b) and (c, d) are in $A \times B$, name four elements in $B \times A$.

8. Show why the sequence that begins $2, 6, \ldots$ could be either an arithmetic or a geometric sequence.

Problem Solving/Application

9. If $n(A) = 71$, $n(B) = 53$, $n(A \cap B) = 27$, what is $n(A \cup B)$?

10. Find the smallest values for a and b so that $21_b = 25_a$.

Whole Numbers: Operations and Properties

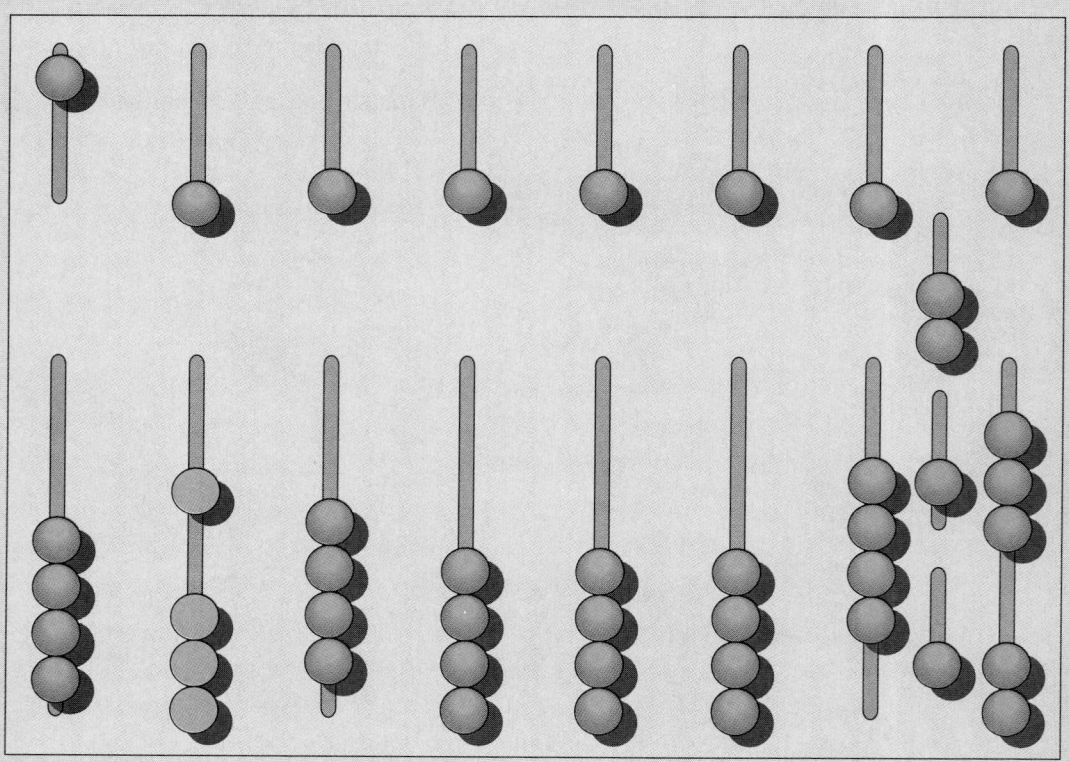

Courtesy, Margaret F. Willerding

FOCUS ON:

Calculation Devices Versus Written Algorithms: A Debate Through Time

The Hindu–Arabic numeration system can be traced back to 250 B.C. However, it was about A.D. 800 when a complete Hindu system was described in a book by the Persian mathematician al-Khowarizimi. Although the Hindu–Arabic numerals, as well as the Roman numeral system, were used to represent numbers, they were not used for computations, mainly because of the lack of inexpensive, convenient writing equipment such as paper and pencil. In fact, the Romans used a sophisticated abacus or "sand tray" made of a board with small pebbles (calculi) that slid in grooves as their calculator. Another form of the abacus was a wooden frame with beads sliding on thin rods, much like those used by the Chinese and Japanese.

From about A.D. 1100 to 1500 there was a great debate among Europeans regarding calculation. Those who advocated the use of Roman numerals along with the abacus were called the **abacists**. Those who advocated using the Hindu–Arabic numeration system together with written algorithms such as the ones we use today were called **algorists**. About 1500, the algorists won the argument and by the eighteenth century, there was no trace of the abacus in western Europe. However, parts of the world—notably, China, Japan, Russia, and some Arabian countries—continued to use a form of the abacus.

It is interesting, though, that in the 1970s and 1980s, technology produced the inexpensive, hand-held calculator, which rendered many forms of written algorithms obsolete. Yet the debate continues regarding what role the calculator should play in arithmetic. Could it be that a debate will be renewed between algorists and the modern-day abacists (or "calculatorists")? Is it possible that we may someday return to being "abacists" by using our Hindu–Arabic system to record numbers while using calculators to perform all but simple mental calculations? Let's hope that it does not take us 400 years to decide the appropriate balance between written and electronic calculations!

STRATEGY 8: USE DIRECT REASONING

The Use Direct Reasoning strategy is used virtually all the time in conjunction with other strategies when solving problems. Direct reasoning is used to reach a valid conclusion from a series of statements. Often, statements involving direct reasoning are of the form "If A then B." Once this statement is shown to be true, statement B will hold whenever statement A does. (An expanded discussion of reasoning is contained in the Logic section near the end of the book). In the following initial problem, no computations are required. That is, a solution can be obtained merely by using direct reasoning, and perhaps by drawing pictures.

Initial Problem

In a group of nine coins, eight weigh the same and the ninth is heavier. Assume that the coins are identical in appearance. Using a pan balance, what is the smallest number of weighings needed to identify the heavy coin?

Clues

The Use Direct Reasoning strategy may be appropriate when:

- A proof is required.
- A statement of the form "If . . . , then . . ." is involved.
- You see a statement that you want to imply from a collection of known conditions.

A solution of the Initial Problem above appears on page 134.

INTRODUCTION

The whole-number operations of addition, subtraction, multiplication, and division and their corresponding properties form the foundation of arithmetic. Because of their primary importance, this entire chapter is devoted to the study of how to introduce and develop these concepts independent of computational procedures. First, addition is introduced by considering the union of disjoint sets. Then the key properties of addition are developed and applied to a sequence for learning the basic addition facts. Then, subtraction is introduced and shown to be closely related to addition. Next, multiplication is introduced as a shortcut for addition and, here again, properties of multiplication are developed and applied to a sequence for learning the basic multiplication facts. Division of whole numbers, without and with remainders, is introduced next, both as an extension of subtraction and as the inverse of multiplication. Finally, exponents are introduced to simplify multiplication and to serve as a convenient notation for representing large numbers.

3.1

ADDITION AND SUBTRACTION

Addition and Its Properties

Finding the sum of two whole numbers is one of the first mathematical ideas a child encounters after learning the counting chant "one, two, three, four, . . ." and the concept of number. In particular, the question "How many is 3 and 2?" can be answered using both a set model and a measurement model.

Set Model

To find "3 + 2," find two *disjoint* sets, one with three objects and one with two objects, form their union, and count the total (Figure 3.1). Care must be taken to use disjoint sets, as Figure 3.2 illustrates. The example in Figure 3.1, which correctly illustrates how to find 3 + 2, suggests the following general definition of addition. Recall that *n(A)* denotes the number of elements in set *A*.

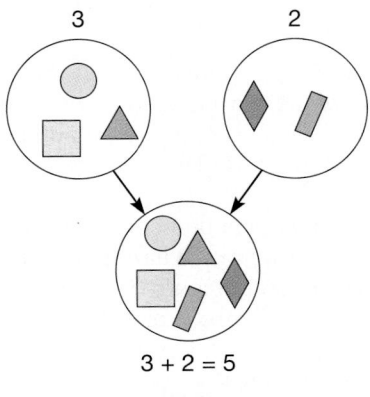

3 + 2 = 5

FIGURE 3.1

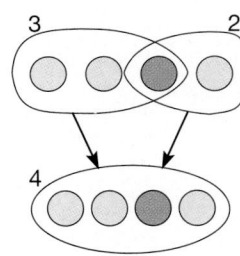

FIGURE 3.2

> **Definition**
>
> ### Addition of Whole Numbers
>
> Let a and b be any two whole numbers. If A and B are disjoint sets with $a = n(A)$ and $b = n(B)$, then $a + b = n(A \cup B)$.

The number $a + b$, read "a plus b," is called the **sum** of a and b, and a and b are called **addends** or **summands** of $a + b$.

EXAMPLE 3.1   Use the definition of addition to compute $4 + 5$.

Solution

Let $A = \{a, b, c, d\}$ and $B = \{e, f, g, h, i\}$.
Then $n(A) = 4$ and $n(B) = 5$.
Also, A and B have been chosen to be disjoint.
Therefore, $4 + 5 = n(A \cup B)$

$$= n(\{a, b, c, d\} \cup \{e, f, g, h, i\})$$
$$= n(\{a, b, c, d, e, f, g, h, i\})$$
$$= 9.$$

Addition is called a **binary operation** because two ("bi") numbers are combined to produce a unique (one and only one) number. Multiplication is another example of a binary operation with numbers. Intersection, union, and set difference are binary operations using sets.

Measurement Model

Addition can also be represented on the whole-number line pictured in Figure 3.3. Even though we have drawn a solid arrow starting at zero and

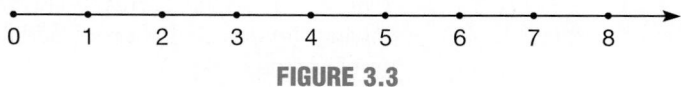

FIGURE 3.3

pointing to the right to indicate that the collection of whole numbers is unending, the whole numbers are represented by the equally spaced points labeled 0, 1, 2, 3, and so on. The magnitude of each number is represented by its distance from 0. The number line will be extended and filled in in later chapters.

Addition of whole numbers is represented by directed arrows of whole-number lengths. The procedure used to find the sum $3 + 4$ using the number line is illustrated in Figure 3.4. Here the sum, 7, of 3 and 4 is found by placing arrows of lengths 3 and 4 end to end, starting at zero.
Notice that the arrows for 3 and 4 are placed end to end and are disjoint just as in the set model.

Next we examine some fundamental properties of addition of whole numbers that can be helpful in simplifying computations. These properties,

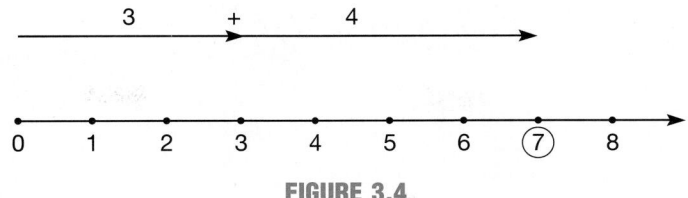

FIGURE 3.4

as well as similar properties in this and other chapters, should become an integral part of the way you view mathematics.

Properties of Whole-Number Addition

The fact that one always obtains a whole number when adding two whole numbers is summarized by the closure property.

Closure Property for Whole-Number Addition

The sum of any two whole numbers is a whole number.

When an operation on a set satisfies a closure property, the set is said to be **closed** with respect to the given operation. Knowing that a set is closed under an operation is helpful when checking certain computations. For example, consider the set of all *even* whole numbers, {0, 2, 4, . . .} the set of all odd whole numbers, {1, 3, 5, . . .}. The set of even numbers is closed under addition since the sum of two even numbers is *even*. Therefore, if one is adding a collection of *even* numbers and obtains an odd sum, an error has been made. The set of odd numbers is *not* closed under addition since the sum 1 + 3 is *not* an odd number.

Many children learn how to add by "counting on." For example, to find 9 + 1 a child will count on 1 more from 9, namely, think "nine, then ten." However, if asked to find 1 + 9, a child might say "1, then 2, 3, 4, 5, 6, 7, 8, 9, 10." Not only is this inefficient, but the child might lose track of counting on 9 more from 1. The fact that 1 + 9 = 9 + 1 is useful in simplifying this computation and is an instance of the following property.

Commutative Property for Whole-Number Addition

Let a and b be any whole numbers. Then

$$a + b = b + a.$$

Note that the root word of "commutative" is "commute," which means to interchange. Figure 3.5 illustrates this property for 3 + 2 and 2 + 3 (see page 100).

Now suppose that a child knows all the addition facts through the fives, but wants to find 6 + 3. A simple way to do this is to rewrite 6 + 3 as 5 + 4 by taking one from 6 and adding it to 3. Since the sum 5 + 4 is known to be 9, the sum 6 + 3 is 9. In summary, this argument shows that 6 + 3 can be thought of as 5 + 4 by following this reasoning: 6 + 3 = (5 + 1) + 3 = 5 + (1 + 3) = 5 + 4. The next property is most useful in simplifying computations in this way.

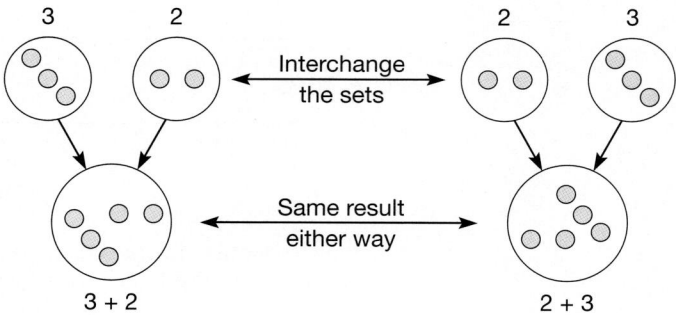

FIGURE 3.5

> ### Associative Property for Whole-Number Addition
>
> Let a, b, and c be any whole numbers. Then
>
> $$(a + b) + c = a + (b + c).$$

The root word of "associative" is "associate," which means to unite, or, in this case, reunite. The example in Figure 3.6 should convince you that this property holds for all whole numbers.

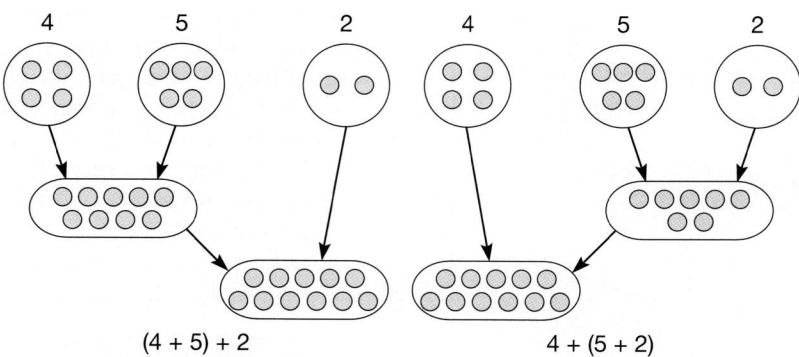

FIGURE 3.6

Since the empty set has no elements, $A \cup \{\ \} = A$. A numerical counterpart to this statement is one such as $7 + 0 = 7$. In general, adding zero to any number results in the same number. This concept is stated in generality in the next property.

> ### Identity Property for Whole-Number Addition
>
> There is a unique whole number, namely 0, such that for all whole numbers a,
>
> $$a + 0 = a = 0 + a.$$

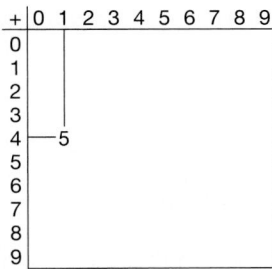

FIGURE 3.7

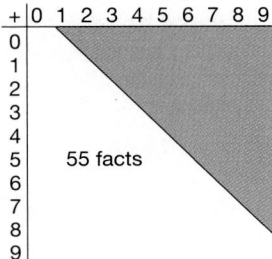

FIGURE 3.8

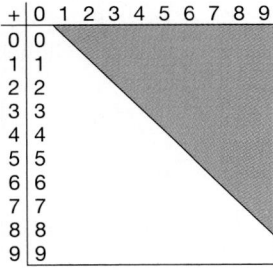

FIGURE 3.9

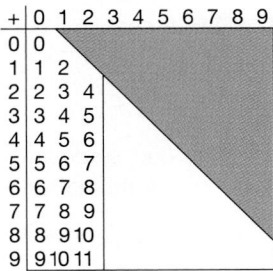

FIGURE 3.10

Because of this property, zero is called the **additive identity** or the **identity for addition**.

The previous properties can be applied to help simplify computations. They are especially useful in learning the basic addition facts, that is, all possible sums of the digits 0 through 9. Although drilling using flash cards or similar electronic devices is helpful for learning the facts, an introduction to learning the facts via the following thinking strategies will pay rich dividends later as students learn to perform multidigit addition mentally.

Thinking Strategies for Learning the Addition Facts

The addition table in Figure 3.7 has 100 empty spaces to be filled. The sum of $a + b$ is placed in the intersection of the row labeled a and the column labeled b. For example, since $4 + 1 = 5$, a 5 appears in the intersection of the row labeled 4 and the column labeled 1.

1. *Commutativity.* Because of commutativity and the symmetry of the table, a child will automatically know the facts in the shaded region of Figure 3.8 as soon as the child learns the remaining 55 facts. For example, notice that the sum $4 + 1$ is in the unshaded region, but its corresponding fact $1 + 4$ is in the shaded region.

2. *Adding zero.* The fact that $a + 0 = a$ for all whole numbers fills in 10 of the remaining blank spaces in the "zero" column (Figure 3.9)—45 spaces to go.

3. *Counting on by 1 and 2.* Children find sums like $7 + 1$, $6 + 2$, $3 + 1$, and $9 + 2$ by counting on. For example, to find $9 + 2$, think 9, then 10, 11. This thinking strategy fills in 17 more spaces in the columns labeled 1 and 2 (Figure 3.10)—28 facts to go.

4. *Combinations to ten.* Combinations of the ten fingers can be used to find $7 + 3$, $6 + 4$, $5 + 5$, and so on. Notice that now we begin to have some overlap. There are 25 facts left to learn (Figure 3.11).

5. *Doubles.* $1 + 1 = \mathbf{2}$, $2 + 2 = \mathbf{4}$, $3 + 3 = \mathbf{6}$, and so on. These sums, which appear on the main left-to-right downward diagonal, are easily learned as a consequence of counting by twos: namely, 2, 4, 6, 8, 10, . . . (Figure 3.12). Now there are 19 facts to be determined.

6. *Adding ten.* When using base ten pieces as a model, adding 10 amounts to laying down a "long" and saying the new name. For example, $3 + 10$ is 3 units and 1 long, or 13; $7 + 10$ is seventeen, and so on.

7. *Associativity.* The sum $9 + 5$ can be thought of as $10 + 4$, or 14, since $9 + 5 = 9 + (1 + 4) = (9 + 1) + 4$. Similarly, $8 + 7 = 10 + 5 = 15$, and so on. The rest of the addition table can be filled using associativity (sometimes called **regrouping**) combined with adding 10.

8. *Doubles ± 1 and ± 2.* This technique overlaps with the others. Many children use it effectively. For example, $7 + 8 = 7 + 7 + 1 = 14 + 1 = 15$, or $8 + 7 = 8 + 8 - 1 = 15$; $5 + 7 = 5 + 5 + 2 = 10 + 2 = 12$, and so on.

By using thinking strategies 6, 7, and 8 described above, the remaining basic addition facts needed to complete the table in Figure 3.12 can be determined.

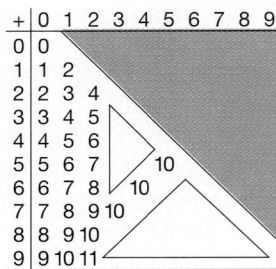

FIGURE 3.11

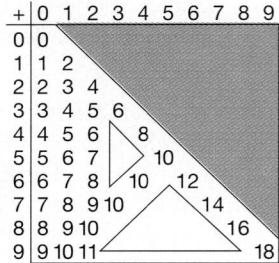

FIGURE 3.12

EXAMPLE 3.2   Use thinking strategies in three different ways to find the sum of $9 + 7$.

Solution
(a) $9 + 7 = 9 + (1 + 6) = (9 + 1) + 6 = 10 + 6 = 16$
(b) $9 + 7 = (8 + 1) + 7 = 8 + (1 + 7) = 8 + 8 = 16$
(c) $9 + 7 = (2 + 7) + 7 = 2 + (7 + 7) = 2 + 14 = 16$ ■

Thus far we have been adding single-digit numbers. However, thinking strategies can be applied to multidigit addition also. Figure 3.13 illustrates how multidigit addition is an extension of single-digit addition. The only difference is that instead of adding units each time, we might be adding longs, flats, and so on. Mentally combine similar pieces, then exchange as necessary.

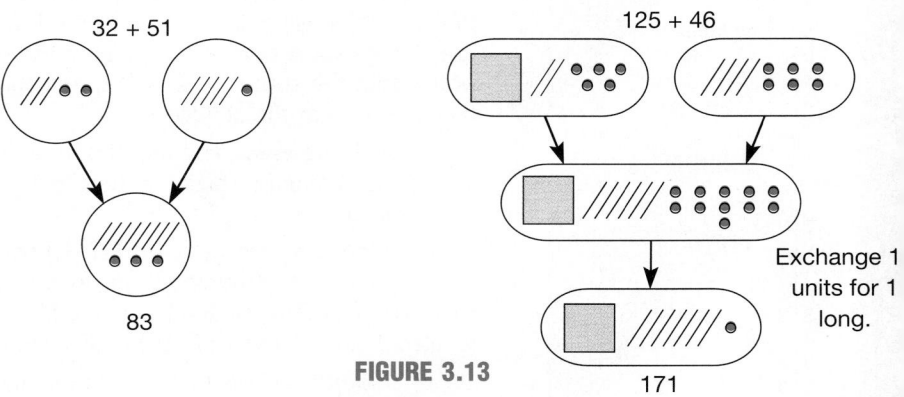

FIGURE 3.13

The next example illustrates how thinking strategies can be applied to multidigit numbers.

EXAMPLE 3.3   Using thinking strategies, find the following sums.
(a) $42 + 18$ **(b)** $37 + (42 + 13)$ **(c)** $51 + 39$

Solution
(a) $42 + 18 = (40 + 2) + (10 + 8)$ Addition
$= (40 + 10) + (2 + 8)$ Commutativity and associativity
$= 50 + 10$ Place value and combination to 10
$= 60$ Addition
(b) $37 + (42 + 13) = 37 + (13 + 42)$
$= (37 + 13) + 42$
$= 50 + 42$
$= 92$
(c) $51 + 39 = (50 + 1) + 39$
$= 50 + (1 + 39)$
$= 50 + 40$
$= 90$

The use of other number bases can help you simulate how these thinking strategies are experienced by students when they learn base ten arithmetic for the first time. Perhaps the two most powerful thinking strategies, especially when used together, are associativity and combinations to the base (base ten above). For example, $7_{nine} + 6_{nine} = 7_{nine} + (2_{nine} + 4_{nine}) = (7_{nine} + 2_{nine}) + 4_{nine} = 14_{nine}$ (since the sum of 7_{nine} and 2_{nine} is one of the base in base nine), $4_{six} + 5_{six} = 3_{six} + 1_{six} + 5_{six} = 13_{six}$ (since $1_{six} + 5_{six}$ is one of the base in base six), and so on.

EXAMPLE 3.4   Compute the following sums using thinking strategies.

(a) $7_{eight} + 3_{eight}$ **(b)** $5_{seven} + 4_{seven}$ **(c)** $9_{twelve} + 9_{twelve}$

Solution

(a) $7_{eight} + 3_{eight} = 7_{eight} + (1_{eight} + 2_{eight}) = (7_{eight} + 1_{eight}) + 2_{eight} = 12_{eight}$

(b) $5_{seven} + 4_{seven} = 5_{seven} + (2_{seven} + 2_{seven}) = (5_{seven} + 2_{seven}) + 2_{seven} = 12_{seven}$

(c) $9_{twelve} + 9_{twelve} = 9_{twelve} + (3_{twelve} + 6_{twelve}) = (9_{twelve} + 3_{twelve}) + 6_{twelve} = 16_{twelve}$

Notice how associativity and combinations to the base are used.   ■

Subtraction

The Take-Away Approach

There are two distinct approaches to subtraction. The take-away approach is often used to introduce children to the concept of subtraction. The problem "If you have 5 coins and spend 2, how many do you have left?" can be solved with a set model using the take-away approach. Also, the problem "If you walk 5 miles from home and turn back to walk 2 miles toward home, how many miles are you from home?" can be solved with a measurement model using the take-away approach (Figure 3.14).

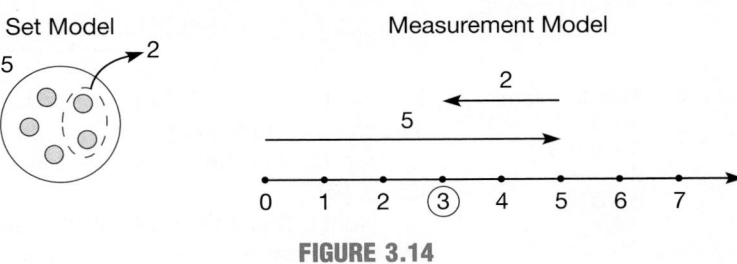

FIGURE 3.14

This approach can be stated using sets.

Definition

Subtraction of Whole Numbers: Take-Away Approach

Let a and b be any whole numbers and A and B be sets such that $a = n(A)$, $b = n(B)$, and $B \subseteq A$. Then

$$a - b = n(A - B).$$

The number "$a - b$" is called the **difference** and is read "a minus b," where a is called the **minuend** and b the **subtrahend**. To find $7 - 3$ using sets, think of a set with seven elements, say $\{a, b, c, d, e, f, g\}$. Then, using set difference, take away a subset of three elements, say $\{a, b, c\}$. The result is the set $\{d, e, f, g\}$, so $7 - 3 = 4$.

The Missing-Addend Approach

The second method of subtraction, called the missing-addend approach, is often used when making change. For example, if an item costs 76 cents and 1 dollar is tendered, a clerk will often hand back the change by adding up and saying "76 plus *four* is 80, and *twenty* is a dollar" as four pennies and two dimes are returned. This method is illustrated in Figure 3.15.

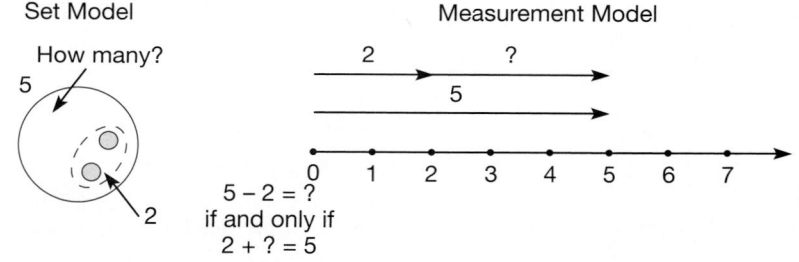

FIGURE 3.15

Since $2 + \mathbf{3} = 5$ in each case in Figure 3.15, we know that $5 - 2 = \mathbf{3}$.

Alternate Definition

Subtraction of Whole Numbers: Missing-Addend Approach

Let a and b be any whole numbers. Then $a - b = c$ if and only if $a = b + c$ for some whole number c.

In this alternate definition of subtraction, c is called the **missing addend**. The missing-addend approach to subtraction is very useful for learning subtraction facts because it shows how to relate them to the addition facts (Figure 3.16).

Notice that this alternative definition of subtraction does not guarantee that there is an answer for *every* whole-number subtraction problem. For example, there is no whole number c such that $3 = 4 + c$, so the

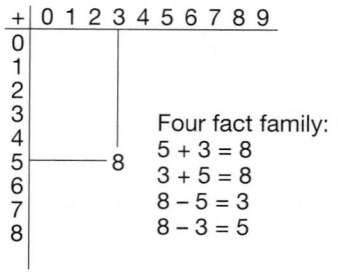

Four fact family:
$5 + 3 = 8$
$3 + 5 = 8$
$8 - 5 = 3$
$8 - 3 = 5$

FIGURE 3.16

problem $3 - 4$ has no whole-number answer. Another way of expressing this idea is to say that the set of whole numbers is *not* closed under subtraction.

Finally, the reason for learning to add and subtract is to be able to solve problems. In particular, it is crucial to decide which operations to use in solving a problem. Consider the problem "If Larry has $7 and Judy has $3, how much more money does Larry have?" Neither the take-away approach nor the missing-addend approach can be applied literally since Judy's $3 is not a subset of Larry's $7. However, Judy's three dollars can be matched with three of Larry's $7, leaving a difference of 4 (Figure 3.17). This approach to subtraction is called the **comparison approach**. In this approach we begin with two distinct sets. Then we match the elements of the set having fewer elements with a subset of the larger set and apply either the take-away or missing-addend approach to find the difference. We can solve the preceding problem by rephrasing it in missing-addend format:

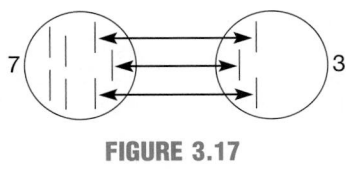

FIGURE 3.17

$$3 + c = 7 \quad \text{so} \quad c = 7 - 3 = 4.$$

MATHEMATICAL MORSEL

Benjamin Franklin was known for his role in politics and as an inventor. One of his mathematical discoveries was an 8-by-8 square made up of the counting numbers from 1 to 64. Check out the following properties:
1. All rows and columns total 260.
2. All half rows and half columns total 130.
3. The four corners total 130.
4. The sum of the corners in any 4-by-4 or 6-by-6 array is 130.
5. Every 2-by-2 array of four numbers totals 130.
(NOTE: There are 49 of these 2-by-2 arrays!)

EXERCISE/PROBLEM SET 3.1—PART A

Exercises

1. Draw a figure similar to Figure 3.1 to illustrate the problem $4 + 3 = 7$.

2. **(a)** Given sets A, B, and C, find the number for each union of sets specified.

$A = \{\text{red, yellow}\}$ $B = \{\text{blue, green, orange}\}$
$C = \{\text{purple, white, blue}\}$
(i) $n(A \cup B)$ (ii) $n(A \cup C)$ (iii) $n(B \cup C)$

(b) In which cases is the number of colors in the union of the two sets equal to the sum of the numbers of colors in each set?

3. Illustrate the problem $3 + 5 = 8$ on the number line.

4. Which of the following sets are closed under addition? Why or why not?
(a) $\{0, 10, 20, 30, \ldots\}$
(b) $\{0\}$
(c) $\{0, 1, 2\}$
(d) $\{1, 2\}$
(e) Whole numbers greater than 17
(f) $\{0, 3, 6, 9, \ldots\}$
(g) $\{1\}$
(h) $\{1, 5, 9, 13, \ldots\}$
(i) $\{8, 12, 16, 20, \ldots\}$
(j) Whole numbers less than 17

5. Identify the property or properties being illustrated.
(a) $1279 + 3847$ must be a whole number.
(b) $7 + 5 = 5 + 7$
(c) $53 + 47 = 50 + 50$
(d) $1 + 0 = 1$
(e) $1 + 0 = 0 + 1$
(f) $(53 + 48) + 7 = 60 + 48$

6. Rewrite the following expression to apply the property specified.
$$(6 + 0) + 3$$
(a) Associative   **(b)** Commutative   **(c)** Identity

7. What property or properties justify that you get the same answer to the following problem whether you add "up" (starting with $9 + 8$) or "down" (starting with $3 + 8$)?
$$\begin{array}{r} 3 \\ 8 \\ +9 \\ \hline \end{array}$$

8. (a) Complete this addition table in base two.

+	0	1
0		
1		

(b) Use the table, if you wish, to determine if the following statements are true.
  (i) $0 + 1 = 1 + 0$
  (ii) $(0 + 1) + 1 = 0 + (1 + 1)$
  (iii) $1 + 1 = 11_{\text{two}}$
  (iv) $10_{\text{two}} - 1 = 1$
(c) Is it necessary to use the table in parts (i) and (ii)? Explain.

9. (a) State the difference $8 - 3$ in terms of both definitions of subtraction given in this section.
(b) Illustrate the missing-addend approach for $8 - 3$ using a measurement model and a set model.

(c) Illustrate the take-away approach for $8 - 3$ using a set model and a measurement model.
(d) Illustrate the comparison approach for $8 - 3$ using a set model.

10. Which of the following subtraction problems can be obtained immediately from an addition facts table?
(a) $\begin{array}{r} 11 \\ -\ 9 \\ \hline \end{array}$ **(b)** $\begin{array}{r} 8 \\ -2 \\ \hline \end{array}$ **(c)** $\begin{array}{r} 34 \\ -16 \\ \hline \end{array}$
(d) $\begin{array}{r} 17 \\ -\ 9 \\ \hline \end{array}$ **(e)** $\begin{array}{r} 111 \\ -\ 52 \\ \hline \end{array}$ **(f)** $\begin{array}{r} 12 \\ -\ 0 \\ \hline \end{array}$

11. Using different-shaped boxes for variables provides a transition to algebra as well as a means of stating problems. Try some whole numbers in the boxes to determine if these properties hold.
(a) Is subtraction closed?

$$\square - \triangle \overset{?}{=} \bigcirc$$

(b) Is subtraction commutative?

$$\square - \triangle \overset{?}{=} \triangle - \square$$

(c) Is subtraction associative?

$$(\square - \triangle) - \bigcirc \overset{?}{=} \square - (\triangle - \bigcirc)$$

(d) Is there an identity element for subtraction?

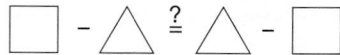

$$\square - \triangle = \square \quad \text{and} \quad \triangle - \square = \square$$

12. Let x, y, and z be whole numbers. For what values of x, y, and z are the following defined?
(a) $x - (y - z)$ **(b)** $(x - y) - z$

13. Each situation described next involves a subtraction problem. In each case, tell whether the problem situation is best represented by the take-away model, the missing-addend model, or the comparison approach, and why. Then write an appropriate equation to fit the situation.
(a) An elementary teacher started the year with a budget of $200 to be spent on manipulatives. By the end of December, $120 had been spent. How much money remained in the budget?
(b) Doreen planted 24 tomato plants in her garden and Justin planted 18 tomato plants in his garden. How many more plants did Doreen plant?

(c) Tami is saving money for a trip to Hawaii over spring break. The package tour she is interested in costs $1795. From her part-time job she has saved $1240 so far. How much more money must she save?

14. (a) Complete the following addition table in base six. Remember to use the thinking strategies.

$$
\begin{array}{c|cccccc}
+ & 0 & 1 & 2 & 3 & 4 & 5 \\
\hline
0 \\
1 \\
2 \\
3 \\
4 \\
5
\end{array}
$$
(base six)

(b) For each of the following subtraction problems in base six, rewrite the problem using the missing-addend approach and find the answer in the table.
 (i) $13_{six} - 5_{six}$ (ii) $5_{six} - 4_{six}$
 (iii) $12_{six} - 4_{six}$ (iv) $10_{six} - 2_{six}$
 (v) $12_{six} - 3_{six}$ (vi) $11_{six} - 3_{six}$

15. Using the addition table for base six given in Exercise 14, complete the following "four-fact families" in base six.
(a) $2_{six} + 3_{six} = 5_{six}$

_____

_____

_____

(b) _____

_____

$11_{six} - 5_{six} = 2_{six}$

_____

Problems

16. A given set contains the number 1. What other numbers must also be in the set if it is closed under addition?

17. The number 100 can be expressed using the nine digits 1, 2, . . . , 9 with plus and minus signs as follows:

$$1 + 2 + 3 - 4 + 5 + 6 + 78 + 9 = 100$$

Find a sum of 100 using each of the nine digits and only three plus or minus signs.

18. Complete the following magic square, in which the sum of each row, each column, and each diagonal is the same. When completed, the magic square should contain each of the numbers 10 to 25 exactly once.

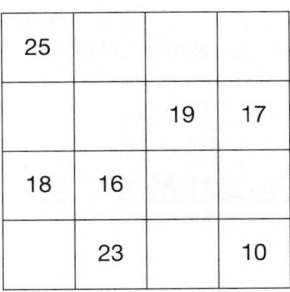

19. Magic squares are not the only magic figures. The following figure is a magic hexagon. What is "magic" about it?

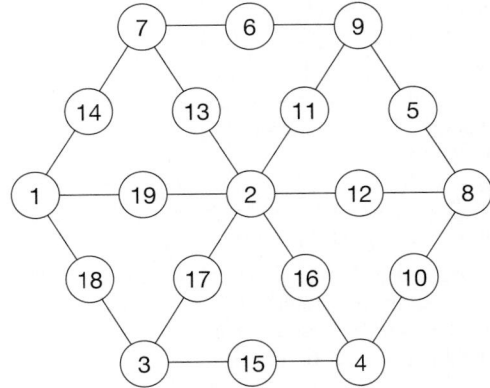

20. A **palindrome** is any number that reads the same backward and forward. For example, 262 and 37673 are palindromes. In the accompanying example, the process of reversing the digits and adding the two numbers has been repeated until a palindrome is obtained.

$$
\begin{array}{r}
67 \\
+76 \\
\hline
143 \\
+341 \\
\hline
484
\end{array}
$$

(a) Try this method with the following numbers.
 (i) 39   (ii) 87   (iii) 32
(b) Find a number for which the procedure takes more than three steps to obtain a palindrome.

21. Mr. Morgan has five daughters. They were all born the number of years apart as the youngest daughter is old. The oldest daughter is 16 years older than the youngest. What are the ages of Mr. Morgan's daughters?

22. Using a Venn diagram, justify this equation:

$$n(A \cup B) = n(A) + n(B) - n(A \cap B)$$

23. The property "If $a + c = b + c$, then $a = b$," is called the **additive cancellation property**. Is this property true for all whole numbers? If "yes," how would you convince your students that it is always true? If "no," give a counterexample.

EXERCISE/PROBLEM SET 3.1—PART B

Exercises

1. Can the sets {0, 3} and {0, 2} be used to demonstrate the sum of two plus two? Why or why not?

2. For which of the following pairs of sets is it true that $n(D) + n(E) = n(D \cup E)$?
(a) $D = \{1, 2, 3, 4\}, E = \{7, 8, 9, 10\}$
(b) $D = \{ \}, E = \{1\}$
(c) $D = \{a, c, e, g\}, E = \{b, d, f, g\}$
(d) $D = \{ \}, E = \{ \}$

3. Tell whether or not the following sets are closed under addition. Why or why not?
(a) $A = \{0\}$
(b) $E = \{0, 2, 4, 6, . . .\}$
(c) $O = \{1, 3, 5, 7, 9, . . .\}$
(d) $F = \{0, 5, 10, 15, 20, . . .\}$

4. Suppose that S is a set of whole numbers closed under addition. S contains 3, 27, and 72.
(a) List six other elements in S.
(b) Why must 24 be in S?

5. (a) Illustrate $3 + 6$ and $6 + 3$ on the same number line. Which property does this demonstrate?
(b) Devise a way of illustrating 0 plus any number on the number line. Then illustrate $4 + 0$ and $0 + 4$ on the same line. Which property is demonstrated?
(c) Illustrate $(5 + 2) + 3$ and $5 + (2 + 3)$ on the same number line. Which property is demonstrated?

6. Each of the following is an example of one of the properties for addition of whole numbers. Fill in the blank to complete the statement, and identify the property.
(a) $5 + \_\_\_\_ = 5$
(b) $7 + 5 = \_\_\_\_ + 7$
(c) $(4 + 3) + 6 = 4 + (\_\_\_\_ + 6)$
(d) $(4 + 3) + 6 = \_\_\_\_ + (4 + 3)$
(e) $(4 + 3) + 6 = (3 + \_\_\_\_) + 6$
(f) $2 + 9$ is a _____ number.

7. Addition can be simplified using the associative property of addition. For example,

$$26 + 57 = 26 + (4 + 53) = (26 + 4) + 53$$
$$= 30 + 53 = 83$$

Complete the following statements.
(a) $39 + 68 = 40 + \_\_\_\_ = \_\_\_\_$
(b) $25 + 56 = 30 + \_\_\_\_ = \_\_\_\_$
(c) $47 + 23 = 50 + \_\_\_\_ = \_\_\_\_$

8. Look for easy combinations of numbers to compute the following sums mentally. Show the groupings you used.
(a) $94 + 27 + 6 + 13$
(b) $5 + 13 + 25 + 31 + 47$

9. Without performing the addition, determine which sum (if either) is larger. What properties are you using?

$$
\begin{array}{cc}
3261 & 4187 \\
4287 & 5291 \\
+5193 & +3263 \\
\end{array}
$$

10. Use a number line (measurement model) to illustrate each of the following problems.
(a) $2 + 5$ (b) $9 + 6$ (c) $12 - 4$
(d) $15 - 8$

11. Rewrite each of the following subtraction problems as an addition problem.
(a) $x - 156 = 279$ (b) $279 - 156 = x$
(c) $279 - x = 156$

12. In the following figure centimeter strips are used to illustrate $3 + 8 = 11$. What two subtraction problems are also being represented? What definition of subtraction is being demonstrated?

	10		1
3		8	

13. Solve $10{,}013 - 4322$ by using the missing-addend method. In other words, find a number so that $4322 + _____ = 10{,}013$. See if you can solve it from left to right: finding the thousands, then the hundreds, and so on.

14. For each of the following, determine whole numbers x, y, and z that make the statement true.
(a) $x - 0 = 0 - x = x$
(b) $x - y = y - x$
(c) $(x - y) - z = x - (y - z)$
Which, if any, are true for all whole numbers x, y, and z?

15. Each situation described next involves a subtraction problem. In each case, tell whether the problem situation is best represented by the take-away model, the missing-addend model, or the comparison approach, and why. Then write an appropriate equation to fit the situation.

(a) Robby has accumulated a collection of 362 sports cards. Chris has a collection of 200 cards. How many more cards than Chris does Robby have?

(b) Jack is driving from St. Louis to Kansas City for a meeting, a total distance of 250 miles. After 2 hours he notices that he has traveled 114 miles. How far is he from Kansas City at that time?

(c) An elementary school library consists of 1095 books. As of May 8, 105 books were checked out of the library. How many books were still available for checkout on May 8?

16. (a) Complete the following addition table in base five. Remember to use the thinking strategies.

+	0	1	2	3	4
0					
1					
2					
3					
4					

(base five)

(b) Using this table, complete the following "four-fact families" in *base five*.

(i) $3_{five} + 4_{five} = 12_{five}$ (ii) _____

_____ $4_{five} + 1_{five} = 10_{five}$

_____   _____

_____   _____

(iii) _____

_____

$11_{five} - 4_{five} = 2_{five}$

_____

17. (a) Complete the following addition table in base four.

+	0	1	2	3
0				
1				
2				
3				

(base four)

(b) For each of the following subtraction problems in base four, rewrite the problem using the missing addend approach and find the answer in the table.

(i) $11_{four} - 2_{four}$

(ii) $10_{four} - 3_{four}$

(iii) $12_{four} - 3_{four}$

Problems

18. A given set contains the number 5. What other numbers must also be in the set if it is closed under addition?

19. Is there a set of whole numbers with more than one element that is closed under subtraction?

20. Using only the digits 1, 2, . . . , 9 and plus signs, the number 99 can be expressed as

$$9 + 8 + 7 + 6 + 5 + 43 + 21$$

Can you find another way?

21. The following figure can provide practice in addition and subtraction.

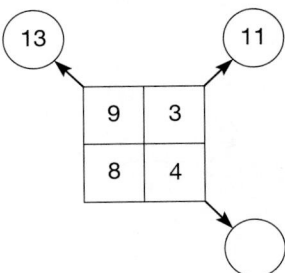

The figure is completed by filling the upper two circles with the sums obtained by adding diagonally.

$$9 + 4 = 13 \quad \text{and} \quad 8 + 3 = 11$$

The circle at the lower right is filled in one of two ways:

1. Adding the numbers in the upper circles:
   13 + 11 = 24
2. Adding across the rows, adding down the columns, and then adding the results in each case:

$$12 + 12 = 24 \quad \text{and} \quad 17 + 7 = 24$$

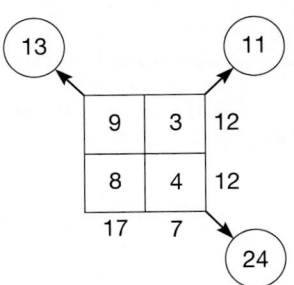

(a) Fill in the missing numbers for the following figure.

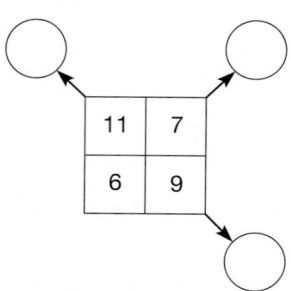

(b) Fill in the missing numbers for the following figure.

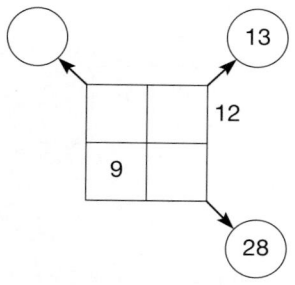

(c) Use variables to show why the sum of the numbers in the upper two circles will always be the same as the sum of the two rows and the sum of the two columns.

22. Arrange the numbers 1 to 10 around the outside of the circle shown so that the sum of any two adjacent numbers is the same as the sum of the two numbers on the other ends of the spokes. As an example, 6 and 9, 8 and 7 might be placed as shown since $6 + 9 = 8 + 7$.

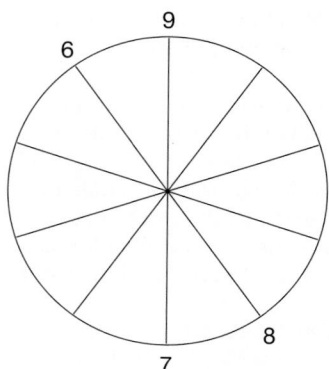

23. Place the numbers 1–16 in the cells of the following magic square so that the sum of each row, column, and diagonal is the same.

	2		
5			8
	7	6	
		15	1

24. Shown here is a magic triangle discovered by the mental calculator Marathe. What is its magic?

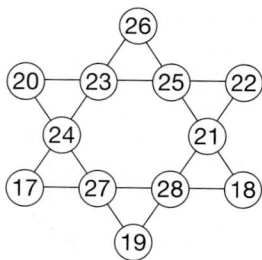

3.2

MULTIPLICATION AND DIVISION

Multiplication and Its Properties

There are many ways to view multiplication.

Repeated-Addition Approach

Consider the following problems: There are five children and each has three silver dollars. How many silver dollars do they have altogether? The silver dollars are about 1 inch wide. If the silver dollars are laid in a single row with each dollar touching the next, what is the length of the row? These problems can be modeled using the set model and the measurement model (Figure 3.18).

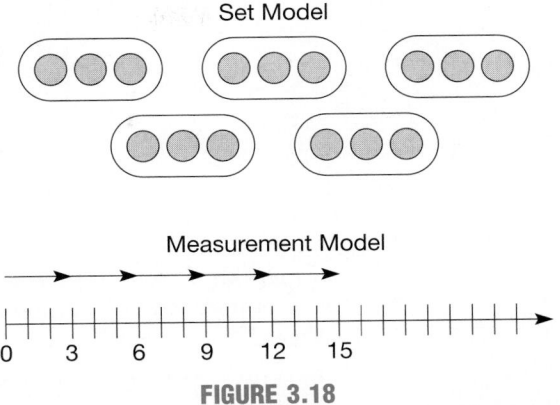

FIGURE 3.18

These models look similar to the ones that we used for addition since we are merely adding repeatedly. They show that $3 + 3 + 3 + 3 + 3 = 15$, or that $5 \times 3 = 15$.

Definition

Multiplication of Whole Numbers: Repeated-Addition Approach

Let a and b be any whole numbers where $a \neq 0$. Then

$$ab = \underbrace{b + b + \cdots + b}_{a \text{ addends}}.$$

If $a = 1$, then $ab = 1 \cdot b = b$; also $0 \cdot b = 0$ for all b.

Since multiplication combines two numbers to form a single number, it is a binary operation. The number **ab**, read "**a times b**," is called the **product** of a and b. The numbers a and b are called **factors** of ab. The product ab can also be written as "**a · b**" and "**a × b**." Notice that $0 \cdot b = 0$ for all b. That is, the product of zero and any whole number is zero.

Rectangular Array Approach

If the silver dollars in the preceding problem are arranged in a rectangular array, multiplication can be viewed in a slightly different way (Figure 3.19, page 112).

Alternate Definition

Multiplication of Whole Numbers: Rectangular Array Approach

Let a and b be any whole numbers. Then ab is the number of elements in a rectangular array having a rows and b columns.

Rectangular Array Approach

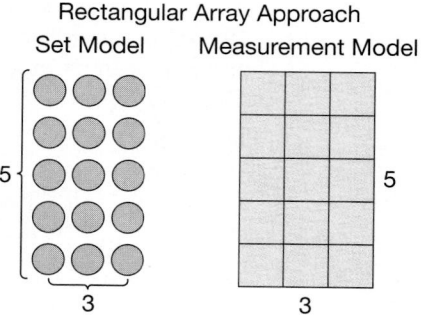

FIGURE 3.19

Cartesian Product Approach

A third way of viewing multiplication is an abstraction of this array approach.

Alternate Definition

Multiplication of Whole Numbers: Cartesian Product Approach

Let a and b be any whole numbers. If $a = n(A)$ and $b = n(B)$, then

$$ab = n(A \times B).$$

For example, to compute $2 \cdot 3$, let $2 = n(\{a, b\})$ and $3 = n(\{x, y, z\})$. Then $2 \cdot 3$ is the number of ordered pairs in the set $\{a, b\} \times \{x, y, z\}$. Because $\{a, b\} \times \{x, y, z\} = \{(a, x), (a, y), (a, z), (b, x), (b, y), (b, z)\}$ has six ordered pairs, we conclude that $2 \cdot 3 = 6$. Actually, by arranging the pairs in an appropriate row and column configuration, this approach can also be viewed as the array approach, as illustrated next.

	x	y	z
a	(a, x)	(a, y)	(a, z)
b	(b, x)	(b, y)	(b, z)

Tree Diagram Approach

Another way of modeling this approach is through the use of a **tree diagram** (Figure 3.20). Tree diagrams are especially useful in the field of probability, which we study in Chapter 12.

Properties of Whole-Number Multiplication

You have probably observed that whenever you multiplied any two whole numbers, your product was always a whole number. This fact is summarized by the following property.

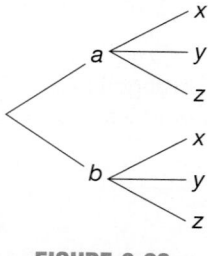

FIGURE 3.20

Closure Property for Multiplication of Whole Numbers

The product of two whole numbers is a whole number.

When two odd whole numbers are multiplied together, the product is odd; thus the set of odd numbers is closed under multiplication. Closure is a useful idea since if we are multiplying two (or more) odd numbers and the product we calculate is even, we can conclude that our product is incorrect. The set {2, 5, 8, 11, 14, . . .} is not closed under multiplication since $2 \cdot 5 = 10$ and 10 is not in the set.

The next property can be used to simplify learning the basic multiplication facts. For example, by the repeated-addition approach, 7×2 represents $2 + 2 + 2 + 2 + 2 + 2 + 2$, whereas 2×7 means $7 + 7$. Since $7 + 7$ was learned as an addition fact, viewing 7×2 as 2×7 makes this computation easier.

> **Commutative Property for Whole-Number Multiplication**
>
> Let a and b be any whole numbers. Then
>
> $$ab = ba.$$

The example in Figure 3.21 should convince you that the commutative property for multiplication is true.

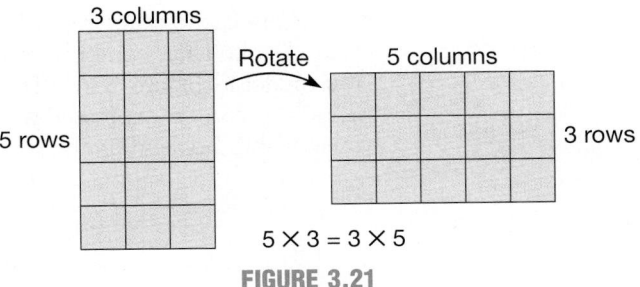

$$5 \times 3 = 3 \times 5$$

FIGURE 3.21

The product $5 \cdot (2 \cdot 13)$ is more easily found if it is viewed as $(5 \cdot 2) \cdot 13$. Regrouping to put the 5 and 2 together can be done because of the next property.

> **Associative Property for Whole-Number Multiplication**
>
> Let a, b, and c be any whole numbers. Then
>
> $$a(bc) = (ab)c.$$

To illustrate the validity of the associative property for multiplication, consider the three-dimensional models in Figure 3.22.

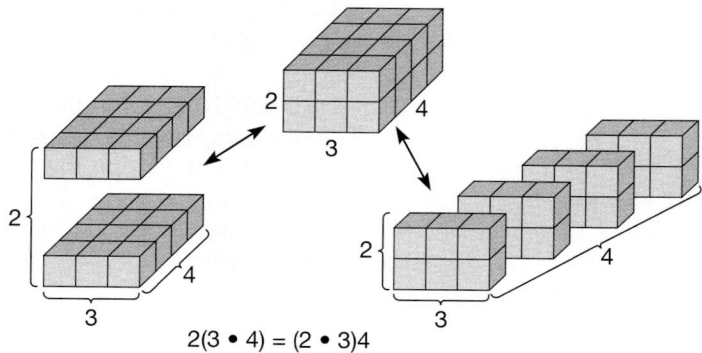

$$2(3 \cdot 4) = (2 \cdot 3)4$$

FIGURE 3.22

The next property is an immediate consequence of each of our definitions of multiplication.

Identity Property for Whole-Number Multiplication

The number 1 is the unique whole number such that for every whole number a,

$$a \cdot 1 = a = 1 \cdot a.$$

Because of this property, the number one is called the **multiplicative identity** or the **identity for multiplication**.

There is one other important property of the whole numbers. This property, distributivity, combines both multiplication and addition. Study the array model in Figure 3.23. This model shows that the *product of a sum*, $3(2 + 4)$, can be expressed as the *sum of products*, $(3 \cdot 2) + (3 \cdot 4)$. This relationship holds in general.

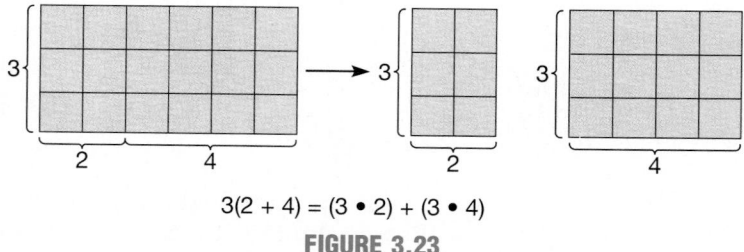

$$3(2 + 4) = (3 \cdot 2) + (3 \cdot 4)$$

FIGURE 3.23

Distributive Property of Multiplication over Addition

Let a, b, and c be any whole numbers. Then

$$a(b + c) = ab + ac.$$

Because of commutativity, we can also write

$$(b + c)a = ba + ca.$$

Notice that the distributive property "distributes" the a to the b *and* the c.

EXAMPLE 3.5 Rewrite each of the following expressions using the distributive property.

(a) $3(4 + 5)$ **(b)** $5 \cdot 7 + 5 \cdot 3$ **(c)** $am + an$
(d) $31 \cdot 76 + 29 \cdot 76$ **(e)** $a(b + c + d)$

Solution
(a) $3(4 + 5) = 3 \cdot 4 + 3 \cdot 5$
(b) $5 \cdot 7 + 5 \cdot 3 = 5(7 + 3)$
(c) $am + an = a(m + n)$
(d) $31 \cdot 76 + 29 \cdot 76 = (31 + 29)76$
(e) $a(b + c + d) = a(b + c) + ad = ab + ac + ad$ ■

Let's summarize the properties of whole-number addition and multiplication.

Whole-Number Properties

Property	Addition	Multiplication
Closure	Yes	Yes
Commutativity	Yes	Yes
Associativity	Yes	Yes
Identity	Yes (zero)	Yes (one)
Distributivity of multiplication over addition		Yes

In addition to these properties, we highlight the following.

Multiplication Property of Zero

For every whole number a,

$$a \cdot 0 = 0 \cdot a = 0.$$

Using the missing-addend approach to subtraction, we will now show that $a(b - c) = ab - ac$ whenever $b - c$ is a whole number. In words, multiplication distributes over subtraction.

Let	$b - c = n$	
Then	$b = c + n$	Missing addend
	$ab = a(c + n)$	Multiplication
	$ab = ac + an$	Distributivity
Therefore,	$ab - ac = an$	Missing addend
But	$b - c = n$	from the first equation

So, substituting $b - c$ for n, we have

$$ab - ac = a(b - c).$$

> **Distributivity of Multiplication over Subtraction**
>
> Let a, b, and c be any whole numbers where $b \geq c$. Then
> $$a(b - c) = ab - ac$$

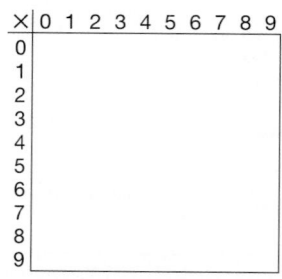

FIGURE 3.24

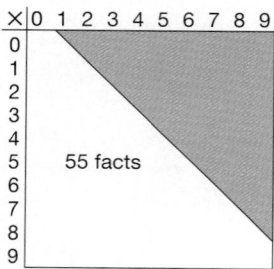

FIGURE 3.25

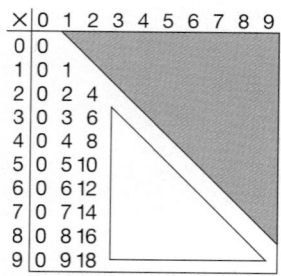

FIGURE 3.26

FIGURE 3.27

The following discussion shows how the properties are used to develop thinking strategies for learning the multiplication facts.

Thinking Strategies for Learning the Multiplication Facts

The multiplication table in Figure 3.24 has $10 \times 10 = 100$ unfilled spaces.

1. *Commutativity.* As in the case of the addition table, because of commutativity, only 55 facts in the unshaded region in Figure 3.25 have to be found.

2. *Multiplication by 0.* $a \cdot 0 = 0$ for all whole numbers a. Thus the first column is all zeros (Figure 3.26).

3. *Multiplication by 1.* $1 \cdot a = a \cdot 1 = a$. Thus the column labeled "1" is the same as the left-hand column outside the table (Figure 3.26).

4. *Multiplication by 2.* $2 \cdot a = a + a$, which are the doubles from addition (Figure 3.26).

We have filled in 27 facts using thinking strategies 1, 2, 3, and 4. Therefore, 28 facts remain to be found out of our original 55.

5. *Multiplication by 5.* The counting chant by fives, namely 5, 10, 15, 20, and so on, can be used to learn these facts (see the column and/or row headed by a 5 in Figure 3.27.

6. *Multiplication by 9.* The multiples of 9 are 9, 18, 27, 36, 45, 54, 63, 72, and 81 (Figure 3.27). Notice how the tens digit is one less than the number we are multiplying by 9. For example, the tens digit of $3 \cdot 9$ is 2 (one less than 3). Also, the sum of the digits of the multiples of 9 is 9. Thus $3 \cdot 9 = 27$ since $2 + 7 = 9$. The multiples of 5 and 9 eliminate 13 more facts, so 15 remain.

7. *Associativity and distributivity.* The remaining facts can be obtained using these two properties. For example, $8 \times 4 = 8 \times (2 \times 2) = (8 \times 2) \times 2 = 16 \times 2 = 32$ or $8 \times 4 = 8(3 + 1) = 8 \cdot 3 + 8 \cdot 1 = 24 + 8 = 32$.

In the next example we consider how the knowledge of the basic facts and the properties can be applied to multiplying a single digit number by a multidigit number.

EXAMPLE 3.6 Compute the following products using thinking strategies.
(a) 2×34 **(b)** $5(37 \cdot 2)$ **(c)** $7(25)$

Solution
(a) $2 \times 34 = 2(30 + 4) = 2 \cdot 30 + 2 \cdot 4 = 60 + 8 = 68$
(b) $5(37 \cdot 2) = 5(2 \cdot 37) = (5 \cdot 2) \cdot 37 = 370$
(c) $7(25) = (4 + 3)25 = 4 \cdot 25 + 3 \cdot 25 = 100 + 75 = 175$ ∎

Division

Just as with addition, subtraction, and multiplication, we can view division in different ways. Consider these two problems.

1. A class of 20 children is to be divided into four teams with the same number of children on each team. How many children are on each team?
2. A class of 20 children is to be divided into teams of four children each. How many teams are there?

Notice how these are different problems, but both can be solved by using division (Figure 3.28).

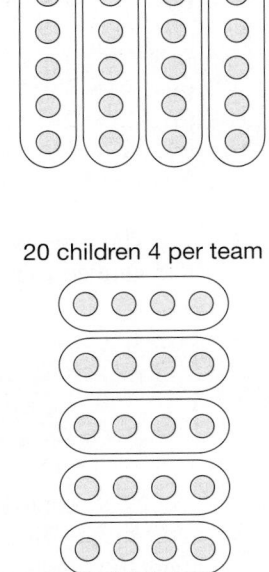

20 children in 4 teams

20 children 4 per team

FIGURE 3.28

Figure 3.29 pictures division using a measurement model.

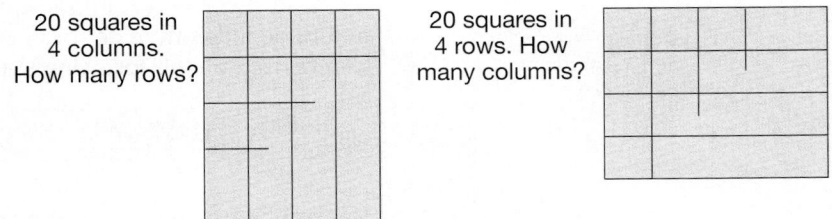

20 squares in 4 columns. How many rows?

20 squares in 4 rows. How many columns?

FIGURE 3.29

Missing-Factor Approach

The answers to the problems in Figure 3.29 can be obtained using multiplication facts. This suggests the following definition of division.

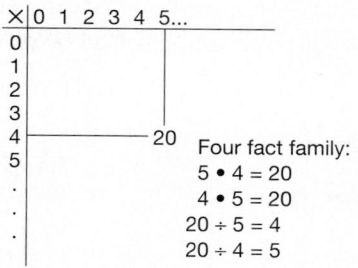

Four fact family:
$5 \cdot 4 = 20$
$4 \cdot 5 = 20$
$20 \div 5 = 4$
$20 \div 4 = 5$

FIGURE 3.30

> **Definition**
>
> ### Division of Whole Numbers: Missing-Factor Approach
>
> If a and b are any whole numbers with $b \neq 0$, then $a \div b = c$ if and only if $a = bc$ for some whole number c.

The symbol $a \div b$ is read "a divided by b." Also, a is called the **dividend**, b is called the **divisor**, and c is called the **quotient** or **missing factor**. The basic facts multiplication table can be used to learn division facts (Figure 3.30).

EXAMPLE 3.7   Find the following quotients.
(a) $24 \div 8$ **(b)** $72 \div 9$ **(c)** $52 \div 4$ **(d)** $0 \div 7$

Solution
(a) $24 \div 8 = 3$ since $24 = 8 \times 3$
(b) $72 \div 9 = 8$ since $72 = 9 \times 8$
(c) $52 \div 4 = 13$ since $52 = 13 \times 4$
(d) $0 \div 7 = 0$ since $0 = 7 \times 0$ ∎

The division problem in Example 3.7(d) can be generalized as follows and verified using the missing-factor approach.

> ### Division Property of Zero
>
> If $a \neq 0$, then $0 \div a = 0$.

Next, consider the situation of *dividing by zero*. Suppose that we extend the missing-factor approach of division to dividing by zero. Then we have the following two cases.

Case 1: $a \div 0$, where $a \neq 0$. If $a \div 0 = c$, then $a = 0 \cdot c$, or $a = 0$. But $a \neq 0$. Therefore, $a \div 0$ is undefined.

Case 2: $0 \div 0$. If $0 \div 0 = c$, then $0 = 0 \cdot c$. But any value can be selected for c, so there is no *unique* quotient c. Thus division by zero is said to be indeterminate, or undefined, here. These two cases are summarized by the following statement.

> ### Division by 0 is undefined.

Now consider the problem $37 \div 4$. Although $37 \div 4$ does not have a whole-number answer, there are applications where it is of interest to know how many groups of 4 are in 37 with the possibility that there is something left over. For example, if there are 37 fruit slices to be divided among four children so that each child gets the same number of slices, how many would each child get? We can find as many as 9 fours in 37 and then have 1 remaining. Thus each child would get nine fruit slices with one left undistributed. This way of looking at division of whole numbers, but with a remainder, is summarized next.

The Division Algorithm

If a and b are any whole numbers with $b \neq 0$, then there exist unique whole numbers q and r such that $a = bq + r$, where $0 \leq r < b$.

Here b is called the **divisor**, q is called the **quotient**, and r is the **remainder**. Notice that the remainder is always less than the divisor. Also, when the remainder is 0, this result coincides with the usual definition of whole-number division.

EXAMPLE 3.8   Find the quotient and remainder for these problems.
(a) $57 \div 9$ **(b)** $44 \div 13$ **(c)** $96 \div 8$

Solution
(a) $9 \times 6 = 54$, so $57 = 6 \cdot 9 + 3$. The quotient is 6 and the remainder is 3 (Figure 3.31).

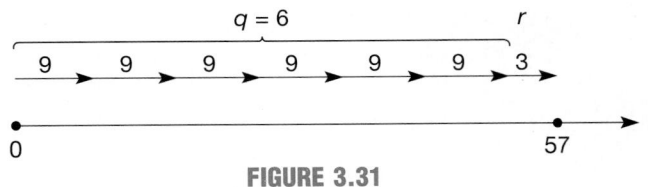

FIGURE 3.31

(b) $13 \times 3 = 39$, so $44 = 3 \cdot 13 + 5$. The quotient is 3 and the remainder is 5.
(c) $8 \times 12 = 96$, so $96 = 12 \cdot 8 + 0$. The quotient is 12 and the remainder is 0. ◼

Repeated-Subtraction Approach

Figure 3.32 suggests an alternative way of viewing division.

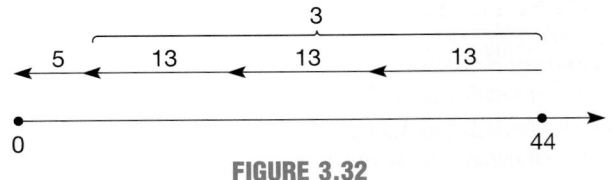

FIGURE 3.32

In the picture, 13 was subtracted from 44 three successive times until a number less than 13 was reached, namely 5. Thus 44 divided by 13 has a quotient of 3 and a remainder of 5. This example shows that division can be viewed as repeated subtraction. In general, to find $a \div b$ using the repeated- subtraction approach, subtract b successively from a and from the

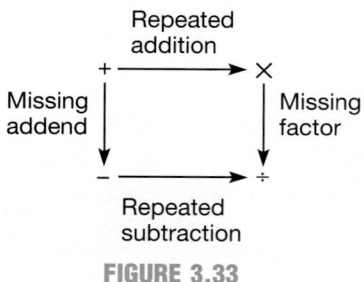

Repeated addition

Missing addend

Missing factor

Repeated subtraction

FIGURE 3.33

resulting differences until a remainder r is reached, where $r < b$. The number of times b is subtracted is the quotient q.

Figure 3.33 provides a visual way to remember the main interconnections among the four basic whole-number operations. For example, multiplication of whole numbers is defined by using the repeated-addition approach, subtraction is defined using the missing-addend approach, and so on. An important message in this diagram is that success in subtraction, multiplication, and division begins with a solid foundation in addition.

MATHEMATICAL MORSEL

The following note appeared in a newspaper:

"What's $241,573,142,393,627,673,576,$ $957,439,048$ times $45,994,811,347,886,846,$ $310,221,728,895,223,034,301,839$? The answer is 71 consecutive 1s—one of the biggest numbers a computer has ever factored. The 71-digit number was factored this month in 9.5 hours of a Cray supercomputer's time at Los Alamos National Laboratory in New Mexico, besting the previous high—69 digits—by two. Why bother? The feat might affect national security. Some computer systems are guarded by cryptographic codes once thought to be beyond factoring. The work at Los Alamos could help intelligence experts break codes."

See if you can find an error in the article and correct it.

EXERCISE/PROBLEM SET 3.2—PART A

Exercises

1. Illustrate 4×6 using each of the following models.
   (a) Set model
   (b) Measurement model
   (c) Rectangular array approach

2. Show how to demonstrate that $3 \cdot (5 \cdot 2) = (3 \cdot 5) \cdot 2$ using a three-dimensional model as suggested by Figure 3.22.

3. Given a set A with $n(A) = a$ and the fact that $A \times \varnothing = \varnothing$, show that $a \cdot 0 = 0$ using the Cartesian product approach to whole-number multiplication.

4. Which of the following sets are closed under multiplication? Why or why not?
   (a) $\{2, 4\}$
   (b) $\{0, 2, 4, 6, \ldots\}$
   (c) $\{0, 3\}$
   (d) $\{0, 1\}$
   (e) $\{1\}$
   (f) $\{0\}$
   (g) $\{5, 7, 9, \ldots\}$
   (h) $\{0, 7, 14, 21, \ldots\}$
   (i) $\{0, 1, 2, 4, 8, 16, \ldots, 2^k, \ldots\}$
   (j) odd whole numbers

5. Identify the property of whole numbers being illustrated.
   (a) $4 \cdot 5 = 5 \cdot 4$
   (b) $6(3 + 2) = (3 + 2)6$
   (c) $5(2 + 9) = 5 \cdot 2 + 5 \cdot 9$

(d) $1(x + y) = x + y$
(e) $3(5 - 2) = 3 \cdot 5 - 3 \cdot 2$
(f) $6(7 \cdot 2) = (6 \cdot 7) \cdot 2$
(g) $(4 + 7) \cdot 0 = 0$
(h) $(5 + 6) \cdot 3 = 5 \cdot 3 + 6 \cdot 3$

6. Rewrite each of the following expressions using the distributive property for multiplication over addition or for multiplication over subtraction. Your answers should contain no parentheses.
   (a) $4(60 + 37)$ **(b)** $(21 + 35) \cdot 6$
   (c) $3(29 + 30 + 6)$ **(d)** $5(x - 2y)$
   (e) $37(60 - 22)$ **(f)** $a(7 - b + z)$

7. Use the distributive property of multiplication over subtraction to find n. For example,

   $$4 \times 58 = (4 \times 60) - (4 \times 2) = 240 - 8 = 232$$

   (a) $6 \times 99 = n$ **(b)** $5 \times 49 = n$
   (c) $7 \times 19 = n$ **(d)** $6 \times 47 = n$

8. **(a)** Evaluate the expression $2n + 5n$ for $n = 6$.
   (b) Evaluate the expression $2n + 5n$ for $n = 13$.
   (c) Evaluate the expression $2n + 5n$ for $n = 20$.
   (d) What do you notice about the answer in each case?

9. The distributive property of multiplication over addition can be used to perform some calculations mentally. For example, to find $13 \cdot 12$, you can think

   $$13(12) = 13(10 + 2) = 13(10) + 13(2)$$
   $$= 130 + 26 = 156$$

   How could each of the following products be rewritten using the distributive property so that it is more easily computed mentally?
   (a) $45(11)$
   (b) $39(102)$
   (c) $23(21)$
   (d) $97(101)$

10. Shirley meant to add $12349 \boxed{+} 29746$ on her calculator. After entering 12349, she pushed the $\boxed{\times}$ button by mistake. What could she do next to keep from reentering 12349? What property are you using?

11. Explain how to find the answer to $56 \div 7$ in a multiplication table.

12. Rewrite each of the following division problems as a multiplication problem.
    (a) $48 \div 6 = 8$ **(b)** $51 \div x = 3$
    (c) $x \div 13 = 5$ **(d)** $24 \div x = 12$
    (e) $x \div 3 = 27$ **(f)** $a \div b = x$

13. How many division problems without remainder are possible where one member of the given set is divided by another (possibly the same) member of the same set? List the problems. Remember, division by zero is not defined. For example, in $\{1, 2, 4\}$ there are six problems: $1 \div 1$, $2 \div 2$, $4 \div 4$, $4 \div 1$, $2 \div 1$, and $4 \div 2$.

(a) $\{0\}$ **(b)** $\{0, 1\}$
(c) $\{0, 1, 2, 3, 4\}$ **(d)** $\{0, 2, 4, 6\}$
(e) $\{0, 1, 2, 3, \ldots, 9\}$ **(f)** $\{3, 4, 5, \ldots, 11\}$

14. Each situation described next involves a multiplication problem. In each case state whether the problem situation is best represented by the repeated-addition approach, the rectangular array approach, or the Cartesian product approach, and why. Then write an appropriate equation to fit the situation.
    (a) At the student snack bar, three sizes of beverages are available: small, medium, and large. Five varieties of soft drinks are available: cola, diet cola, lemon-lime, root beer, and orange. How many different choices of soft drink does a student have including the size that may be selected?
    (b) At graduation students file into the auditorium four abreast. A parent seated near the door counts 72 rows of students who pass him. How many students participated in the graduation exercise?
    (c) Kirsten was in charge of the food for an all-school picnic. She went to the grocery store and purchased 25 eight-packs of hot dog buns for 70 cents each. How much did she spend on the hot dog buns?

15. **(a)** Complete the following multiplication table in *base five*.

$\times$	0	1	2	3	4
0					
1					
2					(base five)
3					
4					

(b) Using the table above, complete the following "four-fact families" in *base five*.
   (i) $2_{five} \times 3_{five} = 11_{five}$
   ─────────────
   ─────────────
   ─────────────
   (ii) ─────────────
   ─────────────
   $22_{five} \div 3_{five} = 4_{five}$
   ─────────────
   (iii) ─────────────
   ─────────────
   ─────────────
   $13_{five} \div 2_{five} = 4_{five}$

16. Show that, in general, each of the following is false if x, y, and z are whole numbers. Give an example (other than dividing by zero) where each statement is false.
    (a) $x \div y$ is a whole number.

(b) $x \div y = y \div x$
(c) $(x \div y) \div z = x \div (y \div z)$
(d) $x \div y = x = y \div x$ for some y
(e) $x \div (y + z) = x \div y + x \div z$

Problems

17. Suppose that A is a set of whole numbers closed under addition. Is A necessarily closed under multiplication? (If you think so, give reasons. If you think not, give a counterexample, that is, a set A that is closed under addition but not multiplication.)

18. (a) Use the numbers from 1 to 9 once each to complete this magic square. (The row, column, and diagonal sums are all equal.) (HINT: First determine the sum of each row.)

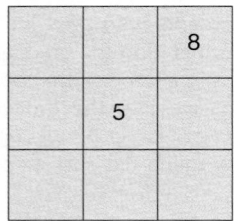

(b) Can you make a multiplicative magic square? (The row, column, and diagonal products are equal.) (NOTE: The numbers 1 through 9 will not work in this case.)

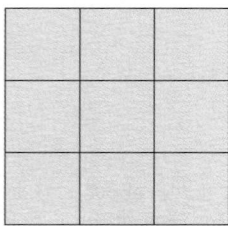

19. Predict the next three lines in this pattern and check your work.

$$
\begin{array}{rcl}
1 & = & 1 \\
3 + 5 & = & 8 \\
7 + 9 + 11 & = & 27 \\
13 + 15 + 17 + 19 & = & 64 \\
21 + 23 + 25 + 27 + 29 & = & 125
\end{array}
$$

20. Using the digits 1 through 9 once each, fill in the boxes to make the equations true.

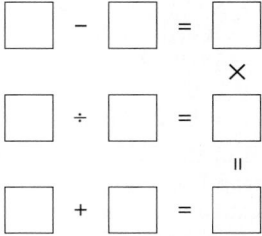

21. Take any number. Add 10, multiply by 2, add 100, divide by 2, and subtract the original number. The answer will be the number of minutes in an hour. Why?

22. Jason, Wendy, Kevin, and Michelle each entered a frog in an annual frog-jumping contest. Each of their frogs, Hippy, Hoppy, Bounce, and Pounce, placed first, second, or third in the contest and earned a blue, red, or white ribbon, respectively. Use the following clues to determine who entered which frog and the order in which the frogs placed.

1. Michelle's frog finished ahead of both Bounce and Hoppy.
2. Hippy and Hoppy tied for second place.
3. Kevin and Wendy recaptured Hoppy when he escaped from his owner.
4. Kevin admired the blue ribbon Pounce received but was quite happy with the red ribbon his frog received.

23. A café sold tea at 30 cents a cup and cakes at 50 cents each. Everyone in a group had the same number of cakes and the same number of cups of tea. (NOTE: This is not to say that the number of cakes is the same as the number of teas.) The bill came to $13.30. How many cups of tea did each have?

24. Find five consecutive whole numbers whose product is 15,120.

25. A creature from Mars lands on Earth. It reproduces itself by dividing into three new creatures each day. How many creatures will populate Earth after 30 days if there is one creature on the first day?

26. There are eight coins and a balance scale. The coins are alike in appearance but one of them is counterfeit and lighter than the other seven. Find the counterfeit coin using two weighings on the balance scale.

27. Determine if the property "If $ac = bc$, then $a = b$" is true for all whole numbers. If not, give a counterexample. (NOTE: This property is called the **multiplicative cancellation property** when $c \neq 0$.)

EXERCISE/PROBLEM SET 3.2—PART B

Exercises

1. What multiplication problems are suggested by the following diagrams?

(a)

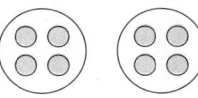

(b)

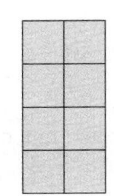

(c)

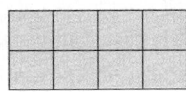

(d)

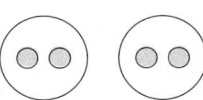

(e)

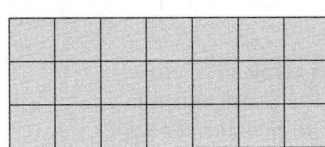

(f)

★ ★ ★
★ ★ ★
★ ★ ★
★ ★ ★
★ ★ ★
★ ★ ★
★ ★ ★

2. The repeated-addition approach can easily be illustrated using a calculator. For example, 4×3 can be found by pressing the following keys:

$$3 \boxed{+} 3 \boxed{+} 3 \boxed{+} 3 \boxed{=} \boxed{12}$$

or if the calculator has a constant key, by pressing

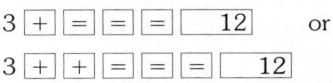

or

$$3 \boxed{+} \boxed{+} \boxed{=} \boxed{=} \boxed{=} \boxed{12}$$

Find the following products using one of these techniques.
(a) 3×12 **(b)** 4×17
(c) 7×93 **(d)** 143×6 (Think!)

3. (a) Is the set of whole numbers with 3 removed
    (i) closed under addition? Why?
    (ii) closed under multiplication? Why?
(b) Answer the same questions for the set of whole numbers with 7 removed.

4. Is the set of whole numbers with 6 removed
(a) closed under addition? Why?
(b) closed under multiplication? Why?

5. Rewrite each of the following using the distributive property and whole-number operations.
(a) $5x + 2x$
(b) $3a + 6a + 4a$
(c) $3(a + 1) + 5(a + 1)$
(d) $x(x + 2) + 3(x + 2)$

6. The distributive property of multiplication over subtraction can be used to perform some calculations mentally. For example, to find 7(99), you can think

$$7(99) = 7(100 - 1) = 7(100) - 7(1)$$
$$= 700 - 7 = 693$$

How could each of the following products be rewritten using the distributive property so that it is more easily computed mentally?
(a) 14(19)   **(b)** 25(38)   **(c)** 35(98)   **(d)** 27(999)

7. Compute mentally.

$$(2348 \times 7{,}653{,}214) + (7652 \times 7{,}653{,}214)$$

(Hint: Use distributivity.)

8. (a) Compute 463×17 on your calculator *without* using the 7 key.
(b) Find another way to do it.
(c) Calculate 473×17 without using the 7 key.

9. Paraphrase the problem "$35 \div 7 = $ _____" in terms of the missing-factor definition of division.

10. Each situation described next involves a multiplication problem. In each case tell whether the problem situation is best represented by the repeated-addition approach, the rectangular array approach, or the Cartesian product approach, and why. Then write an appropriate equation to fit the situation.
(a) A rectangular room has square tiles on the floor.

Along one wall, Kurt counts 15 tiles and along an adjacent wall he counts 12 tiles. How many tiles cover the floor of the room?

(b) Jack has three pairs of athletic shorts and eight different tee shirts. How many different combinations of shorts and tee shirts could he wear to play basketball?

(c) A teacher provided three number 2 pencils to each student taking a standardized test. If a total of 36 students were taking the test, how many pencils did the teacher need to have available?

11. Find the quotient and remainder for each problem.
(a) $7 \div 3$ (b) $3 \div 7$ (c) $7 \div 1$
(d) $1 \div 7$ (e) $15 \div 5$ (f) $8 \div 12$

12. How many possible remainders (including zero) are there when dividing by the following numbers? How many possible quotients are there?
(a) 2   (b) 1   (c) 6   (d) 23

13. (a) Complete the following multiplication table in base eight. Remember to use the thinking strategies.

×	0	1	2	3	4	5	6	7
0								
1								
2								
3								
4								
5								
6								
7								

(base eight)

(b) Rewrite each of the following division problems in *base eight* using the missing-factor approach, and find the answer in the table.

(i) $61_{eight} \div 7_{eight}$
(ii) $17_{eight} \div 3_{eight}$
(iii) $30_{eight} \div 6_{eight}$
(iv) $16_{eight} \div 2_{eight}$
(v) $44_{eight} \div 6_{eight}$
(vi) $25_{eight} \div 7_{eight}$

14. Which of the following properties hold for division of whole numbers?
(a) Closure   (b) Commutativity
(c) Associativity   (d) Identity

15. Fill in the following table with either a "yes" or a "no" (W = {whole numbers}).

Set	Operation	Closure	Com.	Assoc.	Two-Sided Identity
W	+	(a)	Yes	(b)	(c)
W	−	(d)	(e)	(f)	(g)
W	×	(h)	(i)	(j)	(k)
W	÷	(l)	(m)	(n)	(o)
{0, 1}	+	(p)	(q)	(r)	(s)
{0, 1}	−	(t)	(u)	(v)	(w)
{0, 1}	×	(x)	(y)	(z)	(aa)

Problems

16. If a subset of the whole numbers is closed under multiplication, is it necessarily closed under addition? Discuss.

17. Is there a subset of the whole numbers with more than one element that is closed under division? Discuss.

18. Complete the pattern and give a justification for your answers. If necessary, check your answers using your calculator.

$$12,345,679 \times 9 = 111,111,111$$
$$12,345,679 \times 18 = 222,222,222$$
$$12,345,679 \times 27 =$$
$$12,345,679 \times 63 =$$
$$12,345,679 \times 81 =$$

19. Solve this problem posed by this Old English children's rhyme:

As I was going to St. Ives
I met a man with seven wives;
Every wife had seven sacks;
Every sack had seven cats;
Every cat had seven kits.
Kits, cats, sacks, and wives.
How many were going to St. Ives?

How many wives, sacks, cats, and kits were met?

20. Write down your favorite three-digit number twice to form a six-digit number (e.g., 587,587). Is your six-digit number divisible by 7? How about 11? How about 13? Does this always work? Why? (HINT: Expanded form.)

21. Find a four-digit whole number equal to the cube of the sum of its digits.

22. Delete every third counting number starting with 3.

1, 2, 4, 5, 7, 8, 10, 11, 13, 14, 16, 17

Write down the cumulative sums starting with 1.

1, 3, 7, 12, 19, 27, 37, 48, 61, 75, 91, 108

Delete every second number from this last sequence, starting with 3. Then write down the sequence of cumulative sums. Describe the resulting sequence.

23. Write, side by side, the numeral 1 an even number of times. Take away from the number thus formed the number obtained by writing, side by side, a series of 2s half the length of the first number. For example,

$$1111 - 22 = 1089 = 33 \times 33$$

Will you always get a perfect square? Why or why not?

24. Four men, one of whom committed a crime, said the following:

   Bob: Charlie did it.
   Charlie: Eric did it.
   Dave: I didn't do it.
   Eric: Charlie lied when he said I did it.

   (a) If only one of the statements is true, who was guilty?
   (b) If only one of the statements was false, who was guilty?

25. Andrew and Bert met on the street and had the following conversation:

   A: How old are your three children?
   B: The product of their ages is 36.

A: That's not enough information for me to know their ages.
B: The sum of their ages is your house number.
A: That's still not quite enough information.
B: The oldest child plays the piano.
A: Now I know!

Assume that the ages are whole numbers and that twins have the same age. How old are the children? (HINT: Make a list after Bert's first answer.)

26. Three boxes contain black and white marbles. One box has all black marbles, one has all white marbles, and one has a mixture of black and white. All three boxes are mislabeled. By selecting only one marble, determine how you can correctly label the boxes. (HINT: Notice that "all black" and "all white" are the "same" in the sense that they are the same color.)

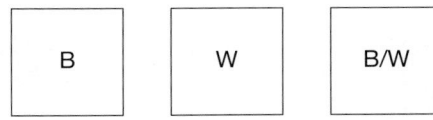

27. If a and b are whole numbers and $ab = 0$, what conclusion can you draw about a or b? Defend your conclusion with a convincing argument.

3.3

ORDERING AND EXPONENTS

Ordering and Whole-Number Operations

In Chapter 2, whole numbers were ordered in three different, though equivalent, ways using (1) the counting chant, (2) the whole-number line, and (3) a 1-1 correspondence. Now that we have defined whole-number addition, there is another, more useful way to define "less than." Notice that $3 < 5$ and $3 + 2 = 5$, $4 < 9$ and $4 + 5 = 9$, and $2 < 11$ and $2 + 9 = 11$. This idea is presented in the next definition of "less than."

> **Definition**
>
> ### "Less Than" for Whole Numbers
>
> For any two whole numbers a and b, $a < b$ (or $b > a$) if and only if there is a nonzero whole number n such that $a + n = b$.

For example, $7 < 9$ since $7 + 2 = 9$ and $13 > 8$ since $8 + 5 = 13$. The symbols "$\leq$" and "$\geq$" mean "less than or equal to" and "greater than or equal to," respectively.

One useful property of "less than" is the transitive property.

> ### Transitive Property of "Less Than" for Whole Numbers
>
> For all whole numbers a, b, and c, if $a < b$ and $b < c$, then $a < c$.

The transitive property can be verified using any of our definitions of "less than." Consider the number line in Figure 3.34.

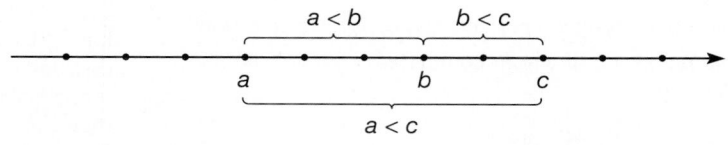

FIGURE 3.34

Since $a < b$, we have a is to the left of b, and since $b < c$, we have b is to the left of c. Hence a is to the left of c, or $a < c$.

The following is a more formal argument to verify the transitive property. It uses the definition of "less than" involving addition.

$a < b$ means $a + n = b$ for some nonzero whole number n.
$b < c$ means $b + m = c$ for some nonzero whole number m.
Adding m to $a + n$ and b, we obtain
$$a + n + m = b + m$$
Thus $\qquad\qquad a + n + m = c$ since $b + m = c$.
Therefore, $a < c$ since $a + (n + m) = c$ and $n + m$ is a nonzero whole number.

NOTE: The transitive property of "less than" holds if "$<$" is replaced with "$>$," "$\leq$," or "$\geq$" throughout.

There are two additional properties involving "less than." The first involves addition (or subtraction).

> ### Property of Less Than and Addition for Whole Numbers
>
> If $a < b$, then $a + c < b + c$.

As was the case with transitivity, this property can be verified formally using the definition of "less than." An informal justification using the whole number line follows (Figure 3.35).

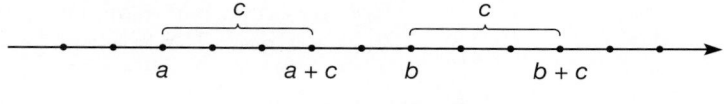

FIGURE 3.35

Notice that $a < b$ since a is to the left of b. Then the same distance, c, is added to each to obtain $a + c$ and $b + c$, respectively. Since $a + c$ is left of $b + c$, we have $a + c < b + c$.

In the case of "less than" and multiplication we have to assume that $c \neq 0$. The proof of this property is left for the problem set.

Property of Less Than and Multiplication for Whole Numbers

If $a < b$ and $c \neq 0$, then $ac < bc$.

Since c is a nonzero whole number, it follows that $c > 0$. In Chapter 8, where negative numbers are first discussed, this property will have to be modified to include negatives.

Exponents

Just as multiplication is a shortcut for addition and division may be viewed as repeated subtraction, the concept of exponent can be used to simplify many multiplication problems.

Definition

Whole-Number Exponent

Let a and m be any two whole numbers where $m \neq 0$. Then

$$a^m = \underbrace{a \cdot a \cdot \cdots a.}_{m \text{ factors}}$$

The number m is called the **exponent** or **power** of a, and a is called the **base**. The number a^m is read "a to the power m" or "a to the mth power." For example, 5^2, read "5 to the second power" or "5 squared," is $5 \cdot 5 = 25$; 2^3, read "2 to the third power" or "2 cubed," equals $2 \cdot 2 \cdot 2 = 8$; and $3^4 = 3 \cdot 3 \cdot 3 \cdot 3 = 81$.

There are several properties of exponents that permit us to represent numbers and to do many calculations quickly.

EXAMPLE 3.9   Rewrite each of the following expressions using a single exponent.
(a) $2^3 \cdot 2^4$ **(b)** $3^5 \cdot 3^7$

Solution
(a) $2^3 \cdot 2^4 = (2 \cdot 2 \cdot 2) \cdot (2 \cdot 2 \cdot 2 \cdot 2) = 2^7$
(b) $3^5 \cdot 3^7 = (3 \cdot 3 \cdot 3 \cdot 3 \cdot 3) \cdot (3 \cdot 3 \cdot 3 \cdot 3 \cdot 3 \cdot 3 \cdot 3) = 3^{12}$ ∎

In Example 3.9(a) the exponents of the factors were 3 and 4, and the exponent of the product is $3 + 4 = 7$. Also, in (b) the exponents 5 and 7 yielded an exponent of $5 + 7 = 12$ in the product.

The fact that exponents are added in this way can be shown to be valid in general. This result is stated next as a theorem. A **theorem** is a statement that can be proved based on known results.

Theorem   Let a, m, and n be any whole numbers where m and n are nonzero. Then

$$a^m \cdot a^n = a^{m+n}.$$

Proof

$$a^m \cdot a^n = \underbrace{a \cdot a \cdots a}_{m \text{ factors}} \cdot \underbrace{a \cdot a \cdots a}_{n \text{ factors}} = \underbrace{a \cdot a \cdots a}_{m+n \text{ factors}} = a^{m+n}.$$

■

STUDENT PAGE SNAPSHOT

UNDERSTANDING A CONCEPT

Using Exponents

A. Jeff did a study about rabbits for a science project. He found that a colony of rabbits doubled in number every month. If there were 2 rabbits at the beginning of the first month, how many were there at the beginning of the 5th month?

Beginning of 1st Month	Beginning of 2nd Month	Beginning of 3rd Month	Beginning of 4th Month	Beginning of 5th Month
2	2×2 $= 4$	$2 \times 2 \times 2$ $= 8$	$2 \times 2 \times 2 \times 2$ $= 16$	$2 \times 2 \times 2 \times 2 \times 2$ $= 32$

There were 32 rabbits at the beginning of the 5th month.

A short way of writing $2 \times 2 \times 2 \times 2 \times 2$, or expressing 2 as a factor 5 times, is to use **exponential form**.

$$2 \times 2 \times 2 \times 2 \times 2 = 2^5 \leftarrow \text{exponent}$$
$$\qquad\qquad\qquad\qquad \uparrow\text{---base}$$

2^5 is read "two to the fifth power."

Some numbers in exponential form can be read in special ways.

For example, 2^2 is read as "2 squared" or "2 to the 2nd power." 2^3 is read as "2 cubed" or "2 to the 3rd power."

1. How would you find the value of 7^4?

2. Express the rabbit population at the beginning of the 12th month in exponential form and in standard form.

3. During which month would the population exceed 50,000?

B. You can use patterns to find the value of any nonzero number to the zero power.

$2^5 = 32$	$2^4 = 32 \div 2 = 16$
$2^4 = 16$	$2^3 = 16 \div 2 = 8$
$2^3 = 8$	$2^2 = 8 \div 2 = 4$
$2^2 = 4$	$2^1 = 4 \div 2 = 2$
$2^1 = 2$	$2^0 = 2 \div 2 = 1$

4. What is 6^0? 12^0? any number greater than zero to the zero power?

TRY OUT   Find the value.

5. 4^3 6. 10^0 7. 5^4 8. 10^7 9. 11^2

The next example illustrates another way of rewriting products of numbers having the same exponent.

EXAMPLE 3.10 Rewrite the following expressions using a single exponent.
(a) $2^3 \cdot 5^3$ **(b)** $3^2 \cdot 7^2 \cdot 11^2$

Solution
(a) $2^3 \cdot 5^3 = (2 \cdot 2 \cdot 2)(5 \cdot 5 \cdot 5) = (2 \cdot 5)(2 \cdot 5)(2 \cdot 5) = (2 \cdot 5)^3$
(b) $3^2 \cdot 7^2 \cdot 11^2 = (3 \cdot 3)(7 \cdot 7)(11 \cdot 11) = (3 \cdot 7 \cdot 11)(3 \cdot 7 \cdot 11) = (3 \cdot 7 \cdot 11)^2$ ■

The results in Example 3.10 suggest the following theorem.

> **Theorem**   Let a, b, and m be any whole numbers where m is nonzero. Then
> $$a^m \cdot b^m = (ab)^m.$$

Proof
$$a^m \cdot b^m = \underbrace{a \cdot a \cdots a}_{m \text{ factors}} \cdot \underbrace{b \cdot b \cdots b}_{m \text{ factors}} = \underbrace{(ab)(ab) \cdots (ab)}_{m \text{ pairs of factors}} = (ab)^m.$$
  ■

The next example shows how to simplify expressions of the form $(a^m)^n$.

EXAMPLE 3.11 Rewrite the following expressions with a single exponent.
(a) $(5^3)^2$ **(b)** $(7^8)^4$

Solution
(a) $(5^3)^2 = 5^3 \cdot 5^3 = 5^{3+3} = 5^6 = 5^{3 \cdot 2}$
(b) $(7^8)^4 = 7^8 \cdot 7^8 \cdot 7^8 \cdot 7^8 = 7^{32} = 7^{8 \cdot 4}$ ■

In general, we have the next theorem.

> **Theorem**   Let a, m, and n be any whole numbers where m and n are nonzero. Then
> $$(a^m)^n = a^{mn}.$$

The proof of this theorem is similar to the proofs of the previous two theorems.

The previous three properties involved exponents and multiplication. However, notice that $(2 + 3)^3 \neq 2^3 + 3^3$, so there is *not* a corresponding property involving sums or differences raised to powers.

The next example concerns the division of numbers involving exponents with the same base number.

EXAMPLE 3.12 Rewrite the following quotients with a single exponent.
(a) $5^7 \div 5^3$ **(b)** $7^8 \div 7^5$

Solution

(a) $5^7 \div 5^3 = 5^4$ since $5^7 = 5^3 \cdot 5^4$. Therefore, $5^7 \div 5^3 = 5^{7-3}$.

(b) $7^8 \div 7^5 = 7^3$ since $7^8 = 7^5 \cdot 7^3$. Therefore, $7^8 \div 7^5 = 7^{8-5}$.   ■

In general, we have the following result.

> **Theorem**   Let a, m, and n be any whole numbers where $m > n$ and n is nonzero. Then
>
> $$a^m \div a^n = a^{m-n}.$$

Proof

$a^m \div a^n = c$ if and only if $a^m = a^n \cdot c$. Since $a^n \cdot a^{m-n} = a^{n+(m-n)} = a^m$, we have $c = a^{m-n}$. Therefore, $a^m \div a^n = a^{m-n}$.   ■

Notice that we have not yet defined a^0. Consider the following pattern:

$$a^3 = a \cdot a \cdot a \quad \searrow \quad \div a$$
$$a^2 = a \cdot a \quad \searrow \quad \div a$$
$$a^1 = a \quad \searrow \quad \div a$$
$$a^0 = 1$$

$$\uparrow \qquad\qquad\qquad \uparrow$$

$$\begin{bmatrix} \text{The exponents} \\ \text{are decreasing} \\ \text{by 1 each time} \end{bmatrix} \quad \text{when} \quad \begin{bmatrix} \text{the numbers are} \\ \text{divided by } a \\ \text{each time} \end{bmatrix}$$

Extending this pattern, we see that the following definition is appropriate.

> **Definition**
>
> ### Zero as an Exponent
>
> $a^0 = 1$ for all whole numbers $a \neq 0$.

Notice that 0^0 is not defined. To see why, consider the following two patterns.

Pattern 1	Pattern 2
$3^0 = 1$	$0^3 = 0$
$2^0 = 1$	$0^2 = 0$
$1^0 = 1$	$0^1 = 0$
$0^0 = ?$	$0^0 = ?$

Pattern 1 suggests that 0^0 should be 1 and pattern 2 suggests that 0^0 should be 0. Thus to avoid such an inconsistency, 0^0 is undefined.

MATHEMATICAL MORSEL

John von Neumann was a brilliant mathematician who made important contributions to several scientific fields, including the theory and application of high-speed computing machines. George Pólya of Stanford University admitted that "Johnny was the only student I was *ever* afraid of. If in the course of a lecture I stated an unsolved problem, the chances were he'd come to me as soon as the lecture was over, with the complete solution in a few scribbles on a slip of paper." At the age of 6, von Neumann could divide two eight-digit numbers in his head, and when he was 8 he had mastered the calculus. When he invented his first electronic computer, someone suggested that he race it. Given a problem like "What is the smallest power of 2 with the property that its decimal digit fourth from the right is a 7," the machine and von Neumann started at the same time and von Neumann won!

EXERCISE/PROBLEM SET 3.3—PART A

Exercises

1. Find the nonzero whole number n in the definition of "less than" that verifies the following statements.
   (a) $12 < 31$ (b) $17 < 26$ (c) $53 > 37$

2. Using the definitions of $<$ and $>$ given in this section, write four inequality statements based on the fact that $2 + 8 = 10$.

3. The statement $a < x < b$ is equivalent to writing $a < x$ and $x < b$ and is called a **compound inequality**. We often read $a < x < b$ as "x is between a and b." For the questions that follow, assume that a, x, and b are whole numbers.

   (a) If $a < x < b$ and c is a nonzero whole number, is it always true that $a + c < x + c < b + c$? Try several examples to test your conjecture.
   (b) If $a < x < b$ and c is a nonzero whole number, is it always true that $ac < xc < bc$? Try several examples to test your conjecture.

4. Using exponents, rewrite the following expressions in a simpler form.
   (a) $3 \cdot 3 \cdot 3 \cdot 3$ (b) $2 \cdot 2 \cdot 3 \cdot 2 \cdot 3 \cdot 2$
   (c) $6 \cdot 7 \cdot 6 \cdot 7 \cdot 6$ (d) $x \cdot y \cdot x \cdot y \cdot y \cdot y$
   (e) $a \cdot b \cdot b \cdot a$ (f) $5 \cdot 6 \cdot 5 \cdot 5 \cdot 6 \cdot 6$

5. Write each of the following expressions in expanded form, without exponents.
   (a) $3x^2y^5z$ (b) $7 \cdot 5^3$ (c) $(7 \cdot 5)^3$

6. Rewrite with a single exponent.
   (a) $5^3 \cdot 5^4$ (b) $3^{12} \div 3^2$ (c) $2^7 \cdot 5^7$
   (d) $8 \cdot 2^5$ (e) $25^3 \div 5^2$ (f) $9^2 \cdot 12^3 \cdot 2$

7. A student asked to simplify the expression $3^2 \cdot 3^4$ wrote $3^2 \cdot 3^4 = 9^6$. How would you convince the student that this answer is incorrect? That is, do not just give the correct answer, but explain *why* the student's method is incorrect.

8. Determine if the statement $(a + b)^n = a^n + b^n$ is true for all whole numbers a and b and for n a whole number such that $n \geq 2$. Try several different examples before drawing a conclusion.

9. The $\boxed{y^x}$ key on a calculator can be used to raise numbers to any power. To calculate 2^5, for example, enter the sequence

$$2 \boxed{y^x} \quad 5 \boxed{=}$$
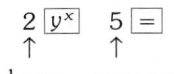
base   exponent

(NOTE: On some calculators the sequence will be 2 $\boxed{\text{ENT}}$ 5 $\boxed{y^x}$. Other calculators have an $\boxed{x^y}$ or $\boxed{\wedge}$ key for raising numbers to powers.) Use your calculator to evaluate the following.

(a) 7^6 (b) 9^0 (c) $10 \cdot 2^3$

(d) $(10 \cdot 2)^3$ (e) $4^3 + 3^5$ (f) $\dfrac{2^8 \cdot 3^4}{4^3}$

10. Find x.
(a) $3^7 \cdot 3^x = 3^{13}$ (b) $(3^x)^4 = 3^{20}$
(c) $3^x \cdot 2^x = 6^x$

Problems

11. Using properties of exponents, *mentally* determine the larger of the following pairs.
(a) 6^{10} and 3^{20} (b) 9^9 and 3^{20}
(c) 12^{10} and 3^{20}

12. The price of a certain candy bar doubled over a period of five years. Suppose that the price continued to double every 5 years and that the candy bar cost 25 cents in 1980.
(a) What would be the price of the candy bar in the year 1995?
(b) What would be the price of the candy bar in the year 2020?
(c) Write an expression representing the price of the candy bar after n five-year periods.

13. Verify the transitive property of "less than" using the 1-1 correspondence definition.

14. Observe the following pattern in the sums of consecutive whole numbers. Use your calculator to verify that the statements are true.

$$2 + 3 + 4 = 1^3 + 2^3$$
$$5 + 6 + 7 + 8 + 9 = 2^3 + 3^3$$
$$10 + 11 + 12 + 13 + 14 + 15 + 16 = 3^3 + 4^3$$

(a) Write the next two lines in this sequence of sums.
(b) Express $9^3 + 10^3$ as a sum of consecutive whole numbers.

(c) Express $12^3 + 13^3$ as a sum of consecutive whole numbers.
(d) Express $n^3 + (n + 1)^3$ as a sum of consecutive whole numbers.

15. Pizzas come in four different sizes, each with or without a choice of four ingredients. How many ways are there to order a pizza?

16. The perfect square 49 is special in that each of the two digits forming the number is itself a perfect square.
(a) Explain why there are no other two-digit squares with this property.
(b) What three-digit perfect squares can you find that are made up of one one-digit square and one two-digit square?
(c) What four-digit perfect squares can you find that are made up of two one-digit squares and one two-digit square?
(d) What four-digit perfect squares can you find that are made up of one three-digit square and one one-digit square?
(e) What four-digit perfect squares can you find that are made up of two two-digit squares?
(f) What four-digit perfect squares can you find that are made up of four one-digit squares?

17. When asked to find four whole numbers such that the product of any two of them is one less than the square of a whole number, one mathematician said, "2, 4, 12, and 22." A second mathematician said, "2, 12, 24, and 2380." Which was correct?

18. 12 is a factor of $10^2 - 2^2$, 27 is a factor of $20^2 - 7^2$, and 84 is a factor of $80^2 - 4^2$. Check to see if these three statements are correct. Using a variable, prove why this works in general.

19. (a) Give a formal proof of the property of less than and addition. (HINT: See the proof in the paragraph following Figure 3.34.)
(b) State and prove the corresponding property for subtraction.

EXERCISE/PROBLEM SET 3.3—PART B

Exercises

1. Fill in the blanks with an appropriate order symbol or whole number to make a true statement.
(a) 2 _____ 7   (b) 13 _____ 12
(c) _____ < 9   (d) _____ ≥ 13
(e) If $a \geq b$ and $b \geq c$, then
a _____ c.

2. Using the definitions of $<$ and $>$ given in this section, write four inequality statements based on the fact that $9 + 5 = 14$.

3. Does the transitive property hold for the following?
(a) $=$ (b) $\neq$ (c) $>$ (d) $\leq$

4. Choose any set of whole numbers, finite or infinite, and call the set S. Let S not be the empty set.
  (a) Is there a smallest element in your set S? Consider other sets S. Is your answer the same?
  (b) Is there a biggest element in your set S? Consider other sets S. Is your answer the same?

5. Using exponents, rewrite the following expressions in a simpler form.
  (a) $4 \cdot 4 \cdot 4 \cdot 4 \cdot 4 \cdot 4 \cdot 4$
  (b) $4 \cdot 3 \cdot 3 \cdot 4 \cdot 4 \cdot 3 \cdot 3 \cdot 3 \cdot 3$
  (c) $y \cdot 2 \cdot x \cdot y \cdot x \cdot x$
  (d) $a \cdot b \cdot a \cdot b \cdot a \cdot b \cdot a \cdot b$

6. Write each of the following expressions in expanded form, without exponents.
  (a) $10ab^4$ **(b)** $(2x)^5$ **(c)** $2x^5$

7. Write the following with only one exponent.
  (a) $x^3 \cdot x^6$ **(b)** $a^{15} \div a^3$ **(c)** $x^5 y^5$
  (d) $2^3 \cdot 16$ **(e)** $128 \div 2^3$ **(f)** $3^7 \cdot 9^5 \div 27^2$

8. A student asked to simplify the expression $8^5 \div 2^2$ wrote $8^5 \div 2^2 = 4^3$. How would you convince the student that this answer is incorrect? That is, do not just give the correct answer, but explain *why* the student's method is incorrect.

9. Express 7^{20} in three different ways using the numbers 7, 2, 5 and exponents. (You may use a number more than once.)

10. Use the $\boxed{y^x}$, $\boxed{x^y}$, or $\boxed{\wedge}$ key on your calculator to evaluate the following. (Refer to Problem 9 in Part A.)
  (a) 6^8 **(b)** $(3 \cdot 5)^4$ **(c)** $3 \cdot 5^4$
  (d) $3^7 + 2^4$ **(e)** $2 \cdot 5^6 - 3 \cdot 2^3$ **(f)** $\dfrac{9^3 \cdot 12^4}{3^8}$

11. Arrange these from the smallest to the largest.
$$5^3 \qquad 6^2 \qquad 3^5 \qquad 2^7$$

12. (a) How does the sum $1 + 2 + 3$ compare to the sum $1^3 + 2^3 + 3^3$?
  (b) Try several more such examples and determine the relationship between $1 + 2 + 3 + \cdots + n$ and $1^3 + 2^3 + 3^3 + \cdots + n^3$.
  (c) Use the pattern you observed to find the sum of the first 10 cubes, $1^3 + 2^3 + 3^3 + \cdots + 10^3$, without evaluating any of the cubes.

Problems

13. A student rewrote $\left(3^2\right)^2$ as $3^{(2^2)}$ (a form of associativity, perhaps). Was the student correct or incorrect? Another rewrote $\left(2^3\right)^2$ as $2^{(3^2)}$. Right or wrong? If a, b, and c are nonzero whole numbers, what about $\left(a^b\right)^c$ and $a^{(bc)}$? Are they always equal? Are they ever equal?

14. Order these numbers from smallest to largest using properties of exponents and mental methods.
$$3^{22} \qquad 4^{14} \qquad 9^{10} \qquad 8^{10}$$

15. A pad of 200 sheets of paper is approximately 15 mm thick. Suppose that one piece of this paper were folded in half, then folded in half again, then folded again, and so on. If this folding process was continued until the piece of paper had been folded in half 30 times, how thick would the folded paper be?

16. Suppose that you can order a submarine sandwich with or without each of seven condiments.
  (a) How many ways are there?
  (b) How many ways can you order exactly two condiments?
  (c) Exactly seven?
  (d) Exactly one?
  (e) Exactly six?

17. (a) If $n^2 = 121$, what is n?
  (b) If $n^2 = 1{,}234{,}321$, what is n?
  (c) If $n^2 = 12{,}345{,}654{,}321$, what is n?
  (d) If $n^2 = 123{,}456{,}787{,}654{,}321$, what is n?

18. (a) Verify that the property of less than and multiplication holds where $a = 3$, $b = 7$, and $c = 5$.
  (b) Show that the property does not hold if $c = 0$.
  (c) Give a formal proof of the property. (HINT: Use the fact that the product of two nonzero whole numbers is nonzero.)
  (d) State the corresponding property for division.

SOLUTION OF INITIAL PROBLEM

In a group of nine coins, eight weigh the same and the ninth is heavier. Assume that the coins are identical in appearance. Using a pan balance, what is the smallest number of weighings needed to identify the heavy coin?

Strategy: Use Direct Reasoning

Two weighings are sufficient. Separate the coins into three groups of three coins each.

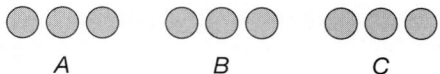

A   B   C

Weigh group A against group B. If they balance, we can deduce that the heavy coin is in group C. In this case, select two coins from group C. Weigh one against the other. If they balance, the remaining coin in group C is heavy. If they do not balance, the heavier coin tips the scales.

If the coins in group A do not balance the coins in group B, one group is heavier and must contain the heavy coin. Suppose that it is in group A. Then choose two coins from group A and weigh one against the other. Use the same reasoning as in the preceding paragraph with coins from group C. In any case, only two weighings are needed.

Additional Problems Where the Strategy "Use Direct Reasoning" Is Useful

1. The sum of the digits of a three-digit palindrome is odd. Determine whether the middle digit is odd or even.
2. Jose's room in a hotel was higher than Michael's but lower than Ralph's. Andre's room is on a floor between Ralph's and Jose's. If it weren't for Michael, Clyde's room would be the lowest. List the rooms from lowest to highest.
3. Given an 8-liter jug of water and empty 3-liter and 5-liter jugs, pour the water so that two of the jugs have 4 liters.

WRITING/DISCUSSING FOR UNDERSTANDING

1. In the 1960s, the era of the "New Math," the properties of the whole-number operations were heavily emphasized. Explain why a knowledge of these properties is important to math students.
2. In the 1970s, students in the United States were described as lacking in their basic math skills. To rectify this situation, we went "back to basics," utilizing drill, timed tests for basic math facts, flashcards, and so on. Discuss the pros and cons of this approach.
3. Explain how the following NCTM Standards are reflected in this chapter.

- Develop meaning for the operations by modeling and discussing a rich variety of problem situations.
- Relate the mathematical language and symbolism of operations to problem situations and informal language.
- Understand how the basic arithmetic operations are related to one another.

PROJECTS

1. How do you suppose that mathematics instruction of whole-number arithmetic differs today from when you were in school? Interview a third- or fourth-grade teacher to find out. In addition, ask him or her what impact the National Council of Teachers of Mathematics *Curriculum and Evaluation Standards* have had, if any, on the way that mathematics is taught in his or her classroom and in the school? (NOTE: A brief summary of the Standards is contained in the *Connections to School Mathematics* section near the end of this book.)
2. Hindu–Arabic numerals have been used as exponents since around 1637, when first employed by René Descartes. Other means of representing powers were used prior to Descartes' time. What other notation has been used to represent a power? Consult a mathematics history book to find out and prepare a summary.

CHAPTER REVIEW

Major Ideas

1. The whole-number binary operations addition and multiplication have their roots in physical models.
2. The four basic operations are interconnected, as shown in the diagram.

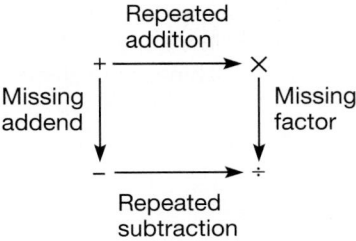

3. Whole-number addition and multiplication satisfy several important properties.

Property	Addition	Multiplication
Closure	Yes	Yes
Commutativity	Yes	Yes
Associativity	Yes	Yes
Identity	Yes (zero)	Yes (one)
Distributivity of multiplication over addition or subtraction	Yes	

4. The addition and multiplication facts for single-digit numbers can be developed meaningfully through the use of thinking strategies.

5. The division of whole numbers may or may not have a remainder.

6. Whole-number exponents and their properties can be used to simplify notation and computations.

Following is a list of key vocabulary, notation, and ideas for this chapter. Mentally review these items and, where appropriate, write down the meaning of each term. Then restudy the material that you are unsure of before proceeding to take the chapter test.

SECTION 3.1:   ADDITION AND SUBTRACTION

Vocabulary/Notation

Sum **98**
Addend **98**
Summand **98**
Binary operation **98**
Closure for addition **99**
Commutativity for addition **99**
Associativity for addition **100**
Identity for addition **100**
Thinking strategies for addition facts **101**

Take-away approach **103**
Difference **104**
Minuend **104**
Subtrahend **104**
Missing-addend approach **104**
Missing addend **104**
Comparison approach **105**

Ideas

Addition of whole numbers using two models **97**
Four main properties of whole-number addition **99**
Thinking strategies for learning basic addition facts **101**
Subtraction of whole numbers using three approaches **103**
The connection between addition and subtraction **104**

SECTION 3.2:   MULTIPLICATION AND DIVISION

Vocabulary/Notation

Repeated-addition approach 110
Product 111
Factor 111
Rectangular array approach 111
Cartesian product approach 112
Tree diagram approach 112
Closure for multiplication 112
Commutativity for multiplication 113
Associativity for multiplication 113
Multiplicative identity 114
Distributive property 114

Multiplication property of zero 115
Thinking strategies for multiplication facts 116
Missing-factor approach 117
Dividend 118
Divisor 118
Quotient 118
Missing factor 118
Division property of zero 118
Division algorithm 119
Remainder 119
Repeated-subtraction approach 119

Ideas

Multiplication of whole numbers using equivalent definitions 110
Four main properties of whole-number multiplication 112
Distributive property connects multiplication and addition/subtraction 114
Thinking strategies for learning the basic multiplication facts 116
Division of whole numbers 117
The connection between multiplication and division 118
The division algorithm 119

SECTION 3.3:   ORDERING AND EXPONENTS

Vocabulary/Notation

Less than 125
Transitive property of less than 126
Property of less than with addition (subtraction) 126
Property of less than with multiplication (division) 126
Exponent 127
Power 127
Base 127
Theorem 127

Ideas

The connection between less than and addition (subtraction) 125
The connection between less than and multiplication 126
Properties of exponents 127
Zero as an exponent 130

PEOPLE IN MATHEMATICS

John von Neumann (1903–1957) was one of the most remarkable mathematicians of this century. His logical power was legendary. It is said that during and after World War II the U.S. government reached many scientific decisions simply by asking von Neumann for his opinion. Paul Halmos, his one-time assistant, said, "The most spectacular thing about Johnny was not his power as a mathematician, which was great, but his rapidity; he was very, very fast. And like the modern computer, which doesn't memorize logarithms, but computes them, Johnny didn't bother to memorize things. He computed them." Appropriately, von Neumann was one of the first to realize how a general-purpose computing machine—a computer—should be designed. In the 1950s he invented a "theory of automata," the basis for subsequent work in artificial intelligence.

Julia Bowman Robinson (1919–1985) spent her early years in Arizona, near Phoenix. She said that one of her earliest memories is of arranging pebbles in the shadow of a giant saguaro—"I've always had a basic liking for the natural numbers." In 1948, Julia earned her doctorate in mathematics at Berkeley; she went on to contribute to the solution of "Hilbert's tenth problem." In 1975 she became the first woman mathematician elected to the prestigious National Academy of Sciences. Julia has also served as president of the American Mathematical Society, the main professional organization for research mathematicians. "Rather than being remembered as the first woman this or that, I would prefer to be remembered simply for the theorems I have proved and the problems I have solved."

CHAPTER 3 TEST

Knowledge

1. True or false?
   (a) $n(A \cup B) = n(A) + n(B)$ for all finite sets A and B.
   (b) If $B \subseteq A$, then $n(A - B) = n(A) - n(B)$ for all finite sets A and B.
   (c) Commutativity does not hold for subtraction of whole numbers.
   (d) Distributivity of multiplication over subtraction does not hold in the set of whole numbers.
   (e) The symbol m^a, where m and a are nonzero whole numbers, represents the product of m factors of a.
   (f) If a is the divisor, b is the dividend, and c is the quotient, then $ab = c$.
   (g) The statement "$a + b = c$ if and only if $c - b = a$" is an example of the take-away approach to subtraction.
   (h) Factors are to multiplication as addends are to addition.
   (i) If $n \neq 0$ and $b + n = a$, then $a < b$.
   (j) If $n(A) = a$ and $n(B) = b$, then $A \times B$ contains exactly ab ordered pairs.

Skill

2. Find the following sums and products using thinking strategies. Show your work.
   (a) $39 + 12$ (b) $47 + 87$
   (c) $5(73 \cdot 2)$ (d) 12×33

3. Find the quotient and remainder when 321 is divided by 5.

4. Rewrite the following using a single exponent in each case.
   (a) $3^7 \cdot 3^{12}$ (b) $5^{31} \div 5^7$
   (c) $(7^3)^5$ (d) $4^5/2^8$
   (e) $7^{12} \cdot 2^{12} \cdot 14^3$ (f) $(12^8/12^5)^4 \cdot (3^6)^2$

5. Perform the following calculations by applying appropriate properties. Which properties are you using?
   (a) $13 \cdot 97 + 13 \cdot 3$ (b) $(194 + 86) + 6$
   (c) $7 \cdot 23 + 23 \cdot 5$ (d) $25(123 \cdot 8)$

Understanding

6. Using the following table, find $A - (B - C)$.

+	A	B	C
A	C	A	B
B	A	B	C
C	B	C	A

7. (a) Using the definition of an exponent, provide an explanation to show that $(7^3)^4 = 7^{12}$.

(b) Use the fact that $a^m \cdot a^n = a^{m+n}$ to explain why $(7^3)^4 = 7^{12}$.

Problem Solving/Application

8. Which is the smallest set of whole numbers that contains 2 and 3 and is closed under addition and multiplication?

9. If the product of two numbers is even and their sum is odd, what can you say about the two numbers?

4

Whole-Number Computation—Mental, Electronic, and Written

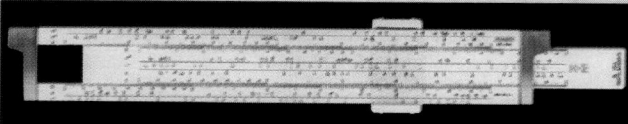

Figure 4

Figure 1

Figure 2

Figure 5

Figure 3

Figure 6

FOCUS ON:

Computational Devices from the Abacus to the Computer

The abacus was one of the earliest computational devices. The Romans used a grooved board as an abacus, with stones in the grooves, which was shown in the Focus On in Chapter 3. The Chinese abacus, or suan-pan (Figure 1), and the Japanese abacus, or saroban (Figure 2), were composed of a frame together with beads on fixed rods.

In 1617, Napier invented lattice rods, called Napier's bones, which could be used to perform multiplication. To multiply, appropriate rods were selected, laid side by side, and then appropriate "columns" were added (Figure 3). This uses the lattice multiplication procedure that is studied in this chapter.

About 1594, Napier also invented logarithms. The most remarkable property of logarithms is that multiplication can be performed simply by adding the respective logarithms. The slide rule, which was used extensively by engineers and scientists through the 1960s, was designed using properties of logarithms (Figure 4).

In 1642, Pascal invented the first mechanical adding machine (Figure 5). In 1671, Leibniz developed his "reckoning machine," which could also multiply and divide (Figure 6). In 1812, Babbage designed and built his Difference Engine, which was the first "computer" (Figure 7). By 1946, ENIAC (Electronic Numerical Integrator and Computer) was developed. It filled a room, weighed over 30 tons, and had nearly 20,000 vacuum tubes. Finally, vacuum tubes gave way to transistors, which, in turn, gave way to integrated circuits, or "chips." Chips permitted the manufacture of microcomputers, such as the Apple computer in the late 1970s and the Apple Macintosh in the late 1980s (Figure 8), and the notebook computers of the early 1990s (Figure 9). These small computers were 5 to 10 times faster than the ENIAC, much more reliable, and cost less than $2000.

Figure 7

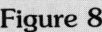

Figure 8

Figure 9

STRATEGY 9: USE INDIRECT REASONING

Occasionally, in mathematics, there are problems that are not easily solved using direct reasoning. In such cases, **indirect reasoning** may be the best way to solve the problem. A simple way of viewing indirect reasoning is to consider an empty room with only two entrances, say A and B. If you want to use direct reasoning to prove that someone entered the room through A, you would watch entrance A. However, you could also prove that someone entered through A by watching entrance B. If a person got into the room and did not go through B, the person had to go through entrance A. In mathematics, to prove that a condition, say "A," is true, one assumes that the condition "not A" is true and shows the latter condition to be impossible.

Initial Problem

The whole numbers 1 through 9 can be used once, each being arranged in a 3 × 3 square array so that the sum of the numbers in each of the rows, columns, and diagonals is fifteen. Show that 1 cannot be in one of the corners.

Clues

The Use Indirect Reasoning strategy may be appropriate when:

- Direct reasoning seems too complex or does not lead to a solution.
- Assuming the negation of what you are trying to prove narrows the scope of the problem.
- A proof is required.

A solution of the Initial Problem above appears on page 180.

INTRODUCTION

In the past, much of elementary school mathematics was devoted to learning written methods for doing addition, subtraction, multiplication, and division. Due to the availability of electronic calculators and computers, less emphasis is being placed on doing written calculations involving numbers with many digits. Instead, an emphasis is being placed on developing skills in the use of all three types of computations: mental, written, and electronic (calculators/computers). Then, depending on the size of the numbers involved, the number of operations to be performed, the accuracy desired in the answer, and the time required to do the calculations, the appropriate mode(s) of calculation will be selected and employed.

In this chapter you will study all three forms of computation: mental, electronic (calculators), and written.

4.1

MENTAL MATH, ESTIMATION, AND CALCULATORS

Mental Math

The availability and widespread use of calculators and computers have permanently changed the way we compute. Consequently, there is an increasing need to develop students' skills in estimating answers when checking the reasonableness of results obtained electronically. Computational estimation, in turn, requires a good working knowledge of mental math. Thus this section begins with several techniques for doing calculations mentally.

In Chapter 3 we saw how the thinking strategies for learning the basic arithmetic facts could be extended to multidigit numbers, as illustrated next.

EXAMPLE 4.1 Calculate the following mentally.
(a) $15 + (27 + 25)$ **(b)** $21 \cdot 17 - 13 \cdot 21$ **(c)** $(8 \times 7) \times 25$
(d) $98 + 59$ **(e)** $87 + 29$ **(f)** $168 \div 3$

Solution
(a) $15 + (27 + 25) = (27 + 25) + 15 = 27 + (25 + 15) = 27 + 40 = 67$. Notice how commutativity and associativity play a key role here.
(b) $21 \cdot 17 - 13 \cdot 21 = 21 \cdot 17 - 21 \cdot 13 = 21(17 - 13) = 21 \cdot 4 = 84$. Observe how commutativity and distributivity are useful here.
(c) $(8 \times 7) \times 25 = (7 \times 8) \times 25 = 7 \times (8 \times 25) = 7 \times 200 = 1400$. Here commutativity is used first, then associativity is used to group the 8 and 25 since their product is 200.
(d) $98 + 59 = 98 + (2 + 57) = (98 + 2) + 57 = 157$. Associativity is used here to form 100.
(e) $87 + 29 = 80 + 20 + 7 + 9 = 100 + 16 = 116$ using associativity and commutativity.
(f) $168 \div 3 = (150 \div 3) + (18 \div 3) = 50 + 6 = 56$. ∎

Observe that part (f) makes use of **right distributivity of division over addition**; that is, whenever the three quotients are whole numbers, $(a + b) \div c = (a \div c) + (b \div c)$. Right distributivity of division over subtraction also holds.

The calculations in Example 4.1 illustrate the following important mental techniques.

Properties

Commutativity, associativity, and distributivity play an important role in simplifying calculations so that they can be performed mentally. Notice how useful these properties were in parts (a), (b), (c), (d), and (e). Also, the solution in part (f) uses right distributivity.

Compatible Numbers

Compatible numbers are number whose sums, differences, products, or quotients are easy to calculate mentally. Examples of compatible numbers are 86 and 14 under addition (since $86 + 14 = 100$), 25 and 8 under multiplication (since $25 \times 8 = 200$), and 600 and 30 under division (since $600 \div 30 = 20$). In part (a) of Example 4.1, adding 15 to 25 produces a number, namely 40, that is easy to add to 27. Notice that numbers are compatible with *respect to an operation*. For example, 86 and 14 are compatible with respect to addition but not with respect to multiplication.

EXAMPLE 4.2   Calculate the following mentally using properties and/or compatible numbers.
(a) $(4 \times 13) \times 25$ **(b)** $1710 \div 9$ **(c)** 86×15

Solution
(a) $(4 \times 13) \times 25 = 13 \times (4 \times 25) = 1300$
(b) $1710 \div 9 = (1800 - 90) \div 9 = (1800 \div 9) - (90 \div 9) = 200 - 10 = 190$
(c) $86 \times 15 = (86 \times 10) + (86 \times 5) = 860 + 430 = 1290$ (Notice that 86×5 is half of 86×10.)   ∎

Compensation

The sum $43 + (38 + 17)$ can be viewed as $38 + 60 = 98$ using commutativity, associativity, and the fact that 43 and 17 are compatible numbers. Finding the answer to $43 + (36 + 19)$ is not as easy. However, by reformulating the sum $36 + 19$ mentally as $37 + 18$, we obtain the sum $(43 + 37) + 18 = 80 + 18 = 98$. This process of reformulating a sum, difference, product, or quotient to one that is more readily obtained mentally is called **compensation**. Some specific techniques using compensation are introduced next.

In the computations of Example 4.1(d), 98 was *increased* by 2 to 100 and then 59 was *decreased* by 2 to 57 (a compensation was made) to maintain the same sum. This technique, **additive compensation**, is an application of associativity. Similarly, additive compensation is used when $98 + 59$ is rewritten as $97 + 60$ or $100 + 57$. The problem $47 - 29$ can be thought of as $48 - 30 (= 18)$. This use of compensation in subtraction is called the **equal additions method** since the same number (here 1) is added to both 47 and 29 to maintain the same difference. This compensation is performed to make the subtraction easier by subtracting 30 from 48. The product 48×5 can be found using **multiplicative compensation** as follows: $48 \times 5 = 24 \times 10 = 240$. Here, again, associativity can be used to justify this method.

Left-to-Right Methods

To add 342 and 136, one can first add the hundreds $(300 + 100)$, then the tens $(40 + 30)$, and then the ones $(2 + 6)$, to obtain 478. To add 158 and 279, one can think as follows: $100 + 200 = 300, 300 + 50 + 70 = 420, 420 + 8 + 9 = 437$. Alternatively, $158 + 279$ can be found as follows: $158 + 200 = 358, 358 + 70 = 428, 428 + 9 = 437$. Subtraction from left to right can be done in a similar manner. Research has found that people who are excellent mental calculators utilize this left-to-right method to reduce memory load, instead of mentally picturing the usual right-to-left written method. The multiplication problem 3×123 can be thought of mentally as $3 \times 100 + 3 \times 20 + 3 \times 3$ using distributivity. Similarly, 4×253 can be thought of mentally as $800 + 200 + 12 = 1012$ or as $4 \times 250 + 4 \times 3 = 1000 + 12 = 1012$.

Multiplying Powers of Ten

These special numbers can be multiplied mentally in either standard or exponential form. For example, $100 \times 1000 = 100,000, 10^4 \times 10^5 = 10^9, 20 \times 300 = 6000$, and $12,000 \times 110,000 = 12 \times 11 \times 10^7 = 1,320,000,000$.

Multiplying by Special Factors

Numbers such as 5, 25, and 99 are regarded as special factors because they are convenient to use mentally. For example, since $5 = 10 \div 2$, we have $38 \times 5 = 38 \times 10 \div 2 = 380 \div 2 = 190$. Similarly, since $25 = 100 \div 4, 36 \times 25 = 3600 \div 4 = 900$. The product 46×99 can be thought of as $46(100 - 1) = 4600 - 46 = 4554$. Also, dividing by 5 can be viewed as dividing by 10, then multiplying by 2. Thus $460 \div 5 = (460 \div 10) \times 2 = 46 \times 2 = 92$.

EXAMPLE 4.3   Calculate mentally using the indicated method.
(a) $197 + 248$ using additive compensation
(b) 125×44 using multiplicative compensation
(c) $273 - 139$ using the equal additions method
(d) $321 + 437$ using a left-to-right method
(e) 3×432 using a left-to-right method
(f) 456×25 using the multiplying by a special factor method

Solution
(a) $197 + 248 = 197 + 3 + 245 = 200 + 245 = 445$
(b) $125 \times 44 = 125 \times 4 \times 11 = 500 \times 11 = 5500$
(c) $273 - 139 = 274 - 140 = 134$
(d) $321 + 437 = 758$ [*Think:* $(300 + 400) + (20 + 30) + (1 + 7)$]

(e) $3 \times 432 = 1296$ [*Think:* $(3 \times 400) + (3 \times 30) + (3 \times 2)$]

(f) $456 \times 25 = 114 \times 100 = 11,400$ (*Think:* $25 \times 4 = 100$. Thus $456 \times 25 = 114 \times 4 \times 25 = 114 \times 100 = 11,400$.)   ■

Computational Estimation

The process of estimation takes on various forms. The number of beans in a jar may be estimated using no mathematics, simply a "guesstimate." Also, one may estimate how long a trip will be, based simply on experience. **Computational estimation** is the process of finding an approximate answer (an estimate) to a computation, often using mental math. With the use of calculators becoming more commonplace, computational estimation is an essential skill. Next we consider various types of computational estimation.

Front-End Estimation

Three types of front-end estimation will be demonstrated.

Range Estimation.   Often it is sufficient to know an interval or **range**, that is, a low value and a high value, that will contain an answer. The following example shows how ranges can be obtained in addition and multiplication.

EXAMPLE 4.4   Find a range for answers to these computations by using only the leading digits.

(a)   257   **(b)**   294
     $+576$ $\times\ 53$

Solution

(a)

Sum	Low Estimate	High Estimate
257	200	300
$+576$	$+500$	$+600$
	700	900

Thus a range for the answer is from 700 to 900. Notice that you have to look at only the digits having the largest place values ($2 + 5 = 7$, or 700) to arrive at the low estimate, and these digits each increased by one ($3 + 6 = 9$, or 900) to find the high estimate.

(b)

Product	Low Estimate	High Estimate
294	200	300
$\times\ 53$	$\times\ 50$	$\times\ 60$
	10,000	18,000

Due to the nature of multiplication, this method gives a wide range, here 10,000 to 18,000. Even so, this method will catch many errors.   ■

One-Column/Two-Column Front-End.   We can estimate the sum $498 + 251$ using the **one-column front-end method** as follows: To estimate $498 + 251$, think $400 + 200 = 600$ (the estimate). Notice that this is simply the low end of the range estimate. The one-column front-end method always provides low estimates in addition problems as well as in multiplication problems. In the case of 376 + 53 + 417, the one-column estimate is 300 + 400 = 700 since there are no hundreds in 53. The two-column front-end method also provides a low estimate for sums and products. However, this estimate is closer to the exact answer than one obtained from using only one column. For example, in the case of 372 + 53 + 417, the **two-column front-end method** yields 370 + 50 + 410 = 830, which is closer to the exact answer 842 than the 700 obtained using the one-column method.

Front-End with Adjustment.   This method enhances the one-column front-end method. For example, to find 498 + 251, think 400 + 200 = 600 and 98 + 51 is about 150. Thus the estimate is 600 + 150 = 750. Unlike one-column or two-column front-end estimates, this technique may produce either a low estimate or a high estimate, as in this example.

Keep in mind that one estimates to obtain a "rough" answer, so all of the forms of front-end estimation above belong in one's estimation repertoire.

EXAMPLE 4.5   Estimate using the method indicated.
(a) 503 × 813 using one-column front-end
(b) 1200 × 35 using range estimation
(c) 4376 − 1889 using two-column front-end
(d) 3257 + 874 using front-end adjustment

Solution
(a) To estimate 503 × 813 using the one-column front-end method, think 500 × 800 = 400,000. Using words, think "5 hundreds times 8 hundreds is 400,000."
(b) To estimate a range for 1200 × 35, think 1200 × 30 = 36,000 and 1200 × 40 = 48,000. Thus a range for the answer is from 36,000 to 48,000. One also could use 1000 × 30 = 30,000 and 2000 × 40 = 80,000. However, this yields a wider range.
(c) To estimate 4376 − 1889 using the two-column front-end method, think 4300 − 1800 = 2500. You also can think "43 − 18 = 25" and then append two zeros after the 25 to obtain 2500.
(d) To estimate 3257 + 874 using front-end with adjustment, think 3000, but since 257 + 874 is about 1000, adjust to 4000. ■

Rounding
Rounding is perhaps the best known computational estimation technique. The purpose of rounding is to replace complicated numbers with simpler numbers. Here, again, since the objective is to obtain an estimate, any of several rounding techniques may be used. However, some may be more appropriate than others, depending on the word problem situation. For example, if you are estimating how much money to take along on a trip, you would round up to be sure that you had enough. When calculating the amount of gas needed for a trip, one would round the miles per gallon es-

timate down to ensure that there would be enough money for gas. Unlike the previous estimation techniques, rounding is often applied to an answer as well as to the individual numbers before a computation is performed.

Several different methods of rounding are illustrated next. What is common, however, is that each method rounds to a particular place. You are asked to formulate rules for the following methods in the problem set.

Round Up (Down).   The number 473 **rounded up** to the nearest tens place is 480 since 473 is between 470 and 480 and 480 is *above* 473 (Figure 4.1). The number 473 **rounded down** to the nearest tens place is 470. Rounding down is also called truncating (**truncate** means to cut off). The number 1276 truncated to the hundreds place is 1200.

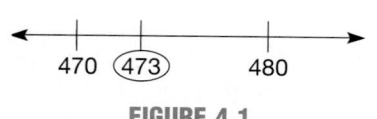

FIGURE 4.1

Round a 5 Up.   The most common rounding technique used in schools is the round a 5 up method. This method can be motivated using a number line. Suppose that we wish to round 475 to the nearest ten (Figure 4.2).

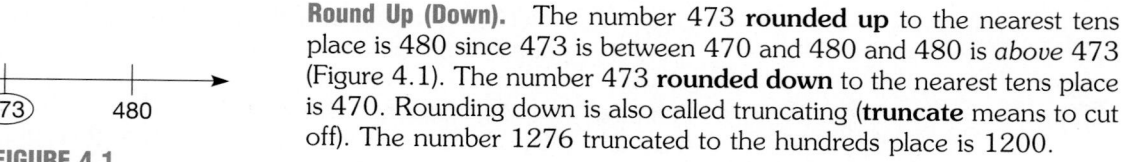

FIGURE 4.2

Since 475 is midway between 470 and 480, we have to make an agreement concerning whether we round 475 to 470 or to 480. The **round a 5 up** method always rounds such numbers up, so 475 rounds to 480. In the case of the numbers 471 to 474, since they are all nearer 470 than 480, they are rounded to 470 when rounding to the nearest ten. The numbers 476 to 479 are rounded to 480.

One disadvantage of this method is that estimates obtained when several 5s are involved tend to be on the high side. For example, the "round a 5 up" to the nearest ten estimate applied to the addends of the sum 35 + 45 + 55 + 65 yields 40 + 50 + 60 + 70 = 220, which is 20 more than the exact sum 200.

Round to the Nearest Even.   Rounding to the nearest even can be used to avoid errors of accumulation in rounding. For example, if 475 + 545 (= 1020) is estimated by rounding up to the tens place or rounding a 5 up, the answer is 480 + 550 = 1030. By rounding down, the estimate is 470 + 540 = 1010. Since 475 is between 480 and 470 and the 8 in the tens place is even, and 545 is between 550 and 540 and the 4 is even, **rounding to the nearest even** method yields 480 + 540 = 1020.

EXAMPLE 4.6   Estimate using the indicated method. (The symbol "≈" means "is approximately.")
(a) Estimate 2173 + 4359 by rounding down to the nearest hundreds place.
(b) Estimate 3250 − 1850 by rounding to the nearest even hundreds place.
(c) Estimate 575 − 398 by rounding a 5 up to the nearest tens place.

Solution

(a) $2173 + 4359 \approx 2100 + 4300 = 6400$

(b) $3250 - 1850 \approx 3200 - 1800 = 1400$

(c) $575 - 398 \approx 580 - 400 = 180$ ∎

Round to Compatible Numbers. Another rounding technique can be applied to estimate products such as 26×37. A reasonable estimate of 26×37 is $25 \times 40 = 1000$. The numbers 25 and 40 were selected since they are estimates of 26 and 37, respectively, and are compatible with respect to multiplication. (Notice that the rounding up technique would have yielded the considerably higher estimate of $30 \times 40 = 1200$, whereas the exact answer is 962). This **round to compatible numbers** technique allows one to round either up or down to compatible numbers to simplify calculations, rather than rounding to specified places. For example, a reasonable estimate of 57×98 is $57 \times 100 (= 5700)$. Here, only the 98 needed to be rounded to obtain an estimate mentally. The division problem $2716 \div 75$ can be estimated mentally by considering $2800 \div 70 (= 40)$. Here 2716 was rounded up to 2800, and 75 was rounded down to 70 because $2800 \div 70$ easily leads to a quotient since 2800 and 70 are compatible numbers with respect to division.

EXAMPLE 4.7 Estimate by rounding to compatible numbers in two different ways.

(a) 43×21 (b) $256 \div 33$

Solution

(a) $43 \times 21 \approx 40 \times 21 = 840$

$43 \times 21 \approx 43 \times 20 = 860$

(The exact answer is 903.)

(b) $256 \div 33 \approx 240 \div 30 = 8$

$256 \div 33 \approx 280 \div 40 = 7$

(The exact answer is 7 with remainder 25.) ∎

Rounding is a most useful and flexible technique. It is important to realize that the main reasons to round are (i) to simplify calculations while obtaining reasonable answers, and (ii) to report numerical results that can be easily understood. Any of the methods illustrated here may be used to estimate.

The ideas involving mental math and estimation in this section were observed in children who were facile in working with numbers. The following suggestions should help develop number sense in all children.

1. Learn the basic facts using thinking strategies, and extend the strategies to multidigit numbers.
2. Master the concept of place value.
3. Master the basic addition and multiplication properties of whole numbers.
4. Develop a habit of using the front-end and left-to-right methods.
5. Practice mental calculations often, daily if possible.

6. Accept approximate answers when exact answers are not needed.

7. Estimate prior to doing exact computations.

8. Be flexible by using a variety of mental math and estimation techniques.

Using a Calculator

Math Explorer.
Figure 4.3(a)

Although a basic calculator that costs less than $10 is sufficient for most elementary school students, there are features on $15 to $30 calculators that simplify many complicated calculations. The keyboards and displays of two calculators are featured here: the *Math Explorer* [Figure 4.3(a)] and the *TI-34* [Figure 4.3(b)], both manufactured by Texas Instruments. The *Math Explorer,* which is designed especially for elementary and middle schools, performs fraction, as well as the usual decimal calculations and can perform long division with remainder directly. The *TI-34* is a standard scientific calculator that also performs fraction calculations.

The $\boxed{\text{ON/AC}}$ key turns the calculator on; the AC is an abbreviation for All Clear. Thus pressing this key clears the calculator, including the memory. The $\boxed{\text{CE/C}}$ key clears the current entry on the calculator display.

There are three main types of logic available in calculators: arithmetic, algebraic, and reverse Polish notation. The following discussion illustrates how these three logics differ.

(NOTE: For ease of reading, we will write numerals without the usual squares around them to indicate that they are keys.)

TI-34.
Figure 4.3(b)

Arithmetic Logic. In arithmetic logic, the calculator performs operations in the order they are entered. For example, if 3 $\boxed{+}$ 4 $\boxed{\times}$ 5 $\boxed{=}$ is entered, the calculations are performed as follows: $(3 + 4) \times 5 = 7 \times 5 = 35$. That is, the operations are performed from left to right as they are entered.

Algebraic Logic. If your calculator has algebraic logic and 3 $\boxed{+}$ 4 $\boxed{\times}$ 5 $\boxed{=}$ is entered, the result is different; here the calculator evaluates expressions according to the usual mathematical convention for **order of operations**.

Within the innermost parentheses,

First: Calculate exponentials.

Second: Perform multiplications and divisions from left to right.

Third: Perform additions and subtractions from left to right.

Repeat until all calculations have been performed. For 3 $\boxed{+}$ 4 $\boxed{\times}$ 5 $\boxed{=}$,

$$3 + (4 \times 5) = 3 + 20 = 23$$

since multiplication takes precedence over addition. If a calculator has parentheses, they can be inserted to be sure that the desired operation is performed first. In a calculator that uses algebraic logic, the calculation $13 - 5 \times 4 \div 2 + 7$ will result in $13 - 10 + 7 = 10$. If one wishes to calculate $13 - 5$ first, parentheses must be inserted. Thus $(13 - 5) \times 4 \div 2 + 7 = 23$. Both the *Math Explorer* and the *TI-34* have algebraic logic.

Reverse Polish Notation (RPN) Logic. RPN is found on more sophisticated scientific calculators (e.g., those made by Hewlett-Packard). Such calculators can easily be recognized by their ENTER key. The calculation (3 + 4) × 5 is performed as follows on an RPN calculator: 3 ENTER 4 + 5 ×. Here the 3 is sent to a memory "stack" by the ENTER key. Then 4 is added to the 3, and 3 + 4 is multiplied by the 5. To find 3 + (4 × 5), the following sequence of keystrokes may be used: 3 ENTER 4 ENTER 5 × +. Here the 3 is entered in the stack first. Then the 4 is also entered in the stack. This moves the 3 to a stack location directly above the location of 4. Then 5 × 4 is found and 3 + (5 × 4) is obtained from the last keystroke. Note that RPN logic does not require the use of an "equals" key.

Now let's consider some features that make a calculator helpful both as a computational and a pedagogical device. Several keystroke sequences will be displayed to simulate the variety of calculator operating systems available.

STUDENT PAGE SNAPSHOT

Multiplying Greater Numbers

A. The manager of a video-store chain figures that the chain's profit averages $1,830 per day. At this rate what would the chain's profit be in a year?

Record your estimate.

Anna uses a calculator, and Louanne uses paper and pencil.

Anna	Louanne
365 ⊗ 1830 ⊜ *667950.*	$1,830
	× 365
	9150
	10980
	5490
	$667,950

The video-store chain's profit would be $667,950.

1. Does the answer seem reasonable? How do you know?

2. Which method would you use to find 207 × 894? Why? Find the product.

B. When using a calculator you need to be careful about entering digits and signs of operation.

Anna and Louanne use calculators to find 368 × 245.

Anna's answer: *90160.*   Louanne's answer: *156400.*

3. Which answer is more reasonable? How do you know?

Parentheses.   As mentioned earlier when we were discussing algebraic logic, one must always be attentive to the order of operations when several operations are present. For example, the product $2 \times (3 + 4)$ can be found in two ways. First, by using commutativity, the following keystrokes will yield the correct answer:

$$3 \boxed{+} 4 \boxed{=} \boxed{\times} 2 \boxed{=} \boxed{\qquad 14}.$$

Alternatively, the parentheses keys may be used as follows:

$$2 \boxed{\times} \boxed{(} 3 \boxed{+} 4 \boxed{)} \boxed{=} \boxed{\qquad 14}.$$

Parentheses are needed, since pressing the keys $2 \boxed{\times} 3 \boxed{+} 4 \boxed{=}$ on a calculator with algebraic logic will result in the answer 10. Distributivity may be used to simplify calculations. For example, $753 \cdot 8 + 753 \cdot 9$ can be found using $753 \boxed{\times} \boxed{(} 8 \boxed{+} 9 \boxed{)} \boxed{=}$ instead of $753 \boxed{\times} 8 \boxed{+} 753 \boxed{\times} 9 \boxed{=}$.

Constant Functions.   In Chapter 3, multiplication was viewed as repeated addition; in particular, $5 \times 3 = 3 + 3 + 3 + 3 + 3 = 15$. Repeated operations are carried out in different ways depending on the model of calculator. For example, the following keystroke sequence is used to calculate 5×3 on one calculator that has a built-in constant function:

$$3 \boxed{+} \boxed{=} \boxed{=} \boxed{=} \boxed{=} \boxed{\qquad 15}.$$

Numbers raised to a whole-number power may be found using a similar technique also. For example, 3^5 can be calculated by replacing the $\boxed{+}$ with a $\boxed{\times}$ in the preceding examples. A constant function can also be used to do repeated subtraction to find a quotient and a remainder in a division problem. For example, the following sequence can be used to find $35 \div 8$:

$$35 \boxed{-} 8 \boxed{=} \boxed{=} \boxed{=} \boxed{=} \boxed{\qquad 3}.$$

The remainder (3 here) is the first number displayed that is less than the divisor (8 here), and the number of times the equal sign was pressed is the quotient (4 here).

Exponent Keys.   There are three common types of exponent keys: $\boxed{10^n}$, $\boxed{x^2}$, and $\boxed{y^x}$. The $\boxed{10^n}$ key finds powers of ten in one of two ways, depending on the make of calculator:

$$\boxed{10^n} 3 \boxed{=} \boxed{\qquad 1000} \quad \text{or} \quad 3 \boxed{10^n} \boxed{\qquad 1000}.$$

The $\boxed{x^2}$ key is used to find squares as follows:

$$3 \boxed{x^2} \boxed{\qquad 9}.$$

The $\boxed{y^x}$ key is used to find more general powers. For example, 7^3 may be found as follows:

$$7 \boxed{y^x} 3 \boxed{=} \boxed{\qquad 343}.$$

Memory Functions. Many calculators have a memory function designated by the keys $\boxed{\text{M+}}$, $\boxed{\text{M−}}$, $\boxed{\text{MR}}$, or $\boxed{\text{STO}}$, $\boxed{\text{RCL}}$, $\boxed{\text{SUM}}$. Your calculator's display will probably show an "M" to remind you that there is a nonzero number in the memory. The problem $5 \times 9 + 7 \times 8$ may be found as follows using the memory keys:

$$5 \boxed{\times} 9 \boxed{=} \boxed{\text{M+}} 7 \boxed{\times} 8 \boxed{=} \boxed{\text{M+}} \boxed{\text{MR}} \boxed{ 101 } \quad \text{or}$$

$$5 \boxed{\times} 9 \boxed{=} \boxed{\text{SUM}} 7 \boxed{\times} 8 \boxed{=} \boxed{\text{SUM}} \boxed{\text{RCL}} \boxed{ 101 }.$$

It is a good practice to clear the memory for each new problem using the all clear key.

Additional special keys will be introduced throughout the book as the need arises.

Scientific Notation. Input and output of a calculator are limited by the number of places in the display (generally 8, 10, or 12). There are two basic responses when there is a number that is too large to fit in the display. Simple calculators either provide a partial answer with an "E" (for "error"), or the word "ERROR" is displayed. Many scientific calculators automatically express the answer in **scientific notation**, that is, as the product of a decimal number greater than or equal to 1 but less than 10, and the appropriate power of 10. For example, on the 10-digit display of the *TI-34,* the product of 123,456,789 and 987 is displayed as $\boxed{1.218518507^{11}}$, which means $1.218518507 \times 10^{11}$. (NOTE: Scientific notation is discussed in more detail in Chapter 9 after decimals and negative numbers have been studied.) If an exact answer is needed, the use of the calculator can be combined with paper/pencil and distributivity as follows:

$$\begin{aligned}
123{,}456{,}789 \times 987 &= 123{,}456{,}789 \times 900 + 123{,}456{,}789 \times 80 \\
&\quad + 123{,}456{,}789 \times 7 \\
&= 111{,}111{,}110{,}100 + 9{,}876{,}543{,}120 \\
&\quad + 864{,}197{,}523.
\end{aligned}$$

Now we can obtain the product by adding:

$$\begin{array}{r}
111{,}111{,}110{,}100 \\
9{,}876{,}543{,}120 \\
+ 864{,}197{,}523 \\
\hline
121{,}851{,}850{,}743
\end{array}$$

As the Student Page Snapshot in this section illustrates, calculations with numbers having three or more digits will probably be performed on a calculator (or computer) to save time and increase accuracy. Even so, it is prudent to estimate your answer when using your calculator.

MATHEMATICAL MORSEL

In his fascinating book *The Great Mental Calculators,* author Steven B. Smith discusses various ways that the great mental calculators did their calculations. In his research, he found that all auditory calculators (people who are given problems verbally and perform computations mentally) *except one* did their multiplications from left to right to minimize their short-term memory load.

EXERCISE/PROBLEM SET 4.1—PART A

Exercises

1. Calculate mentally using properties.
   (a) $(37 + 25) + 43$ **(b)** $47 \cdot 15 + 47 \cdot 85$
   (c) $(4 \times 13) \times 25$ **(d)** $26 \cdot 24 - 21 \cdot 24$

2. Find each of these differences mentally using equal additions. Write out the steps that you thought through.
   (a) $43 - 17$ **(b)** $62 - 39$ **(c)** $132 - 96$
   (d) $250 - 167$

3. Calculate mentally left to right.
   (a) $123 + 456$ **(b)** $342 + 561$
   (c) $587 - 372$ **(d)** $467 - 134$

4. Calculate mentally using the indicated method.
   (a) $198 + 387$ (additive compensation)
   (b) 84×5 (multiplicative compensation)
   (c) 99×53 (special factor)
   (d) $4125 \div 25$ (special factor)

5. The **halving and doubling** method can be used to multiply two numbers when one factor is a power of 2. For example, to find 8×17, find 4×34 or $2 \times 68 = 176$. Find the following products using this method.
   (a) 16×21 **(b)** 4×72 **(c)** 8×123
   (d) 16×211

6. Calculate mentally.
   (a) $58,000 \times 5,000,000$
   (b) $7 \times 10^5 \times 21,000$
   (c) $13,000 \times 7,000,000$
   (d) $4 \times 10^5 \times 3 \times 10^6 \times 7 \times 10^3$
   (e) $5 \times 10^3 \times 7 \times 10^7 \times 4 \times 10^5$
   (f) $17,000,000 \times 6,000,000,000$

7. Estimate each of the following using the four front-end methods: (i) range, (ii) one-column, (iii) two-column, and (iv) with adjustment.

    (a) $\quad 3741$ **(b)** $\quad 1591$ **(c)** $\quad 2347$
    $\quad +1252$ $\quad 346$ $\quad 58$
              $\quad 589$ $\quad 192$
           $+ \quad 163$ $+5783$

8. Find a range estimate for these products.
   (a) 37×24 **(b)** 157×231 **(c)** 491×8

9. Calculate mentally using compatible number estimation.
   (a) 63×97 **(b)** 51×212
   (c) $3112 \div 62$ **(d)** 103×87
   (e) 62×58 **(f)** $4254 \div 68$

10. Round as specified.
    (a) 373 to the nearest tens place
    (b) 650 using "round a 5 up" to the hundreds place
    (c) 1123 up to the tens place
    (d) 457 to the nearest tens place
    (e) 3457 to the nearest thousands place

11. **Cluster estimation** is used to estimate sums and products when there are several numbers that cluster near a single number. For example, the addends in $789 + 810 + 792$ cluster around 800. Thus $3 \times 800 = 2400$ is a good estimate of the sum. Estimate the following using cluster estimation.
    (a) $347 + 362 + 354 + 336$
    (b) $61 \times 62 \times 58$
    (c) $489 \times 475 \times 523 \times 498$
    (d) $782 + 791 + 834 + 812 + 777$

12. The sum $26 + 38 + 55$ can be found mentally as follows: $26 + 30 = 56$, $56 + 8 = 64$, $64 + 50 = 114$, $114 + 5 = 119$. Find the following sums mentally using this technique.

(a) $32 + 29 + 56$ (b) $54 + 28 + 67$
(c) $19 + 66 + 49$ (d) $62 + 84 + 27 + 81$

13. Before granting an operating license, a scientist has to estimate the amount of pollutants that should be allowed to be discharged from an industrial chimney. Should she overestimate or underestimate? Explain.

14. Here are four ways to estimate 26×12:

$$26 \times 10 = 260 \qquad 30 \times 12 = 360$$
$$25 \times 12 = 300 \qquad 30 \times 10 = 300$$

Estimate the following in four ways.
(a) 31×23 (b) 35×46
(c) 48×27 (d) 76×12

15. Estimate the following values and check with a calculator.
(a) 656×74 is between _____ 000 and _____ 000.
(b) 491×3172 is between _____ 00000 and _____ 00000.
(c) 143^2 is between _____ 0000 and _____ 0000.
(d) 35^4 is between _____ 0000 and _____ 0000.

16. Often subtraction can be done more easily in steps. For example, $43 - 37$ can be found as follows: $43 - 37 = (43 - 30) - 7 = 13 - 7 = 6$. Find the following differences using this technique.
(a) $52 - 35$ (b) $173 - 96$
(c) $241 - 159$ (d) $83 - 55$

17. In division you can sometimes simplify the problem by multiplying or dividing both the divisor and dividend by the same number. This is called **division compensation**. For example,

$$72 \div 12 = (72 \div 2) \div (12 \div 2)$$
$$= 36 \div 6 = 6 \qquad \text{and}$$
$$145 \div 5 = (145 \times 2) \div (5 \times 2)$$
$$= 290 \div 10 = 29$$

Calculate the following mentally using this technique.
(a) $84 \div 14$ (b) $234 \div 26$
(c) $120 \div 15$ (d) $168 \div 14$

18. Use properties to calculate the following problems in two different ways on a calculator.
(a) $37(13 + 98)$ (b) $132 + (276 + 498)$
(c) $57(93 \cdot 81)$ (d) $49 \cdot 59 + 59 \cdot 87$

19. Some products can be found most easily using a combination of mental math and a calculator. For example, the product $20 \times 47 \times 139 \times 5$ can be found by calculating 47×139 on a calculator and then multiplying your result by 100 mentally ($20 \times 5 = 100$). Calculate the following using a combination of mental math and a calculator.
(a) $17 \times 25 \times 817 \times 4$
(b) $98 \times 2 \times 673 \times 5$
(c) $674 \times 50 \times 889 \times 4$
(d) $783 \times 8 \times 79 \times 125$

20. Find the following without using the multiplication key.
(a) 374×6 (b) 149×4
(c) 564×11 (d) $12{,}321 \times 9$

21. Find the remainders using repeated subtraction.
(a) $374 \div 83$ (b) $491 \div 97$
(c) $1293 \div 317$ (d) $24{,}984 \div 8976$

22. Guess which is larger. Check with your calculator.
(a) 5^4 or 4^5 (b) 7^3 or 3^7
(c) 7^4 or 4^7 (d) 6^3 or 3^6

23. Compute the quotient and remainder (a whole number) for the following problems on a calculator without using repeated subtraction. Describe the procedure you used.
(a) $8\overline{)103}$ (b) $17\overline{)543}$
(c) $123\overline{)849}$ (d) $894\overline{)107{,}214}$

24. $1233 = 12^2 + 33^2$ and $8833 = 88^2 + 33^2$. How about $10{,}100$ and $5{,}882{,}353$? (HINT: Think 588 2353.)

25. Determine if the following equation is true for $n = 1$, 2, or 3.

$$1^n + 6^n + 8^n = 2^n + 4^n + 9^n$$

26. Notice that $153 = 1^3 + 5^3 + 3^3$. Determine which of the following numbers have the same property.
(a) 370   (b) 371   (c) 407

27. Determine if the following equation is true when n is 1, 2, or 3.

$$1^n + 4^n + 5^n + 5^n + 6^n + 9^n = 2^n + 3^n$$
$$+ 3^n + 7^n + 7^n + 8^n$$

Problems

28. Place a multiplication sign or signs so that the product in each problem is correct; for example, in 1 2 3 4 5 6 = 41,472, the multiplication sign should be placed between the 2 and the 3 since $12 \times 3456 = 41{,}472$.
(a) 1 3 5 7 9 0 = 122,130
(b) 6 6 6 6 6 = 439,956
(c) 7 8 9 3 4 5 6 = 3,307,824
(d) 1 2 3 4 5 6 7 = 370,845

29. Develop a method for finding a range for subtraction problems for three-digit numbers.

30. Find $13{,}333{,}333^2$.

31. Calculate $99 \cdot 36$ and $99 \cdot 23$ and look for a pattern. Then predict $99 \cdot 57$ and $99 \cdot 63$ mentally and check with a calculator.

32. (a) Calculate 25^2, 35^2, 45^2, and 55^2 and look for a pattern. Then find 65^2, 75^2, and 95^2 mentally and check your answers.

(b) Using a variable, prove that your result holds for squaring numbers that have a 5 as their ones digit.

33. George Bidder was a calculating prodigy in England during the nineteenth century. When he was 9, he was asked: If the moon were 123,256 miles from the earth and sound traveled at the rate of 4 miles a minute, how long would it be before inhabitants of the moon could hear the battle of Waterloo? His answer, 21 days, 9 hours, 34 minutes, was given in 1 minute. Was he correct? Try to do this calculation in less than 1 minute using a calculator. (NOTE: The moon is about 240,000 miles from earth and sound travels about 12.5 miles per second.)

34. Found in a newspaper article: What is

241,573,142,393,627,673,576,957,439,048
times   45,994,811,347,886,846,310,221,728,895,
223,034,301,839?

The answer is 71 consecutive 1s—one of the biggest numbers a computer has ever factored. This factorization bested the previous high, the factorization of a 69-digit number. Find a mistake here, and suggest a correction.

35. Some mental calculators use the following fact: $(a + b)(a - b) = a^2 - b^2$. For example, $43 \times 37 = (40 + 3)(40 - 3) = 40^2 - 3^2 = 1600 - 9 = 1591$.

Apply this technique to find the following products mentally.
(a) 54×46 **(b)** 81×79
(c) 122×118 **(d)** 1210×1190

36. Fermat claimed that

$$100,895,598,169 = 898,423 \times 112,303$$

Check this on your calculator.

37. Show how to find $439,268 \times 6852$ using a calculator that displays only eight digits.

38. Insert parentheses (if necessary) to obtain the following results.
(a) $76 \times 54 + 97 = 11,476$
(b) $4 \times 13^2 = 2704$
(c) $13 + 59^2 \times 47 = 163,620$
(d) $79 - 43 \div 2 + 17^2 = 307$

39. (a) Find a shortcut.

$$24 \times 26 = 624$$
$$62 \times 68 = 4216$$
$$73 \times 77 = 5621$$
$$41 \times 49 = 2009$$
$$86 \times 84 = 7224$$
$$57 \times 53 = \underline{\quad\quad}$$

(b) Prove that your result works in general.
(c) How is this problem related to Problem 32?

40. Develop a set of rules for the "round a 5 up" method.

EXERCISE/PROBLEM SET 4.1—PART B

Exercises

1. Calculate mentally using properties.
(a) $52 \cdot 14 - 52 \cdot 4$ **(b)** $(5 \times 37) \times 20$
(c) $(56 + 37) + 44$ **(d)** $23 \cdot 4 + 23 \cdot 5 + 7 \cdot 9$

2. Find each of these differences mentally using equal additions. Write out the steps that you thought through.
(a) $56 - 29$ **(b)** $83 - 37$
(c) $214 - 86$ **(d)** $542 - 279$

3. Calculate mentally using the left-to-right method.
(a) $246 + 352$ **(b)** $49 + 252$
(c) $842 - 521$ **(d)** $751 - 647$

4. Calculate mentally using the method indicated.
(a) $359 + 596$ (additive compensation)
(b) 76×25 (multiplicative compensation)
(c) 4×37 (halving and doubling)
(d) 37×98 (special factor)
(e) $1240 \div 5$ (special factor)

5. Calculate mentally.
(a) $32,000 \times 400$
(b) $6000 \times 12,000$
(c) $4000 \times 5000 \times 70$
(d) $5 \times 10^4 \times 30 \times 10^5$
(e) $12,000 \times 4 \times 10^7$
(f) $23,000,000 \times 5,000,000$

6. Estimate each of the following using the four front-end methods: (i) one-column, (ii) range, (iii) two-column, and (iv) with adjustment.

(a)	4652	**(b)**	2659	**(c)**	15923
	+8134		3752		672
			79		2341
			+ 143		+ 251

7. Find a range estimate for these products.
(a) 257×1924 **(b)** 1349×45
(c) $547 \times 73,951$

8. Estimate using compatible number estimation.
   (a) 84×49 (b) $5527 \div 82$ (c) $2315 \div 59$
   (d) 78×81 (e) 207×73 (f) $6401 \div 93$

9. Round as specified.
   (a) 257 down to the tens place
   (b) 650 to the nearest even hundreds place
   (c) 593 to the nearest tens place
   (d) 4157 to the nearest hundreds place
   (e) 7126 to the nearest thousands place

10. Round 254,755 as specified.
   (a) To the nearest even tens place
   (b) To the nearest hundreds place
   (c) To the nearest thousands place
   (d) To the nearest ten thousands place
   (e) To the nearest hundred thousands place

11. Five of the following six numbers were rounded to the nearest thousand, then added to produce an estimated sum of 87,000. Which number was not included?

   5228   14,286   7782   19,628   9168   39,228

12. Estimate using cluster estimation.
   (a) $547 + 562 + 554 + 556$
   (b) $31 \times 32 \times 35 \times 28$
   (c) $189 + 175 + 193 + 173$
   (d) $562 \times 591 \times 634$

13. Estimate the following values and check with a calculator.
   (a) 324×56 is between _____ 000 and _____ 000.
   (b) 5714×13 is between _____ 000 and _____ 000.
   (c) 256^3 is between _____ 000000 and _____ 000000.

14. A scientist has to estimate the distance that lava from an erupting volcano will flow to determine an evacuation zone. Should she overestimate or underestimate? Explain.

15. Find the quotient and remainder using a calculator. Check your answers.
   (a) $18,114 \div 37$ (b) $381,271 \div 147$
   (c) $9,346,870 \div 1349$ (d) $817,293 \div 749$

16. One student calculated $84 - 28$ as $84 - 30 = 54$ and $54 + 2 = 56$; thus $84 - 28 = 56$. Another student calculated $84 - 28$ as $84 - 30 = 54$, and $54 - 2 = 52$; thus $84 - 28 = 52$. Determine which of these two methods is valid. Explain why students might have trouble with this method.

17. Guess what whole numbers can be used to fill in the blanks. Use your calculator to check.
   (a) $\_\_\_\_^4 = 6561$ (b) $\_\_\_\_^5 = 16,807$
   (c) $\_\_\_\_^6 = 4096$ (d) $\_\_\_\_^4 = 28,561$

18. True or false? $493,827,156^2 = 246,913,578 \times 987,654,312$.

19. What is interesting about the quotient obtained by dividing 987,654,312 by 8? (Do this mentally.)

20. Notice how by starting with 55 and continuing to raise the digits to the third power and adding, 55 reoccurs in three steps.

$$55 \to 5^3 + 5^3 = 250 \to 2^3 + 5^3$$
$$= 133 \to 1^3 + 3^3 + 3^3 = 55$$

Check to see if this phenomenon is also true for these three numbers:
   (a) 136   (b) 160   (c) 919

21. Using distributivity, show that $(a - b)^2 = a^2 - 2ab + b^2$. Use this idea to compute the following squares mentally. (HINT: $99 = 100 - 1$.)
   (a) 99^2 (b) 999^2 (c) 9999^2

22. It is easy to show that $3^2 + 4^2 = 5^2$, and $5^2 + 12^2 = 13^2$. However, in 1966 two mathematicians claimed the following:

$$27^5 + 84^5 + 110^5 + 133^5 = 144^5$$

True or false?

23. Check to see that $1634 = 1^4 + 6^4 + 3^4 + 4^4$. Then determine which of the following four numbers satisfy the same property.
   (a) 8208   (b) 9474   (c) 1138   (d) 2178

24. Verify the following patterns.

$$3^2 + 4^2 = 5^2$$
$$10^2 + 11^2 + 12^2 = 13^2 + 14^2$$
$$21^2 + 22^2 + 23^2 + 24^2 = 25^2 + 26^2 + 27^2$$

25. For which of the values $n = 1, 2, 3, 4$ is the following true?

$$1^n + 5^n + 8^n + 12^n + 18^n + 19^n$$
$$= 2^n + 3^n + 9^n + 13^n + 16^n + 20^n$$

26. Fill in the empty squares to produce true equations.

Problems

27. Develop a method for finding a range for division problems when a five-digit number is divided by a two-digit number.

28. Discuss the similarities/differences of using (i) special factors and (ii) multiplicative compensation when calculating 36×5 mentally.

29. Find $166,666,666^2$.

30. Calculate $999 \cdot 357$ and $999 \cdot 489$ and look for a pattern. Then find $999 \cdot 547$ and $999 \cdot 632$ mentally and check with a calculator.

31. Megan tried to multiply 712,000 by 864,000 on her calculator and got an error message. Explain how she can use her calculator (and a little thought) to find the exact product.

32. What is the product of 777,777,777 and 999,999,999?

33. Explain how you could calculate 342×143 even if the "3" and "4" keys did not work.

34. Find the missing products by completing the pattern. Check your answers with a calculator.

$$11 \times 11 = 121$$
$$111 \times 111 = 12321$$
$$1111 \times 1111 = \underline{\hspace{1cm}}$$
$$11111 \times 11111 = \underline{\hspace{1cm}}$$
$$111111 \times 111111 = \underline{\hspace{1cm}}$$

35. If you count one whole number per second, estimate how long (in hours, minutes, seconds) it will take you to count from 1 to the following numbers.
   (a) 100   **(b)** 1000   **(c)** 100,000
   (d) 1,000,000

36. Use your calculator to find the following products.

$$12 \times 11 \qquad 24 \times 11 \qquad 35 \times 11$$

Look at the middle digit of each product, and at the first and last digits. Write a rule that you can use to multiply by 11. Now try these problems using your rule and check your answers with your calculator.

$$54 \times 11 \qquad 62 \times 11 \qquad 36 \times 11$$

Adapt your rule to handle

$$37 \times 11 \qquad 59 \times 11 \qquad 76 \times 11$$

37. When asked to multiply 987,654,321 by 123,456,789, one mental calculator replied, "I saw in a flash that $987,654,321 \times 81 = 80,000,000,001$, so I multiplied 123,456,789 by 80,000,000,001 and divided by 81." Determine if his reasoning was correct. If it was, see if you can find the answer using your calculator.

38. (a) Find a pattern for multiplying the following pairs:

$$32 \times 72 = 2304 \qquad 43 \times 63 = 2709$$
$$73 \times 33 = 2409$$

Try finding these products mentally.

$$17 \times 97 \qquad 56 \times 56 \qquad 42 \times 62$$

(b) Prove why your method works.

39. Have you always wanted to be a calculating genius? Amaze yourself with the following problems.
   (a) To multiply 4,109,589,041,096 by 83, simply put the 3 in front of it and the 8 at the end of it. Now check your answer.
   (b) After you have patted yourself on the back, see if you can find a fast way to multiply

$$7,894,736,842,105,263,158 \text{ by } 86$$

   (NOTE: This works only in special cases.)

40. Find the ones digits.
   (a) 2^{10} **(b)** 432^{10} **(c)** 3^6 **(d)** 293^6

41. Develop a set of rules for the "round to the nearest even" method.

4.2

WRITTEN ALGORITHMS FOR WHOLE-NUMBER OPERATIONS

Section 4.1 was devoted to mental and calculator computation. This section presents the common written algorithms as well as some alternative ones that have historical interest and can be used to help students better understand how their algorithms work.

Algorithms for the Addition of Whole Numbers

An **algorithm** is a systematic, step-by-step procedure used to find an answer, usually to a computation. The common written algorithm for addition involves two main procedures: (i) adding single digits (thus using the basic facts), and (ii) carrying (regrouping or exchanging).

A development of our **standard addition algorithm** is used in Figure 4.4 to find the sum 134 + 325.

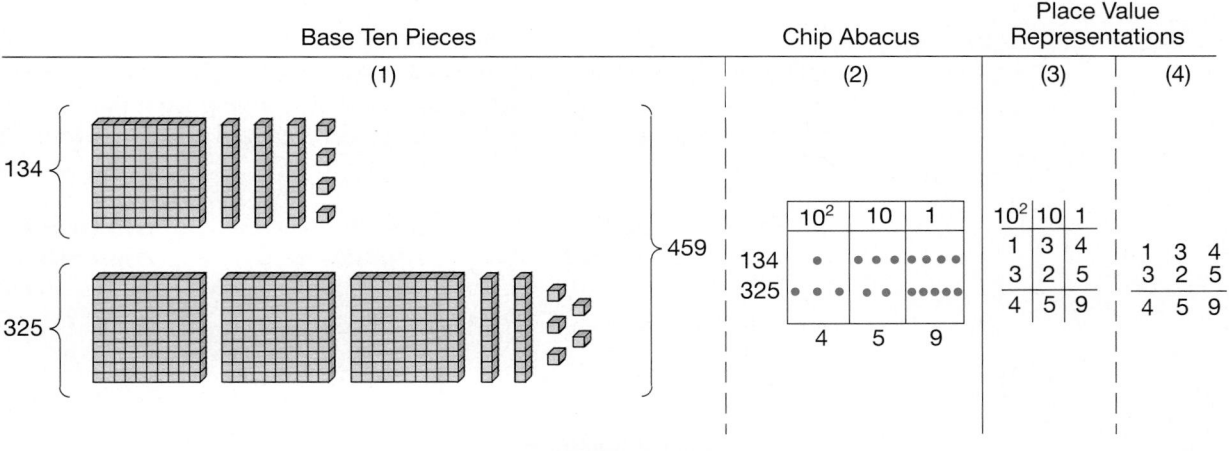

FIGURE 4.4

Observe how the left-to-right sequence in Figure 4.4 becomes progressively more abstract. When one views the base ten pieces (1), the hundreds, tens, and ones are distinguishable due to their sizes and the number of each type of piece. In the chip abacus (2), the chips all look the same. However, representations are distinguished by the number of chips in each column and by the column containing the chips (i.e., place value). In the place-value representation (3), the numbers are distinguished by the digits and the place values of their respective columns. Representation (4) is the common "add in columns" algorithm. The place-value method can be justified using expanded form and properties of whole-number addition as follows:

$$
\begin{aligned}
134 + 325 &= (1 \cdot 10^2 + 3 \cdot 10 + 4) && \text{Expanded form}\\
&\quad + (3 \cdot 10^2 + 2 \cdot 10 + 5)\\
&= (1 \cdot 10^2 + 3 \cdot 10^2) && \text{Associativity and}\\
&\quad + (3 \cdot 10 + 2 \cdot 10) + (4 + 5) && \text{commutativity}\\
&= (1 + 3)10^2 + (3 + 2)10 + (4 + 5) && \text{Distributivity}\\
&= 4 \cdot 10^2 + 5 \cdot 10 + 9 && \text{Addition}\\
&= 459 && \text{Expanded form}
\end{aligned}
$$

Note that 134 + 325 can be found working from left to right (add the hundreds first, etc.) or from right to left (add the ones first, etc.).

An addition problem when regrouping is required is illustrated in Figure 4.5 to find the sum 37 + 46.

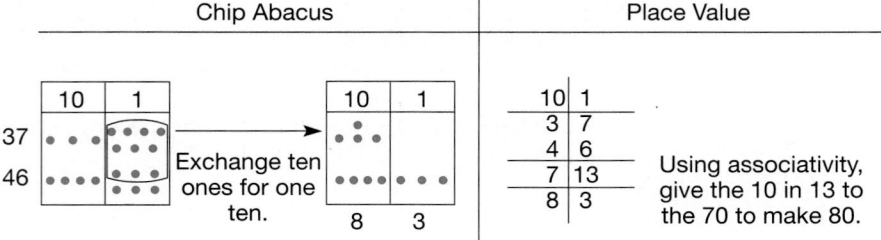

FIGURE 4.5

The procedure illustrated in the place-value representation can be refined in a series of steps to lead to our standard carrying algorithm for addition. Intermediate algorithms that lead to our standard addition algorithm are illustrated next.

(a) **Intermediate Algorithm 1**	(b) **Intermediate Algorithm 2**	(c) **Standard Algorithm**
		$\begin{array}{c} 11 \end{array}$
$\begin{array}{r} 568 \\ +394 \\ \hline 12 \end{array}$ sum of ones	$\begin{array}{r} 568 \\ +394 \\ \hline 12 \end{array}$	$\begin{array}{r} 5\ 6\ 8 \\ +3\ 9\ 4 \\ \hline 9\ 6\ 2 \end{array}$
150 sum of tens	15	
$\underline{800}$ sum of hundreds	$\underline{8}$	
962 final sum	962	

The preceding intermediate algorithms are easier to understand than the standard algorithm. However, they are less efficient and generally require more time and space.

Throughout history there have been many other algorithms for addition. One of these, the **lattice method for addition**, is illustrated next.

Lattice Method

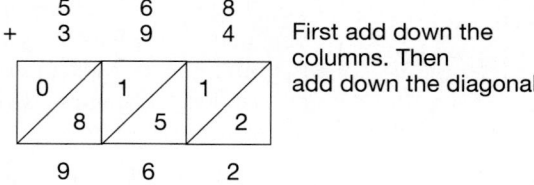

First add down the columns. Then add down the diagonals.

Notice how the lattice method is very much like intermediate algorithm 2. Other interesting algorithms are contained in the problem sets.

Algorithms for the Subtraction of Whole Numbers

The common algorithm for subtraction involves two main procedures: (i) subtracting numbers that are determined by the addition facts table, and (ii) exchanging or regrouping (the reverse of the carrying process for addition). Although this exchanging procedure is commonly called "borrowing," we choose to avoid this term because the numbers that are borrowed are not paid back. Hence the word "borrow" does not represent to children the actual underlying process of exchanging.

A development of our **standard subtraction algorithm** is used in Figure 4.6 to find the difference $357 - 123$.

Concrete Models

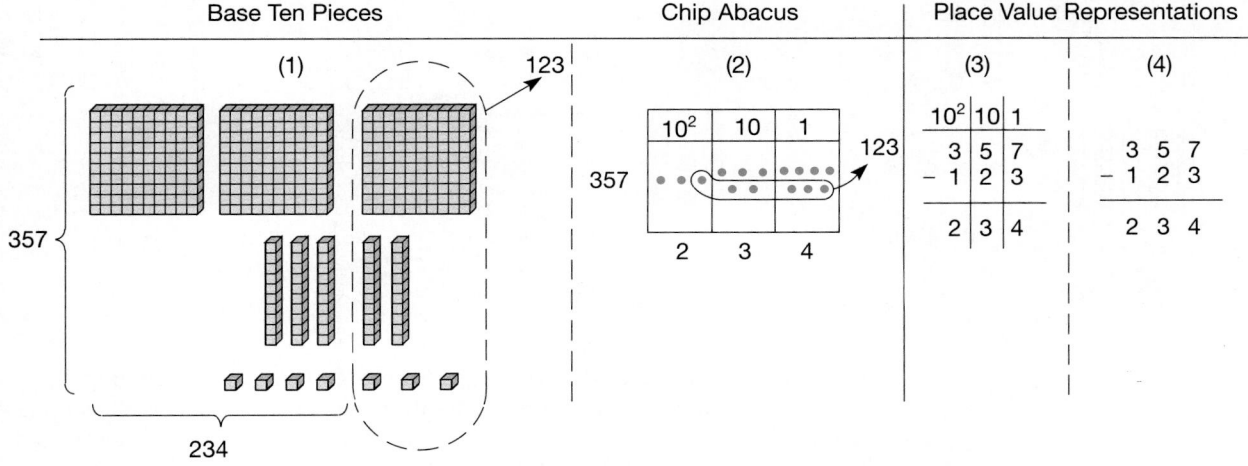

FIGURE 4.6

Notice that in the example in Figure 4.6, the answer will be the same if we subtract from left to right or right to left. The problem $423 - 157$ cannot be done in the same way since we cannot subtract 7 from 3 directly. In such cases, exchanges need to be made to permit us to use this subtraction algorithm. This is illustrated in Figure 4.7.

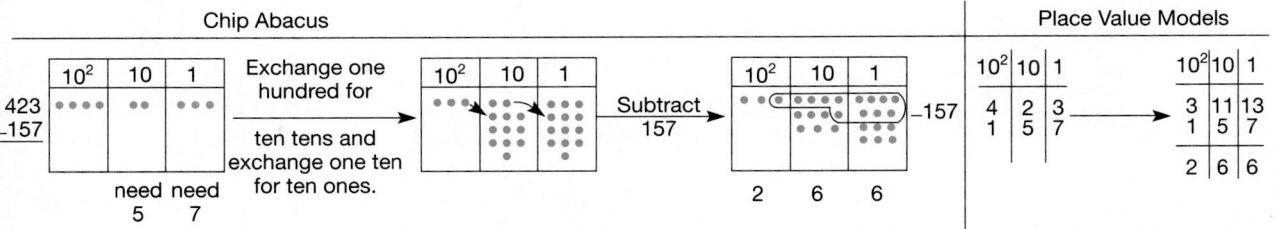

FIGURE 4.7

This place-value procedure is finally shortened to produce our standard subtraction algorithm.

$$
\begin{array}{c}
423 \\
-157 \\
\end{array}
\quad
\begin{array}{c}
\text{make} \\
\text{exchanges} \\
\longrightarrow
\end{array}
\quad
\begin{array}{c}
\overset{3\ \ 11\ \ 13}{\cancel{4}\ \cancel{2}\ \cancel{3}} \\
-1\ \ 5\ \ 7 \\
\hline
2\ \ 6\ \ 6 \\
\end{array}
$$

One nontraditional algorithm that is *especially* effective in any base is called the **subtract-from-the-base algorithm**. This algorithm is illustrated in Figure 4.8 using base ten pieces to find $323 - 64$.

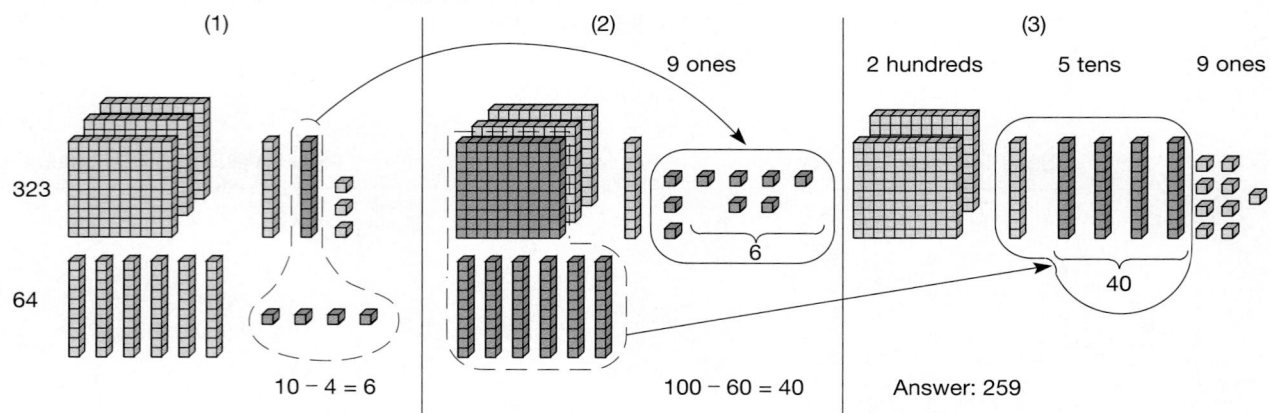

(1)   (2)   (3)

9 ones   2 hundreds   5 tens   9 ones

323

64

$10 - 4 = 6$ $100 - 60 = 40$ Answer: 259

6   40

FIGURE 4.8

In (1), observe that the 4 is subtracted from the 10 (instead of finding $13 - 4$ as in the standard algorithm). The difference $10 - 4 = 6$ is then combined with the 3 units in (2) to form 9 units. Then the 6 longs are subtracted from 1 flat (instead of finding $11 - 6$). The difference, $10 - 6 = 4$ longs, is then combined with the 1 long in (3) to obtain 5 longs (or 50). Thus since two flats remain, $323 - 64 = 259$. The following illustrates this process symbolically.

$$
\begin{array}{ccc}
 & & 10 \\
 & 2\;\;1 & 10 \\
323 & 3\;\;2 & 3 \\
-\;\;64 \;\rightarrow\; & -\;\;6 & 4 \;\rightarrow \\
 & & 9 \\
\end{array}
\quad
\begin{array}{ccc}
 & & 10 \\
 & 2\;\;1 & 10 \\
 & 3\;\;2 & 3 \\
 & -\;\;6 & 4 \;\rightarrow \\
 & 5 & 9 \\
\end{array}
\quad
\begin{array}{ccc}
 & & 10 \\
 & 2\;\;1 & 10 \\
 & 3\;\;2 & 3 \\
 & -\;\;6 & 4 \\
 & 2\;\;5 & 9 \\
\end{array}
$$

$$\underbrace{(10 - 4) + 3}\qquad\underbrace{(10 - 6) + 1}$$

The advantage of this algorithm is that we only need to know the addition facts and *differences from 10* (as opposed to differences from all the teens). As you will see later in this chapter, this method can be used in any base, hence the name "subtract-from-the-base." After a little practice, you may find this algorithm to be easier and faster than our usual algorithm for subtraction.

Algorithms for the Multiplication of Whole Numbers

The standard multiplication algorithm involves the multiplication facts, distributivity, and a thorough understanding of place value. A development of our **standard multiplication algorithm** is used in Figure 4.9 to find the product 3×213.

Concrete Model	Place Value Representations	

Concrete Model	Horizontal Format	Vertical Format

	10^2	10	1
213	• •	•	• • •
213	• •	•	• • •
213	• •	•	• • •
	6	3	9

$3(213) = 3(200 + 10 + 3)$ Expanded form

$= 3 \times 200 + 3 \times 10 + 3 \times 3$ Distributivity

$= 600 + 30 + 9$ Multiplication

$= 639$ Addition

$$\begin{array}{r} 213 \\ \times \quad 3 \\ \hline 9 \\ 30 \\ 600 \\ \hline 639 \end{array}$$

3×3
3×10
3×200

FIGURE 4.9

Next, the product of a two-digit number times a two-digit number is found.

Calculate 34×12.

$$\begin{aligned}
34 \times 12 &= 34(10 + 2) & \text{Expanded form} \\
&= 34 \cdot 10 + 34 \cdot 2 & \text{Distributivity} \\
&= (30 + 4)10 + (30 + 4)2 & \text{Expanded form} \\
&= 30 \cdot 10 + 4 \cdot 10 + 30 \cdot 2 + 4 \cdot 2 & \text{Distributivity} \\
&= 300 + 40 + 60 + 8 & \text{Multiplication} \\
&= 408 & \text{Addition}
\end{aligned}$$

The product 34×12 also can be represented pictorially (Figure 4.10).

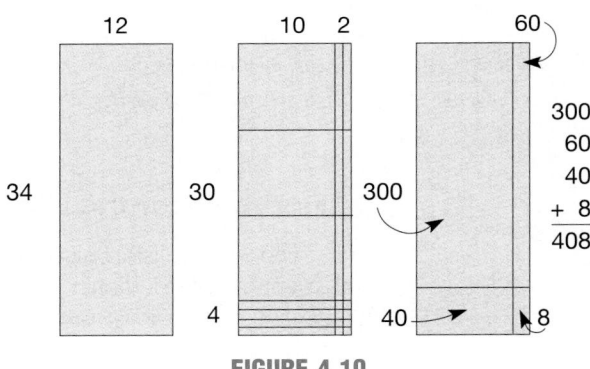

FIGURE 4.10

The following vertical intermediate multiplication algorithms can be used to lead to our standard multiplication algorithm.

Calculate 34×12.

(a) Intermediate Algorithm 1

$$\begin{array}{r} 34 \\ \times 12 \\ \hline 8 \\ 60 \\ 40 \\ 300 \\ \hline 408 \end{array}$$

(b) Intermediate Algorithm 2

$$\begin{array}{r} 34 \\ \times 12 \\ \hline 68 \\ \\ 340 \\ \hline 408 \end{array}$$

Think 2×34

Think 10×34

(c) Standard Algorithm

$$\begin{array}{r} 34 \\ \times 12 \\ \hline 68 \\ 34 \\ \hline 408 \end{array}$$

Think 2×4
Think 2×3

Think 1×4, but in tens place
Think 1×3, but in hundreds place

One final complexity in the standard multiplication algorithm is illustrated next.

Calculate: 857×9.

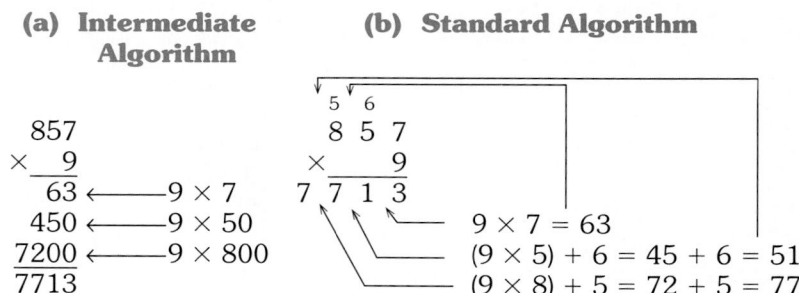

(a) Intermediate Algorithm

$$
\begin{array}{r}
857 \\
\times\quad 9 \\
\hline
63 \longleftarrow 9 \times 7 \\
450 \longleftarrow 9 \times 50 \\
7200 \longleftarrow 9 \times 800 \\
\hline
7713
\end{array}
$$

(b) Standard Algorithm

$$
\begin{array}{r}
\overset{5}{}\ \overset{6}{} \\
8\ 5\ 7 \\
\times\qquad 9 \\
\hline
7\ 7\ 1\ 3
\end{array}
$$

$9 \times 7 = 63$

$(9 \times 5) + 6 = 45 + 6 = 51$

$(9 \times 8) + 5 = 72 + 5 = 77$

Notice the complexity involved in explaining the standard algorithm!

The **lattice method for multiplication** is an example of an extremely simple multiplication algorithm that is no longer used, perhaps because we do not use paper with lattice markings on it and it is too time consuming to draw such lines.

To calculate 35×4967, begin with a blank lattice and find products of the digits in intersecting rows and columns. The 18 in the completed lattice was obtained by multiplying its row value, 3, by its column value, 6 (Figure 4.11). The other values are filled in similarly. Then the numbers are added down the diagonals as in lattice addition. The answer, read counterclockwise from left to right, is 173,845.

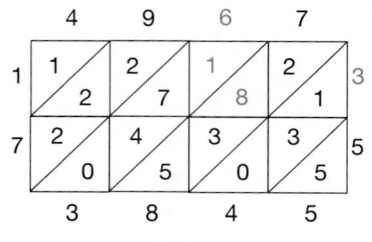

FIGURE 4.11

Algorithms for the Division of Whole Numbers

The long-division algorithm is the most complicated procedure in the elementary mathematics curriculum. Because of calculators, the importance of written long division using multidigit numbers has greatly diminished. However, the long-division algorithm involving one- and, perhaps, two-digit divisors continues to have common applications. The main idea behind the long-division algorithm is the division algorithm, which was given in Section 3.2. It states that if a and b are any whole numbers with $b \neq 0$, there exist unique whole numbers q and r such that $a = bq + r$, where $0 \leq r < b$. For example, if $a = 17$ and $b = 5$, then $q = 3$ and $r = 2$ since $17 = 5 \cdot 3 + 2$. The purpose of the long-division algorithm is to find the quotient, q, and remainder, r, for any given divisor, b, and dividend, a.

We will arrive at the final form of the long-division algorithm by working through various levels of complexity to illustrate how one can gain an understanding of the algorithm by progressing in small steps.

Find the quotient and remainder for $5739 \div 31$.
The **scaffold method** is a good method to use first.

$$
\begin{array}{rl}
31\overline{)5739} \\
-3100 & \quad 100(31) \\
\hline
2639 \\
-1550 & \quad 50(31) \\
\hline
1089 \\
-930 & \quad 30(31) \\
\hline
159 \\
155 & +\underline{\quad 5(31)} \\
\hline
4 & \quad 185
\end{array}
$$

How many 31s in 5739? *Guess:* 100

How many 31s in 2639? *Guess:* 50

How many 31s in 1089? *Guess:* 30

How many 31s in 159? *Guess:* 5

Since 4 is less than 31 we stop and add $100 + 50 + 30 + 5$. Therefore, the quotient is 185 and remainder is 4.

CHECK: $31 \cdot 185 + 4 = 5735 + 4 = 5739$.

As shown above, various multiples of 31 are subtracted successively from 5739 (or the resulting difference) until a remainder less than 31 is found. The key to this method is how well one can estimate the appropriate multiples of 31. In the scaffold method, it is better to estimate too low rather than too high as in the case of the 50. However, 80 would have been the optimal guess at that point. Thus, although the quotient and remainder can be obtained using this method, it can be an inefficient application of the Guess and Test strategy.

The next example illustrates how division by a single digit can be done more efficiently.

Find the quotient and remainder for $3159 \div 7$.

Intermediate Algorithm

$$
\begin{array}{r}
451 \\
1 \\
50 \\
400 \\
\end{array}
$$

Start here:
$$
\begin{array}{rl}
7\overline{)3159} \\
-2800 \\
\hline
359 \\
-350 \\
\hline
9 \\
-7 \\
\hline
2
\end{array}
$$

Think: How many 7s in 3100? 400
Think: How many 7s in 350? 50
Think: How many 7s in 9? 1

Therefore, the quotient is the sum $400 + 50 + 1$, or 451, and the remainder is 2.

CHECK: $7 \cdot 451 + 2 = 3157 + 2 = 3159$.

Now consider division by a two-digit divisor. Find the quotient and remainder for 1976 ÷ 32.

Intermediate Algorithm

$$
\begin{array}{r}
61 \\
\underline{1} \\
60 \\
32\overline{)1976} \\
-1920 \\
\hline
56 \\
-32 \\
\hline
24
\end{array}
$$

Think: How many
32s in 1976? 60
Think: How many
32s in 56? 1

Therefore, the quotient is 61 and the remainder is 24.

Next we will employ rounding to help estimate the appropriate quotients. Find the quotient and remainder for 4238 ÷ 56.

$$
\begin{array}{r}
5 \\
\underline{70} \\
56\overline{)4238} \\
-3920 \\
\hline
318 \\
-280 \\
\hline
38
\end{array}
$$

Think: How many 60s in 4200? 70
$70 \times 56 = 3920$
Think: How many 60s in 310? 5
$5 \times 56 = 280$

Therefore, the quotient is $70 + 5 = 75$ and the remainder is 38.

CHECK: $56 \cdot 75 + 38 = 4200 + 38 = 4238$.

Observe how we rounded the divisor up to 60 and the dividend *down* to 4200 in the first step. This up/down rounding assures us that the quotient at each step will not be too large.

This algorithm can be simplified further to our **standard algorithm for division** by reducing the "think" steps to divisions with single-digit divisors. For example, in place of "How many 60s in 4200?" one could ask equivalently, "How many 6s in 420?" Even easier, "How many 6s in 42?" Notice also that in general, the *divisor should be rounded up and the dividend should be rounded down.*

EXAMPLE 4.8   Find the quotient and remainder for 4238 ÷ 56.

Solution

$$
\begin{array}{r}
75 \\
56\overline{)4238} \\
\underline{392}
\end{array}
$$

$\begin{cases} \textit{Think:} \text{ How many 6s in 42? 7} \\ \text{Put the 7 above the 3 since we} \\ \text{are actually finding } 4230 \div 56. \\ \text{The 392 is } 7 \cdot 56. \end{cases}$

$$
\begin{array}{r}
318 \\
\underline{280} \\
38
\end{array}
$$

$\begin{cases} \textit{Think:} \text{ How many 6s in 31? 5} \\ \text{Put the 5 above the 8 since we} \\ \text{are finding } 318 \div 56. \\ \text{The 280 is } 5 \cdot 56. \end{cases}$

■

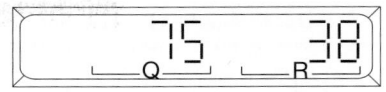

FIGURE 4.12

The quotient and remainder for $4238 \div 56$ can be found using a calculator. The TI Explorer does long division with remainder directly. The result for this problem is shown in Figure 4.12 as it appears on the calculator's display. To find the quotient and remainder using a standard calculator press these keys: $4238 \boxed{\div} 56 \boxed{=}$. Your display should read 75.678571 (perhaps with fewer or more decimal places). Thus the whole-number quotient is 75. From the relationship $a = bq + r$ we see that $r = a - bq$ is the remainder. In this case the remainder is $4238 - 56 \cdot 75$, or 38.

As the preceding calculator example illustrates, calculators virtually eliminate the need for becoming skilled in performing involved long divisions and other tedious calculations.

In this section, each of the four basic operations were illustrated by different algorithms. The problem set contains examples of many other algorithms. Even today, other countries use algorithms different from our "standard" algorithms. Also, students may even invent "new" algorithms. Since computational algorithms are aids for simplifying calculations, it is important to understand that *all correct algorithms are acceptable.* Clearly, computation in the future will rely less and less on written calculations and more and more on mental and electronic calculations.

MATHEMATICAL MORSEL

Have someone write down a three-digit number using three different digits hidden from your view. Then have the person form all of the other five three-digit numbers that can be obtained by rearranging their three digits. Add these six numbers together with a seventh number, which is any other one of the six. The person tells you the sum, and then you, in turn, tell him the seventh number. Here is how. Add the thousands digit of the sum to the remaining three-digit number (if the sum was 2347, you form $347 + 2 = 349$). Then take the remainder upon division of this new number by nine ($349 \div 9$ leaves a remainder of 7). Multiply the remainder by 111 ($7 \times 111 = 777$) and add this to the previous number ($349 + 777 = 1126$). Finally, add the thousands digit (if there is one) to the remaining number (1126 yields $126 + 1 = 127$, the seventh number!).

EXERCISE/PROBLEM SET 4.2—PART A

Exercises

1. The physical models of base ten blocks and chip abacus have been used to demonstrate addition. Using bundling sticks, sketch the solution to the following addition problems.
   (a) $15 + 32$ (b) $63 + 79$

2. Give a reason or reasons for each of the following steps to justify the addition process.

$$
\begin{aligned}
17 + 21 &= (1 \cdot 10 + 7) + (2 \cdot 10 + 1) \\
&= (1 \cdot 10 + 2 \cdot 10) + (7 + 1) \\
&= (1 + 2) \cdot 10 + (7 + 1) \\
&= 3 \cdot 10 + 8 \\
&= 38
\end{aligned}
$$

3. There are many ways of providing intermediate steps between the models for computing sums (base ten blocks, chip abacus, etc.) and the algorithm for addition. One of these is to represent numbers in their expanded forms. Consider the following examples:

$$
\begin{array}{r}
246 = 2 \text{ hundreds} + 4 \text{ tens} + 6 \\
+352 = 3 \text{ hundreds} + 5 \text{ tens} + 2 \\
\hline
5 \text{ hundreds} + 9 \text{ tens} + 8 \\
= 598
\end{array}
$$

$$
\begin{array}{r}
547 = 5(10)^2 + 4(10) + 7 \\
+296 = 2(10)^2 + 9(10) + 6 \\
\hline
7(10)^2 + 13(10) + 13 \\
7(10)^2 + 14(10) + 3 \\
8(10)^2 + 4(10) + 3 \\
= 843
\end{array} \Bigg\} \text{regrouping}
$$

   Use this expanded form of the addition algorithm to compute the following sums.
   (a)   351   (b)   478   (c)   1965
        $+635$ $+269$ $+\ 857$

4. Another intermediate algorithm involves computing partial sums. The digits in each column are summed and written on separate lines. In the example, notice where the partial sums are placed.

$$
\begin{array}{r}
632 \\
+798 \\
\hline
10 \\
12 \\
13 \\
\hline
1430
\end{array}
$$

   Using this method, compute the following sums.
   (a) $598 + 396$
   (b) $322 + 799 + 572$

5. Compute the following sums using the lattice method.
   (a)   482   (b)   567   (c)   982
        $+269$ $+765$ $+659$

6. Name an advantage and disadvantage of each of the following methods for addition.
   (a) Intermediate algorithm
   (b) Expanded form
   (c) Lattice
   (d) Standard algorithm

7. Sketch solutions to the following problems, using bundling sticks.
   (a)   57   (b)   44   (c)   34
        -37 -22 -29

8. 9342 is usually thought of as 9 thousands, 3 hundreds, 4 tens, and 2 ones, but in subtracting 6457 from 9342 using the customary algorithm, we regroup and think of 9342 as

   _____thousands, _____hundreds, _____tens, and _____ones

9. To perform some subtractions, it is necessary to reverse the rename and regroup process of addition. Perform the following subtraction in expanded form and follow regrouping steps.

$$
\begin{array}{cc}
732 & 700 + 30 + 2 \\
-378 & -(300 + 70 + 8) \quad \text{or}
\end{array}
$$

$$
\begin{array}{cc}
700 + 20 + 12 & 600 + 120 + 12 \\
-(300 + 70 + \ 8) \quad \text{or} & -(300 + \ 70 + \ 8) \\
& \overline{300 + \ 50 + \ 4} = 354
\end{array}
$$

   Use expanded form with regrouping as necessary to perform the following subtractions.
   (a) $652 - 175$ (b) $923 - 147$
   (c) $8257 - 6439$

10. Subtraction by **adding the complement** goes as follows:

$$
\begin{array}{rr}
619 & 619 \\
-476 & +523 \\
\hline
& \not{1}\,142 \\
+ \quad 1 \\
\hline
143
\end{array}
$$

   The complement of 476 is 523 since $476 + 523 = 999$. (The sum in each place is 9.) Cross out the leading digit. Add 1. Answer $= 143$

   (a) Find the following differences using this algorithm.

   $$
   \begin{array}{rrr}
   537 & 86{,}124 & 6{,}002{,}005 \\
   -179 & -38{,}759 & -4{,}187{,}269
   \end{array}
   $$

   (b) Explain how the method works with three-digit numbers.

11. Without performing the addition, tell which sum, if either, is greater.

```
23,456      20,002
23,400          32
23,000         432
+20,002     +65,432
```

12. Add the numbers below. Then turn this page upside down and add it again. What did you find? What feature of the numerals 1, 6, 8, 9 accounts for this?

```
986
818
969
989
696
616
```

13. Show how to find 34 × 28 on this grid paper.

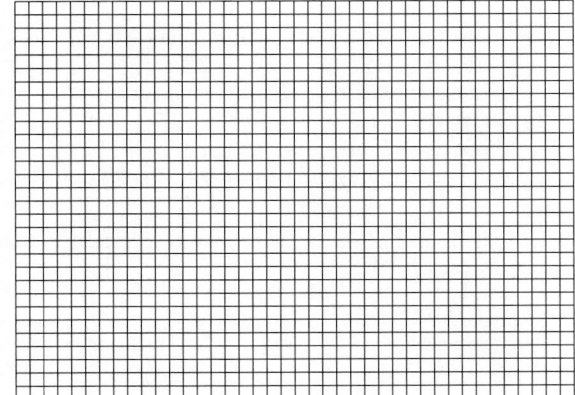

14. Justify each step in the following proof that 72 × 10 = 720.

$$72 \times 10 = (70 + 2) \times 10$$
$$= 70 \times 10 + 2 \times 10$$
$$= (7 \times 10) \times 10 + 2 \times 10$$
$$= 7 \times (10 \times 10) + 2 \times 10$$
$$= 7 \times 100 + 2 \times 10$$
$$= 700 + 20$$
$$= 720$$

15. Estimate the answer to 237 × 40 by doing 200 × 40 mentally. Is this a high or low estimate? What kind of estimate is 300 × 40?

16. Solve the following problems using the lattice method for multiplication and an intermediate algorithm.
(a) 23 × 62   **(b)** 17 × 45
(c) 237 × 48   **(d)** 617 × 896

17. Study the pattern in the left-to-right multiplication below.

```
   731
   238
  1462     (2 · 731)
  2193     (3 · 731)
  5848     (8 · 731)
 173978
```

Use this algorithm to do the following computations.
(a) 75 × 47   **(b)** 364 × 421   **(c)** 768 × 891

18. The use of finger numbers and systems of finger computation have been widespread through the years. One such system for multiplication uses the finger positions shown for computing the products of numbers from 6 through 10.

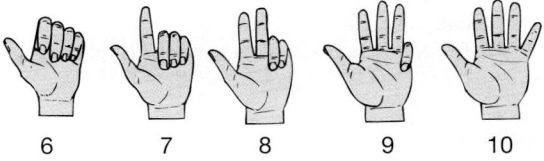

The two numbers to be multiplied are each represented on a different hand. The sum of the raised fingers is the number of tens and the product of the closed fingers is the number of ones. For example, 1 + 3 = 4 fingers raised, and 4 × 2 = 8 (fingers down).

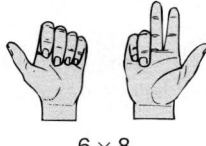

6 × 8

Use this method to compute the following products.
(a) 7 × 8   **(b)** 6 × 7   **(c)** 6 × 10

19. A third-grade teacher prepared her students for division this way:

```
20 ÷ 4        20
            −  4 ✔
              16
            −  4 ✔
              12
            −  4 ✔      20 ÷ 4 = 5
               8
            −  4 ✔
               4
            −  4 ✔
               0
```

How would her students find 42 ÷ 6?

20. Without using the divide key, use a calculator to find the quotient and remainder for each of the following problems.
   (a) $3\overline{)29}$ **(b)** $8\overline{)89}$ **(c)** $6\overline{)75}$

21. When asked to find the quotient and remainder of $431 \div 17$, one student did the following with a calculator:

$$\text{Display}$$
$$431 \;\boxed{\div}\; 17 \;\boxed{=}\; \boxed{25.35294} \;\boxed{-}$$

$$\text{Display}$$
$$25 \;\boxed{=}\; \boxed{\times}\; 17 \;\boxed{=}\; \boxed{6.0000000}$$

He gave a quotient of 25, and a remainder of 6. Is this answer correct?
   (a) Try this method on the following pairs.
      (i) $1379 \div 87$
      (ii) $69{,}431 \div 139$
      (iii) $1{,}111{,}111 \div 333$
   (b) Does this method always work? Explain.

Problems

22. Larry, Curly, and Moe each add incorrectly as follows.

Larry: $\begin{array}{r} \overset{2}{2}9 \\ +83 \\ \hline 1012 \end{array}$ Curly: $\begin{array}{r} 29 \\ +83 \\ \hline 121 \end{array}$ Moe: $\begin{array}{r} 29 \\ +83 \\ \hline 102 \end{array}$

How would you explain their mistakes to each of them?

23. Use the digits 1 to 9 to make an addition problem and answer. Use each digit only once.

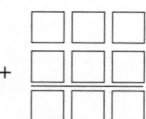

24. Place the digits 2, 3, 4, 6, 7, 8 in the boxes to obtain the following sums.
   (a) The greatest sum
   (b) The least sum

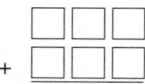

25. Arrange the digits 1, 2, 3, 4, 5, 6, 7 in order to add up to 100. (For example, $12 + 34 + 56 + 7 = 109$.)

26. (a) Given the following addition problem, replace seven digits with 0s so that the sum of the numbers is 1111.

$$\begin{array}{r} 999 \\ 777 \\ 555 \\ 333 \\ \underline{111} \end{array}$$

   (b) Do the same problem by replacing
      (i) eight digits with 0s.
      (ii) nine digits with 0s.
      (iii) ten digits with 0s.

27. Consider the following array:

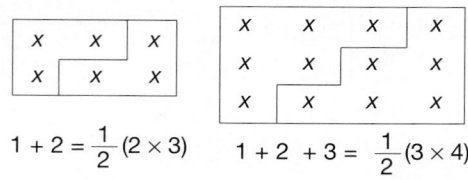

Compare the pair 26, 37 with the pair 36, 27.
   (a) Add: $26 + 37 =$ $36 + 27 =$
      What do you notice about the answers?
   (b) Subtract: $37 - 26 =$ $36 - 27 =$
      What do you notice about the answers?
   (c) Are your findings true for any two such pairs?
   (d) What similar patterns can you find?

28. The x's in half of each figure can be counted in two ways.

x	x	x
x	x	x

x	x	x	x
x	x	x	x
x	x	x	x

$$1 + 2 = \frac{1}{2}(2 \times 3) \qquad 1 + 2 + 3 = \frac{1}{2}(3 \times 4)$$

   (a) Draw a similar figure for $1 + 2 + 3 + 4$.
   (b) Express that sum in a similar way. Is the sum correct?
   (c) Use this idea to find the sum of whole numbers from 1 to 50 and from 1 to 75.

29. In the following problems, each letter represents a different digit and any of the digits 0 through 9 may be used. However, both additions have the same result. What are the problems?

$$\begin{array}{r} ZZZ \\ KKK \\ +\underline{LLL} \\ RSTU \end{array} \qquad \begin{array}{r} ZZZ \\ PPP \\ +\underline{QQQ} \\ RSTU \end{array}$$

30. Following are some problems worked out by students. Each student has a particular error pattern. Find that error and tell what answer that student will get for the last problem.

Bob:

$$\begin{array}{r} 22 \\ \times\ 4 \\ \hline 28 \end{array} \qquad \begin{array}{r} 312 \\ \times\ \ 2 \\ \hline 314 \end{array} \qquad \begin{array}{r} 82 \\ \times 37 \\ \hline 254 \end{array} \qquad \begin{array}{r} 84 \\ \times 26 \\ \hline \end{array}$$

Jennifer:

$$\begin{array}{r} 34 \\ \times\ 2 \\ \hline 68 \end{array} \qquad \begin{array}{r} {}^{2} \\ 26 \\ \times\ 4 \\ \hline 84 \end{array} \qquad \begin{array}{r} {}^{2} \\ 36 \\ \times\ 4 \\ \hline 124 \end{array} \qquad \begin{array}{r} 25 \\ \times\ 6 \\ \hline \end{array}$$

Suzie:

$$\begin{array}{r} {}^{2} \\ 27 \\ \times\ 4 \\ \hline 168 \end{array} \qquad \begin{array}{r} {}^{2} \\ 34 \\ \times\ 5 \\ \hline 250 \end{array} \qquad \begin{array}{r} {}^{3} \\ 54 \\ \times\ 8 \\ \hline 642 \end{array} \qquad \begin{array}{r} 29 \\ \times\ 4 \\ \hline \end{array}$$

Tom:

$$\begin{array}{r} 313 \\ \times\ 4 \\ \hline 1252 \end{array} \qquad \begin{array}{r} 211 \\ \times\ 15 \\ \hline 215 \end{array} \qquad \begin{array}{r} {}^{1} \\ 433 \\ \times 226 \\ \hline 878 \end{array} \qquad \begin{array}{r} 517 \\ \times 463 \\ \hline \end{array}$$

What instructional procedures might you use to help each of these students?

31. The following is an example of the **German Low-Stress Algorithm**. Find 5314×79 using this method and explain how it works.

$$\begin{array}{r} 4967 \times 35 \\ \hline 21 \\ 1835 \\ 2730 \\ 1245 \\ 20 \\ \hline 173845 \end{array}$$

EXERCISE/PROBLEM SET 4.2—PART B

Exercises

1. Sketch the solution to $46 + 55$ using the following objects.
   (a) Bundling sticks   **(b)** Base ten pieces
   (c) Chip abacus

2. Give a reason for each of the following steps to justify the addition process.

$$\begin{aligned} 38 + 56 &= (3 \cdot 10 + 8) + (5 \cdot 10 + 6) \\ &= (3 \cdot 10 + 5 \cdot 10) + (8 + 6) \\ &= (3 \cdot 10 + 5 \cdot 10) + 14 \\ &= (3 \cdot 10 + 5 \cdot 10) + 1 \cdot 10 + 4 \\ &= (3 \cdot 10 + 5 \cdot 10 + 1 \cdot 10) + 4 \\ &= (3 + 5 + 1) \cdot 10 + 4 \\ &= 9 \cdot 10 + 4 \\ &= 94 \end{aligned}$$

3. An alternate algorithm for addition, called **scratch addition**, is shown next. Using it, students can do more complicated additions by doing a series of single-digit additions. This method is sometimes more effective with students having trouble with the standard algorithm. For example, to compute $78 + 56 + 38$:

$$\begin{array}{r} 7\ 8 \\ 5\ \cancel{6} \\ 3\ \cancel{8}^{4} \\ \hline \end{array}$$
Add the number in the units place starting at the top. When the sum is ten or more, scratch a line through the last number added and write down the units. The scratch represents 10.

$$\begin{array}{r} {}_{2} \\ 7\ 8 \\ 5\ \cancel{6} \\ 3\ \cancel{8}^{4} \\ \hline 2 \end{array}$$
Continue adding units (adding 4 and 8). Write the last number of units below the line. Count the number of scratches, and write above the second column.

$$\begin{array}{r} {}_{2} \\ 7\ 8 \\ \cancel{5}\ \cancel{6} \\ 3^{4}\ \cancel{8}^{4} \\ \hline 1\ 7\ 2 \end{array}$$
Repeat the procedure for each column.

Compute the following additions using the scratch algorithm.

(a) $\begin{array}{r} 734 \\ 468 \\ +\ \ 27 \\ \hline \end{array}$ **(b)** $\begin{array}{r} 1364 \\ 7257 \\ +4813 \\ \hline \end{array}$

4. Another scratch method involves adding from left to right, as shown in the following example.

```
  987        9 8 7       9 8 7        987
 +356       +3 5 6      +3 5 6       +356
  12        1 2̸ 3      1 2̸ 3̸ 3       1343
             3           3 4
```

First the hundreds column was added. Then the tens column is added and because of carrying, the "2" was scratched out and replaced by a "3." The process continued until the sum is complete. Apply this method to compute the following sums.

(a) 475   **(b)** 856   **(c)** 179
    +381   +907   +356

5. Sketch the solution to $42 - 27$ using the following objects.
(a) Bundling sticks   **(b)** Base ten blocks
(c) Chip abacus

6. (a) 513 is usually thought of as _____ hundreds, _____ tens, and _____ ones. However, to subtract 29 from 513, we regroup and think of 513 as _____ hundreds, _____ tens, and _____ ones.
(b) To subtract 999 from 1111, regroup and think of 1111 as _____ hundreds, _____ tens, and _____ ones.

7. Order these computations from easiest to hardest.
(a) 81   **(b)** 80   **(c)** 8819
    −36   −30   −3604

(d) 809   **(e)** 8
    −306   −3

8. The **cashier's algorithm** for subtraction is closely related to the missing-addend approach to subtraction; that is, $a - b = c$ if and only if $a = b + c$. For example, you buy $23 of school supplies and give the cashier a $50 bill. While handing you the change, the cashier would say "$23, $24, $25, $30, $40, $50." How much change did you receive?

What cashier said: $23 $24 $25 $30 $40 $50
Money received: 0 $1 $1 $5 $10 $10

Now you are the cashier. The customer owes you $62 and gives you a $100 bill. What will you say to the customer, and how much will you give back?

9. A subtraction algorithm, popular in the past, is called the **equal-additions algorithm**. Consider this example.

```
  436          4 · 10² + 3 · 10 + 6
 −282         −(2 · 10² + 8 · 10 + 2)
                                       13
```

$$4 · 10² + 13 · 10 + 6$$
$$-(3 · 10² + \quad 8 · 10 + 2)$$
$$\overline{1 · 10² + \quad 5 · 10 + 4} = 154$$

```
  4 3̸ 6
 −³2̸ 8 2
  1 5 4
```

To subtract $8 · 10$ from $3 · 10$, add ten 10s to the minuend and $1 · 10²$ (or ten 10s) to the subtrahend. The problem is changed, but the answer is the same. This method is sometimes shortened as shown on the right above. Will this algorithm work in general? Why or why not?

10. Use the equal-additions algorithm to find the following differences.
(a) $421 - 286$ **(b)** $92,863 - 75,387$
(c) $50,004 - 36,289$

11. Gerald added 39,642 and 43,728 on his calculator and got 44,020 as the answer. How could he tell, mentally, that his sum is wrong?

12. Without calculating the actual sums, select the smallest sum, the middle sum, and the largest sum in each group. Mark them A, B, and C, respectively. Use your estimating powers!
(a) _____ 284 + 625
       _____ 593 + 237
       _____ 304 + 980
(b) _____ 427 + 424
       _____ 748 + 611
       _____ 272 + 505
(c) _____ 283 + 109
       _____ 161 + 369
       _____ 403 + 277
(d) _____ 629 + 677
       _____ 723 + 239
       _____ 275 + 631
Now check your estimates with a calculator.

13. Justify each step in the following proof that shows $573 \times 100 = 57,300$.

$$573 \times 100 = (500 + 70 + 3) \times 100$$
$$= 500 \times 100 + 70 \times 100 + 3 \times 100$$
$$= (5 \times 100) \times 100 + (7 \times 10) \times 100 + 3 \times 100$$
$$= 5 \times (100 \times 100) + 7 \times (10 \times 100) + 3 \times 100$$
$$= 5 \times 10,000 + 7 \times 1000 + 300$$
$$= 50,000 + 7000 + 300$$
$$= 57,300$$

14. The pictorial representation of multiplication can be adapted as follows to perform 23×16.

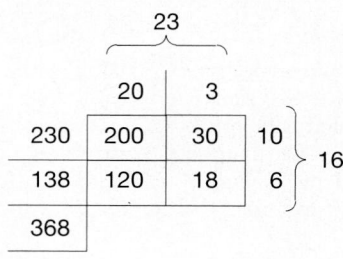

Use this method to find the following products.
(a) 15×36 **(b)** 62×35 **(c)** 23×48
How do the numbers within the grid compare with the steps of intermediate algorithm 1?

15. The **Russian peasant algorithm** for multiplying 27×51 is illustrated as follows:

Halving		Doubling
27	×	51
13	×	102
~~6~~	~~×~~	~~204~~
3	×	408
1	×	816

Notice that the numbers in the first column are halved (disregarding any remainder), and that the numbers in the second column are doubled. When 1 is reached in the halving column, the process is stopped. Next, each row with an even number in the halving column is crossed out and the remaining numbers in the doubling column are added. Thus

$$27 \times 51 = 51 + 102 + 408 + 816 = 1377$$

Use the Russian peasant algorithm to compute the following products.
(a) 68×35 **(b)** 38×62 **(c)** 31×54

16. The **duplication algorithm** for multiplication combines a succession of doubling operations, followed by addition. This algorithm depends on the fact that any number can be written as the sum of numbers that are powers of 2. To compute 28×36, the 36 is repeatedly doubled as shown.

$$\begin{aligned}
1 \times 36 &= 36 \\
2 \times 36 &= 72 \\
\rightarrow \quad 4 \times 36 &= 144 \\
\rightarrow \quad 8 \times 36 &= 288 \\
\rightarrow \quad 16 \times 36 &= 576 \\
&\uparrow \\
&\text{powers} \\
&\text{of 2}
\end{aligned}$$

This process stops when the next power of 2 in the list is greater than the number by which you are multiplying. Here we want 28 of the 36s, and since $28 = (16 + 8 + 4)$, the product of $28 \times 36 = (16 + 8 + 4) \cdot 36$. From the last column, you add $144 + 288 + 576 = 1008$.
(a) Use the duplication algorithm to compute the following products.
    (i) 25×62 (ii) 35×58 (iii) 73×104
(b) Which property justifies the algorithm?

17. Use the scaffold form of the division algorithm to compute the following quotients and remainders.
(a) $32\overline{)1100}$ **(b)** $47\overline{)5062}$ **(c)** $84\overline{)95,809}$

18. Find the quotient and remainder of the following problems using a calculator and the method illustrated following Example 4.8. Check your answers.
(a) $18,114 \div 37$ **(b)** $381,271 \div 147$
(c) $9,346,870 \div 349$

Problems

19. Peter, Jeff, and John each perform subtraction incorrectly as follows.

$$\text{Peter:} \quad \begin{array}{r} 503 \\ -269 \\ \hline 366 \end{array} \qquad \text{Jeff:} \quad \begin{array}{r} {}^{4}\!\!\!\!\!\;{}^{10}\!\!\;{}^{13} \\ \cancel{5}\,\cancel{0}\,\cancel{3} \\ -2\;6\;9 \\ \hline 2\;4\;4 \end{array} \qquad \text{John:} \quad \begin{array}{r} {}^{3}\quad{}^{9} \\ \cancel{4}\cancel{1}\cancel{0}\,13 \\ \cancel{5}\,0\,\cancel{3} \\ -2\;6\;9 \\ \hline 1\;3\;4 \end{array}$$

How would you explain their mistakes to each of them?

20. Let A, B, C, and D represent four consecutive whole numbers. Find the values for A, B, C, and D if the four boxes are replaced with A, B, C, and D in an unknown order.

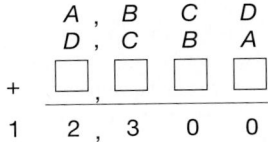

21. Place the digits 3, 5, 6, 2, 4, 8 in the boxes to obtain the following differences.
(a) The greatest difference
(b) The least difference

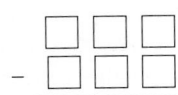

22. Arrange eight 8s so that the sum is 1000.

23. (a) A college student, short of funds and in desperate need, writes the following note to his father:

$$\begin{array}{r} \text{SEND} \\ +\text{MORE} \\ \hline \text{MONEY} \end{array}$$

If each letter in this message represents a different digit, how much MONEY (in cents) is he asking for?

(b) The father, considering the request, decides to send some money along with some important advice.

$$\begin{array}{r} \text{SAVE} \\ +\text{MORE} \\ \hline \text{MONEY} \end{array}$$

However, the father had misplaced the request and could not recall the amount. If he sent the largest amount of MONEY (in cents) represented by this sum, how much did the college student receive?

24. Consider the sums

$$1 + 11 =$$
$$1 + 11 + 111 =$$
$$1 + 11 + 111 + 1111 =$$

(a) What is the pattern?

(b) How many addends are there the first time the pattern no longer works?

25. Select any three-digit number whose first and third digits are different. Reverse the digits and find the difference between the two numbers. By knowing only the hundreds digit in this difference, it is possible to determine the other two digits. How? Explain how the trick works.

26. Choose any four-digit number, reverse its digits, and add the two numbers. Is the sum divisible by 11? Will this always be true?

27. Select any number larger than 100 and multiply it by 9. Select one of the digits of this result as the "missing digit." Find the sum of the remaining digits. Continue adding digits in resulting sums until you have a one-digit number. Subtract that number from 9. Is that your missing digit? Try it again with another number. Determine which missing digits this procedure will find.

28. Select any four-digit number. Arrange the digits to form the largest possible number and the smallest possible number. Subtract the smallest number from the largest number. Use the digits in the difference and start the process over again. Keep repeating the process. What do you discover?

29. Three businesswomen traveling together stopped at a motel to get a room for the night. They were charged $30 for the room and agreed to split the cost equally. The manager later realized that he had overcharged them by $5. He gave the refund to his son to deliver

to the women. This smart son, realizing it would be difficult to split $5 equally, gave the women $3 and kept $2 for himself. Thus it cost each woman $9 for the room. Therefore, they spent $27 for the room plus the $2 "tip." What happened to the other dollar?

30. Following are some division exercises done by students. Determine the error pattern and tell what each student will get for the last problem.

Carol:

$$\begin{array}{c} 233 \\ 2\overline{)176} \end{array} \qquad \begin{array}{c} 221 \\ 4\overline{)824} \end{array} \qquad \begin{array}{c} 231 \\ 3\overline{)813} \end{array} \qquad 4\overline{)581}$$

Steve:

$$\begin{array}{r} 14 \\ 4\overline{)164} \\ 160 \\ \hline 4 \\ 4 \\ \hline \end{array} \qquad \begin{array}{r} 97 \\ 3\overline{)237} \\ 210 \\ \hline 27 \\ 27 \\ \hline \end{array} \qquad \begin{array}{r} 37 \\ 5\overline{)365} \\ 350 \\ \hline 15 \\ \hline \end{array} \qquad 6\overline{)414}$$

Tracy:

$$\begin{array}{r} 75r5 \\ 6\overline{)4235} \\ 42 \\ \hline 35 \\ 30 \\ \hline 5 \\ \end{array} \qquad \begin{array}{r} 47r4 \\ 8\overline{)3260} \\ 32 \\ \hline 60 \\ 56 \\ \hline 4 \\ \end{array} \qquad \begin{array}{r} 53r5 \\ 7\overline{)3526} \\ 35 \\ \hline 26 \\ 21 \\ \hline 5 \\ \end{array} \qquad 9\overline{)3642}$$

What instructional procedures might you use to help each of these students?

31. How can you tell at a glance that

$$563 \times 489 \times 9777$$

cannot be 2,691,676,538?

32. Show that a perfect square is obtained by adding one to the product of two whole numbers that differ by 2. For example, $8(10) + 1 = 9^2$, $11 \times 13 + 1 = 12^2$, etc.

4.3

ALGORITHMS IN OTHER BASES

All of the algorithms you have learned can be used in any base. In this section we apply the algorithms in base five and then let you try them in other bases in the problem set. The purpose for doing this is to help you see where, how, and why your future students might have difficulties in learning the standard algorithms.

Operations in Base Five

Addition

Addition in base five is facilitated using the thinking strategies *in base five*.

EXAMPLE 4.9 Find $342_{\text{five}} + 134_{\text{five}}$ using the following methods.

(a) Lattice method   **(b)** Intermediate algorithm   **(c)** Standard algorithm

Solution

(a) LATTICE METHOD

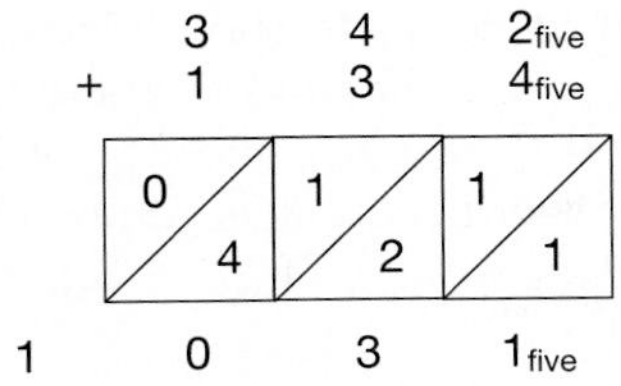

$$
\begin{array}{ccc}
3 & 4 & 2_{\text{five}} \\
+ \quad 1 & 3 & 4_{\text{five}}
\end{array}
$$

0 / 4	1 / 2	1 / 1

$$1 \quad 0 \quad 3 \quad 1_{\text{five}}$$

(b) INTERMEDIATE ALGORITHM

$$
\begin{array}{r}
342_{\text{five}} \\
+ 134_{\text{five}} \\
\hline
11_{\text{five}} \\
120_{\text{five}} \\
400_{\text{five}} \\
\hline
1031_{\text{five}}
\end{array}
$$

(c) STANDARD ALGORITHM

$$
\begin{array}{r}
1 \quad 1 \quad 1 \\
3 \ \ 4 \ \ 2_{\text{five}} \\
+ 1 \ \ 3 \ \ 4_{\text{five}} \\
\hline
1 \ 0 \ 3 \ 1_{\text{five}}
\end{array}
$$

Be sure to use thinking strategies when adding in base five. It is helpful to find sums to five first; for example, think of $4_{\text{five}} + 3_{\text{five}}$ as $4_{\text{five}} + (1_{\text{five}} + 2_{\text{five}}) = (4_{\text{five}} + 1_{\text{five}}) + 2_{\text{five}} = 12_{\text{five}}$ and so on.

Subtraction

There are two ways to apply a subtraction algorithm successfully. One is to know the addition facts table forward and *backward*. The other is to use the missing-addend approach repeatedly. For example, to find $12_{\text{five}} - 4_{\text{five}}$, think "What number plus 4_{five} is 12_{five}?" To answer this, one could count up "$10_{\text{five}}, 11_{\text{five}}, 12_{\text{five}}$." Thus $12_{\text{five}} - 4_{\text{five}} = 3_{\text{five}}$ (one for each of $10_{\text{five}}, 11_{\text{five}}$, and 12_{five}). For convenience, a copy of the addition table for base five is given in Figure 4.13 to assist you in working through Example 4.10. (All numerals in Figure 4.13 are written in base five with the subscripts omitted.)

+	0	1	2	3	4
0	0	1	2	3	4
1	1	2	3	4	10
2	2	3	4	10	11
3	3	4	10	11	12
4	4	10	11	12	13

FIGURE 4.13

EXAMPLE 4.10 Calculate $412_{\text{five}} - 143_{\text{five}}$ using the following methods.
(a) Standard algorithm   **(b)** Subtract-from-the-base algorithm

Solution

(a) STANDARD ALGORITHM

(b) SUBTRACT-FROM-THE-BASE

Think:

$$412_{five} \longrightarrow \begin{array}{c} 3 \ \ 10 \ \ 12 \\ 4 \ \ 1 \ \ 2_{five} \\ \underline{1 \ \ 4 \ \ 3_{five}} \\ 2 \ \ 1 \ \ 4_{five} \end{array}$$
$$-143_{five}$$

Third step $3_{five} - 1_{five}$
Second step $10_{five} - 4_{five}$
First step $12_{five} - 3_{five}$

Think:

$$412_{five} \longrightarrow \begin{array}{c} 3 \ \ 10 \\ 0 \ \ 10 \\ 4 \ \ 1 \ \ 2_{five} \\ \underline{1 \ \ 4 \ \ 3_{five}} \\ 2 \ \ 1 \ \ 4_{five} \end{array}$$
$$-143_{five}$$

Third step $3_{five} - 1_{five}$
Second step $(10_{five} - 4_{five}) + 0_{five}$
First step $(10_{five} - 3_{five}) + 2_{five}$

Notice that to do subtraction in base five using the subtract-from-the-base algorithm, you only need to know two addition combinations to five, namely $1_{five} + 4_{five} = 10_{five}$ and $2_{five} + 3_{five} = 10_{five}$. These two, in turn, lead to the four subtraction facts you need to know, namely $10_{five} - 4_{five} = 1_{five}$, $10_{five} - 1_{five} = 4_{five}$, $10_{five} - 3_{five} = 2_{five}$, and $10_{five} - 2_{five} = 3_{five}$.

Multiplication

To perform multiplication efficiently, one must know the multiplication facts. The multiplication facts for base five are displayed in Figure 4.14. (All numerals are written in base five with subscripts omitted.)

×	0	1	2	3	4
0	0	0	0	0	0
1	0	1	2	3	4
2	0	2	4	11	13
3	0	3	11	14	22
4	0	4	13	22	31

FIGURE 4.14

EXAMPLE 4.11 Calculate $43_{five} \times 123_{five}$ using the following methods.
(a) Lattice method   **(b)** Intermediate algorithm   **(c)** Standard algorithm

Solution

(a) LATTICE METHOD

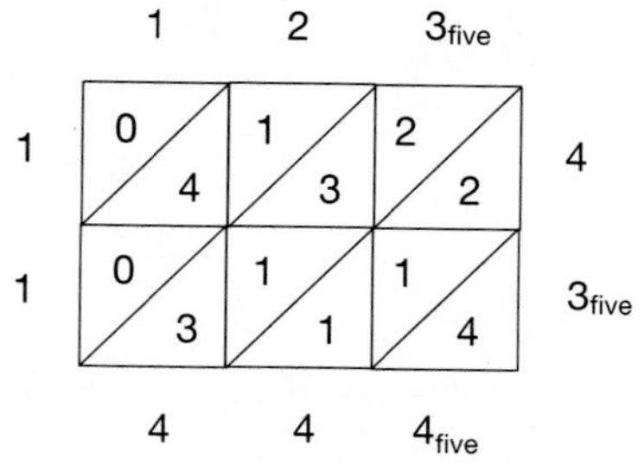

(b) INTERMEDIATE ALGORITHM

$$\begin{array}{r} 123_{five} \\ \times \ 43_{five} \\ \hline 14 \\ 110 \\ 300 \\ 220 \\ 1300 \\ \underline{4000} \\ 11444_{five} \end{array}$$

$3 \cdot 3$
$3 \cdot 20$
$3 \cdot 100$
$40 \cdot 3$
$40 \cdot 20$
$40 \cdot 100$

(c) STANDARD ALGORITHM

$$\begin{array}{r} 123_{five} \\ \times \ 43_{five} \\ \hline 424 \\ \underline{1102} \\ 11444_{five} \end{array}$$

Notice how efficient the lattice method is. Also, instead of using the multiplication table, you could find single-digit products using repeated addition and thinking strategies. For example, you could find $4_{\text{five}} \times 2_{\text{five}}$ as follows:

$$4_{\text{five}} \times 2_{\text{five}} = 2_{\text{five}} \times 4_{\text{five}} = 4_{\text{five}} + 4_{\text{five}} = 4_{\text{five}} + (1 + 3)_{\text{five}}$$
$$= (4 + 1)_{\text{five}} + 3_{\text{five}} = 13_{\text{five}}$$

Although this may look like it would take a lot of time, it would go quickly mentally, especially if you imagine base five pieces.

Division

Doing long division in other bases points out the difficulties of learning this algorithm and, especially, the need to become proficient at approximating multiples of numbers.

EXAMPLE 4.12   Find the quotient and remainder for $1443_{\text{five}} \div 34_{\text{five}}$ using the following methods.
(a) Scaffold method   **(b)** Standard long-division algorithm

Solution
(a) SCAFFOLD METHOD

$$
\begin{array}{r}
34_{\text{five}} \overline{)\, 1443_{\text{five}}} \\
-1230 \\
\hline
213 \\
-212 \\
\hline
1
\end{array}
\quad
\begin{array}{l}
\\
20_{\text{five}} \\
\\
3_{\text{five}} \\
23_{\text{five}}
\end{array}
$$

QUOTIENT: 23_{five}

REMAINDER: 1_{five}

(b) STANDARD LONG-DIVISION ALGORITHM

$$
\begin{array}{r}
23_{\text{five}} \\
34_{\text{five}} \overline{)\, 1443_{\text{five}}} \\
-123 \\
\hline
213 \\
-212 \\
\hline
1
\end{array}
\quad
\begin{array}{l}
\\
\\
(2_{\text{five}} \times 34_{\text{five}}) \\
\\
(3_{\text{five}} \times 34_{\text{five}})
\end{array}
$$

In the scaffold method, the first estimate, namely 20_{five}, was selected because $2_{\text{five}} \times 3_{\text{five}}$ is 11_{five}, which is less than 14_{five}. ∎

In summary, doing computations in other number bases can provide insights into how computational difficulties arise, whereas our own familiarity and competence with our algorithms in base ten tend to mask the trouble spots that children face.

MATHEMATICAL MORSEL

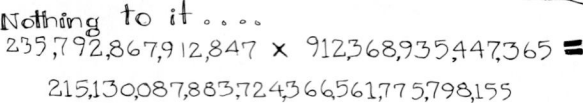

George Parker Bidder (1806–1878), who lived in Devonshire, England, was blessed with an incredible memory as well as being a calculating prodigy. When he was 10 he was read a number backward and he immediately gave the number back in its correct form. An hour later, he repeated the original number, which was

$$2{,}563{,}721{,}987{,}653{,}461{,}598{,}746{,}$$
$$231{,}905{,}607{,}541{,}128{,}975{,}231.$$

Furthermore, his brother memorized the entire Bible and could give the chapter and verse of any quoted text. Also, one of Bidder's sons could multiply 15-digit numbers in his head.

EXERCISE/PROBLEM SET 4.3—PART A

Exercises

1. Draw a sketch, using blocks in the appropriate base, to show the following sums and write the numeral. *Example:*

$$7_{\text{nine}} + 5_{\text{nine}} \longrightarrow \boxed{\quad} \longrightarrow 13_{\text{nine}}$$

   (a) $2_{\text{three}} + 2_{\text{three}}$
   (b) $9_{\text{twelve}} + E_{\text{twelve}}$
   (c) $6_{\text{eight}} + 7_{\text{eight}}$
   (d) $5_{\text{twelve}} + T_{\text{twelve}}$

2. Solve each of the following base four addition problems.
   (a) $1_{\text{four}} + 2_{\text{four}}$ **(b)** $2_{\text{four}} + 3_{\text{four}}$
   (c) $11_{\text{four}} + 23_{\text{four}}$ **(d)** $31_{\text{four}} + 23_{\text{four}}$
   (e) $212_{\text{four}} + 113_{\text{four}}$ **(f)** $312_{\text{four}} + 331_{\text{four}}$
   (g) $2023_{\text{four}} + 3330_{\text{four}}$ **(h)** $3333_{\text{four}} + 3333_{\text{four}}$

3. Use an intermediate algorithm to compute the following sums.
   (a) $78_{\text{nine}} + 65_{\text{nine}}$ **(b)** $TE_{\text{twelve}} + EE_{\text{twelve}}$

4. Use bundling sticks, chips, or multibase pieces for the appropriate base to illustrate the following problems.
   (a) $41_{\text{six}} - 33_{\text{six}}$ **(b)** $555_{\text{seven}} - 66_{\text{seven}}$
   (c) $3030_{\text{four}} - 102_{\text{four}}$

5. Solve each of the following base four subtraction problems using both the standard algorithm and the subtract-from-the-base algorithm.
   (a) $3_{\text{four}} - 1_{\text{four}}$ **(b)** $11_{\text{four}} - 3_{\text{four}}$
   (c) $32_{\text{four}} - 12_{\text{four}}$ **(d)** $31_{\text{four}} - 12_{\text{four}}$
   (e) $123_{\text{four}} - 32_{\text{four}}$ **(f)** $1102_{\text{four}} - 333_{\text{four}}$

6. Find $10201_{\text{three}} - 2122_{\text{three}}$ using "adding the complement." What is the complement of a base three number?

7. Solve the following problems using the lattice method, an intermediate algorithm, and the standard algorithm.

(a) 31_{four}
$\times\ 2_{\text{four}}$

(b) 43_{five}
$\times\ 3_{\text{five}}$

(c) 22_{four}
$\times\ 3_{\text{four}}$

(d) 34_{six}
$\times\ 5_{\text{six}}$

(e) 47_{eight}
$\times 25_{\text{eight}}$

(f) 11011_{two}
$\times\ 1101_{\text{two}}$

(g) 43_{twelve}
$\times 23_{\text{twelve}}$

(h) 666_{seven}
$\times\ 66_{\text{seven}}$

(i) 213_{five}
$\times\ 42_{\text{five}}$

8. Find $4023_{\text{five}} \div 3_{\text{five}}$ using the scaffold method.

Problems

9. $345\_\_\_\_ + 122\_\_\_\_ = 511\_\_\_\_$ is an addition problem done in base $\_\_\_\_\_$.

10. Jane has $10 more than Bill, Bill has $17 more than Tricia, and Tricia has $21 more than Steve. If the total amount of all their money put together is $115, how much money does each have?

11. Without using a calculator, determine which of the five numbers is a perfect square. There is exactly one.

$$39{,}037{,}066{,}087$$
$$39{,}037{,}066{,}084$$
$$39{,}037{,}066{,}082$$
$$38{,}336{,}073{,}623$$
$$38{,}414{,}432{,}028$$

12. What single number can be added separately to 100 and 164 to make them both perfect square numbers?

EXERCISE/PROBLEM SET 4.3—PART B

Exercises

1. Use bundling sticks, chips, or multibase pieces for the appropriate base to illustrate the following problems.

(a) $32_{\text{four}} + 33_{\text{four}}$
(b) $54_{\text{six}} + 55_{\text{six}}$
(c) $65_{\text{seven}} + 66_{\text{seven}}$
(d) $43_{\text{five}} + 44_{\text{five}}$

2. Write out a base six addition table. Use your table to compute the following sums.

(a) $32_{\text{six}} + 23_{\text{six}}$
(b) $45_{\text{six}} + 34_{\text{six}}$
(c) $145_{\text{six}} + 541_{\text{six}}$
(d) $355_{\text{six}} + 211_{\text{six}}$
(e) $2405_{\text{six}} + 5425_{\text{six}}$
(f) $5555_{\text{six}} + 5555_{\text{six}}$

3. Use the lattice method to compute the following sums.

(a) $46_{\text{seven}} + 13_{\text{seven}}$
(b) $13_{\text{four}} + 23_{\text{four}}$

4. Use the standard algorithm to compute the following sums.

(a) $79_{\text{twelve}} + 85_{\text{twelve}}$
(b) $T1_{\text{eleven}} + 99_{\text{eleven}}$

5. Solve the following problems using both the standard algorithm and the subtract-from-the-base algorithm.

(a) $45_{\text{seven}} - 36_{\text{seven}}$
(b) $99_{\text{twelve}} - 7T_{\text{twelve}}$
(c) $100_{\text{eight}} - 77_{\text{eight}}$
(d) $1111_{\text{five}} - 444_{\text{five}}$
(e) $776_{\text{nine}} - 87_{\text{nine}}$
(f) $4443_{\text{six}} - 554_{\text{six}}$

6. Find $1001010_{\text{two}} - 111001_{\text{two}}$ by "adding the complement."

7. Use the scaffold method of division to compute the following numbers. (HINT: Write out a multiplication table in the appropriate base to help you out.)

(a) $14_{\text{five}} \div 3_{\text{five}}$
(b) $22_{\text{six}} \div 2_{\text{six}}$
(c) $2134_{\text{six}} \div 14_{\text{six}}$
(d) $4044_{\text{seven}} \div 51_{\text{seven}}$
(e) $13002_{\text{four}} \div 33_{\text{four}}$
(f) $61245_{\text{seven}} \div 354_{\text{seven}}$

8. Solve the following problems using the missing-factor definition of division. (HINT: Use a multiplication table for the appropriate base.)

(a) $21_{\text{four}} \div 3_{\text{four}}$
(b) $23_{\text{six}} \div 3_{\text{six}}$
(c) $24_{\text{eight}} \div 5_{\text{eight}}$
(d) $42_{\text{seven}} \div 5_{\text{seven}}$
(e) $62_{\text{nine}} \div 7_{\text{nine}}$
(f) $92_{\text{twelve}} \div E_{\text{twelve}}$

Problems

9. $320\_\_\_\_ - 42\_\_\_\_ = 256\_\_\_\_$ is a correct subtraction problem in what base?

10. Betty has three times as much money as her brother Tom. If each of them spends $1.50 to see a movie, Betty will have nine times as much money left over as Tom. How much money does each have before going to the movie?

11. Which whole numbers can be expressed as the difference of two consecutive squares? For example, $3 = 2^2 - 1^2$, $7 = 4^2 - 3^2$, and so on.

12. To stimulate his son in the pursuit of mathematics, a math professor offered to pay his son $8 for every equation correctly solved and to fine him $5 for every incorrect solution. At the end of 26 problems, neither owed any money to the other. How many did the boy solve correctly?

13. Prove: If n is a whole number and n^2 is odd, then n is odd. (HINT: Use indirect reasoning. Either n is even or odd. Assume that n is even and reach a contradiction.)

SOLUTION OF INITIAL PROBLEM

The whole numbers 1 through 9 can be used once each arranged in a 3×3 square array so that the sum of the numbers in each of the rows, columns, and diagonals is 15. Show that 1 cannot be in one of the corners.

Strategy: Use Indirect Reasoning

Suppose that 1 could be in a corner as shown in the figure below. Each row, column, and diagonal containing 1 must have a sum of 15. This means that there must be three pairs of numbers among 2 through 9 whose sum is 14. Hence the sum of all three pairs is 42. However, the largest six numbers, 9, 8, 7, 6, 5, and 4, have a sum of 39, so that it is impossible to find three pairs whose sum is 14. Therefore, it is impossible to have 1 in a corner.

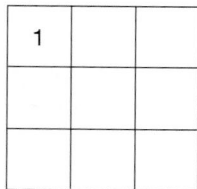

Additional Problems Where the Strategy "Use Indirect Reasoning" Is Useful

1. If x represents a whole number and $x^2 + 2x + 1$ is even, prove that x cannot be even.
2. If n is a whole number and n^4 is even, then n is even.
3. For whole numbers x and y, if $x^2 + y^2$ is a square, then x and y cannot both be odd.

WRITING/DISCUSSING FOR UNDERSTANDING

1. Describe several problem situations that arise in daily life in which an estimate is required. What method might be used to arrive at a reasonable estimate?
2. Discuss how your personal education on computation was balanced among mental math/estimation, calculators, and written algorithms. Compare this balance with how you now do your computations. Based on this comparison, explain how you believe your teaching of computation should be balanced in the future.
3. The following two estimations are known as **Fermi problems**, which request estimates *without* seeking any exact numbers from reference materials.
   (a) Estimate the number of hot dogs sold at all of the major league baseball games played in the United States in one year.
   (b) Estimate the number of days of playing time there are on all the musical compact discs sold in your state in one month.

4. Explain how the following NCTM Standards are reflected in this chapter.
   - Model, explain, and develop reasonable proficiency with basic facts and algorithms.
   - Use a variety of mental computation and estimation techniques.
   - Use calculators in appropriate computational situations.
   - Select and use an appropriate method for computing from among mental arithmetic, paper-and-pencil, calculator, and computer methods.

PROJECTS

1. Collect examples of various computational uses of mathematics in newspapers, on television, and so on. Classify the uses among mental math, estimations, written, or calculator computations.
2. Interview several friends to see what mental methods they use when performing computations.
3. One of the recommendations of the National Council of Teachers of Mathematics' Curriculum and Evaluation Standards is that the K–4 curriculum make "appropriate and ongoing use of calculators." What do you think constitutes "appropriate" use of calculators? Find out what specific recommendations mathematics educators are currently making with regard to the use of calculators.

CHAPTER REVIEW

Major Ideas

1. There are three commonly used modes of computation:
   (a) Mental.
   (b) Electronic (calculators and computers).
   (c) Written algorithms.

   Whenever a computation is to be done, one should strive to use the most efficient mode that leads to a correct answer.

2. Mental math and estimation should be used routinely, especially in conjunction with a calculator.
3. There are a variety of written algorithms for all four operations. Even though most of us have learned the "standard" algorithms, any correct algorithm may be used.
4. Doing computations in other number bases can provide insight into difficulties that others (or even you) may have when doing computations in base ten.

   Following is a list of key vocabulary, notation and ideas for this chapter. Mentally review these items and, where appropriate, write down the meaning of each term. Then restudy the material that you are unsure of before proceeding to take the chapter test.

SECTION 4.1:   MENTAL MATH, ESTIMATION, AND CALCULATORS

Vocabulary/Notation

Ideas

SECTION 4.2: WRITTEN ALGORITHMS FOR WHOLE-NUMBER OPERATIONS

Vocabulary/Notation

Ideas

SECTION 4.3: ALGORITHMS IN OTHER BASES

Ideas

Applying algorithms in bases other than ten 174

PEOPLE IN MATHEMATICS

Grace Brewster Murray Hopper (1906–1992) recalled that as a young girl, she disassembled one of the family's alarm clocks. When she was unable to reassemble the parts, she dismantled another clock to see how those parts fit together. This process continued until she had seven clocks in pieces. This attitude of exploration foreshadowed her innovations in computer programming. Trained in mathematics, Grace worked with some of the first computers, and invented the business language COBOL. After World War II she was active in the Navy, where her experience in computing and programming began. In 1985 she was promoted to the rank of rear admiral. Known for her common sense and spirit of invention, she kept a clock on her desk which ran (and kept time) counterclockwise. Whenever someone argued that a job must be done in the traditional manner, she just pointed to the clock. Also, to encourage risk taking, she once said: "I do have a maxim—I teach it to all youngsters: A ship in port is safe, but that's not what ships are built for."

John Kemeny (1926–1992) created BASIC with Tom Kurtz while both were teaching in the mathematics department at Dartmouth in the mid-1960s. The idea was to design a language much friendlier than anything then available. Today, BASIC continues to be a widely used computer language, and Kemeny has made Dartmouth a leader in the educational uses of computers. John's first faculty position was in philosophy. "The only good job offer I got was from the Princeton philosophy department," he says, explaining that his degree was in logic, and he studied philosophy as a hobby in college. Kemeny has the distinction of having served as Einstein's mathematical assistant while still a young graduate student at Princeton. Einstein's assistants were always mathematicians. Contrary to popular belief, Einstein did need help in mathematics. He was very good at it, but he was not an up-to-date research mathematician.

CHAPTER 4 TEST

Knowledge

1. True or false?
   (a) An algorithm is a technique that is used exclusively for doing algebra.
   (b) Intermediate algorithms are helpful because they require less writing than their corresponding standard algorithms.
   (c) There is only one computational algorithm for each of the four operations, addition, subtraction, multiplication, and division.
   (d) Approximating answers to computations by rounding is useful because it increases the *speed* of computation.

Skill

2. Compute each of the following using an intermediate algorithm.
   (a) $376 + 594$ (b) 56×73

3. Compute the following using the lattice method.
   (a) 568 + 493   **(b)** 37 × 196

4. Compute the following mentally. Then, explain how you did it.
   (a) 54 + 93 + 16 + 47
   (b) 9223 − 1998
   (c) 3497 − 1362
   (d) 25 × 52

5. Find 7496 ÷ 32 using the standard division algorithm and check your results using a calculator.

6. Estimate the following using (i) one-column front-end, (ii) range estimation, (iii) front-end with adjustment, and (iv) rounding to the nearest 100.
   (a) 546 + 971 + 837 + 320
   (b) 731 × 589

Understanding

7. Compute 32 × 21 using expanded form; that is, continue the following:

$$32 \times 21 = (30 + 2)(20 + 1) = \cdots$$

8. In the standard multiplication algorithm, why do we "shift over one to the left" as illustrated in the 642 in the following problem?

$$
\begin{array}{r}
321 \\
\times\ 23 \\
\hline
963 \\
+642 \\
\hline
\end{array}
$$

9. To check an addition problem where one has "added down the column," one can "add up the column." Which properties guarantee that the sum should be the same in both directions?

Problem Solving/Application

10. If each different letter represents a different digit, find the number "HE" such that $(HE)^2 = SHE$. (NOTE: "HE" means $10 \cdot H + E$ due to place value.)

11. Find values for a, b, and c in the lattice multiplication problem shown. Also find the product.

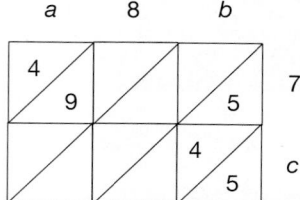

Number Theory

Pierre de Fermat

Famous Unsolved Problems

Number theory provides a rich source of intriguing problems. Interestingly, there are many problems in number theory that have not been solved, yet can be so simply phrased that children of elementary school age can understand the statement of the problem. The following list contains several such problems with some comments and numerical examples to illustrate them. If you can solve any of these problems, you will surely become famous, at least among mathematicians.

1. *Fermat's last theorem. There are no nonzero whole numbers a, b, c, where $a^n + b^n = c^n$, for n a whole number greater than 2.* (This is a generalization of the Pythagorean theorem concerning right triangles with whole-number lengths. That is, $a^2 + b^2 = c^2$, where a and b are the lengths of the sides and c is the length of the hypotenuse. For example, $3^2 + 4^2 = 5^2$, and $5^2 + 12^2 = 13^2$ are two such triples of numbers.) Fermat left a marginal note in a book saying that he did not have room to write up the proof. (A proof of this theorem eluded mathematicians for over 350 years. In June 1993, Andrew Wiles, an English mathematician on the faculty at Princeton, presented a proof at a conference at Cambridge University. However, at the time this book is published, his proof has yet to undergo the careful scrutiny of a wider audience of mathematicians *and* appear in print.)

2. *Goldbach's conjecture. Every even number greater than 4 can be expressed as the sum of two odd primes.* For example, $6 = 3 + 3, 8 = 3 + 5, 10 = 5 + 5, 12 = 5 + 7$, and so on. It is interesting to note that if Goldbach's conjecture is true, then *every* odd number greater than 7 can be written as the sum of three odd primes.

3. *Twin prime conjecture. There is an infinite number of pairs of primes whose difference is two.* For example, (3, 5), (5, 7), and (11, 13), are such prime pairs. Notice that 3, 5, and 7 are three prime numbers where $5 - 3 = 2$ and $7 - 5 = 2$. It can easily be shown that this is the only such triple of primes.

4. *Odd perfect number conjecture. There is no odd perfect number; that is, there is no odd number that is the sum of its proper factors.* For example, $6 = 1 + 2 + 3$, hence 6 is a perfect number. It has been shown that the even perfect numbers are all of the form $2^{p-1}(2^p - 1)$, where $2^p - 1$ is a prime.

5. *Ulam's conjecture. If a nonzero whole number is even, divide it by 2. If a nonzero whole number is odd, multiply it by 3 and add 1. If this process is applied repeatedly to each answer, eventually you will arrive at 1.* For example, the number 7 yields this sequence of numbers: 7, 22, 11, 34, 17, 52, 26, 13, 40, 20, 10, 5, 16, 8, 4, 2, 1. Interestingly, there is a whole number less than 30 that requires at least 100 steps before it arrives at 1. It can be seen that 2^n requires n steps to arrive at 1. Hence one can find numbers with as many steps (finitely many) as one wishes.

The material in this chapter includes a discussion of many of the concepts in these unsolved problems.

STRATEGY 10: USE PROPERTIES OF NUMBERS

Understanding the intrinsic nature of numbers is often helpful in solving problems. For example, knowing that the sum of two even numbers is even and that an odd number squared is odd may simplify checking some computations. The solution of the initial problem will seem to be impossible to a naive problem solver who attempts to solve it using, say, the Guess and Test strategy. On the other hand, the solution is immediate for one who understands the concept of divisibility of numbers.

Initial Problem

A major fast-food chain held a contest to promote sales. With each purchase a customer was given a card with a whole number less than 100 on it. A $100 prize was given to any person who presented cards whose numbers totaled 100. Below are several typical cards. Can you find a winning combination?

$$\boxed{3} \quad \boxed{9} \quad \boxed{12} \quad \boxed{15} \quad \boxed{18} \quad \boxed{27} \quad \boxed{51} \quad \boxed{72} \quad \boxed{84}$$

Can you suggest how the contest could be structured so that there would be at most 1000 winners throughout the country?

Clues

The Use Properties of Numbers strategy may be appropriate when:

- Special types of numbers such as odds, even, primes, and so on, are involved.
- A problem can be simplified by using certain properties.
- A problem involves lots of computation.

A solution of the Initial Problem above appears on page 214.

INTRODUCTION

Number theory is a branch of mathematics that is devoted primarily to the study of the set of counting numbers. In this chapter, those aspects of the counting numbers that are useful in simplifying computations, especially those with fractions (Chapter 6), are studied. The topics central to the elementary curriculum that are covered in this chapter include primes, composites, and divisibility tests as well as the notions of greatest common factor and least common multiple.

5.1

PRIMES, COMPOSITES, AND TESTS FOR DIVISIBILITY

Primes and Composites

Prime numbers are building blocks for the counting numbers 1, 2, 3, 4, ...

Definition

Prime and Composite Numbers

A counting number with exactly two different factors is called a **prime number**, or a **prime**. A counting number with more than two factors is called a **composite number**, or a **composite**.

For example, 2, 3, 5, 7, 11 are primes since they have only themselves and 1 as factors; 4, 6, 8, 9, 10 are composites since they each have more than two factors; and 1 is neither prime nor composite since 1 is its only factor.

An algorithm that can be used to find primes is called the **sieve of Eratosthenes** (Figure 5.1). The directions for using this procedure are as follows: Skip the number 1. Circle 2 and cross out every second number after 2. Circle 3 and cross out every third number after 3 (even if it had been crossed out before). Continue this procedure with 5, 7, and each succeeding number that is not crossed out. The circled numbers will be the

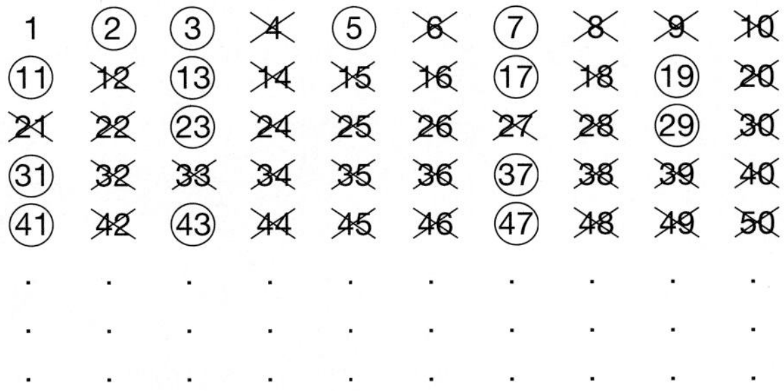

FIGURE 5.1

primes and the crossed-out numbers will be the composites since prime factors cause them to be crossed out. Again, notice that 1 is neither prime nor composite.

Composite numbers have more than two factors and can be expressed as the product of two smaller numbers. Figure 5.2 shows how a composite can be expressed as the product of smaller numbers using **factor trees**.

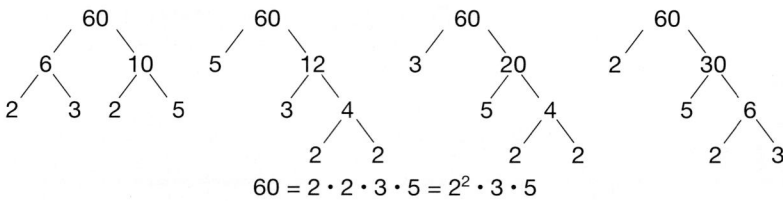

$$60 = 2 \cdot 2 \cdot 3 \cdot 5 = 2^2 \cdot 3 \cdot 5$$

FIGURE 5.2

Notice that 60 was expressed as the product of two factors in several different ways. However, when we kept factoring until we reached primes, each method led us to the same **prime factorization**, namely $60 = 2 \cdot 2 \cdot 3 \cdot 5$. This example illustrates the following important result.

Theorem

Fundamental Theorem of Arithmetic

Each composite number can be expressed as the product of primes in exactly one way (except for the order of the factors).

EXAMPLE 5.1   Express each number as the product of primes.
(a) 84   **(b)** 180   **(c)** 324

Solution
(a) $84 = 4 \times 21 = 2 \cdot 2 \cdot 3 \cdot 7 = 2^2 \cdot 3 \cdot 7$
(b) $180 = 10 \times 18 = 2 \cdot 5 \cdot 2 \cdot 3 \cdot 3 = 2^2 \cdot 3^2 \cdot 5$
(c) $324 = 4 \times 81 = 2 \cdot 2 \cdot 3 \cdot 3 \cdot 3 \cdot 3 = 2^2 \cdot 3^4$ ∎

Next, we will study shortcuts that will help us find prime factors. When division yields a zero remainder, as in the case of $15 \div 3$, for example, we say that 15 is divisible by 3, 3 is a divisor of 15, or 3 divides 15. In general, we have the following definition.

Definition

Divides

Let a and b be any whole numbers with $a \neq 0$. We say that a **divides** b, and write $a \mid b$, if and only if there is a whole number x such that $ax = b$. The symbol $a \nmid b$ means that a **does not divide** b.

In words, a divides b if and only if a is a factor of b. When a divides b we can also say that a is a **divisor** of b, a is a **factor** of b, b is a **multiple** of a, and b is **divisible** by a.

EXAMPLE 5.2 Determine if the following are true or false. Explain.
(a) $3 \mid 12$.   **(b)** 8 is a divisor of 96.
(c) 216 is a multiple of 6.   **(d)** 51 is divisible by 17.
(e) 7 divides 34.   **(f)** $(2^2 \cdot 3) \mid (2^3 \cdot 3^2 \cdot 5)$

Solution
(a) True. $3 \mid 12$ since $3 \cdot 4 = 12$.
(b) True. 8 is a divisor of 96 since $8 \cdot 12 = 96$.
(c) True. 216 is a multiple of 6 since $6 \cdot 36 = 216$.
(d) True. 51 is divisible by 17 since $17 \cdot 3 = 51$.
(e) False. $7 \nmid 34$ since there is no whole number x such that $7x = 34$.
(f) True. $(2^2 \cdot 3) \mid (2^3 \cdot 3^2 \cdot 5)$ since $(2^2 \cdot 3)(2 \cdot 3 \cdot 5) = (2^3 \cdot 3^2 \cdot 5)$. ■

Tests for Divisibility

Some simple tests can be employed to help determine the factors of numbers. For example, which of the numbers 27, 45, 38, 70, and 111,110 are divisible by 2, 5, or 10? If your answers were found simply by looking at the ones digits, you were applying tests for divisibility. The tests for divisibility by 2, 5, and 10 are stated next.

Theorem

Tests for Divisibility by 2, 5, and 10

A number is divisible by 2 if and only if its ones digit is 0, 2, 4, 6, or 8.
A number is divisible by 5 if and only if its ones digit is 0 or 5.
A number is divisible by 10 if and only if its ones digit is 0.

Now notice that $3 \mid 27$ and $3 \mid 9$. It is also true that $3 \mid (27 + 9)$ and $3 \mid (27 - 9)$. This is an instance of the following theorem.

Theorem Let a, m, n, and k be whole numbers where $a \neq 0$.
(a) If $a \mid m$ and $a \mid n$, then $a \mid (m + n)$.
(b) If $a \mid m$ and $a \mid n$, then $a \mid (m - n)$ for $m \geq n$.
(c) If $a \mid m$, then $a \mid km$.

Proof

(a) If $a \mid m$, then $ax = m$ for some whole number x.

If $a \mid n$, then $ay = n$ for some whole number y.

Therefore, adding the respective sides of the two equations, we have $ax + ay = m + n$, or

$$a(x + y) = m + n.$$

Since $x + y$ is a whole number, this last equation implies that $a \mid (m + n)$. Part (b) can be proved simply by replacing the plus signs with minus signs in this discussion. The proof of (c) follows from the definition of "divides." ∎

Using this result, we can verify the tests for divisibility by 2, 5, and 10. The main idea of the proof of the test for 2 is now given for an arbitrary three-digit number (the same idea holds for any number of digits).

Let $r = a \cdot 10^2 + b \cdot 10 + c$ be any three-digit number.
Observe that $a \cdot 10^2 + b \cdot 10 = 10(a \cdot 10 + b)$.
Since $2 \mid 10$, it follows that $2 \mid 10(a \cdot 10 + b)$ or $2 \mid (a \cdot 10^2 + b \cdot 10)$ for any digits a and b.
Thus if $2 \mid c$ (where c is the ones digit), then $2 \mid [10(a \cdot 10 + b) + c]$.
Thus $2 \mid (a \cdot 10^2 + b \cdot 10 + c)$, or $2 \mid r$.
Conversely, let $2 \mid (a \cdot 10^2 + b \cdot 10 + c)$. Since $2 \mid (a \cdot 10^2 + b \cdot 10)$, it follows that $2 \mid [(a \cdot 10^2 + b \cdot 10 + c) - (a \cdot 10^2 + b \cdot 10)]$ or $2 \mid c$.

Therefore, we have shown that 2 divides a number if and only if 2 divides the number's ones digit. One can apply similar reasoning to see why the tests for divisibility for 5 and 10 hold.

The next two tests for divisibility can be verified using arguments similar to the test for 2. Their verifications are left for the problem set.

Theorem

Tests for Divisibility by 4 and 8

A number is divisible by 4 if and only if the number represented by its last two digits is divisible by 4.

A number is divisible by 8 if and only if the number represented by its last three digits is divisible by 8.

Notice that the test for 4 involves two digits and $2^2 = 4$. Also, the test for 8 requires that one consider the last three digits and $2^3 = 8$.

EXAMPLE 5.3 Determine if the following are true or false. Explain.

(a) $4 \mid 1432$ **(b)** $8 \mid 4204$
(c) $4 \mid 2,345,678$ **(d)** $8 \mid 98,765,432$

Solution
(a) True. $4 \mid 1432$ since $4 \mid 32$.
(b) False. $8 \nmid 4204$ since $8 \nmid 204$.
(c) False. $4 \nmid 2{,}345{,}678$ since $4 \nmid 78$.
(d) True. $8 \mid 98{,}765{,}432$ since $8 \mid 432$.

The next two tests for divisibility provide a simple way to test for factors of 3 or 9.

Theorem

Tests for Divisibility by 3 and 9

A number is divisible by 3 if and only if the sum of its digits is divisible by 3.
A number is divisible by 9 if and only if the sum of its digits is divisible by 9.

EXAMPLE 5.4   Determine if the following are true or false. Explain.
(a) $3 \mid 12{,}345$ **(b)** $9 \mid 12{,}345$ **(c)** $9 \mid 6543$

Solution
(a) True. $3 \mid 12{,}345$ since $1 + 2 + 3 + 4 + 5 = 15$ and $3 \mid 15$.
(b) False. $9 \nmid 12{,}345$ since $1 + 2 + 3 + 4 + 5 = 15$ and $9 \nmid 15$.
(c) True. $9 \mid 6543$ since $9 \mid (6 + 5 + 4 + 3)$.   ∎

The following justification of the test for divisibility by 3 in the case of a three-digit number can be extended to prove that this test holds for any whole number.

Let $r = a \cdot 10^2 + b \cdot 10 + c$ be any three-digit number. We will show that if $3 \mid (a + b + c)$, then $3 \mid r$. Rewrite r as follows:

$$r = a \cdot (99 + 1) + b \cdot (9 + 1) + c$$
$$= a \cdot 99 + a \cdot 1 + b \cdot 9 + b \cdot 1 + c$$
$$= a \cdot 99 + b \cdot 9 + a + b + c$$
$$= (a \cdot 11 + b)9 + a + b + c.$$

Since $3 \mid 9$, it follows that $3 \mid (a \cdot 11 + b)9$. Thus if $3 \mid (a + b + c)$, where $a + b + c$ is the sum of the digits of r, then $3 \mid r$ since $3 \mid [(a \cdot 11 + b)9 + (a + b + c)]$. On the other hand, if $3 \mid r$, then $3 \mid (a + b + c)$ since $3 \mid [r - (a \cdot 11 + b)9]$ and $r - (a \cdot 11 + b)9 = a + b + c$.

The test for divisibility by 9 can be justified in a similar manner.

STUDENT PAGE SNAPSHOT

Mental Math: Divisibility

A. Shelley and Marty are planning the ticket sales for the Wheel-a-thon at Johnson School. They have 1,638 tickets, which they want to divide evenly among the school's 9 classrooms. Will they have any tickets left over?

If 1,638 **is divisible by** 9, there will not be any tickets left over.

Shelley recalls that a number is divisible by 9 if the sum of its digits is divisible by 9.

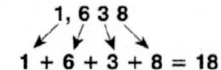

1 + 6 + 3 + 8 = 18

Since 18 is divisible by 9, so is 1,638.

 Marty uses a calculator to divide.

1,638 ⊕ 9 ⊜ [*182.*]

Shelley and Marty find that they will not have any tickets left over.

1. Use Shelley's **divisibility rule** to test if these numbers are divisible by 9. Check with a calculator.
   a. 727   **b.** 6,948   **c.** 5,030,100   **d.** 81,003

2. For each number in Problem 1 that is not divisible by 9, find the two closest numbers that are divisible by 9.

B. Here are a few more divisibility rules.

A number is divisible by:			
2	if the ones digit is 0, 2, 4, 6, or 8.	5	if the ones digit is 0 or 5.
3	if the sum of its digits is divisible by 3.	6	if it is divisible by 2 and by 3.
4	if the last two digits are divisible by 4.	10	if the ones digit is 0.

TRY OUT   Write the letter of the correct answer.

3. Which number is divisible by 9?
   a. 3,499   **c.** 1,070,001
   b. 191,919   **d.** 578

4. Which number is divisible by 6?
   a. 427,616   **c.** 636,363
   b. 12,408   **d.** 38,517

5. Which number is divisible by 5?
   a. 17,340   **c.** 275,396
   b. 5,508   **d.** 515,151

6. Which number is divisible by 4?
   a. 434   **c.** 173,636
   b. 45,405   **d.** 9,462

The following is a test for divisibility by 11.

Theorem

Test for Divisibility by 11

A number is divisible by 11 if and only if 11 divides the difference of the sum of the digits whose place values are odd powers of 10 and the sum of the digits whose place values are even powers of 10.

EXAMPLE 5.5 Determine if the following are true or false. Explain.
(a) 11 | 5346   **(b)** 11 | 909,381   **(c)** 11 | 16,543

Solution
(a) True. 11 | 5346 since $(5 + 4) - (3 + 6) = 0$ and 11 | 0.
(b) True. 11 | 909,381 since $(9 + 9 + 8) - (0 + 3 + 1) = 22$ and 11 | 22.
(c) False. 11 ∤ 16,543 since $(6 + 4) - (1 + 5 + 3) = 1$ and 11 ∤ 1. ■

The justification of this test for divisibility by 11 is left for the problem set. Also a test for divisibility by 7 is given in the problem set.

One can test for divisibility by 6 by applying the tests for 2 and 3.

Theorem

Test for Divisibility by 6

A number is divisible by 6 if and only if both of the tests for divisibility by 2 and 3 hold.

This technique of applying two tests simultaneously can be used in other cases also. For example, the test for 10 can be thought of as applying the tests for 2 and 5 simultaneously. By the test for 2, the ones digit must be 0, 2, 4, 6, or 8, *and* by the test for 5 the ones digit must be 0 or 5. Thus a number is divisible by 10 if and only if its ones digit is zero. Testing for divisibility by applying two tests can be done in general.

Theorem A number is divisible by the product, ab, of two nonzero whole numbers a and b if it is divisible by both a and b, and a and b have only the number 1 as a common factor.

According to this theorem, a test for divisibility by 36 would be to test for 4 and test for 9 since 4 and 9 both divide 36, and 4 and 9 have only 1 as a common factor. However, the test "a number is divisible by 24 if and only if it is divisible by 4 and 6" is *not* valid, since 4 and 6 have a common factor of 2. For example, 4 | 36 and 6 | 36, but 24 ∤ 36. The next example shows how to use tests for divisibility to find the prime factorization of a number.

EXAMPLE 5.6   Find the prime factorization of 5148.

Solution
First, since the sum of the digits of 5148 is 18 (which is a multiple of 9), we know that $5148 = 9 \cdot 572$. Next, since $4 \mid 72$, we know that $4 \mid 572$. Thus $5148 = 9 \cdot 572 = 9 \cdot 4 \cdot 143 = 3^2 \cdot 2^2 \cdot 143$. Finally, since in 143, $1 + 3 - 4 = 0$ is divisible by 11, the number 143 is divisible by 11, so $5148 = 2^2 \cdot 3^2 \cdot 11 \cdot 13$.   ■

We can also use divisibility tests to help decide if a particular counting number is prime. For example, we can determine if 137 is prime or composite by checking to see if it has any prime factors less than 137. None of 2, 3, or 5 divides 137. How about 7? 11? 13? How many prime factors must be considered before we know whether 137 is a prime? Consider the following example.

EXAMPLE 5.7   Determine if 137 is a prime.

Solution
First, by the tests for divisibility, none of 2, 3, or 5 is a factor of 137. Next try 7, 11, 13, and so on.

$$7 \times 19 < 137 \text{ and } 7 \times 20 > 137, \text{ so } 7 \nmid 137$$
$$11 \times 12 < 137 \text{ and } 11 \times 13 > 137, \text{ so } 11 \nmid 137$$
$$13 \times 10 < 137 \text{ and } 13 \times 11 > 137, \text{ so } 13 \nmid 137$$
$$17 \times 8 < 137 \text{ and } 17 \times 9 > 137, \text{ so } 17 \nmid 137$$

column 1

column 2

Notice that the numbers in column 1 form an increasing list of primes and the numbers in column 2 are decreasing. Also the numbers in the two columns "cross over" between 11 and 13. Thus, if there is a prime factor of 137, it will appear in column 1 first and reappear later as a factor of a number in column 2. Thus, as soon as the crossover is reached, there is no need to look any further for prime factors. Since the crossover point was passed in testing 137 and no prime factor of 137 was found, we conclude that 137 is prime.   ■

Example 5.7 suggests that to determine if a number n is prime, we need only search for prime factors p, where $p^2 \leq n$. Recall that $y = \sqrt{x}$ (read "the **square root** of x") means that $y^2 = x$ where $y \geq 0$. For example, $\sqrt{25} = 5$ since $5^2 = 25$. Not all whole numbers have whole-number square roots. For example, using a calculator, $\sqrt{27} \approx 5.196$ since $5.196^2 \approx 27$. (A more complete discussion of the square root is contained in Chapter 9.) Thus the search for prime factors of a number n by considering only those primes p where $p^2 \leq n$ can be simplified even further by using the $\boxed{\sqrt{x}}$ key on a calculator and checking only those primes p where $p \leq \sqrt{n}$.

> **Theorem**
>
> ## Prime Factor Test
>
> To test for prime factors of a number n, one need only search for prime factors p of n, where $p^2 \leq n$ (or $p \leq \sqrt{n}$).

EXAMPLE 5.8 Determine whether the following numbers are prime or composite.
(a) 299   **(b)** 401

Solution
(a) Only the prime factors 2 through 17 need to be checked since $17^2 < 299 < 19^2$ (check this on your calculator). None of 2, 3, 5, 7, or 11 is a factor, but since $299 = 13 \cdot 23$, the number 299 is composite.
(b) Only primes 2 through 19 need to be checked since $\sqrt{401} \approx 20$. Since none of the primes 2 through 19 are factors of 401, we know that 401 is a prime. (The tests for divisibility show that 2, 3, 5, and 11 are not factors of 401. A calculator, tests for divisibility, or long division can be used to check 7, 13, 17, and 19.) ■

MATHEMATICAL MORSEL

Finding large primes is a favorite pastime of some mathematicians. Before the advent of calculators and computers, this was certainly a time-consuming endeavor. Three anecdotes about large primes follow.

- Euler once announced that 1,000,009 was prime. However, he later found that it was the product of 293 and 3413. At the time of this discovery Euler was 70 and blind.
- Fermat was once asked if 100,895,598,169 was prime. He replied shortly that it had two factors, 898,423 and 112,303.
- For more than 200 years the Mersenne number $2^{67} - 1$ was thought to be prime. In 1903, Frank Nelson Cole, in a speech to the American Mathematical Society, went to the blackboard and without uttering a word, raised 2 to the power 67 (by hand, using our usual multiplication algorithm!) and subtracted 1. He then multiplied 193,707,721 by 761,838,257,287 (also by hand). The two numbers agreed! When asked how long it took him to crack the number, he said, "Three years of Sundays."

EXERCISE/PROBLEM SET 5.1—PART A

Exercises

1. Using the sieve of Eratosthenes, find all primes less than 100.

2. Find three factor trees for 48.

3. Find a factor tree for each of the following numbers.
   (a) 36   (b) 54   (c) 102   (d) 1000

4. A factor tree is not the only way to find the prime factorization of a composite number. Another method is to divide the number first by 2 as many times as possible, then by 3, then by 5, and so on, until all possible divisions by prime numbers have been performed. For example, to find the prime factorization of 108 you might organize your work as follows to conclude that $108 = 2^2 \times 3^3$.

$$
\begin{array}{r|r}
 & 3 \\
3 & 9 \\
3 & 27 \\
2 & 54 \\
2 & 108 \\
\end{array}
$$

Use this method to find the prime factorization of the following numbers.
   (a) 216   (b) 2940   (c) 825   (d) 198,198

5. (a) Write 36 in prime factorization form.
   (b) List the divisors of 36.
   (c) Write each divisor of 36 in prime factorization form.
   (d) What relationship exists between your answer to part (a) and each of your answers to part (c)?
   (e) Let $n = 13^2 \times 29^5$. If m divides n, what can you conclude about the prime factorization of m?

6. Determine which of the following are true.
   (a) 3 | 9   (b) 12 | 6
   (c) 3 is a divisor of 21.   (d) 6 is a factor of 3.
   (e) 4 is a factor of 16.   (f) 0 | 5
   (g) 11 | 11   (h) 48 is a multiple of 16.

7. Decide whether the following are true or false using only divisibility ideas given in this section (do not use long division or a calculator). Give a reason for your answers.
   (a) 6 | 80   (b) 15 | 10,000
   (c) 4 | 15,000   (d) 12 | 32,304
   (e) 24 | 325,608   (f) 45 | 13,075
   (g) 40 | 1,732,800   (h) 36 | 677,916

8. If 21 divides m, what else must divide m?

9. If 16 divides n, what else must divide n?

10. (a) Show that 8 | 123,152 using the test for divisibility by 8.

(b) Show that 8 | 123,152 by finding x such that $8x = 123,152$.

(c) Is the x that you found in part (b) a divisor of 123,152? Prove it.

11. Which of the following are multiples of 3? Of 4? Of 9?
   (a) 123,452   (b) 1,114,500
   (c) 2,199,456   (d) 31,020,417

12. True or false? Explain.
   (a) If a counting number is divisible by 9, it must be divisible by 3.
   (b) If a counting number is divisible by 3 and 11, it must be divisible by 33.
   (c) If a counting number is divisible by 6 and 8, it must be divisible by 48.
   (d) If a counting number is divisible by 4, it must be divisible by 8.

13. Use the test for divisibility by 11 to determine which of the following numbers are divisible by 11.
   (a) 2838   (b) 71,992   (c) 172,425

Problems

14. Justify the tests for divisibility by 5 and 10 for any three-digit number by reasoning by analogy from the test for divisibility by 2.

15. The symbol 4! is called four **factorial** and means $4 \times 3 \times 2 \times 1$; thus 4! = 24. Which of the following statements are true?
   (a) 6 | 6!   (b) 5 | 6!   (c) 11 | 6!
   (d) 30 | 30!   (e) 40 | 30!   (f) 30 | (30! + 1)
   [Do not multiply out parts (d) to (f).]

16. (a) Does 8 | 7!?   (b) Does 7 | 6!?
   (c) For what counting numbers n will n divide $(n - 1)!$?

17. There is one composite number in this set: 331, 3331, 33,331, 333,331, 3,333,331, 33,333,331, 333,333,331. Which one is it? (HINT: It has a factor less than 30.)

18. Show that the formula $p(n) = n^2 + n + 17$ yields primes for $n = 0, 1, 2,$ and 3. Find the smallest whole number n for which $p(n) = n^2 + n + 17$ is not a prime.

19. (a) Compute $n^2 + n + 41$, where $n = 0, 1, 2, \ldots ,$ 10, and determine which of these numbers is prime.
   (b) On another piece of paper, continue the following spiral pattern until you reach 151. What do you notice about the main upper left to lower right diagonal?

```
            etc.
53    52    51    50
      43    42    49
      44    41    48
      45    46    47
```

20. In the book *The Canterbury Puzzles* (1907) by Dudeney, he mentioned that 11 was the only number consisting entirely of ones which was known to be prime. In 1918, Oscar Hoppe proved that the number 1,111,111,111,111,111,111 (19 ones) was prime. Later it was shown that the number made up of 23 ones was also prime. Now see how many of these "repunit" numbers up to 19 ones you can factor.

21. Which of the following numbers can be written as the sum of two primes, and why?

$$7, 17, 27, 37, 47, \ldots$$

22. One of the theorems of Fermat states that *every prime of the form* $4x + 1$ *is the sum of two square numbers in one and only one way.* For example, $13 = 4(3) + 1$, and $13 = 4 + 9$, where 4 and 9 are square numbers.
   (a) List the primes less than 100 that are of the form $4x + 1$, where x is a whole number.
   (b) Express each of these primes as the sum of two square numbers.

23. The primes 2 and 3 are consecutive whole numbers. Is there another such pair of consecutive primes? Justify your answer.

24. Two primes that differ by 2 are called **twin primes**. For example, 5 and 7, 11 and 13, and 29 and 31 are twin primes. Find the other twin primes less than 200.

25. One result that mathematicians have been unable to prove true or false is called Goldbach's conjecture. It claims that each even number greater than 2 can be expressed as the sum of two primes. For example,

$$4 = 2 + 2, \quad 6 = 3 + 3, \quad 8 = 3 + 5,$$
$$10 = 5 + 5, \quad 12 = 5 + 7$$

   (a) Verify that it holds for even numbers through 40.
   (b) Assuming that Goldbach's conjecture is true, show how each odd whole number greater than 6 is the sum of three primes.

26. For the numbers greater than 5 and less than 50, are there at least two primes between every number and its double? If not, for which one does it not hold?

27. Find two whole numbers with the smallest possible difference between them that when multiplied together will produce 1,234,567,890.

28. Find the largest counting number that divides every number in the following sets.

(a) $\{1 \cdot 2 \cdot 3, 2 \cdot 3 \cdot 4, 3 \cdot 4 \cdot 5, \ldots\}$
(b) $\{1 \cdot 3 \cdot 5, 2 \cdot 4 \cdot 6, 3 \cdot 5 \cdot 7, \ldots\}$
Can you explain your answer in each case?

29. Find the smallest counting number that is divisible by the numbers 2 through 10.

30. What is the smallest counting number divisible by 2, 4, 5, 6, and 12?

31. Fill in the blank. The sum of three consecutive counting numbers always has a divisor (other than 1) of _____. Prove.

32. Choose any two numbers, say 5 and 7. Form a sequence of numbers as follows: 5, 7, 12, 19, and so on, where each new term is the sum of the two preceding numbers until you have 10 numbers. Add the 10 numbers. Is the seventh number a factor of the sum? Repeat several times, starting with a different pair of numbers each time. What do you notice? Prove that your observation is always true.

33. **(a)** $5! = 5 \cdot 4 \cdot 3 \cdot 2 \cdot 1$ is divisible by 2, 3, 4, and 5. Prove that $5! + 2$, $5! + 3$, $5! + 4$, and $5! + 5$ are all composite.
   (b) Find 1000 consecutive numbers that are composite.

34. The customer said to the cashier, "I have 5 apples at 27 cents each and 2 pounds of potatoes at 78 cents per pound. I also have 3 cantaloupes and 6 lemons, but I don't remember the price for each." The cashier said, "That will be $3.52." The customer said, "You must have made a mistake." The cashier checked and the customer was correct. How did the customer catch the mistake?

35. There is a three-digit number with the following property: If you subtract 7 from it, the difference is divisible by 7; if you subtract 8 from it, the difference is divisible by 8; and if you subtract 9 from it, the difference is divisible by 9. What is the number?

36. Paula and Ricardo are serving cupcakes at a school party. If they arrange the cupcakes in groups of 2, 3, 4, 5, or 6, they always have exactly one cupcake left over. What is the smallest number of cupcakes they could have?

37. Prove that all six-place numbers of the form *abcabc* (e.g., 416,416) are divisible by 13. What other two numbers are always factors of a number of this form?

38. **(a)** Prove that all four-digit palindromes are divisible by 11.
   (b) Is this also true for *every* palindrome with an even number of digits? Prove or disprove.

39. The annual sales for certain calculators were $2567 one year and $4267 the next. Assuming that the price of the calculators was the same each of the two years, how many calculators were sold in each of the two years?

40. Observe that 7 divides 2149. Also check to see that 7 divides 149,002. Try this pattern on another four-digit number using 7. If it works again, try a third. If that one also works, formulate a conjecture based on your three examples and prove it. (HINT: $7 \mid 1001$.)

41. How long does this list continue to yield primes?

$$17 + 2 = 19$$
$$19 + 4 = 23$$
$$23 + 6 = 29$$
$$29 + 8 = 37$$

42. Justify the test for divisibility by 11 for four-digit numbers by completing the following:

Let $a \cdot 10^3 + b \cdot 10^2 + c \cdot 10 + d$ be any four-digit number. Then

$$a \cdot 10^3 + b \cdot 10^2 + c \cdot 10 + d$$
$$= a(1001 - 1) + b(99 + 1) + c(11 - 1) + d$$
$$= \cdots$$

43. If p is a prime greater than 5, then the number $111 \ldots 1$, consisting of $p - 1$ ones, is divisible by p. For example, $7 \mid 111,111$ since $7 \times 15873 = 111,111$. Verify the initial sentence for the next three primes.

44. **(a)** Find the largest n such that $3^n \mid 24!$.
(b) Find the smallest n such that $3^6 \mid n!$.
(c) Find the largest n such that $12^n \mid 24!$.

EXERCISE/PROBLEM SET 5.1—PART B

Exercises

1. An efficient way to find all the primes up to 100 is to arrange the numbers from 1 to 100 in six columns. As with the sieve of Eratosthenes, cross out the multiples of 2, 3, 5, and 7. What pattern do you notice? (HINT: Look at the columns and diagonals.)

1	2	3	4	5	6
7	8	9	10	11	12
13	14	15	16	17	18
19	20	21	22	23	24
25	26	27	28	29	30
31	32	33	34	35	36
37	38	39	40	41	42
43	44	45	46	47	48
49	50	51	52	53	54
55	56	57	58	59	60
61	62	63	64	65	66
67	68	69	70	71	72
73	74	75	76	77	78
79	80	81	82	83	84
85	86	87	88	89	90
91	92	93	94	95	96
97	98	99	100		

2. Find a factor tree for each of the following numbers.
(a) 192   **(b)** 380   **(c)** 1593   **(d)** 3741

3. Each of the following prime factorizations corresponds to a particular number. Determine the number in each case.
(a) $3 \times 5 \times 11 \times 13$
(b) $2^2 \times 7 \times 11 \times 19$
(c) $2^3 \times 3^2 \times 5^2 \times 7$
(d) $2^3 \times 3^2 \times 5^3 \times 13$
(e) $2^4 \times 5^4 \times 7^2 \times 13^2$

4. Factor each of the following numbers into primes.
(a) 39   **(b)** 1131   **(c)** 55   **(d)** 935
(e) 3289   **(f)** 5889

5. Use the definition of "divides" to show that each of the following is true. (HINT: Find x that satisfies the definition of divides.)
(a) $7 \mid 49$
(b) $21 \mid 210$
(c) $3 \mid 9 \times 18$
(d) $2 \mid 2^2 \times 5 \times 7$
(e) $6 \mid 2^4 \times 3^2 \times 7^3 \times 13^5$
(f) $100,000 \mid 2^7 \times 3^9 \times 5^{11} \times 17^8$
(g) $6000 \mid 2^{21} \times 3^{17} \times 5^{89} \times 29^{37}$
(h) $22 \mid 121 \times 4$
(i) $p^3 q^5 r \mid p^5 q^{13} r^7 s^2 t^{27}$
(j) $7 \mid (5 \times 21 + 14)$

6. If 24 divides b, what else must divide b?

7. **(a)** Prove in two different ways that 2 divides 114.
(b) Prove in two different ways that $3 \mid 336$.

8. Justify the test for divisibility by 9 for any four-digit number. (HINT: Reason by analogy from the test for divisibility by 3.)

9. If the variables represent counting numbers, determine whether each of the following is true or false.
(a) If $x \nmid y$ and $x \nmid z$, then $x \nmid (y + z)$.
(b) If $2 \mid a$ and $3 \mid a$, then $6 \mid a$.
(c) If $2 \mid a$ and $6 \mid a$, then $12 \mid a$.
(d) If $6 \mid xy$, then $6 \mid x$ or $6 \mid y$.

10. A test for divisibility by 7 is illustrated below. Does 7 divide 17,276?

$$
\begin{array}{ll}
\textit{Test:} \quad & 17276 \\
& \underline{-\ \ 12} \qquad \text{Subtract } 2 \times 6 \\
& 1715 \qquad \text{from 1727} \\
& \underline{-\ \ 10} \qquad \text{Subtract } 2 \times 5 \\
& 161 \qquad \text{from 171} \\
& \underline{-\ \ 2} \qquad \text{Subtract } 2 \times 1 \\
& 14 \qquad \text{from 16}
\end{array}
$$

Since 7 | 14 we also have 7 | 17,276. Use this test to see if the following numbers are divisible by 7.
(a) 8659   (b) 46,187   (c) 864,197,523

11. A calculator may be used to test for divisibility of one number by another, where n and d represent counting numbers.
(a) If $n \div d$ gives an answer 176, is it necessarily true that $d \mid n$?
(b) If $n \div d$ gives an answer 56.3, is it possible that $d \mid n$?

12. Which of the following numbers are composite? Why?
(a) 12   (b) 123   (c) 1234
(d) 12,345   (e) 123,456   (f) 1,234,567
(g) 123,456,789

13. The numbers 2, 3, 5, 7, 11, and 13 are not factors of 211. Can we conclude that 211 is prime without checking for more factors? Why or why not?

14. In 1845 the French mathematician Bertrand made the following conjecture: Between any whole number greater than 1 and its double there is at least one prime. In 1911, a Russian mathematician Tchebyshev proved the conjecture true. Find a prime between each of the following numbers and its double.
(a) 2   (b) 10   (c) 100

Problems

15. Find the first composite number in this list.

$$
\begin{array}{l}
3! - 2! + 1! = 5 \text{ Prime} \\
4! - 3! + 2! - 1! = 19 \text{ Prime} \\
5! - 4! + 3! - 2! + 1! = 101 \text{ Prime}
\end{array}
$$

Continue this pattern. (HINT: The first composite comes within the first 10 such numbers. Also, you might want to use Computer Program B5.1 from the Technology Section.)

16. It is claimed that the formula $n^2 - n + 41$ yields a prime for all whole-number values for n. Decide if this statement is true or false.

17. In 1644, the French mathematician Mersenne asserted that $2^n - 1$ was prime only when $n = 2, 3, 5, 7, 13, 17, 19, 31, 67, 127,$ and 257. As it turned out, when $n = 67$ and $n = 257$, $2^n - 1$ was a composite and $2^n - 1$ was also prime when $n = 89$ and $n = 107$. Show that Mersenne's assertion was correct concerning $n = 3, 5, 7,$ and 11.

18. It is claimed that every prime greater than 3 is either one more or one less than a multiple of 6. Investigate. If it seems true, prove it. If it does not, find a counterexample.

19. Is it possible for the sum of two odd prime numbers to be a prime number? Why or why not?

20. A mathematician, D. H. Lehmer, found that there are 209 consecutive composites between 20,831,323 and 20,831,533. Pick two numbers at random between 20,831,323 and 20,831,533 and prove that they are composite.

21. **Prime triples** are consecutive primes whose difference is 2. One such triple is 3, 5, 7. Find more or prove that there cannot be any more.

22. A seventh-grade student named Arthur Hamann made the following conjecture: Every even number is the difference of two primes. Express the following even numbers as the difference of two primes.
(a) 12   (b) 20   (c) 28

23. The numbers 1, 7, 13, 31, 37, 43, 61, 67, and 73 form an additive 3×3 magic square. (An **additive magic square** has the same sum in all three rows, three columns, and two main diagonals.) Find it.

24. Can you find whole numbers a and b such that $3^a = 5^b$? Why or why not?

25. I'm a two-digit number less than 40. I'm divisible by only one prime number. The sum of my digits is a prime, and the difference between my digits is another prime. What numbers could I be?

26. What is the smallest counting number divisible by 2, 4, 6, 8, 10, 12, and 14?

27. What is the smallest counting number divisible by the numbers 1, 2, 3, 4, . . . , 24, 25? (HINT: Give your answer in prime factorization form.)

28. The sum of five consecutive counting numbers has a divisor (other than 1) of _____. Prove.

29. Take any number with an even number of digits. Reverse the digits and add the two numbers. Does 11 divide your result? If yes, try to explain why.

30. Take a number. Reverse its digits and subtract the smaller of the two numbers from the larger. Determine what number always divides such differences for the following types of numbers.
(a) A two-digit number   (b) A three-digit number
(c) A four-digit number

31. Choose any three digits. Arrange them three ways to form three numbers. *Claim:* The sum of your three numbers has a factor of 3. True or false?

Example:

$$371$$
$$137$$
$$+713$$
$$\overline{1221}$$

and $1221 = 3 \times 407$

32. Someone spilled ink on a bill for 36 sweatshirts. If only the first and last digits were covered and the other three digits were, in order, 8, 3, 9 as in ?83.9?, how much did each cost?

33. Determine how many zeros are at the end of the numerals for the following numbers in base 10.
   (a) 10!   **(b)** 100!   **(c)** 1000!

34. Find the smallest number n with the following property: If n is divided by 3, the quotient is the number obtained by moving the last digit (ones digit) of n to become the first digit. All of the remaining digits are shifted one to the right.

35. A man and his grandson have the same birthday. If for six consecutive birthdays the man is a whole number of times as old as his grandson, how old is each at the sixth birthday?

36. Let m be any odd whole number. Then m is a divisor of the sum of any m consecutive whole numbers. True or false? If true, prove. If false, provide a counterexample.

37. A merchant marked down some pads of paper from $2 and sold the entire lot. If the gross received from the sale was $603.77, how many pads did she sell?

38. How many prime numbers less than 100 can be written using the digits 1, 2, 3, 4, 5 if
   (a) No digit is used more than once?
   (b) A digit may be used twice?

39. Which of the numbers in the set

$$\{9,\ 99,\ 999,\ 9999,\ .\ .\ .\}$$

are divisible by 7?

40. Two digits of this number were erased: 273*49*5. However, we know that 9 and 11 divide the number. What is it?

41. This problem appeared on a Russian mathematics exam: Show that all the numbers in the sequence 100001, 10000100001, 1000010000100001, . . . are composite. Show that 11 divides the first, third, fifth numbers in this sequence, and so on, and that 111 divides the second. An American engineer claimed that the fourth number was the product of

$$21401 \quad \text{and} \quad 4672725574038601$$

Was he correct?

42. The Fibonacci sequence, 1, 1, 2, 3, 5, 8, 13, . . . , is formed by adding any two consecutive numbers to find the next term. Prove or disprove: The sum of any ten consecutive Fibonacci numbers is a multiple of 11.

43. Justify the tests for divisibility by 4 and 8.

5.2

COUNTING FACTORS, GREATEST COMMON FACTOR, AND LEAST COMMON MULTIPLE

Counting Factors

In addition to finding prime factors, it is sometimes useful to be able to find how many factors (not just prime factors) a number has. The fundamental theorem of arithmetic is helpful in this regard. For example, to find all the factors of 12, consider its prime factorization $12 = 2^2 \cdot 3^1$. All factors of 12 must be made up of products of at most 2 twos and 1 three. All such combinations are contained in the following table.

Exponent of 2	Exponent of 3	Factor
0	0	$2^0 \cdot 3^0 = 1$
1	0	$2^1 \cdot 3^0 = 2$
2	0	$2^2 \cdot 3^0 = 4$
0	1	$2^0 \cdot 3^1 = 3$
1	1	$2^1 \cdot 3^1 = 6$
2	1	$2^2 \cdot 3^1 = 12$

Thus 12 has six factors, namely, 1, 2, 3, 4, 6, and 12.

The technique used in the preceding table can be used with any whole number that is expressed as the product of primes with their respective exponents. To find the number of factors of $2^3 \cdot 5^2$, a similar list could be constructed. The exponents of 2 would range from 0 to 3 (four possibilities), and the exponents of 5 would range from 0 to 2 (three possibilities). In all there would be $4 \cdot 3$ combinations, or 12 factors of $2^3 \cdot 5^2$, as shown in the following table.

Exponents of 5 →	0	1	2
2 ↓			
0	$2^0 5^0$	$2^0 5^1$	$2^0 5^2$
1	$2^1 5^0$	$2^1 5^1$	$2^1 5^2$
2	$2^2 5^0$	$2^2 5^1$	$2^2 5^2$
3	$2^3 5^0$	$2^3 5^1$	$2^3 5^2$

This method for finding the number of factors of any number can be summarized as follows.

> **Theorem** Suppose that a counting number n is expressed as a product of *distinct* primes with their respective exponents, say $n = (p_1^{n_1})(p_2^{n_2}) \cdots (p_m^{n_m})$. Then the number of factors of n is the product $(n_1 + 1) \cdot (n_2 + 1) \cdots (n_m + 1)$.

EXAMPLE 5.9 Find the number of factors.
(a) 144   **(b)** $2^3 \cdot 5^7 \cdot 7^4$ **(c)** $9^5 \cdot 11^2$

Solution
(a) $144 = 2^4 \cdot 3^2$. So, the number of factors of 144 is $(4 + 1)(2 + 1) = 15$.
(b) $2^3 \cdot 5^7 \cdot 7^4$ has $(3 + 1)(7 + 1)(4 + 1) = 160$ factors.
(c) $9^5 \cdot 11^2 = 3^{10} \cdot 11^2$ has $(10 + 1)(2 + 1) = 33$ factors. (NOTE: 9^5 had to be rewritten as 3^{10} since 9 was not prime.) ■

Notice that the number of factors does not depend on the prime factors, but rather, on their respective exponents.

Greatest Common Factor

The concept of greatest common factor is useful when simplifying fractions.

> **Definition**
>
> **Greatest Common Factor**
>
> The **greatest common factor** (GCF) of two (or more) nonzero whole numbers is the largest whole number that is a factor of both (all) of the numbers. The GCF of a and b is written **GCF(a, b)**.

There are two elementary ways to find the greatest common factor of two numbers: the set intersection method and the prime factorization method. The GCF(24, 36) is found next using these two methods.

Set Intersection Method

Step 1: Find all factors of 24 and 36. Since $24 = 2^3 \cdot 3$, there are $4 \cdot 2 = 8$ factors of 24 and since $36 = 2^2 \cdot 3^2$, there are $3 \cdot 3 = 9$ factors of 36. The set of factors of 24 is {1, 2, 3, 4, 6, 8, 12, 24} and the set of factors of 36 is {1, 2, 3, 4, 6, 9, 12, 18, 36}.

Step 2: Find all common factors of 24 and 36 by taking the intersection of the two sets in step 1.

$$\{1, 2, 3, 4, 6, 8, 12, 24\} \cap \{1, 2, 3, 4, 6, 9, 12, 18, 36\}$$
$$= \{1, 2, 3, 4, 6, 12\}.$$

Step 3: Find the largest number in the set of common factors in step 2. The largest number in {1, 2, 3, 4, 6, 12} is 12. Therefore, 12 is the GCF of 24 and 36.

(NOTE: The set intersection method can also be used to find the GCF of more than two numbers in a similar manner.)

Prime Factorization Method

Step 1: Express the numbers 24 and 36 in their prime factor exponential form: $24 = 2^3 \cdot 3$ and $36 = 2^2 \cdot 3^2$.

Step 2: The GCF will be the number $2^m 3^n$ where m is the smaller of the exponents of the 2s and n is the smaller of the exponents of the 3s. For $2^3 \cdot 3^1$ and $2^2 \cdot 3^2$, m is the smaller of 3 and 2, and n is the smaller of 1 and 2. Therefore, the GCF of $2^3 \cdot 3^1$ and $2^2 \cdot 3^2$ is $2^2 \cdot 3^1 = 12$. Review this method so that you see why it always yields the largest number that is a factor of both of the given numbers.

EXAMPLE 5.10 Find the GCF(42, 24) in two ways.

Solution

(a) *Set Intersection Method*

$42 = 2 \cdot 3 \cdot 7$, so 42 has $2 \cdot 2 \cdot 2 = 8$ factors.

$24 = 2^3 \cdot 3$, so 24 has $4 \cdot 2 = 8$ factors.

Factors of 42 are 1, 2, 3, 6, 7, 14, 21, 42.

Factors of 24 are 1, 2, 3, 4, 6, 8, 12, 24.

Common factors are 1, 2, 6.

GCF(42, 24) = 6.

(b) *Prime Factorization Method*

$42 = 2 \cdot 3 \cdot 7$ and $24 = 2^3 \cdot 3$.

GCF (42, 24) = $2 \cdot 3 = 6$.

Notice that only the common primes (2 and 3) are used since the exponent on the 7 is zero in the prime factorization of 24. ■

Earlier in this chapter we obtained the following result: If $a \mid m$, $a \mid n$, and $m \geq n$, then $a \mid (m - n)$. In words, if a number divides each of two numbers, then it divides their difference. Hence, if c is a common factor of a and b, where $a \geq b$, then c is also a common factor of b and $a - b$. Since every common factor of a and b is also a common factor of b and $a - b$, the pairs (a, b) and $(a - b, b)$ have the same common factors. So GCF(a, b) and GCF$(a - b, b)$ must also be the same.

Theorem   If a and b are whole numbers, with $a \geq b$, then

$$\text{GCF}(a, b) = \text{GCF}(a - b, b).$$

The usefulness of this result is illustrated in the next example.

EXAMPLE 5.11   Find the GCF(546, 390).

Solution

$$
\begin{aligned}
\text{GCF}(546, 390) &= \text{GCF}(546 - 390, 390) \\
&= \text{GCF}(156, 390) \\
&= \text{GCF}(390 - 156, 156) \\
&= \text{GCF}(234, 156) \\
&= \text{GCF}(78, 156) \\
&= \text{GCF}(78, 78) \\
&= 78.
\end{aligned}
$$

Using a calculator, we can find the GCF(546, 390) as follows:

$$
\begin{aligned}
546 \;\boxed{-}\; 390 \;\boxed{=}\; 156 \\
390 \;\boxed{-}\; 156 \;\boxed{=}\; 234 \\
234 \;\boxed{-}\; 156 \;\boxed{=}\; 78 \\
156 \;\boxed{-}\; 78 \;\boxed{=}\; 78
\end{aligned}
$$

Therefore, since the last two numbers in the last line are equal, the GCF(546, 390) = 78. Notice that this procedure may be shortened by storing 156 in the calculator's memory.

This calculator method can be refined for very large numbers or in exceptional cases. For example, to find GCF(1417, 26), 26 must be subtracted many times to produce a number that is less than (or equal to) 26. Since division can be viewed as repeated subtraction, long division can be used to shorten this process as follows:

$$
\begin{array}{r}
54 \text{ R } 13 \\
26\overline{)1417}
\end{array}
$$

Here 26 was "subtracted" from 1417 a total of 54 times to produce a remainder of 13. Thus GCF(1417, 26) = GCF(13, 26). Next, divide 13 into 26.

$$
\begin{array}{r}
2 \text{ R } 0 \\
13\overline{)26}
\end{array}
$$

Thus GCF(13, 26) = 13, so GCF(1417, 26) = 13. Each step of this method can be justified by the following theorem.

> **Theorem**   If a and b are whole numbers with $a \geq b$ and $a = bq + r$, where $r < b$, then
>
> $$GCF(a, b) = GCF(r, b).$$

Thus, to find the GCF of any two numbers, this theorem can be applied repeatedly until a remainder of zero is obtained. The final divisor that leads to the zero remainder is the GCF of the two numbers. This method is called the **Euclidean algorithm**.

EXAMPLE 5.12   Find the GCF(840, 3432).

Solution

$$840 \overline{)3432} \quad 4 \text{ R } 72$$

$$72 \overline{)840} \quad 11 \text{ R } 48$$

$$48 \overline{)72} \quad 1 \text{ R } 24$$

$$24 \overline{)48} \quad 2 \text{ R } 0$$

Therefore, GCF(840, 3432) = 24.

A calculator also can be used to calculate the GCF(3432, 840) using the Euclidean algorithm.

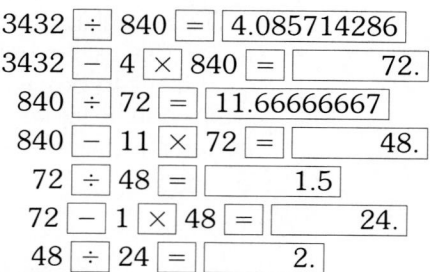

Therefore, 24 is the GCF(3432, 840). Notice how this method parallels the one in Example 5.12.

Least Common Multiple

The least common multiple is useful when adding or subtracting fractions.

Definition

Least Common Multiple

The **least common multiple** (LCM) of two (or more) nonzero whole numbers is the smallest nonzero whole number that is a multiple of each (all) of the numbers. The LCM of a and b is written **LCM(a, b)**.

There are also two elementary ways to find the least common multiple of two numbers: the set intersection method and the prime factorization method. The LCM(24, 36) is found next using these two methods.

Set Intersection Method

Step 1: List the first several nonzero multiples of 24 and 36. The set of nonzero multiples of 24 is {24, 48, 72, 96, 120, 144, . . .} and the set of nonzero multiples of 36 is {36, 72, 108, 144, . . .}. (NOTE: The set of multiples of any nonzero whole number is an infinite set.)

Step 2: Find the first several common multiples of 24 and 36 by taking the intersection of the two sets in step 1. {24, 48, 72, 96, 120, 144, . . .} ∩ {36, 72, 108, 144, . . .} = {72, 144, . . .}.

Step 3: Find the smallest number in the set of common multiples in step 2. The smallest number in {72, 144, . . .} is 72. Therefore, 72 is the LCM of 24 and 36 (Figure 5.3).

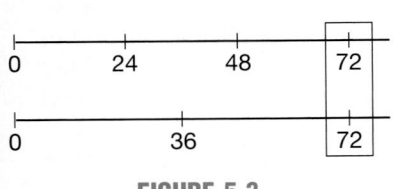

FIGURE 5.3

Prime Factorization Method

Step 1: Express the numbers 24 and 36 in their prime factor exponential form: $24 = 2^3 \cdot 3$ and $36 = 2^2 \cdot 3^2$.

Step 2: The LCM will be the number $2^r 3^s$, where r is the larger of the exponents of the twos and s is the larger of the exponents of the threes. For $2^3 \cdot 3^1$ and $2^2 \cdot 3^2$, r is the larger of 3 and 2 and s is the larger of 1 and 2. That is, the LCM of $2^3 \cdot 3^1$ and $2^2 \cdot 3^2$ is $2^3 \cdot 3^2$, or 72. Review this procedure to see why it always yields the smallest number than is a multiple of both of the given numbers. ■

EXAMPLE 5.13   Find the LCM(42, 24) in two ways.

Solution

Set Intersection Method

Multiples of 42 are 42, 84, 126, 168, ...

Multiples of 24 are 24, 48, 72, 96, 120, 144, 168, ...

Common multiples are 168, ...

LCM(42, 24) = 168.

Prime Factorization Method

$42 = 2 \cdot 3 \cdot 7$ and $24 = 2^3 \cdot 3$.

$LCM(42, 24) = 2^3 \cdot 3 \cdot 7 = 168$.

Notice that *all* primes from either number are used when forming the least common multiple.   ■

The prime factorization method can also be applied to find the GCF and LCM of several numbers.

EXAMPLE 5.14 Find the **(a)** GCF and **(b)** LCM of the three numbers $2^5 \cdot 3^2 \cdot 5^7$, $2^4 \cdot 3^4 \cdot 5^3 \cdot 7$, and $2 \cdot 3^6 \cdot 5^4 \cdot 13^2$.

Solution

(a) The GCF is $2^1 \cdot 3^2 \cdot 5^3$ (use the common primes and the smallest respective exponents).

(b) The LCM is $2^5 \cdot 3^6 \cdot 5^7 \cdot 7 \cdot 13^2$ (use all the primes and the largest respective exponents).   ■

If you are trying to find the GCF of several numbers that are not in prime-factored exponential form, as in Example 5.14, you may want to use a computer program. By considering examples in exponential notation, one can observe that the GCF of a, b, and c can be found by finding GCF(a, b) first and then GCF(GCF(a, b), c). This idea can be extended to as many numbers as you wish. Thus one can use the Euclidean algorithm by finding GCFs of numbers, two at a time. For example, to find GCF(24, 36, 160), find GCF (24, 36), which is 12, and then find GCF(12, 160), which is 4.

Finally, there is a very useful connection between the GCF and LCM of two numbers, as illustrated in the next example.

EXAMPLE 5.15 Find the GCF and LCM of a and b, for the numbers $a = 2^5 \cdot 3^7 \cdot 5^2 \cdot 7$ and $b = 2^3 \cdot 3^2 \cdot 5^6 \cdot 11$.

Solution

Notice that the product of the factors of a and b in bold type below make up the GCF, and the product of the remaining factors, which are circled, make up the LCM.

$$GCF = 2^3 \cdot 3^2 \cdot 5^2$$

$$a = \textcircled{2^5} \cdot \textcircled{3^7} \cdot \mathbf{5^2} \cdot \textcircled{7} \qquad b = \mathbf{2^3} \cdot \mathbf{3^2} \cdot \textcircled{5^6} \cdot \textcircled{11}$$

$$LCM = 2^5 \cdot 3^7 \cdot 5^6 \cdot 7 \cdot 11$$

Hence

$$\begin{aligned}
\text{GCF}(a,\ b) \times \text{LCM}(a,\ b) &= (2^3 \cdot 3^2 \cdot 5^2)(2^5 \cdot 3^7 \cdot 5^6 \cdot 7 \cdot 11)\\
&= (2^5 \cdot 3^7 \cdot 5^2 \cdot 7) \cdot (2^3 \cdot 3^2 \cdot 5^6 \cdot 11)\\
&= a \times b.
\end{aligned}$$ ∎

Example 5.15 illustrates that *all* of the prime factors and their exponents from the original number are accounted for in the GCF and LCM. This relationship is stated below.

> **Theorem**   Let a and b be any two whole numbers. Then
>
> $$\text{GCF}(a,\ b) \times \text{LCM}(a,\ b) = ab.$$

Also, $\text{LCM}(a,\ b) = \dfrac{ab}{\text{GCF}(a,\ b)}$ is a consequence of this theorem. So if the GCF of two numbers is known, the LCM can be found using the GCF.

EXAMPLE 5.16   Find the LCM(36, 56).

Solution

$\text{GCF}(36,\ 56) = 4$. Therefore, $\text{LCM} = \dfrac{36 \cdot 56}{4} = 9 \cdot 56 = 504$. ∎

This technique applies only to the case of finding the GCF and LCM of *two* numbers.

We end this chapter with an important result regarding the primes by proving that there is an infinite number of primes.

> **Theorem**   There is an infinite number of primes.

Proof

Either there is a finite number of primes or there is an infinite number of primes. We will use indirect reasoning. Let us *assume* that there is only a *finite* number of primes, say 2, 3, 5, 7, 11, . . . , p, where p is the greatest prime. Let $N = (2 \cdot 3 \cdot 5 \cdot 7 \cdot 11 \cdots p) + 1$. This number, N, must be 1, prime, or composite. Clearly, N is greater than 1. Also, N is greater than any prime. But then, if N is composite, it must have a prime factor. Yet, whenever N is divided by a prime the remainder is always 1 (think about this!). Therefore, N is neither 1, a prime, nor a composite. But that is impossible. Using indirect reasoning, we conclude that there must be an infinite number of primes. ∎

There are also infinitely many composite numbers: for example, the even numbers greater than 2.

MATHEMATICAL MORSEL

As of March 1992, the largest known prime was $2^{756839} - 1$, about three times the size of the last known one. This prime number has 227,832 digits and, if written out in typical newsprint size, would fill seven pages of a newspaper. Why search for such large primes? One reason is that it requires trillions of calculations and hence can be used to test computer speed and reliability. Also, it is important in writing messages in code. Besides, as a computer expert put it, "It's like Mount Everest; why do people climb mountains?"

EXERCISE/PROBLEM SET 5.2—PART A

Exercises

1. How many factors does each of the following numbers have?
(a) $2^2 \times 3$ (b) $2^2 \times 3^2$
(c) $3^3 \times 5^2$ (d) $7^3 \times 11^3$
(e) $5^2 \times 7^3 \times 11^4$ (f) $7^{11} \times 19^6 \times 79^{23}$

2. (a) Which are larger, divisors of 18 or multiples of 18? Are there any exceptions?
(b) Which is larger, GCF(12, 18) or LCM(12, 18)?
(c) Let a and b represent two nonzero whole numbers. Which is larger, GCF(a, b) or LCM(a, b)?

3. Use the set intersection method to find the GCFs.
(a) GCF(8, 18)   (b) GCF(36, 42)
(c) GCF(24, 66)   (d) GCF(18, 36, 54)
(e) GCF(16, 51)   (f) GCF(136,153)

4. Using a calculator method, find the following.
(a) GCF(138, 102)   (b) GCF(484, 363)
(c) GCF(297, 204)   (d) GCF(222, 2222)

5. Use any method to find the following GCFs.
(a) GCF(12, 60, 90)
(b) GCF(15, 35, 42)
(c) GCF(55, 75, 245)
(d) GCF(28, 98, 154)
(e) GCF(1105, 1729, 3289)
(f) GCF(1421, 1827, 2523)

6. Use the set intersection method to find the LCMs.
(a) LCM(6, 8)   (b) LCM(4, 10)
(c) LCM(7, 9)   (d) LCM(2, 3, 5)
(e) LCM(8, 10)   (f) LCM(8, 12, 18)

7. One method of finding the LCM of two or more numbers is shown below. Find the LCM(27, 36, 45, 60).

2	27 36 45 60
2	27 18 45 30
3	27 9 45 15
3	9 3 15 5
3	3 1 5 5
5	1 1 5 5
	1 1 1 1

Divide all even numbers by 2. If not divisible by 2, bring down. Repeat until none is divisible by 2.

Proceed to the next prime number and repeat the process.

Continue until the last row is all 1s.

LCM = $2^2 \cdot 3^3 \cdot 5$ (see the left column)

Use this method to find the following LCMs.
(a) LCM(21, 24, 63, 70)
(b) LCM(20, 36, 42, 33)
(c) LCM(15, 35, 42, 80)

8. In the following problems, you are given three pieces of information. Use these to answer the question.

(a) GCF(a, b) = 2×3, LCM(a, b) = $2^2 \times 3^3 \times 5$, $b = 2^2 \times 3 \times 5$. What is a?

(b) GCF(a, b) = $2^2 \times 7 \times 11$, LCM(a, b) = $2^5 \times 3^2 \times 5 \times 7^3 \times 11^2$, $b = 2^5 \times 3^2 \times 5 \times 7 \times 11$. What is a?

9. Using the Euclidean algorithm, find the following GCFs.

(a) GCF(24, 54)   (b) GCF(39, 91)
(c) GCF(72, 160)   (d) GCF(5291, 11951)

10. The factors of a number that are less than the number itself are called **proper factors**. The Pythagoreans classified numbers as deficient, abundant, or perfect, depending on the sum of their proper factors.

(a) A number is **deficient** if the sum of its proper factors is less than the number. For example, the proper factors of 4 are 1 and 2. Since $1 + 2 = 3 < 4$, 4 is a deficient number. What other numbers less than 25 are deficient?

(b) A number is **abundant** if the sum of its proper factors is greater than the number. Which numbers less than 25 are abundant?

(c) A number is **perfect** if the sum of its proper factors is equal to the number. Which number less than 25 is perfect?

11. Determine which of the following numbers are perfect.
(a) 48   (b) 96   (c) 496   (d) 2281

12. Two counting numbers are **relatively prime** if the greatest common factor of the two numbers is 1. Which of the following pairs of numbers are relatively prime?
(a) 4 and 9   (b) 24 and 123   (c) 12 and 45

Problems

13. What is the smallest whole number having exactly the following number of divisors?
(a) 1   (b) 2   (c) 3   (d) 4   (e) 5   (f) 6
(g) 7   (h) 8

14. Find six examples of whole numbers that have the following number of factors. Then try to characterize the set of numbers you found in each case.
(a) 2   (b) 3   (c) 4   (d) 5

15. Euclid (300 B.C.) proved that $2^{n-1}(2^n - 1)$ produced a perfect number [see Exercise 10(c)] whenever $2^n - 1$ is prime, where $n = 1, 2, 3, \ldots$. Find the first four such perfect numbers. (NOTE: Some 2000 years later, Euler proved that this formula produces all even perfect numbers.)

16. Find all whole numbers x such that GCF(24, x) = 1 and $1 \leq x \leq 24$.

17. Following recess the 1000 students of a school lined up and entered the school as follows: The first student opened all of the 1000 lockers in the school. The second student closed all lockers with even numbers. The third student "changed" all lockers that were numbered with multiples of 3 by closing those that were open and opening those that were closed. The fourth student changed each locker whose number was a multiple of 4, and so on. After all 1000 students had entered the building in this fashion, which lockers were left open?

18. George made enough money by selling candy bars at 15 cents each to buy several cans of pop at 48 cents each. If he had no money left over, what is the fewest number of candy bars he could have sold?

19. Three chickens and one duck sold for as much as two geese, whereas one chicken, two ducks, and three geese were sold together for $25.00. What was the price of each bird in an exact number of dollars?

20. Which, if any, of the numbers in the set {10, 20, 40, 80, 160, . . .} is a perfect square?

21. What is the largest three-digit prime all of whose digits are prime?

22. Take any four-digit palindrome whose digits are all nonzero and not all the same. Form a new palindrome by interchanging the unlike digits. Add these two numbers.

$$\textit{Example:} \quad \begin{array}{r} 8,448 \\ +4,884 \\ \hline 13,332 \end{array}$$

(a) Find a whole number greater than 1 that divides *every* such sum.

(b) Find the *largest* such whole number.

23. Fill in the following 4×4 additive magic square, which is comprised entirely of primes.

3	61	19	37
43	31	5	—
—	—	—	29
—	—	23	—

24. What is the least number of cards that could satisfy the following three conditions?

If all the cards are put in two equal piles, there is one card left over.

If all the cards are put in three equal piles, there is one card left over.

If all the cards are put in five equal piles, there is one card left over.

25. Show that the number 343 is divisible by 7. Then prove or disprove: Any three-digit number of the form $100a + 10b + a$, where $a + b = 7$, is divisible by 7.

26. In the set {18, 96, 54, 27, 42}, find the pair(s) of numbers with the greatest GCF and the pair(s) with the smallest LCM.

EXERCISE/PROBLEM SET 5.2—PART B

Exercises

1. 12^4 has how many factors?

2. **(a)** Factor 120 into primes.
   (b) Factor each divisor of 120 into primes.
   (c) What relationship exists between the prime factors in part (b) and the prime factors in part (a)?
   (d) Let $x = 11^5 \times 13^3$. If n is a divisor of x, what can you say about the prime factorization of n?

3. Use any method to find the following GCFs.
   (a) GCF(38, 68)
   (b) GCF(60, 126)
   (c) GCF(56, 120)
   (d) GCF(42, 385)
   (e) GCF(117, 195)
   (f) GCF(338, 507)
   (g) GCF(290, 609)
   (h) GCF(714, 1156)

4. Using a calculator method, find the following.
   (a) GCF(276, 54)
   (b) GCF(111, 111111)
   (c) GCF(399, 102)
   (d) (GCF(12345, 54323)

5. Use the prime factorization method to find the following LCMs.
   (a) LCM(15, 21)
   (b) LCM(14, 35)
   (c) LCM(75, 100)
   (d) LCM(66, 88)
   (e) LCM(13, 39)
   (f) LCM(21, 51)
   (g) LCM(130, 182)
   (h) LCM(410, 1024)

6. The GCF of two numbers is 3 and the LCM is 180. If one of the numbers is 45, what is the other number?

7. It is claimed that

   $$GCF(a, b) = GCF(a + b, LCM(a, b)).$$

   Determine if this is true for these pairs of numbers.
   (a) 36, 48   **(b)** 56, 72   **(c)** $2^5 \cdot 3^7$, $2^7 \cdot 3^4$

8. Using the Euclidean algorithm and your calculator, find the greatest common factor for each pair of numbers.
   (a) 2244 and 418   **(b)** 963 and 657
   (c) 7286 and 1684

9. **(a)** Complete the following table by listing the factors for the given numbers. Include 1 and the number itself as factors.
   (b) What kind of numbers have only two factors?
   (c) What kind of numbers have an odd number of factors?

Number	Factors	Number of Factors
1	1	1
2	1, 2	2
3		
4		
5		
6		
7		
8		
9		
10		
11		
12		
13		
14		
15		
16		

10. Identify the following numbers as deficient, abundant, or perfect. [See Exercise 10, Part A.]
    (a) 36   **(b)** 28   **(c)** 60   **(d)** 51

11. A pair of whole numbers is called **amicable** if each is the sum of the proper divisors of the other. For example, 284 and 220 are amicable since the proper divisors of 220 are 1, 2, 4, 5, 10, 11, 20, 22, 44, 55, 110, which sum to 284, whose proper divisors are 1, 2, 4, 71, 142, which sum to 220. Determine which of the following pairs are amicable.
    (a) 1184 and 1210   **(b)** 1254 and 1832
    (c) 2620 and 2924

12. If 17,296 is one of a pair of amicable numbers, what is the other one? Be sure to check your work.

13. Two numbers are said to be **betrothed** if the sum of all proper factors greater than 1 of one number equals the other, and vice versa. For example, 48 and 75 are betrothed since

    $$48 = \underbrace{3 + 5 + 15 + 25}$$

    proper factors of 75 except for 1

    and

    $$75 = \underbrace{2 + 3 + 4 + 6 + 8 + 12 + 16 + 24}$$

    proper factors of 48 except for 1

Determine which of the following pairs are betrothed.

(d) (140, 195)   (e) (1575, 1648)

(f) (2024, 2295)

14. (a) Show that 83,154,367 and 4 are relatively prime.

(b) Show that 165,342,985 and 13 are relatively prime.

(c) Show that 165,342,985 and 33 are relatively prime.

Problems

15. Let the letters p, q, and r represent different primes. Then p^2qr^3 has 24 divisors. So would p^{23}. Use p, q, and r to describe all whole numbers having exactly the following number of divisors.

(a) 2   (b) 3   (c) 4   (d) 5   (e) 6

(f) 12

16. Let a and b represent whole numbers. State the conditions on a and b that make the following statements true.

(a) GCF(a, b) = a (b) LCM(a, b) = a

(c) GCF(a, b) = $a \times b$ (d) LCM(a, b) = $a \times b$

17. If GCF(x, y) = 1, what is GCF(x^2, y^2)? Justify your answer.

18. It is claimed that every perfect number greater than 6 is the sum of consecutive odd cubes beginning with 1. For example, $28 = 1^3 + 3^3$. Determine if the statement above is true for the perfect numbers 496 and 8128.

19. Plato supposedly guessed (and may have proved) that there are only four relatively prime whole numbers that satisfy both of the following equations simultaneously.

$$x^2 + y^2 = z^2 \quad \text{and} \quad x^3 + y^3 + z^3 = w^3$$

If $x = 3$ and $y = 4$ are two of the numbers, what are z and w?

20. Tilda's car gets 34 miles per gallon and Naomi's gets 8 miles per gallon. When traveling from Washington, D.C., to Philadelphia, they both used a whole number of gallons of gasoline. How far is it from Philadelphia to Washington, D.C.?

21. Three neighborhood dogs barked consistently last night. Spot, Patches, and Lady began with a simultaneous bark at 11 P.M. Then Spot barked every 4 minutes, Patches every 3 minutes, and Lady every 5 minutes. Why did Mr. Jones suddenly awaken at midnight?

22. The numbers 2, 5, and 9 are factors of my locker number and there are 12 factors in all. What is my locker number, and why?

23. Which number less than 70 has the greatest number of factors?

24. The theory of biorhythm states that there are three "cycles" to your life:

The physical cycle: 23 days long

The emotional cycle: 28 days long

The intellectual cycle: 33 days long

If your cycles are together one day, in how many days will they be together again?

25. Show that the number 494 is divisible by 13. Then prove or disprove: Any three-digit number of the form $100a + 10b + a$, where $a + b = 13$, is divisible by 13.

26. A **Smith number** is a counting number the sum of whose digits is equal to the sum of all the digits of its prime factors. Prove that 4,937,775 (which was discovered by Harold Smith) is a Smith number.

27. (a) Draw a 2×3 rectangular array of squares. If one diagonal is drawn in, how many squares will the diagonal go through?

(b) Repeat for a 4×6 rectangular array.

(c) Generalize this problem to an $m \times n$ array of squares.

SOLUTION OF INITIAL PROBLEM

A major fast-food chain held a contest to promote sales. With each purchase a customer was given a card with a whole number less than 100 on it. A $100 prize was given to any person who presented cards whose numbers totaled 100. Below are several typical cards. Can you find a winning combination?

| 3 | 9 | 12 | 15 | 18 | 27 | 51 | 72 | 84 |

Can you suggest how the contest could be structured so that there would be at most 1000 winners throughout the country?

Strategy: Use Properties of Numbers

Perhaps you noticed something interesting about the numbers that were on sample cards—they are all multiples of 3. From work in this chapter, we know that the sum of two (hence any number of) multiples of 3 is a multiple of 3. Therefore, any combination of the given numbers will produce a sum that is a multiple of 3. Since 100 is not a multiple of 3, it is impossible to win with the given numbers. Although there are several ways to control the number of winners, a simple way is to include only 1000 cards with the number 1 on them.

Additional Problems Where the Strategy "Use Properties of Numbers" Is Useful

1. How old is Mary?
   - She is younger than 75 years old.
   - Her age is an odd number.
   - The sum of the digits of her age is 8.
   - Her age is a prime number.
   - She has three great-grandchildren.
2. A folding machine folds letters at a rate of 45 per minute and a stamping machine stamps folded letters at a rate of 60 per minute. What is the fewest number of each machine required so that all machines are kept busy?
3. Find infinitely many natural numbers each of which has exactly 91 factors.

WRITING/DISCUSSING FOR UNDERSTANDING

1. Describe the algorithm you use to determine the prime factorization of a large number using a calculator. Be certain to include all of your steps so that a student unfamiliar with your technique would be able to follow your directions.
2. When asked to list the prime numbers, many students will include the number 1. Based on the definition of a prime number, why is 1 not a prime? Could 1 be defined to be a prime? Develop a rationale to explain why 1 is excluded from being a prime number?

PROJECTS

1. Many books of math tables contain tables of prime numbers. Consult a table of primes (or write a computer program) to determine the number of primes between 300 and 399, between 400 and 499, and between 500 and 599. How many twin primes are in each interval? What is the largest gap between two consecutive primes in each of these intervals? Try some other intervals of 100 numbers to see if any patterns emerge.
2. Several unsolved problems are listed in the Focus On at the beginning of this chapter. Write an historical sketch of one of the problems. Also, seek out some of the most up-to-date number theory textbooks or interview a professor who does research in this area of mathematics to see if progress has been made on the solution of the problem.

CHAPTER REVIEW

Major Ideas

1. Primes are "building blocks" for the counting numbers.
2. Divisibility tests are very helpful when factoring.
3. The concepts of GCF and LCM will be useful in doing computations with fractions.
4. Number theory provides a rich source of interesting problems, both solved and unsolved, for students at all levels.

Following is a list of key vocabulary, notation, and ideas for this chapter. Mentally review these items and, where appropriate, write down the meaning of each term. Then restudy the material that you are unsure of before proceeding to take the chapter test.

SECTION 5.1:   PRIMES, COMPOSITES, AND TESTS FOR DIVISIBILITY

Vocabulary/Notation

Prime 185
Composite 189
Factor tree 190
Divides ($a \mid b$) 190
Does not divide ($a \nmid b$) 190

Divisor 191
Factor 191
Multiple 191
Is divisible by 191
Square root 196

Ideas

Sieve of Eratosthenes 189
Fundamental theorem of arithmetic 190
Tests for divisibility 191
Finding prime factorizations 196

SECTION 5.2: COUNTING FACTORS, GREATEST COMMON FACTOR, AND LEAST COMMON MULTIPLE

Vocabulary/Notation

Ideas

PEOPLE IN MATHEMATICS

Srinivasa Ramanujan (1887–1920) developed a passion for mathematics when he was a young man in India. Working from numerical examples, he arrived at astounding results in number theory. Yet he had little formal training beyond high school and had only vague notions of the principles of mathematical proof. In 1913 he sent some of his results to the English mathematician George Hardy, who was astounded at the raw genius of the work. Hardy arranged for the poverty-stricken young man to come to England. Hardy became his mentor and teacher, but later remarked, "I learned from him much more than he learned from me." After several years in England, Ramanujan's health declined. He went home to India in 1919 and died of tuberculosis the following year. On one occasion, Ramanujan was ill in bed. Hardy went to visit, arriving in taxicab number 1729. He remarked to Ramanujan that the number seemed rather dull, and he hoped it wasn't a bad omen. "No," said Ramanujan, "it is a very interesting number; it is the smallest number expressible as a sum of cubes in two different ways."

Constance Bowman Reid (1917–   ), Julia Bowman Robinson's older sister, became a high school English and journalism teacher. She gave up teaching after marriage to become a freelance writer. Constance became fascinated with number theory as a result of discussions with her mathematician sister Julia. Her first popular exposition of mathematics appeared in *Scientific American* in 1952; it was an article about finding perfect numbers using a computer. When it was published, one of the readers complained that *Scientific American* articles should be written by recognized authorities, not by housewives! Constance has written the popular books *From Zero to Infinity, A Long Way from Euclid,* and *Introduction to Higher Mathematics.* In recent years, she has written highly regarded biographies of the mathematicians Hilbert, Courant, and Neyman.

CHAPTER 5 TEST

Knowledge

1. True or false?
   (a) Every prime number is odd.
   (b) The sieve of Eratosthenes is used to find primes.
   (c) A number is divisible by 6 if it is divisible by 2 and 3.
   (d) A number is divisible by 8 if it is divisible by 4 and 2.
   (e) If $a \neq b$, then GCF$(a, b) <$ LCM(a, b).
   (f) The number of factors of n can be determined by the exponents in its prime factorization.
   (g) The prime factorization of a and b can be used to find the GCF and LCM of a and b.
   (h) The larger a number, the more prime factors it has.
   (i) The number 12 is a multiple of 36.
   (j) Every counting number has more multiples than factors.

Skill

2. Find the prime factorization of each of the following numbers.
   (a) 120   (b) 10,800   (c) 819
3. Test the following for divisibility by 2, 3, 4, 5, 6, 8, 9, 10, and 11.
   (a) 11,223,344   (b) 6,543,210   (c) $2^3 \cdot 3^4 \cdot 5^6$

4. Determine the number of factors for each of the following numbers.
   (a) 360   (b) 216   (c) 900
5. Find the GCF and LCM of each of the following pairs of numbers.
   (a) 144, 120   (b) 147, 70
   (c) $2^3 \cdot 3^5 \cdot 5^7$, $2^7 \cdot 3^4 \cdot 5^3$ (d) 2419, 2173

Understanding

6. Explain how the sieve of Eratosthenes can be used to find composite numbers.
7. Is it possible to find nonzero whole numbers x and y such that $7^x = 11^y$? Why or why not?
8. Show that the sum of any four consecutive counting numbers must have a factor of 2.

Problem Solving/Application

9. Find the smallest number that has factors of 2, 3, 4, 5, 6, 7, 8, 9, and 10.
10. The primes 2 and 5 differ by 3. Prove that this is the only pair of primes whose difference is 3.
11. If $a = 2^2 \cdot 3^3$ and the LCM(a, b) is 1080, what is the (a) smallest and (b) the largest that b can be?

Fractions

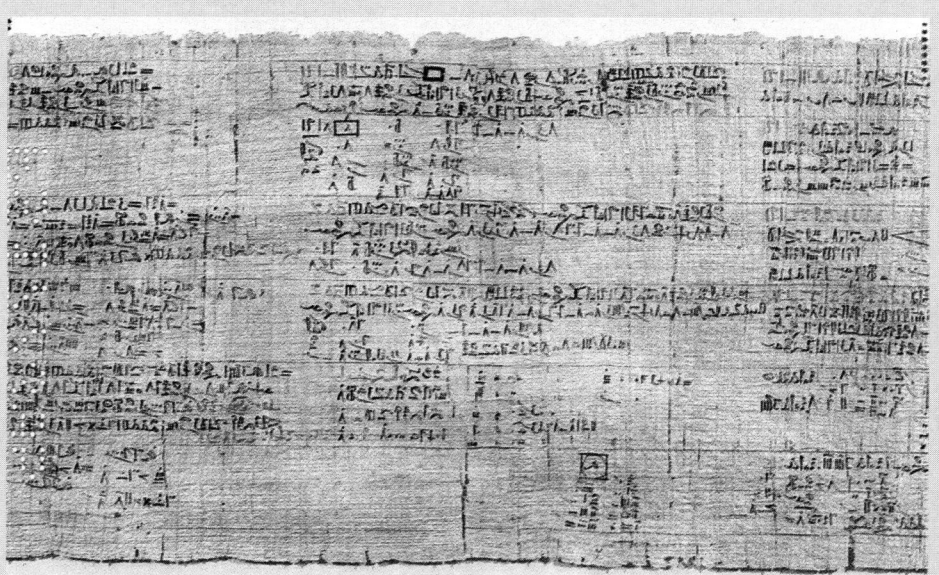

The Rhind Papyrus

Fractions: A Historical Sketch

The first extensive treatment of fractions known to us appears in the Ahmes (or Rhind) Papyrus (1600 B.C.), which contains the work of Egyptian mathematicians. The Egyptians expressed ratios in unit fractions, that is, fractions in which the numerator is 1. For example, the ratio $2:43$ was expressed as $\frac{1}{42} + \frac{1}{86} + \frac{1}{129} + \frac{1}{301}$, rather than our modern fraction $\frac{2}{43}$. Of course, the Egyptians used hieroglyphics to represent these unit fractions; for example,

$$\frac{1}{5} = \quad \frac{1}{10} = \quad \frac{1}{21} = $$

Our present way of expressing fractions is probably due to the Hindus. Brahmagupta (circa A.D. 630) wrote the symbol $\frac{2}{3}$ (with no bar) to represent "two-thirds." The Arabs introduced the "bar" to separate the two parts of a fraction, but this first attempt did not catch on. Later, due to typesetting constraints, the bar was omitted and, at times, the fraction "two-thirds" was written as 2/3.

The name "fraction" came from the Latin word *frangere,* which means "to break." The term "common fraction" was used to refer to fractions employed in trade as opposed to the special collection of fractions used by astronomers. The notion of an improper fraction, such as $\frac{3}{2}$, is a fairly recent development, perhaps arising first in the sixteenth century. The names "numerator" and "denominator" also came to us from Latin writers.

Adding and subtracting fractions was generally done by using the product of the denominators as the common denominator. It was not until the seventeenth century that the "least" common denominator method was used extensively. Although the multiplication of fractions as we know it has been unchanged for centuries, the division of fractions was carried out in two different ways, neither of which is the method currently used.

Method 1 (Common Denominator)

$$\frac{2}{3} \div \frac{3}{4} = \frac{8}{12} \div \frac{9}{12} = \frac{8}{9}.$$

Method 2 (Cross-Multiplication)

$$\frac{2}{3} \quad \frac{3}{4} = \frac{8}{9}.$$

Although the Hindu and Arab writers were aware of the "invert the divisor and multiply" algorithm for division, this method dropped out of sight for 300 to 400 years, only to reappear and then come into favor in the seventeenth century.

STRATEGY 11: SOLVE AN EQUIVALENT PROBLEM

One's point of view or interpretation of a problem can often change a seemingly difficult problem into one that is easily solvable. One way to solve the next problem is by drawing a picture or, perhaps, by actually finding some representative blocks to try various combinations. On the other hand, another approach is to see if the problem can be restated in an equivalent form, say, using numbers. Then if the equivalent problem can be solved, the solution can be interpreted to yield an answer to the original problem.

Initial Problem

A child has a set of 10 cubical blocks. The lengths of the edges are 1 cm, 2 cm, 3 cm, . . . , 10 cm. Using all the cubes, can the child build two towers of the same height by stacking one cube upon another? Why or why not?

Clues

The Solve an Equivalent Problem strategy may be appropriate when:

- You can find an equivalent problem that is easier to solve.
- A problem is related to another problem you have solved previously.
- A problem can be represented in a more familiar setting.
- A geometric problem can be represented algebraically, or vice versa.
- Physical problems can easily be represented with numbers or symbols.

A solution of the Initial Problem above appears on page 261.

INTRODUCTION

Chapters 2 to 5 have been devoted to the study of the system of whole numbers. Understanding the system of whole numbers is necessary to ensure success in mathematics later. This chapter is devoted to the study of fractions. Fractions were invented because it was not convenient to describe many problem situations using only whole numbers. As you study this chapter, note the importance that the whole numbers play in helping to make fraction concepts easy to understand.

6.1

THE SET OF FRACTIONS

The Concept of a Fraction

There are many times when whole numbers do not fully describe a mathematical situation. For example, using whole numbers, try to answer the following questions, which refer to Figure 6.1: (1) How much pizza is left? (2) How much of the stick is shaded? (3) How much paint is left in the can?

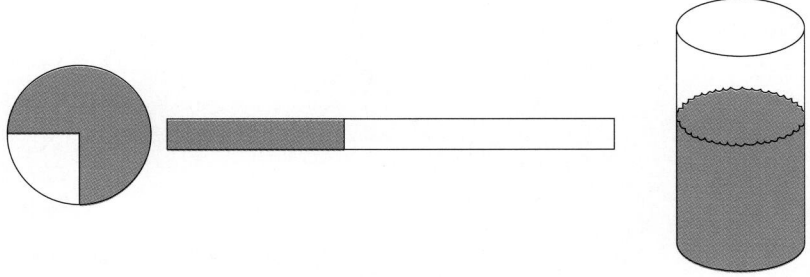

FIGURE 6.1

Although it is not easy to provide whole-number answers to the questions above, the situations in Figure 6.1 can be conveniently described using fractions. Reconsider the questions above in light of the subdivisions added in Figure 6.2. Typical answers to these questions are (1) "Three-fourths of the pizza is left." (2) "Four-tenths of the stick is shaded." (3) "The paint can is three-fifths full."

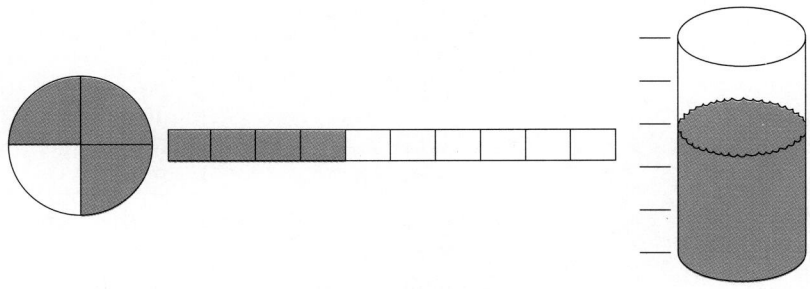

FIGURE 6.2

The term "fraction" is used in two distinct ways in elementary mathematics. Initially, fractions are used as numerals to indicate the number of parts of a whole to be considered. In Figure 6.2, the pizza was cut into 4 equivalent pieces and 3 remain. In this case we use the fraction $\frac{3}{4}$ to represent the 3 out of 4 equivalent pieces (i.e., equivalent in size). The use of a fraction as a numeral in this way is commonly called the "part-to-whole" model. Succinctly, if a and b are whole numbers, where $b \neq 0$, then the fraction $\frac{a}{b}$, or a/b, represents a of b equivalent parts; a is called the **numerator** and b is called the **denominator**. The term "equivalent parts" means equivalent in some attribute, such as length, area, volume, number, or weight, depending on the composition of the whole and appropriate parts. In Figure 6.2, since 4 of 10 equivalent parts of the stick are shaded, the fraction $\frac{4}{10}$ describes the shaded part when it is compared to the whole stick. Also, the fraction $\frac{3}{5}$ describes the filled portion of the paint can in Figure 6.2. The fraction $\frac{7}{2}$ would mean that an object was divided into 2 equivalent parts and 7 such parts are designated.

As with whole numbers, a fraction also has an *abstract* meaning as a number. What do you think of when you look at the relative amounts represented by the shaded regions in Figure 6.3?

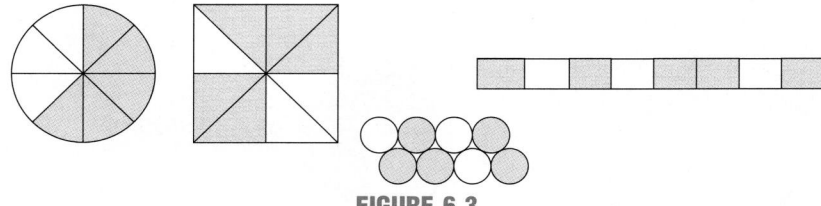

FIGURE 6.3

Although the various diagrams are different in size and shape, they share a common attribute, namely that 5 of 8 equivalent parts are shaded. That is, the same *relative amount* is shaded. This attribute can be represented by the fraction $\frac{5}{8}$. Thus, in addition to representing parts of a whole, a fraction is viewed as a number representing a relative amount. Hence we make the following definition.

Definition

Fractions

A **fraction** is a number that can be represented by an ordered pair of whole numbers $\frac{a}{b}$ (or a/b), where $b \neq 0$. In set notation, the **set of fractions** is

$$F = \left\{ \frac{a}{b} \,\middle|\, a \text{ and } b \text{ are whole numbers, } b \neq 0 \right\}.$$

Before proceeding with the computational aspects of fractions as numbers, it is instructive to comment further on the complexity of this topic, namely, viewing fractions as numerals and as numbers. Recall that the whole number three was the attribute common to all sets that match the set $\{a, b, c\}$. Thus if a child who understands the concept of a whole number is shown a set of three objects, the child will answer the question "How many objects?" with the word "Three" regardless of the size, shape, color, and so on, of the objects themselves. That is, it is the "numerousness" of the set on which the child is focusing.

With fractions, there are two attributes that the child must observe. First, when considering a fraction *as a number,* the focus is on relative amount. For example, in Figure 6.4, the relative amount represented by the various shaded regions is described by the fraction $\frac{1}{4}$ (which is considered as a number). Notice that $\frac{1}{4}$ describes the relative amount shaded without regard to size, shape, arrangement, orientation, number of equivalent parts, and so on; thus it is the "numerousness" of a fraction on which we are focusing.

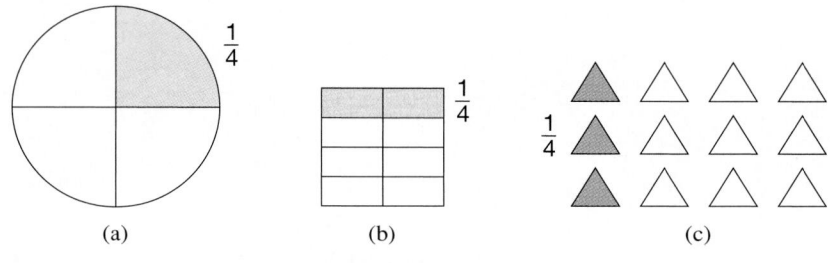

FIGURE 6.4

Second, when considering a fraction *as a numeral* representing a part-to-whole relationship, many numerals can be used for the relationship. For example, the three diagrams in Figure 6.4 can be labeled differently (Figure 6.5).

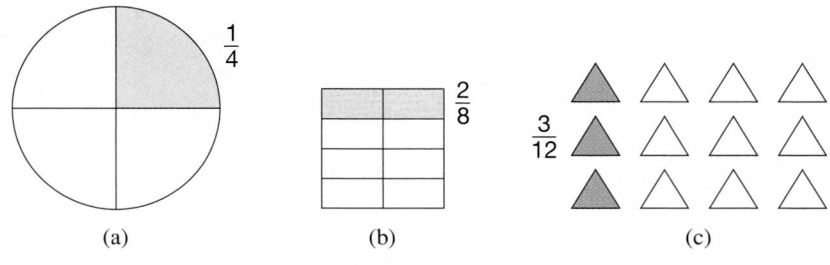

FIGURE 6.5

In Figure 6.5(b) and (c), the shaded regions have been renamed using the fractions $\frac{2}{8}$ and $\frac{3}{12}$, respectively, to call attention to the different subdivisions. The notion of fraction as a numeral displaying a part-to-whole relationship can be merged with the concept of fraction as a number. That is, the fraction (number) $\frac{1}{4}$ can also be thought of and represented by any of the fractions $\frac{2}{18}, \frac{3}{12}, \frac{4}{16}$, and so on. Figure 6.6 brings this into sharper focus.

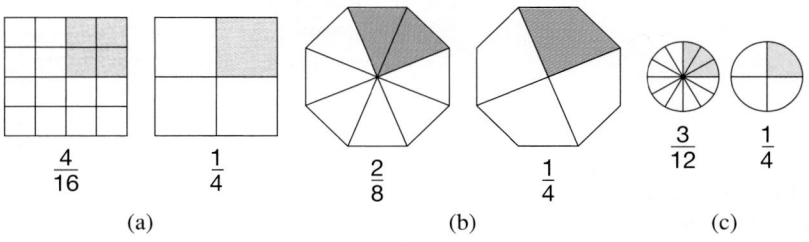

FIGURE 6.6

In each of the pairs of diagrams in Figure 6.6, the same relative amount is shaded, although the subdivisions into equivalent parts and the sizes of the diagrams are different. As suggested by the shaded regions, the fractions $\frac{4}{16}$, $\frac{2}{8}$, and $\frac{3}{12}$ all represent the same relative amount as $\frac{1}{4}$.

The diagrams in Figure 6.6 were different shapes and sizes. **Fraction strips** also can be used to visualize fractional parts (Figure 6.7). The advantage of this model is that the unit strips are the same size—only the shading and number of subdivisions vary.

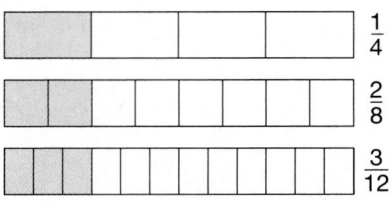

FIGURE 6.7

It is useful to have a simple test to determine if fractions such as $\frac{2}{8}$, $\frac{3}{12}$, and $\frac{4}{16}$ represent the same relative amount without having to draw a picture of each representation. There are two approaches that can be taken. First, observe that $\frac{2}{8} = \frac{1 \cdot 2}{4 \cdot 2}$, $\frac{3}{12} = \frac{1 \cdot 3}{4 \cdot 3}$, and $\frac{4}{16} = \frac{1 \cdot 4}{4 \cdot 4}$. These equations illustrate the fact that $\frac{2}{8}$ can be obtained from $\frac{1}{4}$ by equally subdividing each portion of a representation of $\frac{1}{4}$ by 2 [Figure 6.6(b)]. A similar argument can be applied to the equations $\frac{3}{12} = \frac{1 \cdot 3}{4 \cdot 3}$ [Figure 6.6(c)] and $\frac{4}{16} = \frac{1 \cdot 4}{4 \cdot 4}$ [Figure 6.6(a)]. Thus it appears that any fraction of the form $\frac{1 \cdot n}{4 \cdot n}$, where n is a counting number, represents the same relative amount as $\frac{1}{4}$, or that $\frac{an}{bn} = \frac{a}{b}$, in general. When $\frac{an}{bn}$ is replaced with $\frac{a}{b}$, where $n \neq 1$, we say that $\frac{an}{bn}$ has been **simplified**.

To determine if $\frac{3}{12}$ and $\frac{4}{16}$ are equal, we can simplify each of them: $\frac{3}{12} = \frac{1}{4}$ and $\frac{4}{16} = \frac{1}{4}$. Since they both equal $\frac{1}{4}$, we can write $\frac{3}{12} = \frac{4}{16}$. Alternatively, we can view $\frac{3}{12}$ and $\frac{4}{16}$ as $\frac{3 \cdot 16}{12 \cdot 16}$ and $\frac{4 \cdot 12}{16 \cdot 12}$ instead. Since the numerators $3 \cdot 16 = 48$ and $4 \cdot 12 = 48$ are equal and the denominators are the same, namely $12 \cdot 16$, the two fractions $\frac{3}{12}$ and $\frac{4}{16}$ must be equal. As the next diagram suggests, the numbers $3 \cdot 16$ and $4 \cdot 12$ are called the **cross-products** of the fractions $\frac{3}{12}$ and $\frac{4}{16}$.

$$\frac{3}{12} \diagdown\!\!\!\!\!\diagup \frac{4}{16}$$

This technique, which can be used for any pair of fractions, leads to the following definition of fraction equality.

Definition

Fraction Equality

Let $\dfrac{a}{b}$ and $\dfrac{c}{d}$ be any fractions. Then

$$\dfrac{a}{b} = \dfrac{c}{d} \text{ if and only if } ad = bc.$$

In words, two fractions are equal if and only if their **cross-products**, that is, products ad and bc obtained by **cross-multiplication**, are equal. The first method described above for determining if two fractions are equal is an immediate consequence of this definition since $a(bn) = b(an)$ by associativity and commutativity. This is summarized next.

Theorem   Let $\dfrac{a}{b}$ be any fraction and n a nonzero whole number. Then

$$\dfrac{a}{b} = \dfrac{an}{bn} = \dfrac{na}{nb}.$$

It is important to note that this theorem can be used in two ways: (1) to replace the fraction $\dfrac{a}{b}$ with $\dfrac{an}{bn}$, and (2) to replace the fraction $\dfrac{an}{bn}$ with $\dfrac{a}{b}$. Occasionally, the term "reducing" is used to describe the process in (2). However, the term "reducing" can be misleading since fractions are not reduced in size (the relative amount they represent), but only in complexity (the numerators and denominators are smaller).

EXAMPLE 6.1   Verify the following equations using the definition of fraction equality or the preceding theorem.

(a) $\dfrac{5}{6} = \dfrac{25}{30}$ (b) $\dfrac{27}{36} = \dfrac{54}{72}$ (c) $\dfrac{16}{48} = \dfrac{1}{3}$

Solution

(a) $\dfrac{5}{6} = \dfrac{5 \cdot 5}{6 \cdot 5} = \dfrac{25}{30}$ by the preceding theorem.

(b) $\dfrac{54}{72} = \dfrac{27 \cdot 2}{36 \cdot 2} = \dfrac{27}{36}$ by simplifying. Alternatively, $\dfrac{27}{36} = \dfrac{3 \cdot 9}{4 \cdot 9} = \dfrac{3}{4}$ and $\dfrac{54}{72} = \dfrac{3 \cdot 18}{4 \cdot 18} = \dfrac{3}{4}$, so $\dfrac{27}{36} = \dfrac{54}{72}$.

(c) $\dfrac{16}{48} = \dfrac{1}{3}$ since their cross-products, $16 \cdot 3$ and $48 \cdot 1$, are equal.   ■

Fraction equality can readily be checked on a calculator using an alternate version of cross-multiplication, namely $\frac{a}{b} = \frac{c}{d}$ if and only if $\frac{ad}{b} = c$. Thus the equality of $\frac{20}{36} = \frac{30}{54}$ can be checked by pressing 20 $\boxed{\times}$ 54 $\boxed{\div}$ 36 $\boxed{=}$ $\boxed{}$ 30. Since 30 obtained in this way equals the numerator of $\frac{30}{54}$, the two fractions are equal.

Since $\frac{a}{b} = \frac{an}{bn}$ for $n = 1, 2, 3, \ldots$, every fraction has an infinite number of representations (numerals). For example,

$$\frac{1}{2} = \frac{2}{4} = \frac{3}{6} = \frac{4}{8} = \frac{5}{10} = \frac{6}{12} = \cdots$$

are different numerals for the number $\frac{1}{2}$. In fact, another way to view a fraction as a number is to think of the idea that is common to all of its various representations. That is, the fraction $\frac{2}{3}$, as a *number*, is the idea that one associates with the set of all fractions, as *numerals*, that are equivalent to $\frac{2}{3}$, namely $\frac{2}{3}, \frac{4}{6}, \frac{6}{9}, \frac{8}{12}, \ldots$. Notice that the term "equal" refers to fractions as numbers, while the term "equivalent" refers to fractions as numerals.

Every whole number is a fraction and hence has an infinite number of fraction representations. For example,

$$1 = \frac{1}{1} = \frac{2}{2} = \frac{3}{3} = \cdots, 2 = \frac{2}{1} = \frac{4}{2} = \frac{6}{3} = \cdots, 0 = \frac{0}{1} = \frac{0}{2} = \cdots,$$

and so on. Thus the set of fractions extends the set of whole numbers.

A fraction is written in its **simplest form** or **lowest terms** when its numerator and denominator have no common prime factors.

EXAMPLE 6.2 Find the simplest form of the following fractions.

(a) $\frac{12}{18}$ **(b)** $\frac{36}{56}$ **(c)** $\frac{9}{31}$ **(d)** $(2^3 \cdot 3^5 \cdot 5^7)/(2^6 \cdot 3^4 \cdot 7)$

Solution

(a) $\frac{12}{18} = \frac{2 \cdot 6}{3 \cdot 6} = \frac{2}{3}$

(b) $\frac{36}{56} = \frac{18 \cdot 2}{28 \cdot 2} = \frac{18}{28} = \frac{9 \cdot 2}{14 \cdot 2} = \frac{9}{14}$

(c) $\frac{9}{31}$ is in simplest form since 9 and 31 have only 1 as a common factor.

(d) To write $(2^3 \cdot 3^5 \cdot 5^7)/(2^6 \cdot 3^4 \cdot 7)$ in simplest form, first find the GCF of $2^3 \cdot 3^5 \cdot 5^7$ and $2^6 \cdot 3^4 \cdot 7$:

$$\text{GCF}(2^3 \cdot 3^5 \cdot 5^7, 2^6 \cdot 3^4 \cdot 7) = 2^3 \cdot 3^4.$$

Then

$$\frac{2^3 \cdot 3^5 \cdot 5^7}{2^6 \cdot 3^4 \cdot 7} = \frac{(3 \cdot 5^7)(2^3 \cdot 3^4)}{(2^3 \cdot 7)(2^3 \cdot 3^4)} = \frac{3 \cdot 5^7}{2^3 \cdot 7}.$$

■

Fractions with numerators greater than or equal to their denominators fall into two categories. The fractions $\frac{1}{1}, \frac{2}{2}, \frac{3}{3}, \frac{4}{4}, \ldots$, in which the numerators and denominators are equal, represent the whole number 1. Fractions where the numerators are greater than the denominators are called **improper fractions**. For example, $\frac{7}{2}, \frac{8}{5}$, and $\frac{117}{35}$ are improper fractions. Figure 6.8 illustrates a model for $\frac{7}{2}$ because seven halves are shaded where one shaded circle represents one unit. The diagram in Figure 6.8 illustrates that $\frac{7}{2}$ can also be viewed as 3 wholes plus $\frac{1}{2}$, or $3\frac{1}{2}$. A combination of a whole number with a fraction juxtaposed to its right is called a **mixed number**. Mixed numbers will be studied in Section 6.2.

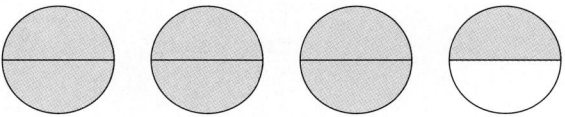

FIGURE 6.8

Scientific/fraction calculators can be used to convert improper fractions to mixed numbers. For example, to convert $\frac{1234}{378}$ to a mixed number in its simplest form on a fraction calculator, press 1234 $\boxed{a\,b/c}$ 378 $\boxed{=}$ $\boxed{3\_50\lrcorner 189}$. The result is $3\frac{50}{189}$ in simplest form. For scientific calculators, 1234 $\boxed{\div}$ 378 $\boxed{=}$ $\boxed{3.2645502}$ shows the whole-number part, namely 3, together with a decimal fraction. The calculation 1234 $\boxed{-}$ 3 $\boxed{\times}$ 378 $\boxed{=}$ $\boxed{100}$ gives the numerator of the fraction part; thus $\frac{1234}{378} = 3\frac{100}{378}$, which is $3\frac{50}{189}$ in simplest form.

Ordering Fractions

The concepts of "less than" and "greater than" in fractions are extensions of the respective whole-number concepts. Fraction strips can be used to order fractions (Figure 6.9).

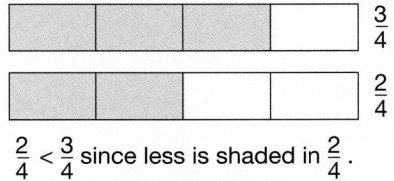

$\frac{2}{4} < \frac{3}{4}$ since less is shaded in $\frac{2}{4}$.

FIGURE 6.9

Next consider the three pairs of fractions on the **fraction number line** in Figure 6.10.

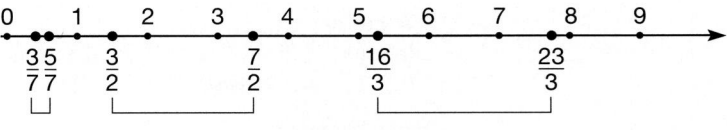

FIGURE 6.10

As it was in the case of whole numbers, the smaller of two fractions is to the left of the larger fraction on the fraction number line. Also, the three examples in Figure 6.10 suggest the following definition, where fractions having common denominators can be compared simply by comparing their numerators (which are whole numbers).

Definition

Less Than for Fractions

Let $\dfrac{a}{c}$ and $\dfrac{b}{c}$ be any fractions. Then $\dfrac{a}{c} < \dfrac{b}{c}$ if and only if $a < b$.

For example, $\frac{3}{7} < \frac{5}{7}$ since $3 < 5$, $\frac{4}{13} < \frac{10}{13}$ since $4 < 10$, and so on. The numbers $\frac{2}{7}$ and $\frac{4}{13}$ can be compared by getting a common denominator.

$$\frac{2}{7} = \frac{2 \cdot 13}{7 \cdot 13} = \frac{26}{91} \quad \text{and} \quad \frac{4}{13} = \frac{4 \cdot 7}{13 \cdot 7} = \frac{28}{91}.$$

NOTE: Although the definition is stated for "less than," a corresponding statement holds for "greater than." Similar statements hold for "less than or equal to" and "greater than or equal to." Since $\frac{26}{91} < \frac{28}{91}$, we conclude that $\frac{2}{7} < \frac{4}{13}$.

This last example suggests a convenient shortcut for comparing any two fractions. To compare $\frac{2}{7}$ and $\frac{4}{13}$, we compared $\frac{26}{91}$ and $\frac{28}{91}$, and eventually, 26 and 28. But $26 = 2 \cdot 13$ and $28 = 7 \cdot 4$. In general, this example suggests the following theorem.

Theorem

Cross Multiplication of Fraction Inequality

Let $\dfrac{a}{b}$ and $\dfrac{c}{d}$ be any fractions. Then $\dfrac{a}{b} < \dfrac{c}{d}$ if and only if $ad < bc$.

Notice that this theorem reduces the ordering of fractions to the ordering of whole numbers. Also, since $\dfrac{a}{b} < \dfrac{c}{d}$ if and only if $\dfrac{c}{d} > \dfrac{a}{b}$, we can observe that $\dfrac{c}{d} > \dfrac{a}{b}$ if and only if $bc > ad$.

EXAMPLE 6.3   Arrange in order.
(a) $\frac{7}{8}$ and $\frac{9}{11}$ **(b)** $\frac{17}{32}$ and $\frac{19}{40}$

Solution
(a) $\frac{7}{8} < \frac{9}{11}$ if and only if $7 \cdot 11 < 8 \cdot 9$. But $77 > 72$; therefore, $\frac{7}{8} > \frac{9}{11}$.
(b) $17 \cdot 40 = 680$ and $32 \cdot 19 = 608$. Since $32 \cdot 19 < 17 \cdot 40$, we have $\frac{19}{40} < \frac{17}{32}$.

Keep in mind that this procedure is just a shortcut for finding common denominators and comparing the numerators.

Cross-multiplication of fraction inequality can also be adapted to a calculator as follows: $\frac{a}{b} < \frac{c}{d}$ if and only if $\frac{ad}{b} < c$ (or $\frac{a}{b} > \frac{c}{d}$ if and only if $\frac{ad}{b} > c$). To order $\frac{17}{32}$ and $\frac{19}{40}$ using a fraction calculator, press 17 $\boxed{a \ ^b/_c}$ 32 $\boxed{\times}$ 40 $\boxed{=}$ $\boxed{\quad 21\_1\_4}$. Since $21\frac{1}{4} > 19$, we conclude that $\frac{17}{32} > \frac{19}{40}$. On a decimal calculator, the following sequence leads to a similar result: 17 $\boxed{\times}$ 40 $\boxed{\div}$ 32 $\boxed{=}$ $\boxed{\quad 21.25}$. Since 21.25 is greater than 19, $\frac{17}{32} > \frac{19}{40}$. Ordering fractions using decimal equivalents, which is shown next, will be covered in Chapter 7. In this case, 17 $\boxed{\div}$ 32 $\boxed{=}$ $\boxed{\quad 0.53125}$ and 19 $\boxed{\div}$ 40 $\boxed{=}$ $\boxed{\quad 0.475}$. Therefore, $\frac{19}{40} < \frac{17}{32}$ since $0.475 < 0.53125$. Finally, one could have ordered these two fractions mentally by observing that $\frac{19}{40}$ is less than $\frac{1}{2}$ ($= \frac{20}{40}$), whereas $\frac{17}{32}$ is greater than $\frac{1}{2}$ ($= \frac{16}{32}$).

On the whole-number line, there are gaps between the whole numbers (Figure 6.11).

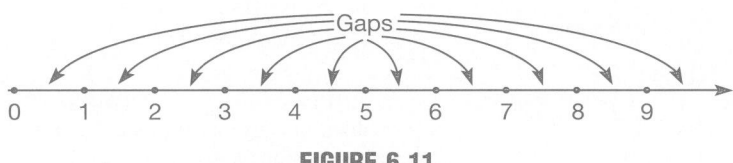

FIGURE 6.11

However, when fractions are introduced to make up the **fraction number line**, many new fractions appear in these gaps (Figure 6.12).

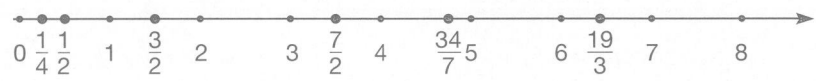

FIGURE 6.12

Unlike the case with whole numbers, it can be shown that there is a fraction between any two fractions. For example, consider $\frac{3}{4}$ and $\frac{5}{6}$. Since $\frac{3}{4} = \frac{18}{24}$ and $\frac{5}{6} = \frac{20}{24}$, we have that $\frac{19}{24}$ is between $\frac{3}{4}$ and $\frac{5}{6}$. Now consider $\frac{18}{24}$ and $\frac{19}{24}$. These equal $\frac{36}{48}$ and $\frac{38}{48}$, respectively; thus $\frac{37}{48}$ is between $\frac{3}{4}$ and $\frac{5}{6}$ also. Continuing in this manner, one can show that there are infinitely many fractions between $\frac{3}{4}$ and $\frac{5}{6}$. From this it follows that there are *infinitely* many fractions between any two different fractions.

EXAMPLE 6.4 Find a fraction between these pairs of fractions.
(a) $\frac{7}{11}$ and $\frac{8}{11}$ **(b)** $\frac{9}{13}$ and $\frac{12}{17}$

Solution
(a) $\frac{7}{11} = \frac{14}{22}$ and $\frac{8}{11} = \frac{16}{22}$. Hence $\frac{15}{22}$ is between $\frac{7}{11}$ and $\frac{8}{11}$.
(b) $\frac{9}{13} = \frac{9 \cdot 17}{13 \cdot 17} = \frac{153}{13 \cdot 17}$ and $\frac{12}{17} = \frac{12 \cdot 13}{17 \cdot 13} = \frac{156}{17 \cdot 13}$. Hence $\frac{154}{13 \cdot 17}$ or $\frac{155}{13 \cdot 17}$ is between $\frac{9}{13}$ and $\frac{12}{17}$.

Sometimes students incorrectly add numerators and denominators to find the sum of two fractions. It is interesting, though, that this simple technique does provide an easy way to find a fraction between two given fractions. For example, for fractions $\frac{2}{3}$ and $\frac{3}{4}$, the number $\frac{5}{7}$ satisfies $\frac{2}{3} < \frac{5}{7} < \frac{3}{4}$ since $2 \cdot 7 < 3 \cdot 5$ and $5 \cdot 4 < 7 \cdot 3$. This idea is generalized next.

> **Theorem** Let $\dfrac{a}{b}$ and $\dfrac{c}{d}$ be any fractions, where $\dfrac{a}{b} < \dfrac{c}{d}$. Then
>
> $$\frac{a}{b} < \frac{a + c}{b + d} < \frac{c}{d}.$$

Proof

Let $\dfrac{a}{b} < \dfrac{c}{d}$. Then we have $ad < bc$. From this inequality, it follows that $ad + ab < bc + ab$, or $a(b + d) < b(a + c)$. By cross-multiplication of fraction inequality, this last inequality implies $\dfrac{a}{b} < \dfrac{a + c}{b + d}$, which is "half" of what we are to prove. The other half can be proved in a similar fashion.   ∎

To find a fraction between $\frac{9}{13}$ and $\frac{12}{17}$ using this theorem, add the numerators and denominators to obtain $\frac{21}{30}$. This theorem shows that there is a fraction between any two fractions. The fact that there is a fraction between any two fractions is called the **density property** of fractions.

MATHEMATICAL MORSEL

Although decimals are prevalent in our monetary system, the stock market continues to use fractions involving sixteenths, eighths, fourths, and halves. It has been suggested that tradition was based on the Spanish milled dollar coin and its fractional parts that were used in our American colonies. Its fractional parts were called "bits" and each bit had a value of $12\frac{1}{2}$ cents (thus a quarter is known as "two bits"). Some also believe that this fraction system evolved from the British shilling and pence. A shilling was one-fourth of a dollar and a sixpence was one-eighth of a dollar, or $12\frac{1}{2}$ cents.

EXERCISE/PROBLEM SET 6.1—PART A

Exercises

1. In this section fractions were represented using equivalent parts. Another representation uses a set model. In the following set of objects, four out of the total of five objects are triangles.

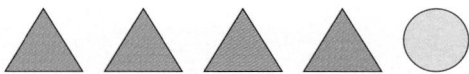

We could say that $\frac{4}{5}$ of the objects are triangles. This interpretation of fractions compares part of a set with all of the set. Draw pictures to represent the following fractions.

(a) $\frac{3}{5}$ (b) $\frac{3}{7}$ (c) $\frac{1}{3}$

2. Fractions can also be represented on the number line by selecting a unit length and subdividing the interval into equal parts. For example, to locate the fraction $\frac{2}{5}$, subdivide the interval from 0 to 1 into five parts and mark off two.

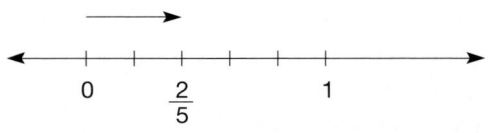

Represent the following fractions on a number line.

(a) $\frac{4}{5}$ (b) $\frac{2}{3}$ (c) $\frac{3}{8}$ (d) $\frac{7}{10}$

3. Does the picture below represent $\frac{3}{4}$? Explain.

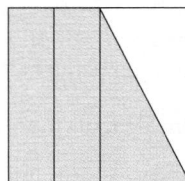

4. Fill in the blank with the correct fraction.
   (a) 10 cents is _____ of a dollar.
   (b) 15 minutes is _____ of an hour.
   (c) If you sleep eight hours each night, you spend _____ of a day sleeping.
   (d) Using the information in part (c), what part of a year do you sleep?

5. Figure 6.3 uses an area model to show the equality of fractions. Use a similar area model to show that $\frac{5}{8} = \frac{15}{24}$.

6. (a) List six different fractions that name the whole number 4.
   (b) List five different fractions that are equivalent to $\frac{4}{9}$.

7. Determine if the following pairs are equal by writing each in simplest form.
   (a) $\frac{5}{8}$ and $\frac{625}{1000}$ (b) $\frac{11}{18}$ and $\frac{275}{450}$
   (c) $\frac{24}{36}$ and $\frac{50}{72}$ (d) $\frac{14}{98}$ and $\frac{8}{56}$

8. Determine if the following pairs are equal by changing both to the same denominator.
   (a) $\frac{3}{25}$ and $\frac{1}{9}$ (b) $\frac{0}{5}$ and $\frac{0}{12}$
   (c) $\frac{21}{86}$ and $\frac{31}{129}$ (d) $\frac{7}{20}$ and $\frac{56}{160}$

9. Rewrite in simplest form.
   (a) $\frac{21}{28}$ (b) $\frac{49}{56}$ (c) $\frac{108}{156}$ (d) $\frac{220}{100}$ (e) $\frac{189}{153}$
   (f) $\frac{294}{63}$ (g) $\frac{480}{672}$ (h) $\frac{3335}{230}$

10. Rewrite as a mixed number in simplest form.
   (a) $\frac{525}{96}$ (b) $\frac{1234}{432}$
   (c) $\frac{2332}{444}$ (d) $\frac{8976}{144}$

11. Determine which of the following pairs are equal.
   (a) $\frac{349}{568}, \frac{569}{928}$ (b) $\frac{734}{957}, \frac{468}{614}$
   (c) $\frac{156}{558}, \frac{52}{186}$ (d) $\frac{882}{552}, \frac{147}{92}$

12. Which is greater, $\frac{4}{27}$ or $\frac{1}{7}$? How did you decide?

13. (a) Arrange each of the following from smallest to largest.
   (i) $\frac{11}{17}, \frac{13}{17}, \frac{12}{17}$ (ii) $\frac{1}{5}, \frac{1}{6}, \frac{1}{7}$
   (iii) $\frac{4}{7}, \frac{7}{13}, \frac{14}{25}$ (iv) $\frac{3}{11}, \frac{7}{23}, \frac{2}{9}, \frac{5}{18}$
   (b) What patterns do you observe in parts (i) and (ii)?

14. Use the cross-multiplication property for fraction inequality to order the following sets of fractions from smallest to largest.
   (a) $\frac{17}{23}, \frac{51}{68}$ (b) $\frac{43}{567}, \frac{50}{687}$
   (c) $\frac{214}{897}, \frac{597}{2511}$ (d) $\frac{93}{2811}, \frac{3}{87}, \frac{531}{16,134}$

15. According to Bureau of the Census data, in 1990 in the United States there were about

92,000,000 households
51,000,000 married-couple households
3,100,000 family households with a male householder
11,000,000 family households with a female householder
23,000,000 households consisting of one person

(Note: Figures have been rounded to make calculations easier.)
   (a) What fraction of U.S. households in 1990 were headed by a married couple? To what fraction with a denominator of 100 is this fraction closest?
   (b) What fraction of U.S. households in 1990 consisted of individuals living alone? To what fraction with a denominator of 100 is this closest?
   (c) What fraction of U.S. family households in 1990 with one head of household were headed by a

woman? To what fraction with a denominator of 100 is this fraction closest?

16. Find a fraction between each of the following pairs of fractions.

(a) $\frac{3}{7}, \frac{3}{8}$

(b) $\frac{1}{17}, \frac{1}{18}$

(c) $\frac{8}{9}, \frac{10}{11}$

(d) $\frac{a}{b}, \frac{c}{d}$

17. What is mathematically inaccurate about the following sales "pitches"?

(a) "Save $\frac{1}{2}, \frac{1}{3}, \frac{1}{4}$, and even more!"

(b) "You'll pay only a fraction of the list price!"

18. As of 1991 the state of Illinois was generating approximately 13,100,000 tons of waste per year, and of that amount, 786,000 tons were being recycled. In 1991 the state of Texas was generating approximately 18,000,000 tons of waste, and of that amount, 1,440,000 tons were being recycled. Which state had the higher recycling rate? (SOURCE: *1991 Environmental Almanac.*)

Problems

19. When possible, replace each of the following with an equivalent fraction whose denominator is a power of 10. For example, $\frac{1}{250} = \frac{4}{1000} = \frac{4}{10^3}$. Give a single explanation for all cases that do not work. Factor the numerators and denominators for those that work. What pattern do you observe?

(a) $\frac{1}{4}$ (b) $\frac{1}{3}$ (c) $\frac{1}{5}$

(d) $\frac{3}{25}$ (e) $\frac{1}{8}$ (f) $\frac{55}{80}$

(g) $\frac{17}{54}$ (h) $\frac{9}{40}$ (i) $\frac{8}{260}$

(j) $\frac{14}{70}$ (k) $\frac{15}{70}$ (l) $\frac{57}{64}$

(m) $\frac{27}{60}$ (n) $\frac{75}{128}$ (o) $\frac{128}{75}$

(p) $\frac{52}{130}$

20. Let x, y, z be counting numbers.

(a) If $\dfrac{x}{z} = \dfrac{y}{z}$, what must be true about $x, y,$ and z?

(b) If $\dfrac{x}{y} = \dfrac{x}{z}$, what must be true about $x, y,$ and z?

21. The shaded regions in the figures above represent the fractions $\frac{1}{2}$ and $\frac{1}{3}$, respectively.

Trace the outline of a figure like those shown and shade in portions that represent the following fractions.

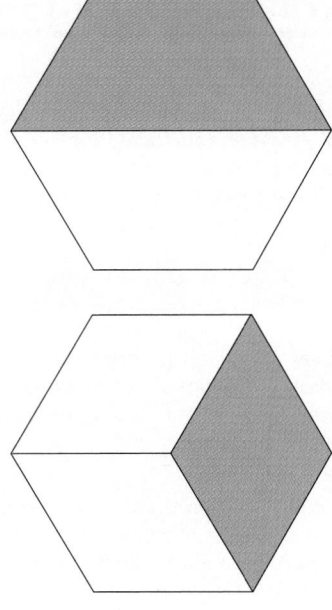

(a) $\frac{1}{2}$ (different from the one shown)

(b) $\frac{1}{3}$ (different from the one shown)

(c) $\frac{1}{4}$ (d) $\frac{1}{6}$ (e) $\frac{1}{12}$ (f) $\frac{1}{24}$

22. A student simplifies $\frac{286}{583}$ by "canceling" the 8s, obtaining $\frac{26}{53}$, which equals $\frac{286}{583}$. He uses the same method with $\frac{28,886}{58,883}$, simplifying it to $\frac{26}{53}$ also. Does this always work with similar fractions? Why or why not?

23. True or false? Explain.

(a) The greater the numerator, the greater the fraction.

(b) The greater the denominator, the smaller the fraction.

(c) If the denominator is fixed, the greater the numerator, the greater the fraction.

(d) If the numerator is fixed, the greater the denominator, the smaller the fraction.

24. I am a proper fraction. The sum of my numerator and denominator is a one-digit square. Their product is a cube. What fraction am I?

EXERCISE/PROBLEM SET 6.1—PART B

Exercises

1. What fraction is represented by the shaded portion of each diagram?

(a)

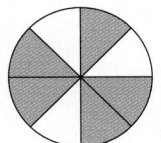

(b)

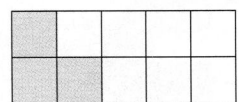

(c)

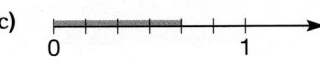

(d)

2. Illustrate $\frac{4}{7}$ using the following models.
   (a) Set model   **(b)** Area model
   (c) Number-line model

3. Using the diagram, represent each of the following as a fraction of all the dots.

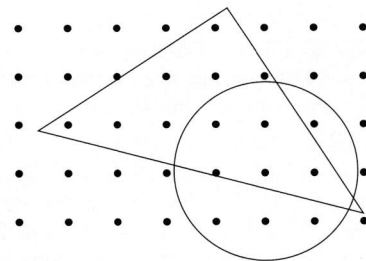

   (a) The part of the collection of dots inside the circle
   (b) The part of the collection of dots inside both the circle and the triangle
   (c) The part of the collection of dots inside the triangle but outside the circle

4. True or false? Explain.
   (a) 5 days is $\frac{1}{6}$ of a month.
   (b) 4 days is $\frac{4}{7}$ of a week.
   (c) 1 month is $\frac{1}{12}$ of a year.

5. Show that $\frac{3}{2} = \frac{9}{6}$ using an area model.

6. The following figure demonstrates that $\frac{6}{10} = \frac{9}{15}$. Using the picture, find two other pairs of fractions that are equal.

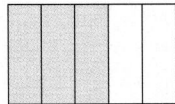

$\frac{6}{10}$

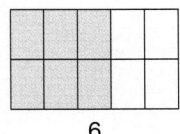

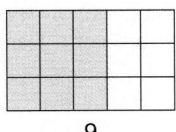

$\frac{9}{15}$

7. Decide which of the following are true. Do this mentally.
   (a) $\frac{7}{6} = \frac{29}{24}$ **(b)** $\frac{3}{12} = \frac{20}{84}$
   (c) $\frac{7}{9} = \frac{63}{81}$ **(d)** $\frac{7}{12} = \frac{105}{180}$

8. Determine which of the following pairs are equal.
   (a) $\frac{693}{858}, \frac{42}{52}$ **(b)** $\frac{873}{954}, \frac{184}{212}$
   (c) $\frac{48}{84}, \frac{756}{1263}$ **(d)** $\frac{468}{891}, \frac{156}{297}$

9. Find the unknown whole number that will make the following statements true.
   (a) $\frac{7}{11} = \frac{?}{88}$ **(b)** $\frac{8}{13} = \frac{40}{?}$
   (c) $\frac{29}{30} = \frac{203}{?}$ **(d)** $\frac{11}{3} = \frac{?}{45}$
   (e) $\frac{42}{?} = \frac{168}{36}$ **(f)** $\frac{?}{6} = \frac{135}{54}$

10. In how many ways can $\frac{35}{49}$ be expressed as a fraction with numerator less than 35 (not necessarily in lowest terms)?

11. **(a)** Is it true that $\dfrac{7 \times 5}{12 \times 5} = \dfrac{35}{60}$?
   (b) Is it true that $\dfrac{7 \times 5}{12 \times 5} = \dfrac{7}{12}$?
   (c) Is it true that $\dfrac{7 + 5}{12 + 5} = \dfrac{12}{17}$?
   (d) Is it true that $\dfrac{7 + 5}{12 + 5} = \dfrac{7}{12}$?
   (e) What conclusion can you draw about "canceling"?

12. Determine if the following pairs are equal. If they are not, order them and find a fraction between them.
   (a) $\frac{231}{654}$ and $\frac{308}{872}$ **(b)** $\frac{1516}{2312}$ and $\frac{2653}{2890}$
   (c) $\frac{516}{892}$ and $\frac{1376}{2376}$

13. Rewrite as a mixed number in simplest form.
   (a) $\frac{128}{72}$ **(b)** $\frac{455}{325}$ **(c)** $\frac{1020}{153}$ **(d)** $\frac{7452}{690}$

14. What is wrong with the following argument?

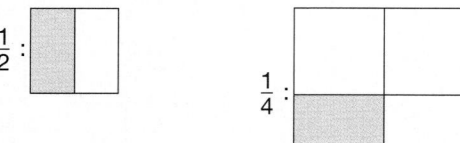

Therefore, $\frac{1}{4} > \frac{1}{2}$ since the area of the shaded square is greater than the area of the shaded rectangle.

15. Compare the following fractions.
  (a) $\frac{3}{4}, \frac{17}{23}$ (b) $\frac{11}{17}, \frac{14}{19}$ (c) $\frac{17}{23}, \frac{14}{19}$
  (d) $\frac{14}{19}, \frac{3}{4}, \frac{17}{23}, \frac{11}{17}$ (e) $\frac{3}{5}, \frac{12}{20}$ (f) $\frac{5}{35}, \frac{2}{14}$

16. According to Bureau of the Census data on living arrangements of children under 18 (not counting persons under 18 who maintained households), in 1990 in the United States there were about

64,000,000 children under 18
46,500,000 children under 18 living with two parents
16,000,000 children under 18 living with one parent
14,000,000 children under 18 living with mother only
2,000,000 children under 18 living with father only
1,400,000 children under 18 living with relatives other than parents

(NOTE: Figures have been rounded to make calculations easier.)
  (a) In 1990 what fraction of children under 18 in the United States lived with two parents? To what fraction with a denominator of 100 is this fraction closest?
  (b) In 1990 what fraction of children under 18 in the United States lived with only one parent? To what fraction with a denominator of 100 is this fraction closest?
  (c) In 1990, of those children under 18 who lived with one parent, what fraction were living with their mother? To what fraction with a denominator of 100 is this fraction closest?
  (d) In 1990, what fraction of children under 18 were living with relatives other than their parents? To what fraction with a denominator of 100 is this fraction closest?

17. Mrs. Wills and Mr. Roberts gave the same test to their fourth-grade classes. In Mrs. Wills's class, 28 out of 36 students passed the test. In Mr. Roberts's class, 26 out of 32 students passed the test. Which class had the higher passing rate?

18. Find three fractions between $\frac{2}{7}$ and $\frac{3}{5}$.

Problems

19. Frank ate 12 pieces of pizza and Dave ate 15 pieces. "I ate $\frac{1}{4}$ more," said Dave. "I ate $\frac{1}{5}$ less," said Frank. Who was right?

20. The shaded regions in the following figures represent the fractions $\frac{1}{2}$ and $\frac{1}{6}$, respectively.

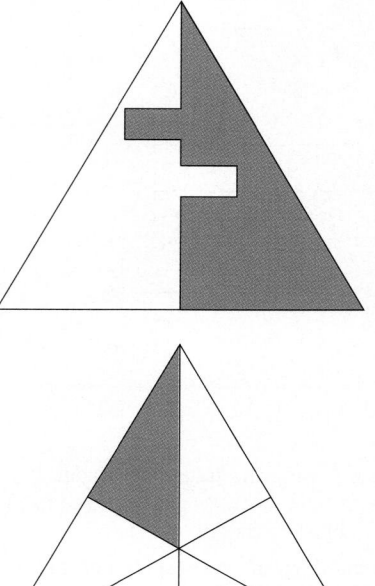

Trace outlines of figures like the ones shown and shade in portions that represent the following fractions.
  (a) $\frac{1}{2}$ (different from the one shown)
  (b) $\frac{1}{3}$ (c) $\frac{1}{4}$ (d) $\frac{1}{8}$ (e) $\frac{1}{9}$

21. If the same number is added to the numerator and denominator of a proper fraction, is the new fraction greater than, less than, or equal to the original fraction? Justify your answer. (Be sure to look at a variety of fractions.)

22. A popular math trick shows that a fraction like $\frac{16}{64}$ can be simplified by "canceling" the 6's and obtaining $\frac{1}{4}$. There are many other fractions for which this technique yields a correct answer.
  (a) Apply this technique to each of the following fractions and verify that the results are correct.
    (i) $\frac{16}{64}$ (ii) $\frac{19}{95}$ (iii) $\frac{26}{65}$
    (iv) $\frac{199}{995}$ (v) $\frac{26666}{66665}$
  (b) Using the pattern established in parts (iv) and (v) of part (a), write three more examples of fractions for which this method of simplification works.

23. Find a fraction less than $\frac{1}{12}$. Find another fraction less than the fraction you found. Can you continue this process? Is there a "smallest" fraction greater than 0? Explain.

24. Find 999 fractions between $\frac{1}{3}$ and $\frac{1}{2}$ so that the difference between pairs of numbers next to each other is the same. (HINT: Find convenient equivalent fractions for $\frac{1}{3}$ and $\frac{1}{2}$.)

6.2

FRACTIONS: ADDITION AND SUBTRACTION

Addition and Its Properties

Addition of fractions is an extension of whole-number addition and can be motivated using models. To find the sum of $\frac{1}{5}$ and $\frac{3}{5}$, consider the following measurement models, the region model and number-line model in Figure 6.13.

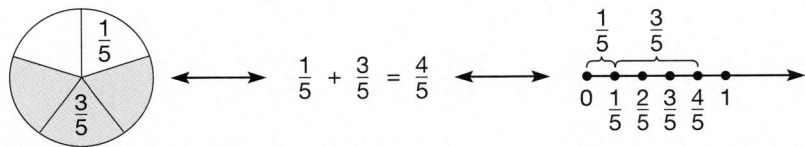

Region Model   Number Line Model

FIGURE 6.13

The idea illustrated in Figure 6.13 can be applied to any pair of fractions that have the same denominator. Figure 6.14 shows how fraction strips, which are a blend of these two models, can be used to find the sum of $\frac{1}{5}$ and $\frac{3}{5}$. That is, the sum of two fractions with the same denominator may be found by adding the numerators as stated next.

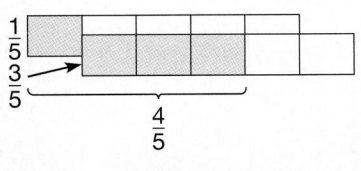

FIGURE 6.14

> **Definition**
>
> #### Addition of Fractions with Common Denominators
>
> Let $\frac{a}{b}$ and $\frac{c}{b}$ be any fractions. Then
>
> $$\frac{a}{b} + \frac{c}{b} = \frac{a + c}{b}.$$

Figure 6.15 illustrates how to add fractions when the denominators are not the same.

Similarly, to find the sum $\frac{2}{7} + \frac{3}{5}$, use the equality of fractions to express the fractions with common denominators as follows.

$$\frac{2}{7} + \frac{3}{5} = \frac{2 \cdot 5}{7 \cdot 5} + \frac{3 \cdot 7}{5 \cdot 7}$$

$$= \frac{10}{35} + \frac{21}{35}$$

$$= \frac{31}{35}.$$

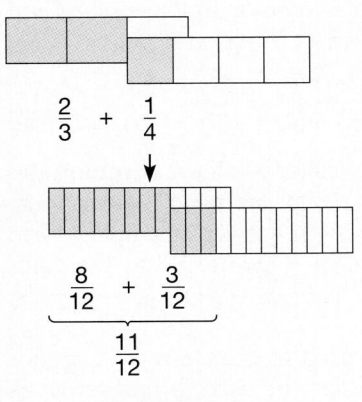

FIGURE 6.15

This procedure can be generalized as follows.

Theorem

Addition of Fractions with Unlike Denominators

Let $\dfrac{a}{b}$ and $\dfrac{c}{d}$ be any fractions. Then

$$\frac{a}{b} + \frac{c}{d} = \frac{ad + bc}{bd}.$$

Proof

$$\frac{a}{b} + \frac{c}{d} = \frac{ad}{bd} + \frac{bc}{bd} \qquad \text{Equality of fractions}$$

$$= \frac{ad + bc}{bd} \qquad \text{Addition with common denominators} \qquad \blacksquare$$

In words, to add fractions with unlike denominators, find equivalent fractions with common denominators. Then the sum will be represented by the sum of the numerators over the common denominator.

EXAMPLE 6.5 Find the following sums and simplify.
(a) $\frac{3}{7} + \frac{2}{7}$ **(b)** $\frac{5}{9} + \frac{3}{4}$ **(c)** $\frac{17}{15} + \frac{5}{12}$

Solution

(a) $\dfrac{3}{7} + \dfrac{2}{7} = \dfrac{3 + 2}{7} = \dfrac{5}{7}$

(b) $\dfrac{5}{9} + \dfrac{3}{4} = \dfrac{5 \cdot 4}{9 \cdot 4} + \dfrac{9 \cdot 3}{9 \cdot 4} = \dfrac{20}{36} + \dfrac{27}{36} = \dfrac{47}{36}$

(c) $\dfrac{17}{15} + \dfrac{5}{12} = \dfrac{17 \cdot 12 + 15 \cdot 5}{15 \cdot 12} = \dfrac{204 + 75}{180} = \dfrac{279}{180} = \dfrac{31}{20}$ $\qquad \blacksquare$

In Example 6.5(c), an alternative method can be used. Rather than use $15 \cdot 12$ as the common denominator, the least common multiple of 12 and 15 can be used. The $\text{LCM}(15, 12) = 2^2 \cdot 3 \cdot 5 = 60$. Therefore,

$$\frac{17}{15} + \frac{5}{12} = \frac{17 \cdot 4}{15 \cdot 4} + \frac{5 \cdot 5}{12 \cdot 5} = \frac{68}{60} + \frac{25}{60} = \frac{93}{60} = \frac{31}{20}.$$

Although using the LCM of the denominators (called the **least common denominator** and abbreviated LCD) simplifies paper-and-pencil calculations, using this method does not necessarily result in an answer in simplest form as in the previous case. For example, to find $\frac{3}{10} + \frac{8}{15}$, use 30 as the common denominator since $\text{LCM}(10, 15) = 30$. Thus $\frac{3}{10} + \frac{8}{15} = \frac{9}{30} + \frac{16}{30} = \frac{25}{30}$, which is not in simplest form.

Calculators and computers can also be used to calculate the sums of fractions. A common four-function calculator can be used to find sums, as in the following example.

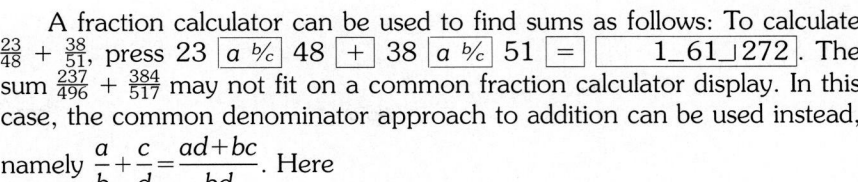

A fraction calculator can be used to find sums as follows: To calculate $\frac{23}{48} + \frac{38}{51}$, press 23 $\boxed{a\ ^b/_c}$ 48 $\boxed{+}$ 38 $\boxed{a\ ^b/_c}$ 51 $\boxed{=}$ $\boxed{\qquad 1\_61\_272}$. The sum $\frac{237}{496} + \frac{384}{517}$ may not fit on a common fraction calculator display. In this case, the common denominator approach to addition can be used instead, namely $\frac{a}{b} + \frac{c}{d} = \frac{ad+bc}{bd}$. Here

$$
\begin{aligned}
ad &= 237 \times 517 & &= 122529 \\
bc &= 496 \times 384 & &= 190464 \\
ad + bc &= 122529 + 190464 &&= 312993 \\
bd &= 496 \times 517 & &= 256432.
\end{aligned}
$$

Therefore, the sum is $\dfrac{312993}{256432}$. Notice that the latter method may be done on any four-function calculator.

The following properties of fraction addition can be used to simplify computations. For simplicity, all properties are stated using common denominators since any two fractions can be expressed with the same denominator.

Closure Property for Fraction Addition

The sum of two fractions is a fraction.

This follows from the equation $\dfrac{a}{c} + \dfrac{b}{c} = \dfrac{a + b}{c}$ since $a + b$ and c are both whole numbers and $c \neq 0$.

Commutative Property for Fraction Addition

Let $\dfrac{a}{b}$ and $\dfrac{c}{b}$ be any fractions. Then

$$\frac{a}{b} + \frac{c}{b} = \frac{c}{b} + \frac{a}{b}.$$

Figure 6.16 provides a visual justification using fraction strips. The following is a formal proof of this commutativity.

$$
\begin{aligned}
\frac{a}{b} + \frac{c}{b} &= \frac{a + c}{b} & &\text{Addition of fractions} \\
&= \frac{c + a}{b} & &\text{Commutative property of} \\
& & &\text{whole-number addition} \\
&= \frac{c}{b} + \frac{a}{b}. & &\text{Addition of fractions}
\end{aligned}
$$

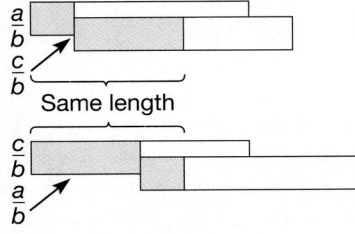

FIGURE 6.16

Associative Property for Fraction Addition

Let $\dfrac{a}{b}$, $\dfrac{c}{b}$, and $\dfrac{e}{b}$ be any fractions. Then

$$\left[\frac{a}{b} + \frac{c}{b}\right] + \frac{e}{b} = \frac{a}{b} + \left[\frac{c}{b} + \frac{e}{b}\right].$$

The associative property for fraction addition is easily justified using the associative property for whole-number addition.

Additive Identity Property for Fraction Addition

Let $\dfrac{a}{b}$ be any fraction. There is a unique fraction, $\dfrac{0}{b}$, such that

$$\frac{a}{b} + \frac{0}{b} = \frac{a}{b} = \frac{0}{b} + \frac{a}{b}.$$

The following equations show how this additive identity property can be justified using the corresponding property in whole numbers.

$$\frac{a}{b} + \frac{0}{b} = \frac{a + 0}{b} \qquad \text{Addition of fractions}$$

$$= \frac{a}{b}. \qquad \begin{array}{l}\text{Additive identity property}\\\text{of whole-number addition}\end{array}$$

The fraction $\dfrac{0}{b}$ is also written as $\dfrac{0}{1}$ or 0. It is shown in the problem set that this is the only fraction that serves as an additive identity.

The preceding properties can be used to simplify computations.

EXAMPLE 6.6   Compute: $\dfrac{3}{5} + \left[\dfrac{4}{7} + \dfrac{2}{5}\right]$.

Solution

$$\frac{3}{5} + \left[\frac{4}{7} + \frac{2}{5}\right] = \frac{3}{5} + \left[\frac{2}{5} + \frac{4}{7}\right] \qquad \text{Commutativity}$$

$$= \left[\frac{3}{5} + \frac{2}{5}\right] + \frac{4}{7} \qquad \text{Associativity}$$

$$= 1 + \frac{4}{7}. \qquad \text{Addition} \qquad ■$$

The number $1 + \frac{4}{7}$ can be expressed as the mixed number $1\frac{4}{7}$. As in Example 6.6, any mixed number can be expressed as a sum. For example,

$3\frac{2}{5} = 3 + \frac{2}{5}$. Also, any mixed number can be changed to an improper fraction, and vice versa, as shown in the next example.

EXAMPLE 6.7
(a) Express $3\frac{2}{5}$ as an improper fraction.
(b) Express $\frac{36}{7}$ as a mixed number.

Solution

(a) $3\dfrac{2}{5} = 3 + \dfrac{2}{5} = \dfrac{15}{5} + \dfrac{2}{5} = \dfrac{17}{5}$

$\left[\text{Shortcut: } 3\dfrac{2}{5} = \dfrac{5 \cdot 3 + 2}{5} = \dfrac{17}{5} \right]$

(b) $\dfrac{36}{7} = \dfrac{35}{7} + \dfrac{1}{7} = 5 + \dfrac{1}{7} = 5\dfrac{1}{7}$ ∎

Subtraction

Subtraction of fractions can be viewed in two ways as we did with whole-number subtraction—either as (1) take-away or (2) using the missing-addend approach.

EXAMPLE 6.8   Find: $\frac{4}{7} - \frac{1}{7}$.

Solution
From Figure 6.17, $\frac{4}{7} - \frac{1}{7} = \frac{3}{7}$. ∎

This example suggests the following definition.

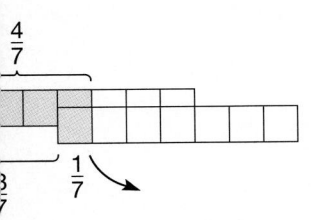

FIGURE 6.17

Definition
Subtraction of Fractions with Common Denominators
Let $\dfrac{a}{b}$ and $\dfrac{c}{b}$ be any fractions with $a \ge c$. Then
$$\dfrac{a}{b} - \dfrac{c}{b} = \dfrac{a-c}{b}.$$

Now consider the subtraction of fractions using the missing-addend approach. For example, to find $\dfrac{4}{7} - \dfrac{1}{7}$, find a fraction $\dfrac{n}{7}$ such that $\dfrac{4}{7} = \dfrac{1}{7} + \dfrac{n}{7}$. The following argument shows that the missing-addend approach leads to the take-away approach.

If $\dfrac{a}{b} - \dfrac{c}{b} = \dfrac{n}{b}$, and the missing-addend approach holds, then $\dfrac{a}{b} = \dfrac{c}{b} + \dfrac{n}{b}$ or $\dfrac{a}{b} = \dfrac{c+n}{b}$. This implies that $a = c + n$ or $a - c = n$. That is, $\dfrac{a}{b} - \dfrac{c}{b} = \dfrac{a-c}{b}$.

Also, it can be shown that the missing-addend approach is a consequence of the take-away approach.

If fractions have different denominators, subtraction is done by first finding common denominators, then subtracting as before.

Suppose that $\dfrac{a}{b} \geq \dfrac{c}{d}$. Then $\dfrac{a}{b} - \dfrac{c}{d} = \dfrac{ad}{bd} - \dfrac{bc}{bd} = \dfrac{ad - bc}{bd}$.

Therefore, fractions with unlike denominators may be subtracted as follows.

Theorem

Subtraction of Fractions with Unlike Denominators

Let $\dfrac{a}{b}$ and $\dfrac{c}{d}$ be any fractions, where $\dfrac{a}{b} \geq \dfrac{c}{d}$. Then

$$\frac{a}{b} - \frac{c}{d} = \frac{ad - bc}{bd}.$$

EXAMPLE 6.9   Find the following differences.

(a) $\dfrac{4}{7} - \dfrac{3}{8}$ (b) $\dfrac{25}{12} - \dfrac{7}{18}$ (c) $\dfrac{7}{10} - \dfrac{8}{15}$

Solution

(a) $\dfrac{4}{7} - \dfrac{3}{8} = \dfrac{4 \cdot 8}{7 \cdot 8} - \dfrac{3 \cdot 7}{8 \cdot 7} = \dfrac{31 - 21}{56} = \dfrac{11}{56}$

(b) $\dfrac{25}{12} - \dfrac{7}{18}$. Note: LCM(12, 18) = 36.

$\dfrac{25}{12} - \dfrac{7}{18} = \dfrac{25 \cdot 3}{12 \cdot 3} - \dfrac{7 \cdot 2}{18 \cdot 2} = \dfrac{75 - 14}{36} = \dfrac{61}{36}$

(c) $\dfrac{7}{10} - \dfrac{8}{15} = \dfrac{21}{30} - \dfrac{16}{30} = \dfrac{5}{30} = \dfrac{1}{6}$

STUDENT PAGE SNAPSHOT

Estimating Sums and Differences

A. Fernando received one share of each of four stocks in the table at the right for his thirteenth birthday. The next day he checked the stock prices in the local newspaper to estimate the value of his stocks.

STOCK PRICES (in dollars)		
Stock	Open	Close
ESTv	$14\frac{1}{8}$	$13\frac{3}{8}$
MfrCo	$8\frac{3}{4}$	$8\frac{3}{4}$
NatToy	1	$\frac{7}{8}$
VTL	$6\frac{1}{8}$	$6\frac{5}{8}$

Estimate: $13\frac{3}{8} + 8\frac{3}{4} + \frac{7}{8} + 6\frac{5}{8}$

Here are two ways to estimate:

Round to the Nearest Whole Number

$13\frac{3}{8} \longrightarrow$ 13   *Think:* $\frac{3}{8} < \frac{1}{2}$ Round down.

$8\frac{3}{4} \longrightarrow$ 9   *Think:* $\frac{3}{4} > \frac{1}{2}$ Round up.

$\frac{7}{8} \longrightarrow$ 1

$+ 6\frac{5}{8} \longrightarrow + \ 7$

$\overline{\hspace{1.5cm} 30}$

Use Front-End Estimation

$13\frac{3}{8}$ *Think:* Use the whole-number part.

$8\frac{3}{4}$

$\frac{7}{8}$

$+ 6\frac{5}{8}$

$\overline{\hspace{1.2cm} 27}$

1. Which method gives an estimate less than the exact answer? Why?

2. Adjust the front-end estimate to make it closer to the exact sum.

B. You can also use these methods to estimate differences.

Estimate: $15\frac{3}{4} - 13\frac{3}{8}$

Round to the Nearest Whole Number

$15\frac{3}{4} \longrightarrow$ 16

$- 13\frac{3}{8} \longrightarrow - 13$

$\overline{\hspace{1.5cm} 3}$

Use Front-End Estimation

$15\frac{3}{4}$

$- 13\frac{3}{8}$

$\overline{\hspace{1.2cm} 2}$

3. How does the exact answer compare to the front-end estimate of 2?

4. How would you estimate $25\frac{3}{8} - 20\frac{7}{8}$ using both methods?

TRY OUT   Estimate first by rounding and then by using the front digits.

5. $\frac{7}{10} + 5\frac{5}{7} + 8\frac{3}{4}$

6. $16\frac{2}{7} - 6\frac{4}{7}$

7. $2\frac{2}{3} + \frac{4}{9} + 12\frac{7}{8}$

8. $22\frac{5}{7} - 12\frac{1}{8}$

Mental Math and Estimation for Addition and Subtraction

Mental math and estimation techniques similar to those used with whole numbers can be used with fractions.

EXAMPLE 6.10   Calculate mentally.

(a) $\left(\dfrac{1}{5} + \dfrac{3}{4} \right) + \dfrac{4}{5}$ **(b)** $3\dfrac{4}{5} + 2\dfrac{2}{5}$ **(c)** $40 - 8\dfrac{3}{7}$

Solution

(a) $\left(\dfrac{1}{5} + \dfrac{3}{4} \right) + \dfrac{4}{5} = \dfrac{4}{5} + \left(\dfrac{1}{5} + \dfrac{3}{4} \right) = \left(\dfrac{4}{5} + \dfrac{1}{5} \right) + \dfrac{3}{4} = 1\dfrac{3}{4}$

Commutativity and associativity were used to be able to add $\dfrac{4}{5}$ and $\dfrac{1}{5}$ since they are compatible fractions (their sum is 1).

(b) $3\dfrac{4}{5} + 2\dfrac{2}{5} = 4 + 2\dfrac{1}{5} = 6\dfrac{1}{5}$

This is an example of additive compensation where $3\dfrac{4}{5}$ was increased by $\dfrac{1}{5}$ to 4 and consequently $2\dfrac{2}{5}$ was decreased by $\dfrac{1}{5}$ to $2\dfrac{1}{5}$.

(c) $40 - 8\dfrac{3}{7} = 40\dfrac{4}{7} - 9 = 31\dfrac{4}{7}$

Here $\dfrac{4}{7}$ was added to both 40 and $8\dfrac{3}{7}$ (since $8\dfrac{3}{7} + \dfrac{4}{7} = 9$), an example of the equal-additions method of subtraction.   ◼

EXAMPLE 6.11   Estimate using the indicated techniques.

(a) $3\dfrac{3}{7} + 6\dfrac{2}{5}$ using range estimation

(b) $15\dfrac{1}{4} + 7\dfrac{3}{5}$ using front-end with adjustment

(c) $3\dfrac{5}{6} + 5\dfrac{1}{8} + 8\dfrac{3}{8}$ rounding to the nearest $\frac{1}{2}$ or whole

Solution

(a) $3\dfrac{3}{7} + 6\dfrac{2}{5}$ is between $3 + 6 = 9$ and $4 + 7 = 11$.

(b) $15\dfrac{1}{4} + 7\dfrac{3}{5} \approx 23$ since $15 + 7 = 22$ and $\dfrac{1}{4} + \dfrac{3}{5} \approx 1$.

(c) $3\dfrac{5}{6} + 5\dfrac{1}{8} + 8\dfrac{3}{8} \approx 4 + 5 + 8\dfrac{1}{2} = 17\dfrac{1}{2}$.   ◼

MATHEMATICAL MORSEL

Around 2900 B.C. the great Pyramid of Gizeh was constructed. It covered 13 acres and contained over 2,000,000 stone blocks averaging 2.5 tons each. Some chamber roofs are made of 54-ton granite blocks, 27 feet long and 4 feet thick, hauled from a quarry 600 miles away and set into place 200 feet above the ground. The relative error in the lengths of the sides of the square base was $\frac{1}{14,000}$ and in the right angles was $\frac{1}{27,000}$. This construction was estimated to have required 100,000 laborers working for about 30 years.

EXERCISE/PROBLEM SET 6.2—PART A

Exercises

1. Illustrate the problem $\frac{2}{5} + \frac{1}{3}$ using the following models.
   (a) A region model   **(b)** A number-line model

2. Find the following sums and express your answer in simplest form.
   (a) $\frac{1}{8} + \frac{5}{8}$ **(b)** $\frac{1}{4} + \frac{1}{2}$
   (c) $\frac{3}{7} + \frac{1}{3}$ **(d)** $\frac{8}{9} + \frac{1}{12} + \frac{3}{16}$
   (e) $\frac{8}{13} + \frac{4}{51}$ **(f)** $\frac{9}{22} + \frac{89}{121}$
   (g) $\frac{61}{100} + \frac{7}{1000}$ **(h)** $\frac{7}{10} + \frac{29}{100}$
   (i) $\frac{143}{1000} + \frac{759}{100,000}$

3. If one of your students wrote $\frac{1}{4} + \frac{2}{3} = \frac{3}{7}$, how would you convince him/her that this is incorrect?

4. Change the following mixed numbers to improper fractions.
   (a) $3\frac{5}{6}$ **(b)** $2\frac{7}{8}$ **(c)** $5\frac{1}{5}$ **(d)** $7\frac{1}{9}$

5. On a number line, demonstrate the following problems using the take-away approach.
   (a) $\frac{7}{10} - \frac{3}{10}$ **(b)** $\frac{5}{12} - \frac{1}{12}$ **(c)** $\frac{2}{3} - \frac{1}{4}$

6. Perform the following subtractions when the differences exist.
   (a) $\frac{9}{11} - \frac{5}{11}$ **(b)** $\frac{3}{7} - \frac{2}{9}$
   (c) $\frac{1}{12} - \frac{1}{11}$ **(d)** $\frac{4}{5} - \frac{3}{4}$
   (e) $\frac{13}{18} - \frac{8}{27}$ **(f)** $\frac{21}{51} - \frac{7}{39}$
   (g) $\frac{11}{100} - \frac{99}{1000}$ **(h)** $\frac{453}{1,000,000} - \frac{3}{10,000}$
   (i) $\frac{1}{5251} - \frac{2}{18,821}$

7. Find the sum and difference (first minus second) for the following pairs of mixed numbers. Answers should be written as mixed numbers.
   (a) $2\frac{2}{3}$, $1\frac{1}{4}$ **(b)** $7\frac{5}{7}$, $5\frac{2}{3}$ **(c)** $22\frac{1}{6}$, $15\frac{11}{12}$

8. Use the properties of fraction addition to calculate each of the following sums mentally.
   (a) $(\frac{3}{7} + \frac{1}{9}) + \frac{4}{7}$ **(b)** $1\frac{9}{13} + (\frac{5}{6} + \frac{4}{13})$
   (c) $(2\frac{2}{5} + 3\frac{5}{8}) + (1\frac{4}{5} + 2\frac{3}{8})$

9. Find each of these differences mentally using the equal-additions method. Write out the steps that you thought through.
   (a) $8\frac{2}{7} - 2\frac{6}{7}$ **(b)** $9\frac{1}{8} - 2\frac{5}{8}$
   (c) $11\frac{3}{7} - 6\frac{5}{7}$ **(d)** $8\frac{1}{6} - 3\frac{5}{6}$

10. Estimate each of the following using (i) range and (ii) front-end with adjustment estimation.
   (a) $6\frac{7}{11} + 7\frac{3}{9}$ **(b)** $7\frac{4}{6} + 6\frac{6}{7}$ **(c)** $8\frac{2}{11} + 2\frac{7}{11} + 5\frac{2}{9}$

11. Estimate each of the following using "rounding to the nearest whole number or $\frac{1}{2}$."
   (a) $9\frac{7}{9} + 3\frac{6}{13}$ **(b)** $9\frac{5}{8} + 5\frac{4}{9}$
   (c) $7\frac{2}{11} + 5\frac{3}{13} + 2\frac{7}{12}$

12. An alternative definition of "less than" for fractions is as follows:

$$\frac{a}{b} < \frac{c}{d} \text{ if and only if } \frac{a}{b} + \frac{m}{n} = \frac{c}{d} \text{ for a nonzero } \frac{m}{n}$$

244 Chapter 6: Fractions

Use this definition to confirm the following statements.
(a) $\frac{3}{7} < \frac{5}{7}$ (b) $\frac{1}{3} < \frac{1}{2}$ (c) $\frac{2}{5} < \frac{5}{8}$

13. Calculate using a fraction calculator.
   (a) $\frac{3}{4} + \frac{7}{10}$ (b) $\frac{8}{9} - \frac{3}{5}$ (c) $\frac{7}{6} + \frac{4}{5}$ (d) $\frac{4}{5} - \frac{2}{7}$

14. To find the sum $\frac{2}{5} + \frac{3}{4}$ on a scientific calculator, press
$2 \div 5 + 3 \div 4 =$ ⬚ 1.15 . The whole-number part of the sum is 1. Subtract it: $- 1 =$ ⬚ 0.15 . This represents the fraction part of the answer in decimal form. Since the denominator of the sum should be $5 \times 4 = 20$, multiply by 20: $\times 20 =$ ⬚ 3 . This is the numerator of the fraction part of the sum. Thus $\frac{2}{5} + \frac{3}{4} = 1\frac{3}{20}$. Find the simplest form of the sums/differences using this method.
(a) $\frac{3}{7} + \frac{5}{8}$ (b) $\frac{19}{135} + \frac{51}{75}$
(c) $\frac{3}{5} - \frac{4}{7}$ (d) $\frac{37}{52} - \frac{19}{78}$

Problems

15. Using the alternative definition of "less than," prove the following statements. Assume that the product of two fractions is a fraction in part (c).
(a) If $\frac{a}{b} < \frac{c}{d}$ and $\frac{c}{d} < \frac{e}{f}$, then $\frac{a}{b} < \frac{e}{f}$.
(b) If $\frac{a}{b} < \frac{c}{d}$, then $\frac{a}{b} + \frac{e}{f} < \frac{c}{d} + \frac{e}{f}$.
(c) If $\frac{a}{b} < \frac{c}{d}$, then $\frac{a}{b} \cdot \frac{e}{f} < \frac{c}{d} \cdot \frac{e}{f}$ for any nonzero $\frac{e}{f}$.

16. Find this sum: $\frac{1}{2} + \frac{1}{2^2} + \frac{1}{2^3} + \cdots + \frac{1}{2^{100}}$.

17. Sally, her brother, and another partner own a pizza restaurant. If Sally owns $\frac{1}{3}$ and her brother owns $\frac{1}{4}$ of the restaurant, what part does the third partner own?

18. John spent a quarter of his life as a boy growing up, one-sixth of his life in college, and one-half of his life as a teacher. He spent his last six years in retirement. How old was he when he died?

19. In the first 10 games of the baseball season, Jim has 15 hits in 50 times at bat. The fraction of his times at bat that were hits is $\frac{15}{50}$. In the next game he is at bat 6 times and gets 3 hits.
(a) What fraction of at-bats are hits in this game?
(b) How many hits does he now have this season?
(c) How many at-bats does he now have this season?
(d) What is his record of hits/at-bats this season?
(e) In this setting "baseball addition" can be defined as
$$\frac{a}{b} \oplus \frac{c}{d} = \frac{a+c}{b+d}$$
(Use $\oplus$ to distinguish from ordinary $+$.)

Using this definition of addition, do you get an equivalent answer when fractions are replaced by equivalent fractions?

20. (a) The divisors (other than 1) of 6 are 2, 3, and 6. Compute $\frac{1}{2} + \frac{1}{3} + \frac{1}{6}$.
(b) The divisors (other than 1) of 28 are 2, 4, 7, 14, and 28. Compute $\frac{1}{2} + \frac{1}{4} + \frac{1}{7} + \frac{1}{14} + \frac{1}{28}$.
(c) Will this result be true for 496? What other numbers will have this property?

21. David is having trouble when subtracting mixed numbers. What might be causing his difficulty? How might you help David?

$$3\frac{2}{5} = 2\frac{12}{5}$$
$$-\frac{3}{5} = \frac{3}{5}$$
$$\overline{2\frac{9}{5} = 3\frac{4}{5}}$$

22. Fractions whose numerators are 1 are called **unitary fractions**. Do you think that it is possible to add unitary fractions with different odd denominators to obtain 1? For example, $\frac{1}{2} + \frac{1}{3} + \frac{1}{6} = 1$, but 2 and 6 are even. How about the following sum?

$$\frac{1}{3} + \frac{1}{5} + \frac{1}{7} + \frac{1}{9} + \frac{1}{15} + \frac{1}{21} + \frac{1}{27}$$
$$+ \frac{1}{35} + \frac{1}{63} + \frac{1}{105} + \frac{1}{135}$$

23. The Egyptians were said to use only unitary fractions with the exception of $\frac{2}{3}$. It is known that every unitary fraction can be expressed as the sum of two unitary fractions in more than one way. Represent the following fractions as the sum of two different unitary fractions. (NOTE: $\frac{1}{2} = \frac{1}{4} + \frac{1}{4}$, but $\frac{1}{2} = \frac{1}{3} + \frac{1}{6}$ is requested.)
(a) $\frac{1}{5}$ (b) $\frac{1}{7}$ (c) $\frac{1}{17}$

24. Determine if $\dfrac{1+3}{5+7} = \dfrac{1+3+5}{7+9+11}$.

Is $\dfrac{1+3+5+7}{9+11+13+15}$

also the same fraction? Find two other such fractions. Prove why this works. (HINT: $1 + 3 = 2^2$, $1 + 3 + 5 = 3^2$, etc.)

25. At a round-robin tennis tournament, each of eight players plays every other player once. How many matches are there?

EXERCISE/PROBLEM SET 6.2—PART B

Exercises

1. Give four different common denominators, including the least common denominator, for each pair of fractions.
   (a) $\frac{1}{3}, \frac{1}{4}$ (b) $\frac{11}{20}, \frac{5}{12}$ (c) $\frac{5}{9}, \frac{7}{12}$
   (d) $\frac{2}{13}, \frac{25}{39}$ (e) $\frac{7}{10}, \frac{13}{15}$ (f) $\frac{11}{12}, \frac{41}{63}$

2. Find the following sums and express your answer in simplest form. (Leave your answers in prime factorization form.)
   (a) $\dfrac{1}{2^2 \times 3^2} + \dfrac{1}{2 \times 3^3}$

   (b) $\dfrac{1}{3^2 + 7^3} + \dfrac{1}{5^3 \times 7^2 \times 29}$

   (c) $\dfrac{1}{5^4 \times 7^5 \times 13^2} + \dfrac{1}{3^2 \times 5 \times 13^3}$

   (d) $\dfrac{1}{17^3 \times 53^5 \times 67^{13}} + \dfrac{1}{11^5 \times 17^2 \times 67^9}$

3. Change the following improper fractions to mixed numbers.
   (a) $\frac{35}{3}$ (b) $\frac{19}{4}$ (c) $\frac{49}{6}$ (d) $\frac{17}{5}$

4. On a number line, demonstrate the following problems using the missing-addend approach.
   (a) $\frac{9}{12} - \frac{5}{12}$ (b) $\frac{2}{3} - \frac{1}{5}$ (c) $\frac{3}{4} - \frac{1}{3}$

5. (a) Compute the following problems.
   (i) $\frac{7}{8} + \left(\frac{2}{3} + \frac{1}{6}\right)$ (ii) $\left(\frac{7}{8} + \frac{2}{3}\right) + \frac{1}{6}$
   (iii) $\frac{7}{8} - \left(\frac{2}{3} - \frac{1}{6}\right)$ (iv) $\left(\frac{7}{8} - \frac{2}{3}\right) - \frac{1}{6}$
   (b) What property of addition is illustrated in parts (i) and (ii)?

6. Calculate the following and express as mixed numbers in simplest form.
   (a) $11\frac{3}{5} - 9\frac{8}{9}$ (b) $7\frac{5}{8} + 13\frac{2}{3}$
   (c) $11\frac{3}{5} + 9\frac{8}{9}$ (d) $13\frac{2}{3} - 7\frac{5}{8}$

7. Use properties of fraction addition to calculate each of the following sums mentally.
   (a) $\left(\frac{2}{5} + \frac{5}{8}\right) + \frac{3}{5}$ (b) $\frac{4}{9} + \left(\frac{2}{15} + 2\frac{5}{9}\right)$
   (c) $\left(1\frac{3}{4} + 3\frac{5}{11}\right) + \left(1\frac{8}{11} + 2\frac{1}{4}\right)$

8. A man measures a room for a wallpaper border and finds he needs lengths of 10 ft. $6\frac{3}{8}$ in., 14 ft. $9\frac{3}{4}$ in., 6 ft. $5\frac{1}{2}$ in., and 3 ft. $2\frac{7}{8}$ in. What total length of wallpaper border does he need to purchase? (Ignore amount needed for matching and overlap.)

9. Find each of these differences mentally using the equal-additions method. Write out the steps that you thought through.
   (a) $5\frac{2}{9} - 2\frac{7}{9}$ (b) $9\frac{1}{6} - 2\frac{5}{6}$ (c) $21\frac{3}{7} - 8\frac{5}{7}$
   (d) $5\frac{3}{11} - 2\frac{6}{11}$

10. Estimate each of the following using (i) range and (ii) front-end with adjustment estimation.
    (a) $5\frac{8}{9} + 6\frac{3}{13}$ (b) $7\frac{4}{5} + 5\frac{6}{7}$ (c) $8\frac{2}{11} + 2\frac{8}{9} + 7\frac{3}{13}$

11. Estimate each of the following using "rounding to the nearest whole number or $\frac{1}{2}$" estimation.
    (a) $5\frac{8}{9} + 6\frac{4}{7}$ (b) $7\frac{4}{5} + 5\frac{5}{9}$ (c) $8\frac{4}{11} + 2\frac{7}{12} + 7\frac{3}{13}$

12. Estimate using cluster estimation.
    (a) $5\frac{1}{3} + 4\frac{4}{5} + 5\frac{6}{7}$
    (b) $6\frac{1}{8} + 6\frac{2}{11} + 5\frac{8}{9} + 6\frac{3}{13}$

Problems

13. Using the definition of fraction addition and the properties of whole numbers, verify the associative property for fraction addition.

14. Show that $\dfrac{0}{b}$ is the only identity for addition. (HINT: Suppose that $\dfrac{a}{b} + \dfrac{x}{b} = \dfrac{a}{b}$ and show that $x = 0$.)

15. Separate the set of fractions given below into two sets so that the sum of each set is the same.

$$\frac{1}{6} \quad \frac{1}{12} \quad \frac{1}{18} \quad \frac{1}{9} \quad \frac{1}{36}$$

16. By giving a counterexample, show for fractions that
    (a) subtraction is not closed.
    (b) subtraction is not commutative.
    (c) subtraction is not associative.

17. Take the denominator of the fraction $\frac{1}{3}$ and add it to both the numerator and the denominator. Notice that the fraction is doubled. Find a fraction that will triple when its denominator is added to its numerator and denominator.

18. Following are some problems worked by students. Identify their errors and determine how they would answer the final question.

Amy:

$$7\frac{1}{6} = 7\overset{6\,6}{\cancel{\frac{1}{6}}}$$
$$-5\frac{2}{3} = 5\frac{4}{6}$$
$$\overline{\phantom{-5\frac{2}{3} = }} \; 1\frac{2}{6} = 1\frac{1}{3}$$

$$5\frac{1}{3} = \overset{4\,6}{\cancel{5}}\frac{2}{6}$$
$$-2\frac{1}{2} = 2\frac{3}{6}$$
$$\overline{\phantom{-2\frac{1}{2} = }} \; 2\frac{3}{6} = 2\frac{1}{2}$$

$$5\frac{3}{8}$$
$$-2\frac{1}{2}$$

Robert: $9\frac{1}{6} = 9\frac{55}{48}$ $6\frac{1}{3} = 6\frac{19}{3}$ $5\frac{1}{3}$

$-2\frac{7}{8} = 2\frac{23}{48}$ $-1\frac{2}{3} = 1\frac{5}{3}$ $-1\frac{4}{5}$

$\overline{\phantom{-2\frac{7}{8}}7\frac{32}{48}}$ $\overline{\phantom{-1\frac{2}{3}}5\frac{14}{3}}$

What property of fractions might you use to help these students?

19. The triangle shown next is called the **harmonic triangle**. Observe the pattern in the rows of the triangle and then answer the questions that follow.

$$1$$
$$\frac{1}{2} \qquad \frac{1}{2}$$
$$\frac{1}{3} \qquad \frac{1}{6} \qquad \frac{1}{3}$$
$$\frac{1}{4} \qquad \frac{1}{12} \qquad \frac{1}{12} \qquad \frac{1}{4}$$
$$\frac{1}{5} \qquad \frac{1}{20} \qquad \frac{1}{30} \qquad \frac{1}{20} \qquad \frac{1}{5}$$

(a) Write down the next two rows of the triangle.
(b) Describe the pattern in the numbers that are first in each row.
(c) Describe how each fraction in the triangle is related to the two fractions directly below it.

20. Consider the sum of fractions shown next.

$$\frac{1}{3} + \frac{1}{5} = \frac{8}{15}$$

The denominators of the first two fractions differ by two.
(a) Verify that 8 and 15 are two parts of a Pythagorean triple. What is the third number of the triple?
(b) Verify that the same result holds true for the following sums:
   (i) $\frac{1}{7} + \frac{1}{9}$ (ii) $\frac{1}{11} + \frac{1}{13}$ (iii) $\frac{1}{19} + \frac{1}{21}$

(c) How is the third number in the Pythagorean triple related to the other two numbers?
(d) Use a variable to explain why this result holds. For example, you might represent the two denominators by n and $n + 2$.

21. The unending sum $\frac{1}{2} + \frac{1}{4} + \frac{1}{8} + \frac{1}{16} + \cdots$ where each term is a fixed multiple (here $\frac{1}{2}$) of the preceding term is called an **infinite geometric series**. The sum of the first two terms is $\frac{3}{4}$.
(a) Find the sum of the first three terms, first four terms, first five terms.
(b) How many terms must be added in order for the sum to exceed $\frac{99}{100}$?
(c) Guess the sum of the geometric series.

22. Find this sum: $\dfrac{1}{1 \times 3} + \dfrac{1}{3 \times 5} + \dfrac{1}{5 \times 7} + \cdots + \dfrac{1}{21 \times 23}$.

23. A classroom of 25 students was arranged in a square with five rows and five columns. The teacher told the students that they could rearrange themselves by having each student move to a new seat directly in front, back, or directly to the right or left—no diagonal moves were permitted. Determine how this could be accomplished (if at all). (HINT: Solve an equivalent problem—consider a 5 × 5 checkerboard.)

24. There is at least one correct subtraction equation of the form $a - b = c$ in each of the following. Find all such equations. For example, in the row $\frac{1}{4} \frac{2}{3} \frac{1}{7} \frac{11}{21} \frac{2}{15}$, a correct equation is $\frac{2}{3} - \frac{1}{7} = \frac{11}{21}$.
(a) $\frac{11}{12} \frac{7}{12} \frac{3}{4} \frac{5}{9} \frac{4}{5} \frac{5}{12} \frac{1}{3} \frac{1}{12}$ (b) $\frac{2}{3} \frac{3}{5} \frac{3}{7} \frac{6}{12} \frac{1}{6} \frac{1}{3} \frac{1}{9}$

25. The following fractions use all ten digits and yield 9:
$\dfrac{97,524}{10,836}$ and $\dfrac{95,823}{10,647}$. See if you can find one more.

6.3

FRACTIONS: MULTIPLICATION AND DIVISION

Multiplication and Its Properties

Extending the repeated-addition approach of whole-number multiplication to fraction multiplication is an interesting challenge. Consider the following cases.

Case 1: A whole number times a fraction:

$$3 \times \frac{1}{4} = \frac{1}{4} + \frac{1}{4} + \frac{1}{4} = \frac{3}{4}$$

$$6 \times \frac{1}{2} = \frac{1}{2} + \frac{1}{2} + \frac{1}{2} + \frac{1}{2} + \frac{1}{2} + \frac{1}{2} = 3.$$

Here repeated addition works well since the first factor is a whole number.

Case 2: A fraction times a whole number:

$$\frac{1}{2} \times 6.$$

Here, we cannot apply the repeated-addition approach directly since that would literally say to add 6 one-half times. But if multiplication is to be commutative, then $\frac{1}{2} \times 6$ would have to be equal to $6 \times \frac{1}{2}$, or 3, as in case 1. Thus a way of interpreting $\frac{1}{2} \times 6$ would be to view the $\frac{1}{2}$ as taking "one-half of 6" or "one of two equal parts of 6," namely 3. Similarly, $\frac{1}{4} \times 3$ could be modeled by finding "one-fourth of 3" on the fraction number line to obtain $\frac{3}{4}$ (Figure 6.18).

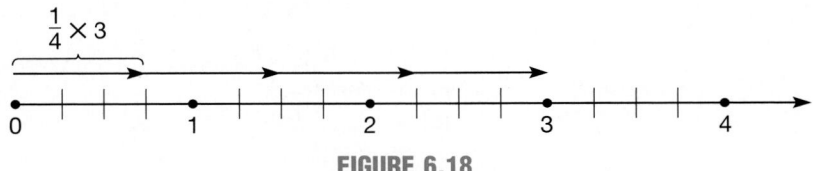

FIGURE 6.18

In the following final case, it is impossible to use the repeated-addition approach, so we apply the new technique of case 2.

Case 3: A fraction of a fraction:

$$\frac{1}{3} \times \frac{5}{7} \text{ means } \frac{1}{3} \text{ of } \frac{5}{7}.$$

First picture $\frac{5}{7}$. Then take one of the three equivalent parts of $\frac{5}{7}$ (Figure 6.19).

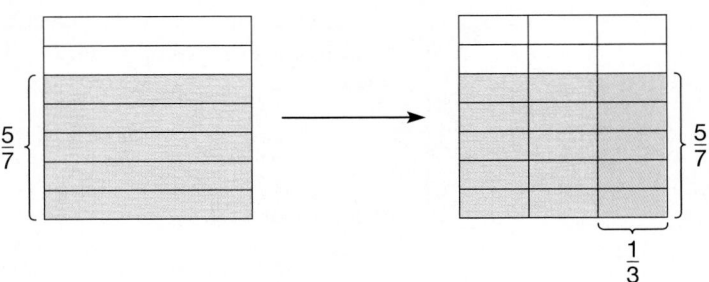

FIGURE 6.19

After subdividing the region in Figure 6.19 horizontally into seven equivalent parts and vertically into three equal parts, the crosshatched region consists of 5 of the 21 smallest rectangles (each small rectangle represents $\frac{1}{21}$). Therefore,

$$\frac{1}{3} \times \frac{5}{7} = \frac{5}{21}.$$

Similarly, $\frac{2}{3} \times \frac{5}{7}$ would comprise 10 of the smallest rectangles, so

$$\frac{2}{3} \times \frac{5}{7} = \frac{10}{21}.$$

This discussion should make the following definition of fraction multiplication seem reasonable.

Definition

Multiplication of Fractions

Let $\dfrac{a}{b}$ and $\dfrac{c}{d}$ be any fractions. Then

$$\frac{a}{b} \cdot \frac{c}{d} = \frac{ac}{bd}.$$

EXAMPLE 6.12 Compute the following products and express the answers in simplest form.
(a) $\frac{2}{3} \cdot \frac{5}{13}$ **(b)** $\frac{3}{4} \cdot \frac{28}{15}$ **(c)** $2\frac{1}{3} \times 7\frac{2}{5}$

Solution

(a) $\dfrac{2}{3} \cdot \dfrac{5}{13} = \dfrac{2 \cdot 5}{3 \cdot 13} = \dfrac{10}{39}$

(b) $\dfrac{3}{4} \cdot \dfrac{28}{15} = \dfrac{3 \cdot 28}{4 \cdot 15} = \dfrac{84}{60} = \dfrac{21 \cdot 4}{15 \cdot 4} = \dfrac{21}{15} = \dfrac{7 \cdot 3}{5 \cdot 3} = \dfrac{7}{5}$

(c) $2\dfrac{1}{3} \cdot 7\dfrac{2}{5} = \dfrac{7}{3} \cdot \dfrac{37}{5} = \dfrac{259}{15}$, or $17\dfrac{4}{15}$

In Example 6.12(b), the product was easy to find but the process of simplification required several steps.

When using a fraction calculator, the answers are often given in simplest form. For example, on the TI-34, Example 6.12(b) is obtained as follows:

$$3 \boxed{a\,^b/_c}\, 4 \boxed{\times} 28 \boxed{a\,^b/_c} 15 \boxed{=}$$
$$\boxed{1\_2\lrcorner5}$$

which means $1\frac{2}{5}$.

The next example shows how one can simplify first (a good habit to cultivate) and then multiply.

EXAMPLE 6.13 Compute and simplify: $\frac{3}{4} \cdot \frac{28}{15}$.

Solution
Instead, simplify, and then compute.

$$\frac{3}{4} \cdot \frac{28}{15} = \frac{3 \cdot 28}{4 \cdot 15} = \frac{3 \cdot 28}{15 \cdot 4} = \frac{3}{15} \cdot \frac{28}{4} = \frac{1}{5} \cdot \frac{7}{1} = \frac{7}{5}.$$

The equation $\dfrac{a}{b} \cdot \dfrac{c}{d} = \dfrac{a}{d} \cdot \dfrac{c}{b}$ is a simplification of the essence of the procedure in Example 6.13. That is, we simply interchange the two denominators to expedite the simplification process. This can be justified as follows:

$$\frac{a}{b} \cdot \frac{c}{d} = \frac{ac}{bd} \qquad \text{Multiplication of fractions}$$

$$= \frac{ac}{db} \qquad \begin{array}{l}\text{Commutativity for} \\ \text{whole-number multiplication}\end{array}$$

$$= \frac{a}{d} \cdot \frac{c}{b}. \qquad \text{Multiplication of fractions}$$

You may have seen the following even shorter method.

EXAMPLE 6.14   Compute and simplify.
(a) $\frac{18}{13} \cdot \frac{39}{72}$
(b) $\frac{50}{15} \cdot \frac{39}{55}$

Solution

(a) $\dfrac{18}{13} \cdot \dfrac{39}{72} = \dfrac{18}{13} \cdot \dfrac{\overset{3}{39}}{72} = \dfrac{\overset{1}{18}}{13} \cdot \dfrac{\overset{3}{39}}{\underset{4}{72}} = \dfrac{3}{4}$

(b) $\dfrac{50}{15} \cdot \dfrac{39}{55} = \dfrac{\overset{10}{50}}{\underset{3}{15}} \cdot \dfrac{39}{55} = \dfrac{\overset{2}{10}}{3} \cdot \dfrac{39}{\underset{11}{55}} = \dfrac{2}{3} \cdot \dfrac{\overset{13}{39}}{\underset{1}{11}} = \dfrac{26}{11}$

The definition of fraction multiplication together with the corresponding properties for whole-number multiplication can be used to verify properties of fraction multiplication. A verification in the multiplicative identity property for fraction multiplication is shown next.

$$\frac{a}{b} \cdot 1 = \frac{a}{b} \cdot \frac{1}{1} \qquad \text{Recall that } 1 = \frac{1}{1} = \frac{2}{2} = \frac{3}{3} = \cdots$$

$$= \frac{a \cdot 1}{b \cdot 1} \qquad \text{Fraction multiplication}$$

$$= \frac{a}{b}. \qquad \text{Identity for whole-number multiplication}$$

It is shown in the problem set that 1 is the only multiplicative identity.

The properties of fraction multiplication are summarized next. Notice that fraction multiplication has an additional property, different from any whole-number properties, namely the multiplicative inverse property.

Properties of Fraction Multiplication

Let $\dfrac{a}{b}$, $\dfrac{c}{d}$, and $\dfrac{e}{f}$ be any fractions.

Closure Property for Fraction Multiplication

The product of two fractions is a fraction.

Commutative Property for Fraction Multiplication

$$\frac{a}{b} \cdot \frac{c}{d} = \frac{c}{d} \cdot \frac{a}{b}.$$

Associative Property for Fraction Multiplication

$$\left(\frac{a}{b} \cdot \frac{c}{d} \right) \cdot \frac{e}{f} = \frac{a}{b} \cdot \left(\frac{c}{d} \cdot \frac{e}{f} \right).$$

Multiplicative Identity Property for Fraction Multiplication

$$\frac{a}{b} \cdot 1 = \frac{a}{b} = 1 \cdot \frac{a}{b}. \quad \left(1 = \frac{m}{m}, m \neq 0. \right)$$

Multiplicative Inverse Property for Fraction Multiplication

For every *nonzero* fraction $\dfrac{a}{b}$, there is a unique fraction $\dfrac{b}{a}$ such that

$$\frac{a}{b} \cdot \frac{b}{a} = 1.$$

When $\dfrac{a}{b} \neq 0$, the number $\dfrac{b}{a}$ is called the **multiplicative inverse** or **reciprocal** of $\dfrac{a}{b}$. The multiplicative inverse property is useful for solving equations involving fractions.

EXAMPLE 6.15 Solve: $\frac{3}{7}x = \frac{5}{8}$.

Solution

$$\frac{3}{7}x = \frac{5}{8}$$

$$\frac{7}{3}\left(\frac{3}{7}x\right) = \frac{7}{3} \cdot \frac{5}{8} \qquad \text{Multiplication}$$

$$\left(\frac{7}{3} \cdot \frac{3}{7}\right)x = \frac{7}{3} \cdot \frac{5}{8} \qquad \text{Associative property}$$

$$1 \cdot x = \frac{35}{24} \qquad \text{Multiplicative inverse property}$$

$$x = \frac{35}{24}. \qquad \text{Multiplicative identity property}$$

Finally, as with whole numbers, distributivity holds for fractions. This property can be verified using distributivity in the whole numbers.

Distributive Property of Fraction Multiplication over Addition

Let $\dfrac{a}{b}$, $\dfrac{c}{d}$, and $\dfrac{e}{f}$ be any fractions. Then

$$\frac{a}{b}\left(\frac{c}{d} + \frac{e}{f}\right) = \frac{a}{b} \times \frac{c}{d} + \frac{a}{b} \times \frac{e}{f}.$$

Distributivity of multiplication over subtraction also holds; that is,

$$\frac{a}{b}\left(\frac{c}{d} - \frac{e}{f}\right) = \frac{a}{b} \times \frac{c}{d} - \frac{a}{b} \times \frac{e}{f}.$$

Division

Division of fractions is a difficult concept for many children (and adults), in part because of the lack of simple concrete models. We will view division of fractions as an *extension* of whole-number division. Several other approaches will be used in this section and in the problem set. These approaches provide a *meaningful way* of learning fraction division. Such approaches are a departure from simply memorizing the rote procedure of "invert and multiply," which offers no insight into fraction division.

By using common denominators, division of fractions can be viewed as an extension of whole-number division. For example, the answer to the problem $\frac{6}{7} \div \frac{2}{7}$ can be obtained by answering the question: "How many $\frac{2}{7}$ are in $\frac{6}{7}$?" The answer to this question is equivalent to asking "How many 2s are in 6?" Since there are *three* 2s in 6, so there are *three* $\frac{2}{7}$ in $\frac{6}{7}$ because $\frac{2}{7} + \frac{2}{7} + \frac{2}{7} = \frac{6}{7}$. Figure 6.20 illustrates this visually.

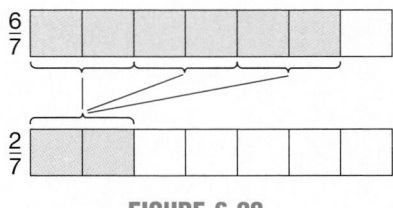

FIGURE 6.20

EXAMPLE 6.16   Find the following quotients.
(a) $\frac{12}{13} \div \frac{4}{13}$ **(b)** $\frac{6}{17} \div \frac{3}{17}$ **(c)** $\frac{16}{19} \div \frac{2}{19}$

Solution
(a) $\frac{12}{13} \div \frac{4}{13} = 3$ since there are three $\frac{4}{13}$ in $\frac{12}{13}$.
(b) $\frac{6}{17} \div \frac{3}{17} = 2$ since there are two $\frac{3}{17}$ in $\frac{6}{17}$.
(c) $\frac{16}{19} \div \frac{2}{19} = 8$ since there are eight $\frac{2}{19}$ in $\frac{16}{19}$.

Notice that the answers to all three of these problems can be found simply by dividing the numerators in the correct order. ∎

In the case of $\frac{12}{13} \div \frac{5}{13}$, we ask ourselves, "How many $\frac{5}{13}$ make $\frac{12}{13}$?" But this is the same as asking, "How many 5s (including fractional parts) are in 12?" The answer is 2 and $\frac{2}{5}$ fives or $\frac{12}{5}$ fives. Thus $\frac{12}{13} \div \frac{5}{13} = \frac{12}{5}$. Generalizing this idea and Example 6.16, we define fraction division as follows:

Definition

Division of Fractions with Common Denominators

Let $\dfrac{a}{b}$ and $\dfrac{c}{b}$ be any fractions with $c \neq 0$. Then

$$\frac{a}{b} \div \frac{c}{b} = \frac{a}{c}.$$

To divide fractions with different denominators, we can rewrite the fractions so that they have the same denominator. Thus we see that

$$\frac{a}{b} \div \frac{c}{d} = \frac{ad}{bd} \div \frac{bc}{bd} = \frac{ad}{bc} \quad \left(= \frac{a}{b} \times \frac{d}{c} \right)$$

using division with common denominators. For example, $\dfrac{3}{7} \div \dfrac{5}{9} = \dfrac{27}{63} \div \dfrac{35}{63} = \dfrac{27}{35}$.

Notice that the quotient $\dfrac{a}{b} \div \dfrac{c}{d}$ is equal to the product $\dfrac{a}{b} \times \dfrac{d}{c}$ since they are both equal to $\dfrac{ad}{bc}$. Thus a procedure for dividing fractions is to invert the divisor and multiply.

Another interpretation of division of fractions using the missing-factor approach refers directly to multiplication of fractions.

EXAMPLE 6.17 Find: $\frac{21}{20} \div \frac{7}{8}$.

Solution

Let $\dfrac{21}{40} \div \dfrac{7}{8} = \dfrac{e}{f}$. If the missing-factor approach holds, then $\dfrac{21}{40} = \dfrac{7}{8} \times \dfrac{e}{f}$. Then $\dfrac{7 \times e}{8 \times f} = \dfrac{21}{40}$ and we can take $e = 3$ and $f = 5$. Therefore, $\dfrac{e}{f} = \dfrac{3}{5}$, or $\dfrac{21}{40} \div \dfrac{7}{8} = \dfrac{3}{5}$. ■

In Example 6.17 we have the convenient situation where one set of numerators and denominators divides evenly into the other set. Thus a short way of doing this problem is

$$\frac{21}{40} \div \frac{7}{8} = \frac{21 \div 7}{40 \div 8} = \frac{3}{5}$$

since $21 \div 7 = 3$ and $40 \div 8 = 5$. This "divide the numerators and denominators approach" can be adapted to a more general case, as the following example shows.

EXAMPLE 6.18   Find: $\frac{21}{40} \div \frac{6}{11}$.

Solution

$$\frac{21}{40} \div \frac{6}{11} = \frac{21 \times 6 \times 11}{40 \times 6 \times 11} \div \frac{6}{11}$$

$$= \frac{(21 \times 6 \times 11) \div 6}{(40 \times 6 \times 11) \div 11}$$

$$= \frac{21 \times 11}{40 \times 6}$$

$$= \frac{231}{240} = \frac{21}{40} \times \frac{11}{6} \ .$$

Notice that this approach leads us to conclude that $\frac{21}{40} \div \frac{6}{11} = \frac{21}{40} \times \frac{11}{6}$. Generalizing from these examples and results using the common-denominator approach, we are led to the following familiar "invert the divisor and multiply" procedure.

Theorem

Division of Fractions with Unlike Denominators— Invert the Divisor and Multiply

Let $\frac{a}{b}$ and $\frac{c}{d}$ be any fractions with $c \neq 0$. Then

$$\frac{a}{b} \div \frac{c}{d} = \frac{a}{b} \times \frac{d}{c}.$$

EXAMPLE 6.19   Find the following quotients using the most convenient division method.
(a) $\frac{17}{11} \div \frac{4}{11}$ **(b)** $\frac{3}{4} \div \frac{5}{7}$ **(c)** $\frac{6}{25} \div \frac{2}{5}$ **(d)** $\frac{5}{19} \div \frac{13}{11}$

Solution

(a) $\dfrac{17}{11} \div \dfrac{4}{11} = \dfrac{17}{4}$, using the common-denominator approach.

(b) $\dfrac{3}{4} \div \dfrac{5}{7} = \dfrac{3}{4} \times \dfrac{7}{5} = \dfrac{21}{20}$,   using the invert-the-divisor-and-multiply approach.

(c) $\dfrac{6}{25} \div \dfrac{2}{5} = \dfrac{6 \div 2}{25 \div 5} = \dfrac{3}{5}$,   using the divide-numerators-and-denominators approach.

(d) $\dfrac{5}{19} \div \dfrac{13}{11} = \dfrac{5}{19} \times \dfrac{11}{13} = \dfrac{55}{247}$,   using the invert-the-divisor-and-multiply approach.

In summary, there are three equivalent ways to view the division of fractions:

1. The common-denominator approach.
2. The divide-the-numerators-and-denominators approach.
3. The invert-the-divisor-and-multiply approach.

Now, through the division of fractions, we can perform the division of any whole numbers without having to use remainders. (Of course, we still cannot divide by zero.) That is, if a and b are whole numbers and $b \neq 0$, then $a \div b = \dfrac{a}{1} \div \dfrac{b}{1} = \dfrac{a}{1} \times \dfrac{1}{b} = \dfrac{a}{b}$. This is summarized next.

For all whole numbers a and b, b ≠ 0,

$$a \div b = \frac{a}{b}.$$

EXAMPLE 6.20   Find $17 \div 6$ using fractions.

Solution
$17 \div 6 = \frac{17}{6} = 2\frac{5}{6}$.   ■

There are many situations in which the answer $2\frac{5}{6}$ is more useful than 2 with a remainder of 5. For example, suppose that 17 acres of land were to be divided among 6 families. Each family would receive $2\frac{5}{6}$ acres, rather than each receiving 2 acres with 5 acres remaining unassigned.

Expressing a division problem as a fraction is a useful idea. For example, **complex fractions** such as $\dfrac{\frac{1}{2}}{\frac{3}{5}}$ may be written in place of $\frac{1}{2} \div \frac{3}{5}$. Although fractions are comprised of whole numbers in elementary school mathematics, numbers other than whole numbers are used in numerators and denominators of "fractions" later. For example, the "fraction" $\dfrac{\sqrt{2}}{\pi}$ is simply a symbolic way of writing the quotient $\sqrt{2} \div \pi$ (numbers such as $\sqrt{2}$ and π are discussed in Chapter 9).

Mental Math and Estimation for Multiplication and Division

Mental math and estimation techniques similar to those used with whole numbers can be used with fractions.

EXAMPLE 6.21   Calculate mentally.

(a) $(25 \times 16) \times \dfrac{1}{4}$ **(b)** $3\dfrac{1}{8} \times 24$ **(c)** $\dfrac{4}{5} \times 15$

Solution
(a) $(25 \times 16) \times \dfrac{1}{4} = 25 \times \left(16 \times \dfrac{1}{4} \right) = 25 \times 4 = 100.$

Associativity was used to group 16 and $\frac{1}{4}$ together since they are compatible numbers. Also, 25 and 4 are compatible with respect to multiplication.

(b) $3\frac{1}{8} \times 24 = \left(3 + \frac{1}{8}\right) \times 24 = 3 \times 24 + \frac{1}{8} \times 24 = 72 + 3 = 75.$

Distributivity can often be used when multiplying mixed numbers as illustrated here.

(c) $\frac{4}{5} \times 15 = \left(4 \times \frac{1}{5}\right) \times 15 = 4 \times \left(\frac{1}{5} \times 15\right) = 4 \times 3 = 12.$

The calculation also can be written as $\frac{4}{5} \times 15 = 4 \times \frac{15}{5} = 4 \times 3 = 12.$ This product also can be found as follows: $\frac{4}{5} \times 15 = \left(\frac{4}{5} \times 5\right) \times 3 = 4 \times 3 = 12.$ ∎

EXAMPLE 6.22   Estimate using the indicated techniques.

(a) $5\frac{1}{8} \times 7\frac{5}{6}$ using range estimation

(b) $4\frac{3}{8} \times 9\frac{1}{16}$ rounding to the nearest $\frac{1}{2}$ or whole

Solution

(a) $5\frac{1}{8} \times 7\frac{5}{6}$ is between $5 \times 7 = 35$ and $6 \times 8 = 48.$

(b) $4\frac{3}{8} \times 9\frac{1}{16} \approx 4\frac{1}{2} \times 9 = 36 + 4\frac{1}{2} = 40\frac{1}{2}.$ ∎

MATHEMATICAL MORSEL

The Hindu mathematician Bhaskara (1119–1185) wrote an arithmetic text called the *Lilavat* (named after his wife). The following is one of the problems contained in this text. "A necklace was broken during an amorous struggle. One-third of the pearls fell to the ground, one-fifth stayed on the couch, one-sixth were found by the girl, and one-tenth were recovered by her lover; six pearls remained on the string. Say of how many pearls the necklace was composed."

EXERCISE/PROBLEM SET 6.3—PART A

Exercises

1. Illustrate the following using repeated addition.
   (a) $5 \times \frac{1}{2}$ (b) $8 \times \frac{1}{3}$

2. Illustrate the following products using the rectangular area model.
   (a) $\frac{1}{3} \times \frac{2}{5}$ (b) $\frac{3}{8} \times \frac{5}{6}$ (c) $\frac{2}{3} \times \frac{7}{10}$

3. What multiplication problems are represented by each of the following area models? What are the products?
   (a)

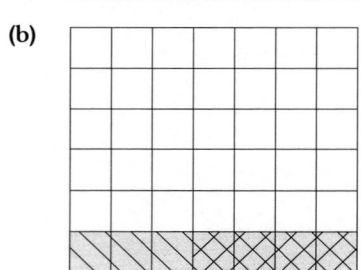

   (b)

4. Find reciprocals for the following numbers.
   (a) $\frac{11}{21}$ (b) $\frac{9}{3}$ (c) $13\frac{4}{9}$ (d) 108

5. (a) Insert the appropriate equality or inequality symbol in the following statement:

   $$\frac{3}{4} \_\_\_\_ \frac{3}{2}$$

   (b) Find the reciprocals of $\frac{3}{4}$ and $\frac{3}{2}$ and complete the following statement, inserting either $<$ or $>$ in the center blank.

   $$\underline{\hspace{2cm}} \_\_\_\_ \underline{\hspace{2cm}}$$
   reciprocal of $\frac{3}{4}$ reciprocal of $\frac{3}{2}$

   (c) What do you notice about ordering reciprocals?

6. Use the common-denominator method to divide the following fractions.
   (a) $\frac{15}{17} \div \frac{3}{17}$ (b) $\frac{4}{7} \div \frac{3}{7}$ (c) $\frac{33}{51} \div \frac{39}{51}$

7. Use the fact that the numerators and denominators divide evenly to simplify the following quotients.
   (a) $\frac{15}{16} \div \frac{3}{4}$ (b) $\frac{21}{27} \div \frac{7}{9}$ (c) $\frac{39}{56} \div \frac{3}{8}$
   (d) $\frac{17}{24} \div \frac{17}{12}$

8. Perform the following operations and express your answers in simplest form.

   (a) $\frac{4}{7} \cdot \frac{3}{8}$
   (b) $\frac{6}{25} \cdot \frac{5}{9} \cdot \frac{3}{2}$
   (c) $\frac{2}{5} \cdot \frac{9}{13} + \frac{2}{5} \cdot \frac{4}{13}$
   (d) $\frac{11}{12} \cdot \frac{5}{13} + \frac{5}{13} \cdot \frac{7}{12}$
   (e) $\frac{4}{7} \div \frac{3}{14}$
   (f) $\frac{2}{9} \div \frac{4}{3} \cdot \frac{5}{7}$
   (g) $\frac{7}{15} \div 3\frac{1}{2} \div \frac{3}{5}$
   (h) $\frac{1}{3} \cdot \frac{5}{4} + \frac{1}{4} \cdot \frac{5}{6}$
   (i) $\frac{1}{3} \cdot (\frac{5}{4} - \frac{1}{4}) \cdot \frac{5}{6}$
   (j) $\frac{1}{3} + \frac{5}{4}(\frac{1}{4} \div \frac{5}{6})$

9. Find the following products and quotients.
   (a) $5\frac{1}{3} \cdot 2\frac{1}{6}$ (b) $3\frac{7}{8} \cdot 2\frac{3}{4}$ (c) $3\frac{3}{4} \cdot 2\frac{2}{5}$
   (d) $8\frac{1}{3} \div 2\frac{1}{10}$ (e) $6\frac{1}{4} \div 1\frac{2}{3}$ (f) $16\frac{2}{3} \div 2\frac{7}{9}$

10. Calculate mentally using properties.
    (a) $15 \cdot \frac{3}{7} + 6 \cdot \frac{3}{7}$ (b) $35 \cdot \frac{6}{7} - 35 \cdot \frac{3}{7}$
    (c) $(\frac{3}{7} + \frac{1}{9}) + \frac{4}{7}$ (d) $3\frac{5}{9} \times 54$

11. Suppose that the following unit square represents the whole number 1.

    We can use squares like this one to represent division problems like $3 \div \frac{1}{2}$, by asking how many $\frac{1}{2}$'s are in 3.

    $3 \div \frac{1}{2} = 6$ since there are six one-half squares in the three squares. Draw similar figures and calculate the quotients for the following division problems.
    (a) $4 \div \frac{1}{3}$ (b) $2\frac{1}{2} \div \frac{1}{4}$ (c) $3 \div \frac{3}{4}$

12. Estimate using compatible numbers.
    (a) $29\frac{1}{3} \times 4\frac{2}{3}$ (b) $57\frac{1}{5} \div 7\frac{4}{5}$
    (c) $70\frac{3}{5} \div 8\frac{5}{8}$ (d) $31\frac{1}{4} \times 5\frac{3}{4}$

13. Estimate using cluster estimation.
    (a) $12\frac{1}{4} \times 11\frac{5}{6}$ (b) $5\frac{1}{10} \times 4\frac{8}{9} \times 5\frac{4}{11}$

14. Change each of the following complex fractions into ordinary fractions.
    (a) $\dfrac{\frac{7}{9}}{\frac{13}{14}}$ (b) $\dfrac{\frac{2}{3}}{\frac{3}{2}}$ (c) $\dfrac{\frac{2}{3}}{\frac{2}{3}}$ (d) $\dfrac{1\frac{4}{7}}{3\frac{7}{8}}$

15. Identify which of the properties of fractions could be applied to simplify each of the following computations.
    (a) $\frac{2}{7} + (\frac{5}{7} + \frac{2}{9})$ (b) $(\frac{3}{5} \times \frac{2}{11}) + (\frac{2}{5} \times \frac{2}{11})$
    (c) $(\frac{8}{5} \times \frac{3}{13}) \times \frac{13}{3}$

16. Justify each line in the following proof of the distributive property for fractions.

    $$\frac{a}{b} \times \left(\frac{c}{b} + \frac{d}{b}\right) = \frac{a}{b} \times \left(\frac{c + d}{b}\right)$$

    $$= \frac{a \times (c + d)}{b^2}$$

$$= \frac{a \times c + a \times d}{b^2}$$

$$= \frac{a \times c}{b^2} + \frac{a \times d}{b^2}$$

$$= \frac{a}{b} \times \frac{c}{b} + \frac{a}{b} \times \frac{d}{b}.$$

17. We usually think of the distributive property for fractions as "multiplication of fractions distributes over addition of fractions." Which of the following variations of the distributive property for fractions holds for arbitrary fractions?
(a) Addition over subtraction
(b) Division over multiplication
(c) Multiplication over subtraction
(d) Subtraction over addition

18. Are fractions closed under the following operations?
(a) Addition
(b) Subtraction
(c) Multiplication
(d) Division by nonzero fractions

19. Calculate using a fraction calculator.
(a) $\frac{7}{6} \times \frac{4}{5}$ (b) $\frac{4}{5} \div \frac{2}{7}$ (c) $2 \times \frac{3}{8}$
(d) $12 \div \frac{2}{3}$

20. The introduction of fractions allows us to solve equations of the form $ax = b$ by dividing whole numbers. For example, $5x = 16$ has as its solution $x = \frac{16}{5}$ (which is 16 divided by 5). Solve each of the following equations and check your results.
(a) $31x = 15$ (b) $67x = 56$ (c) $102x = 231$

Problems

21. You buy a family-size box of laundry detergent that contains 40 cups. If your washing machine calls for $1\frac{1}{4}$ cups per wash load, how many loads of wash can you do?

22. In 1989 the total U.S. petroleum production was only about $\frac{5}{7}$ of the amount of petroleum used in the United States for transportation purposes. If U.S. petroleum production in 1989 was 7,630,000 barrels per day, how much petroleum was being used for transportation at that time? (SOURCE: *1992 Environmental Almanac.*)

23. All but $\frac{1}{16}$ of the students enrolled at a particular elementary school participated in "Family Fun Night" activities. If a total of 405 students were involved in the evening's activities, how many students attend the school?

24. The directions for Weed-Do-In weed killer recommend mixing $2\frac{1}{2}$ ounces of the concentrate with 1 gallon of water. The bottle of Weed-Do-In contains 32 ounces of concentrate.

(a) How many gallons of mixture can be made from the bottle of concentrate?
(b) Since the weed killer is rather expensive, one gardener decided to stretch his dollar by mixing only $1\frac{3}{4}$ ounces of concentrate with a gallon of water. How many more gallons of mixture can be made this way?

25. During one evening Kathleen devoted $\frac{2}{5}$ of her study time to mathematics, $\frac{3}{20}$ of her time to Spanish, $\frac{1}{3}$ of her time to biology, and the remaining 35 minutes to English. How much time did she spend studying her Spanish?

26. A number of employees of a company enrolled in a fitness program on January 2. By March 2, $\frac{4}{5}$ of them were still participating. Of those, $\frac{5}{6}$ were still participating on May 2 and of those, $\frac{9}{10}$ were still participating on July 2. Determine the number of employees who originally enrolled in the program if 36 of the original participants were still active on July 2.

27. Each morning Tammy walks to school. At one-third of the way she passes a grocery store and halfway to school she passes a bicycle shop. At the grocery store, her watch says 7:40 and at the bicycle shop it says 7:45. When does Tammy reach her school?

28. A recipe that makes 3 dozen peanut butter cookies calls for $1\frac{1}{4}$ cups of flour.
(a) How much flour would you need if you doubled the recipe?
(b) How much flour would you need for half the recipe?
(c) How much flour would you need to make 5 dozen cookies?

29. A softball team had three pitchers: Gale, Ruth, and Sandy. Gale started in $\frac{3}{8}$ of the games played in one season. Sandy started in one more game than Gale, and Ruth started in half as many games as Sandy. In how many of the season's games did each pitcher start?

30. A piece of office equipment purchased for $60,000 depreciates in value each year. Suppose that each year the value of the equipment is $\frac{1}{20}$ less than its value the preceding year.
(a) Calculate the value of the equipment after 2 years.
(b) When will the piece of equipment first have a value less than $40,000?

31. If a nonzero number is divided by one more than itself, the result is one-fifth. If a second nonzero number is divided by one more than itself, the answer is one-fifth of the number itself. What is the product of the two numbers?

32. Carpenters divide fractions by 2 in the following way:

$$\frac{11}{16} \div 2 = \frac{11}{16 \times 2} = \frac{11}{32} \text{ (doubling the denominator)}$$

(a) How would they find $\frac{11}{16} \div 5$?

(b) Does $\dfrac{a}{b} \div n = \dfrac{a}{b \times n}$ always?

(c) Find a quick mental method for finding $5\frac{3}{8} \div 2$. Do the same for $10\frac{9}{16} \div 2$.

33. (a) Following are examples of student work in multiplying fractions. In each case, identify the error and answer the given problem as the student would.

Sam: $\frac{1}{2} \times \frac{2}{3} = \frac{3}{6} \times \frac{4}{6} = \frac{12}{6} = 2$

   $\frac{3}{4} \times \frac{1}{8} = \frac{6}{8} \times \frac{1}{8} = \frac{6}{8} = \frac{3}{4}$ $\frac{3}{4} \times \frac{1}{6} = ?$

Sandy: $\frac{3}{8} \times \frac{5}{6} = \frac{3}{8} \times \frac{6}{5} = \frac{18}{40} = \frac{9}{20}$

   $\frac{2}{5} \times \frac{2}{3} = \frac{2}{5} \times \frac{3}{2} = \frac{6}{10} = \frac{3}{5}$ $\frac{5}{6} \times \frac{3}{8} = ?$

(b) Each student is confusing the multiplication algorithm with another algorithm. Which one?

34. Arrange the digits 3, 4, 5, 6, 8, 9 to produce equations.

(a) $\dfrac{\square}{\square} \times \dfrac{\square}{\square} = \dfrac{8}{15}$ **(b)** $\dfrac{\square}{\square} \div \dfrac{\square}{\square} = \dfrac{5}{4}$

(c) $\dfrac{\square}{\square} \times \dfrac{\square}{\square} = \dfrac{6}{5}$ **(d)** $\dfrac{\square}{\square} \div \dfrac{\square}{\square} = \dfrac{16}{5}$

35. Mr. Horne wanted to buy all the grocer's apples for a church picnic. When he asked how many apples the store had, the grocer replied, "If you added $\frac{1}{4}$, $\frac{1}{5}$, and $\frac{1}{6}$ of them, it would make 37." How many apples were in the store?

36. An organization has five elected officers. Two of the officers will attend a statewide meeting as voting delegates. In how many different ways can two delegates be selected from the five officers?

EXERCISE/PROBLEM SET 6.3—PART B

Exercises

1. Illustrate the following products using the rectangular area model.
   (a) $\frac{1}{4} \times \frac{3}{5}$ **(b)** $\frac{4}{7} \times \frac{2}{3}$ **(c)** $\frac{3}{4} \times \frac{5}{6}$

2. What multiplication problems are represented by each of the following area models. What are the products?
   (a)

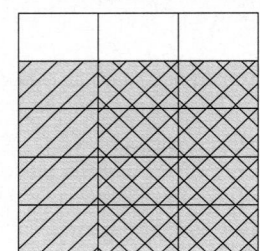

   (b)

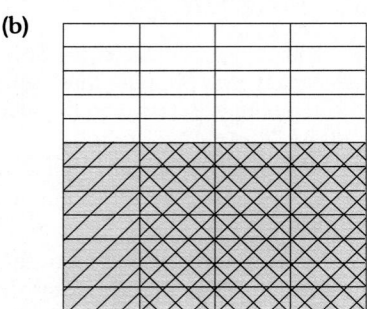

3. (a) What is the reciprocal of the reciprocal of $\frac{4}{13}$?
   (b) What is the reciprocal of the multiplicative inverse of $\frac{4}{13}$?

4. (a) Order the following numbers from smallest to largest.

$$\frac{5}{8} \qquad \frac{3}{16} \qquad \frac{7}{5} \qquad \frac{9}{10}$$

   (b) Find the reciprocals of the given numbers and order them from smallest to largest.
   (c) What do you observe about these two orders?

5. The missing-factor approach can be applied to fraction division, as illustrated.

$$\frac{4}{7} \div \frac{2}{5} = \boxed{} \quad \text{so} \quad \frac{2}{5} \times \boxed{} = \frac{4}{7}$$

Since we want $\frac{4}{7}$ to be the result, we insert that in the box. Then if we put in the reciprocal of $\frac{2}{5}$, we have

$$\frac{2}{5} \times \boxed{\frac{5}{2} \times \frac{4}{7}} = \frac{4}{7} \quad \text{so}$$

$$\frac{4}{7} \div \frac{2}{5} = \boxed{\frac{5}{2} \times \frac{4}{7}} = \frac{20}{14} = \frac{10}{7}$$

Use this approach to do the following division problems.
   (a) $\frac{3}{5} \div \frac{2}{7}$ **(b)** $\frac{13}{6} \div \frac{3}{7}$ **(c)** $\frac{12}{13} \div \frac{6}{5}$

6. Find the following quotients using the most convenient of the three methods for division. Express your answer in simplest form.
   (a) $\frac{5}{7} \div \frac{4}{9}$ **(b)** $\frac{33}{14} \div \frac{11}{7}$
   (c) $\frac{5}{13} \div \frac{3}{13}$ **(d)** $\frac{3}{11} \div \frac{8}{22}$

7. Perform the following operations and express your answer in simplest form.
   (a) $\frac{3}{5} \times \frac{4}{9}$ **(b)** $\frac{2}{7} \times \frac{21}{10}$

(c) $\frac{7}{100} \times \frac{11}{10,000}$ **(d)** $\frac{4}{9} \times \frac{8}{11} + \frac{7}{9} \times \frac{8}{11}$

(e) $\frac{3}{5} \times \frac{2}{3} + \frac{4}{7}$ **(f)** $\frac{3}{5} + \frac{2}{3} \times \frac{4}{7}$

(g) $\frac{3}{5} \times (\frac{2}{3} + \frac{4}{7})$ **(h)** $7\frac{2}{5} \times 5\frac{4}{7}$

(i) $8\frac{1}{4} \times 3\frac{4}{5}$ **(j)** $\frac{9}{11} \div \frac{2}{3}$

(k) $4\frac{3}{7} \div 3\frac{8}{11}$ **(l)** $\frac{17}{100} \div \frac{9}{10,000}$

8. Calculate the following and express as mixed numbers in simplest form.
  (a) $11\frac{3}{5} \div 9\frac{8}{9}$ **(b)** $7\frac{5}{8} \times 13\frac{2}{3}$
  (c) $11\frac{3}{5} \times 9\frac{8}{9}$ **(d)** $7\frac{5}{8} \div 13\frac{2}{3}$

9. If the following square represents 1, draw figures to represent each of the following division problems. Then find the quotients. (See Problem 11 in Part A.)

  (a) $2 \div \frac{1}{4}$ **(b)** $6 \div \frac{3}{5}$ **(c)** $3\frac{1}{3} \div \frac{2}{3}$

10. (a) Does $2\frac{3}{4} + 5\frac{7}{8} = 2\frac{7}{8} + 5\frac{3}{4}$? Explain.
  (b) Does $2\frac{3}{4} \times 5\frac{7}{8} = 2\frac{7}{8} \times 5\frac{3}{4}$? Explain.

11. Calculate mentally using properties.
  (a) $52 \cdot \frac{7}{8} - 52 \cdot \frac{3}{8}$ **(b)** $(\frac{2}{5} + \frac{5}{8}) + \frac{3}{5}$
  (c) $36 \times 2\frac{3}{4}$ **(d)** $23 \cdot \frac{3}{7} + 7 + 23 \cdot \frac{4}{7}$

12. Estimate using compatible numbers.
  (a) $19\frac{1}{3} \times 5\frac{3}{5}$ **(b)** $77\frac{1}{5} \div 23\frac{4}{5}$
  (c) $54\frac{3}{5} \div 7\frac{5}{8}$ **(d)** $25\frac{2}{3} \times 3\frac{3}{4}$

13. Estimate using cluster estimation.
  (a) $5\frac{2}{3} \times 6\frac{1}{8}$ **(b)** $3\frac{1}{10} \times 2\frac{8}{9} \times 3\frac{2}{11}$

14. Using the definition of fraction multiplication and the properties of whole numbers, verify the following properties.
  (a) Closure property for fraction multiplication
  (b) Commutative property for fraction multiplication
  (c) Associative property for fraction multiplication

15. Do the following properties hold for division of fractions? Explain.
  (a) Commutativity **(b)** Associativity

16. Another way to find a fraction between two given fractions $\frac{a}{b}$ and $\frac{c}{d}$ is to find the average of the two fractions. For example, the average of $\frac{1}{2}$ and $\frac{2}{3}$ is $\frac{1}{2}(\frac{1}{2} + \frac{2}{3}) = \frac{7}{12}$. Use this method to find a fraction between each of the given pairs.
  (a) $\frac{7}{8}, \frac{8}{9}$ **(b)** $\frac{7}{12}, \frac{11}{16}$

17. Here is a shortcut for multiplying by 25:

$$25 \times 36 = \frac{100}{4} \times 36 = 100 \times \frac{36}{4} = 900.$$

Use this idea to find the following products mentally.
  (a) 25×44 **(b)** 25×120
  (c) 25×488 **(d)** 1248×25

Now make up your own shortcuts for multiplying by 50 and 75 and use them to compute the following products mentally.
  (e) 50×246 **(f)** $84,602 \times 50$
  (g) 75×848 **(h)** 420×75

18. Solve the following equations involving fractions.
  (a) $\frac{2}{5}x = \frac{3}{7}$ **(b)** $\frac{1}{6}x = \frac{5}{12}$
  (c) $\frac{2}{9}x = \frac{7}{9}$ **(d)** $\frac{5}{3}x = \frac{1}{10}$

Problems

19. Show that 1 $\left(\text{or } \frac{b}{b} \right)$ is the only identity for multiplication. (HINT: Suppose that $\frac{a}{b} \cdot \frac{c}{d} = \frac{a}{b}$ for all fractions $\frac{a}{b}$ and show that $\frac{c}{d} = 1$.)

20. Which of the following is true? If true, prove. If false, give a counterexample. Let $\frac{a}{b}, \frac{c}{d},$ and $\frac{e}{f}$ be nonzero fractions.

  (a) $\left(\frac{a}{b} + \frac{c}{d} \right) \div \frac{e}{f} = \left(\frac{a}{b} \div \frac{e}{f} \right) + \left(\frac{c}{d} \div \frac{e}{f} \right)$

  (b) $\frac{e}{f} \div \left(\frac{a}{b} + \frac{c}{d} \right) = \left(\frac{e}{f} \div \frac{a}{b} \right) + \left(\frac{e}{f} \div \frac{c}{d} \right)$

21. According to U.S. industry estimates, 55 billion aluminum cans were recycled in 1990. That amount was $\frac{5}{8}$ of the total number of beverage cans produced in 1990. How many beverage cans were produced in the United States in 1990? (SOURCE: *1992 Environmental Almanac.*)

22. Kids belonging to a Boys and Girls Club collected cans and bottles to raise money by returning them for the deposit. If 54 more cans than bottles were collected and the number of bottles was $\frac{5}{11}$ of the total number of beverage containers collected, how many bottles were collected?

23. Mrs. Martin bought $20\frac{1}{4}$ yards of material to make 4 bridesmaid dresses and 1 dress for the flower girl. The flower girl's dress needs only half as much material as a bridesmaid dress. How much material is needed for a bridesmaid dress? For the flower girl's dress?

24. Karl wants to fertilize his $6\frac{3}{5}$ acres. If it takes $8\frac{2}{3}$ bags of fertilizer for each acre, how much fertilizer does Karl need to buy?

25. In a cost-saving measure, Chuck's company reduced all salaries by $\frac{1}{8}$ of their present salaries. If Chuck's monthly salary was $2400, what will he now receive? If his new salary is $2800, what was his old salary?

26. (a) A chicken and a half lays an egg and a half in a day and a half. How many eggs do 12 chickens lay in 12 days?

(b) How long will it take 3 chickens to lay 2 dozen eggs?

(c) How many chickens will it take to lay 36 eggs in 6 days?

27. The following students are having difficulty with division of fractions. Determine what procedure they are using and answer their final question as they would.

Abigail:
$$\frac{4}{6} \div \frac{2}{6} = \frac{2}{6}$$
$$\frac{6}{10} - \frac{6}{10} \div \frac{2}{10} = \frac{3}{10}$$
$$\frac{8}{12} - \frac{8}{12} \div \frac{2}{12} =$$

Harold:
$$\frac{2}{3} \div \frac{3}{8} = \frac{2}{3} \times \frac{3}{8} = \frac{9}{16}$$
$$\frac{3}{4} \div \frac{5}{6} = \frac{4}{3} \times \frac{5}{6} = \frac{20}{18}$$
$$\frac{5}{8} \div \frac{3}{4} =$$

28. Use numbers from this set $\{2, 3\frac{1}{4}, \frac{1}{2}, \frac{5}{6}, 4\}$ to fill in the following blanks to produce true equations.

(a) ____ + ____ − ____ = $2\frac{1}{12}$

(b) ____ − ____ + ____ = $6\frac{5}{12}$

(c) ____ × ____ + ____ = $2\frac{11}{24}$

(d) ____ ÷ ____ − ____ = $2\frac{1}{2}$

(e) ____ × ____ ÷ ____ = $\frac{1}{4}$

(f) ____ ÷ ____ − ____ = $\frac{19}{24}$

29. If you place one full container of flour on one pan of a balance scale and a similar container $\frac{3}{4}$ full and a $\frac{1}{3}$-pound weight on the other pan, the pans balance. How much does the full container of flour weigh?

30. A young man spent $\frac{1}{4}$ of his allowance on a movie. He spent $\frac{11}{18}$ of the remainder on after-school snacks. Then from the money remaining, he spent $3.00 on a magazine, which left him $\frac{1}{24}$ of his original allowance to put into savings. How much of his allowance did he save?

31. An airline passenger fell asleep halfway to her destination. When she awoke, the distance remaining was half the distance traveled while she slept. How much of the entire trip was she asleep?

32. Fill in the empty squares to produce equations.

$$\boxed{1\frac{1}{2}} \times \boxed{1\frac{1}{3}} \times \boxed{} = \boxed{5\frac{1}{3}}$$
$$\times \qquad \times \qquad \times \qquad \times$$
$$\boxed{} \times \boxed{} \times \boxed{} = \boxed{2\frac{3}{16}}$$
$$\times \qquad \times \qquad \times \qquad \times$$
$$\boxed{} \times \boxed{\frac{2}{3}} \times \boxed{4} = \boxed{1\frac{1}{3}}$$
$$= \qquad = \qquad = \qquad =$$
$$\boxed{1\frac{7}{8}} \times \boxed{3\frac{1}{9}} \times \boxed{2\frac{2}{3}} = \boxed{}$$

33. Observe the following pattern:

$$3 + 1\frac{1}{2} = 3 \times 1\frac{1}{2}$$
$$4 + 1\frac{1}{3} = 4 \times 1\frac{1}{3}$$
$$5 + 1\frac{1}{4} = 5 \times 1\frac{1}{4}$$

(a) Write the next two equations in the list.

(b) Determine whether this pattern will always hold true. If so, explain why.

34. To what pages must a book be opened if the product of the two facing pages is 4032? What if the product is 13,806?

35. If the sum of two numbers is 18 and their product is 40, find the following without finding the two numbers.

(a) The sum of the reciprocals of the two numbers

(b) The sum of the squares of the two numbers [HINT: What is $(x + y)^2$?]

36. A recipe calls for $\frac{2}{3}$ of a cup of sugar. You find that you only have $\frac{1}{2}$ a cup of sugar left. What fraction of the recipe can you make?

SOLUTION OF INITIAL PROBLEM

A child has a set of 10 cubical blocks. The lengths of the edges are 1 cm, 2 cm, 3 cm, . . . , 10 cm. Using all the cubes, can the child build two towers of the same height by stacking one cube upon another? Why or why not?

Strategy: Solve an Equivalent Problem

This problem can be restated as an equivalent problem: Can the numbers 1 through 10 be put into two sets whose sums are equal? Answer— No! If the sums are *equal* in each set and if these two sums are added together, the resulting sum would be even. However, the sum of 1 through 10 is 55, an odd number!

Additional Problems Where the Strategy "Solve an Equivalent Problem" Is Useful

1. How many numbers are in the set {11, 18, 25, . . . , 396}?
2. Which is larger: 2^{30} or 3^{20}?
3. Find eight fractions equally spaced between 0 and $\frac{1}{3}$ on the number line.

WRITING/DISCUSSING FOR UNDERSTANDING

1. A student comments that when dividing one whole number by another, the result is smaller than the dividend. For example, $10 \div 2 = 5$ and $5 < 10$. He wants to know how it is possible that when you divide by a fraction like $\frac{1}{2}$, the result is *larger* than the dividend. In other words, how can you get a bigger answer than what you started with? Can you make sense of this seeming contradiction for the student?
2. With the availability of calculators and, in particular, calculators that perform fraction arithmetic, what skill level with fraction operations do you think students need to develop? Is it sufficient for students to be able to add and subtract halves, fourths, eighths, sixteenths, thirty-seconds, and sixty-fourths since those are the fractions we use for measuring? Is there value in students' learning to find common denominators for fractions with "large" denominators?
3. Carefully examine the three equivalent ways of doing fraction division as presented in this chapter. Discuss the strengths and weaknesses of each approach. Based on this discussion, describe how you will teach fraction division when you introduce it.
4. Explain how the following NCTM Standards are reflected in this chapter.
  • Develop concepts of fractions and mixed numbers.
  • Develop number sense for fractions.

- Use models to find equivalent fractions.
- Use models to explore operations on fractions.
- Apply fractions to problem situations.

PROJECTS

1. Collect many examples of fractions and their contexts as they appear in newspapers, magazines, on television, and so on.
2. Examine an elementary mathematics textbook series to see what models are used to introduce the concept of a fraction. Also, look at several catalogs of educational materials to see what manipulatives are available for developing the concept of a fraction. Then explain how you would use manipulatives to introduce the topic in a way related to the students' experiences.

CHAPTER REVIEW

Major Ideas

1. The set of fractions is useful in solving problems where whole numbers are inadequate.
2. The set of fractions can be ordered according to "less than" and "greater than" and there is always a fraction between any two fractions.
3. Fraction addition, subtraction, multiplication, and division have their roots in appropriate physical models.
4. The operations of addition, subtraction, multiplication, and division are extensions of the respective whole-number operations.
5. Fraction addition and multiplication satisfy several important properties:

	Addition	Multiplication
Closure	Yes	Yes
Commutativity	Yes	Yes
Associativity	Yes	Yes
Identity	Yes	Yes
Inverse	No	Yes
Distributivity of multiplication over addition (subtraction)	Yes	

Following is a list of key vocabulary, notation, and ideas for this chapter. Mentally review these items and, where appropriate, write down the meaning of each term. Then restudy the material that you are unsure of before proceeding to take the chapter test.

SECTION 6.1: THE SET OF FRACTIONS

Vocabulary/Notation

Ideas

SECTION 6.2: FRACTIONS: ADDITION AND SUBTRACTION

Vocabulary/Notation

Ideas

SECTION 6.3: FRACTIONS: MULTIPLICATION AND DIVISION

Vocabulary/Notation

Ideas

PEOPLE IN MATHEMATICS

Evelyn Boyd Granville (1924–) was a mathematician in the Mercury and Apollo space programs, specializing in orbit and trajectory computations and computer techniques. She says that if she had foreseen the space program and her role in it, she would have been an astronomer. Evelyn grew up in Washington, D.C. at a time when the public schools were racially segregated. She was fortunate to attend a black high school with high standards and was encouraged to apply to the best colleges. In 1949 she graduated from Yale with a Ph.D. in mathematics, one of two black women to receive doctorates in mathematics that year and the first ever to do so. Following her work with the space program, she joined the mathematics faculty at California State University. She has written (with Jason Frand) the text *Theory and Application of Mathematics for Teachers.* "I never encountered any problems in combining career and private life. Black women have always had to work."

Paul Erdos (1913–) is one of the most prolific of mathematicians. Erdos (pronounced "air-dish") has authored or coauthored approximately 900 research papers. He has been called an "itinerant mathematician" because of his penchant for traveling to mathematical conferences around the world. His achievements in number theory are legendary. At one mathematical conference, he was dozing during a lecture of no particular interest to him. When the speaker mentioned a problem in number theory, Erdos perked up and asked him to explain the problem again. The lecture then proceeded, and a few minutes later Erdos interrupted to announce that he had the solution! Erdos is also known for posing problems and offering monetary awards for their solution, from $25 to $10,000. He also is known for the many mathematical prodigies he has discovered and "fed" problems.

CHAPTER 6 TEST

Knowledge

1. True or false?
   (a) Every whole number is a fraction.
   (b) The fraction $\frac{17}{51}$ is in simplest form.
   (c) The fractions $\frac{2}{12}$ and $\frac{15}{20}$ are equivalent.
   (d) Improper fractions are always greater than 1.
   (e) There is a fraction less than $\frac{2}{1,000,000}$ and greater than $\frac{1}{1,000,000}$.
   (f) The sum of $\frac{5}{7}$ and $\frac{3}{8}$ is $\frac{8}{15}$.
   (g) The difference $\frac{4}{7} - \frac{5}{6}$ does not exist in the set of fractions.
   (h) The quotient $\frac{6}{11} \div \frac{7}{13}$ is the same as the product $\frac{11}{6} \cdot \frac{7}{13}$.

Skill

2. Write the following fractions in simplest form.
   (a) $\frac{12}{18}$ (b) $\frac{34}{36}$ (c) $\frac{34}{85}$ (d) $\frac{123,123}{567,567}$

3. Write the following mixed numbers as improper fractions, and vice versa.
   (a) $3\frac{5}{11}$ (b) $\frac{91}{16}$ (c) $5\frac{2}{7}$ (d) $\frac{123}{11}$

4. Determine the smaller of each of the following pairs of fractions.
   (a) $\frac{3}{4}, \frac{10}{13}$ (b) $\frac{7}{2}, \frac{7}{3}$ (c) $\frac{16}{92}, \frac{18}{94}$

5. Perform the following operations and write your answer in simplest form.
   (a) $\frac{4}{9} + \frac{5}{12}$ (b) $\frac{7}{15} - \frac{8}{25}$ (c) $\frac{4}{5} \cdot \frac{15}{16}$ (d) $\frac{8}{7} \div \frac{7}{8}$

6. Use properties of fractions to perform the following computations in the easiest way. Write answers in simplest form.
   (a) $\frac{5}{2} \cdot (\frac{3}{4} \cdot \frac{2}{5})$
   (b) $\frac{4}{7} \cdot \frac{3}{5} + \frac{4}{5} \cdot \frac{3}{5}$
   (c) $(\frac{13}{17} + \frac{5}{11}) + \frac{4}{17}$
   (d) $\frac{3}{8} \cdot \frac{5}{7} - \frac{4}{9} \cdot \frac{3}{8}$

Understanding

7. Using a carton of twelve eggs as a model, explain how the fractions $\frac{6}{12}$ and $\frac{12}{24}$ are distinguishable.

8. Show how the statement "$\frac{a}{c} < \frac{b}{c}$ if and only if $a < b$" can be used to verify the statement "$\frac{a}{b} < \frac{c}{d}$ if and only if $ad < bc$," where b and d are nonzero.

9. Verify the distributive property of fraction multiplication over subtraction using the distributive property of whole-number multiplication over subtraction.

Problem Solving/Application

10. Notice that $\frac{2}{3} < \frac{3}{4} < \frac{4}{5}$. Show that this sequence continues indefinitely, namely that $\frac{n}{n+1} < \frac{n+1}{n+2}$ when $n \geq 0$.

11. An auditorium contains 315 occupied seats and was $\frac{7}{9}$ filled. How many empty seats were there?

12. Upon his death, Mr. Freespender left $\frac{1}{2}$ of his estate to his wife, $\frac{1}{8}$ to each of his two children, $\frac{1}{16}$ to each of his three grandchildren, and the remaining \$15,000 to his favorite university. What was the value of his entire estate?

Decimals, Ratio, Proportion, and Percent

The Parthenon

The Golden Ratio

The **golden ratio**, also called the **divine proportion**, was known to the Pythagoreans in 500 B.C. and has many interesting applications in geometry. The golden ratio may be found using the Fibonacci sequence, 1, 1, 2, 3, 5, 8, . . ., a_n, . . ., where a_n is obtained by adding the previous two numbers. That is, $1 + 1 = 2$, $1 + 2 = 3$, $2 + 3 = 5$, and so on. If the quotient of each consecutive pair of numbers, $\dfrac{a_n}{a_{n-1}}$, is formed, the numbers produce a new sequence. The first several terms of this new sequence are 1, 2, 1.5, 1.66. . ., 1.6, 1.625, 1.61538. . ., 1.61904 . . ., ... These numbers approach a decimal 1.61803 . . . , which is the golden ratio, ϕ. Technically, $\phi = \dfrac{1 + \sqrt{5}}{2}$. (Square roots are discussed in Chapter 9.)

Here are a few of the remarkable properties associated with the golden ratio.

1. *Aesthetics.* In a golden rectangle, the ratio of the length to the width is the golden ratio, ϕ. Golden rectangles were deemed by the Greeks to be especially pleasing to the eye. The Parthenon at Athens can be surrounded by such a rectangle (Figure 1). Along these lines, notice how index cards are usually dimensioned 3×5 and 5×8, two pairs of numbers in the Fibonacci sequence whose quotients approximate ϕ.

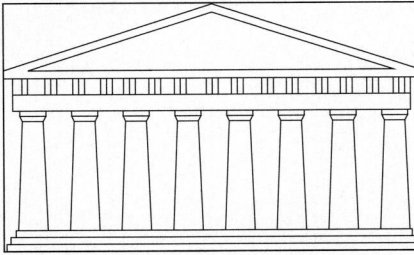

FIGURE 1

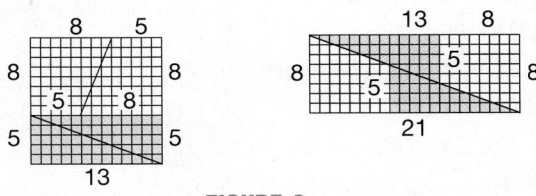

FIGURE 2

2. *Geometric fallacy.* If one cuts out the square in Figure 2 and rearranges it into the rectangle, a surprising result regarding the areas is obtained. (Check this!) Notice that the numbers 5, 8, 13, and 21 occur. If these numbers from the Fibonacci sequence are replaced by 8, 13, 21, and 34, respectively, an even more surprising result occurs. These surprises continue when using the Fibonacci sequence. However, if the four numbers are replaced with 1, ϕ, $\phi + 1$, and $2\phi + 1$, respectively, all is in harmony.

3. *Surprising places.* Part of Pascal's triangle is shown in Figure 3. However, if carefully rearranged, the Fibonacci sequence reappears (Figure 4).

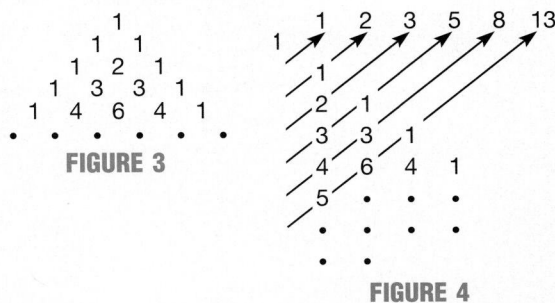

FIGURE 3

FIGURE 4

These are but a few of the many interesting relationships that arise from the golden ratio and its counterpart, the Fibonacci sequence.

STRATEGY 12: WORK BACKWARD

Normally, when you begin to solve a problem, you probably start at the beginning of a problem and proceed "forward" until you arrive at an answer by applying appropriate strategies. At times, though, rather than start at the beginning of a problem statement, it is more productive to begin at the end of the problem statement and work backward. The following problem can be solved quite easily by this strategy.

Initial Problem

A street vendor had a basket of apples. Feeling generous one day, he gave away one-half of his apples plus one to the first stranger he met, one-half of his remaining apples plus one to the next stranger he met, and one-half of his remaining apples plus one to the third stranger he met. If the vendor had one left for himself, with how many apples did he start?

Clues

The Work Backward strategy may be appropriate when:

- The final result is clear and the initial portion of a problem is obscure.
- A problem proceeds from being complex initially to being simple at the end.
- A direct approach involves a complicated equation.
- A problem involves a sequence of reversible actions.

A solution of the Initial Problem above appears on page 317.

INTRODUCTION

In Chapter 6, the set of fractions was introduced to permit us to deal with parts of a whole. In this chapter we introduce decimals, which are a convenient numeration system for the fractions, and percents, which are representations of fractions convenient for commerce. Then the concepts of ratio and proportion are developed because of their importance in applications throughout mathematics.

7.1

DECIMALS

Decimals

Decimals are used to represent fractions in our usual base ten place-value notation. The method used to express decimals is shown in Figure 7.1. In the figure, the number 3457.968 shows that the **decimal**

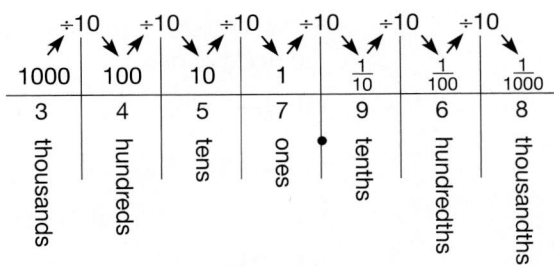

FIGURE 7.1

point is placed between the ones column and the tenths column to show where the whole-number portion ends and where the decimal (or fractional) portion begins. Decimals are read as if they were written as fractions and the decimal point is read "and." The number 3457.968 is written in its **expanded form** as

$$3(1000) + 4(100) + 5(10) + 7(1) + 9\left(\frac{1}{10}\right) + 6\left(\frac{1}{100}\right) + 8\left(\frac{1}{1000}\right).$$

From this form one can see that $3457.968 = 3457\frac{968}{1000}$ and hence is read "three thousand four hundred fifty-seven *and* nine hundred sixty-eight thousandths." Notice that the word "and" should only be used to indicate where the decimal point is located.

Figure 7.2 shows how a **hundreds square** can be used to represent tenths and hundredths.

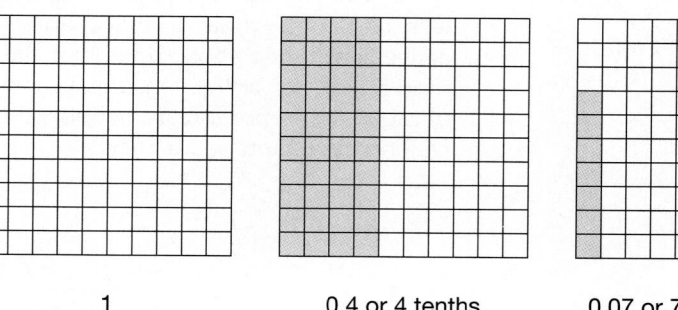

1   0.4 or 4 tenths   0.07 or 7 hundredths

FIGURE 7.2

A number line can also be used to picture decimals. The number line in Figure 7.3 shows the location of various decimals between 0 and 1.

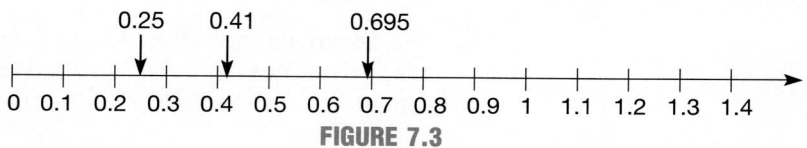

FIGURE 7.3

EXAMPLE 7.1   Rewrite each of these numbers in decimal form and state the decimal name.

(a) $\frac{7}{100}$ **(b)** $\frac{123}{10,000}$ **(c)** $1\frac{7}{8}$

Solution

(a) $\frac{7}{100} = 0.07$, read "seven hundredths"

(b) $\frac{123}{10,000} = \frac{100}{10,000} + \frac{20}{10,000} + \frac{3}{10,000} = \frac{1}{100} + \frac{2}{1000} + \frac{3}{10,000} = 0.0123$, read "one hundred twenty-three ten thousandths"

(c) $1\frac{7}{8} = 1 + \frac{7}{8} = 1 + \frac{7 \cdot 5 \cdot 5 \cdot 5}{2 \cdot 2 \cdot 2 \cdot 5 \cdot 5 \cdot 5} = 1 + \frac{875}{1000} =$

$1 + \frac{800}{1000} + \frac{70}{1000} + \frac{5}{1000} = 1 + \frac{8}{10} + \frac{7}{100} + \frac{5}{1000} = 1.875$, read "one and eight hundred seventy-five thousandths" ■

All of the fractions in Example 7.1 have denominators whose only prime factors are 2 or 5. Such fractions can always be expressed in decimal form since they have equivalent fractional forms whose denominators are powers of 10. This idea is illustrated in Example 7.2.

EXAMPLE 7.2   Express as decimals.

(a) $\frac{3}{2^4}$ **(b)** $\frac{7}{2^3 \cdot 5}$ **(c)** $\frac{43}{1250}$

Solution

(a) $\dfrac{3}{2^4} = \dfrac{3 \cdot 5^4}{2^4 \cdot 5^4} = \dfrac{1875}{10,000} = 0.1875$

(b) $\dfrac{7}{2^3 \cdot 5} = \dfrac{7 \cdot 5^2}{2^3 \cdot 5^3} = \dfrac{175}{1000} = 0.175$

(c) $\dfrac{43}{1250} = \dfrac{43}{2 \cdot 5^4} = \dfrac{43 \cdot 2^3}{2^4 \cdot 5^4} = \dfrac{344}{10,000} = 0.0344$ ◼

The decimals we have been studying thus far are called **terminating decimals**, since they can be represented using a finite number of nonzero digits to the right of the decimal point. We will study nonterminating decimals later in this chapter. The following result should be clear, based on the work we have done in Example 7.2.

Theorem

Fractions with Terminating Decimal Representations

Let $\dfrac{a}{b}$ be a fraction in *simplest form*. Then $\dfrac{a}{b}$ has a terminating decimal representation if and only if b contains only 2s and/or 5s in its prime factorization.

Ordering Decimals

Terminating decimals can be compared using a hundreds square, using a number line, by comparing them in their fraction form, or by comparing place values one at a time from left to right just as we compare whole numbers.

EXAMPLE 7.3 Determine the larger of each of the following pairs of numbers in the four ways mentioned in the preceding paragraph.
(a) 0.7, 0.23   (b) 0.135, 0.14

Solution
(a) *Hundreds Square:* See Figure 7.4.
   Since more is shaded in the 0.7 square, we conclude that $0.7 > 0.23$.

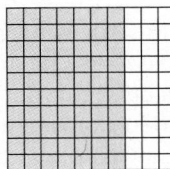
0.7

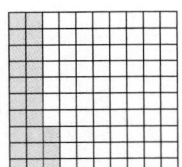
0.23

FIGURE 7.4

Number Line: See Figure 7.5.

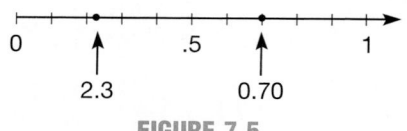

FIGURE 7.5

Since 0.7 is to the right of 0.23, we have 0.7 > 0.23.

Fraction Method: First, $0.7 = \frac{7}{10}$, $0.23 = \frac{23}{100}$. Now $\frac{7}{10} = \frac{70}{100}$ and $\frac{70}{100} > \frac{23}{100}$ since 70 > 23. Therefore, 0.7 > 0.23.

Place-Value Method: 0.7 > 0.23 since 7 > 2. The reasoning behind this method is that since 7 > 2, we have 0.7 > 0.2. Furthermore, in a terminating decimal, the digits that appear after the 2 cannot contribute enough to make a decimal as large as 0.3, yet having 2 in its tenths place. This technique holds for all terminating decimals.

(b) ***Hundreds Square:*** The number 0.135 is one tenth plus three hundredths plus five thousandths. Since $\frac{5}{1000} = \frac{1}{200} = \frac{1}{2} \cdot \frac{1}{100}$, $13\frac{1}{2}$ squares on a hundreds square must be shaded to represent 0.135. The number 0.14 is represented by 14 squares on a hundreds square. See Figure 7.6.

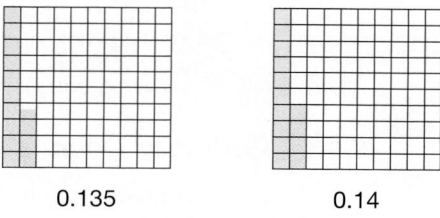

0.135   0.14

FIGURE 7.6

Since an extra half of a square is shaded in 0.14, we have 0.14 > 0.135.

Number Line: See Figure 7.7.

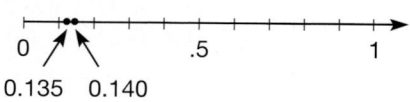

0.135   0.140

FIGURE 7.7

Since 0.14 is to the right of 0.135 on the number line, 0.14 > 0.135.

Fraction Method: $0.135 = \frac{135}{1000}$ and $0.14 = \frac{14}{100} = \frac{140}{1000}$. Since 140 > 135, we have 0.14 > 0.135. Many times children will write 0.135 > 0.14 because they know 135 > 14 and believe that this situation is the same. It is not! Here we are comparing *decimals,* not whole numbers. A decimal comparison can be turned into a whole-number comparison by getting common denominators or, equivalently, by having the same number of decimal places. For example, 0.14 > 0.135 since $\frac{140}{1000} > \frac{135}{1000}$, or 0.140 > 0.135.

Place-Value Method: 0.14 > 0.135 since (1) the tenths are equal (both are 1), but (2) the hundredths place in 0.14, namely 4, is greater than the hundredths place in 0.135, namely 3. ∎

Mental Math and Estimation

The operations of addition, subtraction, multiplication, and division involving decimals are similar to the corresponding operations with whole numbers. In particular, place value plays a key role. For example, to find the sum $3.2 + 5.7$ mentally, one may add the whole number parts, $3 + 5 = 8$, and then the tenths, $0.2 + 0.7 = 0.9$ to obtain 8.9. Observe that the whole number parts were added first, then the tenths—that is, the addition took place from left-to-right. In the case of finding the sum $7.6 + 2.5$, one could add the tenths first, $0.6 + 0.5 = 1.1$, then combine this sum with $7 + 2 = 9$ to obtain the sum $9 + 1.1 = 10.1$. Thus, as with whole numbers, decimals may be added from left-to-right or right-to-left.

Before developing algorithms for operations involving decimals, some mental math and estimation techniques similar to those that were used with whole numbers and fractions will be extended to decimal calculations.

EXAMPLE 7.4 Use compatible (decimal) numbers, properties, and/or compensation to calculate the following mentally.

(a) $1.7 + (3.2 + 4.3)$ **(b)** $(0.5 \times 6.7) \times 4$
(c) 6×8.5 **(d)** $3.76 + 1.98$
(e) $7.32 - 4.94$ **(f)** $17 \times 0.25 + 0.25 \times 23$

Solution
(a) $1.7 + (3.2 + 4.3) = (1.7 + 4.3) + 3.2 = 6 + 3.2 = 9.2$. Here 1.7 and 4.3 are compatible numbers with respect to addition since their sum is 6.
(b) $(0.5 \times 6.7) \times 4 = 6.7 \times (0.5 \times 4) = 6.7 \times 2 = 13.4$. Since $0.5 \times 4 = 2$, it is more convenient to use commutativity and associativity to find 0.5×4 rather than to find 0.5×6.7 first.
(c) Using distributivity, $6 \times 8.5 = 6(8 + 0.5) = 6 \times 8 + 6 \times 0.5 = 48 + 3 = 51$.
(d) $3.76 + 1.98 = 3.74 + 2 = 5.74$ using additive compensation.
(e) $7.32 - 4.94 = 7.38 - 5 = 2.38$ by equal additions.
(f) $17 \times 0.25 + 0.25 \times 23 = 17 \times 0.25 + 23 \times 0.25 = (17 + 23) \times 0.25 = 40 \times 0.25 = 10$ using distributivity and the fact that 40 and 0.25 are compatible numbers with respect to multiplication. ■

Since common decimals have fraction representations, the **fraction equivalents** shown in Table 7.1 can often be used to simplify decimal calculations.

TABLE 7.1

Decimal	Fraction	Decimal	Fraction
0.05	$\frac{1}{20}$	0.5	$\frac{1}{2}$
0.1	$\frac{1}{10}$	0.6	$\frac{3}{5}$
0.125	$\frac{1}{8}$	0.625	$\frac{5}{8}$
0.2	$\frac{1}{5}$	0.75	$\frac{3}{4}$
0.25	$\frac{1}{4}$	0.8	$\frac{4}{5}$
0.375	$\frac{3}{8}$	0.875	$\frac{7}{8}$
0.4	$\frac{2}{5}$		

EXAMPLE 7.5   Find these products using fraction equivalents.

(a) 68×0.5 (b) 0.25×48
(c) 0.2×375 (d) 0.05×280
(e) 56×0.125 (f) 0.75×72

Solution

(a) $68 \times 0.5 = 68 \times \frac{1}{2} = 34$
(b) $0.25 \times 48 = \frac{1}{4} \times 48 = 12$
(c) $0.2 \times 375 = \frac{1}{5} \times 375 = 75$
(d) $0.05 \times 280 = \frac{1}{20} \times 280 = \frac{1}{2} \times 28 = 14$
(e) $56 \times 0.125 = 56 \times \frac{1}{8} = 7$
(f) $0.75 \times 72 = \frac{3}{4} \times 72 = 3 \times \frac{1}{4} \times 72 = 3 \times 18 = 54$ ∎

Multiplying and dividing decimals by powers of 10 can be performed mentally in a fashion similar to the way we multiplied and divided whole numbers by powers of 10.

EXAMPLE 7.6   Find the following products and quotients by converting to fractions.

(a) 3.75×10^4 (b) 62.013×10^5
(c) $127.9 \div 10$ (d) $0.53 \div 10^4$

Solution

(a) $3.75 \times 10^4 = \frac{375}{100} \times \frac{10,000}{1} = 37,500$
(b) $62.013 \times 10^5 = \frac{62,013}{1000} \times \frac{100,000}{1} = 6,201,300$
(c) $127.9 \div 10 = \frac{1279}{10} \div 10 = \frac{1279}{10} \times \frac{1}{10} = 12.79$
(d) $0.53 \div 10^4 = \frac{53}{100} \div 10^4 = \frac{53}{100} \times \frac{1}{10,000} = 0.000053$ ∎

Notice that in Example 7.6(a), multiplying by 10^4 was equivalent to moving the decimal point of 3.75 four places to the right to obtain 37,500. Similarly, in part (b), because of the 5 in 10^5, moving the decimal point five places to the right in 62.013 results in the correct answer, 6,201,300. When dividing by a power of 10, the decimal point is moved to the left an appropriate number of places. These ideas are summarized next.

Theorem

Multiplying/Dividing Decimals by Powers of 10

Let n be any decimal number and m represent any nonzero whole number. *Multiplying* a number n by 10^m is equivalent to forming a new number by moving the decimal point of n to the right m places. *Dividing* a number n by 10^m is equivalent to forming a new number by moving the decimal point of n to the left m places.

Multiplying/dividing by powers of 10 can be used with multiplicative compensation to multiply some decimals mentally. For example, to find the product $0.003 \times 41,000$, one can multiply 0.003 by 1000 (yielding 3) and then divide 41,000 by 1000 (yielding 41) to obtain the product $3 \times 41 = 123$.

Previous work with whole-number and fraction computational estimation can also be applied to estimate the results of decimal operations.

EXAMPLE 7.7 Estimate each of the following using the indicated estimation techniques.
(a) $1.57 + $4.36 + $8.78 using (i) range, (ii) front-end with adjustment, and (iii) rounding techniques
(b) 39.37 × 5.5 using (i) range and (ii) rounding techniques

Solution
(a) *Range:* A low estimate for the range is $1 + $4 + $8 = $13, and a high estimate is $2 + $5 + $9 = $16. Thus a range estimate of the sum is $13 to $16.
Front-end: The one-column front-end estimate is simply the low estimate of the range, namely $13. The sum of 0.57, 0.36, and 0.78 is about $1.50, so a good estimate is $14.50.
Rounding: Rounding to the nearest whole or half yields an estimate of $1.50 + $4.50 + $9.00 = $15.00.
(b) *Range:* A low estimate is 30 × 5 = 150, and a high estimate is 40 × 6 = 240. Hence a range estimate is 150 to 240.
Rounding: One choice for estimating this product is to round 39.37 × 5.5 to 40 × 6 to obtain 240. A better estimate would be to round to 40 × 5.5 = 220. ■

Decimals can be rounded to any specified place as was done with whole numbers.

EXAMPLE 7.8 Round 56.94352 to the nearest
(a) tenth   **(b)** hundredth   **(c)** thousandth   **(d)** ten thousandth

Solution
(a) First, 56.9 < 56.94352 < 57.0. Since 56.94352 is closer to 56.9 than to 57.0, we round to 56.9 (Figure 7.8).

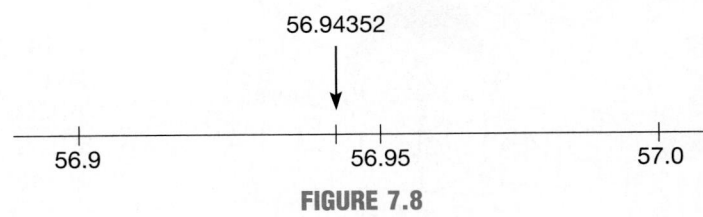

FIGURE 7.8

(b) 56.94 < 56.94352 < 56.95 and 56.94352 is closer to 56.94 (since 352 < 500), so we round to 56.94.
(c) 56.943 < 56.94352 < 56.944 and 56.94352 is closer to 56.944 since 52 > 50. Thus we round up to 56.944.
(d) 56.9435 < 56.94352 < 56.9436. Since 56.94352 < 56.94355, and 56.94355 is the halfway point between 56.94350 and 56.94360, we round down to 56.9435. ■

For decimals ending in a five, we can use the "round a 5 up" method, as is usually done in elementary school. For example, 1.835, rounded to hundredths, would round to 1.84.

Perhaps the most useful estimation technique for decimals is rounding to numbers that will, in turn, yield compatible whole numbers or fractions.

EXAMPLE 7.9 Estimate.
(a) 203.4×47.8 **(b)** $31 \div 1.93$
(c) 75×0.24 **(d)** $124 \div 0.74$
(e) $0.0021 \times 44{,}123$ **(f)** $3847.6 \div 51.3$

Solution
(a) $203.4 \times 47.8 \approx 200 \times 50 = 10{,}000$
(b) $31 \div 1.93 \approx 30 \div 2 = 15$
(c) $75 \times 0.24 \approx 75 \times \frac{1}{4} \approx 76 \times \frac{1}{4} = 19$. (Note that 76 and $\frac{1}{4}$ are compatible, since 76 has a factor of 4.)
(d) $124 \div 0.74 \approx 124 \div \frac{3}{4} = 124 \times \frac{4}{3} \approx 123 \times \frac{4}{3} = 164$. (123 and $\frac{1}{3}$, hence $\frac{4}{3}$, are compatible since 123 has a factor of 3.)
(e) $0.0021 \times 44{,}123 = 0.21 \times 441.23 \approx \frac{1}{5} \times 450 = 90$. (Here multiplicative compensation was used by *multiplying* 0.0021 by 100 and *dividing* 44,123 by 100.)
(f) $3847.6 \div 51.3 \approx 38.476 \div 0.513 \approx 38 \div \frac{1}{2} = 76$; alternately, $3847.6 \div 51.3 \approx 3500 \div 50 = 70$ ∎

MATHEMATICAL MORSEL

Decimal notation has evolved over the years without universal agreement. Consider the following list of decimal expressions for the fraction $\frac{3142}{1000}$.

Notation	Date Introduced
3 142	1522, Adam Riese (German)
3 | 142 3,142	1579, François Vieta (French)
0|1|2|3 3|1|4|2	1585, Simon Stevin (Dutch)
3 · 142	1614, John Napier (Scottish)

Today, Americans use a version of Napier's "decimal point" notation (3.142, where the point is on the line), the English retain the original version (3 · 142, where the point is in the middle of the line), and the French and Germans retain Vieta's "decimal comma" notation (3,142). Hence the issue of establishing a universal decimal notation remains unresolved to this day.

EXERCISE/PROBLEM SET 7.1—PART A

Exercises

1. Express each of the following decimals as a fraction.
   (a) 0.064   (b) 1.3578   (c) 0.00051

2. Write each of the following numbers in its expanded form.
   (a) 351.26   (b) 7654.321   (c) 62.35475

3. Write the following numbers in words.
   (a) 0.013
   (b) 0.0082
   (c) 0.0000000092
   (d) 68,485,532
   (e) 7,589,632.12345
   (f) 859.080509
   (g) 23,187,213.020030004
   (h) 111,001,002,003.0010000200003

4. A student reads the number 3147 as "three thousand one hundred and forty-seven." What is wrong with this reading?

5. Determine, without converting to decimals, which of the following fractions has a terminating decimal representation.
   (a) $\frac{21}{45}$ (b) $\frac{62}{125}$ (c) $\frac{63}{90}$
   (d) $\frac{326}{400}$ (e) $\frac{39}{60}$ (f) $\frac{54}{130}$

6. Arrange the following numbers in order from smallest to largest.
   (a) 0.58, 0.085, 0.85
   (b) 781.345, 781.354, 780.9999
   (c) 4.9, 4.09, 4.99, 4.099
   (d) 8.01002, 8.010019, 8.0019929
   (e) 0.5, 0.505, 0.5005, 0.55

7. One method of comparing two fractions is to find their decimal representations by calculator and compare them. For example, divide the numerator by the denominator.

$$\frac{7}{12} = \boxed{0.58333333} \qquad \frac{9}{16} = \boxed{0.56250000}$$

Thus $\frac{9}{16} < \frac{7}{12}$. Use this method to compare the following fractions.
   (a) $\frac{5}{9}$ and $\frac{19}{34}$ (b) $\frac{38}{52}$ and $\frac{18}{25}$

8. Calculate mentally. Describe your method.
   (a) 18.43 − 9.96
   (b) 1.3 × 5.9 + 64.1 × 1.3
   (c) 4.6 + (5.8 + 2.4)
   (d) (0.25 × 17) × 8
   (e) 51.24 ÷ 10^3
   (f) 21.28 + 17.79
   (g) 8(9.5)
   (h) 0.15 × 10^5

9. It is possible to write any decimal as a number between 1 and 10 (including 1) times a power of 10. This scientific notation is particularly useful in expressing large numbers. For example,

$$6321 = 6.321 \times 10^3 \qquad \text{and}$$
$$760,000,000 = 7.6 \times 10^8$$

Write each of the following in scientific notation.
   (a) 59   (b) 4326
   (c) 97,000   (d) 1,000,000
   (e) 64,020,000   (f) 71,000,000,000

10. Find each of the following products and quotients. For parts (e) to (h), express answers in scientific notation.
   (a) (6.75)(1,000,000)
   (b) 0.00125 × 10,000
   (c) 19.514 ÷ 100,000
   (d) $\dfrac{0.044}{1000}$
   (e) $(1.5 \times 10^5) \times 100$
   (f) $(2.96 \times 10^{16})(10^{12})$
   (g) $(1.5 \times 10^5) \div 100$
   (h) $\dfrac{2.96 \times 10^{16}}{10^{12}}$

11. The nearest star (other than the sun) is Alpha Centauri, which is the brightest star in the constellation Centaurus.
   (a) Alpha Centauri is 41,600,000,000,000,000 meters from our sun. Express this distance in scientific notation.
   (b) While it appears to the naked eye to be one star, Alpha Centauri is actually a double star. The two stars that comprise it are an average distance of 3,500,000,000 meters apart. Express this distance in scientific notation.

12. Calculate by using fraction equivalents.
   (a) 0.25 × 44   (b) 0.75 × 80
   (c) 35 × 0.4   (d) 0.2 × 65
   (e) 65 × 0.8   (f) 380 × 0.05

13. Estimate, using the indicated techniques.
   (a) 4.75 + 5.91 + 7.36; range and rounding to the nearest whole number
   (b) 74.5 × 6.1; range and rounding
   (c) 3.18 + 4.39 + 2.73; front-end with adjustment
   (d) 4.3 × 9.7; rounding to the nearest whole number

14. Estimate by rounding to compatible numbers and fraction equivalents.
   (a) 47.1 ÷ 2.9   (b) 0.23 × 88
   (c) 126 × 0.21   (d) 56,324 × 0.25
   (e) 14,897 ÷ 750   (f) 0.59 × 474

15. Round the following numbers.
   (a) 97.26 to the nearest tenth
   (b) 345.51 to the nearest ten
   (c) 345.00 to the nearest ten
   (d) 0.01826 to the nearest thousandth
   (e) 0.01826 to the nearest ten thousandth
   (f) 0.498 to the nearest tenth
   (g) 0.498 to the nearest hundredth

Problems

16. The numbers shown next can be used to form an additive magic square:

   10.48, 15.72, 20.96, 26.2, 31.44,
   36.68, 41.92, 47.16, 52.4

Use your calculator to determine where to place the numbers in the nine cells of the magic square.

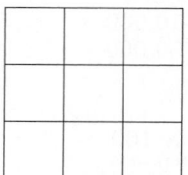

17. Gary cashed a check from Joan for $29.35. Then he bought two magazines for $1.95 each, a book for $5.95, and a record for $5.98. He had $21.45 left. How much money did he have before cashing the check?

18. Each year a car depreciates to about $\frac{4}{5}$ of its value the year before. What was the original value of a car that is worth $16,000 at the end of 3 years?

19. Todd bought a large bag of miniature candy bars to distribute to Halloween trick-or-treaters. He made the mistake of opening the bag five days before Halloween to have a "few" for a snack. Feeling less and less guilty, each day he ate two more candy bars than he had on the preceding day. He realized that he ate as many candy bars on the last two days as he had on the first three days. How many candy bars did Todd eat on each of the five days before Halloween?

EXERCISE/PROBLEM SET 7.1—PART B

Exercises

1. Write each of the following sums in decimal form.
   (a) $7(10) + 5 + 6(\frac{1}{10}) + 3(\frac{1}{1000})$
   (b) $6(\frac{1}{10})^2 + 3(\frac{1}{10})^3$
   (c) $3(10)^2 + 6 + 4(\frac{1}{10})^2 + 2(\frac{1}{10})^3$
   (d) $5(\frac{1}{10})^2 + 7(10) + 3(\frac{1}{10})^5$
   (e) $8(\frac{1}{10}) + 3(10)^3 + 9(\frac{1}{10})^2$
   (f) $5(\frac{1}{10})^3 + 2(\frac{1}{10})^2 + (\frac{1}{10})^6$

2. Write the following expressions as decimal numerals.
   (a) Seven hundred forty-six thousand
   (b) Seven hundred forty-six thousandths
   (c) Seven hundred forty-six million
   (d) Seven hundred forty-six millionths
   (e) Seven hundred forty-six thousand and seven hundred forty-six millionths
   (f) Seven hundred forty-six million and seven hundred forty-six thousandths

3. In Chapter 6, region models were used to represent fractions. What decimal is represented by each of the region models that follow?

(a)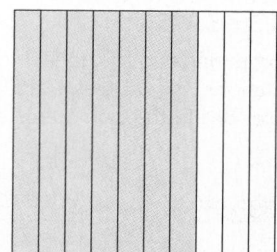

(b)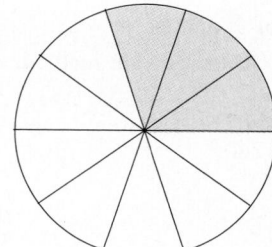

(c)

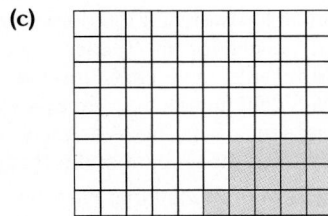

4. Determine which of the following fractions have terminating decimal representations.

(a) $\dfrac{2^4 \cdot 11^{16} \cdot 17^{19}}{5^{12}}$ (b) $\dfrac{2^3 \cdot 3^{11} \cdot 7^9 \cdot 11^{16}}{7^{13} \cdot 11^9 \cdot 5^7}$

(c) $\dfrac{2^3 \cdot 3^9 \cdot 11^{17}}{2^8 \cdot 3^4 \cdot 5^7}$

5. Decide whether or not the following fractions terminate in their decimal form. If a fraction terminates, tell in how many places and explain how you can tell from the fraction form.

(a) $\dfrac{4}{3}$ (b) $\dfrac{7}{8}$ (c) $\dfrac{1}{15}$

(d) $\dfrac{3}{16}$ (e) $\dfrac{1}{11}$ (f) $\dfrac{3}{110}$

(g) $\dfrac{17}{625}$ (h) $\dfrac{1}{60}$ (i) $\dfrac{3}{12,800}$

(j) $\dfrac{5}{64,000}$ (k) $\dfrac{11}{2^4 \times 3^2 \times 5^3}$ (l) $\dfrac{17}{2^{19} \times 5^{23}}$

6. Order each of the following from smallest to largest by changing each fraction to a decimal.

(a) $\frac{5}{7}, \frac{4}{5}, \frac{10}{13}$ (b) $\frac{4}{11}, \frac{3}{7}, \frac{2}{5}$

(c) $\frac{5}{9}, \frac{7}{13}, \frac{11}{18}$ (d) $\frac{3}{5}, \frac{11}{18}, \frac{17}{29}$

7. Order each of the following from smallest to largest as simply as possible by using any combinations of the three following methods: (1) common denominators, (2) cross-multiplication, and (3) converting to a decimal.

(a) $\frac{5}{8}, \frac{1}{2}, \frac{17}{23}$

(b) $\frac{13}{16}, \frac{2}{3}, \frac{3}{4}$

(c) $\frac{8}{5}, \frac{26}{15}, \frac{50}{31}$

8. According to state law, the amount of radon released from wastes cannot exceed a 0.033 working level. A study of two locations reported a 0.0095 working level at one location and 0.0039 at a second location. Does either of these locations fail to meet state standards?

9. Calculate mentally.

(a) $7 \times 3.4 + 6.6 \times 7$ (b) $26.53 - 8.95$

(c) $0.491 \div 10^2$ (d) $5.89 + 6.27$

(e) $(5.7 + 4.8) + 3.2$ (f) 67.32×10^3

(g) $0.5 \times (639 \times 2)$ (h) 6.5×12

10. Write each of the following numbers in scientific notation.

(a) 860
(b) 4520
(c) 26,000,000
(d) 315,000
(e) 1,084,000,000
(f) 54,000,000,000,000

11. Find each of the following products and quotients. For parts (e) to (h), express your answers in scientific notation.

(a) $(375.995)(100,000)$ (b) 12.6416×100

(c) $46.088 \div 10,000$ (d) $\dfrac{7.8752}{10,000,000}$

(e) $(2.64 \times 10^{10}) \times 1000$ (f) $(8.25 \times 10^{20})(10^7)$

(g) $(2.64 \times 10^{10}) \div 1000$ (h) $\dfrac{8.25 \times 10^{20}}{10^7}$

12. (a) The longest human life on record was more than 113 years, or about 3,574,000,000 seconds. Express this number of seconds in scientific notation.

(b) Some tortoises have been known to live more than 150 years, or about 4,730,000,000 seconds. Express this number of seconds in scientific notation.

(c) The oldest living plant is probably a bristlecone pine tree in Nevada; it is about 4900 years old. Its age in seconds would be about 1.545×10^{11} seconds. Express this number of seconds in standard form and write a name for it.

13. Calculate using fraction equivalents.

(a) 230×0.1 (b) 36×0.25

(c) 82×0.5 (d) 125×0.8

(e) 175×0.2 (f) 0.6×35

14. Estimate, using the indicated techniques.

(a) 34.7×3.9; range and rounding to the nearest whole number

(b) $15.71 + 3.23 + 21.95$; two-column front-end

(c) 13.7×6.1; one-column front-end and range

(d) $3.61 + 4.91 + 1.3$; front-end with adjustment

15. Estimate by rounding to compatible numbers and fraction equivalents.

(a) $123.9 \div 5.3$ (b) 87.4×7.9

(c) $402 \div 1.25$ (d) $34,546 \times 0.004$

(e) $0.0024 \times 470,000$ (f) $3591 \div 0.61$

16. Round the following decimal numbers to the appropriate place.

(a) 321.0864 to the nearest hundredth
(b) 12.16231 to the nearest thousandth
(c) 4.009055 to the nearest thousandth
(d) 1.9984 to the nearest tenth
(e) 1.9984 to the nearest hundredth

17. The weight in grams, to the nearest hundredth, of a particular sample of toxic waste was 28.67 grams.
   (a) What is the minimum amount the sample could have weighed? (Write out your answer to the ten-thousandths place.)
   (b) What is the maximum amount? (Write out your answer to the ten-thousandths place.)

Problems

18. Determine if each of the following is an additive magic square. If not, change one entry so that your resulting square is magic.

(a)

2.4	5.4	1.2
1.8	3	4.2
4.8	1.4	3.6

(b)

0.438	0.073	0.584
0.511	0.365	0.219
0.146	0.657	0.292

19. An absentminded bank teller switched the dollars and cents when he cashed a check for Mr. Spencer, giving him dollars instead of cents, and cents instead of dollars. After buying a 5-cent newspaper, Mr. Spencer discovered that he had left exactly twice as much as his original check. What was the amount of the check?

20. The total value of any sum of money that earns interest at 9% per year doubles about every 8 years. What amount of money invested now at 9% per year will accumulate to about $120,000 in about 40 years (assuming no taxes are paid on the earnings and no money is withdrawn)?

7.2

OPERATIONS WITH DECIMALS

Algorithms for Operations with Decimals

Algorithms for adding, subtracting, multiplying, and dividing decimals are simple extensions of the corresponding whole-number algorithms.

Addition

EXAMPLE 7.10 Add:
(a) $3.56 + 7.95$ **(b)** $0.0094 + 80.183$

Solution
We will find these sums in two ways: (1) using fractions and (2) using a decimal algorithm.
(1) **Fraction Approach**

(a)

$$3.56 + 7.95 = \frac{356}{100} + \frac{795}{100}$$

$$= \frac{1151}{100}$$

$$= 11.51$$

(b)

$$0.0094 + 80.183 = \frac{94}{10,000} + \frac{80,183}{1000}$$

$$= \frac{94}{10,000} + \frac{801,830}{10,000}$$

$$= \frac{801,924}{10,000}$$

$$= 80.1924$$

(2) **Decimal Approach:** As with whole-number addition, arrange the digits in columns according to their corresponding place values and add the numbers in each column, regrouping when necessary (Figure 7.9).   ■

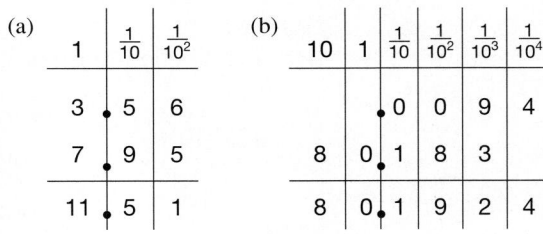

FIGURE 7.9

This decimal algorithm can be stated more simply as "align the decimal points, add the numbers in columns as if they were whole numbers, and insert a decimal point in the answer immediately beneath the decimal points in the numbers being added." This algorithm can easily be justified by writing the two summands in their expanded form and applying the various properties for fraction addition and/or multiplication.

Subtraction

EXAMPLE 7.11   Subtract:
(a) $14.793 - 8.95$ **(b)** $7.56 - 0.0008$

Solution
Here we could again use the fraction approach as we did with addition. However, the usual subtraction algorithm is more efficient.

(a)

STEP 1: ALIGN DECIMAL POINTS	STEP 2: SUBTRACT AS IF WHOLE NUMBERS	STEP 3: INSERT DECIMAL POINT IN ANSWER
14.793	14793	14.793
− 8.95	− 8950	− 8.95
	5843	5.843

(NOTE: Step 2 is performed mentally—there is no need to rewrite the numbers without the decimal points.)

(b) Rewrite 7.56 as 7.5600.

$$
\begin{array}{r}
7.5600 \\
-0.0008 \\
\hline
7.5592
\end{array}
$$

■

Now let's consider how to multiply decimals.

Multiplication

EXAMPLE 7.12   Multiply 437.09×3.8.

Solution
Refer to fraction multiplication.

$$437.09 \times 3.8 = \frac{43709}{100} \times \frac{38}{10} = \frac{43709 \times 38}{100 \times 10}$$

$$= \frac{1{,}660{,}942}{1000} = 1660.942$$

Observe that when multiplying the two fractions in Example 7.12, we multiplied 43,709 and 38 (the original numbers "without the decimal points"). Thus the procedure illustrated in Example 7.12 suggests the following algorithm for multiplication.
Multiply the numbers "without the decimal points":

$$
\begin{array}{r}
43{,}709 \\
\times\quad 38 \\
\hline
1{,}660{,}942
\end{array}
$$

Insert a decimal point in the answer as follows: The number of digits to the right of the decimal point in the answer is the sum of the number of digits to the right of the decimal points in the numbers being multiplied.

$$
\begin{array}{r}
437.09 \\
\times\quad 3.8 \\
\hline
1660.942
\end{array}
$$
(2 digits to the right of the decimal point)
(1 digit to the right of the decimal point)
(2 + 1 digits to the right of the decimal point)

Notice that there are three decimal places in the answer since the product of the two denominators (100 and 10) is 10^3. This procedure can be justified by writing the decimals in expanded form and applying appropriate properties.
    An alternative way to place the decimal point in the answer of a decimal multiplication problem is to do an approximate calculation. For example, 437.09×3.8 is approximately 400×4 or 1600. Hence the answer should be in the thousands, namely 1660.942, not 16,609.42 or 16.60942, and so on.

EXAMPLE 7.13   Compute: 57.98×1.371 using a calculator.

Solution
First, the answer should be a little less than 60×1.4, or 84. Using a calculator we find $57.98 \boxed{\times} 1.371 \boxed{=} 79.49058$. Notice that the answer is close to the estimate of 84.

Division

EXAMPLE 7.14   Divide: $154.63 \div 4.7$.

Solution
First let's estimate the answer: $155 \div 5 = 31$, so the answer should be approximately 31.

Next, we divide using fractions.

$$154.63 \div 4.7 = \frac{15{,}463}{100} \div \frac{47}{10} = \frac{15{,}463}{100} \div \frac{470}{100}$$

$$= \frac{15{,}463}{470} = 32.9.$$ ∎

Notice that in the fraction m-ethod, we replaced our original problem in decimals with an equivalent problem involving whole numbers:

$$154.63 \div 4.7 \rightarrow 15{,}463 \div 470.$$

Similarly, the problem $1546.3 \div 47$ also has the answer 32.9 by the missing-factor approach. Thus, as this example suggests, any decimal division problem can be replaced with an equivalent one having a whole-number divisor. This technique is usually used when performing the long-division algorithm with decimals, as illustrated next.

EXAMPLE 7.15   Compute: $4.7 \overline{)154.63}$.

Solution
Replace with an equivalent problem where the divisor is a whole number.

$$47 \overline{)1546.3}$$

Note: Both the divisor and dividend have been multiplied by 10. Now divide as if it is whole-number division. The decimal point in the dividend is temporarily omitted.

$$\begin{array}{r} 329 \\ 47 \overline{)15463} \\ -141 \\ \hline 136 \\ -94 \\ \hline 423 \\ -423 \\ \hline 0 \end{array}$$

Replace the decimal point in the dividend, and place a decimal point in the quotient directly above the decimal point in the dividend. This can be justified using division of fractions.

$$\begin{array}{r} 32.9 \\ 47 \overline{)1546\!\cdot\!3} \end{array}$$

CHECK: $4.7 \times 32.9 = 154.63$. ∎

The "moving the decimal points" step to obtain a whole-number divisor in Example 7.15 can be justified as follows:

Let a and b be decimals.
If $a \div b = c$, then $a = bc$.
Then $a \cdot 10^n = bc \cdot 10^n = (b \cdot 10^n)c$ for any n.
Thus $(a \cdot 10^n) \div (b \cdot 10^n) = c$.

This last equation shows we can multiply both a and b (the dividend and divisor) by the same power of 10 to make the divisor a whole number. This technique is similar to equal-additions subtraction except that division and multiplication are involved here.

Classifying Repeating Decimals

In Example 7.2 we observed that fractions in simplest form whose denominators are of the form $2^m \cdot 5^n$ have terminating decimal representations. Fractions of this type can also be converted into decimals using a calculator or the long-division algorithm for decimals.

EXAMPLE 7.16   Express $\frac{7}{40}$ in decimal form **(a)** using a calculator and **(b)** using the long-division algorithm.

Solution

(a) $7 \boxed{\div} 40 \boxed{=} \boxed{0.175}$

(b)
$$
\begin{array}{r}
0.175 \\
40\overline{)7.000} \\
-4\,0 \\
\hline
3\,00 \\
-2\,80 \\
\hline
200 \\
-200 \\
\hline
0
\end{array}
$$

Therefore, $\frac{7}{40} = 0.175$.   ∎

Now let's express $\frac{1}{3}$ as a decimal. Using a calculator we obtain

$$1 \boxed{\div} 3 \boxed{=} \boxed{0.333333333}$$

This display shows $\frac{1}{3}$ as a terminating decimal since the calculator can display only finitely many decimal places. However, the long-division method adds some additional insight to this situation.

$$
\begin{array}{r}
0.333 \ldots \\
3\overline{)1.000} \\
-9 \\
\hline
10 \\
-9 \\
\hline
10 \\
-9 \\
\hline
1
\end{array}
$$

Using long division, we see that the decimal in the quotient will *never* terminate since every remainder is 1. Similarly, the decimal for $\frac{1}{11}$ is 0.0909. . . . Instead of writing dots, a horizontal bar may be placed above the **repetend**, the first string of repeating digits. Thus

$$\frac{1}{3} = 0.\overline{3}, \quad \frac{1}{11} = 0.\overline{09}, \quad \frac{2}{7} = 0.\overline{285714}, \quad \frac{2}{9} = 0.\overline{2}, \text{ and } \frac{40}{99} = 0.\overline{40}.$$

(Use your calculator or the long-division algorithm to check that these are correct.) Decimals having a repetend are called **repeating decimals**. (NOTE: Terminating decimals are those repeating decimals whose repetend is zero.) The number of digits in the repetend is called the **period** of the decimal. For example, the period of $\frac{1}{11}$ is 2. To gain additional insight into why certain decimals repeat, consider the next example.

EXAMPLE 7.17   Express $\frac{6}{7}$ as a decimal.

Solution

$$
\begin{array}{r}
0.857142 \\
7\overline{)6.000000} \\
-5\,6 \\
\hline
40 \\
-35 \\
\hline
50 \\
-49 \\
\hline
10 \\
-\,7 \\
\hline
30 \\
-28 \\
\hline
20 \\
-14 \\
\hline
6
\end{array}
$$

When dividing by 7, there are seven possible remainders—0, 1, 2, 3, 4, 5, 6. Thus, when dividing by 7, either a 0 will appear as a remainder (and the decimal terminates) or one of the other nonzero remainders must eventually *reappear* as a remainder. At that point, the decimal will begin to repeat. Notice that the remainder 6 appears for a second time, so the decimal will begin to repeat at that point. Therefore, $\frac{6}{7} = 0.\overline{857142}$. Similarly, $\frac{1}{13}$ will begin repeating no later than the 13th remainder, $\frac{7}{23}$ will begin repeating *by* the 23rd remainder, and so on.   ■

STUDENT PAGE SNAPSHOT

Fractions, Mixed Numbers, and Decimals

A. Twenty-four students were surveyed to find out how each travels to school. How can you write a decimal to express the portion of students who travel by bicycle?

Think: 15 out of 24 students travel by bicycle. ⟶ $\frac{15}{24}$

To rename a fraction as a decimal, divide the numerator by the denominator.   ⟶ **15 ÷ 24**

TRANSPORTATION TO SCHOOL

Type	Number of Students
Bicycle	15
Bus	5
Car	3
Foot	1

Calculator

15 ⊕ 24 ⊜ $\boxed{0.625}$

The decimal 0.625 is a **terminating decimal.**
The remainder after division is 0.

So 0.625 of the students travel to school by bicycle.

Paper and Pencil

$$\begin{array}{r} 0.6\,2\,5 \\ 24\overline{)15.000} \\ \underline{14\,4} \\ 6\,0 \\ \underline{4\,8} \\ 12\,0 \\ \underline{12\,0} \\ 0 \end{array}$$

1. If you use paper and pencil, why does writing $\frac{15}{24}$ in simplest form lead to an easier division?

B. Sometimes when you rename a fraction as a decimal you get a **repeating decimal.**

Think: 5 out of 24 students travel by bus. ⟶ $\frac{5}{24}$

Divide 5 by 24 to rename $\frac{5}{24}$ as a decimal. ⟶ **5 ÷ 24**

Calculator

5 ⊕ 24 ⊜ $\boxed{0.2083333}$

The decimal 0.2083333 . . . is a repeating decimal. The remainder is never 0. Use a bar to show which digit or digits repeat:
$\frac{5}{24} = 0.208\overline{3}$.

So 0.208$\overline{3}$ of the students travel to school by bus.

Paper and Pencil

$$\begin{array}{r} 0.2\,0\,8\,3\,3 \\ 24\overline{)5.00000} \\ \underline{4\,8} \\ 2\,0\,0 \\ \underline{1\,9\,2} \\ 8\,0 \\ \underline{7\,2} \\ 8\,0 \\ \underline{7\,2} \\ 8 \end{array}$$

2. When dividing using paper and pencil, how can you tell that the 3 will continue to repeat?

3. How can you rename $2\frac{13}{33}$ as a repeating decimal?

By considering several examples where the denominator has factors other than 2 or 5, the following statement will be apparent.

Theorem

Fractions with Repeating, Nonterminating Decimal Representations

Let $\frac{a}{b}$ be a fraction written in *simplest form*. Then $\frac{a}{b}$ has a repeating decimal representation that does not terminate if and only if b has a prime factor other than 2 or 5.

Earlier we saw that it was easy to express any terminating decimal as a fraction. But suppose that a number has a repeating, nonterminating decimal representation. Can we find a fractional representation for that number?

EXAMPLE 7.18   Express $0.\overline{34}$ in its fractional form.

Solution
Let $n = 0.\overline{34}$. Thus $100n = 34.\overline{34}$.

$$\text{Then} \qquad 100n = 34.343434\ldots$$
$$-\qquad n = .343434\ldots$$
$$\text{so} \qquad \overline{99n = 34}$$

$$\text{or} \qquad n = \frac{34}{99} \qquad\blacksquare$$

This procedure can be applied to any repeating decimal that does not terminate, except that instead of multiplying n by 100 each time, you must multiply n by 10^m, where m is the number of digits in the repetend. For example, to express $17.\overline{531}$ in its fractional form, let $n = 17.\overline{531}$ and multiply both n and $17.\overline{531}$ by 10^3 since the repetend $.\overline{531}$ has three digits. Then $10^3 n - n = 17{,}531.\overline{531} - 17.\overline{531} = 17{,}514$. From this we find that $n = \frac{17{,}514}{999}$.

Finally, we can state the following important result that links fractions and repeating decimals.

Theorem   Every fraction has a repeating decimal representation and every repeating decimal has a fraction representation.

The following diagram provides a visual summary of this theorem.

Fractions $\leftrightarrow$ Repeating Decimals

Terminating (decimals whose repetend is zero)   Nonterminating (decimals whose repetend is not zero)

MATHEMATICAL MORSEL

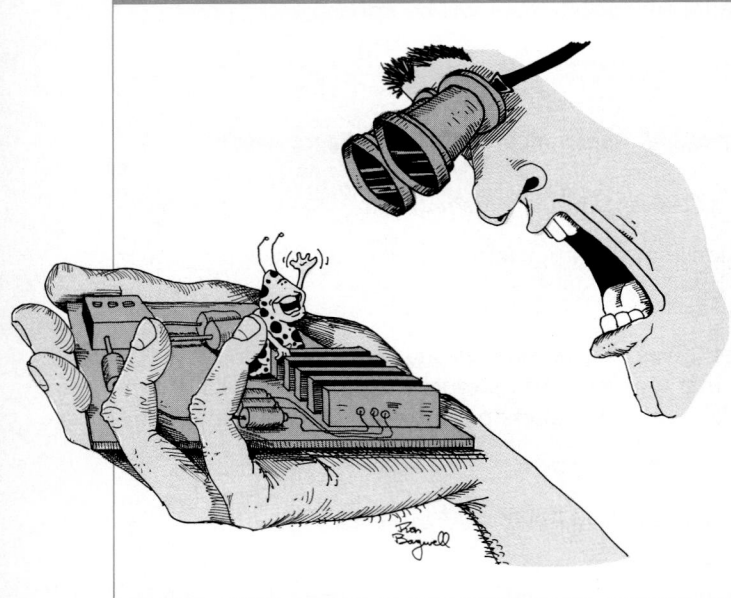

Debugging is a term used to describe the process of checking a computer program for errors and then correcting the errors. According to legend, the process of debugging was adopted by Grace Hopper, who designed the computer language COBOL. When one of her programs was not running as it should, it was found that one of the computer components had malfunctioned and that a real bug found among the components was the culprit. Since then, if a program did not run as it was designed to, it was said to have a "bug" in it. Thus it had to be "debugged."

EXERCISE/PROBLEM SET 7.2—PART A

Exercises

1. **(a)** Perform the following operations using the decimal algorithms of this section.
   (i) 38.52 + 9.251   (ii) 0.58 + 0.006
   (iii) 534.51 − 48.67
   (b) Change the decimals in part (a) to fractions, perform the computations, and express the answers as decimals.

2. **(a)** Perform the following operations using the algorithms of this section.
   (i) 5.23×0.034 (ii) 6.007×2.38
   (iii) $35.466 \div 0.23$ (iv) $8.272 \div 1.76$
   (b) Change the decimals in part (a) to fractions, perform the computations, and express the answers as decimals.

3. Use the algorithm taught in the text to compute $0.05 \times 0.263 \times 350$ and then verify your answer by multiplying the numbers above as fractions.

4. What two division problems are suggested by $0.273 \times 5.7 = 1.5561$?

5. Using the properties of numbers and exponents, it is possible to do multiplication in scientific notation. For example,
$$3100 \times 460 = (3.1 \times 10^3) \times (4.6 \times 10^2)$$
$$= (3.1 \times 4.6) \times (10^3 \times 10^2)$$
$$= 14.26 \times 10^5$$
$$= 1.426 \times 10^1 \times 10^5$$
$$= 1.426 \times 10^6$$

Find the following products and express answers in scientific notation.
(a) $(6.2 \times 10^1) \times (5.9 \times 10^4)$
(b) $(7.1 \times 10^2) \times (8.3 \times 10^6)$

6. Quotients in scientific notation can be found as follows:
$$\frac{5.27 \times 10^6}{8.5 \times 10^2} = \frac{5.27}{8.5} \times \frac{10^6}{10^2}$$
$$= 0.62 \times 10^4$$
$$= 0.62 \times 10 \times 10^3$$
$$= 6.2 \times 10^3$$

Find the following quotients and express the answers in scientific notation.
(a) $\dfrac{1.612 \times 10^5}{3.1 \times 10^2}$ **(b)** $\dfrac{8.019 \times 10^9}{9.9 \times 10^5}$

7. A scientific calculator can be used to perform calculations with numbers written in scientific notation. The $\boxed{\text{SCI}}$ key or $\boxed{\text{EE}}$ key is used as shown in the following multiplication example: $(3.41 \times 10^{12})(4.95 \times 10^8)$.

3.41 $\boxed{\text{SCI}}$ 12 $\boxed{\times}$ 4.95 $\boxed{\text{SCI}}$ 8 $\boxed{=}$ $\boxed{1.68795 \quad 21}$

So the product is 1.68795×10^{21}.

(a) Try this example on your calculator. The sequence of steps and the appearance of the result may differ slightly from what was shown. Consult your manual if necessary.

(b) Use your calculator to find the following products and quotients. Express your answers in scientific notation.

(i) $(7.19 \times 10^6)(1.4 \times 10^8)$

(ii) $\dfrac{6.4 \times 10^{24}}{5.0 \times 10^{10}}$

(iii) $(1.2 \times 10^{10})(3.4 \times 10^{12})(8.5 \times 10^{17})$

(iv) $\dfrac{(4.56 \times 10^9)(7.0 \times 10^{21})}{(1.2 \times 10^6)(2.8 \times 10^{10})}$

(v) $(3.6 \times 10^{18})^3$

8. The diameter of Jupiter, the largest of the planets, is 143,800,000 meters.

(a) | | Express the diameter of Jupiter in scientific notation.

(b) If the diameter of Jupiter is about 1.2 times that of Saturn, what is the diameter of the Saturn? Express your answer in scientific notation.

9. Write each of the following using a bar over the repetend.

(a) 0.7777 . . .   (b) 0.47121212 . . .
(c) 0.181818 . . .   (d) 0.35
(e) 0.14141414 . . .   (f) 0.45315961596 . . .

10. Write out the first 14 decimal places of each of the following.

(a) $0.\overline{3174}$ (b) $0.3\overline{174}$
(c) $0.31\overline{74}$ (d) $0.317\overline{4}$
(e) 0.3174 (f) $0.\overline{1159123}$

11. Express each of the following repeating decimals as a fraction in simplest form.

(a) $0.\overline{16}$ (b) $0.3\overline{87}$
(c) $0.7\overline{25}$ (d) $0.3\overline{015}$
(e) $0.52\overline{1}$ (f) $0.00\overline{184}$

12. To write a number in base two, we define place values to the right of the decimal point as shown next.

2^2	2^1	2^0	$\dfrac{1}{2}$	$\dfrac{1}{2^2}$	$\dfrac{1}{2^3}$
1	0	1	0	1	1

So 101.011 in expanded form is $1(2^2) + 0(2^1) + 1(2^0) + 0\left(\dfrac{1}{2}\right) + 1\left(\dfrac{1}{2^2}\right) + 1\left(\dfrac{1}{2^3}\right) = 5\dfrac{3}{8}$. Find the equivalent base ten fraction for each of the following numerals in base two.

(a) 1.001_{two} (b) 111.11_{two} (c) 0.0011_{two}

13. To find the "decimal" representation of a fraction in base two, we can divide the numerator by the denomi-

nator as in base 10. For example, $\dfrac{1}{4} = \dfrac{1}{100_{\text{two}}} = 0.01_{\text{two}}$ since $1 \div 100_{\text{two}} = 0.01_{\text{two}}$.

$$\begin{array}{r} .01 \\ 100\overline{)1.00} \\ 1.00 \\ \hline \end{array}$$

Find the "decimal" equivalents in base two for each of the following fractions.

(a) $\dfrac{1}{2} = \dfrac{1}{10_{\text{two}}}$ (b) $\dfrac{1}{16} = \dfrac{1}{1000_{\text{two}}}$

(c) $\dfrac{1}{3} = \dfrac{1}{11_{\text{two}}}$ (d) $\dfrac{1}{5} = \dfrac{1}{101_{\text{two}}}$

Problems

14. The star Deneb is approximately 1.5×10^{19} meters from Earth. A light year, the distance that light travels in one year, is about 9.46×10^{15} meters. What is the distance from Earth to Deneb measured in light years?

15. Is the decimal expansion of $151/7,018,923,456,413$ terminating or nonterminating? How can you tell without computing the decimal expansion?

16. Give an example of a fraction whose decimal expansion terminates in the following numbers of places.

(a) 3   (b) 4   (c) 8   (d) 17

17. From the fact that $0.\overline{1} = \frac{1}{9}$, mentally convert the following decimals into fractions.

(a) $0.\overline{3}$ (b) $0.\overline{5}$ (c) $0.\overline{7}$ (d) $2.\overline{8}$
(e) $5.\overline{9}$

18. From the fact that $0.\overline{01} = \frac{1}{99}$, mentally convert the following decimals into fractions.

(a) $0.\overline{03}$ (b) $0.\overline{05}$ (c) $0.\overline{07}$
(d) $0.\overline{37}$ (e) $0.\overline{64}$ (f) $5.\overline{97}$

19. From the fact that $0.\overline{001} = \frac{1}{999}$, mentally convert the following decimals into fractions.

(a) $0.\overline{003}$ (b) $0.\overline{005}$ (c) $0.\overline{007}$
(d) $0.\overline{019}$ (e) $0.\overline{827}$ (f) $3.\overline{217}$

20. (a) Use the pattern you have discovered in Problems 17 to 19 to convert the following decimals into fractions. Do mentally.

(i) $0.\overline{23}$ (ii) $0.\overline{010}$
(iii) $0.\overline{769}$ (iv) $0.\overline{9}$
(v) $0.\overline{57}$ (vi) $0.\overline{1827}$

(b) Verify your answers by using the method taught in the text for converting repeating decimals into fractions using a calculator.

21. (a) Give an example of a fraction whose decimal representation has a repetend containing exactly five digits.

(b) Characterize all fractions whose decimal representations are of the form $0.\overline{abcde}$, where a, b, c, d, and e are arbitrary digits 0 through 9 and not all five digits are the same.

22. (a) What is the eleventh digit to the right of the decimal in the decimal expansion of $\frac{1}{13}$?
(b) 33rd digit of $\frac{1}{13}$?
(c) 2731st digit of $\frac{1}{13}$?
(d) 11,000,000th digit of $\frac{1}{13}$?

23. From the observation that $100 \times \frac{1}{71} = \frac{100}{71} = 1\frac{29}{71}$, what conclusion can you draw about the relationship between the decimal expansions of $\frac{1}{71}$ and $\frac{29}{71}$?

24. It may require some ingenuity to calculate the following number on an inexpensive four-function calculator. Explain why, and show how one can, in fact, calculate it.

$$\frac{364 \times 363 \times 362 \times 361 \times 360 \times 359}{365 \times 365 \times 365 \times 365 \times 365 \times 365}$$

EXERCISE/PROBLEM SET 7.2—PART B

Exercises

1. Perform the following operations using the decimal algorithms of this section.
(a) $7.482 + 94.3$ **(b)** $100.63 - 72.495$
(c) $0.08 + 0.1234$ **(d)** $24 - 2.099$
(e) 16.4×2.8 **(f)** 0.065×1.92
(g) $44.4 \div 0.3$ **(h)** $129.168 \div 4.14$

2. (a) Show in detail that $9.3 \div 0.7 = 93 \div 7$. (Do not use the fact that the algorithm allows you to move the decimal point; you are trying to show that the algorithm is reasonable.) (HINT: Use fractions.)
(b) Repeat for $18.71 \div 3.18 = 1871 \div 318$.
(c) Repeat for $8.375 \div 7.2 = 83.75 \div 72$.

3. Find these products on your calculator *without* using the decimal-point key. (HINT: Locate the decimal point by doing approximate calculations.)
(a) 3.92×4.12
(b) 7.77×82.3
(c) 48.62×52.7
(d) 147.21×39.7

4. Mentally determine which of the following division problems have the same quotient.
(a) $5.6\overline{)16.8}$ **(b)** $0.056\overline{)1.68}$
(c) $0.56\overline{)16.8}$ **(d)** $56\overline{)1680}$
(e) $0.056\overline{)0.168}$ **(f)** $0.56\overline{)0.168}$

5. Perform the following calculations.
(a) $\frac{1}{4} + 0.373$ **(b)** $5.21 + 3\frac{2}{5}$ **(c)** $0.923 - \frac{1}{8}$
(d) $2.16 \times \frac{1}{3}$ **(e)** $2\frac{1}{5} \times 1.55$ **(f)** $16.4 \div \frac{4}{9}$

6. Perform the following operations and express answers in scientific notation.
(a) $(2.3 \times 10^2) \times (3.5 \times 10^4)$
(b) $(7.3 \times 10^3) \times (8.6 \times 10^6)$
(c) $\dfrac{9.02 \times 10^5}{2.2 \times 10^3}$ **(d)** $\dfrac{5.561 \times 10^7}{6.7 \times 10^2}$

7. At a height of 8.488 kilometers, the highest mountain in the world is Mount Everest in the Himalayas. The deepest part of the oceans is the Marianas Trench in the Pacific Ocean, with a depth of 11.034 kilometers. What is the vertical distance from the top of the highest mountain in the world to the deepest part of the oceans?

8. The earth's oceans have a total volume of approximately 1,286,000,000 cubic kilometers. The volume of fresh water on the earth is approximately 35,000,000 cubic kilometers.
(a) Express each of these volumes in scientific notation.
(b) The volume of salt water in the oceans is about how many times greater than the volume of fresh water on the earth?

9. The amount of gold in the earth's crust is about 120,000,000,000,000 kilograms.
(a) Express this amount of gold in scientific notation.
(b) The market value of gold in July 1992 was about $11,500 per kilogram. What was the total market value of all the gold in the earth's crust at that time?
(c) The total U.S. national debt in July 1992 was about 4×10^{12}. How many times would the value of the gold pay off the national debt?
(d) If there were about 250,000,000 people in the United States in July 1992, how much do each of us owe on the national debt?

10. Determine if the following are equal. If not, which is smaller, and why?

$$0.25\overline{25} \qquad 0.2\overline{525}$$

11. Finding the decimal expansion for a fraction like $\frac{19}{31}$ is extremely tedious using long division and cannot be done directly on a calculator that displays only seven, eight, or nine decimal places. (Remember that the repetend for $\frac{19}{31}$ may have as many as 30 digits!) But a calculator can be used to find the decimal expansion of $\frac{19}{31}$ in the following way. Assume, for this example, that your calculator displays seven decimal places.

Step 1: Divide 19 by 31.

$$19 \boxed{\div} 31 \boxed{=} \boxed{0.6129032}$$

Since the calculator rounds the display to seven places, we do not know whether the seventh digit is really a 1 or a 2. But we do know that the first six places in the expansion are 0.612903; so we have

$$31\overline{)19.000000}^{.612903}$$

Step 2: To continue the process, multiply and subtract as shown next.

$$0.612903 \boxed{\times} 31 \boxed{=} \boxed{18.999993}$$

$$\begin{array}{r} .612903 \\ 31\overline{)19.000000} \\ 18.999993 \\ \hline 7 \end{array}$$

Step 3: Now divide 7 by 31, as in step 1, and record the first six digits in the quotient.

$$7 \boxed{\div} 31 \boxed{=} \boxed{0.2258064}$$

$$\begin{array}{r} .612903225806 \\ 31\overline{)19.000000000000} \\ 18.999993 \\ \hline 7000000 \end{array}$$

By continuing this process, we eventually obtain

$$\begin{array}{r} .61290322580645161290 3225 \\ 31\overline{)19.00000000000000000000000000} \\ 18.999993 \\ \hline 7000000 \\ 6999986 \\ \hline 14000000 \\ 13999972 \\ \hline 28 \end{array}$$

Now the repetend can be identified, and we have $\frac{19}{31} =$ 0.$\overline{612903225806451}$.

Use your calculator to determine the decimal representation for each of the following fractions. (NOTE: You can adjust the process described to allow for the number of decimal places displayed on your calculator.)

(a) $\frac{1}{26}$ (b) $\frac{4}{17}$ (c) $\frac{1}{42}$

12. Express each of the following decimals as fractions.
(a) 0.$\overline{5}$ (b) 0.$\overline{78}$ (c) 0.$\overline{123}$
(d) 0.1$\overline{24}$ (e) 0.01$\overline{78}$ (f) 0.123456

13. Find the equivalent base ten fraction for each of the following "decimals" in other bases. (Refer to Problem 12 in Part A.)
(a) 21.11_{three} (b) 104.13_{five}
(c) 0.012_{four} (d) 0.1234_{six}

Problems

14. Without doing any written work or using a calculator, order the following numbers from largest to smallest.

$$x = 0.00000456789 \div 0.00000987654$$
$$y = 0.00000456789 \times 0.00000987654$$
$$z = 0.00000456789 + 0.00000987654$$

15. Look for a pattern in each of the following sequences of decimal numbers. For each one, write what you think the next two terms would be.
(a) 11.5, 14.7, 17.9, 21.1, . . .
(b) 24, 33.6, 47.04, 65.856, . . .
(c) 0.5, 0.05, 0.055, 0.0055, 0.00555, . . .
(d) 0.5, 0.6, 1.0, 1.9, 3.5, 6.0, . . .
(e) 1.0, 0.5, 0.$\overline{6}$, 0.75, 0.8, . . .

16. In Chapter 3 a palindrome was defined to be a number such as 343 that reads the same forward and backward. A process of reversing the digits of any number and adding until a palindrome is obtained was described. The same technique works for decimal numbers, as shown next.

$$\begin{array}{rl} 7.95 & \\ +\ \underline{59.7} & \text{(step 1)} \\ 67.65 & \\ +\ \underline{56.76} & \text{(step 2)} \\ 124.41 & \\ +\ \underline{14.421} & \text{(step 3)} \\ 138.831 & \text{(a palindrome)} \end{array}$$

(a) Determine the number of steps required to obtain a palindrome from each of the following numbers.
  (i) 16.58   (ii) 217.8
  (iii) 1.0097   (iv) 9.63
(b) Find a decimal number that requires exactly four steps to give a palindrome.

17. (a) Express each of the following as fractions.
  (i) 0.$\overline{1}$ (ii) 0.$\overline{01}$
  (iii) 0.$\overline{001}$ (iv) 0.$\overline{0001}$
(b) What fraction would you expect to be given by 0.$\overline{000000001}$?
(c) What would you expect the decimal expansion of $\frac{1}{90}$ to be?

18. Change 0.$\overline{9}$ to a fraction. Can you explain your result?

19. Consider the decimals: $a_1 = 0.9$, $a_2 = 0.99$, $a_3 = 0.999$, $a_4 = 0.9999$, . . ., $a_n = 0.999 \ldots 9$ (with n digits of 9).
(a) Give an argument that $0 < a_n < a_{n+1} < 1$ for each n.
(b) Show that there is a term a_n in the sequence such that

$$1 - a_n < \frac{1}{10^{100}}$$

(Find a value of n that works.)

(c) Give an argument that the sequence of terms gets arbitrarily close to 1. That is, for any distance d, no matter how small, there is a term a_n in the sequence such that $1 - d < a_n < 1$.

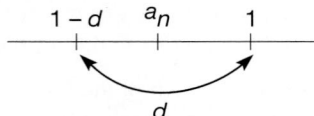

(d) Use parts (a) to (c) to explain why $0.\overline{9} = 1$.

20. (a) Write $\frac{1}{7}, \frac{2}{7}, \frac{3}{7}, \frac{4}{7}, \frac{5}{7}$, and $\frac{6}{7}$ in their decimal expansion form. What do the repetends for each expansion have in common?

(b) Write $\frac{1}{13}, \frac{2}{13}, \frac{3}{13}, \ldots, \frac{11}{13}$, and $\frac{12}{13}$ in decimal expansion form. What observations can you make about the repetends in these expansions?

21. Characterize all fractions a/b, $a < b$, whose decimal expansions consist of n random digits to the right of the decimal followed by a five-digit repetend. For example, suppose that $n = 7$; then $0.213567\overline{451139}$ would be the decimal expansion of such a fraction.

22. When the following fractions (written with base ten numerals) are written in the given bases, which will have "decimal" representations that terminate?

$$\frac{1}{2}, \frac{1}{3}, \frac{1}{4}, \frac{1}{5}, \frac{1}{6}, \frac{1}{14}, \frac{1}{16}, \frac{1}{20}, \frac{1}{21}$$

(a) Base ten   **(b)** Base six   **(c)** Base twelve
(d) Base seven

23. If $\frac{9}{23} = 0.\overline{3913043478260869565217}$, what is the 999th digit to the right of the decimal?

24. Name the digit in the 4321st place of each of the following decimals.
(a) $0.\overline{142857}$
(b) $0.1234567891011121314 \ldots$

25. What happened to the other $\frac{1}{4}$?

$$
\begin{array}{r}
16.5 \\
\times 12.5 \\
\hline
8.25 \\
33 \\
165 \\
\hline
206.25
\end{array}
\qquad
\begin{array}{r}
16\frac{1}{2} \\
\times 12\frac{1}{2} \\
\hline
32 \\
160 \\
8\frac{1}{4} \\
6\frac{1}{4} \\
\hline
206\frac{1}{2}
\end{array}
\quad
\begin{array}{l}
\\
\\
\text{(one-half of } 16\frac{1}{2}\text{)} \\
\text{(one-half of } 12\frac{1}{2}\text{)}
\end{array}
$$

7.3

RATIO AND PROPORTION

Ratio

The concept of ratio occurs in many places in mathematics and in everyday life, as the next example illustrates.

EXAMPLE 7.19
(a) In Washington School, the ratio of students to teachers is $17:1$, read "17 to 1."
(b) In Smithville, the ratio of girls to boys is $3:2$.
(c) A paint mixture calls for a $5:3$ ratio of blue paint to red paint.
(d) The ratio of centimeters to inches is $2.54:1$.   ■

In this chapter the numbers used in ratios will be whole numbers, fractions, or decimals representing fractions. Ratios involving real numbers are studied in Chapter 9.

In English, the word "per" means "for every" and indicates a ratio. For example, rates such as miles per gallon (gasoline mileage), kilometers per hour (speed), dollars per hour (wages), cents per ounce (unit price), people per square mile (population density), and percent are all ratios.

> **Definition**
>
> ### Ratio
>
> A **ratio** is an ordered pair of numbers, written $a:b$, with $b \neq 0$.

Unlike fractions, there are instances of ratios in which b could be zero. For example, the ratio of men to women on a starting major league baseball team could be reported as $9:0$. However, since such applications as this are rare, the definition of the ratio $a:b$ excludes cases in which $b = 0$.

Ratios allow us to compare the relative sizes of two quantities. This comparison can be represented by the ratio symbol $a:b$ or as the quotient $\dfrac{a}{b}$.

Quotients occur quite naturally when we interpret ratios. In Example 7.19(a), there are $\frac{1}{17}$ as many teachers as students in Washington School. In part (b) there are $\frac{3}{2}$ as many girls as boys in Smithville. We could also say that there are $\frac{2}{3}$ as many boys as girls, or that the ratio of boys to girls is $2:3$. This is illustrated in Figure 7.10.

Notice that there are several ratios that we can form when comparing the population of boys and girls in Smithville, namely $2:3$ (boys to girls), $3:2$ (girls to boys), $2:5$ (boys to children), $5:3$ (children to girls), and so on. Some ratios give a **part-to-part** comparison, as in Example 7.19(c). In mixing the paint, we would use 5 units of blue paint and 3 units of red paint. (A unit could be any size—milliliter, teaspoon, cup, and so on.) Ratios can also represent the comparison of **part to whole** or **whole to part**. In Example 7.19(b) the ratio of boys (part) to children (whole) is $2:5$. Notice that the part-to-whole ratio, $2:5$, is the same concept as the fraction of the children that are boys, namely $\frac{2}{5}$. The comparison of all the children to the boys can be expressed in a whole-to-part ratio as $5:2$, or as the fraction $\frac{5}{2}$.

In Example 7.19(b), the ratio of girls to boys indicates only the *relative* sizes of the populations of girls and boys in Smithville. There could be 30 girls and 20 boys, 300 girls and 200 boys, or some other pair of numbers whose ratio is equivalent. It is important to note that ratios always represent relative, rather than absolute, amounts. In many applications, it is useful to know which ratios represent the same relative amounts. Consider the following example.

EXAMPLE 7.20   In class 1 the ratio of girls to boys is $8:6$. In class 2 the ratio is $4:3$. Suppose that each class has 28 students. Do these ratios represent the same relative amounts?

Solution

Notice that the classes can be grouped in different ways (Figure 7.11). The subdivisions shown in Figure 7.11 do not change the relative number of

G G G
B B

FIGURE 7.10

| Class 1: | *GGGG* | *GGGG* | *GGGG* | *GGGG* | |
| | *BBB* | *BBB* | *BBB* | *BBB* | Ratio 8:6 |

| Class 2: | *GGGG* | *GGGG* | *GGGG* | *GGGG* | |
| | *BBB* | *BBB* | *BBB* | *BBB* | Ratio 4:3 |

FIGURE 7.11

girls to boys in the groups. We see that in both classes there are 4 girls for every 3 boys. Hence we say that, as ordered pairs, the ratios $4:3$ and $8:6$ are equivalent since they represent the same relative amount. They are equivalent to the ratio $16:12$. ∎

From Example 7.20 it should be clear that the ratios $a:b$ and $ar:br$, where $r \neq 0$, represent the same relative amounts. Using an argument similar to the one used with fractions, we can show that the ratios $a:b$ and $c:d$ represent the same relative amounts if and only if $ad = bc$. Thus we have the following definition.

Definition

Equality of Ratios

Let $\dfrac{a}{b}$ and $\dfrac{c}{d}$ be any two ratios. Then $\dfrac{a}{b} = \dfrac{c}{d}$ if and only if $ad = bc$.

Just as with fractions, this definition can be used to show that if n is a nonzero number, then $\dfrac{an}{bn} = \dfrac{a}{b}$, or $an:bn = a:b$. In the equation $\dfrac{a}{b} = \dfrac{c}{d}$, a and d are called the **extremes** since a and d are at the "extremes" of the equation $a:b = c:d$, while b and c are called the **means**. Thus the equality of ratios states that two ratios are equal if and only if the product of the means equals the product of the extremes.

Proportion

The concept of proportion is useful in solving problems involving ratios.

Definition

Proportion

A **proportion** is a statement that two given ratios are equal.

The equation $\dfrac{10}{12} = \dfrac{5}{6}$ is a proportion since $\dfrac{10}{12} = \dfrac{5 \cdot 2}{6 \cdot 2} = \dfrac{5}{6}$. Also, the equation $\frac{14}{21} = \frac{22}{33}$ is an example of a proportion since $14 \cdot 33 = 21 \cdot 22$. In general, $\dfrac{a}{b} = \dfrac{c}{d}$ is a proportion if and only if $ad = bc$. The next example shows how proportions are used to solve everyday problems.

EXAMPLE 7.21   Adams School orders 3 cartons of chocolate milk for *every* 7 students. If there are 581 students in the school, how many cartons of chocolate milk should be ordered?

Solution
Set up a proportion using the ratio of cartons to students. Let n be the unknown number of cartons. Then

$$\frac{3 \text{ (cartons)}}{7 \text{ (students)}} = \frac{n \text{ (cartons)}}{581 \text{ (students)}}$$

Using the cross-multiplication property of ratios, we have that

$$3 \times 581 = 7 \times n,$$

so

$$n = \frac{3 \times 581}{7} = 249.$$

The school should order 249 cartons of chocolate milk.   ■

In Example 7.21, the number of cartons of milk were compared with the number of students. Ratios involving different units (here cartons to students) are called **rates**. Commonly used rates include miles per gallon, cents per ounce, and so on.

When solving proportions like the one in Example 7.21, it is important to set up the ratios in a consistent way according to the units associated with the numbers. In our solution, the ratios 3:7 and n:581 represented ratios of *cartons of chocolate milk* to *students in the school*. The following proportion could also have been used.

$$\frac{3 \left(\begin{array}{c} \text{cartons of chocolate} \\ \text{milk in the ratio} \end{array} \right)}{n \left(\begin{array}{c} \text{cartons of chocolate} \\ \text{milk in school} \end{array} \right)} = \frac{7 \left(\begin{array}{c} \text{students} \\ \text{in the ratio} \end{array} \right)}{581 \left(\begin{array}{c} \text{students} \\ \text{in school} \end{array} \right)}.$$

Here the numerators show the original ratio. (Notice that the proportion $\frac{3}{n} = \frac{581}{7}$ would *not* correctly represent the problem, since the units in the numerators and denominators would not correspond.)

In general, the following proportions are equivalent (i.e., have the same solutions). This can be justified by cross-multiplication.

$$\frac{a}{b} = \frac{c}{d} \qquad \frac{a}{c} = \frac{b}{d} \qquad \frac{b}{a} = \frac{d}{c} \qquad \frac{c}{a} = \frac{d}{b}.$$

Thus there are several possible correct proportions that can be established when equating ratios.

EXAMPLE 7.22   A recipe calls for 1 cup of mix, 1 cup of milk, the whites from 4 eggs, and 3 teaspoons of oil. If this recipe serves six people, how many eggs are needed to make enough for 15 people?

Solution

When solving proportions, it is useful to list the various pieces of information as follows:

	Original Recipe	New Recipe
Number of Eggs	4	x
Number of People	6	15

Thus $\dfrac{4}{6} = \dfrac{x}{15}$. This proportion can be solved in two ways:

Cross-Multiplication	Equivalent Ratios
$\dfrac{4}{6} = \dfrac{x}{15}$	$\dfrac{4}{6} = \dfrac{x}{15}$
$4 \cdot 15 = 6x$	$\dfrac{4}{6} = \dfrac{2 \cdot 2}{2 \cdot 3} = \dfrac{2}{3} = \dfrac{2 \cdot 5}{3 \cdot 5} = \dfrac{10}{15} = \dfrac{x}{15}$
$60 = 6x$	Thus $x = 10$.
$10 = x$	

Notice that the table in Example 7.22 showing the number of eggs and people can be used to set up three other equivalent proportions:

$$\frac{4}{x} = \frac{6}{15} \qquad \frac{x}{4} = \frac{15}{6} \qquad \frac{6}{4} = \frac{15}{x}.$$

EXAMPLE 7.23   If your car averages 29 miles per gallon, how many gallons should you expect to buy for a 609-mile trip?

Solution

	Average	Trip
Miles	29	609
Gallons	1	x

Therefore, $\dfrac{29}{1} = \dfrac{609}{x}$, or $\dfrac{x}{1} = \dfrac{609}{29}$. Thus $x = 21$.

EXAMPLE 7.24 In a scale drawing, 0.5 centimeter represents 35 miles.
(a) How many miles will 4 centimeters represent?
(b) How many centimeters will represent 420 miles?

Solution
(a)

	Scale	Actual
Centimeters	0.5	4
Miles	35	x

Thus $\dfrac{0.5}{35} = \dfrac{4}{x}$. Solving, we obtain $x = \dfrac{35 \cdot 4}{0.5}$, or $x = 280$.

(b)

	Scale	Actual
Centimeters	0.5	y
Miles	35	420

Thus $\dfrac{0.5}{35} = \dfrac{y}{420}$, or $\dfrac{0.5 \times 420}{35} = y$. Therefore, $y = \dfrac{210}{35} = 6$ centimeters.

Example 7.24 could have been solved mentally by using the following mental technique called **scaling up/scaling down**; that is, by multiplying/dividing each number in a ratio by the same number. In Example 7.24(a) we can scale up as follows:

$$0.5 \text{ centimeter} : 35 \text{ miles} = 1 \text{ centimeter} : 70 \text{ miles}$$
$$= 2 \text{ centimeters} : 140 \text{ miles}$$
$$= 4 \text{ centimeters} : 280 \text{ miles}.$$

Similarly, the number of centimeters representing 420 miles in Example 7.24(b) could have been found mentally by scaling up as follows:

$$35 \text{ miles} : 0.5 \text{ centimeter} = 70 \text{ miles} \quad : 1 \text{ centimeter}$$
$$= 6 \times 70 \text{ miles} : 6 \times 1 \text{ centimeters}.$$

Thus 420 miles is represented by 6 centimeters.
In Example 7.22, to solve the proportion $4:6 = x:15$, the ratio $4:6$ was scaled down to $2:3$, then $2:3$ was scaled up to $10:15$. Thus $x = 10$.

EXAMPLE 7.25 Two neighbors were trying to decide if their property taxes were fair. The assessed value of one house was \$79,900 and its tax bill was \$1893.63. The other house had a tax bill of \$2391.48 and was assessed at \$87,600. Were the two houses taxed at the same rate?

Solution

Since the ratio of property taxes to assessed values should be the same, the following equation should be a proportion:

$$\frac{1893.63}{79,900} = \frac{2391.48}{87,600}.$$

Equivalently, we should have $1893.63 \times 87,600 = 79,900 \times 2391.48$. Using a calculator, $1893.63 \times 87,600 = 165,881,988$, and $79,900 \times 2391.48 = 191,079,252$. Thus the two houses are not taxed the same, since $165,881,988 \neq 191,079,252$.

An alternative solution to this problem would be actually to determine the tax rate per $1000 for each house.

First house: $\dfrac{1893.63}{79,900} = \dfrac{r}{1000}$ yields $r = \$23.70$ per $1000.

Second house: $\dfrac{2391.48}{87,600} = \dfrac{r}{1000}$ yields $r = \$27.30$ per $1000.

Thus it is likely that two digits of one of the tax rates were accidentally interchanged when calculating one of the bills. ■

MATHEMATICAL MORSEL

The famous mathematician Pythagoras founded a school that bore his name. As lore has it, to lure a young student to study at this school, he agreed to pay the student a penny for every theorem the student mastered. The student, motivated by the penny-a-theorem offer, studied intently and accumulated a huge sum of pennies. However, he so enjoyed the geometry that he begged Pythagoras for more theorems to prove. Pythagoras agreed to provide him with more theorems, but for a price, namely, a penny a theorem. Soon, Pythagoras had all his pennies back, in addition to a sterling student.

EXERCISE/PROBLEM SET 7.3—PART A

Exercises

1. The ratio of girls to boys in a particular classroom is 6:5.
   (a) What is the ratio of boys to girls?
   (b) What fraction of the total number of students are boys?
   (c) How many boys are in the class?
   (d) How many boys are in the class if there are 33 students?

2. Explain how each of the following rates satisfies the definition of ratio. Give an example of how each is used.
   (a) 250 miles/11.6 gallons
   (b) 25 dollars/3.5 hours
   (c) 1 dollar (American)/0.85 dollar (Canadian)
   (d) 2.5 dollars/0.96 pound
   (e) 1580 people/square mile
   (f) 450 people/year
   (g) 360 kilowatt-hours/4 months
   (h) 355 calories/6 ounces

3. Write a fraction in the simplest form that is equivalent to each ratio.
   (a) 16 to 64   (b) 30 to 75   (c) 82.5 to 16.5

4. When blood cholesterol levels are tested, sometimes a cardiac risk ratio is calculated.

Cardiac Risk Ratio =

$$\frac{\text{total cholesterol level}}{\text{high density lipoprotein level (HDL)}}$$

For women, a ratio between 3.0 and 4.5 is desirable. A woman's blood test yields an HDL cholesterol level of 60 mg/dL and a total cholesterol level of 225 mg/dL. What is her cardiac risk ratio, expressed as a one-place decimal? Is her ratio in the normal range?

5. Solve each proportion for n.
   (a) $\dfrac{57}{95} = \dfrac{18}{n}$ **(b)** $\dfrac{2}{130} = \dfrac{9}{n}$ **(c)** $\dfrac{n}{70} = \dfrac{6}{21}$

   (d) $\dfrac{n}{84} = \dfrac{3}{14}$ **(e)** $\dfrac{7}{n} = \dfrac{42}{48}$ **(f)** $\dfrac{12}{n} = \dfrac{18}{45}$

6. Solve each proportion for x. Round each answer to two decimal places.
   (a) $16:125 = x:5$ **(b)** $\dfrac{9}{7} = \dfrac{10.8}{x}$

   (c) $\dfrac{35.2}{19.6} = \dfrac{5}{3x}$ **(d)** $\dfrac{x}{4-x} = \dfrac{3}{4}$

   (e) $\dfrac{3\frac{1}{4}}{2\frac{1}{4}} = \dfrac{x}{1\frac{1}{2}}$ **(f)** $\dfrac{2x}{x+10} = \dfrac{0.04}{1.85}$

7. Solve these proportions mentally by scaling up or scaling down.
   (a) 24 miles for 2 gallons is equal to _____ miles for 16 gallons.
   (b) \$13.50 for 1 day is equal to _____ for 6 days.
   (c) 300 miles in 12 hours is equal to _____ miles in 8 hours. (Hint: Scale down to 4 hours, then scale up to 8 hours.)
   (d) 20 inches in 15 hours is equal to 16 inches in _____ hours.
   (e) 32 cents for 8 ounces is equal to _____ cents for 12 ounces.

8. For this exercise, use 50 mph = 80 kph (kilometers per hour). (The exact metric equivalent is 80.4672 kph.)
   (a) If you are traveling 100 kilometers per hour, how fast are you traveling in mph?
   (b) If you are traveling 55 mph, how fast are you traveling in kph?

9. Solve the problem stated in Example 7.21 by using the proportion of cartons:cartons = students:students.

10. Which of the following is the best buy?
   (a) 67 cents for 58 ounces or 17 cents for 15 ounces
   (b) 29 ounces for 13 cents or 56 ounces for 27 cents
   (c) 17 ounces for 23 cents, 25 ounces for 34 cents, or 73 ounces for 96 cents

Problems

11. Grape juice concentrate is mixed with water in a ratio of 1 part concentrate to 3 parts water. How much grape juice can be made from a 10-ounce can of concentrate?   40

12. A crew clears brush from $\frac{1}{2}$ acre of land in 3 days. How long will it take the same crew to clear the entire plot of $2\frac{3}{4}$ acres?

13. A recipe for peach cobbler calls for six small peaches for four servings. If a large quantity is to be prepared to serve 10 people, about how many peaches would be needed?

14. Dan used a 128-ounce bottle of liquid laundry detergent over a period of $6\frac{1}{2}$ weeks. About how many ounces of liquid laundry detergent will he probably purchase in a year's time if this use of detergent is typical?

15. If a 92-year-old man has averaged 8 hours per 24-hour day sleeping, how many years of his life has he been asleep?

16. A man who weighs 175 pounds on earth would weigh 28 pounds on the moon. How much would his 30-pound dog weigh on the moon?

17. Suppose that you drive an average of 4460 miles every half-year in your car. At the end of $2\frac{3}{4}$ years, how far will your car have gone?

18. Becky is climbing a hill that has a 17° slope. For every 5 feet she gains in altitude, she travels about 16.37 horizontal feet. If at the end of her uphill climb she has traveled 1 mile horizontally, how much altitude has she gained?

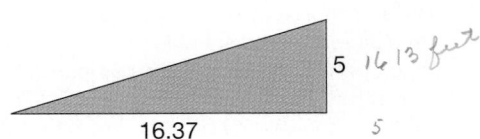
5   16.13 feet

16.37   5

19. The "Spruce Goose," a wooden flying boat built for Howard Hughes, had the world's largest wing span of 319 ft 11 in., according to the *Guinness Book of World Records*. It few only once in 1947 for a distance of about 1000 yards. Shelly wants to build a scale model of the 218 ft 8 in.–long Spruce Goose. If her model will be 20 inches long, what will its wing span be (to the nearest inch)?   about 29"

20. Jefferson School has 1400 students. The teacher–pupil ratio is $1:35$.
   (a) How many additional teachers will have to be hired to reduce the ratio to $1:20$?   30
   (b) If the teacher-pupil ratio remains at $1:35$ and if the cost to the district for one teacher is \$33,000 per year, how much will be spent per pupil per year?   \$314.29
   (c) Answer part (b) for a ratio of $1:20$.   \$550

21. Two triangles are **similar** if their sides are "proportional," meaning that there is a 1-1 correspondence between the sides of the first triangle and the sides of the second triangle such that the ratios of the corresponding lengths are equal. For example, if $\triangle RST$ is similar to $\triangle XYZ$, we have the following correspondences.

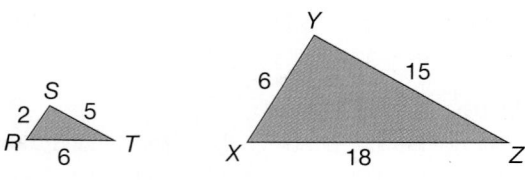

Correspondences		Ratio
$R \longleftrightarrow X$	$\overline{RS} \longleftrightarrow \overline{XY}$	$2:6 = 1:3$
$S \longleftrightarrow Y$	$\overline{ST} \longleftrightarrow \overline{YZ}$	$5:15 = 1:3$
$T \longleftrightarrow Z$	$\overline{TR} \longleftrightarrow \overline{ZX}$	$6:18 = 1:3$

Given that $\triangle ABC$ is similar to $\triangle DEF$, find the lengths of $\overline{BC}$ and $\overline{DE}$.

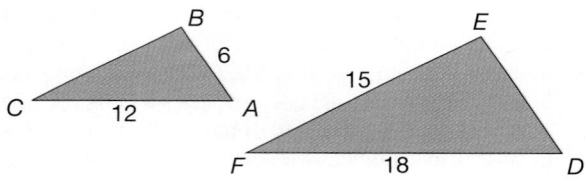

22. An **astronomical unit** (AU) is a measure of distance used by astronomers. In October 1985 the relative distance from Earth to Mars in comparison with the distance from Earth to Pluto was $1:12.37$.
   (a) If Pluto was 30.67 AU from Earth in October 1985, how many astronomical units from Earth was Mars?
   (b) Earth is always about 1 AU from the sun (in fact, this is the basis of this unit of measure). In October 1985, Pluto was about 2.85231×10^9 miles from Earth. About how many miles is Earth from the sun?
   (c) In October 1985 about how many miles was Mars from Earth?

23. According to the "big-bang" hypothesis, the universe was formed approximately 10^{10} years ago. The analogy of a 24-hour day is often used to put the passage of this amount of time into perspective. Imagine that the universe was formed at midnight 24 hours ago and answer the following questions.
   (a) To how many years of actual time does 1 hour correspond?
   (b) To how many years of actual time does 1 minute correspond?
   (c) To how many years of actual time does 1 second correspond?
   (d) The earth was formed, according to the hypothesis, approximately 5 billion years ago. To what time in the 24-hour day does this correspond?
   (e) Earliest known manlike remains have been determined by radioactive dating to be approximately 2.6 million years old. At what time of the 24-hour day did the creatures die who left these remains?
   (f) Intensive agriculture and the growth of modern civilization may have begun as early as 10,000 years ago. To what time of the 24-hour day does this correspond?

24. Cary was going to meet Jane at the airport. If he traveled 60 mph, he would arrive 1 hour early, and if he traveled 30 mph, he would arrive 1 hour late. How far was the airport? (Recall: Distance = rate · time.)

25. A man walked into a store to buy a hat. The hat he selected cost $20. He said to his father, "If you will lend me as much money as I have in my pocket, I will buy that $20 hat." The father agreed. Then they did it again with a $20 pair of slacks and again with a $20 pair of shoes. The man was finally out of money. How much did he have when he walked into the store?

26. What is the largest sum of money in U.S. coins that you could have without being able to give change for a nickel, dime, quarter, half-dollar, or dollar?

27. Beginning with 100, each of two persons, in turn, subtracts a single-digit number. The player who ends at zero is the loser. Can you explain how to play so that one player always wins?

28. How can you cook something for exactly 15 minutes if all you have are a 7-minute and an 11-minute egg timer?

29. Twelve posts stand equidistant along a race track. Starting at the first post, a runner reaches the eighth post in 8 seconds. If she runs at a constant velocity, how many seconds are needed to reach the twelfth post?

30. Seven children each had a different number of pennies. The ratio of each child's total to the next richer was a whole number. Altogether they had $28.79. How much did each have?

31. A box contains three different varieties of apples. What is the smallest number of apples that must be taken to be sure of getting at least 2 of one kind? How about at least 3 of one kind? How about at least 10 of a kind? How about at least n of a kind?

EXERCISE/PROBLEM SET 7.3—PART B

Exercises

1. Write a ratio based on each of the following.
   (a) Two-fifths of Ted's garden is planted in tomatoes.
   (b) The certificate of deposit you purchased earns $6.18 interest on every $100 you deposit.
   (c) Three out of every four voters surveyed favor ballot measure 5.
   (d) There are five times as many boys as girls in Mr. Wright's physics class.
   (e) There are half as many sixth graders in Fremont School as eighth graders.
   (f) Nine of every 16 students in the hot-lunch line are girls.

2. Determine whether the given ratios are equal.
   (a) 3:4 and 15:22
   (b) 11:6 and 66:36
   (c) 5:8 and 15:25
   (d) 7:12 and 36:60

3. In one analysis of people of the world, it was reported that of every 1000 people of the world,
   165 speak Mandarin
   86 speak English
   83 speak Hindi/Urdu
   64 speak Spanish
   58 speak Russian
   37 speak Arabic
   as their *native* language
   (a) Find the ratio of Spanish speakers to Russian speakers.
   (b) Find the ratio of Arabic speakers to English speakers.
   (c) The ratio of which two groups is nearly 2:1?
   (d) Find the ratio of persons who speak Mandarin, English, or Hindi/Urdu to the total group of 1000 people.
   (e) What fraction of persons in the group of 1000 world citizens are *not* accounted for in this list? These persons speak one of the more than 200 other languages spoken in the world today.

4. Solve for the unknown in each of the following proportions.
   (a) $\dfrac{\frac{3}{5}}{6} = \dfrac{D}{25}$
   (b) $\dfrac{B}{8} = \dfrac{2\frac{1}{4}}{18}$
   (c) $\dfrac{X}{100} = \dfrac{4.8}{1.5}$
   (d) $\dfrac{57.4}{39.6} = \dfrac{7.4}{P}$ (to one decimal place)

5. Solve each proportion for x. Round your answers to two decimal places where decimal answers do not terminate.
   (a) $\dfrac{7}{5} = \dfrac{x}{40}$
   (b) $\dfrac{12}{35} = \dfrac{40}{x}$
   (c) $2:9 = x:3$
   (d) $\dfrac{3}{4}:8 = 9:x$

   (e) $\dfrac{15}{32} = \dfrac{x}{x+2}$
   (f) $\dfrac{3x}{4} = \dfrac{12-x}{6}$

6. Write three other proportions for each given proportion.
   (a) $\dfrac{36 \text{ cents}}{18 \text{ ounces}} = \dfrac{42 \text{ cents}}{21 \text{ ounces}}$
   (b) $\dfrac{35 \text{ miles}}{2 \text{ hours}} = \dfrac{87.5 \text{ miles}}{5 \text{ hours}}$

7. Solve these proportions mentally by scaling up or scaling down.
   (a) 26 miles for 6 hours is equal to _____ miles for 24 hours.
   (b) 84 ounces for each 6 square inches is equal to _____ ounces for each 15 square inches.
   (c) 40 inches in 12 hours is equal to _____ inches in 9 hours.
   (d) $27.50 for 1.5 days is equal to _____ for 6 days.
   (e) 750 people for each 12 square miles is equal to _____ people for each 16 square miles.

8. Ms. Price has three times as many girls as boys in her class. Ms. Lippy has twice as many girls as boys. Ms. Price has 60 students in her class and Ms. Lippy has 135 students. If the classes were combined into one, what would be the ratio of girls to boys?

9. Mentally determine which of the following is the best buy.
   (a) 60 ounces for 29 cents or 84 ounces for 47 cents
   (b) $45 for 10 yards of material or $79 for 15 yards
   (c) 18 ounces for 40 cents, 20 ounces for 50 cents, or 30 ounces for 75 cents (HINT: How much does $1 purchase in each case?)

Problems

10. Three car batteries are advertised with warranties as follow.

    Model *XA*: 40-month warranty, $34.95
    Model *XL*: 50-month warranty, $39.95
    Model *XT*: 60-month warranty, $49.95

    Considering only the warranties and the prices, which model of car battery is the best buy?

11. Cari walked 3.4 kilometers in 45 minutes. At that rate, how long will it take her to walk 11.2 kilometers? Round to the nearest minute.

12. A family uses 5 gallons of milk every 3 weeks. At that rate how many gallons of milk will they need to purchase in a year's time?

13. A couple was assessed property taxes of $1623 on a home valued at $67,500. What might Frank expect to pay in property taxes on a home he hopes to purchase in the same neighborhood if it has a value of $79,600? Round to the nearest dollar.

14. By reading just a few pages at night before falling asleep, Randy finished a 248-page book in $4\frac{1}{2}$ weeks. He just started a new book of 676 pages. About how long should it take him to finish the new book if he reads at the same rate?

15. (a) If 1 inch on a map represents 35 miles, how many miles are represented by 3 inches? 10 inches? n inches?

(b) Los Angeles is about 1000 miles from Portland. About how many inches apart would Portland and Los Angeles be on this map?

16. A farmer calculates that out of every 100 seeds of corn he plants, he harvests 84 ears of corn. If he wants to harvest 7200 ears of corn, how many seeds must he plant?

17. A map is drawn to scale such that $\frac{1}{8}$ inch represents 65 feet. If the shortest route from your house to the grocery store measures $23\frac{7}{16}$ inches, how many miles is it to the grocery store?

18. (a) If $1\frac{3}{4}$ cups of flour are required to make 28 cookies, how many cups are required for 88 cookies?

(b) If your car gets 32 miles per gallon, how many gallons do you use on a 160-mile trip?

(c) If your mechanic suggests 3 parts antifreeze to 4 parts water, and if your radiator is 14 liters, how many liters of antifreeze should you use?

(d) If 11 ounces of roast beef costs $1.86, how much does roast beef cost per pound?

19. Two professional drag racers are speeding down a $\frac{1}{4}$-mile track. If the lead driver is traveling 1.738 feet for every 1.670 feet that the trailing car travels, and if the trailing car is going 198 mph, how fast in miles per hour is the lead car traveling?

20. In 1989 the Internal Revenue Service audited 92 of every 10,000 individual returns.

(a) In a community in which 12,500 people filed returns, how many returns might be expected to be audited?

(b) In 1990 only 80 returns per 10,000 were audited. How many fewer of the 12,500 returns would be expected to be audited for 1990 than for 1989?

21. (a) A baseball pitcher has pitched a total of 25 innings so far during the season and has allowed 18 runs. At this rate, how many runs, to the nearest hundredth, would he allow in nine innings? This number is called the pitcher's **earned run average** or ERA.

(b) Orel Hershiser of the Los Angeles Dodgers had an ERA of 2.26 in 1988. At that rate, how many runs would he be expected to allow in 100 innings pitched? Round your answer to the nearest whole number.

22. Many tires come with $\frac{13}{32}$ inch of tread of them. The first $\frac{2}{32}$ inch wears off quickly (say, during the first 1000 miles). From then on the tire wears uniformly (and more slowly). A tire is considered "worn out" when only $\frac{2}{32}$ inch of tread is left.

(a) How many 32nds of an inch of usable tread does a tire have after 1000 miles?

(b) A tire has traveled 20,000 miles and has $\frac{5}{32}$ inch of tread remaining. At this rate, how many total miles should the tire last before it is considered worn out?

23. In classroom A, there are 12 boys and 15 girls. In classroom B, there are 8 boys and 6 girls. In classroom C, there are 4 boys and 5 girls.

(a) Which two classrooms have the same boys-to-girls ratio?

(b) On one occasion classroom A joined classroom B. What was the resulting boys-to-girls ratio?

(c) On another occasion classroom C joined classroom B. What was the resulting ratio of boys to girls?

(d) Are your answers to parts (b) and (c) equivalent? What does this tell you about adding ratios?

24. An old picture frame has dimensions 33 inches by 24 inches. What one length must be cut from each dimension so that the ratio of the shorter side to the longer side is $\frac{2}{3}$?

25. The Greek musical scale, which very closely resembles the 12-note tempered scale used today, is based on ratios of frequencies. To hear the first and fifth tones of the scale is equivalent to hearing the ratio $\frac{3}{2}$, which is the ratio of their frequencies.

(a) If the frequency of middle C is 256 vibrations per second, find the frequencies of each of the other notes given. For example, since G is a fifth above middle C, it follows that G:256 = 3:2 or G = 384 vibrations/second. (NOTE: Proceeding beyond B would give sharps, below F, flats.)

(b) Two notes are an octave apart if the frequency of one is double the frequency of the other. For example, the frequency of C above middle C is 512 vibrations per second. Using the values found in part (a), find the frequencies of the corresponding notes in the octave above middle C (in the range given below).

256   512
C   D   E   F   G   A   B   C

(c) The aesthetic effect of a chord depends on the ratio of its frequencies. Find the following ratios of seconds.

D:C   E:D   A:G

What simple ratio are these equivalent to?
(d) Find the following ratios of fourths.

F:C   G:D   A:E

What simple ratio are these equivalent to?

26. Ferne, Donna, and Susan have just finished playing three games. There was only one loser in each game. Ferne lost the first game, Donna lost the second game, and Susan lost the third game. After each game, the loser was required to double the money of the other two. After three rounds, each woman had $24. How much did each have at the start?

27. A ball, when dropped from any height, bounces $\frac{1}{3}$ of the original height. If the ball is dropped, bounces back up, and continues to bounce up and down so that it has traveled 106 feet when it strikes the ground for the fourth time, what is the original height from which it was dropped?

28. Take 92,471.
(a) Drop one digit and rearrange the others to form a perfect cube.
(b) Drop one digit from your perfect cube in part (a) and rearrange to form another perfect cube.
(c) Drop one digit from your cube in part (b) and form yet another perfect cube.

29. Mary had a basket of hard-boiled eggs to sell. She first sold half her eggs plus half an egg. Next she sold half her eggs and half an egg. The same thing occurred on her third, fourth, and fifth times. When she finished, she had no eggs in her basket. How many did she have when she started?

30. A woman has equal numbers of pennies, nickels, and dimes. If the total value of the coins is $12.96, how many dimes does she have?

31. Joleen had a higher batting average than Maureen for the first half of the season, and Joleen also had a higher batting average than Maureen for the second half of the season. Does it follow that Joleen had a better batting average than Maureen for the entire season? Why or why not?

32. Two baseball batters, Eric and Morgan, each get 31 hits in 69 at bats. In the next week, Eric slumps to 1 hit in 27 at bats and Morgan bats 4 for 36 (1 out of 9). Without doing any calculations, which batter do you think has the higher average? Check your answer by calculating the two averages (the number of hits divided by the number of times at bat).

7.4

PERCENT

Converting Percents

Percents provide another common way of representing fractions. The word **percent** has a Latin origin that means "per hundred." Thus 25 percent means 25 per hundred, $\frac{25}{100}$, or 0.25. The symbol "%" is used to represent percent. So 420% means $\frac{420}{100}$, 4.20, or 420 per hundred. In general, $n\%$ represents the ratio $\dfrac{n}{100}$.

Since percents are alternative representations of fractions and decimals, it is important to be able to convert among all three forms, as suggested in

Figure 7.12. Since we have studied converting fractions to decimals, and vice versa, there are only four cases of conversion left to consider in Figure 7.12.

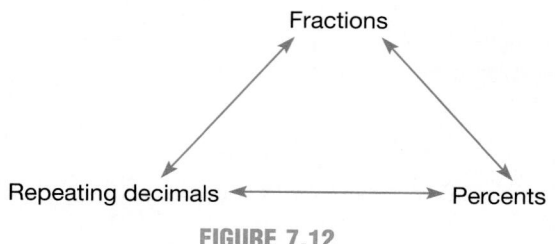

FIGURE 7.12

Case 1: Percents to Fractions

Use the definition of percent. For example, $63\% = \frac{63}{100}$ by the meaning of percent.

Case 2: Percents to Decimals

Since we know how to convert fractions to decimals, we can use this skill to convert percents to fractions and then to decimals. For example, $63\% = \frac{63}{100} = 0.63$ and $27\% = \frac{27}{100} = 0.27$. These two examples suggest the following shortcut, which eliminates the conversion to a fraction step. Namely, to convert a percent directly to a decimal, "drop the % symbol and move the number's decimal point two places to the *left*." Thus $31\% = 0.31$, $813\% = 8.13$, $0.0001\% = 0.000001$, and so on.

Case 3: Decimals to Percents

Here we merely reverse the shortcut in Case 2. For example, $0.83 = 83\%$, $5.1 = 510\%$, and $0.0001 = 0.01\%$ where the percents are obtained from the decimals by "moving the decimal point two places to the *right* and writing the % symbol on the *right* side."

Case 4: Fractions to Percents

Some fractions that have terminating decimals can be converted to percents by expressing the fraction with a denominator of 100. For example, $\frac{17}{100} = 17\%$, $\frac{2}{5} = \frac{4}{10} = \frac{40}{100} = 40\%$, $\frac{3}{25} = \frac{12}{100} = 12\%$, and so on. Also, fractions can be converted to decimals (using a calculator or long division), and then Case 3 can be applied.

A calculator is useful when converting fractions to percents. For example,

$$3 \boxed{\div} 13 \boxed{=} \boxed{0.23076923}$$

shows that $\frac{3}{13} \approx 0.23$ or 23%. Also,

$$5 \boxed{\div} 9 \boxed{=} \boxed{0.555555555}$$

shows that $\frac{5}{9} \approx 56\%$.

EXAMPLE 7.26   Write each of the following in all three forms: decimal, percent, fraction (in simplest form).

(a) 32% **(b)** 0.24 **(c)** 450% **(d)** $\frac{1}{16}$

Solution

(a) $32\% = 0.32 = \frac{8}{25}$

(b) $0.24 = 24\% = \frac{6}{25}$

(c) $450\% = 4.5 = 4\frac{1}{2}$

(d) $\dfrac{1}{16} = \dfrac{1}{2^4} = \dfrac{1 \cdot 5^4}{2^4 \cdot 5^4} = \dfrac{625}{10,000} = 0.0625 = 6.25\%$ ■

Mental Math and Estimation Using Fraction Equivalents

Since many commonly used percents have convenient fraction equivalents, it is often easier to find the percent of a number mentally, using fractions (Table 7.2). Also, as was the case with proportions, percentages of numbers can be estimated by choosing compatible fractions.

TABLE 7.2

Percent	5%	10%	20%	25%	$33\frac{1}{3}$%	50%	$66\frac{2}{3}$%	75%
Fraction	$\frac{1}{20}$	$\frac{1}{10}$	$\frac{1}{5}$	$\frac{1}{4}$	$\frac{1}{3}$	$\frac{1}{2}$	$\frac{2}{3}$	$\frac{3}{4}$

EXAMPLE 7.27   Find the following percents mentally, using fraction equivalents.

(a) $25\% \times 44$ **(b)** $75\% \times 24$ **(c)** $50\% \times 76$
(d) $33\frac{1}{3}\% \times 93$ **(e)** $38\% \times 50$ **(f)** $84\% \times 25$

Solution

(a) $25\% \times 44 = \frac{1}{4} \times 44 = 11$

(b) $75\% \times 24 = \frac{3}{4} \times 24 = 18$

(c) $50\% \times 76 = \frac{1}{2} \times 76 = 38$

(d) $33\frac{1}{3}\% \times 93 = \frac{1}{3} \times 93 = 31$

(e) $38\% \times 50 = 38 \times 50\% = 38 \times \frac{1}{2} = 19$

(f) $84\% \times 25 = 84 \times 25\% = 84 \times \frac{1}{4} = 21$ ■

EXAMPLE 7.28   Estimate the following percents mentally, using fraction equivalents.

(a) $48\% \times 73$ **(b)** $32\% \times 95$ **(c)** $24\% \times 71$
(d) $123\% \times 54$ **(e)** $0.45\% \times 57$ **(f)** $59\% \times 81$

Solution

(a) $48\% \times 73 \approx 50\% \times 72 = 36$. (Since $50\% > 48\%$, 73 was rounded down to 72 to compensate.)

(b) $32\% \times 95 \approx 33\frac{1}{3} \times 93 = \frac{1}{3} \times 93 = 31$. (Since $33\frac{1}{3}\% > 32\%$, 95 was rounded down to 93, which is a multiple of 3.)

(c) $24\% \times 71 \approx \frac{1}{4} \times 72 = \frac{1}{4} \times 8 \times 9 = 18$

(d) $123\% \times 54 \approx 125\% \times 54 \approx \frac{5}{4} \times 56 = 5 \times 14 = 70$; alternatively, $123\% \times 54 = 123 \times 54\% \approx 130 \times 50\% = 130 \times \frac{1}{2} = 65$

(e) $0.45\% \times 57 \approx 0.5\% \times 50 = 0.5 \times 50\% = 0.25$

(f) $59\% \times 81 \approx 60\% \times 81 \approx \frac{3}{5} \times 80 = 3 \times 16 = 48$ ■

Solving Percent Problems

The following questions illustrate three common types of problems involving percents.

1. A car was purchased for $13,000 with a 20% down payment. How much was the down payment?

2. One hundred sixty-two seniors, 90% of the senior class, are going on the class trip. How many seniors are there?

3. Susan scored 48 points on a 60-point test. What percent did she get correct?

There are two common approaches to solving percent problems such as the preceding three problems: solving proportions and solving equations.

Proportion Approach

Since percent means "per hundred," a percent can be viewed as a ratio. Therefore, solving problems to find a missing percent may be done using proportions, as illustrated next.

EXAMPLE 7.29 Answer the preceding three problems using the proportion approach.

Solution

(a) A car was purchased for $13,000 with a 20% down payment. How much was the down payment?

	Dollars	Percent
Down Payment	x	20
Purchase Price	13,000	100

Thus $\dfrac{x}{13,000} = \dfrac{20}{100}$, or $x = \dfrac{13,000}{5} = \$2600$.

(b) One hundred sixty-two seniors, 90% of the senior class, are going on the class trip. How many seniors are there?

	Seniors	Percent
Class Trip	162	90
Class Total	x	100

Thus $\dfrac{162}{x} = \dfrac{90}{100}$, or $x = 162\left(\dfrac{10}{9}\right) = 180$.

(c) Susan scored 48 points on a 60-point test. What percent did she get correct?

	Test	Percent
Score	48	x
Total	60	100

Thus $\dfrac{48}{60} = \dfrac{x}{100}$, or $x = 100 \cdot \dfrac{4}{5} = 80$.

Notice how (a), (b), and (c) above lead to the following generalization:

$$\frac{\text{part}}{\text{whole}} = \frac{\text{percent}}{100}$$

In other examples, if the "part" is larger than the "whole," the percent is larger than 100%.

Equation Approach

An equation can be used to represent each of the problems in Example 7.29 as follows:

(a) $20\% \cdot 13,000 = x$

(b) $90\% \cdot x = 162$

(c) $x\% \cdot 60 = 48$

In fact, many percent problems can be solved easily by expressing the problem in an equation in one of the three forms above and then by solving the equation. The following equations illustrate these three forms, where x represents an unknown, and p, n, and a are fixed numbers.

Translation of Problem	**Equation**
(a) $p\%$ of n is x	$\left(\dfrac{p}{100}\right)n = x$
(b) $p\%$ of x is a	$\left(\dfrac{p}{100}\right)x = a$
(c) $x\%$ of n is a	$\left(\dfrac{x}{100}\right)n = a$

Once we have obtained one of these three equations, the solution, x, can be found. In equation (a), we multiply $\dfrac{p}{100}$ and n. In equations (b) and (c) we solve for the missing factor x.

EXAMPLE 7.30   Solve the problems in Example 7.29 using the equation approach.

Solution
(a) $20\% \cdot 13{,}000 = 0.20(13{,}000) = \$2600$
(b) $90\% \cdot x = 162$ or $0.9x = 162$. Thus, by the missing-factor approach,
$x = 162 \div (0.9)$, or $x = 180$

CHECK: $90\%(180) = 0.9(180) = 162$.

(c) $x\% \cdot 60 = 48$, or $\dfrac{x}{100}(60) = 48$. By the missing-factor approach,

$\dfrac{x}{100} = \dfrac{48}{60} = \dfrac{8}{10}$, or $x = 80$

CHECK: $80\%(60) = 0.8(60) = 48$.   ■

A calculator can also be used to solve percent problems once the correct equations or proportions are set up. (Problems can be done using fewer keystrokes if your calculator has a percent key.) The following key sequences can be used to solve the following equations arising from Example 7.30.
(a) $20\% \times 13000 = x$.

$$20 \boxed{\%} \boxed{\times} 13000 \boxed{=} \boxed{2600}$$

NOTE: With some calculators, the 13000 must be keyed in before the 20%. Also, the $\boxed{=}$ may not be needed in this case.
(b) $90\% \times x = 162$ (or $x = 162 \div 90\%$)

$$162 \boxed{\div} 90 \boxed{\%} \boxed{=} \boxed{180}$$

Note: Some calculators do not require the $\boxed{=}$ here.
(c) $x\% \times 60 = 48$ (or $\dfrac{x}{100} = 48 \div 60$)

$$48 \boxed{\div} 60 \boxed{\times} 100 \boxed{=} \boxed{80}$$

We end this section on percent with several applications.

EXAMPLE 7.31   Rachelle bought a dress whose original price was \$125 but was discounted 10%. What was the discounted price? Also, what is a quick way to mark down several items 10% using a calculator?

Solution
The original price is \$125. The discount is $(10\%)(125)$, or \$12.50. The new price is $\$125 - \$12.50 = \$112.50$. In general, if the original price was n, the discount would be $(10\%)n$. Then the new price would be $n - (10\%)n = n - (0.1)n = 0.9n$.   ■

If many prices were to be discounted 10%, the new prices could be found by multiplying the old price by 0.9, or 90%. If your calculator has a percent key, the solution to the original problem would be

$$125 \boxed{\times} 90 \boxed{\%} \boxed{112.50}$$

(NOTE: It is not necessary to use the percent key; we could simply multiply by 0.9.)

EXAMPLE 7.32   A television set is put on sale at 28% off the regular price. The sale price is $379. What was the regular price?

Solution
The sale price is 72% of the regular price (since 100% − 28% = 72%). Let P be the regular price. Then, in proportion form,

$$\frac{72}{100} = \frac{379}{P} \left(\frac{\text{sale price}}{\text{regular price}} \right)$$
$$72 \times P = 379 \times 100 = 37{,}900$$
$$P = \frac{37{,}900}{72} = \$526.39, \text{ rounding to the nearest cent.}$$

CHECK: $(0.72)(526.39) = 379$, rounding to the nearest dollar.   ■

EXAMPLE 7.33   Suppose that Irene's credit-card balance is $576. If the monthly interest rate is 1.5% (i.e., 18% per year), what will this debt be at the end of 5 months if she makes no payments to reduce her balance?

Solution
The amount of interest accruing by the end of the first month is 1.5% × 576, or $8.64, so the balance at the end of the first month is $576 + $8.64, or $584.64. The interest at the end of the second month would be (1.5%)(584.64) or $8.77, so the balance at the end of the second month would be $593.41. Continuing in this manner, the balance at the end of the fifth month would be $620.52. Can you see why this is called compound interest?   ■

A much faster way to solve this problem is to use the technique illustrated in Example 7.31. The balance at the end of a month can be found by multiplying the balance from the end of the previous month by 1.015 (this is equal to 100% + 1.5%). Then, using your calculator, the computation for the balance after five months would be

$$576(1.015)(1.015)(1.015)(1.015)(1.015) = 576(1.015)^5 = 620.52.$$

If your calculator has a constant function, your number of key presses would be reduced considerably. Here is a sequence of steps that works on many calculators.

$$1.015 \; \boxed{\times} \; \boxed{=} \; \boxed{=} \; \boxed{=} \; \boxed{=} \; \boxed{\times} \; 576 \; \boxed{=} \; \boxed{620.5155862}$$

(On some calculators you may have to press the $\boxed{\times}$ key twice after entering 1.015 to implement the constant function to repeat multiplication.) Better yet, if your calculator has a $\boxed{y^x}$ (or $\boxed{x^y}$ or $\boxed{\wedge}$) key, the following keystrokes can be used.

$$1.015 \; \boxed{y^x} \; 5 \; \boxed{\times} \; 576 \; \boxed{=} \; \boxed{620.5155862}$$

The balance at the end of a year is

$$1.015 \; \boxed{y^x} \; 12 \; \boxed{\times} \; 576 \; \boxed{=} \; \boxed{688.6760668}$$

or $688.68.

Example 7.33 illustrates a problem involving interest. Most of us encounter interest through savings, loans, credit cards, and so on. With a calculator that has an exponential key, such as y^x or x^y, calculations that formerly were too time consuming for the average consumer are now merely a short sequence of keystrokes. However, it is important that one understand how to set up a problem so that the calculator can be correctly used.Our last two examples illustrate how a calculator with an exponential key can be used to show the effect of compound interest.

EXAMPLE 7.34   Parents want to establish a college fund for their 8-year-old daughter. The father received a bonus of $10,000. The $10,000 is deposited in a tax-deferred account guaranteed to yield at least $7\frac{3}{4}\%$ compounded quarterly. How much will be available from this account when the child is 18?

Solution
There are several aspects to this problem. First, one needs to understand what "compounded quarterly" means. Compounded quarterly means that earned interest is added to the principal amount every 3 months. Since the annual rate is $7\frac{3}{4}\%$, the quarterly rate is $\frac{1}{4}(7\frac{3}{4}\%) = 1.9375\%$. Following the ideas in Example 7.33, the principal, which is $10,000, will amount to $10,000(1.019375) = \$10,193.75$ at the end of the first quarter.

Next, one needs to determine the number of quarters (of a year) that the $10,000 will earn interest. Since the child is 8 and the money is needed when she is 18, this account will grow for 10 years (or 40 quarters). Again, following Example 7.33, after 40 quarters the $10,000 will amount to $10,000(1.019375)^{40} = \$21,545.63$. If the interest rate had simply been $7\frac{3}{4}\%$ per year not compounded, the $10,000 would have earned $10,000(7\frac{3}{4}\%) = \$775$ per year for each of the 10 years, or would have amounted to $10,000 + 10(\$775) = \$17,750$. Thus the compounding amounted to an extra $3795.63. ■

Our last example shows you how to determine how much to save now for a specific amount at a future date.

EXAMPLE 7.35   You project that you will need $20,000 before taxes in 15 years. If you find a tax-deferred investment that guarantees you 10% interest, compounded semiannually, how much should you set aside now?

Solution
As you may have observed while working through Examples 7.33 and 7.34, if P is the amount of your initial principal, r is the interest rate for a given period, and n is the number of payment periods for the given rate, then your final amount, A, will be given by the equation $A = P(1 + r)^n$. In this example, $A = \$20,000$, $r = \frac{1}{2}(10\%)$, since semiannual means every half-year, and $n = 2 \times 15$, since there are $2 \times 15 = 30$ half-years in 15 years. Thus

$$20{,}000 = P\left[1 + \tfrac{1}{2}(0.10)\right]^{30} \quad \text{or} \quad P = \frac{20{,}000}{\left[1 + \tfrac{1}{2}(0.10)\right]^{30}}. \quad ■$$

A calculator can be used to find the dollar value for P.

$$20000 \;\boxed{\div}\; \boxed{(} \; 1.05 \;\boxed{y^x}\; 30 \;\boxed{)} \; \boxed{=} \; \boxed{4627.548973}.$$

Thus $4627.55 needs to be set aside now at 10% interest compounded semiannually to have $20,000 available in 15 years.

MATHEMATICAL MORSEL

Two students were finalists in a free-throw shooting contest. In the two parts of the contest, the challenger had to shoot 25 free-throws in the first part, then 50 in the second part, while the champion shot 50 free-throws first and 25 second. In the first part, Vivian made 20 of 25, or 80%, and Joan made 26 of 50, or 52%. Then Vivian made 9 of 50, or 18%, and Joan made 4 of 25, or 16%. Since Vivian had a higher percentage in both parts, she declared herself to be the winner. However, Joan cried "Foul!" and claimed the totals should be counted. In that case, Vivian made 29 of 75 and Joan made 30 of 75. Who should win? This mathematical oddity can arise when data involving ratios are combined.

EXERCISE/PROBLEM SET 7.4—PART A

Exercises

1. Convert the following percents to decimals.
   (a) 37%   **(b)** 52.7%   **(c)** 79.21%
   (d) 302%   **(e)** 0.3%   **(f)** 0.065%

2. Convert the following decimals to percents.
   (a) 5.3   **(b)** 0.72   **(c)** 0.192
   (d) 25   **(e)** 0.075   **(f)** 0.0038

3. Convert the following percents to fractions written in simplest form.
   (a) 72%   **(b)** 65.3%
   (c) 542%   **(d)** 0.03%

4. Convert the following fractions to percents.
   (a) $\frac{3}{4}$ **(b)** $\frac{5}{3}$ **(c)** $\frac{4}{5}$
   (d) $\frac{3}{20}$ **(e)** $\frac{7}{25}$ **(f)** $\frac{7}{8}$

5. (a) Mentally calculate each of the following.
   (i) 10% of 50   (ii) 10% of 68.7
   (iii) 10% of 4.58   (iv) 10% of 32,900

(b) Mentally calculate each of the following. Use the fact that 5% is half of 10%.
   (i) 5% of 240   (ii) 5% of 18.6
   (iii) 5% of 12,000   (iv) 5% of 62.56

(c) Mentally calculate each of the following. Use the fact that 15% is 10% + 5%.
   (i) 15% of 90   (ii) 15% of 50,400
   (iii) 15% of 7.2   (iv) 15% of 0.066

6. It is common practice to leave a 15% tip when eating in a restaurant. Mentally estimate the amount of tip to leave for each of the following check amounts.
   (a) $11.00   **(b)** $14.87
   (c) $35.06   **(d)** $23.78

7. Mentally find the following percents.
   (a) 50% of 64   **(b)** 25% of 148
   (c) 75% of 244   **(d)** $33\frac{1}{3}$% of 210
   (e) 20% of 610   **(f)** 60% of 450

8. Complete the following statements mentally.
  (a) 126 is 50% of _____.
  (b) 36 is 25% of _____.
  (c) 154 is $66\frac{2}{3}$% of _____.
  (d) 78 is 40% of _____.
  (e) 50 is 125% of _____.
  (f) 240 is 300% of _____.

9. Mentally solve these problems.
  (a) 56 is _____% of 100.
  (b) 38 is _____% of 50.
  (c) 17 is _____% of 25.
  (d) 7.5 is _____% of 20.
  (e) 75 is _____% of 50.
  (f) 40 is _____% of 30.

10. Estimate.
  (a) 39% of 72   **(b)** 58.7% of 31
  (c) 123% of 59   **(d)** 0.48% of 207
  (e) 18% of 76   **(f)** 9.3% of 315
  (g) 0.97% of 63   **(h)** 412% of 185

11. As discussed in this section, percent problems can be solved using a proportion like the following:

$$\frac{\text{part}}{\text{whole}} = \frac{\text{percent}}{100}$$

Many students who are comfortable with proportions prefer this method. Write a proportion that could be used to solve each of the following percent problems.
  (a) 42 is what percent of 75?
  (b) 17% of 964 is what number?
  (c) 156.6 is 37% of what number?
  (d) $8\frac{3}{4}$ is what percent of $12\frac{1}{3}$?
  (e) 225% of what number is $12\frac{1}{3}$?

12. Answer the following and round to one decimal place.
  (a) Find 24% of 140.
  (b) Find $3\frac{1}{2}$% of 78.
  (c) Find 32.7% of 252.
  (d) What percent of 23 is 11.2?
  (e) What percent of 1.47 is 0.816?
  (f) 21 is 17% of what number?
  (g) What percent of $\frac{1}{4}$ is $\frac{1}{12}$?
  (h) 512 is 240% of what number?
  (i) 140% of a number is 0.65. Find the number.
  (j) Find $\frac{1}{2}$% of 24.6.

13. Use your calculator to find the following percents.
  (a) 63% of 90   **(b)** 27.5% of 420
  (c) 31.3% of 1200

14. Solve.
  (a) 147 is 42% of _____.
  (b) 3648 is 128% of _____.
  (c) 0.5% of _____ is 78.4.
  (d) 3.5% of _____ is 154.

15. Solve.
  (a) 36.3 is _____% of 165.
  (b) 7.5 is _____% of 1250.
  (c) 87.5 is _____% of 125.
  (d) 221 is _____% of 34.

16. A 4200-pound automobile contains 357 pounds of rubber. What percent of the car's total weight is rubber?

17. The senior class consists of 2780 students. If 70% of the students will graduate, how many students will graduate?

Problems

18. An investor earned $208.76 in interest in one year on an account that paid 4.25% simple interest.
  (a) What was the value of the account at the end of that year?
  (b) How much more interest would the account have earned at a rate of 5.33%?

19. Suppose that you have borrowed $100 at the daily interest rate of 0.04839%. How much would you save by paying the entire $100.00 fifteen days before it is due?

20. A basketball team played 35 games. They lost 2 games. What percent of the games played did they lose? What percent did they win?

21. In 1991 total charitable contributions increased by 6.2% from the preceding year.
  (a) If a total of 1.25×10^{11} was donated to charity in 1991, what amount was donated to charity in 1990?
  (b) Of the total amount donated to charity in 1991, individuals contributed 1.03×10^{11}. What percent of all charitable contributions were made by individuals?

22. The following pie graph shows the sources of U.S. energy production in 1988.

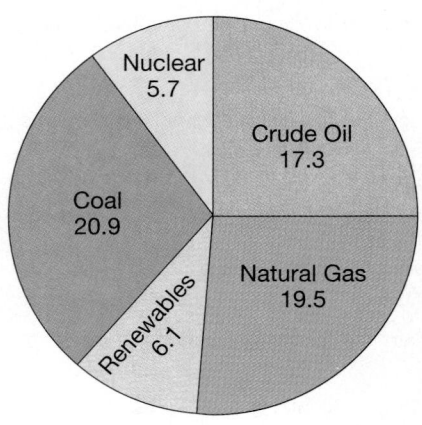

U.S. Energy Production by Source, 1988
(Quadrillion Btu)

Source: 1992 Environmental Almanac

  (a) How much energy was produced, from all sources, in the United States in 1988?

(b) What percent of the energy produced in the United States in 1988 came from each of the sources? Round your answers to the nearest tenth of a percent.

23. A clothing store advertised a coat at a 15% discount. The original price was $115.00, and the sale price was $100. Was the price consistent with the ad? Explain.

24. Rosemary sold a car and made a profit of $850, which was 17% of the selling price. What was the selling price?

25. Complete the following. Try to solve them mentally before using written or calculator methods.
   (a) 30% of 50 is 6% of _____.
   (b) 40% of 60 is 5% of _____.
   (c) 30% of 80 is _____% of 160.

26. A car lot is advertising an 8% discount on a particular automobile. You pay $4485.00 for the car. What was the original price of the car?

27. **(a)** The continents of Asia, Africa, and Europe together have an area of 8.5×10^{13} square meters. What percent of the surface area of the Earth do these three continents comprise if the total surface area of the Earth is about 5.2×10^{14} square meters?
   (b) The Pacific Ocean has an area of about 1.81×10^{14} square meters. What percent of the surface of the Earth is covered by the Pacific Ocean?
   (c) If all of the oceans are taken together, they make up about 70% of the surface of the Earth. How many square meters of the Earth's surface are covered by ocean?
   (d) What percent of the land mass of the earth is contained in the state of Texas, with an area of about 6.92×10^{11} square meters?

28. The nutritional information on a box of cereal indicates that one serving provides 3 grams of protein or 4% of U.S. recommended daily allowances (RDA). One serving with milk provides 7 grams or 15% U.S. RDA. Is the information provided consistent? Explain.

29. A pair of slacks was made of material that was expected to shrink 10%. If the manufacturer makes the 32-inch inseam of the slacks 10% longer, what will the inseam measure after shrinkage?

30. Which results in a higher price: a 10% markup followed by a 10% discount, or a 10% discount followed by a 10% markup? Explain.

31. Joseph has 64% as many baseball cards as Cathy. Martin has 50% as many cards as Joseph. Martin has _____% as many cards as Cathy.

32. Your optimal exercise heart rate for cardiovascular benefits is calculated as follows: Subtract your age from 220. Then find 70% of this difference and 80% of this difference. The optimal rate is between the latter two numbers. Find the optimal heart rate range for a 50-year-old.

33. In an advertisement for a surround sound decoder it was stated that "our unit provides six outputs of audio information—that's 40% more than the competition." Explain why the person writing this ad does not understand the mathematics involved.

34. A heart doctor in Florida offers patients discounts for adopting good health habits. He offers 10% off if a patient stops smoking and another 5% off if a patient lowers her blood pressure or cholesterol a certain percentage. If you qualify for both discounts, would you rather the doctor (i) add them together and take 15% off your bill, or (ii) take 10% off first and then take 5% off the resulting discounted amount? Explain.

35. The population in one country increased by 4.2% during 1990, increased by 2.8% in 1991, and then decreased by 2.1% in 1992. What was the net percent change in population over the three-year period? Round your answer to the nearest tenth of a percent.

36. Monica has a daisy with nine petals. She asks Jerry to play the following game: They will take turns picking either one petal or two petals that are next to each other. The player who picks the last petal wins. Does the first player always win? Can the first player ever win? Discuss.

37. A clothing store was preparing for its semiannual 20% off sale. When it came to marking down the items, the salespeople wondered if they should (i) deduct the 20% from the selling price and then add the 6% sales tax, or (ii) add the 6% tax and then deduct the 20% from the total. Which way is correct, and why?

38. Elaine wants to deposit her summer earnings of $12,000 in a savings account to save for retirement. The bank pays 7% interest per year compounded semiannually (every 6 months). How much will her tax-deferred account be worth at the end of 3 years?

39. Assuming an inflation rate of 11%, how much would a woman earning $35,000 per year today need to earn five years from now to have the same buying power? Round your answer to the nearest thousand.

40. A couple wants to increase their savings for their daughter's college education. How much money must they invest now at 8.25% compounded annually in order to have accumulated $20,000 at the end of 10 years?

41. The consumer price index (CPI) is used by the government to relate prices to inflation. At the end of 1986 the CPI was 115.7, which means that prices were 15.7% higher than prices for the 1982–1983 period. If the CPI at the end of 1985 was 111.2, what was the percent of increase from 1985 to 1986?

42. The city of Taxaphobia imposed a progressive income tax rate; that is, the more you earn, the higher the rate you pay. The rate they chose is equal to the number of thousands of dollars you earn. For example, a person who earns $13,000 pays 13% of her earnings in taxes. If you could name your own salary less than $100,000, what would you want to earn? Explain.

EXERCISE/PROBLEM SET 7.4—PART B

Exercises

1. Fill in this chart.

Fraction	Decimal	Percent
——	——	50%
——	0.35	——
$\frac{1}{4}$	——	——
$\frac{1}{8}$	——	——
——	0.0125	——
——	——	125%
——	0.75	——
——	——	66.66%
——	0.003	——
$\frac{1}{40}$	——	——
——	0.05	——
——	——	$1.\overline{6}$%
$\frac{1}{100}$	——	——
——	0.00001	——
——	——	0.0085%

2. Mentally complete the following sets of information.
  (a) A school's enrollment of seventh, eighth, and ninth graders is 1000 students.
  40% are seventh graders = ——— of 1000 students.
  35% are eighth graders = ——— of 1000 students.
  ——% are ninth graders = ——— of 1000 students.
  (b) 10% interest rate:
  10 cents on every ———
  $1.50 on every ———
  $4.00 on every ———
  (c) 6% sales tax:
  $——— on $1.00
  $——— on $6.00
  $——— on $0.50
  $——— on $7.50

3. Mentally complete the following statements.
  (a) 196 is 200% of ———.
  (b) 25% of 244 is ———.
  (c) 39 is ———% of 78.
  (d) 731 is 50% of ———.
  (e) 40 is ———% of 32.
  (f) 40% of 355 is ———.
  (g) $166\frac{2}{3}$% of 300 is ———.
  (h) 4.2 is ———% of 4200.

  (i) 210 is 60% of ———.

4. Find mentally, using fraction equivalents.
  (a) 50% of 180
  (b) 25% of 440
  (c) 75% of 320
  (d) $33\frac{1}{3}$% of 210
  (e) 40% of 250
  (f) $12\frac{1}{2}$% of 400
  (g) $66\frac{2}{3}$% of 660
  (h) 20% of 120

5. Find mentally.
  (a) 10% of 16
  (b) 1% of 1000
  (c) 20% of 150
  (d) 200% of 75
  (e) 15% of 40
  (f) 10% of 440
  (g) 15% of 50
  (h) 300% of 120

6. Estimate.
  (a) 21% of 34
  (b) 42% of 61
  (c) 24% of 57
  (d) 211% of 82
  (e) 16% of 42
  (f) 11.2% of 431
  (g) 48% of 26
  (h) 39.4% of 147

7. Write a percent problem for each proportion.
  (a) $\dfrac{67}{95} = \dfrac{x}{100}$
  (b) $\dfrac{18.4}{x} = \dfrac{112}{100}$
  (c) $\dfrac{x}{3.5} = \dfrac{16\frac{2}{3}}{100}$
  (d) $\dfrac{2.8}{0.46} = \dfrac{x}{100}$
  (e) $\dfrac{4200}{x} = \dfrac{0.05}{100}$

8. Find each missing number in the following percent problems. Round to the nearest tenth.
  (a) 48% of what number is 178?
  (b) 14.36 is what percent of 35?
  (c) What percent of 2.4 is 5.2?
  (d) $83\frac{1}{3}$% of 420 is what number?
  (e) 6 is $\frac{1}{4}$% of what number?
  (f) What percent of $16\frac{3}{4}$ is $12\frac{2}{3}$?

9. Calculate, using a percent key.
  (a) 34% of 90
  (b) 126% of 72
  (c) 30% of what number is 57?
  (d) 50 is what percent of 80?
  (e) $90 marked up 13%
  (f) $120 discounted 12%

10. Compute each of the following to the nearest cent.
  (a) 65% of $298.54
  (b) 52.7% of $211.53
  (c) 35.2% of $2874.65
  (d) 49.5% of $632.09

11. A mathematics test had 80 questions, each worth the same value. Wendy was correct on 55 of the questions. What percent of the questions did she get correct?

12. A retailer sells a shirt for $21.95. If the retailer marked up the shirt about 70%, what was his cost for the shirt?

13. In 1980, 4414 U.S. taxpayers reported incomes of more than $1,000,000. In 1990, the number of taxpayers reporting incomes of more than $1,000,000 had increased to 64,000. By what percent did the number of taxpayers earning more than $1,000,000 increase between 1980 and 1990? Round your answer to the nearest whole number.

14. Frank's salary is $240 per week. He saves $28 a week. What percent of his salary does he save?

15. It is common practice to pay salespeople extra money, called a **commission**, on the amount of sales. Bill is paid $315.00 a week, plus 6% commission on sales. Find his total earnings if his sales are $575.

16. The pie graph (or circle graph) shows a student's relative expenditures. If the student's resources are $8000.00, how much is spent on each item?

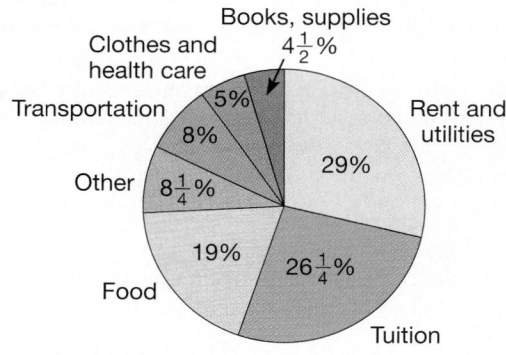

17. In a class of 36 students, 13 were absent on Friday. What percent of the class was absent?

18. A volleyball team wins 105 games, which is 70% of the games played. How many games were played?

Problems

19. The mass of all the bodies in our solar system, excluding the Sun, is about 2.67×10^{27} kg. The mass of Jupiter is about 1.9×10^{27} kg.
    (a) What percent of the total mass of the solar system, excluding the Sun, does Jupiter contain?
    (b) The four largest planets together (Jupiter, Saturn, Neptune, and Uranus) account for nearly all the mass of the solar system, excluding the Sun. If the masses of Saturn, Neptune, and Uranus are 5.7 $\times$ 10^{26} kg, 1.03×10^{26} kg, and $8.69 \times$

10^{25} kg, respectively, what percent of the total mass of the solar system, excluding the Sun, do these four planets contain?

20. Henry got a raise of $80, which was 5% of his salary. What was his salary? Do mentally.

21. A record store is advertising all records at up to 35% off. What would be the price range for records originally priced at $12.00?

22. Shown in the following table are data on the number of registered motor vehicles in the United States and fuel consumption in the United States in 1979 and 1989.

	Vehicle Registrations (millions)	Motor Fuel Consumption (thousands of barrels per day)
1979	159.6	8204
1989	191.7	8882

   (a) By what percent did the number of vehicle registrations increase between 1979 and 1989?
   (b) By what percent did the consumption of motor fuel increase between 1979 and 1989?
   (c) Are these increases proportional? Explain.

23. A refrigerator and range were purchased and a 5% sales tax was added to the purchase price. If the total bill was $834.75, how much did the refrigerator and range cost?

24. Susan has $20.00. Sharon has $25.00. Susan claims that she has 20% less than Sharon. Sharon replies, "No. I have 25% more than you." Who is right?

25. Following is one tax table from a recent income tax form.

If Your Taxable Income Is:	Your Tax Is:
Not over $500	4.2% of taxable income
Over $500 but not over $1000	$21.00 + 5.3% of excess over $500
Over $1000 but not over $2000	$47.50 + 6.5% of excess over $1000
Over $2000 but not over $3000	$112.50 + 7.6% of excess over $2000
Over $3000 but not over $4000	$188.50 + 8.7% of excess over $3000
Over $4000 but not over $5000	$275.50 + 9.8% of excess over $4000
Over $5000	$373.50 + 10.8% of excess over $5000

(a) Given the following taxable income figures, compute the tax owed (to the nearest cent).
(i) $3560   (ii) $8945   (iii) $2990
(b) If your tax was $324.99, what was your taxable income?

26. The price of coffee was 50 cents a pound 10 years ago. If the current price of coffee is $4.25 a pound, what percent increase in price does this represent?

27. A bookstore had a spring sale. All items were reduced by 20%. After the sale, prices were marked up at 20% over sale price. How do prices after the sale differ from prices before the sale?

28. A department store marked down all of its summer clothing 25%. The following week the remaining items were marked down again 15% off the sale price. When Jorge bought two tank tops on sale, he presented a coupon that gave him an additional 20% off. What percent of the original price did Jorge save?

29. A fishing crew is paid 43% of the value of their catch.
(a) If they catch $10,500 worth of fish, what is the crew paid?
(b) If the crew is paid $75,000 for a year's work, what was the total catch worth?
(c) Suppose that the owner has the following expenses for a year:

Item	Expense
Insurance	$12,000
Fuel	20,000
Maintenance	7,500
Miscellaneous	5,000

How much does he need to make to pay all his expenses and the crew?
(d) If the fish are selling to the processors for an average of 22 cents/pound, how many pounds of fish does the owner need to sell to pay his expenses in part (c)?

30. Alan has thrown 24 passes and completed 37.5% of them. How many consecutive passes will Alan have to complete if he wants to have a completion average above 58%?

31. Beaker A has a quantity of water and beaker B has an equal quantity of wine. A milliliter of A is placed in B and B is mixed thoroughly. Then a milliliter of the mixture in B is placed in A and mixed. Which is greater, the percentage of wine in A or the percentage of water in B? Explain.

32. A girl bought some pencils, erasers, and paper clips at the stationery store. The pencils cost 10 cents each,

the erasers cost 5 cents each, and the clips cost 2 for 1 cent. If she bought 100 items altogether at a total cost of $1, how many of each item did she buy?

33. If you add the square of Tom's age to the age of Carol, the sum is 62; but if you add the square of Carol's age to the age of Tom, the result is 176. Determine the ages of Tom and Carol.

34. Suppose that you have five chains each consisting of three links. If a single chain of fifteen links is to be formed by cutting and welding, what is the fewest number of cuts that need to be made?

35. A pollster found that 36.72$\overline{3672}$% of her sample voted Republican. What is the smallest number of people that could have been in the sample?

36. Think of any whole number. Add 20. Multiply by 10. Find 20% of your last result. Find 50% of the last number. Subtract the number you started with. What is your result? Repeat. Did you get a similar result? If yes, prove that this procedure will always lead to a certain result.

37. Eric deposited $32,000 in a savings account to save for his children's college education. The bank pays 8% tax-deferred interest per year compounded quarterly. How much will his account be worth at the end of 18 years?

38. Jim wants to deposit money in an account to save for a new stereo system in two years. He wants to have $4000 available at that time. The following rates are available to him:

1. 6.2% simple interest
2. 6.1% compounded annually
3. 5.8% compounded semiannually
4. 5.75% compounded quarterly

(a) Which account(s) should he choose if he wants to invest the smallest amount of money now?
(b) How much money must he invest to accumulate $4000 in two years' time?

39. Suppose that you have $1000 in a savings account that pays 4.8% interest per year. Suppose, also, that you owe $500 at 1.5% per month interest.
(a) If you pay the interest on your loan for one month so that you can collect one month's interest on $500 in your savings account, what is your net gain or loss?
(b) If you pay the loan back with $500 from your savings account rather than pay one month's interest on the loan, what is your net gain or loss?
(c) What strategy do you recommend?

40. One-fourth of the world's population is Chinese and one-fifth of the rest is Indian. What percent of the world's population is Indian?

41. In the square below, the object is to start at square 1 and move to square 100 by moving to an adjacent square (horizontally, vertically, or diagonally) whenever you can add, subtract, multiply, or divide the number in your present square by 2 or 5 to get the number in the adjacent square. For example, from square 6, one could move to 30 (6 × 5) or 8 (6 + 2). Find a path from 1 to 100.

1	5	7	20	30
2	3	22	6	28
4	25	8	14	19
20	16	13	55	95
18	9	50	59	100

SOLUTION OF INITIAL PROBLEM

A street vendor had a basket of apples. Feeling generous one day, he gave away one-half of his apples plus one to the first stranger he met, one-half of his remaining apples plus one to the next stranger he met, and one-half of his remaining apples plus one to the third stranger he met. If the vendor had one left for himself, with how many apples did he start?

Strategy: Work Backward

The vendor ended up with 1 apple. In the previous step, he gave away half of his apples plus 1 more. Thus he must have had 4 apples since the one he had plus the one he gave away was 2, and 2 is half of 4. Repeating this procedure, 4 + 1 = 5 and 2 · 5 = 10; thus he must have had 10 apples when he met the second stranger. Repeating this procedure once more, 10 + 1 = 11 and 2 · 11 = 22. Thus he had 22 apples when he met the first stranger.

CHECK:

Start with 22.
Give away one-half (11) plus one, or 12.
10 remain.
Give away one-half (5) plus one, or 6.
4 remain.
Give away one-half (2) plus one, or 3.
1 remains.

Additional Problems Where the Strategy "Work Backward" Is Useful

1. On a class trip to the world's tallest building, the class rode up several floors, then rode down 18 floors, rode up 59 floors, rode down 87 floors, and ended up on the first floor. How many floors did they ride up initially?

2. At a sports card trading show, one trader gave 3 cards for 5. Then she traded 7 cards for 2. Finally, she bought 4 and traded 2 for 9. If she ended up with 473 cards, how many did she bring to the show?

3. Try the following "magic" trick: Multiply a number by 6. Then add 9. Double this result. Divide by 3. Subtract 6. Then divide by 4. If the answer is 13, what was your original number?

WRITING/DISCUSSING FOR UNDERSTANDING

1. In what ways are ratios and proportions used in everyday life? List as many examples as you can.
2. Make several descriptive statements involving percent about the students in your math class.
3. Think about how you usually calculate sales tax, tips, discounts, and so on, mentally. Describe your method. Compare your method with the methods in the text.
4. Explain how the following NCTM Standards are reflected in this chapter.

   - Develop concepts of decimals.
   - Develop number sense for decimals.
   - Use models to relate fractions to decimals.
   - Use models to explore operations on decimals.
   - Apply decimals to problem situations.
   - Understand and apply ratios, proportions, and percents in a wide variety of situations.
   - Investigate relationships among fractions, decimals, and percents.

PROJECTS

1. Using newspapers, including advertising supplements, find several applied problems using percent. Based on your findings, write problems that you think would be interesting and relevant to the students solving them.
2. Find several uses of decimals in the print media. Discuss why decimals were used in these situations instead of fractions or percents.

CHAPTER REVIEW

Major Ideas

1. Decimals are a useful representation of fractions, especially in commerce and in the age of calculators.
2. Every fraction has a repeating decimal representation, and vice versa.
3. The algorithms for decimal arithmetic (addition, subtraction, multiplication, and division) are extensions of the respective whole-number algorithms and can be developed using the arithmetic of fractions.
4. Ratios and proportions are useful in solving problems such as mixture and rate problems.
5. Rules involving equivalence of ratios and solving proportions are extensions of the respective rules involving fractions.
6. Percents are a convenient form of decimals and fractions, and are especially useful in commerce.
7. Problems involving percents can be solved via proportions or equation approaches.
8. Calculators are especially useful in solving problems involving compound interest.

Following is a list of key vocabulary, notation, and ideas for this chapter. Mentally review and, where appropriate, write down the meaning of each term. Then restudy the material that you are unsure of before proceeding to take the chapter test.

SECTION 7.1: DECIMALS

Vocabulary/Notation

Decimal 269
Decimal point 269
Expanded form 269

Terminating decimal 271
Fraction equivalents 273

Ideas

Naming and ordering decimals and expressing them in expanded form 269
Mental math and estimation techniques for decimals 273

SECTION 7.2: OPERATIONS WITH DECIMALS

Vocabulary/Notation

Repetend (.$\overline{abcd}$) 285   Repeating decimal 285

Ideas

Adding, subtracting, multiplying, and dividing using decimals 280
The equivalence of fractions and repeating decimals 284
Fractions corresponding to terminating and nonterminating decimals 287

SECTION 7.3: RATIO AND PROPORTION

Vocabulary/Notation

Ratio 293
Part to part 293
Part to whole 293
Whole to part 293
Extremes 294

Means 294
Proportion 294
Rates 297
Scaling up/scaling down 297

Ideas

Equality of ratios 294
Solving problems involving ratios and proportions 295
Solving proportions mentally 297

SECTION 7.4: PERCENT

Vocabulary/Notation

Percent 303

Ideas

PEOPLE IN MATHEMATICS

When David Blackwell (1919–   ) entered college at age 16, David's ambition was to earn a bachelor's degree and become an elementary teacher. Six years later, he had a doctorate in mathematics and was nominated for a fellowship at the Institute for Advanced Study at Princeton. The position included an honorary membership in the faculty at nearby Princeton University, but the university objected to the appointment of a black man as a faculty member. The director of the institute insisted on appointing Blackwell, and eventually won out. From Princeton, David went on to teach for ten years at Howard University, then at Berkeley. He has made important contributions to statistics, probability, game theory, and set theory. "Why do you want to share something beautiful with someone else? It's because of the pleasure he will get, and in transmitting it you will appreciate its beauty all over gain. My high school geometry teacher really got me interested in mathematics. I hear it suggested from time to time that geometry might be dropped from the curriculum. I would really hate to see that happen. It is a beautiful subject."

Sonya Kovalevskaya (1850–1891), as a young woman, hoped to study in Berlin under the great mathematician Karl Weierstrass. But women were barred from attending the university. She approached Weierstrass directly. Skeptical, he assigned her a set of difficult problems. When Sonya returned the following week with solutions, he agreed to teach her privately and was influential in seeing that she was granted her degree—even though she never officially attended the university. Kovalevskaya is known for her work in differential equations and for her mathematical theory of the rotation of solid bodies. In addition, she was editor of a mathematical journal, wrote two plays (with Swedish writer Anne Charlotte Leffler), a novella, and memoirs of her childhood. Of her literary and mathematical talents, Sonya wrote, "The poet has to perceive that which others do not perceive, to look deeper than others look. And the mathematician must do the same thing."

CHAPTER 7 TEST

Knowledge

1. True or false?
   (a) The decimal 0.034 is read "thirty-four hundredths."
   (b) The expanded form of 0.0271 is $\frac{2}{100} + \frac{7}{1000} + \frac{1}{10,000}$.
   (c) The fraction $\frac{27}{125}$ has a terminating decimal representation.
   (d) The repetend of $0.03\overline{74}$ is "374."
   (e) The fraction $\frac{27}{225}$ has a repeating, nonterminating decimal representation.
   (f) Forty percent equals two-fifths.
   (g) The ratios $m:n$ and $p:q$ are equal if and only if $mq = np$.
   (h) If $p\%$ of n is x, then $p = \dfrac{100x}{n}$.

Skill

2. Compute the following problems without a calculator. Find approximate answers first.
   (a) $3.71 + 13.809$ (b) $14.3 - 7.961$
   (c) 7.3×11.41 (d) $6.5 \div 0.013$

3. Determine which number in the following pairs is larger using (i) the fraction representation, and (ii) the decimal representation.
   (a) 0.103 and 0.4   (b) 0.0997 and 0.1

4. Express each of the following fractions in its decimal form.
   (a) $\frac{2}{7}$ (b) $\frac{5}{8}$ (c) $\frac{7}{48}$ (d) $\frac{4}{9}$

5. Without converting, determine if the following fractions will have a terminating or nonterminating decimal representation.
   (a) $\dfrac{9}{16}$ (b) $\dfrac{17}{78}$ (c) $\dfrac{2^3}{2^7 \cdot 5^3}$

6. Express each of the following decimals in its simplest fraction form.
   (a) $0.\overline{36}$ (b) $0.3\overline{6}$ (c) 0.3636

7. Express each of the following in all three forms: decimal, fraction, and percent.
   (a) 52%   (b) 1.25   (c) $\frac{17}{25}$

8. The ratio of boys to girls is $3:2$ and there are 30 boys and girls altogether. How many boys are there?

Understanding

9. Without performing any calculations, explain why $\frac{1}{123456789}$ must have a repeating, nonterminating decimal representation.

10. Suppose that the percent key and the decimal point key on your calculator are both broken. Explain how you could still use your calculator to solve problems like "Find 37% of 58" and "Find 312% of 45."

Problem-Solving/Application

11. What is the 100th digit in $0.\overline{564793}$?

12. If the cost of a new car is $12,000 (plus 5% sales tax) and a down payment of 20% (including the tax) is required, how much money will a customer need to drive out in a new car?

13. A television set was to be sold at a 13% discount, which amounted to $78. How much would the set sell for after the discount?

14. A photograph measuring 3 inches by $2\frac{1}{2}$ inches is to be enlarged so that the smaller side, when enlarged, will be 8 inches. How long will the enlarged longer side be?

Integers

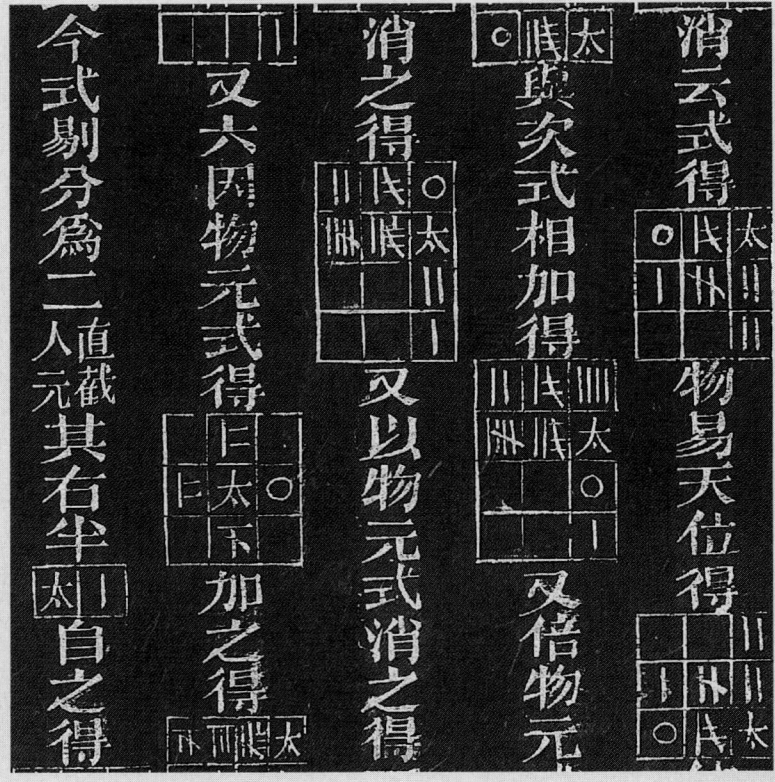

Both zeros and negative terms occur in this page from Chu Shih-Chieh's book on algebra, *Precious Mirror of the Four Elements,* published in 1303. Each box, consisting of a group of squares containing signs, represents a "matrix" form of writing an algebraic expression. The frequent occurrence of the sign "0" for zero may be clearly seen. (In these cases it means that terms corresponding for those squares do not occur in the equation.) The diagonal lines slashed through some of the numbers in the squares indicate that they are negative terms. (The number "one" is one vertical line, the number "two" is two vertical lines, etc.)

A Brief History of Negative Numbers

No trace of the recognition of negative numbers can be found in any of the early writings of the Egyptians, Babylonians, Hindus, Chinese, or Greeks. Even so, computations involving subtraction, such as $(10 - 6) \cdot (5 - 2)$, were performed correctly where rules for multiplying negatives were applied. The first mention of negative numbers can be traced to the Chinese in 200 B.C.

In the fourth century in his text *Arithmetica,* Diophantus spoke of the equation $4x + 20 = 4$ as "absurd" since x would have to be -4! The Hindu Brahmagupta (circa A.D. 630) spoke of "negative" and "affirmative" quantities, although these numbers always appeared as subtrahends. Around 1300, the Chinese mathematician Chu Shi-Ku gave the "rule of signs" in his algebra text. Also, in his text *Ars Magna* (1545) the Italian mathematician Cardano recognized negative roots and clearly stated rules of negatives.

Various notations have been used to designate negative numbers. The Hindus placed a dot or small circle over or beside a number to denote that it was negative; for example, 6̇ or 6̥ represented -6. The Chinese used red to denote positive and black to denote negative integers, and indicated negative numbers by drawing a slash through a portion of the numeral; for example, $-10,200$ was written 10,200. Cardano used the symbol m: (probably for "minus") for negatives; for example, -3 was written m:3.

In this chapter we use black chips and red chips to motivate the concepts underlying positive ("in the black") and negative ("in the red") numbers much as the Chinese may have done, although with the colors reversed.

STRATEGY 13: USE CASES

Many problems can be solved more easily by breaking the problem into various cases. For example, consider the following statement: The square of any whole number n is a multiple of 4 or one more than a multiple of 4. To prove this, we need only consider two cases: n is even or n is odd. If n is even, then $n = 2x$ and $n^2 = 4x^2$, which is a multiple of 4. If n is odd, then $n = 2x + 1$ and $n^2 = 4x^2 + 4x + 1$, which is one more than a multiple of 4. The following problem can be solved easily by considering various cases for a, b, and c.

Initial Problem

Prove or disprove: 2 is a factor of $(a - b)(b - c)(c - a)$ for any integers a, b, c. (Hint: Try a few examples first.)

$a = 8$, $b = 5$, $c = 1$.
$(a - b)(b - c)(c - a) = -84$.
$2 \mid -84$.

Clues

The Use Cases strategy may be appropriate when:

- A problem can be separated into several distinct cases.
- A problem involves distinct collections of numbers such as odds and evens, primes and composites, and positives and negatives.
- Investigations in specific cases can be generalized.

A solution of the Initial Problem above appears on page 355.

INTRODUCTION

Whole numbers and fractions are useful in solving many problems and applications in society. However, there are many situations where negative numbers are useful. For example, negative numbers are very helpful in describing temperature below zero, elevation below sea level, losses in the stock market, and an overdrawn checking account. In this chapter we study the integers, the set of numbers that consists of the whole numbers, together with the negative numbers that are the opposites of the nonzero whole numbers. The four basic operations of the integers are introduced together with order relationships.

8.1

ADDITION AND SUBTRACTION

Integers and the Integer Number Line

The introduction to this chapter lists several situations in which negative numbers are useful. There are other situations in mathematics in which negative numbers are needed. For example, the subtraction problem $4 - 7$ has no answer when using whole numbers. Also, the equation $x + 7 = 4$ has no whole-number solution. To remedy these situations, we introduce a new set of numbers, the integers. Our approach here will be to introduce the integers using a physical model. This model is related to a procedure that was used in accounting. Numerals written in black ink represent amounts above zero ("in the black" is positive) and in red ink represent accounts below zero ("in the red" is negative). We will use the integers to represent these situations.

Definition

Integers

The set of **integers** is the set

$$I = \{. . . , -3, -2, -1, 0, 1, 2, 3, . . .\}.$$

The numbers $1, 2, 3, . . .$ are called **positive integers** and the numbers $-1, -2, -3, . . .$ are called **negative integers**. Zero is neither a positive nor a negative integer.

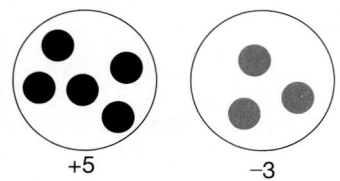

+5   −3
Five black chips Three red chips

FIGURE 8.1

In a set model, chips can be used to represent integers. However, *two colors of chips must be used*, one color to represent positive integers (black) and a second to represent negative integers (red) (Figure 8.1). One black chip represents a credit of 1 and one red chip represents a debit of 1. Thus *one black chip and one red chip cancel each other* or "make a zero"

[Figure 8.2(a)]. Using this concept, each integer can be represented by chips in many different ways [Figure 8.2(b)].

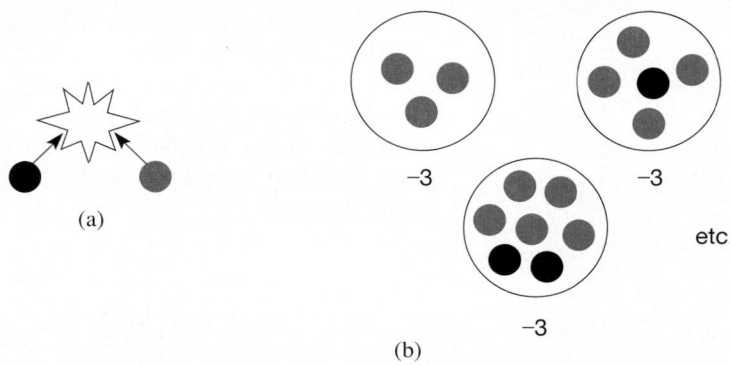

FIGURE 8.2

An extension from the examples in Figure 8.2 is that each integer has infinitely many representations using chips. (Recall that every fraction also has an infinite number of representations.)

Another way to represent the integers is to use a measurement model, the **integer number line** (Figure 8.3). The integers are equally spaced and arranged symmetrically to the right and left of zero on the number line. This

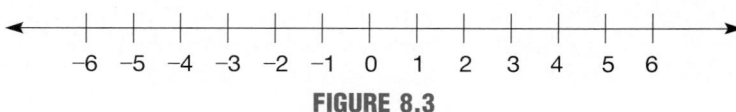

FIGURE 8.3

symmetry leads to a useful concept associated with positive and negative numbers. This concept, the opposite of a number, can be defined using either the measurement model or the set model of integers. The **opposite** of the integer a, written $-a$ or $(-a)$, is defined as follows:

Set Model.   The opposite of a is the integer that is represented by the same number of chips as a, but of the opposite color (Figure 8.4).

Measurement Model.   The opposite of a is the integer that is its mirror image about 0 on the integer number line (Figure 8.5).

The opposite of a positive integer is negative and the opposite of a negative integer is positive. Also, the opposite of zero is zero. The concept of opposite will be seen to be very useful later in this section when we study subtraction.

4 and −4 are opposites of each other.

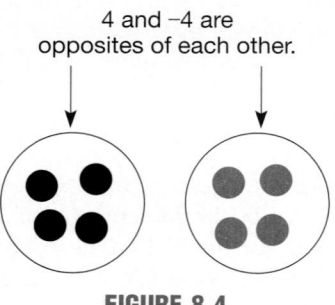

FIGURE 8.4

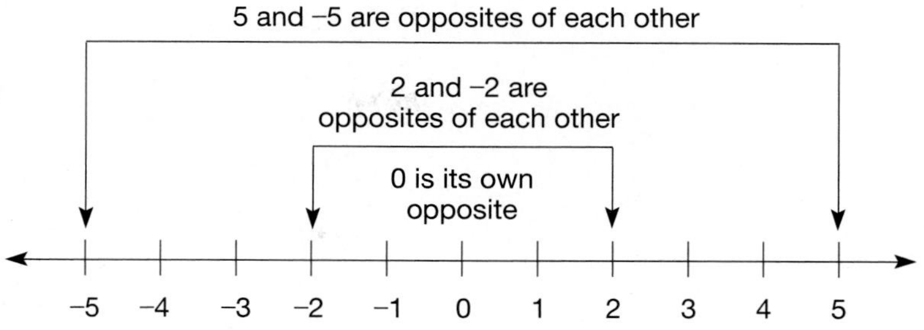

5 and −5 are opposites of each other

2 and −2 are
opposites of each other

0 is its own
opposite

FIGURE 8.5

Addition and Its Properties

Consider the following situation. In a football game, a running back made 12 running attempts and was credited with the following yardage for each attempt: 12, 7, −6, 8, 13, −1, 17, −5, 32, 16, 14, −7. What was his total yardage for the game? Integer addition can be used to answer this question. The definition of addition of integers can be motivated using both the set model and the measurement model.

Set Model.   Addition means to put together or form the union of two disjoint sets (Figure 8.6).

Measurement Model.   Addition means to put directed arrows end to end starting at zero. Note that positive integers are represented by arrows pointing to the right and negative integers by arrows pointing to the left (Figure 8.7).

(a) 3 + 1 = 4   (b) (−2) + (−1) = −3   (c) 3 + (−4) = −1

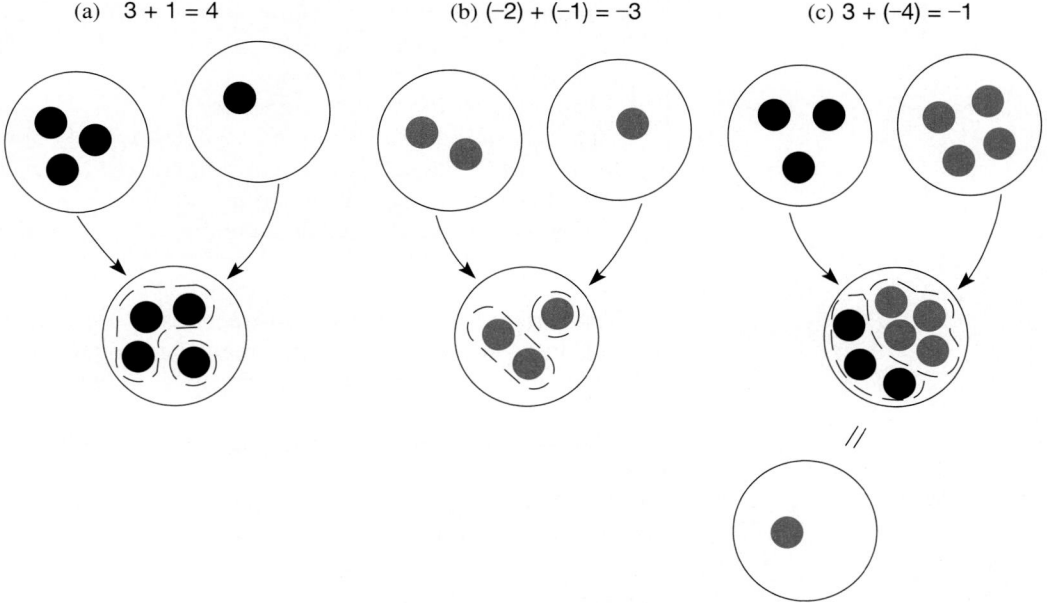

FIGURE 8.6

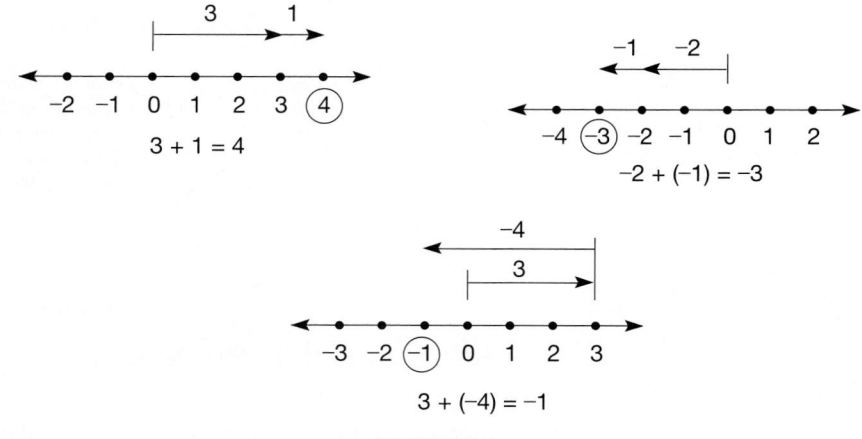

$$3 + 1 = 4$$

$$-2 + (-1) = -3$$

$$3 + (-4) = -1$$

FIGURE 8.7

The examples in Figures 8.6 and 8.7 lead to the following definition of integer addition.

Definition

Addition of integers

Let a and b be any integers.

1. *Adding zero.* $a + 0 = 0 + a = a$.
2. *Adding two positives.* If a and b are positive, they are added as whole numbers.
3. *Adding two negatives.* If a and b are positive (hence $-a$ and $-b$ are negative), then $(-a) + (-b) = -(a + b)$, where $a + b$ is the whole-number sum of a and b.
4. *Adding a positive and a negative.*
   (a) If a and b are positive and $a \geq b$, then $a + (-b) = a - b$, where $a - b$ is the whole-number difference of a and b.
   (b) If a and b are positive and $a < b$, then $a + (-b) = -(b - a)$, where $b - a$ is the whole-number difference of a and b.

These rules for addition are abstractions of what most people do when they add integers, namely, compute mentally using whole numbers and then determine if the answer is positive, negative, or zero.

EXAMPLE 8.1   Calculate the following using the definition of integer addition.

(a) $3 + 0$ (b) $3 + 4$ (c) $(-3) + (-4)$
(d) $7 + (-3)$ (e) $3 + (-7)$ (f) $5 + (-5)$

Solution
(a) *Adding zero:* $3 + 0 = 3$
(b) *Adding two positives:* $3 + 4 = 7$

(c) *Adding two negatives:* $(-3) + (-4) = -(3 + 4) = -7$
(d) *Adding a positive and a negative:* $7 + (-3) = 7 - 3 = 4$
(e) *Adding a positive and a negative:* $3 + (-7) = -(7 - 3) = -4$
(f) *Adding a number and its opposite:* $5 + (-5) = 0$ ■

The integer models and the rules for the addition of integers can be used to justify the following properties of integers.

Properties of Integer Addition

Let a, b, and c be any integers.

Closure Property for Integer Addition

$a + b$ is an integer.

Commutative Property for Integer Addition

$a + b = b + a$.

Associative Property for Integer Addition

$(a + b) + c = a + (b + c)$.

Identity Property for Integer Addition

0 is the unique integer such that $a + 0 = a = 0 + a$ for all a.

Additive Inverse Property for Integer Addition

For each integer a there is a unique integer, written $-a$, such that $a + (-a) = 0$.

The integer $-a$ is called the **additive inverse** of or the **opposite** of a. In words, this property states that any number plus its additive inverse is zero. A useful result that is a consequence of the additive inverse property is **additive cancellation.**

Theorem

Additive Cancellation for Integers

Let a, b, and c be any integers. If $a + c = b + c$, then $a = b$.

Proof
Let $a + c = b + c$. Then

$$(a + c) + (-c) = (b + c) + (-c) \qquad \text{Addition}$$
$$a + [c + (-c)] = b + [c + (-c)] \qquad \text{Associativity}$$
$$a + 0 = b + 0 \qquad \text{Additive inverse}$$
$$a = b \qquad \text{Additive identity}$$

Thus, if $a + c = b + c$, then $a = b$.   ■

Observe that $-a$ need not be negative. For example, the opposite of -7, written $-(-7)$, is 7, a positive number. In general, if a is positive, then $-a$ is negative; if a is negative, then $-a$ is positive; and if a is zero, then $-a$ is zero. As shown in Figure 8.8, using colored chips or a number line, it can be seen that $-(-a) = a$ for any integer a. (NOTE: The three small dots are used to allow for enough chips to represent any integer a, not necessarily just -3 and 3 as suggested by the black and red chips.)

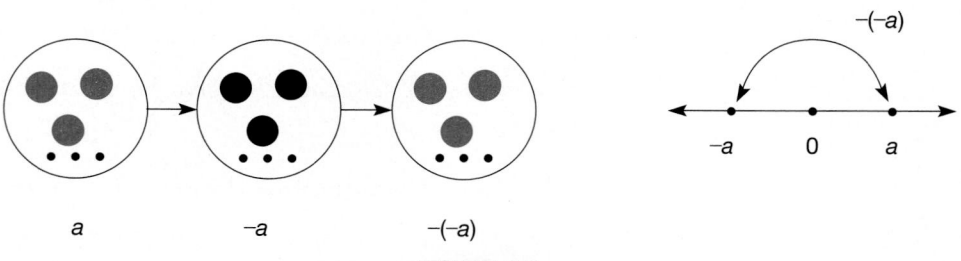

FIGURE 8.8

> **Theorem** Let a be any integer. Then $-(-a) = a$.

Proof
Notice that $a + (-a) = 0$ and $-(-a) + (-a) = 0$.
Therefore, $a + (-a) = -(-a) + (-a)$.
Finally, $a = -(-a)$, since the $(-a)$s can be canceled by additive cancellation. ∎

Properties of integer addition, together with thinking strategies, are helpful in doing computations. For example,

$$3 + (-10) = 3 + [(-3) + (-7)]$$
$$= [3 + (-3)] + (-7) = 0 + (-7) = -7$$

and

$$(-7) + 21 = (-7) + (7 + 14)$$
$$= [(-7) + 7] + 14 = 0 + 14 = 14.$$

Each step above can be justified using a property or the definition of integer addition. When one does the problem above mentally, not all the steps need to be carried out. However, it is important to understand how the properties are being applied.

Subtraction

Subtraction of integers can be viewed in several ways.

Take Away

EXAMPLE 8.2   Calculate the following differences.
(a) $6 - 2$ **(b)** $-4 - (-1)$ **(c)** $-2 - (-3)$ **(d)** $2 - 5$

Solution.   See Figure 8.9.

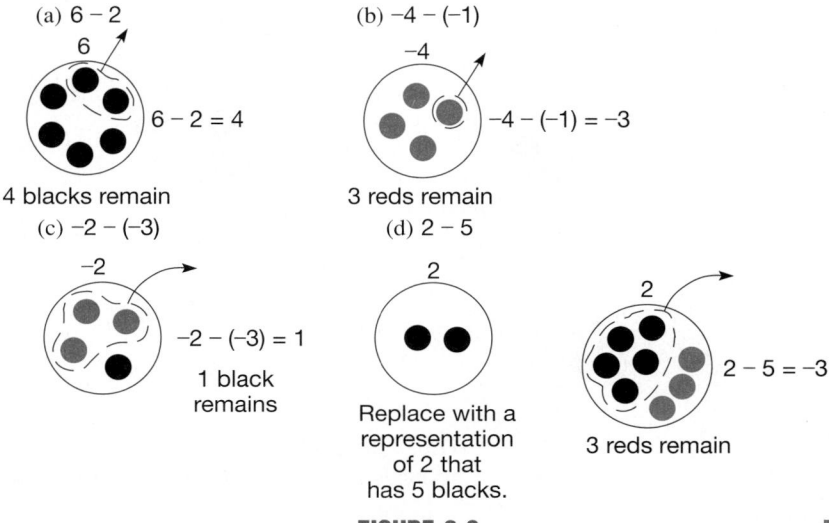

(a) $6 - 2$

6

$6 - 2 = 4$

4 blacks remain

(b) $-4 - (-1)$

-4

$-4 - (-1) = -3$

3 reds remain

(c) $-2 - (-3)$

-2

$-2 - (-3) = 1$

1 black remains

(d) $2 - 5$

2

Replace with a representation of 2 that has 5 blacks.

2

$2 - 5 = -3$

3 reds remain

FIGURE 8.9

Adding the Opposite
Let's reexamine the problem in Example 8.2(d). The difference $2 - 5$ can be found in yet another way using the chip model (Figure 8.10).

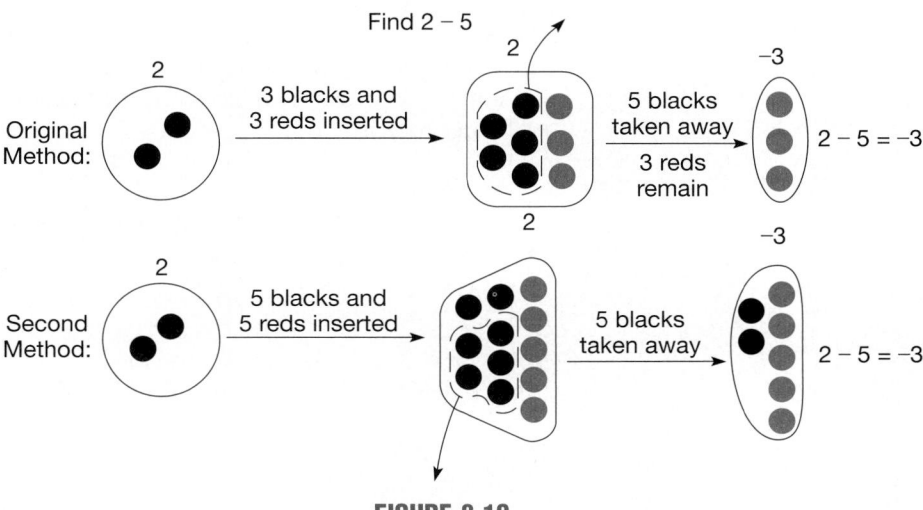

Find $2 - 5$

Original Method:

2

3 blacks and 3 reds inserted

2

5 blacks taken away
3 reds remain

-3

$2 - 5 = -3$

Second Method:

2

5 blacks and 5 reds inserted

2

5 blacks taken away

-3

$2 - 5 = -3$

FIGURE 8.10

This second method can be simplified. The process of inserting 5 blacks and 5 reds and then removing 5 blacks can be accomplished more simply by inserting 5 reds, since we would just turn around and take the 5 blacks away once they were inserted.

Simplified Second Method.   Find $2 - 5$. Notice that the simplified method in Figure 8.11 finds $2 - 5$ by finding $2 + (-5)$.

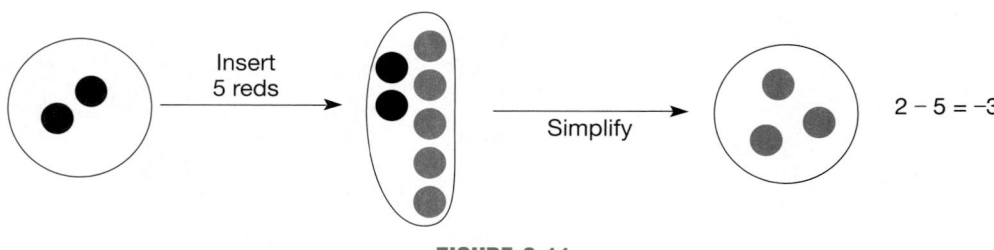

FIGURE 8.11

Thus this method of subtraction replaces a subtraction problem with an equivalent addition problem, namely, adding the opposite.

Definition

Subtraction of Integers: Adding the Opposite

Let a and b be any integers. Then
$$a - b = a + (-b).$$

Adding the opposite is perhaps the most efficient method for subtracting integers because it replaces any subtraction problem with an equivalent addition problem.

EXAMPLE 8.3   Find the following differences by adding the opposite.
(a) $(-8) - 3$ **(b)** $4 - (-5)$

Solution
(a) $(-8) - 3 = (-8) + (-3) = -11$
(b) $4 - (-5) = 4 + [-(-5)] = 4 + 5 = 9$ ■

Missing Addend
Recall that another approach to subtraction, the missing-addend approach, was used in whole-number subtraction. For example,

$$7 - 3 = n \quad \text{if and only if} \quad 7 = 3 + n.$$

In this way, subtraction can be done by referring to addition. This method can also be extended to integer subtraction.

EXAMPLE 8.4   Find $7 - (-3)$.

Solution
$7 - (-3) = n$ if and only if $7 = -3 + n$. But $-3 + 10 = 7$. Therefore, $7 - (-3) = 10$.   ■

Using variables, we can state the following.

Alternate Definition

Subtraction of Integers: Missing-Addend Approach

Let a, b, and c be any integers. Then $a - b = c$ if and only if $a = b + c$.

In summary, there are three equivalent ways to view subtraction in the integers.

(a) Take-away.   **(b)** Adding the opposite.   **(c)** Missing addend.

Notice that both the take-away and the missing-addend approaches are extensions of whole-number subtraction. The adding-the-opposite approach is new because the additive inverse property is a property the integers have but the whole numbers do not. As one should expect, all of these methods yield the same answer. The following argument shows that adding the opposite is a consequence of the missing-addend approach.

Let $a - b = c$.
Then $a = b + c$ by the missing-addend approach.
Hence $a + (-b) = b + c + (-b) = c$, or
$$a + (-b) = c.$$
Therefore, $a - b = a + (-b)$.

It can also be shown that the missing-addend approach follows from adding the opposite.

EXAMPLE 8.5   Find $4 - (-2)$ using all three methods of subtraction.

Solution
(a) *Take-Away:* See Figure 8.12.
(b) *Adding the Opposite:* $4 - (-2) = 4 + [-(-2)] = 4 + 2 = 6$.
(c) *Missing Addend:* $4 - (-2) = c$ if and only if $4 = (-2) + c$. But $4 = -2 + 6$. Therefore, $c = 6$.   ■

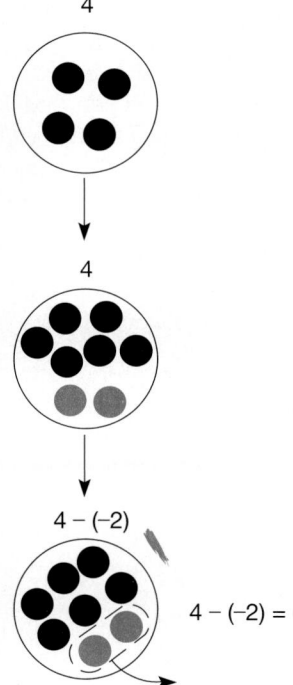

4

4

$4 - (-2)$

$4 - (-2) = 6$

FIGURE 8.12

The change-of-sign key $\boxed{+/-}$ or $\boxed{\text{CHS}}$ is used for integer calculations. The number -9 is found as follows: $9 \boxed{+/-} \boxed{ -9}$. To calculate $(-18) - (-3)$ press these keys: $18 \boxed{+/-} \boxed{-} 3 \boxed{+/-} \boxed{=} \boxed{ -15}$. Notice that the change-of-sign key is pressed *following* the number you want to change the sign of, *not* preceding the number.

As you may have noticed, the "$-$" symbol has three different meanings. Therefore, it should be read in a way that distinguishes among its uses. First, the symbol "-7" is read "negative 7" (negative means less than zero). Second, since it also represents the opposite or additive inverse of 7, "-7" can be read "the opposite of 7" or "the additive inverse of 7." Remember that "opposite" and "additive inverse" are not synonymous with "negative integers." For example, the opposite or additive inverse of -5 is 5 and 5 is a positive integer. In general, the symbol "$-a$" should be read "the opposite of a" or "the additive inverse of a." It is confusing to children to call it "negative a" since $-a$ may be positive, zero, or negative, depending on the value of a. Third, "$a - b$" is usually read "a minus b" to indicate subtraction.

MATHEMATICAL MORSEL

Often, very surprising results in mathematics spring from simple problems. One such result is the following: Take any collection of seven integers, say $a, b, c, d, e, f,$ and g. Form all consecutive sums from the left; $a, a + b, a + b + c, \ldots, a + b + \cdots + g; b, b + c, b + c + d, \ldots, b + c + \cdots + g;$ and so on. Then one of these sums must have a factor of 7. For example, in the set $\{2, -3, 5, -1, 3, -4, -5\}$, the consecutive sum $(-1) + 3 + (-4) + (-5)$ is $7(-1)$, hence has a factor of 7. It is interesting that the result above holds for *any* collection of integers, not just 7. That is, if one takes any collection of n integers, there is always a consecutive sum of these integers that has a factor of n.

EXERCISE/PROBLEM SET 8.1—PART A

Exercises

1. Using the set model, represent each of the following numbers in three different ways.
   (a) 3   (b) −5   (c) 0

2. Draw an integer number line and locate the following points.
   (a) −2   (b) −6   (c) 3   (d) −10

3. Represent the opposites of each of the numbers represented by the following models, where B = black chip and R = red chip.
   (a) *BBBBR*
   (b) *RBBRRRRR*
   (c)
   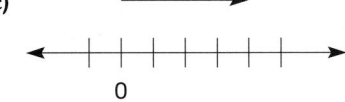
   (d)
   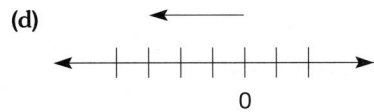

4. Write the opposite of each integer.
   (a) 3   (b) −4   (c) 0
   (d) −168   (e) 56   (f) −1235

5. Show how you could find the following sums (i) using a number-line model, and (ii) using black chips and red chips.
   (a) 5 + (−3)   (b) 3 + (−5)   (c) (−3) + (−2)

6. Dixie had a balance of $115 in her checking account at the beginning of the month. She deposited $384 in the account and then wrote checks for $153, $86, $196, $34, and $79. Then she made a deposit of $123. If at any time during the month the account is overdrawn, a $10 service charge is deducted. At the end of the month, what was Dixie's balance?

7. Use thinking strategies to compute the following sums. Identify your strategy.
   (a) −14 + 6   (b) 17 + (−3)   (c) −21 + 11

8. Use the chip model to compute the following differences.
   (a) 3 − 7   (b) 4 − (−5)
   (c) (−3) − (−6)   (d) 0 − (−4)

9. Find the following differences using the missing-addend approach.
   (a) 7 − (−3)   (b) (−5) − (−8)   (c) −2 − 7

10. Rewrite each of the following subtraction problems as an addition problem. Compute the solution.
    (a) 15 − 6   (b) −5 − 7
    (c) 5 − (−2)   (d) −3 − (−7)

11. Calculate.
    (a) 3 − 7   (b) 8 − (−4)
    (c) (−2) + 3   (d) (−7) − (−8)
    (e) (−3) + (−5)   (f) 3 + (−9)

12. Find the following using your calculator and the ⊞ +/− key. Check mentally.
    (a) −27 + 53   (b) (−51) − (−46)
    (c) 123 − (−247)   (d) −56 − 72

13. Fill in each empty square so that the number in the square will be the sum of the pair of numbers beneath the square.

    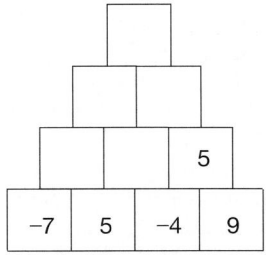

14. The existence of additive inverses in the set of integers enables us to solve equations of the form $x + b = c$ or $x − b = c$. For example, to solve $x + 15 = 8$, add (−15) to both sides; $x + 15 + (−15) = 8 + (−15)$ or $x = −7$. Solve the following equations using this technique.
    (a) $x + 21 = 16$ (b) $(−5) + x = 7$
    (c) $65 + x = −13$ (d) $x − 6 = −5$
    (e) $x − (−8) = 17$ (f) $x − 53 = −45$

15. True or false?
    (a) Every whole number is an integer.
    (b) The set of additive inverses of the whole numbers is equal to the set of integers.
    (c) Every integer is a whole number.
    (d) The set of additive inverses of the negative integers is a proper subset of the whole numbers.

16. Write out in words (use minus, negative, opposite).
    (a) 5 − 2   (b) −6 (two possible answers)
    (c) −3   (d) −(−5)
    (e) 10 − [−(−2)]   (f) −p

17. Is −x positive or negative if x is
    (a) positive?   (b) negative?   (c) zero?

18. The **absolute value** of an integer a, written $|a|$, is defined to be the distance from a to the zero on the integer number line. For example, $|3| = 3$, $|0| = 0$, and $|−7| = 7$. Evaluate the following absolute values.
    (a) $|5|$ (b) $|−17|$
    (c) $|5 − 7|$ (d) $|5| − |7|$
    (e) $−|7 − 5|$ (f) $|−(7 − 5)|$

Problems

19. Which of the following properties hold for integer subtraction? If the property holds, give an example. If it does not hold, disprove it by a counterexample.
  (a) Closure   **(b)** Commutative
  (c) Associative   **(d)** Identity

20. Assume that the adding-the-opposite approach is true and prove that the missing-addend approach is a consequence of it. (HINT: Assume that $a - b = c$ and show that $a = b + c$ using the adding-the-opposite approach.)

21. (a) If possible, for each of the following statements find a pair of integers a and b that satisfy the equation or inequality.
  (i) $|a + b| = |a| + |b|$
  (ii) $|a + b| < |a| + |b|$
  (iii) $|a + b| > |a| + |b|$
  (iv) $|a + b| \leq |a| + |b|$
  (b) Which of the conditions above will hold for all pairs of integers?

22. (a) Let A be a set that is closed under subtraction. If 4 and 9 are elements of A, show that each of the following are also elements of A.
  (i) 5   (ii) -5 (iii) 0
  (iv) 13   (v) 1   (vi) -3
  (b) List all members of A.

(c) Repeat part (b) if 4 and 8 are given as elements of A.
(d) Make a generalization about your findings.

23. Fill in each empty square so that the number in a square will be the sum of the pair of numbers beneath the square.

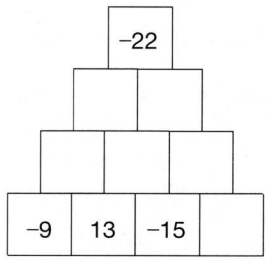

24. A student suggests the following algorithm for calculating $72 - 38$.

$$\begin{array}{r} 72 \\ -38 \\ \hline -6 \\ 40 \\ \hline 34 \end{array}$$

Two minus eight equals negative six.

Seventy minus thirty equals forty.

Forty plus negative six equals thirty-four, which therefore is the result.

As a teacher, what is your response? Does this procedure always work? Explain.

EXERCISE/PROBLEM SET 8.1—PART B

Exercises

1. Which of the following are integers? If they are, identify as positive, negative, or neither.
  (a) 25   **(b)** -7 **(c)** 0
  (d) $\frac{3}{4}$ **(e)** $231 - 556$ **(f)** $-252/5$

2. Identify each of the integers represented by the following models where B = black chip and R = red chip.
  (a) BBBRR
  (b) BRRRRBRR
  (c) BRRRBBRB
  (d)

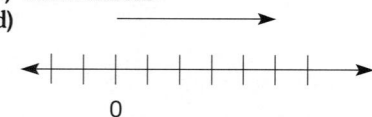

  (e)

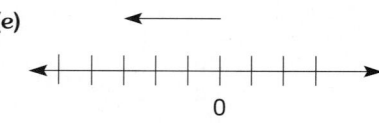

(f)

3. What is the opposite or additive inverse of each of the following (a and b represent integers)?
  (a) a **(b)** $-b$ **(c)** $a + b$ **(d)** $a - b$

4. Given I = integers
$$N = \{-1, -2, -3, -4, \ldots\}$$
$$P = \{1, 2, 3, 4, \ldots\}$$
$$W = \text{whole numbers}$$
list the members of the following sets.
  (a) $N \cup W$ **(b)** $N \cup P$ **(c)** $N \cap P$
  (d) $N \cap I$ **(e)** $P \cap I$ **(f)** $I \cap W$

5. Write an addition statement for each of the following sentences, and then find the answer.
  (a) In a series of downs, a football team gained 7 yards, lost 4 yards, lost 2 yards, and gained 8 yards. What was the total gain or loss?

(b) In a week, a given stock gained 5 points, dropped 12 points, dropped 3 points, gained 18 points, and dropped 10 points. What was the net change in the stock's worth?

(c) A visitor in an Atlantic City casino won $300, lost $250, and then won $150. Find the gambler's overall gain or loss.

6. Identify the property illustrated by the following equations.
   (a) $3 + [6 + (-3)] = 3 + (-3 + 6)$
   (b) $3 + (-3 + 6) = [3 + (-3)] + 6$
   (c) $[3 + (-3)] + 6 = 0 + 6$
   (d) $0 + 6 = 6$

7. Apply the properties and thinking strategies to compute the following sums mentally.
   (a) $-126 + (635 + 126)$
   (b) $84 + (-67) + (-34)$
   (c) $-165 + 3217 + 65$
   (d) $173 + (-43) + (-97)$

8. What problems are illustrated by the following models of black chips (B) and red chips (R)?
   (a) BB RRR   **(b)** BBB RR
   (c) B RR RR   **(d)** BRBRB BB

9. What is the smallest number of black chips and red chips needed to model the problem $6 - (-2)$ using the following approaches?
   (a) Adding the opposite   **(b)** Take-away

10. Calculate the following sums and differences.
    (a) $13 - 27$ **(b)** $38 - (-14)$
    (c) $(-21) + 35$ **(d)** $-26 - (-32)$

11. Find the following using your calculator and the $\boxed{+/-}$ key. Check mentally.
    (a) $-119 + 351 + (-463)$
    (b) $-98 - (-42)$
    (c) $632 - (-354)$
    (d) $-752 - (-549) + (-352)$

12. On a given day, the following Fahrenheit temperature extremes were recorded. Find the range between the high and low temperature in each location.

City	High	Low
Philadelphia	65	37
Cheyenne	35	-9
Bismarck	-2	-13

13. For each of the following equations, find the integer that satisfies the equation.
    (a) $-x = 5$ **(b)** $x + (-3) = -10$
    (c) $x - (-5) = -8$ **(d)** $6 - x = -3$
    (e) $-5 - x = -2$ **(f)** $x = -x$

14. If p and q are arbitrary negative integers, which of the following is true?

(a) $-p$ is negative   **(b)** $p - q = q - p$
(c) $-(p + q) = q - p$ **(d)** $-p$ is positive

15. Fill in each empty square so that the number in the square will be the sum of the pair of numbers beneath the square.

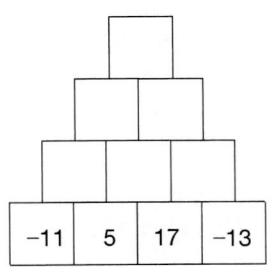

16. Is it always true for integers a and b that $a - b$ and $b - a$ are opposites? What if $a = b$?

17. Under what conditions is the following equation true?

$$(a - b) - c = (a - c) - b$$

(a) Never   **(b)** Always
(c) Only when $b = c$ **(d)** Only when $b = c = 0$

18. An alternate definition of absolute value is

$$|a| = \begin{cases} a & \text{if } a \text{ is positive or zero} \\ -a & \text{if } a \text{ is negative} \end{cases}$$

(NOTE: $-a$ is the opposite of a.) Using this definition, calculate the following values.
(a) $|-3|$ **(b)** $|7|$
(c) $|x|$ if $x < 0$ **(d)** $|-x|$ if $-x > 0$
(e) $-|x|$ if $x < 0$ **(f)** $-|-x|$ if $x > 0$

19. A student claims that if $a \neq 0$, then $|a| = -a$ is never true since absolute value is always positive. Explain why the student is wrong. What two concepts is the student confusing?

20. Complete the magic square using the following integers:

$$10, 7, 4, 1, -5, -8, -11, -14$$

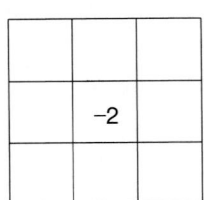

21. If a is an element of $\{-3, -2, -1, 0, 1, 2\}$ and b is an element of $\{-5, -4, -3, -2, -1, 0, 1\}$, find the

smallest and largest values for the following expressions.

(a) $a + b$ **(b)** $b - a$ **(c)** $|a + b|$

22. Switch two numbers to produce an additive magic square.

140	−56	−42	−28
−14	70	56	28
42	14	0	84
98	112	126	−70

23. Fill in each empty square so that a number in a square will be the sum of the pair of numbers beneath the square.

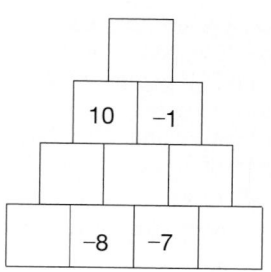

24. (a) Demonstrate a 1-1 correspondence between the sets given.
   (i) Positive integers and negative integers
   (ii) Positive integers and whole numbers
   (iii) Whole numbers and integers
(b) What does part (iii) tell you about the number of whole numbers compared to the number of integers?

8.2

MULTIPLICATION, DIVISION, AND ORDER

Multiplication and Its Properties

Integer multiplication can be viewed as extending whole-number multiplication. Recall that the first model for whole-number multiplication was repeated addition, as illustrated below.

$$3 \times 4 = 4 + 4 + 4 = 12.$$

Now suppose that you were selling tickets and you accepted three bad checks worth four dollars each. A natural way to think of your situation would be $3 \times (-4) = (-4) + (-4) + (-4) = -12$ (Figure 8.13).

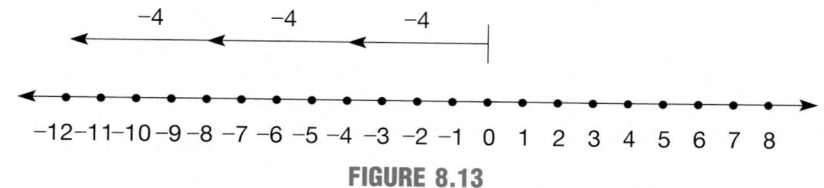

FIGURE 8.13

Rules for integer multiplication can be motivated using the following pattern.

The first column remains 3 throughout.
The second column is decreasing by one each time.

$3 \times 4 = 12$
$3 \times 3 = 9$ ↙ 3 less
$3 \times 2 = 6$ ↙ 3 less
$3 \times 1 = 3$ ↙ 3 less
$3 \times 0 = 0$ ↙ etc.
$3 \times (-1) = ?$ ↙
$3 \times (-2) = ?$ ↙
$3 \times (-3) = ?$ ↙
$3 \times (-4) = ?$ ↙

This pattern extended suggests that $3 \times (-1) = -3$, $3 \times (-2) = -6$, $3 \times (-3) = -9$, and so on. A similar pattern can be used to suggest what the product of two negative integers should be, as follows.

The first column
remains (-3).

The second column
decreases by 1 each
time.

$(-3) \times 3 = -9$
$(-3) \times 2 = -6$ 3 more
$(-3) \times 1 = -3$ 3 more
$(-3) \times 0 = 0$ 3 more
$(-3) \times (-1) = ?$ etc.
$(-3) \times (-2) = ?$
$(-3) \times (-3) = ?$

This pattern suggests that $(-3)(-1) = 3$, $(-3)(-2) = 6$, $(-3)(-3) = 9$, and so on. Such patterns lead to the following definition.

Definition

Multiplication of Integers

Let a and b be any integers.

1. *Multiplying by 0.* $a \cdot 0 = 0 = 0 \cdot a$.
2. *Multiplying two positives.* If a and b are positive, they are multiplied as whole numbers.
3. *Multiplying a positive and a negative.* If a is positive and b is positive (thus $-b$ is negative), then

$$a(-b) = -(ab),$$

where ab is the whole-number product of a and b. That is, the product of a positive and a negative is negative.
4. *Multiplying two negatives.* If a and b are positive, then

$$(-a)(-b) = ab,$$

where ab is the whole-number product of a and b. That is, the product of two negatives is positive.

NOTE: This definition of integer multiplication can also be motivated using the black/red chip model. See the problem set for this approach.

EXAMPLE 8.6 Calculate the following using the definition of integer multiplication.
(a) $5 \cdot 0$ **(b)** $5 \cdot 8$ **(c)** $5(-8)$ **(d)** $(-5)(-8)$

Solution
(a) *Multiplying by zero:* $5 \cdot 0 = 0$
(b) *Multiplying two positives:* $5 \cdot 8 = 40$
(c) *Multiplying a positive and a negative:* $5(-8) = -(5 \cdot 8) = -(40)$
(d) *Multiplying two negatives:* $(-5)(-8) = 5 \cdot 8 = 40$ ∎

The definition of multiplication of integers can be used to justify the following properties.

Properties of Integer Multiplication

Let a, b, and c be any integers.

Closure Property for Integer Multiplication

ab is an integer.

Commutative Property for Integer Multiplication

$ab = ba.$

Associative Property for Integer Multiplication

$(ab)c = a(bc).$

Identity Property for Integer Multiplication

1 is the unique integer such that $a \cdot 1 = a = 1 \cdot a$ for all a.

As in the system of whole numbers, our final property, the distributive property, connects addition and multiplication.

Distributivity of Multiplication over Addition of Integers

Let a, b, and c be any integers. Then

$$a(b + c) = ab + ac.$$

Using the preceding properties of addition and multiplication of integers, some important results that are useful in computations can be justified.

Theorem   Let a be any integer. Then

$$a(-1) = -a.$$

Proof
First, $a \cdot 0 = 0$ by definition.
But $a \cdot 0 = a[1 + (-1)]$ Additive inverse
$\qquad\quad = a(1) + a(-1)$ Distributivity
$\qquad\quad = a + a(-1)$ Multiplicative identity
Therefore, $a + a(-1) = 0$
Then $a + a(-1) = a + (-a)$ Additive inverse
Finally, $a(-1) = -a$ Additive cancellation   ■

Stating the preceding result in words, we have "the product of negative one and any integer is the opposite (or additive inverse) of that integer." Notice that, on the integer number line, multiplication by -1 is equivalent geometrically to reflecting an integer about the origin (Figure 8.14).

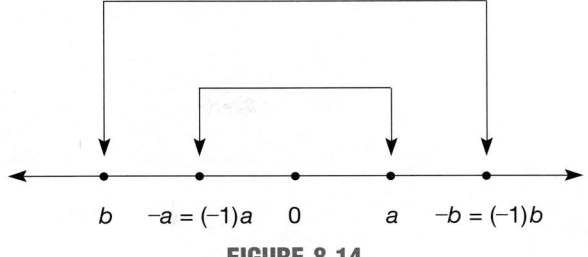

$$b \quad -a = (-1)a \quad 0 \quad a \quad -b = (-1)b$$

FIGURE 8.14

Theorem   Let a and b be any integers. Then

$$(-a)b = -(ab).$$

Proof

$$
\begin{aligned}
(-a)b &= [(-1)a]b & & (-1)a = -a \\
&= (-1)(ab) & & \text{Associativity for multiplication} \\
&= -(ab) & & (-1)a = -a
\end{aligned}
$$

Using commutativity with this result gives $a(-b) = -(ab)$.   ■

Theorem   Let a and b be any integers. Then

$$(-a)(-b) = ab \text{ for all integers } a, b.$$

Proof

$$
\begin{aligned}
(-a)(-b) &= [(-1)a][(-1)b] & & (-1)a = -a \\
&= [(-1)(-1)](ab) & & \text{Associativity and commutativity} \\
&= 1ab & & \text{Definition of integer multiplication} \\
&= ab & & \text{Multiplicative identity}
\end{aligned}
$$ ■

NOTE: The three preceding results encompass more than just statements about multiplying by negative numbers. For example, $(-a)(-b) = ab$ is read "the opposite of a times the opposite of b is ab." The numbers a and b may be positive, negative, or zero, hence $(-a)$ and $(-b)$ also may be negative, positive, or zero. Thus there is a subtle but important difference between these results and parts 3 and 4 of the definition of multiplication of integers.

EXAMPLE 8.7   Calculate the following products.
(a) $3(-1)$ **(b)** $(-3)5$ **(c)** $(-3)(-4)$ **(d)** $(-1)(-7)$
(e) $(-x)(-y)(-z)$

Solution
(a) $3(-1) = -3$ since $a(-1) = -a$.
(b) $(-3)5 = -(3 \cdot 5) = -15$ since $(-a)b = -(ab)$.
(c) $(-3)(-4) = (3 \cdot 4)$ since $(-a)(-b) = ab$.
(d) $(-1)(-7)$ can be found in two ways: $(-1)(-7) = -(-7) = 7$ since $(-1)a = -a$, and $(-1)(-7) = 1 \cdot 7 = 7$ since $(-a)(-b) = ab$.
(e) $(-x)(-y)(-z) = xy(-z)$ since $(-a)(-b) = ab$, and $xy(-z) = -(xyz)$ since $a(-b) = -(ab)$.   ■

Finally, the next property will be useful in integer division.

> **Multiplicative Cancellation Property**
>
> Let a, b, c be any integers with $c \neq 0$. If $ac = bc$, then $a = b$.

Notice that the condition $c \neq 0$ is necessary since $3 \cdot 0 = 2 \cdot 0$, but $3 \neq 2$.

The multiplicative cancellation property is truly a *property* of the integers (and whole numbers and counting numbers) because it cannot be proven from any of our previous properties. However, in a system where nonzero numbers have multiplicative inverses (such as the fractions), it is a theorem. The following property is equivalent to the multiplicative cancellation property.

> **Zero Divisors Property**
>
> Let a and b be integers. Then $ab = 0$ if and only if $a = 0$ or $b = 0$.

Division

Recall that to find $6 \div 3$ in the whole numbers, we sought the whole number c, where $6 = 3 \cdot c$. Division of integers can be viewed as an extension of whole-number division using the missing-factor approach.

> **Definition**
>
> **Division of Integers**
>
> Let a and b be any integers, where $b \neq 0$. Then $a \div b = c$ if and only if $a = b \cdot c$ for a unique integer c.

EXAMPLE 8.8   Find the following quotients (if possible).
(a) $12 \div (-3)$ **(b)** $(-15) \div (-5)$ **(c)** $(-8) \div 2$ **(d)** $7 \div (-2)$

Solution
(a) $12 \div (-3) = c$ if and only if $12 = (-3) \cdot c$. From multiplication, $12 = (-3)(-4)$. Since $(-3) \cdot c = (-3)(-4)$, by multiplicative cancellation, $c = -4$.
(b) $(-15) \div (-5) = c$ if and only if $-15 = (-5) \cdot c$. From multiplication, $-15 = (-5) \cdot 3$. Since $(-5) \cdot c = (-5) \cdot 3$, by multiplicative cancellation, $c = 3$.
(c) $(-8) \div 2 = c$ if and only if $(-8) = 2 \cdot c$. Thus $c = -4$ since $2(-4) = -8$.
(d) $7 \div (-2) = c$ if and only if $7 = (-2) \cdot c$. There is no such integer c. Therefore, $7 \div (-2)$ is undefined in the integers.   ■

Considering the results of this example, the following generalizations can be made about the division of integers: Assume that b divides a, that is, that b is a factor of a.

1. *Dividing by 1.* $a \div 1 = a$.
2. *Dividing two positives (negatives).* If *a* and *b* are both positive (or both negative), then $a \div b$ is positive.
3. *Dividing a positive and a negative.* If one of *a* or *b* is positive and the other is negative, then $a \div b$ *is negative*.
4. *Dividing zero by a nonzero integer.* $0 \div b = 0$, where $b \neq 0$ since $0 = b \cdot 0$. As with whole numbers, division by zero is undefined for integers.

EXAMPLE 8.9   Calculate.
(a) $0 \div 5$ **(b)** $40 \div 5$ **(c)** $40 \div (-5)$ **(d)** $(-40) \div (-5)$

Solution
(a) *Dividing into zero:* $0 \div 5 = 0$
(b) *Dividing two positives:* $40 \div 5 = 8$
(c) *Dividing a positive and negative:* $40 \div (-5) = -8$ and $(-40) \div 5 = -8$
(d) *Dividing two negatives:* $(-40) \div (-5) = 8$ ∎

The change-of-sign key can be used to find $-306 \times (-76) \div 12$ as follows:

$$306 \boxed{+/-} \boxed{\times} 76 \boxed{+/-} \boxed{\div} 12 \boxed{=} \boxed{1938}.$$

However, this calculation can be performed without the change-of-sign key by observing that there are an even number (two) of negative integers multiplied together. Thus the product is positive. In the case of an odd number of negative factors, the product is negative.

Negative Exponents and Scientific Notation

When studying whole numbers, exponents were introduced as a shortcut for multiplication. As the following pattern suggests, there is a way to extend our current definition of exponents to include integer exponents.

$$a^3 = a \cdot a \cdot a$$
$$a^2 = a \cdot a \qquad \Big) \div a$$
$$a^1 = a \qquad \Big) \div a$$
$$a^0 = 1 \qquad \Big) \div a$$
$$a^{-1} = \frac{1}{a} \qquad \Big) \div a$$
$$a^{-2} = \frac{1}{a^2} \qquad \Big) \div a$$
$$a^{-3} = \frac{1}{a^3} \qquad \Big) \div a$$

etc.

This pattern leads to the next definition.

Definition

Negative Integer Exponent

Let a be any nonzero number and n be a positive integer. Then

$$a^{-n} = \frac{1}{a^n}.$$

For example, $7^{-3} = \frac{1}{7^3}$, $2^{-5} = \frac{1}{2^5}$, $3^{-10} = \frac{1}{3^{10}}$, and so on. Also, $\frac{1}{4^{-3}} = \frac{1}{1/4^3} = 4^3$. The last sentence indicates how the definition leads to the statement $a^{-n} = \frac{1}{a^n}$ for all integers n.

It can be shown that the theorems on whole-number exponents given in Section 3.3 can be extended to integer exponents. That is, for any nonzero numbers a and b, and integers m and n, we have

$$a^m \cdot a^n = a^{m+n}$$
$$a^m \cdot b^m = (ab)^m$$
$$(a^m)^n = a^{mn}$$
$$\frac{a^m}{a^n} = a^{m-n}$$

In Section 4.1 scientific notation was discussed in the context of using a scientific calculator. Numbers are said to be in **scientific notation** when expressed in the form $a \times 10^n$, where $1 \le a < 10$ and n is any integer. The number a is called the **mantissa** and n the **characteristic** of $a \times 10^n$. The following list provides some examples of numbers written in scientific notation.

	Scientific Notation	Standard Notation
Diameter of Jupiter	1.438×10^8 meters	143,800,000 meters
Total amount of gold in Earth's crust	1.2×10^{16} kilograms	12,000,000,000,000,000 kilograms
Mass of a human egg	1.5×10^{-9} kilogram	0.0000000015 kilogram
Diameter of a proton	1×10^{-11} meter	0.00000000001 meter

EXAMPLE 8.10   Convert as indicated.
(a) 38,500,000 to scientific notation
(b) 7.2×10^{-14} to standard notation
(c) 4.135×10^{11} to standard notation
(d) 0.0000961 to scientific notation

Solution
(a) $38,500,000 = 3.85 \times 10^7$
(b) $7.2 \times 10^{-14} = 0.000000000000072$
(c) $4.135 \times 10^{11} = 413,500,000,000$
(d) $0.0000961 = 9.61 \times 10^{-5}$ ■

Conversions from standard notation to scientific notation can be performed on most scientific calculators. For example, on the TI-34 calculator, the following keystrokes convert 38,500,000 to scientific notation.

$$38500000 \boxed{\text{2nd}}\ \boxed{\text{Sci}}\ \boxed{\qquad 3.85^{07}\qquad}$$

The raised "07" represents 10^7. Since the number of digits displayed by calculators differs, one needs to keep these limitations in mind when converting between scientific and standard notations.

Scientific notation is used to solve problems involving very large and very small numbers, especially in science and engineering.

EXAMPLE 8.11   The diameter of Jupiter is about 1.438×10^8 meters and the diameter of Earth is about 1.27×10^7 meters. What is the ratio of the diameter of Jupiter to the diameter of Earth?

Solution

$$\frac{1.438 \times 10^8}{1.27 \times 10^7} = \frac{1.438}{1.27} \times \frac{10^8}{10^7} \approx 1.13 \times 10 = 11.3.$$ ■

When performing calculations involving numbers written in scientific notation, it is customary to express the answer in scientific notation. For example, the product $(5.4 \times 10^7)(3.5 \times 10^6)$ is written as follows:

$$(5.4 \times 10^7)(3.5 \times 10^6) = 18.9 \times 10^{13} = 1.89 \times 10^{14}.$$

STUDENT PAGE SNAPSHOT

Scientific Notation: Integer Exponents

A. Wavelengths of light are too short to be measured using standard units of length. Scientists use an extremely small unit called a *nanometer (nm)* to measure light wavelengths.

1 nm = 0.000000001 m

How can 1 nm be written using scientific notation?

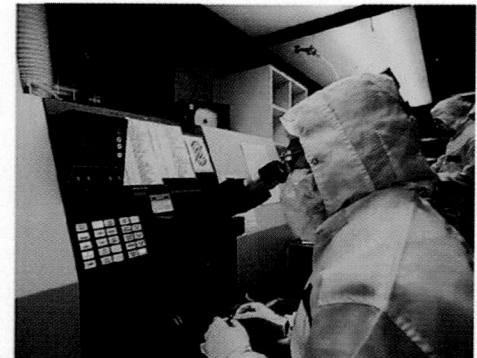

Recall how to write a number in scientific notation:

a number from 1 to 10

$42,000,000 = 42,000,000 = 4.2 \times 10^7$ a power of 10

Move decimal point 7 places to left.

When a number is less than 1, use a negative exponent to write it in scientific notation.

tenths	hundredths	thousandths	ten-thousandths	hundred-thousandths	millionths	ten-millionths	hundred-millionths	billionths
10^{-1}	10^{-2}	10^{-3}	10^{-4}	10^{-5}	10^{-6}	10^{-7}	10^{-8}	10^{-9}

1 nm = 0.000000001 m = 0.000000001 m = 1×10^{-9} m

9 decimal places

1. The light produced by a sample of burning sodium has a wavelength of 0.000000573 m. Write the wavelength in scientific notation.

B. It takes 5.3×10^{-6} seconds for light to travel 1 mi. How can you write the time in standard form?

5.3×10^{-6} seconds = 5.3×0.000001 seconds
= 0000005.3 seconds = 0.0000053 seconds

Move decimal point 6 places to left.

TRY OUT

2. Write 0.00000000045 in scientific notation.

3. Write 9.73×10^{-4} in standard form.

Ordering Integers

The concepts of "greater than" and "less than" in the integers are defined to be extensions of ordering in the whole numbers. In the following, ordering is viewed in two equivalent ways, (1) the number-line approach and (2) the addition approach. Let a and b be any integers.

Number-Line Approach

The integer a is less than the integer b, written $a < b$, if a is to the left of b on the integer number line. Thus, by viewing the number line, one can see that $-3 < 2$ (Figure 8.15). Also, $-4 < -1$, $-2 < 3$, and so on.

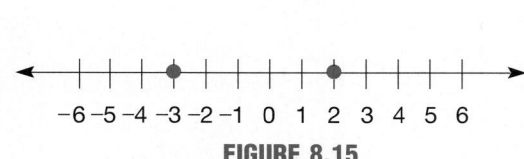

$$-3 < 2$$

FIGURE 8.15

Addition Approach

The integer a **is less than** the integer b, written $a < b$, if and only if there is a *positive* integer p such that $a + p = b$. Thus $-5 < -3$ since $-5 + 2 = -3$, and $-7 < 2$ since $-7 + 9 = 2$. Equivalently, $a < b$ if and only if $b - a$ is positive (since $b - a = p$). For example, $-27 < -13$ since $-13 - (-27) = 14$, which is positive. Similar definitions can be made for $\leq$, $>$, and $\geq$.

EXAMPLE 8.12 Order the following integers from the smallest to largest using the number-line approach.

$$2, 11, -7, 0, 5, -8, -13.$$

Solution
See Figure 8.16.

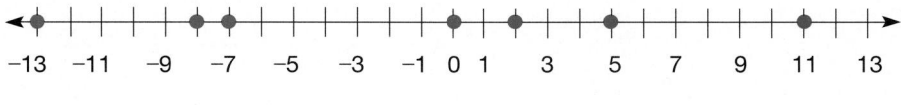

$$-13 < -8 < -7 < 0 < 2 < 5 < 11$$

FIGURE 8.16 ■

EXAMPLE 8.13 Determine the smallest integer in the set $\{3, 0, -5, 9, -8\}$ using the addition approach.

Solution
$-8 < -5$ since $(-8) + 3 = -5$. Also, since any negative integer is less than 0 or any positive integer, -8 must be the smallest. ■

The following results involving ordering, addition, and multiplication extend similar ones for whole numbers.

> ### Properties of Ordering Integers
>
> Let a, b, c be any integers, p a positive integer, and n a negative integer.
>
> #### *Transitive Property for Less Than*
>
> If $a < b$ and $b < c$, then $a < c$.
>
> #### *Property of Less Than and Addition*
>
> If $a < b$, then $a + c < b + c$.
>
> #### *Property of Less Than and Multiplication by a Positive*
>
> If $a < b$, then $ap < bp$.
>
> #### *Property of Less Than and Multiplication by a Negative*
>
> If $a < b$, then $an > bn$.

The first three properties for ordering integers are extensions of similar statements in the whole numbers. However, the fourth property deserves special attention because it involves multiplying both sides of an inequality by a *negative* integer. For example, $2 < 5$ but $2(-3) > 5(-3)$. [Note that *2 is less than* 5 but that $2(-3)$ *is greater than* $5(-3)$.] Similar properties hold where $<$ is replaced by $\leq$, $>$, and $\geq$. The last two properties which involve multiplication and ordering are illustrated in Example 8.14 using the number-line approach.

EXAMPLE 8.14

(a) $-2 < 3$ and $4 > 0$, thus $(-2) \cdot 4 < 3 \cdot 4$ by the property of less than and multiplication by a positive (Figure 8.17).

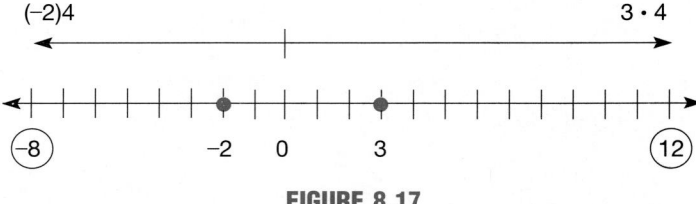

FIGURE 8.17

(b) $-2 < 3$ and $-4 < 0$, thus $(-2)(-4) > 3(-4)$ by the property of less than and multiplication by a negative (Figure 8.18).

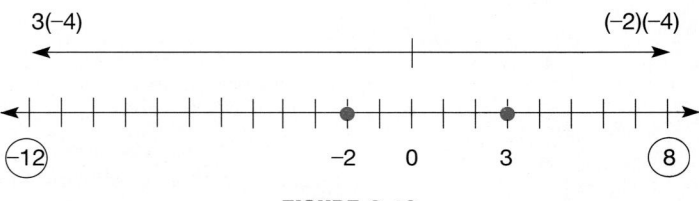

FIGURE 8.18

Notice how −2 was to the left of 3, *but* (−2)(−4) is to the *right* of (3)(−4). ∎

To see why the property of less than and multiplication by a negative is true, recall that multiplying an integer *a* by −1 is geometrically the same as reflecting *a* across the origin on the integer number line. Using this idea in all cases leads to the following general result.

If $a < b$, then $(-1)a > (-1)b$ (Figure 8.19).

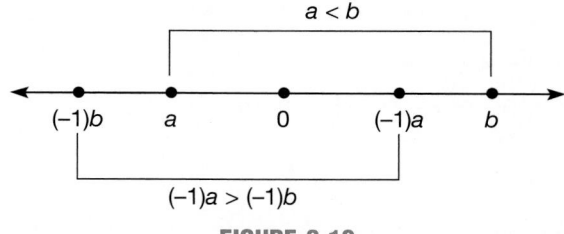

FIGURE 8.19

Now, to justify the statement "if $a < b$ and $n < 0$, then $an > bn$," suppose that $a < b$ and $n < 0$. Since n is negative, we can express n as $(-1)p$, where p is positive. Then $ap < bp$ by the property of less than and multiplication by a positive. But if $ap < bp$, then $(-1)ap > (-1)bp$, or $a[(-1)p] > b[(-1)p]$, which, in turn, yields $an > bn$. Informally, this result says that "multiplying an inequality by a negative number 'reverses' the inequality."

MATHEMATICAL MORSEL

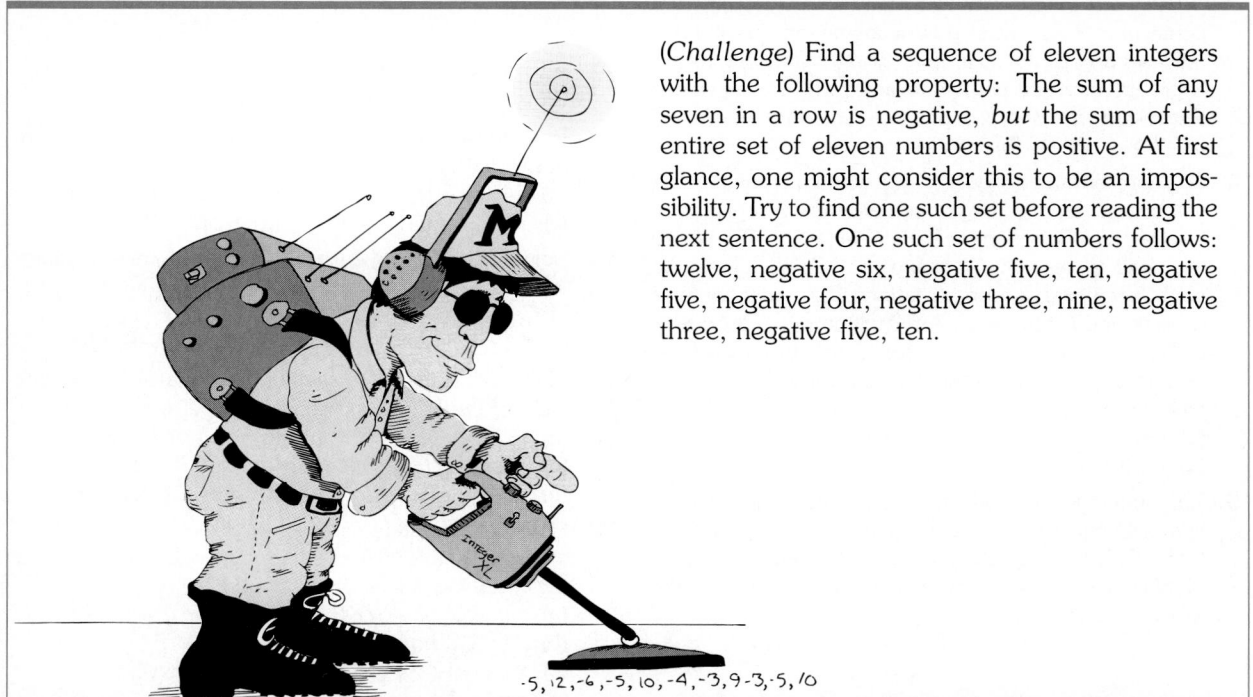

(*Challenge*) Find a sequence of eleven integers with the following property: The sum of any seven in a row is negative, *but* the sum of the entire set of eleven numbers is positive. At first glance, one might consider this to be an impossibility. Try to find one such set before reading the next sentence. One such set of numbers follows: twelve, negative six, negative five, ten, negative five, negative four, negative three, nine, negative three, negative five, ten.

EXERCISE/PROBLEM SET 8.2—PART A

Exercises

1. Write one addition and one multiplication equation represented by each number-line model given.

(a)

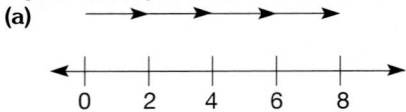

(b)

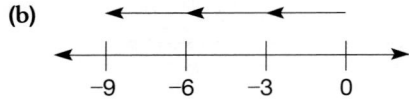

(c)

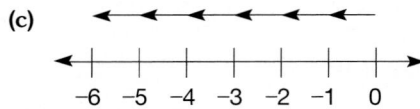

2. (a) Extend the patterns below by writing the next three equations.

(i) $6 \times 3 = 18$ (ii) $9 \times 3 = 27$
$6 \times 2 = 12$ $9 \times 2 = 18$
$6 \times 1 = 6$ $9 \times 1 = 9$
$6 \times 0 = 0$ $9 \times 0 = 0$

(b) What rule of multiplication of negative numbers is suggested by the equations you have written?

3. Integer multiplication may be modeled with black and red chips. Beginning with a set representing zero, the product $a \times b$ tells you how many times to add (if a is positive) or take out (if a is negative) groups of chips representing b. For example, $2 \times (-3)$ means to put 2 groups of 3 red chips into a set with no elements. Represent the following products and give the result.

(a) $3 \times (-2)$ **(b)** $3 \times (-4)$ **(c)** $5 \times (-2)$

4. To represent the product $a \times b$ when a is negative, it will be necessary to begin with a different representation of zero. For example, to model $(-2) \times (3)$, where we need to take out 2 groups of 3 black chips, we might begin with a representation of zero that contains 6 black and 6 red chips. After taking out 2 groups of 3 black chips, we have 6 red chips left; therefore, $(-2) \times 3 = -6$. Represent the following products and give the result.

(a) $(-3) \times 4$ **(b)** $(-2) \times (-4)$
(c) $(-2) \times (-1)$

5. The uniqueness of additive inverses and other properties of integers enable us to give another justification that $-3(4) = -12$. By definition, the additive inverse of $3(4)$ is $-(3 \cdot 4)$. Provide reasons for each of the following equations.

$$-3 \cdot 4 + 3 \cdot 4 = (-3 + 3) \cdot 4$$
$$= 0 \cdot 4$$
$$= 0.$$

Thus we have shown that $(-3)4$ is also the additive inverse of $3 \cdot 4$ and hence is equal to $-(3 \cdot 4) = -12$.

6. The following argument shows another justification for $(-3)(-4) = 12$ using the ideas in the previous problem. Provide reasons for each of the following equations.

$$(-3)(-4) + (-3) \cdot 4 = (-3)(-4 + 4)$$
$$= (-3) \cdot 0$$
$$= 0.$$

Therefore, $(-3)(-4)$ is the additive inverse of $(-3)4 = -12$. But the additive inverse of -12 is 12, so $(-3)(-4) = 12$.

7. Extend the meaning of a whole-number exponent.

$$a^n = \underbrace{a \cdot a \cdot a \cdots a,}_{n \text{ factors}}$$

where a is any integer. Use this definition to find the following values.

(a) 2^4 **(b)** $(-3)^3$ **(c)** $(-2)^4$
(d) $(-5)^2$ **(e)** $(-3)^5$ **(f)** $(-2)^6$

8. Provide reasons for each step below.

$$a(b - c) = a[b + (-c)]$$
$$= ab + a(-c)$$
$$= ab + [-(ac)]$$
$$= ab - ac.$$

Which property have you justified?

9. Rewrite the following division equations as multiplication equations.

(a) $24 \div (-4) = n$ **(b)** $-42 \div (-6) = n$
(c) $-48 \div (-12) = n$ **(d)** $-56 \div 7 = n$

10. Solve the following equations using the missing-factor approach.

(a) $-3x = -9$ **(b)** $-15x = 1290$
(c) $11x = -374$ **(d)** $-9x = -8163$

11. Make use of the ⬚ +/− ⬚ key on a calculator to calculate each of the following problems.

(a) -36×72 **(b)** $-51 \times (-38)$
(c) $-128 \times (-765)$ **(d)** $-658 \div 14$
(e) $3588 \div (-23)$ **(f)** $-108{,}697 \div (-73)$

12. Consider the statement $(x + y) \div z = (x \div z) + (y \div z)$. Is this a true statement in the integers for the following values of x, y, and z?

(a) $x = 16, y = -12, z = 4$
(b) $x = -20, y = 36, z = -4$
(c) $x = -42, y = -18, z = -6$
(d) $x = -12, y = -8, z = 3$

13. Write each of the following as a rational number in simplest form (without exponents).
(a) 10^{-2} (b) 4^{-3} (c) 2^{-6} (d) 5^{-3}

14. (a) Simplify $4^{-2} \cdot 4^6$ by expressing it in terms of whole-number exponents and simplifying.
(b) Simplify $4^{-2} \cdot 4^6$ by applying $a^m \cdot a^n = a^{m+n}$.
(c) Repeat parts (a) and (b) to simplify $5^{-4} \cdot 5^{-2}$.
(d) Does it appear that the property $a^m \cdot a^n = a^{m+n}$ still applies for integer exponents?

15. (a) Simplify $\dfrac{3^{-2}}{3^5}$ by expressing it in terms of whole-number exponents and simplifying.
(b) Simplify the expression above by applying $\dfrac{a^m}{a^n} = a^{m-n}$.
(c) Repeat parts (a) and (b) to simplify $\dfrac{6^3}{6^{-7}}$.
(d) Does it appear that the property $\dfrac{a^m}{a^n} = a^{m-n}$ still applies for integer exponents?

16. (a) Simplify $(3^2)^{-3}$ by expressing it in terms of whole-number exponents and simplifying.
(b) Simplify $(3^2)^{-3}$ by applying $(a^m)^n = a^{mn}$.
(c) Repeat parts (a) and (b) to simplify $(5^{-3})^{-2}$.
(d) Does it appear that the property $(a^m)^n = a^{mn}$ still applies for integer exponents?

17. Use the definition of integer exponents and properties of exponents to find a numerical value for the following expressions.
(a) $3^{-2} \cdot 3^5$ (b) $\dfrac{6^{-3}}{6^{-4}}$ (c) $(3^{-4})^{-2}$

18. Express each of the following numbers in scientific notation.
(a) 0.0004
(b) 0.0000016
(c) 0.000000000495
(d) 0.000000000000000000008071

19. You can use a scientific calculator to perform arithmetic operations with numbers written in scientific notation. If the exponent is negative, use your $\boxed{+/-}$ or $\boxed{\text{CHS}}$ or $\boxed{(-)}$ key to change the sign. For example, see the following multiplication problem.

$$(1.6 \times 10^{-4})(2.7 \times 10^{-8})$$

1.6 $\boxed{\text{SCI}}$ 4 $\boxed{+/-}$ $\boxed{\times}$ 2.7 $\boxed{\text{SCI}}$ 8 $\boxed{+/-}$ $\boxed{=}$
$\boxed{4.32 \qquad -12}$

(NOTE: The sequence of steps or appearance of the answer in the display window may be slightly different on your calculator.)

Use your calculator to evaluate each of the following. Express your results in scientific notation.

(a) $(7.6 \times 10^{10})(9.5 \times 10^{-36})$
(b) $(2.4 \times 10^{-6})(3.45 \times 10^{-20})$
(c) $\dfrac{1.2 \times 10^{-15}}{4.8 \times 10^{-6}}$
(d) $\dfrac{(7.5 \times 10^{-12})(8 \times 10^{-17})}{(1.5 \times 10^9)}$
(e) $\dfrac{480{,}000{,}000}{0.0000006}$
(f) $\dfrac{0.000000000000123}{0.0000006}$

20. A mercury atom measures approximately 3×10^{-10} meter across. Express this distance in decimal form.

21. Show that each of the following is true by using the number-line approach.
(a) $-3 < 2$ (b) $-6 < -2$ (c) $-3 > -12$

22. Write each of the following lists of integers in increasing order from left to right.
(a) $-5, 5, 2, -2, 0$ (b) $12, -6, -8, 3, -5$
(c) $-2, -3, -5, -8, -11$
(d) $23, -36, 45, -72, -108$

Problems

23. Fill in each empty square so that a number in a square is the product of the two numbers beneath it.

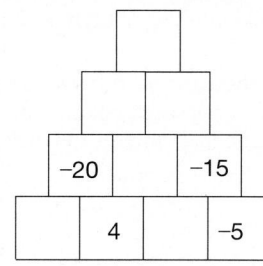

24. (a) Which of the following integers when substituted for x make the given inequality true?
$$3x + 5 < -16$$
$$-6 \qquad -10 \qquad -8 \qquad -7$$
(b) Is there a largest integer value for x that makes the inequality true?
(c) Is there a smallest integer value for x that makes the inequality true?

25. (a) The rules of integer addition can be summarized in a table as follows:

+	+	−
+	+	?
−		

Positive + positive = positive (+ sign)
Positive + negative = positive or negative or zero (? sign)
Complete the table.

(b) Make a similar table for
    (i) Subtraction   (ii) Multiplication
    (iii) Division (when possible)

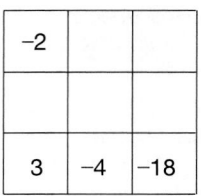

26. There are 6.022×10^{23} atoms in 12.01 grams of carbon. Find the mass of one atom of carbon. Express your answer in scientific notation.

27. Hair on the human body can grow as fast as 0.0000000043 meter per second.
    (a) At this rate, how much would a strand of hair grow in one month of 30 days? Express your answer in scientific notation.
    (b) About how long would it take for a strand of hair to grow to be 1 meter in length?

28. (a) If possible, find an integer x to satisfy the following conditions.
        (i) $|x| > x$ (ii) $|x| = x$
        (iii) $|x| < x$ (iv) $|x| \geq x$
    (b) Which, if any, of the conditions in part (a) will hold for all integers?

29. A student suggests that she can show $(-1)(-1) = 1$ using the fact that $-(-1) = 1$. Is her reasoning correct? If yes, what result will she apply? If not, why not?

30. A student does not believe that $-10 < -5$. He argues that a debt of $10 is greater than a debt of $5. How would you convince him that the inequality is true?

31. In a multiplication magic square, the product of the integers in each row, each column, and each diagonal is the same number. Complete the multiplication magic square given.

32. If $0 < x < y$ where x and y are integers, prove that $x^2 < y^2$.

33. A farmer goes to market and buys one hundred animals at a total cost of $1000. If cows cost $50 each, sheep cost $10 each, and rabbits cost 50 cents each, how many of each kind does he buy?

34. Prove or disprove: The square of any whole number is a multiple of 3 or one more than a multiple of 3.

35. Find the "cell sums" for the numbers in the top row and the numbers in the left-hand column. Does this procedure produce a square whose diagonal sums are the same? Will this procedure always work? If yes, prove, if no, give a counterexample.

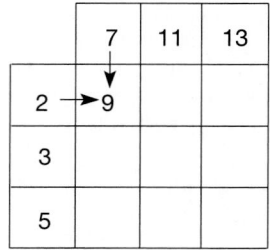

36. Assume that if $ac = bc$ and $c \neq 0$, then $a = b$. Prove that if $ab = 0$, then $a = 0$ or $b = 0$. (HINT: Assume that $b \neq 0$. Then $ab = 0 = 0 \cdot b$ . . . .)

EXERCISE/PROBLEM SET 8.2—PART B

Exercises

1. Illustrate the following products on an integer number line.
   (a) $2 \times (-5)$ (b) $3 \times (-4)$ (c) $5 \times (-2)$

2. Evaluate each of the following products.
   (a) $6(-5)$ (b) $(-2)(-16)$
   (c) $-(-3)(-5)$ (d) $-3(-7 - 6)$
   (e) $(-2)(-5)(-3)$ (f) $(-10)(7)(-6)$
   (g) $5[(-2)(13) + 5(-4)]$
   (h) $-23[(-2)(6) + (-3)(-4)]$

3. Extend the patterns below by writing the next three equations. What rule of multiplication of negative numbers is suggested by the equations you have written?
   (a) $-5 \times 3 = -15$ (b) $-8 \times 3 = -24$
       $-5 \times 2 = -10$ $-8 \times 2 = -16$
       $-5 \times 1 = -5$ $-8 \times 1 = -8$
       $-5 \times 0 = 0$ $-8 \times 0 = 0$

4. Represent the following integer multiplication problems with black and red chips and give the result.
   (a) $4 \times (-3)$
   (b) $(-2) \times (-3)$
   (c) $(-3) \times 3$
   (d) $(-4) \times (-3)$

5. Identify whether the following numbers are positive or negative.
   (a) $(-2)^5$
   (b) $(-2)^8$
   (c) $(-5)^3$
   (d) $(-5)^{16}$
   (e) $(-1)^{20}$
   (f) $(-1)^{33}$
   (g) a^n if $a < 0$ and n is even
   (h) a^n if $a < 0$ and n is odd

6. If a is an integer and $a \neq 0$, which of the following expressions are always positive and which are always negative?
   (a) a
   (b) $-a$
   (c) a^2
   (d) $(-a)^2$
   (e) $-(a)^2$ (also written $-a^2$)
   (f) a^3
   (g) $(-a)^3$
   (h) $-(a^3)$
   (i) a^4
   (j) $(-a)^4$
   (k) $-(a^4)$ (also $-a^4$)

7. Expand each of the following products.
   (a) $-6(x + 2)$
   (b) $-5(x - 11)$
   (c) $-3(x - y)$
   (d) $x(a - b)$
   (e) $-x(a - b)$
   (f) $(x - 3)(x + 2)$

8. Evaluate each quotient.
   (a) $-18 \div 3$
   (b) $-45 \div (-9)$
   (c) $75 \div (-5)$
   (d) $(-5 + 5) \div (-2)$
   (e) $[144 \div (-12)] \div (-3)$
   (f) $144 \div [-12 \div (-3)]$

9. (a) Start with zero and subtract 4 eight times. What multiplication problem (and answer) does this computation suggest?
   (b) How many 5s need to be added on the calculator to get 65? This suggests the question $65 \div 5 =$ _____? How many -5s need to be added to get -65? What division problem (and answer) does this suggest?

10. Compute the following.
   (a) $(-36)(52)$
   (b) $(-83)(-98)$
   (c) $(127)(-31)(-57)$
   (d) $(-39)(-92)(-68)$
   (e) $-899 \div 29$
   (f) $-5904 \div (-48)$
   (g) $7308 \div (-126)$
   (h) $[-1848 \div (-56)] \div (-33)$

11. Consider the statement $x \div (y + z) = (x \div y) + (x \div z)$. Is this statement true for the following values of x, y, and z?
   (a) $x = 12$, $y = -2$, $z = -4$
   (b) $x = 18$, $y = 2$, $z = -3$

12. Complete the following table (by entering yes or no) indicating properties of integer operations.

Property	+	−	×	÷
Closure				
Commutativity				
Associativity				
Identity				
Inverse				
Distributive over addition	╳	╳		
Distributive over subtraction	╳	╳		

(header: Operation)

13. Write the following values in simplest form.
   (a) 4^{-2}
   (b) 2^{-5}
   (c) 7^{-3}

14. Apply the properties of exponents to express the following values in a simpler form.
   (a) $\dfrac{5^{-2} \cdot 5^3}{5^{-4}}$
   (b) $\dfrac{(3^{-2})^{-5}}{3^{-6}}$
   (c) $\dfrac{8^3}{2^3 \cdot 4^{-2}}$
   (d) $\dfrac{2^6 \cdot 3^2}{(3^{-3})^{-2} \cdot 4^5}$

15. Each of the following numbers is written in scientific notation. Rewrite each in standard decimal form.
   (a) 3.7×10^{-5}
   (b) 2.45×10^{-8}
   (c) 9.0×10^{-6}
   (d) 1.26×10^{-13}

16. Express each of the following numbers in scientific notation.
   (a) 0.078
   (b) 0.000000691
   (c) 0.0000000000003048

17. Using scientific notation, calculate the following. Express answers in scientific notation.
   (a) 0.0000032×0.03
   (b) 1500×0.000006
   (c) $\dfrac{4500}{0.009}$
   (d) $\dfrac{0.00036}{0.0003}$

18. Use your calculator to evaluate each of the following. Express your answers in scientific notation.
   (a) $(9.62 \times 10^{-12})(2.8 \times 10^{-9})$
   (b) $\dfrac{3.74 \times 10^{-6}}{8.5 \times 10^{-30}}$
   (c) $(4.35 \times 10^{-40})(7.8 \times 10^{19})$
   (d) $\dfrac{(1.38 \times 10^{12})(4.5 \times 10^{-16})}{1.15 \times 10^{10}}$
   (e) $(62{,}000)(0.00000000000033)$
   (f) $\dfrac{0.000000000000000232}{0.000000145}$

19. Show that each of the following inequalities is true by using the addition approach.
   (a) $-7 < -3$
   (b) $-6 < 5$
   (c) $-17 > -23$
   (d) $4 > -13$

20. Fill in the blanks with the appropriate symbol $<$, $>$, or $=$, to produce true statements.
 (a) -4 ____ 9
 (b) 3 ____ -2
 (c) -4 ____ -5
 (d) 0 ____ -2
 (e) $3 + (-5)$ ____ $2 \times (-3)$
 (f) $(-12) \div (-2)$ ____ $-2 - (-3)$
 (g) $15 - (-6)$ ____ $(-3) \times (-7)$
 (h) $5 + (-5)$ ____ $(-3) \times (-6)$

21. Complete the following statements by inserting $<$, $=$, or $>$ in the blanks to produce true statements.
 (a) If $x < 4$, then $x + 2$ ____ 6.
 (b) If $x > -2$, then $x - 6$ ____ -8.
 (c) If $x < -3$, then $4x$ ____ -12.
 (d) If $x > -6$, then $-2x$ ____ 12.

Problems

22. Fill in each empty square so that a number in a square is the product of the two numbers beneath it.

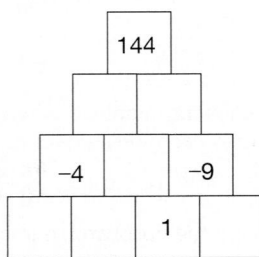

23. (a) Which of the following integers when substituted for x make the given inequality true?
$$5x - 3 \geq -18$$
$$-4 \qquad -3 \qquad -2 \qquad -1$$
 (b) Is there a largest integer value for x that makes the inequality true?
 (c) Is there a smallest integer value for x that makes the inequality true?

24. (a) Is there a largest whole number? Integer? Negative integer? Positive integer? If yes, what is it?
 (b) Is there a smallest whole number? Integer? Negative integer? Positive integer? If yes, what is it?

25. The mass of one electron is 9.11×10^{-28} gram. A uranium atom contains 92 electrons. Find the total mass of the electrons in a uranium atom. Express your answer in scientific notation.

26. A rare gas named "krypton" glows orange when heated by an electric current. The wavelength of the light it emits is about 605.8 nanometers and this wavelength is used to define the exact length of a meter. If one nanometer is 0.000000001 meter, what is the wavelength of krypton in meters? Express your answer in scientific notation.

27. The mass of one molecule of hemoglobin can be described as 0.11 attogram.
 (a) If 1 attogram $= 10^{-21}$ kilogram, what is the mass in kilograms of one molecule of hemoglobin?
 (b) The mass of a molecule of hemoglobin can be specified in terms of other units, too. For example, the mass of a molecule of hemoglobin might be given as 68,000 daltons. Determine the number of kilograms in 1 dalton.

28. Red blood corpuscles in the human body are constantly disintegrating and being replaced. About 73,000 of them disintegrate and are replaced every 3.16×10^{-2} second.
 (a) How many red blood corpuscles break down in 1 second? Express your answer in scientific notation.
 (b) There are approximately 25,000,000,000,000 red blood corpuscles in the blood of an adult male at any given time. About how long does it take for all of these red blood corpuscles to break down and be replaced?

29. Use the absolute-value notation to complete the following two parts of the definition of integer multiplication.
 (a) If p is positive and q is negative, then $pq =$ _____.
 (b) If p is negative and q is negative, then $pq =$ _____.

30. Use the absolute-value notation to express the answers for these division problems.
 (a) If p is positive and q is negative, then $p \div q =$ _____.
 (b) If both of p and q are negative, then $p \div q =$ _____.

31. If $x < y$, where x and y are integers, is it always true that $x^2 < y^2$? Prove or give a counterexample.

32. If $x < y$, where x and y are integers, is it always true that $z - y < z - x$, if z is an integer? Prove or give a counterexample.

33. A shopper asked for 50 cents worth of apples. The shopper was surprised when she received five more than the previous week. Then she noticed that the price had dropped 10 cents per dozen. What was the new price per dozen?

34. Prove or disprove: If $x^2 + y^2 = z^2$ for whole numbers x, y, and z, either x or y is a multiple of 3.

35. A woman born in the first half of the nineteenth century (1800 to 1849) was X years old in the year X^2. In what year was she born?

36. Assume that the statement "If $ab = 0$, then $a = 0$ or $b = 0$" is true. Prove the multiplication cancellation property. [HINT: If $ac = bc$, where $c \neq 0$, then $ac - bc = 0$, or $(a - b)c = 0$. Since $(a - b)c = 0$, what can you conclude based on the statement assumed above?]

SOLUTION OF INITIAL PROBLEM

Prove or disprove: 2 is a factor of $(a - b)(b - c)(c - a)$ for any integers a, b, c.

Strategy: Use Cases

Note that if a and b are integers with $a \neq 0$, then $a \mid b$ means $an = b$ for some integer n.

Case 1: Assume that at least two of a, b, or c are even (say, a and b are even). Then $a = 2m$, $b = 2n$, and $a - b = 2m - 2n = 2(m - n)$. Thus $2 \mid (a - b)$, so $2 \mid (a - b)(b - c)(c - a)$.

Case 2: Assume that at least two of a, b, or c are odd (say, a and b are odd). Then $a = 2m + 1$, $b = 2n + 1$, and $a - b = (2m + 1) - (2n + 1) = 2(m - n)$. Thus $2 \mid (a - b)$, so $2 \mid (a - b)(b - c)(c - a)$.

Since either at least two of a, b, or c are even or at least two are odd, we have covered all cases.

Additional Problems Where the Strategy "Use Cases" Is Useful

1. If the sum of three consecutive numbers is even, prove that two of the numbers must be odd.
2. If m and n are integers, under what circumstances will $m^2 - n^2$ be positive?
3. Show that the square of any whole number is either a multiple of 5, one more than a multiple of 5, or one less than a multiple of 5.

WRITING/DISCUSSING FOR UNDERSTANDING

1. What real-life applications of negative integers can you think of? Which of those might be useful models for introducing the concept of negative integers to students?
2. Students sometimes have difficulty with multiplication of negative integers. Describe as many arguments or models as you can to demonstrate that $(-3)(-5) = 15$.
3. Describe three different uses of the "minus sign" and how a student can determine from the context what meaning is intended.
4. A student performing the subtraction problem $4 - (-3)$ says "a negative times a negative is a positive, so this problem means $4 + 3$." How would you respond to this explanation?

PROJECTS

1. Examine several series of mathematics textbooks to determine at what stage in students' mathematical development integers are introduced and what models for integers are used in the textbooks.

2. Look for uses of negative numbers in newspapers, magazines, and so on.
3. Find more data written in scientific notation that can be used in creating problems for sixth graders.

CHAPTER REVIEW

Major Ideas

1. The set of integers includes negative numbers. Hence we are able to solve some problems that were impossible to solve in the set of fractions.
2. Integer addition and subtraction can be motivated through physical models.
3. In the set of integers, subtraction can be viewed using the following approaches: take away, adding an opposite, or missing addend.
4. The operations of integer addition, subtraction, multiplication, and division are extensions of the respective whole-number operations.
5. Integer addition and multiplication satisfy the following properties.

	Addition	Multiplication
Closure	Yes	Yes
Commutativity	Yes	Yes
Associativity	Yes	Yes
Identity	Yes	Yes
Inverse	Yes	No
Distributivity of multiplication over addition/subtraction	Yes	

6. Thinking strategies can be used to perform mental computations with integers.
7. Scientific notation is useful in solving problems involving very large or very small numbers.
8. Ordering using "less than" and "greater than" can be extended from whole numbers to integers. The following properties involving "less than" are true. The last property in the following list merits special attention.
   (a) If $a < b$ and $b < c$, then $a < c$.
   (b) If $a < b$, then $a + c < b + c$.
   (c) If $a < b$ and $p > 0$, then $ap < bp$.
   (d) If $a < b$ and $n < 0$, then $an > bn$.

Following is a list of key vocabulary, notation, and ideas for this chapter. Mentally review these items and, where appropriate, write down the meaning of each term. Then restudy the material that you are unsure of before proceeding to take the chapter test.

SECTION 8.1: ADDITION AND SUBTRACTION

Vocabulary/Notation

Integers 325
Positive integers 325
Negative integers 325
Integer number line 326
Opposite 326

Additive inverse 329
Additive cancellation 329
Take away 331
Adding the opposite 331
Missing addend 333

Ideas

Addition of integers 327
Five properties of integer addition 329
Additive cancellation 329
Subtraction of integers 330

SECTION 8.2: MULTIPLICATION, DIVISION, AND ORDER

Vocabulary/Notation

Scientific notation 344
Mantissa 344

Characteristic 344
Less than, greater than 347

Ideas

Multiplication of integers 338
Four properties of integer multiplication 340
Distributive property 340
Multiplying by opposites 341
Multiplicative cancellation 342
Zero divisors property 342
Division of integers 342
Integer exponents 343
Scientific notation 343
Ordering integers using less than 347
Four properties of less than 348

PEOPLE IN MATHEMATICS

In 1895, Grace Chisholm Young (1868–1944), who was born in England, became the first woman to receive a doctoral degree in Germany. She married William Young, a mathematician who had been her tutor in England. A curious collaboration developed between the two. Both had done important mathematical research independently, but together they produced 220 mathematical papers, several books, and six children. Their joint papers were usually published under Will's name alone because of prejudice against women mathematicians. In a letter to Grace, Will wrote, "Our papers ought to be published under our joint names, but if this were done neither of us get the benefit of it." Their daughter Cecily describes their collaboration: "My mother had decision and initiative and the stamina to carry an undertaking to its conclusion. If not for [her skill] my father's genius would probably have been abortive, and would not have eclipsed hers and the name she had already made for herself."

Martin Gardner (1914–) wrote the lively and thoughtful "Mathematical Games" column in *Scientific American* magazine for more than 20 years. Readers were served an eclectic blend of diversions—logical puzzles, number problems, card tricks, game theory, and much more. Perhaps more than anyone else in our time, Martin has succeeded in popularizing mathematics, which he calls "a kind of game that we play with the universe." There are now 14 book collections of his *Scientific American* features, and he has written more than 50 books in all. He wrote "A good mathematical puzzle, paradox, or magic trick can stimulate a child's imagination much faster than a practical application (especially if the application is remote from the child's experience), and if the game is chosen carefully, it can lead almost effortlessly into significant mathematical ideas."

CHAPTER 8 TEST

Knowledge

1. True or false?
   (a) The sum of any two negative integers is negative.
   (b) The product of any two negative integers is negative.
   (c) The difference of any two negative integers is negative.
   (d) The result of any positive integer subtracted from any negative integer is negative.
   (e) If $a < b$, then $ac < bc$ for integers a, b, and nonzero integer c.
   (f) The opposite of an integer is negative.
   (g) If $c = 0$ and $ac = bc$, then $a = b$.
   (h) The sum of an integer and its additive inverse is zero.

Skill

2. Compute each of the following problems without using a calculator.
   (a) $37 + (-43)$ (b) $(-7)(-6)$
   (c) $45 - (-3)$ (d) $16 \div (-2)$
   (e) $(-13) - 17$ (f) $(-24) \div (-8)$
   (g) $(-13)(4)$ (h) $[-24 - (-27)] \times (-4)$

3. Evaluate each of the following expressions in two ways to check the fact that $a(b + c)$ and $ab + ac$ are equal.
   (a) $a = 3, b = -4, c = 2$
   (b) $a = -3, b = -5, c = -2$

4. Express the following in scientific notation.
   (a) $(9.7 \times 10^8)(8.5 \times 10^3)$
   (b) $(5.5 \times 10^{-7}) \div (9.1 \times 10^{-2})$

Understanding

5. Name the property or properties that can be used to simplify these computations.
  (a) $(-37 + 91) + (-91)$ **(b)** $[(-2)17] \cdot 5$
  (c) $(-31)17 + (-31)83$ **(d)** $(-7)13 + 13(17)$

6. Compute using each of the three approaches: (i) take-away, (ii) adding the opposite, and (iii) missing addend.
  (a) $8 - (-5)$ **(b)** $(-2) - (-7)$

7. If a and b are negative and c is positive, determine whether the following are positive or negative.
  (a) $(-a)(-c)$ **(b)** $(-a)(b)$
  (c) $(c - b)(c - a)$ **(d)** $a(b - c)$

Problem Solving/Application

8. If $30 \leq a \leq 60$ and $-60 \leq b \leq -30$, where a and b are integers, find the largest and smallest possible *integer* values for the following expressions.
  (a) $a + b$ **(b)** $a - b$
  (c) ab **(d)** $a \div b$

9. Complete this *additive* magic square of integers using $9, -12, 3, -6, 6, -3, 12, -9$.

	0	

10. Complete this *multiplicative* magic square of integers.

		−64
	32	128
		−4

9

Rational Numbers and Real Numbers, with an Introduction to Algebra

Pythagoras

The Pythagoreans and Irrational Numbers

Pythagoras (circa 570 B.C.) was one of the most famous of all Greek mathematicians. After his studies and travels, he founded a school in southern Italy. This school, an academy for the study of philosophy, mathematics, and natural science, developed into a closely knit brotherhood with secret rites and observances. The society was dispersed, but the brotherhood continued to exist for at least two centuries after the death of Pythagoras.

Much of the work of the Pythagoreans was done using whole numbers, but they also felt that all measurements could be done with fractions. However, the hypotenuse of the unit right triangle caused them some alarm since they could not find a fraction to measure it and have consistency with the Pythagorean theorem. One feeble attempt was to say that $c = \frac{7}{5}$. Then $c^2 = \frac{49}{25}$ (which is almost 2).

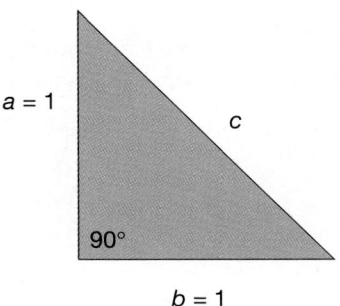

Pythagorean Theorem: $a^2 + b^2 = c^2$

Hippasus is attributed with the discovery of incommensurable ratios, that is, numbers not expressible as the ratio of two whole numbers. However, this discovery caused a great scandal among the Pythagoreans since their theory did not allow for such a number. Legend has it that Hippasus, a Pythagorean, was thrown into the sea and perished because he shared the secret of incommensurables with others outside the society. Actually, according to Aristotle, the Pythagoreans gave the first proof (using an indirect proof) that there is no fraction whose square is 2. However, they still would not accept the existence of a number whose square is 2.

By 300 B.C. many other irrational numbers were known, such as $\sqrt{3}$, $\sqrt{5}$, $\sqrt{6}$, and $\sqrt{8}$. Eudoxus, a Greek mathematician, developed a theory of incommensurables which was a geometric way of handling irrationals. This treatment was presented in Euclid's *Elements*. (See the *"Focus On"* section for Chapter 14.)

In the first century A.D. the Hindus began to manipulate irrationals like other numbers, replacing expressions such as $5\sqrt{2} + 4\sqrt{2}$ with $9\sqrt{2}$, and so on. Finally, in the late nineteenth century, irrationals were fully accepted as numbers.

3000 B.C.	Babylonians and Egyptians
500 B.C.	Pythagoreans
300 B.C.	Greeks
A.D. 100	Hindus
A.D. 1880	Acceptance of irrationals

One of the stumbling blocks in their acceptance was the fact that, as decimals, irrationals could never be expressed exactly. For example, $\pi = 3.141592654 \ldots$ has been calculated to over one billion places, but we will never know its exact decimal representation.

In this chapter, the rational and irrational numbers are developed. If you have difficulty grasping the concept of an irrational number, keep in mind that many famous mathematicians throughout history had similar difficulties.

STRATEGY 14: SOLVE AN EQUATION

Often, when applying the Use a Variable strategy to solve a problem, the representation of the problem will be an equation. The following problem yields such an equation. Techniques for solving simple equations are given in Section 9.2.

Initial Problem

A man's boyhood lasted for $\frac{1}{6}$ of his life, he played soccer for the next $\frac{1}{12}$ of his life, and he married after $\frac{1}{7}$ more of his life. A daughter was born 5 years after his marriage, and the daughter lived $\frac{1}{2}$ as many years as her father did. If the man died four years after his daughter did, how old was the man when he died?

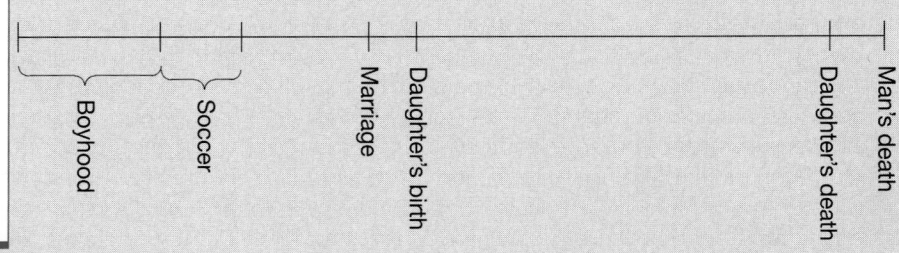

Clues

The Solve an Equation strategy may be appropriate when:

- A variable has been introduced.
- The words "is," "is equal to," or "equals" appear in a problem.
- The stated conditions can easily be represented with an equation.

A solution of the Initial Problem above appears on page 419.

INTRODUCTION

In this book we have introduced number systems much the same as they are developed in the school curriculum. The counting numbers came first. Then zero was included to form the whole numbers. Because of the need to deal with parts of a whole, fractions were introduced. Since there was a need to have numbers to represent amounts less than zero, the set of integers was introduced. The relationships among these sets are illustrated in Figure 9.1, where each arrow represents "is a subset of." For example, the set of counting numbers is a subset of the set of whole numbers, and so on. Recall that as number systems, both the fractions and integers extend the system of whole numbers.

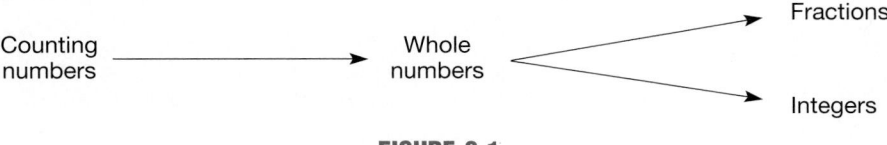

FIGURE 9.1

It is the objective of this chapter to introduce our final number systems, first the rational numbers and then the real numbers. Both of these are extensions of our existing number systems. The set of rational numbers is composed of the fractions and their opposites, and the real numbers include all of the rational numbers together with additional numbers such as π and $\sqrt{2}$. Finally, we use the real numbers to solve equations and inequalities, and graph functions.

9.1

THE RATIONAL NUMBERS

Rational Numbers: An Extension of Fractions and Integers

There are many reasons for needing numbers that have both reciprocals, as fractions do, and opposites, as integers do. For example, the fraction $\frac{2}{3}$ satisfies the equation $3x = 2$ since $3(\frac{2}{3}) = 2$ and -3 satisfies the equation $x + 3 = 0$ since $-3 + 3 = 0$. However, there is neither a fraction nor an integer that satisfies the equation $3x = -2$. To find such a number, we need the set of rational numbers.

There are various ways to introduce a set of numbers that extends both the fractions and the integers. Using models, one could merge the shaded-region model for fractions with the black and red chip model for integers. The resulting model would represent rational numbers by shading parts of wholes—models with black shaded parts to represent positive rational numbers and with red shaded parts to represent negative rational numbers.

For the sake of efficiency and mathematical clarity, we will introduce the rational numbers abstractly by focusing on the two properties we wish to extend; namely, that every nonzero number has a reciprocal and that every number has an opposite. There are two directions we can take. First, we could take all the fractions together with their opposites. This would give us a new collection of numbers, namely the fractions and numbers such as $-\frac{2}{3}$, $-\frac{5}{7}$, $-\frac{11}{2}$. A second approach would be to take the integers and form all possible "fractions" where the numerators are *integers* and the denominators are *nonzero integers*. We adopt this second approach, in which a rational number will be defined to be a *ratio* of integers. The set of rational numbers defined in this way will include the opposites of the fractions.

Definition

Rational Numbers

The set of **rational numbers** is the set

$$Q = \left\{ \frac{a}{b} \ \middle| \ a \text{ and } b \text{ are integers, } b \neq 0 \right\}.$$

Examples of rational numbers are $\frac{2}{3}$, $\frac{-5}{7}$, $\frac{4}{-9}$, $\frac{0}{1}$, and $\frac{-7}{-9}$. Mixed numbers such as $-3\frac{1}{4} = \frac{-13}{4}$, $-5\frac{2}{7} = \frac{-37}{7}$, and $2\frac{1}{3} = \frac{7}{3}$ are also rational numbers since they can be expressed in the form $\frac{a}{b}$, where a and b are integers, $b \neq 0$. Notice that every fraction is a rational number: for example, in the case when $a \geq 0$ and $b > 0$ in $\frac{a}{b}$. Also, every integer is a rational number: for example, in the case when $b = 1$ in $\frac{a}{b}$. Thus we can extend our diagram in Figure 9.1 to include the set of rational numbers (Figure 9.2).

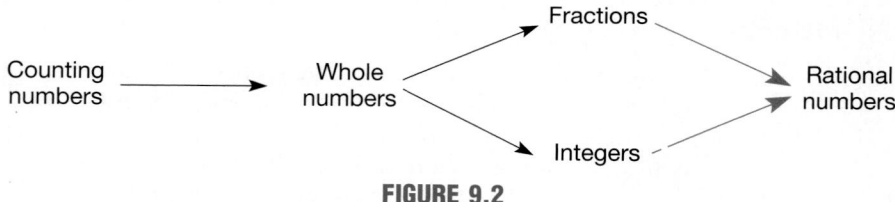

FIGURE 9.2

Equality of rational numbers and the four basic operations are defined as natural extensions of their counterparts for fractions and integers.

Definition

Equality of Rational Numbers

Let $\frac{a}{b}$ and $\frac{c}{d}$ be any rational numbers. Then $\frac{a}{b} = \frac{c}{d}$ if and only if $ad = bc$.

The equality-of-rational-numbers definition is used to find equivalent representations of rational numbers (1) to simplify rational numbers and (2) to obtain common denominators to facilitate addition, subtraction, and comparing rational numbers.

As with fractions, each rational number has an infinite number of representations. That is, by the definition of equality of rational numbers, $\frac{1}{2} = \frac{2}{4} = \frac{3}{6} = \cdots = \frac{-1}{-2} = \frac{-2}{-4} = \frac{-3}{-6} = \cdots$. The rational number $\frac{1}{2}$ can then be viewed as the idea represented by all of its various representations. Similarly, the number $\frac{-2}{3}$ should come to mind when any of the representations $\frac{-2}{3}, \frac{2}{-3}, \frac{-4}{6}, \frac{4}{-6}, \frac{-6}{9}, \frac{6}{-9}, \cdots$ are considered.

By using the definition of equality of rational numbers, it can be shown that the following theorem holds for rational numbers.

Theorem   Let $\frac{a}{b}$ be any rational number and n any nonzero integer.

Then

$$\frac{a}{b} = \frac{an}{bn} = \frac{na}{nb}.$$

A rational number $\frac{a}{b}$ is said to be in **simplest form** or in **lowest terms** if a and b have no common prime factors and b is *positive*. For example, $\frac{2}{3}, \frac{-5}{7}$, and $\frac{-3}{10}$ are in simplest form, whereas $\frac{5}{-7}, \frac{4}{6}$, and $\frac{-3}{81}$ are not because of the -7 in $\frac{5}{-7}$, and because $\frac{4}{6} = \frac{2}{3}$ and $\frac{-3}{81} = \frac{-1}{27}$.

EXAMPLE 9.1   Determine if the following pairs are equal. Then express them in simplest form.

(a) $\frac{5}{-7}, \frac{-5}{7}$ (b) $\frac{-20}{-12}, \frac{5}{3}$ (c) $\frac{16}{-30}, \frac{-8}{15}$ (d) $\frac{-15}{36}, \frac{20}{-48}$

Solution

(a) $\frac{5}{-7} = \frac{-5}{7}$ since $5 \cdot 7 = (-7)(-5)$. The simplest form is $\frac{-5}{7}$.

(b) $\frac{-20}{-12} = \frac{(-4)5}{(-4)3} = \frac{5}{3}$ due to simplification. The simplest form is $\frac{5}{3}$.

(c) $\frac{16}{-30} = \frac{-8}{15}$ since $16 \cdot 15 = 240$ and $(-30)(-8) = 240$. The simplest form is $\frac{-8}{15}$.

(d) $\dfrac{-15}{36} = \dfrac{20}{-48}$, since $(-15)(-48) = 720 = 36 \times 20$. The simplest form is $\dfrac{-5}{12}$. ∎

Addition and Its Properties

Addition of rational numbers is defined as an extension of fraction addition.

Definition

Addition of Rational Numbers

Let $\dfrac{a}{b}$ and $\dfrac{c}{d}$ be any rational numbers. Then

$$\frac{a}{b} + \frac{c}{d} = \frac{ad + bc}{bd}.$$

It follows from this definition that $\dfrac{a}{b} + \dfrac{c}{b} = \dfrac{a + c}{b}$ also.

EXAMPLE 9.2 Find these sums.

(a) $\dfrac{3}{7} + \dfrac{-5}{7}$ **(b)** $\dfrac{-2}{5} + \dfrac{4}{-7}$ **(c)** $\dfrac{-2}{5} + \dfrac{0}{5}$ **(d)** $\dfrac{5}{6} + \dfrac{-5}{6}$

Solution

(a) $\dfrac{3}{7} + \dfrac{-5}{7} = \dfrac{3 + (-5)}{7} = \dfrac{-2}{7}$

(b) $\dfrac{-2}{5} + \dfrac{4}{-7} = \dfrac{(-2)(-7) + 5 \cdot 4}{5(-7)} = \dfrac{14 + 20}{-35} = \dfrac{34}{-35} = \dfrac{-34}{35}$

(c) $\dfrac{-2}{5} + \dfrac{0}{5} = \dfrac{-2 + 0}{5} = \dfrac{-2}{5}$

(d) $\dfrac{5}{6} + \dfrac{-5}{6} = \dfrac{5 + (-5)}{6} = \dfrac{0}{6}$ ∎

Example 9.2(c) suggests that just as with the integers, the rationals have an additive identity. Also, Example 9.2(d) suggests that there is an additive inverse for each rational number. These two observations will be substantiated in the rest of this paragraph.

$$\frac{a}{b} + \frac{0}{b} = \frac{a + 0}{b} \qquad \text{Addition of rational numbers}$$

$$= \frac{a}{b} \qquad \text{Identity property for } integer \text{ addition}$$

Thus $\dfrac{0}{b}$ is an identity for addition of rational numbers; moreover, it can be shown to be unique. Because of this we write $\dfrac{0}{b}$ as 0, where b can represent any nonzero integer.

Next, let's consider additive inverses.

$$\frac{a}{b} + \frac{-a}{b} = \frac{a + (-a)}{b} \qquad \text{Addition of rational numbers}$$

$$= \frac{0}{b}. \qquad\qquad \text{Additive inverse property for } \textit{integer} \text{ addition}$$

Thus the rational number $\dfrac{-a}{b}$ is an additive inverse of $\dfrac{a}{b}$. Moreover, it can be shown that each rational number has a unique additive inverse.

Notice that $\dfrac{-a}{b} = \dfrac{a}{-b}$ since $(-a)(-b) = ab = ba$. Therefore, $\dfrac{a}{-b}$ is the additive inverse of $\dfrac{a}{b}$ also. The symbol $-\dfrac{a}{b}$ is used to represent this additive inverse. We summarize this in the following result.

Theorem   Let $\dfrac{a}{b}$ be any rational number. Then

$$-\frac{a}{b} = \frac{-a}{b} = \frac{a}{-b}.$$

We can represent the rational numbers on a line that extends both the fraction number line and the integer number line. Since every fraction and every integer is a rational number, we can begin to form the rational number line from the combination of the fraction number line and the integer number line (Figure 9.3).

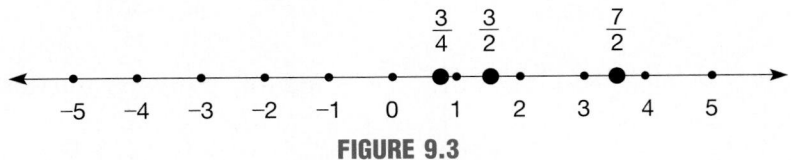

FIGURE 9.3

Just as in the case of fractions, we cannot label the entire fraction portion of the line since there are infinitely many fractions between each pair of fractions. Furthermore, this line does not represent the rational numbers since the additive inverses of the fractions are not yet represented. The additive inverses of the nonzero fractions, called the negative rational numbers, can be located by reflecting each nonzero fraction across zero

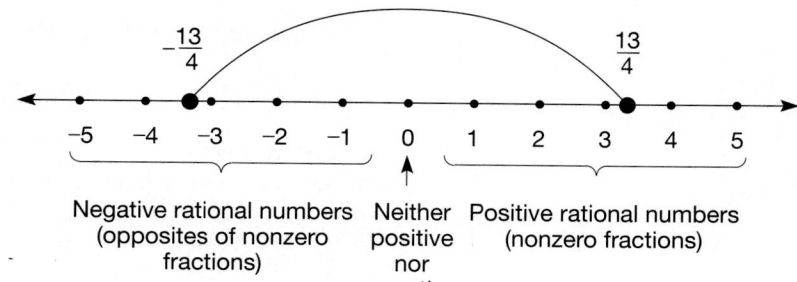

Negative rational numbers   Neither   Positive rational numbers
(opposites of nonzero   positive   (nonzero fractions)
fractions)   nor
                            negative

FIGURE 9.4

(Figure 9.4). In particular, $-\frac{2}{3}$, $-\frac{5}{7}$, $-\frac{13}{4}$, and so on, are examples of negative rational numbers. In general, $\frac{a}{b}$ is a **positive rational number** if a and b are both positive or both negative integers, and $\frac{a}{b}$ is a **negative rational number** if one of a or b is positive and the other is negative.

Next we list all the properties of rational-number addition. These properties can be verified using similar properties of integers.

Properties of Rational-Number Addition

Let $\frac{a}{b}$, $\frac{c}{d}$, and $\frac{e}{f}$ be any rational numbers.

Closure Property for Rational-Number Addition

$\frac{a}{b} + \frac{c}{d}$ is a rational number.

Commutative Property for Rational-Number Addition

$$\frac{a}{b} + \frac{c}{d} = \frac{c}{d} + \frac{a}{b}.$$

Associative Property for Rational-Number Addition

$$\left(\frac{a}{b} + \frac{c}{d}\right) + \frac{e}{f} = \frac{a}{b} + \left(\frac{c}{d} + \frac{e}{f}\right).$$

Identity Property for Rational-Number Addition

$$\frac{a}{b} + 0 = \frac{a}{b} = 0 + \frac{a}{b} \left(0 = \frac{0}{m}, m \neq 0\right).$$

Additive Inverse Property for Rational-Number Addition

For every rational number $\frac{a}{b}$ there exists a unique rational number $-\frac{a}{b}$ such that $\frac{a}{b} + \left(-\frac{a}{b}\right) = 0 = \left(-\frac{a}{b}\right) + \frac{a}{b}.$

EXAMPLE 9.3 Apply properties of rational-number addition to calculate the following sums. Try to do them mentally before looking at the solutions.

(a) $\left(\dfrac{3}{4} + \dfrac{5}{6}\right) + \dfrac{1}{4}$

(b) $\left(\dfrac{5}{7} + \dfrac{3}{8}\right) + \dfrac{-6}{16}$

Solution

(a) $\left(\dfrac{3}{4} + \dfrac{5}{6}\right) + \dfrac{1}{4} = \dfrac{1}{4} + \left(\dfrac{3}{4} + \dfrac{5}{6}\right)$ Commutativity

$= \left(\dfrac{1}{4} + \dfrac{3}{4}\right) + \dfrac{5}{6}$ Associativity

$= 1 + \dfrac{5}{6}$ Addition

$= 1\dfrac{5}{6}$ or $\dfrac{11}{6}$ Addition

(b) $\left(\dfrac{5}{7} + \dfrac{3}{8}\right) + \dfrac{-6}{16} = \dfrac{5}{7} + \left(\dfrac{3}{8} + \dfrac{-6}{16}\right)$ Associativity

$= \dfrac{5}{7} + 0$ Additive inverse

$= \dfrac{5}{7}$ Additive identity ∎

The following two consequences of the rational number properties are extensions of corresponding integer results. Their verifications are left for the problem set.

Theorem

Additive Cancellation for Rational Numbers

Let $\dfrac{a}{b}, \dfrac{c}{d}$, and $\dfrac{e}{f}$ be any rational numbers.

$$\text{If } \dfrac{a}{b} + \dfrac{e}{f} = \dfrac{c}{d} + \dfrac{e}{f}, \text{ then } \dfrac{a}{b} = \dfrac{c}{d}.$$

Theorem

Opposite of the Opposite for Rational Numbers

Let $\dfrac{a}{b}$ be any rational number. Then

$$-\left(-\dfrac{a}{b}\right) = \dfrac{a}{b}.$$

Subtraction

Since there is an additive inverse for each rational number, subtraction can be defined as an extension of integer subtraction.

Definition

Subtraction of Rational Numbers: Adding the Opposite

Let $\dfrac{a}{b}$ and $\dfrac{c}{d}$ be any rational numbers. Then

$$\frac{a}{b} - \frac{c}{d} = \frac{a}{b} + \left(-\frac{c}{d}\right)$$

The following discussion shows that this definition is also an extension of fraction subtraction.

Common Denominators

$$\frac{a}{b} - \frac{c}{b} = \frac{a}{b} + \left(-\frac{c}{b}\right) = \frac{a}{b} + \left(\frac{-c}{b}\right) = \frac{a + (-c)}{b} = \frac{a - c}{b}.$$

That is,

$$\frac{a}{b} - \frac{c}{b} = \frac{a - c}{b}.$$

Thus rational numbers with common denominators can be subtracted as is done with fractions that have common denominators, namely by subtracting numerators.

Unlike Denominators

$$\frac{a}{b} - \frac{c}{d} = \frac{ad}{bd} - \frac{bc}{bd} = \frac{ad - bc}{bd}. \qquad \text{Using common denominators}$$

EXAMPLE 9.4   Calculate the following differences and express the answers in simplest form.

(a) $\dfrac{3}{10} - \dfrac{4}{5}$

(b) $\dfrac{8}{27} - \dfrac{-1}{12}$

Solution

(a) $\dfrac{3}{10} - \dfrac{4}{5} = \dfrac{3}{10} - \dfrac{8}{10} = \dfrac{3 - 8}{10} = \dfrac{-5}{10} = \dfrac{-1}{2}$

(b) $\dfrac{8}{27} - \left(\dfrac{-1}{12}\right) = \dfrac{32}{108} - \left(\dfrac{-9}{108}\right) = \dfrac{32}{108} + \left(-\left(\dfrac{-9}{108}\right)\right) = \dfrac{41}{108}$ ■

The fact that the missing-addend approach to subtraction is equivalent to the adding-the-opposite approach is discussed in the problem set.

A fraction calculator can be used to find sums and differences of rational numbers just as we did with fractions, except that the $\boxed{+/-}$ key may have to be used. For example, $\dfrac{5}{27} - \left(\dfrac{-7}{15}\right)$ can be found as follows: 5 $\boxed{a\,b/c}$ 27 $-\backslash$ 7 $\boxed{+/-}$ $\boxed{a\,b/c}$ 15 $\boxed{=}$ $\boxed{88\rfloor135}$. Note that the $\boxed{+/-}$ key and the $\boxed{a\,b/c}$ key are pressed after the 7 to lead to $\dfrac{-7}{15}$. However, the keystrokes 7 $\boxed{a\,b/c}$ 15 $\boxed{+/-}$ would also be correct since $\dfrac{-7}{15} = \dfrac{7}{-15}$. Using a decimal calculator, the numerator, $5 \cdot 15 + 27 \cdot 7$, and the denominator, $27 \cdot 15$, can be calculated. The result, $\frac{264}{405}$ can be simplified to $\frac{88}{135}$.

Multiplication and Its Properties

Multiplication of rational numbers is defined as an extension of fraction multiplication as follows.

Definition

Multiplication of Rational Numbers

Let $\dfrac{a}{b}$ and $\dfrac{c}{d}$ be any rational numbers. Then

$$\frac{a}{b} \cdot \frac{c}{d} = \frac{ac}{bd}.$$

A fraction calculator can be used to find products of rational numbers. For example, $\dfrac{-24}{35} \cdot \dfrac{-15}{16}$ can be found as follows: 24 $\boxed{+/-}$ $\boxed{a\,b/c}$ 35 $\boxed{\times}$ 15 $\boxed{+/-}$ $\boxed{a\,b/c}$ 16 $\boxed{=}$ $\boxed{9\rfloor14}$. Also, this product can be found as follows using a decimal calculator: 24 $\boxed{\times}$ 15 $\boxed{=}$ $\boxed{360}$ (the numerator) and 35 $\boxed{\times}$ 16 $\boxed{=}$ $\boxed{560}$ (the denominator); the product is 360/560 (since the product of two negative numbers is positive, the two $\boxed{+/-}$ keys were omitted). Notice that one advantage in using most fraction calculators is that the answer appears in simplest form.

Reasoning by analogy to fraction multiplication, the following properties can be verified using the definition of rational-number multiplication and the corresponding properties of integer multiplication.

> ### Properties of Rational-Number Multiplication
>
> Let $\dfrac{a}{b}, \dfrac{c}{d}$, and $\dfrac{e}{f}$ be any rational numbers.
>
> #### Closure Property for Rational-Number Multiplication
>
> $$\frac{a}{b} \cdot \frac{c}{d} = \frac{ac}{bd} \text{ is a rational number.}$$
>
> #### Commutative Property for Rational-Number Multiplication
>
> $$\frac{a}{b} \cdot \frac{c}{d} = \frac{c}{d} \cdot \frac{a}{b}.$$
>
> #### Associative Property for Rational-Number Multiplication
>
> $$\left(\frac{a}{b} \cdot \frac{c}{d} \right) \frac{e}{f} = \frac{a}{b} \left(\frac{c}{d} \cdot \frac{e}{f} \right).$$
>
> #### Identity Property for Rational-Number Multiplication
>
> $$\frac{a}{b} \cdot 1 = \frac{a}{b} = 1 \cdot \frac{a}{b} \left(1 = \frac{m}{m}, m \neq 0 \right).$$
>
> #### Multiplicative Inverse Property for Rational-Number Multiplication
>
> For every nonzero rational number $\dfrac{a}{b}$ there exists a unique rational number $\dfrac{b}{a}$ such that $\dfrac{a}{b} \cdot \dfrac{b}{a} = 1$.

Recall that the multiplicative inverse of a number is also called the **reciprocal** of the number. Notice that the reciprocal of the reciprocal of any nonzero rational number is the original number.

It can be shown that distributivity also holds in the set of rational numbers. The verification of this fact takes precisely the same form as it did in the set of fractions and will be left for the problem set.

> ### Distributive Property of Multiplication over Addition of Rational Numbers
>
> Let $\dfrac{a}{b}, \dfrac{c}{d}$, and $\dfrac{e}{f}$ be any rational numbers. Then
>
> $$\frac{a}{b} \left(\frac{c}{d} + \frac{e}{f} \right) = \frac{a}{b} \cdot \frac{c}{d} + \frac{a}{b} \cdot \frac{e}{f}.$$

The distributive property of multiplication over subtraction also holds.

EXAMPLE 9.5   Use properties of rational numbers to compute the following problems (mentally if possible).

(a) $\dfrac{2}{3} \cdot \dfrac{5}{7} + \dfrac{2}{3} \cdot \dfrac{2}{7}$ (b) $\dfrac{-3}{5}\left(\dfrac{13}{37} \cdot \dfrac{10}{3}\right)$ (c) $\dfrac{4}{5} \cdot \dfrac{7}{8} - \dfrac{1}{4} \cdot \dfrac{4}{5}$

Solution

(a) $\dfrac{2}{3} \cdot \dfrac{5}{7} + \dfrac{2}{3} \cdot \dfrac{2}{7} = \dfrac{2}{3}\left(\dfrac{5}{7} + \dfrac{2}{7}\right) = \dfrac{2}{3}\left(\dfrac{7}{7}\right) = \dfrac{2}{3}$

(b) $\dfrac{-3}{5}\left(\dfrac{13}{37} \cdot \dfrac{10}{3}\right) = \left(\dfrac{13}{37} \cdot \dfrac{10}{3}\right)\left(\dfrac{-3}{5}\right) = \dfrac{13}{37}\left(\dfrac{10}{3} \cdot \dfrac{-3}{5}\right) = \dfrac{-26}{37}$

NOTE: Just as with fractions, we could simplify before multiplying as follows:

$$\dfrac{-3}{5}\left(\dfrac{13}{37} \cdot \dfrac{10}{3}\right) = \dfrac{-\overset{-1}{\cancel{3}}}{\cancel{5}}\left(\dfrac{13}{37} \cdot \dfrac{\overset{2}{\cancel{10}}}{\cancel{3}}\right) = \dfrac{-26}{37}$$

(c) $\dfrac{4}{5} \cdot \dfrac{7}{8} - \dfrac{1}{4} \cdot \dfrac{4}{5} = \dfrac{4}{5} \cdot \dfrac{7}{8} - \dfrac{4}{5} \cdot \dfrac{1}{4} = \dfrac{4}{5}\left(\dfrac{7}{8} - \dfrac{1}{4}\right) = \dfrac{4}{5} \cdot \dfrac{5}{8} = \dfrac{1}{2}$ ■

Division

Division of rational numbers is the natural extension of fraction division, namely, "invert the divisor and multiply" or "multiply by the reciprocal of the divisor."

Definition

Division of Rational Numbers

Let $\dfrac{a}{b}$ and $\dfrac{c}{d}$ be any rational numbers where $\dfrac{c}{d}$ is nonzero. Then

$$\dfrac{a}{b} \div \dfrac{c}{d} = \dfrac{a}{b} \times \dfrac{d}{c}.$$

The common-denominator approach to fraction division also holds for rational-number division, as illustrated next.

$$\dfrac{a}{b} \div \dfrac{c}{b} = \dfrac{a}{b} \times \dfrac{b}{c} = \dfrac{a}{c}, \text{ that is, } \dfrac{a}{b} \div \dfrac{c}{b} = \dfrac{a}{c}$$

Also, since $a \div b$ can be represented as $\dfrac{a}{b}$, the numerator and denominator of the quotient of two rationals can also be found by dividing numerators and denominators in order from left to right. That is,

$$\dfrac{a}{b} \div \dfrac{c}{d} = \dfrac{a}{b} \times \dfrac{d}{c} = \dfrac{a}{c} \times \dfrac{d}{b} = \dfrac{a}{c} \div \dfrac{b}{d} = \dfrac{a \div c}{b \div d};$$

in summary, $\dfrac{a}{b} \div \dfrac{c}{d} = \dfrac{a \div c}{b \div d}$. When c is a divisor of a, the rational number $\dfrac{a}{c}$ equals the integer $a \div c$ and, if d is a divisor of b, $\dfrac{b}{d}$ equals $b \div d$.

Thus, just as with fractions, there are three equivalent ways to divide rational numbers.

Theorem

Three Methods of Rational-Number Division

Let $\dfrac{a}{b}$ and $\dfrac{c}{d}$ be any rational numbers where $\dfrac{c}{d}$ is nonzero. Then the following are equivalent.

$$\textbf{1.} \quad \frac{a}{b} \div \frac{c}{d} = \frac{a}{b} \times \frac{d}{c}.$$

$$\textbf{2.} \quad \frac{a}{b} \div \frac{c}{b} = \frac{a}{c}.$$

$$\textbf{3.} \quad \frac{a}{b} \div \frac{c}{d} = \frac{a \div c}{b \div d}.$$

EXAMPLE 9.6 Express the following quotients in simplest form using the most appropriate of the three methods of rational-number division.

(a) $\dfrac{12}{-25} \div \dfrac{4}{5}$ **(b)** $\dfrac{13}{17} \div \dfrac{-4}{9}$ **(c)** $\dfrac{-18}{23} \div \dfrac{-6}{23}$

Solution

(a) $\dfrac{12}{-25} \div \dfrac{4}{5} = \dfrac{12 \div 4}{-25 \div 5} = \dfrac{3}{-5} = \dfrac{-3}{5}$ by dividing the numerators and denominators using method (3) of the previous theorem since $4 | 12$ and $5 | 25$.

(b) $\dfrac{13}{17} \div \dfrac{-4}{9} = \dfrac{13}{17} \times \dfrac{-9}{4} = \dfrac{-117}{68}$ by multiplying by the reciprocal using method (1).

(c) $\dfrac{-18}{23} \div \dfrac{-6}{23} = \dfrac{-18}{-6} = 3$ by the common-denominator approach using method (2) since the denominators are equal.   ■

Figure 9.5 shows how rational numbers are extensions of the fractions and the integers.

Ordering Rational Numbers

There are three equivalent ways to order rationals in much the same way as the fractions were ordered.

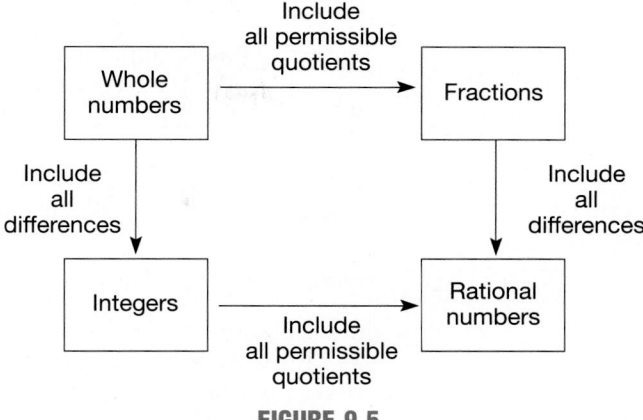

FIGURE 9.5

Number-Line Approach

$$\frac{a}{b} < \frac{c}{d}\left(\text{or } \frac{c}{d} > \frac{a}{b}\right) \text{ if and only if } \frac{a}{b} \text{ is to the left of } \frac{c}{d} \text{ on the rational}$$
number line.

Common-*Positive*-Denominator Approach

$\frac{a}{b} < \frac{c}{b}$ if and only if $a < c$ and $b > 0$. Look at some examples where

$a < c$ and $b < 0$. What can be said about $\frac{a}{b}$ and $\frac{c}{b}$ in these cases? In par-

ticular, consider the pair $\frac{3}{-5}$ and $\frac{4}{-5}$ to see why a positive denominator is

required in this approach.

Addition Approach

$\frac{a}{b} < \frac{c}{d}$ if and only if there is a *positive* rational number $\frac{p}{q}$ such that

$\frac{a}{b} + \frac{p}{q} = \frac{c}{d}$. An equivalent form of the addition approach is $\frac{a}{b} < \frac{c}{d}$ if and

only if $\frac{c}{d} - \frac{a}{b}$ is positive.

EXAMPLE 9.7 Order the following pairs of numbers using one of the three
approaches to ordering.

(a) $\frac{-3}{7}, \frac{5}{2}$ (b) $\frac{-7}{13}, \frac{-2}{13}$ (c) $\frac{-5}{7}, \frac{-3}{4}$

Solution

(a) Using the number line, all negatives are to the left of all positives, hence

$$\frac{-3}{7} < \frac{5}{2}.$$

(b) Since $-7 < -2$, we have $\dfrac{-7}{13} < \dfrac{-2}{13}$ by the common-positive-denominator approach.

(c) $\dfrac{-5}{7} - \left(-\dfrac{3}{4}\right) = \dfrac{-5}{7} + \dfrac{3}{4} = \dfrac{-20}{28} + \dfrac{21}{28} = \dfrac{1}{28}$, which is positive.

Therefore, $\dfrac{-3}{4} < \dfrac{-5}{7}$ by the addition approach. Alternately, using the common-positive-denominator approach, $\dfrac{-3}{4} = \dfrac{-21}{28} < \dfrac{-20}{28} = \dfrac{-5}{7}$. ∎

As was done with fractions, the common-positive-denominator approach to ordering can be used to develop a shortcut for determining which of two rationals is smaller.

Suppose that $\dfrac{a}{b} < \dfrac{c}{d}$, where $b > 0$ and $d > 0$.

Then $\dfrac{ad}{bd} < \dfrac{bc}{bd}$. Since $bd > 0$, we conclude that $ad < bc$.

Similarly, if $ad < bc$, where $b > 0$ and $d > 0$, then $\dfrac{ad}{bd} < \dfrac{bc}{bd}$, so

$\dfrac{a}{b} < \dfrac{c}{d}$.

We can summarize this as follows.

Theorem

Cross-Multiplication of Rational-Number Inequality

Let $\dfrac{a}{b}$ and $\dfrac{c}{d}$ be any rational numbers, where $b > 0$ and $d > 0$. Then

$$\frac{a}{b} < \frac{c}{d} \text{ if and only if } ad < bc.$$

Cross-multiplication of inequality can be applied immediately when the two rational numbers involved are in simplest form, since their denominators will be positive.

To compare $\dfrac{-37}{56}$ and $\dfrac{63}{-95}$, first rewrite both numbers with a positive denominator: $\dfrac{-37}{56}$ and $\dfrac{-63}{95}$. Now $(-37)95 = -3515$, and $(-63)(56) = -3528$, and $-3528 < -3515$. Therefore, $\dfrac{-63}{95} < \dfrac{-37}{56}$. Of course, one could also compare the two numbers using their decimal representations: $\dfrac{-37}{56} \approx -0.6607$, $\dfrac{63}{-95} \approx -0.6632$, and $-0.6632 < -0.6607$. Therefore, $\dfrac{63}{-95} < \dfrac{-37}{56}$. One could also use the fact that $\dfrac{a}{b} < \dfrac{c}{d}$ if and only if $\dfrac{ad}{b} < c$ $\left(\dfrac{a}{b} > \dfrac{c}{d} \text{ if and only if } \dfrac{ad}{b} > c\right)$, where $b, d > 0$, as we did with fractions.

The following relationships involving order, addition, and multiplication are extensions of similar ones involving fractions and integers. The verification of these is left for the problem set.

Properties of Ordering Rational Numbers

Transitive Property for Less Than
Property of Less Than and Addition
Property of Less Than and Multiplication by a Positive
Property of Less Than and Multiplication by a Negative
Density Property

Similar properties hold for $>$, $\leq$, and $\geq$. Applications of these properties are given in Section 9.2.

MATHEMATICAL MORSEL

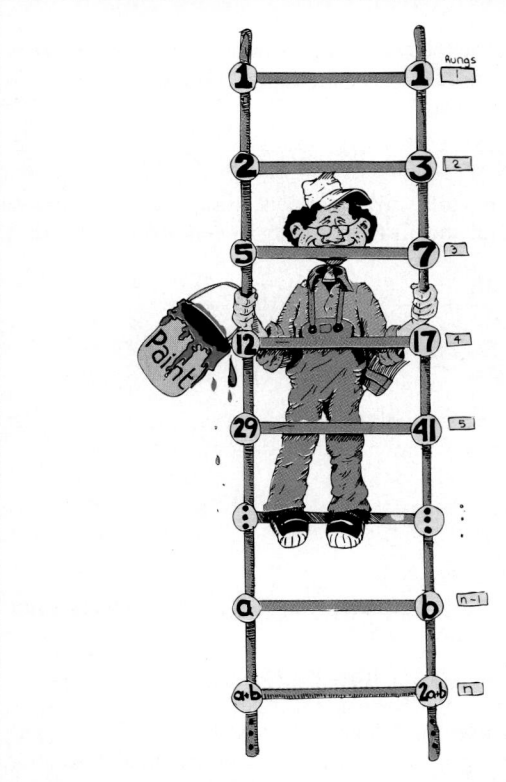

To approximate $\sqrt{2}$, the Greeks built the "ladder" of numbers below. The fourth rung "12, 17" is obtained from the third rung as follows: $12 = 5 + 7$, and $17 = 12 + 5$. In general, the nth rung, obtained by the $(n - 1)$st rung "a, b" is "$a + b, 2a + b$." The ratio of the number in the second column to the number in the first column (like 7/5 in rung 3) approaches $\sqrt{2}$.

Column 1	Column 2	Ratio	Rung
1	1	$1{:}1 = 1$	1
2	3	$3{:}2 = 1.5$	2
5	7	$7{:}5 = 1.4$	3
12	17	$17{:}12 = 1.41\overline{6}$	4
29	41	$41{:}29 = 1.413\cdots$	5
.	.	.	.
.	.	.	.
.	.	.	.
a	b	$b{:}a$	$n - 1$
$a + b$	$2a + b$	$(2a + b){:}(a + b)$	n
.	.	.	.
.	.	.	.

EXERCISE/PROBLEM SET 9.1—PART A

Exercises

1. Demonstrate how the following numbers satisfy the definition of a rational number.
(a) $-\frac{2}{3}$ (b) $-5\frac{1}{6}$ (c) 10

2. Determine which of the following pairs of rational numbers are equal (try to do mentally first).
(a) $\frac{-3}{5}$ and $\frac{63}{-105}$ (b) $\frac{-18}{-24}$ and $\frac{45}{60}$
(c) $-\frac{10}{6}$ and $\frac{-30}{-18}$ (d) $\frac{6}{-14}$ and $\frac{18}{-42}$

3. Rewrite each of the following rational numbers in simplest form.
(a) $\frac{5}{-7}$ (b) $\frac{21}{-35}$ (c) $\frac{-8}{-20}$ (d) $\frac{-144}{180}$

4. Add the following rational numbers. Express your answers in simplest form.
(a) $\frac{4}{9} + \frac{-5}{9}$ (b) $\frac{-5}{12} + \frac{11}{-12}$
(c) $\frac{-2}{5} + \frac{13}{20}$ (d) $\frac{-5}{6} + \frac{30}{36}$
(e) $\frac{8}{11} + \frac{-5}{7}$ (f) $\frac{-7}{8} + \frac{1}{12} + \frac{2}{3}$

5. Find the additive inverses of each of the following numbers.
(a) -2 (b) $\frac{5}{3}$ (c) $\frac{2}{-7}$ (d) $-\frac{5}{16}$

6. Perform the following subtractions. Express your answers in simplest form.
(a) $\frac{5}{6} - \frac{1}{6}$ (b) $\frac{3}{4} - \frac{-5}{4}$
(c) $\frac{-4}{7} - \frac{-9}{7}$ (d) $\frac{-7}{12} - \frac{5}{18}$
(e) $\frac{5}{6} - \frac{-3}{8}$ (f) $\frac{5}{24} - \frac{27}{40} - \frac{-1}{2}$

7. Perform each of the following multiplications. Express your answers in simplest form.
(a) $\frac{2}{3} \cdot \frac{7}{9}$ (b) $\frac{-5}{6} \cdot \frac{7}{3}$
(c) $\frac{-3}{10} \cdot \frac{-25}{27}$ (d) $\frac{-2}{5} \cdot \frac{-15}{24}$
(e) $\frac{-13}{49} \cdot \frac{-35}{65}$ (f) $\frac{12}{25} \cdot \frac{45}{-66}$

8. Use the properties of rational numbers to compute the following (mentally, if possible).
(a) $-\frac{3}{5} \cdot \left(\frac{11}{17} \cdot \frac{5}{3} \right)$ (b) $\left(-\frac{3}{7} \cdot \frac{10}{12} \right) \cdot \frac{6}{10}$

(c) $\frac{2}{3} \cdot \left(\frac{3}{2} + \frac{5}{7} \right)$ **(d)** $\frac{5}{9} \cdot \frac{2}{7} + \frac{2}{7} \cdot \frac{4}{9}$

(e) $\frac{7}{6} \cdot \frac{-3}{5} + \frac{3}{5} \cdot \frac{1}{6}$

(f) $\frac{-5}{6} \cdot \frac{-11}{12} - \frac{1}{3} \cdot \frac{11}{12}$

9. Divide the following rational numbers using the common-denominator approach. Express your answers in simplest form.
(a) $\frac{-12}{17} \div \frac{4}{17}$ (b) $\frac{4}{7} \div \frac{-6}{7}$ (c) $\frac{-7}{24} \div \frac{-5}{12}$

10. Divide the following rational numbers by dividing numerators and denominators. Express your answers in simplest form.
(a) $\frac{-8}{15} \div \frac{-4}{5}$ (b) $\frac{-21}{24} \div \frac{7}{8}$ (c) $\frac{33}{65} \div \frac{-11}{13}$

11. Find the multiplicative inverse (reciprocal) of the following numbers.
(a) -3 (b) $\frac{6}{7}$ (c) $\frac{-2}{5}$ (d) $\frac{11}{-17}$

12. Divide the following rational numbers by multiplying by the reciprocal of the divisor. Express your answers in simplest form.
(a) $\frac{-3}{4} \div \frac{7}{12}$ (b) $\frac{-3}{2} \div \frac{-9}{8}$ (c) $\frac{-3}{5} \div \frac{-6}{7}$

13. Find the following quotients using the most appropriate of the three methods of rational-number division.
(a) $\frac{-40}{27} \div \frac{-10}{9}$ (b) $\frac{-1}{4} \div \frac{3}{2}$
(c) $\frac{-3}{8} \div \frac{5}{6}$ (d) $\frac{21}{25} \div \frac{-3}{5}$

14. Arrange each of the following in increasing order using the common-positive-denominator approach.
(a) $\frac{-1}{6}, \frac{-5}{6}, \frac{3}{6}$ (b) $\frac{-5}{8}, \frac{7}{-8}, \frac{-9}{8}$
(c) $\frac{-2}{3}, \frac{-7}{12}, \frac{5}{-6}$

15. Order the following pairs of rational numbers using cross-multiplication.
(a) $\frac{-2}{3}, \frac{-5}{8}$ (b) $\frac{-17}{12}, \frac{-7}{5}$ (c) $\frac{-5}{7}, \frac{-7}{9}$

16. Show that the following inequalities are true by finding the positive rational number p/q in the addition approach.

(a) $\dfrac{3}{7} < \dfrac{10}{21}$ (b) $\dfrac{-3}{4} < \dfrac{-1}{6}$ (c) $\dfrac{-2}{3} > \dfrac{-3}{2}$

17. Order the following pairs of rational numbers using any of the approaches.

(a) $\dfrac{-9}{11}, \dfrac{-3}{11}$ (b) $\dfrac{-1}{3}, \dfrac{2}{5}$

(c) $\dfrac{-5}{6}, \dfrac{-9}{10}$ (d) $\dfrac{-10}{9}, \dfrac{-9}{8}$

18. The property of less than and addition for ordering rational numbers can be used to solve simple inequalities. For example,

$$x + \dfrac{3}{5} < \dfrac{-7}{10}$$

$$x + \dfrac{3}{5} + \left(-\dfrac{3}{5}\right) < \dfrac{-7}{10} + \left(-\dfrac{3}{5}\right)$$

$$x < -\dfrac{13}{10}$$

Solve the following inequalities.

(a) $x + \dfrac{1}{2} < -\dfrac{5}{6}$ (b) $x - \dfrac{2}{3} < \dfrac{-3}{4}$

(c) $x - \dfrac{6}{5} < \dfrac{-12}{7}$ (d) $x + \left(\dfrac{-3}{7}\right) > \dfrac{-4}{5}$

19. Some inequalities with rational numbers can be solved by applying the property of less than and multiplication by a positive for ordering rational numbers. For example,

$$\dfrac{2}{3}x < -\dfrac{5}{6}$$

$$\left(\dfrac{3}{2}\right)\left(\dfrac{2}{3}x\right) < \left(\dfrac{3}{2}\right)\left(-\dfrac{5}{6}\right)$$

$$x < -\dfrac{5}{4}$$

Solve the following inequalities.

(a) $\dfrac{5}{4}x < \dfrac{15}{8}$ (b) $\dfrac{3}{2}x < -\dfrac{9}{8}$ (c) $\dfrac{1}{6}x < \dfrac{-5}{12}$

20. When the property of less than and multiplication by a negative for ordering rational numbers is applied to solve inequalities, we need to be careful to change the inequality sign. For example,

$$-\dfrac{2}{3}x < -\dfrac{5}{6}$$

$$\left(-\dfrac{3}{2}\right)\left(-\dfrac{2}{3}x\right) > \left(-\dfrac{3}{2}\right)\left(-\dfrac{5}{6}\right)$$

$$x > \dfrac{5}{4}$$

Solve each of the following inequalities.

(a) $-\dfrac{3}{4}x < -\dfrac{15}{16}$ (b) $-\dfrac{3}{5}x < \dfrac{9}{10}$

(c) $-\dfrac{1}{3}x < -\dfrac{5}{6}$ (d) $\dfrac{-3}{7}x > \dfrac{8}{5}$

21. Use the properties of ordering rational numbers to solve these inequalities.

(a) $x + \dfrac{2}{3} < \dfrac{5}{6}$ (b) $x - \dfrac{3}{5} < \dfrac{-2}{5}$

(c) $\dfrac{3}{4}x < -\dfrac{5}{6}$ (d) $-\dfrac{5}{8}x < -\dfrac{15}{16}$

22. State the property that justifies each statement.

(a) $\dfrac{-2}{3} + \left(\dfrac{1}{6} + \dfrac{3}{4}\right) = \left(\dfrac{-2}{3} + \dfrac{1}{6}\right) + \dfrac{3}{4}$

(b) $\left(\dfrac{5}{6} \cdot \dfrac{7}{8}\right) \cdot \dfrac{-8}{3} = \left(\dfrac{7}{8} \cdot \dfrac{5}{6}\right) \cdot \dfrac{-8}{3}$

(c) $\dfrac{1}{4}\left(\dfrac{8}{3} + \dfrac{-5}{4}\right) = \dfrac{1}{4}\left(\dfrac{8}{3}\right) + \dfrac{1}{4}\left(\dfrac{-5}{4}\right)$

(d) $\dfrac{4}{9} + \dfrac{3}{5} < \dfrac{5}{9} + \dfrac{3}{5}$, since $\dfrac{4}{9} < \dfrac{5}{9}$

(e) $\dfrac{5}{11} \cdot \left(\dfrac{-1}{3}\right) > \dfrac{6}{11} \cdot \left(\dfrac{-1}{3}\right)$, since $\dfrac{5}{11} < \dfrac{6}{11}$

23. Calculate the following in two ways: (i) exactly as written, and (ii) calculating an answer using all positive numbers and then determining if the answer is positive or negative.

(a) $(-37)(-43)(-57)$ (b) $\dfrac{(-55)(-49)}{-35}$

(c) $\dfrac{(-1111)(-23)(49)}{-77}$ (d) $(-43)^2(-36)^3$

24. Calculate and express in simplest form.

(a) $\dfrac{13}{27} + \dfrac{-21}{31}$ (b) $\dfrac{-15}{22} - \dfrac{-31}{48}$

(c) $\dfrac{-65}{72} \times \dfrac{7}{48}$ (d) $\dfrac{43}{57} \div \dfrac{37}{72}$

25. Order the following pairs of numbers and find a number between each pair.

(a) $\dfrac{-37}{76}, \dfrac{-43}{88}$ (b) $\dfrac{59}{-97}, \dfrac{-68}{113}$

(c) $\dfrac{-113}{217}, \dfrac{-163}{314}$ (d) $\dfrac{-812}{779}, \dfrac{545}{-522}$

Problems

26. Using the definition of equality of rational numbers, prove that $\dfrac{a}{b} = \dfrac{an}{bn}$, where n is any nonzero integer.

27. Using the corresponding properties of integers and reasoning by analogy from fraction properties, prove the following properties of rational-number multiplication.

(a) Closure **(b)** Commutativity
(c) Associativity **(d)** Identity
(e) Inverse

28. (a) Complete the following statement for the missing-addend approach to subtraction.

$$\frac{a}{b} - \frac{c}{d} = \frac{e}{f} \text{ if and only if } \underline{\hspace{3cm}}.$$

(b) Assuming the adding-the-opposite approach, prove that the missing-addend approach is true.

(c) Assume that the missing-addend approach is true and prove that the adding-the-opposite approach is true.

29. Verify the distributive property of multiplication over addition for rational numbers: If $\frac{a}{b}, \frac{c}{d}$, and $\frac{e}{f}$ are rational numbers, then

$$\frac{a}{b}\left(\frac{c}{d} + \frac{e}{f}\right) = \frac{a}{b} \cdot \frac{c}{d} + \frac{a}{b} \cdot \frac{e}{f}.$$

30. Verify the following statement.

$$\text{If } \frac{a}{b} < \frac{c}{d}, \text{ then } \frac{a}{b} + \frac{e}{f} < \frac{c}{d} + \frac{e}{f}.$$

EXERCISE/PROBLEM SET 9.1—PART B

Exercises

1. (a) Which of the following are equal to -3?

$$\frac{-3}{1}, \frac{3}{1}, \frac{3}{-1}, -\frac{3}{1}, \frac{-3}{-1}, -\frac{-3}{1}, -\frac{-3}{-1}$$

(b) Which of the following are equal to $\frac{5}{6}$?

$$-\frac{5}{6}, \frac{-5}{6}, \frac{5}{-6}, \frac{-5}{-6}, -\frac{-5}{6}, -\frac{5}{-6}$$

2. Determine if the following statements are true or false.

(a) $\dfrac{-32}{22} = \dfrac{48}{-33}$ **(b)** $\dfrac{-75}{-65} = \dfrac{21}{18}$

3. Rewrite each of the following rational numbers in simplest form.

(a) $\dfrac{4}{-6}$ **(b)** $\dfrac{-60}{-84}$ **(c)** $\dfrac{64}{-144}$

4. Add the following rational numbers. Express your answers in simplest form.

(a) $\dfrac{3}{10} + \dfrac{-8}{10}$ **(b)** $\dfrac{-5}{4} + \dfrac{1}{9}$

(c) $\dfrac{-5}{6} + \dfrac{5}{12} + \dfrac{-1}{4}$ **(d)** $\dfrac{-3}{8} + \dfrac{5}{12}$

5. Apply the properties of rational-number addition to calculate the following sums. Do as many as you can mentally.

(a) $\dfrac{5}{7} + \left(\dfrac{9}{7} + \dfrac{5}{8}\right)$ **(b)** $\left(\dfrac{5}{9} + \dfrac{3}{5}\right) + \dfrac{4}{9}$

(c) $\left(\dfrac{3}{11} + \dfrac{-18}{66}\right) + \dfrac{17}{23}$ **(d)** $\left(\dfrac{3}{17} + \dfrac{6}{29}\right) + \dfrac{3}{-17}$

6. Perform the following subtractions. Express your answers in simplest form.

(a) $\dfrac{8}{9} - \dfrac{2}{9}$ **(b)** $\dfrac{-3}{7} - \dfrac{3}{4}$ **(c)** $\dfrac{2}{9} - \dfrac{-7}{12}$

7. Multiply the following rational numbers. Express your answers in simplest form.

(a) $\dfrac{3}{5} \cdot \dfrac{-10}{21}$ **(b)** $\dfrac{-6}{11} \cdot -\dfrac{-33}{18}$

(c) $\dfrac{5}{12} \cdot \dfrac{48}{-15} \cdot \dfrac{-9}{8}$ **(d)** $\dfrac{-6}{11} \cdot \dfrac{-22}{21} \cdot \dfrac{7}{-12}$

8. Apply the properties of rational numbers to compute the following (mentally, if possible).

(a) $\dfrac{2}{9} + \left(\dfrac{3}{5} + \dfrac{7}{9}\right)$

(b) $\dfrac{3}{7}\left(\dfrac{-11}{21}\right) + \left(\dfrac{-3}{7}\right)\left(\dfrac{-11}{21}\right)$

(c) $\dfrac{3}{7} + \left(\dfrac{5}{6} + \dfrac{-3}{7}\right)$

(d) $\left(\dfrac{-9}{7} \cdot \dfrac{23}{-27}\right) \cdot \left(\dfrac{-7}{9}\right)$

9. (a) Find the opposite of the reciprocal of $-\frac{6}{5}$.
(b) Find the reciprocal of the opposite of $-\frac{6}{5}$.
(c) Repeat parts (a) and (b) using $-\frac{13}{17}$ in place of $-\frac{6}{5}$.
(d) What do you conclude?

10. Find the following quotients. Express your answer in simplest form.

(a) $\dfrac{-8}{9} \div \dfrac{2}{9}$ **(b)** $\dfrac{12}{15} \div \dfrac{-4}{3}$ **(c)** $\dfrac{-10}{9} \div \dfrac{-5}{4}$

11. Locate the following points on the rational number line. Then list them in increasing order.

$$-\frac{3}{5}, \frac{7}{6}, -\frac{14}{5}, -\frac{3}{2}, -6, \frac{7}{3}$$

12. Put the appropriate symbol, $<$, $=$, or $>$, between each pair of rational numbers to make a true statement.

(a) $-\frac{5}{6}$ ___ $-\frac{11}{12}$ **(b)** $-\frac{1}{3}$ ___ $\frac{5}{4}$

(c) $\frac{-12}{15}$ ___ $\frac{36}{-45}$ **(d)** $-\frac{3}{12}$ ___ $\frac{-4}{20}$

13. Using a calculator and cross-multiplication of inequality, order the following pairs of rational numbers.

(a) $\frac{-231}{356}, \frac{-152}{201}$ **(b)** $\frac{-761}{532}, \frac{-637}{315}$

(c) $\frac{475}{652}, \frac{-308}{-421}$

14. Calculate and express in simplest form.

(a) $\frac{25}{33} + \frac{-23}{39}$ **(b)** $\frac{47}{49} - \frac{19}{-35}$

(c) $\frac{67}{42} \times \frac{51}{59}$ **(d)** $\frac{213}{76} \div \frac{-99}{68}$

15. Let W = the set of whole numbers
F = the set of (nonnegative) fractions
I = the set of integers
N = the set of negative integers
Q = the set of rational numbers
List all the sets that have the following properties.
(a) -5 is an element of the set.
(b) $-\frac{3}{4}$ is an element of the set.
(c) The set is closed under addition.
(d) The set is closed under subtraction.
(e) The set is closed under multiplication.
(f) The set is closed under division.
(g) The set has an additive identity.
(h) The set has a multiplicative identity.
(i) The set has additive inverses for each element.
(j) The set has multiplicative inverses for each nonzero element.

16. State the property that justifies each statement.

(a) $-\frac{2}{3}\left(\frac{3}{2} \cdot \frac{3}{5}\right) = \left(-\frac{2}{3} \cdot \frac{3}{2}\right) \cdot \frac{3}{5}$

(b) $\frac{-7}{9}\left(\frac{3}{2} + \frac{-4}{5}\right) = \frac{-7}{9}\left(\frac{-4}{5} + \frac{3}{2}\right)$

(c) $\left(\frac{-3}{5}\right) + \left(\frac{-5}{6}\right) < \left(\frac{-1}{5}\right) + \left(\frac{-5}{6}\right)$, since

$\frac{-3}{5} < \frac{-1}{5}$

17. Given that the first part of each of the following statements is true, does the conclusion necessarily follow?

(a) If $\frac{-3}{4} < \frac{-2}{3}$ and $\frac{-2}{3} < \frac{-1}{3}$, then

$\frac{-3}{4} < \frac{-1}{3}$.

(b) If $\frac{11}{23} + \frac{1}{4} < \frac{7}{8}$, then $\frac{11}{23} < \frac{7}{8} - \frac{1}{4}$.

(c) If $\frac{5}{6} > \frac{3}{4}$, then $\frac{-5}{6} > \frac{-3}{4}$.

(d) If $\frac{-3}{2} < \frac{-7}{8}$, then

$\left(\frac{-3}{2}\right)\left(\frac{-5}{11}\right) > \left(\frac{-7}{8}\right)\left(\frac{-5}{11}\right)$.

18. The set of rational numbers also has the density property. Recall some of the methods we used for fractions and find three rational numbers between each pair of given numbers.

(a) $\frac{-3}{4}$ and $\frac{-1}{2}$ **(b)** $\frac{-5}{6}$ and $\frac{-7}{8}$

(c) $\frac{-5}{4}$ and $\frac{-6}{5}$

19. Use the properties of ordering rational numbers to solve these inequalities.

(a) $x - \frac{5}{6} < \frac{9}{10}$ **(b)** $-\frac{3}{4}x > \frac{9}{16}$

Problems

20. The closure property for rational-number addition can be verified as follows.

$$\frac{a}{b} + \frac{c}{d} = \frac{ad + bc}{bd} \qquad \text{by definition of addition}$$

$ad + bc$ and bd are both integers by closure properties of integer addition and multiplication and $bd \neq 0$. Therefore, by the definition of rational number,

$$\frac{ad + bc}{bd} \text{ is a rational number.}$$

In a similar way, verify the following properties of rational-number addition.
(a) Commutative **(b)** Associative

21. Which of the following properties hold for subtraction of rational numbers? Verify the property or give a counterexample.
(a) Closure **(b)** Commutative
(c) Associative **(d)** Identity
(e) Inverse

22. Prove that additive cancellation holds for the rational numbers:

$$\text{If } \frac{a}{b} + \frac{e}{f} = \frac{c}{d} + \frac{e}{f}, \quad \text{then } \frac{a}{b} = \frac{c}{d}.$$

23. The positive rational numbers can be defined as those a/b where $ab > 0$. Determine if the following are true or false. If true, prove; if false, give a counterexample.
  (a) The sum of two positive rationals is a positive rational.
  (b) The difference of two positive rationals is a positive rational.
  (c) The product of two positive rationals is a positive rational.
  (d) The quotient of two positive rationals is a positive rational.

24. Using additive cancellation, prove $-\left(-\dfrac{a}{b}\right) = \dfrac{a}{b}$.

25. Given: $\dfrac{a}{b} \cdot \left(\dfrac{c}{d} + \dfrac{e}{f}\right) = \dfrac{a}{b} \cdot \dfrac{c}{d} + \dfrac{a}{b} \cdot \dfrac{e}{f}$

Prove: $\dfrac{a}{b} \cdot \left(\dfrac{c}{d} - \dfrac{e}{f}\right) = \dfrac{a}{b} \cdot \dfrac{c}{d} - \dfrac{a}{b} \cdot \dfrac{e}{f}$

26. Prove: If $\dfrac{a}{b} < \dfrac{c}{d}$ and $\dfrac{c}{d} < \dfrac{e}{f}$, then $\dfrac{a}{b} < \dfrac{e}{f}$.

27. Prove each of the following statements.
  (a) If $\dfrac{a}{b} < \dfrac{c}{d}$ and $\dfrac{e}{f} > 0$, then $\dfrac{a}{b} \cdot \dfrac{e}{f} < \dfrac{c}{d} \cdot \dfrac{e}{f}$.
  (b) If $\dfrac{a}{b} < \dfrac{c}{d}$ and $\dfrac{e}{f} < 0$, then $\dfrac{a}{b} \cdot \dfrac{e}{f} > \dfrac{c}{d} \cdot \dfrac{e}{f}$.

9.2

THE REAL NUMBERS

Real Numbers: An Extension of Rational Numbers

You may have surmised that as with fractions, each rational number has a repeating decimal representation. (Remember that terminating decimals are those decimals that repeat zero.) The only difference is that the rational numbers include negative repeating decimals. But what about the number 0.2020020002 . . . , where after each successive 2 the number of zeros is increased by one? This is certainly an infinite decimal, but it is *not* repeating since the number of zeros continues to increase. Therefore, it is not a rational number. Then what type of number is it? Let's approach this question from another point of view.

The equation $x - 3 = 0$ has a whole-number solution, namely 3. However, the equation $x + 3 = 0$ does not have a *whole* number solution. But the equation $x + 3 = 0$ does have an *integer* solution, namely -3. Now consider the equation $3x = 2$. This equation has neither a whole number nor an integer solution. But the *fraction* $\frac{2}{3}$ is a solution of $3x = 2$. What about the equation $-3x = 2$? We must move to the set of *rationals* to find its solution, namely $-\frac{2}{3}$. Since solving equations plays an important role in mathematics, we want to have a number system that will allow us to solve many types of equations. Mathematicians encountered great difficulty when attempting to solve the equation $x^2 = 2$ using rational numbers. Because of its historical significance, we give a proof to show that it is actually *impossible* to find a rational number whose square is 2.

Theorem   There is no rational number whose square is 2.

Proof

Use indirect reasoning. Suppose that there is a rational number $\dfrac{a}{b}$ such that $\left(\dfrac{a}{b}\right)^2 = 2$. Then we have the following.

$$\left(\frac{a}{b}\right)^2 = 2$$

$$\frac{a^2}{b^2} = 2$$

$$a^2 = 2b^2.$$

Now the argument will become a little subtle. By the fundamental theorem of arithmetic, the numbers a^2 and $2b^2$ have the same prime factorization. Because squares have prime factors that occur in pairs, a^2 must have an *even* number of prime factors in its prime factorization. Similarly, b^2 has an even number of prime factors in its prime factorization. But 2 is a prime also, so $2 \cdot b^2$ has an *odd* number of prime factors in its prime factorization. (Note that b^2 contributes an even number of prime factors, and the factor 2 produces one more, hence an odd number of prime factors.) Recapping, $a^2 = 2b^2$, a^2 has an even number of prime factors in its prime factorization and $2b^2$ has an odd number of prime factors in its prime factorization. According to the fundamental theorem of arithmetic, it is impossible for a number to have an even number of prime factors *and* an odd number of prime factors in its prime factorization. Thus there is *no* rational number whose square is 2. ■

Using similar reasoning, it can be shown that for *every* prime p there is no rational number, $\dfrac{a}{b}$, whose square is p. We leave that verification for the problem set.

Using a calculator, one can show that the square of the rational number 1.414213562 is very close to 2. However, we have proved that *no* rational number squared is exactly 2. Consequently, we have a need for a new system of numbers that will include infinite nonrepeating decimals, such as 0.020020002 . . . , as well as numbers that are solutions to equations such as $x^2 = p$, where p is a prime.

Definition

Real Numbers

The set of **real numbers**, R, is the set of all numbers that have an infinite decimal representation.

Thus the real numbers contain all the rationals (which are the infinite *repeating* decimals, positive, negative, or zero) together with a new set of numbers called appropriately, the irrational numbers. The set of **irrational numbers** is the set of numbers that have infinite *nonrepeating* decimal representations. Figure 9.6 shows the different types of decimals. Since irrational numbers have infinite nonrepeating decimal representations, rational-number approximations (using finite decimals) have to be used to perform approximate computations in some cases.

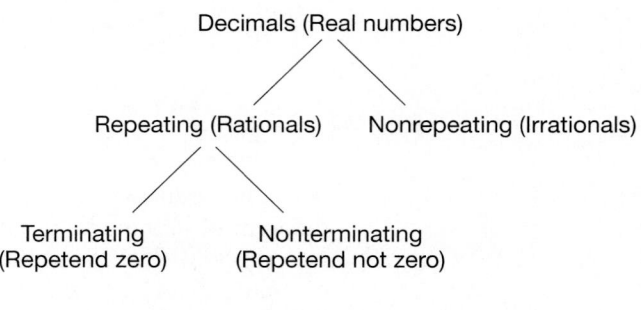

FIGURE 9.6

EXAMPLE 9.8   Determine if the following decimals represent rational or irrational numbers.

(a) 0.273 **(b)** $3.14159.\,.\,.$ **(c)** $-15.7\overline{6}$

Solution

(a) 0.273 is a rational number since it is a terminating decimal.

(b) $3.14159.\,.\,.$ should be considered to be irrational since the three dots indicate an infinite decimal and there is no repetend indicated.

(c) $-15.7\overline{6}$ is rational since it is a repeating decimal.   ■

Now we can extend our diagram in Figure 9.2 to include the real numbers (Figure 9.7).

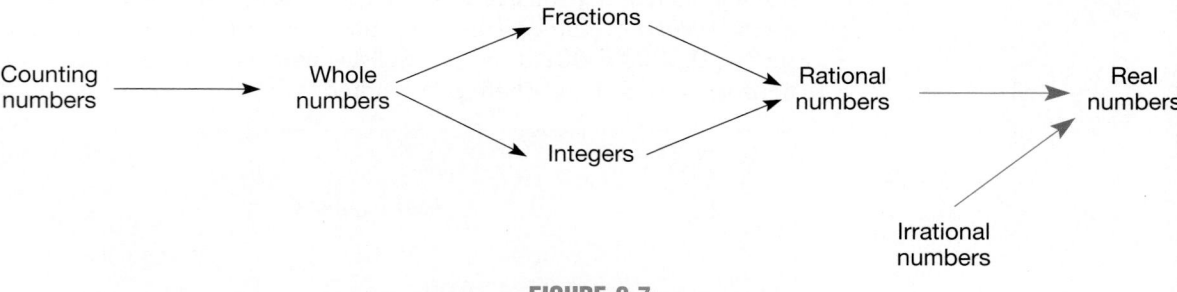

FIGURE 9.7

In terms of a number line, the points representing real numbers completely fill in the gaps in the rational number line. In fact, the points in the gaps represent irrational numbers (Figure 9.8).

Real Number Line

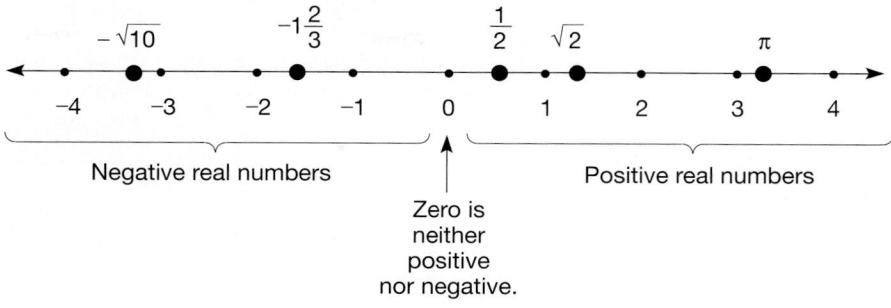

FIGURE 9.8

Let's take this geometric representation of the real numbers one step further. The Pythagorean theorem from geometry states that in a right triangle whose sides have lengths a and b and whose hypotenuse has length c, the equation $a^2 + b^2 = c^2$ holds (Figure 9.9).

Now consider the construction in Figure 9.10. The length c is found by using the Pythagorean theorem:

$$1^2 + 1^2 = c^2 \quad \text{or} \quad c^2 = 2.$$

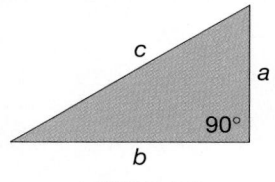

FIGURE 9.9

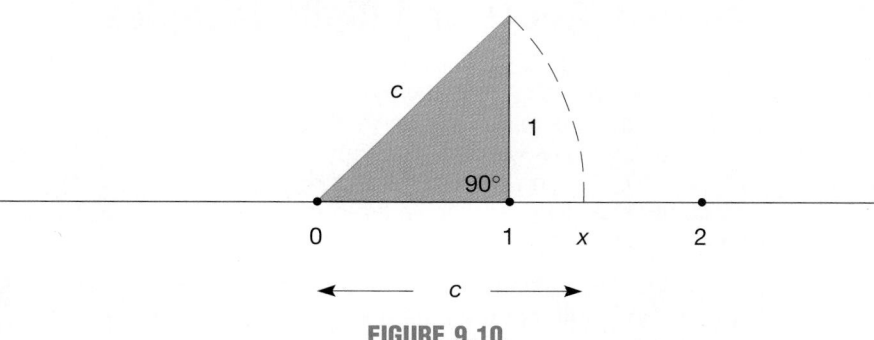

FIGURE 9.10

Moreover, the length of the segment from 0 to x is c also, since the dashed arc in Figure 9.10 is a portion of a circle. Thus $x = c$ where $c^2 = 2$. Since we know the number whose square is 2 is not rational, c must have an infinite *nonrepeating* decimal representation. To represent c with numerals other than an infinite nonrepeating decimal, we need the concept of square root.

Since both $(-3)^2$ and 3^2 equal 9, -3 and 3 are called **square roots** of 9. The symbol $\sqrt{a}$ represents the *nonnegative* square root of a, called the **principal square root**. For example, $\sqrt{4} = 2$, $\sqrt{25} = 5$, $\sqrt{144} = 12$, and so on. We can also write symbols such as $\sqrt{2}$, $\sqrt{3}$, and $\sqrt{17}$. These numbers are not rational, so they have infinite nonrepeating decimal representations. Thus it is necessary to leave them written as $\sqrt{2}$, $\sqrt{3}$, $\sqrt{17}$, and so on. According to the definition, though, we know that $(\sqrt{2})^2 = 2$, $(\sqrt{3})^2 = 3$, and $(\sqrt{17})^2 = 17$.

> **Definition**
>
> ### Square Root
>
> Let a be a nonnegative real number. Then the **square root** of a (i.e., the principal square root of a), written $\sqrt{a}$, is defined as
>
> $$\sqrt{a} = b \qquad \text{where } b^2 = a \text{ and } b \geq 0.$$

Calculators can be used to find square roots. First, a $\boxed{\sqrt{}}$ key can be used. For example, to find $\sqrt{3}$, press 3 $\boxed{\sqrt{}}$ $\boxed{=}$ $\boxed{1.732050808}$ or perhaps simply 3 $\boxed{\sqrt{}}$. (Some calculators have "$\sqrt{}$" as a second function.) The $\boxed{\sqrt[x]{y}}$ may also be used where the x is 2 for square root. To find $\sqrt{3}$ using $\boxed{\sqrt[x]{y}}$, press 3 $\boxed{\sqrt[x]{y}}$ 2 $\boxed{=}$ $\boxed{1.732050808}$. Generally, the first number entered is the y and the second is x.

STUDENT PAGE SNAPSHOT

MATH *CONNECTION:* GEOMETRY

Square Roots and Right Triangles

A. The world's longest aerial tramway climbs to the summit of Sandia Peak in Albuquerque, New Mexico. The tram wires rise 0.7 mi in a horizontal distance of 2.6 mi. How long are the wires to the nearest tenth of a mile?

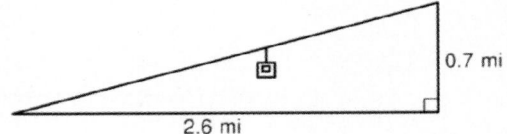

Recall that the Pythagorean Theorem relates the lengths of the legs and the hypotenuse of a right triangle.

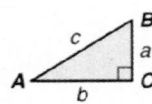

In $\triangle ABC$, $a^2 + b^2 = c^2$.

Substitute to find the length of the tram wires.

$$a^2 + b^2 = c^2$$
$$(0.7)^2 + (2.6)^2 = c^2$$
$$0.49 + 6.76 = c^2$$
$$7.25 = c^2$$
$$\sqrt{7.25} = c$$

$\boxed{2.6925824} \approx c$

Think: A number, c, squared is 7.25. Find $\sqrt{7.25}$.

The wires are about 2.7 mi long.

One can observe that there are infinitely many irrational numbers, namely $\sqrt{p}$, where p is a prime. However, the fact that there are many more irrationals will be developed in the problem set. The number pi (π), of circle fame, was proved to be irrational around 1870; π is the ratio of the circumference to the diameter in any circle.

Using the decimal representation of real numbers, addition, multiplication, subtraction, and division of real numbers can be defined as extensions of similar operations in the rationals. The following properties hold (although it is beyond the scope of this book to prove them).

Properties of Real-Number Operations

Addition	**Multiplication**
Closure	*Closure*
Commutativity	*Commutativity*
Associativity	*Associativity*
Identity (**0**)	*Identity* (**1**)
Inverse ($-a$)	*Inverse* $\left(\dfrac{1}{a} \text{ for } a \neq 0\right)$

Distributivity of Multiplication over Addition

Also, subtraction is defined by $a - b = a + (-b)$, and division is defined by $a \div b = a \cdot \dfrac{1}{b}$, where $b \neq 0$. "Less than" and "greater than" can be defined as extensions of ordering in the rationals, namely $a < b$ if and only if $a + p = b$ for some positive real number p. The following order properties also hold. Similar properties hold for $>$, $\leq$, and $\geq$.

Properties of Ordering Real Numbers

Transitive Property of Less Than
Property of Less Than and Addition
Property of Less Than and Multiplication by a Positive
Property of Less Than and Multiplication by a Negative
Density Property

You may have observed that the system of real numbers satisfies all of the properties that we have identified for the system of rational numbers. The main property that distinguishes the two systems is that the real numbers are "complete" in the sense that this is the set of numbers that finally fills up the entire number line. Even though the rational numbers are dense, there are still infinitely many gaps in the rational number line, namely, the points that represent the irrationals. Together, the rationals and irrationals comprise the entire real number line.

Rational Exponents

Now that we have the set of real numbers, we can extend our study of exponents to rational exponents. We begin by generalizing the definition of square root to more general types of roots. For example, since $(-2)^3 = -8$, -2 is called the cube root of -8. Because of negative numbers, the definition must be stated in two parts.

Definition

nth Root

Let a be a real number and n be a positive integer.

1. If $a \geq 0$, then $\sqrt[n]{a} = b$ if and only if $b^n = a$ and $b \geq 0$.
2. If $a < 0$ and n is odd, then $\sqrt[n]{a} = b$ if and only if $b^n = a$.

EXAMPLE 9.9   Where possible, write the following values in simplest form by applying the previous two definitions.

(a) $\sqrt[4]{81}$

(b) $\sqrt[5]{-32}$

(c) $\sqrt[6]{-64}$

Solution

(a) $\sqrt[4]{81} = b$ if and only if $b^4 = 81$. Since $3^4 = 81$, we have $\sqrt[4]{81} = 3$.

(b) $\sqrt[5]{-32} = b$ if and only if $b^5 = -32$. Since $(-2)^5 = -32$, we have $\sqrt[5]{-32} = -2$.

(c) It is tempting to begin to apply the definition and write $\sqrt[6]{-64} = b$ if and only if $b^6 = -64$. However, since b^6 must always be positive or zero, there is no real number b such that $\sqrt[6]{-64} = b$. ■

The number a in $\sqrt[n]{a}$ is called the **radicand** and n is called the **index**. The symbol $\sqrt[n]{a}$ is read **the nth root of a** and is called a **radical**. Notice that $\sqrt[n]{a}$ has not been defined for the case when n is even and a is negative. This is because $b^n \geq 0$ for any real number b and n an even positive integer. For example, there is no real number b such that $b = \sqrt{-1}$. For if there were, then $b^2 = -1$. This is impossible since, by the property of less than and multiplication by a positive (or negative), it can be shown that the square of any nonzero real number is positive.

Roots of real numbers can be calculated by using a $\boxed{\sqrt[x]{y}}$ key. For example, to find $\sqrt[5]{30}$, press 30 $\boxed{\sqrt[x]{y}}$ 5 $\boxed{=}$ $\boxed{1.9743505}$. (NOTE: Some calculators require that you press a second function key to get to the $\boxed{\sqrt[x]{y}}$ function.) Also, a mental check, since $2^5 = 32$, a good estimate of $\sqrt[5]{30}$ is a number somewhat less than 2. Hence the answer 1.9743505 is a reasonable approximation for $\sqrt[5]{30}$.

Using the concept of radicals, we can now proceed to define rational exponents. What would be a good definition of $3^{1/2}$? If the usual additive property of exponents is to hold, then $3^{1/2} \cdot 3^{1/2} = 3^{1/2+1/2} = 3^1 = 3$. But $\sqrt{3} \cdot \sqrt{3} = 3$. Thus $3^{1/2}$ should represent $\sqrt{3}$. Similarly, $5^{1/3} = \sqrt[3]{5}$, $2^{1/7} = \sqrt[7]{2}$, and so on. We summarize this idea in the next definition.

Definition

Unit Fraction Exponent

Let a be any real number and n any positive integer. Then

$$a^{1/n} = \sqrt[n]{a}$$

where

    1. n is arbitrary when $a \geq 0$, and
    2. n must be odd when $a < 0$.

For example, $(-8)^{1/3} = \sqrt[3]{-8} = -2$, and $81^{1/4} = \sqrt[4]{81} = 3$.

The combination of this last definition with the definitions for integer exponents leads us to this final definition of **rational exponent**. For example, taking into account the previous definition and our earlier work with exponents, a natural way to think of $27^{2/3}$ would be $(27^{1/3})^2$. For the sake of simplicity, we restrict our definition to rational exponents of nonnegative real numbers.

Definition

Rational Exponent

Let a be a nonnegative real number, and $\dfrac{m}{n}$ be a rational number in simplest form. Then $a^{m/n} = (a^{1/n})^m = (a^m)^{1/n}$.

EXAMPLE 9.10 Express the following values without exponents.
(a) $9^{3/2}$ **(b)** $16^{5/4}$ **(c)** $125^{-4/3}$

Solution
(a) $9^{3/2} = (9^{1/2})^3 = 3^3 = 27$
(b) $16^{5/4} = (16^{1/4})^5 = 2^5 = 32$
(c) $125^{-4/3} = (125^{1/3})^{-4} = 5^{-4} = \dfrac{1}{5^4} = \dfrac{1}{625}$ ■

The following properties hold for rational exponents.

Properties of Rational Exponents

Let a, b represent positive real numbers and m, n positive rational exponents. Then

$$a^m a^n = a^{m+n}$$
$$a^m b^m = (ab)^m$$
$$(a^m)^n = a^{mn}$$
$$a^m \div a^n = a^{m-n}.$$

Real-number exponents are defined using more advanced mathematics, and they have the same properties as rational exponents.

An exponent key such as $\boxed{y^x}$ or $\boxed{x^y}$ can be used to calculate real exponents. For example, to calculate $3^{\sqrt{2}}$, press 3 $\boxed{y^x}$ 2 $\boxed{\sqrt{}}$ $\boxed{=}$ $\boxed{4.7288044}$.

Introduction to Algebra

Solving equations and inequalities is one of the most important processes in mathematics. Traditionally, this topic represents a substantial portion of an entire course in introductory algebra. An **equation** is a sentence involving numbers, or symbols representing numbers where the verb is "equals" (=); an **inequality** is a sentence whose verb is one of the following: $<$, $\leq$, $>$, $\geq$, or $\neq$. Examples of equations and inequalities follow.

Equations	**Inequalities**
$x + 3 = 7$	$2x + 4 < -17$
$\dfrac{1}{3}x + \dfrac{2}{5} = \dfrac{2}{7}x - \dfrac{4}{13}$	$(\sqrt{2})x - \dfrac{2}{5} \leq 8x - \dfrac{1}{\sqrt{3}}$

The following treatment will be limited to solving equations of the form $ax + b = cx + d$, where a, b, c, d, and x are real numbers, as well as inequalities of the form $ax + b \leq cx + d$. The symbol x is a **variable**. We will permit variables to represent real numbers. When a particular number replaces a variable to produce a true equation (or inequality), that number is called a **solution**. The set of all solutions for a given equation (inequality) is called the **solution set** of the equation (inequality). For example, the solution set of the equation $x + 3 = 7$ is $\{4\}$, of $x + 4 < 7$ is $\{x \mid x < 3\}$, and so on. To **solve** an equation or inequality means to find its solution set.

Solving Equations

Before we solve equations of the form $ax + b = cx + d$, the next example shows three different ways to solve equations of the form $ax + b = c$.

EXAMPLE 9.11   Solve the equation $3x + 4 = 19$.

Solution

Guess and Test: As the name of this method suggests, one guesses values for the variable and substitutes to see if a true equation results.

Try $x = 1$: $3(1) + 4 = 7 \neq 19$.
Try $x = 4$: $3(4) + 4 = 16 \neq 19$.
Try $x = 5$: $3(5) + 4 = 19$. Therefore, 5 is a solution of the equation.

Cover Up: In this method we cover up the term with the variable: $\square + 4 = 19$. To make a true equation, the $\square$ must be 15. Thus $3x = 15$. Since $3 \cdot 5 = 15$, x must be 5.

Work Backward: The left side of the equation shows that x was *multiplied* by 3 and then 4 was *added* to obtain 19. Thus if we *subtract* 4 from 19 and *divide* by 3, we can work backward to the value of x. Here $19 - 4 = 15$ and $15 \div 3 = 5$, so $x = 5$. The diagram to the left summarizes this approach.   ■

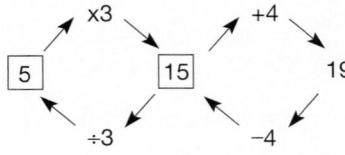

Next we develop a systematic approach for solving more complex equations and inequalities. Consider equations of the form $ax + b = cx + d$, where x is a variable and a, b, c, and d are fixed real numbers. Here, a and c are called **coefficients** of the variable x; they are numbers multiplied by a variable. We begin with an elementary form and proceed to more complex forms.

Form 1. $x + a = b$

Solve: $x + 4 = 7$.

Concrete/Pictorial Representation	Abstract Representation

$$x + 4 = 7$$

There are four coins and some more hidden from view behind the square. Altogether they balance seven coins. How many coins are hidden?
(NOTE: Throughout this section we are assuming that the coins are identical.)

Add (-4) to both sides.
$$x + 4 + (-4) = 7 + (-4)$$
$$x + 0 = 3$$
$$x = 3$$

Remove four coins from each side. There are three coins hidden.

Form 2. $ax + b = c$

Solve: $3x + 6 = 12$.

Concrete/Pictorial Representation	Abstract Representation

$$3x + 6 = 12$$

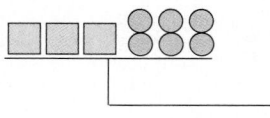
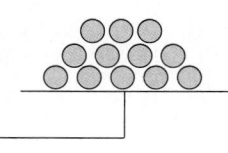

Remove six coins from each side.

Add (-6) to both sides (equivalently, subtract 6 from both sides).

$$3x + 6 + (-6) = 12 + (-6)$$
$$3x = 6$$

Divide the coins into three equal piles (one pile for each square). Each square hides two coins.

Multiply both sides by $\frac{1}{3}$ (equivalently, divide both sides by 3).

$$\left(\frac{1}{3}\right)3x = \left(\frac{1}{3}\right)6$$

$$\left(\frac{1}{3} \cdot 3\right)x = 2$$

$$1 \cdot x = 2$$
$$x = 2$$

Form 3. $ax + b = cx + d$
   Solve: $4x + 5 = 2x + 13$.

Concrete/Pictorial Representation

Abstract Representation

$$4x + 5 = 2x + 13$$

Remove five coins from each pan. (We could have removed the coins behind two squares from each pan also.)

Add (-5) to both sides (equivalently, subtract 5 from both sides).

$$4x + 5 + (-5) = 2x + 13 + (-5)$$
$$4x = 2x + 8$$

Remove all the coins behind two squares from each pan. Remember, all squares hide the same number of coins.

Add $(-2x)$ to both sides (equivalently, subtract $-2x$ from both sides).

$$4x = 2x + 8$$
$$-2x + 4x = -2x + 2x + 8$$
$$2x = 8$$

Divide the coins into two equal piles (one for each square). Each square hides four coins.

Multiply both sides by $\frac{1}{2}$ (equivalently, divide both sides by 2).

$$2x = 8$$
$$\frac{1}{2}(2x) = \frac{1}{2} \cdot 8$$
$$x = 4$$

(NOTE: In the preceding three examples, all the coefficients of x were chosen to be positive. However, the same techniques we have applied hold for negative coefficients also.)

The previous examples show that to solve equations of the form $ax + b = cx + d$, you should add the appropriate values to each side to obtain another equation of the form $mx = n$. Then multiply both sides by $\frac{1}{m}$ (or, equivalently, divide by m) to yield the solution $x = \frac{n}{m}$.

EXAMPLE 9.12   Solve these equations.

(a) $5x + 11 = 7x + 5$

(b) $\dfrac{2}{3}x + \dfrac{5}{7} = \dfrac{9}{4}x - \dfrac{2}{11}$

Solution

(a)
$$5x + 11 = 7x + 5$$
$$(-5x) + 5x + 11 = (-5x) + 7x + 5$$
$$11 = 2x + 5$$
$$11 + (-5) = 2x + 5 + (-5)$$
$$6 = 2x$$
$$\frac{1}{2} \cdot 6 = \frac{1}{2} \cdot 2x$$
$$3 = x$$

To check, substitute 3 for x into the initial equation:

CHECK: $5 \cdot 3 + 11 = \mathbf{26}$, and $7 \cdot 3 + 5 = \mathbf{26}$.

(b) This solution incorporates some shortcuts.

$$\frac{2}{3}x + \frac{5}{7} = \frac{9}{4}x - \frac{2}{11}$$
$$\frac{2}{3}x = \frac{9}{4}x - \frac{2}{11} - \frac{5}{7}$$
$$\frac{2}{3}x - \frac{9}{4}x = -\frac{69}{77}$$
$$\frac{-19}{12}x = \frac{-69}{77}$$
$$x = \left(-\frac{12}{19}\right)\left(-\frac{69}{77}\right) = \frac{828}{1463}$$

$$\text{CHECK: } \frac{2}{3} \cdot \frac{828}{1463} + \frac{5}{7} = \frac{552}{1463} + \frac{5}{7} = \frac{1597}{1463} \quad \text{and}$$

$$\frac{9}{4} \cdot \frac{828}{1463} - \frac{2}{11} = \frac{1863}{1463} - \frac{2}{11} = \frac{1597}{1463}. \quad \blacksquare$$

In the solution of Example 9.12(a), the same term was added to both sides of the equation or both sides were multiplied by the same number until an equation of the form $x = a$ (or $a = x$) resulted. In the solution of Example 9.12(b), terms were moved from one side to the other, changing signs when addition was involved and inverting when multiplication was involved. This method is called **transposing**.

Solving Inequalities

Inequalities can be solved in much the same manner using the following properties of order.

Property of less than and addition: If $a < b$, then $a + c < b + c$.

Property of less than and multiplication by a positive: If $a < b$ and $c > 0$, then $ac < bc$.

Property of less than and multiplication by a negative: If $a < b$ and $c < 0$, then $ac > bc$.

Notice that in the third property, the property of less than and multiplication by a negative, the inequality $a < b$ "reverses" to the inequality $ac > bc$ since c is *negative*. Also, similar corresponding properties hold for "greater than," "less than or equal to," and "greater than or equal to."

EXAMPLE 9.13   Solve these inequalities.
(a) $3x - 4 < x + 12$ **(b)** $\frac{1}{3}x - 7 > \frac{3}{5}x + 3$

Solution
(a)

$$3x - 4 < x + 12$$
$$3x + (-4) + 4 < x + 12 + 4 \qquad \left(\begin{array}{c}\text{Property of less}\\\text{than and addition}\end{array}\right)$$
$$3x < x + 16$$
$$(-x) + 3x < (-x) + x + 16 \qquad \left(\begin{array}{c}\text{Property of less}\\\text{than and addition}\end{array}\right)$$
$$2x < 16$$
$$\frac{1}{2}(2x) < \frac{1}{2}(16) \qquad \left(\begin{array}{c}\text{Property of less than and}\\\text{multiplication by a positive}\end{array}\right)$$
$$x < 8$$

(b)

$$\frac{1}{3}x - 7 > \frac{3}{5}x + 3$$
$$\frac{1}{3}x - 7 + 7 > \frac{3}{5}x + 3 + 7 \qquad \left(\begin{array}{c}\text{Property of less}\\\text{than and addition}\end{array}\right)$$
$$\frac{1}{3}x > \frac{3}{5}x + 10$$
$$-\frac{3}{5}x + \frac{1}{3}x > -\frac{3}{5}x + \frac{3}{5}x + 10 \qquad \left(\begin{array}{c}\text{Property of less}\\\text{than and addition}\end{array}\right)$$

$$-\frac{4}{15}x > 10$$

$$\left(-\frac{15}{4}\right)\left(-\frac{4}{15}x\right) < \left(-\frac{15}{4}\right)10 \qquad \left(\begin{array}{l}\text{Property of less than and}\\ \text{multiplication by a negative}\end{array}\right)$$

$$x < \frac{-75}{2} = -37.5 \qquad\qquad\qquad\qquad \blacksquare$$

Solutions of equations can be checked by substituting the solutions back into the initial equation. In Example 9.12(a), the substitution of 3 into the equation $5x + 11 = 7x + 5$ yields $5 \cdot 3 + 11 = 7 \cdot 3 + 5$, or $26 = 26$. Thus 3 is a solution of this equation. The process of checking inequalities is more involved. Usually, there are infinitely many numbers in the solution set of an inequality. Since there are infinitely many numbers to check, it is reasonable to check only a few (perhaps two or three) well-chosen numbers. For example, let's consider Example 9.13(b). The solution set for the inequality $\frac{1}{3}x - 7 > \frac{3}{5}x + 3$ is $\{x \mid x < -37.5\}$ (Figure 9.11).

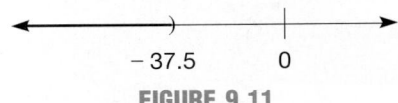

-37.5 0

FIGURE 9.11

To check the solution, substitute into the inequality one "convenient" number from the solution set and one outside the solution set. Here -45 (in the solution set) and 0 (not in the solution set) are two convenient values.

1. In $\frac{1}{3}x - 7 > \frac{3}{5}x + 3$, substitute 0 for x: $\frac{1}{3} \cdot 0 - 7 > \frac{3}{5} \cdot 0 + 3$, or $-7 > 3$, which is false. Therefore, 0 does *not* belong to the solution set.
2. To test -45: $\frac{1}{3}(-45) - 7 > \frac{3}{5}(-45) + 3$, or $-22 > -24$, which is true. Therefore, -45 does belong to the solution set.

You may want to check several other numbers. Although this method is not a complete check, it should add to your confidence that your solution set is correct.

Algebra has important uses in addition to solving equations and inequalities. For example, the problem-solving strategy Use a Variable is another application of algebra that is very useful.

EXAMPLE 9.14 Prove that the sum of any five consecutive whole numbers has a factor of 5.

Solution
Let $x, x + 1, x + 2, x + 3, x + 4$ represent any five consecutive whole numbers. Then

$$x + (x + 1) + (x + 2) + (x + 3) + (x + 4) = 5x + 10 = 5(x + 2),$$

which has a factor of 5. $\blacksquare$

MATHEMATICAL MORSEL

Throughout history there have been many interesting approximations of π as well as many ways of computing them. The value of pi to seven decimal places can easily be remembered using the mnemonic "May I have a large container of coffee?", where the number of letters in each word yields 3.1415926.

1. Found in an Egyptian papyrus: $\pi \approx \left(2 \times \dfrac{8}{9}\right)^2.$

2. Due to Archimedes: $\pi \approx \dfrac{22}{7}, \pi \approx \dfrac{355}{113}.$

3. Due to Wallis:
$$\pi = 2 \cdot \frac{2}{1} \cdot \frac{2}{3} \cdot \frac{4}{3} \cdot \frac{4}{5} \cdot \frac{6}{5} \cdot \frac{6}{7} \cdot \frac{8}{7} \cdots$$

4. Due to Gregory:
$$\pi = 4\left(1 - \frac{1}{3} + \frac{1}{5} - \frac{1}{7} + \cdots\right).$$

5. Due to Euler and Bernoulli:
$$\pi^2 = 6\left(\frac{1}{1^2} + \frac{1}{2^2} + \frac{1}{3^2} + \cdots\right).$$

6. In 1989, Gregory V. and David V. Chudnovsky calculated π to 1,011,196,691 places.

EXERCISE/PROBLEM SET 9.2—PART A

Exercises

1. Which of the following numbers are rational and which are irrational? Assume that the decimal patterns continue.
   (a) 6.233233323333 . . .
   (b) −5.235723572357 . . .
   (c) 7.121231234 . . .
   (d) 4.233233233 . . .

2. Which of the following are irrational numbers?
   (a) $\sqrt{49}$ (b) $\sqrt{61}$ (c) $\sqrt{37}$ (d) $\sqrt{64}$

3. The number π is given as an example of an irrational number. Often the value $\frac{22}{7}$ is used for π. Does $\pi = \frac{22}{7}$? Why or why not?

4. Arrange the following real numbers in increasing order.

0.56   0.$\overline{56}$ 0.5$\overline{66}$ 0.565565556 . . .
0.$\overline{566}$ 0.56656665 . . .
0.565566555666 . . .

5. Find four irrational numbers between 3 and 4.

6. (a) Which property of real numbers justifies the following statement?
$$2\sqrt{3} + 5\sqrt{3} = (2 + 5)\sqrt{3} = 7\sqrt{3}$$

   (b) Can this property be used to simplify $5\pi + 3\pi$? Explain.

   (c) Can this property be used to simplify $2\sqrt{3} + 7\sqrt{5}$? Explain.

7. Compute the following pairs of expressions.
   (a) $\sqrt{4} \times \sqrt{9}$, $\sqrt{4 \times 9}$
   (b) $\sqrt{4} \times \sqrt{25}$, $\sqrt{4 \times 25}$
   (c) $\sqrt{9} \times \sqrt{16}$, $\sqrt{9 \times 16}$
   (d) $\sqrt{9} \times \sqrt{25}$, $\sqrt{9 \times 25}$
   (e) What conclusion do you draw about $\sqrt{a}$ and $\sqrt{b}$ and $\sqrt{a \times b}$? (NOTE: a and b must be nonnegative.)

8. Estimate the following values, then check with a calculator.
   (a) $\sqrt{361}$ (b) $\sqrt{729}$
   (c) $\sqrt{3136}$ (d) $\sqrt{5041}$

9. Calculate the following values and determine a pattern.
   (a) $\sqrt{576}$, $\sqrt{5.76}$ (b) $\sqrt{1369}$, $\sqrt{13.69}$
   (c) $\sqrt{3721}$, $\sqrt{0.3721}$ (d) $\sqrt{8649}$, $\sqrt{0.8649}$

10. The result that $\sqrt{a} \times \sqrt{b} = \sqrt{a \times b}$ may be used to simplify square roots. For example, $\sqrt{20} = \sqrt{4 \times 5} = \sqrt{4} \times \sqrt{5} = 2\sqrt{5}$. Simplify the following square roots so that the radicand is as small as possible.
    (a) $\sqrt{48}$ (b) $\sqrt{32}$ (c) $\sqrt{50}$

11. Compute each of the following products and simplify the resulting square roots.
    (a) $\sqrt{20} \times \sqrt{5}$ (b) $\sqrt{11} \times \sqrt{44}$
    (c) $\sqrt{6} \times \sqrt{18}$

12. The lengths $\sqrt{2}$, $\sqrt{3}$, $\sqrt{4}$, $\sqrt{5}$, . . . can be constructed as follows.
    (a) First construct a right triangle with both legs of length 1. What is the length of the hypotenuse?
    (b) This hypotenuse is a leg of the next right triangle. The other leg has length 1. What is the length of the hypotenuse of this triangle?
    (c) Continue drawing right triangles, using the hypotenuse of the preceding triangle as a leg of the next triangle until you have constructed one with length $\sqrt{7}$.

13. Use the Pythagorean theorem to find the length of the indicated side of the following right triangles. (NOTE: The square-like symbol indicates the 90° angle.)
    (a)   (b)

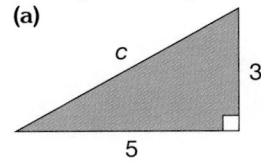

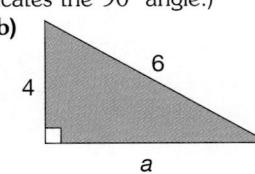

    (c)

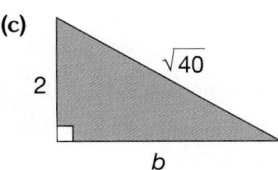

14. Find the square roots of the following numbers. Indicate whether the result is exact or an approximation.
    (a) 841   (b) 790   (c) 1332.25   (d) 665.86

15. Using the square root key on your calculator, find the square roots of the following numbers. Then order the given number and its square root in increasing order. What do you observe?
    (a) 0.3   (b) 0.5   (c) 0.7   (d) 0.98

16. Express the following values without exponents.
    (a) $25^{1/2}$ (b) $32^{1/5}$ (c) $9^{5/2}$
    (d) $(-27)^{4/3}$ (e) $16^{3/4}$ (f) $25^{-3/2}$

17. Calculate the following to three decimal places.
    (a) $625^{0.5}$ (b) $37^{0.37}$ (c) $11111^{1.7}$
    (d) $7^{8.23}$

18. Write the following values as integers if possible.
    (a) $\quad$ (b) $\sqrt[5]{243}$ (c) $\sqrt[4]{-81}$
    (d) $\sqrt[3]{4096}$

19. Find the following roots on a calculator.
    (a) $\sqrt[4]{731.162}$ (b) $\sqrt[5]{826.79}$
    (c) $\sqrt[3]{753.571}$ (d) $\sqrt[3]{314.432}$

20. Solve the following equations using any method.
    (a) $x + 15 = 7$ (b) $x + (-21) = -16$
    (c) $x + \frac{11}{9} = \frac{2}{3}$ (d) $x + 2\sqrt{2} = 5\sqrt{2}$

21. Solve the following equations using each of the three methods of Example 9.11.
    (a) $2x - 5 = 13$ (b) $3x + 7 = 22$
    (c) $-5x + 13 = -12$ (d) $\frac{2}{3}x + \frac{1}{6} = \frac{11}{12}$
    (e) $-\frac{3}{5}x - \frac{1}{4} = \frac{9}{20}$ (f) $3x + \pi = 7\pi$

22. Solve the following equations.
    (a) $2x + 5 = 3x - 6$ (b) $4x - 3 = 6x - 9$
    (c) $9x + 13 = 3x + 1$ (d) $\frac{2}{5}x + 5 = \frac{1}{3}x - 1$
    (e) $\frac{1}{4}x - \frac{3}{10} = \frac{2}{5}x + \frac{3}{4}$ (f) $\frac{2}{3}x - \frac{5}{9} = \frac{1}{4}x + \frac{1}{6}$

23. Solve the following inequalities.
    (a) $x + 5 < 9$ (b) $x - \frac{2}{3} \leq \frac{6}{7}$
    (c) $x - 3\sqrt{2} < 6\sqrt{5}$ (d) $x + 6\pi > -3\pi$

24. Find the solution sets of these inequalities.
    (a) $2x + 5 < -2$ (b) $-3x + 4 < -6$
    (c) $-5x - 2 \geq -12$ (d) $-\frac{1}{3}x - 6 < \frac{3}{2}$
    (e) $\frac{2}{3}x + \frac{1}{4} > \frac{5}{2}$ (f) $-\frac{2}{5}x + \frac{1}{10} > \frac{1}{2}$

25. Solve these inequalities.
    (a) $3x - 6 < 6x + 5$ (b) $2x + 3 \geq 5x - 9$
    (c) $\frac{2}{3}x - \frac{1}{4} > \frac{1}{9}x + \frac{3}{4}$ (d) $\frac{6}{5}x - \frac{1}{3} \leq \frac{3}{10}x + \frac{2}{5}$

Problems

26. Prove that $\sqrt{3}$ is not rational. (HINT: Reason by analogy from the proof that there is no rational number whose square is 2.)

27. Show why, when reasoning by analogy from the proof that $\sqrt{2}$ is irrational, an indirect proof does not lead

to a contradiction when you try to show that $\sqrt{9}$ is irrational.

28. Prove that $\sqrt[3]{2}$ is irrational.

29. (a) Show that $5\sqrt{3}$ is an irrational number. (HINT: Assume that it is rational, say a/b, isolate $\sqrt{3}$, and show that a contradiction occurs.)

(b) Using a similar argument, show that the product of any nonzero rational number with an irrational number is an irrational number.

30. (a) Prove that $1 + \sqrt{3}$ is an irrational number.
(b) Show, similarly, that $m + n\sqrt{3}$ is an irrational number for all rational numbers m and n ($n \neq 0$).

31. Show that the following are irrational numbers.
(a) $6\sqrt{2}$ **(b)** $2 + \sqrt{3}$ **(c)** $5 + 2\sqrt{3}$

32. A student says to the teacher, "You proved to us that $\sqrt{a} \cdot \sqrt{b} = \sqrt{ab}$. Reasoning by analogy, we get $\sqrt{a} + \sqrt{b} = \sqrt{a + b}$. Therefore, $\sqrt{9} + \sqrt{16} = \sqrt{25}$ or $3 + 4 = 5$. Right?" Comment!

33. A student says to the teacher,

"You proved that $\sqrt{a} \cdot \sqrt{b} = \sqrt{ab}$.

Therefore,

$-1 = (\sqrt{-1})^2 = \sqrt{-1}\sqrt{-1} = \sqrt{(-1)(-1)} = \sqrt{1} = 1$,

so that $-1 = 1$." What do you say?

34. A **Pythagorean triple** is a set of three nonzero whole numbers (a, b, c) where $a^2 + b^2 = c^2$. For example, $(3, 4, 5)$ is a Pythagorean triple. Show that there are infinitely many Pythagorean triples.

35. A **primitive Pythagorean triple** is a Pythagorean triple whose members have only 1 as a common prime factor. For example, $(3, 4, 5)$ is primitive, whereas $(6, 8, 10)$ is not. It has been shown that all such primitive Pythagorean triples are given by the three equations.

$$a = 2uv \qquad b = u^2 - v^2 \qquad c = u^2 + v^2$$

where u and v are relatively prime, one of u or v is even and the other is odd, and $u > v$. Generate five primitive triples using these equations.

36. You have three consecutive integers less than twenty. Add two of them together, divide by the third, and the answer is the smallest of the three integers. What are the numbers?

37. Greg has 1002 meters of fencing. He wants to fence a rectangular region that is four times as long as it is wide when one of the longer sides is bordered by a river. What is the area of the region? (Use a variable and solve an equation; recall that the area of a rectangle is the product of its length and its width.)

38. Can a rational number plus its reciprocal ever be an integer? If yes, say precisely when.

39. If you are given two straight pieces of wire, is it possible to cut one of them into two pieces so that the length of one of the three pieces is the average of the lengths of the other two? Explain.

EXERCISE/PROBLEM SET 9.2—PART B

Exercises

1. Which of the following numbers are rational and which are irrational?
(a) $2.375375\ldots$ **(b)** $3.0120123\ldots$
(c) $\sqrt{169}$ **(d)** 2π
(e) $3.\overline{12}$ **(f)** $\sqrt{7}$
(g) $\dfrac{35}{0.72}$ **(h)** $5.626626662\ldots$

2. Using decimal notation, write two different irrational numbers using only the digits 3 and 5.

3. Complete the following chart. For each given number, determine what type of number it is and put checks in the appropriate columns. The first one has been done as an example.

Number	Rational	Irrational	Real
-6	✔		✔
$3.\overline{56}$			
$1/12$			
$0.35335\ldots$			
$2.4/0.6$			
$\sqrt{3}$			

4. Find an irrational number between $0.\overline{37}$ and $0.\overline{38}$.

5. Find three irrational numbers between 2 and 3.

6. Simplify the following square roots.
(a) $\sqrt{40}$ **(b)** $\sqrt{80}$ **(c)** $\sqrt{180}$

7. Compute and simplify the following expressions.
   (a) $\sqrt{18} \times \sqrt{2}$ (b) $\sqrt{27} \times \sqrt{3}$
   (c) $\sqrt{60} \times \sqrt{12}$ (d) $5\sqrt{2} - 9\sqrt{2}$
   (e) $\sqrt{18} + \sqrt{32}$ (f) $\sqrt{20} - \sqrt{5} + \sqrt{45}$

8. Use the Pythagorean theorem to find the lengths of the given segments drawn on the following square lattices.

   (a) 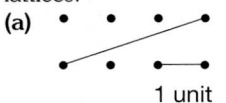 (b)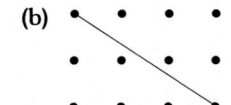

   1 unit

   (c)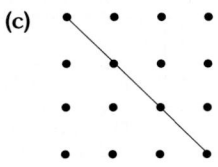

9. Use the Pythagorean theorem to find the missing lengths in the following diagrams.

   (a) 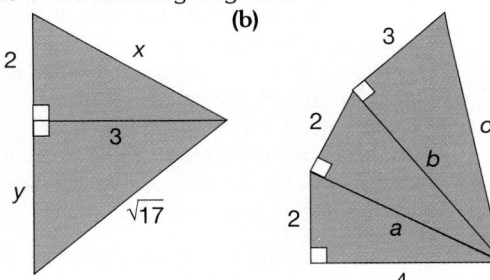 (b)

10. Since the square roots of some numbers are irrational, their decimal representations do not repeat. Approximations of these decimal representations can be made by a process of squeezing. For example, from Figure 9.9, we see that $1 < \sqrt{2} < 2$. To improve this approximation, find two numbers between 1 and 2 that "squeeze" $\sqrt{2}$. Since $(1.4)^2 = 1.96$, and $(1.5)^2 = 2.25$, $1.4 < \sqrt{2} < 1.5$. To obtain a closer approximation, we could continue the squeezing process by choosing numbers close to 1.4 (since 1.96 is closer to 2 than 2.25). Since $(1.41)^2 = 1.9981$, and $(1.42)^2 = 2.0164$, $1.41 < \sqrt{2} < 1.42$ or $\sqrt{2} \approx 1.41$. Use the squeezing process to approximate square roots of the following to the nearest hundredth.
    (a) 7 (b) 15.6 (c) 0.036

11. Find $\sqrt{13}$ using the following method: Make a guess, say r_1. Then find $13 \div r_1 = s_1$. Then find the average of r_1 and s_1 by computing $(r_1 + s_1)/2 = r_2$. Now find $13 \div r_2 = s_2$. Continue this procedure until r_n and s_n differ by less than 0.00001.

12. Using a calculator with a square-root key, enter the number 2. Press the square-root key several times consecutively. What do you observe about the numbers displayed? Continue to press the square-root key until no new numbers appear in the display. What is this number?

13. On your calculator, enter a positive number less than 1. Repeatedly press the square-root key. The displayed numbers should be increasing. Will they ever reach 1?

14. Express the following values without exponents.
    (a) $36^{1/2}$ (b) $9^{3/2}$ (c) $27^{2/3}$

15. Write the following radicals in simplest form if they are real numbers.
    (a) $\sqrt[3]{-27}$ (b) $\sqrt[4]{-16}$ (c) $\sqrt[5]{32}$

16. Use a scientific calculator to calculate approximations of the following values. (These will require several steps and/or the use of the memory.)
    (a) $(\sqrt{2})^{4/3}$ (b) $\sqrt{3}^{\sqrt{2}}$ (c) $\sqrt{17}^{\sqrt{17}}$
    (d) $391^{0.31}$

17. Determine the larger of each pair.
    (a) $\pi, \frac{22}{7}$ (b) $\sqrt[3]{37}, 1.35^4$
    (c) $\sqrt[5]{7^2}, \sqrt[13]{7^5}$ (d) $\pi^{\sqrt{2}}, (\sqrt{2})^\pi$

18. Solve the following equations.
    (a) $x + 9 = -5$ (b) $x - (-\frac{3}{4}) = \frac{5}{6}$
    (c) $3x - 4 = 9$ (d) $\frac{1}{2}x + 1 = \frac{5}{2}$
    (e) $6 = 3x - 9$ (f) $-2 = (\frac{-5}{12})x + 3$

19. Solve the following equations.
    (a) $3x + \sqrt{6} = 2x - 3\sqrt{6}$
    (b) $x - \sqrt{2} = 9\sqrt{3}$
    (c) $5x - \sqrt{3} = 4\sqrt{3}$
    (d) $2\pi x - 6 = 5\pi x + 9$

20. Solve the following inequalities.
    (a) $x - \frac{2}{3} > \frac{5}{6}$ (b) $-2x + 4 \leq 11$
    (c) $3x + 5 \geq 6x - 7$ (d) $\frac{3}{2}x - 3 < \frac{5}{6}x + \frac{1}{3}$

Problems

21. True or false? $\sqrt{p}$ is irrational for any prime p. If true, prove. If false, give a counterexample.

22. Prove that $\sqrt{6}$ is irrational. (HINT: You should use an indirect proof as we did for $\sqrt{2}$; however, this case requires a little additional reasoning.)

23. Prove that $\sqrt{p^7 q^5}$ is not rational where p and q are primes.

24. Prove or disprove: $\sqrt[n]{2}$ is irrational for any whole number $n \geq 2$.

25. Let p represent any prime. Determine if the following are rational or irrational and prove your assertion.
    (a) $\sqrt[3]{p}$ (b) $\sqrt[3]{p^2}$

26. (a) Let r be a nonzero rational number and p and q be two irrational numbers. Determine if the follow-

ing expressions are rational or irrational. Prove your assertion in each case.

(i) $r + p$ (ii) $r \cdot p$ (iii) $p + q$ (iv) $p \cdot q$

(b) What if $r = 0$? Would this change your answers in part (a)? Explain.

27. Give an example which shows that each of the following can occur.
   (a) The sum of two irrational numbers may be an irrational number.
   (b) The sum of two irrational numbers may be a rational number.
   (c) The product of two irrational numbers may be an irrational number.
   (d) The product of two irrational numbers may be a rational number.

28. Is the set of irrational numbers
   (a) closed under addition?
   (b) closed under subtraction?
   (c) closed under multiplication?
   (d) closed under division?

29. Take *any* two real numbers whose sum is 1 (fractions, decimals, integers, etc., are appropriate). Square the larger and add the smaller. Then square the smaller and add the larger.
   (a) What will be true?
   (b) Prove your assertion.

30. The tempered musical scale, first employed by Johann Sebastian Bach, divides the octave into 12 equally spaced intervals.

$$\text{C C}^{\#} \text{ D D}^{\#} \text{ E F F}^{\#} \text{ G G}^{\#} \text{ A A}^{\#} \text{ B C}^{\text{oct}}$$

The fact that the intervals are equally spaced means that the ratios of the frequencies between any adjacent notes are the same. For example,

$$\text{C}^{\#}\text{:C} = k \quad \text{and} \quad \text{D:C}^{\#} = k$$

From this we see that $\text{C}^{\#} = k \cdot \text{C}$ and $\text{D} = k \cdot \text{C}^{\#} = k(k \cdot \text{C}) = k^2\text{C}$. Continuing this pattern, we can show that $\text{C}^{\text{oct}} = k^{12} \cdot \text{C}$ (verify this). It is also true that two notes are an octave apart if the frequency of one is double the other. Thus $\text{C}^{\text{oct}} = 2 \cdot \text{C}$. Therefore, $k^{12} = 2$ or $k = \sqrt[12]{2}$. In tuning instruments, the frequency of A above middle C is 440 cycles per second. From this we can find the other frequencies of the octave

$$\text{A}^{\#} = \sqrt[12]{2} \cdot 440 = 466.16$$
$$\text{G}^{\#} = 440/(\sqrt[12]{2}) = 415.31$$

(a) Find the remaining frequencies to the nearest hundredth of a cycle.
(b) In the Greek scale, a fifth (C to G, F to C) had a ratio of $\frac{3}{2}$. How does the tempered scale compare?

(c) Also in the Greek scale, a fourth (C to F, D to G) had a ratio of $\frac{4}{3}$. How close is the tempered scale to this ratio?

31. Two towns A and B are 3 miles apart. It is proposed to build a new school to serve 200 students in town A and 100 students in town B. How far from A should the school be built if the total distance traveled by all 300 students is to be as small as possible?

32. *Calendar calculus:*

   1. Mark any 4×4 array of dates on a calendar.

		1	2	3	4	5
6	7	8	9	10	11	12
13	14	15	16	17	18	19
20	21	22	23	24	25	26
27	28	29	30	31		

   2. Circle any numeral in the 4×4 array, say 15. Then cross out all other numerals in the same row and column as 15.
   3. Circle any numeral not crossed out, say 21. Then cross out all other numerals in the same row and column as 21.
   4. Continue until there are four circled numbers. Their sum should be 76 (this is true for this particular 4×4 array).

   Try this with another 4×4 calendar array. Are all such sums the same there? Does this work for 3×3 calendar arrays? How about $n \times n$ arrays if we make bigger calendars?

33. Two numbers are reciprocals of each other. One number is 9 times as large as the other. Find the two numbers.

34. The following problem was given as a challenge to Fibonacci: Three men share a pile of money in the fractions $\frac{1}{2}, \frac{1}{3}, \frac{1}{6}$. Each man takes some money from the pile until there is nothing left. The first man returns one-half of what he took, the second returns one-third, and the third one-sixth. When the returned amount is divided equally among the men it is found that they each have what they are entitled to. How much money was in the original pile, and how much did each man take from the original pile?

35. Chad was the same age as Shelly, and Holly was four years older than both of them. Chad's dad was 20 when Chad was born and the average age of the four of them is 39. How old is Chad?

36. There are only two consecutive primes between 0 and 1000 that differ by 20. If their sum is 1794, what are

the two primes? Be sure to check to see that the two numbers are primes!

37. Mr. Carter, Mr. Farrell, Mr. Milne, and Mr. Smith serve the little town of Milford as architect, banker, druggist, and grocer, though not necessarily respectively. The druggist earns exactly twice as much as the grocer, the architect earns exactly twice as much as the druggist, and the banker earns exactly twice as much as the architect. Although Mr. Carter is older than anyone who makes more money than Mr. Farrell, Mr. Farrell

does not make twice as much as Mr. Carter. Mr. Smith earns exactly $3776 more than Mr. Milne. What is each man's occupation?

38. At a contest, two persons were asked their ages. Then, to test their arithmetical powers, they were asked to add the two ages together. One gave me 44 as the answer and the other gave 1280. The first had subtracted one age from the other, while the second person had multiplied them together. What were their ages?

9.3

FUNCTIONS AND THEIR GRAPHS

The Cartesian Coordinate System

The concept of a function was introduced in Section 2.4. Here we see how functions can be displayed using graphs on a coordinate system. This section has several goals: to emphasize the importance of functions by showing how they represent many types of physical situations, to help develop skills in graphing functions, and to help you learn how to use a graph to develop a better understanding of the corresponding function.

Suppose that we choose two perpendicular real number lines l and m in the plane and use their point of intersection, O, as a reference point called the **origin** [Figure 9.12(a)]. To locate a point P relative to point O, we use the directed real-number distances x and y that indicate the position of P left/right of and above/below the origin O, respectively. If P is to the right of line m, then x is positive [Figure 9.12(b)]. If P is to the left of line m,

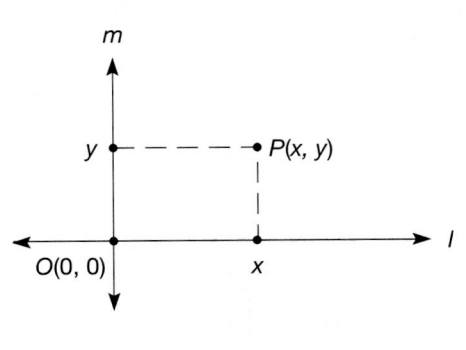

(a)

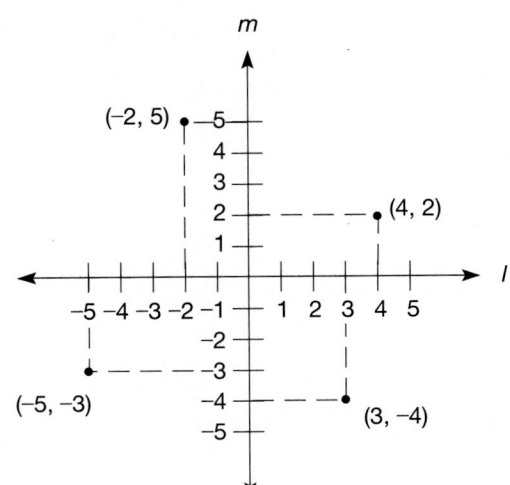

(b)

FIGURE 9.12

then x is negative. If P is on line m, then x is zero. Similarly, y is positive, negative, or zero, respectively, according to whether P is above, below, or on line l. The pair of real numbers x and y are called the **coordinates** of point P. We identify a point simply by giving its coordinates in an ordered pair (x, y). That is, by "the point (x, y)" we mean the point whose coordinates are x and y, respectively. In an ordered pair of coordinates, the first number is called the **x-coordinate**, and the second is the **y-coordinate**. Figure 9.13 shows the various possible cases for the coordinates of points in the plane.

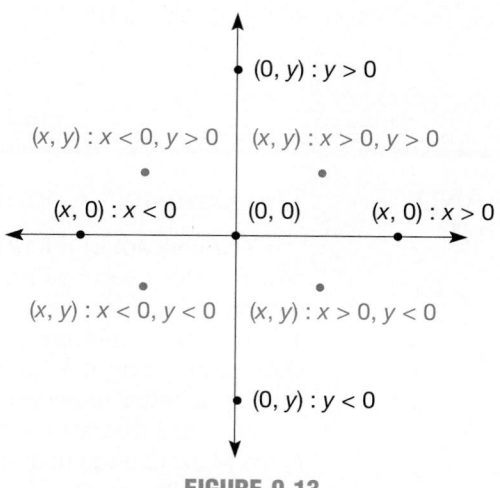

FIGURE 9.13

We say that lines l and m determine a **coordinate system** for the plane. Customarily, the horizontal line l is called the **x-axis**, and the vertical line m is called the **y-axis** for the coordinate system. Observe in Figure 9.14 that l and m have been relabeled as the x-axis and y-axis and that they divide the plane into four disjoint regions, called **quadrants**. (The axes are not part of any of the quadrants.) The points in quadrants I and IV have positive x-coordinates, while the points in quadrants II and III have negative x-coordinates. Similarly, the points in quadrants I and II have positive

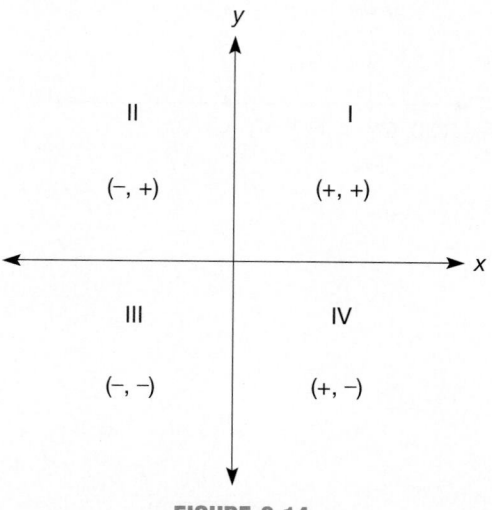

FIGURE 9.14

y-coordinates, while the points in quadrants III and IV have negative y-coordinates (Figure 9.14).

The following example provides a simple application of coordinates in mapmaking.

EXAMPLE 9.15   Plot the points with the following coordinates.

P_1 (−7, 5), P_2 (−5, 5), P_3 (−4, 3), P_4 (0, 3), P_5 (3, 4), P_6 (6, 4), P_7 (7, 3), P_8 (5, −1), P_9 (6, −2), P_{10} (6, −7), P_{11} (−8, −7), P_{12} (−8, −3)

Connect the points, in succession, P_1 to P_2, P_2 to P_3, . . . , P_{12} to P_1 with line segments to form a polygon (Figure 9.15).

Solution

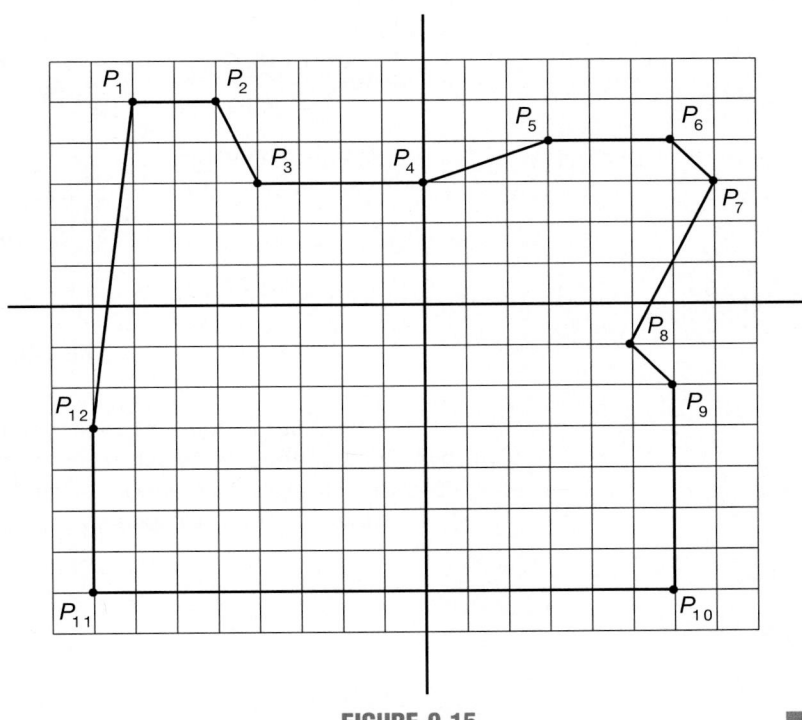

FIGURE 9.15   ■

Notice that the polygon in Figure 9.15 is a simplified map of the state of Oregon. Cartographers use computers to store maps of regions in coordinate form. They can then print maps in a variety of sizes. In the problem set we will investigate altering the size of a two-dimensional figure using coordinates.

Graphs of Linear Functions

As the name suggests, **linear functions** are functions whose graphs are lines. The next example involves a linear function and its graph.

EXAMPLE 9.16   A salesperson is given a monthly salary of $1200 plus a 5% commission on sales. Graph the salesperson's total earnings as a function of sales.

TABLE 9.1

Sales, s	Earnings, $E(s)$
1000	1250
2000	1300
3000	1350
4000	1400
5000	1450

Solution

Let s represent the dollar amount of the salesperson's monthly sales. The total earnings can be represented as a function of sales, s, as follows: $E(s) = 1200 + (0.05)s$. Several values of this function are shown in Table 9.1. Using these values we can plot the function $E(s)$ (Figure 9.16). The mark on the vertical axis below 1200 is used to indicate that this portion of the graph is not the same scale as on the rest of the axis.

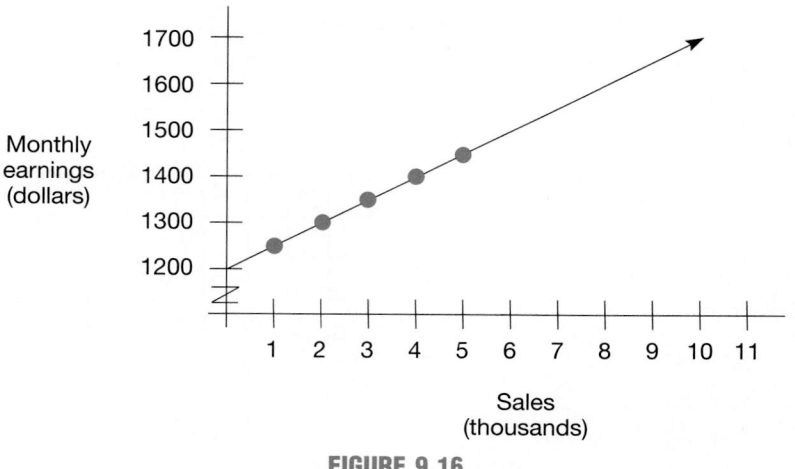

FIGURE 9.16

Notice that the points representing the pairs of values lie on a line. Thus, by extending the line, which is the graph of the function, we can see what salaries will result from various sales. For example, to earn $1650, Figure 9.17 shows that the salesperson must have sales of $9000.

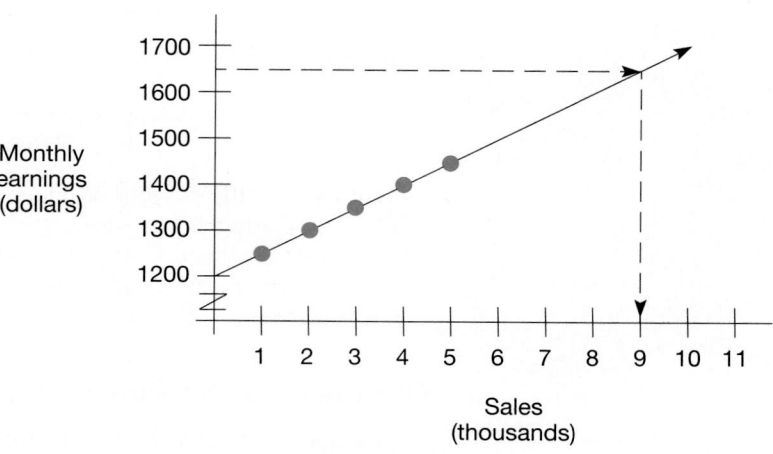

FIGURE 9.17

A **linear function** has the algebraic form $f(x) = ax + b$, where a and b are constants. In the function $E(s) = (0.05)s + 1200$, the value of a is 0.05 and of b is 1200.

Graphs of Quadratic Functions

A **quadratic function** is a function of the form $f(x) = ax^2 + bx + c$, where a, b, and c are constants and $a \neq 0$. The next example presents a problem involving a quadratic function.

EXAMPLE 9.17   A ball is tossed up vertically at a velocity of 50 feet per second from a point 5 feet above the ground. It is known from physics that the height of the ball above the ground, in feet, is given by the position function $p(t) = -16t^2 + 50t + 5$, where t is the time in seconds. At what time, t, is the ball at its highest point?

TABLE 9.2

t	$p(t)$
0	5
1	39
2	41
3	6

Solution

Table 9.2 lists several values for t with the corresponding function values from $p(t) = -16t^2 + 50t + 5$. Figure 9.18 shows a graph of the points in the table.

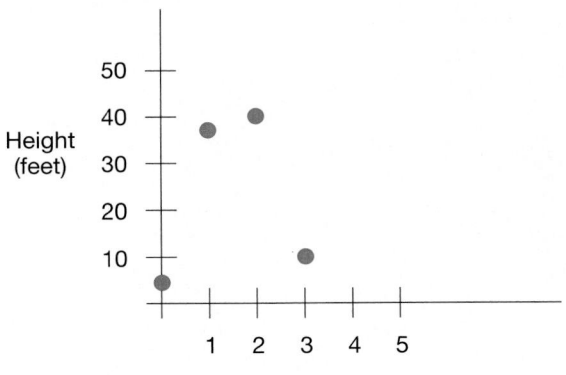

FIGURE 9.18

Unfortunately, it is unclear from the graph of these four points what the highest point will be. One way of getting a better view of this situation would be to plot several more points between 1 and 2, say $t = 1.1, 1.2, 1.3,$ . . . , 1.9. However, this can be tedious. Instead, Figure 9.19 shows how a graphics calculator can be used to get an estimate of this point.

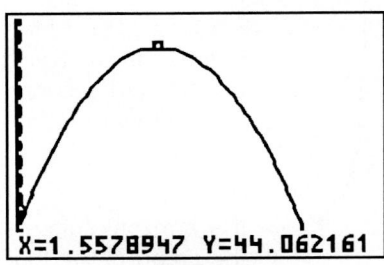

X=1.5578947 Y=44.062161

FIGURE 9.19

By moving the cursor (the "+") to what appears to be the highest point on the graph, the calculator's display screen shows that the value $t = 1.5578947$ corresponds to that point. It can be shown *mathematically* that $t = \frac{25}{16} = 1.5625$ seconds is the exact time when the ball is at its highest point, 44.0625 feet. ∎

Graphs of Exponential Functions

Exponential Functions

Amoebas have the interesting property that they split in two over time intervals. Therefore, the number of amoebas is a function of the number of splits. Table 9.3 lists the first several ordered pairs of this function, and Figure 9.20 shows the corresponding graph.

TABLE 9.3

Number of Splits	Number of Amoebas
0	1
1	2 (= 2^1)
2	4 (= 2^2)
3	8 (= 2^3)
4	16 (= 2^4)
5	32 (= 2^5)

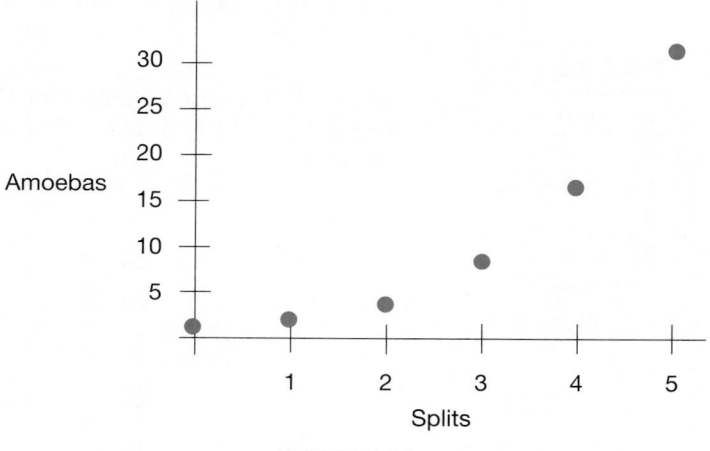

FIGURE 9.20

This functional relationship can be represented as the formula $f(x) = 2^x$, where $x = 0, 1, 2, \ldots$. This is an example of an **exponential function** since, in the function rule, the variable appears as the exponent.

Exponential growth also appears in the study of compound interest. In Section 8.3 it was shown that for an initial principal of P_0, an interest rate of r, compounded annually, and time t, in years, the amount of principal is given by the equation $P(t) = P_0(1 + r)^t$. In particular, if $100 is deposited at 6% interest, the value of the investment after t years is given by $P(t) = 100(1.06)^t$. Figure 9.21 shows a portion of the graph of this function.

EXAMPLE 9.18   How long does it take to double your money when the interest rate is 6% compounded annually? (Assume that your money is a tax-deferred account so that you don't have to pay taxes until the money is withdrawn.)

Solution

If a horizontal line is drawn through $200 in Figure 9.21, it will intersect the graph of the function approximately above the 12. Thus it takes about

12 years to double the $100 investment. (A more precise estimate that can be obtained from the formula is 11.9 years.)

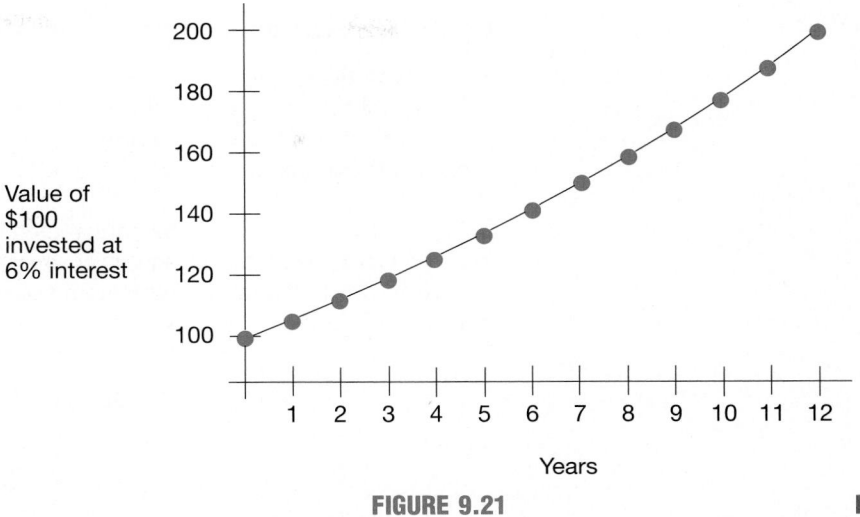

Value of $100 invested at 6% interest

Years

FIGURE 9.21

Interestingly, it takes only seven more years to add another $100 to the account and five more to add the next $100. This acceleration in accumulating principal illustrates the power of compounding, in particular, and of exponential growth, in general.

A similar phenomenon, decay, occurs in nature. Radioactive materials decay at an exponential rate. For example, the half-life of uranium 238 is 4.5 billion years. The formula for calculating the amount of ^{238}U after t years is $U(t) = (0.86)^t$. Figure 9.22 shows part of the graph of this function.

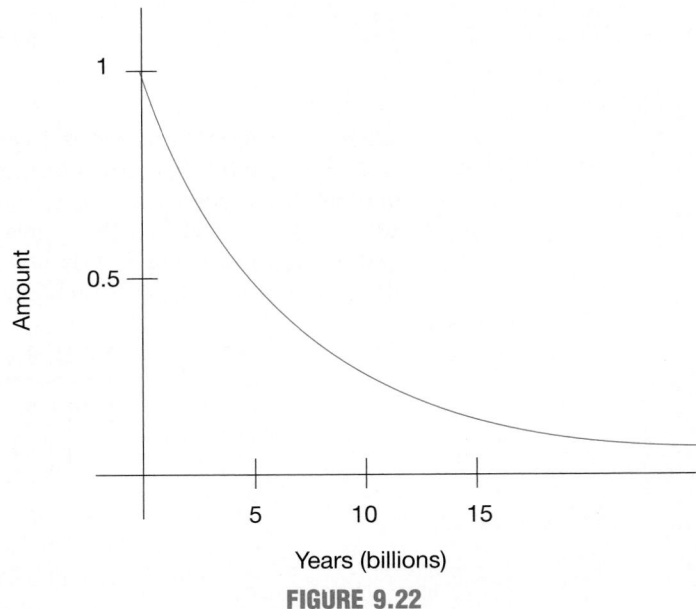

Amount

Years (billions)

FIGURE 9.22

This graph shows that although uranium decays rapidly at first, relatively speaking, it lingers around a long time.

Graphs of Other Common Functions

Cubic Functions

The following example illustrates a cubic function that arises from a problem posed in the *Connections to School Mathematics* section which precedes the index at the end of the book.

EXAMPLE 9.19   A box is to be constructed from a piece of cardboard 20 by 20 cm square by cutting out square corners and folding up the resulting sides (Figure 9.23). Estimate the maximum volume of a box that can be formed in this way.

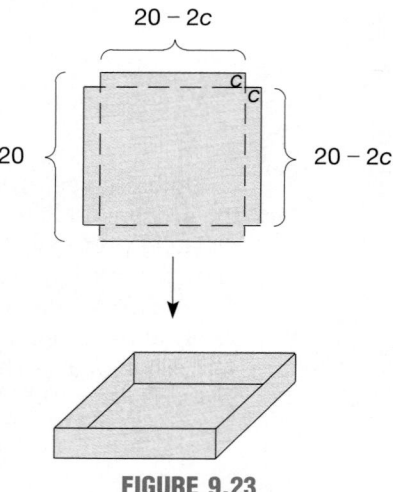

FIGURE 9.23

Solution

When a corner of dimensions 1 cm by 1 cm is cut out, a box of dimensions 1 cm by 18 cm by 18 cm is formed. Its volume is $1 \times 18 \times 18 = 324$. In general, if the corner is c by c, the volume of the resulting box is given by $V(c) = c(20 - 2c)(20 - 2c)$. Table 9.4 shows several sizes of corners together with the resulting box volumes. Using these values we can sketch the graph of the function $V(c)$ (Figure 9.24).

TABLE 9.4

Corners	Volume
1 cm by 1cm	324 cm^3
2 cm by 2 cm	512 cm^3
3 cm by 3 cm	588 cm^3
4 cm by 4 cm	576 cm^3
5 cm by 5 cm	500 cm^3

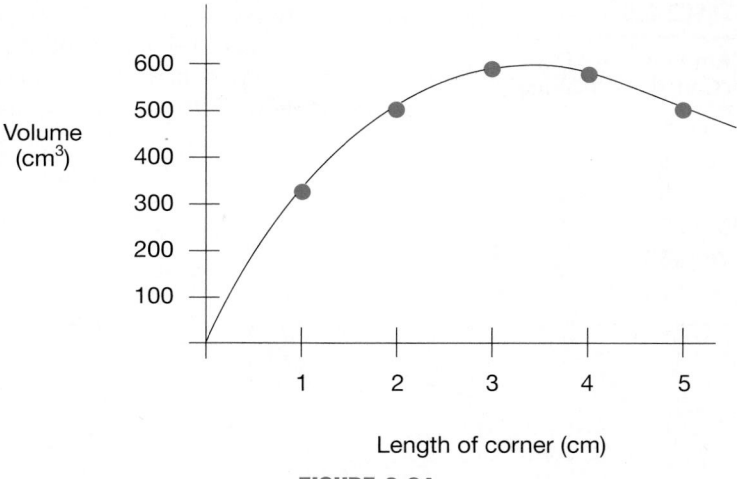

Volume (cm³)

Length of corner (cm)

FIGURE 9.24

The five points in the table are shown in the graph in Figure 9.24. From the graph it appears that when the corner measures about 3.5 by 3.5, the maximum volume is achieved, $V(3.5) = (3.5)(13)(13) \approx 592$ cm³. It can be shown mathematically that the value $c = 3\frac{1}{3}$ actually leads to the maximum volume of about 593. ■

The function $V(c) = c(20 - 2c)(20 - 2c)$ can be rewritten as $V(c) = 4c^3 - 80c^2 + 400c$, a **cubic function**. Actually, the graph in Figure 9.24 looks similar to the quadratic function pictured earlier in this section. However, if the function $V(c) = 4c^3 - 80c^2 + 400c$ were allowed to take on all real number values, its graph would take the shape as shown from a graphics calculator in Figure 9.25. (This shape is characteristic of all cubic functions.)

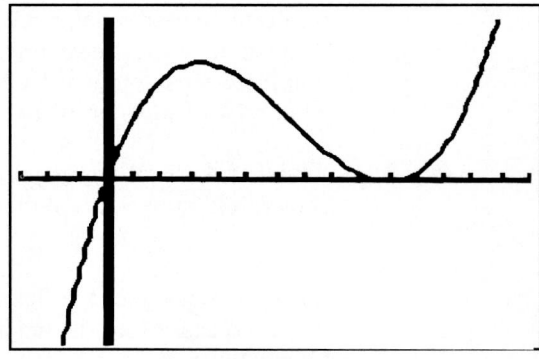

FIGURE 9.25

However, in Example 9.19, only a portion of this graph is shown since the values of c are limited to $0 < c < 10$, the only lengths which produce corners that lead to a box.

TABLE 9.5

Amount (Cents)	Tax (Cents)
0–15	0
16–35	1
36–55	2
56–75	3
76–95	4
96–115	5

Step Functions

The sales tax or the amount of postage are examples of step functions. Table 9.5 shows a typical sales tax, in cents, for sales up to $1.15. The graph in Figure 9.26 displays this information.

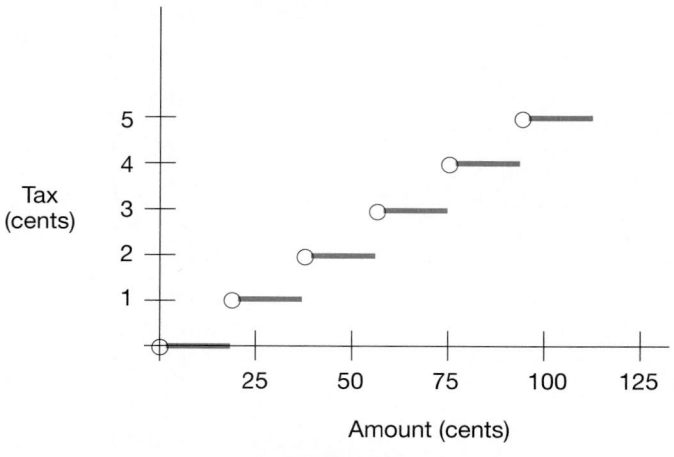

FIGURE 9.26

The open circles indicate that those points are *not* part of the graph. Otherwise, the endpoints are included in a segment. Notice that although the steps in this function are pictured as line segments, they could actually be pictured as a series of dots, one for each cent in the amount. A similar graph, which can be drawn for postage stamp rates, must use a line segment since the weights of envelopes vary continuously. A function such as the one pictured in Figure 9.26 is called a **step function** since its values are pictured in a series of line segments, or steps.

Graphs and Their Functions

Thus far we have studied several special types of functions: linear, quadratic, exponential, cubic, and step functions. Rather than starting with a function and constructing the graph, this subsection will develop your graphical sense by first displaying a graph and then analyzing it to predict what type of function would produce the graph.

EXAMPLE 9.20   Water is poured at a constant rate into the three containers shown in Figure 9.27. Which graph corresponds to which container?

Solution

Since the bottom of the figure in (a) is the narrowest, if water is poured into it at a constant rate, its height will rise faster initially and will slow in time. Graph (ii) is steeper initially to indicate that water is rising faster. Then it levels off slowly as the container is being filled. Thus graph (ii) best represents the height of water in container (a) as it is being filled. Container (b) should fill at a constant rate; thus graph (i) best represents its situation. Since the bottom of (c) is larger than its top, the water's height will rise more slowly at first, as in (iii).

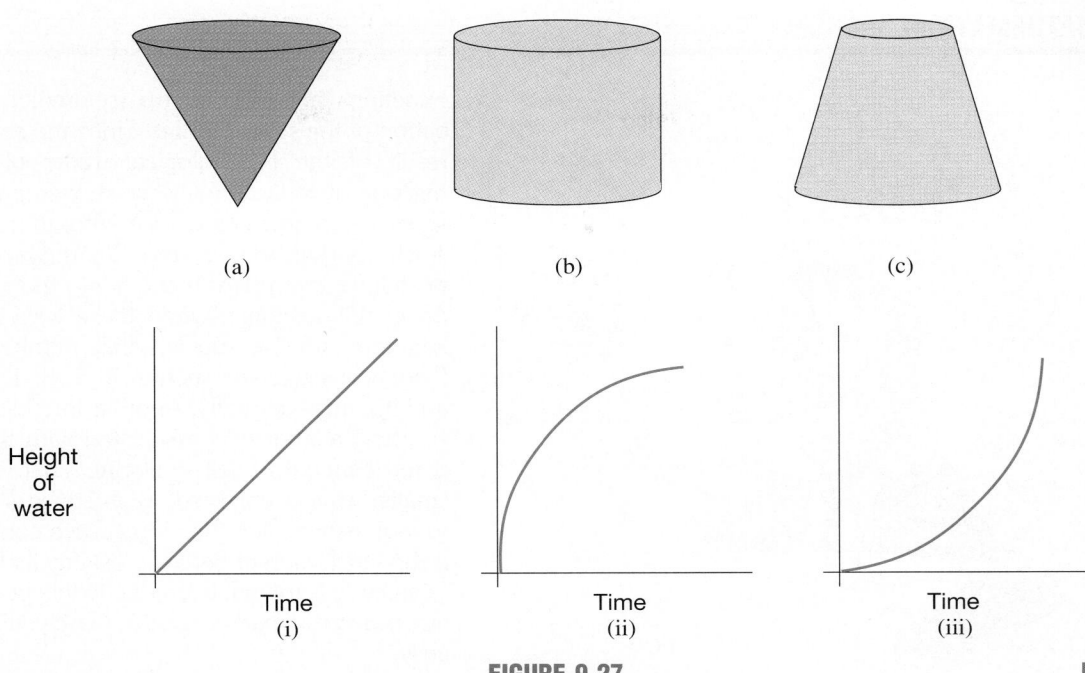

Height
of
water

Time
(i)

Time
(ii)

Time
(iii)

FIGURE 9.27

Finally, since a function assigns to each element in its domain only one element in its codomain, there is a simple visual test to see if a graph represents a function. The **vertical line test** states that a graph can represent a function if every vertical line that can be drawn intersects the graph in at most one point. Review the graphs of functions in this section to see that they pass this test by moving a vertical pencil across the graph as suggested in Figure 9.28.

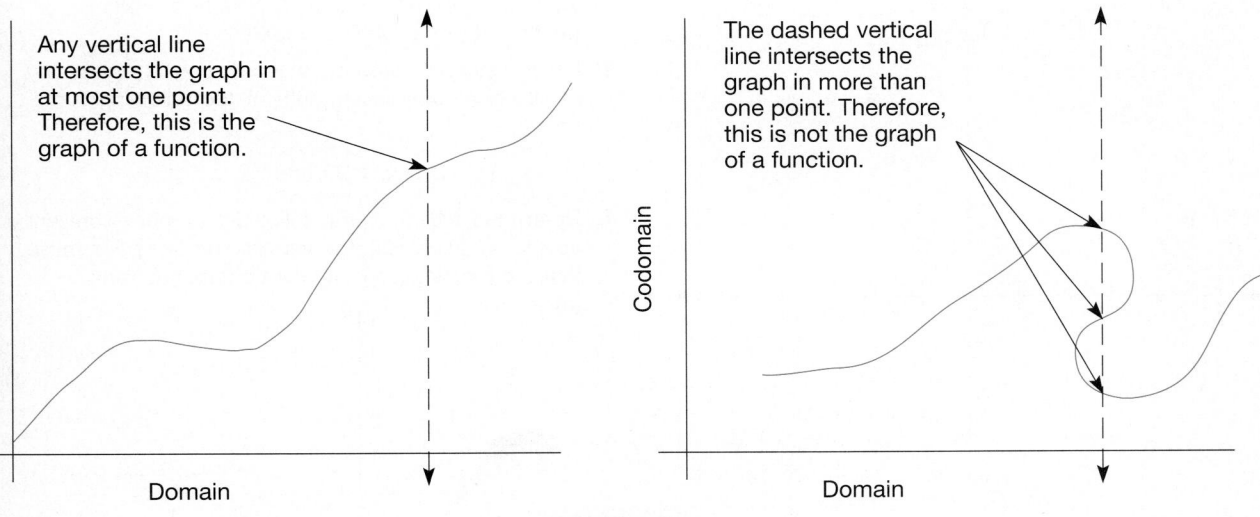

Any vertical line intersects the graph in at most one point. Therefore, this is the graph of a function.

Domain

The dashed vertical line intersects the graph in more than one point. Therefore, this is not the graph of a function.

Codomain

Domain

FIGURE 9.28

MATHEMATICAL MORSEL

Functions are used to try to predict the price action of the stock market. Since the action is the result of the psychological frame of mind of millions of individuals, price movements do not seem to conform to a nice smooth curve. One stock market theory, the Elliott wave theory, postulates that prices move in waves, 5 up and 3 down. Interestingly, when these waves are broken into smaller subdivisions, numbers of the Fibonacci sequence, such as 3, 5, 8, 13, 21, 34, and 55, arise naturally. Another interesting mathematical relationship associated with this theory is the concept of self-similarity. That is, when a smaller wave is enlarged, its structure is supposed to look exactly like the larger wave containing it. If the stock market behaved exactly as Elliott had postulated it should, everyone would become rich by playing the market. Unfortunately, it is not that easy.

EXERCISE/PROBLEM SET 9.3—PART A

Exercises

1. Given the graph shown here, find the coordinates of points A, B, C, D, E, and F.

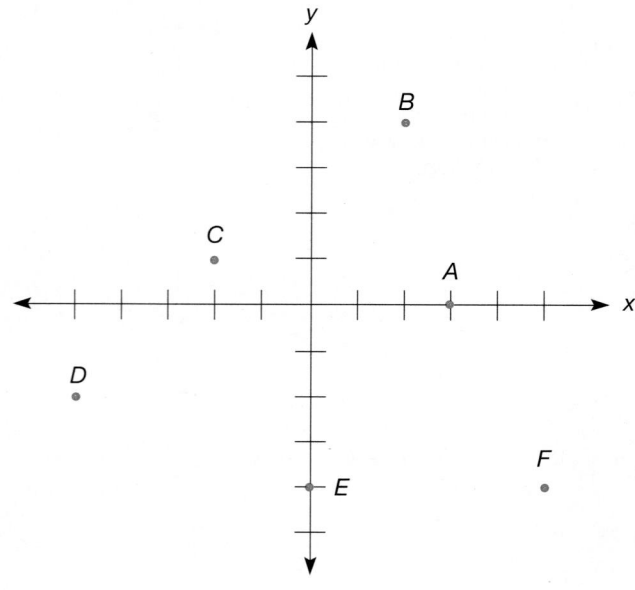

2. Plot the following points on graph paper.
   (a) (3, 2), (−3, 2), (−3, −2), (3, −2)
   (b) (0, 5), (5, 0), (3, −6), (−2, 1)
   (c) (−1, −3), (−2, −3), (−3, −4), (−5, −2)
   (d) (2, −4), (−2, 5), (−2, −3), (1, −2)

3. On a coordinate system, shade the region consisting of all points that satisfy both of the following conditions:

$$-3 \leq x \leq 2 \quad \text{and} \quad 2 \leq y \leq 4$$

4. Determine which of the following graphs represent functions. (HINT: Use the vertical line test.) For those that are functions, specify the domain and range.
   (a)

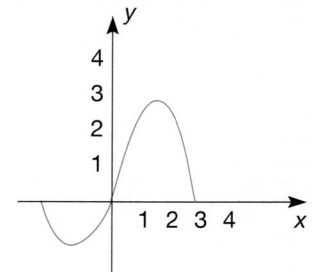

(b)

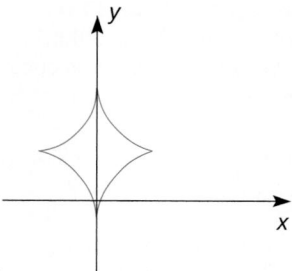

(c)

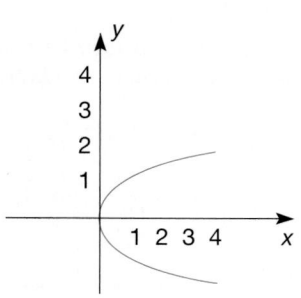

(d)

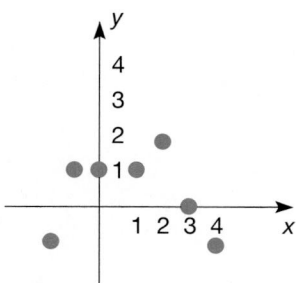

(e)

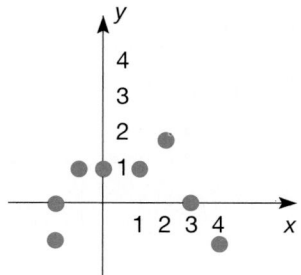

(f)

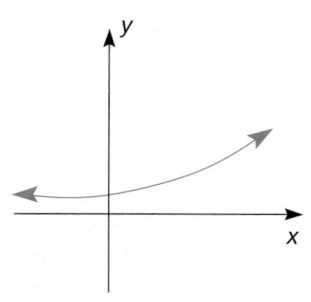

5. Consider the function f whose graph is shown next.

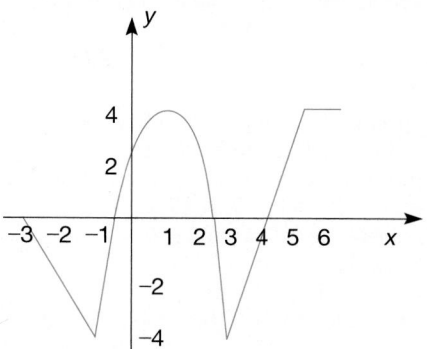

(a) Find the following.
(i) $f(1)$ (ii) $f(-1)$ (iii) $f(4.5)$
(b) Specify the domain and range of the function.
(c) For which value(s) of x is $f(x) = 2$?

6. As you stand on a beach and look out toward the ocean, the distance that you can see is a function of the height of your eyes about sea level. The following formula and graph represent this relationship, where h is the height of your eyes *in feet* and d is the distance you can see *in miles*.

$$d(h) = 1.2\sqrt{h}$$

(a) Use the formula to calculate the approximate values of $d(4)$ and $d(5.5)$. Use the graph to check your answers.
(b) A child's eyes are about 3 feet 3 inches from the ground. How far can she see out to the horizon?
(c) Specify the domain and range of the function as described above.

7. Make a table of at least five values for each of the following linear functions and sketch the graph of each function. How does the coefficient of the x affect the graph? How does the constant term affect the graph?
(a) $f(x) = 2x + 3$
(b) $m(x) = 40 - 5x$
(c) $g(x) = 7.2x - 4.5$

8. Make a table of at least five values for each of the following functions and sketch their graphs.
   (a) $h(x) = \frac{1}{2}x^2 + x$
   (b) $r(x) = 3^x$
   (c) $s(x) = 2 - x^3$

9. The **greatest integer function** of x, denoted $f(x) = [\![x]\!]$, is defined to be the greatest integer that is less than or equal to x. For example, $[\![3.5]\!] = 3$, $[\![-3.9]\!] = -4$, and $[\![17]\!] = 17$.
   (a) Evaluate the following.
       (i) $[\![2.4]\!]$ (ii) $[\![7.98]\!]$
       (iii) $[\![-4.2]\!]$ (iv) $[\![0.3]\!]$
   (b) Sketch the graph of $f(x) = [\![x]\!]$ for $-3 \le x \le 3$.

10. (a) Sketch the graph of each function. Use a graphics calculator if available.
       (i) $f(x) = x^2$ (ii) $f(x) = x^2 + 2$
       (iii) $f(x) = x^2 - 2$ (iv) $f(x) = (x - 2)^2$
       (v) $f(x) = (x + 2)^2$
    (b) Taking the graph in part (i) as a standard, what effect does the constant 2 have on the graph in each of the other parts of part (a).
    (c) Use the pattern you observed in part (a) to sketch graphs of $f(x) = x^2 + 4$ and $f(x) = (x - 3)^2$. Use a graphics calculator to check your prediction.

11. (a) Sketch a graph of each of the following quadratic equations. Use a graphics calculator if available.
       (i) $f(x) = x^2$ (ii) $f(x) = 2x^2$
       (iii) $f(x) = \frac{1}{2}x^2$ (iv) $f(x) = -3x^2$
    (b) What role does the coefficient of x^2 play in determining the shape of the graph?
    (c) Use the pattern you observed in part (a) and in Exercise 10 to predict the shaped of the graphs of $f(x) = -5x^2$ and $f(x) = \frac{1}{3}x^2 + 2$.

12. In 1992, postal rates for single mailings of third-class mail were as follows:

    29 cents for the first oz or less
    52 cents for over 1 oz and up to 2 oz
    75 cents for over 2 oz and up to 3 oz
    98 cents for over 3 oz and up to 4 oz
    $1.21 for over 4 oz and up to 6 oz
    $1.33 for over 6 oz and up to 8 oz
    $1.44 for over 8 oz and up to 10 oz
    $1.56 for over 10 oz and up to 12 oz
    $1.67 for over 12 oz and up to 14 oz
    $1.79 for over 14 oz, but less than 16 oz

    (a) If $P(w)$ gives the rate for a parcel weighing w ounces, find each of the following.
        (i) $P(0.5)$ (ii) $P(5.5)$
        (iii) $P(13.9)$ (iv) $P(14.1)$
    (b) Specify the domain and range for P based on the previous list.
    (c) Sketch the graph of third-class rates as a function of weight.

(d) Suppose that you have 20 pieces weighing $\frac{3}{4}$ oz each that you wish to mail third class to the same destination. Explain why it is cheaper to package them together in one bundle than to mail them separately.

13. Sketch the graph of each of the following step functions.
    (a) $f(x) = [\![x + 1]\!]$ for $0 \le x \le 4$
    (b) $f(x) = [\![2 - x]\!]$ for $-1 \le x \le 3$
    (c) $f(x) = 5 - [\![x]\!]$ for $0 \le x \le 5$
    (d) $f(x) = 6 \left[\!\left[\dfrac{x}{2} \right]\!\right]$ for $2 \le x \le 6$

14. Which type function listed next best fits each of the following graphs? (i) Linear, (ii) quadratic, (iii) cubic, (iv) exponential, or (v) step.
    (a)
    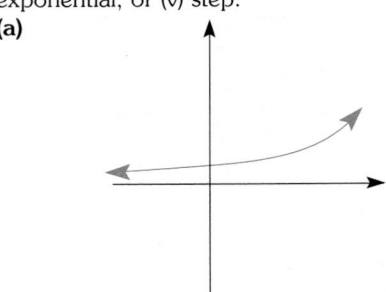
    (b)
    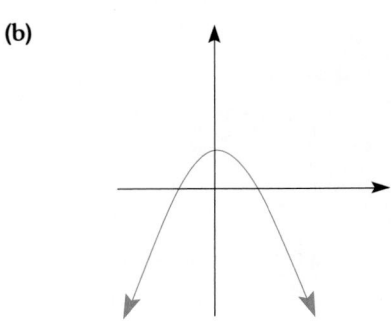
    (c)
    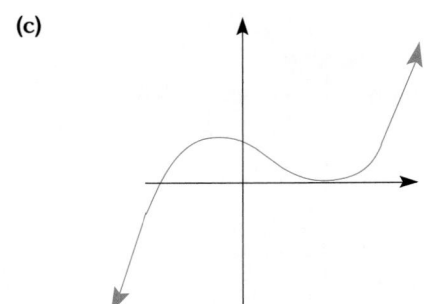

Problems

15. The following graph shows the relationship between the length of the shadow of a 100-meter-tall building and the number of hours that have passed since noon.

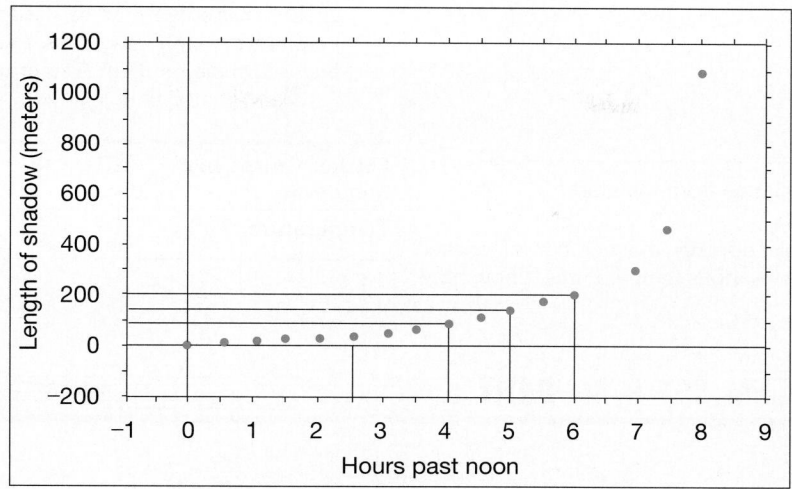

(a) If L represents the length of the shadow and n represents the number of hours since noon, why is L a function of n? What type of function does the graph appear to represent?

(b) Use the graph to approximate $L(5)$, $L(8)$, and $L(2.5)$ to the nearest 50.

(c) After how many hours is the shadow 100 meters long? When is it twice as long?

(d) Why do you think the graph stops at $n = 8$?

16. A man standing at a window 55 feet above the ground leans out and throws a ball straight up into the air with a speed of 70 feet per second. The height, s, of the ball above the ground, as a function of the number of seconds elapsed, t, is given as

$$s(t) = -16t^2 + 70t + 55$$

(a) Sketch a graph of the function for $0 \le t \le 6$. If available, use a graphics calculator.

(b) Use your graph to determine when the ball is about 90 feet above the ground. (NOTE: There are two times when this occurs. Use the formula as a check.)

(c) About when does the ball hit the ground?

(d) About how high does the ball go before it starts back down?

17. The population of the world is growing exponentially. A formula that can be used to make rough predictions of world population based on the population in 1980 and 1991 is given as

$$P(t) = 4.473e^{0.01685t}$$

where $P(t)$ is the world population in billions, t is the number of years since 1980, and e is an irrational number approximately equal to 2.718. (NOTE: Scientific calculators have e as one of their keys.)

(a) Sketch the graph of the function P. A graphics calculator will be helpful.

(b) Use the formula to predict the world population in 1996 to two decimal places.

(c) Use your graph to predict when the world population will reach 8 billion.

(d) Use your graph to estimate the current doubling time for the world population. That is, about how many years are required for the population to double?

18. A bicyclist pedals at a constant rate along a route that is essentially flat, but has one hill as shown in the next figure.

Which of the following graphs best describes what happens to the speed of the cyclist as she travels along the route?

(a)

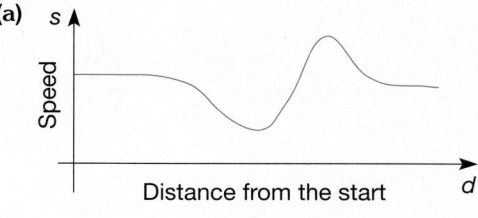

(b)

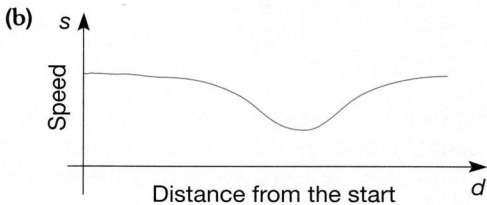

(c)

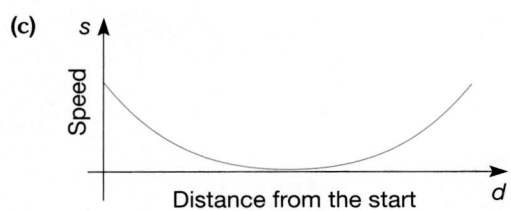

19. The following table displays the number of cricket chirps per minute at various temperatures. Show how cricket chirps can thus be used to measure the temperature by expressing T as a function of n; that is, find a formula for $T(n)$. Also graph your function.

Cricket Chirps per Minute, n	20	40	60	80	100
Temperature, T (°F)	45	50	55	60	65

EXERCISE/PROBLEM SET 9.3—PART B

Exercises

1. Plot the following points on graph paper. Indicate in which quadrant or on which axis the point lies.
   (a) $(-3, 0)$ **(b)** $(6, 4)$ **(c)** $(-2, 3)$
   (d) $(0, 5)$ **(e)** $(-1, -4)$ **(f)** $(3, -2)$

2. In which of the four quadrants will a point have the following characteristics?
   (a) Negative y-coordinate
   (b) Positive x-coordinate and negative y-coordinate
   (c) Negative x-coordinate and negative y-coordinate
   (d) Negative x-coordinate and positive y-coordinate
   (e) Positive x-coordinate and positive y-coordinate

3. A region in the coordinate plane is shaded where each mark on the axes represents one unit. Describe this region algebraically. That is, describe the values of the coordinates of the region using equations and/or inequalities.

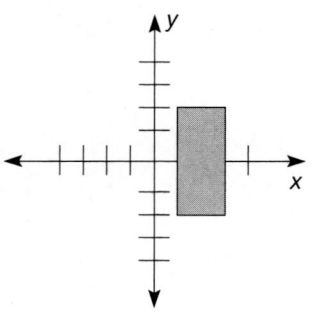

4. Determine which of the following graphs represent functions. That is, in which cases is y a function of x? For those that are functions, specify the domain and range.

(a)

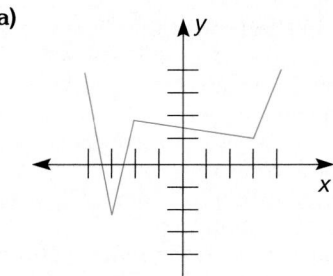

(b)

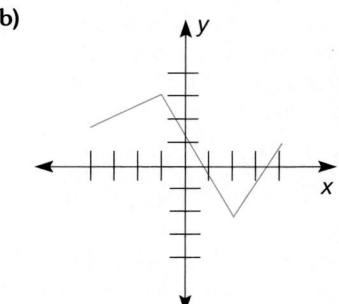

(c)

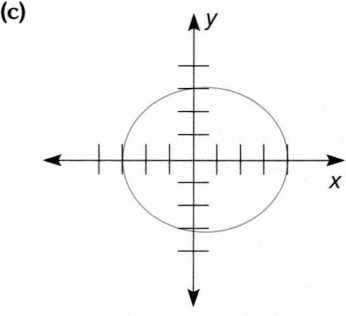

(d)

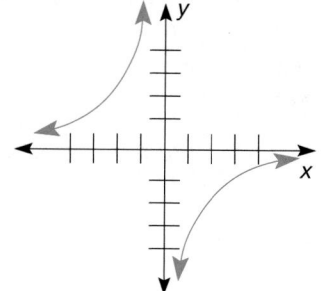

(e)

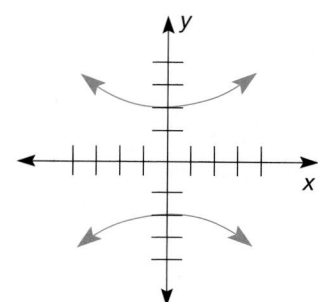

(f)

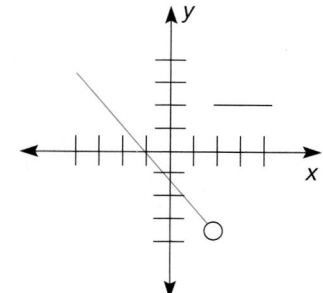

5. Consider the function f whose graph follows.

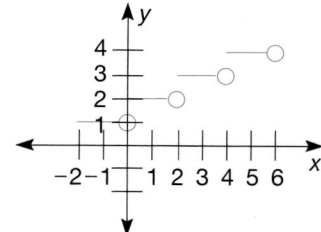

(a) Use the graph to find the following.
(i) $f(-1)$ (ii) $f(2)$ (iii) $f(3.75)$
(b) Specify the domain and range of f.
(c) For what value(s) of x is $f(x) = 3$? For what value(s) of x is $f(x) = 1.5$?
(d) What type of function is f?

6. The following graph shows the relationship between the diameter of a circular cake, d, and the area of the top of the cake, A.

$$A(d) \approx 0.7854d^2$$

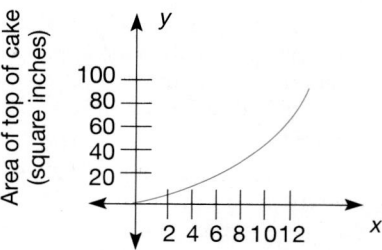

Diameter of cake (inches)

(a) Which type of function is A?
(b) Find $A(4)$ and $A(12)$ from the graph. Check your estimate using the formula.
(c) Sketch the graph of $A(d) = 0.7854d^2$ for values of d between -5 and 5. A graphics calculator would be helpful.
(d) Why are no points in the second quadrant included in the original graph?

7. Make a table of at least five values for each of the following linear functions and sketch their graphs.
(a) $f(x) = 3x - 2$
(b) $g(x) = -\frac{3}{4}x + 9$
(c) $h(x) = 120x + 25$

8. Make a table of at least five values for each of the following functions and sketch their graphs.
(a) $f(x) = x^2 - 4x$
(b) $f(x) = (\frac{1}{2})^x$
(c) $f(x) = \frac{2}{3}x^3 - 4$

9. (a) Sketch the graph of each of the following linear functions. Compare your graphs. A graphics calculator would be helpful.
(i) $f(x) = 2x - 3$ (ii) $f(x) = \frac{1}{2}x - 3$
(iii) $f(x) = 4x - 3$ (iv) $f(x) = \frac{2}{3}x - 3$
(b) How is the graph of the line affected by the coefficient of x?
(c) How would a negative coefficient of x affect the graph of the line? Try graphing the following functions to test your conjecture.
(i) $f(x) = (-2)x - 3$ (ii) $f(x) = (-\frac{3}{4})x - 3$

10. (a) Sketch the graph of each of the following linear equations. Use a graphics calculator if available. Compare your graphs.
(i) $f(x) = x + 2$ (ii) $f(x) = x - 4$
(iii) $f(x) = x + 6.5$ (iv) $f(x) = x$
(b) How is the graph of the line affected by the value of the constant term of the function?

11. **(a)** Sketch the graph of each of the following exponential functions. Use a graphics calculator if available. Compare your graphs.

    (i) $f(x) = 2^x$ (ii) $f(x) = 5^x$

    (iii) $f(x) = (\frac{1}{2})^x$ (iv) $f(x) = (\frac{3}{4})^x$

  (b) How is the shape of the graph of each function affected by the value of the base of the function?

  (c) Use the pattern you observed in part (a) to predict the shapes of the graphs of $f(x) = 10^x$ and $f(x) = (0.95)^x$. Check your prediction by sketching their graphs.

12. **(a)** Draw graphs of each of the following pairs of exponential functions. Compare the graphs you obtain. Use a graphics calculator if available.

    (i) $f(x) = (\frac{1}{3})^x$ and $f(x) = 3^{-x}$

    (ii) $f(x) = (\frac{2}{5})^x$ and $f(x) = 2.5^{-x}$

    (iii) $f(x) = 10^x$ and $f(x) = (0.1)^{-x}$

  (b) What interesting observation can be made about the pairs in part (a)?

13. The Institute for Aerobics Research recommends an optimal heart rate for exercisers who want to get the maximum benefit from their workouts. The rate is a function of the age of the exerciser and should be between 65% and 80% of the difference between 220 and the person's age. That is, if a is the age in years, then the minimum heart rate for 1 minute is

$$r(a) = 0.65(220 - a)$$

and the maximum is

$$R(a) = 0.8(220 - a)$$

  (a) Sketch the graphs of the functions r and R on the same set of axes.

  (b) A woman 30 years old begins a new exercise program. To benefit from the program, into what range should her heart rate fall?

  (c) How are the recommended heart rates affected as the age of the exerciser increases? How does your graph display this information?

14. Sketch the graph of each of the following step functions.

  (a) $f(x) = [\![x + 3]\!]$ for $0 \le x \le 5$

  (b) $f(x) = [\![4 - x]\!]$ for $-2 \le x \le 2$

  (c) $f(x) = 4 - [\![2 - x]\!]$ for $0 \le x \le 4$

  (d) $f(x) = 10 \left[\!\left[\dfrac{x}{4} \right]\!\right]$ for $-4 \le x \le 8$

15. Which type of function listed next best fits each of the following graphs? (i) Linear, (ii) quadratic, (iii) cubic, (iv) exponential, or (v) step.

(a)

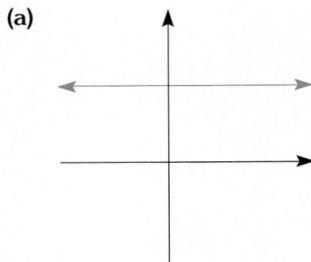

(b)

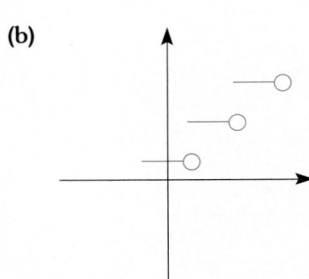

(c)

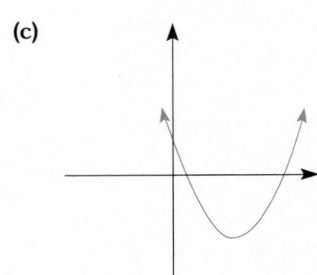

(d)

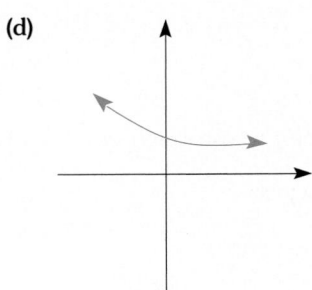

Problems

16. The length of time that passes between the time you see a flash of lightning and the time you hear the clap of thunder is related directly to your distance from the lightning. The following graph displays this relationship.

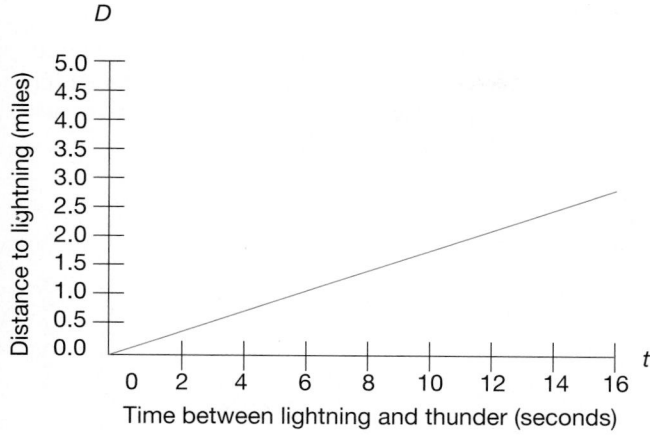

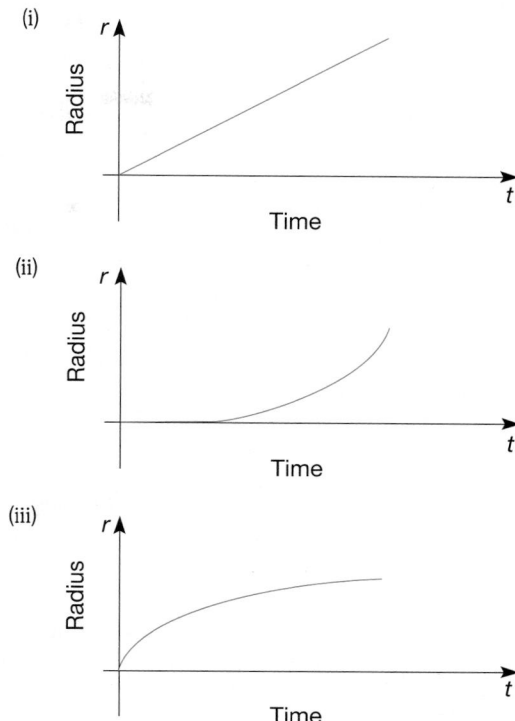

(a) If D represents your distance from the lightning and t represents the elapsed time between the lightning and thunder, is D a function of t? Explain.

(b) Use the graph to determine the approximate value of $D(8)$. Describe in words what this $D(8)$ means.

(c) Write a formula for $D(t)$.

17. If interest is compounded, the value of an investment increases exponentially. The following formula gives the value, V, of an investment of $250 after t years, where the interest rate is 6.25% and interest is compounded continuously:

$$V(t) = 250e^{0.0625t}$$

(a) Sketch the graph of V. A graphics calculator will be helpful here.

(b) Use the formula and your calculator to calculate the value of the $250 investment after 5 years.

(c) Use your graph and your calculator to predict when the investment will be worth $700.

(d) Use your graph to estimate the doubling time for this investment. That is, how long does it take to accumulate a total of $500?

18. A man is inflating a spherical balloon by blowing air into the balloon at a constant rate. Which of the following graphs best represents the radius of the balloon as a function of time?

19. In an effort to boost sales, an employer offers each sales associate a $20 bonus for every $500 of sales. However, no credit is given for amounts less than a multiple of $500.

(a) Two sales associates have sales totaling $758 and $1625. Calculate the amount of bonus each earned.

(b) One sales associate was paid a bonus of $80. Give a range for the dollar amount of merchandise that he or she sold.

(c) Make a table of values and sketch the graph of the bonus paid by the employer as a function of the dollar value of the merchandise.

(d) Write a function $B(n)$ that gives the bonus earned by an employee in terms of n, the number of dollars of merchandise sold. (HINT: Use the greatest integer function.)

SOLUTION OF INITIAL PROBLEM

A man's boyhood lasted for $\frac{1}{6}$ of his life, he played soccer for the next $\frac{1}{12}$ of his life, and he married after $\frac{1}{7}$ more of his life. A daughter was born 5 years after his marriage, and the daughter lived $\frac{1}{2}$ as many years as her father did. If the man died four years after his daughter did, how old was the man when he died?

Strategy: Solve an Equation

Let a represent the age of the father when he died. Then his boyhood was $\frac{1}{6}a$, he played soccer $\frac{1}{12}a$, and he married $\frac{1}{7}a$ years later. His daughter was born 5 years after his marriage. She lived $\frac{1}{2}$ as many years as her father, and he died four years after her, as shown below.

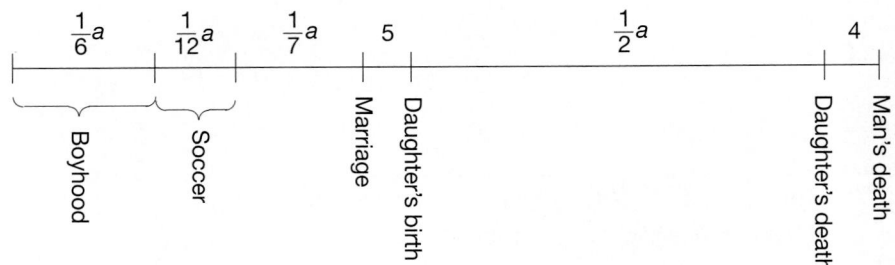

The diagram leads to the following equation.

$$\frac{1}{6}a + \frac{1}{12}a + \frac{1}{7}a + 5 + \frac{1}{2}a + 4 = a.$$

Solving this equation, we obtain

$$\frac{25}{28}a + 9 = a$$

$$9 = \frac{3}{28}a$$

$$84 = a.$$

Therefore, the father lived to be 84 years old. Check this solution back in the story to convince yourself that it is correct.

Additional Problems Where the Strategy "Solve an Equation" Is Useful

1. A saver opened a savings account and increased the account by one-third at the beginning of each year. At the end of the third year, she buys a $10,000 car and still has $54,000. If interest earned is not considered, how much did she have at the end of the first year?
2. Albert Einstein was once asked how many students he had had. He replied, "One-half of them study only arithmetic, one-third of them study only geometry, one-seventh of them study only chemistry, and there are 20 who study nothing at all." How many students did he have?
3. In an insect collection, centipedes had 100 legs and spiders had eight legs. There were 824 legs altogether and 49 more spiders than centipedes. How many centipedes were there?

WRITING/DISCUSSING FOR UNDERSTANDING

1. Contrast the system of real numbers with all the other systems we have studied, stating similarities and differences.
2. Discuss the strengths and shortcomings of the various approaches to solving equations as presented in Section 9.2.

3. Students find it easy to accept that $\frac{1}{3} = 0.\overline{33}$. However, many find it difficult to see that $0.\overline{9} = 1$. Develop two or three arguments to make this seem plausible.

4. Explain how the following NCTM Standards are reflected in this chapter.

- Extend their understanding of whole-number operations to fractions, decimals, integers, and rational numbers.
- Analyze functional relationships to explain how a change in one quantity results in a change in another.
- Use patterns and functions to represent and solve problems.
- Represent situations and number patterns with tables, graphs, verbal rules, and equations and explore the interrelationships of these representations.
- Represent numerical relationships in one- and two-dimensional graphs.

PROJECTS

1. Consult college algebra books to find a discussion about complex numbers. Explain how the complex numbers are an extension of the real numbers and how the equation $x^2 + 1 = 0$ has a solution in the complex numbers but not in the real numbers.

2. Peruse other college-level mathematics, physics, chemistry, biology, and business textbooks to find several examples of functions.

CHAPTER REVIEW

Major Ideas

1. The rational numbers are extensions of the fractions and the integers as displayed in the following diagram.

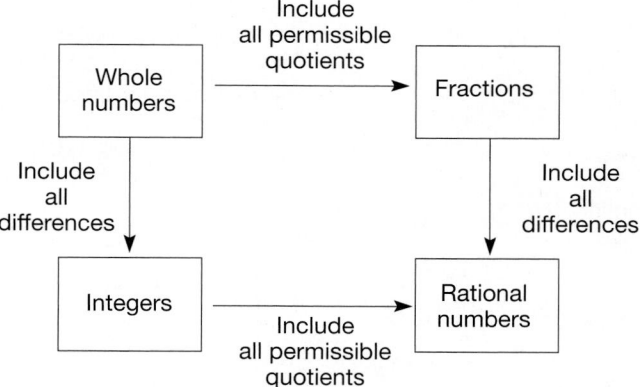

2. The operations of rational-number addition, subtraction, multiplication, and division are extensions of the respective operations on both the set of fractions and the set of integers.

3. Rational- and real-number addition and multiplication satisfy the following properties.

	Addition	**Multiplication**
Closure	Yes	Yes
Commutativity	Yes	Yes
Associativity	Yes	Yes
Identity	Yes	Yes
Inverse	Yes	Yes
Distributivity of multiplication over addition/subtraction		Yes

4. Ordering using "less than" and "greater than" can be extended from both fractions and integers to the rational numbers. The following properties following "less than" are true.

   (a) If $\frac{a}{b} < \frac{c}{d}$ and $\frac{c}{d} < \frac{e}{f}$, then $\frac{a}{b} < \frac{e}{f}$.

   (b) If $\frac{a}{b} < \frac{c}{d}$, then $\frac{a}{b} + \frac{e}{f} < \frac{c}{d} + \frac{e}{f}$.

   (c) If $\frac{a}{b} < \frac{c}{d}$ and $\frac{e}{f} > 0$, then $\frac{a}{b} \cdot \frac{e}{f} < \frac{c}{d} \cdot \frac{e}{f}$.

   (d) If $\frac{a}{b} < \frac{c}{d}$ and $\frac{e}{f} < 0$, then $\frac{a}{b} \cdot \frac{e}{f} > \frac{c}{d} \cdot \frac{e}{f}$.

   (e) If $\frac{a}{b} < \frac{c}{d}$, then there is an $\frac{e}{f}$ such that $\frac{a}{b} < \frac{e}{f} < \frac{c}{d}$.

5. The solutions of equations of the form $x^2 = p$, where p is a prime, are not rational numbers. Yet these solutions can be located precisely on the number line using the Pythagorean theorem.

6. The real numbers are all numbers that have infinite decimal representations. Real numbers with repeating decimal representations are the rational numbers. Irrational numbers are those real numbers that have infinite nonrepeating decimal representations. The real numbers correspond to all the points on the number line. The following diagram displays the relationships among the various sets studied in this book.

7. The real numbers are complete in the sense that they completely fill in the real number line.

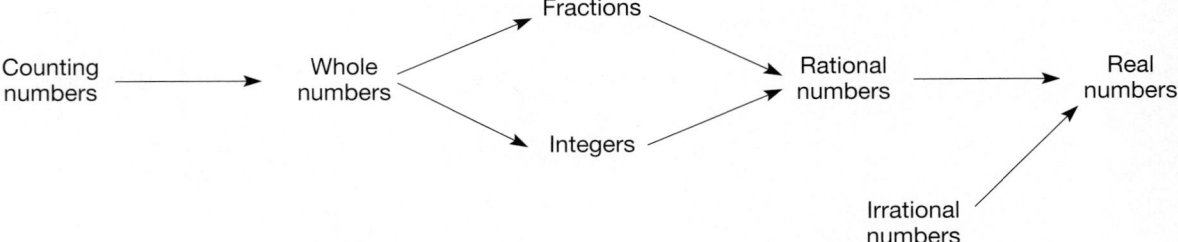

8. The square root of any nonnegative real number exists. Furthermore, the concept of square root ($\sqrt{a}$) can be extended to any nth root ($\sqrt[n]{a}$) of any nonnegative real number, a, where $n > 0$ and any negative real number, a, where n is an odd number.

9. Rational exponents can be defined on all positive real numbers.

10. Equations and inequalities of the form $ax + b = cx + d$ and $ax + b < cx + d$ can be solved using properties of real numbers.

11. Graphs of functions are useful for solving problems.

Following is a list of key vocabulary, notation, and ideas for this chapter. Mentally review these items and, where appropriate, write down the meaning of each term. Then restudy the material that you are unsure of before proceeding to take the chapter test.

SECTION 9.1: THE RATIONAL NUMBERS

Vocabulary/Notation

Rational number 364
Simplest form (lowest terms) 365
Positive rational number 368

Negative rational number 368
Opposite of a rational number 369
Reciprocal of a rational number 373

Ideas

Equality of rational numbers 364
Addition of rational numbers 366
Five properties of rational-number addition 368
Subtraction of rational numbers 369
Multiplication of rational numbers 371
Five properties of rational-number multiplication 372
Distributive property 372
Three methods of rational-number division 374
Three ways of ordering rational numbers 375
Cross-multiplication of inequality of rational numbers 376
Five properties of rational numbers using "less than" 377

SECTION 9.2: THE REAL NUMBERS

Vocabulary/Notation

Real numbers 383
Irrational numbers 384
Principal square root 385
Square root ($\sqrt{}$) 386
Radicand 388
Index 388
Radical 388
nth root ($\sqrt[n]{}$) 389
Rational exponent 389

Equation 390
Inequality 390
Variable 390
Solution 390
Solution set 390
Guess and test method 390
Cover-up method 390
Work backward method 390
Equivalent equation method 391

Ideas

SECTION 9.3: FUNCTIONS AND THEIR GRAPHS

Vocabulary/Notation

Ideas

PEOPLE IN MATHEMATICS

Paul Cohen (1934–) has won two of the most prestigious awards in mathematics: the Fields medal and the Bocher Prize. In 1963, he solved the so-called "continuum hypothesis," the first problem in David Hilbert's famous list of 23 unsolved problems. As a youngster in Brooklyn, Paul was intensely curious about math and science. Children were not allowed in the main section of the public library, but he would sneak in to browse the math section. At age 9 he proved the converse of the Pythagorean theorem, and by age 11 his older sister was bringing him math books from the college library. A major influence was his attendance at Stuyvesant High School, a competitive math–science school in Manhattan. "When my proof [of the continuum hypothesis] was first presented, some people thought it was wrong. Then it was thought to be extremely complicated. Then it was thought to be easy. But of course it is easy in the sense that there is a clear philosophical idea."

Rozsa Peter (1905–1977) was a pioneer in the field of mathematical logic, writing two books and more than 50 papers on the subject. She was also known as a consummate teacher who engaged her students in the joint discovery of mathematics. She served for 10 years at a teacher's college in Budapest, where she wrote mathematics textbooks and proposed reforms in mathematics education. She fought against elitism and urged mathematicians to visit primary schools to communicate the spirit of their work. Her popularized account of mathematics, *Playing with Infinity* was published in 1945 and has been translated into 12 languages. Rozsa wrote that she would like others to see that "mathematics and the arts are not so different from each other. I love mathematics not only for its technical applications, but principally because it is beautiful."

CHAPTER 9 TEST

Knowledge

1. True or false?
   (a) The fractions together with the integers comprise the rational numbers.
   (b) Every rational number is a real number.
   (c) The square root of any positive rational number is irrational.
   (d) 7^{-3} means $(-7)(-7)(-7)$.
   (e) $25^{5/2}$ means $(\sqrt{25})^5$.
   (f) If a, b, and c are real numbers and $a < b$, then $ac < bc$.
   (g) If $(-3)x + 7 = 13$, then $x = -2$.
   (h) If F is a function, the graph of F can be intersected at most once by any horizontal line.

Skill

2. Compute the following problems and express the answers in simplest form.
   (a) $\dfrac{-5}{3} + \dfrac{4}{7}$ (b) $\dfrac{-3}{11} \div \dfrac{5}{2}$ (c) $\dfrac{3}{(-4)} - \dfrac{(-5)}{7}$

3. Which properties can be used to simplify these computations?
   (a) $\dfrac{2}{3} + \left(\dfrac{5}{7} + \dfrac{-2}{3}\right)$ (b) $\dfrac{3}{4} \cdot \dfrac{5}{11} + \dfrac{5}{11} \cdot \dfrac{1}{4}$

4. Solve for x.
   (a) $\left(\dfrac{-3}{5}\right)x + \dfrac{4}{7} < \dfrac{8}{5}$ (b) $\dfrac{5}{4}x - \dfrac{3}{7} = \dfrac{2}{3}x + \dfrac{5}{8}$

5. Express the following values without using exponents.
   (a) $(3^{10})^{3/5}$ (b) $8^{7/3}$ (c) $81^{-5/4}$

6. Sketch the graph of each of the following functions.
   (a) $f(x) = 3x + 4$
   (b) $g(x) = x^2 - 3$
   (c) $h(x) = 1.5^x$

Understanding

7. Using the fact that $\dfrac{a}{b} \cdot \dfrac{c}{d} = \dfrac{ac}{bd}$, show that $\dfrac{-3}{7} = \dfrac{3}{-7}$.
   (HINT: Make a clever choice for $\dfrac{c}{d}$.)

8. Cross-multiplication of inequality states: If $b > 0$ and $d > 0$, then $\dfrac{a}{b} < \dfrac{c}{d}$ if and only if $ad < bc$. Would this property still hold if $b < 0$ and $d > 0$? Why or why not?

9. By definition $a^{-m} = \dfrac{1}{a^m}$, where m is a positive integer. Using this definition, carefully explain why $\dfrac{1}{5^{-7}} = 5^7$.

Problem Solving/Application

10. Extending the argument used to show that $\sqrt{2}$ is not rational, show that $\sqrt{8}$ is not rational.

11. Four-sevenths of a school's faculty are women. Four-fifths of the male faculty members are married and 9 of the male faculty members are unmarried. How many faculty members are there?

12. Some students *incorrectly* simplify fractions as follows: $\dfrac{3+4}{5+4} = \dfrac{3}{5}$. Determine all possible values for x such that $\dfrac{a+x}{b+x} = \dfrac{a}{b}$; that is, find all values for x for which this *incorrect* process works.

13. For the function $f(t) = (0.5)^t$, its value when $t = 0$ is $f(0) = (0.5)^0 = 1$. For what value of t is $f(t) = 0.125$?

Statistics

USA SNAPSHOTS®

A look at statistics that shape the sports world

California's racket

Since the NCAA Div. I tennis championships began, California colleges have dominated. The score to date:

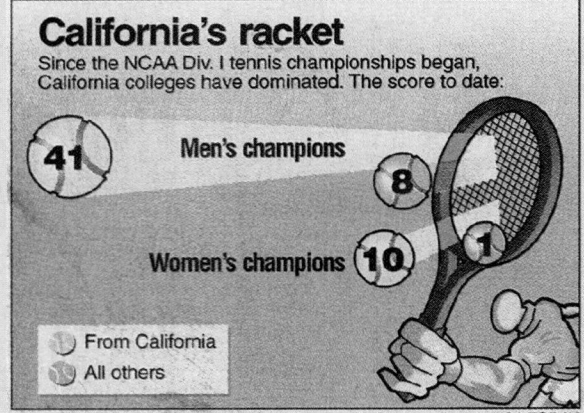

41 Men's champions **8**

Women's champions **10** **1**

- From California
- All others

Source: USA TODAY research by John Riley   By Stephen Conley, USA TODAY

USA SNAPSHOTS®

A look at statistics that shape our lives

College seniors' plans for five years down the road

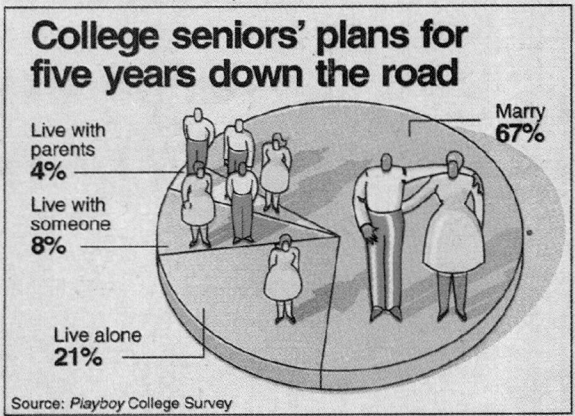

Live with parents **4%**

Live with someone **8%**

Marry **67%**

Live alone **21%**

Source: *Playboy* College Survey

By Elys A. McLean, USA TODAY

USA SNAPSHOTS®

A look at statistics that shape the nation

World's population is soaring

The world's population adds the equivalent of a Mexico every year and will top 5.5 billion this year. Population projections:

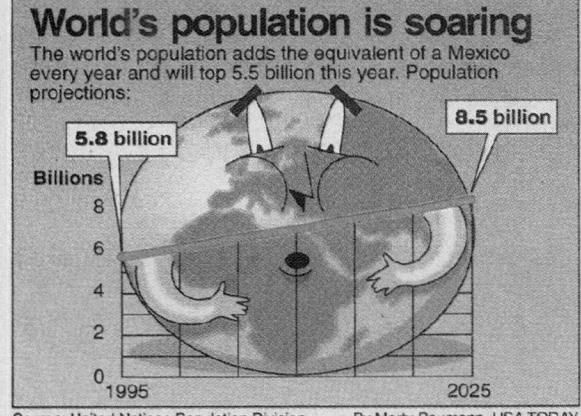

5.8 billion

8.5 billion

Billions

8	
6	
4	
2	
0	

1995   2025

Source: United Nations Population Division   By Marty Baumann, USA TODAY

USA SNAPSHOTS®

A look at statistics that shape the sports world

Dominating college lacrosse

A few colleges have dominated men's lacrosse, but on the women's side, no such group has surfaced. Leading NCAA Division I lacrosse champions:

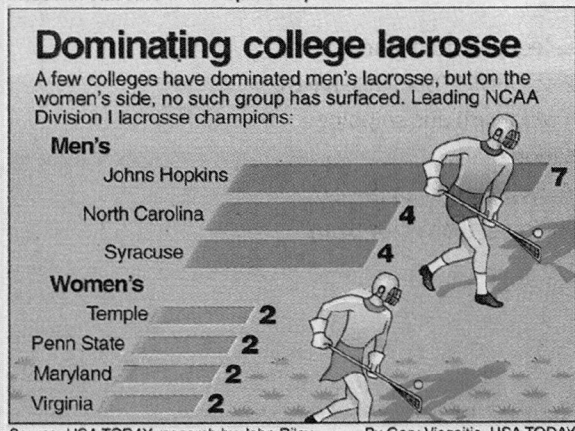

Men's

Johns Hopkins **7**

North Carolina **4**

Syracuse **4**

Women's

Temple **2**

Penn State **2**

Maryland **2**

Virginia **2**

Source: USA TODAY research by John Riley   By Gary Visgaitis, USA TODAY

Four Graphs from USA Today

Statistics in the Everyday World

Statistics influence our daily lives in many ways: in presidential elections, weather forecasting, television programming, and advertising, to name a few. H. G. Wells once said: "Statistical thinking will one day be as necessary as the ability to read and write." The accompanying graphs from USA Today are testimony to Wells's statement.

One of the real challenges in interpreting everyday statistically based information is to keep alert to "misinformation" derived through the judicious misuse of statistics. Several examples of such misinformation follow.

1. An advertisement stated that "Over 95% of our cars registered in the past 11 years are still on the road." This is an interesting statistic, but what if most of these cars were sold within the past two or three years? The inference in the ad was that the cars are durable. However, no additional statistics were provided from which the readers could draw conclusions.

2. The advertisement of another company claimed that only 1% of the more than half million people who used their product were unsatisfied and applied for their double-your-money-back guarantee. The inference is that 99% of their customers are happy, when it could be that many customers were unhappy, but only 1% chose to apply for the refund.

3. In an effort to boost its image, a company claimed that its sales had increased by 50% while its competitor's had increased by only 20%. There was no mention made of earnings or of the absolute magnitude of the increases. After all, if one's sales are $100, it is easier to push them to $150 than it is to increase, say $1 billion of sales by 20%.

4. A stockbroker who lets an account balance drop by 25% says to a client, "We'll easily be able to make a 25% recovery in your account." Unfortunately, a $33\frac{1}{3}$% increase is required to reach the break-even point.

Additional creative ways to influence you through the misuse of statistics via graphs are presented in this chapter.

STRATEGY 15: LOOK FOR A FORMULA

The strategy Look for a Formula is especially appropriate in problems involving number patterns. Often it extends and refines the strategy Look for a Pattern and gives more general information. For example, in the number sequence 1, 4, 7, 10, 13, . . . we observe many patterns. If we wanted to know the 100th term in the sequence, we could eventually generate it by using patterns. However, with some additional investigation, we can establish that the formula $T = 3n - 2$ gives the value of the nth term in the sequence, for $n = 1, 2, 3$, and so on. Hence the 100th term can be found directly to be $3 \cdot 100 - 2 = 298$. We will make use of the Look for a Formula strategy in this chapter and subsequent chapters. For example, in Chapter 13 we look for formulas for various measurement aspects of geometrical figures.

Initial Problem

A servant was asked to perform a job that would take 30 days. The servant would be paid 1000 gold coins. The servant replied, "I will happily complete the job, but I would rather be paid 1 copper coin on the first day, 2 copper coins on the second day, 4 on the third day, and so on, with the payment of copper coins doubling each day." The king agreed to the servant's method of payment. If a gold coin is worth 100 copper coins, did the king make the right decision? How much was the servant paid?

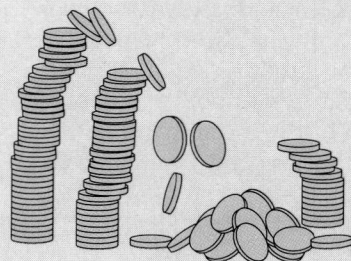

Clues

The Look for a Formula strategy may be appropriate when:

- A problem suggests a pattern that can be generalized.
- Ideas such as percent, rate, distance, area, volume, or other measurable attributes are involved.
- Applications in science, business, and so on, are involved.
- Solving problems involving such topics as statistics, probability, and so on.

A solution of the Initial Problem above appears on page 470.

INTRODUCTION

After World War II, W. Edwards Deming, an American statistician, was sent to Japan to aid in its reconstruction. Deming worked with the Japanese to establish quality control in their manufacturing system. If a problem arose, they would (1) formulate questions, (2) design a study, (3) collect data, (4) organize and analyze the data, (5) present the data, and finally (6), interpret the data to identify the cause of the problem. It is interesting to note that the most prestigious award given for quality manufacturing in Japan is the Deming Award. In the past several years, many of his techniques have also been adapted by American manufacturers. In Section 10.1, ways of organizing and presenting data are studied. Then, in Section 10.2, data are analyzed and interpreted using such concepts as various types of averages, dispersion, and distribution of data.

10.1

ORGANIZING AND PICTURING INFORMATION

Organizing Information

Line Plots

Suppose that 30 fourth-graders took a science test and made the following scores: 22, 23, 14, 45, 39, 11, 9, 46, 22, 25, 6, 28, 33, 36, 16, 39, 49, 17, 22, 32, 34, 22, 18, 21, 27, 34, 26, 41, 28, 25. What can we conclude about the students' performance? At the outset, we can say very little, since the data are so disorganized. First, let us put them in increasing order (Table 10.1).

TABLE 10.1   SCIENCE TEST SCORES

6, 9, 11, 14, 16, 17, 18, 21, 22, 22, 22, 22, 23, 25, 25, 26, 27, 28, 28, 32, 33, 34, 34, 36, 39, 39, 41, 45, 46, 49

From the table we can make the general observation that the scores range from 6 to 49 and seem rather spread out. With the **line plot** in Figure 10.1 we can graph the scores and obtain a more visual representation of the data.

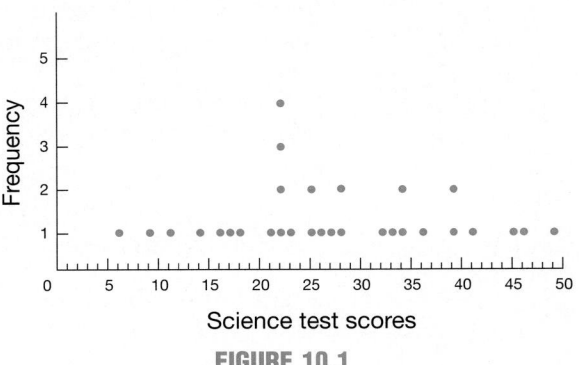

FIGURE 10.1

Each dot corresponds to one score. The **frequency** of a number is the number of times it occurs in a collection of data. From the line plot, we see that five scores occurred more than once and that the score 22 had the greatest frequency.

Stem and Leaf Plots

One popular method of organizing data is to use a **stem and leaf plot**. To illustrate this method, refer to the list of the science test scores:

22, 23, 14, 45, 39, 11, 9, 46, 22, 25, 6, 28, 33, 36, 16,
39, 49, 17, 22, 32, 34, 22, 18, 21, 27, 34, 26, 41, 28, 25

A stem and leaf plot for the scores appears in Table 10.2. The stems are the tens digits of the science test scores, and the leaves are the ones digits. For example, 0 | 6 represents a score of 6, and 1 | 4 represents a score of 14.

Notice that the leaves are recorded in the order in which they appear in the list of science test scores, not in increasing order. We can refine the stem and leaf plot by listing the leaves in increasing order, as in Table 10.3.

EXAMPLE 10.1 Make a stem and leaf plot for the following children's heights, in centimeters.

94, 105, 107, 108, 108, 120, 121, 122, 122, 123

Solution
Use the numbers in the 100s and 10s places as the stems and the 1s digits as the leaves (Table 10.4). For example, 10 | 5 represents 105 cm. ▪

From the stem and leaf plot in Table 10.4 we see that no data occur between 108 and 120. A large empty interval such as this is called a **gap** in the data. We also see that several values of the data lie close together—namely, those with stems "10" and "12." Several values of the data that lie in close proximity form a **cluster**. Thus one gap and two clusters are evident in Table 10.4. The presence or absence of gaps and clusters is often revealed by stem and leaf plots as well as in line plots. "Gap" and "cluster" are imprecise terms describing general breaks or groupings in data and may be interpreted differently by different people. However, such phenomena often reveal useful information. For example, clusters of data separated by gaps in reading test scores for a class can help in the formation of reading groups.

Suppose that a second class of fourth-graders took the same science test as the class represented in Table 10.3 and had the following scores:

5, 7, 12, 13, 14, 22, 25, 26, 27, 28, 28, 29, 31, 32, 33,
34, 34, 35, 36, 37, 38, 39, 42, 43, 45, 46, 47, 48, 49, 49

Using a **back-to-back stem and leaf plot**, we can compare the two classes by listing the leaves for the classes on either side of the stem (Table 10.5).

TABLE 10.2

Stems	Leaves
0	9 6
1	4 1 6 7 8
2	2 3 2 5 8 2 2 1 7 6 8 5
3	9 3 6 9 2 4 4
4	5 6 9 1

TABLE 10.3

Stems	Leaves
0	6 9
1	1 4 6 7 8
2	1 2 2 2 2 3 5 5 6 7 8 8
3	2 3 4 4 6 9 9
4	1 5 6 9

TABLE 10.4

Stems	Leaves
9	4
10	5 7 8 8
11	
12	0 1 2 2 3

TABLE 10.5

Class 1		Class 2
9 6	0	5 7
8 7 6 4 1	1	2 3 4
8 8 7 6 5 5 3 2 2 2 2 1	2	2 5 6 7 8 8 9
9 9 6 4 4 3 2	3	1 2 3 4 4 5 6 7 8 9
9 6 5 1	4	2 3 5 6 7 8 9 9

Notice that the leaves increase as they move away from the stems. By comparing the corresponding leaves for the two classes in Table 10.5, we see that class 2 seems to have performed better than class 1. For example, there are fewer scores in the 10s and 20s in class 2 and more scores in the 30s and 40s.

Histograms

Another common method of representing data is to group it in intervals and plot the frequencies of the data in each interval. For example, in Table 10.3, we see that the interval from 20 to 29 had more scores than any other, and that relatively few scores fell in the extreme intervals 0–9 and 40–49. To make this visually apparent, we can make a **histogram**, which shows the number of scores that occur in each interval (Figure 10.2). We determine the height of each rectangular bar of the histogram by using the frequency of the scores in the intervals. Bars are centered above the midpoints of the intervals. The vertical axis of the histogram shows the frequency of the scores in each of the intervals on the horizontal axis. Here we see that a cluster of scores occurs in the interval from 20 to 29 and that there are relatively few extremely high or low scores.

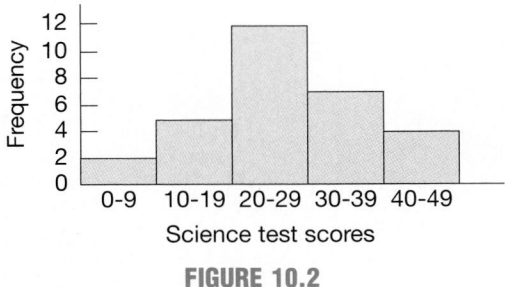

FIGURE 10.2

Notice that if we turn the stem and leaf plot in Table 10.3 counterclockwise through one-quarter of a turn, we will have a diagram resembling the histogram in Figure 10.2. An advantage of a stem and leaf plot is that each value of the data can be retrieved. With a histogram, only approximate data can be retrieved.

Charts and Graphs

Pictographs

There are many common types of charts and graphs used for picturing data. A **pictograph**, like the one in Figure 10.3, uses a picture, or icon, to symbolize the quantities being represented. From a pictograph we can observe the change in a quantity over time. We can also make comparisons between similar situations. For example, in Figure 10.4 we can compare the numbers of microcomputers in American elementary, middle, and high schools in 1986. Notice that Figures 10.3 and 10.4 are equivalent to line plots with pictures of computers instead of dots.

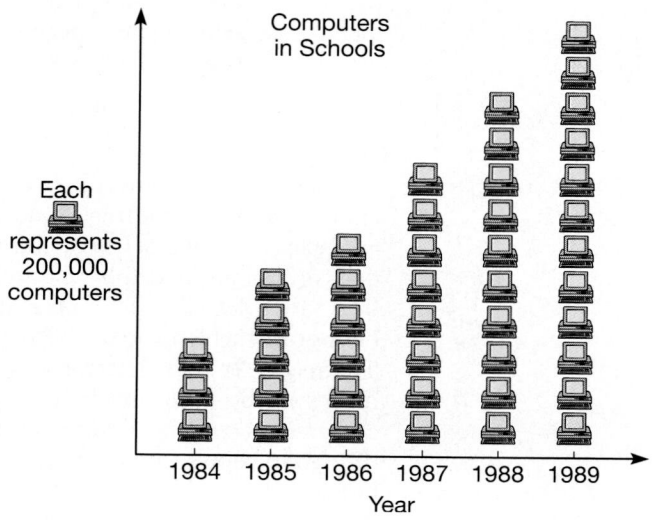

FIGURE 10.3
Source: Center for the Social Organization of Schools.

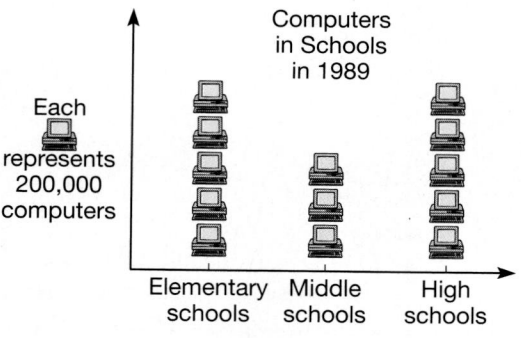

FIGURE 10.4
Source: Center for the Social Organization of Schools.

STUDENT PAGE SNAPSHOT

Deceptive Graphs

If one or more parts of a graph are distorted, a deceptive graph can result. When reading a graph check to see that scales are not condensed or expanded, that labels are truthful, and that data is plotted accurately.

WORKING TOGETHER

The Best Bolt Co. produced this graph from the data comparing bolt sales of the three largest manufacturers.

BOLT SALES (in millions)

Acme	11.2
Reliable	11.1
Best	11.8

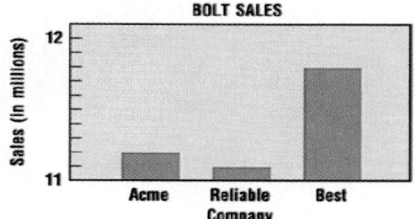

1. What impression is given by the graph? How has it been created?

2. Draw a graph to accurately depict the data.

Candidate Jones published this graph from the data showing the results of voter-preference polls of candidate Smith.

PERCENTAGE OF VOTERS CHOOSING SMITH

July	Aug.	Sept.	Oct.
20	30	40	50

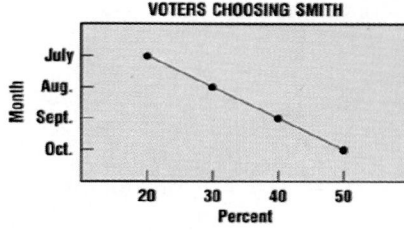

3. According to the polls is Smith gaining or losing popularity?

4. What impression is given by the graph? How has it been created?

5. Draw a graph that gives the correct impression of the data.

SHARING IDEAS

6. Describe three ways you can create a misleading impression using a bar graph.

7. Describe three ways you can create a misleading impression using a line graph.

8. Describe how you could draw a graph to create the misleading impression that Mason has been rising steadily in the polls since July.

PERCENTAGE OF VOTERS CHOOSING MASON

July 1	July 15	Aug. 1	Sept. 1	Oct. 1
20	21	22	22	22

The pictograph map of the United States in Figure 10.5 displays municipal waste *per person* by state. Notice how quickly one can scan this graph for absolute amounts for each state as well as comparisons between states.

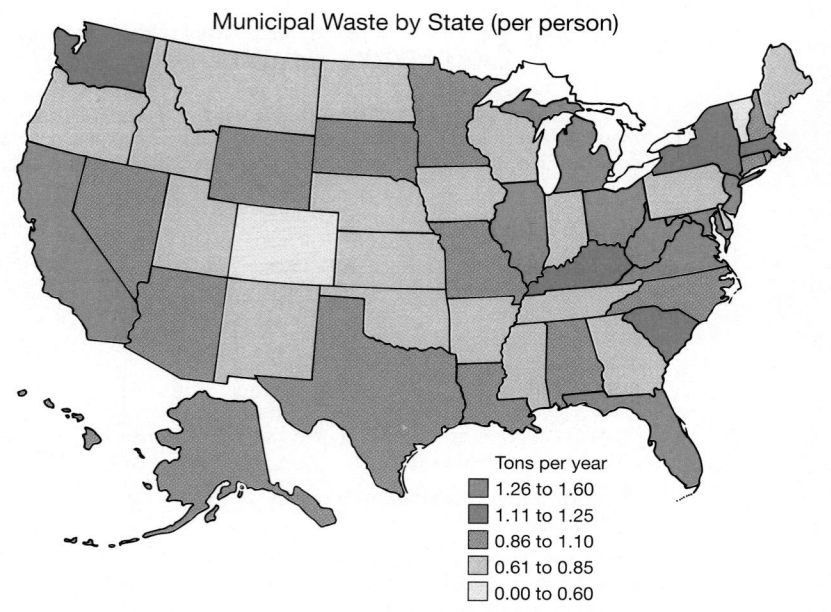

Municipal Waste by State (per person)

Tons per year
- ■ 1.26 to 1.60
- ■ 1.11 to 1.25
- ■ 0.86 to 1.10
- ■ 0.61 to 0.85
- □ 0.00 to 0.60

FIGURE 10.5
Source: *Biocycle*, March 1990.

Pictographs can be deceptive, particularly if drawn to represent three-dimensional objects. Figure 10.6 gives an example of a deceptive comparison. From the vertical scale, we see that milk sales doubled from 1985 to 1991. Yet because *each* dimension in the 1985 icon is doubled to make

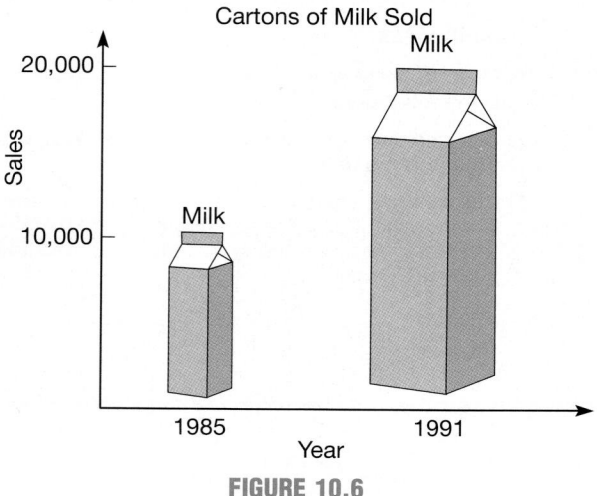

Cartons of Milk Sold

FIGURE 10.6

the 1991 icon, it appears that milk consumption in 1991 was considerably more than twice that of 1985. In fact, the milk carton shown for 1991 would have eight times the capacity of the 1985 carton—very deceptive. If only one dimension of the icon is changed to show the correct ratio, the pictograph will not be deceptive; however, the icons will not have the same shape. But if two or more dimensions are multiplied by this ratio, the pictograph will be misleading.

Bar Graphs

A bar graph is useful for making direct visual comparisons over a period of time. The **bar graph** in Figure 10.7 shows the amount of school funding for a district over a five-year period. The bar graph in Figure 10.8 shows the same data as the bar graph in Figure 10.7. When the bars in the graph in Figure 10.8 are compared, they visually suggest a much larger increase in funding from 1986 to 1987 than does the graph in Figure 10.7. This is due to the vertical scale change in the graph in Figure 10.8. Notice that the vertical scale begins at zero in the graph in Figure 10.7, but the vertical scale begins at 10 in Figure 10.8. NOTE: The mark on the vertical axis is used to indicate that this part of the scale is not consistent with the rest of the scale.

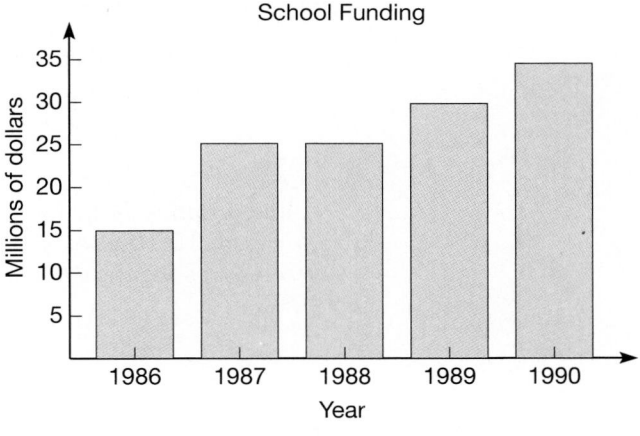

FIGURE 10.7

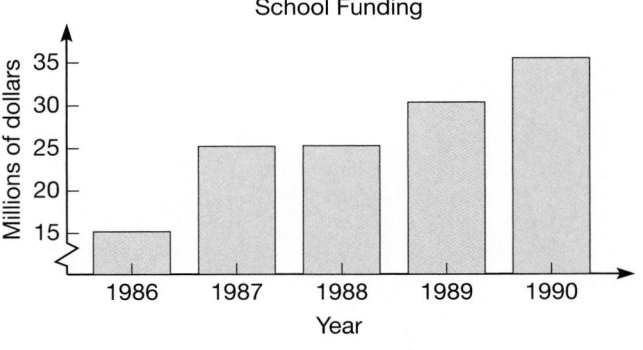

FIGURE 10.8

Multiple-bar graphs can be used to show comparisons of data. In Figure 10.9 the enrollments in two school districts, A and B, are shown for the years 1980, 1985, and 1990. We see that enrollments in each district grew, but those in district A grew more.

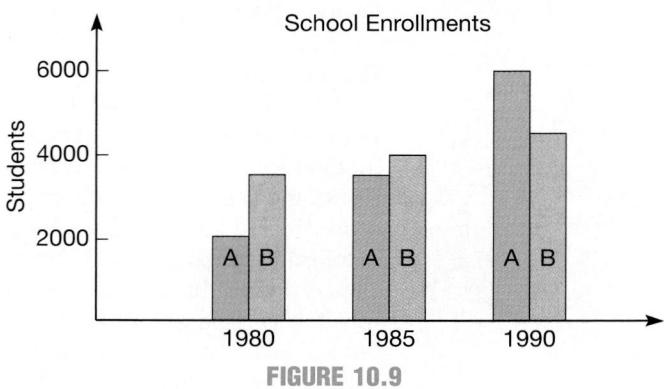

FIGURE 10.9

A histogram, such as the one in Figure 10.2, is a special type of bar graph. Histograms are useful for picturing grouped or rounded data. The method by which the data are grouped, however, can lead to differently shaped histograms.

Line Graphs

A **line graph** is useful for plotting data over a period of time to indicate trends. Figure 10.10 gives an example.

By compressing the vertical scale, a very different graph results (see Figure 10.11).

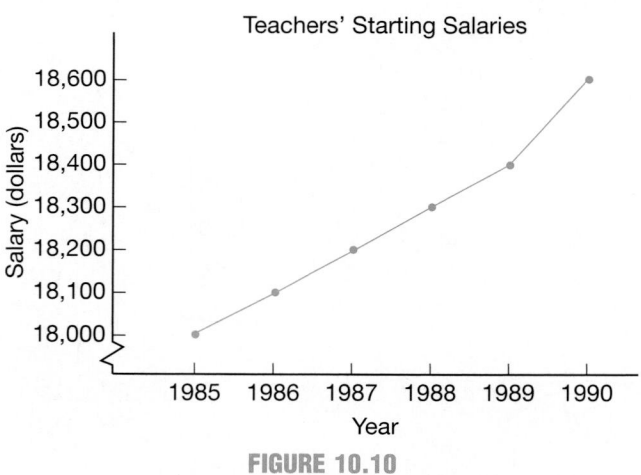

FIGURE 10.10

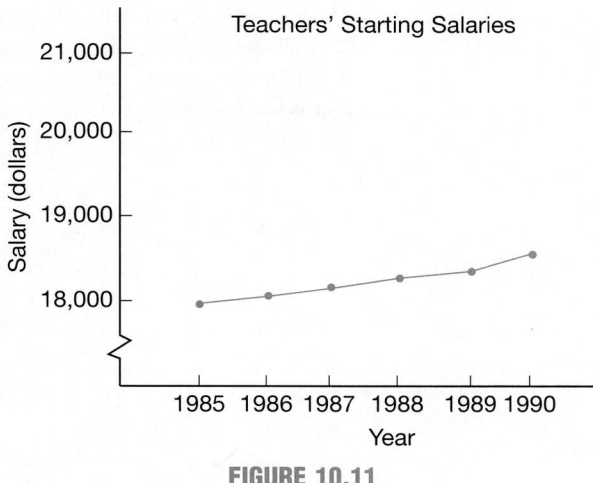

FIGURE 10.11

The salary increases appear much more modest in the line graph in Figure 10.11 than they do in Figure 10.10 because of the change in the vertical scale.

Multiple-line graphs can be used to show trends and comparisons simultaneously. For example, Figure 10.12 shows milk prices each month for the years 1987–1989. Notice that prices generally fell from January through April. In 1988 and 1989 they then rose steadily to the end of the year, while in 1987 they fell again from October on. Prices in 1988 were lower than in the same months in 1987 until October, when they crossed over and stayed higher. Prices in 1989 were consistently higher than in 1988. Notice that the break in the vertical scale (to save space) does not affect the analysis of comparisons and trends.

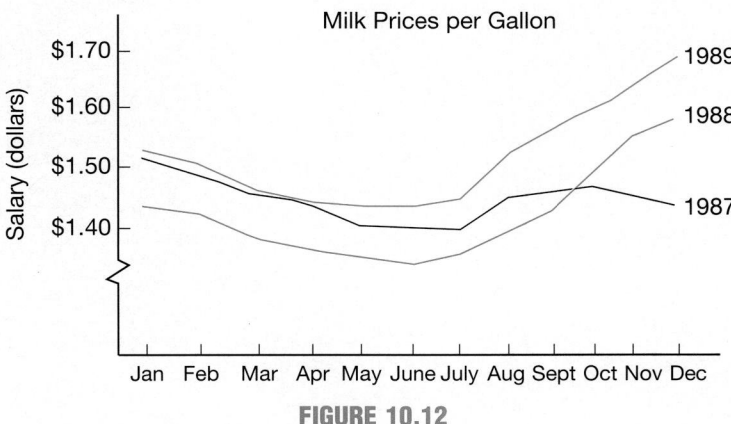

FIGURE 10.12

Line graphs also can be used to display two different pieces of information simultaneously. For example, the graph in Figure 10.13 shows world fertilizer use and grain area per person from 1950 to 1985. By graphing this information together, it is noticeable that as fertilizer use was increased, the amount of area devoted to grain production was decreased.

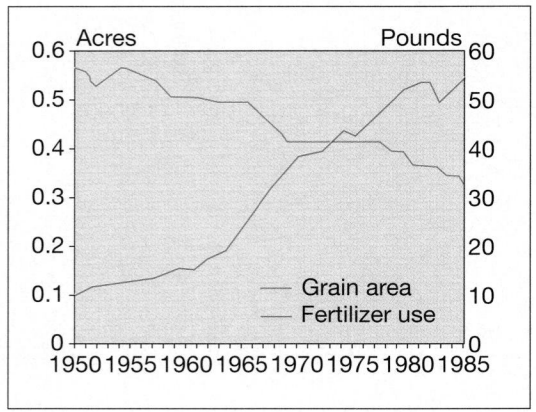

FIGURE 10.13
World fertilizer use and grain area per person, 1950–1986. *Source*: U.S. Department of Agriculture.

Circle Graphs

The last type of graph we will consider is a **circle graph** or **pie chart**. Circle graphs are used for comparing parts of a whole. Figure 10.14 shows the percentages of people working in a certain community.

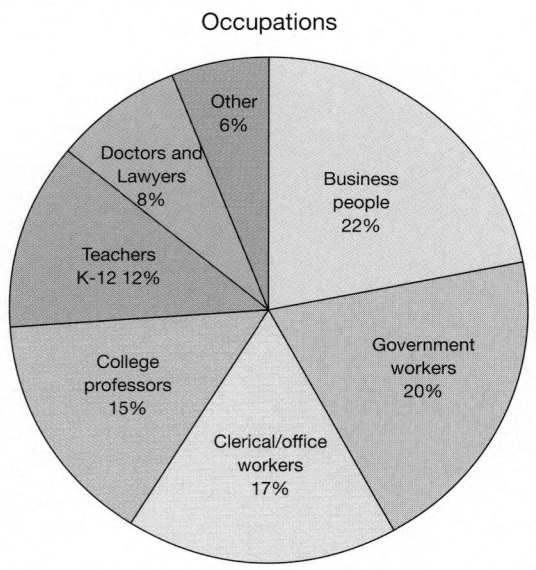

FIGURE 10.14

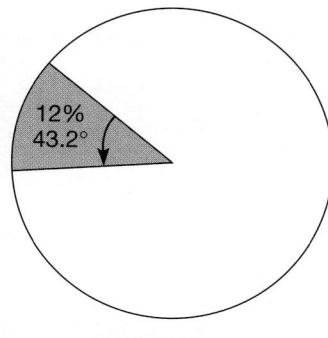

FIGURE 10.15

In making a circle graph, the area of a sector is proportional to the fraction or percentage that it represents. The central angle in the sector is equal to the given percentage of 360°. For example, in Figure 10.14, the central angle for the teachers' sector is 12% of 360°, or 43.2° (Figure 10.15).

Multiple circle graphs can be used to show trends. For example, Figure 10.16 shows the changes in meat consumption between the two years 1971 and 1989. One can see that the relative amount of red meat consumed per person has declined and the relative amounts of both poultry and seafood has increased.

Changes in Meat Consumption per Person, 1971 and 1989 (in percentages)

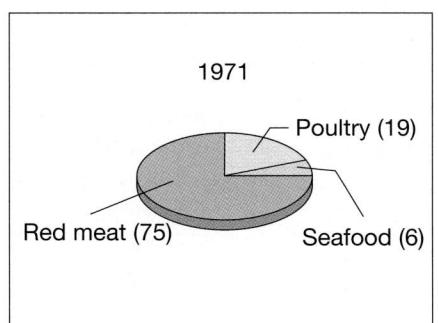
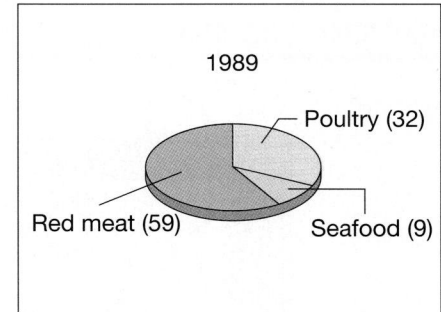

FIGURE 10.16
Source: U.S. Department of Agriculture, 1990.

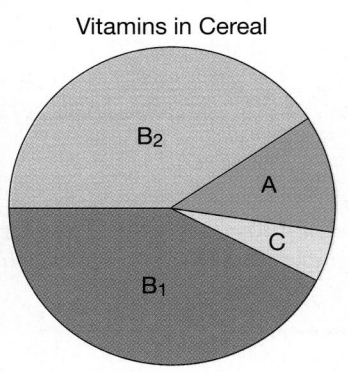

FIGURE 10.17

Circle graphs allow for visual comparisons of the relative sizes of fractional parts. The graph in Figure 10.17 shows the relative sizes of the vitamin content in a serving of cornflakes and milk. Four vitamins are present, B_1, B_2, A, and C. We can conclude that most of the vitamin content is B_1 and B_2, that less vitamin A is present, and that the vitamin C content is the least. However, the graph is deceptive, in that it gives no indication whatsoever of the actual amount of these four vitamins, either by weight (say in grams) or by percentage of minimum daily requirement. Thus, although the circle graph is excellent for picturing relative amounts, it does not necessarily indicate absolute amounts.

From the examples above, we see that there are many useful methods of organizing and picturing data, but that each method has limitations and can be misleading. Table 10.6 on page 440 gives a summary of our observations about charts and graphs. Notice that although *individual* circle graphs are not designed to show trends, multiple circle graphs may be used for that purpose as illustrated in Figure 10.16.

TABLE 10.6

Graphs	Good for Picturing:	Not *as* Good for Picturing:	Can Mislead by:
Pictograph	Totals, trends, and comparisons	Relative amounts	Dimensional changes
Bar	Totals and trends	Relative amounts	Altering scales
Line	Trends and comparisons of several quantities simultaneously	Relative amounts	Altering scales
Circle	Relative amounts	Trends	Representing absolute amounts

MATHEMATICAL MORSEL

There is statistical evidence to indicate that some people postpone death so that they can witness an important birthday or anniversary. For example, there is a dip in U.S. deaths before U.S. Presidential elections. Also, Presidents Jefferson and Adams died on the 4th of July, 50 years after signing the Declaration of Independence. This extending-death phenomenon is further reinforced by Jefferson's doctor, who quoted Jefferson on his deathbed as asking, "Is it the Fourth?" The doctor replied, "It soon will be." These were the last words spoken by Thomas Jefferson.

EXERCISE/PROBLEM SET 10.1—PART A

Exercises

1. A class of 30 students made the following scores on a 100-point test:

63, 76, 82, 85, 65, 95, 98, 92, 76,
80, 72, 76, 80, 78, 72, 69, 92, 72,
74, 85, 58, 86, 76, 74, 67, 78, 88,
93, 80, 70

  (a) Arrange the scores in increasing order.
  (b) What is the lowest score? The highest score?
  (c) What score occurs most often?
  (d) Make a line plot to represent these data.
  (e) Make a frequency table, grouping the data in increments of 10 (91–100, 81–90, etc.).
  (f) From the information in the frequency table, make a histogram.

  (g) Which interval has the most scores?

2. A six-sided die is tossed 100 times and the number showing on top is recorded. The following distribution is given.

Number	1	2	3	4	5	6
Frequency	5	5	10	25	25	30

  (a) Draw a histogram for these data.
  (b) Does this appear to be a fair die? Explain how you decided.

3. The following pictograph represents the mining production in a given state.

Mining Production

= $10 million

Bauxite

Sand and gravel

Petroleum and
natural gas

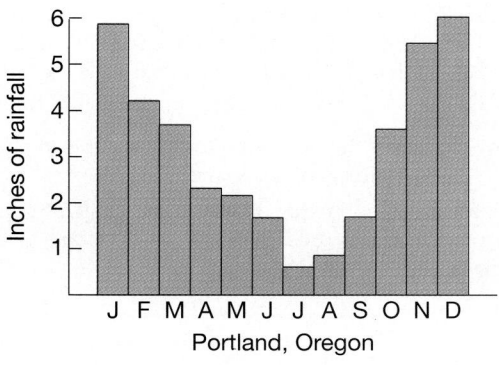

(a) About how much bauxite was mined?
(b) About how much sand and gravel?
(c) About how much petroleum and natural gas?

4. Given below are data on public school enrollments during this century.

1900	15,503,110	1910	17,813,852
1920	21,578,316	1930	25,678,015
1940	25,433,542	1950	25,111,427
1960	36,086,771	1970	45,909,088
1980	40,984,093		

(a) Choose an appropriate icon, a reasonable amount for it to represent, and draw a pictograph.
(b) In which decades were there increases in enrollment?
(c) What other types of graphs could we use to represent these data?

5. The given bar graphs represent the average monthly precipitation in Portland, Oregon, and New York City.

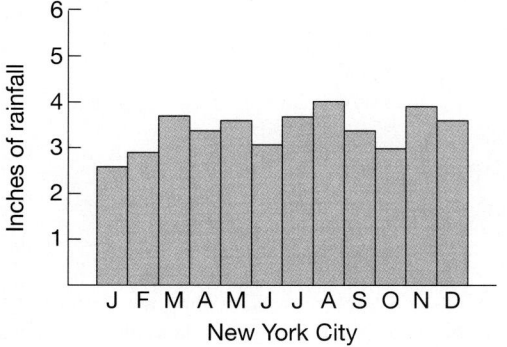

Portland, Oregon

New York City

(a) Which city receives more precipitation, on the average, in January?
(b) In how many months is there less than 2 inches precipitation in Portland? In New York City?
(c) In which month does the greatest amount of precipitation occur in Portland? The least?
(d) In which month does the greatest amount of precipitation occur in New York City? The least?
(e) Which city has the greater annual precipitation?

6. Given below are several gasoline vehicles and their fuel consumption averages.

Chevrolet Cavalier	27 mpg
Datsun 200SX	28 mpg
Nissan Pulsar	35 mpg
Honda Civic Coupe	51 mpg
Dodge Colt	41 mpg
Buick Riviera	16 mpg

(a) Draw a bar graph to represent these data.
(b) Which model gets the least miles per gallon? The most?
(c) _____ gets about twice as many miles per gallon as _____.
(d) What is the cost of fuel for 80,000 miles of driving at $1.05 per gallon for each car?

7. The circle graphs here represent the revenues and expenditures of a state government. Use them to answer the following questions.

Expenditures by Function

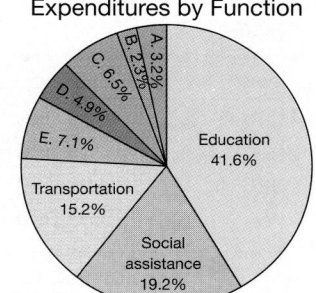

A. 3.2%
B. 2.3%
C. 6.5%
D. 4.9%
E. 7.1%
Education 41.6%
Transportation 15.2%
Social assistance 19.2%

A. Justice
B. Natural Resources
C. Business, Community and Consumer Affairs
D. Health and Rehabilitation
E. General government

Revenues by Source

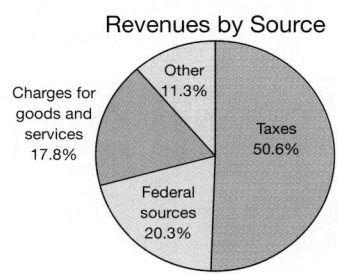

Other 11.3%
Charges for goods and services 17.8%
Taxes 50.6%
Federal sources 20.3%

(a) What is the largest source of revenue?

(b) What percent of the revenue comes from federal sources?

(c) Find the central angle of the sector "charges for goods and services."

(d) What category of expenditures is smallest?

(e) Which four categories, when combined, have the same expenditures as education?

(f) Find the central angles of the sectors for "business, community, and consumer affairs" and "general government."

8. The following circle graph shows how a state spends its revenue of $4,500,000,000. Find out how much was spent on each category.

Expenditures by Object

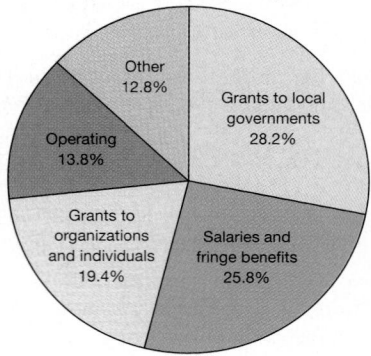

9. The table gives projections for the world's population.

WORLD POPULATION PROJECTIONS

Year	Population
1990	5,319,719,000
2000	6,240,748,000
2025	8,675,128,000
2050	10,805,207,000

Source: U.S. Bureau of the Census.

(a) Draw a pictograph representing the data. (Round the data first.)

(b) Draw a bar graph representing the data.

(c) Draw a line graph with the vertical scale starting at 0.

(d) Draw a second line graph in which the vertical scale starts at 5,000,000,000 and is the same otherwise. Which line graph suggests a more dramatic increase in the population?

10. The populations of the world's 12 largest urban areas in 1990 and their populations in 1970 are given in the following table.

WORLD'S LARGEST URBAN AREAS, 1990

Urban Area	Population (millions) 1970	Population (millions) 1990
Tokyo/Yokohama	14.91	19.28
Mexico City	9.12	20.25
Sao Paulo	8.22	18.77
New York	16.29	15.69
Shanghai	11.41	12.35
Calcutta	7.12	12.54
Buenos Aires	8.55	11.71
Rio de Janeiro	7.17	11.37
London	10.59	10.40
Seoul	5.42	11.66
Bombay	5.98	11.79
Los Angeles	8.43	10.48

Source: United Nations.

(a) Draw a double bar graph of the data with two bars for each urban area.

(b) Which urban area has the largest percentage growth?

(c) Which area has the largest percentage loss in population?

11. (a) Make a stem and leaf plot for the following weights of children in kilograms. Use two-digit stems.

17.0, 18.1, 19.2, 20.2, 21.1, 15.8, 22.0, 16.1, 15.9, 18.2, 18.5, 22.0, 16.3, 20.3, 20.9, 18.5, 22.1, 21.4, 17.5, 19.4, 21.8, 16.4, 20.9, 18.5, 20.6

(b) Construct the histogram for the weights in part (a), using intervals of 1 kilogram.

12. Public education expenditures in the United States, as a percentage of gross national product, are given in the table.

Year	Expenditure (%)
1940	3.6
1950	3.5
1960	4.8
1970	7.1
1980	6.7
1990	7.2

Source: National Center for Education Statistics.

(a) Make a line graph illustrating the data.

(b) Make another line graph illustrating the data, but

with vertical scale unit interval twice as long as that of part (a) and the same otherwise.

(c) Which of your graphs would be used to lobby for more funds for education? Which graph would be used to oppose budget increases?

13. (a) Make a two-sided stem and leaf plot for the following test scores.

Class 1: 57, 62, 76, 80, 93, 87, 76, 86, 75, 60,
   59, 86, 72, 80, 93, 79, 58, 86, 93, 81
Class 2: 68, 79, 75, 87, 92, 90, 83, 77, 95, 67,
   84, 92, 85, 77, 66, 87, 92, 82, 90, 85

(b) Which class seems to have performed better?

Problems

14. The number of public and private schools in the United States in 1988 is given in the table. "Combined" schools have elementary and secondary grades.

Type of School	Public	Private
Elementary	59,311	15,303
Secondary	20,758	2,438
Combined	2,179	4,949
Other	1,000	2,926

Source: National Center for Education Statistics.

(a) What is an appropriate type of graph for displaying the data? Explain.
(b) Make a graph of the data using your chosen type.

15. The federal budget is derived from several sources, as listed in the table.

FEDERAL BUDGET REVENUE, 1992

Source	Percent
Individual income taxes	47
Social insurance receipts	31
Corporate income taxes	13
Excise taxes	5
Other	4
	100

Source: Office of Management and Budget.

(a) What is an appropriate type of graph for displaying the data? Explain.
(b) Make a graph of the data using your chosen type.

16. Given in the table is the average cost of tuition and fees at an American four-year college.

U.S. COLLEGE TUITION AND FEES

	Public	Private
1983	1031	4639
1984	1148	5093
1985	1228	5556
1986	1318	6121
1987	1414	6658
1988	1537	7116
1989	1646	7722
1990	1780	8396
1991	1888	9083
1992	2134	9841

Source: The College Board.

(a) What is an appropriate type of graph for displaying the data? Explain.
(b) Make a graph of the data using your chosen type.
(c) For the 10-year period, which college costs increased at the greater rate—public or private?

17. The five U.S. cities receiving the most mail are listed in the table.

U.S. CITIES RECEIVING THE MOST MAIL, 1988

City	Total Pieces of Mail (billions)
New York	5.69
Los Angeles	3.77
Philadelphia	2.53
Chicago	2.51
San Francisco	2.49

Source: U.S. Postal Service.

(a) What is an appropriate type of graph for displaying the data? Explain.
(b) Make a graph of the data using your chosen type.

18. The table gives the percentages of U.S. households with videocassette recorders.

Year	Percent of U.S. Households with Videocassette Recorders
1987	48.7
1989	64.6
1991	71.9

Source: A. C. Nielsen.

(a) What is an appropriate type of graph for displaying the data? Explain.

(b) Make a graph of the data using your chosen type.

19. Given in the table are revenues for public elementary and secondary schools from federal, state, and local sources.

SOURCE OF SCHOOL FUNDS BY PERCENT, 1920–1990

School Year	Federal	State	Local
1920	0.3	16.5	83.2
1930	0.4	16.9	82.7
1940	1.8	30.3	68.0
1950	2.9	39.8	57.3
1960	4.4	39.1	56.5
1970	8.0	39.9	52.1
1980	9.8	46.8	43.4
1990	6.1	47.2	46.6

Source: National Center for Education Statistics.

(a) What is an appropriate type of graph for displaying the data? Explain.

(b) Make a graph of the data using your chosen type.

(c) What trends does your graph display?

20. The table gives the percentage of first births per 1000 women by the age of the mother from ages 18 to 44. For example, in 1985, 47% of firstborn children had mothers from 18 to 24 years of age.

PERCENTAGES OF FIRST BIRTHS BY AGE OF MOTHER

Age	1985	1990
18–24	47	43
25–29	34	32
30–34	14	19
35–39	4	5
40–44	1	1

Source: U.S. Bureau of the Census.

(a) What is an appropriate type of graph for displaying the data? Explain.

(b) Make a graph of the data using your chosen type.

21. Six coins are tossed 60 times. A distribution for the number of heads obtained is given.

Number of Heads	0	1	2	3	4	5	6
Frequency	1	6	14	18	15	4	2

(a) Draw a histogram for these data.

(b) Draw a circle graph for these data.

(c) If the experiment were repeated and the coins were tossed 100 times, about how many times would you expect to get just one head?

22. Two coins are tossed and how they land is recorded. For example, HT means head on the first coin and tail on the second.

(a) List all the possible outcomes for tossing two coins.

(b) If each of these outcomes is as likely as the others to occur, how many times would you expect to get both heads when the two coins are tossed 20 times?

(c) How many times would you expect to get exactly one head in 20 tosses?

(d) How many times would you expect to get two tails (no heads) in 20 tosses?

(e) Draw a histogram for these expected results for 20 tosses.

23. (a) Check to see if the first equation is true.

$$4^2 + 5^2 + 6^2 = 2^2 + 3^2 + 8^2$$
$$42^2 + 53^2 + 68^2 = 24^2 + 35^2 + 86^2$$

(b) The numbers on each side of the first equation were rearranged to form the resulting second equation. Is the second equation true?

(c) Determine if similar equations always hold.

24. Find all four-digit squares whose digits are all even.

EXERCISE/PROBLEM SET 10.1—PART B

Exercises

1. The following data from a major city hospital give the number of flame burns where children's sleepwear was involved.

Year	Number of Burns
1969	10
1970	8
1971	17
1972	15
1973	11
1974	10
1975	3
1976	1
1977	2
1978	6
1979	2

(a) Draw a line graph to represent these data.

(b) Government regulations regarding flammability of material used in children's sleepwear were adopted in 1972. When did the effects of these regulations appear to be felt?

(c) What was the average number of burns per year prior to 1975? From 1975 to 1979?

2. Roger has totaled his expenses for the last school year and represented his findings in a circle graph.

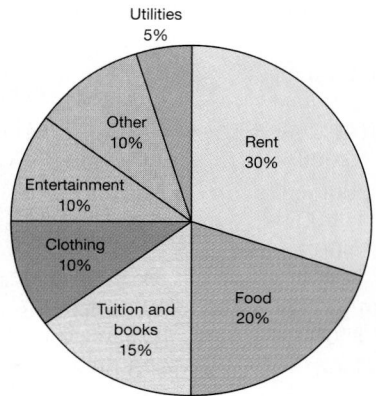

(a) What is the central angle of the rent sector?

(b) For the food sector?

(c) For tuition and books?

(d) If his total expenses were $6000, what amount was spent on rent? On entertainment? On clothing?

3. Given below are data for American automobile factory sales.

Year	Number of Passenger Cars (thousands)
1900	4
1910	181
1920	1,906
1930	2,787
1940	3,717
1950	6,666
1960	6,675
1970	6,547
1980	6,400
1990	6,050

(a) What problem would you encounter in trying to make a pictograph?

(b) Construct a line graph representing these data.

4. The bar graph represents the Dow-Jones Industrial Average for a 12-week period. Use it to answer the following questions.

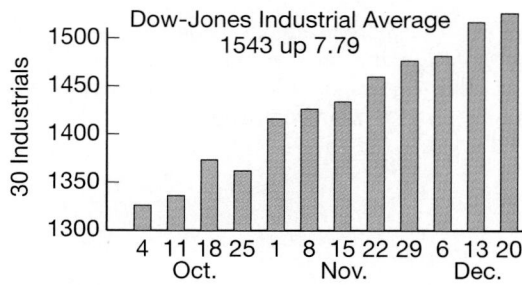

(a) Does it appear that the average on December 20 was more than eight times the average on October 4? Is this true?

(b) Does it appear that the average doubled from October 25 to November 8? Did it double?

(c) Why is this graph misleading?

5. What is wrong with the line graph shown?

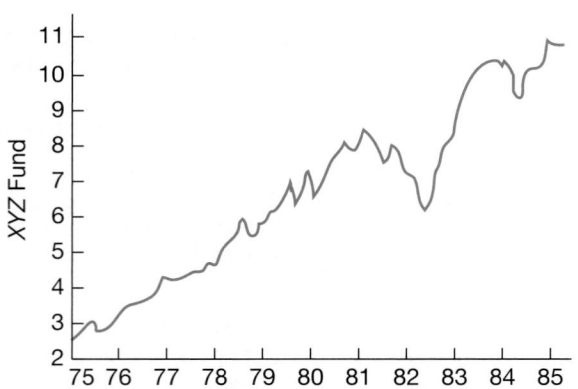

6. Of a total population of 135,525,000 people 25 years and over, 39,357,000 had completed less than 4 years of high school, 51,426,000 had completed 4 years of high school, 20,692,000 had completed 1 to 3 years of college, and 24,050,000 had completed 4 or more years of college.

    (a) To construct a circle graph, find the percentage (to nearest percent) and central angle (to nearest degree) for each category.

       (i) Less than 4 years of high school

      (ii) 4 years of high school

      (iii) 1 to 3 years of college

      (iv) 4 or more years of college

    (b) Construct the circle graph.

7. The following graphs represent the average wages of employees in a given company.

(i)

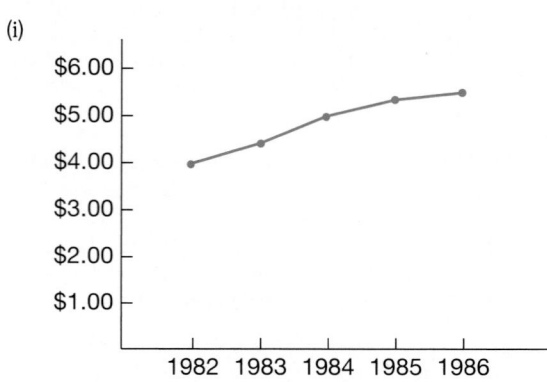

(ii)

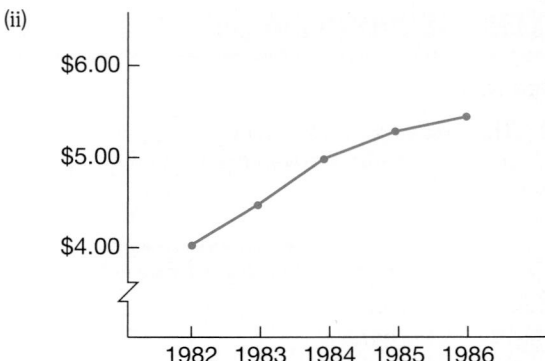

    (a) Do these graphs represent the same data?

    (b) What is the difference between these graphs?

    (c) Which graph would you use if you were the leader of a labor union seeking increased wages?

    (d) Which graph would you use if you were seeking to impress prospective employees with wages?

8. The data given represent energy consumption (in quadrillion Btu) according to type.

Coal	15.461
Natural gas	20.394
Petroleum	34.202
Hydroelectric power	3.107
Nuclear electric power	2.672

    (a) Draw a bar graph for these data.

    (b) Draw a circle graph for these data.

9. Below is one tax table from a recent state income tax form.

If Your Taxable Income Is:	Your Tax Is:
Not over $500	4.2% of taxable income
Over $500 but not over $1000	$21.00 + 5.3% of excess over $500
Over $1000 but not over $2000	$47.50 + 6.5% of excess over $1000
Over $2000 but not over $3000	$112.50 + 7.6% of excess over $2000
Over $3000 but not over $4000	$188.50 + 8.7% of excess over $3000
Over $4000 but not over $5000	$275.50 + 9.8% of excess over $4000
Over $5000	$373.50 + 10.8% of excess over $5000

    (a) Compute the tax when taxable income is $0, $500, $1000, $2000, $3000, $4000, $5000, $6000.

(b) Use these data to construct a line graph of tax versus income.

10. (a) Which of the following pictographs would be correct to show that sales have doubled from the left figure to the right figure?

(i)

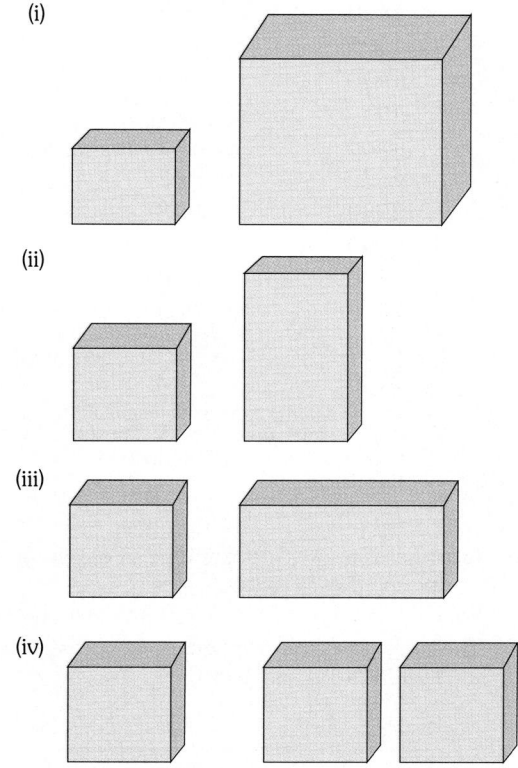

(ii)

(iii)

(iv)

(b) What is misleading about the other(s)?

11. Consider the following data, representing interest rates in percent.

12.50, 12.45, 12.25, 12.80, 12.50, 12.15, 12.80, 12.40, 12.50, 12.85

(a) Make a stem and leaf plot using two-digit stems.
(b) Make a stem and leaf plot using three-digit stems.
(c) Which stem and leaf plot is more informative?

12. Consider the following stem and leaf plots where the stems are the tens digits of the data.

```
2 | 0 0 1 1 7
3 | 1 3 5 5 5
4 | 2 3 3 3 5 8 9
5 | 4 7
```

(a) Construct the line plot for the data.
(b) Construct the histogram for the data grouped by tens.

13. A circle graph with equal-sized sectors is shown in (i). The same graph is shown in (ii), but drawn as if three-dimensional and in perspective.

(i)

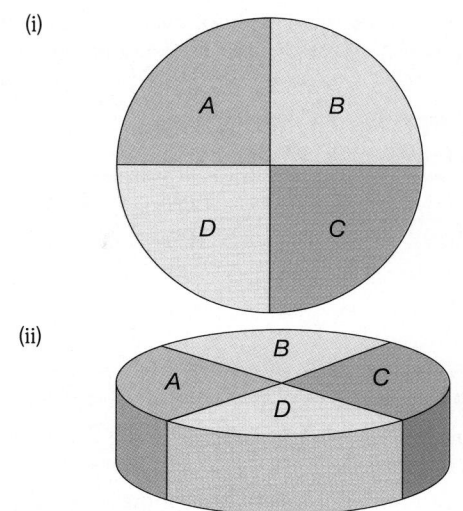

(ii)

Explain how the perspective version is deceptive.

14. Fall school enrollments are given in the table.

FALL ENROLLMENT (MILLIONS OF STUDENTS)

	1970	1975	1980	1985	1990
Elementary	36.7	34.2	31.7	31.2	33.6
Secondary	14.6	15.6	14.6	13.9	12.6
College	8.6	11.2	12.1	12.3	13.1

Source: National Center for Education Statistics.

(a) Make line graphs for the data on the same axes.
(b) What changes in school populations are shown by your graphs? Explain.

Problems

15. Given is the volume of all types of mail handled by the U.S. Postal Service in 1988.

VOLUME OF MAIL HANDLED, 1988

Type	Pieces (billions)
First class	89.92
Second class	10.68
Third class	63.73
Fourth class	0.66
International	0.80
Priority	0.52

Source: U.S. Postal Service.

(a) What is an appropriate type of graph for displaying the data? Explain.
(b) Make a graph of the data using your chosen type.

16. Projections of the population of the United States, by race and Hispanic origin, are given in the table.

U.S. POPULATION PROJECTIONS 1990–2000 (MILLIONS)

	1990	1995	2000
White	192	195	198
Black	31	33	35
Hispanic	22	26	30
Other races	8	10	11

Source: U.S. Bureau of the Census.

(a) What is an appropriate type of graph for displaying the data? Explain.

(b) Make a graph of the data using your chosen type.

17. The federal budget is spent on several categories of expense, as listed in the table.

FEDERAL BUDGET EXPENSES, 1992

Expense Category	Percent
Human resources	52
National defense	20
Net interest	13
Physical resources	10
Other federal operations	5
	100

Source: Office of Management and Budget.

(a) What is an appropriate type of graph for displaying the data? Explain.

(b) Make a graph of the data using your chosen type.

18. The growth of the U.S. population age 65 and over is given in the table.

Year	Percent of Population Age 65 and Over
1900	4.1
1910	4.3
1920	4.7
1930	5.5
1940	6.9
1950	8.1
1960	9.2
1970	9.8
1980	11.3
1990	12.7[a]
2000	13.0
2010	13.8
2020	17.3
2030	21.2

Source: U.S. Bureau of the Census.
[a]Percentages from 1990 on are projections.

(a) What is an appropriate type of graph for displaying the data? Explain.

(b) Make a graph of the data using your chosen type.

19. The table gives the numbers of videocassettes rented for 1982, 1985, and 1988.

Year	Number of Prerecorded Videocassette Rentals
1982	201,240
1985	1,224,250
1988	2,512,800

Source: Paul Kagan Associates, Inc.

(a) What is an appropriate type of graph for displaying the data? Explain.

(b) Make a graph of the data using your chosen type.

20. The table gives the percentages of various types of solid waste in the United States in 1984.

Type	Percent of Total
Paper	37.1
Yard wastes	17.9
Glass	9.7
Metals	9.6
Food	8.1
Plastics	7.2
Wood	3.8
Rubber and leather	2.5
Textiles	2.1
Other	1.9

Source: Environmental Protection Agency.

(a) What is an appropriate type of graph for displaying the data?
(b) Make a graph of the data using your chosen type.

21. Three coins are tossed 24 times.
  (a) List the possible outcomes for each toss.
  (b) How many times would you expect to get no heads? (Assume that the outcomes are equally likely.)
  (c) How many times would you expect to get one head?
  (d) Two heads? Three heads?
  (e) Draw a histogram for these expected results.

22. The spinner is spun 24 times.

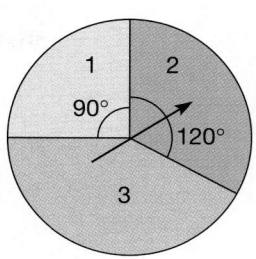

(a) How many times would you expect it to stop in sector 1?
(b) How many times would you expect it to stop in sector 2?
(c) How many times would you expect it to stop in sector 3?
(d) Draw a histogram for these expected results.

23. What is the 100th term in each sequence?
  (a) 1, 4, 7, 10, 13, 16, . . .
  (b) 1, 3, 6, 10, 15, 21, 28, . . .
  (c) $\frac{1}{2} - \frac{1}{3}, \frac{1}{3} - \frac{1}{4}, \frac{1}{4} - \frac{1}{5}, \ldots$

24. What is the smallest number that ends in a 4 and is multiplied by 4 by moving the last digit (a 4) to be the first digit? (HINT: It is a six-digit number.)

10.2

ANALYZING DATA   Measuring Central Tendency

Suppose that two fifth-grade classes take a reading test, yielding the following scores. Scores are given in year–month equivalent form. For example, a score of 5.3 means that the student is reading at the fifth-year, third-month level, where years mean years in school.

Class 1: 5.3, 4.9, 5.2, 5.4, 5.6, 5.1, 5.8, 5.3, 4.9, 6.1, 6.2, 5.7, 5.4, 6.9, 4.3, 5.2, 5.6, 5.9, 5.3, 5.8

Class 2: 4.7, 5.0, 5.5, 4.1, 6.8, 5.0, 4.7, 5.6, 4.9, 6.3, 7.8, 3.6, 8.4, 5.4, 4.7, 4.4, 5.6, 3.7, 6.2, 7.5

How did the two classes compare on the reading test? This question is complicated since there are many ways to compare the classes. To answer it, we need several new concepts.

Since we wish to compare the classes as a whole, we need to take the overall performances into account rather than individual scores. Numbers that give some indication of the overall "average" of some data are called **measures of central tendency**. The three measures of central tendency that we study in this chapter are the mode, median, and mean.

Mode, Median, Mean

To compare these two classes, we first begin by putting the scores from the two classes in increasing order.

Class 1:   4.3, 4.9, 4.9, 5.1, 5.2, 5.2, 5.3, 5.3, 5.3, 5.4, 5.4,
            5.6, 5.6, 5.7, 5.8, 5.8, 5.9, 6.1, 6.2, 6.9

Class 2:   3.6, 3.7, 4.1, 4.4, 4.7, 4.7, 4.7, 4.9, 5.0, 5.0, 5.4,
            5.5, 5.6, 5.6, 6.2, 6.3, 6.8, 7.5, 7.8, 8.4

The most frequently occurring score in class 1 is 5.3 (it occurs three times), while in class 2 it is 4.7 (it also occurs three times). Each of the numbers 5.3 and 4.7 is called the mode score for its respective list of scores.

Definition

Mode

In a list of numbers, the number that occurs most frequently is called the **mode**. There can be more than one mode, for example, if several numbers occur most frequently. If each number appears equally often, there is no mode.

The mode for a class gives us some very rough information about the general performance of the class. It is unaffected by all the other scores. On the basis of the mode scores *only,* it appears that class 1 scored higher than class 2.

The median score for a class is the "middle score" or "halfway" point in a list of the scores that is arranged in increasing (or decreasing) order.

Definition

Median

Suppose that x_1, x_2, x_3, . . . , x_n is a collection of numbers in increasing order; that is, $x_1 \leq x_2 \leq x_3 \leq \cdot \cdot \cdot \leq x_n$. If n is odd, the **median** of the numbers is the middle score in the list; that is, the median is the number with subscript $\dfrac{n+1}{2}$. If n is even, the **median** is the arithmetic average of the two middle scores; that is, the median is one-half of the sum of the two numbers with subscripts $\dfrac{n}{2}$ and $\dfrac{n}{2} + 1$.

Since there is an even number of scores (20) in each class, we average the tenth and eleventh scores. The median for class 1 is 5.4. For class 2, the median is 5.2 (verify). On the basis of the median scores *only,* it appears that class 1 scored higher than class 2. Notice that the median does not take into account the magnitude of any scores except the score (or scores) in the middle. Hence it is not affected by extreme scores. Also, the median is not necessarily a member of the original set of scores if there are an even number of scores.

EXAMPLE 10.2   Find the mode and median for each collection of numbers.
(a) 1, 2, 3, 3, 4, 6, 9   **(b)** 1, 1, 2, 3, 4, 5, 10
(c) 0, 1, 2, 3, 4, 4, 5, 5   **(d)** 1, 2, 3, 4

Solution
(a) The mode is 3 since it occurs more often than any other number. The median is also 3, since it is the middle score in this ordered list of numbers.
(b) The mode is 1 and the median is 3.
(c) There are two modes, 4 and 5. Here we have an even number of scores. Hence we average the two middle scores to compute the median. The median is $\dfrac{3 + 4}{2} = 3.5$. Note that the median is not one of the scores in this case.
(d) The median is $\dfrac{2 + 3}{2} = 2.5$. There is no mode since each number occurs equally often.   ■

From Example 10.2 we observe that the mode can be equal to, less than, or greater than the median [see (a), (b), and (c), respectively].

A third, and perhaps the most useful measure of central tendency is the mean, also called the **arithmetic average**.

Definition

Mean

Suppose that $x_1, x_2, \ldots, x_n$ is a collection of numbers. The **mean** of the collection is

$$\frac{x_1 + x_2 + \cdots + x_n}{n}.$$

The mean for each class is obtained by summing all the scores and dividing the sum by the total number of scores. For our two fifth-grade classes, we can compute the means as in Table 10.7.

TABLE 10.7

Class	Sum of Scores	Mean
1	109.9	$\dfrac{109.9}{20} = 5.495$
2	109.9	$\dfrac{109.9}{20} = 5.495$

On the basis of the mean scores, the classes performed equivalently. That is, the "average student" in each class scored 5.495 on the reading test. This means that if all the students had equal scores (and the class total was the same), each student would have a score of 5.495. The mean takes every score into account and hence is affected by extremely high or low scores. Among the mean, median, and mode, any one of the three can be the largest or smallest measure of central tendency.

Box and Whisker Plots

A popular application of the median is a **box and whisker plot** or simply a **box plot**. To construct a box and whisker plot, we first find the lowest score, the median, the highest score, and two additional statistics, namely the lower and upper quartiles. We define the lower and upper quartiles using the median. To find the lower and upper quartiles, arrange the scores in increasing order. With an even number of scores, say $2n$, the **lower quartile** is the median of the n smallest scores. The **upper quartile** is the median of the n largest scores. With an odd number of scores, say $2n + 1$, the lower quartile is the median of the n smallest scores, and the upper quartile is the median of the n largest scores.

We will use the reading test scores from class 1 as an illustration:

$$4.3, 4.9, 4.9, 5.1, 5.2, 5.2, 5.3, 5.3, 5.3, 5.4,$$
$$5.4, 5.6, 5.6, 5.7, 5.8, 5.8, 5.9, 6.1, 6.2, 6.9$$

Lowest score = 4.3
Lower quartile = median of 10 lowest scores = 5.2
Median = 5.4
Upper quartile = median of 10 highest scores = 5.8
Highest score = 6.9

Next, we plot these five statistics on a number line, then make a box from the lower quartile to the upper quartile, indicating the median with a line crossing the box. Finally, we connect the lowest score to the lower quartile with a line segment, one "whisker," and the upper quartile to the highest score with another line segment, the other whisker (Figure 10.18). The box represents about 50% of the scores, and each whisker represents about 25%.

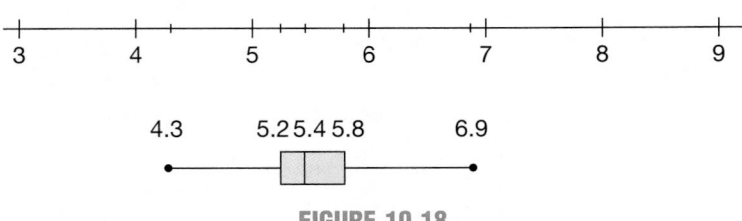

FIGURE 10.18

The difference between the upper and lower quartiles is called the **interquartile range** (IQR). This statistic is useful for identifying extremely small or large values of the data, called outliers. An **outlier** is commonly defined as any value of the data that lies more than 1.5 IQR units below the lower quartile or more than 1.5 IQR units above the upper quartile. For the class scores, IQR = 5.8 − 5.2 = 0.6, so that 1.5 IQR units = (1.5)(0.6) = 0.9. Hence any score below 5.2 − 0.9 = 4.3 or above

$5.8 + 0.9 = 6.7$ is an outlier. Thus 6.9 is an outlier for these data; that is, it is an unusually large value given the relative closeness of the rest of the data. Later in this section, we will see an explanation of outliers using z-scores. Often outliers are indicated using an asterisk. In the case of the reading test scores above, 6.9 was identified to be an outlier. This is indicated in Figure 10.19. When there are outliers, the whiskers end at the value farthest away from the box that is still within 1.5 IQR units from the end.

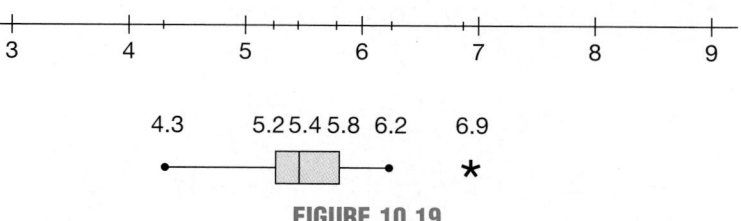

FIGURE 10.19

We can visually compare the performances of class 1 and class 2 on the reading test by comparing their box and whisker plots. The reading scores from class 2 are 3.6, 3.7, 4.1, 4.4, 4.7, 4.7, 4.7, 4.9, 5.0, 5.0, 5.4, 5.5, 5.6, 5.6, 6.2, 6.3, 6.8, 7.5, 7.8, and 8.4. Thus we have

Lowest score = 3.6
Lower quartile = 4.7
Median = 5.2
Upper quartile = 6.25
Highest score = 8.4
1.5 IQR = 2.3

The box and whisker plots for both classes appear with outliers in Figure 10.20.

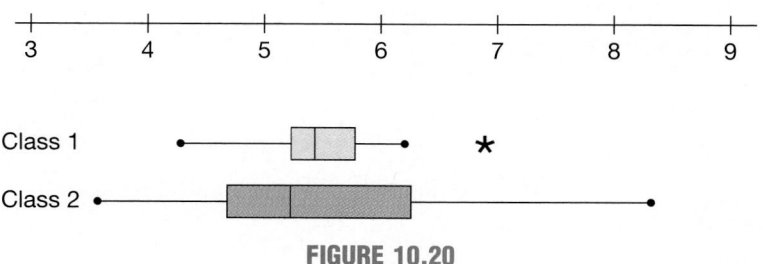

FIGURE 10.20

From the two box and whisker plots, we see that the scores for class 2 are considerably more widely spread; the box is wider and the distances to the extreme scores are greater.

EXAMPLE 10.3   Teacher salary averages for 1991 are given in Table 10.8. Construct a stem and leaf plot as well as box and whisker plots for the data. How do the salaries compare?

TABLE 10.8   TEACHER SALARY AVERAGES IN 1991 ($\times$ $1000)

State	Elementary Teachers	Secondary Teachers	State	Elementary Teachers	Secondary Teachers
AK	43.3	44.1	MT	26.1	28.2
AL	27.3	27.3	NC	29.0	29.4
AR	22.4	23.7	ND	23.5	23.7
AZ	30.8	31.3	NE	26.6	26.6
CA	38.7	41.1	NH	31.3	31.3
CO	31.1	32.6	NJ	37.6	39.7
CT	43.3	45.0	NM	25.5	26.9
DC	39.6	39.6	NV	31.2	33.7
DE	34.0	36.2	NY	40.4	43.7
FL	30.5	30.5	OH	31.7	33.8
GA	29.2	29.2	OK	23.5	25.2
HI	32.5	32.5	OR	31.6	33.3
IA	26.9	29.0	PA	35.4	36.7
ID	25.0	26.0	RI	37.2	38.4
IL	33.1	38.3	SC	27.7	29.5
IN	31.7	32.4	SD	22.1	23.0
KS	29.8	29.8	TN	27.8	29.4
KY	28.4	30.6	TX	27.7	28.9
LA	26.2	26.2	UT	24.6	25.6
MA	36.1	36.1	VA	31.3	33.9
MD	37.0	39.8	VT	30.3	31.6
ME	27.9	29.9	WA	32.4	34.0
MI	38.2	38.6	WI	31.8	34.3
MN	32.4	34.0	WV	25.6	26.4
MO	27.6	29.5	WY	28.8	29.1
MS	23.9	25.0			

Source: National Education Association.

Solution

The stem and leaf plot is given in Table 10.9, where the statistics for constructing the box and whisker plots are shown in boldface type.

TABLE 10.9

Elementary Teachers		Secondary Teachers
4 **1**	22.	
9 5 5	23.	**0** 7 7
6	24.	
6 5 0	25.	0 2 6
9 6 2 1	26.	0 2 4 6 9
9 8 7 7 6 3	27.	3
8 4	28.	**2** 9
8 2 0	29.	0 1 2 4 4 5 5 8 9
8 **5** 3	30.	2 6
8 7 7 6 3 3 2 1	31.	3 3 6
5 4 4	32.	4 5 6
1	33.	3 7 8 9
0	34.	0 0 3
4	35.	
1	36.	**1** 2 7
6 2 0	37.	
7 2	38.	3 4 6
6	39.	6 7 8
4	40.	
	41.	1
	42.	
3 3	43.	7
	44.	1
	45.	**0**

Thus we have the following quartile statistics for constructing the box and whisker plots (Table 10.10). Using the statistics in Table 10.10, we can construct the box and whisker plots (Figure 10.21).

TABLE 10.10

	Elementary Teachers	Secondary Teachers
Lowest data value	22.1	23.0
Lower quartile	26.9	28.2
Median	30.5	31.3
Upper quartile	33.1	36.1
Highest data value	43.3	45.0
Interquartile range	6.2	7.9
1.5 IQR	9.3	11.85
Outliers	$< 26.9 - 9.3 = 18.3$	$< 28.2 - 11.85 = 16.35$
	$> 33.1 + 9.3 = 42.4$	$> 36.1 + 11.85 = 47.95$

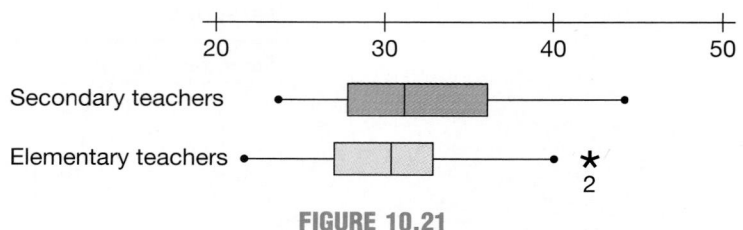

FIGURE 10.21

Since the box and whisker plot for the secondary teachers lies to the right of that of the elementary teachers, we see that secondary teachers were generally paid more.   ■

Notice how the box and whisker plots of Figure 10.21 give us a *direct visual comparison* of the statistics in Table 10.10. In the next section we will investigate methods of actually measuring the spread, of data.

Measuring Dispersion

Statistics that give an indication of how the data are "spread out" or distributed are called **measures of dispersion**. The **range** of the scores is simply the difference of the largest and smallest scores. For the class 1 scores at the beginning of this section, the range is $6.9 - 4.3 = 2.6$. For class 2, the range of the scores is $8.4 - 3.6 = 4.8$. The range gives us limited information about the distribution of scores since it takes only the extremes into account, ignoring the intervening scores.

Variance and Standard Deviation

Perhaps the most common measures of dispersion are the variance and the standard deviation.

Definition

Variance

The **variance** of a collection of numbers is the arithmetic average of the squared differences between each number and the mean of the collection of numbers. Symbolically, for the numbers, x_1, x_2, . . . , x_n, with mean $\bar{x}$, the variance is

$$\frac{(x_1 - \bar{x})^2 + (x_2 - \bar{x})^2 + \cdots + (x_n - \bar{x})^2}{n}.$$

To find the variance of a set of numbers, use the following procedure.

1. Find the mean, $\bar{x}$.
2. For each number x, find the difference between the number and the mean, namely $x - \bar{x}$.
3. Square all the differences in step 2, namely $(x - \bar{x})^2$.
4. Find the arithmetic average of all the squares in step 3. This average is the variance.

EXAMPLE 10.4 Find the variance for the numbers 5, 7, 7, 8, 10, 11.

Solution

The mean, $\bar{x} = \dfrac{5 + 7 + 7 + 8 + 10 + 11}{6} = 8$.

	Step 1 $\bar{x}$	Step 2 $x - \bar{x}$	Step 3 $(x - \bar{x})^2$
5	8	-3	9
7	8	-1	1
7	8	-1	1
8	8	0	0
10	8	2	4
11	8	3	9

(Step 4): $\dfrac{9 + 1 + 1 + 0 + 4 + 9}{6} = 4$, the variance.   ■

Definition

Standard Deviation

The **standard deviation** is the square root of the variance.

EXAMPLE 10.5 Find the standard deviation for the data in Example 10.4.

Solution

The standard deviation is the square root of the variance, 4. Hence the standard deviation is 2.   ■

In general, the greater the standard deviation, the more the scores are spread out.

Finding the standard deviation for a collection of data is a straightforward task when using a calculator that possesses the appropriate statistical keys. Usually, a calculator must be set in its statistics or standard deviation mode. Then, after the data are entered one at a time, the mean and standard deviation can be found simply by pressing appropriate keys. For example, assuming that the calculator is in its statistics mode, enter the data 3, 4, 7, 8, 9 using the $\boxed{\Sigma+}$ key as follows:

$$3 \boxed{\Sigma+} \; 4 \boxed{\Sigma+} \; 7 \boxed{\Sigma+} \; 8 \boxed{\Sigma+} \; 9 \boxed{\Sigma+}$$

Pressing the $\boxed{n}$ key yields the number 5, which is the number of data entered. Pressing $\boxed{\bar{x}}$ yields 6.2, the mean of our data. Pressing $\boxed{\sigma_n}$ yields 2.315167381, the standard deviation. Squaring this result yields the variance, 5.36.

NOTE: When the key representing standard deviation is pressed in the example above, a number greater than 2.315167381 appears on some calculators. This is because there are two different interpretations of standard deviation. If *all n* of the data for some experiment are used in calculating the standard deviation, then $\boxed{\sigma_n}$ is the correct choice. However, if only *n* pieces of data from a large collection of numbers (more than *n*) is used, the variance is calculated with an $n - 1$ in the denominator. Some calculators have a $\boxed{\sigma_{n-1}}$ key to distinguish this case.

Let us return to our comparison of the two fifth-grade classes on their reading test. Table 10.11 gives the variance and standard deviation for each class, rounded to two decimal places.

TABLE 10.11

Class	Variance	Standard Deviation
1	0.29	0.54
2	1.65	1.28

Comparing the classes on the basis of the standard deviation shows that the scores in class 2 were more widely distributed than were the scores in class 1 since the greater the standard deviation, the larger the spread of scores. Hence class 2 is more heterogeneous in reading ability than is class 1. This finding may mean that more reading groups are needed in class 2 than in class 1, if students are grouped by ability. Although it is difficult to give a general rule of thumb about interpreting the standard deviation, it does allow us to compare several sets of data to see which set is more homogeneous. In summary, comparing the two classes on the basis of the mean scores, the classes performed equivalently on the reading. However, on the basis of the standard deviation, class 2 is more heterogeneous than class 1.

In addition to obtaining information about the entire class, we can use the mean and standard deviation to compare an individual student's performances on different tests relative to the class as a whole. Example 10.6 illustrates how we might do this.

EXAMPLE 10.6   Adrienne made the following scores on two achievement tests. On which test did she perform better relative to the class?

	Test 1	Test 2
Adrienne	45	40
Mean	30	25
Standard deviation	10	15

Solution

Comparing Adrienne's scores only to the means seems to suggest that she performed equally well on both tests since her score is 15 points higher than the mean in each case. However, using the standard deviation as a unit of distance, we see that she was 1.5 (15 divided by 10) standard deviations above the mean on test 1 and only 1 (15 divided by 15) standard deviation above the mean on test 2. Hence she performed better on test 1, relative to the whole class.   ■

We are able to make comparisons as in Example 10.6 more easily if we use *z*-scores.

Definition

z-score

The **z-score**, z, for a particular score, x, is

$$z = \frac{x - \overline{x}}{s},$$

where $\overline{x}$ is the mean of all the scores and s is the standard deviation.

The *z*-score of a number indicates how many standard deviations the number is away from the mean. Numbers above the mean have positive *z*-scores and numbers below the mean have negative *z*-scores.

EXAMPLE 10.7   Compute Adrienne's *z*-score for tests 1 and 2 in Example 10.6.

Solution

For test 1, her *z*-score is $\dfrac{45 - 30}{10} = 1.5$, and for test 2, her *z*-score is

$\dfrac{40 - 25}{15} = 1$.   ■

Notice that Adrienne's *z*-score tells us how far her score was above the mean, measured in multiples of the standard deviation. Example 10.8 illustrates several other features of *z*-scores.

EXAMPLE 10.8   Find the *z*-scores for the data 1, 1, 2, 3, 4, 9, 12, 18.

Solution
We first find the mean, $\overline{x}$, and the standard deviation, s.

$$\overline{x} = \frac{1 + 1 + 2 + 3 + 4 + 9 + 12 + 18}{8} = \frac{50}{8} = 6.25$$

$s = 5.78$ to two places (verify)

Hence we can find the *z*-scores for each number in the set of data (Table 10.12).

TABLE 10.12

Score	z-Score
1	$\dfrac{1 - 6.25}{5.78} = -0.91$
2	$\dfrac{2 - 6.25}{5.78} = -0.74$
3	$\dfrac{3 - 6.25}{5.78} = -0.56$
4	$\dfrac{4 - 6.25}{5.78} = -0.39$
9	$\dfrac{9 - 6.25}{5.78} = 0.48$
12	$\dfrac{12 - 6.25}{5.78} = 0.99$
18	$\dfrac{18 - 6.25}{5.78} = 2.03$

The computations in Table 10.12 suggest the following observations.

Case 1: If $x > \bar{x}$, then $x - \bar{x} > 0$, so $z = \dfrac{x - \bar{x}}{s} > 0$.

Conclusion: x is greater than the mean if and only if the z-score of x is positive.

Case 2: If $x = \bar{x}$, then $z = \dfrac{x - \bar{x}}{s} = \dfrac{\bar{x} - \bar{x}}{s} = 0$.

Conclusion: The z-score of the mean is 0.

Case 3: If $x < \bar{x}$, then $x - \bar{x} < 0$, so $z = \dfrac{x - \bar{x}}{s} < 0$.

Conclusion: x is less than the mean if and only if the z-score of x is negative.

We will use z-scores to provide even more defined information later in this section.

Distributions

Large amounts of data are commonly organized in increasing order and pictured in relative frequency form in a histogram. The **relative frequency** that a number occurs is the percentage of the total amount of data that the number represents. For example, in a collection of 100 numbers, if the number 14 appears 6 times, the relative frequency of 14 is 6%. A graph of the data versus the relative frequency of each number in the data is called a **distribution**. Two hypothetical distributions are discussed in Example 10.9.

EXAMPLE 10.9 The distribution in Figure 10.22 has two modes, 34 and 36 kilograms. The modes are indicated by the "peaks" of the histogram. The distribution is also symmetrical, since there is a vertical line that would

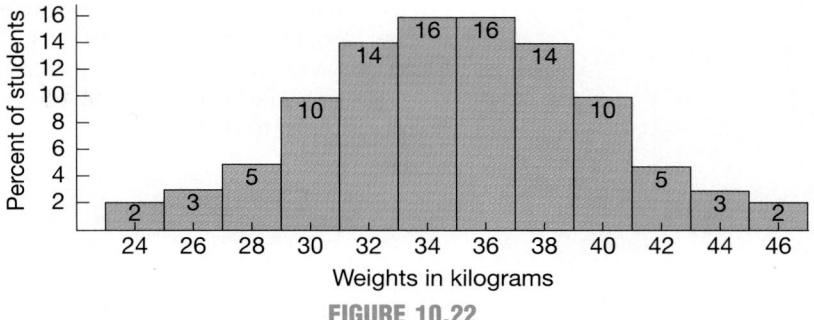

FIGURE 10.22

serve as a "mirror" line of symmetry, namely a line through 35 on the horizontal axis. The distribution in Figure 10.23 has only one mode (4 hours) and is not symmetrical.

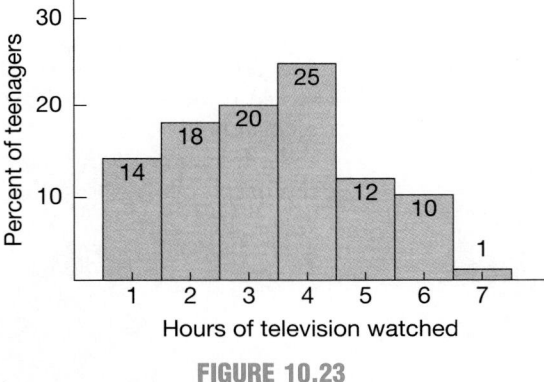

FIGURE 10.23

In Figure 10.22 the students' weights were rounded to the nearest 2 kilograms, producing 12 possible values from 24 to 46. Suppose, instead, that very accurate weights were obtained for the students, say to the nearest gram (one one-thousandth of a kilogram). Suppose, also, that a smooth curve was used to connect the midpoints of the "steps" of the histogram. One possibility is shown in Figure 10.24. The curve shows a symmetrical "bell-shaped" distribution with one mode.

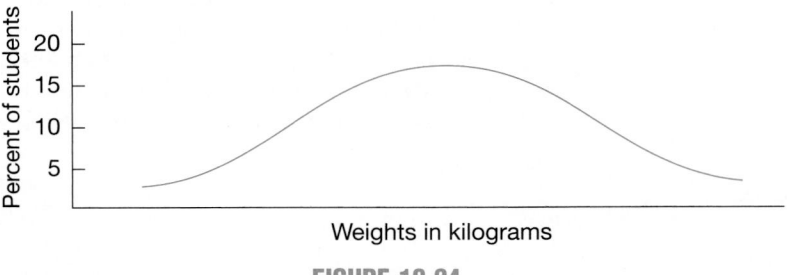

FIGURE 10.24

Distributions of physical measurements such as heights and weights for one sex, for large groups of data, frequently are smooth bell-shaped curves, such as the curve in Figure 10.24. There is a geometrical, or visual, way to interpret the median, mean, and mode for such smooth distributions. The vertical line through the median cuts the region between the curve and the horizontal axis into two regions of equal area (Figure 10.25). (NOTE: This characterization of the median does not always hold for histograms because they are not "smooth.")

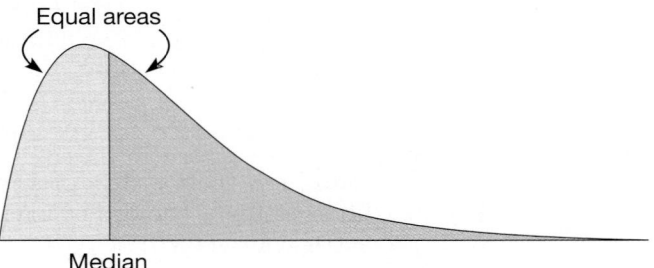

FIGURE 10.25

The mean is the point on the horizontal axis where the distribution would balance (Figure 10.26). This characterization of the mean holds for all distributions, histograms as well as smooth curves. Since the mode is the most frequently occurring value of the data, the highest point or points of the graph occur above the mode(s).

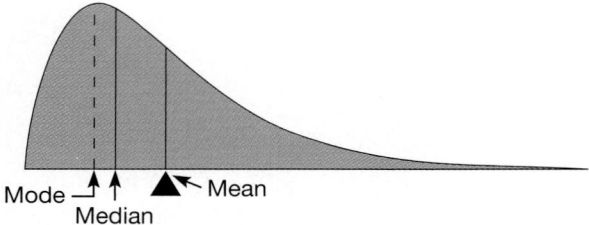

FIGURE 10.26

A special type of smooth, bell-shaped distribution is the **normal distribution**. The normal distribution is symmetrical, with the mean, median, and mode all being equal. Figure 10.27 shows the general shape of the normal distribution. (The technical definition of the normal distribution is more complicated than we can go into here.) An interesting feature of the normal distribution is that it is completely determined by the mean, $\bar{x}$, and the standard deviation, s. The "peak" is always directly above the mean. The standard deviation determines the shape, in the following way. The larger

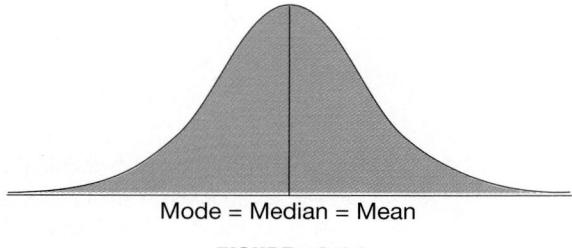

FIGURE 10.27

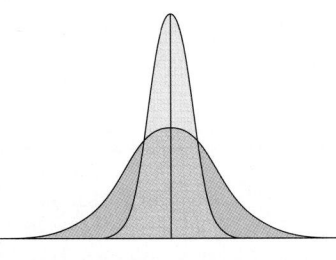

FIGURE 10.28

the standard deviation, the lower and flatter is the curve. That is, if two normal distributions are represented using the same horizontal and vertical scales, the one with the larger standard deviation will be lower and flatter (Figure 10.28).

The distribution of the weights in Figure 10.22 is essentially normal, so we could determine everything about the curve from the mean and the standard deviation. For example, the interval within one standard deviation of the mean contains about 68% of the data. We can see this and other features of the normal distribution in Figure 10.29. Notice that for a normal distribution, about 95% of the data are between $\bar{x} - 2s$ and $\bar{x} + 2s$, and that 99.7% of the data are between $\bar{x} - 3s$ and $\bar{x} + 3s$.

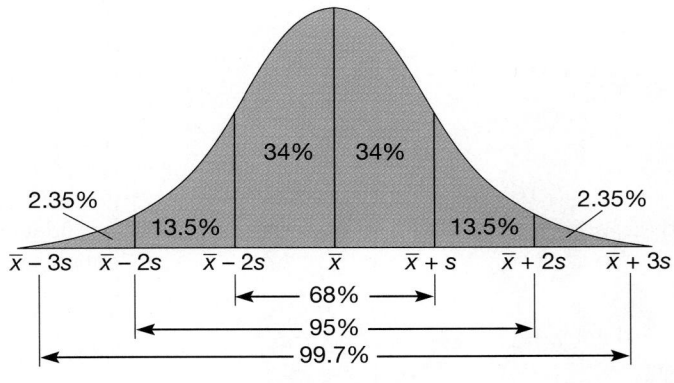

FIGURE 10.29

We can picture our results about z-scores for normal distributions in Figure 10.30. From Figures 10.29 and 10.30, we see that z-scores of 2 or more in a normal distribution are very high (higher than 97.5% of all other scores—50% below the mean plus 47.5% up to $z = 2$). Also, z-scores of 3 or more are extremely high. On the other hand, z-scores of -2 or less from a normal distribution are lower than 97.5% of all scores.

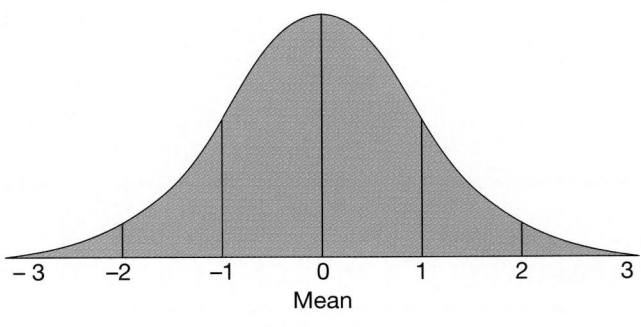

FIGURE 10.30

Tabulated values of z-scores for a normal distribution can be used to explain the relatively unlikely occurrence of outliers. For example, for data from a normal distribution, small outliers have z-scores less than -2.7 and are smaller than 99.5% of the data. Similarly, large outliers from a normal distribution have z-scores greater than 2.7 and are larger than 99.5% of the data. Thus outliers represent very rare observations. The normal distribution is a very commonly occurring distribution for many large collections of data. Hence the mean, standard deviation, and *z*-scores are especially important statistics.

MATHEMATICAL MORSEL

Several presidential election polls went statistically awry in this century. A spectacular failure was the 1935 *Literary Digest* poll predicting that Alfred Landon would defeat Franklin Roosevelt in the 1936 election. So devastated was the *Literary Digest* by its false prediction that it subsequently ceased publication. The *Literary Digest* poll used voluntary responses from a preselected sample—but only 23% of the people in the sample responded. Evidently, the majority of those who did were more enthusiastic about their candidate (Landon) than were the majority of the entire sample. Thus the sampling error was so large that a false prediction resulted. A study by J. H. Powell showed that if the data were analyzed and weighted according to how the respondents represented the general population, they would have picked Roosevelt.

The Dewey–Truman 1948 Gallup poll also used a biased sample. Interviewers were allowed to select individuals based on certain quotas (e.g., sex, race, and age). However, the people selected tended to be more prosperous than average, which produced a sample biased toward Republican candidates. Also, the poll was conducted 3 weeks before the election, when Truman was gaining support and Dewey was slipping. Nowadays, sampling procedures are done with extreme care to produce representative samples of public opinion.

EXERCISE/PROBLEM SET 10.2—PART A

Exercises

1. Calculate the mean, median, and mode for each collection of data.
  (a) 8, 9, 9, 10, 11, 12
  (b) 17, 2, 10, 29, 14, 13
  (c) 4.2, 3.8, 9.7, −4.8, 0, −10.0
  (d) 29, 42, −65, −73, 48, 17, 0, 0, −36

2. Calculate the mean, median, and mode for each collection of data.
  (a) 1, 2, 3, 4, 5, 5
  (b) 2, 4, 6, 8, 10
  (c) 22, 24, 26, 28, 30
  (d) 12, 14, 10, 9, 7, 13, 16, 19, 15, 10, 2

(e) 14.8, 17.9, 16.3, 15.4, 18.7, 17.9, 16.2, 15.4, 17.0, 18.1

(f) −20, 9, 5, −8, 5, −1, 0

3. Suppose that 1234 students all scored 47 on their science tests. Find the mean, median, and mode of the scores.

4. Scores for Mrs. McClellan's class on mathematics and reading tests are given in the following tables. Which student is the "average" student for the group?

Student	Mathematics Test Score	Reading Test Score
Rob	73	87
Doug	83	58
Myron	62	90
Alan	89	70
Ed	96	98

5. At a shoe store, which statistic would be most helpful to the manager when reordering shoes: mean, median, or mode? Explain.

6. Make a box and whisker plot for the following heights of children, in centimeters.

120, 121, 121, 124, 126, 128, 130, 134, 140, 142, 147, 150, 152, 160

7. (a) Make box and whisker plots on the same number line for the following test scores.

Class 1:   57, 58, 59, 60, 62, 72, 75, 76, 76, 79, 80, 80, 81, 86, 86, 86, 87, 93, 93, 93

Class 2:   66, 67, 68, 75, 77, 77, 79, 82, 83, 84, 85, 85, 87, 87, 90, 90, 92, 92, 92, 95

(b) Which class performed better on the test? Explain.

8. Compute the variance and standard deviation for each collection of data.

(a) 4, 4, 4, 4, 4

(b) 1, 2, 3, 4, 5

(c) −4, −3, −2, −1, 0, 1, 2, 3, 4

(d) 14.6, −18.7, 29.3, 15.4, −17.5

9. Compute the variance and standard deviation for each collection of data. What do you observe?

(a) 1, 2, 3, 4, 5

(b) 3, 6, 9, 12, 15

(c) 5, 10, 15, 20, 25

(d) −6, −12, −18, −24, −30

10. (a) Compute the variance and standard deviation for the data 2, 4, 6, 8, and 10.

(b) Add 0.7 to each element of the data in part (a) and compute the variance and standard deviation.

(c) Subtract 0.5 from each data value in part (a) and compute the variance and standard deviation.

(d) Given that the variance and standard deviation of the set of data a, b, c, and d is 16 and 4, respectively, what are the variance and standard deviation of the set $a + x$, $b + x$, $c + x$, $d + x$, where x is any real number?

11. Compute the mean, median, mode, variance, and standard deviation for the distribution represented by this histogram.

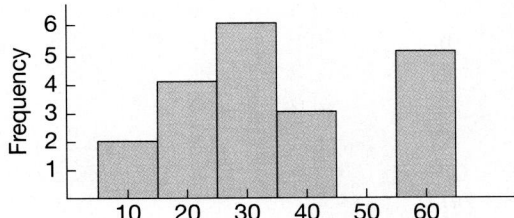

12. Compute the z-scores for the following test scores.

Student	Score
Larry	59
Curly	43
Moe	71
Bud	89
Lou	62
Jerry	65
Dean	75

13. Given in the table are projected changes in the U.S. population for the period 1986–2010. For example, the population of Alaska is expected to increase 38.7%.

PROJECTED POPULATION CHANGES (1986–2010)

State	Percent Change	State	Percent Change
AK	38.7	MT	−3.1
AL	13.2	**NC**	26.5
AR	10.3	ND	−10.4
AZ	51.4	NE	−4.3
CA	34.4	**NH**	37.5
CO	23.6	**NJ**	16.0
CT	10.4	NM	45.0
DE	23.3	NV	46.7
FL	43.8	**NY**	2.1
GA	42.3	**OH**	−3.3
HI	41.2	OK	6.2
IA	−17.4	OR	10.5
ID	7.4	**PA**	−6.4
IL	−0.5	**RI**	10.9
IN	−1.8	**SC**	22.9
KS	4.2	SD	1.9
KY	−0.5	**TN**	13.8
LA	1.0	TX	30.3
MA	7.1	UT	27.8
MD	25.2	**VA**	25.9
ME	11.1	**VT**	12.0
MI	−0.6	WA	17.4
MN	8.4	**WI**	−4.1
MO	8.6	**WV**	−16.5
MS	14.6	WY	−4.1

Source: U.S. Bureau of the Census.

Make a box and whisker plot for states east of the Mississippi River (in boldface) and beneath it a box and whisker plot for states west of the Mississippi River. What trends, if any, do your box and whisker plots reveal?

14. Twenty-two major league baseball players have hit more than 400 home runs in their careers, as of 1990.
    (a) Make a stem and leaf plot and a box and whisker plot of the data.
    (b) Outliers between 1.5 and 3.0 IQR are called **mild outliers**, and those greater than 3.0 IQR are called **extreme outliers**. What outliers, mild or extreme, occur?

Player	Home Runs
Hank Aaron	755
Babe Ruth	714
Willie Mays	660
Frank Robinson	586
Harmon Killebrew	573
Reggie Jackson	563
Mike Schmidt	548
Mickey Mantle	536
Jimmie Foxx	534
Willie McCovey	521
Ted Williams	521
Ernie Banks	512
Eddie Mathews	512
Mel Ott	511
Lou Gehrig	493
Stan Musial	475
Willie Stargell	475
Carl Yastrzemski	452
Dave Kingman	442
Billy Williams	426
Darrell Evans	414
Duke Snider	407

Source: The Baseball Encyclopedia.

15. The table gives the percentages of American families having 0, 1, 2, 3, 4, or more than 4 children in 1970 and 1990.

PERCENT OF FAMILIES HAVING 0–4 CHILDREN UNDER 18

Year	None	1	2	3	4 or More
1970	44.1	18.2	17.4	10.6	9.8
1990	41.9	23.3	21.2	8.9	4.7

Source: U.S. Bureau of the Census.

(a) What is an appropriate type of graph for displaying the data?
(b) Make a graph of the data using your chosen type.
(c) What trends, if any, are displayed by your graph?

(d) What was the average number of children (to one decimal place) in a family in 1970? 1990? Use 4 children for the "4 or more" category.

Problems

16. The class average on a reading test was 27.5 out of 40 possible points. The 19 girls in the class scored 532 points. How many total points did the 11 boys score?

17. When 100 students took a test, the average score was 77.1. Two more students took the test. The sum of their scores was 125. What is the new average?

18. The mean score for a set of 35 mathematics tests was 41.6, with a standard deviation of 4.2. What was the sum of all the scores?

19. Percentiles are scores indicating the fractional part of a distribution that is less than a certain score. For example, the 20th percentile is the score greater than or equal to exactly 20% of the scores. The 75th percentile is the score greater than or equal to 75% of the scores.
(a) What percentile is the median score?
(b) In a normal distribution what percentile has a z-score of 1? 2? -1? -2?
(c) Assume a certain distribution is normal with mean 65 and standard deviation 10. Find the 50th percentile score. Find the 16th percentile, the 84th percentile, and the 99.85th percentile.

20. Here are Mr. Emery's class scores for two tests. On which test did Lora do better relative to the entire class?

Student	Test 1 Score	Test 2 Score
Lora	85	89
Verne	72	93
Harvey	89	96
Loma	75	65
Jim	79	79
Betty	86	60

21. (a) On the same axes, draw a graph of two normal distributions with the same means but different variances. Which graph has a higher "peak"?

(b) On the same axes, draw a graph of two normal distributions with different means but equal variances. Which graph is farther to the right?

22. Reading test scores for Smithville had an average of 69.2. Nationally, the average was 60.3 with a standard deviation of 7.82. In Miss Brown's class, the average was 75.9.
(a) What is the z-score for Smithville's average score?
(b) What is the z-score for Miss Brown's class average?
(c) Assume that the distribution of all scores was a normal distribution. Approximately what percent of students in the country scored lower than Miss Brown's average?

23. (a) For the distribution given here by the histogram, find the median according to the following definition: The median is the number through which a vertical line divides the area under the graph into two equal areas. (Recall that the area of a rectangle is the product of the length of the base and the height.)
(b) Find the median according to the definition in Section 10.1. Are the two "medians" equal?

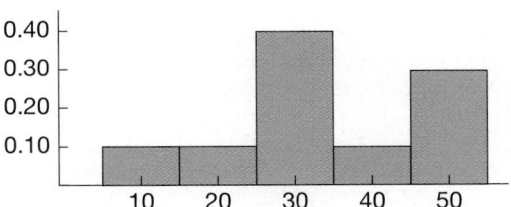

24. A dirt biker must circle a 5-mile track twice. His average speed must be 60 mph. On his first lap, he averaged 30 mph. How fast must he travel on his second lap in order to qualify?

25. A $3 \times 3 \times 3$ cube was painted on all faces, then cut apart into 27 little $1 \times 1 \times 1$ cubes.
(a) How many $1 \times 1 \times 1$ cubes had no faces painted? One face painted? Two faces painted? Three faces painted? Four or more faces painted?
(b) Answer the same questions for a $4 \times 4 \times 4$ and a $5 \times 5 \times 5$ cube.
(c) Answer the same questions for an $n \times n \times n$ cube, where n is any whole number greater than 1.

EXERCISE/PROBLEM SET 10.2—PART B

Exercises

1. Calculate the mean, median, and mode for each collection of data. Give exact answers.
   (a) $-10, -9, -8, -7, 0, 0, 7, 8, 9, 10$
   (b) $-5, -3, -1, 0, 3, 6$
   (c) $-6.5, -6.3, -6.1, 6.0, 6.3, 6.6$
   (d) $3 + \sqrt{2}, 4 + \sqrt{2}, 5 + \sqrt{2}, 6 + \sqrt{2}, 7 + \sqrt{2}$

2. Calculate the mean, median, and mode for each collection of data. Give exact answers.
   (a) $\sqrt{2}, 3\sqrt{2}, -8\sqrt{2}, 4\sqrt{2}, 3\sqrt{2}, 0$
   (b) $-2\pi, 4\pi, 0, 6\pi, 10\pi, 4\pi$
   (c) $-3 + \pi, -8 + \pi, -15 + \pi, \pi, 4 + \pi, 4 + \pi, 18 + \pi$
   (d) $\sqrt{2} + \pi, 2\sqrt{2} + \pi, \pi, -3\sqrt{2} + \pi, \sqrt{3} + \pi, -\sqrt{3} + \pi$

3. Suppose that 950 students in a state took a reading test and each scored 63. Find the mean, median, and mode for the scores.

4. All the students in a school were weighed. Their average weight was 31.4 kilograms. Their total weight was 18,337.6 kilograms. How many students are in the school?

5. Jamie made the following grades during fall term at State University. What was his grade-point average? (A = 4 points, B = 3 points, C = 2, D = 1, F = 0.)

Course	Credits	Grade
English	2	B
Chemistry	3	C
Mathematics	4	A
History	3	B
French	3	C

6. Which of the following situations are possible regarding the mean, median, and mode for a set of data? Give examples.
   (a) Mean = median = mode
   (b) Mean < median = mode
   (c) Mean < median < mode
   (d) Mean = median < mode

7. **(a)** From the box and whisker plot for 80 test scores, find the lowest score, the highest score, the lower quartile, the upper quartile, and the median.

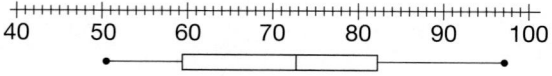

   (b) Approximately how many scores are between the lowest score and the lower quartile? Between the lower quartile and the upper quartile? Between the lower quartile and the highest score?

8. (a) Consider the following double stem and leaf plot (Table 10.5).

Class 1		Class 2
9 6	0	5 7
8 7 6 4 1	1	2 3 4
8 8 7 6 5 5 3 2 2 2 2 1	2	2 5 6 7 8 8 9
9 9 6 4 4 3 2	3	1 2 3 4 4 5 6 7 8 9
9 6 5 1	4	2 3 5 6 7 8 9 9

   Construct box and whisker plots on the same number line for the test scores.
   (b) Which class performed better? Explain.
   (c) From the box and whisker plots below, which class performed the best? Explain.

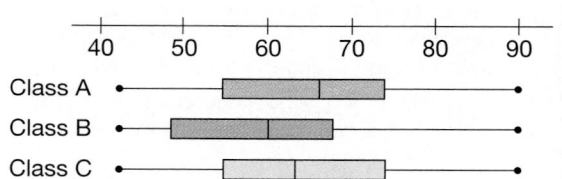

9. Compute the variance and standard deviation for each collection of data.
   (a) 5, 5, 5, 5, 5, 5, 5
   (b) 8.7, 3.8, 9.2, 14.7, 26.3
   (c) 1, 3, 5, 7, 9, 11
   (d) $-13.8, -12.3, -9.7, -15.4, -19.7$

10. Compute the z-scores for the following data:

$$8, 10, 4, 3, 6, 9, 2, 1, 15, 20$$

11. Compute the mean, median, mode, variance, and standard deviation for the data in the following table.

Number	Frequency
15	2
18	3
19	4
20	1
25	5

MEDIAN AGE IN THE UNITED STATES

Year	Age
1820	16.7
1830	17.2
1840	17.8
1850	18.9
1860	19.4
1870	20.2
1880	20.9
1890	22.0
1900	22.9
1910	24.1
1920	25.3
1930	26.4
1940	29.0
1950	30.2
1960	29.5
1970	28.0
1980	30.0
1990	33.0[a]
2000	36.4
2010	38.9
2020	40.2
2030	41.8

Source: U.S. Bureau of the Census.
[a]Ages from 1990 on are projections.

SCHOOL EXPENDITURES, 1991 (×100)

State	Expenditures per Student	State	Expenditures per Student
AK	79	MT	52
AL	32	NC	48
AR	33	ND	37
AZ	42	NE	44
CA	48	NH	55
CO	48	NJ	91
CT	79	NM	44
DC	82	NV	46
DE	60	NY	85
FL	51	OH	56
GA	49	OK	37
HI	50	OR	53
IA	48	PA	65
ID	32	RI	70
IL	51	SC	43
IN	51	SD	37
KS	50	TN	37
KY	44	TX	42
LA	40	UT	30
MA	64	VA	54
MD	62	VT	57
ME	59	WA	50
MI	53	WI	59
MN	53	WV	50
MO	44	WY	53
MS	33		

Source: U.S. Department of Education.

12. The median age of the U.S. population is given in the table.
   (a) What is an appropriate type of graph for displaying the data over a period of time?
   (b) Make a graph of the data using your chosen type.

13. Given in the table are school expenditures per student by state in 1991.
   (a) Make a stem and leaf plot of the data, using one-digit stems.
   (b) What gaps or clusters occur?
   (c) Which, if any, data values are outliers (using IQR units)? What explanation is there for the occurrence of outliers in these data?

   (d) Make a box and whisker plot for states east of the Mississippi River (see Exercise 13 in Part A), and beneath it a box and whisker plot for states west of the Mississippi River. What trends, if any, do your box and whisker plots reveal?

14. Nineteen baseball pitchers have won 300 or more games in their careers, as of 1992.

Pitcher	Victories
Cy Young	511
Walter Johnson	416
Grover Alexander	373
Christy Mathewson	373
Warren Spahn	363
James Galvin	361
Charles Nichols	361
Tim Keefe	342
Steve Carlton	329
Eddie Plank	327
John Clarkson	326
Don Sutton	324
Nolan Ryan	324
Phil Niekro	318
Gaylord Perry	314
Tom Seaver	311
Charles Radbourne	311
Mickey Welch	308
"Lefty" Grove	300
Early Wynn	300

Source: The Baseball Encyclopedia.

(a) Make a stem and leaf plot and a box and whisker plot of the data.

(b) What outliers, mild or extreme, occur?

Problems

15. The average height of a class of students is 134.7 cm. The sum of all the heights is 3771.6 cm. There are 17 boys in the class. How many girls are in the class?

16. The average score on a reading test for 58 students was 87.3. Twelve more students took the test. The average of the 12 students was 90.7. What was the average for all students?

17. Suppose that the variance for a set of data is zero. What can you say about the data?

18. (a) Give two sets of data with the same means but different variances.

(b) Give two sets of data with the same variances but different means.

19. Amy's z-score on her reading test was 1.27. The class average was 60, the median was 58.5, and the variance was 6.2. What was Amy's "raw" score (i.e., her score before converting to z-scores)?

20. (a) Can two different numbers in a distribution have the same z-score?

(b) Can all of the z-scores for a distribution be equal?

21. Suppose that a, b, c, d, and e are real numbers. In this problem, we will show that the variance for the set of data a, b, c, d, e is

$$v = \frac{a^2 + b^2 + c^2 + d^2 + e^2}{5} - \bar{x}^2$$

where $\bar{x}$ is the mean of a, b, c, d, and e.

(a) Write an expression of $\bar{x}$ in terms of a, b, c, d, and e.

(b) Show that $(a - \bar{x})^2 = a^2 - 2a\bar{x} + \bar{x}^2$.

(c) Show that $v = \dfrac{a^2 + b^2 + c^2 + d^2 + e^2}{5} - \bar{x}^2$.

(d) Write a formula, similar to the formula in part (c), for the variance of the data x_1, x_2, x_3, . . . , x_n.

(e) Verify this formula for the variance using the data 1, 2, 3, 4, 5.

22. The **unbiased standard deviation,** s_{n-1}, is computed in exactly the same way as the standard deviation, s, except that instead of dividing by n, we divide by $n - 1$. That is, s_{n-1} is equal to

$$\sqrt{\frac{(x_1 - \bar{x})^2 + (x_2 - \bar{x})^2 + \cdots + (x_n - \bar{x})^2}{n - 1}}$$

where x_1, . . . , x_n are the data and $\bar{x}$ is the mean. The unbiased standard deviation of a sample is a better estimate of the true standard deviation for a normal distribution.

(a) Compute s_{n-1} and s for the following data: 1, 2, 3, 4, 5.

(b) True or false: $s_{n-1} \geq s$ for all sets of data. Explain.

23. Amy deposited $1000 in the bank at 8% annual interest. If she leaves her money on deposit for 10 years, how much will she have at the end of 10 years?

SOLUTION OF INITIAL PROBLEM

A servant was asked to perform a job that would take 30 days. The servant would be paid 1000 gold coins. The servant replied, "I will happily complete the job, but I would rather be paid 1 copper coin on the first day, 2 copper coins on the second day, 4 on the third day, and so on, with the payment of copper coins doubling each day." The king agreed to the servant's method of payment. If a gold coin is worth 1000 copper coins, did the king make the right decision? How much was the servant paid?

Strategy: Look for a Formula

Make a table.

Day	Payment (Copper Coins)	Total Payment to Date
1	$1 = 2^0$	1
2	$2 = 2^1$	$1 + 2 = 3$
3	$4 = 2^2$	$1 + 2 + 4 = 7$
4	$8 = 2^3$	$1 + 2 + 4 + 8 = 15$
5	$16 = 2^4$	$1 + 2 + 4 + 8 + 16 = 31$
.	.	.
.	.	.
.	.	.
n	2^{n-1}	$1 + 2 + 4 + 8 + \cdots + 2^{n-1} = S$

From our table we see that on the nth day, where n is a whole number from 1 to 30, the servant is paid 2^{n-1} copper coins. His total payment through n days is $1 + 2 + 4 + \cdots + 2^{n-1}$ copper coins. Hence we wish to find a formula for $1 + 2 + \cdots + 2^{n-1}$. From the table it appears that this sum is $2^n - 1$. (Check this for $n = 1, 2, 3, 4, 5$.) Notice that this formula allows us quickly to compute the value of S for any whole number n. In particular, for $n = 30$, $S = 2^{30} - 1$, so the servant would be paid $2^{30} - 1$ copper coins altogether. Using a calculator, $2^{30} - 1 = 1,073,741,823$. Hence the servant is paid the equivalent of 1,073,741.823 gold coins. The king made a very costly error!

Additional Problems Where the Strategy "Look for a Formula" Is Useful

1. Hector's parents suggest the following allowance arrangements for a 30-week period: a penny a day for the first week, 3 cents a day for the second week, 5 cents a day for the third week, and so on or $2 a week. Which deal should he take?

2. Jack's beanstalk increases its height by $\frac{1}{2}$ the first day, $\frac{1}{3}$ the second day, $\frac{1}{4}$ the third day, and so on. What is the smallest number of days it would take to become at least 100 times as tall as its original height?

3. How many different (nonzero) angles are formed in a fan of rays like the one pictured on the left, but one having 100 rays?

WRITING/DISCUSSING FOR UNDERSTANDING

1. For purposes of comparing two sets of scores, what advantages do you think a box and whisker plot has over a double stem and leaf plot? What do you think are the disadvantages of a box and whisker plot?

2. Suppose that you wished to describe the number of miles driven per day by each 30-year-old driver in your state. What information would you need, how would you collect it, and how would you present your results? Are there any restrictions that you would impose or assumptions that you would make?

3. Think of the objects and people around you and the events taking place at this time. What examples can you give of data (numbers, scores, measurements, times, etc.) that are normally distributed?

4. Explain how the following NCTM standards are reflected in this chapter.
   • Systematically collect, organize, and describe data.
   • Construct, read, and interpret tables, charts, and graphs.

PROJECTS

1. Collect as many examples as you can find in newspapers, magazines, books, and so on, of circle graphs, bar graphs, line graphs, and pictographs. Evaluate the appropriateness of the type of graph chosen to represent the data. Also, examine your graphs to see if they contain any misleading information.

2. What kinds of statistics are typically used to describe student performances on achievement tests?

3. Find several examples in the media where the term *average* is used. Which of the three averages described in this chapter do you think is being referred to in each case, and why?

CHAPTER REVIEW

Major Ideas

1. Statistics is the study of methods for collecting, organizing, representing, and interpreting data.

2. Graphs are useful for picturing information.

3. Graphs can be misleading if only portions of complete graphs are displayed or if scales are chosen inappropriately, or if multidimensional drawings are used.

4. Data can be described by their measures of central tendency and measures of dispersion.

5. Distributions can be conveniently represented graphically using histograms or curves and provide geometrical interpretations of measures of central tendencies and dispersions.

Following is a list of key vocabulary, notation, and ideas for this chapter. Mentally review these items and, where appropriate, write down the meaning of each term. Then restudy the material that you are unsure of before proceeding to take the chapter test.

SECTION 10.1: ORGANIZING AND PICTURING INFORMATION

Vocabulary/Notation

Data 429	Histogram 431
Line plot 429	Pictograph 432
Frequency 430	Bar graph 435
Stem and leaf plot 430	Line graph 436
Gap 430	Circle graph 438
Cluster 430	Pie chart 438

Ideas

Using line plots, stem and leaf plots, pictographs, bar graphs, line graphs, and circle graphs for picturing information 429
Analyzing dimensional and scale changes to determine if information is being misrepresented 435, 437, 439

SECTION 10.2: ANALYZING DATA

Vocabulary/Notation

Measures of central tendency 449	Outlier 452
Mode 450	Measures of dispersion 456
Median 450	Range 456
Mean 451	Variance 456
Arithmetic average 451	Standard deviation 457
Box and whisker plot 452	z-score 459
Lower quartile 452	Relative frequency 460
Upper quartile 452	Distribution 460
Interquartile range (IQR) 452	Normal distribution 462

Ideas

Using measures of central tendency to describe data 449
Using box and whisker plots to picture central tendency and dispersion 452
Using measures of dispersion to describe data 456
Using distributions to provide geometrical interpretations of data 460

PEOPLE IN MATHEMATICS

Mina Rees (1902–) graduated from Hunter College, a women's school where mathematics was one of the most popular majors. "I wanted to be in the mathematics department, not because of its practical uses at all; it was because it was such fun!" Ironically, much of her recognition in mathematics has been for practical results. During World War II, she served on the National Defense Research Committee, working on wartime applications of mathematics. Later, she was director of mathematical sciences in the Office of Naval Research. Mina also taught for many years at Hunter College and City College of New York, where she served as president. Since her retirement, she has been active in the applications of research to social problems. "I have always found that mathematics was an advantage when I was dean or president of a college. If your habit is to organize things a certain way, the way a mathematician does, then you are apt to have an organization that is easier to present and explain."

Leonhard Euler (1707–1783) was one of the most prolific of all mathematicians. He published 530 books and papers during his lifetime and left much unpublished work at the time of his death. From 1771 on, he was totally blind, yet his mathematical discoveries continued. He would work mentally, then dictate to assistants, sometimes using a large chalkboard on which to write the formulas for them. His writings are a model of clear exposition, and much of our modern mathematical notation has been influenced by his style. For instance, the modern use of the symbol π is due to Euler. In geometry, he is best known for the Euler line of a triangle and the formula $V - E + F = 2$, which relates the number of vertices, edges, and faces of any simple closed polyhedron.

CHAPTER 10 TEST

Knowledge

1. True or false?
   (a) The mode of a collection of data is the middle score.
   (b) The range is the last number minus the first number in a collection of data.
   (c) A z-score is the number of standard deviations away from the median.
   (d) The median is always greater than the mean.
   (e) A circle graph is effective in displaying relative amounts.
   (f) Pictographs can be used to mislead by displaying two dimensions when only one of the dimensions represents the data.
   (g) Every large group of data has a normal distribution.
   (h) In a normal distribution, most of the data are contained within one standard deviation from the mean.

Skill

2. If a portion of a circle graph is to represent 30%, what will be the measure of the corresponding central angle?

3. Find the mean, median, mode, and range of the following data: 5, 7, 3, 8, 10, 3.

4. If a collection of data has a mean of 17 and a standard deviation of 3, what numbers would have z-scores of -2, -1, 1, and 2?

5. Calculate the standard deviation for the following data: 15, 1, 9, 13, 17, 8, 3.

Understanding

6. If possible, give a single list of data such that the mean equals the mode and the mode is less than the median. If impossible, explain why.

7. If possible, give a collection of data for which the standard deviation is zero and the mean is nonzero. If impossible, explain why.

Problem Solving/Application

8. In a distribution, the number 7 has a z-score of -2 and the number 19 has a z-score of 1. What is the mean of the distribution?

9. If the mean of the numbers 1, 3, x, 7, 11 is 9, what is x?

10. On which test did Ms. Brown's students perform the best compared to the national averages? Explain.

	Ms. Brown's Class Average	National Average	Standard Deviation
Reading	77.9	75.2	12.3
Mathematics	75.2	74.1	14.2
Science	74.3	70.3	13.6
Social studies	71.7	69.3	10.9

11 Probability

Blaise Pascal

Probability in the Everyday World

It is generally agreed that the science of probability began in the sixteenth century from the so-called "problem of the points." The problem is to determine the division of the stakes of two equally skilled players when a game of chance is interrupted before either player has obtained the required number of points in order to win. However, real progress on this subject began in 1654 when Chevalier de Mere, an experienced gambler, whose theoretical understanding of the problem did not match his observations, approached the mathematician Blaise Pascal for assistance. Pascal communicated with Fermat about the problem and, remarkably, each solved the problem by different means. Thus, in this correspondence, Pascal and Fermat laid the foundations of probability.

Now, probability is recognized in many aspects of our lives. For example, when you were conceived, you could have had any of 8,388,608 different sets of characteristics based on 23 pairs of chromosomes. In school, if you guess at random on a 10-item true/false test, there is only about a 17% probability that you will answer 7 or more questions correctly. In the manufacturing process, quality control is becoming the buzzword. Thus it is important to know the probability that certain parts will fail when deciding to revamp a production process or offer a warranty. In investments, advisors assign probabilities to future prices in an effort to decide among various investment opportunities. Another important use of probability is in actuarial science, which is used to determine insurance premiums. Probability also continues to play a role in games of chance such as dice and cards.

One very popular application of probability is the famous "birthday problem." Simply stated, in a group of people, what is the probability of two people having the same month and day of birth? Surprisingly, the probability of such matching birthdates is about 0.5 when there are 23 people and almost 0.9 when there are 40 people. An interesting application of this problem is the birthdays of the 39 American presidents through Reagan. Presidents Polk and Harding were both born on November 2 and Presidents Andrew Johnson and Wilson were both born on December 29. The surprising solution of this problem will be possible using the concepts developed in this chapter.

PROBLEM-SOLVING STRATEGIES

1. Guess and Test
2. Use a Variable
3. Draw a Picture
4. Look for a Pattern
5. Make a List
6. Solve a Simpler Problem
7. Draw a Diagram
8. Use Direct Reasoning
9. Use Indirect Reasoning
10. Use Properties of Numbers
11. Solve an Equivalent Problem
12. Work Backward
13. Use Cases
14. Solve an Equation
15. Look for a Formula
16. *Do a Simulation*

STRATEGY 16: DO A SIMULATION

A simulation is a representation of an experiment using some appropriate objects (slips of paper, dice, etc.) or perhaps a computer program. The purpose of a simulation is to run many replications of an experiment that may be difficult or impossible to perform. As you will see, to solve the following initial problem, it is easier to simulate the problem rather than to perform the actual experiment many times by questioning five strangers repeatedly.

Initial Problem

At a party, a friend bets you that at least two people in a group of five strangers will have the same astrological sign. Should you take the bet? Why or why not?

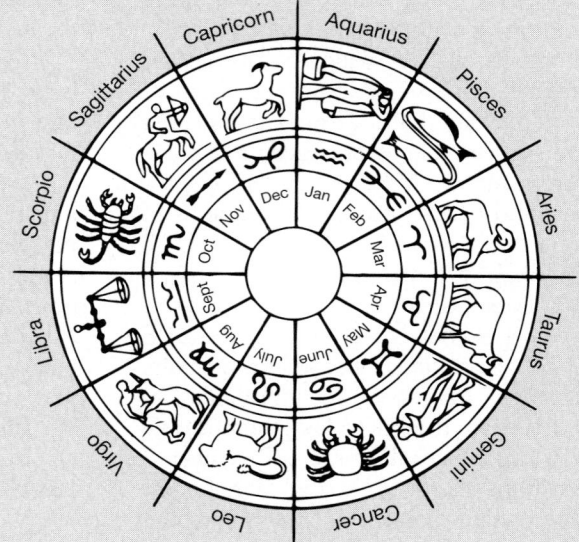

Clues

The Do a Simulation strategy may be appropriate when:

- A problem involves a complicated probability experiment.
- An actual experiment is too difficult or impossible to perform.
- A problem has a repeatable process that can be done experimentally.
- Finding the actual answer requires techniques not previously developed.

A solution of the Initial Problem above appears on page 521.

INTRODUCTION

In this chapter we discuss the fundamental concepts and principles of probability. Probability is the branch of mathematics that enables us to predict the likelihood of uncertain occurrences. There are many applications and uses of probability in the sciences (meteorology and medicine, for example), in sports and games, and in business, to name a few areas. Because of its widespread usefulness, the study of probability is an essential component of a comprehensive mathematics curriculum. In the first section of this chapter we develop the main concepts of probability. In the second section some counting procedures are introduced which lead to more sophisticated methods for computing probabilities. Finally, in the last section, simulations are developed and several applications of probability are presented.

11.1

PROBABILITY AND SIMPLE EXPERIMENTS

Simple Experiments

Probability is the mathematics of chance. Example 11.1 illustrates how probability is commonly used and reported.

EXAMPLE 11.1

(a) The probability of precipitation today is 80%.
   Interpretation: On days in the past with atmospheric conditions like today's, it rained at some time on 80% of the days.
(b) The odds that a patient improves using drug X are 60:40.
   Interpretation: In a group of 100 patients who have had the same symptoms as the patient being treated, 60 of them improved when administered drug X, and 40 did not.
(c) The chances of winning the lottery game "Find the Winning Ticket" are 1 in 150,000.
   Interpretation: If 150,000 lottery tickets are printed, only one of the tickets is the winning ticket. If more tickets are printed, the fraction of winning tickets is approximately $\frac{1}{150,000}$. ■

Probability tells us the relative frequency with which we expect an event to occur. Thus, it can be reported as a fraction, decimal, percent, or ratio. The greater the probability, the more likely the event is to occur. Conversely, the smaller the probability, the less likely the event is to occur.

To study probability in a mathematically precise way, we need special terminology and notation. An **experiment** is the act of making an observation or taking a measurement. An **outcome** is one of the possible things that can occur as a result of an experiment. The set of all the possible outcomes is called the **sample space**. Finally, an **event** is any subset of the sample space. These concepts are illustrated in Example 11.2.

EXAMPLE 11.2

(a) *Experiment:* Roll a standard six-sided die with 1, 2, 3, 4, 5, 6 dots, respectively, on the six faces (Figure 11.1). Record the number of dots showing on the top face.

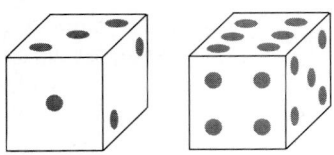

FIGURE 11.1

Sample Space: There are six outcomes: {1, 2, 3, 4, 5, 6}, where numerals represent the number of dots.

Event: For example, {2, 4, 6} is the event of getting an even number of dots, and {2, 3, 5} is the event of getting a prime number of dots. There are $2^6 = 64$ events in total, each event being a subset of {1, 2, 3, 4, 5, 6}.

(b) *Experiment:* Toss a coin three times and record the results.

Sample Space: Use three-letter sequences to represent the outcomes, as illustrated next.

HHH	3 heads	TTT	3 tails
HHT		TTH	
HTH	2 heads, 1 tail	THT	1 head, 2 tails
THH		HTT	

Thus there are eight possible outcomes in the sample space.

Event: The sample space of eight elements has many subsets (256 subsets, in fact). Any one of its subsets is an event. For example, {HTH, HTT, TTH, TTT} is the event of getting a tail on the second coin, since it contains all the possible outcomes matching this condition. (Not all events have such simple descriptions, however.)

(c) *Experiment:* Spin the spinner in Figure 11.2 twice and record the colors of the indicated regions.

Sample Space: Using pairs of letters to represent the outcomes:

RR	YR	GR	BR
RY	YY	GY	BY
RG	YG	GG	BG
RB	YB	GB	BB

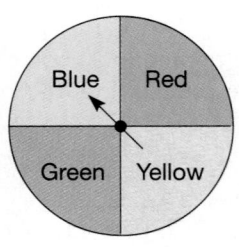

FIGURE 11.2

Event: For example, the event that the colors match is {RR, YY, GG, BB}. The event that one of the spins is green is {RG, YG, GG, BG, GR, GY, GB}.

(d) *Experiment:* Roll two dice and record the number of dots showing on each die.

Sample Space: Using ordered pairs to represent the outcomes, namely the number of dots on the faces of the two dice. For example, (1, 2) represents one dot on the first die and two dots on the second.

(1, 1)	(1, 2)	(1, 3)	(1, 4)	(1, 5)	(1, 6)
(2, 1)	(2, 2)	(2, 3)	(2, 4)	(2, 5)	(2, 6)
(3, 1)	(3, 2)	(3, 3)	(3, 4)	(3, 5)	(3, 6)
(4, 1)	(4, 2)	(4, 3)	(4, 4)	(4, 5)	(4, 6)
(5, 1)	(5, 2)	(5, 3)	(5, 4)	(5, 5)	(5, 6)
(6, 1)	(6, 2)	(6, 3)	(6, 4)	(6, 5)	(6, 6)

Event: For example, the event of getting a total of seven dots on the two dice is {(6, 1), (5, 2), (4, 3), (3, 4), (2, 5), (1, 6)}. The event of getting more than nine dots is {(6, 4), (5, 5), (4, 6), (6, 5), (5, 6), (6, 6)}. ■

Computing Probabilities in Simple Experiments

The probability of an event, *E,* is the fraction (decimal, percent, or ratio) indicating the relative frequency with which event *E* should occur in a given sample space *S.* Two events are **equally likely** if they occur with equal relative frequency (i.e., equally often).

> **Definition**
>
> ### Probability of an Event with Equally Likely Outcomes
>
> Suppose that all of the outcomes in the nonempty sample space *S* of an experiment are equally likely to occur. Let *E* be an event, $n(E)$ be the number of outcomes in *E,* and $n(S)$ the number of outcomes in *S.* Then the **probability of event *E*,** denoted **$P(E)$**, is
>
> $$P(E) = \frac{n(E)}{n(S)}.$$

By using the fact that $\varnothing \subseteq E \subseteq S$, we can determine the range for $P(E)$. In particular, $\varnothing \subseteq E \subseteq S$, so

$$0 = n(\varnothing) \le n(E) \le n(S)$$

hence

$$\frac{0}{n(S)} \le \frac{n(E)}{n(S)} \le \frac{n(S)}{n(S)}$$

so that

$$0 \le P(E) \le 1.$$

The last inequality tells us that the probability of an event must be between 0 and 1, inclusive. If $P(E) = 0$, the event *E* contains no outcomes (hence *E* is an **impossible event**); if $P(E) = 1$, the event *E* equals the entire sample space *S* (hence *E* is a **certain event**).

One way to find $P(E)$ is to make many repetitions of the experiment and simply determine the frequency that event *E* occurs. The relative frequency that event *E* occurs is called its **experimental probability**. Experimental probability may vary from observation to observation.

STUDENT PAGE SNAPSHOT

Probability of Simple Events

A. Winona is going to pick a card from the five cards without looking. This is choosing a card at **random.** The set of all possible outcomes is called the **sample space.** The sample space for Winona's experiment is 1, 2, 3, 4, 5. Any part of the sample space is called an **event.** One event for this experiment is picking a 4. An event can be one or more outcomes or no outcome.

If all events are equally likely, you can find the chance, or **probability,** that an event will occur by using the following ratio.

Probability (event) $= \frac{\text{number of favorable outcomes}}{\text{number of possible outcomes}}$

Winona wants to find the probability of picking a 4.

$$P(4) = \tfrac{1}{5}$$

The probability of picking a 4 is $\tfrac{1}{5}$.

Probability can also be expressed as a decimal or as a percent.

So $P(4) = \tfrac{1}{5}$ or 0.2 or 20%.

1. What is P(even number)? P(odd number)? Write each as a ratio.

2. **What if** a sixth card, labeled 6, were included among the cards? What would be P(even number)? Write the answer as a ratio in simplest form.

B. Look at the spinner at the right. Are all the events equally likely?

What is P(even number)?

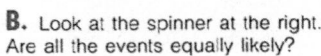

Think: All five numbers are even.

P(even number) $= \tfrac{5}{5}$, or 1

What is P(odd number)?

Think: None of the numbers are odd.

P(odd) $= \tfrac{0}{5}$, or 0

The probability of an event that is **certain** is 1. The probability of an event that is **impossible** is 0.

3. Using the same spinner, find P(multiples of 2) and P(not an even number).

EXAMPLE 11.3 An experiment consists of tossing two coins 500 times and recording the results. Table 11.1 gives the observed results and experimental probabilities. Let E be the event of getting a head on the first coin. Then $E = \{HH, HT\}$. From the table, the experimental probability of E is $\dfrac{137 + 115}{500}$. Hence $P(E) = \dfrac{252}{500} = 0.504$.

TABLE 11.1

Outcome	Frequency	Relative Frequency
HH	137	$\dfrac{137}{500}$
HT	115	$\dfrac{115}{500}$
TH	108	$\dfrac{108}{500}$
TT	140	$\dfrac{140}{500}$
Total: 500		Total: $\dfrac{500}{500} = 1.00$

Experimental probability has the advantage of being established via observations. The obvious disadvantage is that it depends on a particular set of repetitions of an experiment and hence may not generalize to other repetitions of the same type of experiment. To overcome this disadvantage, we assign **theoretical probabilities** to the events in a sample space based on *ideal* occurrences. Example 11.4 illustrates how to assign theoretical probabilities.

EXAMPLE 11.4 An experiment consists of tossing two fair coins. Find theoretical probabilities of the outcomes and the event of getting at least one head.

Solution
There are four outcomes $\{HH, HT, TH, TT\}$. If the coins are fair, all outcomes should be equally likely to occur, so that each outcome should occur $\frac{1}{4}$ of the time. Hence we make the assignments listed in Table 11.2.

TABLE 11.2

Outcome	Theoretical Probability
HH	$\frac{1}{4} = 0.25$
HT	$\frac{1}{4} = 0.25$
TH	$\frac{1}{4} = 0.25$
TT	$\frac{1}{4} = 0.25$

Let E be the event of getting at least one head, that is, $E = \{HH, HT, TH\}$.
The theoretical probability of E is $\frac{n(E)}{n(S)} = \frac{3}{4}$. That is, $P(E) = 0.75$, so we expect to get at least one head approximately 75% of the time when tossing two coins. ∎

When we refer to probability we usually mean theoretical probability. The definition of probability for equally likely outcomes tells us that we can compute the probability of an event E using the ratio of the number of ways that E can occur to the total number of outcomes in the sample space. Examples 11.5 and 11.6 illustrate ways of computing probabilities in simple experiments.

EXAMPLE 11.5   Refer to the experiment of tossing two dice in Example 11.2(d). Assume that the dice are fair. Let A be the event of getting a total of 7 dots, B be the event of getting 8 dots, and C be the event of getting at least 4 dots. Then, using the probability for equally likely outcomes, we can compute $P(A)$, $P(B)$, and $P(C)$ [recall that $n(S) = 36$]. These are recorded in Table 11.3.

TABLE 11.3

Event E	$n(E)$	$P(E)$
A	$n(A) = 6$	$P(A) = \frac{6}{36} = \frac{1}{6}$
B	$n(B) = 5$	$P(B) = \frac{5}{36}$
C	$n(C) = 33$	$P(C) = \frac{33}{36} = \frac{11}{12}$

∎

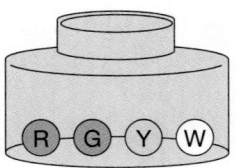

FIGURE 11.3

EXAMPLE 11.6   A jar contains four marbles, one red, one green, one yellow, and one white (Figure 11.3). If we draw two marbles from the jar, one after the other, without replacing the first one drawn, what is the probability of each of the following events?

A: One of the marbles is red.
B: The first marble is red or yellow.
C: The marbles are the same color.
D: The first marble is not white.
E: Neither marble is blue.

Solution
The sample space consists of the following outcomes. ("RG," for example, means that the first marble is red and the second marble is green.)

RG	GR	YR	WR
RY	GY	YG	WG
RW	GW	YW	WY

Thus $n(S) = 12$. Since there is exactly one marble of each color, we assume that all the outcomes are equally likely. Then

$A = \{RG, RY, RW, GR, YR, WR\}$, so $P(A) = \frac{6}{12} = \frac{1}{2}$.

$B = \{RG, RY, RW, YR, YG, YW\}$, so $P(B) = \frac{6}{12} = \frac{1}{2}$.

$C = \varnothing$, the empty event. That is, C is impossible, so $P(C) = \frac{0}{12} = 0$.

$D = \{RG, RY, RW, GR, GY, GW, YR, YG, YW\}$, so $P(D) = \frac{9}{12} = \frac{3}{4}$.

$E =$ the entire sample space, S. So $P(E) = \frac{12}{12} = 1$. ■

Notice that event B in Example 11.6 can be represented as the union of two events corresponding to drawing red on the first marble or yellow on the first marble. That is, if we let $L = \{RG, RY, RW\}$ and $M = \{YR, YG, YW\}$, then $B = L \cup M$. Observe that $L \cap M = \varnothing$. If we compute $P(L \cup M)$, $P(L)$, and $P(M)$, we find $P(L \cup M) = P(B) = \frac{1}{2}$, while $P(L) + P(M) = \frac{3}{12} + \frac{3}{12} = \frac{1}{2}$. Hence $P(L \cup M) = P(L) + P(M)$. Thus the probability of B can be found by adding the probabilities of two *disjoint* events whose union is event B, that is, $P(B) = P(L) + P(M)$.

The set of outcomes in the sample space S but not in event D is called the **complement of the event** D, written $\overline{D}$. Because $S = D \cup \overline{D}$ and $D \cap \overline{D} = \varnothing$, we see that $n(D) + n(\overline{D}) = n(S)$ or $n(\overline{D}) = n(S) - n(D)$. Therefore,

$$P(\overline{D}) = \frac{n(\overline{D})}{n(S)} = \frac{n(S) - n(D)}{n(S)} = \frac{n(S)}{n(S)} - \frac{n(D)}{n(S)} = 1 - P(D).$$

Similarly, $P(D) = 1 - P(\overline{D})$. Thus $P(\overline{D})$ in Example 11.6 is the probability that the first marble is white, namely $\frac{3}{12}$ or $\frac{1}{4}$. So $P(D) = 1 - P(\overline{D}) = 1 - \frac{1}{4} = \frac{3}{4}$, as we found directly.

EXAMPLE 11.7 Figure 11.4 shows a diagram of a sample space S of an experiment with equally likely outcomes. Events A, B, and C are indicated, their outcomes represented by points. Find the probability of each of the following events: $S, \varnothing, A, B, C, A \cup B, A \cap B, A \cup C, \overline{C}$.

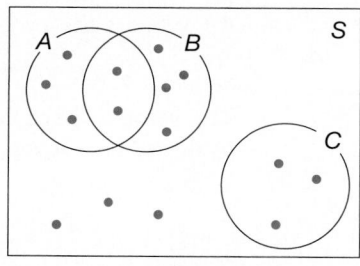

FIGURE 11.4

Solution
We can tabulate the number of outcomes in each event, and the probabilities, as follows. For example, $n(A) = 5$ and $n(S) = 15$, so $P(A) = \frac{5}{15} = \frac{1}{3}$.

Event, E	$n(E)$	$P(E) = \dfrac{n(E)}{n(S)}$
S	15	$\frac{15}{15} = 1$
$\varnothing$	0	$\frac{0}{15} = 0$
A	5	$\frac{5}{15} = \frac{1}{3}$
B	6	$\frac{6}{15} = \frac{2}{5}$
C	3	$\frac{3}{15} = \frac{1}{5}$
$A \cup B$	9	$\frac{9}{15} = \frac{3}{5}$
$A \cap B$	2	$\frac{2}{15}$
$A \cup C$	8	$\frac{8}{15}$
$\overline{C}$	12	$\frac{12}{15} = \frac{4}{5}$

In Example 11.7, observe that $P(A \cup B) = \frac{9}{15}$, while $P(A) + P(B) - P(A \cap B) = \frac{5}{15} + \frac{6}{15} - \frac{2}{15} = \frac{9}{15} = P(A \cup B)$. Hence $P(A \cup B) = P(A) + P(B) - P(A \cap B)$. This result is true for *all* events A and B. In Figure 11.5, observe how the region $A \cap B$ is shaded *twice*, once from A and once from B. Thus to find the number of elements in $A \cup B$, we can calculate $n(A) + n(B)$. *But* we have to subtract $n(A \cap B)$ so that we do not count the elements in $A \cap B$ twice. Hence $n(A \cup B) = n(A) + n(B) - n(A \cap B)$ for sets A and B.

In Example 11.7, events A and C are disjoint, also called **mutually exclusive**. That is, they have no outcomes in common. In such cases, $P(A \cup C) = P(A) + P(C)$, since $A \cap C = \varnothing$. Verify this in Example 11.7. Also, observe that $P(C) + P(\overline{C}) = 1$. Occasionally, it is simpler to compute the probability of an event indirectly, using the complement. That is, $P(C) = 1 - P(\overline{C})$.

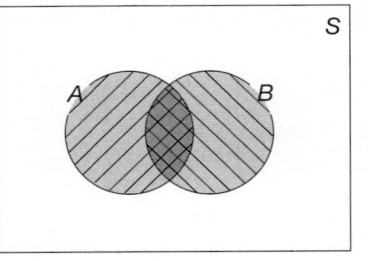

FIGURE 11.5

EXAMPLE 11.8 Carolan and Mary are playing a number matching game. Carolan chooses a whole number between 1 and 4 but does not tell Mary, who then guesses a number between 1 and 4. Assume that all numbers are equally likely to be chosen by each player.
(a) What is the probability that the numbers are equal?
(b) What is the probability that the numbers are unequal?

Solution
The sample space can be represented as ordered pairs of numbers from 1 to 4, the first being Carolan's number, the second Mary's.

$$\begin{array}{cccc}
(\mathbf{1,\ 1}) & (1,\ 2) & (1,\ 3) & (1,\ 4) \\
(2,\ 1) & (\mathbf{2,\ 2}) & (2,\ 3) & (2,\ 4) \\
(3,\ 1) & (3,\ 2) & (\mathbf{3,\ 3}) & (3,\ 4) \\
(4,\ 1) & (4,\ 2) & (4,\ 3) & (\mathbf{4,\ 4})
\end{array}$$

(a) Let E be the event that the numbers are equal. Outcomes for E are in boldface. Assuming all outcomes are equally likely, $P(E) = \frac{4}{16} = \frac{1}{4}$.

(b) Notice that the event here is $\overline{E}$. Hence the probability that the numbers are unequal is $1 - \frac{1}{4} = \frac{3}{4}$. (We can verify this directly by counting the 12 outcomes not in E. Hence $P(\overline{E}) = \frac{12}{16} = \frac{3}{4}$.) ∎

We can summarize our observations about probabilities as follows.

> **Properties of Probability**
>
> **1.** For any event A, $0 \leq P(A) \leq 1$.
> **2.** $P(\varnothing) = 0$.
> **3.** $P(S) = 1$, where S is the sample space.
> **4.** For all events A and B, $P(A \cup B) = P(A) + P(B) - P(A \cap B)$.
> **5.** If $\overline{A}$ denotes the complement of event A, then $P(\overline{A}) = 1 - P(A)$.

Observe in item 4, when $A \cap B = \varnothing$, that is, A and B are mutually exclusive, we have $P(A \cup B) = P(A) + P(B)$. The properties of probability apply to all experiments and sample spaces.

MATHEMATICAL MORSEL

The following true story was reported in a newspaper article. A teacher was giving a standardized true–false achievement test when she noticed that Johnny was busily flipping a coin in the back of the room and then marking his answers. When asked what he was doing he replied, "I didn't have time to study, so instead I'm using a coin. If it comes up heads, I mark true, and if it comes up tails, I mark false." A half-hour later, when the rest of the students were done, the teacher saw Johnny still flipping away. She asked, "Johnny, what's taking you so long?" He replied, "It's like you always tell us. I'm just checking my answers."

EXERCISE/PROBLEM SET 11.1—PART A

Exercises

1. According to the weather report, there is a 20% chance of snow in the county tomorrow. Which of the following statements would be appropriate?
   (a) Out of the next five days, it will snow one of those days.
   (b) Of the 24 hours, snow will fall for 4.8 hours.I
   (c) Of past days when conditions were similar, one out of five had some snow.
   (d) It will snow on 20% of the area of the county.

2. List the elements of the sample space for each of the following experiments.
   (a) A quarter is tossed.
   (b) A single die is rolled with faces labeled A, B, C, D, E, and F.
   (c) A regular tetrahedron die (with four faces labeled 1, 2, 3, 4) is rolled and the number on the bottom face is recorded.
   (d) The following "Red–Blue–Yellow" spinner is spun once. (All central angles are 120°.)

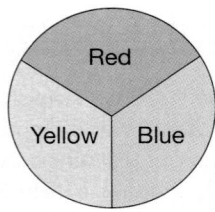

3. An experiment consists of tossing four coins. List each of the following.
   (a) The sample space
   (b) The event of a head on the first coin
   (c) The event of three heads
   (d) The event of a head or a tail on the fourth coin
   (e) The event of a head on the second coin and a tail on the third coin

4. An experiment consists of tossing a regular dodecahedron die (with 12 congruent faces). List the following.
   (a) The sample space
   (b) The event of an even number
   (c) The event of a number less than 8
   (d) The event of a number divisible by 2 and 3
   (e) The event of a number greater than 12

5. One way to find the sample space of an experiment involving two parts is to use the Cartesian product. For example, an experiment consists of tossing a dime and a quarter.

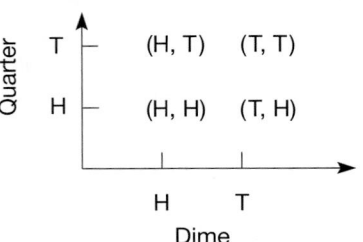

sample space for dime $D = \{H, T\}$
sample space for quarter $Q = \{H, T\}$

The sample space of the experiment is

$$D \times Q = \{(H, H), (H, T), (T, H), (T, T)\}.$$

Using this method, construct the sample space of the following experiments.
   (a) Tossing a coin and rolling a tetrahedron die (four faces)
   (b) Tossing a coin and drawing a marble from a bag containing purple, green, and yellow marbles

6. A die is rolled 60 times with the following results recorded.

Outcome	1	2	3	4	5	6
Frequency	10	9	10	12	8	11

Find the experimental probability of the following events.
   (a) Getting a 4
   (b) Getting an odd number
   (c) Getting a number greater than 3

7. A dropped thumbtack will land point up or point down.
   (a) Do you think one outcome will happen more often than the other? Which one?
   (b) The results for tossing a thumbtack 60 times are as follows.

   Point up: 42 times
   Point down: 18 times

   What is the experimental probability that it lands point up? Point down?
   (c) If the thumbtack was tossed 100 times, about how many times would you expect it to land point up? Point down?

8. Refer to Example 11.2(d), which gives the sample space for the experiment of rolling two dice, and give the probabilities of the following events.
   (a) A four on the second die
   (b) An even number on each die
   (c) At least 7 dots in total
   (d) A total of 15 dots
   (e) A total greater than 1

9. You have a key ring with five keys on it.
   (a) One of the keys is a car key. What is the probability of picking that one?
   (b) Two of the keys are for your apartment. What is the probability of selecting an apartment key?
   (c) What is the probability of selecting either the car key or an apartment key?
   (d) What is the probability of selecting neither the car key nor an apartment key?

10. What is the probability of getting yellow on each of the following spinners?
   (a)

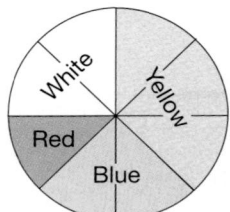

   All central angles
   are 45°

   (b)

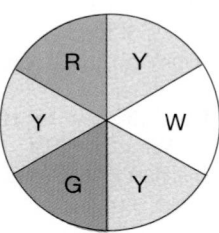

   All central angles
   are 60°

   (c)

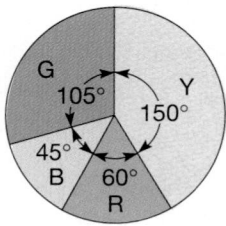

11. A die is made that has two faces marked with 2s, three faces marked with 3s, one face marked with a 5. If this die is thrown once, find the following probabilities.

   (a) Getting a 2
   (b) Not getting a 2
   (c) Getting an odd number
   (d) Not getting an odd number

12. A card is drawn from a standard deck of cards. Find $P(A \cup B)$ in each part.
   (a) A = {getting a black card}, B = {getting a heart}
   (b) A = {getting a diamond}, B = {getting an ace}
   (c) A = {getting a face card}, B = {getting a spade}
   (d) A = {getting a face card}, B = {getting a 7}

13. Consider the sample space for Example 11.2(c) and the following events.

   A: getting a green on the first spin
   B: getting a yellow on the second spin
   $A \cup B$: getting a green on the first spin or a yellow on the second spin

			A	
	RR	YR	GR	BR
B	RY	YY	GY	BY
	RG	YG	GG	BG
	RB	YB	GB	BB

   Verify the following:

$$n(S) = 16, \ n(A) = 4, \ n(B) = 4$$
$$n(A \cup B) = 7, \ n(A \cap B) = 1$$
$$P(A) = \frac{4}{16}, \ P(B) = \frac{4}{16},$$
$$P(A \cup B) = \frac{7}{16}, \text{ and } P(A \cap B) = \frac{1}{16}$$

   Show that $P(A \cup B) = P(A) + P(B) - P(A \cap B)$. Apply this to find $P(A \cup B)$ in the following cases.
   (a) A: getting a red on first spin
       B: getting same color on both spins
   (b) A: getting a yellow or blue on first spin
       B: getting a red or green on second spin

14. The spinner with three sectors is spun once.

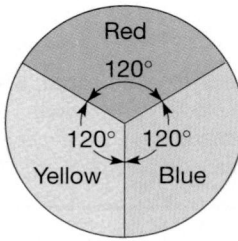

   (a) What is the probability of spinning red (R)?
   (b) What is the probability of spinning blue (B)?

(c) What is the probability of spinning yellow (Y)?

(d) Here the sample space is divided into three different events, R, B, and Y. Find the sum, $P(R) + P(B) + P(Y)$.

(e) Repeat the parts above with the spinner with eight sectors. Do you get the same result in part (d)?

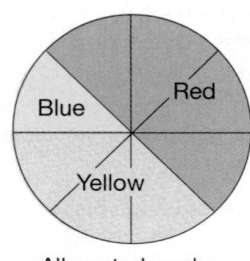

All central angles
are 45°

15. Consider the experiment in Example 11.2(c) where a spinner is spun twice. Consider the following events:

A: getting a blue on the first spin
B: getting a yellow on one spin
C: getting the same color on both spins

Describe the following events and find their probabilities.

(a) $A \cup B$ **(b)** $B \cap C$ **(c)** $\overline{B}$

16. A student is selected at random. Let A be the event that the selected student is a sophomore and B be the event that the selected student is taking English. Write in words what is meant by each of the following probabilities.

(a) $P(A \cup B)$ **(b)** $P(A \cap B)$ **(c)** $1 - P(A)$

17. A bag contains an unknown number of balls, some red, some blue, and some green. Find the smallest number of balls in the bag if the following probabilities are given. Give the P(green) for each situation.

(a) $P(\text{red}) = \frac{1}{6}$, $P(\text{blue}) = \frac{1}{3}$

(b) $P(\text{red}) = \frac{3}{5}$, $P(\text{blue}) = \frac{1}{6}$

(c) $P(\text{red}) = \frac{1}{5}$, $P(\text{blue}) = \frac{3}{4}$

Problems

18. Two fair six-sided dice are rolled, and the sum of the dots on the top faces is recorded.

(a) Complete the table, showing the number of ways each sum can occur.

Sum	2	3	4	5	6	7	8	9	10	11	12
Ways	1	2	3								

(b) Use the table to find the probability of the following events.

A: The sum is prime.
B: The sum is a divisor of 12.
C: The sum is a power of 2.
D: The sum is greater than 3.

19. The probability of a "geometric" event involving the concept of measure (length, area, volume) is determined as follows. Let $m(A)$ and $m(S)$ represent the measures of the event A and the sample space S, respectively. Then

$$P(A) = \frac{m(A)}{m(S)}$$

For example, in the first figure, if the length of S is 12 cm and the length of A is 4 cm, then $P(A) = \frac{4}{12} = \frac{1}{3}$. Similarly, in the second figure, if the area of region B is 10 cm^2 and the area of region S is 60 cm^2, then $P(B) = \frac{10}{60} = \frac{1}{6}$.

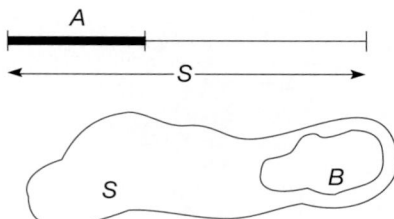

A bus travels between Albany and Binghamton, a distance of 100 miles. If the bus has broken down, we want to find the probability that it has broken down within 10 miles of either city.

(a) The road from Albany to Binghamton is the sample space. What is $m(S)$?

(b) Event A is that part of the road within 10 miles of either city. What is $m(A)$?

(c) Find $P(A)$.

20. The dartboard illustrated is made up of circles with radii of 1, 2, 3, and 4 units. A dart hits the target randomly. What is the probability that the dart hits the bull's-eye?

(HINT: The area of a circle with radius r is πr^2.)

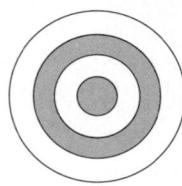

EXERCISE/PROBLEM SET 11.1—PART B

Exercises

1. For visiting a resort area you will receive a special gift.

Category I	Category II
A. A new car	D. 25-inch color TV
B. Food processor	E. AM/FM stereo
C. $2500 cash	F. $1000 cash

Category III
G. Meat smoker
H. Toaster oven
I. $25 cash

The probabilities are as follows: A, 1 in 52,000; B, 25,736 in 52,000; C, 1 in 52,000; D, 3 in 52,000; E, 25,736 in 52,000; F, 3 in 52,000; G, 180 in 52,000; H, 180 in 52,000; I, 160 in 52,000.
   (a) Which gifts are you most likely to receive?
   (b) Which gifts are you least likely to receive?
   (c) If 5000 people visit the resort, how many would be expected to receive a new car?

2. List the sample space for each experiment.
   (a) Tossing a dime and a penny
   (b) Tossing a nickel and rolling a die
   (c) Drawing a marble from a bag containing one red and one blue marble and drawing a second marble from a bag containing one green and one white marble

3. A bag contains one each of red, green, blue, yellow, and white marbles. Give the sample space of the following experiments.
   (a) One marble is drawn.
   (b) One marble is drawn, then replaced, and a second one is then drawn.
   (c) One marble is drawn, but not replaced, and a second one is drawn.

4. An experiment consists of tossing a coin and rolling a die. List each of the following.
   (a) The sample space
   (b) The event of getting a head
   (c) The event of getting a 3
   (d) The event of getting an even number
   (e) The event of getting a head and a number greater than 4
   (f) The event of getting a tail or a 5

5. Identify which of the following events are certain (C), possible (P), or impossible (I).

(a) You throw a 2 on a die.
(b) A student in this class is under 2 years old.
(c) Next week has only 5 days.
(d) There are at least 4 Sundays this month.
(e) It will rain today.
(f) You will get an A in this class.
(g) You throw a head on a die.

6. A loaded die (one in which outcomes are not equally likely) is tossed 1000 times with the following results.

Outcome	1	2	3	4	5	6
Number of Times	125	75	350	250	150	50

Find the experimental probability of the following events.
(a) Getting a 2
(b) Getting a 5
(c) Getting a 1 or a 5
(d) Getting an even number

7. Refer to Example 11.4, in which two fair coins are tossed. Assign theoretical probabilities to the following events.
(a) Getting a head on the first coin
(b) Getting a head on the first coin and a tail on the second coin
(c) Getting at least one tail
(d) Getting exactly one tail

8. A snack pack of colored candies contained the following:

Color	Brown	Tan	Yellow	Green	Orange
Number	7	3	5	3	4

One candy is selected at random. Find the experimental probability that it is of the following color.
(a) Brown   (b) Tan
(c) Yellow   (d) Green
(e) Not brown   (f) Yellow or orange

9. An American roulette wheel has 38 slots around the rim. Two of these are numbered 0 and 00 and are green; the others are numbered from 1 to 36 and half are red, half are black. As the wheel is spun in one direction, a small ivory ball is rolled along the rim in the opposite direction. The ball has an equally likely chance of falling into any one of the 38 slots, assum-

ing that the wheel is fair. Find the probability of each of the following.
(a) The ball lands on 0 or 00.
(b) The ball lands on 23.
(c) The ball lands on a red number.
(d) The ball does not land on 20–36.
(e) The ball lands on an even number or a green slot.

10. Two dice are thrown. If each face is equally likely to turn up, find the following probabilities.
(a) The sum is even.
(b) The sum is not 10.
(c) The sum is a prime.
(d) The sum is less than 9.
(e) The sum is not less than 9.

11. A card is drawn at random from a deck of 52 playing cards. What is the probability of drawing each of the following?
(a) A black card
(b) A face card
(c) Not a face card
(d) A black face card
(e) A black or a face card
(f) An ace or a face card
(g) Neither an ace nor a face card
(h) Not an ace

12. One die is thrown. If each face is equally likely to turn up, find the following probabilities.
(a) Getting a 6
(b) Not getting a 6
(c) An even number turns up.
(d) An even number does not turn up.
(e) The number divides 6.
(f) The number does not divide 6.

13. A bag contains six balls on which are the letters a, a, a, b, b, and c. One ball is drawn at random from the bag. Let A, B, and C be the events that balls a, b, or c are drawn, respectively.

(a) What is $P(A)$?
(b) What is $P(B)$?
(c) What is $P(C)$?
(d) Find $P(A) + P(B) + P(C)$.
(e) An unknown number of balls, each lettered c, are added to the bag. It is known that now $P(A) = \frac{1}{4}$ and $P(B) = \frac{1}{6}$. What is $P(C)$?

14. Consider the experiment in Example 11.2(b) where a coin is tossed three times. Consider the following events:

A: The number of heads is 3.
B: The number of heads is 2.
C: The second toss lands heads.

Describe the following events and find their probabilities.
(a) $A \cup B$ (b) $\overline{B}$
(c) $\overline{C}$ (d) $B \cap C$

15. A bag contains 2 red balls, 3 blue balls, and 1 yellow ball.
(a) What is the probability of drawing a red ball?
(b) How many red balls must be added to the bag so that the probability of drawing a red ball is $\frac{1}{2}$?
(c) How many blue balls must be added to the bag so that the probability of drawing a red ball is $\frac{1}{5}$?

16. What is false about the following statements?
(a) Since there are 50 states, the probability of being born in Pennsylvania is $\frac{1}{50}$.
(b) The probability that I am taking math is 0.80 and the probability that I am taking English is 0.50, so the probability that I am taking math and/or English is 1.30.
(c) The probability that the basketball team wins its next game is $\frac{1}{3}$, the probability that it loses is $\frac{1}{2}$.
(d) The probability that I get an A in this course is 1.5.

Problems

17. A paraglider wants to land in the unshaded region in the square field illustrated, since the shaded regions (four quarter circles) are briar patches. If he lost control and was going to hit the field randomly, what is the probability that he would miss the briar patch?

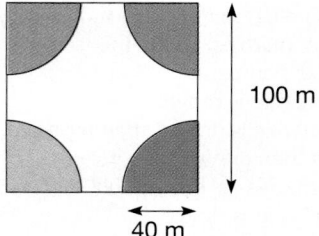

100 m

40 m

18. A microscopic worm is eating its way around the inside of a spherical apple of radius 6 cm. What is the probability that the worm is within 1 cm of the surface of the apple? (HINT: $V = \frac{4}{3}\pi r^3$, where r is the radius.)

11.2

PROBABILITY AND COMPLEX EXPERIMENTS

Tree Diagrams and Counting Techniques

In some experiments it is inefficient to list all the outcomes in the sample space. Therefore, we develop alternative procedures to compute probabilities.

A **tree diagram** can be used to represent the outcomes of an experiment. The experiment of drawing two marbles, one at a time, from a jar of four marbles without replacement, which was illustrated in Example 11.6, can be conveniently represented by the outcome tree diagram shown in Figure 11.6.

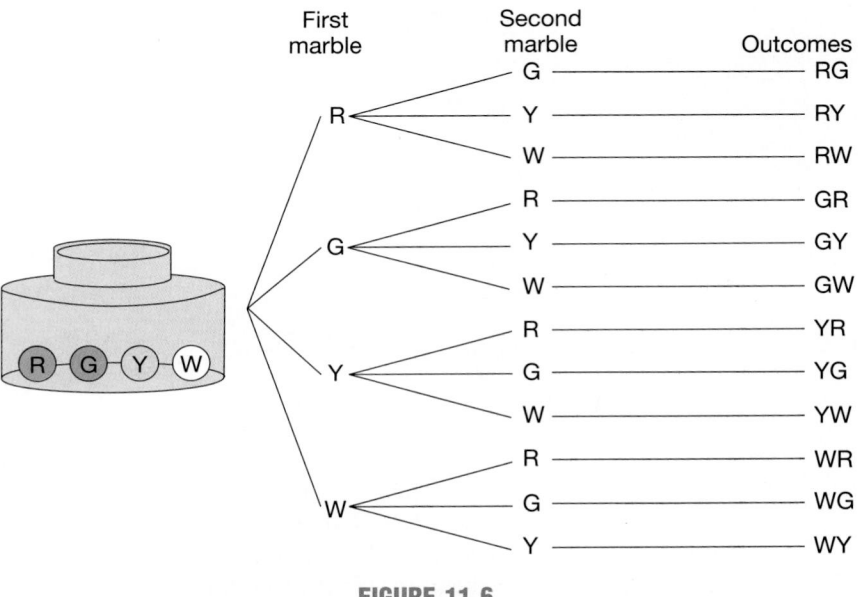

FIGURE 11.6

The diagram in Figure 11.6 shows that there are 12 outcomes in the sample space since there are 12 right-hand endpoints on the tree. To find the probability that the *first* marble is red *or* the *second* marble is white, examine the tree to count the number of pairs where R appears first or W appears second. (*Warning:* Do not count RW twice!) Since there are five equally likely outcomes, RG, RY, RW, GW, and YW, in which the correct combination appears, the probability of getting red first or white second is $\frac{5}{12}$. A tree diagram can also be used in the next example.

EXAMPLE 11.9 Suppose that you can order a new sports car in a choice of five colors, red, white, green, black, or silver (R, W, G, B, S), and two types of transmissions, manual or automatic (M, A). How many different types of cars can you order?

Solution

Figure 11.7 shows that there are 10 types of cars corresponding to the 10 outcomes.

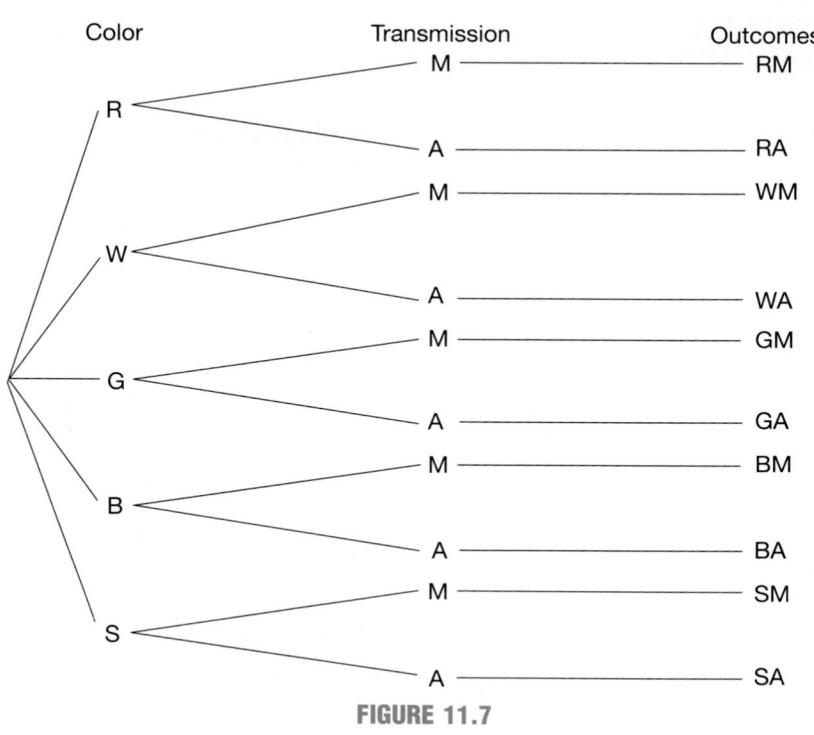

FIGURE 11.7

There are 10 different paths, or outcomes, for selecting cars in Example 11.9. Rather than count all the outcomes, we can actually compute the number of outcomes by making a simple observation about the tree diagram. Notice that there are five colors (five primary branches) and two transmission types (two secondary branches for each of the original five) or 10 (5 · 2) different combinations. This counting procedure suggests the following property.

Fundamental Counting Property

If an event A can occur in r ways, and for each of these r ways, an event B can occur in s ways, then events A and B can occur, in succession, in $r \cdot s$ ways.

The fundamental counting property can be generalized to more than two events occurring in succession. This is illustrated in the next example.

EXAMPLE 11.10 Suppose that pizzas can be ordered in 3 sizes (small, medium, large), 2 crust choices (thick or thin), 4 choices of meat toppings (sausage only, pepperoni only, both, or neither), and 2 cheese toppings (regular or double cheese). How many different ways can a pizza be ordered?

Solution
Since there are 3 size choices, 2 crust choices, 4 meat choices, and 2 cheese choices, by the fundamental counting property, there are $3 \cdot 2 \cdot 4 \cdot 2 = 48$ different types of pizzas altogether. ■

Now let's apply the fundamental counting property to compute the probability of an event in a simple experiment.

EXAMPLE 11.11   Find the probability of getting a sum of 11 when tossing a pair of fair dice.

Solution
Since each die has six faces and there are two dice, there are $6 \cdot 6 = 36$ possible outcomes according to the fundamental counting property. There are two ways of tossing an 11, namely (5, 6) and (6, 5). Therefore, the probability of tossing an eleven is $\frac{2}{36}$, or $\frac{1}{18}$. ■

EXAMPLE 11.12   A local hamburger outlet offers patrons a choice of four condiments: catsup, mustard, pickles, and onions. If the condiments are added or omitted in a random fashion, what is the probability that you will get one of the following types: catsup and onion, mustard and pickles, or one with everything?

Solution
Since we can view each condiment in two ways, namely as being either on or off a hamburger, there are $2^4 = 16$ various possible hamburgers (list them or draw a tree diagram to check this). Since there are three combinations you are interested in, the probability of getting one of the three combinations is $\frac{3}{16}$. ■

The fundamental counting property can be applied to a wide variety of problems involving counting. However, there is a certain class of experiments whose outcomes can be counted using a more convenient procedure. Such experiments consist of a sequence of smaller identical experiments *each having two outcomes*. Coin-tossing experiments are in this general class since there are only two outcomes (head/tail) on each toss.

EXAMPLE 11.13
(a) Three coins are tossed. How many outcomes are there?
(b) Repeat for 4, 5, and 6 coins.
(c) Repeat for n coins, where n is a counting number.

Solution
(a) For each coin there are two outcomes. Thus, by the fundamental counting property, there are $2 \times 2 \times 2 = 2^3 = 8$ total outcomes.
(b) For 4 coins, by the fundamental counting property, there are $2^4 = 16$ outcomes. For 5 and 6 coins, there are $2^5 = 32$ and $2^6 = 64$ outcomes, respectively.
(c) For n coins, there are 2^n outcomes. ■

Counting outcomes in experiments such as coin tossings can be done systematically. Figure 11.8 shows all the outcomes for the experiments in which 1, 2, or 3 coins are tossed.

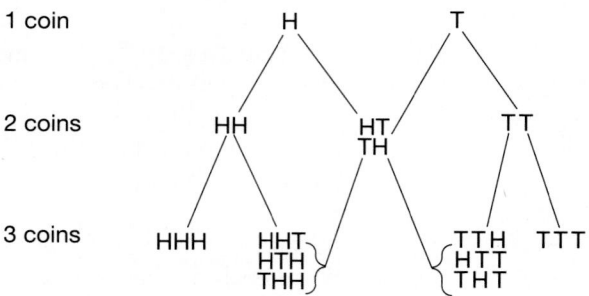

Outcomes in coin experiments

FIGURE 11.8

From the sample space for the experiment of tossing 1 coin we can determine the outcomes for an experiment of tossing 2 coins (Figure 11.8, second row). The two ways of getting exactly 1 head (middle two entries) are derived from the outcomes for tossing 1 coin. The outcome H for 1 coin yields the outcomes HT for two coins, while the outcome T for one coin yields TH for two coins.

In a similar way, the outcomes for tossing 3 coins (Figure 11.8, third row) are derived from the outcomes for tossing 2 coins. For example, the three ways of getting 2 heads when tossing 3 coins is the *sum* of the number of ways of getting 2 or 1 heads when tossing 2 coins. This can be seen by taking the 1 arrangement for getting 2 heads with 2 coins and making the third coin a tail. Similarly, take the arrangements of getting 1 head with 2 coins, and make the third coin a head. This gives all 3 possibilities.

We can abbreviate this counting procedure, as shown in Figure 11.9.

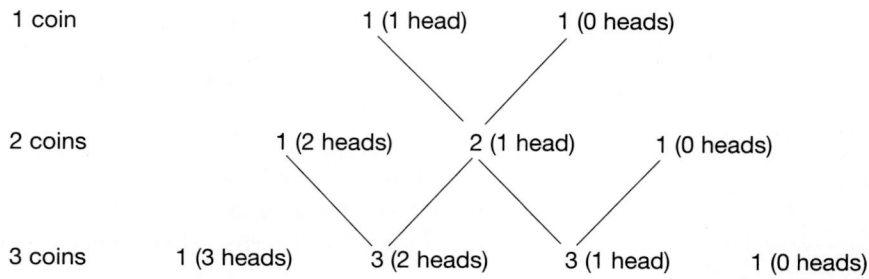

Counting coin outcomes with
a given number of heads

FIGURE 11.9

Notice that the row of possible arrangements when tossing 3 coins begins with 1. Thereafter each entry is the sum of the two entries immediately above it until the final 1 on the right. This pattern generalizes to any whole number of coins. The number array that we obtain is **Pascal's triangle**. Figure 11.10 shows seven rows of Pascal's triangle.

											Sum
					1						2^0
1 coin					1	1					2^1
2 coins				1	2	1					$4 = 2^2$
3 coins			1	3	3	1				$8 = 2^3$
4 coins		1	4	6	4	1			$16 = 2^4$
5 coins	1	5	10	10	5	1		$32 = 2^5$
6 coins	1	6	15	20	15	6	1	$64 = 2^6$

FIGURE 11.10

Notice that the sum of the entries in the nth row is 2^n.

EXAMPLE 11.14   Six fair coins are tossed. Find the probability of getting exactly 3 heads.

Solution
From Example 11.13 there are $2^6 = 64$ outcomes. Furthermore, the 6-coins row of Pascal's triangle (Figure 11.10) may be interpreted as follows:

1(6H)   6(5H)   15(4H)   20(3H)   15(2H)   6(1H)   1(0H).

Thus there are 20 ways of getting exactly 3 heads, and the probability of 3 heads is $\frac{20}{64} = \frac{5}{16}$. ∎

Notice in Example 11.14 that even though half the coins are heads, the probability is not $\frac{1}{2}$, as one might initially guess.

EXAMPLE 11.15   Use Pascal's triangle to find the probability of getting at least four heads when tossing seven coins.

Solution
First, by the fundamental counting property, there are 2^7 possible outcomes when tossing 7 coins. Next, construct the row that begins 1, 7, 21, . . . in Pascal's triangle in Figure 11.10.

$$1 \quad 7 \quad 21 \quad 35 \quad 35 \quad 21 \quad 7 \quad 1$$

The first four numbers, 1, 7, 21, and 35, represent the number of outcomes where there are at least four heads. Thus the probability of tossing at least four heads with seven coins is $\dfrac{(1 + 7 + 21 + 35)}{2^7} = \dfrac{64}{128} = \dfrac{1}{2}$. ∎

Pascal's triangle provides a useful way of counting coin arrangements or outcomes in any experiment in which only two equally likely possibilities exist. For example, births (male/female), true/false exams, and target shooting (hit/miss) are sources of such experiments.

Probability Tree Diagrams

In addition to helping to display and count outcomes, tree diagrams can be used to determine probabilities in complex experiments. In the next example, a marble is drawn and replaced. This is referred to as **drawing with replacement**. If the marble had *not* been replaced, it is called **drawing without replacement**.

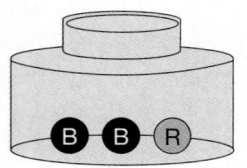

FIGURE 11.11

EXAMPLE 11.16   A jar contains 3 marbles, 2 black and 1 red (Figure 11.11). A marble is drawn, replaced, and a second marble is drawn. What is the probability that both marbles are black? Assume that the marbles are equally likely to be drawn.

Solution
Figure 11.12(a) shows $3 \cdot 3 = 9$ equally likely branches in the tree, of which 4 correspond to the event "two black marbles are drawn." Thus the probability of drawing two black marbles with replacement is $\frac{4}{9}$. Instead of comparing the number of successful outcomes (4 here) with the total number of outcomes (9 here), we could have simply *added* the individual probabilities at the ends of the branches in Figure 11.12(b). That is, the probability is $\frac{1}{9} + \frac{1}{9} + \frac{1}{9} + \frac{1}{9} = \frac{4}{9}$. [Notice that the end of each branch is weighted with a probability of $\frac{1}{9}$ since there are 9 equally likely outcomes in the tree in Figure 11.12(a).]

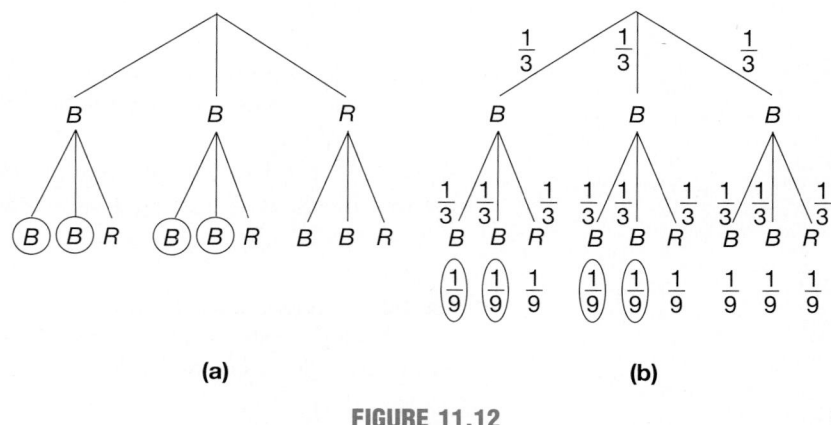

(a)   **(b)**

FIGURE 11.12

The same notion applies to the first stage of the tree in Figure 11.12(b), which has its branches labeled with probability $\frac{1}{3}$. That is, in the top tree in Figure 11.12(b), $P(B) = \frac{2}{3}$ since there are two black marbles out of three marbles. Also, by adding the probabilities of the B branches in the top tree in Figure 11.12(b), we obtain $P(B) = \frac{1}{3} + \frac{1}{3} = \frac{2}{3}$. Thus, by weighting branches using appropriate probabilities, we can form **probability tree diagrams**, which in turn can be used to find the probabilities of various events. The concept of adding the probabilities at the ends of branches in a probability tree is summarized next.

> ### Additive Property of Probability Tree Diagrams
>
> Suppose that an event E is a union of pairwise mutually exclusive simpler events $E_1, E_2, \ldots, E_n$, where $E_1, E_2, \ldots, E_n$ are from a sample space S. Then
>
> $$P(E) = P(E_1) + P(E_2) + \cdots + P(E_n).$$
>
> The probabilities of the events $E_1, E_2, \ldots, E_n$ can be viewed as those associated with the ends of branches in a probability tree diagram.

Notice that this property is an extension of the property

$$P(A \cup B) = P(A) + P(B) - P(A \cap B)$$

where $A \cap B = \emptyset$.

This technique of labeling probability tree diagrams to calculate probabilities can be simplified further. The following figure illustrates how the number of branches in Figure 11.12(b) can be reduced by collapsing similar branches and by then weighting them accordingly [Figure 11.13(a) and (b)].

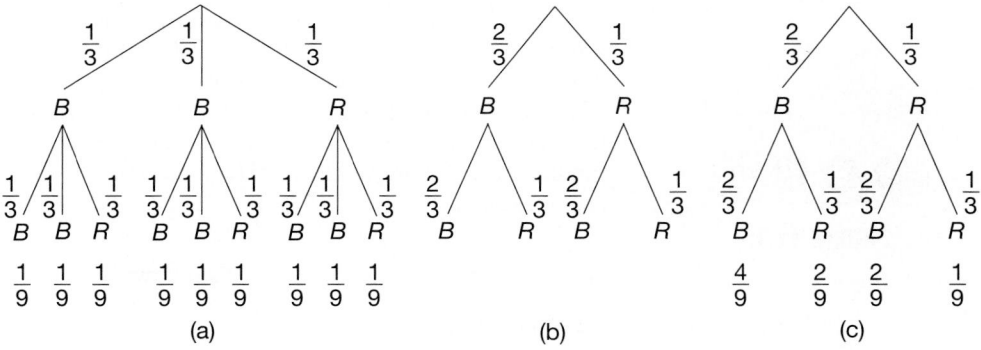

(a)   (b)   (c)

FIGURE 11.13

Next we must decide what weights to assign to the ends of the branches in Figure 11.13(b). This information can be obtained by adding the corresponding probabilities on the ends of the corresponding branches in Figure 11.13(a). Using Figure 11.13(a) we can see that $P(BB) = \frac{1}{9} + \frac{1}{9} + \frac{1}{9} + \frac{1}{9} = \frac{4}{9}$, $P(BR) = \frac{1}{9} + \frac{1}{9} = \frac{2}{9}$, $P(RB) = \frac{1}{9} + \frac{1}{9} = \frac{2}{9}$, and $P(RR) = \frac{1}{9}$. These values are inserted in Figure 11.13(b) to form Figure 11.13(c). Notice that the $\frac{4}{9}$ obtained for $P(BB)$ is located at the end of the two branches labeled $\frac{2}{3}$ and $\frac{2}{3}$, and $\frac{2}{3} \times \frac{2}{3} = \frac{4}{9}$. This multiplicative procedure also holds for the remaining three branches. The property of multiplying the probabilities along a series of branches to find the probability at the end of a branch is stated in general terms next. This property is based on the fundamental counting property.

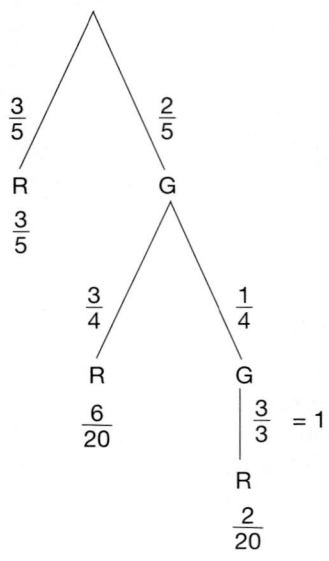

$$\frac{3}{5} \qquad \frac{2}{5}$$

R   G

$$\frac{3}{5}$$

$$\frac{3}{4} \qquad \frac{1}{4}$$

R   G

$$\frac{6}{20} \qquad \frac{3}{3} = 1$$

R

$$\frac{2}{20}$$

FIGURE 11.14

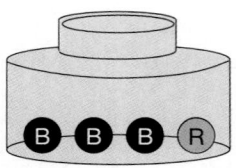

FIGURE 11.15

> ### Multiplicative Property of Probability Tree Diagrams
>
> Suppose that an experiment consists of a sequence of simpler experiments that are represented by branches of a probability tree diagram. Then the probability of any of the simpler experiments is the product of all the probabilities on its branch.

EXAMPLE 11.17   A jar contains three red gumballs and two green gumballs. An experiment consists of drawing gumballs, one at a time from the jar, without replacement, until a red one is obtained. Find the probability of the following events.

A: Only one draw is needed.
B: Exactly two draws are needed.
C: Exactly three draws are needed.

Solution
Make the probability tree diagram (Figure 11.14). Hence $P(A) = \frac{3}{5}$, $P(B) = \frac{2}{5} \cdot \frac{3}{4} = \frac{6}{20} = \frac{3}{10}$, and $P(C) = \frac{2}{5} \cdot \frac{1}{4} \cdot 1 = \frac{2}{20} = \frac{1}{10}$. ∎

In every probability tree diagram, the sum of the probabilities at the end of the branches is 1. (This sum is the probability of the entire sample space.) For example, in Figure 11.14, $\frac{3}{5} + \frac{6}{20} + \frac{2}{20} = 1$.

The following discussion illustrates another way to see why this multiplication property holds for probability tree diagrams. Consider a jar with 3 black marbles and 1 red marble (Figure 11.15), the experiment of drawing two marbles with replacement, and the event of drawing a black marble first, then drawing a red marble. The entries in the 4-by-4 array in Figure 11.16(a) show all possible outcomes of drawing two marbles with replacement.

		All possible draws			First draw B				First draw B Second draw R		

Second draw

		B	B	B	R
	B	BB	BB	BB	BR
First draw	B	BB	BB	BB	BR
	B	BB	BB	BB	BR
	R	RB	RB	RB	RR

(a)

First draw B

	B	B	B	R
B	BB	BB	BB	BR
B	BB	BB	BB	BR
B	BB	BB	BB	BR
R	RB	RB	RB	RR

(b)

First draw B
Second draw R

	B	B	B	R
B	BB	BB	BB	BR
B	BB	BB	BB	BR
B	BB	BB	BB	BR
R	RB	RB	RB	RR

(c)

FIGURE 11.16

The outcomes in which B was drawn first, namely those with a B on the left, are surrounded by a rectangle in Figure 11.16(b). Notice that $\frac{3}{4}$ of the pairs are included in the rectangle since 3 out of 4 of the marbles are black. In Figure 11.16(c), a dashed rectangle is drawn around those pairs

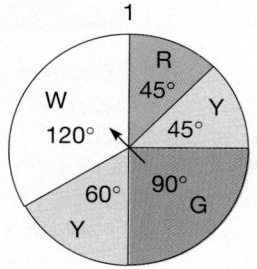

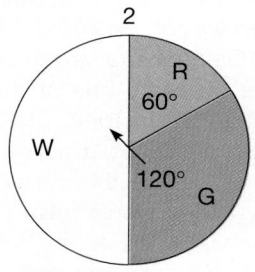

FIGURE 11.17(a)

where a B is drawn first and an R is drawn second. Observe that the portion surrounded by the dashed rectangle is $\frac{1}{4}$ of the pairs inside the rectangle, since $\frac{1}{4}$ of the marbles in the jar are red. The procedure used to find the fraction of pairs that are BR in Figure 11.16(c) is analogous to the model we used to find the product of two fractions. Thus the probability of drawing a B then an R with replacement in this experiment is $\frac{3}{4} \times \frac{1}{4} = \frac{3}{16}$, the *products* of the individual probabilities.

In the next example we illustrate how to calculate the probability of a complex experiment using both the additive and multiplicative properties of probability tree diagrams.

EXAMPLE 11.18 Both spinners shown in Figure 11.17(a) are spun. Find the probability that they stop on the same color.

Solution
Draw an appropriate probability tree diagram [Figure 11.17(b)]. The color

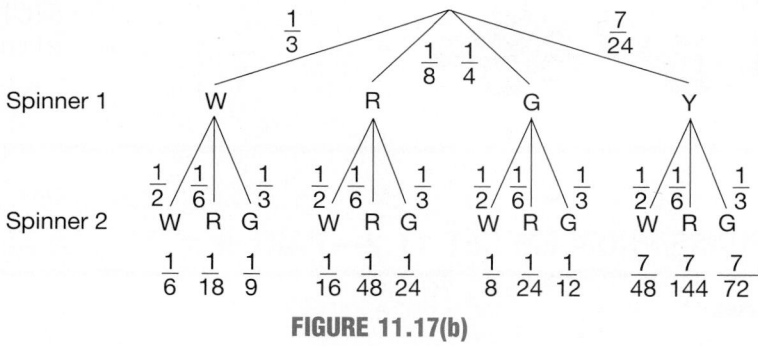

FIGURE 11.17(b)

names are abbreviated by first letter. The desired event is {WW, RR, GG}. By the multiplicative property of probability tree diagrams $P(WW) = \frac{1}{3} \cdot \frac{1}{2} = \frac{1}{6}$, $P(RR) = \frac{1}{8} \cdot \frac{1}{6} = \frac{1}{48}$, and $P(GG) = \frac{1}{4} \cdot \frac{1}{3} = \frac{1}{12}$. By the additive property of probability tree diagrams, $P(\{WW, RR, GG\}) = \frac{1}{6} + \frac{1}{48} + \frac{1}{12} = \frac{13}{48}$. ■

In summary, the probability of a complex event can be found as follows:

1. Construct the appropriate probability tree diagram.
2. Assign probabilities to each branch.
3. Multiply the probabilities along individual branches to find the probability of the outcome at the end of each branch.
4. Add the probabilities of the relevant outcomes, depending on the event.

MATHEMATICAL MORSEL

The following story of the $500,000 "sure thing" appeared in a national news magazine. A popular wagering device at several racetracks and jai alai frontons was called Pick Six. To win, one had to pick the winners of six races or games. The jackpot prize would continue to grow until someone won. At one fronton, the pot reached $551,331. Since there were eight possible winners in each of six games, the number of ways that six winners could occur was 8^6, or 262,144. To cover all of these combinations, a group of bettors bought a $2 ticket on every one of the combinations, betting $524,288 in total. Their risk was that someone else would do the same thing or be lucky enough to guess the correct combination, in which case they would have to split the pot. Neither event happened, so the betting group won $988,326.20, for a net pretax profit of $464, 038.20. (The jai lai club kept part of the total amount of money bet.)

EXERCISE/PROBLEM SET 11.2—PART A

Exercises

1. Tree diagrams are useful in determining the number of outcomes in an experiment. The simplest tree diagrams have **one stage** (when the experiment involves just one action). For example, consider drawing one ball from a box containing a red, a white, and a blue ball. To draw the tree, follow these steps.

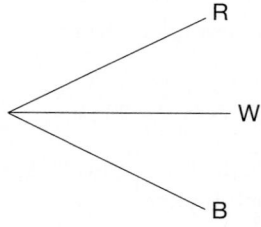

1. Draw a single dot.
2. Draw one branch for each outcome.
3. At the end of the branch, label it by listing the outcome.

Draw one-stage trees to represent each of the following experiments.

(a) Tossing a dime
(b) Drawing a marble from a bag containing one red, one green, one black, and one white marble
(c) Choosing a TV program from among channels 2, 6, 9, 12, and 13
(d) Spinning the spinner, where all central angles are 120°

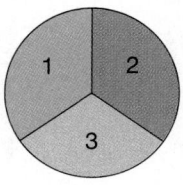

2. In each part, draw **two-stage** trees to represent the following experiments which involve a sequence of two experiments.

1. Draw the one-stage tree for the outcomes of the first experiment.
2. Starting at the end of *each branch* of the tree in step 1, draw the (one-stage) tree for the outcomes of the second experiment.

   (a) Tossing a coin twice
   (b) Drawing a marble from a box containing one yellow and one green marble, then drawing a marble from a box containing one yellow, one red, and one blue marble
   (c) Having two children in the family

3. Trees may have more than two stages. Draw outcome trees to represent the following experiments.
   (a) Tossing a coin three times
   (b) Having four children in the family (Use *B* for boy and *G* for girl.)

4. In some cases, what happens at the first stage of the tree affects what can happen at the next stage. For example, one ball is drawn from the box containing one red, one white, and one blue ball, but not replaced before the second ball is drawn.
   (a) Draw the first stage of the tree.
   (b) If the red ball was selected and not replaced, what possible outcomes are possible on the second draw? Starting at *R*, draw a branch to represent these outcomes.
   (c) If the white was drawn first, what outcomes are possible on the second draw? Draw these branches.
   (d) Do likewise for the case that blue was drawn first.
   (e) How many total outcomes are possible?

5. Outcome tree diagrams may not necessarily be symmetrical. For example, from the box containing one red, one white, and one blue ball, we will draw balls (without replacing) until the red ball is chosen. Draw the outcome tree.

6. An experiment consists of tossing a coin and two dice. How many outcomes are there for the following?
   (a) The coin   (b) The first die
   (c) The second die   (d) The experiment

7. For your vacation, you will travel from your home to New York City, then to London. You may travel to New York City by car, train, bus, or plane, and from New York to London by ship or plane.
   (a) Draw a tree diagram to represent possible travel arrangements.
   (b) How many different routes are possible?
   (c) Apply the fundamental counting property to find the number of possible routes. Does your answer agree with part (b)?

8. The row of Pascal's triangle that starts 1, 4, . . . would be useful in finding probabilities for an experiment of tossing 4 coins.
   (a) Interpret the meaning of each number in the row.
   (b) Find the probability of exactly 1 head and 3 tails.
   (c) Find the probability of at least 1 tail turning up.
   (d) Should you bet in favor of getting exactly 2 heads or should you bet against it?

9. Draw the probability tree diagram for drawing a ball from the following containers.

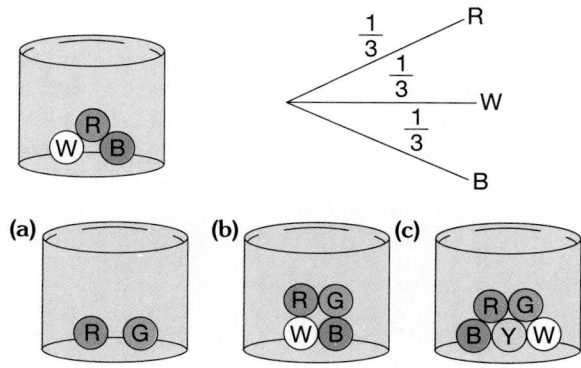

(a)   (b)   (c)

10. Another white ball is added to the container with 1 red, 1 white, and 1 blue ball. Since there are 4 balls, we could draw a tree with 4 branches, as illustrated. Each of these branches is equally likely, so we label them with probability $\frac{1}{4}$. However, we could combine the branches, as illustrated. Since 2 out of the 4 balls are white, $P(W) = \frac{2}{4} = \frac{1}{2}$, and the branch is so labeled.

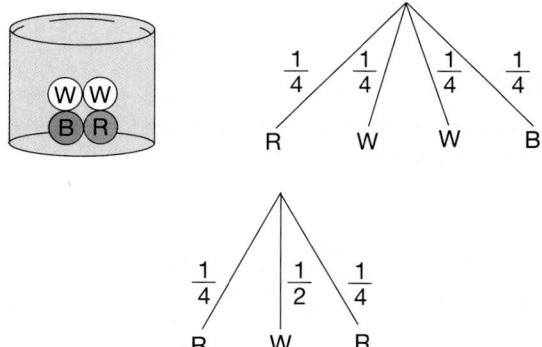

Draw a probability tree representing drawing one ball from the following containers. Combine branches where possible.

(a)

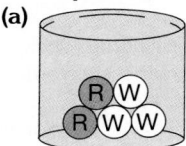

(b)

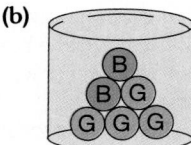

11. The branches of a probability tree diagram may or may not represent equally likely outcomes. The given probability tree diagram represents the outcome for each of the given spinners.

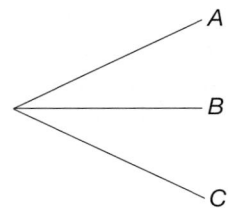

Write the appropriate probabilities along each branch in each case.

(a)   **(b)**

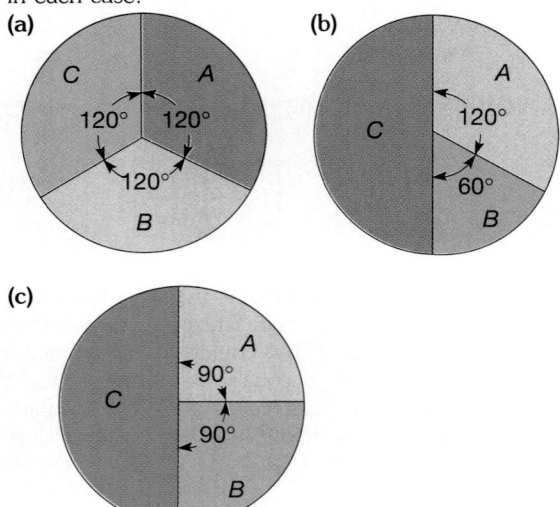

(c)

Problems

12. If each of the 10 digits is chosen at random, how many ways can you choose the following numbers?
  (a) A two-digit code number, repeated digits permitted
  (b) A three-digit identification card number, for which the first digit cannot be a 0
  (c) A four-digit bicycle lock number, where no digit can be used twice
  (d) A five-digit zip code number, with the first digit not zero

13. (a) If eight horses are entered in a race and three finishing places are considered, how many finishing orders are possible?
  (b) If the top three horses are Lucky One, Lucky Two, and Lucky Three, in how many possible orders can they finish?
  (c) What is the probability that these three horses are the top finishers in the race?

14. Three children are born to a family.
  (a) Draw a tree diagram to represent the possible order of boys (B) and girls (G).
  (b) How many of the outcomes involve all girls? 2 girls, 1 boy? 1 girl, 2 boys? No girls?
  (c) How do these results relate to Pascal's triangle?

15. In shooting at a target three times, on each shot you either hit or miss (and we assume these are equally likely). The 1, 3, 3, 1 row of Pascal's triangle can be used to find the probabilities of hits and misses.

Number of Hits	3	2	1	0
Number of Ways (8 Total)	1	3	3	1
Probability	$\frac{1}{8}$	$\frac{3}{8}$	$\frac{3}{8}$	$\frac{1}{8}$

  (a) Use Pascal's triangle to fill in the entries in the following table for shooting 4 times.

Number of Hits	4	3	2	1	0
Number of Ways					
Probability					

  (b) Which is more likely, that in 3 shots you will have 3 hits or that in 4 shots you will have 3 hits and 1 miss?

16. The Boston Celtics and Milwaukee Bucks are going to play a "best two out of three" series. The tree shows the possible outcomes.

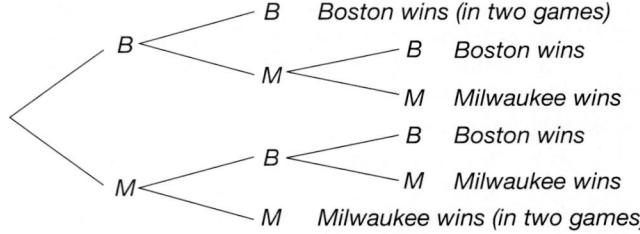

  (a) If the teams are evenly matched, each has a probability of $\frac{1}{2}$ of winning any game. Label each branch of the tree with the appropriate probability.
  (b) Find the probability that Boston wins the series in two straight games and that Milwaukee wins the series after losing the first game.
  (c) Find the following probabilities.
    (i) Boston wins when three games are played.
    (ii) Milwaukee wins the series.
    (iii) The series requires three games to decide a winner.

17. Suppose that the Boston Celtics and the Milwaukee

Bucks are not quite evenly matched in their "best two out of three" series. Let the probability that the Celtics win an individual game with Milwaukee be $\frac{3}{5}$.

(a) What is the probability that Milwaukee wins an individual game?

(b) Label the branches of the probability tree with the appropriate probability.

(c) What is the probability that Milwaukee wins in two straight games?

(d) What is the probability that Boston wins the series when losing the second game?

(e) What is the probability that the series goes for three games?

(f) What is the probability that Boston wins the series?

18. Team A and team B are playing a "best three out of five" series to determine a champion. Team A is the stronger team with an estimated probability of $\frac{2}{3}$ of winning any game.

(a) Team A can win the series by winning three straight games. That path of the tree would look like this:

Label the branches with probabilities and find the probability that this occurs.

(b) Team A can win the series in four games, losing one game and winning 3 games. This could occur as *BAAA, ABAA,* or *AABA* (why not *AAAB*?). Compare the probabilities of the following paths.

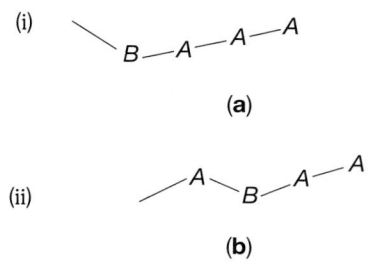

(i)

(a)

(ii)

(b)

What do you observe? What is the probability that team A wins the series in four games?

(a) The series could go to five games. Team A could win in this case by winning three games and losing two games (they must win the last game). List the ways in which this could be done. What is the probability of each of these ways? What is the

probability of team A winning the series in five games?

(d) What is the probability that team A will be the winner of the series? That team B will be the winner?

19. (a) Complete the tree diagram to show the possible ways of answering a true–false test with three questions.

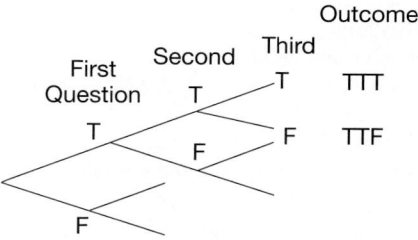

(b) How many possible outcomes are there?

(c) How many of these outcomes give the correct answers?

(d) What is the probability of guessing all the correct answers?

20. Your drawer contains 2 blue socks, 2 brown socks, and 2 black socks. Without looking, you pull out 2 socks.

(a) Draw a probability tree diagram (use E for blue, N for brown, K for black).

(b) List the sample space.

(c) List the event that you have a matched pair.

(d) What is the probability of getting a matched pair?

(e) What is the probability of getting a matched blue pair?

21. Your drawer contains 2 blue socks, 2 brown socks, and 2 black socks. What is the minimum number of socks that you would need to pull, at random, from the drawer to be sure that you have a matched pair?

22. A customer calls a pet store seeking a male puppy. An assistant, who is bathing three puppies, is asked if one is a male. The assistant looks at the one he is toweling and says "This one is a female." What is the probability that either one of the other two is a male?

23. A box contains 4 white and 6 black balls. A second box contains 7 white and 3 black balls. A ball is picked at random from the first box and placed in the second box. A ball is then picked from the second box. What is the probability that it is white?

EXERCISE/PROBLEM SET 11.2—PART B

Exercises

1. Draw outcome trees to represent the following situations.
   (a) Hits or misses in three foul shots in basketball
   (b) Ways that a four-question true/false test may be answered

2. Draw one-stage trees to represent each of the following situations.
   (a) Having one child
   (b) Choosing to go to Boston, Miami, or Los Angeles for vacation
   (c) Hitting a free throw or missing
   (d) Drawing a ball from a bag containing balls labeled A, B, C, D, and E

3. A container has in it three chips, labeled A, B, and C. One chip will be drawn at a time and not returned to the container until all chips have been selected. Draw a tree to represent the outcomes of this experiment.

4. (a) Draw a two-stage tree to represent the experiment of tossing one coin and rolling one die.
   (b) How many possible outcomes are there?
   (c) In how many ways can the first event (tossing one coin) occur?
   (d) In how many ways can the second event (rolling one die) occur?
   (e) According to the fundamental counting property, how many outcomes are possible for this experiment?

5. A coin is tossed. If it lands heads up, a die will be tossed. If it lands tails up, a spinner with equal sections of blue, red, and yellow is spun. Draw a two-stage tree for the experiment.

6. Bob has just left town A. There are five roads leading from town A to town B and four roads leading from town B to C. How many possible ways does he have to travel from A to C?

7. Four coins are tossed.
   (a) Draw a tree diagram to represent the arrangements of heads (H) and tails (T).
   (b) How many outcomes involve all heads? 3 heads, 1 tail? 2 heads, 2 tails? 1 head, 3 tails? No heads?
   (c) How do these results relate to Pascal's triangle?

8. The given tree represents the outcomes for each of the following experiments in which one ball is taken from the container. Write the appropriate probabilities along each branch for each case.

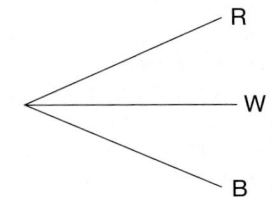

(a)

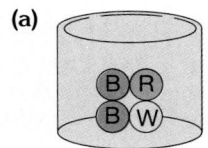

(b)

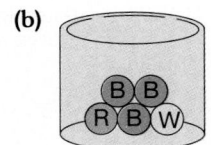

(c)

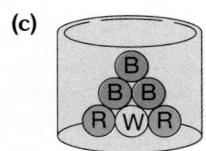

9. Draw probability tree diagrams for the following experiments.
   (a) Spinner A spun once   (b) Spinner B spun once
   (c) Spinner A spun, then spinner B spun [HINT: Draw a two-stage tree combining results of parts (a) and (b).]

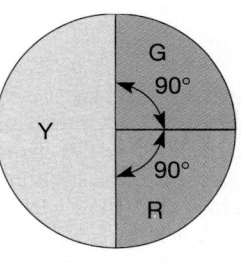

Spinner A

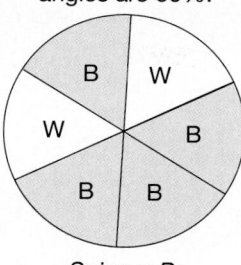

All central
angles are 60%.

Spinner B

10. A container holds two yellow and three red balls. A ball will be drawn, its color noted, and then replaced. A second ball will be drawn and its color recorded. A tree diagram representing the outcomes is given.

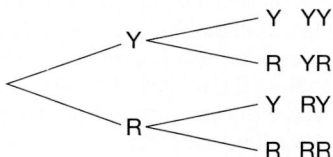

(a) On the diagram, indicate the probability of each branch.
(b) What is the probability of drawing YY? Of drawing RY?
(c) What is the probability of drawing at least one yellow?
(d) Show a different way of computing part (c), using the complement event.

Problems

11. A given locality has the telephone prefix of 237.
(a) How many seven-digit phone numbers are possible with this prefix?
(b) How many of these possibilities have four ending numbers that are all equal?
(c) What is the probability of having one of the numbers in part (b)?
(d) What is the probability that the last four digits are consecutive (i.e., 1234)?

12. Many radio stations in the United States have call letters that begin with a W or a K and have four letters.
(a) How many arrangements of four letters are possible as call letters?
(b) What is the probability of having call letters KIDS?

13. A local menu offers choices from 8 entrées, 3 varieties of potatoes, either salad or soup, and 5 beverages.
(a) If you select an entrée with potatoes, salad or soup, and beverage, how many different meals are possible?

(b) How many of these meals have soup?
(c) What is the probability that a patron has a meal with soup?
(d) What is the probability that a patron has a meal with french fries (one of the potato choices), and cola (one of the beverage choices)?

14. A family decides to have five children. Since there are just two outcomes, boy (B) and girl (G), for each birth and since we will assume that each outcome is equally likely (this is not exactly true), Pascal's triangle can be applied.
(a) Which row of Pascal's triangle would give the pertinent information?
(b) In how many ways can the family have one boy and four girls?
(c) In how many ways can the family have three boys and two girls?
(d) What is the probability of having three boys? Of having at least three boys?

15. You are taking a true–false test. Of the 10 questions, you know the answers to six problems but decide to guess on the remaining four questions. Those guesses may be either right (R) or wrong (W). The possible outcomes are shown below.

RRRR WRRR WWRR WWWR WWWW
      RWRR WRWR WWRW
      RRWR WRRW WRWW
      RRRW RWRW RWWW
            RRWW
            RWWR

(a) To which row of Pascal's triangle does this correspond?
(b) What number of correct answers is most likely to be guessed? Least likely to be guessed?
(c) What is the probability of getting at least 80% correct on the test, assuming that the six you knew are all correct?

16. The Houston Rockets and Los Angeles Lakers will play a "best two out of three" series. Assume that Houston has a probability of $\frac{1}{3}$ of winning any game.
(a) Draw a probability tree showing possible outcomes of the series. Label the branches with appropriate probabilities.
(b) What is the probability that Houston wins in two straight games? L.A. wins in two straight games?
(c) What is the probability that the series goes to three games?
(d) What is the probability that Houston wins the series after losing the first game?
(e) What is the probability that L.A. wins the series?

17. (a) Make a tree diagram to show all the ways that you can choose answers to a multiple-choice test with 3 questions. The first question has 4 possible answers, a, b, c, and d; the second has 3 possible answers, a, b, and c; the third has 2 possible answers, a and b.

(b) How many possible outcomes are there?

(c) Apply the fundamental counting property to find the number of possible ways. Does your answer agree with part (b)?

(d) If all the answer possibilities are equally likely, what is the probability of guessing the right set of answers?

18. Babe Ruth's lifetime batting average was .343. In three times at bat, what is the probability of the following? (HINT: Draw a probability tree diagram.)

(a) He gets three hits.

(b) He gets no hits.

(c) He gets at least one hit.

(d) He gets exactly one hit.

19. A coin will be thrown until it lands heads up or until the coin has been thrown five times.

(a) Draw a probability tree to represent this experiment.

(b) What is the probability that the coin is tossed just once? Just twice? Just three times? Just four times?

(c) What is the probability of tossing the coin five times without getting a head?

20. You come home on a dark night and find the porch-light burned out. Since you cannot tell which key is which, you randomly try the five keys on your key ring until you find one that opens your apartment door. Two of the keys on your key ring unlock the door. Find the probability of opening the door on the first or second try.

(a) Draw the tree diagram for the experiment.

(b) Compute the probability of opening the door with the first or second key.

21. The ski lift of a ski resort takes skiers to the top of the mountain. As the skiers head down the trails, they have a variety of choices. Assume that at each intersection of trails, the skier is equally likely to go left or right. Find the percent (to the nearest whole percent) of the skiers that end up at each lettered location at the bottom of the hill.

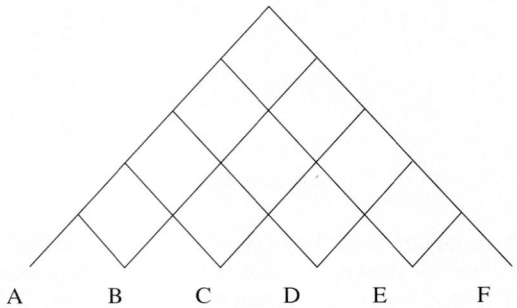

A   B   C   D   E   F

22. A prisoner is given 10 white balls, 10 black balls, and 2 boxes. He is told that his fate depends on drawing a ball from one of the two boxes. If it is white, the prisoner will go free; if it is black, he will remain in prison. How should the prisoner arrange the balls in the boxes to give himself the best chance for freedom?

23. In a television game show, a major prize is hidden behind one of three curtains. A contestant selects a curtain. Then one of the other curtains is opened and the prize is *not* there. The contestant can pick again. Should she switch or stay with her original choice?

24. A box contains 4 white and 8 black balls. You pick out a ball with your left hand and don't look at it. Then you pick out a ball with your right hand and don't look at it.

(a) What is the probability the ball in your left hand is white?

(b) Next, you look at the ball in your right hand and it is black. Now what is the probability that the ball in your left hand is white?

11.3

ODDS, CONDITIONAL PROBABILITY, EXPECTED VALUE, AND SIMULATION

Odds

When people speak about odds in favor of an event in the case of equally likely outcomes, they are comparing the total number of outcomes favorable to an event with the total number of outcomes unfavorable to the event. In this section we are assuming that outcomes are equally likely. For example, if a basketball team had won 10 games and lost 2 games against fairly uniform opponents, the odds of winning the next game may be considered to be the ratio $10:2$, or $5:1$.

In general, let E be an event in the sample space S and $\overline{E}$ be the event complementary to E. Then odds are defined formally as follows.

> **Definition**
>
> ### Odds for Events with Equally Likely Outcomes
>
> If $n(E) = a$ and $n(\overline{E}) = b$, then the **odds in favor** of event E are $a:b$. The **odds against** event E are $b:a$.

EXAMPLE 11.19   If a six-sided die is tossed, what are the odds in favor of the following events?
(a) Getting a 4   **(b)** Getting a prime
(c) Getting a number greater than 0   **(d)** Getting a number greater than 6

Solution
(a) $1:5$ since there is 1 four and 5 other numbers
(b) $3:3 = 1:1$ since there are 3 primes (2, 3, and 5) and 3 nonprimes
(c) $6:0$ since all numbers are favorable to this event
(d) $0:6$ since no numbers are favorable to this event   ■

Notice that in Example 11.19(c) it is reasonable to allow the second number in the odds ratio to be zero.

It is possible to determine the odds in favor of an event E directly from its probability. For example, if $P(E) = \frac{5}{7}$, we would expect that, in the long run, E would occur 5 out of 7 times and not occur 2 of the 7 times. Thus the odds in favor of E would be $5:2$. When determining the odds in favor of E we compare $n(E)$ and $n(\overline{E})$. Now consider $P(E) = \frac{5}{7}$ and $P(\overline{E}) = \frac{2}{7}$. If we compare these two probabilities in the same order, we have $P(E):P(\overline{E}) = \frac{5}{7}:\frac{2}{7} = \frac{5}{7} \div \frac{2}{7} = \frac{5}{2} = 5:2$, the odds in favor of E. The following discussion justifies the latter method of calculating odds. The odds in favor of E are

$$\frac{n(E)}{n(\overline{E})} = \frac{\dfrac{n(E)}{n(S)}}{\dfrac{n(\overline{E})}{n(S)}}$$

$$= \frac{P(E)}{P(\overline{E})} = \frac{P(E)}{1 - P(E)}$$

Thus we can find the odds in favor of an event directly from the probability of an event.

> **Theorem**   The odds in favor of the event E are
>
> $$P(E):1 - P(E) \qquad \text{or} \qquad P(E):P(\overline{E}).$$
>
> The odds against a are
>
> $$1 - P(E):P(E) \qquad \text{or} \qquad P(\overline{E}):P(E).$$

In fact, this result is used to define odds using probabilities in the case of unequally likely outcomes as well as equally likely outcomes.

EXAMPLE 11.20   Find the odds in favor of event E, where E has the following probabilities.
(a) $P(E) = \frac{1}{2}$ **(b)** $P(E) = \frac{3}{4}$ **(c)** $P(E) = \frac{5}{13}$

Solution
(a) Odds in favor of $E = \frac{1}{2}:(1 - \frac{1}{2}) = \frac{1}{2}:\frac{1}{2} = 1:1$
(b) Odds in favor of $E = \frac{3}{4}:(1 - \frac{3}{4}) = \frac{3}{4}:\frac{1}{4} = 3:1$
(c) Odds in favor of $E = \frac{5}{13}:(1 - \frac{5}{13}) = \frac{5}{13}:\frac{8}{13} = 5:8$

Now suppose that you know the odds in favor of an event E. Can the probability of E be found? The answer is "yes!" For example, if the odds in favor of E are $2:3$, this means that the ratio of favorable outcomes to unfavorable outcomes is $2:3$. Thus in a sample space with 5 elements with 2 outcomes favorable to E and 3 unfavorable, $P(E) = \dfrac{2}{5} = \dfrac{2}{2+3}$. In general, we have the following.

> **Theorem**   If the odds in favor of E are $a:b$, then
> $$P(E) = \frac{a}{a+b}.$$

EXAMPLE 11.21   Find $P(E)$ given that the odds in favor of (or against) E are as follows.
(a) Odds in favor of E are $3:4$.   **(b)** Odds in favor of E are $9:2$.
(c) Odds against E are $7:3$.   **(d)** Odds against E are $2:13$.

Solution
(a) $P(E) = \dfrac{3}{3+4} = \dfrac{3}{7}$ **(b)** $P(E) = \dfrac{9}{9+2} = \dfrac{9}{11}$
(c) $P(E) = \dfrac{3}{7+3} = \dfrac{3}{10}$ **(d)** $P(E) = \dfrac{13}{2+13} = \dfrac{13}{15}$

Conditional Probability

The sample space of an experiment is often reduced in size, based on a particular condition. That is, certain information is known about the experiment that affects the possible outcomes. Such "given" information is illustrated in Example 11.22.

EXAMPLE 11.22   Describe the sample space for the experiment "the first coin came up heads when tossing three fair coins."

Solution
When tossing three coins, there are eight outcomes: HHH, HHT, HTH, THH, HTT, THT, TTH, TTT. However, there are only four of these outcomes where the first coin is a head, namely HHH, HHT, HTH, HTT. Thus these four outcomes alone comprise the sample space.

In Example 11.22 the original sample space is reduced to those outcomes having the given condition, namely H on the first coin. Let A be the event that exactly two tails appear among the three coins, and let B be the event that the first coin comes up heads. That is, $A = \{HTT, THT, TTH\}$ and $B = \{HHH, HHT, HTH, HTT\}$, the reduced sample space. We see that there is only one way for A to occur given that B occurs, namely HTT. (Note that $A \cap B = \{HTT\}$.) Thus the probability of A given B is $\frac{1}{4}$. The notation $P(A \mid B)$ means "the probability of A given B." Hence, $P(A \mid B) = \frac{1}{4}$.

Notice that $P(A \mid B) = \dfrac{1}{4} = \dfrac{1/8}{4/8} = \dfrac{P(A \cap B)}{P(B)}$. That is, $P(A \mid B)$ is the relative frequency of event A *within* event B. This suggests the following.

Definition

Conditional Probability

Suppose A and B are events in a sample space S such that $P(B) \neq 0$. The **conditional probability** that event A occurs, given that event B occurs, denoted $P(A \mid B)$, is

$$P(A \mid B) = \frac{P(A \cap B)}{P(B)}.$$

A Venn diagram can be used to illustrate the definition of conditional probability. A sample space S of equally likely outcomes is shown in Figure 11.18(a). The reduced sample space, given that event B occurs, appears in Figure 11.18(b).

From Figure 11.18(a) we see that $\dfrac{P(A \cap B)}{P(B)} = \dfrac{2/12}{7/12} = \dfrac{2}{7}$. From Figure 11.18(b) we see that $P(A \mid B) = \frac{2}{7}$. Thus $P(A \mid B) = \dfrac{P(A \cap B)}{P(B)}$.

The next example illustrates conditional probability in the case of unequally likely outcomes.

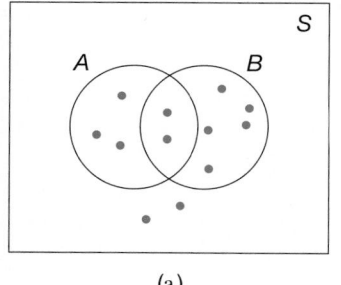

(a)

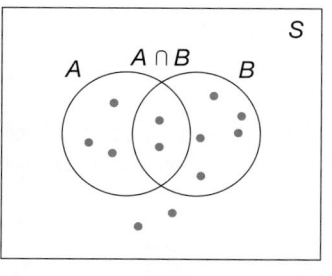

(b)

FIGURE 11.18

EXAMPLE 11.23   Suppose that a 20-sided die has the following numerals on its faces: 1, 1, 2, 2, 2, 3, 3, 4, 5, 6, 7, 8, 9, 10, 11, 12, 13, 14, 15, 16. The die is rolled once and the number on the top face is recorded. Let A be the event that the number is prime, and let B be the event that the number is odd. Find $P(A \mid B)$ and $P(B \mid A)$.

Solution
Assuming that the die is balanced, $P(A) = \frac{9}{20}$ since there are 9 ways that a prime can appear. Similarly, $P(B) = \frac{10}{20}$ since there are 10 ways that an odd number can occur. Also, $P(A \cap B) = P(B \cap A) = \frac{6}{20}$ since an odd prime can appear in 6 ways. Thus

$$P(A \mid B) = \frac{P(A \cap B)}{P(B)} = \frac{6/20}{10/20} = \frac{3}{5}$$

and

$$P(B \mid A) = \frac{P(B \cap A)}{P(A)} = \frac{6/20}{9/20} = \frac{2}{3}.$$

These results can be checked by reducing the sample space to reflect the given information, then assigning probabilities to the events as they occur as subsets of the *reduced* sample space. ∎

Expected Value

Probability can be used to determine values such as admission to games (with payoffs) and insurance premiums, using the idea of *expected value*.

EXAMPLE 11.24   A cube has 3 red faces, 2 green faces, and a blue face. A game consists of rolling the cube twice. You pay $2 to play. If both faces are the same color, you are paid $5 (you win $3). If not, you lose the $2 it costs to play. Will you win money in the long run?

Solution
Use a probability tree diagram (Figure 11.19). Let W be the event that you win. Then $W = \{RR, GG, BB\}$, and $P(W) = \frac{1}{2} \cdot \frac{1}{2} + \frac{1}{3} \cdot \frac{1}{3} + \frac{1}{6} \cdot \frac{1}{6} = \frac{7}{18}$. Hence $\frac{7}{18}$ (about 39%) of the time you will win, and $\frac{11}{18}$ (about 61%) of the time you will lose. If you play the game 18 times, you can expect to win 7 times and lose 11 times on average. Hence, your winnings, in dollars, will be $3 \times 7 + (-2) \times 11 = -1$. That is, you can expect to lose $1 if you play the game 18 times. On the average, you will lose $1/18$ per game (about 6¢).

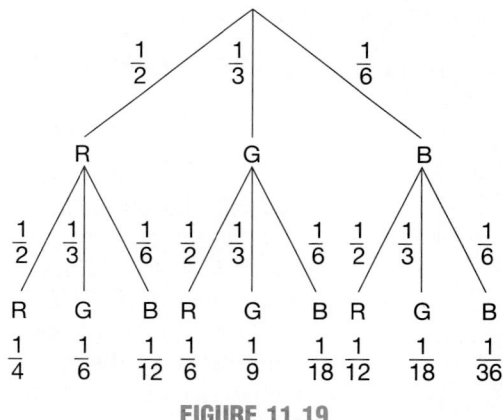

FIGURE 11.19 ∎

In Example 11.24, the amount in dollars that we expect to "win" on each play of the game is $3 \times \frac{7}{18} + (-2) \times \frac{11}{18} = -\frac{1}{18}$, called the *expected value*. Expected value is defined as follows.

Definition
Expected Value

Suppose that the outcomes of an experiment are real numbers (values) called $v_1, v_2, \ldots, v_n$, and suppose that the outcomes have probabilities $p_1, p_2, \ldots, p_n$ respectively. The **expected value**, E, of the experiment is the sum

$$E = v_1 \cdot p_1 + v_2 \cdot p_2 + \cdots + v_n \cdot p_n.$$

TABLE 11.4

Amount of Claim (Nearest $2000)	Probability
0	0.80
$ 2,000	0.10
4,000	0.05
6,000	0.03
8,000	0.01
10,000	0.01

TABLE 11.5

v	p
$v_1 = 0$	$p_1 = 0.80$
$v_2 = 2000$	$p_2 = 0.10$
$v_3 = 4000$	$p_3 = 0.05$
$v_4 = 6000$	$p_4 = 0.03$
$v_5 = 8000$	$p_5 = 0.01$
$v_6 = 10,000$	$p_6 = 0.01$

The expected value of an experiment is the average value of the outcomes over many repetitions. The next example shows how insurance companies use expected values.

EXAMPLE 11.25 Suppose that an insurance company has broken down yearly automobile claims for drivers from age 16 through 21, as shown in Table 11.4. How much should the company charge as its average premium in order to break even on its costs for claims?

Solution
Use the notation from the definition for expectation. Let $n = 6$ (the number of claim categories), and let the values $v_1, v_2, \ldots, v_n$ and the probabilities $p_1, p_2, \ldots, p_n$ be as listed in Table 11.5.
Thus the expected value, $E = 0(0.80) + 2000(0.10) + 4000(0.05) + 6000(0.03) + 8000(0.01) + 10{,}000(0.01) = 760$. Since the average claim value is $760, the average automobile insurance premium should be set at $760 per year for the insurance company to break even on its claims costs. ■

Simulation

Occasionally, an experiment is difficult to analyze theoretically, but it can be modeled or simulated in some way. We can use simulations to estimate theoretical probabilities in such cases.

A **simulation** is a representation of an experiment using a random number generator or some similar device. There is a one-to-one correspondence between outcomes in the original experiment and outcomes in the simulated experiment. The probability that an outcome in the original experiment occurs is estimated to be the probability of its corresponding outcome in the simulated experiment. Random number generators are built into many calculators and computers. More simply, we can use dice tossing, numbered slips of paper, or a table of random digits to simulate an experiment.

EXAMPLE 11.26 A cereal company has put six types of toy cars in its cereal boxes, one car per box. If the cars are distributed uniformly, what is the probability that you will get all six types of cars if you buy 10 boxes?

Solution
Simulate the experiment by using the whole numbers from 1 through 6 to represent the different cars. Use a table of random digits as the random number generator (Figure 11.20 on page 514). (Six numbered slips of paper or chips, drawn at random from a hat, or a six-sided die would also work. In this example we disregard 0, 7, 8, 9 since there are six types of toy cars.) Start anywhere in the table. (We started at the upper left.) Read until 10 numbers from 1 through 6 occur, ignoring 0, 7, 8, and 9. Record the sequence of numbers [Figure 11.20(b)]. Each such sequence of 10 numbers is a simulated outcome. (Simulated outcomes are separated by a vertical bar.) Six of these sequences appear in Figure 11.20(b). Successful outcomes contain 1,

2, 3, 4, 5, and 6 (corresponding to the six cars) and are marked "yes." Based on the simulation, our estimate of the probability is $\frac{2}{6} = 0.\overline{3}$. Using a computer to simulate the experiment yields an estimate of 0.257 (see the Technology Section).

```
2  2  9  8  5  3  5  1  8  7   ─────▶   2  2  5  3  5  1  5  4  3  6   yes
7  5  0  4  3  9  6 │3  6  4   ─────▶   3  6  4  6  1  5  3  3  5  6   no
7  7  7  6  1  9  5  9  3  3
5  6 │1  7  2  3  9  6  5  1   ─────▶   1  2  3  6  5  1  5  6  2  3   no
5  6  2  0  3 │2  8  0  5  9   ─────▶   2  5  3  3  4  6  5  6  6  5   no
3  3  4  8  0  8  6  5  6  6
9  5 │6  7  9  1  3  6  8  3   ─────▶   6  1  3  6  3  4  4  4  2  5   yes
0  4  4  8  4  2  5 │5  9  1   ─────▶   5  1  1  3  1  2  5  5  1  6   no
8  1  8  7  3  1  8  2  5  5
1  9  7  6 │0  3  2  5  2  3
              ·
              ·
              ·
```

(a) Random digits   **(b)** Simulated outcomes

FIGURE 11.20

EXAMPLE 11.27   When planning for a family, a husband and wife plan to stop having children after they have either two girls or four children. Since they want to begin saving for their childrens' college educations, they want to predict how many children they should expect to have. If the chances are equally likely of having a girl or a boy, what is the probability that they will have four children?

Solution
By assumption, since having a girl or a boy is equally likely, this situation can be simulated using a coin (H is boy, T is girl), using a spinner where it is divided into two equal parts, drawing two pieces of paper (one marked B and the other G), or using a random number table. We will use the table in Figure 11.20 where the even numbers represent boys and the odd numbers represent girls since the appearance of evens and odds should be equally likely. With this representation, our "family" will be complete when we have two odd numbers but no more than four numbers. The list of all families represented in Figure 11.20 follows (families of four children appear in bold-face type).

2298	53	51	877	**5043**	963
6477	761	969	33	561	723
965	13	**6203**	**2805**	93	**3480**
8656	695	679	13	**6830**	**4484**
255	91	**8187**	31	**8255**	19
7603	**2523**				

There are 32 families and of these, 13 have four children. Thus the probability that the husband and wife have four children is $\frac{13}{32}$, or about 41%. Note: If this same simulation is carried out using the first five columns of the random number table in Problem 20 of part A at the end of this section, a similar ratio results.

MATHEMATICAL MORSEL

If I drop this needle on those lines, I get a pi?

The French naturalist Buffon devised his famous needle problem from which π may be determined using probability methods. The method is as follows. Draw a number of parallel lines at a distance of d units apart. Then a needle, whose length l is less than d, is dropped *at random* onto the parallel lines. Buffon showed that the probability P that the needle will touch one of the lines is given by $P = 2l/\pi d$. Thus, if this experiment is performed a large number of times, an approximate value of π can be found using the equation $\pi = 2l/Pd$, where here P represents the probability obtained in this experiment.

EXERCISE/PROBLEM SET 11.3—PART A

Exercises

ODDS

1. **(a)** Which, if either, are more favorable odds, 50:50 or 100:100? Explain.
   (b) Which, if either, are more favorable odds, 60:40 or 65:45? Explain?

2. Two dice are thrown.
   (a) Find the odds in favor of the following events.
      (i) Getting a sum of 7
      (ii) Getting a sum greater than 3
      (iii) Getting a sum that is an even number
   (b) Find the odds against each of the events in part (a).

3. A die is thrown once.
   (a) If each face is equally likely to turn up, what is the probability of getting a 5?
   (b) What are the odds in favor of getting a 5?
   (c) What are the odds against getting a 5?

4. In each part, you are given the probability of event E. Find the odds in favor of event E and the odds against event E.
   (a) $\frac{3}{5}$ **(b)** $\frac{1}{4}$ **(c)** $\frac{5}{6}$

5. In each part, you are given the following odds in favor of event E. Find $P(E)$.
   (a) 9:1   **(b)** 2:5   **(c)** 12:5

6. In each part, you are given the following odds *against* event E. Find $P(E)$.
   (a) 8:1   **(b)** 5:3   **(c)** 6:5

7. The odds posted by racetracks are the odds against the horse. For example, if the odds against Long Shot are 8:1, the racetrack expects Long Shot to win only one out of every nine races. For every dollar you bet on Long Shot, the racetrack matches it with $8. If Long Shot wins, you receive $9 (your bet plus $8 matched by the racetrack). Suppose that you bet $2 on horses with the following odds. How much do you receive if they win?
   (a) 5:1   **(b)** 5:4   **(c)** 3:2   **(d)** 1:2

CONDITIONAL PROBABILITY

8. The spinner is spun once. (All central angles equal 60°.)

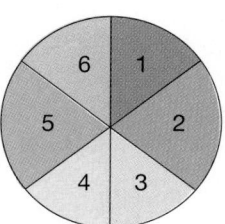

   (a) What is the probability that it lands on 4?
   (b) If you are told it has landed on an even number, what is the probability that it landed on 4?

(c) If you are told it has landed on an odd number, what is the probability that it landed on 4?

9. A container holds three red balls and five blue balls. One ball will be drawn and discarded. Then a second ball is drawn.
  (a) What is the probability that the second ball drawn is red if you drew a red ball the first time?
  (b) What is the probability of drawing a blue ball second if the first ball was red?
  (c) What is the probability of drawing a blue ball second if the first ball was blue?

10. The diagram shows a sample space S of equally likely outcomes and events A and B.

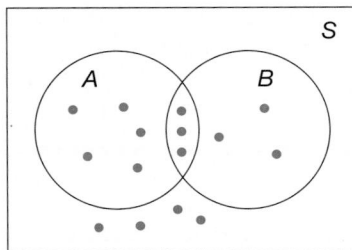

Find the following probabilities.
  (a) $P(A)$ **(b)** $P(B)$ **(c)** $P(A \mid B)$ **(d)** $P(B \mid A)$

11. Given is the probability tree diagram for an experiment.

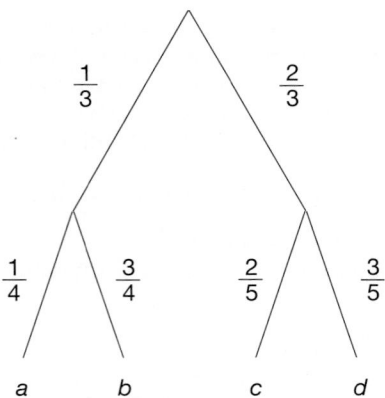

The sample space, $S = \{a, b, c, d\}$. Also, event $A = \{a, b, c\}$ and event $B = \{b, c, d\}$. Find the following probabilities.
  (a) $P(A)$ **(b)** $P(B)$ **(c)** $P(A \cap B)$
  (d) $P(A \cup B)$ **(e)** $P(A \mid B)$ **(f)** $P(B \mid A)$

12. An experiment consists of tossing 6 coins. Let A be the event that at least 3 heads appear. Let B be the event that the first coin shows heads. Let C be the event that the first and last coins show heads. Find the following probabilities.

  (a) $P(A \mid B)$ **(b)** $P(B \mid A)$ **(c)** $P(A \mid C)$
  (d) $P(C \mid A)$ **(e)** $P(B \mid C)$ **(f)** $P(C \mid B)$

EXPECTED VALUE

13. From the data given, compute the expected value.

Outcome	-2000	0	1000	3000
Probability	$\frac{1}{4}$	$\frac{1}{6}$	$\frac{1}{4}$	$\frac{1}{3}$

14. A study of attendance at a football game shows the following pattern:

Weather	Attendance	Weather Probability
Extremely cold	30,000	0.06
Cold	40,000	0.44
Moderate	52,000	0.35
Warm	65,000	0.15

What is the expected value of the attendance?

15. A player rolls a fair die and receives a number of dollars equal to the number of dots showing on the face of the die.
  (a) If the game costs $1.00 to play, how much should the player expect to win for each play?
  (b) If the game costs $2.00 to play, how much should the player expect to win per play?
  (c) What is the most the player should be willing to pay to play the game and not lose money in the long run?

16. A student is considering applying for two scholarships. Scholarship A is worth $1000 and scholarship B is worth $5000. Costs involved in applying for scholarship A are $10 and for scholarship B are $25. The probability of receiving scholarship A is 0.05 and for scholarship B is 0.01.
  (a) What is the student's expected value for applying for scholarship A?
  (b) For applying for scholarship B?
  (c) If the student can apply for only one scholarship, which should she apply for?

SIMULATION

17. A family wants to have five children. To determine the probability that they will have at least four the same sex, perform the following simulation.

  1. Use five coins, where H = girl and T = boy.
  2. Toss the five coins and record how they land.
  3. Repeat step 2 a total of 30 times.
  4. Count the outcomes that have at least four of the same sex.

What is the approximate probability of having at least four of the same sex?

18. A candy bar company is having a contest. On the inside of each package, N, U, or T is printed in ratios 3:2:1. To determine how many packages you should buy to spell NUT, perform the following simulation.

1. Using a die, let 1, 2, 3 represent N, let 4, 5 represent U, and let 6 represent T.
2. Roll the die and record the corresponding letter. Repeat rolling the die until each letter has been obtained.
3. Repeat step 2 a total of 20 times.

Average the number of packages purchased in each case.

19. A cloakroom attendant receives five fur coats from five women and gets them mixed up. She returns the coats at random. Follow the steps below to find the probability that at least one woman receives her own coat.

1. Cut out five pieces of paper, all the same size and label them A, B, C, D, and E.
2. Put the pieces in a container and mix them up.
3. Draw the pieces out, one at a time, without replacing them, and record the order.
4. Repeat the steps (2) and (3) a total of 25 times.
5. Count the number of times at least one letter is in the appropriate place (A in first place, B in second place, etc.).

From this simulation, what is the approximate probability that at least one woman receives her own coat?

20. You are going to bake a batch of 100 oatmeal cookies. Because raisins are expensive, you will only put 150 raisins in the batter and mix the batter well. Follow the steps below to find out the probability that a cookie will end up without a raisin.

1. Draw a 10 × 10 grid as illustrated. Each cell is represented by a two-digit number. The first digit is the horizontal scale and the second digit is the vertical scale. For example, 06 and 73 are shown.

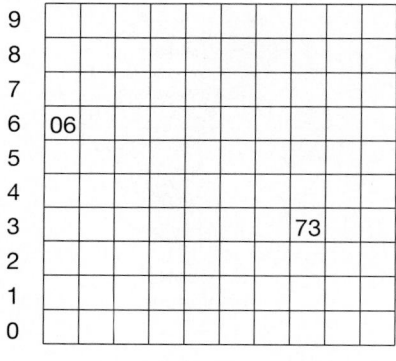

2. Given is a portion of a table of random digits. For each two-digit number in the table, place an x in the appropriate cell of your grid.

15	77	01	64	69	69	58	40	81	16
85	40	51	40	10	15	33	94	11	65
47	69	35	90	95	16	17	45	86	29
13	26	87	40	20	40	81	46	08	09
10	55	33	20	47	54	16	86	11	16
60	20	00	84	22	05	06	67	26	77
57	62	94	04	99	65	50	89	18	74
16	70	48	02	00	59	68	53	31	55
74	99	16	92	99	31	31	05	36	48
59	34	71	55	84	91	59	46	44	45
14	85	40	52	68	60	41	94	98	18
42	07	50	15	69	86	97	40	25	88
73	47	16	49	79	69	80	76	16	60
75	16	00	21	11	42	44	84	46	84
49	25	36	12	07	25	90	89	55	25

(a) Tally the number of squares that have no raisin indicated. What is the probability of selecting a cookie without a raisin?

(b) If your calculator can generate random numbers, generate another set of 150 numbers and repeat this experiment.

Problems

21. In the World Series, the team who wins 4 out of 7 games is the winner.
(a) Would you agree or disagree with the following statement? The prospects for a long series decrease when the teams are closely matched.
(b) If the probability that the American league team wins any game is p, what is the probability that they win the series in 4 games?
(c) If the probability that the National league team wins any game is q, what is the probability that they win the series in 4 games? (NOTE: $q = 1 - p$.)
(d) What is the probability that the series ends at 4 games?
(e) Complete the following table for the given odds.

Odds favoring American League	1:1	2:1	3:1	3:2
p				
q				
P(American in 4 Games)				
P(National in 4 Games)				
P(4-Game Series)				

(f) What conclusion can you state from this evidence about the statement in part (a)?

22. (a) In a 5-game World Series, there are 4 ways the American league could win (*NAAAA, ANAAA, AANAA,* and *AAANA*). Here, event *A* is an American league win, event *N* a National league victory. If $P(A) = p$ and $P(N) = q$, what is the probability of each sequence? What is the probability of the American league winning the series in 5 games?

(b) Similarly, there are 4 ways the National league could win (verify this). What is the probability of the National league winning in 5 games?

(c) What is the probability the series will end at 5 games?

23. (a) There are 10 ways the American league can win a 6-game World Series. (There are 10 branches that contain 4*A*s and 2*N*s, where the last one is *A*.) If $P(A) = p$ and $P(N) = q$, what is the probability of the American league winning the World Series in 6 games? (NOTE: $q = 1 - p$.)

(b) There are also 10 ways the National league team can win a 6-game series. What is the probability of that event?

(c) What is the probability that the World Series will end at 6 games?

24. (a) There are 20 ways each for the American league team or National league team to win a 7-game World Series. If $P(A) = p$ and $P(N) = q$, what is the probability of the American league winning? (NOTE: $q = 1 - p$.)

(b) What is the probability of the National league winning?

(c) What is the probability of the World Series going all 7 games?

25. Summarize the results from Problems 21 to 24. Here **(a)** $P(A) = p$ and $P(N) = q$, where $p + q = 1$.

X = Number of Games	4	5	6	7
P(American Wins)				
P(National Wins)				
P(X Games in Series)				

(b) If the odds in favor of the American league are 1 : 1, complete the following table.

X = Number of Games	4	5	6	7
P(X)				

(c) Find the expected value for the length of the series.

26. A snack company has put 5 different prizes in its snack boxes, one per box. Assuming that the same number of each toy has been used, how many boxes of snacks should you expect to buy in order to get all 5 toys? (Do a simulation; use at least 100 trials.)

EXERCISE/PROBLEM SET 11.3—PART B

Exercises

ODDS

1. A card is drawn at random from a standard 52-card deck. Find the following odds.
   (a) In favor of drawing a face card (king, queen, or jack)
   (b) Against drawing a diamond
   (c) In favor of drawing the ace of spades
   (d) Against drawing a 2, 3, or 4

2. Find the odds in favor of each of these events.
   (a) Probability of rain today is 60%.
   (b) Probability of living to age 20 is 97%.
   (c) Probability of Democratic victory in the next presidential election is 45%.
   (d) Probability of winning the lottery drawing is 0.01%.

3. Given are the odds in favor of event *E*. Find $P(E)$.
   (a) 1 : 5   **(b)** 6 : 11

4. The spinner shown below is spun once. Find the following odds.

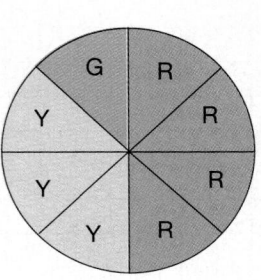

All central angles are 45°

(a) In favor of getting yellow

(b) Against getting green

(c) In favor of getting a primary color (blue, red, or yellow)

(d) Against getting red or green

5. You are given the probability of event E. Find the odds in favor of event E and the odds against event E.

(a) $\frac{1}{8}$ **(b)** $\frac{2}{5}$

6. Two fair dice are rolled, and the sum of the dots is recorded. In each part, give an example of an event having the given odds in its favor.

(a) 1:1   **(b)** 1:5   **(c)** 1:3

(d) 2:1   **(e)** 4:5   **(f)** 35:1

CONDITIONAL PROBABILITY

7. The diagram shows a sample space S of equally likely outcomes and events A, B, and C.

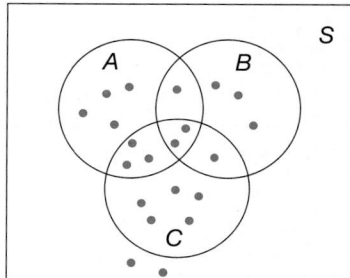

Find the following probabilities.

(a) $P(A)$ **(b)** $P(B)$ **(c)** $P(C)$

(d) $P(A \mid B)$ **(e)** $P(B \mid A)$ **(f)** $P(A \mid C)$

(g) $P(C \mid A)$ **(h)** $P(B \mid C)$ **(i)** $P(C \mid B)$

8. A spinner is spun whose central angles are all 45°. What is the probability that it lands on 5 if you know the following?

(a) It lands on an odd number.

(b) It lands on a number greater than 3.

(c) It does not land on 7 or 8.

(d) It lands on a factor of 10.

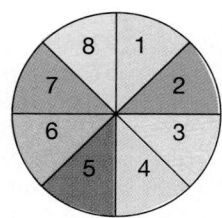

9. A six-sided die is tossed. What is the probability that it shows 2 if you know the following?

(a) It shows an even number.

(b) It shows a number less than 5.

(c) It does not show a 6.

(d) It shows 1 or 2.

(e) It shows an even number less than 4.

(f) It shows a number greater than 3.

10. One container holds the letters DAD and a second container holds the letters ADD. One letter is chosen randomly from the first container and added to the second container. Then a letter will be chosen from the second container.

(a) What is the probability that the second letter chosen is D if the first letter was A? If the first letter was D?

(b) What is the probability that the second chosen letter is A if the first letter was A? If the first letter was D?

11. Given is a tabulation of academic award winners in a school.

	Number of Students Receiving Awards	Number of Math Awards
Class 1	15	7
Class 2	16	8
Class 3	14	9
Class 4	20	11
Class 5	19	12
Class 6	21	14
Boys	52	29
Girls	53	32

A student is chosen at random from the award winners. Find the probabilities of the following events.

(a) The student is in class 1.

(b) The student is in class 4, 5, or 6.

(c) The student won a math award.

(d) The student is a girl.

(e) The student is a boy who won a math award.

(f) The student won a math award given that he or she is in class 1.

(g) The student won a math award given that he or she is in class 1, 2, or 3.

(h) The student is a girl, given that he or she won a math award.

(i) The student won a math award, given that she is a girl.

EXPECTED VALUE

12. From the data given below, compute the expected value.

Payoff	−2	0	2	3
Probability	0.3	0.1	0.4	0.2

13. A laboratory contains 10 electronic microscopes, of which 2 are defective. Four microscopes are to be tested. All microscopes are equally likely to be chosen.

A sample of 4 microscopes can have 0, 1, or 2 defective ones, with the probabilities given.

Number of Defectives	0	1	2
Probability	$\frac{1}{3}$	$\frac{8}{15}$	$\frac{2}{15}$

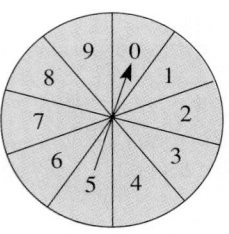

What is the expected number of defective microscopes in the sample?

14. For visiting a resort, you will receive one gift. The probabilities and manufacturer's suggested retail values of each gift are: gift A, 1 in 52,000 ($9272.00); gift B, 25,736 in 52,000 ($44.95); gift C, 1 in 52,000 ($2500.00); gift D, 3 in 52,000 ($729.95); gift E, 25,736 in 52,000 ($26.99); gift F, 3 in 52,000 ($1000.00); gift G, 180 in 52,000 ($44.99); gift H, 180 in 52,000 ($63.98); gift I, 160 in 52,000 ($25.00). Find the expected value of your gift.

15. According to a publisher's records, 20% of the books published break even, 30% lose $1000, 25% lose $10,000, and 25% earn $20,000. When a book is published, what is the expected income for the book?

16. A teacher has a pile of test papers. The paper for a particular student is equally likely to be any of the papers. How many papers should the teacher expect to look through to find the particular paper if the pile contains the following number of papers?
(a) 10   **(b)** 25   **(c)** 50   **(d)** 100   **(e)** n

$$\left[\text{HINT: } 1 + 2 + \cdots + n = \frac{n(n + 1)}{2}. \right]$$

SIMULATION

17. A gumball machine contains gumballs in eight different colors. Assume that there are a large number of gumballs equally divided among the eight colors.
(a) Estimate how many pennies you will have to use to get one of each color.
(b) Cut out eight identical pieces of paper and mark them with the digits 1–8. Put the pieces of paper in a container. Without looking, draw one piece and record its number. Replace the piece; mix the pieces up, and draw again. Repeat this process until all digits have appeared. Record how many draws it took. Repeat this experiment a total of 10 times and average the number of draws needed.

18. (a) Make a table of random digits using the spinner. Place your pencil point at the center, and spin a paper clip around your pencil. Record the number of the sector containing most of the paper clip. Spin 100 times and record the digits in order of appearance.

(b) Consider the following experiment. A committee of 4 people is selected at random from a group of you and 9 others. What is the probability that you are on the committee? Use your table of random digits to simulate the experiment 20 times. Estimate the probability based on your simulations. Explain your procedures.

19. A bus company overbooks the 22 seats on its bus to the coast. It regularly sells 25 tickets. Assuming that there is a 0.1 chance of any passenger not showing up, follow the steps below to find the probability that at least one passenger will not have a seat.

1. Let the digit 0 represent not showing up and the digits 1–9 represent showing up. Is $P(0) = 0.1$?
2. Given below is a portion of a random number table. Each row of 25 numbers represents the 25 tickets sold on a given day. In the first row, how many passengers did not show up (how many zeros appear)?
3. Count the number of rows that have two or fewer zeros. These represent days in which someone will not have a seat.

(a) From this simulation, what is the probability that at least one passenger will not have a seat?
(b) If your calculator can generate random numbers, generate another five sets of 25 numbers and repeat the experiment.

07018	31172	12572	23968	55216
52444	65625	97918	46794	62370
72161	57299	87521	44351	99981
17918	75071	91057	46829	47992
13623	76165	43195	50205	75736
27426	97534	89707	97453	90836
96039	21338	88169	69530	53300
68282	98888	25545	69406	29470
54262	21477	33097	48125	92982
66920	27544	72780	91384	47296
53348	39044	04072	62210	01209
34482	42758	40128	48136	30254
99268	98715	07545	27317	52459
95342	97178	10401	31615	95784
38556	60373	77935	64608	28949
39159	04795	51163	84475	60722

41786	18169	96649	92406	42733
95627	30768	30607	89023	60730
98738	15548	42263	79489	85118
75214	61575	27805	21930	94726
73904	89123	19271	15792	72675
33329	08896	94662	05781	59187
66364	94799	62211	37539	80172
68349	16984	86532	96186	53893
19193	99621	66899	12351	72438

Problems

20. Since you do not like to study for your science test, a 10-question true–false test, you decide to guess on each question. To determine your chances of getting a score of 70% or better, perform the following simulation.

1. Use a coin where H = true and T = false.
2. Toss the coin 10 times, recording the corresponding answers.
3. Repeat step 2 a total of 20 times.
4. Repeat step 2 one more time. This is the answer key of correct answers. Correct each of the 20 "tests."

(a) How many times was the score 70% or better?

(b) What is the probability of a score of 70% or better?

(c) Use Pascal's triangle to compute the probability that you will score 70% or more.

21. How many cards would we expect to draw from a standard deck in order to get two aces? (Do a simulation; use at least 100 trials.)

22. You are among 20 people called for jury duty. If there are to be two cases tried in succession and a jury consists of 12 people, what are your chances of serving on the jury for at least one trial? Assume that all potential jurors have the same chance of being called for each trial. [Do a simulation; use an icosahedron die (20 faces), 20 playing cards, 20 numbered slips of paper, or better yet, a computer program, and at least 100 trials.]

23. Using a spinner with three equal sectors, do a simulation to solve Problem 23 in Exercise/Problem Set 11.2, Part B.

24. Eight points are evenly spaced around a circle. How many segments can be formed by joining these points?

25. True or false? The sum of all the numbers in a 3×3 additive magic square of whole numbers must be a multiple of 3. If true, prove. If false, give a counterexample. (HINT: What can you say about the sums of the three rows?)

SOLUTION OF INITIAL PROBLEM

At a party, a friend bets you that at least two people in a group of five strangers will have the same astrological sign. Should you take the bet? Why or why not?

Strategy: Do a Simulation

Use a six-sided die and a coin. Make these correspondences.

Outcome		Sign
1H	1	Capricorn
2H	2	Aquarius
3H	3	Pisces
4H	4	Aries
5H	5	Taurus
6H	6	Gemini
1T	7	Cancer
2T	8	Leo
3T	9	Virgo
4T	10	Libra
5T	11	Scorpio
6T	12	Sagittarius

Toss both the die and the coin five times. Record your results as a sequence of numbers from 1 to 12, using the correspondences given in the outcome and sign columns. An example sequence might be 7, 6, 4, 3, 8 (meaning that the die and coin came up 1T, 6H, 4H, 3H, and 2T).

Repeat the experiment 100 times and determine the percentage of times that two or more matches occur. (A computer program would be an ideal way to do this.) This gives an estimation of the theoretical probability that two or more people in a group of five have the same astrological sign. More repetitions of the experiment should give a more accurate estimation. Your estimate should be around 60%, which means that your friend will win 60% of the time. No, you should not take the bet.

Additional Problems Where the Strategy "Do a Simulation" Is Useful

1. A game is played as follows: One player starts at one vertex of a regular hexagon and tosses a coin. When a head is tossed, the player moves clockwise two vertices. When a tail is tossed, the player moves counterclockwise one vertex. What is the probability that the player goes around the hexagon in less than 10 moves?

2. At a restaurant, three couples check their coats using one ticket. What is the probability that one couple gets their coats back if the checker gives them a man's and woman's coat at random?

3. At a bazaar to raise money for the library, parents take a chance to win a prize. They win if they open a book and the hundreds digits of facing pages are the same. What is the probability that they win?

WRITING/DISCUSSING FOR UNDERSTANDING

1. A student makes the statement that when two coins are flipped the result will be 0 heads, 1 head, or 2 heads. Therefore, the probability of 2 heads is $\frac{1}{3}$. How should you respond?

2. If you wished to calculate the probability that the next batter in a baseball game gets a hit, describe what information you would use and how you would use it.

3. Explain how the following NCTM Standards are reflected in this chapter.
- Model situations by devising and carrying out experiments or simulations to determine probabilities.
- Model situations by constructing a sample space to determine probabilities.
- Appreciate the power of using a probability model by comparing experimental results with mathematical expectations.
- Make predictions that are based on experimental or theoretical probabilities.

PROJECTS

1. Find a state that has a lottery and obtain information regarding payouts and the like. Then write a description of how you would explain the chances of winning to another person.

2. Investigate ways in which probability is applied in another discipline. For example, in genetics, insurance, weather forecasting, and so on.
3. The NCTM Standards recommend that students in grades 5 through 8 should "develop an appreciation for the pervasive use of probability in the real world." Find several examples of the use of probability in the real world.

CHAPTER REVIEW

Major Ideas

1. Probability is used to estimate the likelihood of uncertain events.
2. Tree diagrams are helpful in representing sample spaces and computing probabilities.
3. The fundamental counting property and Pascal's triangle are useful for calculating the number of outcomes in events and sample spaces, hence in calculating probabilities.
4. Odds are an alternative form for reporting probabilities.
5. Conditional probability is used to compute the probability that an event occurs, given that some other event also occurs.
6. Expected value is used to determine the most likely average value for experiments with numerical outcomes.
7. Simulations are useful in estimating probabilities for complex events.

Following is a list of key vocabulary, notation, and ideas for this chapter. Mentally review these items and, where appropriate, write down the meaning of each term. Then restudy the material that you are unsure of before proceeding to take the chapter test.

SECTION 11.1: PROBABILITY AND SIMPLE EXPERIMENTS

Vocabulary/Notation

Experiment 479   Impossible event 481
Outcome 479   Certain event 481
Sample space 479   Experimental probability 481
Event 479   Theoretical probability 483
Probability of an event A,   Complement of an event A, ($\overline{A}$) 485
  P(A) 481

Ideas

Finding the probability of a simple event 481
Probability of events with equally likely outcomes 481
Five properties of probability 487

SECTION 11.2: PROBABILITY AND COMPLEX EXPERIMENTS

Vocabulary/Notation

Tree diagram 493   Drawing with/without replacement 498
Pascal's triangle 497   Probability tree diagram 498

Ideas

SECTION 11.3:   ODDS, CONDITIONAL PROBABILITY, EXPECTED VALUE, AND SIMULATION

Vocabulary/Notation

Ideas

PEOPLE IN MATHEMATICS

Olga Taussky-Todd (1906–   ) first met Emmy Noether at the University of Gottingen, where, she recalls, Emmy had "a crowd of students." Quite by chance, Olga, who was 24 years younger than Emmy, came to Bryn Mawr on a graduate scholarship. Emmy was there on a Rockefeller fellowship, and Olga recalls that "she was almost frightened that I would obtain a position before her." Unlike Emmy, Olga has been fortunate to receive widespread recognition during her lifetime. Her major work has been in matrix theory, and she won a Ford prize for her paper "Sums of squares." In 1966, she was proclaimed "Woman of the Year" by the *Los Angeles Times,* and she lectured at the prestigious Emmy Noether 100th birthday symposium at Bryn Mawr. "I developed rather early a great desire to see the links between the various branches of mathematics. This struck me with great force when I drifted into topological algebra, a subject where one studies mathematical structures from an algebraic and a geometric point of view simultaneously."

Stanislaw Ulam (1909–1984) helped develop the atomic bomb in Los Alamos, New Mexico during World War II. After the war, he did further work at Los Alamos and for a time had the dubious distinction of being known as "The Father of the H-Bomb." The title eventually stuck with Edward Teller rather than Ulam. Unlike Teller, he subsequently campaigned in favor of the ban on atmospheric testing of nuclear weapons. In the mathematical world, Ulam is known for his theoretical work in set theory, probability, and topology. The unsolved problem known as "Ulam's conjecture" is discussed on page 187. Ulam has written an autobiography called *Adventures of a Mathematician,* and also a book of unsolved mathematics problems. "In learning mathematics, many people—including myself—need examples, practical cases, and not purely formal abstractions and rules, even though mathematics consists of that. We need contact with intuition."

CHAPTER 11 TEST

Knowledge

1. True or false?
   (a) The experimental probability and theoretical probability of an event are the same.
   (b) $P(\overline{A}) = 1 - P(A)$.
   (c) The row of Pascal's triangle that begins 1 10 · · · has 10 numbers in it.
   (d) The sum of the numbers in the row of Pascal's triangle that begins 1 12 · · · is 12^2.
   (e) If three dice are tossed, there are 216 outcomes.
   (f) If A and B are events of some sample space S, then $P(A \cup B) = P(A) + P(B)$.
   (g) $P(A \mid B) = P(A)/P(B)$.
   (h) For any event A, $0 < P(A) < 1$.

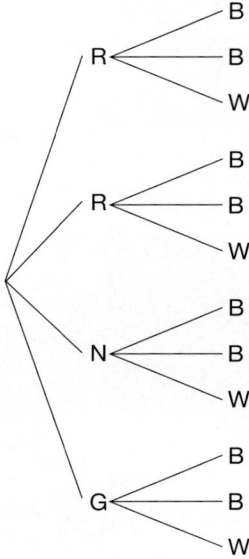

Skill

2. How many outcomes are in the event "Toss two dice and two coins"?

3. Given that $P(A) = \frac{5}{7}$ and $P(B) = \frac{1}{8}$ and $A \cap B = \varnothing$, what is $P(A \cup B)$?

4. Find the probability of tossing a sum that is a prime number when tossing a pair of dice.

5. What is the probability of tossing at least 3 heads when tossing 4 coins *given* that at least 2 heads turn up?

Understanding

6. Given that "If $A \cap B = \varnothing$, then $P(A \cup B) = P(A) + P(B)$," verify that "$P(\overline{A}) = 1 - P(A)$."

7. Explain how tree diagrams and the fundamental counting property are related.

8. Convert the tree diagram of equally likely outcomes into the corresponding probability tree diagram.

Problem Solving/Application

9. Find the probability of tossing a prime number of heads when tossing 10 coins.

10. Show that when tossing a pair of dice, the probability of getting the sum n, where $2 \le n \le 12$, is the same as the probability of getting the sum $14 - n$.

11. Suppose that $P(A) = \frac{2}{3}$, $P(B) = \frac{1}{2}$, and $P(A \mid B) = \frac{1}{3}$. What is $P(B \mid A)$?

Geometric Shapes

Dr. Pierre M. van Hiele

Dieke van Hiele-Geldof

FOCUS ON:

The van Hieles and Learning Geometry

In 1959 in the Netherlands, a short paper appeared entitled "The Child's Thought and Geometry." In it, Pierre van Hiele summarized the collaborative work that he and his wife Dieke van Hiele-Geldof had done on describing students' difficulties in learning geometry concepts. The van Hieles were mathematics teachers at about our middle-school level. Dutch students study a considerable amount of informal geometry before high school, and the van Hieles observed consistent difficulties from year to year as their geometry course progressed. Based on observations of their classes, they stated that learning progresses through five stages or "levels" as they called them, and that, at each level, students reason in a specific, discernible way about geometric concepts.

At the lowest level, level 0, reasoning is visual or wholistic, with no particular significance attached to attributes of shapes, except in gross terms. A square is a square at level 0 because of its general shape and resemblance to other objects that have been labeled "squares." Hands-on materials are essential in rounding out level 0 study. An analysis of shapes occurs at level 1, a refinement of the wholistic thinking of level 0, in that attributes of shapes become explicitly important. A student who is thinking analytically about a shape can list many of its relevant properties and can compare them with those of another shape. Sorting and drawing activities and the use of manipulatives, such as geoboards, are useful at level 1.

Abstraction and ordering of properties occur at level 2. That is, properties and their relationships become the objects of study. Environments such as dot arrays and grids are very helpful for students who are making the transition from level 1 to level 2. At level 3, formal mathematical deduction is used to establish an orderly mathematical system of geometric results. Deduction, or proof, is the final authority in deciding the validity of a conjecture, yet drawings and constructions are helpful in suggesting methods of proof. The last level, level 4, is that of modern-day mathematical rigor, usually saved for university study.

The van Hieles revised their geometry curriculum based on their studies. Dina van Hiele-Geldof published her work in her doctoral dissertation in 1957 before her untimely death a year later. Pierre van Hiele went on to write many papers on the teaching of mathematics and continues his activity today. He has also developed a variety of classroom materials based on the level theory. In the late 1960s, Soviet mathematics educators revised their school geometry curriculum, using the work of the van Hieles. In the 1970s and 1980s interest in the van Hieles' work led to many efforts in the United States to improve geometry teaching.

STRATEGY 17: USE A MODEL

The strategy "Use a Model" is useful in problems involving geometric figures or their applications. Often, we acquire mathematical insight about a problem by seeing a physical embodiment of it. A model, then, is any physical object that resembles the object of inquiry in the problem. It may be as simple as a paper, wooden, or plastic shape, or as complicated as a carefully constructed replica that an architect or engineer might use.

Initial Problem

Describe a solid shape that will fill each of the holes in this template as well as pass through each hole.

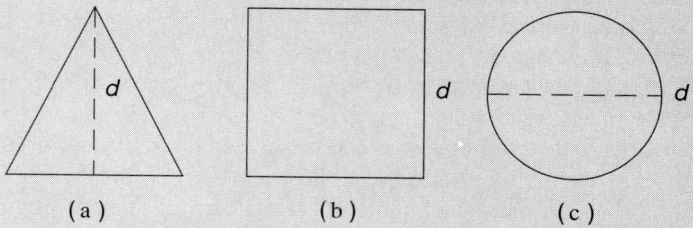

(a)   (b)   (c)

Clues

The Use a Model strategy may be appropriate when:

- Physical objects can be used to represent the ideas involved.
- A drawing is either too complex or inadequate to provide insight into the problem.
- A problem involves three-dimensional objects.

A solution of the Initial Problem above appears on page 605.

INTRODUCTION

The study of geometric shapes and their properties is an essential component of a comprehensive elementary mathematics curriculum. Geometry is rich in concepts, problem-solving experiences, and applications. In this chapter we study simple geometric shapes and their properties from a teacher's point of view. Research in geometry teaching and learning has given strong support to the van Hiele theory that students learn geometry by progressing through a sequence of reasoning levels. The material in this chapter is organized and presented according to the van Hiele theory.

12.1

RECOGNIZING GEOMETRIC SHAPES AND DEFINITIONS

(a) Triangles according to some children.

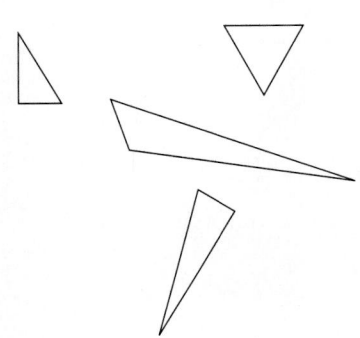

(b) Not triangles according to some children.

FIGURE 12.1

The van Hiele Theory

In the late 1950s in the Netherlands, two mathematics teachers, Pierre van Hiele and Dieke van Hiele-Geldof, husband and wife, put forth a theory of development in geometry based on their own teaching and research. They observed that in learning geometry, students seem to progress through a sequence of five reasoning levels, from wholistic thinking to analytical thinking to rigorous abstract mathematical deduction. The van Hieles described the five levels of reasoning in the following way.

Level 0 (Recognition)

A child who is reasoning at level 0 recognizes certain shapes wholistically without paying attention to their component parts. For example, a rectangle may be recognized because it "looks like a door" and not because it has four straight sides and four right angles. At level 0 some relevant attributes of a shape, such as straightness of sides, might be ignored by a child, and some irrelevant attributes, such as the orientation of the figure on the page, might be stressed. Figure 12.1(a) shows some figures that were classified as triangles by children reasoning wholistically. Can you pick out the ones that do not belong according to a relevant attribute? Figure 12.1(b) shows some figures *not* considered triangles by students reasoning wholistically. Can you identify the irrelevant attributes that should be ignored?

Level 1 (Analysis)

At this level, the child focuses analytically on the component parts of a figure, such as its sides and angles. Component parts and their attributes are used to describe and characterize figures. Relevant attributes are understood and are differentiated from irrelevant attributes. For example, a child who is reasoning analytically would say that a square has four "equal" sides and four "square" corners. The child also knows that turning a square on

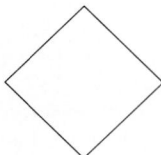

(a) Not a square according to some children thinking wholistically

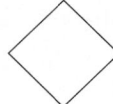

(b) Squares according to children thinking analytically.

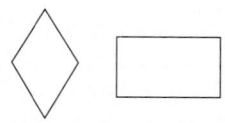

(c) Not squares according to children thinking analytically.

FIGURE 12.2

the page does not affect its "squareness." Figure 12.2 on page 530 illustrates how aspects of the concept "square" change from level 0 to level 1.

The shape in Figure 12.2(a) is not considered a square by some children who are thinking wholistically because of its orientation on the page. They may call it a "diamond." However, if it is turned so that the sides are horizontal and vertical, then the same children may consider it a square. The shapes in Figure 12.2(b) are considered squares by children thinking analytically. These children focus on the relevant attributes (four "equal" sides and four "square corners") and ignore the irrelevant attribute of orientation on the page. The shapes in Figure 12.2(c) are not considered squares by children thinking analytically. These shapes do not have all the relevant attributes. The shape on the left does not have square corners, and the shape on the right does not have four equal sides.

A child thinking analytically might not believe that a figure can belong to several general classes, and hence have several names. For example, a square is also a rectangle since a rectangle has four sides and four square corners, but a child reasoning analytically may object, thinking that square and rectangle are entirely separate types even though they share many attributes.

Level 2 (Relationships)

There are two general types of thinking at this level. First, a child understands abstract *relationships* among figures. For example, a rhombus is a four-sided figure with equal sides and a rectangle is a four-sided figure with square corners (Figure 12.3). A child who is reasoning at level 2 realizes that a square is both a rhombus and a rectangle, since a square has four equal sides and four square corners. Second, at level 2 a child can use *deduction* to justify observations made at level 1. In our treatment of geometry we will use informal deduction (i.e., the chaining of ideas together to verify general properties of shapes). This is analogous to our observations about properties of number systems in earlier chapters. For example, we will make extensive use of informal deduction in Section 12.2.

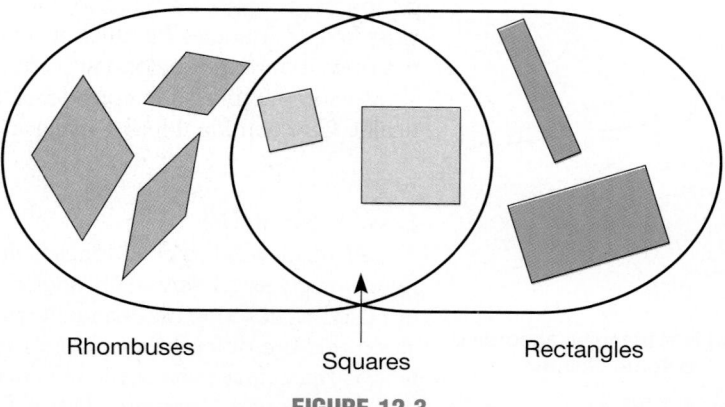

Rhombuses   Squares   Rectangles

FIGURE 12.3

Level 3 (Deduction)

Reasoning at this level includes the study of geometry as a formal mathematical system. A child who reasons at level 3 understands the notions of mathematical postulates and theorems and can write formal proofs of theorems.

Level 4 (Axiomatics)

The study of geometry at level 4 is highly abstract and does not necessarily involve concrete or pictorial models. At this level, the postulates or axioms themselves become the object of intense, rigorous scrutiny. This level of study is not suitable for elementary, middle school, or even most high school students, but is usually the level of study in geometry courses in college.

Recognizing Geometric Shapes

In the primary grades, children are taught to recognize several types of geometric shapes, such as triangles, squares, rectangles, and circles. Shape identification items frequently occur on worksheets and on mathematics achievement tests. For example, a child may be asked to "pick out the triangle, the square, the rectangle, and the circle." Children are taught to look for prototype shapes—shapes like those they have seen in their textbook or in physical models.

Often, however, children have seen only special cases of shapes and do not have a complete idea of the important attributes that a shape must have in order to represent a general type. Referring to the van Hiele theory, we would say that they have recognition ability but not analytic understanding. For example, Figure 12.4 shows a selection of shapes difficult to identify when thinking wholistically. Can you see why some children consider shape 1 to be a triangle, shape 2 a square, shape 6 a rectangle, and shape 8 a circle?

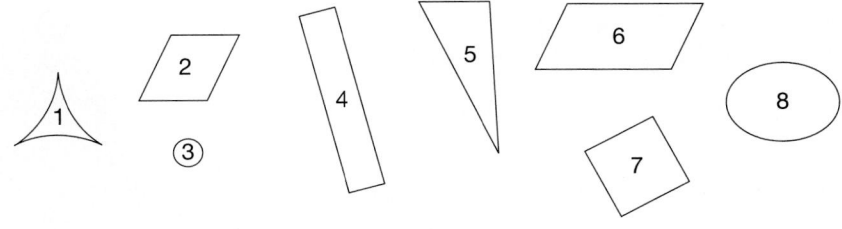

FIGURE 12.4

Wholistic thinking is an important first step in learning about geometrical shapes. It lays the groundwork for the analysis of shapes by properties of their components. Students' wholistic thinking abilities can be developed by means of visualization activities. For example, finding "hidden" figures can help students visually focus on particular shapes as a whole. Example 12.1 gives an illustration.

EXAMPLE 12.1   How many different rectangles are formed by the heavy-line segments in this figure?

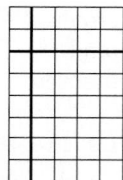

Solution
Looking for "vertical" rectangles, we find seven.

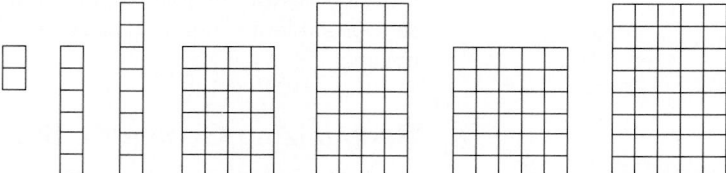

Looking for "horizontal" rectangles, we find two.

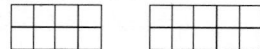

Hence there are nine rectangles altogether.

Making new shapes by rearranging other shapes is also a good way for students to develop visualization skills. Tangram puzzles are examples of this kind of activity. Example 12.2 shows a rearrangement activity that provides a "proof" of the Pythagorean theorem, namely that the sum of the squares on the sides of a right triangle is equal to the square on the hypotenuse.

EXAMPLE 12.2   Figure 12.5 shows a right triangle with squares on each of its two sides, labeled a and b, and on its hypotenuse, labeled c. Trace and cut out the squares on the sides and cut the larger one into four pieces along

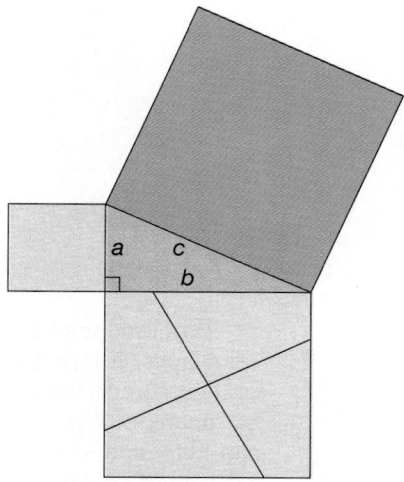

FIGURE 12.5

the dashed lines. Then rearrange these five pieces to cover the square on the hypotenuse exactly.

Solution
See Figure 12.6. ■

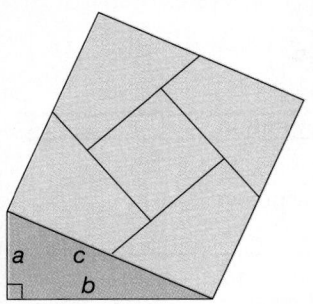

FIGURE 12.6

The problem set contains some additional rearrangement activities.

The ability to manipulate images is an important visualization skill. Example 12.3 provides an illustration.

EXAMPLE 12.3 Fold a square piece of paper in half so that the fold is on the dashed line, as shown in Figure 12.7. Then, punch a hole in the folded paper. How will the paper look when unfolded?

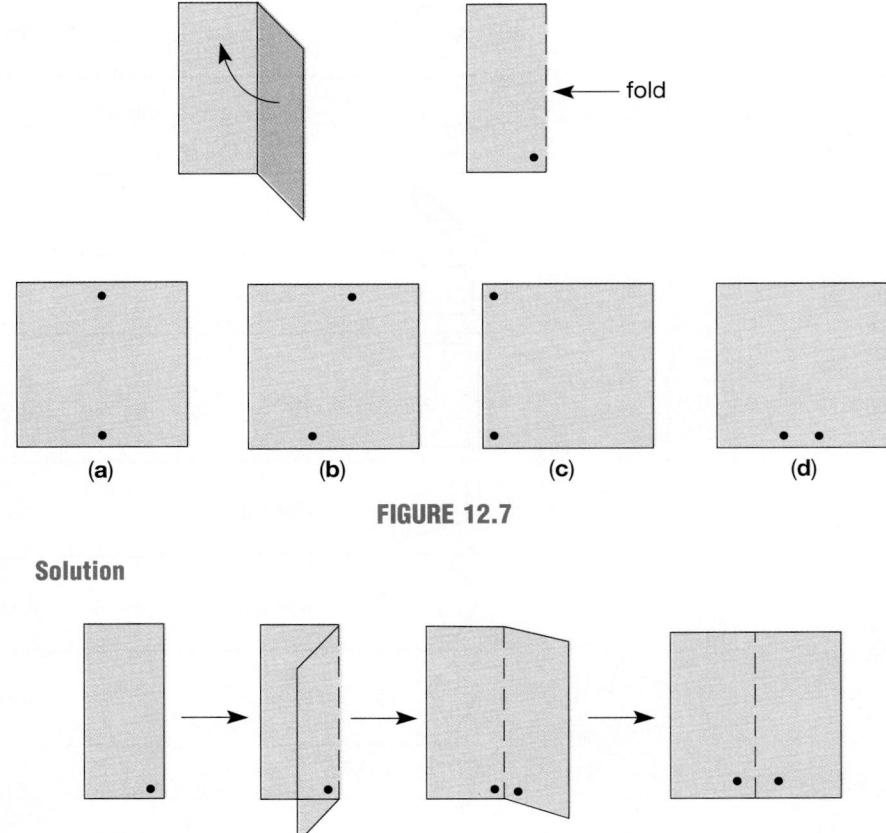

FIGURE 12.7

Solution

Thus figure (d) is correct. ■

Defining Common Geometric Shapes

Next we study parts of geometric figures using informal methods. For example, we will use activities with dot paper, paper folding, and tracings to reveal characteristics of geometric figures, methods that are currently used when introducing these concepts to children.

The geometric shapes defined in this section are abstractions of physical models from our everyday world. Table 12.1 illustrates many of these shapes.

TABLE 12.1

Model		Abstraction
	Top of a window	Line segment
	Vertical flagpole	Right angle (perpendicular segments)
	Yield sign	Triangle (equilateral)
	Opening in a pair of scissors	Angle
	Railroad tracks	Parallel lines
	Floor tile	Square
	Door	Rectangle (that is not a square)
	Railing	Parallelogram
	Diamond	Rhombus
	Kite	Kite
	Water glass silhouette	Trapezoid (isosceles)

Sides and Angles

The points of a **square lattice** (i.e., a square array of dots) serve as an effective environment in which to analyze figures such as those in Table 12.1. A geoboard or square dot paper provide concrete representations for such investigations. By joining two points in the shortest possible way, we form a set of points called a (straight) **line segment**. Figure 12.8 shows on a square lattice, several types of figures whose sides are line segments. The shapes in parts (a) to (c) are all **triangles** because they are closed figures composed of exactly three line segments, called **sides**. The shapes in parts (d) to (h) are

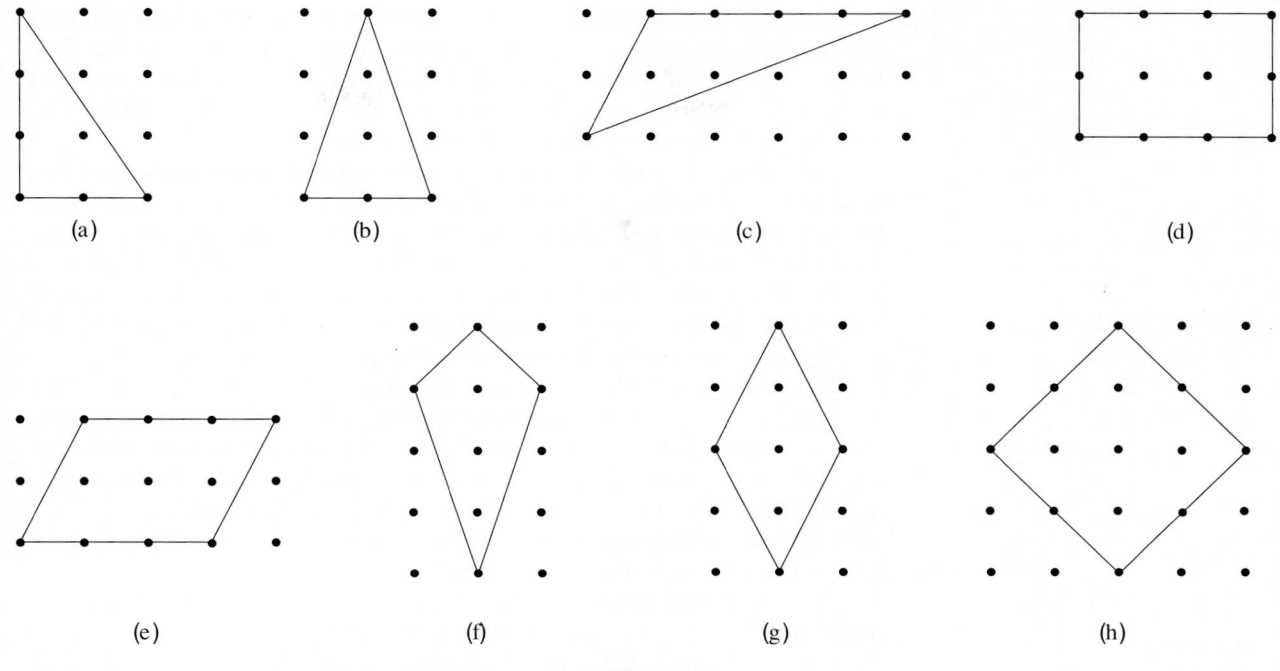

(a)   (b)   (c)   (d)

(e)   (f)   (g)   (h)

FIGURE 12.8

quadrilaterals because they are closed figures composed of four line segments (sides). Triangles have three angles. An **angle** is the union of two line segments with a common endpoint called a **vertex**. (The plural of vertex is **vertices**.) Quadrilaterals have four angles. (Literally, "triangle" means "three angles" and "quadrilateral" means "four sides." Perhaps "trilateral," meaning "three sides," would have been a more useful name for a triangle.)

In the remainder of this section, we will describe figures using the concepts of "length," "right angle," and "parallel." We will use these terms informally for now and give precise definitions of them in Section 12.2.

If we consider the triangles in Figure 12.8, we notice several differences among them. For example, the triangle in part (a) has an angle formed by horizontal and vertical sides. Any angle identical to an angle formed by horizontal and vertical line segments is called a **right angle**. In parts (d) and (h) of Figure 12.8, the quadrilaterals each have four right angles. We discuss general procedures for identifying right angles later in this subsection. Two line segments that form a right angle are called **perpendicular**. Triangle (b) has two sides that are the same length. A triangle with two or three sides the same length is called an **isosceles** triangle. A triangle with three sides the same length is called an **equilateral** triangle. An equilateral triangle is shown on *triangular* dot paper in Figure 12.9. Triangle (c) has three sides that are all different lengths. Such triangles are called **scalene** triangles. Thus we can compare and name types of triangles according to their sides.

Figure 12.8 contains a variety of quadrilaterals. For example, the shape in part (h) is a square. A **square** is a quadrilateral with four sides the same length and four right angles. The shape in part (d) is a rectangle. A **rectangle** is a quadrilateral with four right angles. The shape in part (e) is a parallelogram. A **parallelogram** is a quadrilateral with two pairs of parallel sides

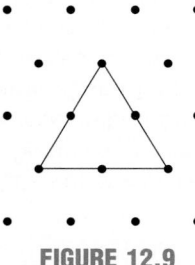

FIGURE 12.9

(point in the same direction). The shape in part (f) is a kite. A **kite** is a quadrilateral with two nonoverlapping pairs of adjacent sides that are the same length. Finally, the shape in part (g) is a rhombus. A **rhombus** is a quadrilateral with four sides the same length. It is also true that shape (h) has four sides the same length and has four right angles.

We will say that two line segments are **congruent line segments** if they have the same length. Any figure whose sides are congruent is called **equilateral**. Two angles are **congruent angles** if they have the same "opening," that is, one angle is an exact copy of the other, except possibly for the lengths of the sides. For example, in a square all four sides are congruent and all four angles are congruent. A figure is said to be **equiangular** if all of its angles are congruent. A square is both equilateral and equiangular.

We notice that rectangle (d) and rhombus (g) in Figure 12.8 also have two pairs of parallel sides. Hence they, too, are parallelograms. Students who are thinking at the analysis level sometimes have difficulty understanding that a figure can represent several types simultaneously. An analogy to membership criteria for clubs can help explain this. For example, shape (h) qualifies for membership in at least five "clubs": the rectangles, parallelograms, kites, rhombuses, and squares.

A quadrilateral with *exactly one pair* of parallel sides is called a **trapezoid** [Figure 12.10(a)]. If the nonparallel sides of a trapezoid are congruent, it is called an **isosceles trapezoid** [Figure 12.10(b)]. Thus a parallelogram is *not* a trapezoid, since it has two pairs of parallel sides.

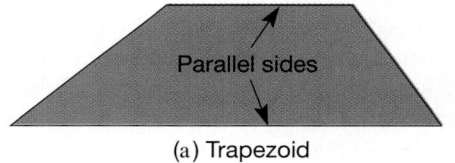

(a) Trapezoid   (b) Isosceles trapezoid

FIGURE 12.10

MATHEMATICAL MORSEL

The game of chess offers a myriad of changing patterns. To settle an old chess problem, a 25-year-old computer science student, Lewis Stiller, used a computer to perform one of the largest such computer searches. His search found that a king, a rook, and a bishop can defeat a king and two knights in 223 moves. Stiller's program ran for five hours and made 100 billion moves by working backward. Although this search, which was reported in *Scientific American,* was directed to solving a chess problem, the techniques Stiller developed can be used in solving other problems in mathematics.

EXERCISE/PROBLEM SET 12.1—PART A

Exercises

1. Answer the following questions visually first. Then devise a way to check your answer.
   (a) If the arrow *A* were continued downward, which arrow would it meet?

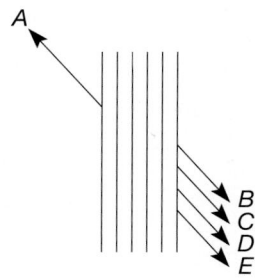

   (b) Are the following curved shapes circles?

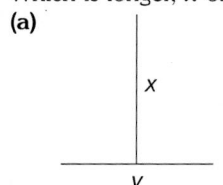

2. Which is longer, *x* or *y*?
   (a)

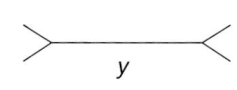

   (b)

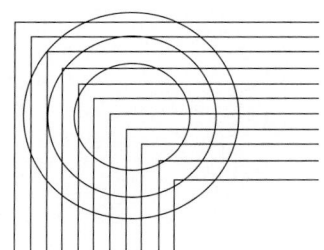

   (c)

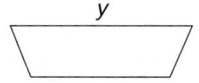

3. How many of the indicated shapes are in the following designs?
   (a) Triangles

   (b) Parallelograms

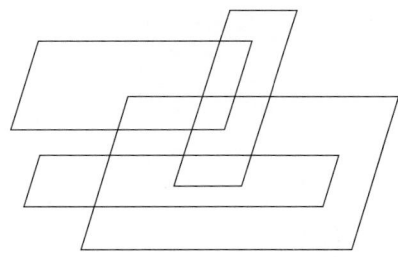

4. How many squares are found in each of the following figures?
   (a)   (b)

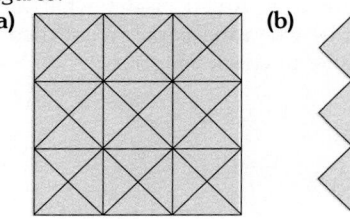

5. Given below are a variety of triangles. Sides with the same length are indicated. Right angles are indicated.

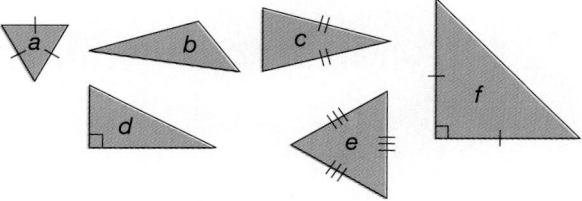

   (a) Name the triangles that are scalene.
   (b) Name the triangles that are isosceles.
   (c) Name the triangles that are equilateral.
   (d) Name the triangles that contain a right angle.

6. Trace the following figure and cut it into five pieces along the lines indicated. Rearrange the pieces to form a square. You must use all five pieces, have no gaps or overlaps, and you cannot turn the pieces over.

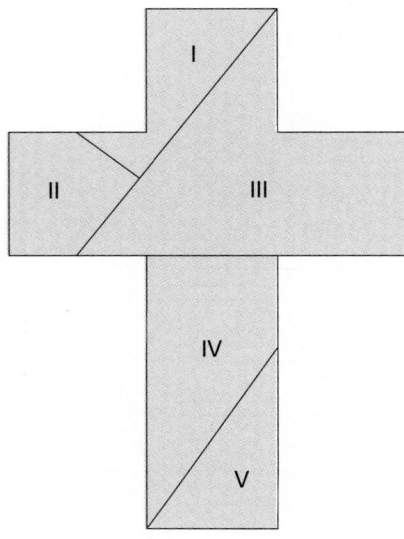

7. Fold a rectangular piece of paper on the dashed line as shown in each of the following figures. Then make cuts in the paper as indicated. Sketch what you think the shape will be when the paper is unfolded. Then unfold your paper to check your picture.

(a)

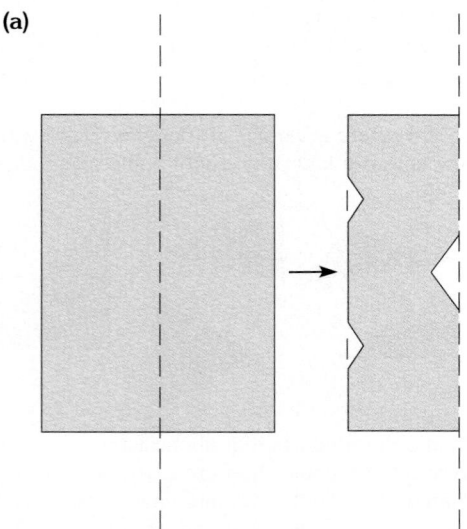

(b)

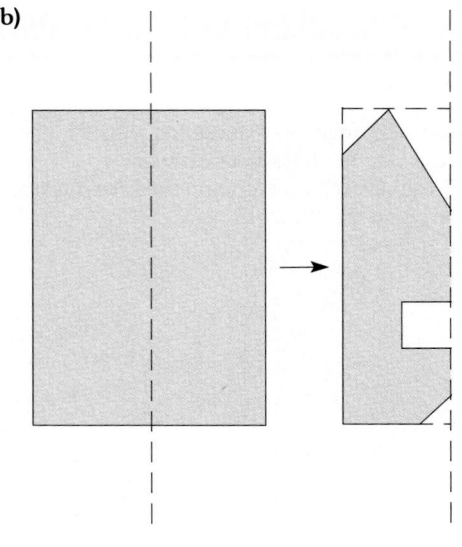

(c)

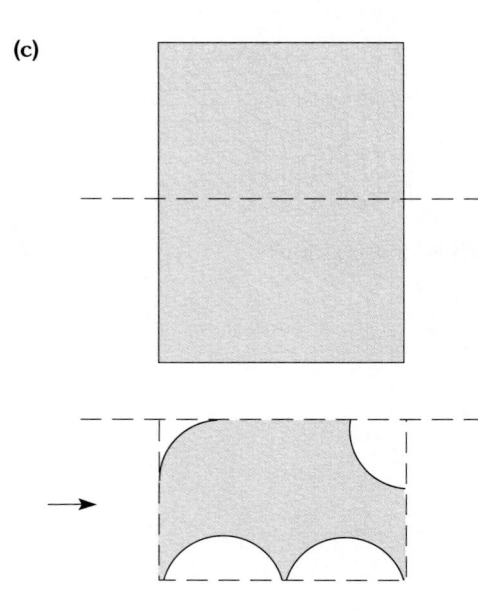

8. Each of the following shapes was obtained by folding a rectangular piece of paper in half vertically (length-wise) and then making appropriate cuts in the paper. For each figure, draw the folded paper and show the cuts that must be made to make the figure. Try folding and cutting a piece of paper to check your answer.

(a)

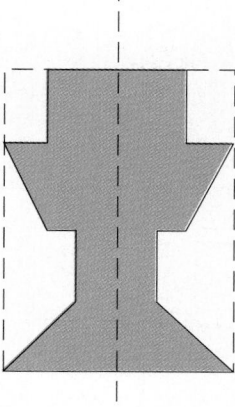

(b)

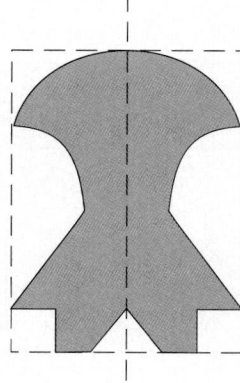

(c)

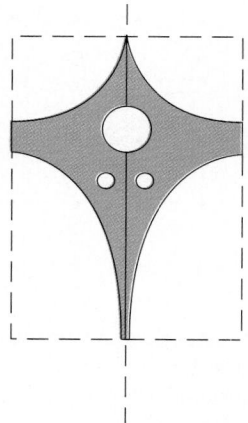

9. Fold the square first on line 1, then on line 2. Next, punch a hole, as indicated. Draw what you think the resulting shape will be. Unfold to check.

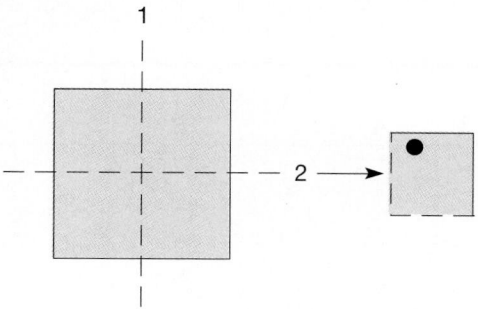

10. To produce each figure, a square was folded twice, punched once, then unfolded. Find the fold lines and where the hole was punched.

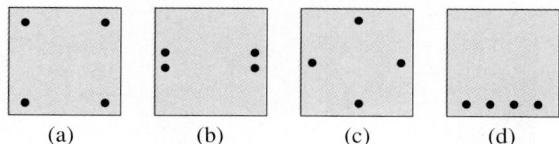

    (a)   (b)   (c)   (d)

11. Find the following shapes in the figure.
- **(a)** A square
- **(b)** A rectangle that is not a square
- **(c)** A parallelogram that is not a rectangle
- **(d)** An isosceles right triangle
- **(e)** An isosceles triangle with no right angles
- **(f)** A rhombus that is not a square
- **(g)** A kite that is not a rhombus
- **(h)** A scalene triangle with no right angles
- **(i)** A right scalene triangle
- **(j)** A trapezoid that is not isosceles
- **(k)** An isosceles trapezoid

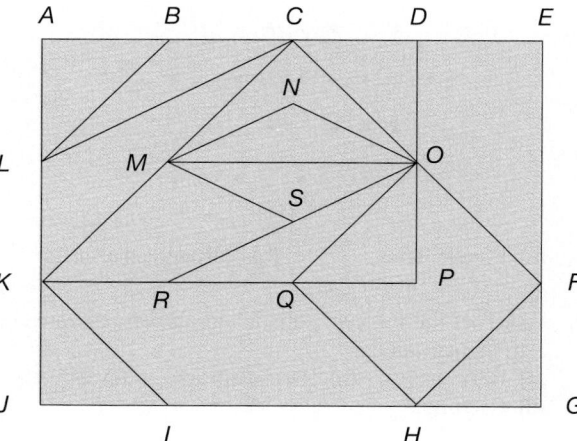

Problems

12. If *A* belongs with *B,* then *X* belongs with *Y.* Which of
(i), (ii), or (iii) is the best choice for *Y?*

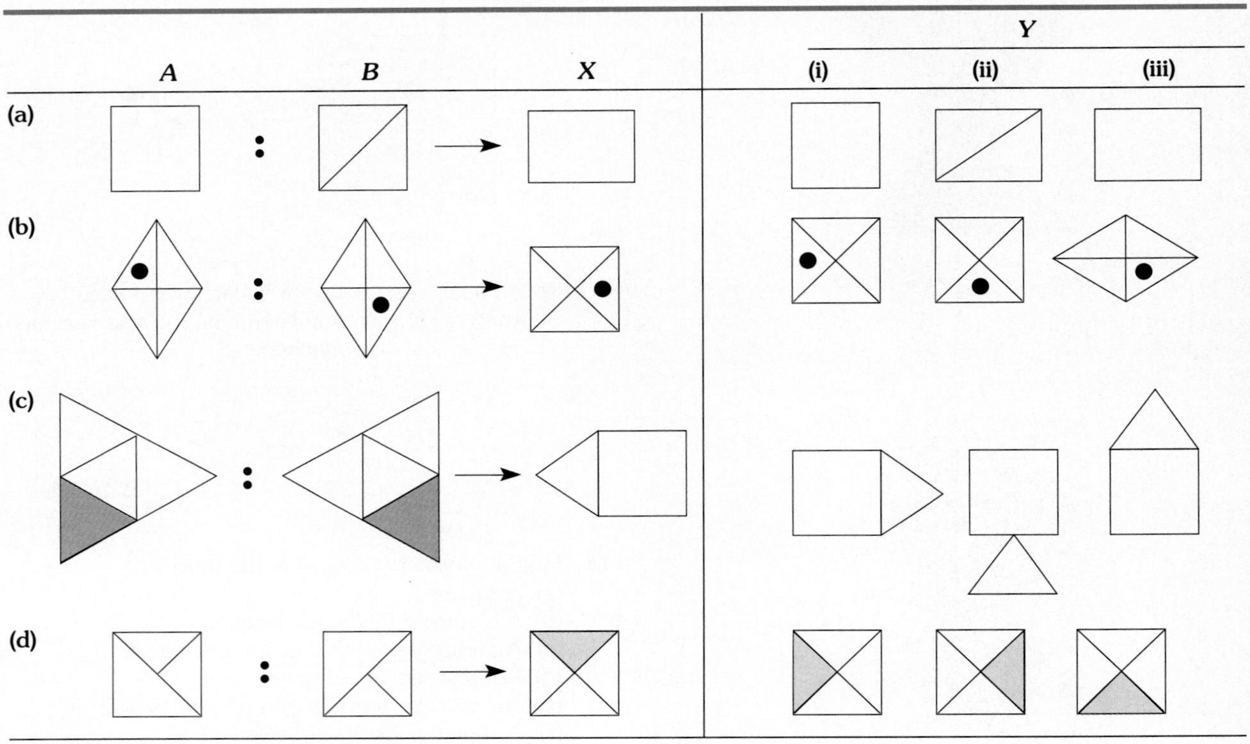

13. A portion of a triangular lattice is given. Which of the
following can be drawn on it?

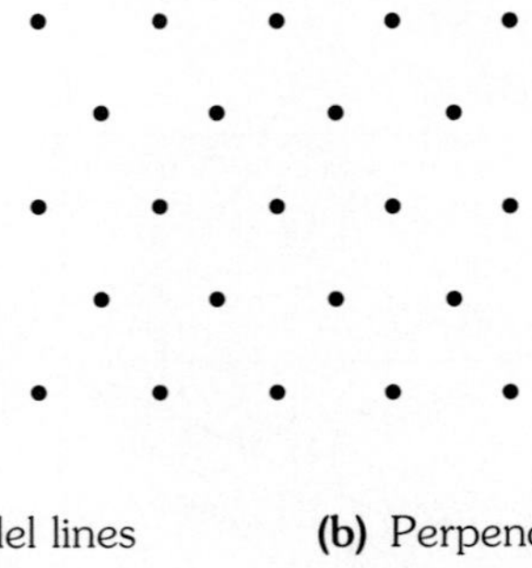

(a) Parallel lines   **(b)** Perpendicular lines

14. Which of the following quadrilaterals can be drawn on
a triangular lattice?
  (a) Rhombus   **(b)** Parallelogram   **(c)** Square
  (d) Rectangle

15. Given the square lattice shown, draw quadrilaterals
having $\overline{AB}$ as a side.

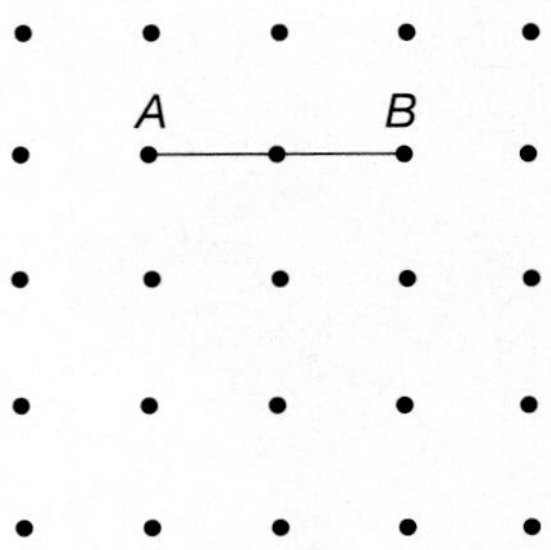

(a) How many parallelograms are possible?
(b) How many rectangles?
(c) How many rhombuses?
(d) How many squares?

16. Trace the following hexagon twice.

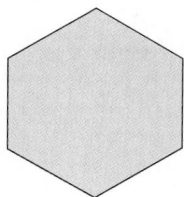

(a) Divide one hexagon into three identical parts so that each part is a rhombus.

(b) Divide the other hexagon into six identical kites.

EXERCISE/PROBLEM SET 12.1—PART B

Exercises

1. Are the lines labeled *l* and *m* parallel?

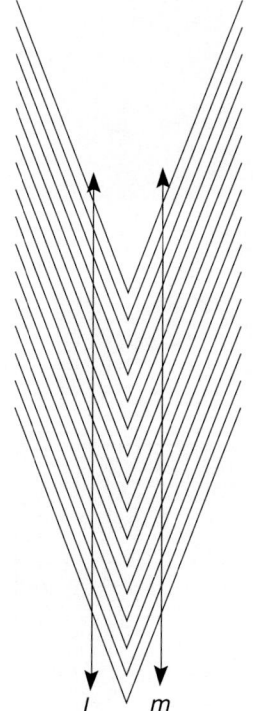

l   *m*

2. Which is longer: *x* or *y*?

(a)

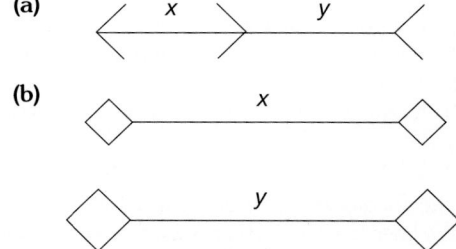

x   *y*

(b)   *x*

y

3. How many rectangles are found in the following design?

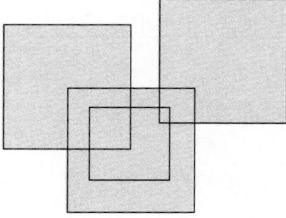

4. (a) How many triangles are in the figure?

(b) How many parallelograms?

(c) How many trapezoids?

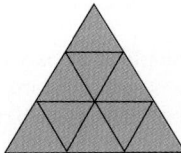

5. Several shapes are pictured below. Sides with the same length are indicated, as are right angles.

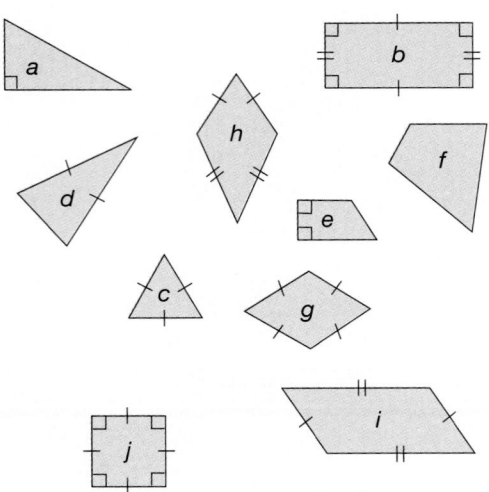

(a) Which figures have a right angle?
(b) Which figures have at least one pair of parallel sides?
(c) Which figures have at least two sides with the same length?
(d) Which figures have all sides the same length?

6. Trace the following figure and cut it into five pieces along the lines indicated. Rearrange the pieces to form a square. You must use all five pieces, have no gaps or overlaps, and you cannot turn the pieces over.

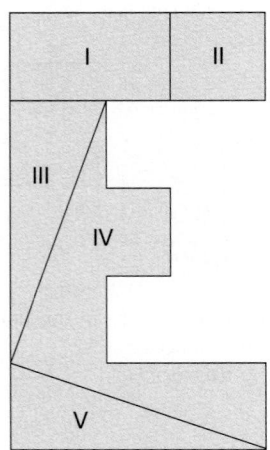

7. Fold a rectangular piece of paper on the dashed line as shown in each of the following figures. Then make cuts in the paper as indicated. Sketch what you think the shape will be when the paper is unfolded. Then unfold your paper to check your picture.

(a)

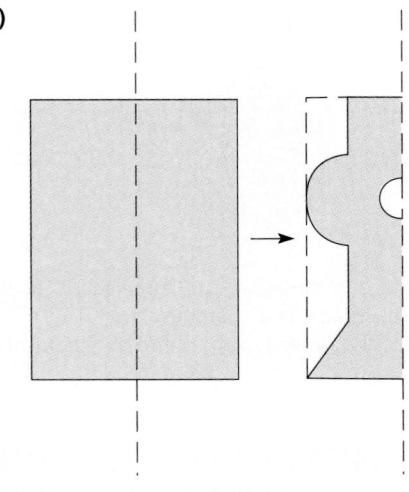

(b)

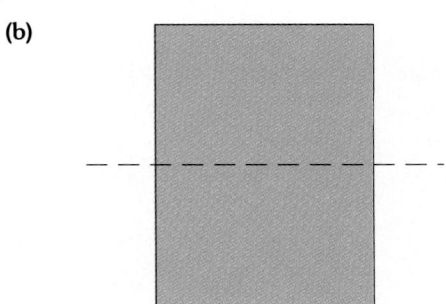

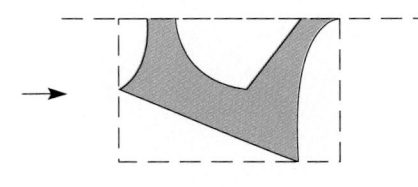

(c)

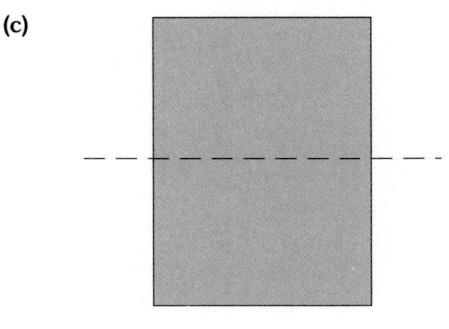

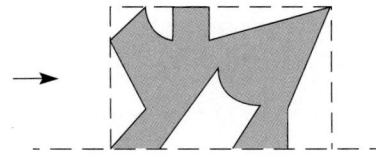

8. Each of the following shapes was obtained by folding a rectangular piece of paper in half horizontally and then making appropriate cuts in the paper. For each figure, draw the folded paper and show the cuts that must be made to make the figure. Try folding and cutting a piece of paper to check your answer.

(a)

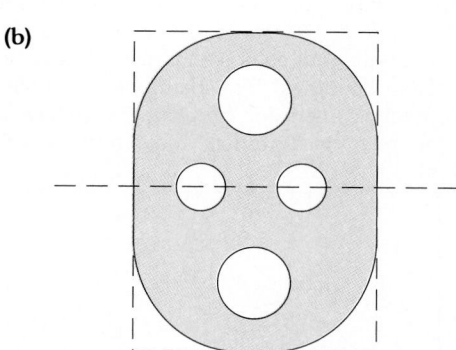

(b)

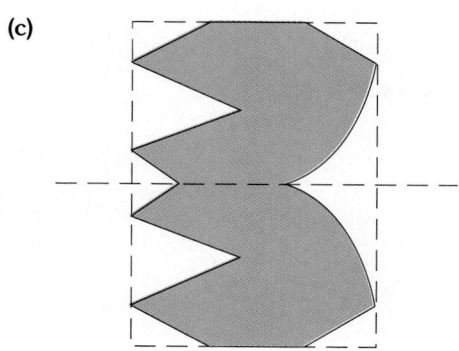

(c)

(a)

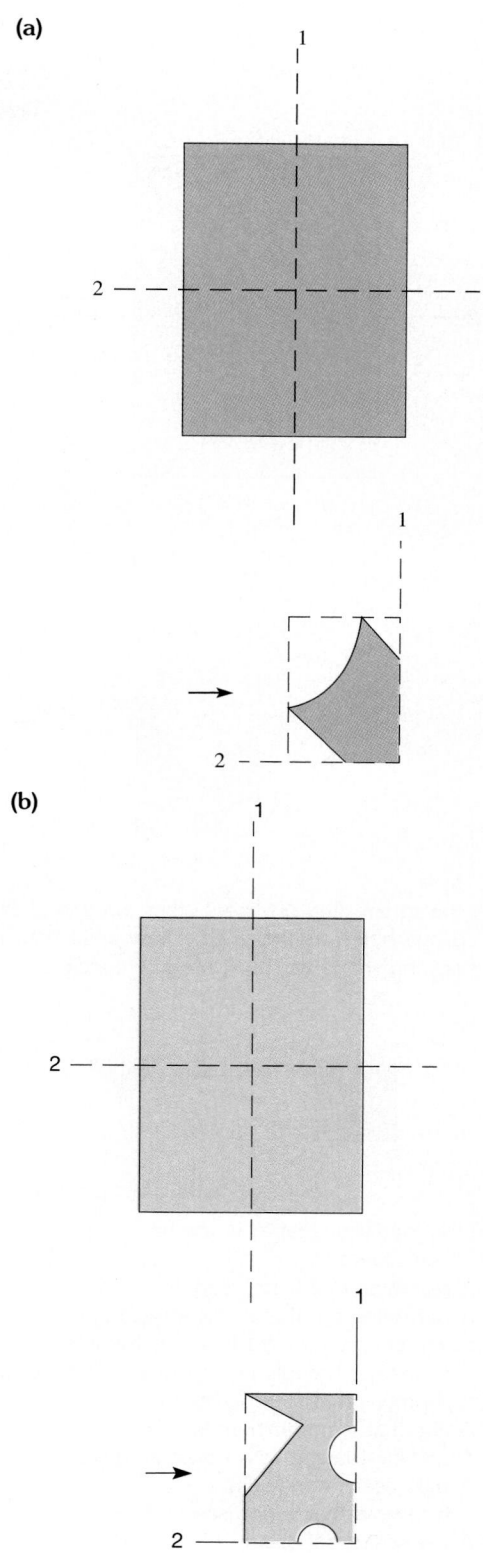

(b)

9. Fold a rectangular piece of paper in half vertically (dashed line 1) and then in half again horizontally (dashed line 2). Then make cuts in the paper as indicated. Sketch what you think the shape will be when the paper is unfolded. Unfold your paper to check your picture.

(c)

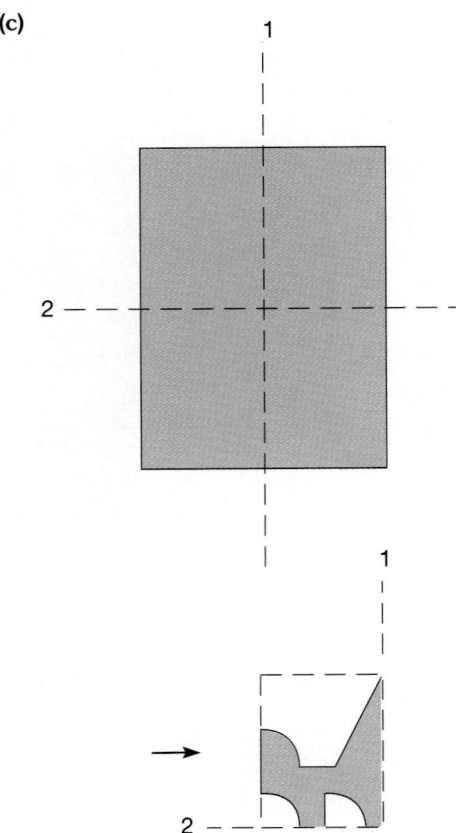

10. Fold the square first on line 1, then on line 2. Next, punch two holes, as indicated. Draw what you think the resulting shape will be. Unfold to check.

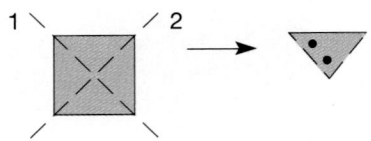

11. Find the following shapes in the figure.
  (a) Three squares
  (b) A rectangle that is not a square
  (c) A parallelogram that is not a rectangle
  (d) Seven congruent right isosceles triangles
  (e) An isosceles triangle not congruent to those in (d)
  (f) A rhombus that is not a square
  (g) A kite that is not a rhombus
  (h) A scalene triangle with no right angles
  (i) A right scalene triangle.
  (j) A trapezoid that is not isosceles
  (k) An isosceles trapezoid

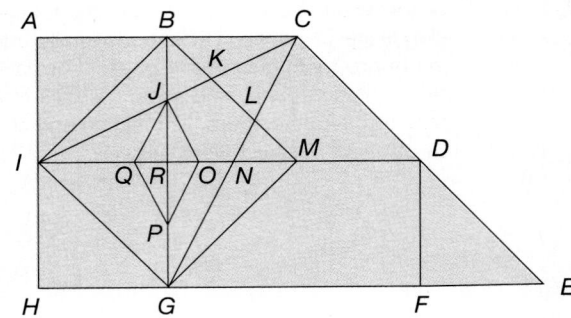

Problems

12. A problem that challenged mathematicians for many years concerns the coloring of maps. That is, what is the minimum number of colors necessary to color *any* map? Just recently it was finally proved with the aid of a computer that no map requires more than four colors. Some maps, however, can be colored with fewer than four colors. Determine the smallest number of colors necessary to color each map shown below. (NOTE: Two "countries" that share only one point can be colored the same color; however, if they have more than one point in common, they must be colored differently.)

(a)

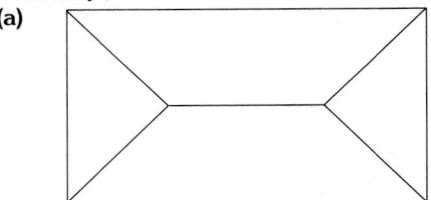

(b)

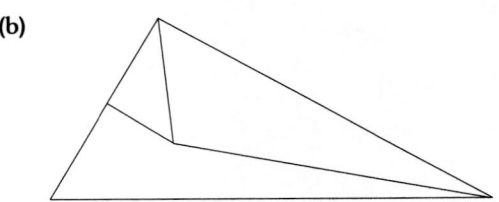

(c)

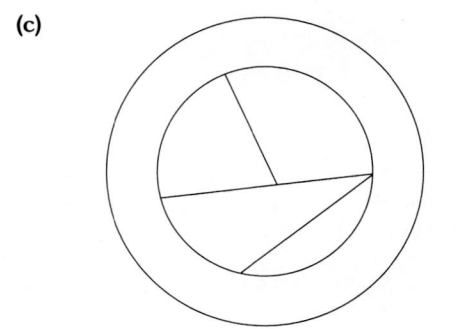

(a)

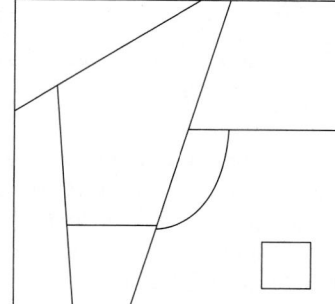

(b)

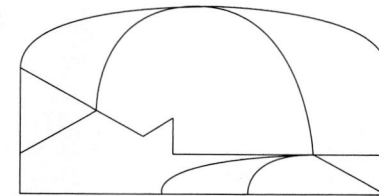

13. A portion of a triangular lattice is shown here.

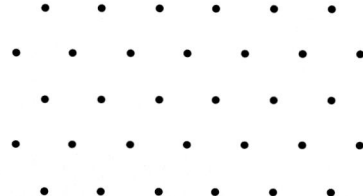

Which of the following can be drawn on it?
(a) Equilateral triangle
(b) Isosceles triangle
(c) Scalene triangle

14. Find the maximal finite number of points of intersection for the following pairs of regular polygons.
(a) A square and a triangle
(b) A triangle and a hexagon
(c) A square and an octagon
(d) An n-gon and an m-gon

15. Trace the hexagon twice.

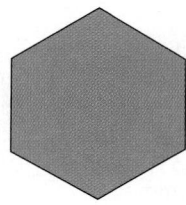

(a) Divide one hexagon into four identical trapezoids.
(b) Divide the other hexagon into eight identical polygons.

16. (a) Make copies of the following large, uncut square. Find ways to cut the squares into each of the following numbers of smaller squares: 7, 8, 9, 11, 12, 13, 14, 15, 16.

If you start with a large square

then you can cut it into 4 smaller squares like this

1	2
3	4

or into 6 smaller squares like this.

You can cut a square into 10 smaller squares this way

or this way.

(b) Can you find more than one way to cut the squares for some numbers? Which numbers?
(c) For which numbers can you cut the square into equal-sized smaller squares?

12.2

ANALYZING SHAPES

Symmetry

The concept of symmetry can be used in analyzing figures. Two-dimensional figures can have two distinct types of symmetry: reflection symmetry and rotation symmetry. Informally, a figure has **reflection symmetry** if there is a line that the figure can be "folded over" so that one-half of the figure matches the other half perfectly (Figure 12.11).

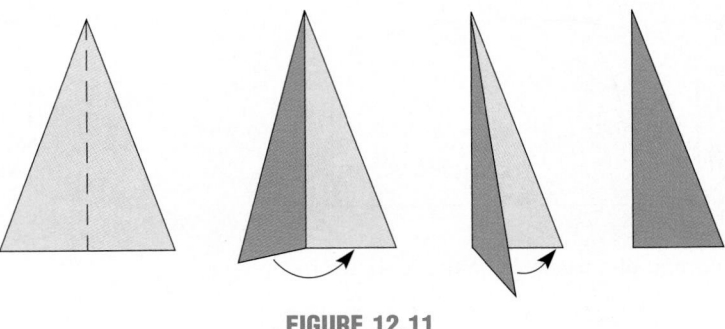

FIGURE 12.11

The "fold line" described above is called the figure's **line (axis) of symmetry**.

Figure 12.12 shows several figures and their lines of reflection symmetry. The lines of symmetry are dashed. Many properties of figures, such as symmetry, can be demonstrated using tracings and paper folding.

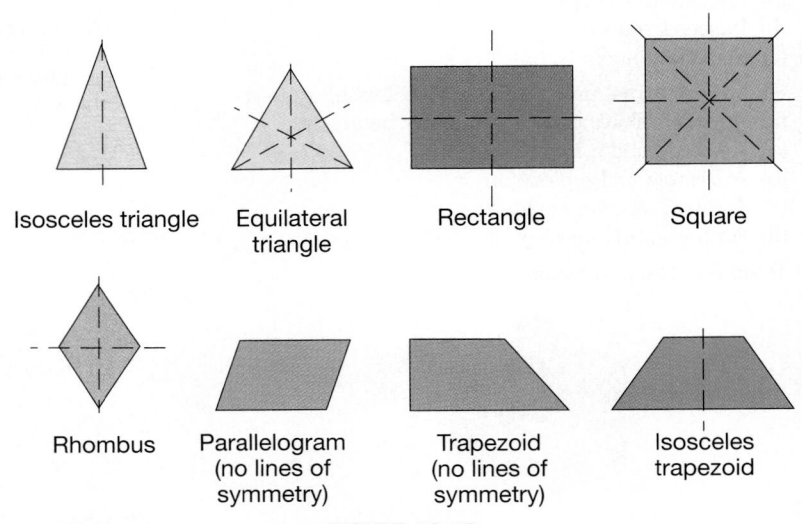

| Isosceles triangle | Equilateral triangle | Rectangle | Square |

| Rhombus | Parallelogram (no lines of symmetry) | Trapezoid (no lines of symmetry) | Isosceles trapezoid |

FIGURE 12.12

Next, we introduce some convenient notation to help describe geometric shapes and their symmetry properties.

Symbol	Meaning
$\overline{AB}$	Line segment with endpoints A and B [Figure 12.13(a)]
$\angle ABC$	Angle with vertex at B and sides $\overline{AB}$ and $\overline{BC}$ [Figure 12.13(b)]
$\triangle ABC$	Triangle with vertices A, B, and C [Figure 12.13(c)]

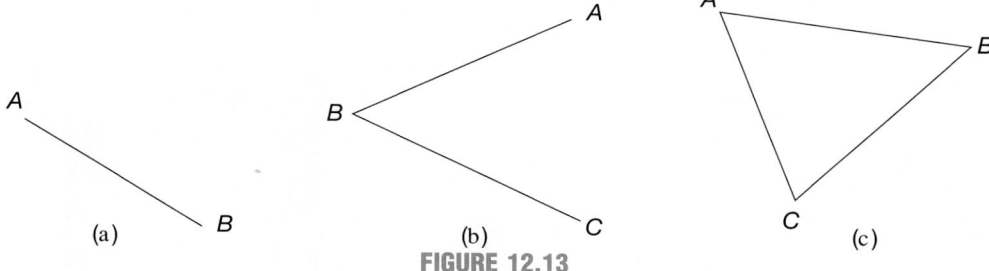

(a) (b) (c)

FIGURE 12.13

Example 12.4 uses symmetry to show a property of isosceles triangles.

EXAMPLE 12.4   Suppose that $\triangle ABC$ is isosceles with side $\overline{AB}$ congruent to side $\overline{AC}$ (Figure 12.14). Show that $\angle ABC$ is congruent to $\angle ACB$.

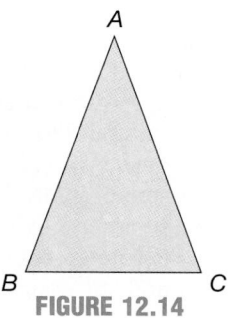

FIGURE 12.14

Solution

Fold the triangle so that vertex A remains fixed while vertex B folds onto vertex C. Semitransparent paper works well for this (Figure 12.15).

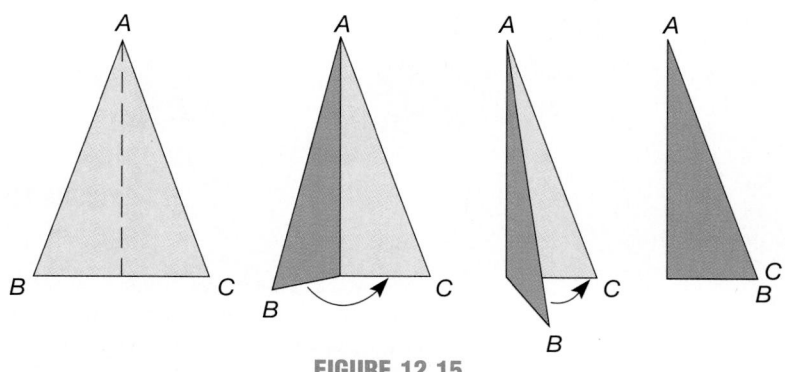

FIGURE 12.15

Observe that, after folding, side $\overline{AB}$ coincides with side $\overline{AC}$. Since $\angle ABC$ folds onto and exactly matches $\angle ACB$, they are congruent. ■

In an isosceles triangle, the angles opposite the congruent sides are called **base angles**. Example 12.4 shows that the base angles of an isosceles triangle are congruent. A similar property holds for isosceles trapezoids.

A useful device for finding lines of symmetry is a **Mira®**, a plexiglass "two-way" mirror. You can see reflections in it, and also see through it. Hence, in the case of a reflection symmetry, the reflection image appears to be superimposed on the figure itself. Figure 12.16 shows how to find lines of symmetry in a rhombus using a Mira. The beveled edge must be down and toward you.

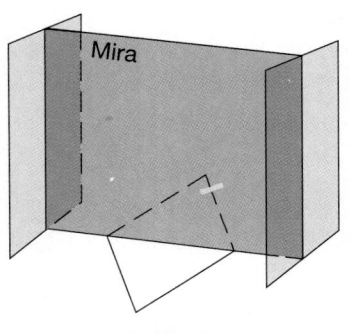

FIGURE 12.16

The second type of symmetry of figures is rotation symmetry. A figure has **rotation symmetry** if there is a point around which the figure can be rotated, *less than a full turn,* so that the image matches the original figure perfectly. (We will see more precise definitions of reflection and rotation symmetry in Chapter 16.) Figure 12.17 shows an investigation of rotation symmetry for an equilateral triangle. In Figure 12.17 the equilateral triangle is rotated counterclockwise $\frac{1}{3}$ of a turn. It could also be rotated $\frac{2}{3}$ of a turn and, of course, through a full turn to produce a matching image. Every figure can be rotated through a full turn using any point as the center of rotation to produce a matching image. Figures for which only a full turn produces an identical image do *not* have rotation symmetry.

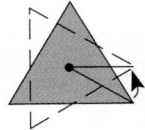 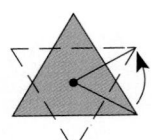 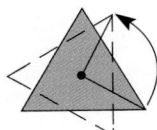 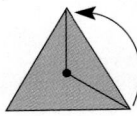

FIGURE 12.17

Figure 12.18 shows several types of figures and the number of turns up to and including one full turn that make the image match the figure. See if you can verify the numbers given. Tracing the figure and rotating your drawing may help you. In Figure 12.18, all figures except the trapezoid have rotation symmetry.

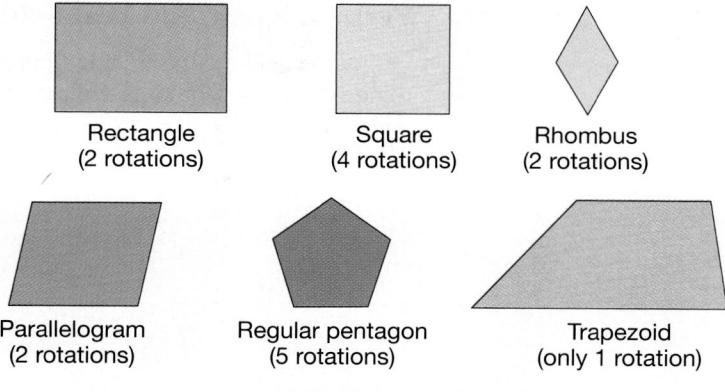

FIGURE 12.18

We see that shapes can have reflection symmetry without rotation symmetry (e.g., Figure 12.12 shows an isosceles triangle that is not equilateral) and rotation symmetry without reflection symmetry (e.g., Figure 12.18 shows a parallelogram that is not a rectangle).

Example 12.5 shows how we can use a rotation to establish a property of parallelograms.

EXAMPLE 12.5 Show that the opposite sides of a parallelogram are congruent.

Solution

Trace the parallelogram and turn the (shaded) tracing one-half turn around its center, the intersection of the diagonals [Figure 12.19(a), (b), (c)]. Observe that side $\overline{AB}$ of the tracing coincides with side $\overline{CD}$ and that side $\overline{AD}$ of the tracing coincides with side $\overline{CB}$ [Figure 12.19(d)].

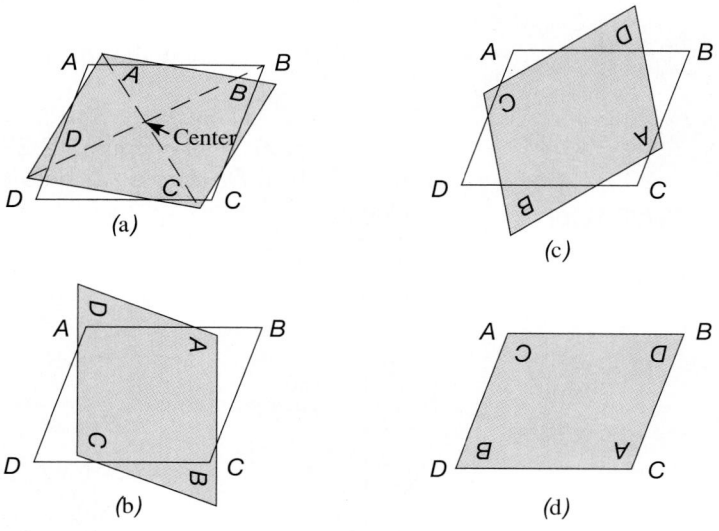

FIGURE 12.19

Thus both pairs of opposite sides are congruent. ■

Perpendicular and Parallel Line Segments

When folding and tracing figures, it is convenient to have tests to determine when line segments are perpendicular or parallel. To determine if two line segments *l* and *m* are perpendicular, we use the following test (Figure 12.20).

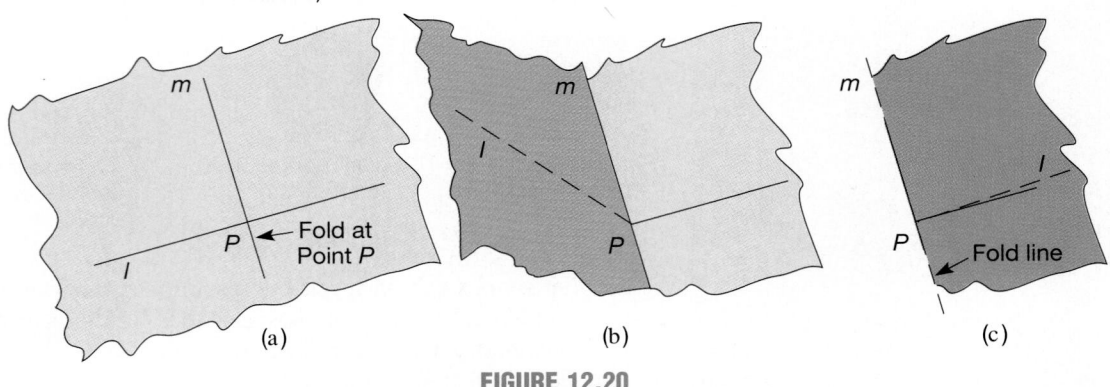

FIGURE 12.20

Perpendicular Line Segments Test

Let *P* be the point of intersection of *l* and *m* [Figure 12.20(a)]. Fold *l* at point *P* so that *l* folds across *P* onto itself [Figure 12.20(b) and (c)]. Then *l* and *m* are perpendicular if and only if *m* lies along the fold line [Figure 12.20(c)].

We can analyze properties of figures using diagonals, also. A **diagonal** is a line segment formed by connecting nonadjacent vertices (i.e., not on the same side) (Figure 12.21).

Example 12.6 demonstrates a property of the diagonals of a kite.

EXAMPLE 12.6   Show that the diagonals of a kite are perpendicular.

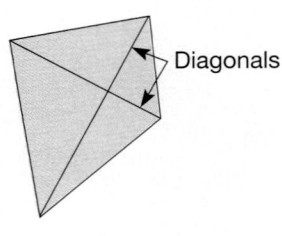

FIGURE 12.21

Solution
Let *ABCD* be a kite [Figure 12.22(a)]. Diagonals $\overline{AC}$ and $\overline{DB}$ intersect at point *E*. Fold $\overline{DE}$ across $\overline{AC}$ onto $\overline{EB}$ [Figure 12.22(b) and (c)]. Notice that diagonal $\overline{AC}$ is on the fold line [Figure 12.22(d)]. Thus the diagonals are perpendicular.

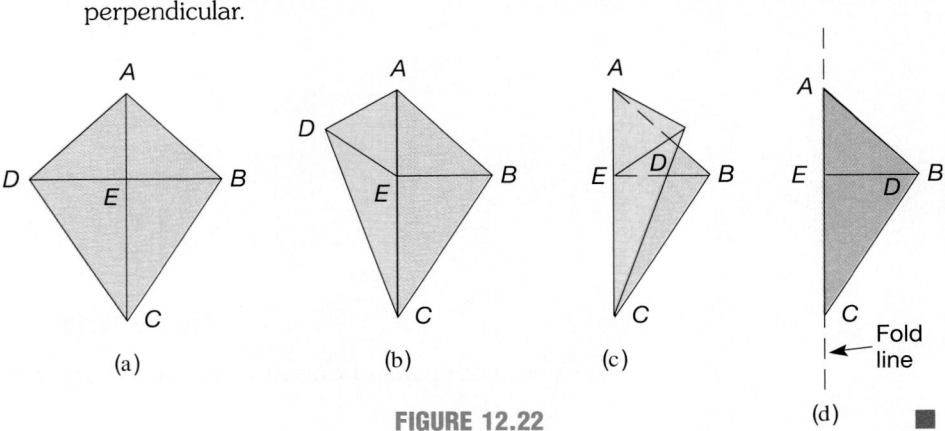

FIGURE 12.22

To determine if two line segments *l* and *m* are parallel, we use the following test (Figure 12.23).

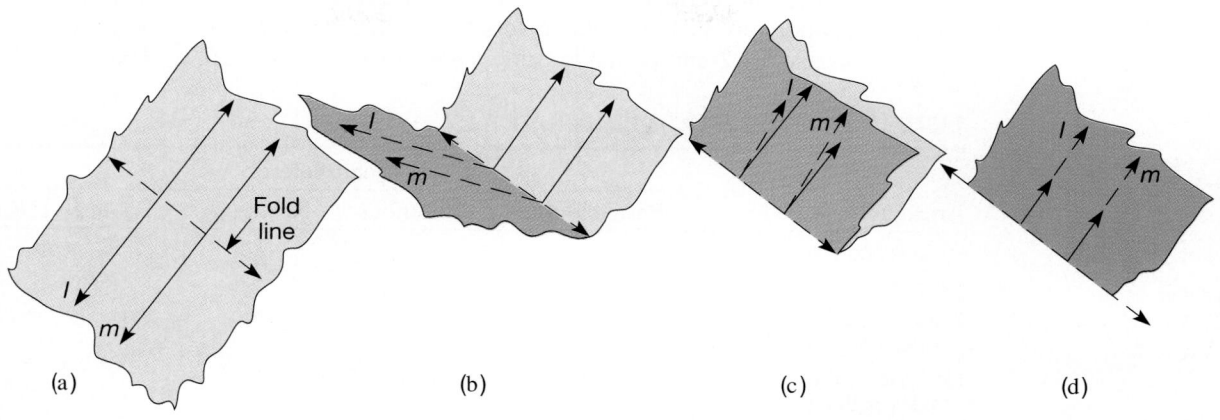

(a)   (b)   (c)   (d)

FIGURE 12.23

> **Parallel Line Segments Test**
>
> Fold so that *l* folds onto itself [Figure 12.23(a) to (c)]. (Any fold line can be used, as long as *l* folds onto itself.) Then *l* and *m* are parallel if and only if *m* folds onto itself or an extension of *m* [Figure 12.23(d)].

Example 12.7 is an application of the test for parallel line segments.

EXAMPLE 12.7   Show that the opposite sides of a rhombus are parallel.

Solution
Let *ABCD* be a rhombus [Figure 12.24(a)]. Fold so that side $\overline{AB}$ is folded onto itself [Figure 12.24(b)]. (Extend $\overline{AB}$ and/or $\overline{DC}$, if necessary.) Observe that side $\overline{DC}$ also folds onto itself. Thus $\overline{AB}$ and $\overline{DC}$ are parallel. Similarly, it can be shown that $\overline{AD}$ is parallel to $\overline{BC}$.

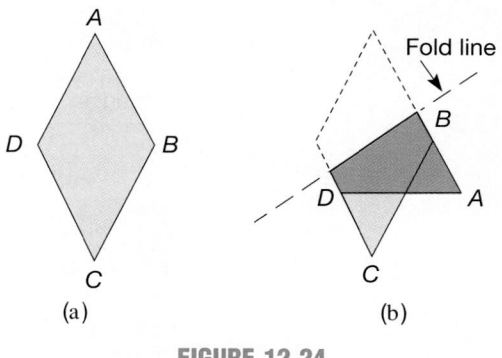

(a)   (b)

FIGURE 12.24   ■

Notice that Example 12.7 demonstrates that *every* rhombus is a parallelogram.

We can tabulate properties of figures and use them to make general comparisons. For example, Table 12.2 gives a list of properties of several types of quadrilaterals. We have demonstrated some of these attributes. Others are in the problem sets. Deductive verifications of the attributes in Table 12.2 can be made using ideas in Chapter 14, 15, or 16.

TABLE 12.2   ATTRIBUTES OF QUADRILATERALS

Attribute	Quadrilateral				
	Parallelogram	Rhombus	Rectangle	Square	Kite
All sides congruent		×		×	
All angles congruent			×	×	
Both pairs of opposite sides congruent	×	×	×	×	
Both pairs of opposite sides parallel	×	×	×	×	
Adjacent sides perpendicular			×	×	
Diagonals perpendicular		×		×	×
Has reflection symmetry		×	×	×	×
Has rotation symmetry	×	×	×	×	

Regular Polygons

A **simple closed curve** in the plane is a curve that can be traced with the same starting and stopping points, and without crossing or retracing any part of the curve (Figure 12.25). A simple closed "curve" made up of line segments is called a **polygon** (which means "many angles"). A polygon in which all sides are congruent and all angles are congruent is called a **regular polygon** or **regular n-gon**. Figure 12.26 shows several types of regular n-gons. The reflection and rotation symmetries of regular polygons are studied in the problem set. Notice that n denotes the number of sides and the

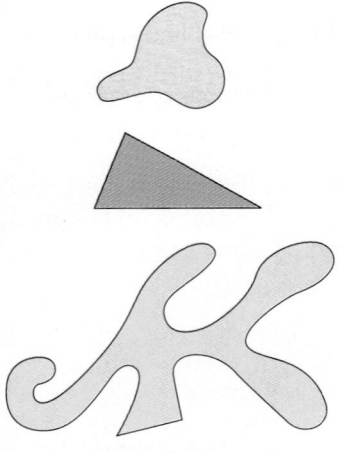

FIGURE 12.25

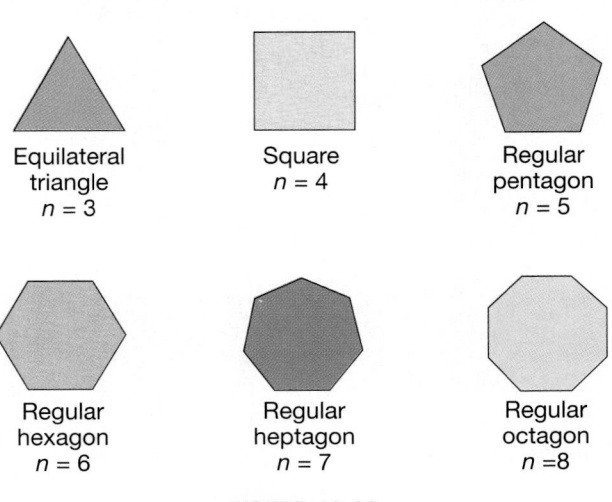

Equilateral triangle
$n = 3$

Square
$n = 4$

Regular pentagon
$n = 5$

Regular hexagon
$n = 6$

Regular heptagon
$n = 7$

Regular octagon
$n = 8$

FIGURE 12.26

number of angles. Since the number of sides in the figure can be any whole number greater than 2, there are infinitely many regular polygons.

The shapes in Figure 12.26 are called **convex**, since each has the following property: A line segment joining any two points inside the figure lies completely inside the figure. Figure 12.27 shows some convex, and nonconvex, called **concave**, two-dimensional shapes. It can be seen that all regular *n*-gons are convex.

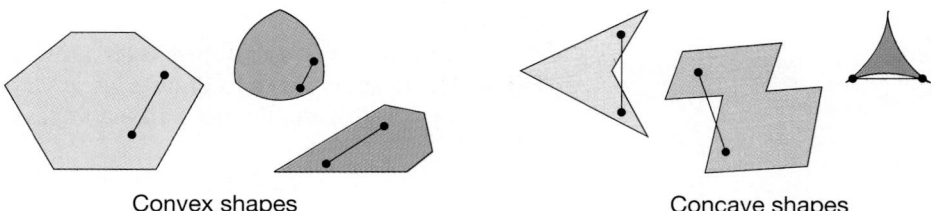

Convex shapes   Concave shapes

FIGURE 12.27

There are several angles of interest in regular *n*-gons. Figure 12.28 shows three of them: vertex angles, central angles, and exterior angles.

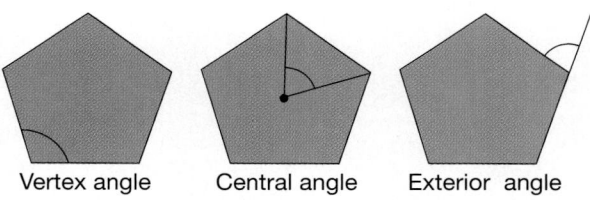

Vertex angle   Central angle   Exterior angle

FIGURE 12.28

A **vertex angle** (also called an **interior angle**) is formed by two consecutive sides. A **central angle** is formed by the segments connecting consecutive vertices to the center of the regular *n*-gon. An **exterior angle** is formed by one side together with an extension of an adjacent side of the regular *n*-gon, as pictured in Figure 12.28. Notice that the number of vertex angles and the sides of a regular polygon are the same. But there are twice as many exterior angles as interior angles. Vertex angles and exterior angles are formed in all convex shapes whose sides are line segments.

Circles

If we consider regular *n*-gons in which *n* is very large, we can obtain figures with many vertices, all of which are the same distance from the center. Figure 12.29 shows a regular 24-gon, for example. A **circle** is the set of *all* points in the plane that are a fixed distance from a given point (called the **center**). The distance from the center to a point on the circle is called the **radius** of the circle. Any segment whose endpoints are the center and a point of the circle is also called a radius. The length of a line segment whose endpoints are on the circle and which contains the center is called a **diameter** of the circle. The line segment itself is also called a diameter. Figure 12.30 shows several circles and their centers.

FIGURE 12.29

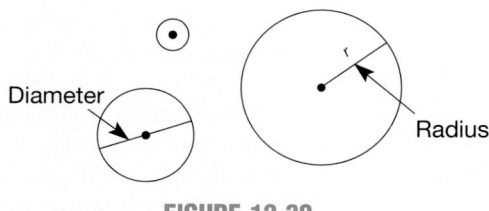

FIGURE 12.30

A **compass** is a useful device for drawing circles with different radii. Figure 12.31 shows how to draw a circle with a compass. We study techniques for constructing figures with a compass and straightedge in Chapter 14.

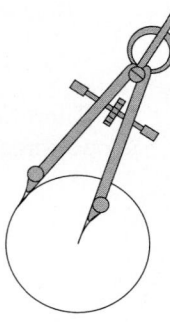

FIGURE 12.31

If we analyze a circle according to its symmetry properties, we find it has infinitely many lines of symmetry. Every line through the center the circle is a line of symmetry (Figure 12.32). Also, a circle has infini many rotation symmetries, since every angle whose vertex is the center the circle is an angle of rotation symmetry (Figure 12.33).

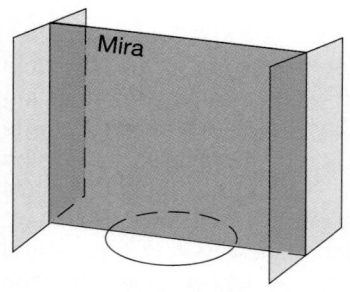

FIGURE 12.32

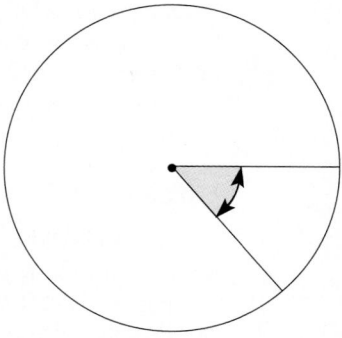

FIGURE 12.33

Many properties of a circle, including its area, are obtained by comparing the circle to regular n-gons with increasingly large values of n. We investigate several measurement properties of circles and other curved shapes in Chapter 13.

MATHEMATICAL MORSEL

Graph theory, originated by the Swiss mathematician Leonhard Euler, is a modern branch of mathematics that got its start in a most interesting way. In Euler's time, there were seven bridges crossing the Pregel River in Königsberg, Germany. Walking over the bridges from the riverbanks to the island and back was a favorite Sunday pastime. The question posed and answered by Euler, which supposedly led to the subject of graph theory, was: "Can one traverse all seven bridges without crossing any bridge twice?"

EXERCISE/PROBLEM SET 12.2—PART A

Exercises

1. Three of these figures are identical except for reflecting and/or rotating. Which figure is different from the others? Explain.

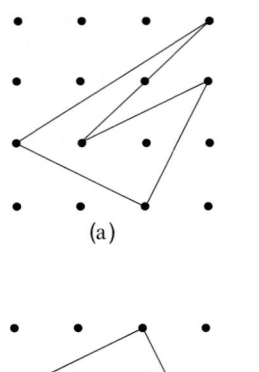
(a)

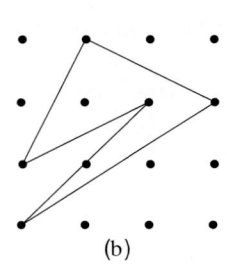
(b)

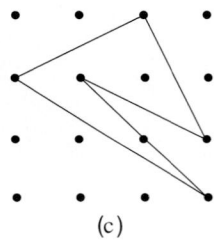
(c)

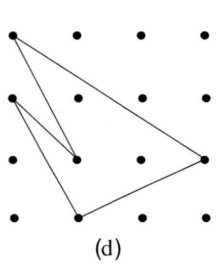
(d)

2. A square is a rectangle and a rhombus. List some properties of a square.

3. Draw the lines of symmetry in the following regular *n*-gons. How many does each have?

(a)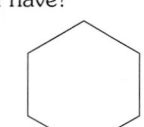

(b)

(c)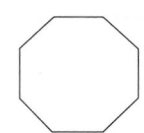

(d)

(e) This illustrates that a regular *n*-gon has how many lines of symmetry?

4. Given a regular *n*-gon, complete the following statements.
(a) If *n* is odd, each line of symmetry goes through a _____ and the _____ of the opposite side.
(b) If *n* is even, half of the lines of symmetry connect a _____ to the opposite _____. The other half connect the _____ of one side to the _____ of the opposite side.

5. How many lines of symmetry are there for each of the following national flags? Colors are indicated and should be considered.

(a) Argentina

Blue
white
blue

(b) Honduras

Blue
white
blue

(c) Israel

Blue design on white background

(d) Senegal

Green
yellow
red

6. Which of the following national flags have rotation symmetry? What are angles in each case (list measures between 0 and 360°)?

(a) United Kingdom

(b) Japan
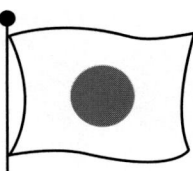

(c) Guatemala

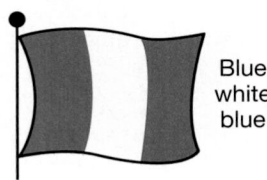

Blue
white
blue

7. For each of the following shapes, determine which of the following descriptions apply.

      S: simple closed curve
      C: convex, simple closed curve
      N: n-gon

(a)

(b)

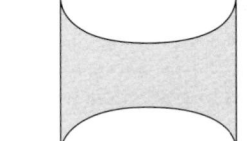

(c)

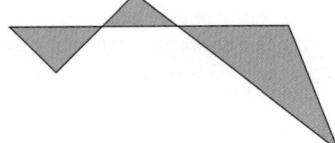

(d)

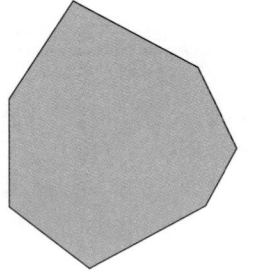

Problems

8. A **tetromino** is formed by connecting four squares so that connecting squares share a complete edge.

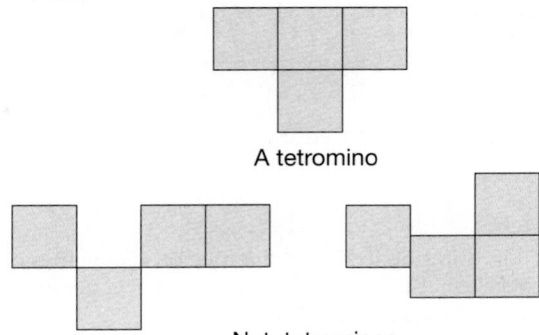

A tetromino

Not tetrominos

Find all the different tetrominos. That is, no two of your tetrominos can be superimposed by reflecting and/or rotating.

9. Make two copies of each tetromino shape. Arrange all of those pieces to cover a 5×8 rectangle.

10. (a) Which of the following pictures of sets best represents the relationship between isosceles triangles and scalene triangles? Label the sets and intersection (if it exists).

   (i)

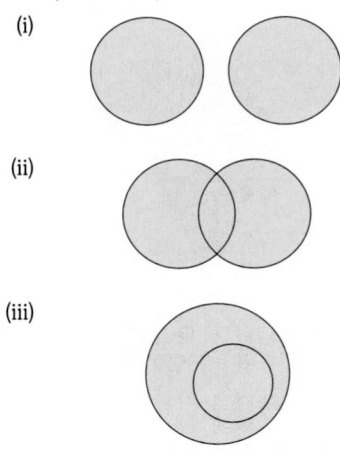

   (ii)

   (iii)

(b) Which represents the relationship between isosceles triangles and equilateral triangles?
(c) Which represents the relationship between isosceles triangles and right triangles?
(d) Which represents the relationship between equilateral triangles and right triangles?

11. Use a tracing to show that the diagonals of a rectangle are congruent.

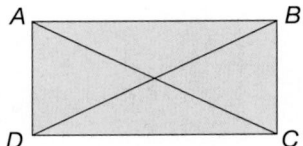

12. Use a tracing to find all the rotation symmetries of a square.

13. Use a tracing to find all the rotation symmetries of an equilateral triangle. (Hɪɴᴛ: The center is the intersection of the reflection lines.)

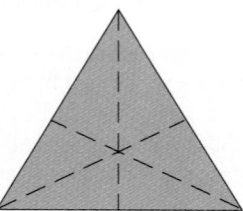

14. (a) Use paper folding to show that two of the opposite angles of a kite are congruent. Are the other angles congruent?

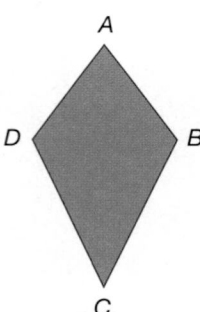

(b) What does the result in part (a) tell us about the opposite angles of a rhombus?

15. Use a tracing to show that the diagonals of a rhombus bisect each other.

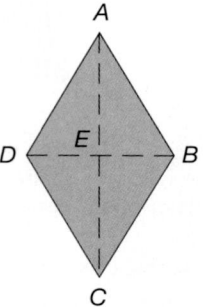

16. Use paper folding to show that the diagonals of a rhombus are perpendicular.

17. The following scalene triangle is formed from 14 toothpicks. We can describe this triangle as a 3–5–6 triangle.

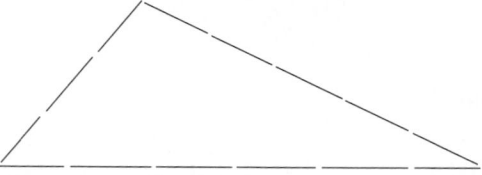

Use toothpicks to answer each of the following questions.

(a) How many different isosceles triangles can be formed using 20 toothpicks? (Nᴏᴛᴇ: You should have no gaps or overlapping toothpicks, nor can toothpicks be broken.) With 24 toothpicks?

(b) How many different scalene triangles can be formed using 20 toothpicks? With 24 toothpicks?

(c) How many different equilateral triangles can be formed using 20 toothpicks? With 24 toothpicks?

EXERCISE/PROBLEM SET 12.2—PART B

Exercises

1. Three of these shapes are identical except for reflecting and/or rotating. Which figure is different from the others? Explain.

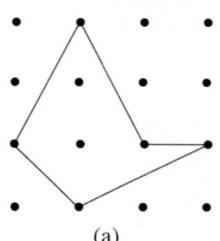

(a)

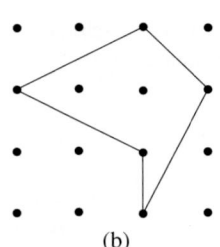

(b)

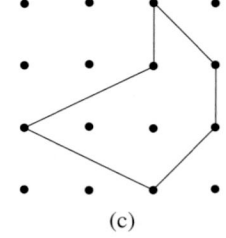

(c)

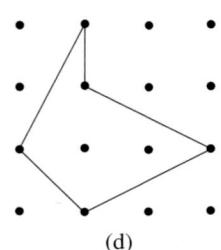

(d)

2. Determine the type(s) of symmetry for each figure. Indicate the lines of reflection symmetry and describe the turn symmetries.

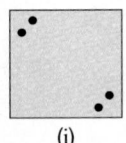 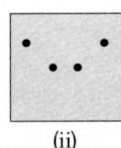 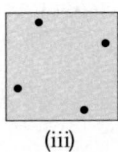 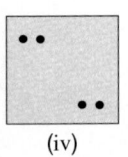

(i)   (ii)   (iii)   (iv)

3. Which capital letters of our alphabet have the following symmetry?
(a) Reflection symmetry in vertical line
(b) Reflection symmetry in horizontal line
(c) Rotation symmetry

4. If the 50 stars on the flag of the United States were considered as single points and arranged as illustrated, what symmetry does the arrangement have? Indicate lines or centers and turn angles.

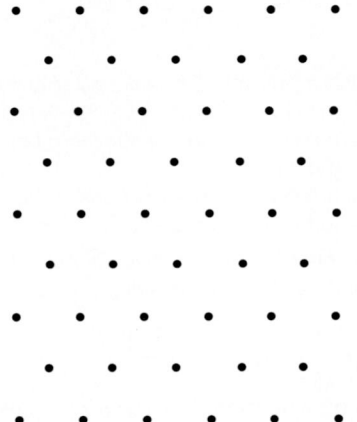

5. Given below are emblems from national flags. What types of symmetry do they have if color is ignored? Give lines or center and turn angle.
(a) Korea

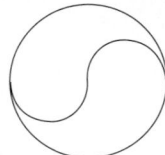

(b) Burundi

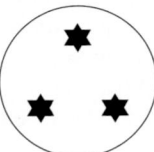

(c) Canada

(d) Taiwan

6. For each of the following shapes, determine which of the following descriptions apply.

    S: simple closed curve
    C: convex, simple closed curve
    N: *n*-gon

(a)

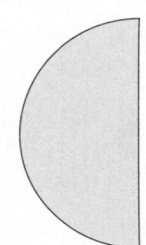

(b)

(c)

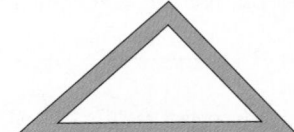

(d)

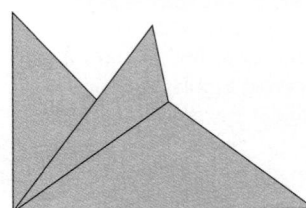

(e)

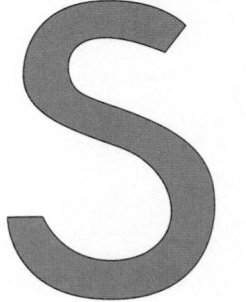

Problems

7. (a) Use paper folding to show that an isosceles trapezoid has reflection symmetry.

(b) In a trapezoid, the **bases** are the parallel sides. **Base angles** are a pair of angles that share a base as a common side. What does part (a) show about both pairs of base angles of an isosceles trapezoid?

8. Use a tracing to show that a rectangle has rotation symmetry.

9. Use a tracing to show that the opposite sides of a rectangle are congruent.

10. Use a tracing to show that the diagonals of a parallelogram bisect each other. That is, show that $\overline{AE}$ is congruent to $\overline{CE}$, and $\overline{DE}$ is congruent to $\overline{BE}$.

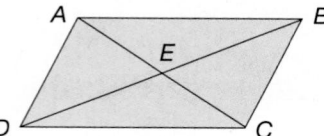

11. (a) Use a tracing to find all the rotation symmetries of the following regular n-gons.
  (i) Regular pentagon

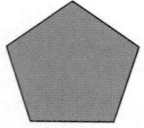

  (ii) Regular hexagon

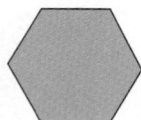

(b) How many rotation symmetries does each regular n-gon have?

12. (a) Which of the following pictures of sets best represents the relationship between rectangles and parallelograms? Label the sets and intersection (if it exists) appropriately.

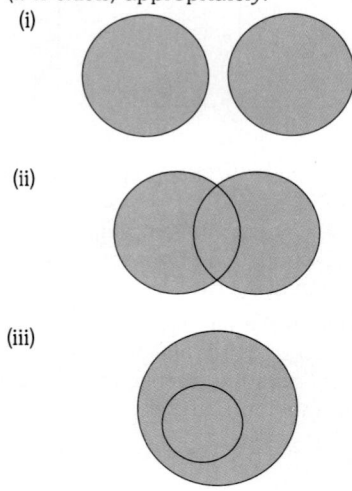

(b) Which represents the relationship between rectangles and rhombuses?
(c) Which represents the relationship between rectangles and squares?
(d) Which represents the relationship between rectangles and isosceles triangles?

13. A **pentomino** is made by five connected squares that touch only on a complete side.

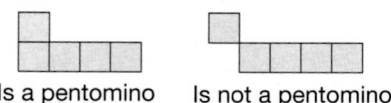

Two pentominoes are the same if they can be matched by turning or flipping.

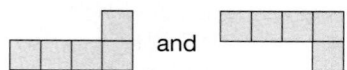

are the same as the one shown above. Find the twelve different pentomino shapes.

14. (a) Which of the pentominoes have reflection symmetry? Indicate the line(s) of reflection.
(b) Which of the pentominoes have rotation symmetry? Indicate the center and angle(s).

15. Look at your set of pentominoes. Which of the shapes can be folded into a cubical box without a top?

16. Find 3 pentomino shapes that can fit together to form a 3×5 rectangle.

17. Using 5 of the pentominoes, cover a 5×5 square.

18. Using each of the pentomino pieces once, make a 6×10 rectangle.

12.3

PROPERTIES OF GEOMETRIC SHAPES: LINES AND ANGLES

Points and Lines in a Plane

Imagine that our square lattice is made with more and more points, so that the points are closer and closer together. Imagine also that a point takes up no space. Figure 12.34 gives a conceptual idea of this "ideal" collection of points. Finally, imagine that our lattice extends in every direction in two dimensions, without restriction. This infinitely large flat surface is called a **plane**. We can think of the **points** as locations in the plane. If a line segment $\overline{AB}$ is extended infinitely in two directions as illustrated in Figure 12.35, the resulting figure is called a **line**. Lines are considered to be straight and extend infinitely in each direction [Figure 12.35(a)]. The notation $\overleftrightarrow{AB}$ denotes the line containing points A and B. The intuitive notions of point, line, and plane serve as the basis for the precise definitions that follow.

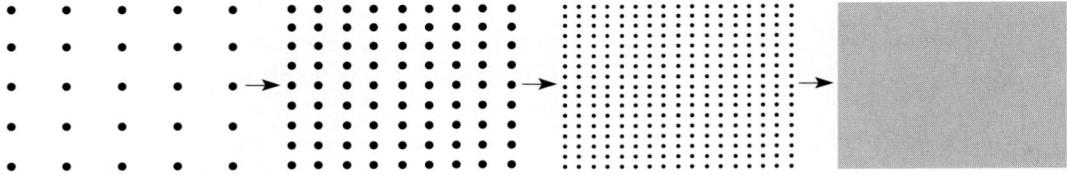

FIGURE 12.34

Points that lie on the same line are called **collinear points** [C, D, and E are collinear in Figure 12.35(b)]. Two lines *in the plane* are called **parallel lines** if they do not intersect [Figure 12.35(c)] or are the same. Thus a line is parallel to itself. Three or more lines that contain the same point are called **concurrent lines**. Lines l, m, and n in Figure 12.35(d) are concurrent, since they all contain point F. Lines r, s, and t in Figure 12.35(e) are not concurrent since no point in the plane belongs to all three lines.

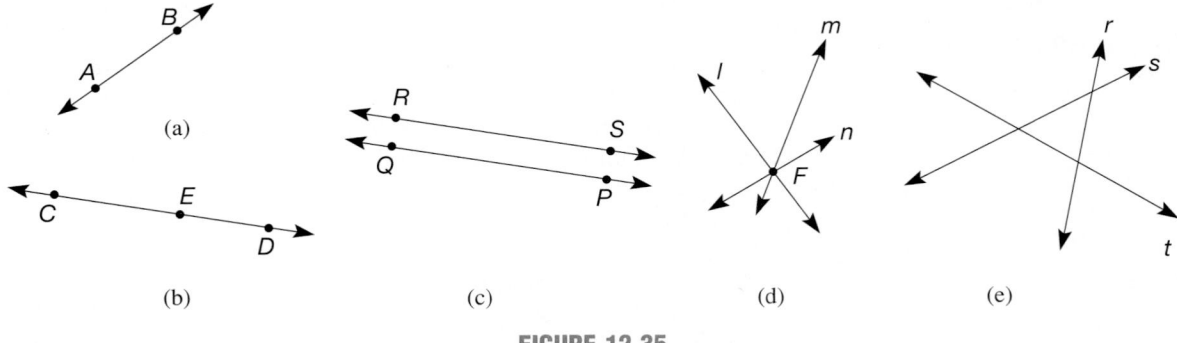

FIGURE 12.35

Because we cannot literally see the plane and its points, the geometric shapes that we will now study are abstractions. However, we can draw pictures and make models to help us imagine shapes, keeping in mind that the shapes exist only in our minds, just as numbers do. We will make certain assumptions about the plane and points in it. These have to do with lines in the plane and the distance between points.

Properties of Points and Lines

1. For each pair of points A, B $(A \neq B)$ in the plane, there is a unique line $\overleftrightarrow{AB}$ containing them.

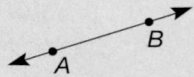

2. Each line can be viewed as a copy of the real number line. The **distance** between two points A and B is the nonnegative difference of the real numbers a and b to which A and B correspond. The distance from A to B is written AB or BA. The numbers a and b are called the **coordinates** of A and B on $\overleftrightarrow{AB}$.

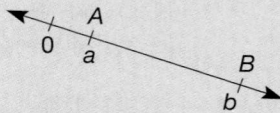

3. If a point P is not on a line l, there is a unique line m, $m \neq l$, such that P is on m and m is parallel to l. We write $m \parallel l$ to mean m is parallel to l.

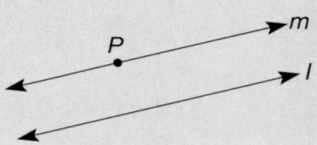

Line segment $\overline{AB}$

Ray $\overrightarrow{CD}$

FIGURE 12.36

FIGURE 12.37

We can use our properties of lines to define line segments, rays, and angles. A point P is between A and B if the coordinate of P with reference to line $\overleftrightarrow{AB}$ is numerically between the coordinates of A and B. In Figure 12.36, M and P are between A and B. The **line segment**, $\overline{AB}$, consists of all the points between A and B on line together with points A and B. Points A and B are called the **endpoints** of $\overline{AB}$. The **length** of line segment $\overline{AB}$ is the distance between A and B. The **midpoint**, M, of a line segment $\overline{AB}$ is the point of $\overline{AB}$ that is **equidistant** from A and B, that is, $AM = MB$. The **ray** $\overrightarrow{CD}$ consists of all points of line $\overleftrightarrow{CD}$ on the same side of C as point D, together with the endpoint C (Figure 12.36).

Angles

An **angle** is the union of two line segments with a common endpoint *or* the union of two rays with a common endpoint (Figure 12.37). The common endpoint is called the **vertex** of the angle. The line segments or rays comprising the angle are called its **sides**. Angles can be denoted by naming a nonvertex point on one side, then the vertex, followed by a nonvertex point on the other side. For example, Figure 12.37 shows angle BAC and angle EDF. Recall that the symbol $\angle BAC$ is used to denote angle BAC. (We could also call it $\angle CAB$.) We will use line segments and angles in studying various types of shapes in the plane, such as triangles and quadrilaterals.

An angle formed by two rays divides the plane into three regions: (1) the angle itself, (2) the **interior** of the angle (i.e., all the points in the plane between the two rays), and (3) the **exterior** of the angle (i.e., all points in the plane not in the angle or its interior). Figure 12.38 illustrates this.

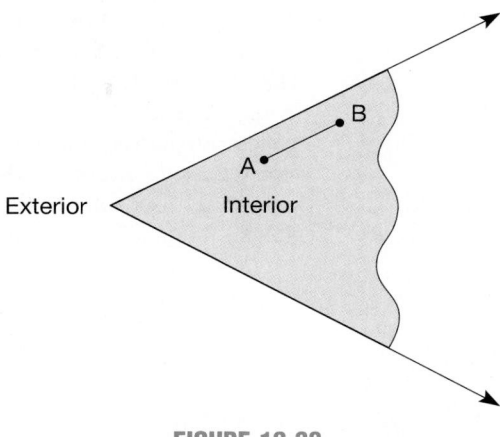

FIGURE 12.38

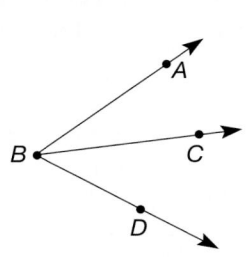

FIGURE 12.39

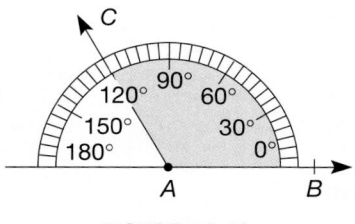

FIGURE 12.40

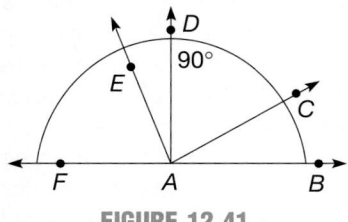

FIGURE 12.41

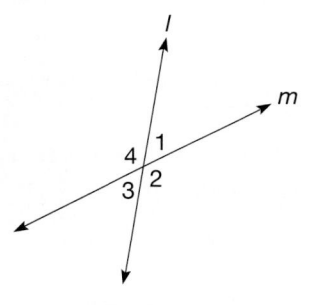

FIGURE 12.42

Notice that the interior of the angle is convex, whereas its exterior is concave. (If the two rays form a line, then the angle has no interior.) Two angles that share a vertex, have a side in common, but whose interiors do not intersect are called **adjacent angles**. In Figure 12.39, $\angle ABC$ and $\angle CBD$ are adjacent angles.

To measure angles, we use a semicircular device called a **protractor**. We place the center of the protractor at the vertex of the angle to be measured, with one side of the angle passing through the zero-degree (0°) mark (Figure 12.40). The protractor is evenly marked from 0 to 180°. (Degrees can be further subdivided into 60 minutes, and each minute into 60 seconds, or we can use nonnegative real numbers to report degrees, such as 27.428°.) The **measure of the angle** is equal to the real number on the protractor that the second side of the angle intersects. For example, the measure of $\angle BAC$ in Figure 12.40 is 120°. The measure of $\angle BAC$ will be denoted $m(\angle BAC)$. An angle measuring less than 90° is called an **acute angle**, an angle measuring 90° is called a **right angle**, and an angle measuring greater than 90° but less than 180° is an **obtuse angle**. An angle measuring 180° is called a **straight angle**. An angle whose measure is greater than 180° is called a **reflex angle**. In Figure 12.41, $\angle BAC$ is acute, $\angle BAD$ is a right angle, $\angle BAE$ is obtuse, and $\angle BAF$ is a straight angle.

When two lines intersect, several angles are formed. In Figure 12.42, lines l and m form four angles, $\angle 1$, $\angle 2$, $\angle 3$, and $\angle 4$. We see that

$$m(\angle 1) + m(\angle 2) = 180° \text{ and } m(\angle 3) + m(\angle 2) = 180°.$$

Hence

$$m(\angle 1) + m(\angle 2) = m(\angle 3) + m(\angle 2),$$

so that

$$m(\angle 1) = m(\angle 3).$$

Similarly, $m(\angle 2) = m(\angle 4)$. Angles 1 and 3 are called a pair of **vertical angles**; they are opposite each other and formed by a pair of intersecting lines. Similarly, angles 2 and 4 are a pair of vertical angles. We have demonstrated that vertical angles have the same measure. Recall that angles having the same opening, that is, the same measure, are called congruent; similarly, line segments having the same length are called congruent.

Two angles, the sum of whose measures is 180°, are called **supplementary angles**. In Figure 12.42 angles 1 and 2 are supplementary, as are angles 2 and 3. If two lines intersect to form a right angle, the lines are called **perpendicular**. Lines l and m in Figure 12.43 are perpendicular lines. We will write $l \perp m$ to denote that line l is perpendicular to line m. Two angles whose sum is 90° are called **complementary angles**. In Figure 12.43, angles 1 and 2 are complementary, as are angles 3 and 4.

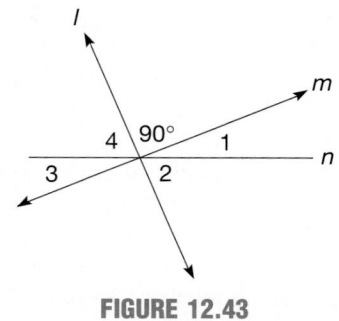

FIGURE 12.43

Angles Associated with Parallel Lines

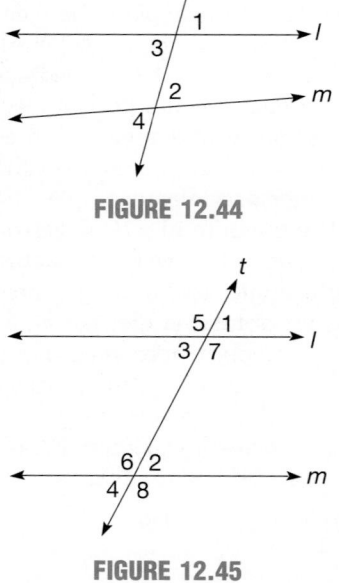

FIGURE 12.44

FIGURE 12.45

If two lines l and m are intersected by a third line, t, we call line t a **transversal** (Figure 12.44). The three lines in Figure 12.44 form many angles. Angles 1 and 2 are called **corresponding angles** since they are in the same locations relative to l, m, and t. Angles 3 and 4 are also corresponding angles. Our intuition tells us that if line l is parallel to line m (i.e., they point in the same direction), corresponding angles will have the same measure (Figure 12.45). Look at the various pairs of corresponding angles in Figure 12.45, where $l \parallel m$. Do they appear to have the same measure? Examples such as those in Figure 12.45 suggest the following property.

Corresponding Angles Property

Suppose that lines l and m are intersected by a transversal t. Then $l \parallel m$ if and only if corresponding angles formed by l, m, and t are congruent.

Using the corresponding angles property, we can prove that every rectangle is a parallelogram. This is left for the problem set.

EXAMPLE 12.8 In Figure 12.46, lines l and m are parallel. Show that $m(\angle 2) = m(\angle 3)$ using the corresponding angles property.

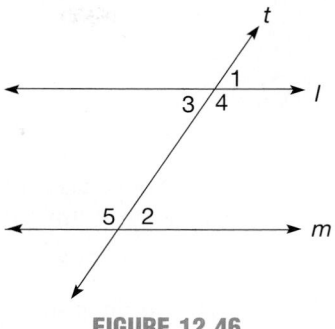

FIGURE 12.46

Solution
Since $l \parallel m$, by the corresponding angles property, $m(\angle 1) = m(\angle 2)$. But also, because $\angle 1$ and $\angle 3$ are vertical angles, we know that $m(\angle 1) = m(\angle 3)$. Hence $m(\angle 2) = m(\angle 3)$. ∎

In the configuration in Figure 12.46, the pair $\angle 2$ and $\angle 3$, and the pair $\angle 4$ and $\angle 5$ are called **alternate interior angles**, since they are nonadjacent angles formed by l, m, and t, the union of whose interiors contains the region between l and m. Similarly, $\angle 4$ and $\angle 5$ are alternate interior angles. Example 12.8 suggests another property of parallel lines and alternate interior angles.

Theorem

Alternate Interior Angles

Suppose that lines l and m are intersected by a transversal t. Then $l \parallel m$ if and only if alternate interior angles formed by l, m, and t are congruent.

The complete verification of this result is left for the problem set.
We can use this result to prove a very important property of triangles. Suppose that we have a triangle, $\triangle ABC$. (The notation $\triangle \textbf{ABC}$ denotes the triangle that is the union of line segments $\overline{AB}$, $\overline{BC}$, and $\overline{CA}$.) Let line $l = \overleftrightarrow{AC}$ (Figure 12.47). By part three of the properties of points and lines, there is

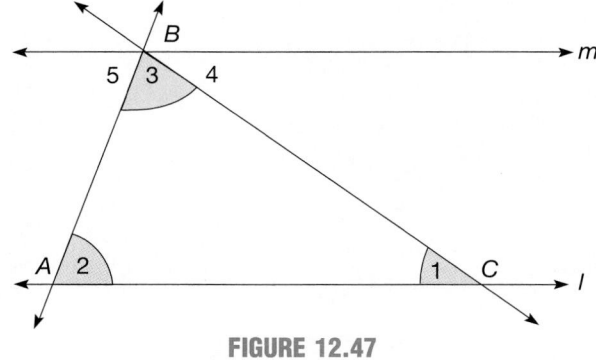

FIGURE 12.47

a line m parallel to l through point B in Figure 12.47. Then lines $\overleftrightarrow{AB}$ and $\overleftrightarrow{BC}$ are transversals for the parallel lines l and m. Hence $\angle 1$ and $\angle 4$ are congruent alternate interior angles. Similarly $m(\angle 2) = m(\angle 5)$. Summarizing, we have the following results:

$$m(\angle 1) = m(\angle 4),$$
$$m(\angle 2) = m(\angle 5),$$
$$m(\angle 3) = m(\angle 3).$$

Notice also that $m(\angle 5) + m(\angle 3) + m(\angle 4) = 180°$, since $\angle 5$, $\angle 3$, and $\angle 4$ form a straight angle. But from the observations above, we see that

$$m(\angle 1) + m(\angle 2) + m(\angle 3) = m(\angle 4) + m(\angle 5) + m(\angle 3) = 180°.$$

This result is summarized next.

> **Theorem**
>
> ### Angle Sum in a Triangle
>
> The sum of the measures of the three vertex angles in a triangle is 180°.

As a consequence of this result, a triangle can have at most one right angle or at most one obtuse angle. A triangle with a right angle is called a **right triangle**, a triangle with an obtuse angle is called an **obtuse triangle**, and a triangle in which *all* angles are acute is called an **acute triangle**. For right triangles, we note that two of the vertex angles must be acute and their sum is 90°. Hence they are complementary. In Figure 12.48, $\angle 1$ and $\angle 2$ are complementary, as are $\angle 3$ and $\angle 4$. Notice in Figure 12.48 that a small symbol "⌐" is used to indicate a right angle.

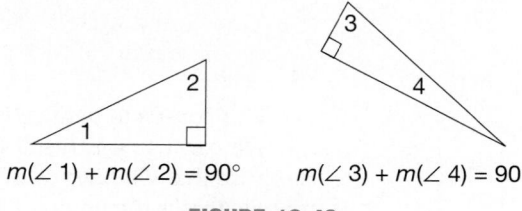

$$m(\angle\, 1) + m(\angle\, 2) = 90° \qquad m(\angle\, 3) + m(\angle\, 4) = 90°$$

FIGURE 12.48

MATHEMATICAL MORSEL

Euler's formula, which relates the number of vertices, edges, and faces of simple polyhedra such as the cube, regular tetrahedron, and so on, is an interesting result about surfaces. Another result about surfaces is due to A. F. Moebius. Start with a rectangular strip *ABCD*. Twist the strip one-half turn to form the "twisted" strip *ABCD*. Then tape the two ends *AB* to *CD* to form a "twisted loop." Then draw a continuous line down the middle of one side of the loop. What did you find? Next, cut the loop on the line you drew. What did you find? Repeat drawing a line down the middle of the new loop and cutting one more time. Surprise!

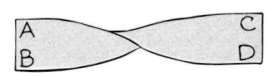
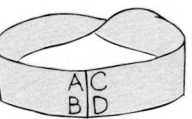

EXERCISE/PROBLEM SET 12.3—PART A

Exercises

1. (a) How many angles are shown in the following figure?

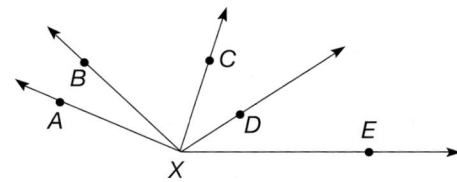

(b) How many are obtuse?
(c) How many are acute?

2. Given the following, how many other segments could be drawn that are parallel to the given segment (but not collinear with it)?

(a)

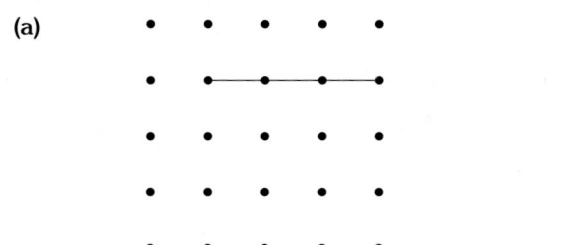

(b)

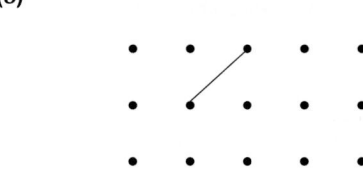

(c)

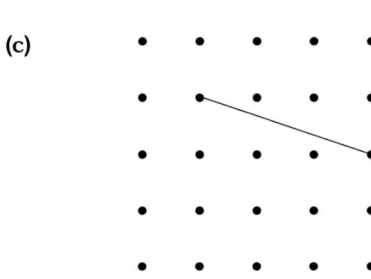

3. Determine which of the following angles represented on a square lattice are right angles. If one isn't, is it acute or obtuse?

(a)

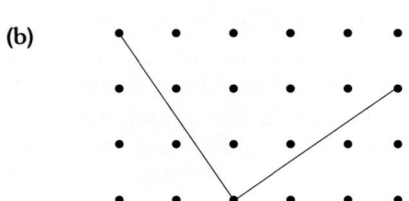

(b)

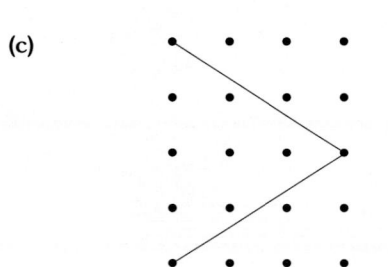

(c)

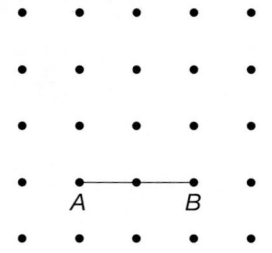

4. Consider the square lattice shown here.

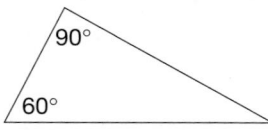

(a) How many triangles have $\overline{AB}$ as one side?
(b) How many of these are isosceles?
(c) How many are right triangles?
(d) How many are acute?
(e) How many are obtuse?

5. Find the missing angle measure in the following triangles.

(a)

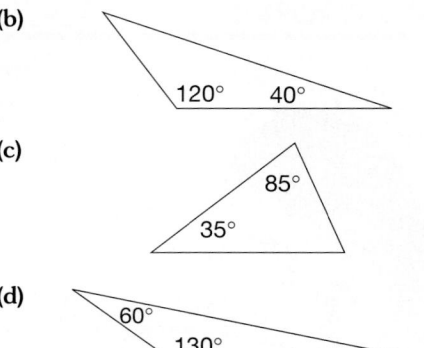

(b)

(c)

(d)

6. Use your ruler and protractor to draw each of the following shapes. Then measure ∠C and diagonal $\overline{AC}$.

(a)

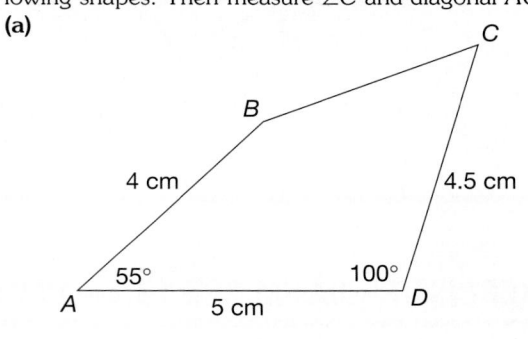

(b)

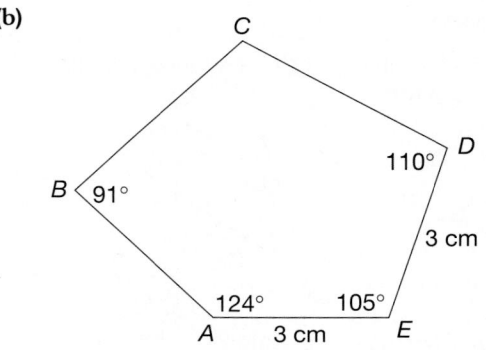

7. Use your protractor to measure angles with dots on their vertices in the following semicircle. Make a conjecture based on your findings.

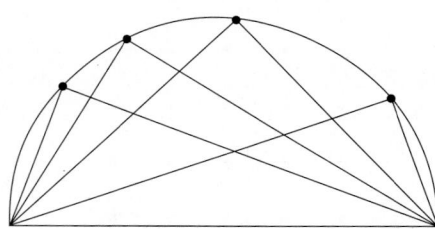

Problems

8. In the figure, $m(\angle BFC) = 55°$, $m(\angle AFD) = 150°$, and $m(\angle BFE) = 120°$. Determine the measures of $\angle AFB$ and $\angle CFD$. (NOTE: Do *not* measure the angles with your protractor to determine these measures.)

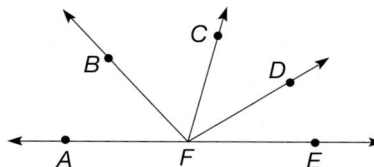

9. In the following figure, the measure of $\angle 1$ is 9° less than half the measure of $\angle 2$. Determine the measures of $\angle 1$ and $\angle 2$.

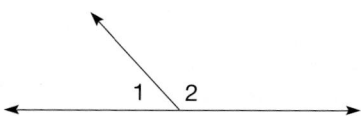

10. Determine the measures of the numbered angles if $m(\angle 1) = 80°$ and $m(\angle 4) = 125°$, and l is parallel to m.

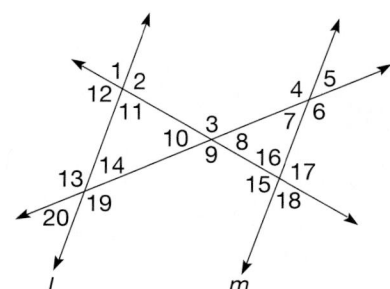

11. The first part of the alternate interior angles theorem was verified in Example 12.8. Verify the second part of the alternate interior angles theorem. In particular, assume that $m(\angle 1) = m(\angle 2)$ and show that $l \parallel m$.

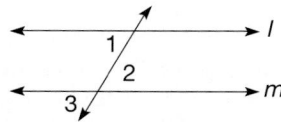

12. Angles 1 and 6 are called **alternate exterior angles**. (Can you see why?) Prove the following statements.

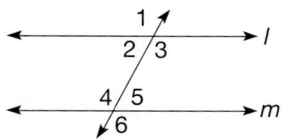

(a) If $m(\angle 1) = m(\angle 6)$, then $l \parallel m$.

(b) If $l \parallel m$, then $m(\angle 1) = m(\angle 6)$.

(c) State the results of parts (a) and (b) as a general property.

13. If $\angle A$ and $\angle B$ are complementary, but $m(\angle A)$ is four times as large as $m(\angle B)$ find the measure of $\angle A$.

14. Using the corresponding angles property, prove that rectangle $ABCD$ is a parallelogram.

15. (a) Given a square and a circle, draw an example where they intersect in exactly the number of points given.
  (i) No points   (ii) One point
  (iii) Two points   (iv) Three points
  (b) What is the greatest number of possible points of intersection?

16. (a) Given a triangle and a circle, draw an example where they intersect in exactly the number of points given.
  (i) No points   (ii) One point
  (iii) Two points   (iv) Three points
  (b) What is the greatest number of possible points of intersection?

17. Two lines drawn in a plane separate the plane into three different regions if the lines are parallel.

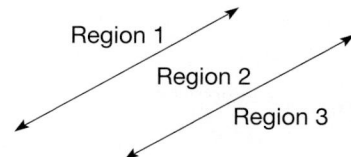

If the lines are intersecting, then they will divide the plane into four regions.

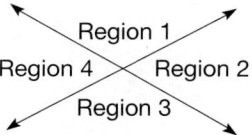

Thus, the greatest number of regions two lines may divide a plane into is four. Determine the greatest number of regions into which a plane can be divided by three lines, four lines, five lines, and ten lines. Generalize to n lines.

EXERCISE/PROBLEM SET 12.3—PART B

Exercises

1. How many different line segments are contained in the following portion of a line?

A   B   C D   E   F

2. Find the angle measure of the following angles drawn on triangular lattices. Use your protractor if necessary.

(a)

(b)

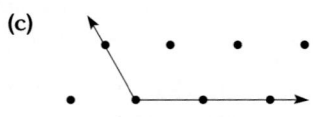

(c)

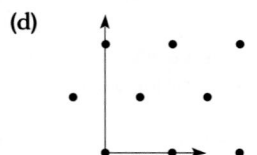

(d)

3. Given the square lattice shown, answer the following questions.

(a) How many triangles have $\overline{AB}$ as one side?
(b) How many of these are right triangles?
(c) How many are acute triangles?
(d) How many are obtuse triangles? [HINT: Use your answers to parts (a) to (c).]

4. Consider the following sets.

T = all triangles   A = acute triangles
S = scalene triangles   R = right triangles
I = isosceles triangles   O = obtuse triangles
E = equilateral triangles

Draw an example of an element of the following sets, if possible.
(a) $S \cap A$ **(b)** $I \cap O$ **(c)** $O \cap E$
(d) $S \cap R$ **(e)** $T - (A \cup O)$ **(f)** $T - (R \cup S)$

5. Given below are the measures of $\angle A$, $\angle B$, and $\angle C$. Can a triangle $\triangle ABC$ be made that has the given angles? Explain.
(a) $m(\angle A) = 36$, $m(\angle B) = 78$, $m(\angle C) = 66$
(b) $m(\angle A) = 124$, $m(\angle B) = 56$, $m(\angle C) = 20$
(c) $m(\angle A) = 90$, $m(\angle B) = 74$, $m(\angle C) = 18$

6. Use your ruler and protractor to draw each of the following shapes. Then measure $\angle C$ and $\overline{AC}$.

(a)

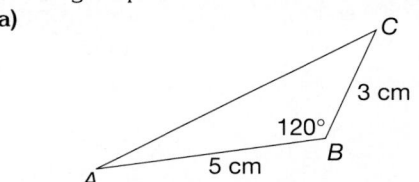

(b)

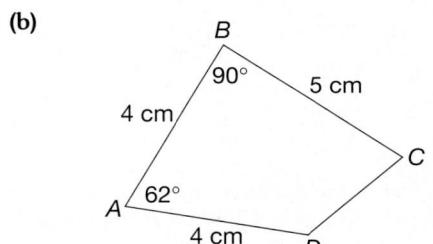

Problems

7. In the following figure $\overline{AO}$ is perpendicular to $\overline{CO}$. If $m(\angle AOD) = 165°$ and $m(\angle BOD) = 82°$, determine the measures of $\angle AOB$ and $\angle BOC$. (NOTE: Do not measure the angles with your protractor to determine these measures.)

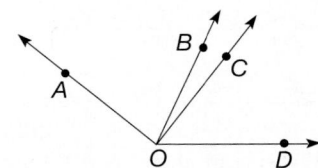

8. In the following figure, the measure of ∠1 is 14° less than twice the measure of ∠2. Without using a protractor, determine the measures of ∠1 and ∠2. Round your answers to the nearest hundredth of a degree.

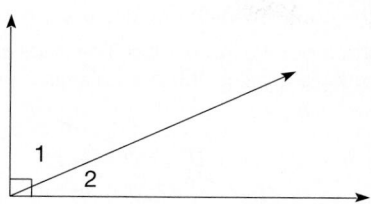

9. The measure of ∠X is 9° more than twice the measure of ∠Y. If ∠X and ∠Y are supplementary angles, find the measure of ∠X.

10. In this section we assumed that the corresponding angles property was true. Then we verified the alternate interior angles theorem. Some geometry books assume the alternate interior angles theorem to be true and build results from there. Assume that the only parallel line test we have is the alternate interior angles theorem and show the following to be true.

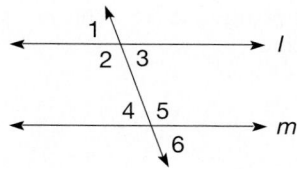

(a) If $l \parallel m$, then corresponding angles have the same measure, namely, $m(\angle 1) = m(\angle 4)$.
(b) If $m(\angle 3) = m(\angle 6)$, then $l \parallel m$.

11. Angles 1 and 3 are called **interior angles on the same side of the transversal**.

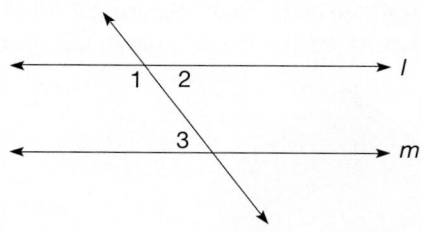

(a) If $l \parallel m$, what is true about $m(\angle 1) + m(\angle 3)$?
(b) Can you show the converse of the result in part (a), that if your conclusion about $m(\angle 1) + m(\angle 3)$ is satisfied, then $l \parallel m$?

12. Find the measures of ∠1, ∠2, ∠3, and ∠4 if some angles formed are related as shown.

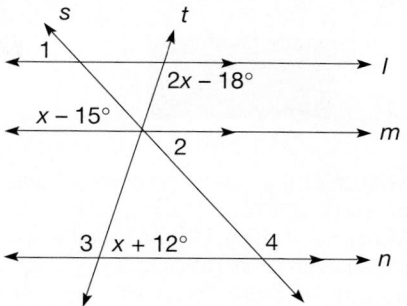

13. In parallelogram $ABCD$, ∠1 and ∠2 are called **consecutive angles**, as are ∠2 and ∠3, ∠3 and ∠4, ∠4 and ∠1. using the results of Problem 11, what can you conclude about any two consecutive angles of a parallelogram? What can you conclude about two opposite angles (e.g., ∠1 and ∠3)?

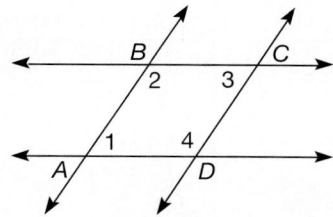

14. Draw a large copy of △ABC on scratch paper and cut it out.

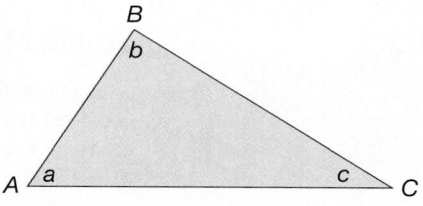

Fold down vertex B so that it lies on $\overline{AC}$ and so that the fold line is parallel to $\overline{AC}$.

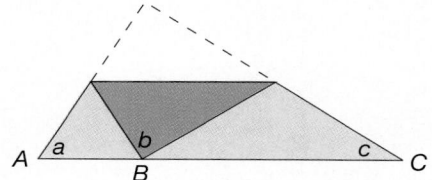

Now fold vertices A and C into point B.

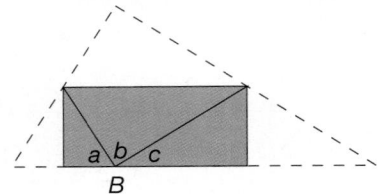

(a) What does the resulting figure tell you about the measures of $\angle A$, $\angle B$, and $\angle C$? Explain.
(b) What kind of polygon is the folded shape, and what is the length of its base?
(c) Try this same procedure with two other types of triangles. Are the results the same?

15. A famous problem, posed by puzzler Henry Dudenay, presented the following situation. Suppose that houses are located at points A, B, and C. We want to connect each house to water, electricity, and gas located at points W, G, and E, without any of the pipes/wires crossing each other.

(a) Try making all of the connections. Can it be done? If so, how?
(b) Suppose that the owner of one of the houses, say B, is willing to let the pipe for one of his neighbors' connections pass through his house. Then can all of the connections be made? If so, how?

16. Given three points, there is one line that can be drawn through them if the points are collinear.

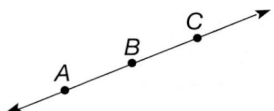

If the three points are noncollinear, there are three lines that can be drawn through pairs of points.

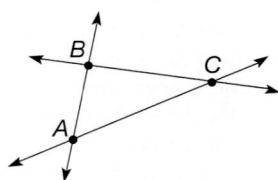

For three points, three is the greatest number of lines that can be drawn through pairs of points. Determine the greatest number of lines that can be drawn for four points, five points, and six points in a plane. Generalize to n points.

12.4

REGULAR POLYGONS AND TESSELLATIONS

Angle Measures in Regular Polygons

A regular polygon (or regular n-gon) is both equilateral and equiangular. To find the measure of a central angle in a regular n-gon, notice that the sum of the measures of n central angles is $360°$. Figure 12.49 illustrates this for $n = 5$. Hence the measure of each central angle in a regular n-gon is $\dfrac{360°}{n}$.

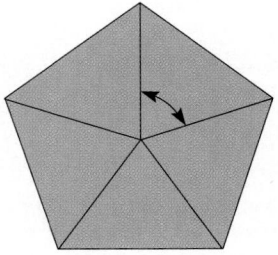

FIGURE 12.49

We can find the measure of the vertex angles in a regular n-gon by using the angle sum in a triangle property. Consider a regular pentagon ($n = 5$; Figure 12.50). Let us call the vertex angles $\angle v_1$, $\angle v_2$, $\angle v_3$, $\angle v_4$, and $\angle v_5$.

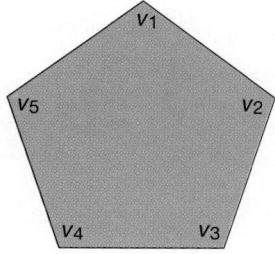

FIGURE 12.50

Since all the vertex angles have the same measure, it suffices to find the vertex angle *sum* in the regular pentagon. The measure of each vertex angle, then, is one-fifth of this sum.

To find this sum, subdivide the pentagon into triangles using diagonals $\overline{AC}$ and $\overline{AD}$ (Figure 12.51). For example, vertices A, B, and C are the

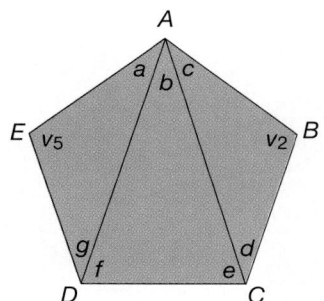

FIGURE 12.51

vertices of a triangle, specifically $\triangle ABC$. Several new angles are formed, namely $\angle a$, $\angle b$, $\angle c$, $\angle d$, $\angle e$, $\angle f$, and $\angle g$. Notice that

$$m(\angle v_1) = m(\angle a) + m(\angle b) + m(\angle c),$$
$$m(\angle v_3) = m(\angle d) + m(\angle e),$$

and

$$m(\angle v_4) = m(\angle f) + m(\angle g).$$

Within each triangle ($\triangle ABC$, $\triangle ACD$, and $\triangle ADE$), we know that the angle sum is $180°$. Hence

$$m(\angle v_1) + m(\angle v_2) + m(\angle v_3) + m(\angle v_4) + m(\angle v_5)$$
$$= m(\angle a) + m(\angle b) + m(\angle c) + m(\angle v_2) + m(\angle d)$$
$$+ m(\angle e) + m(\angle f) + m(\angle g) + m(\angle v_5)$$
$$= [m(\angle c) + m(\angle v_2) + m(\angle d)] + [m(\angle b) + m(\angle e) + m(\angle f)]$$
$$+ [m(\angle g) + m(\angle v_5) + m(\angle a)]$$
$$= 180° + 180° + 180°$$

since each bracketed sum is the angle sum in a triangle. Hence the angle sum in a regular pentagon is $3 \times 180° = 540°$. Finally, the measure of each vertex angle in the regular pentagon is $540° ÷ 5 = 108°$. The technique used here of forming triangles within the polygon can be used to find the sum of the vertex angles in any polygon.

Table 12.3 suggests a way of computing the measure of a vertex angle in a regular n-gon, for $n = 3, 4, 5, 6, 7, 8$. Verify the entries.

TABLE 12.3

	n	Angle Sum in a Regular n-gon	Measure of a Vertex Angle
▲	3	$1 \cdot 180°$	$180° ÷ 3 = 60°$
◻	4	$2 \cdot 180°$	$(2 \times 180°) ÷ 4 = 90°$
⬠	5	$3 \cdot 180°$	$(3 \times 180°) ÷ 5 = 108°$
⬡	6	$4 \cdot 180°$	$(4 \times 180°) ÷ 6 = 120°$
⬣	7	$5 \cdot 180°$	$(5 \times 180°) ÷ 7 = 128\frac{4}{7}°$
⯃	8	$6 \cdot 180°$	$(6 \times 180°) ÷ 8 = 135°$

The entries in Table 12.3 suggest a formula for the measure of the vertex angle in a regular n-gon. In particular, we can subdivide any n-gon into $(n - 2)$ triangles. Since each triangle has an angle sum of $180°$, the angle sum in a regular n-gon is $(n - 2) \cdot 180°$. Thus each vertex angle will measure $\dfrac{(n - 2) \cdot 180°}{n}$. We can also express this as $\dfrac{180°n - 360°}{n} = 180° - \dfrac{360°}{n}$. Thus any vertex angle is supplementary to any central angle.

To measure the exterior angles in a regular n-gon, notice that the sum of a vertex angle and an exterior angle will be $180°$, by the way the exterior angle is formed (Figure 12.52). Hence, each exterior angle will measure $180° - \left[180° - \dfrac{360°}{n} \right] = 180° - 180° + \dfrac{360°}{n} = \dfrac{360°}{n}$. Therefore, the measure of any exterior angle is the same as the measure of a central angle!

We can summarize our results about angle measures in regular polygons as follows.

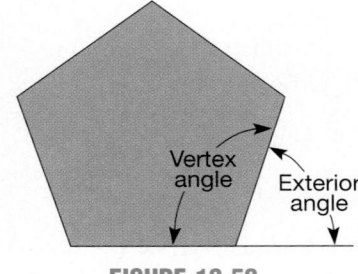

Vertex angle

Exterior angle

FIGURE 12.52

Theorem		
Angle Measures in a Regular n-gon		
Vertex Angle $\dfrac{(n-2) \cdot 180°}{n}$	Central Angle $\dfrac{360°}{n}$	Exterior Angle $\dfrac{360°}{n}$

Remember that these results hold only for angles in *regular* polygons—not necessarily in arbitrary polygons. In the problem set, the central angle measure will be used when discussing rotation symmetry of polygons. We will use the vertex angle measure in the next section on tessellations.

Tessellations

A **polygonal region** is a polygon together with its interior. An arrangement of polygonal regions having only sides in common that completely covers the plane is called a **tessellation**. We can form tessellations with arbitrary triangles, as Figure 12.53 shows. Pattern (a) shows a tessellation with a scalene right triangle, pattern (b) shows a tessellation with an acute isosceles triangle, and pattern (c) shows a tessellation with an obtuse scalene triangle. Note that angles measuring *x, y,* and *z* meet at each vertex to form a straight angle. As suggested by Figure 12.53, every triangle will tessellate the plane.

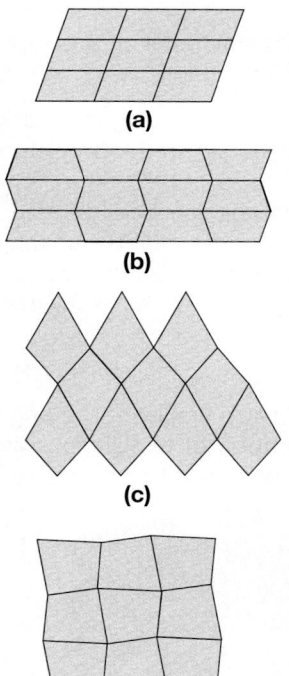

(a)

(b)

(c)

(d)

FIGURE 12.54

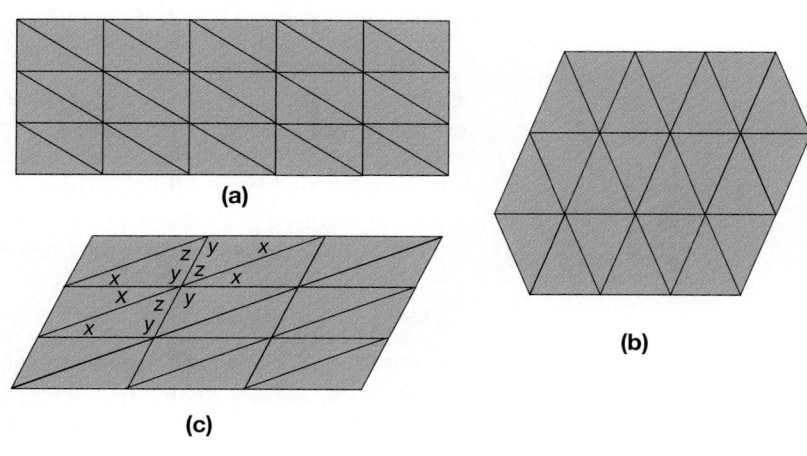

(a)

(c)

(b)

FIGURE 12.53

Every quadrilateral will form a tessellation also. Figure 12.54 shows several tessellations with quadrilaterals. In pattern (a) we see a tessellation with a parallelogram, in pattern (b), a tessellation with a trapezoid, and in pattern (c), a tessellation with a kite. Pattern (d) shows a tessellation with an arbitrary quadrilateral of no special type. We can form a tessellation, starting with *any* quadrilateral, by using the following procedure (Figure 12.55).

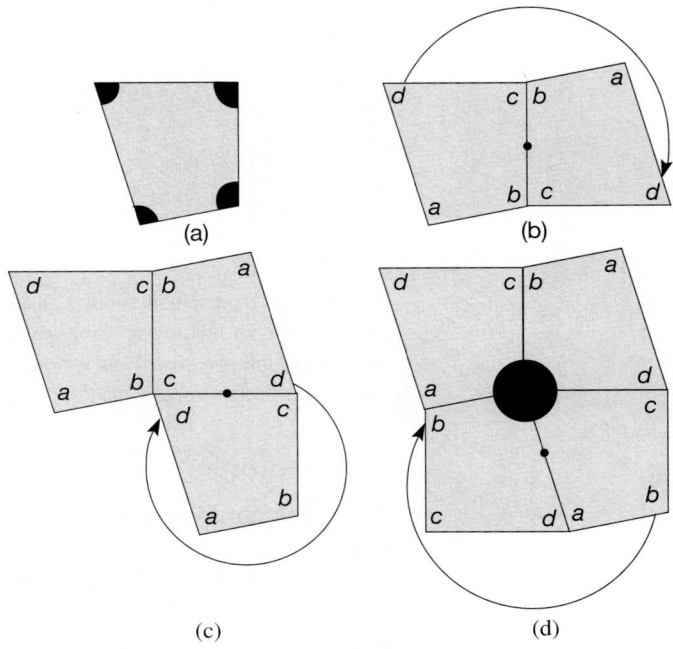

FIGURE 12.55

1. Trace the quadrilateral [Figure 12.55(a)].
2. Rotate the quadrilateral 180° around the midpoint of any side. Trace the image [Figure 12.55(b)].
3. Continue rotating the image 180° around the midpoint of each of its sides and trace the new image [Figure 12.55(c) and (d)].

The rotation procedure described here can be applied to any triangle and to any quadrilateral, even nonconvex quadrilaterals. In the problem set we will investigate such tessellations.

Several results about triangles and quadrilaterals can be illustrated by tessellations. In Figure 12.53(c) we see that $x + y + z = 180°$, a straight angle. In Figure 12.55(d) we see that $a + b + c + d = 360°$ for the quadrilateral. Other results illustrated by tessellations appear in the problem set.

Tessellations with Regular Polygons

Figure 12.56 shows some tessellations with equilateral triangles, squares, and regular hexagons. These are examples of tessellations each composed of copies of one regular polygon. Such tessellations are called

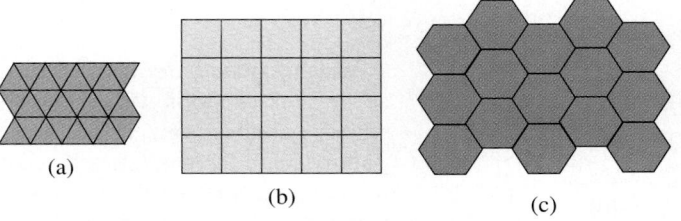

FIGURE 12.56

regular tessellations. Notice that in pattern (a), six equilateral triangles meet at each vertex, in pattern (b) four squares meet at each vertex, and in pattern (c), three hexagons meet at each vertex. We say that the **vertex arrangement** in pattern (a), that is, the configuration of regular polygons meeting at a vertex, is (3, 3, 3, 3, 3, 3). This sequence of six 3s indicates that six equilateral triangles meet at each vertex. Similarly, the vertex arrangement in pattern (b) is (4, 4, 4, 4), and in pattern (c) it is (6,6,6), for three hexagons.

Consider the measures of vertex angles in several regular polygons (Table 12.4). In order for a regular polygon to form a tessellation, its vertex angle must be a divisor of 360, since a whole number of copies of the polygon must meet at a vertex to form a 360° angle. Clearly, regular 3-gons (equilateral triangles), 4-gons (squares), and 6-gons (regular hexagons) will work. Their vertex angles measure 60°, 90°, and 120°, respectively, each measure being a divisor of 360°. For a regular pentagon, the vertex angle measures 108°, and since 108 is not a divisor of 360, we know that regular pentagons will not fit together without gaps or overlapping. Figure 12.57 illustrates this fact.

TABLE 12.4

n	Measure of Vertex Angle in a Regular n-gon
3	60°
4	90°
5	108°
6	120°
7	$128\frac{4}{7}°$
8	135°
9	140°
10	144°
11	$147\frac{3}{11}°$
12	150°

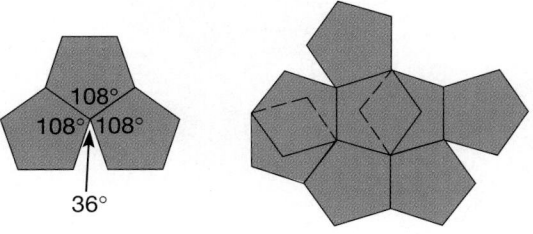

FIGURE 12.57

For regular polygons with more than six sides, the vertex angles are larger than 120° (and less than 180°). At least three regular polygons must meet at each vertex, yet the vertex angles in such polygons are too large to make exactly 360° with three or more of them fitting together. Hence we have the following result.

Theorem

Tessellations with Regular n-gons

Only regular 3-gons, 4-gons, or 6-gons form tessellations of the plane by themselves.

If we allow several different regular polygons with sides the same length to form a tessellation, many other possibilities result, as Figure 12.58 on page 578 shows. Notice in Figure 12.58(d) that several different vertex arrangements are possible. Tessellations such as those in Figure 12.58 appear in patterns for floor and wall coverings and other symmetrical designs. These tessellations using two or more regular polygons are called **semiregular tessellations** if their vertex arrangements are identical. In Chapter 16 we see how the artist M. C. Escher made use of tessellations with polygons to create exotic tessellating patterns.

(4, 8, 8)

(a)

(3, 6, 3, 6)

(b)

(4, 6, 12)

(c)

(3, 3, 3, 3, 3, 3)
(3, 3, 4, 3, 4), (3, 3, 4, 12)

(d)

FIGURE 12.58

MATHEMATICAL MORSEL

So, what do you think? Have you ever seen anything like this shape?

One of the more exciting discoveries in chemistry in modern time is the third pure form of carbon, after graphite and diamonds. These molecules, called Buckyballs since they resemble the geodesic domes of Buckminister Fuller, are like a chicken–wire "sphere" composed of 12 regular pentagons and 20 regular hexagons. As one story goes, a chemist who was working on this discovery called a mathematician to see if he had ever seen anything like this shape. The mathematician replied "You've discovered the exterior of a soccer ball" (the technical name of the shape is a truncated icosahedron). Many times throughout history, mathematicians have studied structures and their properties in the absence of a context, only to find later that their discoveries lead to significant practical applications.

EXERCISE/PROBLEM SET 12.4—PART A

Exercises

1. Use your protractor to measure each vertex angle in each polygon shown below. Extend the sides of the polygon, if necessary. Then find the sum of the measures of the vertex angles. What *should* the sum be in each case?

(a)

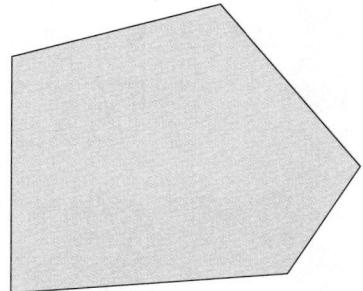

(b)

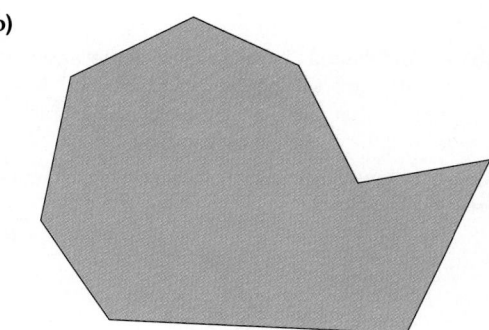

2. Find the missing angle measures in each of the quadrilaterals shown below.

(a)

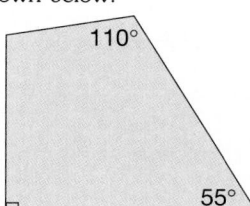

(b)

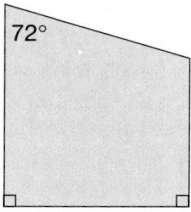

(c)

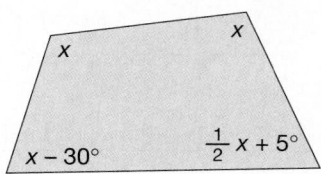

3. For the following regular *n*-gons, give the measure of a vertex angle, a central angle, and an exterior angle.
(a) 12-gon   **(b)** 16-gon   **(c)** 10-gon
(d) 20-gon   **(e)** 18-gon   **(f)** 36-gon

4. Given are the measures of the vertex angles of regular polygons. What is the measure of the central angle of each one?
(a) 90°   **(b)** 176°   **(c)** 150°   **(d)** $x°$

5. Each vertex angle of a regular polygon measures 165.6°. How many sides does the polygon have?

6. Given are the measures of the exterior angles of regular polygons. How many sides does each one have?
(a) 9°   **(b)** 45°   **(c)** 10°   **(d)** 3°

7. The formula given for the vertex angle of a regular polygon is $\dfrac{(n-2)}{n} \cdot 180$.

(a) Is $\dfrac{n-2}{n}$ greater than 1 or less than 1?

(b) Is $\dfrac{(n-2)}{n} \cdot 180$ greater than 180 or less than 180?

(c) What does this tell you about the measures of vertex angles of regular polygons?

8. On a square lattice, draw a tessellation with each of the following triangles.

(a)   **(b)**

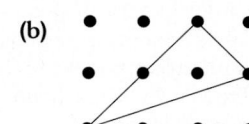

9. Explain how the shaded portion of the tessellation illustrates the Pythagorean theorem.

10. Given is a portion of a tessellation based on a scalene triangle. The angles are labeled from the basic tile.

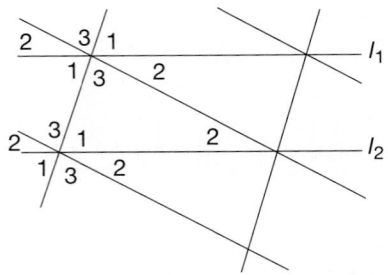

(a) Are lines l_1 and l_2 parallel?
(b) What does the tessellation illustrate about corresponding angles?

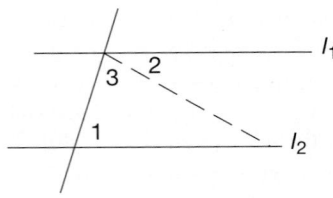

(c) What is illustrated about alternate interior angles?
(d) Angle 1 is an interior angle on the right of the transversal. Angles 2 and 3 together form the other interior angle on the right of the transversal. From the tessellation, what is true about $m(\angle 1) + [m(\angle 2) + m(\angle 3)]$? This result suggests two lines are parallel if and only if the interior angles on the same side of a transversal are _____ angles.

11. One theorem in geometry states the following: The line segment connecting the midpoints of two sides of a triangle is parallel to the third side and half its length. Explain how the figure in the given tessellation suggests this result.

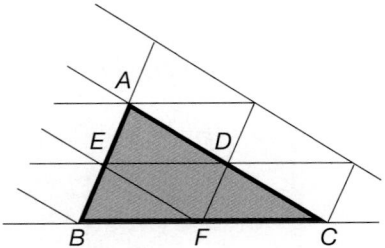

12. (a) Given below are portions of the (3, 3, 3, 3, 3, 3), (4, 4, 4, 4), and (6, 6, 6) tessellations. In the first, we have selected a vertex point and then connected the midpoints of the sides of polygons meeting at that vertex. The resulting figure is called the **vertex figure.** Draw the vertex figure for each of the other tessellations.

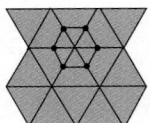
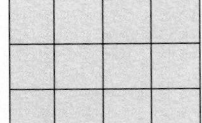

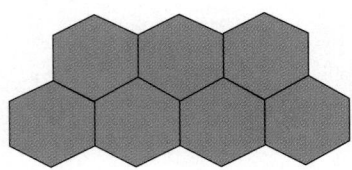

(b) A tessellation is a regular tessellation if it is constructed of regular polygons and has vertex figures that are regular polygons. Which of the tessellations above are regular?

13. Given below are other tessellations with equilateral triangles and squares.

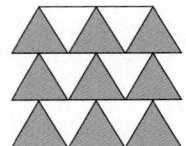

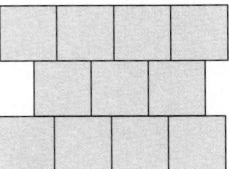

(a) Draw the vertex figure for each tessellation.
(b) Are these tessellations regular tessellations?

14. (a) The **dual** of a tessellation is formed by connecting the centers of polygons that share a common side. The dual tessellation of the equilateral triangle tessellation is shown. Find the dual of the other tessellations.

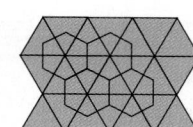

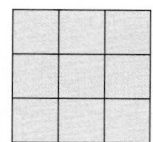

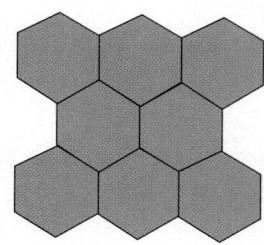

(b) Complete the following statements.
  (i) The dual of the regular tessellation with tri-
      angles is a regular tessellation with _____.
  (ii) The dual of the regular tessellation with
       squares is a regular tessellation with _____.
  (iii) The dual of the regular tessellation with hexa-
        gons is a regular tessellation with _____.

15. Complete the following table. Let V represent the
number of vertices, D the number of diagonals from
each vertex, and T the total number of diagonals.

Polygon	V	D	T
Triangle			
Quadrilateral			
Pentagon			
Hexagon			
Heptagon			
Octagon			
.			
.			
.			
n-gon			

Problems

16. Suppose that there are 20 people in a meeting room.
If every person in the room shakes hands once with
every other person in the room, how many handshakes would there be?

17. Calculate the measure of each lettered angle. Congruent angles and right angles are indicated.

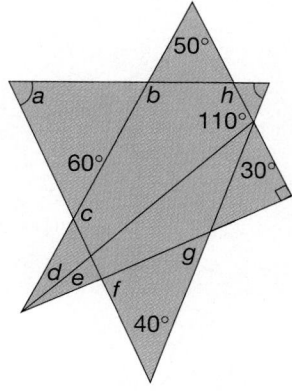

18. In the five-pointed star shown, what is the sum of the
angle measures at A, B, C, D, and E? Assume that
the pentagon is regular.

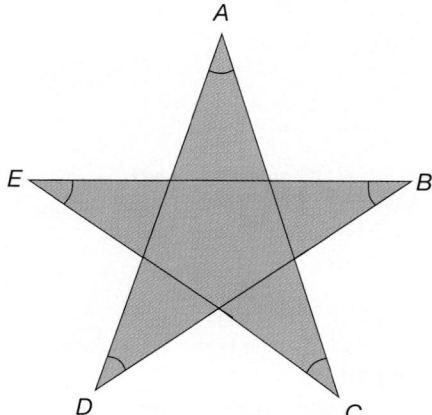

EXERCISE/PROBLEM SET 12.4—PART B

Exercises

1. Use your protractor to measure each vertex angle in each polygon shown. Extend the sides of the polygon if necessary. Then find the sum of the measures of the vertex angles. What *should* the sum be in each case?

(a)

(b)

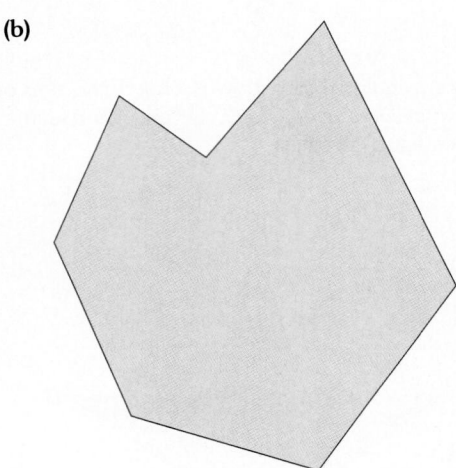

2. Find the missing angle measures in each of the following polygons.

(a)

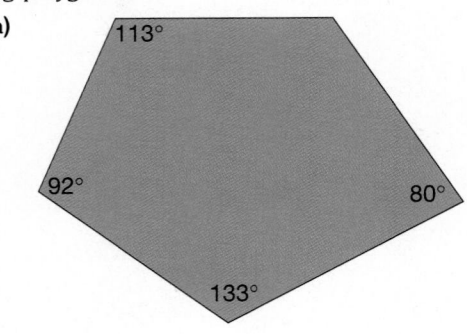

(b)

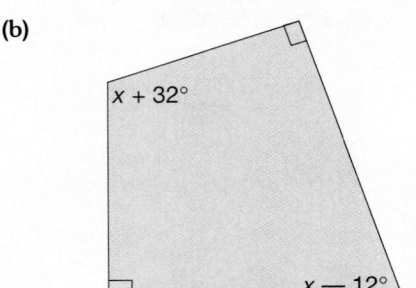

(c)

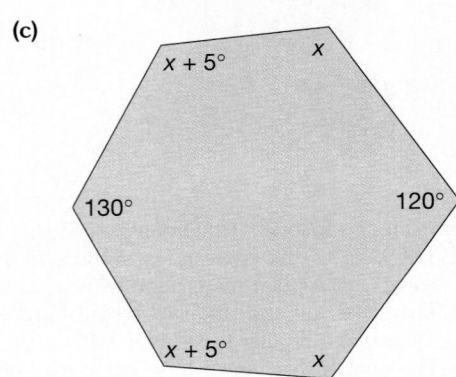

3. Given are the measures of the central angles of regular polygons. How many sides does each one have?
   (a) 120°   **(b)** 12°   **(c)** 15°   **(d)** 5°

4. Given are the measures of the exterior angles of regular polygons. What is the measure of the vertex angle of each one?
   (a) 36°   **(b)** 120°   **(c)** 2°   **(d)** $a°$

5. The sum of the measures of the vertex angles of a certain polygon is 2880°. How many sides does the polygon have?

6. Given the following measures of a vertex angle of a regular polygon, determine how many sides it has.
   (a) 150°   **(b)** 156°   **(c)** 174°   **(d)** 178°

7. On a square lattice, draw a tessellation with each of the following quadrilaterals.

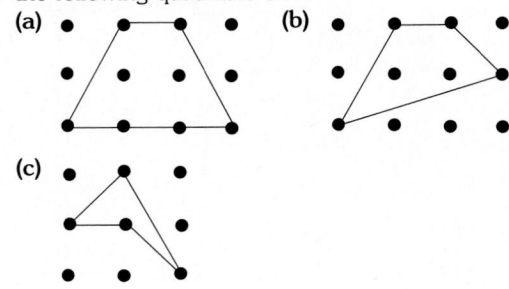

8. (a) Show that it is possible to tessellate with the following pentominoes.

(i)

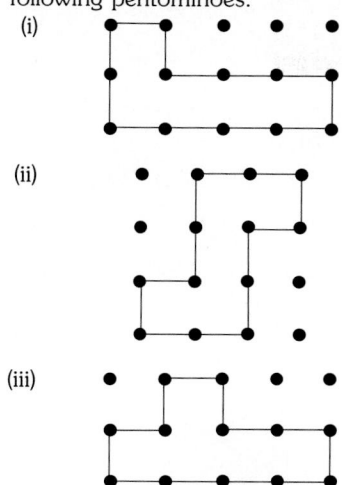

(ii)

(iii)

(b) Which of the other pentominoes will tessellate the plane?

9. The given scalene triangle is used as the basic tile for the illustrated tessellation.

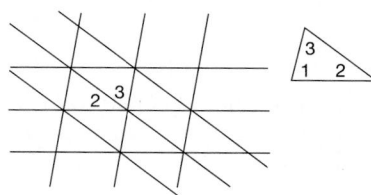

(a) Two of the angles have been labeled around the indicated point. Label the other angles (from basic tile).

(b) What geometric results that you have studied in this chapter are illustrated?

10. Illustrated is a tessellation based on a scalene triangle with sides a, b, and c. The two shaded triangles are similar (have the same shape). For each of the corresponding three sides, find the ratio of the length of one side of the smaller triangle to the length of corresponding side of the larger triangle. What do you observe about corresponding sides of similar triangles?

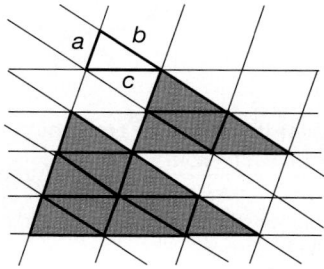

11. A man observed the semiregular floor tiling shown below and concluded after studying it that each angle of a *regular* octagon measures 135°. What was his possible reasoning?

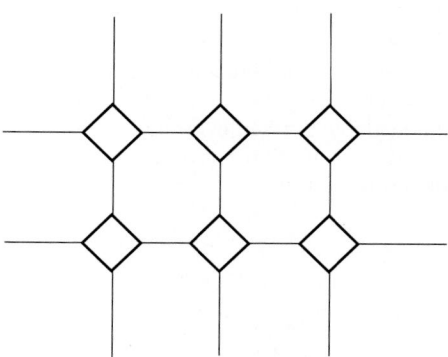

12. A theorem in geometry states the following: Parallel lines intersect proportional segments on all common transversals. In the portion of the tessellation given, lines l_1, l_2, and l_3 are parallel and t_1 and t_2 are transversals. Explain what this geometric result means and use the portion of the tessellation to illustrate it.

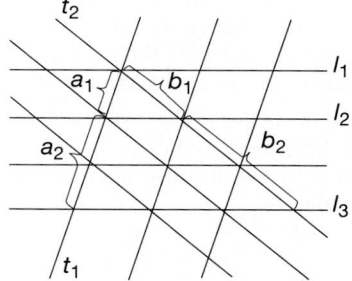

13. Below are copies of an equilateral triangle, a square, a regular hexagon, a regular octagon, and a regular dodecagon.

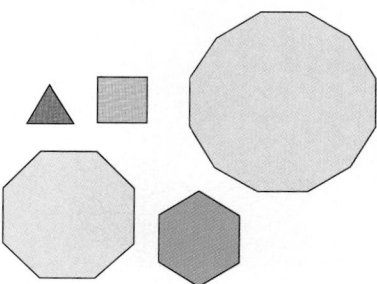

(a) Label one vertex angle of each with its measure.

(b) Find the number of ways that you can combine three of these figures (they may be repeated) to surround a point without gaps and overlaps.

(c) Using tracing paper, record each way you found.

14. Using the polygons in Exercise 13, find the ways that you can combine the specified numbers of polygons to surround a point without gaps and overlaps. Using tracing paper, record each way you found.
  (a) Four polygons   **(b)** Five polygons
  (c) Six polygons   **(d)** Seven polygons

15. A tessellation is a semiregular tessellation if it is made with regular polygons such that each vertex is surrounded by the same arrangement of polygons. The previous questions have shown us ways that a point can be surrounded by regular polygons.

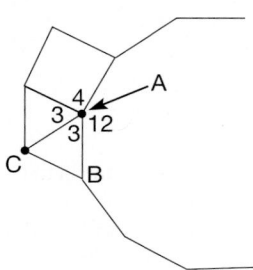

  (a) One of these arrangements was (3, 3, 4, 12), as shown. Can point *B* be surrounded by the same arrangement of polygons as point *A*? What happens to the arrangement at point *C*?
  (b) Find which of the arrangements *cannot* be extended to form a semiregular tessellation.

16. It will be shown later in this exercise/problem set that there are only eight semiregular tessellations. These are pictured below. Identify each by giving its vertex arrangement.
  (a)

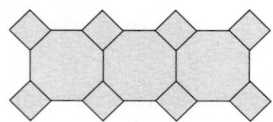

  (b)

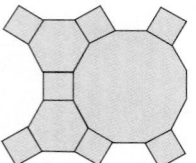

  (c)

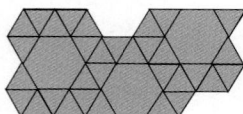

  (d)

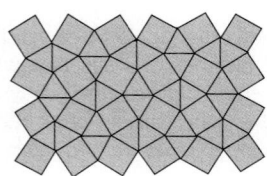

  (e)

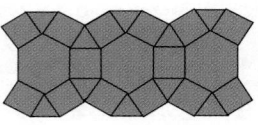

  (f)

  (g)

  (h)

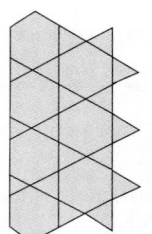

Problems

17. Find the maximum number of points of intersection for the following figures. Assume that no two sides coincide exactly.
  (a) A triangle and a square
  (b) A triangle and a hexagon
  (c) A square and a pentagon
  (d) An *n*-gon (*n* > 2) and a *p*-gon (*p* > 2)

18. Calculate the measure of each lettered angle. Congruent angles and right angles are indicated.

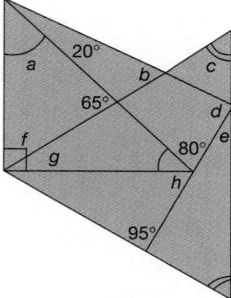

19. It was shown that a vertex angle of a regular *n*-gon measures $\dfrac{(n-2) \cdot 180}{n}$ degrees. If there are three regular polygons completely surrounding the vertex of a tessellation, then

$$\frac{(a-2)\cdot 180}{a} + \frac{(b-2)\cdot 180}{b} + \frac{(c-2)\cdot 180}{c} = 360$$

where the three polygons have a, b, and c sides. Justify each step in the following simplification of the given equation.

$$\frac{a-2}{a} + \frac{b-2}{b} + \frac{c-2}{c} = 2$$

$$1 - \frac{2}{a} + 1 - \frac{2}{b} + 1 - \frac{2}{c} = 2$$

$$1 = \frac{2}{a} + \frac{2}{b} + \frac{2}{c}$$

$$\frac{1}{2} = \frac{1}{a} + \frac{1}{b} + \frac{1}{c}$$

20. Problem 19 gives an equation that whole numbers a, b, and c must satisfy if an a-gon, a b-gon, and a c-gon will completely surround a point.

(a) Let $a = 3$. Find all possible whole-number values of b and c that satisfy the equation.

(b) Repeat part (a) with $a = 4$.

(c) Repeat part (a) with $a = 5$.

(d) Repeat part (a) with $a = 6$.

(e) This gives all possible arrangements of three polygons that will completely surround a point. How many did you find?

21. The following data summarize the possible arrangements of three polygons surrounding a vertex point of a tessellation.

3, 7, 42   4, 5, 20   5, 5, 10   6, 6, 6
3, 8, 24   4, 6, 12
3, 9, 18   4, 8, 4
3, 10, 15
3, 12, 12

The (6, 6, 6) arrangement yields a regular tessellation. It has been shown that (3, 12, 12), (4, 6, 12), and (4, 8, 8) can be extended to form a semiregular tessellation. Consider the (5, 5, 10) arrangement.

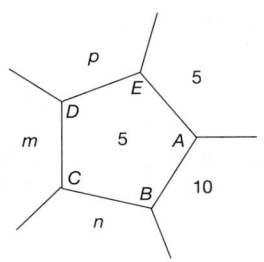

(a) Point A is surrounded by (5, 5, 10). If point B is surrounded similarly, what is n?

(b) If point C is surrounded similarly, what is m?

(c) If point D is surrounded similarly, what is p?

(d) What is the arrangement around point E? This shows that (5, 5, 10) cannot be extended to a semiregular tessellation.

(e) Show, in general, that this argument illustrates that the rest of the arrangements in the table cannot be extended to semiregular tessellations.

22. In a similar way, when four polygons, an a-gon, b-gon, c-gon, and d-gon, surround a point, it can be shown that the following equation is satisfied.

$$\frac{1}{a} + \frac{1}{b} + \frac{1}{c} + \frac{1}{d} = 1$$

(a) Find the four combinations of whole numbers that satisfy this equation.

(b) One of these arrangements gives a regular tessellation. Which arrangement is it?

(c) The remaining three combinations can each surround a vertex in two different ways. Of those six arrangements, four cannot be extended to a semiregular tessellation. Which are they?

(d) The remaining two can be extended to a semiregular tessellation. Which are they?

23. (a) When five polygons surround a point, they satisfy the following equation.

$$\frac{1}{a} + \frac{1}{b} + \frac{1}{c} + \frac{1}{d} + \frac{1}{e} = \frac{3}{2}$$

Find the two combinations of whole numbers that satisfy this equation.

(b) These solutions yield three different arrangements of polygons which can be extended to semiregular tessellations. Illustrate those patterns.

(c) When six polygons surround a point, they satisfy the following equation.

$$\frac{1}{a} + \frac{1}{b} + \frac{1}{c} + \frac{1}{d} + \frac{1}{e} + \frac{1}{f} = 2$$

Find the one combination that satisfies this equation. What type of tessellation is formed by this arrangement?

(d) Can more than six regular polygons surround a point? Why or why not?

12.5

DESCRIBING THREE-DIMENSIONAL SHAPES

Planes, Skew Lines, and Dihedral Angles

We now consider three-dimensional space and investigate various three-dimensional shapes (i.e., shapes having length, width, *and* height). There are infinitely many planes in three-dimensional space. Figure 12.59 shows several possible relationships among planes in three-dimensional space. The shapes in Figure 12.59 are actually portions of planes, since planes extend infinitely in two dimensions. Notice in Figure 12.59(b) and (c) that two intersecting planes meet in a line. In three-dimensional space, two planes are either parallel as in Figure 12.59(a) or they intersect as in Figure 12.59(b).

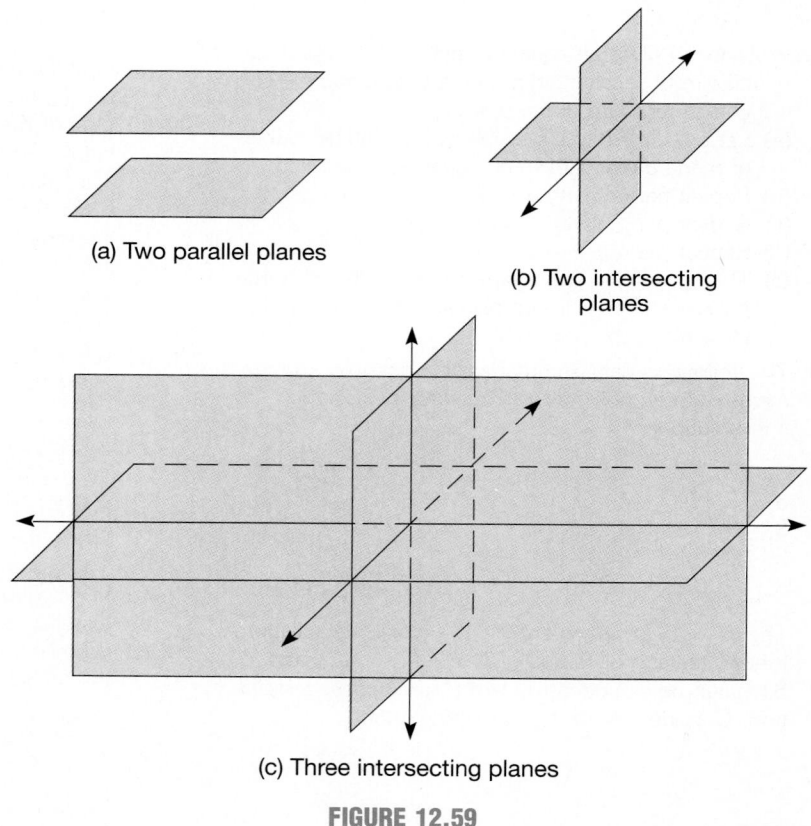

(a) Two parallel planes

(b) Two intersecting planes

(c) Three intersecting planes

FIGURE 12.59

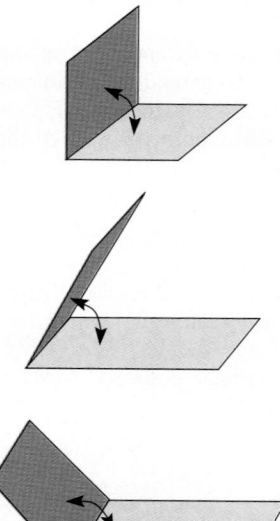

FIGURE 12.60

We can define the angle formed by polygonal regions, much as we defined angles in two dimensions. A **dihedral angle** is formed by the union of polygonal regions in space that share an edge. The polygonal regions forming the dihedral angle are called **faces** of the dihedral angle. Figure 12.60 shows several dihedral angles formed by intersecting rectangular regions. (Dihedral angles are also formed when planes intersect, but we will not investigate this situation.)

We can measure dihedral angles by measuring an angle between two line segments or rays contained in the faces (Figure 12.61). Notice that the

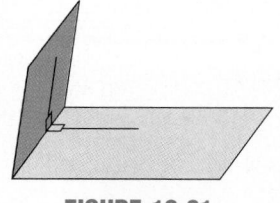

FIGURE 12.61

line segments forming the sides of the angle in Figure 12.61 are *perpendicular* to the line segment that is the intersection of the faces of the dihedral angle. Figure 12.62 shows the measurements of several dihedral angles.

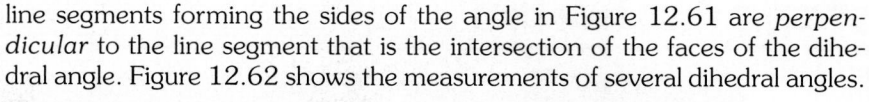

FIGURE 12.62

From our discussion above, we see that planes act in three-dimensional space much as lines do in two-dimensional space. On the other hand, lines in three-dimensional space do not have to intersect if they are not parallel. Such nonintersecting, nonparallel lines are called **skew lines**. Figure 12.63 shows a pair of skew lines, *l* and *m*.

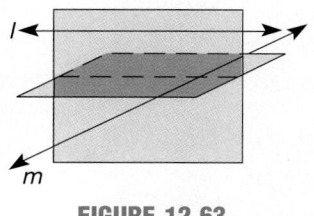

FIGURE 12.63

Thus in three-dimensional space, there are three possible relationships between two lines: they are parallel, they intersect, or they are skew lines. Figure 12.64 shows these relationships among the edges of a cube. Notice that lines *p* and *r* are parallel, lines *p* and *q* intersect, and lines *q* and *s* are skew lines (as are lines *r* and *s,* and lines *p* and *s*).

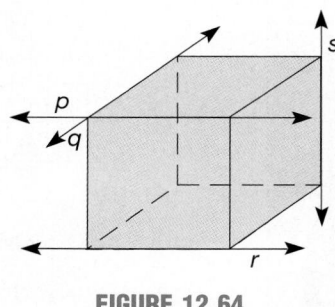

FIGURE 12.64

In three-dimensional space a line *l* is parallel to a plane $\mathcal{P}$ if *l* and $\mathcal{P}$ do not intersect [Figure 12.65(a)]. A line *l* is perpendicular to a plane $\mathcal{P}$ if *l* is perpendicular to *every* line in $\mathcal{P}$ that *l* intersects [Figure 12.65(b)].

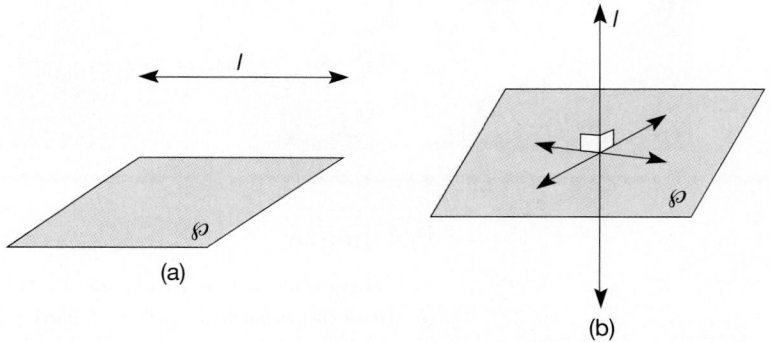

FIGURE 12.65

STUDENT PAGE SNAPSHOT

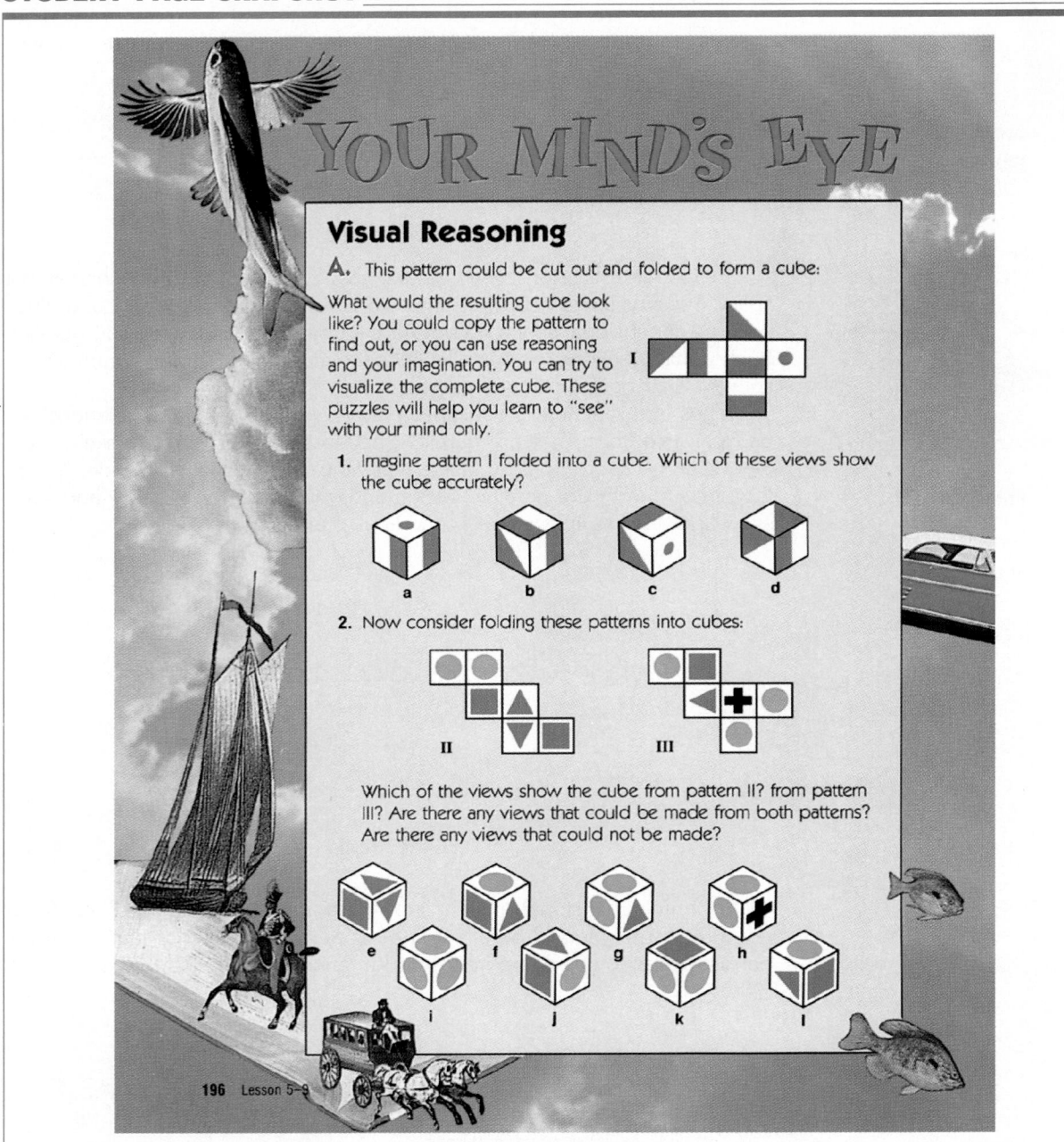

Polyhedra

The cube shown in Figure 12.64 is an example of a general category of three-dimensional shapes called polyhedra. A polyhedron is the three-dimensional analog of a polygon. A **polyhedron** (plural *polyhedra*) is the union of polygonal regions, any two of which have at most a side in common, such that a connected finite region in space is enclosed without holes. Figure 12.66(a) shows examples of polyhedra. Figure 12.66(b) contains shapes that are not polyhedra. In Figure 12.66(b), shape (i) is not a polyhedron since it has a hole, shape (ii) is not a polyhedron since it is curved, and shape (iii) is not a polyhedron since it does not enclose a finite region in space.

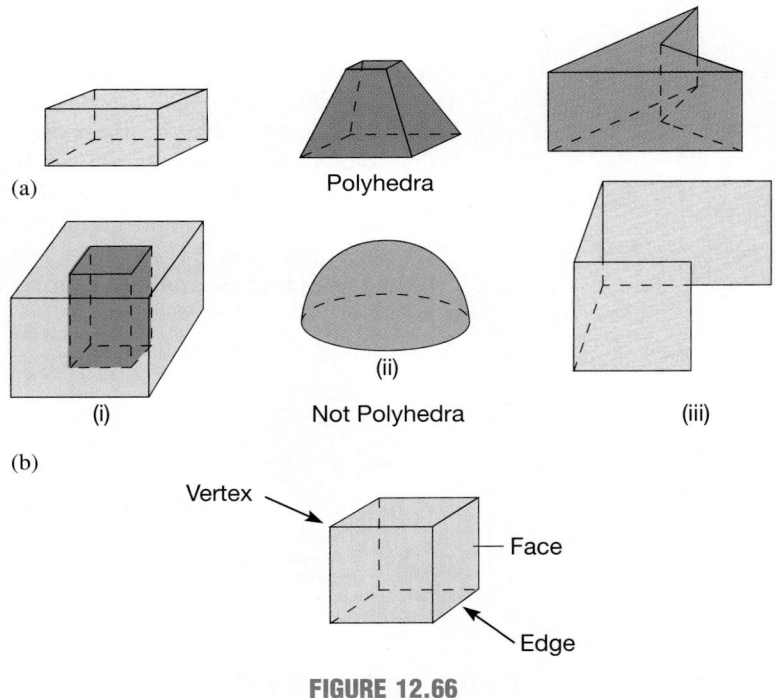

FIGURE 12.66

A polyhedron is **convex** if every line segment joining two of its points is contained inside the polyhedron or is on one of the polygonal regions. The first two polyhedra in Figure 12.66(a) are convex; the third is not. The polygonal regions of a polyhedron are called **faces**, the line segments common to a pair of faces are called **edges**, and the points of intersection of the edges are called **vertices** [Figure 12.66(c)].

Polyhedra can be classified into several general types. For example, **prisms** are polyhedra with two opposite faces that are identical polygons. These faces are called the **bases**. The vertices of the bases are joined to form **lateral faces** that must be parallelograms. If the lateral faces are rectangles, the prism is called a **right prism**, and the dihedral angle formed by a base and a lateral face is a right angle. Otherwise, the prism is called an **oblique prism**. Figure 12.67 shows a variety of prisms, named according to the types of polygons forming the bases and whether they are right or oblique.

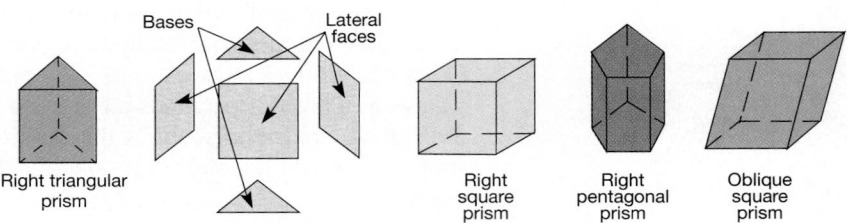

FIGURE 12.67

Since there are infinitely many types of polygons to use as the bases, there are infinitely many types of prisms.

Pyramids are polyhedra formed by using a polygon for the base and a point not in the plane of the base, called the **apex**, that is connected with line segments to each vertex of the base. Figure 12.68 shows several pyramids, named according to the types of polygon forming the base. Pyramids whose bases are regular polygons fall into two categories. Those whose lateral faces are isosceles triangles are called **right regular pyramids**. Otherwise, they are **oblique regular pyramids**.

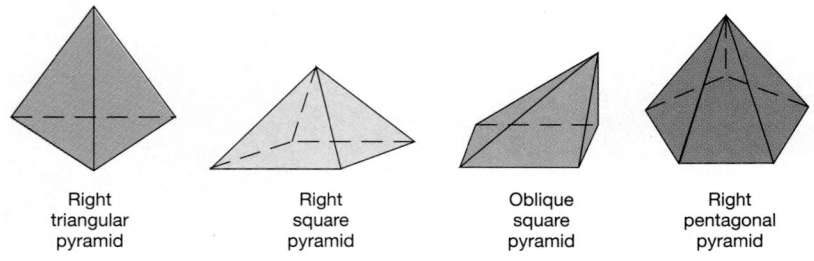

FIGURE 12.68

Polyhedra with regular polygons for faces have been studied since the time of the ancient Greeks. A **regular polyhedron** is one in which all faces are identical regular polygonal regions and all dihedral angles have the same measure. The ancient Greeks were able to show that there are exactly five regular convex polyhedra, called the **Platonic solids**. These are shown in Figure 12.69.

Table 12.5 shows an analysis of the regular polyhedra according to number of faces, vertices, and edges.

TABLE 12.5

Polyhedron	Faces, F	Vertices, V	Edges, E
Tetrahedron	4	4	6
Hexahedron	6	8	12
Octahedron	8	6	12
Dodecahedron	12	20	30
Icosahedron	20	12	30

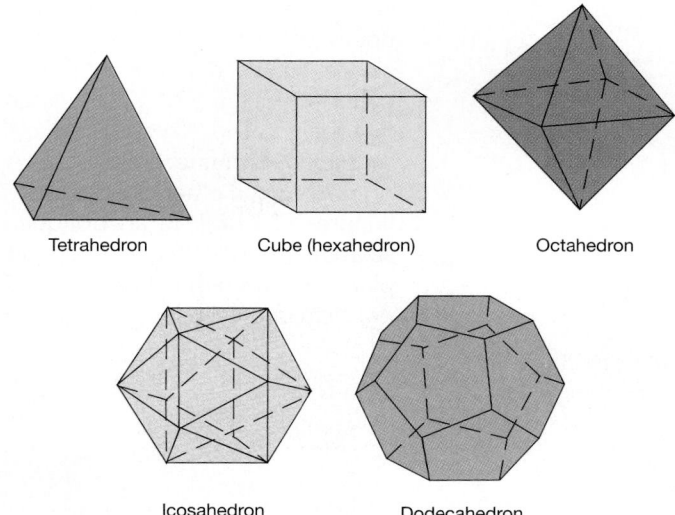

Tetrahedron   Cube (hexahedron)   Octahedron

Icosahedron   Dodecahedron

FIGURE 12.69

An interesting pattern in Table 12.5 is that $F + V = E + 2$ for all five regular polyhedra. That is, the number of faces plus vertices equals the number of edges plus 2. This result, known as **Euler's formula**, holds for *all* convex polyhedra, not just regular polyhedra. For example, verify Euler's formula for each of the polyhedra in Figures 12.66, 12.67, and 12.68.

If we allow several different regular polygonal regions to serve as the faces, then we can investigate a new family of polyhedra, called semiregular polyhedra. A **semiregular polyhedron** is a polyhedron with several different regular polygonal regions for faces but with the same arrangement of polygons at each vertex. Prisms with square faces and regular polygons for bases are semiregular polyhedra. Figure 12.70 shows several types of semiregular polyhedra.

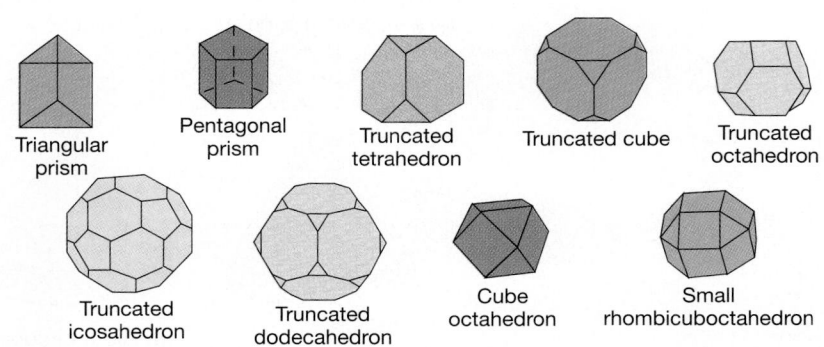

Triangular prism   Pentagonal prism   Truncated tetrahedron   Truncated cube   Truncated octahedron

Truncated icosahedron   Truncated dodecahedron   Cube octahedron   Small rhombicuboctahedron

FIGURE 12.70

Curved Shapes in Three Dimensions

There are three-dimensional curved shapes analogous to prisms and pyramids, namely cylinders and cones. Consider two identical simple closed curves having the same orientation and contained in parallel planes. The union of the line segments joining corresponding points on the simple closed curves and the interiors of the simple closed curves is called a **cylinder** [Figure 12.71(a)]. Each simple closed curve together with its interior is called a base of the cylinder. In a **right circular cylinder**, a line segment $\overline{AB}$ connecting a point A on one circular base to its corresponding point B on the other circular base is perpendicular to the planes of the bases [Figure 12.71(b)]. In an **oblique cylinder**, the bases are parallel, yet line segments connecting corresponding points are not perpendicular to the planes of the bases [Figure 12.71(c)]. In this book we restrict our study to right circular cylinders.

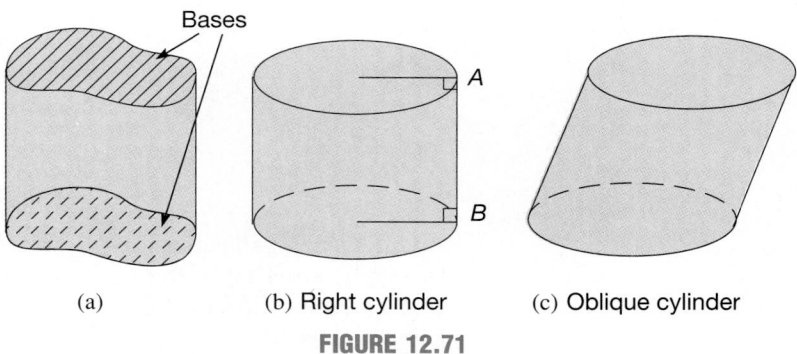

Bases

(a)   (b) Right cylinder   (c) Oblique cylinder

FIGURE 12.71

A **cone** is the union of the interior of a simple closed curve and all line segments joining points of the curve to a point, called the **apex**, that is not in the plane of the curve. The plane curve together with its interior is called the **base** [(Figure 12.72(a)]. We will restrict our attention to circular cones (bases are circles). In a **right circular cone**, the line segment joining the apex and the center of the circular base is perpendicular to the plane of the base [Figure 12.72(b)]. In an **oblique circular cone**, this line segment is not perpendicular to the plane of the base [Figure 12.72(c)]. Cones and cylinders appear frequently in construction and design.

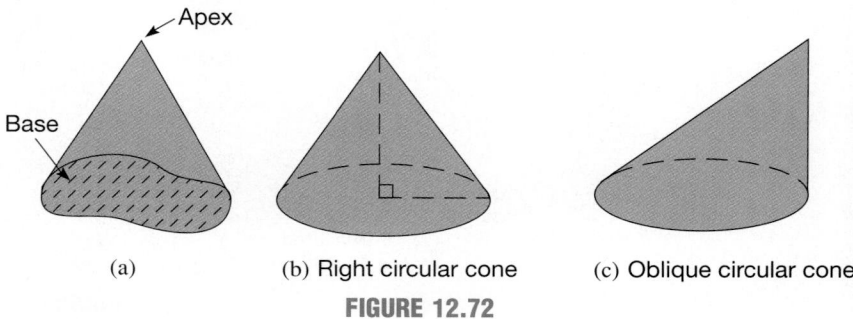

Apex

Base

(a)   (b) Right circular cone   (c) Oblique circular cone

FIGURE 12.72

The three-dimensional analog of a circle is a sphere. A **sphere** is defined as the set of all points in three-dimensional space that are the same distance from a fixed point, called the **center** (Figure 12.73). Any line

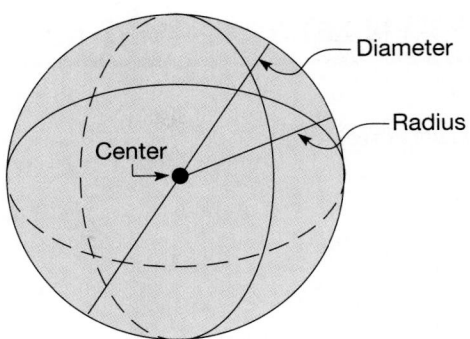

FIGURE 12.73

segment joining the center to a point on the sphere is also called a **radius** of the sphere; its *length* is also called *the* radius of the sphere. A segment joining two points of the sphere and containing the center is called a **diameter** of the sphere; its *length* is also called *the* diameter of the sphere. Spherical shapes are important in many areas. Planets, moons, and stars are essentially spherical. Thus measurement aspects of spheres are very important in science. We consider measurement aspects of cones, cylinders, spheres, and other shapes in Chapter 13.

MATHEMATICAL MORSEL

When Memphis, Tennessee, officials wanted an eye-catching new sports arena, they decided to take a page from the book on their sister city, Memphis, Egypt. A $52,000,000 stainless-steel clad pyramid, two-thirds the size of the world's largest pyramid, the Great Pyramid of Cheops, was the result. The square pyramid is 321 feet, or 32 stories, high and its base covers 300,000 square feet, or about six football fields. In addition to housing sporting events and circuses, the pyramid houses a museum of American music.

EXERCISE/PROBLEM SET 12.5—PART A

Exercises

1. (a) Describe what you see.

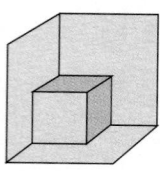

(b) Which is the highest step?

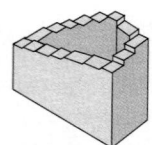

2. How many $1 \times 1 \times 1$ cubes are in the following stacks?

(a)

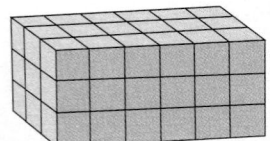

(b)

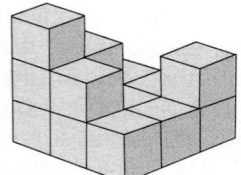

(c)

3. Pictured is a stack of cubes. Also given are the top view, the front view, and the right-side view. (Assume that the only hidden cubes are ones that support a pictured cube.)

 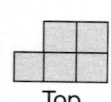 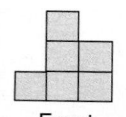 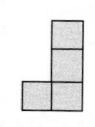

Top   Front   Right side

Give the three views of each of the following stacks of cubes.

(a)    **(b)** 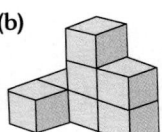   **(c)**

4. In the figure, the drawing on the left shows a shape. The drawing on the right tells you how many cubes are on each base square. The drawing on the right is called a **base design**.

2	2	3
1	1	1

Front

(a) Which is the correct base design for this shape?

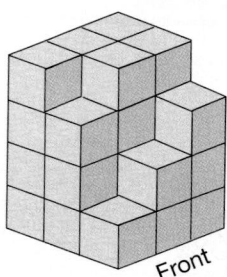

Front

(i)

4	4	4
3	3	3
1	2	4

(ii)

4	4	4
3	4	4
1	2	3

(iii)

4	4	4
3	4	5
1	1	1

(b) Make a base design for each shape.
(i)

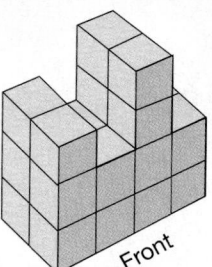

Front

(ii)

(iii)

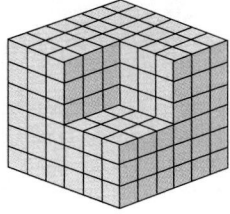

(c) Draw a cube picture from each base design.

(i)

2	3	2
1	1	1

(ii)

3	4
2	3
1	1

(iii)

3	4	3
2	2	2
1	2	1

5. For each of the following prisms:
   (i) Name the bases of the prism.
   (ii) Name the lateral faces of the prism.
   (iii) Name the faces that are hidden from view.
   (iv) Name the prism by type.

(a)

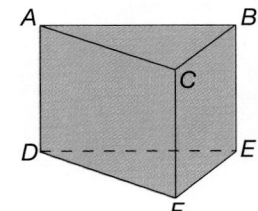

(b)

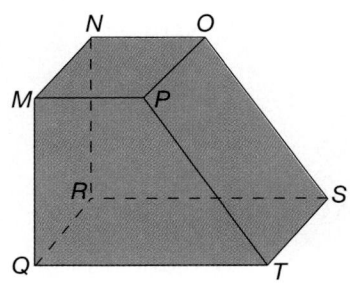

6. Name the following pyramids according to type.
   (a) The base is a square.

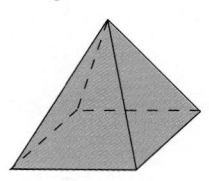

(b)

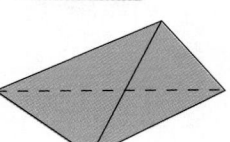

(c)

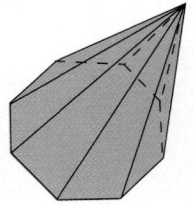

7. Identify the following figures.

(a)

(b)

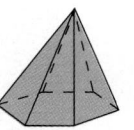

(c) All faces are squares.   **(d)**

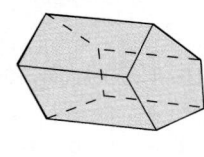

(e) The bases are circular.   **(f)**

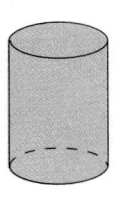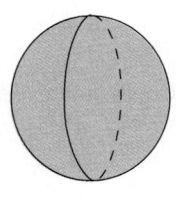

8. Which of the following patterns folds into a cube? If one does, what number will be opposite the X?

(a)

1			
4	X	2	5
3			

(b)

1	X	3		
	2	4	5	

(c)

	3	X	1
5	2	4	

(d)

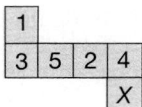

1			
3	5	2	4
			X

(e)

1	3	X	
	2	4	
	5		

(f)

3	X	
1	4	
	2	5

9. All faces of the following cube are different.

Which of these cubes represents a different view of the cube above?

(a)   **(b)**

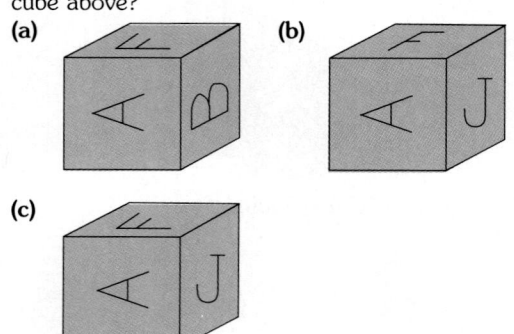

(c)

10. Drawing a prism can be done by following these steps:

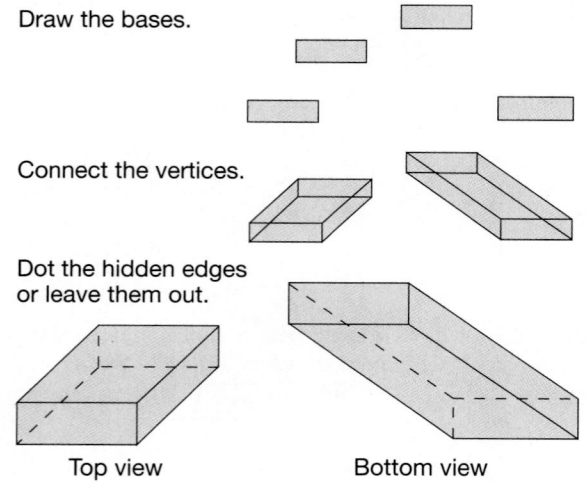

Draw the bases.

Connect the vertices.

Dot the hidden edges or leave them out.

Top view   Bottom view

Draw the following prisms.
(a) Square prism
(b) Pentagonal prism (bottom view)

11. Given is a prism with bases that are regular pentagons.

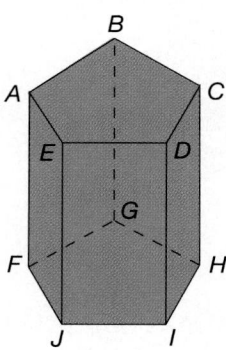

(a) Is there a plane in the picture that is parallel to the plane containing points *A, B, C, D,* and *E*? If so, name the points it contains.
(b) Is there a plane in the picture that is parallel to the plane containing points *C, D, I,* and *H*? If so, name the points that it contains.
(c) What is the measure of the dihedral angle between plane *AEJF* and plane *ABGF*?

12. Shown are patterns or nets for several three-dimensional figures. Copy and cut each one out. Then fold each one up to form the figure. Name the three-dimensional figure you have made in each case.
(a)

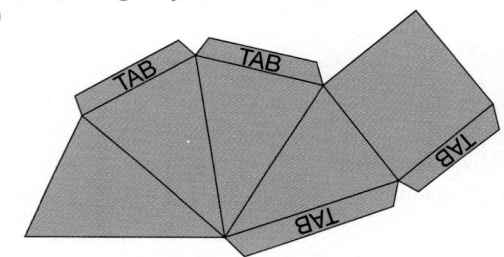

(b)

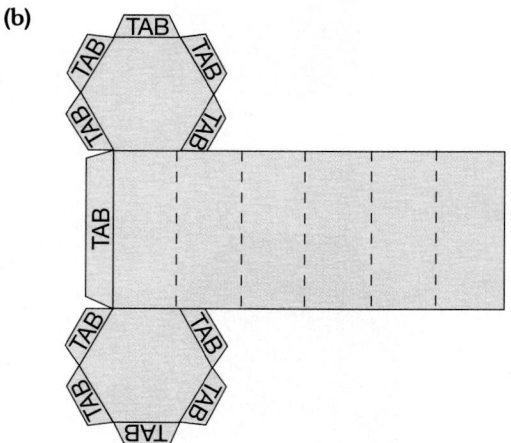

(c)

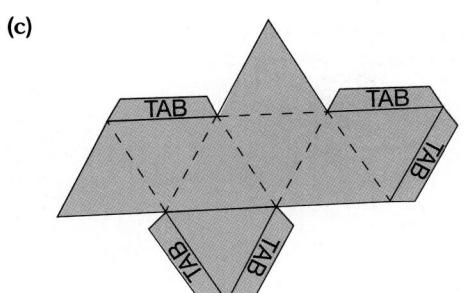

(d) Most nets for three-dimensional shapes are not unique. Sketch another net for each shape you made above. Be sure to include tabs for folding. Try each one to check your answer.

13. Draw a net for each of the following polyhedra. Be sure to include tabs for folding. Cut out and fold your patterns to check your answers.

(a)

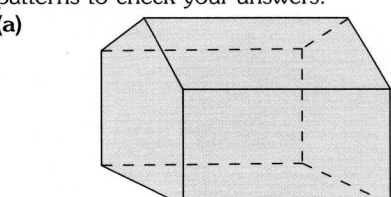

(b) A right hexagonal pyramid

14. (a) Given below are arrangements of polygons that tessellate the plane. Around each vertex, the sum of the measures of the angle is 360°. Can these figures be folded to form faces of a polyhedron without bending or distorting the faces?

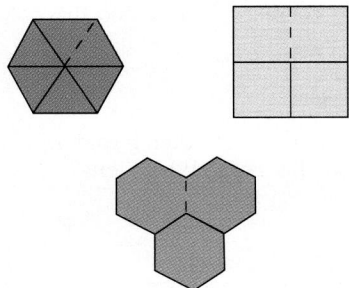

(b) If the figure were cut on the dashed line, could it then be folded to form some faces of a polyhedron without overlapping faces?

(c) Complete the following statement: The sum of the measures of the angles at any vertex of a convex polyhedron is _____ 360°.

15. (a) If the two triangles or two squares illustrated are folded, would a rigid vertex of a polyhedron be formed?

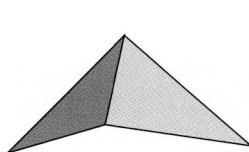   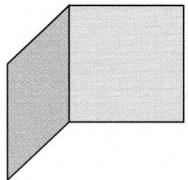

(b) Would a third triangle or a third square make the vertex points above rigid?

(c) Complete the following statement: At least _____ intersecting planes are needed to form the vertex of a polyhedra.

16. (a) Exercises 14 and 15 have established conditions required in forming regular convex polyhedra. What arrangements of triangles will satisfy these two conditions?

(b) What arrangements of squares are possible?

(c) What arrangements of pentagons are possible?

(d) Are there any other arrangements with hexagons, heptagons, and so on, possible?

(e) In parts (a) to (c), you should have found five possible arrangements. Which regular polyhedra correspond to these arrangements? You have just shown that these are the only regular convex polyhedra possible.

17. When the centers of the adjacent faces (i.e., those that share an edge) of a convex regular polyhedron are connected, another convex regular polyhedron is formed. This is called the **dual** of the original polyhedron.

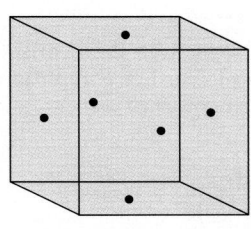   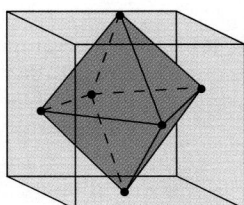

(a) Consider the cube made of wire illustrated to the right. The vertices of the dual are the centers of the faces of the cube. How many are there?

(b) If centers of adjacent faces are connected to form the dual, how many edges are there?

(c) Which regular polyhedron has the appropriate number of vertices and edges? This is the dual of a cube.

18. (a) Vertex A of the pictured tetrahedron is surrounded by the angles of three equilateral triangles. What is the total measure of these three angles?

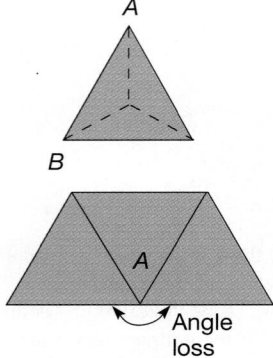

(b) If the three triangles were laid out flat, they would look like the picture shown here. Of the 360° surrounding vertex A in this arrangement, the angle measure not included in parts of the polyhedra is called the "angle loss" at vertex A. What is the angle loss?

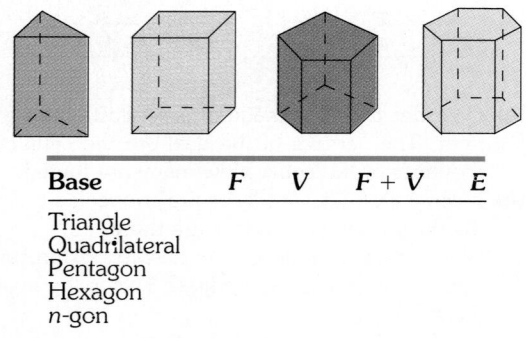

(c) What is the angle loss at vertex B?

(d) What is the total angle loss of the tetrahedron?

19. Complete the following table to find the angle loss for each of the regular polyhedron. Let V represent the number of vertices, A the angle loss at each vertex, and P the angle loss for the polyhedron.

Polyhedron	V	A	P
Tetrahedron	4	180°	720°
Cube			
Octahedron			
Dodecahedron			
Icosahedron			

20. (a) Given are samples of prisms. Use these prisms to complete the following table. Let F represent the number of faces, V the number of vertices, and E the number of edges.

Base	F	V	F + V	E
Triangle				
Quadrilateral				
Pentagon				
Hexagon				
n-gon				

(b) Is Euler's formula satisfied for prisms?

21. The right cylinder is cut by a plane as indicated. Identify the resulting cross section.

(a)   **(b)**

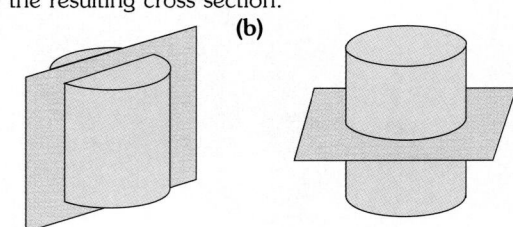

22. When a three-dimensional shape is cut by a plane, the figure that results is a cross section. Identify the cross section formed in the following cases.

(a)

(b)

(c)

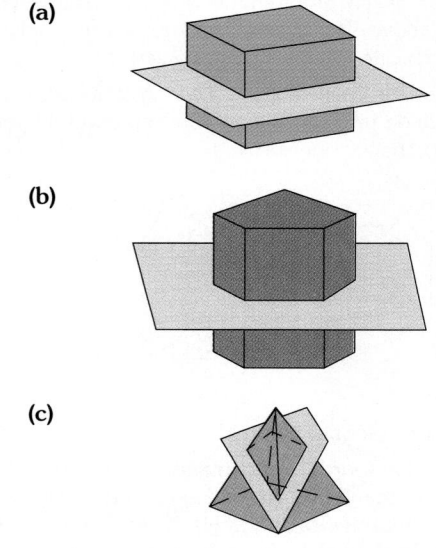

23. A polyhedron has 18 edges and 8 faces. How many vertices does it have? Sketch a polyhedron that satisfies these conditions and name the polyhedron you drew.

Problems

24. The figures on the left when folded become one of the figures on the right. Which one? Make models to check.

(a)   (i)

(ii)

(iii)

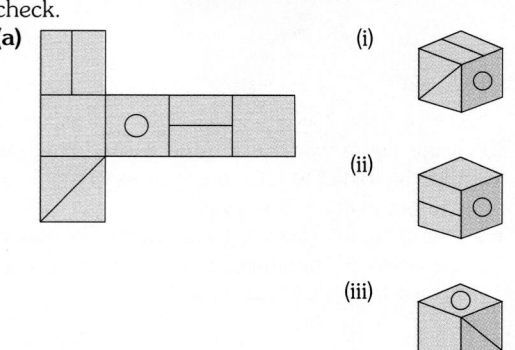

(b)

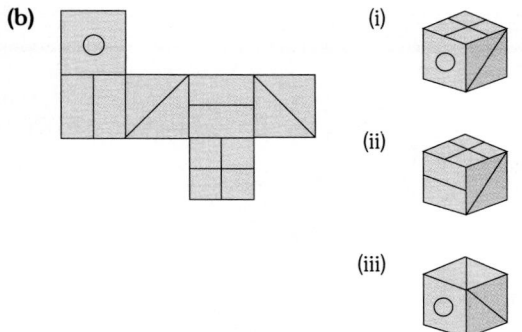

(i)

(ii)

(iii)

25. If the cube illustrated is cut by a plane midway between opposite faces and the front portion is placed against a mirror, the entire cube appears to be formed. The cutting plane is called a **plane of symmetry**, and the figure is said to have **reflection symmetry**.

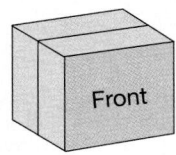

(a) How many planes of symmetry of this type are there for a cube?

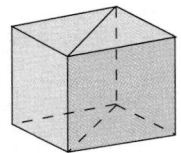

(b) A plane passing through pairs of opposite edges is also a plane of symmetry, as illustrated. How many planes of symmetry of this type are there in a cube?

(c) How many planes of symmetry are there for a cube?

26. The line connecting centers of opposite faces of a cube is an **axis** (plural **axes**) of **rotational symmetry**, since the cube can be turned about the axis and appears to be in the same position. In fact, the cube can be turned about that axis four times before returning to its original position, as shown below.

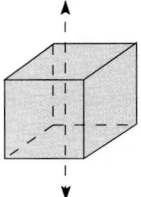

This axis of symmetry is said to have order 4. How many axes of symmetry of order 4 are there in a cube?

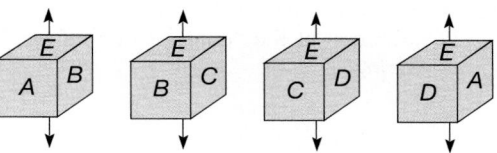

27. The line connecting opposite pairs of vertices of a cube is also an axis of symmetry.

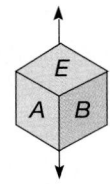

(a) What is the order of this axis (how many turns are needed to return it to the original arrangement)?

(b) How many axes of this order are there in a cube?

28. The line connecting midpoints of opposite edges is an axis of symmetry of a cube.

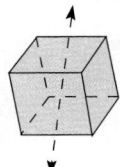

(a) What is the order of this axis?

(b) How many axes of this order are there in a cube?

29. What is the shape of a piece of cardboard that is made into a center tube for a paper towel roll?

30. (a) Can an infinite number of copies of the pictured box be stacked so that they totally fill space without gaps or overlaps? This is called a **tessellation of space**.

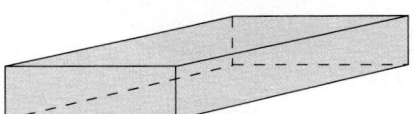

(b) Name some other polyhedra that will tessellate space. (HINT: Consider figures that tessellated the plane.)

(c) Which of the regular polyhedra tessellate spaces by themselves?

EXERCISE/PROBLEM SET 12.5—PART B

Exercises

1. **(a)** Which dark circle is behind the others in the figure? Look at the figure for one minute before answering.

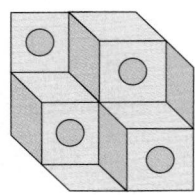

(b) Is the small cube attached to the front or the back of the large cube?

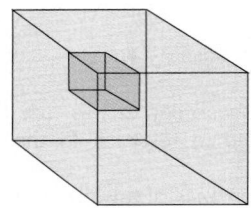

2. All the faces of the cube on the left have different figures on them. Which of the three other cubes represents a different view? Explain.

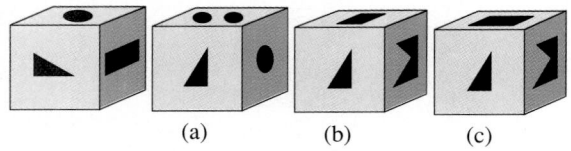

     (a)   (b)   (c)

3. Name the following prisms by type.
(a)

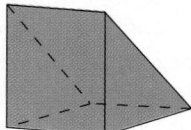

(b)

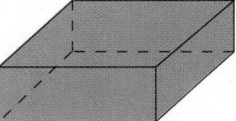

(c)

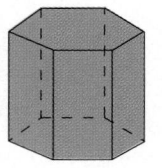

4. Which of the following figures are prisms? Which are pyramids?
(a)

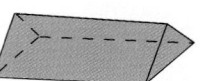

(b)

(c)

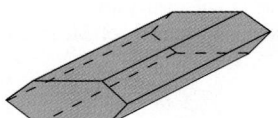

5. Which of the pentominoes that you drew in Exercise/Problem Set 12.1 will fold up to make a box with no lid? Mark the bottom of the box with an X.

6. Following is pictured a stack of cubes. (Assume that the only hidden cubes are ones that support a pictured cube; see Exercise 3 in Part A, for example.) Give three views of each of the following stacks of cubes.
(a)

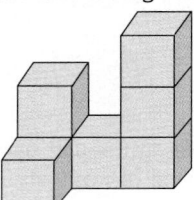

(b)

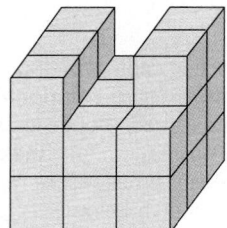

7. Following are shown three views of a stack of cubes. Determine the largest possible number of cubes in the stack. What is the smallest number of cubes that could be in the stack? Make a base design for each answer (see Exercise 3 in Part A).

Top:

Front:

Right side:

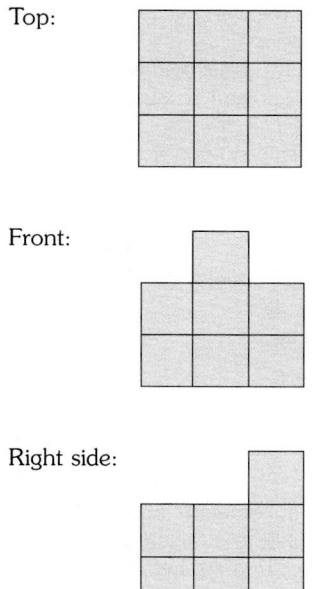

8. Drawing a pyramid can be done by following these steps:

Draw a base.

Draw a point for the apex.

Connect the apex to the vertices of the base.

Draw the hidden edges or leave them out.

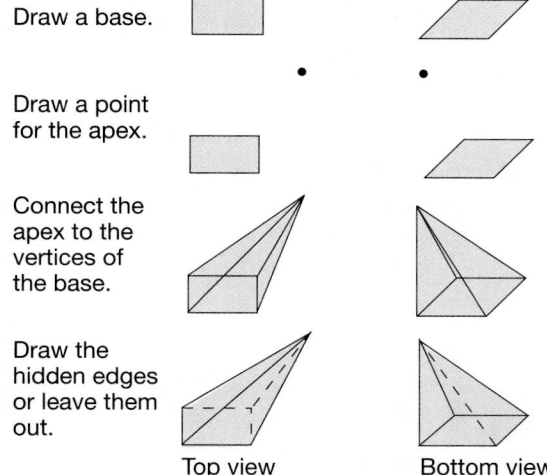

Top view   Bottom view

Draw the following pyramids.
(a) Triangular pyramid
(b) Hexagonal pyramid (bottom view)

9. Following are patterns or nets for several three-dimensional figures. Copy and cut each one out. Then fold each one up to form the figure. Name the three-dimensional figure you have made in each case.

(a)

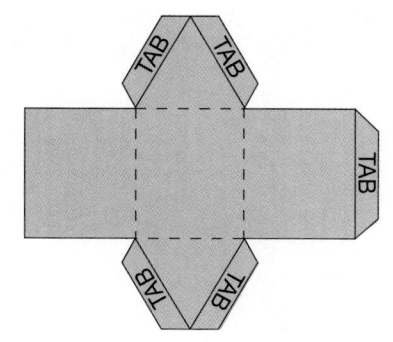

(b)

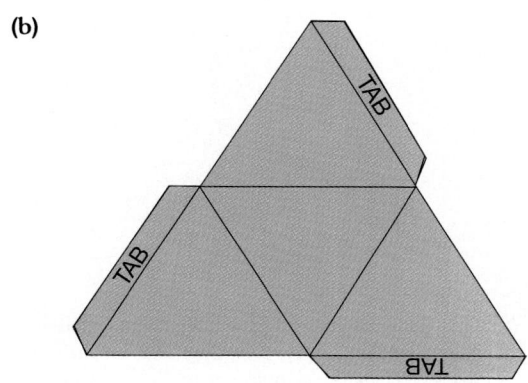

(c)

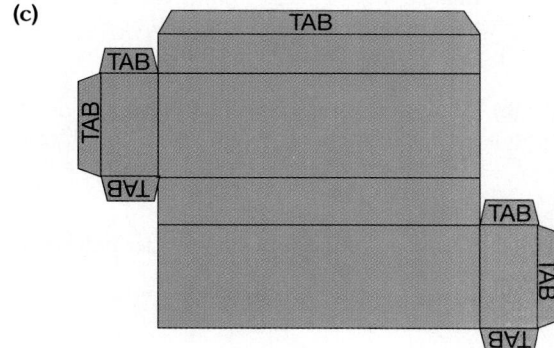

(d) Most nets for three-dimensional shapes are not unique. Sketch another net for each shape you made above. Be sure to include tabs for folding. Try each one to check your answer.

10. Draw a net for the following polyhedron. Be sure to include tabs for folding. Cut out and fold your pattern to check your answer.

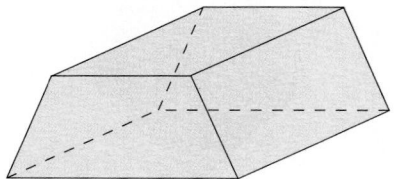

11. The dihedral angle, $\angle AED$, of the tetrahedron pictured can be found by the following procedure.

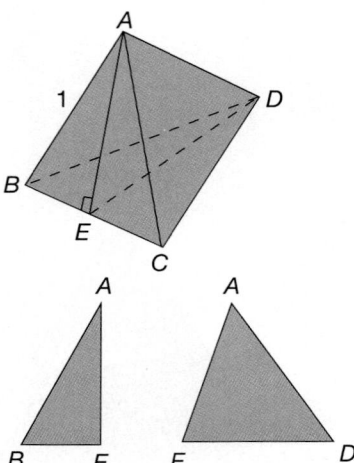

(a) The face of the tetrahedron is an equilateral triangle, $\triangle ABC$. As one segment of the dihedral angle, $\overline{AE}$ is perpendicular to $\overline{BC}$. In an equilateral triangle, the segment from a vertex to a side cuts the side in half. Find the length of $\overline{BE}$ and $\overline{AE}$, if we assume the edges of the tetrahedron have length 1.

(b) Using similar reasoning find the length of $\overline{DE}$.

(c) Label the length of the sides of $\triangle AED$. Use a scale drawing and a protractor to approximate the measure of $\angle AED$.

12. Find the duals of the following regular polyhedra.

(a)

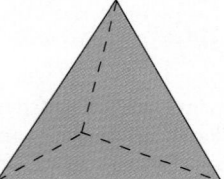

(b)

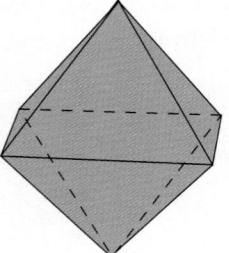

13. (a) Complete the following statements about duals of regular polyhedra.
   (i) The _____ is its own dual.
   (ii) The _____ and _____ are duals of each other.

(b) What relationship do you notice between duals in the following table?

Polyhedron	Number of Vertices	Number of Faces	Number of Edges
Tetrahedron	4	4	6
Cube	8	6	12
Octahedron	6	8	12

(c) Using the relationship observed in part (b), find the dual of a dodecahedron and of an icosahedron.

14. Given is vertex information about four semiregular polyhedra. Complete the table concerning angle loss (see Exercise 18 of Part A). Let N represent the number of vertices, V the vertex arrangement, A the angle loss at each vertex, and P the angle loss for the polyhedron.

Polyhedron		N	V	A	P
(a)	Truncated cube	24	(3, 8, 8)		
(b)	Rhombicub-octohedron	24	(3, 4, 4, 4)		
(c)	Truncated icosahedron	60	(5, 6, 6)		
(d)	Rhombicosido-decahedron	60	(3, 4, 5, 4)		

15. (a) Given are samples of pyramids. Use these to complete the following table. Let F represent the number of faces, V the number of vertices, and E the number of edges.

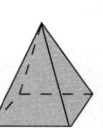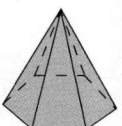

Base	F	V	$F + V$	E
Triangle				
Quadrilateral				
Pentagon				
Hexagon				
n-gon				

(b) Is Euler's formula satisfied for pyramids?

16. (a) Given are pictures of three-dimensional shapes. Use these to complete the following table. Let *F* represent the number of faces, *V* the number of vertices, and *E* the number of edges.

(i)

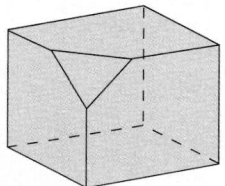

(ii)

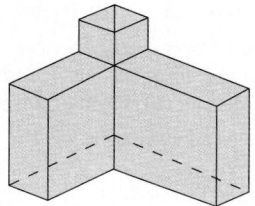

(iii)

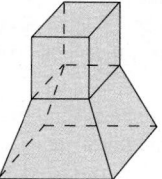

(iv)

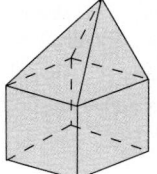

Figure	F	V	F + V	E
(i)				
(ii)				
(iii)				
(iv)				

(b) Is Euler's formula satisfied for these figures?

17. An **antiprism** is a polyhedron like a prism except that the lateral faces are triangles. An example is shown. Notice how the bases are rotated.

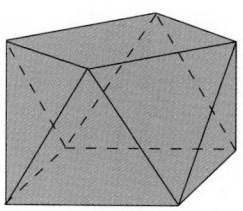

(a) An antiprism with equilateral triangular bases and faces is a regular polyhedron. Which one?
(b) Explain why the antiprism pictured is a semiregular polyhedron. (Note that the top and bottom faces are squares and the other faces are equilateral triangles.)

18. (a) Given below are pictures of some antiprisms. Use these to complete the following table. Let *F* represent the number of faces, *V* the number of vertices, and *E* the number of edges.

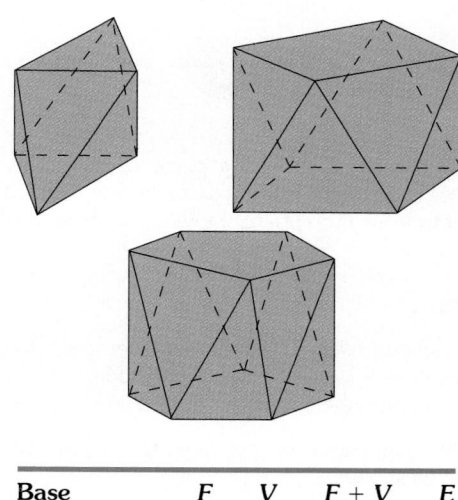

Base	F	V	F + V	E
Triangle				
Quadrilateral				
Pentagon				
n-gon				

(b) Is Euler's formula satisfied for these figures?

19. The cone below is cut by a plane as indicated. Identify the resulting cross section.

(a)

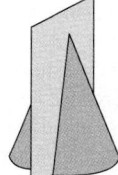

(b)

(c)

20. (a) The picture illustrates the intersection between a sphere and a plane. What is true about all such intersections?

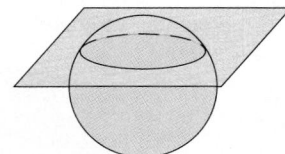

(b) When the intersecting plane contains the center of the sphere, the cross section is called a **great circle** of the sphere. How many great circles are there for a sphere?

Problems

21. A polyhedron has 10 edges and 6 vertices. How many faces does it have? Sketch a polyhedron that satisfies these conditions and name the polyhedron you drew.

22. Eight small cubes are put together to form one large cube as shown.

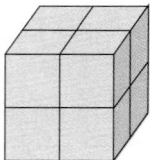

Suppose that all six sides of this larger cube are painted, the paint is allowed to dry, and the cube is taken apart.

(a) How many of the small cubes will have paint on just one side? On two sides? On three sides? On no sides?

(b) Answer the same questions as in part (a) if the large cube is formed from 27 small cubes.

(c) Answer the same questions as in part (a) if the large cube is formed from 64 small cubes.

(d) Answer the same questions as in part (a) if the large cube is formed from n^3 small cubes.

23. Which of the following cross sections are possible when a plane cuts a cube?
   (a) A square
   (b) A rectangle
   (c) An isosceles triangle
   (d) An equilateral triangle
   (e) A trapezoid
   (f) A parallelogram
   (g) A pentagon
   (h) A regular hexagon

24. How many planes of symmetry do the following figures have? (Models may help.)
   (a) Tetrahedron   **(b)** Square pyramid
   (c) Pentagonal prism   **(d)** Right circular cylinder

25. Find the axes of symmetry for the following figures. Indicate the order of each axis. (Models may help.)
   (a) Tetrahedron   **(b)** Pentagonal prism

26. How many axes of symmetry do the following figures have?
   (a) Right square pyramid   **(b)** Right circular cone
   (c) Sphere

27. Show how to slice a cube with four cuts to make a regular tetrahedron. (HINT: Slice a clay cube with a cheese cutter, or draw lines on a paper or plastic cube.)

28. A regular tetrahedron is attached to a face of a square pyramid with equilateral faces where the faces of the tetrahedron and the pyramid are identical triangles. What is the fewest number of faces possible for the resulting polyhedron? (Use a model—it will suggest a surprising answer. However, a complete mathematical solution is difficult.)

29. Imagine a tetrahedron cut with a plane through the midpoints of three edges as shown. Describe the shape of each intersection.

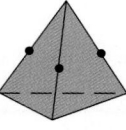 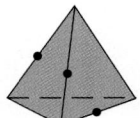

30. Imagine a cube cut with a plane through the midpoints of three edges as shown. Describe the shape of each intersection.

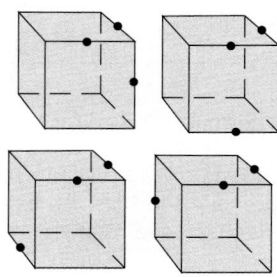

31. A lawyer has some bookcase sections with the following heights:

> 4 sections, each 11 inches high
> 9 sections, each 13 inches high
> 5 sections, each 15 inches high

Assuming that each section can be stacked on top of any other section, how can the lawyer arrange the sections to make three bookcases as nearly equal in height as possible?

SOLUTION OF INITIAL PROBLEM

Describe a solid shape that will fill each of the holes in this template as well as pass through each hole.

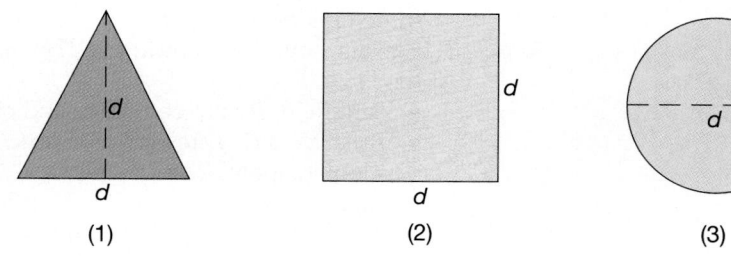

(1)   (2)   (3)

Strategy: Use a Model

A cylinder whose base has diameter d and whose height is d will pass through the square and circle exactly [Figure 12.74(a)]. We will modify a model of this cylinder to get a shape with a triangular cross-section.

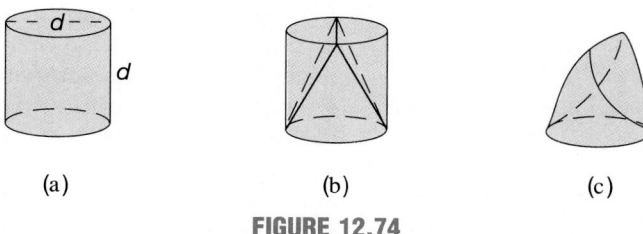

(a)   (b)   (c)

FIGURE 12.74

If we slice the cylinder along the heavy lines in Figure 12.74(b), the resulting model will pass through the triangular hole exactly. Figure 12.74(c) shows the resulting model that will pass through all three holes exactly.

Additional Problems Where the Strategy "Use a Model" Is Useful

1. Which of the following can be folded into a closed box?

(a)   **(b)**   **(c)**

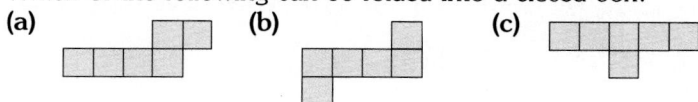

2. If a penny is placed on a table, how many pennies can be placed around it, where each new penny touches the penny in the center and two other pennies?

3. Twenty-five cannonballs are stacked in a 5×5 square rack on the floor. What is the greatest number of cannonballs that can be stacked on these 25 to form a stable pyramid of cannonballs?

WRITING/DISCUSSING FOR UNDERSTANDING

1. Given that we live in a three-dimensional world, is it more natural to introduce students first to three-dimensional shapes and then proceed to two-dimensional shapes? Discuss the advantages and disadvantages of this order of presentation.

2. Describe the types of symmetry you see in the room around you. Be sure to consider both types of symmetry and consider both two- and three-dimensional shapes.

3. Explain how the following NCTM Standards are reflected in this chapter.
- Identify, describe, compare, and classify geometric figures.
- Visualize and represent geometric figures with special attention to developing spatial sense.
- Represent and solve problems using geometric models.
- Understand and apply geometric properties and relationships.
- Develop an appreciation of geometry as a means of describing the physical world.

PROJECTS

1. Put together a collection of pictures from magazines, newspapers, and so on, of objects having shapes like those discussed in this chapter. You might look for shapes in nature or man-made objects. Be sure to consider both two- and three-dimensional shapes. Discuss the symmetries of the objects you find.

2. The unit for angle measure discussed in this chapter is the degree. Other units can be used. In trigonometry and calculus, angles are often measured in radians, which are related to arc length in a circle. A metric unit for angle measure, the grade or grad, was commonly used in the nineteenth century. Find out more about these units of measure and prepare a summary, comparing measures of several angles.

3. Construct models from clay, wire, cardboard, straws, and so on, to represent visually the possible cross sections when a cube is sliced once with a plane (see Problem 23 in Exercise/Problem Set 12.5—Part B).

CHAPTER REVIEW

Major Ideas

1. The van Hiele theory describes learning levels in geometry from recognition to analysis to relationships/deduction to formalism to axiomatics.

2. A shape can simultaneously represent several general types.
3. Paper folding can be used to identify perpendicular and parallel line segments.
4. Shapes can have reflection symmetry, rotation symmetry, both, or neither.
5. In two-dimensional space, using parallel lines, we can compute the angle sum in a triangle. This, in turn, allows us to compute the measures of various angles in a regular n-gon.
6. The plane can be tessellated by certain regular polygonal regions.
7. There are many analogies between two- and three-dimensional shapes, such as

$$line \leftrightarrow plane$$

$$angle \leftrightarrow dihedral\ angle$$

$$polygon \leftrightarrow polyhedron$$

$$circle \leftrightarrow sphere$$

Following is a list of key vocabulary, notation, and ideas for this chapter. Mentally review these items and, where appropriate, write down the meaning of each term. Then restudy the material that you are unsure of before proceeding to take the chapter test.

SECTION 12.1: RECOGNIZING GEOMETRIC SHAPES AND DEFINITIONS

Vocabulary/Notation

Line segment 534	Square 535
Triangle 534	Rectangle 535
Side 534	Parallelogram 535
Quadrilateral 535	Kite 536
Angle 535	Rhombus 536
Vertex (vertices) 535	Congruent line segments 536
Right angle 535	Congruent angles 536
Perpendicular line segments 535	Equilateral 536
Isosceles triangle 535	Equiangular 536
Equilateral triangle 535	Trapezoid 536
Scalene triangle 535	Isosceles trapezoid 536

Ideas

Recognizing shapes and stating definitions 531–536

SECTION 12.2: ANALYZING SHAPES

Vocabulary/Notation

Reflection symmetry 546	Concave 553
Line of symmetry 546	Vertex angle 553
Axis of symmetry 546	Interior angle 553
Base angles 548	Central angle 553
Rotation symmetry 548	Exterior angle 553

Ideas

SECTION 12.3:   PROPERTIES OF GEOMETRIC SHAPES: LINES AND ANGLES

Vocabulary/Notation

Ideas

SECTION 12.4:   REGULAR POLYGONS AND TESSELLATIONS

Vocabulary/Notation

Ideas

SECTION 12.5:   DESCRIBING THREE-DIMENSIONAL SHAPES

Vocabulary/Notation

Ideas

PEOPLE IN MATHEMATICS

Cathleen Synge Morawetz (1923–) said that she liked to construct "engines and levers" as a youngster, but wasn't good in arithmetic. "I used to get bad marks in mental arithmetic." Her father is the Irish mathematician J. L. Synge, and her mother studied mathematics at Trinity College. In college, she gravitated from engineering to mathematics and did her doctoral thesis on the analysis of shock waves. Her professional research has focused on the applications of differential equations. She became the first woman in the United States to head a mathematics institute, the Courant Institute of Mathematical Sciences in New York. "The burden of raising children still falls on the woman, at a time that's very important in her career. I'm about to institute a new plan of life, according to which women would have their children in their late teens and their mothers would bring them up. I don't mean the grandmother would give up her career, but she's already established, so she can afford to take time off to look after the children."

R. L. Moore (1882–1974), a Texan to the core, was a rugged individualist whose specialty was topology. His methods were highly original, both in research and teaching. As a professor at the University of Texas, he encouraged originality in his students by discouraging them from reading standard expositions and requiring them to work things out for themselves, in true pioneer spirit. His Socratic style became known as the "Moore method." One of his students, Mary Ellen Rudin, describes it this way: "He always looked for people who had not been influenced by other mathematical experiences. His technique was to feed all kinds of problems to us. He gave us lists of mathematical statements. Some were true, some were false, some were very easy to prove or disprove, others very hard. We worked on whatever we jolly well pleased."

CHAPTER 12 TEST

Knowledge

1. True or false?
   (a) Every isosceles triangle is equilateral.
   (b) Every rhombus is a kite.
   (c) A circle is convex.
   (d) Vertical angles have the same measure.
   (e) A triangle has at most one right angle or one obtuse angle.
   (f) A regular pentagon has five diagonals.
   (g) A cube has 6 faces, 8 vertices, and 12 edges.
   (h) There are exactly three different regular tessellations each using congruent regular n-gons, where $n = 3, 4,$ or 6.
   (i) A pyramid has a square base.
   (j) Skew lines are the same as parallel lines.
   (k) A regular hexagon has exactly three reflection symmetries.
   (l) The vertex angle of any regular n-gon has the same measure as any exterior angle of the same n-gon.
   (m) A circle has infinitely many rotation symmetries.
   (n) It is possible to have a right scalene triangle.

Skill

2. Explain how to use paper folding to show that the diagonals of a rhombus are perpendicular.

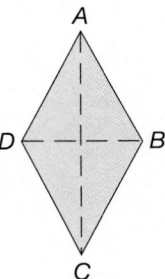

3. Determine the measures of all the dihedral angles of a right prism whose bases are regular octagons.

4. What is the measure of a vertex angle in a regular 10-gon?

5. Determine the number of reflection symmetries a regular 9-gon has. How many rotations less than 360° map a regular 13-gon onto itself?

6. If *l* ∥ *m* in the figure, determine the measures of the following angles: ∠1, ∠2, ∠3, ∠4.

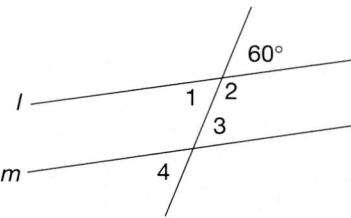

7. Determine the number of faces, vertices, and edges for the hexagonal pyramid shown.

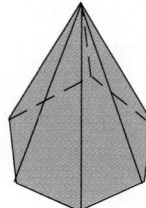

Understanding

8. The corresponding angles property states that $m(\angle 1) = m(\angle 2)$ in the figure. Angles ∠3 and ∠4 are called interior angles on the same side of the transversal. Prove that $m(\angle 3) + m(\angle 4) = 180°$.

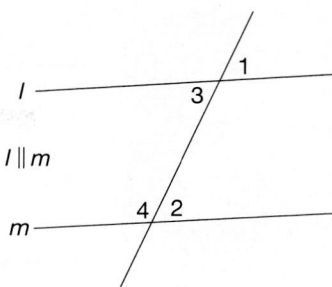

l ∥ *m*

9. Using the result of Problem 8, show that if a parallelogram has one right angle, then the parallelogram must be a rectangle.

Problem Solving/Application

10. A prism has 96 edges. How many vertices and faces does it have? Explain.

11. Use the figure to show that any convex 7-gon has the sum of its vertex angles equal to 900°.

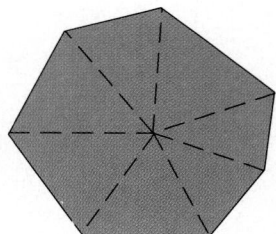

12. Determine if it is possible to tessellate the plane using a combination of regular 5-gons and regular 7-gons only.

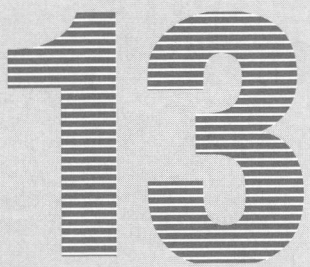

13

Measurement

Archimedes

Archimedes: Mathematical Genius from Antiquity

Archimedes (287–212 B.C.) is considered to have been the greatest mathematician in antiquity. In fact, he is ranked by many with Sir Isaac Newton and Carl Friedrich Gauss as one of the three greatest mathematicians of all time.

Archimedes made significant contributions to mathematics and physics. He computed the centers of gravity of many plane and solid geometric shapes and described properties of levers. He invented a pump for raising water from a river and developed mechanical devices, such as catapults, for protection against Roman invasions. His parabolic "burning mirrors" were used to focus the sun's rays on attacking wooden ships, thereby igniting them. Perhaps the most famous story about Archimedes is that of his discovery of the principle of buoyancy. (A body immersed or floating in water is buoyed up by a force equal to the weight of the water displaced. Thus a steel ship can float if it displaces a quantity of water whose weight exceeds the weight of the ship.) Legend has it that Archimedes discovered the buoyancy principle while bathing, and was so excited by his discovery that he ran naked into the street shouting "Eureka!"

In mathematics, Archimedes discovered and verified formulas for the surface area and volume of a sphere. His method for deriving the volume of a sphere, called the *Archimedean method,* involved a lever principle. He compared a sphere of radius r, a cone of radius $2r$ and height $2r$, to a cylinder also of radius $2r$ and height $2r$. See the figure below.

Using cross sections, Archimedes deduced that the cone and sphere as solids, placed two units from the fulcrum of the lever, would balance the solid cylinder placed one unit from the fulcrum.

Hence the volume of the cone plus the volume of the sphere equals $\frac{1}{2}$ the volume of the cylinder. But the volume of the cone was known to be $\frac{1}{3}$ the volume of the cylinder, so that the volume of the sphere must be $\frac{1}{6}$ the volume of the cylinder. Thus the volume of the sphere is $\frac{1}{6}(8\pi r^3)$, or $\frac{4}{3}\pi r^3$. The original description of the *Archimedean method* was thought to be permanently lost until its rediscovery in Constantinople, now Istanbul, in 1906.

Archimedes viewed his *method* as a means to suggest mathematical results, but not as a rigorous proof. Remarkably, Archimedes was able to verify his derivation of the volume of the sphere, using mathematical reasoning as rigorous as that of calculus-level mathematics. Consequently, he is credited with anticipating the development of some of the ideas of calculus, nearly 2000 years before its creation by Sir Isaac Newton (1642–1727) and Gottfried Wilhelm Leibniz (1646–1716).

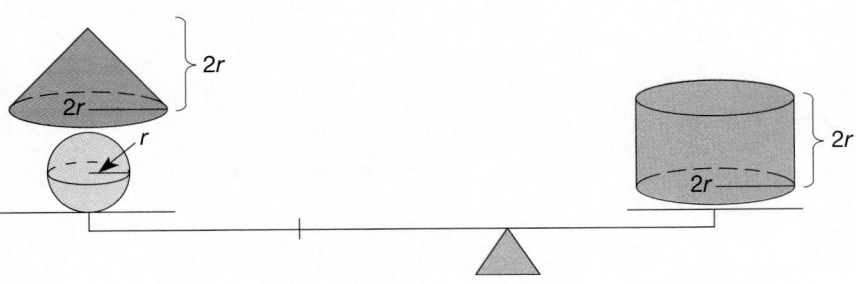

STRATEGY 18: USE DIMENSIONAL ANALYSIS

The strategy Use Dimensional Analysis is useful in applied problems that involve conversions among measurement units. For example, distance–rate–time problems or problems involving several rates (ratios) are sometimes easier to analyze via dimensional analysis. Additionally, dimensional analysis allows us to check our answer to see if we have reported it in the correct measurement units.

Initial Problem

David was planning a motorcycle trip across Canada. He drew his route on a map and estimated the length of his route to be 115 centimeters. The scale on his map is 1 centimeter = 39 kilometers. His motorcycle's gasoline consumption is 75 miles per gallon of gasoline on the average. If gasoline costs $1.25 per gallon, how much should he plan to spend for gasoline? (What additional information does he need?)

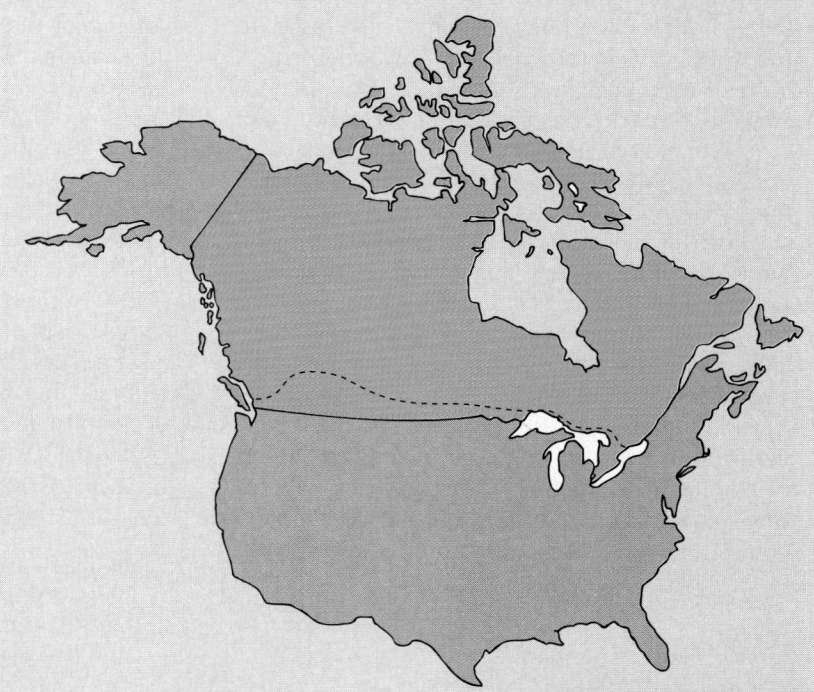

Clues

The Use Dimensional Analysis strategy may be appropriate when:

- Units of measure are involved.
- The problem involves physical quantities.
- Conversions are required.

A solution of the Initial Problem above appears on page 687.

INTRODUCTION

The measurement process allows us to analyze geometric figures using real numbers. For example, suppose that we use a sphere to model the earth (Figure 13.1). Then we can ask many questions about the sphere, such as "How far is it around the equator? How much surface area does it have? How much space does it take up?" Questions such as these can lead us to the study of the measurement of length, area, and volume of geometrical figures, as well as other attributes. In the first section of this chapter we introduce wholistic measurement, using natural or nonstandard units such as "hands" and "paces." We also study two systems of standard units, namely the English system or customary system of units that we Americans use, and the metric system or *Système International* (SI), which virtually all other countries use. In the other sections, we study abstract mathematical measurement of geometric shapes, exploring length, area, surface area, and volume.

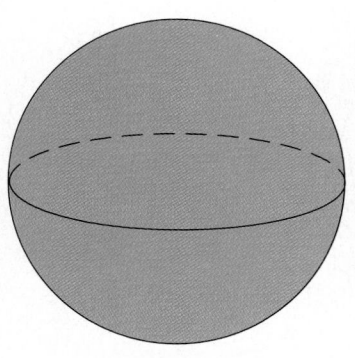

FIGURE 13.1

13.1

MEASUREMENT WITH NONSTANDARD AND STANDARD UNITS

Nonstandard Units

The measurement process is defined as follows.

> **Definition**
>
> ### The Measurement Process
>
> 1. Select an object and an attribute of the object to measure, such as its length, area, volume, weight, or temperature.
> 2. Select an appropriate unit with which to measure the attribute.
> 3. Determine the number of units needed to measure the attribute. (This may require a measurement device.)

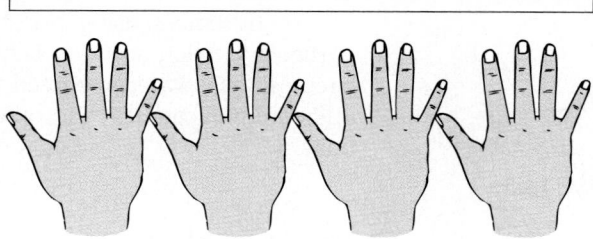

FIGURE 13.2

For example, to measure the length of an object, we might see how many times our hand will span the object. Figure 13.2 shows a stick that is four "hand spans" long. "Hands" are still used as a unit to measure the height of horses. For measuring longer distances, we might use the length of our feet placed heel to toe or our pace as our unit of measurement. For shorter

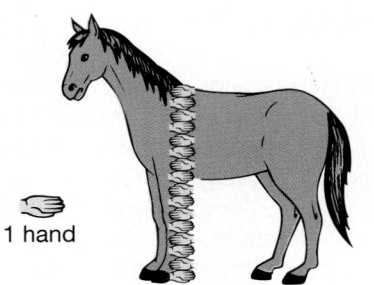

A horse that is 16 hands tall   Stepping off a room   A flower that is 5 fingers wide

FIGURE 13.3

distances, we might use the width of a finger as our unit (Figure 13.3). Regardless, in every case, we can select some appropriate unit and determine how many units are needed to span the object. This is an *informal measurement* method of measuring length, since it involves naturally occurring units and is done in a relatively imprecise way.

To measure the area of a region informally, we select a convenient two-dimensional shape as our unit and determine how many such units are needed to cover the region. Figure 13.4 shows how to measure the area of a rectangular rug, using square floor tiles as the unit of measure. By counting the number of squares inside the rectangular border, and estimating the fractional parts of the other squares that are partly inside the border, it appears that the area of the rug is between 15 and 16 square units (certainly, between 12 and 20).

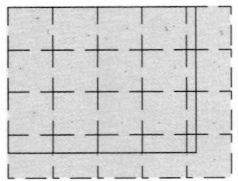

FIGURE 13.4

To measure the capacity of water that a vase will hold, we can select a convenient container, such as a water glass, to use as our unit, and see how many glassfuls are required to fill the vase (see Figure 13.5). This is an informal method of measuring volume. (Strictly speaking, we are measuring the *capacity* of the vase, namely the amount that it will hold. The volume of the vase would be the amount of material comprising the vase itself.) Other wholistic volume measures are found in recipes: a "dash" of hot sauce, a "pinch" of salt, or a "few shakes" of a spice, for example.

Measurement using nonstandard units is adequate for many needs, particularly when accuracy is not essential. However, there are many other circumstances when we need to determine measurements more precisely and communicate them to others. That is, we need standard measurement units.

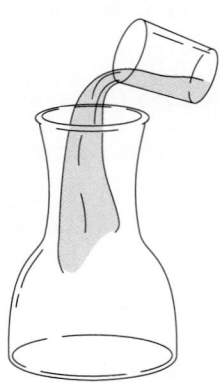

FIGURE 13.5

Standard Units

The English System

The **English system** of units arose from natural, nonstandard units. For example, the foot was literally the length of a human foot and the yard was the distance from the tip of the nose to the end of an outstretched arm (useful in measuring cloth or "'yard goods"). The inch was the length of three barley corns, the fathom was the length of a full arm span (for measuring rope), and the acre was the amount of land that a horse could plow in one day (Figure 13.6).

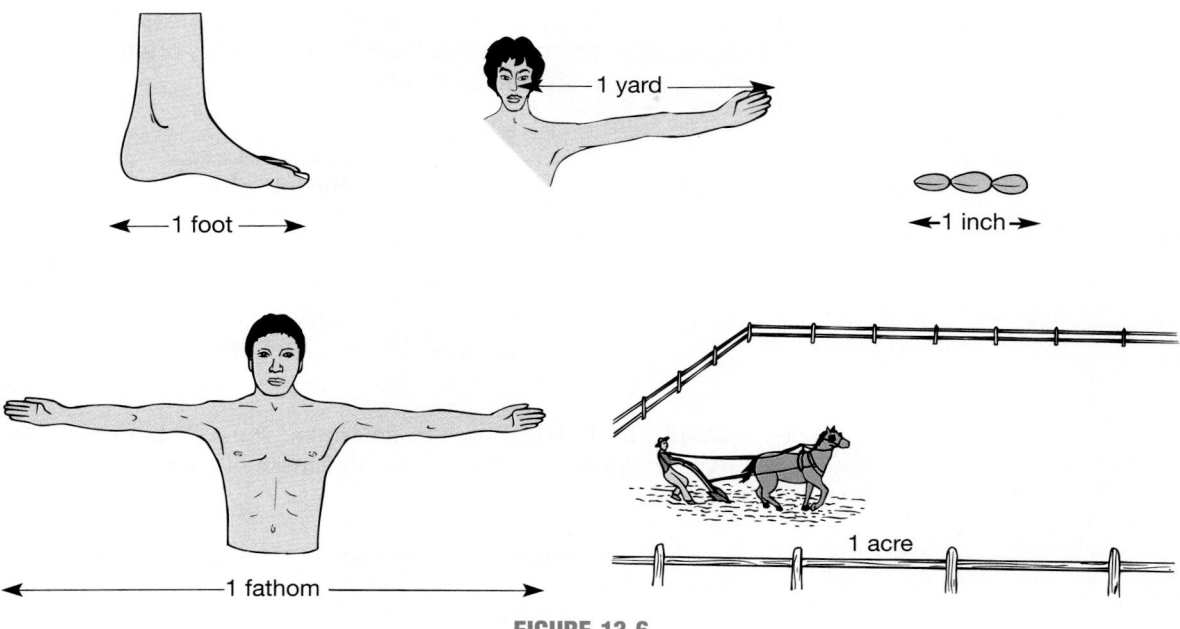

FIGURE 13.6

Length: The natural English units were standardized so that the foot was defined by a prototype metal bar, and the inch defined as $\frac{1}{12}$ of a foot, the yard the length of 3 feet, and so on for other lengths (Table 13.1). A variety of ratios occurs among the English units of length. For example, the ratio of inches to feet is $12:1$, of feet to yards is $3:1$, of yards to rods is $5\frac{1}{2}:1$, and of furlongs to miles is $8:1$. A considerable amount of memorization is needed in learning the English system of measurement.

TABLE 13.1

Unit	Fraction or Multiple of 1 Foot
Inch	$\frac{1}{12}$ ft
Foot	1 ft
Yard	3 ft
Rod	$16\frac{1}{2}$ ft
Furlong	660 ft
Mile	5280 ft

Area: Area is measured in the English system using the square foot (written ft^2) as the fundamental unit. That is, to measure the area of a region, the number of squares, 1 foot on a side, that are needed to cover the region is determined. This is an application of tessellating the plane with squares (see Chapter 12). Other polygons could, in fact, be used as fundamental units of area. For example, a right triangle, an equilateral triangle, or a regular hexagon could also be used as a fundamental unit of area. For large regions, square yards are used to measure areas, and for very large regions, acres and square miles are used to measure areas. Table 13.2 gives the relationships among various English system units of area. Here, again, the ratios between area units are not uniform.

TABLE 13.2

Unit	Multiple of 1 Square Foot
Square foot	1 ft^2
Square yard	9 ft^2
Acre	$43{,}560 \text{ ft}^2$
Square mile	$27{,}878{,}400 \text{ ft}^2$

Example 13.1 shows how to determine some of the entries in Table 13.2. A more general strategy, called dimensional analysis, appears later in this section.

EXAMPLE 13.1   Compute the ratios square feet:square yards and square feet:square miles.

Solution
Since there are 3 feet in 1 yard and one square yard measures one yard by one yard, we see that there are 9 square feet in 1 square yard [Figure 13.7(a)]. Therefore, the ratio of square feet to square yards is 9:1.

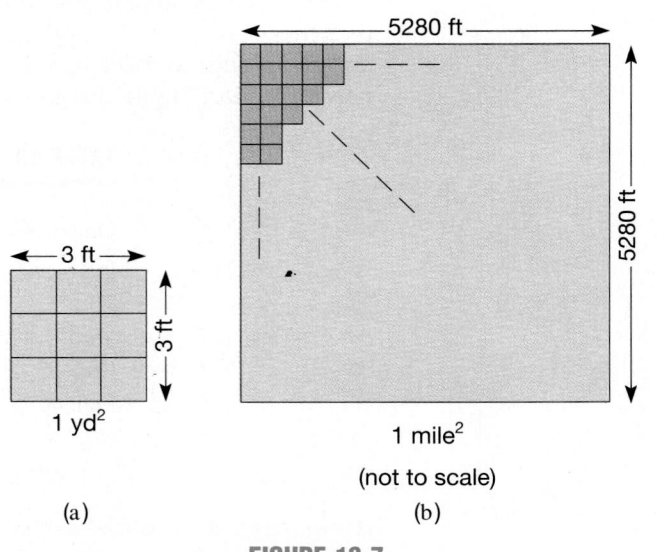

1 yd²

(a)

1 mile²

(not to scale)

(b)

FIGURE 13.7

Next imagine covering a square, 1 mile on each side, with square tiles, each 1 foot on a side [Figure 13.7(b)]. It would take an array of squares with 5280 rows, each row having 5280 tiles. Hence it would take $5280 \times 5280 = 27,878,400$ square feet to cover 1 square mile. So the ratio of square feet to square miles is $27,878,400:1$. ∎

Volume: In the English system, volume is measured using the cubic foot as the fundamental unit (Figure 13.8). To find the volume of a cubical box that is 3 feet on each side, imagine stacking as many cubic feet inside the box as possible (Figure 13.9). The box could be filled with $3 \times 3 \times 3 = 27$ cubes, each measuring 1 foot on an edge. Each of the smaller cubes has a volume of 1 cubic foot (written ft^3) so that the larger cube has a volume of 27 ft^3. The larger cube is, of course, 1 cubic yard (1 yd^3). It is common for top soil and concrete to be sold by the cubic yard, for example. In the English system, we have several cubic units used for measuring volume. Table 13.3 shows some relationships among them. Note the variety of volume ratios in the English system.

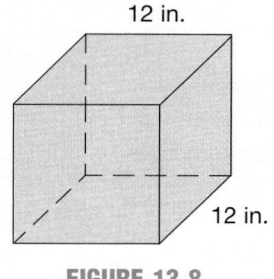

12 in.

12 in.

FIGURE 13.8

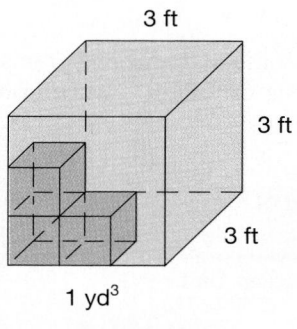

3 ft

3 ft

3 ft

1 yd^3

FIGURE 13.9

TABLE 13.3

Unit	Fraction or Multiple of a Cubic Foot
Cubic inch (1 in^3)	1/1728 ft^3
Cubic foot	1 ft^3
Cubic yard (1 yd^3)	27 ft^3

EXAMPLE 13.2   Verify the ratio of $in^3:ft^3$ given in Table 13.3.

Solution

Since there are 12 inches in each foot, we could fill a cubic foot with $12 \times 12 \times 12$ smaller cubes, each 1 inch on an edge. Hence there are $12^3 = 1728$ cubic inches in 1 cubic foot. Consequently, each cubic inch is $\frac{1}{1728}$ of a cubic foot. ∎

Figure 13.9 shows cubes, one foot on each side, being stacked *inside* the cubic yard to show that the volume of the box is 27 ft^3. If the larger box were a solid, we would still say that its volume is 27 ft^3. Notice that 27 ft^3 of water can be poured into the open box but no water can be poured *into* a solid cube. To distinguish between these two physical situations, we use the words *capacity* (how much the box will hold) and *volume* (how much material makes up the box). Often, however, the word *volume* is used for capacity. The English system uses the units shown in Table 13.4 to measure capacity for liquids. In addition to these liquid measures of capacity, there are similar dry measures.

Weight: In the English system, weight is measured in pounds and ounces. In fact, there are two types of measures of weight—troy ounces and pounds (mainly for precious metals), and avoirdupois ounces and pounds, the latter being more common. We will use the avoirdupois units. The weight of 2000

TABLE 13.4

Unit	Abbreviation	Relation to Preceding Unit
1 teaspoon	tsp	
1 tablespoon	tbs	3 teaspoons
1 liquid ounce	oz	2 tablespoons
1 cup	cp	8 liquid ounces
1 pint	pt	2 cups
1 quart	qt	2 pints
1 gallon	gal	4 quarts
1 barrel	bar	31.5 gallons

pounds is 1 English ton. Smaller weights are measured in drams and grains. Table 13.5 summarizes these English system units of weight. Notice how inconsistent the ratios are between consecutive units.

TABLE 13.5   ENGLISH SYSTEM UNITS OF WEIGHT (Avoirdupois)

Unit	Relation to Preceding Unit
1 grain	
1 dram	$27\frac{11}{32}$ grains
1 ounce	16 drams
1 pound	16 ounces
1 ton	2000 pounds

Technically, the concepts of weight and mass are different. Informally, mass is the measure of the amount of matter of an object and weight is a measure of the force with which gravity attracts the object. Thus although your mass is the same on Earth and on the Moon, you weigh more on Earth since the attraction of gravity is greater on Earth. We will not make a distinction between weight and mass. We will use English units of weight and metric units of mass, both of which are used to weigh objects.

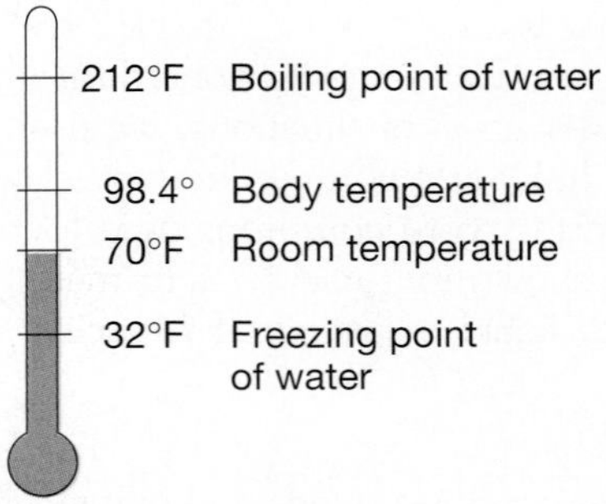

Temperature: Temperature is measured in **degrees Fahrenheit** in the English system. The Fahrenheit temperature scale is named for Gabriel Fahrenheit, a German instrument maker, who invented the mercury thermometer in 1714. The freezing point and boiling point of water are used as reference temperatures. The freezing point is arbitrarily defined to be 32° Fahrenheit, and the boiling point 212° Fahrenheit. This gives an interval of exactly 180° from freezing to boiling (Figure 13.10).

The Metric System

In contrast to the English system of measurement units, the **metric system** of units (or Système International d'Unités) incorporates all of the following features of an ideal system of units.

212°F   Boiling point of water

98.4°   Body temperature

70°F   Room temperature

32°F   Freezing point of water

FIGURE 13.10

> **An Ideal System of Units**
>
> **1.** The fundamental unit can be accurately reproduced without reference to a prototype. (Portability)
> **2.** There are simple (e.g., decimal) ratios among units of the same type. (Convertibility)
> **3.** Different types of units (e.g., those for length, area, and volume) are defined in terms of each other, using simple relationships. (Interrelatedness)

Length: In the metric system, the fundamental unit of length is the **meter** (about $39\frac{1}{2}$ inches). The meter was originally defined to be one ten-millionth of the distance from the equator to the North Pole along the Greenwich meridian. A prototype platinum–iridium bar representing a meter was maintained in the International Bureau of Weights and Measures in France. However, as science advanced, this definition was changed so that the meter could be reproduced anywhere in the world. Since 1960, the meter has been defined to be precisely 1,650,763.73 wavelengths of orange-red light in the spectrum of the element krypton 86. Although this definition may seem highly technical, it has the advantage of being reproducible in a laboratory anywhere. That is, no standard meter prototype need be kept. This is a clear advantage over older versions of the English system. We shall see that there are many more.

The metric system is a decimal system of measurement in which multiples and fractions of the fundamental unit correspond to powers of ten. For example, one thousand meters is a **kilometer**, one-tenth of a meter is a **decimeter**, one-hundredth of a meter is a **centimeter**, and one-thousandth of a meter is a **millimeter**. Table 13.6 shows some relationships among metric units of length. Notice the simple ratios among units of length in the metric system. (Compare Table 13.6 to Table 13.1 for the English system, for example.) From Table 13.6 we see that 1 **dekameter** is equivalent to 10 meters, 1 **hectometer** is equivalent to 100 meters, and so on. Also, 1 dekameter is equivalent to 100 decimeters, 1 kilometer is equivalent to 1,000,000 millimeters, and so on. (Check these.)

TABLE 13.6

Unit	Symbol	Fraction or Multiple of 1 Meter
1 millimeter	1 mm	0.001 m
1 centimeter	1 cm	0.01 m
1 decimeter	1 dm	0.1 m
1 meter	1 m	1 m
1 dekameter	1 dam	10 m
1 hectometer	1 hm	100 m
1 kilometer	1 km	1000 m

From the information in Table 13.6, we can make a metric "converter" diagram to simplify changing units of length. Locate consecutive metric abbreviations for units of length starting with the largest prefix on the left (Figure 13.11). To convert from, say, hectometers to centimeters, count spaces from "hm" to "cm" in the diagram, and move the decimal point in the same direction as many spaces as are indicated in the diagram (here, 4 to the right). For example, 13.23685 hm = 132,368.5 cm. Similarly, 4326.9 mm = 4.3269 m since we move three spaces to the left in the diagram when going from "mm" to "m." It is good practice to use measurement sense as a check. For example, when converting from mm to hm, we have fewer "hm's" than "mm's" since 1 hm is longer than 1 mm.

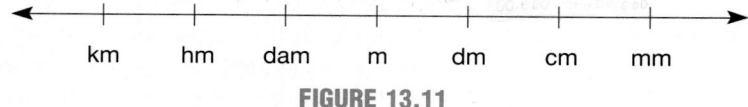

km   hm   dam   m   dm   cm   mm

FIGURE 13.11

Figure 13.12 shows *relative* comparisons of lengths in English and metric systems. Lengths that are measured in feet or yards in the English system are commonly measured in meters in the metric system. Lengths measured in inches in the English system are measured in centimeters in the metric system. (By definition, 1 in. is exactly 2.54 cm.) For example, in metric countries, track and field events use meters instead of yards for the lengths of races. Snowfall is measured in centimeters in metric countries, not inches.

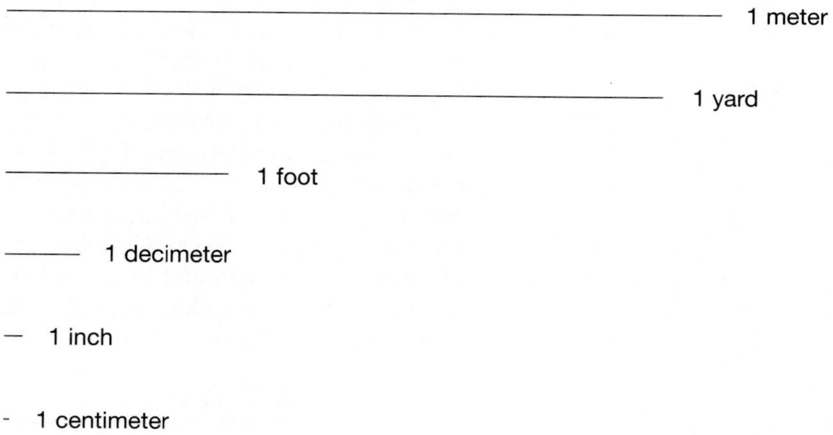

———————————————————————————— 1 meter

———————————————————————— 1 yard

———————————— 1 foot

——————— 1 decimeter

— 1 inch

- 1 centimeter

FIGURE 13.12

From Table 13.6 we see that certain prefixes are used in the metric system to indicate fractions or multiples of the fundamental unit. Table 13.7 gives the meanings of many of the metric prefixes. The three most commonly used prefixes are in italics. We will see that these prefixes are also used with measures of area, volume, and weight. Compare the descriptions of the prefixes in Table 13.7 with their uses in Table 13.6. Notice how the prefixes signify the ratios to the fundamental unit.

Area: In the metric system, the fundamental unit of area is the square meter. A square that is 1 meter long on each side has an area of **1 square meter,** written 1 m^2 (Figure 13.13). Areas measured in square feet or square

TABLE 13.7

Prefix	Multiple or Fraction	
atto-	10^{-18}	
femto-	10^{-15}	
pico-	10^{-12}	Science
nano-	10^{-9}	
micro-	10^{-6}	
milli-	$10^{-3} = \frac{1}{1000}$	
centi-	$10^{-2} = \frac{1}{100}$	
deci-	$10^{-1} = \frac{1}{10}$	Everyday life
deka-	10	
hecto-	$10^2 = 100$	
kilo-	$10^3 = 1000$	
mega-	10^6	
giga-	10^9	
tera-	10^{12}	Science
peta-	10^{15}	
exa-	10^{18}	

yards in the English system are measured in square meters in the metric system. For example, carpeting would be measured in square meters.

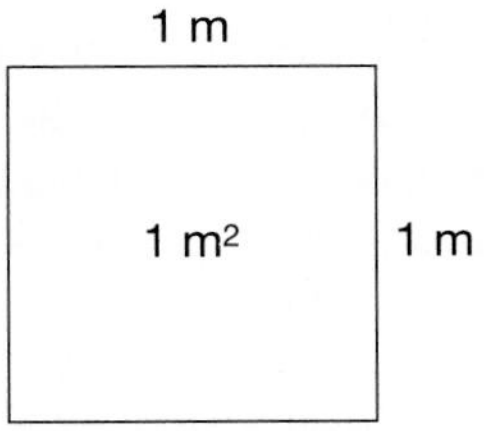

Smaller areas are measured in square centimeters. A **square centimeter** is the area of a square that is 1 centimeter long on each side. For example, the area of a piece of notebook paper or a photograph would be measured in square centimeters (cm^2). Example 13.3 shows the relationship between square centimeters and square meters.

1 m

1 m²   1 m

FIGURE 13.13

EXAMPLE 13.3   Determine the number of square centimeters in 1 square meter.

Solution
A square with area 1 square meter can be covered with an array of square centimeters. In Figure 13.14 we see part of the array. There are 100 rows,

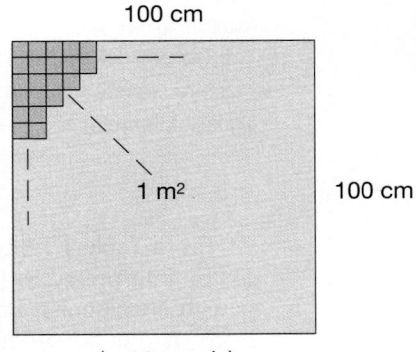

100 cm

1 m²   100 cm

(not to scale)

FIGURE 13.14

each row having 100 square centimeters. Hence there are $100 \times 100 = 10\ 000$ square centimeters needed to cover the square meter. Thus $1\ m^2 = 10\ 000\ cm^2$. (NOTE: Spaces are used instead of commas to show groupings in large numbers.) ■

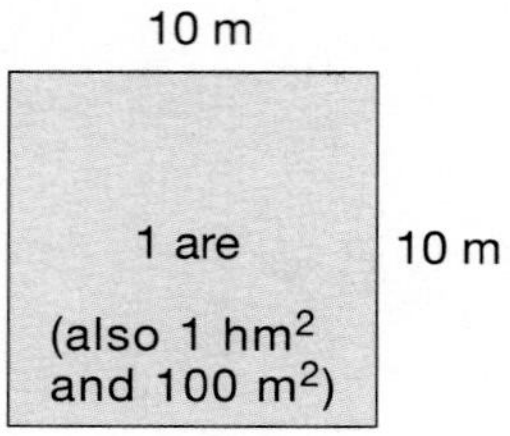

Very small areas, such as on a microscope slide, are measured using square millimeters. A **square millimeter** is the area of a square whose sides are each 1 millimeter long.

In the metric system the area of a square that is 10 m on each side is given the special name **are** (pronounced "air"). Figure 13.15 illustrates this definition. An are is approximately the area of the floor of a large two-car garage. It is a convenient unit for measuring the area of building lots. There are $100\ m^2$ in 1 are.

An area equivalent to 100 ares is called a **hectare**, written 1 ha. Notice the use of the prefix "hect" (meaning 100). The hectare is useful for measuring areas of farms and ranches. We can show that 1 hectare is 1 square hectometer by converting each to square meters, as follows.

$$1\ ha = 100\ ares = 100 \times (100\ m^2) = 10\ 000\ m^2.$$

Also,

$$1\ hm^2 = (100\ m) \times (100\ m) = 10\ 000\ m^2.$$

Thus $1\ ha = 1\ hm^2$.

Finally, very large areas are measured in the metric system using square kilometers. One **square kilometer** is the area of a square that is 1 kilometer on each side. Areas of cities or states, for example, are reported in square kilometers. Table 13.8 gives the ratios among various units of area in the metric system. See if you can verify the entries in the table.

10 m

1 are

(also 1 hm²
and 100 m²)

10 m

FIGURE 13.15

TABLE 13.8

Unit	Abbreviation	Fraction or Multiple 1 Square Meter
Square millimeter	mm²	0.000001 m²
Square centimeter	cm²	0.0001 m²
Square decimeter	dm²	0.01 m²
Square meter	m²	1 m²
Are (square dekameter)	a (dam²)	100 m²
Hectare (square hectometer)	ha (hm²)	10 000 m²
Square kilometer	km²	1 000 000 m²

From Table 13.8 we see that the metric prefixes for square units should *not* be interpreted in the abbreviated forms as having the same meanings as with linear units. For example, $1\ dm^2$ is not one-tenth of $1\ m^2$, rather $1\ dm^2$ is one-hundredth of $1\ m^2$. Conversions among units of area can be done if we use the metric converter in Figure 13.16, but move the decimal point *twice* the number of spaces that we move between units. This is due to the fact that area involves *two* dimensions. For example, suppose that we wish to convert 3.7 m² to mm². From Figure 13.16, we move three spaces to the right from "m" to "mm," so we will move the decimal point $3 \cdot 2 = 6$ (the "2" is due to the *two* dimensions) places to the right. Thus $3.7 \text{ m}^2 = 3\,700\,000 \text{ mm}^2$. Since $1 \text{ m}^2 = (1000 \text{ mm})^2 = 1\,000\,000 \text{ mm}^2$, we have $3.7 \text{ m}^2 = 3.7 \times (1\,000\,000) \text{ mm}^2 = 3\,700\,000 \text{ mm}^2$, which is the same result that we obtained using the metric converter.

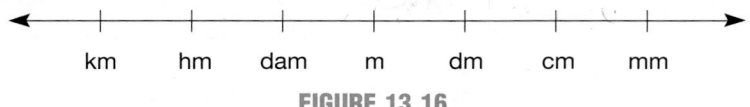

km   hm   dam   m   dm   cm   mm

FIGURE 13.16

Volume: The fundamental unit of volume in the metric system is the liter. A **liter**, abbreviated L, is the volume of a cube that measures 10 cm on each edge (Figure 13.17). We can also say that a liter is 1 **cubic decimeter**, since the cube in Figure 13.17 measures 1 dm on each edge. Notice that the liter is defined with reference to the meter, which is the fundamental unit of length. The liter is slightly larger than a quart. Many soft-drink containers have capacities of 1 or 2 liters.

Imagine filling the liter cube in Figure 13.17 with smaller cubes, 1 centimeter on each edge. Figure 13.18 illustrates this. Each small cube has a volume of 1 **cubic centimeter** (1 cm³). It will take a 10 × 10 array (hence 100) of the centimeter cubes to cover the bottom of the liter cube. Finally, it takes 10 layers, each with 100 centimeter cubes, to fill the liter cube to the top. Thus 1 liter is equivalent to 1000 cm³. Recall that the prefix "milli-" in the metric system means one-thousandth. Thus we see that 1 **milliliter** is equivalent to 1 cubic centimeter, since there are 1000 cm³ in 1 liter. Small volumes in the metric system are measured in milliliters (cubic centimeters). Containers of liquid are frequently labeled in milliliters.

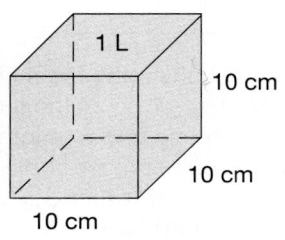

1 L

10 cm

10 cm

10 cm

FIGURE 13.17

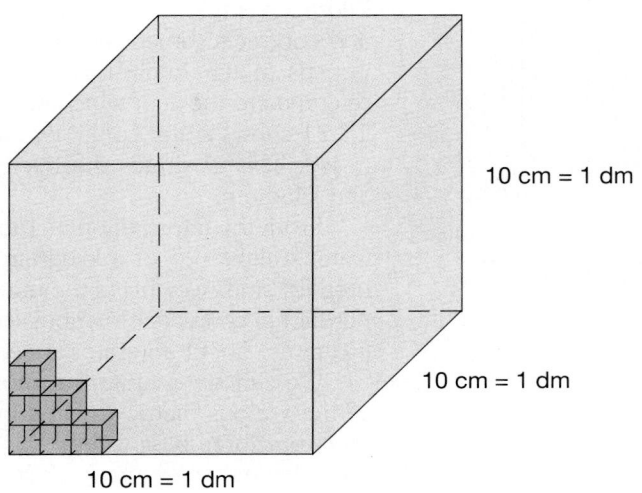

10 cm = 1 dm

10 cm = 1 dm

10 cm = 1 dm

FIGURE 13.18

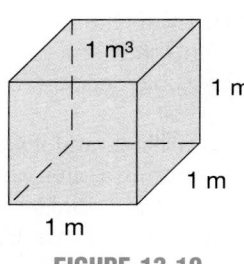

1 m³

1 m

1 m

1 m

FIGURE 13.19

Large volumes in the metric system are measured using cubic meters. A **cubic meter** is the volume of a cube that measures 1 meter on each edge (Figure 13.19). Capacities of large containers such as water tanks, reservoirs, or swimming pools are measured using cubic meters. Table 13.9 gives the relationships among commonly used volume units in the metric system. In the metric system, capacity is usually recorded in liters, milliliters, and so on.

TABLE 13.9

Unit	Abbreviation	Fraction or Multiple of 1 Liter
Milliliter (cubic centimeter)	mL (cm^3)	0.001 L
Liter (cubic decimeter)	L (dm^3)	1 L
Kiloliter (cubic meter)	kL (m^3)	1000 L

We can make conversions among metric volume units using the metric converter (Figure 13.20). To convert among volume units we count the number of spaces that we move left or right in going from one unit to another. Then we move the decimal point exactly *three* times that number of places since volume involves three dimensions. For example, in converting 187.68 cm^3 to m^3, we count two spaces to the left in Figure 13.20 (from cm to m). Then we move the decimal point $2 \cdot 3 = 6$ (the "3" is due to *three* dimensions) places to the left, so that 187.68 cm^3 = 0.00018768 m^3. The justification for this procedure is left to the problem set.

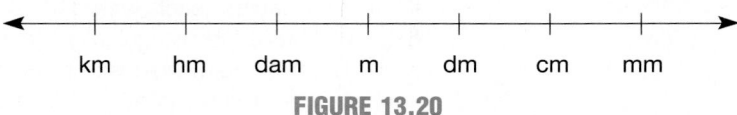

km   hm   dam   m   dm   cm   mm

FIGURE 13.20

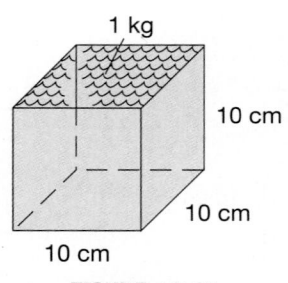

1 kg

10 cm

10 cm

10 cm

FIGURE 13.21

Mass: In the metric system, a basic unit of mass is the kilogram. One **kilogram** is the mass of 1 liter of water in its densest state. (Water expands and contracts somewhat when heated or cooled.) A kilogram is about 2.2 pounds in the English system. Notice that the kilogram is defined with reference to the liter, which in turn was defined relative to the meter. Figure 13.21 shows a liter container filled with water, hence a mass of 1 kilogram (1 kg). This illustrates the interrelatedness of the metric units meter, liter, and kilogram.

From the information in Table 13.9, we can conclude that 1 milliliter of water weighs $\frac{1}{1000}$ of a kilogram. This weight is called a **gram**. Grams are used for small weights in the metric system, such as ingredients in recipes or nutritional contents of various foods. Many foods are packaged and labeled by grams. About 28 grams are equivalent to 1 ounce in the English system.

We can summarize the information in Table 13.9 with the definitions of the various metric weights in the following way. In the metric system, there are three basic cubes: the cubic centimeter, the cubic decimeter, and the cubic meter (Figure 13.22).

The cubic centimeter is equivalent in volume to 1 milliliter, and if water, it weighs 1 gram. Similarly, 1 cubic decimeter of volume is 1 liter and, if water, weighs 1 kilogram. Finally, 1 cubic meter of volume is 1 kiloliter and, if water, weighs 1000 kilograms, called a **metric ton** (tonne). Table 13.10 summarizes these relationships.

TABLE 13.10

Cube	Volume	Mass (water)
1 m³	1 kL	1 tonne
1 dm³	1 L	1 kg
1 cm³	1 mL	1 g

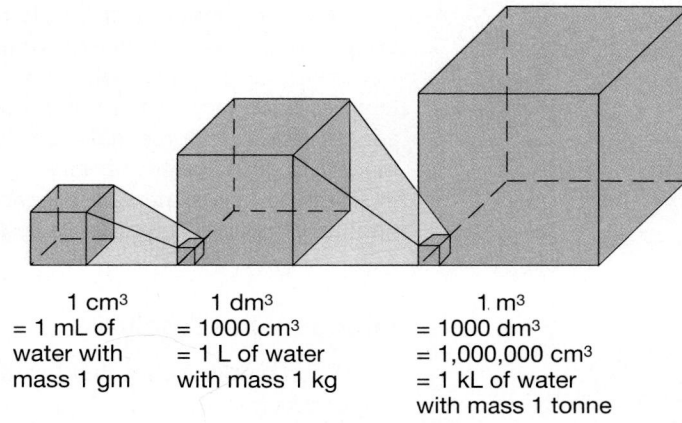

1 cm³
= 1 mL of
water with
mass 1 gm

1 dm³
= 1000 cm³
= 1 L of water
with mass 1 kg

1 m³
= 1000 dm³
= 1,000,000 cm³
= 1 kL of water
with mass 1 tonne

(Drawing not to scale)

FIGURE 13.22

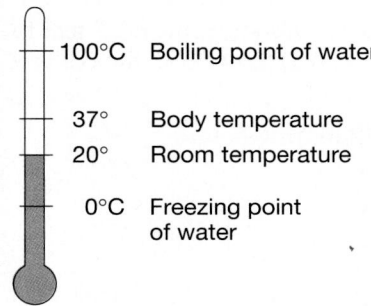

100°C   Boiling point of water

37°   Body temperature
20°   Room temperature

0°C   Freezing point
of water

FIGURE 13.23

Temperature: In the metric system, temperature is measured in **degrees Celsius**. The Celsius scale is named after the Swedish astronomer, Anders Celsius, who devised it in 1742. This scale was originally called "centigrade." Two reference temperatures are used, the freezing point of water and the boiling point of water. These are defined to be, respectively, zero degrees Celsius (0°C) and 100 degrees Celsius (100°C). A metric thermometer is made by dividing the interval from freezing to boiling into 100 degrees Celsius. Figure 13.23 shows a metric thermometer and some useful metric temperatures.

The relationship between degrees Celsius and degrees Fahrenheit (used in the English system) is derived next.

EXAMPLE 13.4
(a) Derive a conversion formula for degrees Celsius to degrees Fahrenheit.
(b) Convert 37°C to degrees Fahrenheit.
(c) Convert 68°F to degrees Celsius.

Solution
(a) Suppose that C represents a Celsius temperature and F the equivalent Fahrenheit temperature. Since there are 100° Celsius for each 180° Fahrenheit (Figure 13.24), there is 1° Celsius for each 1.8° Fahrenheit. If C is a temperature above freezing, then the equivalent Fahrenheit temperature, F, is 1.8C degrees Fahrenheit above 32° Fahrenheit, or 1.8C + 32. Thus 1.8C + 32 = F is the desired formula. (This also applies to temperatures at freezing or below, hence to all temperatures.)
(b) Using 1.8C + 32 = F, we have 1.8(37) + 32 = 98.6° Fahrenheit, which is normal human body temperature.
(c) Using 1.8C + 32 = F and solving for C, we find $C = \dfrac{F - 32}{1.8}$. Hence room temperature of 68° Fahrenheit is equivalent to $C = \dfrac{68 - 32}{1.8} = 20°$ Celsius. ∎

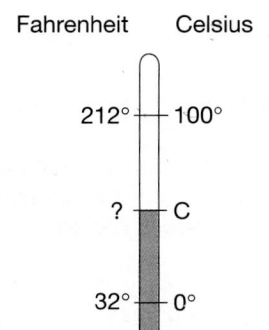

Fahrenheit   Celsius

212°   100°

?   C

32°   0°

FIGURE 13.24

Water is densest at 4°C. Therefore, the precise definition of the kilogram is the mass of 1 liter of water at 4°C.

From our discussion above, we see that the metric system has all of the features of an ideal system of units: portability, convertibility, and interrelatedness. These features make learning the metric system simpler than learning the English system of units. The metric system is the preferred system in science and commerce throughout the world. Moreover, there are only a handful of countries that use a system other than the metric system.

Dimensional Analysis

When working with two (or more) systems of measurement, there are many circumstances requiring conversions among units. The procedure known as dimensional analysis can help simplify the conversion. In **dimensional analysis**, we use unit ratios that are equivalent to 1 and treat these ratios as fractions. For example, suppose that we wish to convert 17 feet to inches. We use the unit ratio 12 in./1 ft (which is 1) to perform the conversion.

$$17 \text{ ft} = 17 \text{ ft} \times \frac{12 \text{ in.}}{1 \text{ ft}}$$
$$= 17 \times 12 \text{ in.}$$
$$= 204 \text{ in.}$$

Hence a length of 17 ft is the same as 204 inches. Dimensional analysis is especially useful if several conversions must be made. Example 13.5 provides an illustration.

EXAMPLE 13.5   A vase holds 4286 grams of water. What is its capacity in liters?

Solution
Since 1 mL of water weighs 1 gm and 1 L = 1000 mL, we have

$$4286 \text{ g} = 4286 \text{ g} \times \frac{1 \text{ mL}}{1 \text{ g}} \times \frac{1 \text{ L}}{1000 \text{ mL}}$$
$$= \frac{4286}{1000} \text{ L} = 4.286 \text{ L}.$$

Consequently, the capacity of the vase is 4.286 liters.   ■

In Example 13.6 we see a more complicated application of dimensional analysis. Notice that treating the ratios as fractions allows us to use multiplication of fractions. Thus we can be sure that our answer has the proper units.

EXAMPLE 13.6   The area of a rectangular lot is 25,375 ft^2. What is the area of the lot in acres? Use the fact that 640 acres = 1 square mile.

Solution

We wish to convert from square feet to acres. Since 1 mile = 5280 ft, we can convert from square feet to square miles. That is, 1 mile^2 = 5280 ft $\times$ 5280 ft = 27,878,400 ft^2. Hence

$$25{,}375 \text{ ft}^2 = 25{,}375 \text{ ft}^2 \times \frac{1 \text{ mile}^2}{27{,}878{,}400 \text{ ft}^2} \times \frac{640 \text{ acres}}{1 \text{ mile}^2}$$

$$= \frac{25{,}375 \times 640}{27{,}878{,}400} \text{ acres} = 0.58 \text{ acre (to two places).} \quad \blacksquare$$

Example 13.7 shows how to make conversions between English and metric system units. We do not advocate memorizing such conversion ratios, since rough approximations serve in most circumstances. However, there are occasions when accuracy is needed. In fact, the English system units are now legally defined *in terms* of metric system units. Recall that the basic conversion ratio for lengths is 1 inch : 2.54 centimeters, exactly.

EXAMPLE 13.7   A pole vaulter vaulted 19 ft $4\frac{1}{2}$ in. Find the height in meters.

Solution

Since 1 meter is a little longer than 1 yard and the vault is about 6 yards, we estimate the vault to be 6 meters. Actually,

$$19 \text{ ft } 4\frac{1}{2} \text{ in.} = 232.5 \text{ in.}$$

$$= 232.5 \text{ in.} \times \frac{2.54 \text{ cm}}{1 \text{ in.}} \times \frac{1 \text{ m}}{100 \text{ cm}}$$

$$= \frac{232.5 \times 2.54}{100} \text{ m} = 5.9055 \text{ m.} \quad \blacksquare$$

Our final example illustrates how we can make conversions involving different types of units, here distance and time.

EXAMPLE 13.8   Suppose that a bullet train is traveling 200 mph. How many feet per second is it traveling?

Solution

$$200 \, \frac{\text{mi}}{\text{hr}} \cdot \frac{5280 \text{ ft}}{1 \text{ mi}} \cdot \frac{1 \text{ hr}}{3600 \text{ sec}} = 293\frac{1}{3} \text{ ft/sec.} \quad \blacksquare$$

MATHEMATICAL MORSEL

In 1958, fraternity pledges at M.I.T. (where "Math Is Truth") were ordered to measure the length of Harvard Bridge—not in feet or meters, but in "Smoots," one Smoot being the height of their 5-foot 7-inch classmate, Oliver Smoot. Handling him like a ruler, the pledges found the bridge to be precisely 364.4 Smoots long. Thus began a tradition: The bridge has been faithfully "re-Smooted" each year since, and its new sidewalk is permanently scored in 10-Smoot intervals. Oliver Smoot went on to become an executive with a trade group in Washington, D.C.

EXERCISE/PROBLEM SET 13.1—PART A

Exercises

1. In your elementary classroom, you find the following objects. For each object, list attributes that could be measured and how you could measure them.
   (a) A student's chair   **(b)** A wastebasket
   (c) A bulletin board   **(d)** An aquarium

2. There are many attributes of the human body that are measured in the normal activities of life. Name some of these attributes that would be measured by the following people.
   (a) A dressmaker   **(b)** A shoe salesman
   (c) A doctor   **(d)** An athletic coach

3. Use Table 13.1 to compute the following conversions.
   (a) How many inches in a mile?
   (b) How many furlongs in a mile?
   (c) How many rods in a furlong?
   (d) How many yards in a mile?

4. Use Table 13.5 to complete the following conversions.
   (a) 1 ounce = _____ grains
   (b) 1 pound = _____ drams
   (c) 1 pound = _____ grains
   (d) 1 ton = _____ ounces

5. Find the area of each figure illustrated on a square lattice. Use the unit square shown as the fundamental unit of area.

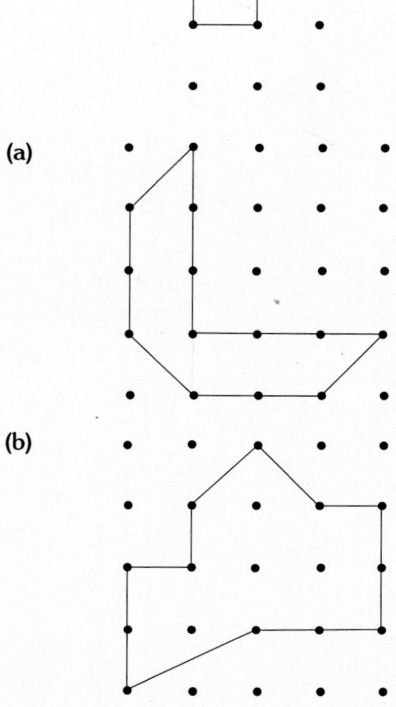

(a)

(b)

(c)

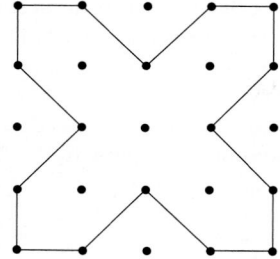

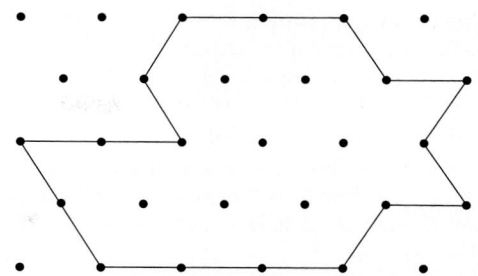

6. Using the grids drawn over the map, estimate the area of Connecticut.

(a)

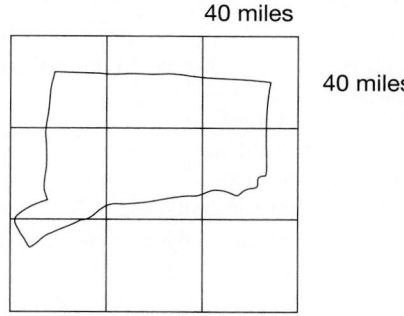

40 miles

40 miles

(b)

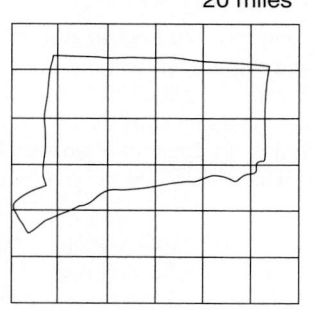

20 miles

20 miles

7. Any figure that tessellates a plane could be used as a unit measuring area. For example, here you are given a triangular, a hexagonal, and a parallelogram unit of area. Using each of the given units, find the area of the large figure.

(a)   **(b)**   **(c)**

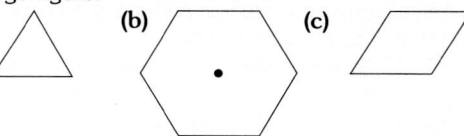

8. Use the metric converter to complete the following statements.

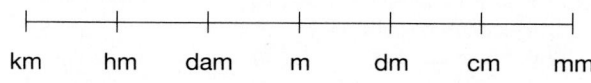

km   hm   dam   m   dm   cm   mm

(a) 1 dm = ____ mm   (b) 7.5 cm = ____ mm
(c) 31 m = ____ cm   (d) 3.06 m = ____ mm
(e) 0.76 hm = ____ m   (f) 0.93 cm = ____ m
(g) 230 mm = ____ dm   (h) 3.5 m = ____ hm
(i) 125 dm = ____ hm   (j) 764 m = ____ km

9. (a) Verify that 1 square millimeter equals 0.000001 square meter.
   (b) Verify that 1 square kilometer equals 1 000 000 square meters.

10. Give the missing numbers.
   (a) 1 cm^2 = ____ mm^2
   (b) 610 dam^2 = ____ hm^2
   (c) 564 m^2 = ____ km^2
   (d) 821 dm^2 = ____ m^2
   (e) 0.382 km^2 = ____ m^2
   (f) 9.5 dm^2 = ____ cm^2
   (g) $6\,540\,000 \text{ m}^2$ = ____ km^2
   (h) 9610 mm^2 = ____ m^2

11. Use the metric converter to answer the following questions.

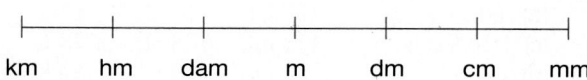

km   hm   dam   m   dm   cm   mm

   (a) One cubic meter contains how many cubic decimeters?
   (b) Based on your answer in part (a), how do we move the decimal point for each step to the right on the metric converter above?
   (c) How should we move the decimal point for each step left?

12. Using a metric converter, if necessary, convert the following measurements of mass.
 (a) 95 mg = _____ cg   (b) 7 kg = _____ g
 (c) 940 mg = _____ g   (d) 475 cg = _____ mg
 (e) 57 dg = _____ hg   (f) 32 g = _____ mg

13. The metric prefixes are also used with measurement of time. If "second" is the fundamental unit of time, what multiple or fraction of a second are the following measurements?
 (a) Megasecond   (b) Millisecond
 (c) Microsecond   (d) Kilosecond
 (e) Centisecond   (f) Picosecond

14. Using a converter if necessary, convert the following measurements of time (s = second).
 (a) 6 s = _____ cs   (b) 13 ms = _____ cs
 (c) 1560 s = _____ ks   (d) 3 ks = _____ cs
 (e) 136 s = _____ ms   (f) 5600 cs = _____ s

15. Using the meanings of the metric prefixes, how do the following units compare to a meter? If it exists, give an equivalent name.
 (a) "Kilomegameter"   (b) "Hectodekameter"
 (c) "Millimillimicrometer"   (d) "Megananometer"

16. Choose the most realistic measures of the following objects.
 (a) Length of a small paper clip   28 mm   28 cm   28 m
 (b) Height of a 12-year-old boy   148 mm   148 cm   148 m
 (c) Length of a shoe   27 mm   27 cm   27 m
 (d) Height of a building   205 cm   205 m   205 km
 (e) Height of a giant redwood tree   72 cm   72 m   72 km
 (f) Distance between two cities   512 cm   512 m   512 km

17. Choose the most realistic measures of the volume of the following objects.
 (a) Juice container   900 mL   900 cL   900 L
 (b) Tablespoon   15 mL   15 cL   15 L
 (c) Pop bottle   473 mL   473 cL   473 L
 (d) Bucket   10 mL   10 L   10 kL
 (e) Coffee cup   2 mL   20 mL   200 mL
 (f) Bath tub   5 L   20 L   200 L

18. Convert the following temperatures into degrees Celsius (to the nearest degree).
 (a) Moderate oven (350°F)
 (b) A spring day (60°F)
 (c) Ice-skating weather (0°F)
 (d) World's highest temperature recorded (136°F) at Azizia, Tripolitania, in northern Africa on September 13, 1922
 (e) World's record low temperature (−126.9°F) at the Soviet Antarctic station Vostok on August 24, 1960

19. A container holds water at its densest state. Give the missing numbers or missing units in the table below.

	Volume	Capacity	Mass
(a)	? cm^3	34 mL	34 g
(b)	? dm^3	? L	18 kg
(c)	23 cm^3	23 ?	23 g
(d)	750 dm^3	750 L	750 ?
(e)	19 ?	19 L	19 ?
(f)	72 cm^3	72 ?	72 ?

20. Give the appropriate unit ratio to convert the following measures.
 (a) 17 hours to minutes
 (b) 360 seconds to hours
 (c) 720 inches to yards
 (d) 1440 man-hours to man-days

21. By using dimensional analysis, make the following conversions:
 (a) 3.6 lb to oz
 (b) 55 mi/hr to ft/min
 (c) 35 mi/hr to in./sec
 (d) $575 per day to dollars per minute

22. Answer the following for the English system.
 (a) How many cups in a quart?
 (b) How many cups in a gallon?
 (c) A half-pint is how many cups?
 (d) Doctors recommend drinking 8 glasses (1 cup = 1 glass) of water daily. How many quarts is this?

23. Prior to conversion to a decimal monetary system, the United Kingdom used the following coins.
 1 pound = 20 shillings   1 penny = 2 half-pennies
 1 shilling = 12 pence   1 penny = 4 farthings
 (Pence is the plural of penny.)
 (a) How many pence were there in a pound?
 (b) How many half-pennies in a pound?
 (c) How many farthings were equal to a shilling?

24. One inch is defined to be exactly 2.54 cm. Using this ratio, convert the following measurements.
 (a) 6-inch snowfall to cm
 (b) 100-yard football field to m
 (c) 440-yard race to m
 (d) 1 km racetrack to mi

25. The speed of sound is 1100 ft/sec at sea level.
 (a) Express the speed of sound in mi/hr.
 (b) Change the speed of sound to mi/year. Let 365 days = 1 year.

Problems

26. A gallon of water weighs about 8.3 pounds. A cubic foot of water weighs about 62 pounds. How many gallons of water (to one decimal place) would fill a cubic foot container?

27. An adult male weighing about 70 kg has a red blood cell count of about 5.4×10^6 cells per microliter of blood and a blood volume of approximately 5 liters. Determine the approximate number of red blood cells in the body of an adult male.

28. The density of a substance is the ratio of its mass to its volume:

$$\text{density} = \frac{\text{mass}}{\text{volume}}$$

Density is usually expressed in terms of grams per cubic centimeter (g/cm^3). For example, the density of copper is 8.94 g/cm^3.

(a) Express the density of copper in kg/dm^3.

(b) A chunk of oak firewood weighs about 2.85 kg and has a volume of 4100 cm^3. Determine the density of oak in g/cm^3, rounding to the nearest thousandth.

(c) A piece of iron weighs 45 ounces and has a volume of 10 in^3. Determine the density of iron in g/cm^3, rounding to the nearest tenth.

29. The features of portability, convertibility, and interrelatedness were described as features of an ideal measurement system. Through an example, explain why the English system has none of these features.

30. Light travels 186,282 miles per second.

(a) Based on a 365-day year, how far in miles will light travel in one year? This unit of *distance* is called a **light-year**.

(b) If a star in Andromeda is 76 light-years away from earth, how many miles will light from the star travel on its way to earth?

(c) The planet Jupiter is approximately 480,000,000 miles from the sun. How long does it take for light to travel from the sun to Jupiter?

31. A train moving 50 miles per hour meets and passes a train moving 50 miles per hour in the opposite direction. A passenger in the first train sees the second train pass in 5 seconds. How long is the second train?

32. (a) If 1 inch of rainfall fell over 1 acre of ground, how many cubic inches of water would that be? How many cubic feet?

(b) If 1 cubic foot of water weighs approximately 62 pounds, what is the weight of a uniform coating of 1 inch of rain over 1 acre of ground?

(c) The weight of 1 gallon of water is about 8.3 pounds. A rainfall of 1 inch over 1 acre of ground means about how many gallons of water?

33. A ruler has marks placed at every unit. For example, an 8-unit ruler has a length of 8 and has seven marks on it to designate the unit lengths.

This ruler provides three direct ways to measure a length of 6: from the left end to the 6 mark, from the 1 mark to the 7 mark, and from the 2 to the 8.

(a) Show how all lengths from 1 through 8 can be measured using only the marks at 1, 4, and 6.

(b) Using a blank ruler 9 units in length, what is the fewest number of marks necessary to be able to measure lengths from 1 to 10 units? How would marks be placed on the ruler?

(c) Repeat for a ruler 10 units in length.

34. A father and his son working together can cut 48 ft^3 of firewood per hour.

(a) If they work an 8-hour day and are able to sell all the wood they cut at $100 per cord, how much money can they earn? A cord is defined as 4 feet $\times$ 4 feet $\times$ 8 feet.

(b) If they split the money evenly, at what hourly rate should the father pay his son?

(c) If the delivery truck can hold 100 cubic feet, how many trips would it take to deliver all the wood cut in a day?

(d) If they sell their wood for $85 per truckload, what price are they getting per cord?

35. A hiker can average 2 km per hour uphill and 6 km per hour downhill. What will be his average speed for the entire trip if he spends no time at the summit?

EXERCISE/PROBLEM SET 13.1—PART B

Exercises

1. A student brings a small rectangular prism to class and wants to find its measure.

(a) What attributes of the container could be measured?

(b) What units might be reasonable to measure each attribute?

(c) Another student has a large sack of marbles which she says she can use to measure the container. What attribute would she be measuring?

(d) What difficulties might be encountered in using the "marble" units?

2. A teacher and her students established the following system of measurements for the Land of Names.

$$1 \text{ jack} = 24 \text{ jills}$$
$$1 \text{ james} = 8 \text{ jacks}$$
$$1 \text{ jennifer} = 60 \text{ james}$$
$$1 \text{ jessica} = 12 \text{ jennifers}$$

Complete the following table.

	jill	jack	james	jennifer	jessica
1 jack =	24	1			
1 james =		8	1		
1 jennifer =			60	1	
1 jessica =				12	1

3. Use Table 13.2 to complete the following statements.
   (a) 1 square mile = ____ square yards
   (b) 1 square mile = ____ acres
   (c) 1 acre = ____ square yards

4. Find the area of each figure illustrated on the square lattice below. Use the unit square shown as the fundamental unit of area.

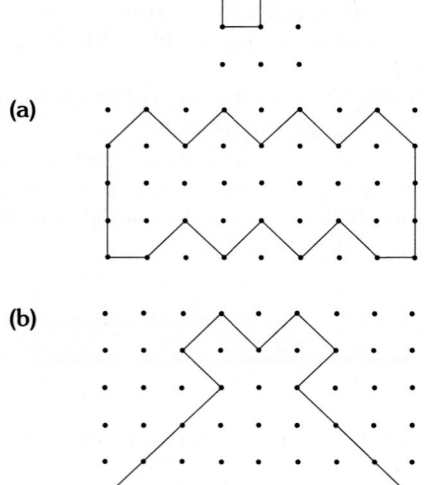

(a)

(b)

(c)

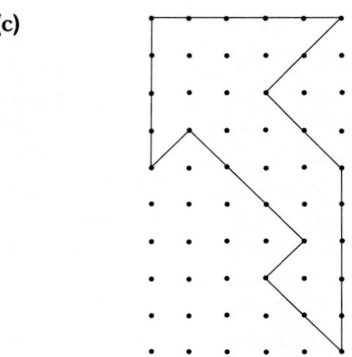

5. Using the triangular unit shown as the fundamental area unit, find the area of the following figures.

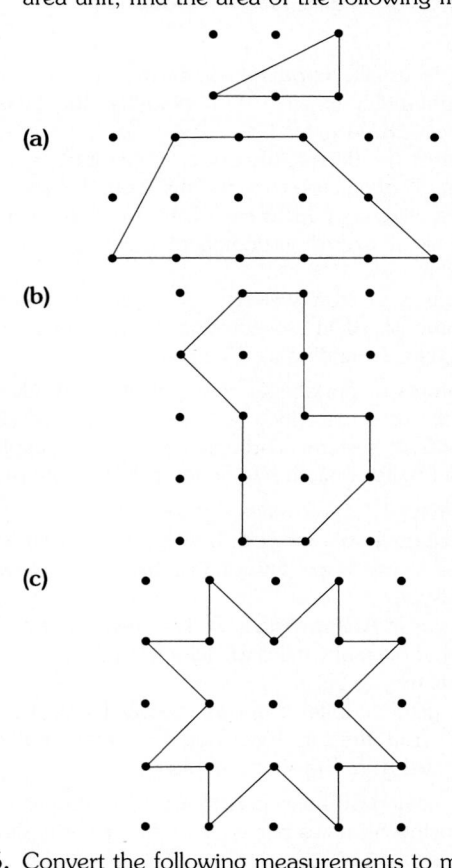

(a)

(b)

(c)

6. Convert the following measurements to meters.
   (a) 1200 cm   **(b)** 35 690 mm   **(c)** 260 km
   (d) 786 mm   **(e)** 32 560 cm   **(f)** 0.63 km

7. Convert the following measurements to centimeters.
   (a) 384 mm   **(b)** 12 m   **(c)** 630 km
   (d) 0.54 km   **(e)** 0.16 m   **(f)** 0.49 mm

8. Convert the following measurements to kilometers.
   (a) 13 450 m   **(b)** 1900 cm
   (c) 46 780 000 mm   **(d)** 89 000 cm

9. The metric converter shown can be used to convert metric measurements of area.

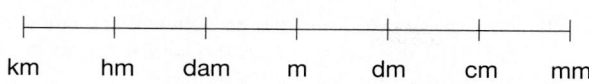

km   hm   dam   m   dm   cm   mm

(a) Each square meter is equivalent to how many square centimeters?

(b) To move from m^2 to cm^2, how many decimal places do we need to move?

(c) For each step *right*, how do we move the decimal point?

(d) For each step *left*, how do we move the decimal point?

(e) What are more common names for dam^2 and hm^2?

10. Convert the following measures.
(a) $2\ m^3 = \underline{\quad} cm^3$
(b) $5\ m^3 = \underline{\quad} mm^3$
(c) $16\ dm^3 = \underline{\quad} cm^3$
(d) $620\ cm^3 = \underline{\quad} dm^3$
(e) $56\ 000\ cm^3 = \underline{\quad} m^3$
(f) $1\ 200\ 000\ mm^3 = \underline{\quad} cm^3$

11. Convert the following measures of volume.
(a) $5\ L = \underline{\quad} cL$
(b) $53\ L = \underline{\quad} daL$
(c) $4.6\ L = \underline{\quad} mL$
(d) $350\ mL = \underline{\quad} dL$
(e) $56\ cL = \underline{\quad} L$
(f) $520\ L = \underline{\quad} kL$

12. Identify the following amounts.
(a) "Decidollar"
(b) "Centidollar"
(c) "Dekadollar"
(d) "Kilodollar"

13. A state lottery contest is called "Megabucks." What does this imply about the prize?

14. Choose the most realistic measures of the mass of the following objects.
(a) A 6-year-old boy   23 mg   23 g   23 kg
(b) A pencil   10 mg   10 g   10 kg
(c) An eyelash   305 mg   305 g   305 kg
(d) A tennis ball   25 mg   25 g   25 kg
(e) An envelope   7 mg   7 g   7 kg
(f) A car   1715 mg   1715 g   1715 kg

15. Choose the best estimate for the following temperatures.
(a) Water temperature for going swimming   22°C   39°C   80°C
(b) A glass of lemonade   −10°C   5°C   40°C
(c) A good day to go skiing   − 5°C   15°C   35°C
(d) Treat yourself for a fever   29°C   39°C   99°C

16. (a) A rectangular prism that measures 24 inches by 18 inches by 9 inches is filled with water. How much does the water weigh? (1 gallon equals 231 cubic inches and weighs 8.3 pounds.)
(b) A similar container measuring 64 cm by 48 cm by 12 cm is filled with water. What is the weight of the water in grams?
(c) Which of the preceding questions involved less work in finding the answer?

17. In performing a dimensional analysis problem, a student does the following:

$$22\ \text{ft} = 22\ \text{ft} \times \frac{1\ \text{ft}}{12\ \text{in.}} = \frac{22}{12}\ \text{in.} = 1.83\ \text{in.}$$

(a) What has the student done wrong?
(b) How would you explain to the student a way of checking that units are correct?

18. Change the following measurements to the given units.
(a) 40 kg/m to g/cm
(b) 65 kg/L to g/cm^3
(c) 72 lb/ft^3 to ton/yd^3
(d) 144 ft/sec to mi/hr
(e) $96/day to cents/hr
(f) 320 mi/hr to ft/sec

19. The **horsepower** is a nonmetric unit of power used in mechanics. It is equal to 746 watts. How many watts of power does a 350-horsepower engine generate?

20. A midwestern farmer has about 210 acres planted in wheat. Express this cultivated area to the nearest hectare.

21. Recipes that use the English system of measurement call for teaspoons (t), tablespoons (T), cups (c), and ounces (oz) of ingredients. Using 3 teaspoons = 1 tablespoon and 16 tablespoons = 1 cup, answer the following questions.
(a) How many teaspoons are in 1 cup?
(b) How many tablespoons in $\frac{1}{2}$ cup?
(c) How many tablespoons in $\frac{1}{3}$ cup?
(d) How many teaspoons in $\frac{1}{3}$ cup?
(e) Fill in the following table, giving volume conversions in the English system. Refer to Exercise 22 of Exercise Problem Set 13.1—Part A.

	gal	qt	pt	c	T	t	oz
1 gal =							
1 qt =							
1 pt =							
1 c =							
1 T =							
1 t =							
1 oz =							

22. The speed limit on some U.S. highways is 55 mph. If metric highway speed limit signs are posted, what will they read? Use 1 inch = 2.54 cm, the official link between the English and metric system.

Problems

23. Glaciers on coastal Greenland are relatively fast moving and have been observed to flow at a rate of 20 m per day.
   (a) How long does it take at this rate for a glacier to move 1 kilometer?
   (b) Use dimensional analysis to express the speed of the glacier in feet/hour to the nearest tenth of a foot.

24. Energy is sold by the **joule**, but in common practice, bills for electrical energy are expressed in terms of a kilowatt-hour (kWh), which is 3,600,000 joules.
   (a) If a household uses 1744 kWh in a month, how many joules are used?
   (b) The first 300 kWh are charged at a rate of 4.237 cents per kWh. Energy above 300 kWh is charged at a rate of 5.241 cents per kWh. What is the monthly charge for 1744 kWh?

25. What temperature is numerically the same in degrees Celsius and degrees Fahrenheit?

26. The Pioneer 10 spacecraft passed the planet Jupiter on December 12, 1973 and exited the solar system on June 14, 1983. The craft traveled from Mars to Jupiter, a distance of approximately 1 billion kilometers, in one year and nine months.
   (a) Calculate the approximate speed of the craft in kilometers per second.
   (b) Assuming a constant speed, approximately how many kilometers did Pioneer 10 travel between the time it passed Jupiter and the time it left the solar system?

27. An astronomical unit used to measure distance is a **parsec**, which is approximately 1.92×10^{13} miles. A parsec is equivalent to how many light-years?

28. A car travels 20 km per hour between two cities. How fast must the car travel on the return trip to average 40 km per hour for the round-trip?

29. The production of plastic fiber involves several steps. Each roll measures 400 feet and weighs 100 pounds.
   (a) The plastic formulation process takes 15 hr per 0.75 ton. Find the ratio of hr/roll.
   (b) The cold sheeting process produces 120 ft/min. How many hours does each roll take?
   (c) If the maximum production is 130 tons, how many rolls can be produced?

30. Noah's ark was 300 cubits long, 50 cubits wide, and 30 cubits high. Use a rectangular prism with no top as an approximation to the shape of the ark. What is the surface area of the ark in square meters? What is the capacity of the ark in cubic meters? (A cubit equals 21 inches, and 1 inch = 2.54 cm.)

31. There are about 1 billion people in China. If they lined up four to a row and marched past you at the rate of 25 rows per minute, how long would it take the parade to pass you?

32. A restaurant chain has sold over 80 billion hamburgers. A hamburger is about one-half inch thick. If the moon is 240 thousand miles away, what percent of the distance to the moon is the height of a stack of 80 billion hamburgers.

33. Kim claims to be over 1 billion seconds old. Lindsay claims to be over 1 billion minutes old. Whom can we believe? Explain.

13.2

LENGTH AND AREA   Length

In Section 13.1 we discussed measurement from a scientific point of view. That is, the measurements we used would be obtained by means of measuring instruments, such as rulers, tape measures, balance scales, thermometers, and so on. In this section we consider measurement from an abstract point of view, in which no physical measuring devices would be required. In fact, none would be accurate enough to suit us! We begin with length and area.

From Chapter 12 we know that every line can be viewed as a copy of the real number line (Figure 13.25). Suppose that P and Q are points on a line such that P corresponds to the real number p, and Q corresponds to the real number q. Recall that the numbers p and q are called coordinates of points P and Q, respectively. The **distance** from P to Q, written PQ, is the real number obtained as the nonnegative difference of p and q.

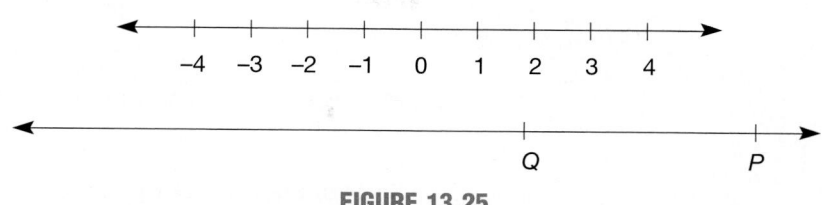

FIGURE 13.25

EXAMPLE 13.9 Suppose that P, Q, and R are points on a line such that P corresponds to -4.628. Q corresponds to 18.75, and R corresponds to 27.5941. Find PQ, QR, and PR.

Solution
In this situation, $p = -4.628$, $q = 18.75$, and $r = 27.5941$. Hence

$$PQ = 18.75 - (-4.628) = 23.378$$
$$QR = 27.5941 - (18.75) = 8.8441$$
$$PR = 27.5941 - (-4.628) = 32.2221$$

Notice that here, since Q is between P and R, we have $PQ + QR = PR$. ∎

From Example 13.9 and similar examples we can observe several properties of distance.

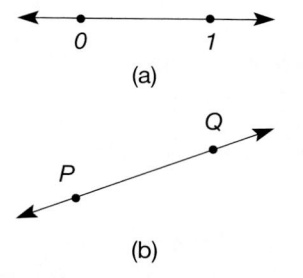

FIGURE 13.26

Properties of Distance on a Line

1. The distance from 0 to 1 on the number line is 1 and is called the **unit distance** [Figure 13.26(a)].
2. For all points P and Q, $PQ = QP$ [Figure 13.26(b)].
3. If P, Q, and R are points on a line and Q is between P and R, then $PQ + QR = PR$ [Figure 13.26(c)].

Property 1 establishes a unit of distance on a line. All distances are thus expressed in terms of this unit. For instance, in Example 13.9, the distance PQ is 23.378 units. Property 1 follows from our definition of distance since $1 - 0 = 1$.

Property 2 states that the distance from point P to point Q is equal to the distance from Q to P. Property 2 also follows from our definition of distance, since in calculating PQ and QP we use the *unique* nonnegative difference of p and q.

In property 3, point Q is between P and R if and only if its coordinate q is numerically between p and r, the coordinates of P and R, respectively. Property 3 states that distances between *consecutive* points on a line segment can be added to determine the total length of the segment.

To verify property 3, suppose that Q is between P and R, and P, Q, and R have coordinates p, q, and r, respectively. Suppose also that $p < q < r$. Then $PQ = q - p$, $PR = r - p$, and $QR = r - q$. Hence

$$PQ + QR = (q - p) + (r - q)$$
$$= q + (-p) + r + (-q)\ \ \ = r - p = PR.$$

Thus $PQ + QR = PR$. The case that $r < q < p$ is similar.

Perimeter

The **perimeter** of a polygon is the sum of the lengths of its sides. "Peri" means around and "meter" represents measure; hence perimeter literally means the measure around. Perimeter formulas can be developed for some common quadrilaterals. A square and a rhombus both have four sides of equal length. If one side is of length s, then the perimeter of each of them can be represented by $4s$ (Figure 13.27).

In rectangles and parallelograms, pairs of opposite sides are congruent. This will be verified formally in Chapter 14. Thus, if the lengths of their sides are a and b, then the perimeter of a rectangle or a parallelogram is $2a + 2b$. A similar formula can be used to find the perimeter of a kite (Figure 13.28).

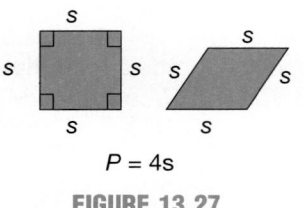

$P = 4s$

FIGURE 13.27

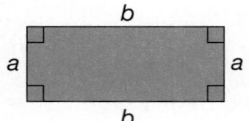

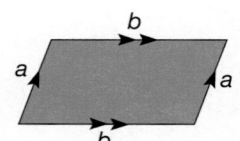

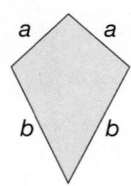

$P = 2a + 2b$

FIGURE 13.28

Perimeters of Common Quadrilaterals	
Figure	**Perimeter**
Square with sides of length s	$4s$
Rhombus with sides of length s	$4s$
Rectangle with sides of lengths a and b	$2a + 2b$
Parallelogram with sides of lengths a and b	$2a + 2b$
Kite with sides of lengths a and b	$2a + 2b$

EXAMPLE 13.10

Find the perimeters of the following (Figure 13.29).

(a) A triangle whose sides have length 5 cm, 7 cm, and 9 cm
(b) A square with sides of length 8 ft
(c) A rectangle with one side of length 9 mm and another side of length 5 mm
(d) A rhombus one of whose sides has length 7 in.
(e) A parallelogram with sides of length 7.3 cm and 9.4 cm
(f) A kite whose shorter sides are $2\frac{2}{3}$ yd and whose longer sides are $6\frac{1}{5}$ yd
(g) A trapezoid whose bases have lengths 13.5 ft and 7.9 ft and whose other sides have lengths 4.7 ft and 8.3 ft

Solution

(a) $P = 5\text{ cm} + 7\text{ cm} + 9\text{ cm} = 21\text{ cm}$
(b) $P = 4 \times 8\text{ ft} = 32\text{ ft}$
(c) $P = 2(9\text{ mm}) + 2(5\text{ mm}) = 28\text{ mm}$
(d) $P = 4 \times 7\text{ in.} = 28\text{ in.}$
(e) $P = 2(7.3\text{ cm}) + 2(9.4\text{ cm}) = 33.4\text{ cm}$
(f) $P = 2(2\frac{2}{3}\text{ yd}) + 2(6\frac{1}{5}\text{ yd}) = 5\frac{1}{3}\text{ yd} + 12\frac{2}{5}\text{ yd} = 17\frac{11}{15}\text{ yd}$
(g) $P = 13.5\text{ ft} + 7.9\text{ ft} + 4.7\text{ ft} + 8.3\text{ ft} = 34.4\text{ ft}$

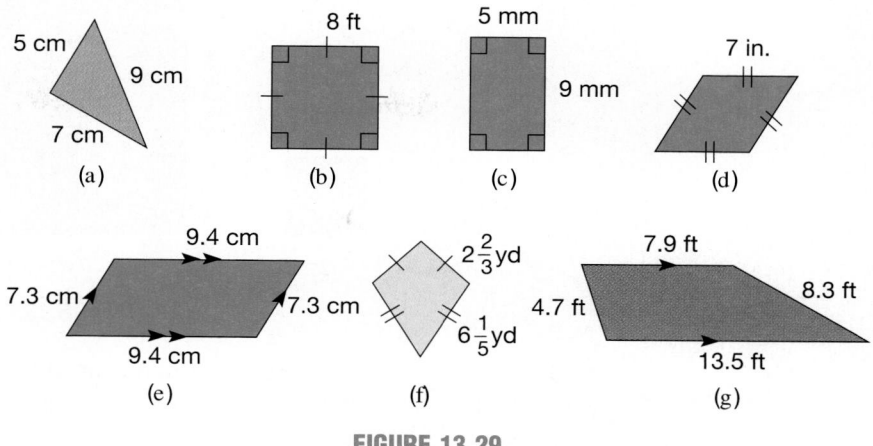

FIGURE 13.29

Circumference

The "perimeter" of a circle, namely the length of the circle, is given the special name **circumference** (Figure 13.30). In every circle, the ratio of the circumference C to the diameter d, namely C/d, is a constant, called π (the Greek letter "pi"). We can approximate π by measuring the circumferences and diameters of several cylindrical cans, then averaging the ratios of circumference to diameter. For example, the can shown in Figure 13.31 measures $C = 19.8$ cm and $d = 6.2$ cm. Thus in this case our approximation of π is the ratio $\dfrac{19.8 \text{ cm}}{6.2 \text{ cm}} = 3.2$ (to one decimal place). Actually, $\pi = 3.14159 \ldots$ and is an irrational number. In every circle, the following relationships hold.

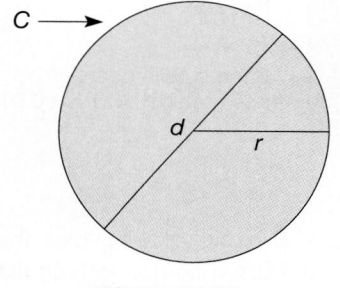

FIGURE 13.30

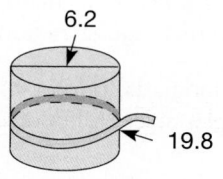

FIGURE 13.31

Distances in a Circle

Let r, d, and C be the radius, diameter, and circumference of a circle, respectively. Then $d = 2r$ and $C = \pi d = 2\pi r$.

Area

Rectangles

To determine the area of a two-dimensional figure, we imagine the interior of the figure completely filled with square regions called **square units** [Figure 13.32(a)]. To find the area of a rectangle whose sides have whole number lengths, as in Figure 13.32(b), we determine the number of unit squares needed to fill the rectangle. In Figure 13.32(b), the rectangle is composed of $4 \times 3 = 12$ square units. This procedure can be extended to rectangles whose dimensions are decimals, as illustrated next.

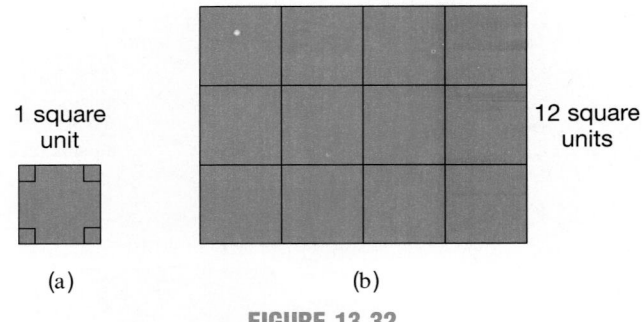

1 square unit   12 square units

(a)   (b)

FIGURE 13.32

EXAMPLE 13.11 Suppose that a rectangle has length 4.2 units and width 2.5 units. Find the area of the rectangle in square units (Figure 13.33).

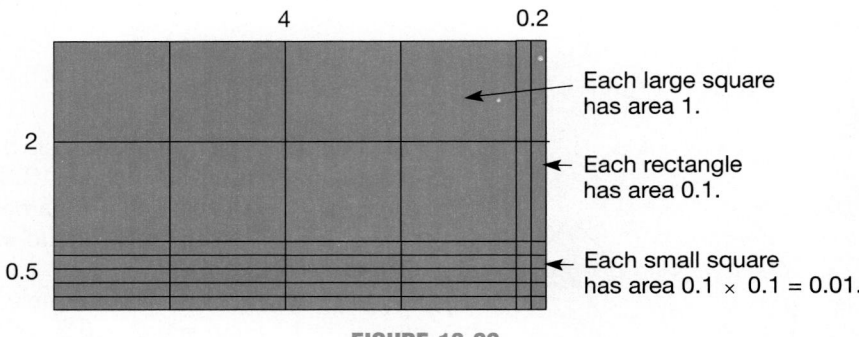

Each large square has area 1.

Each rectangle has area 0.1.

Each small square has area $0.1 \times 0.1 = 0.01$.

FIGURE 13.33

Solution

In Figure 13.33 notice that there are $4 \times 2 = 8$ large squares, plus the equivalent of 2 more large squares made up of 20 horizontal rectangular strips. Also, there are 4 vertical strips plus 10 small squares (i.e., the equivalent of 5 strips altogether). Hence the area is $8 + 2 + 0.5 = 10.5$. Notice that the 8 large squares were found by multiplying 4 times 2. Similarly, the product $4.2 \times 2.5 = 10.5$ is the area of the entire rectangular region. ■

As Example 13.11 suggests, the area of a rectangle is found by multiplying the lengths (real numbers) of two perpendicular sides. Of course, the area would be reported in square units.

Definition

Area of a Rectangle

The area A of a rectangle with perpendicular sides of lengths a and b is

$$A = ab.$$

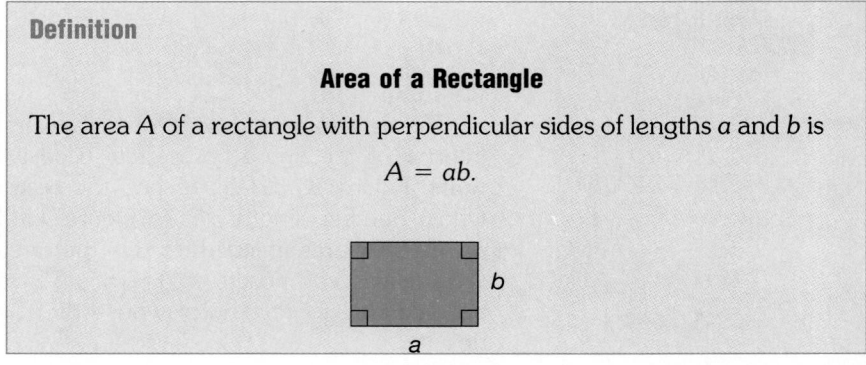

The formula for the area of a square is an immediate consequence of the area of a rectangle formula, since *every* square is a rectangle.

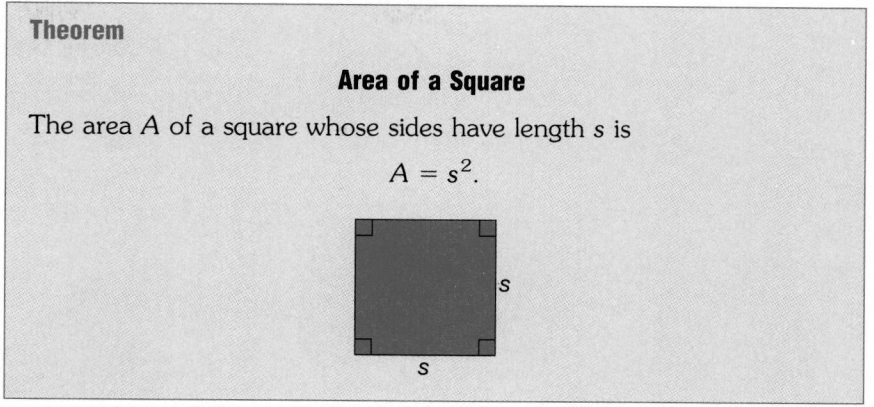

Theorem

Area of a Square

The area A of a square whose sides have length s is

$$A = s^2.$$

Probably the reason that we read s^2 as "s squared" is that it gives the area of a square with side length s.

Triangles

The formula for the area of a triangle also can be determined from the area of a rectangle. Consider first a right triangle $\triangle ABC$ [Figure 13.34(a)]. Construct rectangle $ABDC$ where $\triangle DCB$ is a copy of $\triangle ABC$ [Figure 13.34(b)]. The area of rectangle $ABDC$ is bh, and the area of $\triangle ABC$ is one-half the area of the rectangle. Hence the area of $\triangle ABC = \frac{1}{2}bh$.

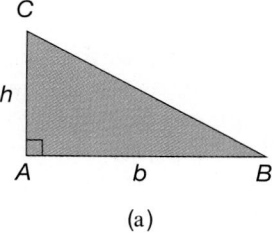

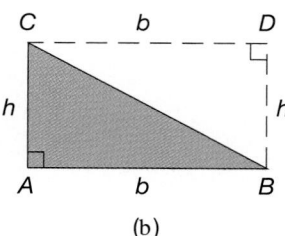

(a)   (b)

FIGURE 13.34

More generally, suppose that we have an arbitrary triangle, $\triangle ABC$ (Figure 13.35). In our figure, $\overline{BD} \perp \overline{AC}$. Consider the right triangles $\triangle ADB$ and $\triangle CDB$. The area of $\triangle ADB$ is $\frac{1}{2}rh$, where $r = AD$. Similarly, the area of $\triangle CDB = \frac{1}{2}sh$, where $s = DC$. Hence

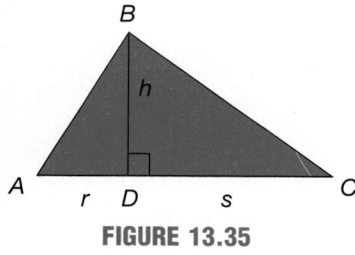

FIGURE 13.35

$$\text{area of } \triangle ABC = \frac{1}{2}rh + \frac{1}{2}sh$$

$$= \frac{1}{2}(r + s)h$$

$$= \frac{1}{2}bh \qquad \text{where } b = r + s, \text{ the length of } \overline{AC}.$$

We have verified the following formula.

> **Theorem**
>
> ## Area of a Triangle
>
> The area A of a triangle with base of length b and corresponding height h is
>
> $$A = \frac{1}{2}\,bh.$$
>
>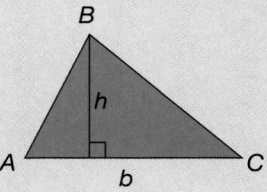

When calculating the area of a triangle, any side may serve as a **base**. The perpendicular distance from the opposite vertex to the line containing the base is the **height** corresponding to this base. Hence each triangle has *three* bases and *three* corresponding heights. In the case of an obtuse triangle, the line segment used to find the height may lie outside the triangle as in $\triangle ABC$ in Figure 13.36.

In this case, the area of $\triangle ABC$ is $\frac{1}{2}h(x + b) - \frac{1}{2}hx = \frac{1}{2}bh$, the same as in the preceding theorem.

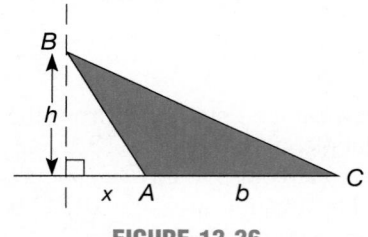

FIGURE 13.36

Parallelograms

We can determine the area of a parallelogram by drawing in a diagonal to form two triangles with the same height (Figure 13.37). Notice that in $\triangle ACD$, if we use AD as a base, then h, the distance between lines $\overleftrightarrow{AD}$ and $\overleftrightarrow{BC}$, is the **height** corresponding to $\overline{AD}$. Similarly, in $\triangle ABC$, if we use BC as a base, then h is also the corresponding height. Observe also that $BC = AD = b$, since opposite sides of the parallelogram $ABCD$ have the same length. Hence

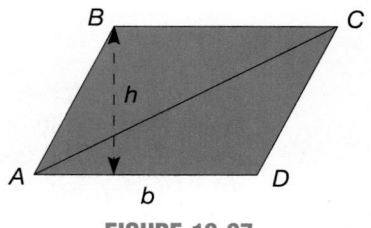

FIGURE 13.37

$$\text{area of } ABCD = \text{area of } \triangle ABC + \text{area of } \triangle ACD$$
$$= \frac{1}{2}\,bh + \frac{1}{2}\,bh$$
$$= bh.$$

Theorem

Area of a Parallelogram

The area A of a parallelogram with base b and height h is

$$A = bh.$$

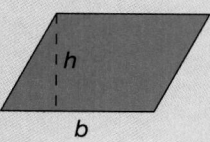

Trapezoids

The area of a trapezoid can also be derived from the area of a triangle. Suppose that we have a trapezoid $PQRS$ whose bases have lengths a and b and whose height is h, the distance between the parallel bases (Figure 13.38).

The diagonal $\overline{PR}$ divides the trapezoid into two triangles with the same height, h, since $QR \parallel PS$. Hence the area of the trapezoid is the sum of the areas of the two triangles, or $\frac{1}{2}ah + \frac{1}{2}bh = \frac{1}{2}(a + b)h$.

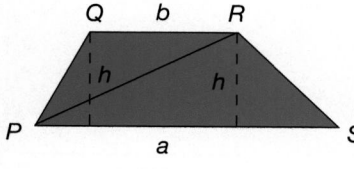

FIGURE 13.38

Theorem

Area of a Trapezoid

The area A of a trapezoid with parallel sides of lengths a and b and height h is

$$A = \frac{1}{2}(a + b)h.$$

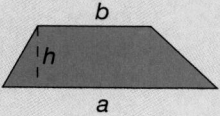

Circles

Our final area formula will be for a circle. Imagine a circle of radius r inscribed in a regular polygon. Figure 13.39 shows an example using a regular octagon with O the center of the inscribed circle.

Let s be the length of each side of the regular octagon. Then the area of $\triangle ABO$ is $\frac{1}{2}sr$. Since there are eight such triangles within the octagon, the area of the entire octagon is $8(\frac{1}{2}sr) = \frac{1}{2}r \times 8s$. Notice that $8s$ is the perimeter of the octagon. In fact, the area of every circumscribed regular polygon is $\frac{1}{2}r \times P$, where P is the perimeter of the polygon. As the number of sides in the circumscribed regular polygon increases, the closer P is to the circumference of the circle, C, and the closer the polygon's area is to

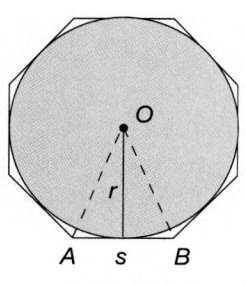

FIGURE 13.39

that of the circle. Thus we expect the area of the circle to be $\frac{1}{2}r \times C = \frac{1}{2}r \times (2\pi r) = \pi r^2$. This is, indeed, the area of a circle with radius r.

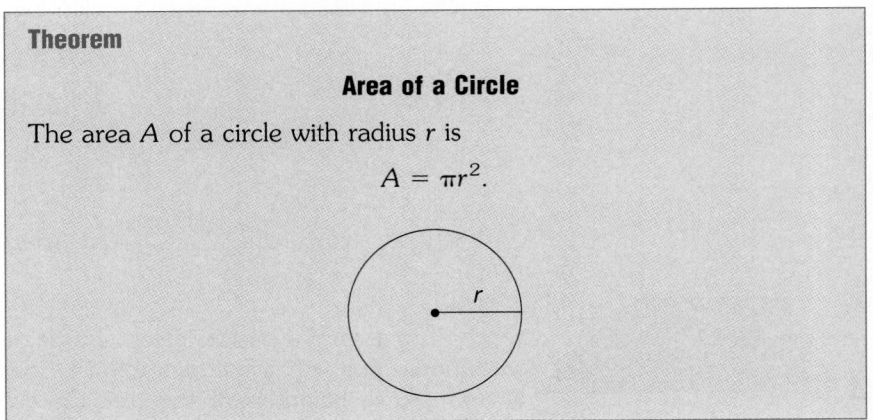

Theorem

Area of a Circle

The area A of a circle with radius r is

$$A = \pi r^2.$$

A rigorous verification of this formula cannot be done without calculus-level mathematics.

Areas of irregular two-dimensional regions can be approximated by covering the region with a grid. This method is illustrated in the *Connections to School Mathematics* section.

The Pythagorean Theorem

The Pythagorean theorem, perhaps the most spectacular result in geometry, relates the lengths of the sides in a right triangle; the longest side is called the **hypotenuse** and the other two sides are called **legs**. Figure 13.40 shows a special instance of the Pythagorean theorem in an arrangement involving isosceles right triangles. Notice that the area of the large square, c^2, is equal to the area of four of the shaded triangles, which, in turn, is equal to the sum of the areas of the two smaller squares, $a^2 + b^2$. Therefore, $a^2 + b^2 = c^2$. In the particular case shown, $a = b$. This result generalizes to all right triangles. In words, it says "the area of the square on the hypotenuse is equal to the sum of the areas of the squares on the two sides."

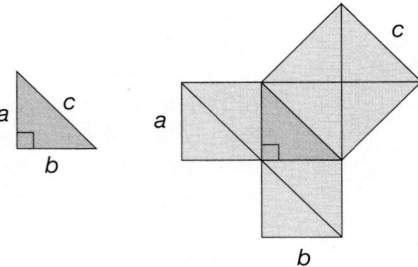

FIGURE 13.40

Theorem

The Pythagorean Theorem

In a right triangle, if the legs have lengths a and b and the hypotenuse has length c, then

$$a^2 + b^2 = c^2.$$

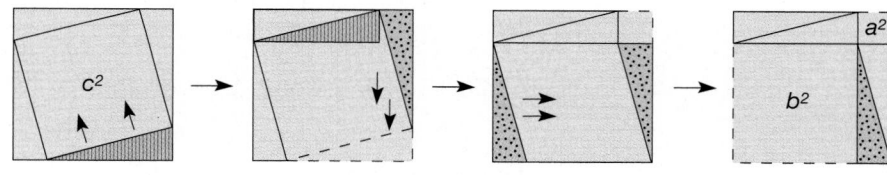

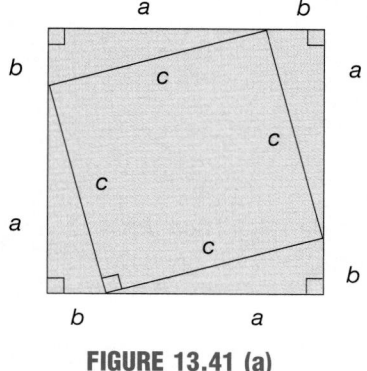

FIGURE 13.41 (a)

To prove the Pythagorean theorem, we construct a square figure consisting of four right triangles surrounding a smaller square [Figure 13.41(a)]. First, the sequence of pictures in Figure 13.41(b) shows a visual "proof." Since the amount of space occupied by the four triangles is constant, the areas of the square region(s) must be. Thus $c^2 = a^2 + b^2$.

FIGURE 13.41 (b)

Next we give an algebraic justification. Observe that the legs of the four right triangles combine to form a large square. The area of the large square is $(a + b)^2$ by the area of a square formula. On the other hand, the area of each triangle is $\frac{1}{2}ab$ and the area of the smaller square (verify that it is a square) is c^2. Thus the area of the large square is also $4(\frac{1}{2}ab) + c^2 = 2ab + c^2$. Thus $(a + b)^2 = 2ab + c^2$. But

$$(a + b)^2 = (a + b)(a + b)$$
$$= (a + b) \cdot a + (a + b) \cdot b$$
$$= a^2 + ba + ab + b^2$$
$$= a^2 + ab + ab + b^2$$
$$= a^2 + 2ab + b^2.$$

Combining these results, we find that

$$a^2 + 2ab + b^2 = 2ab + c^2, \text{ so that}$$
$$a^2 + b^2 = c^2.$$

This proves the Pythagorean theorem. The Pythagorean theorem enables us to find lengths in the plane. Example 13.12 illustrates this.

EXAMPLE 13.12 Suppose that we have points in the plane arranged in a square lattice. Find the length of $\overline{PQ}$ (Figure 13.42).

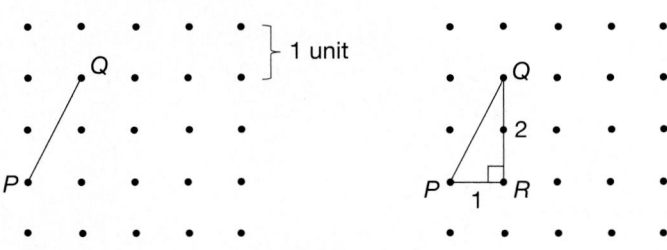

FIGURE 13.42

Solution
Draw the right triangle $\triangle PRQ$ with right angle $\angle R$. Then $PR = 1$ and $QR = 2$. We use the Pythagorean theorem to find PQ, namely, $PQ^2 = 1^2 + 2^2 = 5$, or $PQ = \sqrt{5}$.   ■

Example 13.13 shows how the Pythagorean theorem can be used to construct a line segment whose length is the square root of a whole number.

EXAMPLE 13.13 Construct a length of $\sqrt{13}$ in the plane.

Solution
Observe that $13 = 2^2 + 3^2$. Thus, in a right triangle whose legs have lengths 2 and 3, the hypotenuse will have length $\sqrt{13}$, by the Pythagorean theorem (Figure 13.43). Hence the construction of such a right triangle will yield a segment of length $\sqrt{13}$.   ■

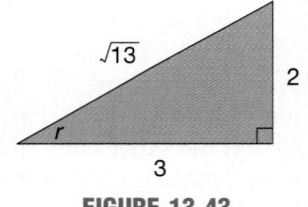

FIGURE 13.43

A final observation that we can make about distance in the plane is called the triangle inequality.

> **Theorem**
>
> ### Triangle Inequality
>
> If P, Q, and R are points in the plane, then $PQ + QR \geq PR$.

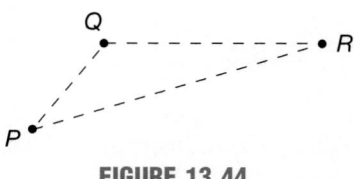

FIGURE 13.44

The triangle inequality states that the distance from P to Q plus the distance from Q to R is always greater than or equal to the distance from P to R (see Figure 13.44). That is, the sum of the lengths of two sides of a triangle is always greater than the length of the third side. (We will have $PQ + QR = PR$ if and only if P, Q, and R are collinear with Q between P and R.) The verification of the triangle inequality is left to the problem set.

MATHEMATICAL MORSEL

The United States remains an island in a metric world. At present, the only nonmetric country in the world other than the United States is Burma. Actually, our units of measure are defined in terms of the metric units. For example, in 1959 one inch was defined to be exactly 2.54 centimeters. Even though many industries in the United States, including the automobile and pharmaceutical industries, already use metric tools and measures, the change to everyday use of the metric system has been very gradual. In 1988, President Reagan signed a bill that required all government agencies to be metric by 1992.

EXERCISE/PROBLEM SET 13.2—PART A

Exercises

1. Points P, Q, R, and S are located on line l illustrated below.

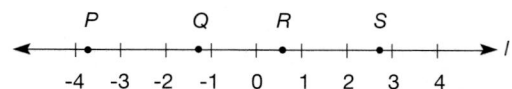

The corresponding real numbers are $p = -3.78$, $q = -1.35$, $r = 0.56$, and $s = 2.87$. Find each of the following lengths.
(a) PR (b) RQ (c) PS (d) QS

2. Points P, Q, R, and S are described in Exercise 1.
(a) Does $PQ + QR = PR$?
(b) Does $PR + QS = PS$?
(c) Does $PQ + QR + RS = PS$?

3. Given is information about points P and Q on line l. Assume that $p < q$, where p and q are the real numbers corresponding to points P and Q. Complete the table.

	p	q	$\overline{PQ}$
(a)		$\sqrt{5}$	$3\sqrt{5}$
(b)	$-\frac{9}{4}$	$\frac{7}{12}$	
(c)	-3π		10π
(d)		$5.3\overline{3}$	7.5

4. Let points P and Q be points on a line l with corresponding real numbers p and q, respectively.
(a) If $p < q$, find the distance between points P and Q.
(b) If $p < q$, then find $\frac{1}{2}PQ$.
(c) Add the value in part (b) to p and simplify. This gives the real number corresponding to the midpoint of segment $\overline{PQ}$.
(d) Repeat parts (a) to (c) if $q < p$, except add the value in part (b) to q. Do you get the same result?
(e) Use the formula you found in part (c) to find the real number corresponding to the midpoint if $p = -2.5$ and $q = 13.9$.

5. Find the real number corresponding to the midpoints of the segments whose endpoints correspond to the following real numbers.
(a) $p = 3.7$, $q = 15.9$
(b) $p = -0.3$, $q = 6.2$
(c) $p = -16.3$, $q = -5.5$
(d) $p = 2.3$, $q = -7.1$

6. Let points P and Q be points on a line with corresponding real numbers p and q, respectively.
(a) Let $p < q$ and find the distance between points P and Q.
(b) Find $m = p + \frac{1}{3}PQ$ and simplify your result.
(c) Find $n = p + \frac{2}{3}PQ$ and simplify.
(d) Use your results from parts (b) and (c) to find the real numbers corresponding to the points that divide $\overline{PQ}$ into three segments which are the same length if $p = -3.6$ and $q = 15.9$.

7. Verify the third property of distances on a line when $r < q < p$.

8. Given below is the real number corresponding to the midpoint M of segment PQ. Also given is the real number corresponding to one of the endpoints. Find the real number corresponding to the other endpoint.
(a) $m = 12.1$, $p = 6.5$
(b) $m = -2.5$, $q = 3.5$
(c) $m = -5.8$, $p = -1.4$
(d) $m = -13.2$, $q = -37.5$

9. Information is given about the illustrated rectangle. Find the information indicated. P = perimeter, A = area.

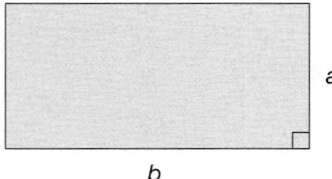

(a) $P = 45.6$, $b = 15.2$. Find a and A.
(b) $P = 37.6$, $a = 6.8$. Find b and A.
(c) $a = 14.1$, $A = 501.96$. Find b and P.

10. After measuring the room she wants to carpet (illustrated here), Sally proceeds to compute how much carpet is needed as shown in the following calculation.

$$
\begin{array}{ll}
10 \text{ ft} \times 8 \text{ ft} & = 80 \quad \text{ft}^2 \\
9 \text{ in.} \times 6 \text{ in.} \quad = 54 \text{ in}^2 & = \underline{0.375 \text{ ft}^2} \\
& 80.375 \text{ ft}^2
\end{array}
$$

If Sally buys 81 square feet of carpet, will she have enough? If not, what part of the room will not be carpeted?

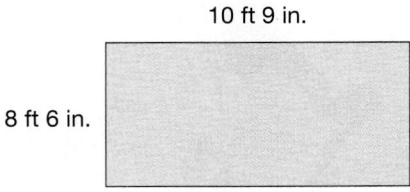

10 ft 9 in.

8 ft 6 in.

11. A group wants to carpet a ramp measuring 60 ft 6 in. by 4 ft 4 in. How many square yards of carpet should they buy?

12. Find the perimeter and area of each parallelogram.
(a)

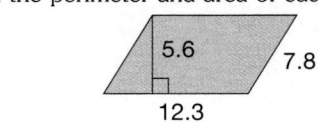

5.6   7.8
12.3

(b)

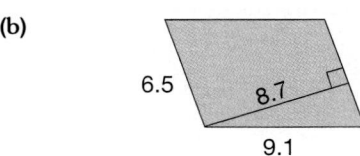

6.5   8.7
9.1

(c)

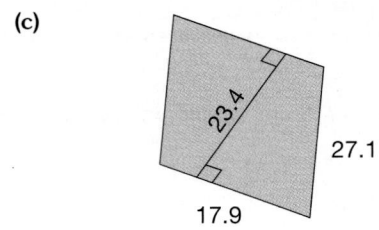

23.4   27.1
17.9

13. Find the perimeter and area of each triangle.
(a)

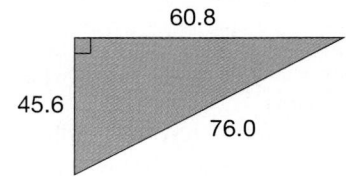

60.8
45.6   76.0

(b)

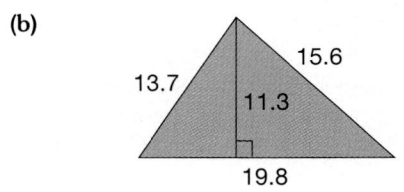

15.6
13.7   11.3
19.8

(c)

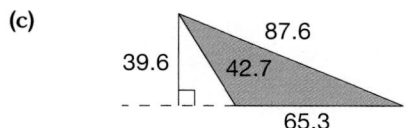

14. Find the circumference and area of each circle.

(a)

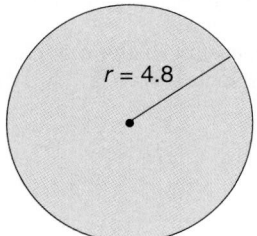

$r = 4.8$

(b)

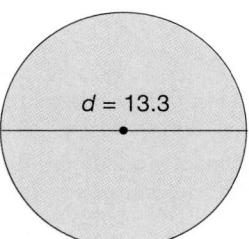

$d = 13.3$

(c)

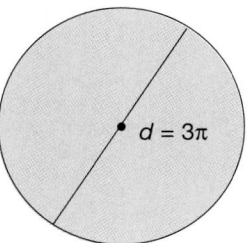

$d = 3\pi$

15. Triangle *ABC* is shown on a square lattice.

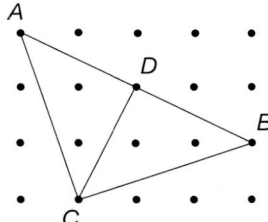

(a) Consider $\overline{AB}$ as the base of the triangle. Which segment gives the corresponding height? Verify that it is perpendicular to $\overline{AB}$ using a square corner of a piece of paper.

(b) Find the area of $\triangle ABC$ using this base and height.

(c) Consider $\overline{BC}$ as the base of the triangle. Which segment gives the corresponding height? Verify.

(d) Find the area of $\triangle ABC$ using this base and height.

(e) Do parts (b) and (d) give the same area?

16. Kathy leaves Kansas City traveling due west on a train with speed 50 mph. At the same time, Bob leaves the same location traveling north in a small plane with speed of 120 mph. After 4 hours, how far apart are they?

17. **Hero's formula** can be used to find the area of a triangle if the lengths of the three sides are known. According to this formula, the area of a triangle is $\sqrt{s(s - a)(s - b)(s - c)}$, where *a*, *b*, and *c* are the lengths of the three sides and $s = (a + b + c)/2$. Use Hero's formula to find the area of the triangle whose sides are given (round to one decimal place).

(a) 5 cm, 12 cm, 13 cm   **(b)** 4 m, 5 m, 6 m

(c) 4 km, 5 km, 8 km   **(d)** 8 m, 15 m, 17 m

18. Find the area of a right triangle with sides of length 6, 8, and 10 by using the following formulas.

(a) $A = \frac{1}{2}bh$

(b) Hero's formula

19. A trapezoid is sometimes defined as a quadrilateral with at *least* one pair of parallel sides. This definition allows parallelograms to be considered trapezoids. A parallelogram is shown.

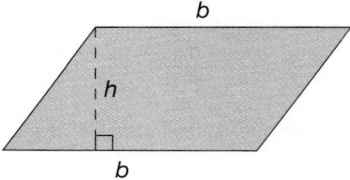

(a) Using the area of a parallelogram formula, find the area of the given parallelogram.

(b) Using the area of a trapezoid formula, find the area of the given parallelogram.

(c) Do both formulas yield the same results?

20. (a) Given below are four rhombuses that all have the same perimeter. Using the fact that diagonals of a rhombus are perpendicular and bisect each other, find the area of each rhombus.

(i)

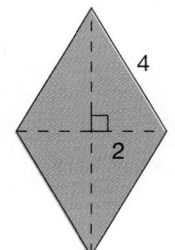

(ii)

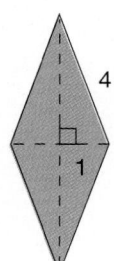

(iii) (iv)

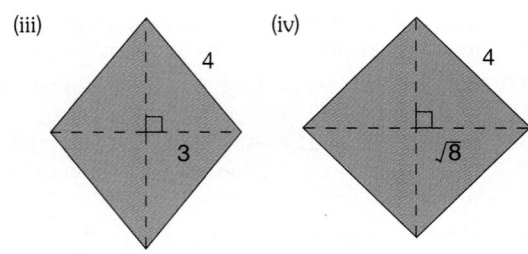

(b) Which one has the largest area?

21. A **sector** of a circle is a pie-shaped wedge of a circle formed by two radii of the circle and the arc of the circle between them.

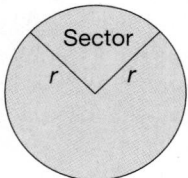

The area of a sector of a circle can be determined by using the angle between the two radii and a proportion. If the angle between the two radii measures n degrees, the sector is $\dfrac{n}{360}$th of the circle. So the area of the sector, A, can be found as follows:

$$\frac{n}{360} = \frac{A}{\pi r^2}.$$

Use this technique to find areas of the sectors below. Round to three digits.

(a)

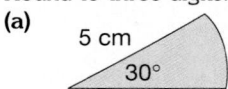

(b)

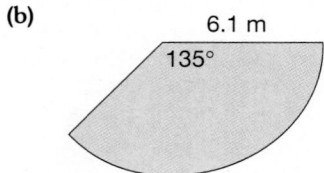

(c)

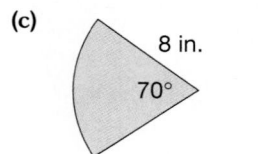

22. (a) Triangle ABC is shown here on a square lattice. What is its area?

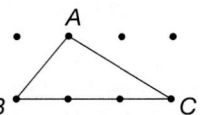

(b) Each dimension of the triangle is doubled in the second triangle shown. What is the area of triangle DEF?

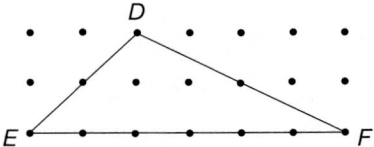

(c) The ratio of the lengths of the sides of triangle ABC to the lengths of sides of triangle DEF is $1:2$. What is the ratio of their areas?

23. Apply the Pythagorean theorem to find the following lengths represented on a square lattice.

(a)   **(b)**

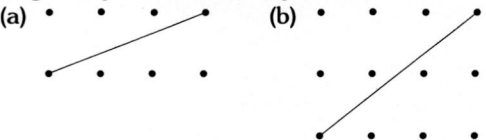

24. Find the length of the side not given.

(a)

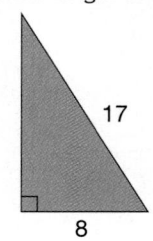

(b)

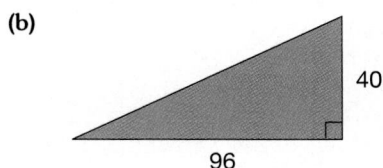

(c)

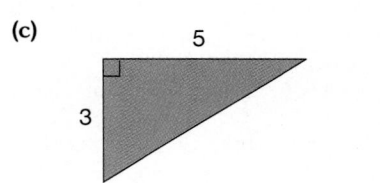

(d)

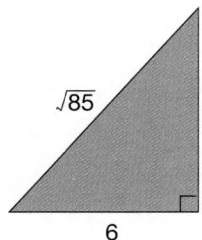

Problems

25. A ladder is leaning against a building. If the ladder reaches 20 feet high on the building and the base of the ladder is 15 feet from the bottom of the building, how long is the ladder?

26. A small pasture is to be fenced off with 96 meters of new fencing along an existing fence, using the existing fence as one side of a rectangular enclosure. What whole-number dimensions yield the largest area that can be enclosed by the new fencing?

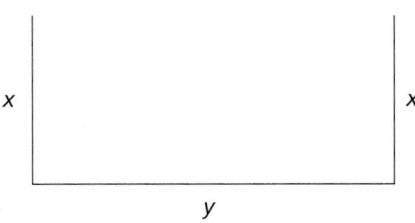

27. George is building a large model airplane in his workshop. If the door to his workshop is 3 feet wide and $6\frac{1}{2}$ feet high and the airplane has a wingspan of 7.1 feet, will George be able to get his airplane out of the workshop?

28. The proof of the Pythagorean theorem that was presented in this section depended on a figure containing squares and right triangles. Another famous proof of the Pythagorean theorem also uses squares and right triangles. It is attributed to a Hindu mathematician, Bhaskara (1114–1185), and it is said that he simply wrote the word "Behold" above the figure, believing that the proof was evident from the drawing. Use algebra and the areas of the right triangles and squares in the figure to verify the Pythagorean theorem.

Behold!

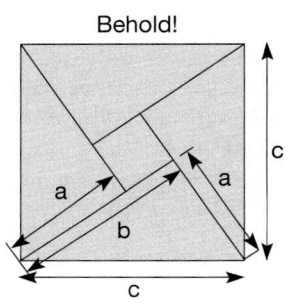

29. Shown is a rectangular prism with length l, width w, and height h.

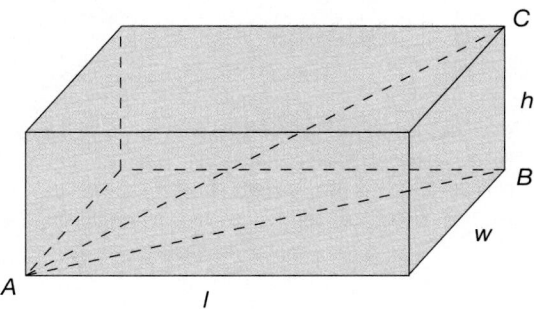

(a) Find the length of the diagonal from A to B.
(b) Using the result of part (a), find the length of the diagonal from A to C.
(c) Use the result of part (b) to find the length of the longest diagonal of a rectangular box 40 cm by 60 cm by 20 cm.

30. Jason has an old trunk that is 16 inches wide, 30 inches long, and 12 inches high. Which of the following objects would he be able to store in his trunk?
(a) Telescope measuring 40 inches
(b) Baseball bat measuring 34 inches
(c) Tennis racket measuring 32 inches

31. Information is given about the right triangle illustrated. Fill in the missing entries of the table. P = perimeter, A = area.

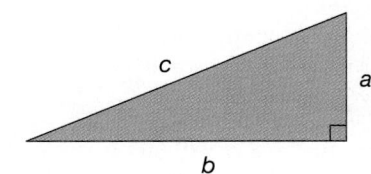

	a	b	c	P	A
(a)	24.9				413.34
(b)	125.5		326.3		
(c)		141.6			7518.96

32. Find the perimeter and area of the following trapezoids.
(a)

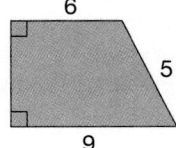

(b)

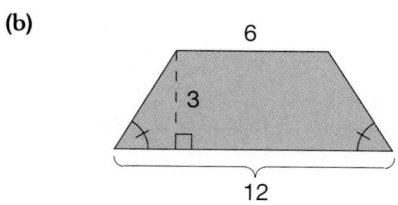

33. Consider the regular octagon *ABCDEFGH* shown. Each side of the octagon is tangent (touches at one point) to the inscribed circle, and the radius to the point of tangency is perpendicular to the side.

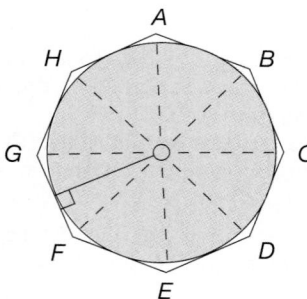

(a) If the radius of the circle is *r* (called an **apothem** of the octagon), find the area of triangle *OGF* in terms of *r* and *FG*.

(b) Use the areas of the other triangles to find the area of the regular octagon.

(c) Express the area in terms of the apothem and perimeter of the regular polygon.

34. Find the area of each regular polygon, given the length of its side (*s*) and its apothem (*r*).

(a) Equilateral triangle, $s = 6$, $r = \sqrt{3}$

(b) Square, $s = 2\sqrt{2}$, $r = \sqrt{2}$

(c) Hexagon, $s = 10$, $r = 5\sqrt{3}$

(d) Octagon, $s = 8$, $r = 9.66$

(e) 20-gon, $s = 50$, $r = 157.8$

(f) 100-gon, $s = 1$, $r = 15.9$

35. Which of the following are lengths of sides of a right triangle?

(a) 7, 24, 25   **(b)** 12, 24, 26   **(c)** 28, 21, 35

(d) 11, 60, 61   **(e)** 8, 9, 15   **(f)** 10, 22, 26

36. The following result, known as **Pick's theorem**, gives a method of finding the area of a polygon on a square lattice, such as on square dot paper or a geoboard. Let *b* be the number of lattice points on the polygon (i.e., on the "boundary"), and let *i* be the number of lattice points inside the polygon. Then the area of the polygon is ($b/2 + i − 1$) square units. For example, for the polygon below, $b = 12$ and $i = 8$. Hence the area of the polygon is $\frac{12}{2} + 8 − 1 = 13$ square units.

(a) Verify, without using Pick's theorem, that the area of the following polygon is 13 square units.

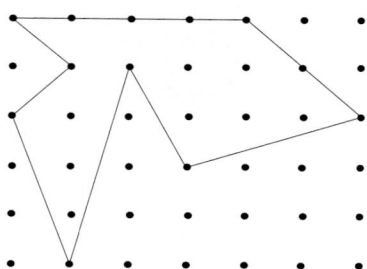

(b) Find the area of each of the following polygons using Pick's theorem.

(i)

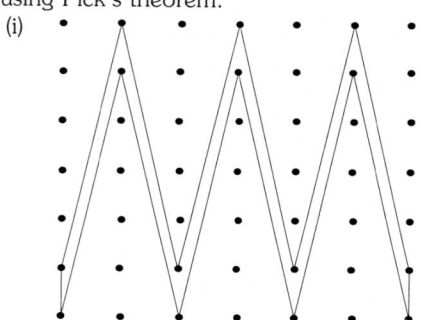

(ii)

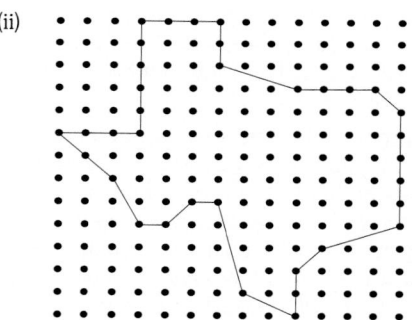

37. Arrange the following lengths in order from smallest to largest.

1. Perimeter of a square with area 100
2. Circumference of a circle with radius 5
3. Perimeter of a triangle with two sides of lengths 10 and one of length 9

38. A rectangle whose length is 3 cm more than its width has an area of 40 square centimeters. Find the length and width.

39. Can an equilateral triangle be constructed on the portion of a square lattice shown here? Show why or why not.

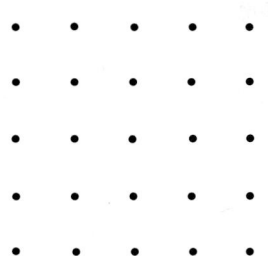

40. In building the pyramids and temples, Egyptian builders were faced with the problem of making the base perfectly square. One method involved using a rope 12 units long with knots equally spaced at each unit. Explain how this rope could serve as a guide to building square corners.

41. Given below are the lengths of the sides of a triangle. Indicate if the triangle is a right triangle. If not a right triangle, indicate whether it is an acute triangle or an obtuse triangle.
(a) 70, 54, 90   (b) 63, 16, 65   (c) 24, 48, 52
(d) 27, 36, 45   (e) 48, 46, 50   (f) 9, 40, 46

42. Given are three segments whose lengths are a, b, and c, where $a < b < c$.
(a) Under what conditions on a, b, and c will these three segments form a triangle?
(b) When will the triangle be a right triangle?
(c) When will the triangle be an acute triangle?
(d) When will the triangle be an obtuse triangle?

43. Find the area of the quadrilateral given. Give the answer to one decimal place. (HINT: Apply Hero's formula from Exercise 17.)

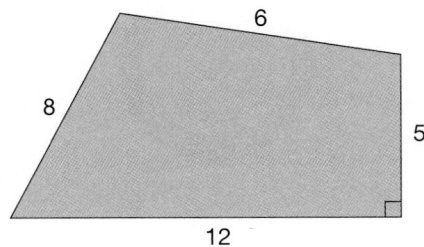

44. The Greek mathematician Eratosthenes, who lived about 225 B.C., was the first person known to have calculated the circumference of the earth. At Syene, it was possible to see the sun's reflection in a deep well on a certain day of the year. At the same time on the same day, the sun cast a shadow of 7.5° in Alexandria, some 500 miles to the north.

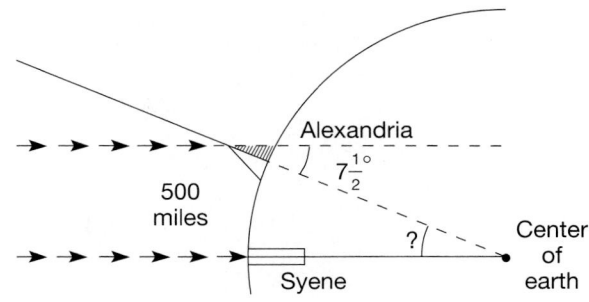

(a) What is the measure of the indicated angle at the center of the earth? By what property?
(b) Using this angle, find the circumference of the earth.
(c) With today's precision instruments, the earth's equatorial circumference has been calculated at 24,901.55 miles. How close was Eratosthenes in miles?

45. Square plugs are often used to check the diameter of a hole. What must the length of the side of the square be to test a hole with diameter 3.16 cm? Round *down* to the nearest 0.01 cm.

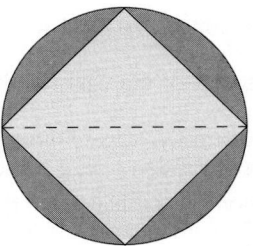

46. Segment $\overline{AB}$, which is 1 unit long, is tangent to the inner circle at A and touches the outer circle at B. What is the area of the region between the two circles? (HINT: The radius of the inner circle that has endpoint A is also perpendicular to $\overline{AB}$.)

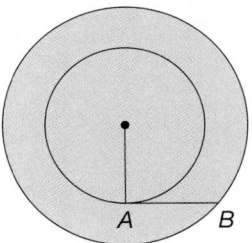

47. Find the area of the shaded region where the petals are formed by constructing semicircles. For each semicircle, the center is the midpoint of a side.

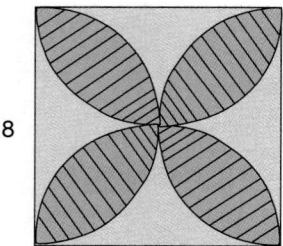

8

48. A farmer has a square field that measures 100 m on a side. He has a choice of using one large circular irrigation system or four smaller ones, as illustrated.

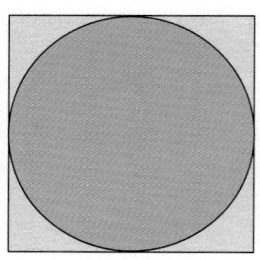 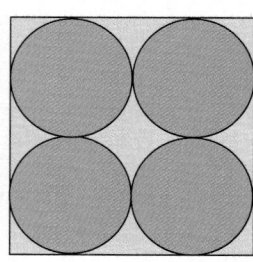

  (a) What percent of the field will the larger system irrigate?
  (b) What percent of the field will the smaller system irrigate?
  (c) Which system will irrigate more land?
  (d) What generalization does your solution suggest?

49. All the polygons in the figure are regular. The length of the side of the triangle is 1 unit. Find the total area of the figure in square units.

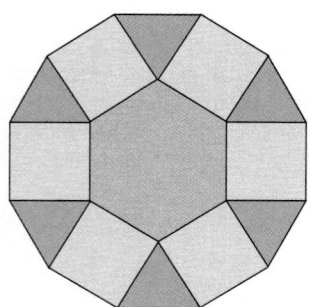

50. Portland, Oregon, is located near 45° north latitude, or halfway between the equator and the North Pole. At similar latitude and halfway around the world is located the Aral Sea. To travel from Portland to the Aral Sea, would it be a shorter distance to travel along the 45° north latitude route or to travel over the North Pole? Use 6380 km as the radius of the earth.

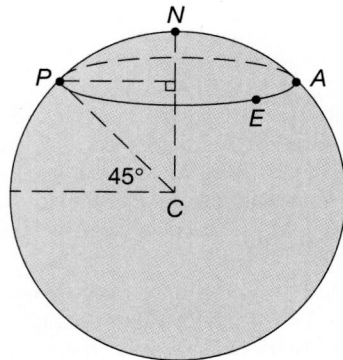

51. (a) Two **concentric circles** (i.e., having the same center) have radii of 10 and 14, respectively. Which is larger, the area inside the smaller circle or the area between the two circles?
  (b) What would the radius of the larger circle have to be to have the area of the inner circle equal to the area between the two circles?

52. The following figure shows five concentric circles. If the width of each of the rings formed is the same, how do the areas of the two shaded regions compare?

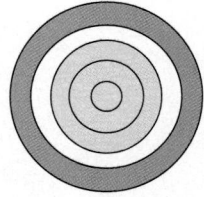

EXERCISE/PROBLEM SET 13.2—PART B

Exercises

1. Given below are points on line *l* and their corresponding real number. Find the distances specified.

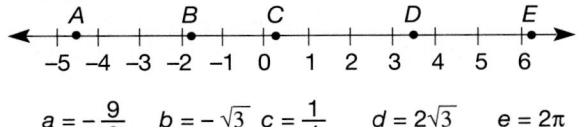

$$a = -\frac{9}{2} \quad b = -\sqrt{3} \quad c = \frac{1}{4} \quad d = 2\sqrt{3} \quad e = 2\pi$$

(a) *AB*
(b) *DB*
(c) *AD* (to two decimal places)
(d) *CE* (to two decimal places)

2. Let points *P* and *Q* be points on a line *l* with corresponding real numbers $p = -6$ and $q = 12$.
(a) Find the distance between points *P* and *Q*.
(b) Find $\frac{1}{2}PQ$.
(c) Add the value in part (b) to *p*. This gives the real number corresponding to the midpoint, M, of segment *PQ*. What is that real number?
(d) Verify that this point is the midpoint *M*, by finding *PM* and *QM*.

3. Let points *P* and *Q* be points on a line *l* with corresponding real numbers $p = 3$ and $q = 27$.
(a) Find the distance between points *P* and *Q*.
(b) Let *M* be the point with real number $m = p + \frac{1}{3}PQ$ and *N* be the point corresponding to $n = p + \frac{2}{3}PQ$. Find *m* and *n*.
(c) Points *M* and *N* divide segment $\overline{PQ}$ into how many equal pieces?
(d) Explain how you could divide $\overline{PQ}$ into four segments of equal length.

4. Find the area and perimeter of the following figures illustrated on a square lattice. The curves are **semicircles** (half-circles).

(a) 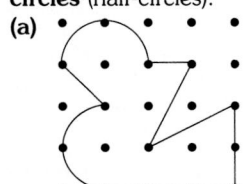   (b)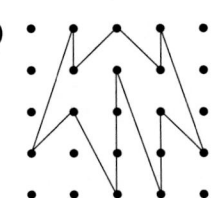

5. How many pieces of square floor tile, 1 foot on a side, would you have to buy to tile a floor that is 11 feet 6 inches by 8 feet?

6. Find the perimeter and area of each rectangle.

(a)

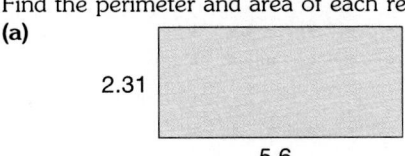

2.31

5.6

(b)

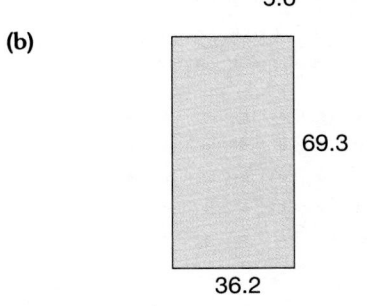

69.3

36.2

(c)

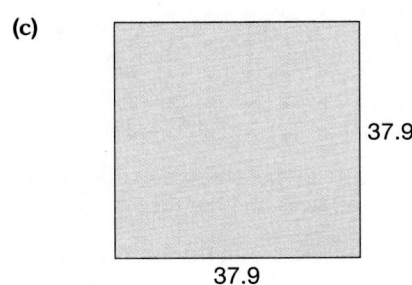

37.9

37.9

7. Information is given about a circle in the following table. Fill in the missing entries of the table. *r* = radius, *d* = diameter, *C* = circumference, *A* = area. Use a calculator and give answers to two decimal places.

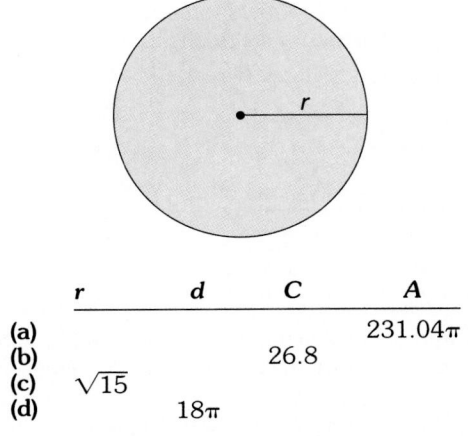

	r	*d*	*C*	*A*
(a)				231.04π
(b)			26.8	
(c)	$\sqrt{15}$			
(d)		18π		

8. Shown are two pairs of parallelograms. In each case, the pairs are drawn with sides of the same length.

(i)

(ii)

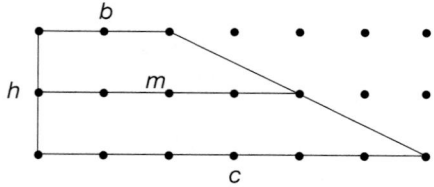

(a) For each pair of parallelograms, determine the lengths of the sides and the area of the parallelograms.

(b) Based on what you found in part (a), how would you respond to the statement "The area of a parallelogram is the product of the lengths of its sides?"

9. (a) Find the area of an equilateral triangle whose sides have a length of 6 units.

(b) If an equilateral triangle has sides of length a, apply Hero's formula to derive a formula for the area of an equilateral triangle.

10. A trapezoid is pictured here.

(a) Part of the area formula for a trapezoid is $\frac{1}{2}(b + c)$, the average of the two parallel sides. Find $\frac{1}{2}(b + c)$ for this trapezoid.

(b) The segment pictured with length m is called the **midsegment** of a trapezoid because it connects midpoints of the nonparallel sides. Find m.

(c) How do the results to parts (a) and (b) compare?

11. (a) A trapezoid is illustrated on a square lattice. What is its area?

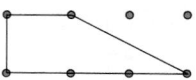

(b) If all dimensions of the trapezoid are tripled, what is the area of the resulting trapezoid?

(c) If the ratio of lengths of sides of two trapezoids is $1:3$, what is the ratio of the areas of the trapezoids?

12. Represent the following lengths on a square lattice.
(a) $\sqrt{5}$ **(b)** $\sqrt{17}$ **(c)** $\sqrt{18}$ **(d)** $\sqrt{29}$

13. A rectangle with sides a and b is shown.

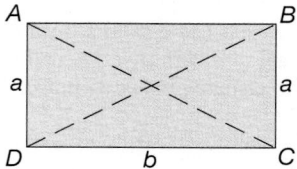

(a) Find the length of diagonal $\overline{AC}$.
(b) Find the length of diagonal $\overline{BC}$.
(c) What property of rectangles has been shown?

14. (a) In building roofs, it is common for each 12 feet of horizontal distance to rise 5 feet in vertical distance. Why might this be more common than one that rises 6 feet for each 12 feet? (Consider distance measured along the roof.)

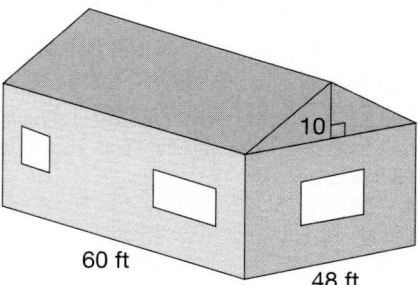

(b) Find the area of the roof on the pictured building.
(c) How many sheets of 4 feet × 8 feet plywood would be needed to cover the roof?
(d) Into what dimensions would you cut the plywood?

15. There is an empty lot on a corner that is 80 m long and 30 m wide. When coming home from school, Gail cuts across the lot diagonally. How much distance (to the nearest meter) does she save?

16. Suppose that you are setting up forms for a rectangular patio and want to be certain that each corner of the patio is "square." Describe how you could accomplish this if the only tools you have at your disposal are a roll of string and a measuring tape.

17. A room is 8 meters long, 5 meters wide, and 3 meters high. Find the following lengths.
  (a) Diagonal of the floor
  (b) Diagonal of a side wall
  (c) Diagonal of an end wall
  (d) Diagonal from one corner of the floor to the opposite corner of the ceiling

18. The length of each edge of the cube is 1. Find the following values.

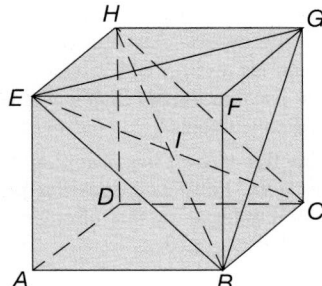

  (a) Length of $\overline{BE}$ **(b)** Length of $\overline{BH}$
  (c) Area of $\triangle BEG$ **(d)** Area of rectangle $BCHE$
  (e) Area of $\triangle BIC$ **(f)** Area of $\triangle BEI$

19. Consecutive terms in a Fibonacci sequence can be used to generate Pythagorean triples, whole numbers that could represent the lengths of the three sides in a right triangle. The process works as follows:

  1. Choose any four consecutive terms of any Fibonacci sequence.
  2. Let a be the product of the first and last of these four terms.
  3. Let b be twice the product of the middle two terms.
  4. Then a and b are the legs of a right triangle. To find the length of the hypotenuse, use $c = \sqrt{a^2 + b^2}$.

  Use the Fibonacci sequence 1, 1, 2, 3, 5, 8, 13, 21, . . . to answer the following questions.

  (a) Using the terms 2, 3, 5, and 8, find values of a, b, and c.
  (b) Using the terms 5, 8, 13, and 21, find values of a, b, and c.
  (c) Using the terms starting with 13, find values of a, b, and c.
  (d) Write out more terms of the sequence. Is c one of the terms in this sequence in each of (a), (b), and (c)? Check to see that a, b, and c in (a), (b), and (c) satisfy $a^2 + b^2 = c^2$.

20. Find the perimeter and area of each triangle.
  (a)

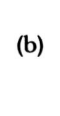
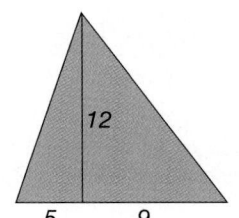

  (b)

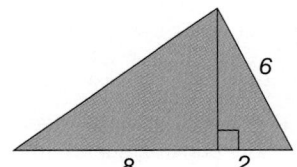

  (c)

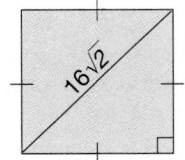

21. Find the perimeter and area of each quadrilateral.
  (a)

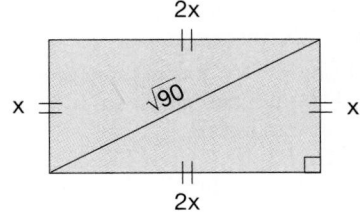

  (b)

  (c)

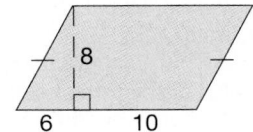

22. A regular hexagon can be divided into six equilateral triangles.

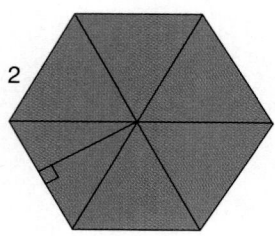

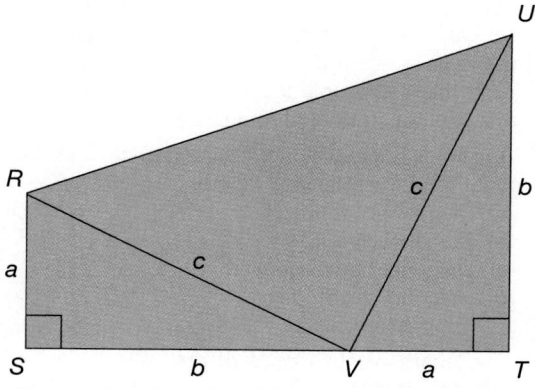

(a) The altitude of an equilateral triangle bisects the base. If each side has length 2, find the length of the altitude.

(b) What is the area of one triangle?

(c) What is the area of the regular hexagon?

23. In each part, three lengths are given. Does there exist a triangle having sides of those lengths?

(a) 4, 5, 17   **(b)** 23, 21, 37   **(c)** 15, 8, 25
(d) 34, 17, 17   **(e)** 36, 52, 15   **(f)** 9, 40, 41

24. An artist is drawing a scale model of the design plan for a new park. If she is using a scale of 1 inch = 12 feet, and the area of the park is 36,000 square feet, what area of the paper will the scale model cover?

Problems

25. There are only two rectangles whose sides are whole numbers and whose area and perimeter are the same numbers. What are they?

26. A baseball diamond is a square 90 feet on a side. To pick off a player stealing second base, how far must the catcher throw the ball?

27. A man has a garden 10 meters square to fence. How many fence posts are needed if each post is 1 meter from the adjacent posts?

28. Given below are lengths of three segments. Will these segments form a triangle? If so, is it a right, an acute, or an obtuse triangle?

(a) 48, 14, 56   **(b)** 54, 12, 37   **(c)** 21, 22, 23
(d) 15, 8, 16   **(e)** 61, 11, 60   **(f)** 84, 13, 100

29. The diagram here was used by President James Garfield to prove the Pythagorean theorem.

(a) Explain why quadrilateral $RSTU$ is a trapezoid.

(b) What is its area?

(c) Show that $\triangle RVU$ is a right triangle.

(d) Find the areas of the three triangles.

(e) Prove the Pythagorean theorem using parts (a) to (d).

30. Alice and Bob took a 20-mile bicycle ride together. Alice rode a touring bicycle and Bob rode his mountain bike. If the outside diameter of the tires on Alice's bike is 27 inches and on Bob's bike is 26 inches, how many more revolutions did Bob's wheels make on the trip than Alice's wheels?

31. (a) Imagine the largest square plug that fits into a circular hole. How well does the plug fit? That is, what percentage of the circular hole does the square plug occupy?

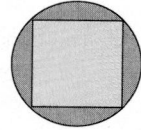

(b) Now imagine the largest circular plug that fits into a square hole. How well does this plug fit? That is, what percentage of the square hole does the circular plug occupy?

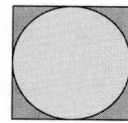

(c) Which of the two plugs described above fits the hole better?

32. Find x.

33. The regular hexagon pictured is inscribed in the circle. The length of the side of the hexagon is 1 unit. Find the circumference of the circle.

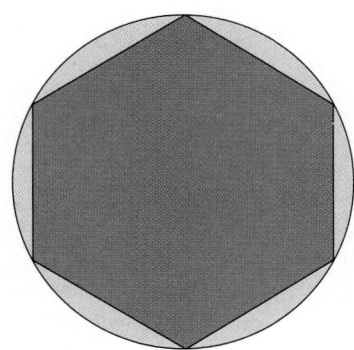

34. A spider and a fly are in a room that has length 8 m, width 4 m, and height 4 m. The spider is on one end wall 1 cm from the floor midway from the two side walls. The fly is caught in the spider's web on the other end wall 1 cm from the ceiling and also midway from the two side walls. What is the shortest distance the spider can walk to enjoy his meal? (HINT: Draw a two-dimensional picture.)

35. (a) Trace the square, cut along the solid lines, and rearrange the four pieces into a rectangle (that is not a square). Find the areas of the square and the rectangle. Is your result surprising?

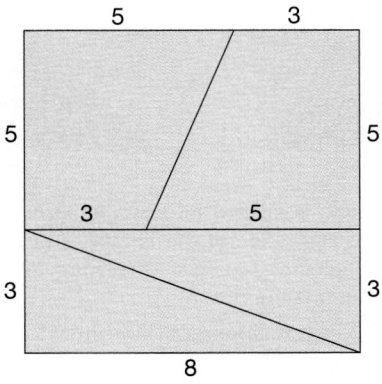

(b) Change the dimensions 3, 5, 8 in the square in part (a) to 5, 8, 13, respectively. Now what is the area of the square? The rectangle? In connection with part (a), are these results even more surprising? Try again with 8, 13, 21, and so on.

36. Find the area of the shaded region.

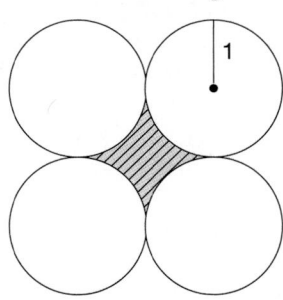

37. A **hexafoil** is inscribed in a circle of radius 1. Find its area. (The petals are formed by swinging a compass of radius 1 with the center at the endpoints of the petals.)

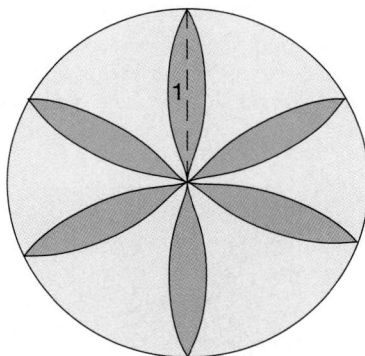

38. The circles in the figure have radii 6, 4, 4, and 2. Which is larger—the shaded area inside the big circle or the shaded area outside the big circle?

39. Compare the total shaded area outside the circles to the total blackened area inside the circles.

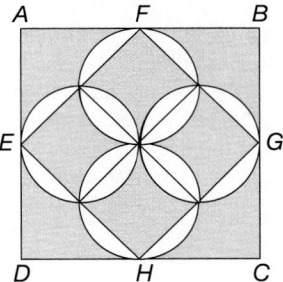

40. Suppose that there are three spherical planets in space with diameters 1000 km, 100 km, and 1 km, respectively. Suppose that each has a satellite revolving about it in a circular orbit. Each orbit is 10 km longer than the circumference of the planet that the satellite revolves about.

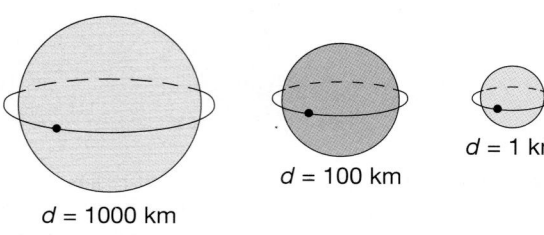

$d = 1000$ km $d = 100$ km $d = 1$ km

Which satellite has the highest altitude from its planet?

41. *(Challenge)* Triangle *PQR* is shown here. Right triangles having *PQ, QR,* and *PR* as hypotenuses have been drawn. Lengths *a, b, c,* and *d* are given.

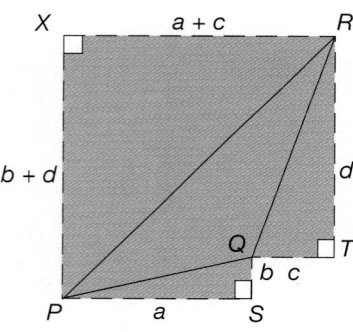

(a) Convince yourself that $PX = b + d$ and $XR = a + c$.

(b) Find the length of *PQ, QR,* and *PR*.

(c) Verify that the triangle inequality is true. (This involves quite a bit of algebra.)

42. There are about 5 billion people on earth. Suppose that they all lined up and held hands, each person taking about 2 yards of space.

(a) How long a line would the people form?

(b) The circumference of the earth is about 25,000 miles at the equator. How many times would the line of people wrap around the earth?

43. Dick and Tyler have collected 82,944 bottle caps. The average bottle cap is 1 inch in diameter, and a stack of six caps is 1 inch high.

(a) If they line them all up, how long is the line of caps?

(b) If they arrange them in a square array, how long is a side of the square?

(c) If they make a cubical array (i.e., square arrays stacked on each other to make a cube), how high is the array?

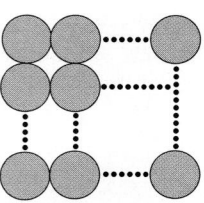

44. Suppose that every week the average American eats one-fourth of a pizza. The average pizza has a diameter of 14 inches and costs $8.00. There are about 250,000,000 Americans, and there are 640 acres in a square mile.

(a) About how many acres of pizza do Americans eat every week?

(b) What is the cost per acre of pizza in America?

45. If the price per square centimeter is the same, which is the better buy—a 10-centimeter-diameter circular pie or a square pie 9 centimeters on each side?

46. A goat is tied to the corner of a grassy pen that is in the shape of an equilateral triangle with sides of length 10 meters each. How long should the goat's tether be so that only one-half of the grass in the pen is available for the goat to eat?

47. (a) Compare the numerical value of the perimeter and area of a square with sides of length 4 units. Are there other squares with this property?

(b) Find three other rectangles with this property.

(c) Find a relationship between the dimensions of each such rectangle.

(d) Is there a circle whose area and circumference have the same numerical value? Explain.

48. Which, if either, of the following two triangles has the larger area?

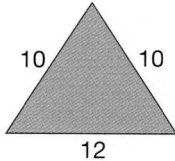
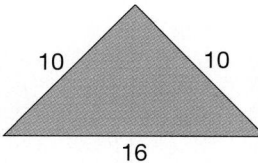

49. A rectangle is divided into two congruent rectangles such that the ratios of the lengths and widths of the original rectangle and the smaller rectangles are the same. What is the ratio?

50. Point *D* is the midpoint of $\overline{AC}$. Show that $\overline{BD}$ divides the triangle into two triangles of equal area.

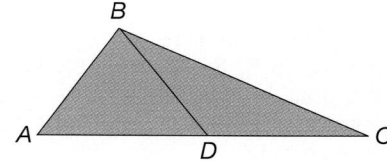

51. In the square *ABCD,* the two other squares pictured have their vertices at the midpoints of the sides of the next largest square.
   (a) Compare the area of the smallest square to the area of the largest square.
   (b) If the indicated process of forming squares is continued indefinitely, what would be the sum of the areas of all the squares if $AB = 1$? Explain.

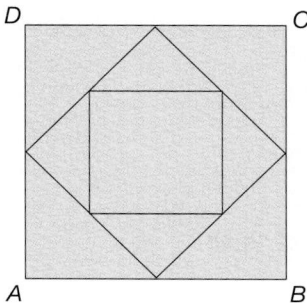

52. (a) In the dart board shown, the radius of circle *A* is 1, of circle *B* is 2, and of circle *C* is 3. Hitting *A* is worth 20 points; region *B,* 10 points; and region *C,* 5 points. Is this a fair dart board? Discuss.

(b) What point structure would make it a fair board if region *A* is worth 30 points?

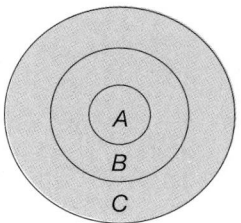

53. Let $\overline{AC}$ be a diagonal of the following rectangle *ABCD.* Show for all points *P* on $\overline{AC}$, $a^2 + c^2 = b^2 + d^2$.

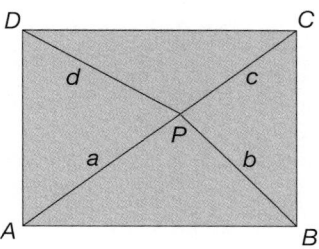

13.3

SURFACE AREA

Surface Area

The **surface area** of a three-dimensional figure is, literally, the total area of its exterior surfaces. For three-dimensional figures having bases, the **lateral surface area** is the surface area minus the areas of the bases. For polyhedra such as prisms and pyramids, the surface area is the sum of the areas of the polygonal faces.

Prisms

Example 13.14 shows how to find the surface area of a right rectangular prism.

EXAMPLE 13.14   Find the surface area of a box in the shape of a right prism whose bases are rectangles with side lengths 5 and 8, and whose height is 3 (Figure 13.45).

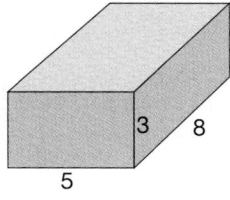

FIGURE 13.45

Solution

We can "disassemble" this box into six rectangles (Figure 13.46). If we consider the 5×8 faces to be the bases, the lateral surface area of this box is $2[(3 \times 5) + (3 \times 8)] = 78$ square units. Since each base has area $5 \times 8 = 40$ square units, the surface area is $78 + 80 = 158$ square units.

8

5

5   5   8

3   3

5

8

FIGURE 13.46

Observe that the lateral surface area in Example 13.14 also can be viewed as $3 \times (5 + 8 + 5 + 8)$, or 3 times the perimeter of the base. In general, let h be the height of a prism, P the perimeter of its base, and A the area of each base. Then, according to Example 13.14, the surface area of the prism is $2A + Ph$.

Theorem

Surface Area of a Right Prism

The surface area S of a right prism with height h whose bases each have area A and perimeter P is

$$S = 2A + Ph.$$

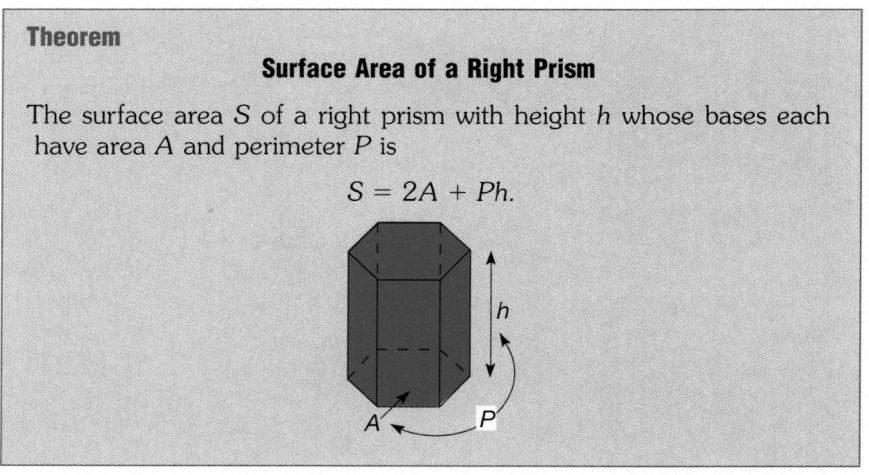

Cylinders

The surface area of a right circular cylinder can be approximated using a sequence of right regular prisms with increasingly many faces (Figure 13.47).

For each prism, the surface area is $2A + Ph$, where A and P are the area and perimeter, respectively, of the base, and h is the height of the prism. As the number of sides of the base increases, the perimeter P more and more closely approximates the circumference, C, of the base of the cylinder (Figure 13.47). Thus we have the following result.

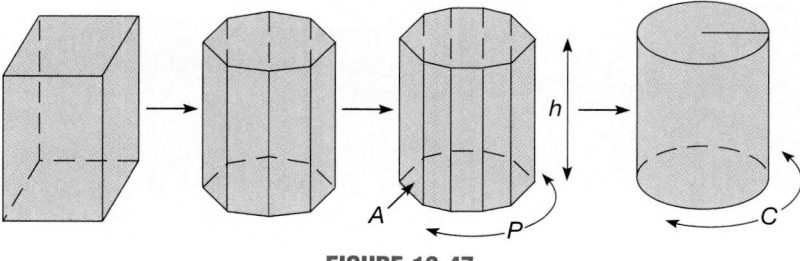

FIGURE 13.47

> **Theorem**
>
> ### Surface Area of a Right Circular Cylinder
>
> The surface area S of a right circular cylinder whose base has area A, radius r, and circumference C, and whose height is h is
>
> $$S = 2A + Ch$$
> $$= 2(\pi r^2) + (2\pi r)h = 2\pi r(r + h).$$
>
>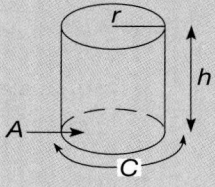

We can verify the formula for the surface area of a right circular cylinder by "slicing" the cylinder open and "unrolling" it to form a rectangle plus the two circular bases (Figure 13.48). The area of each circular base is πr^2. The area of the rectangle is $2\pi rh$, since the length of the rectangle is the circumference of the cylinder. Thus the total surface area is $2\pi r^2 + 2\pi rh$.

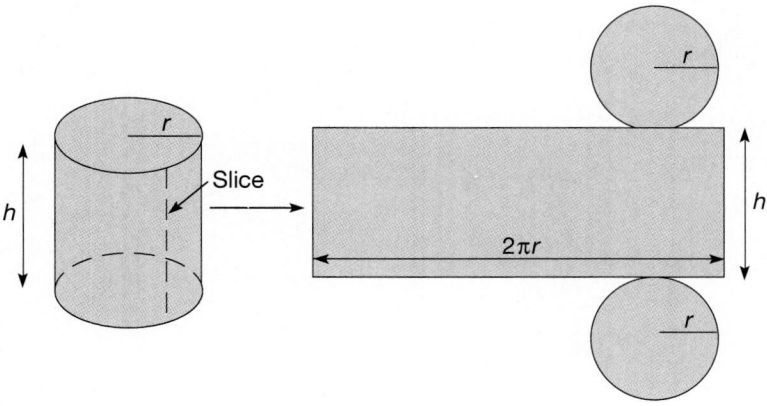

FIGURE 13.48

NOTE: Rather than attempt to memorize this formula, it is easier to imagine the cylinder sliced open to form a rectangle and two circles and then use area formulas for rectangles and circles, as we have just done.

Pyramids

The surface area of a pyramid is obtained by summing the areas of the triangular faces and the base. Example 13.15 illustrates this for a square pyramid.

EXAMPLE 13.15   Find the surface area of a right square pyramid whose base measures 20 units on each side and whose faces are isosceles triangles with edges of length 26 units [Figure 13.49(a)].

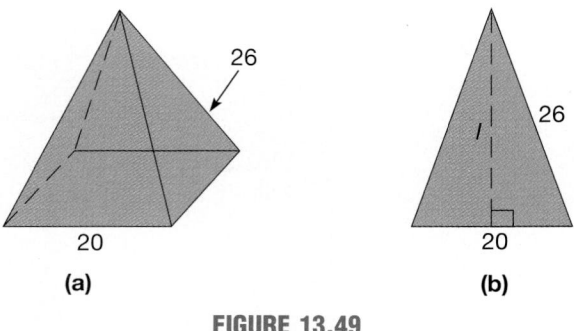

(a)   (b)

FIGURE 13.49

Solution
The area of the square base is $20^2 = 400$ square units. Each face is an isosceles triangle whose height, l, we must determine [Figure 13.49(b)]. By the Pythagorean theorem, $l^2 + 10^2 = 26^2 = 676$, so $l^2 = 576$. Hence $l = \sqrt{576} = 24$. Thus the area of each face is $\frac{1}{2}(20 \cdot 24) = 240$ square units. Finally, the surface area of the prism is the area of the base plus the areas of the triangular faces, or $400 + 4(240) = 1360$ square units   ∎

The height, l, as in Figure 13.49(b) of each triangular face of a right regular pyramid is called the **slant height** of the pyramid. In general, the surface area of a right regular pyramid is determined by the slant height and the base. Recall that a right regular pyramid has a regular n-gon as its base.

The sum of the areas of the triangular faces of a right regular pyramid is $\frac{1}{2}Pl$. This follows from the fact that each face has height l and base of length P/n, where n is the number of sides in the base. So each face has area $\frac{1}{2}(P/n)l$. Since there are n of these faces, the sum of the areas is $n[\frac{1}{2}(P/n)l] = \frac{1}{2}Pl$. Thus we have the following result.

Theorem

Surface Area of a Right Regular Pyramid

The surface area S of a right regular pyramid whose base has area A and perimeter P, and whose slant height is l is

$$S = A + \tfrac{1}{2}Pl.$$

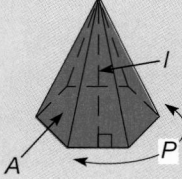

Cones

The surface area of a right circular cone can be obtained by considering a sequence of right regular pyramids with increasing numbers of sides in the bases (Figure 13.50).

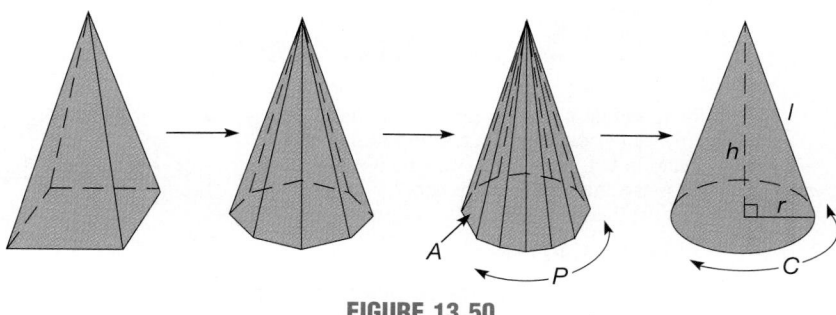

FIGURE 13.50

The surface area of each right pyramid is $A + \frac{1}{2}Pl$, where A is the area of the base of the pyramid, P is the perimeter of the base, and l is the slant height. As the number of sides in the bases of the pyramids increases, the perimeters of the bases approach the circumference of the base of the cone (Figure 13.50). For the right circular cone, the **slant height** is the distance from the apex of the cone to the base of the cone measured along the surface of the cone (Figure 13.51). If the height of the cone is h and the radius of the base is r, then the slant height, l, is $\sqrt{h^2 + r^2}$. The lateral surface area of the cone is one-half the product of the circumference of the base $(2\pi r)$ and the slant height. This is analogous to the sum of the areas of the triangular faces of the pyramids. Combining the area of the base and the lateral surface area, we obtain the formula for the surface area of a right circular cone.

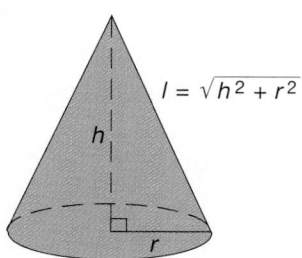

$$l = \sqrt{h^2 + r^2}$$

FIGURE 13.51

STUDENT PAGE SNAPSHOT

ACTIVITY Surface Area: Cones

Meg wants to build a tent in the shape of a tepee. The slant height is 8 ft and the radius of the base is 6 ft. How much canvas will she need to make the tent and the floor?

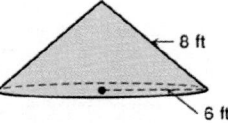

8 ft

6 ft

WORKING TOGETHER

The tepee is a cone. The surface area is the sum of the areas of its circular base and the lateral surface.

1. What is the area of the circular base of a cone with radius r?

2. The diagram shows the pattern for the lateral surface of a cone. Why is the length of the curve equal to $2\pi r$?

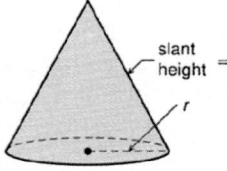

slant height = ℓ

r

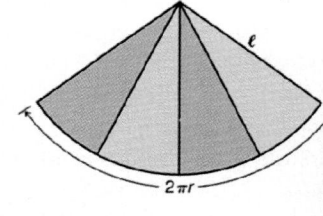

ℓ

$2\pi r$

3. Trace and cut out the pattern of the lateral surface of the cone. Cut the pattern into its four sections. Arrange the sections into a shape that approximates a parallelogram. How can you find the area of the parallelogram? How can you find the area of the lateral surface?

4. Write a formula for the total surface area of a cone.

Here is how Meg found the surface area of the tepee's cone shape.

$S = \pi r^2 \quad + \pi r \ell$

$\approx 3.14(6^2) + 3.14(6)(8)$

≈ 263.76

Meg will need 263.76 ft² of canvas to make the tepee and the floor.

SHARING IDEAS

5. How does your formula compare with Meg's?

> **Theorem**
>
> ### Surface Area of a Right Circular Cone
>
> The surface area S of a right circular cone whose base has area A and circumference C, and whose slant height is l is
>
> $$S = A + \tfrac{1}{2}Cl.$$
>
> If the radius of the base is r and the height of the cone is h, then
>
> $$S = \pi r^2 + \tfrac{1}{2}(2\pi r)l = \pi r^2 + \pi r\sqrt{h^2 + r^2}.$$
>
>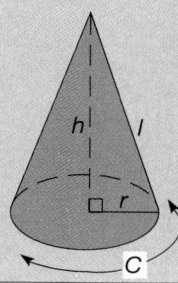

The lateral surface area of a cone is the surface area minus the area of the base. Thus the formula for the lateral surface of a cone is $\pi r\sqrt{h^2 + r^2}$.

Spheres

Archimedes made a fascinating observation regarding the surface area and volume of a sphere. Namely, the surface area (volume) of a sphere is two-thirds the surface area (volume) of the smallest cylinder containing the sphere. (Archimedes was so proud of this observation that he had it inscribed on his tombstone.) The formula for the surface area of a sphere is derived next and the formula for the volume will be derived in the next section.

Figure 13.52 shows a sphere of radius r contained in a cylinder whose base has radius r and whose height is $2r$. The surface area of the cylinder is $2\pi r^2 + 2\pi r(2r) = 6\pi r^2$. Thus, from Archimedes' observation, the formula for the surface area of a sphere of radius r is $\tfrac{2}{3}(6\pi r^2) = 4\pi r^2$.

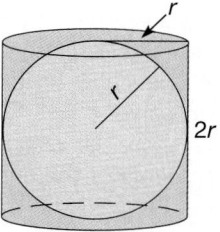

FIGURE 13.52

> **Theorem**
>
> ### Surface Area of a Sphere
>
> The surface area S of a sphere of radius r is
>
> $$S = 4\pi r^2.$$
>
>

A **great circle** of a sphere is a circle on the sphere whose radius is equal to the radius of the sphere. It is interesting that the surface area of a sphere, $4\pi r^2$, is exactly *four* times the area of a great circle of the sphere, πr^2. A great circle is the intersection of the sphere with a plane through the center of the sphere (Figure 13.53). If the earth were a perfect sphere, the equator and the circles formed by the meridians would be great circles. There are infinitely many great circles of a sphere (Figure 13.54).

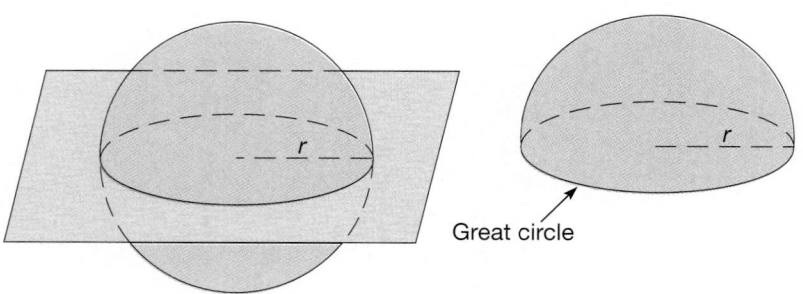

Great circle

FIGURE 13.53

FIGURE 13.54

MATHEMATICAL MORSEL

Let's see... That's eight .. or was that my ninth move?

Rubik's cube was one of the most popular toys in the 1980s. It was developed by a Hungarian design professor, Erno Rubic, to help his students better understand three-dimensional solids. Each face of the cube is made up of nine squares. The nine squares on each of the six faces are the same color *in their initial position,* six colors in all. The cube can be twisted in such a way as to move the smaller square faces around to other faces. In fact, with as few as four twists of an original cube, the faces can be so completely scrambled that most cannot rearrange the cube back to where the faces all have the same color. This should not be surprising since there are over 43 quintillion (!) different arrangements of the cube.

EXERCISE/PROBLEM SET 13.3—PART A

Exercises

1. Find the surface area of the following prisms.

(a)

(b)

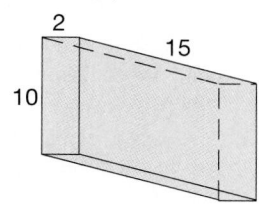

(c)

(d)

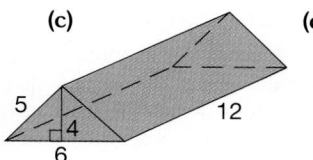
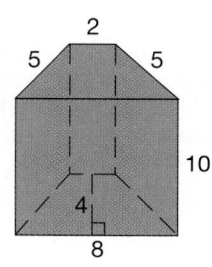

2. Find the surface area of the following square pyramids and cones.

(a)

(b)

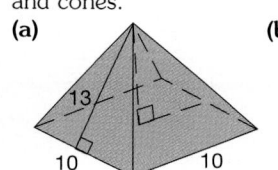
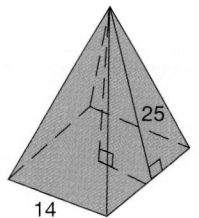

(c)

(d)

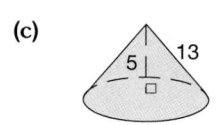
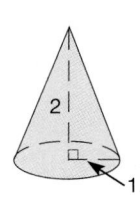

3. Find the surface area of the following cans to the nearest square centimeter.

(a) Coffee can
  $r = 7.6$ cm
  $h = 16.3$ cm
(b) Soup can
  $r = 3.3$ cm
  $h = 10$ cm
(c) Juice can
  \$r = 5.3$ cm
  $h = 17.7$ cm
(d) Shortening can
  $r = 6.5$ cm
  $h = 14.7$ cm

4. Find the surface area of the following spheres (to the nearest whole square unit).

(a) $r = 6$ **(b)** $r = 2.3$
(c) $d = 24$ **(d)** $d = 6.7$

5. Find the surface area of the following regular polyhedra (to the nearest cm^2).
(a) Tetrahedron with edge length of 5 cm
(b) Octahedron with edge length of $4\sqrt{3}$ cm
(c) Icosahedron with edge length of 12 cm

6. A room measures 4 meters by 7 meters and the ceiling is 3 meters high. A liter of paint covers 20 square meters. How many liters of paint will it take to paint all but the floor of the room?

7. Find the surface area of each right prism with the given features.
(a) The bases are equilateral triangles with sides of length 8; height = 10.
(b) The bases are trapezoids with bases of lengths 7 and 9 perpendicular to one side of length 6; height = 12.
(c) The base is a right triangle with legs of length 5 and 12; height = 20.

Problems

8. Refer to the following figure.

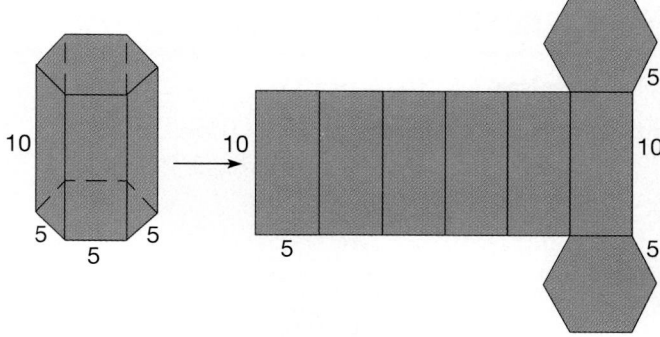

(a) Find the area of each hexagonal base.
(b) Find the total surface area of the prism.

9. A new jumbo-sized cereal box is to be produced. Each dimension of the regular-sized box will be doubled. How will the amount of cardboard required to make the new box compare to the amount of cardboard required to make the old box?

10. Suppose that you have 36 unit cubes like the one shown. Those cubes could be arranged to form right rectangular prisms of various sizes.

(a) Sketch an arrangement of the cubes in the shape of a right rectangular prism that has a surface area of exactly 96 square units.

(b) Sketch an arrangement of the cubes in the shape of a right rectangular prism that has a surface area of exactly 80 square units.

(c) What arrangement of the cubes gives a right rectangular prism with the smallest possible surface area? What is this minimum surface area?

(d) What arrangement of the cubes gives a right rectangular prism with the largest possible surface area? What is this maximum surface area?

11. A scale model of a new engineering building is being built for display. A scale of 5 cm = 3 m is being used. It took 27,900 square centimeters of cardboard to construct the exposed surfaces of the model. What will be the area of the exposed surfaces of the building in square meters?

12. The top of a rectangular box has an area of 96 square inches. Its side has area 72 square inches and its end has area 48 square inches. What are the dimensions of the box?

13. (a) Assuming that the earth is a sphere with an equatorial diameter of 12,760 kilometers, what is a radius of the earth?

(b) What is the surface area of the earth?

(c) If the land area is 135,781,867 square kilometers, what percent of the earth's surface is land?

14. Suppose that the radius of a sphere is reduced by half. What happens to the surface area of the sphere?

15. A square 6 centimeters on a side is rolled up to form the lateral surface of a right circular cylinder. What is the surface area of the cylinder, including the top and the bottom?

16. Given a sphere with diameter 10, find the surface area of the smallest cylinder containing the sphere.

17. A barber pole consists of a cylinder of radius 10 cm on which 1 red, 1 white, and 1 blue helix, each of equal width, are painted. The cylinder is 1 meter high. If each stripe makes a constant angle of 60° with the vertical axis of the cylinder, how much surface area is covered by the red stripe?

EXERCISE/PROBLEM SET 13.3—PART B

Exercises

1. Find the surface area of each prism.

(a)

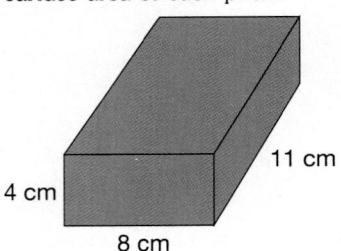

(b)

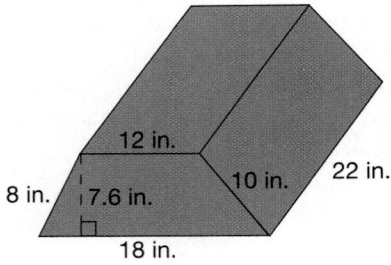

(c)

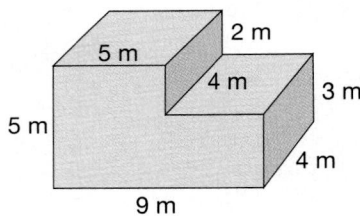

(d)

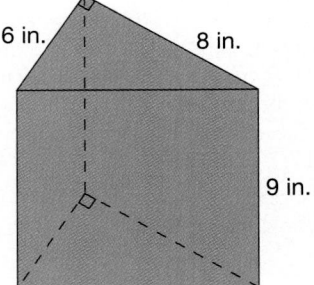

2. Find the surface area of the following cylinders. Round your answers to the nearest square centimeter.

(a)

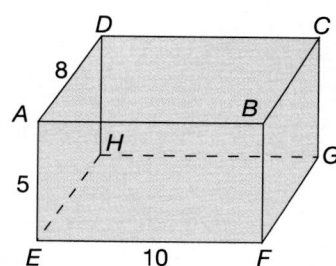

6 cm

15 cm

(b)

10 cm

0.5 cm

3. A right rectangular prism is shown.

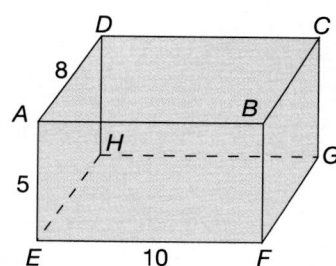

D   C

8

A   B

H   G

5

E   10   F

(a) Apply the formula for the surface area of a right prism to find the surface area of the pictured prism where *ABCD* and *EFGH* are the bases.

(b) Repeat part (a) where *BCGF* and *ADHE* are the bases.

(c) Repeat part (a) where *ABFE* and *DCGH* are the bases.

(d) What conclusion do you draw about applying the formula to a right rectangular prism?

4. Find the surface area of each cone and rectangular pyramid (to the nearest whole square unit).

(a)

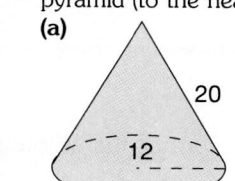

20

12

(b)

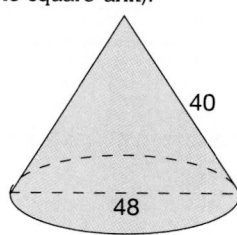

40

48

(c)

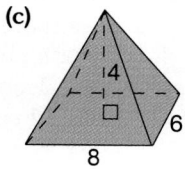

4

6

8

(d)

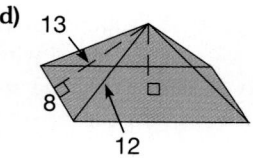

13

8

12

5. **(a)** Find the surface area of a sphere with radius 3 cm in terms of π.

(b) Find the surface area of a sphere with diameter 24.7 cm.

(c) Find the diameter, to the nearest centimeter, of a sphere with surface area 215.8 cm^2.

6. Arrange the surface areas of the following figures from smallest to largest.

1. A cube with edge length 1
2. A sphere with diameter 1
3. A right circular cone with diameter of base 1 and height $\frac{1}{2}$
4. A right circular cylinder with diameter of base 1 and height 1

7. Find the surface area of each solid figure shown below. Round your answers to the nearest square inch.

(a)

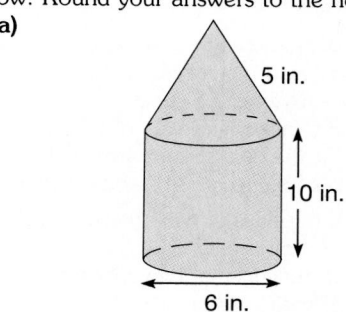

5 in.

10 in.

6 in.

(b)

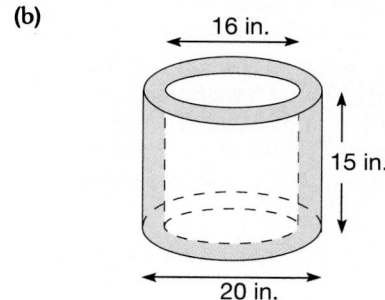

16 in.

15 in.

20 in.

8. A right prism has a base in the shape of a regular hexagon with a 12 cm side and apothem of $6\sqrt{3}$ cm. If the sides of the prism are all squares, determine the total surface area of the prism.

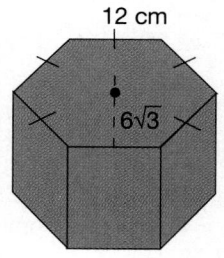

12 cm

$6\sqrt{3}$

9. A right circular cylinder has a surface area of 112π. If the height of the cylinder is 10, find the diameter of the base.

10. Find the surface area of each right pyramid with the given features.
  (a) The base is a regular hexagon with sides of length 12; height = 14.
  (b) The base is a 10 by 18 rectangle; height = 12.

Problems

11. Thirty unit cubes are stacked in square layers to form a tower. The bottom layer measures 4 cubes × 4 cubes, the next layer 3 cubes × 3 cubes, the next layer 2 cubes × 2 cubes, and the top layer a single cube.
  (a) Determine the total surface area of the tower of cubes.
  (b) Suppose that the number of cubes and the height of the tower were increased so that the bottom layer of cubes measured 8 cubes × 8 cubes. What would be the total surface area of this tower?
  (c) What would be the total surface area of the tower if the bottom layer measured 20 cubes × 20 cubes?

12. **(a)** If the ratio of the sides of two squares is $2:5$, what is the ratio of their areas?
  (b) If the ratio of the edges of two cubes is $2:5$, what is the ratio of their surface areas?
  (c) If all the dimensions of a rectangular box are doubled, what happens to its surface area?

13. A tank for storing natural gas is in the shape of a right circular cylinder. The tank is approximately 380 feet high and 250 feet in diameter. The sides and top of the cylinder must be coated with a special primer. How many square feet of surface must be painted?

14. A paper cup has the shape shown in the following drawing (called a **frustum** of a right circular cone).

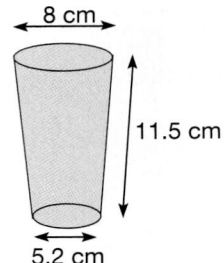

8 cm

11.5 cm

5.2 cm

If the cup is sliced open and flattened, the sides of the cup have the shape below.

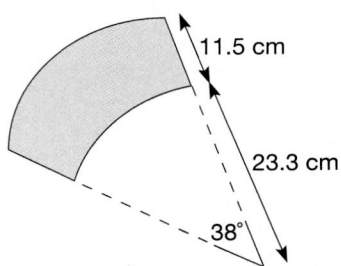

11.5 cm

23.3 cm

38°

Use the dimensions given to calculate the number of square meters of paper used in the construction of 10,000 of these cups. (Hɪɴᴛ: See Problem 21 in Exercise/Problem Set 13.2—Part A.)

15. Let a sphere with surface area 64π be given.
  (a) Find the surface area of the smallest cube containing the sphere.
  (b) Find the surface area of the largest cube contained in the sphere.

13.4

VOLUME

Volume

The **volume** of a three-dimensional figure is a measure of the amount of space that it occupies.

Prisms

To determine the volume of a three-dimensional figure, we imagine the figure filled with unit cubes. A rectangular prism whose sides measure 2, 3, and 4 units, respectively, can be filled with $2 \cdot 3 \cdot 4 = 24$ unit cubes (Figure 13.55). The volume of a cube that is 1 unit on each edge is 1 **cubic unit**. Hence the volume of the rectangular prism in Figure 13.55 is 24 cubic units.

As with units of area, we can subdivide 1 cubic unit into smaller cubes

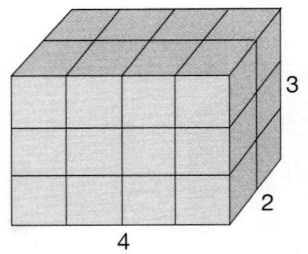

3

2

4

FIGURE 13.55

FIGURE 13.56

to determine volumes of rectangular prisms with dimensions that are terminating decimals. For example, we can subdivide our unit of length into 10 parts and make a tiny cube whose sides are $\frac{1}{10}$ of a unit on each side (Figure 13.56). It would take $10 \cdot 10 \cdot 10 = 1000$ of these tiny cubes to fill our unit cube. Hence the volume of our tiny cube is 0.001 cubic unit. This subdivision procedure can be used to motivate the following volume formula, which holds for any right rectangular prism whose sides have real number lengths.

Definition

Volume of a Right Rectangular Prism

The volume V of a right rectangular prism whose dimensions are positive real numbers a, b, and c is

$$V = abc.$$

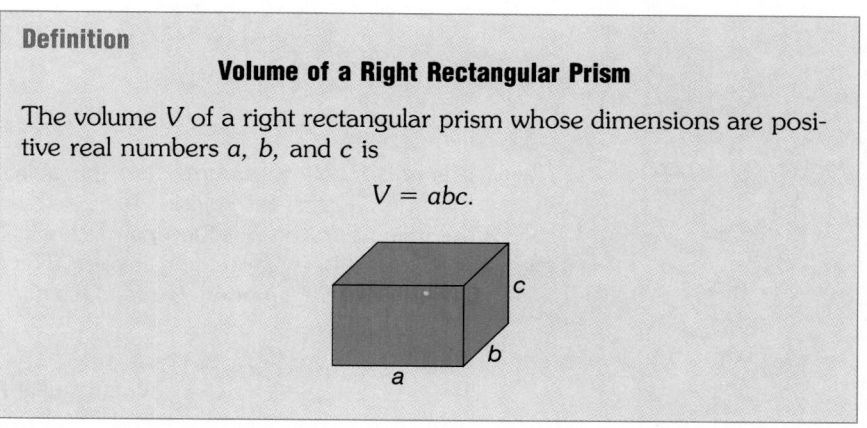

From the formula for the volume of a right rectangular prism, we can immediately determine the volume of a cube, since every cube is a special right rectangular prism with all edges the same length. Volume is reported in cubic units.

Theorem

Volume of a Cube

The volume V of a cube whose edges have length s is

$$V = s^3.$$

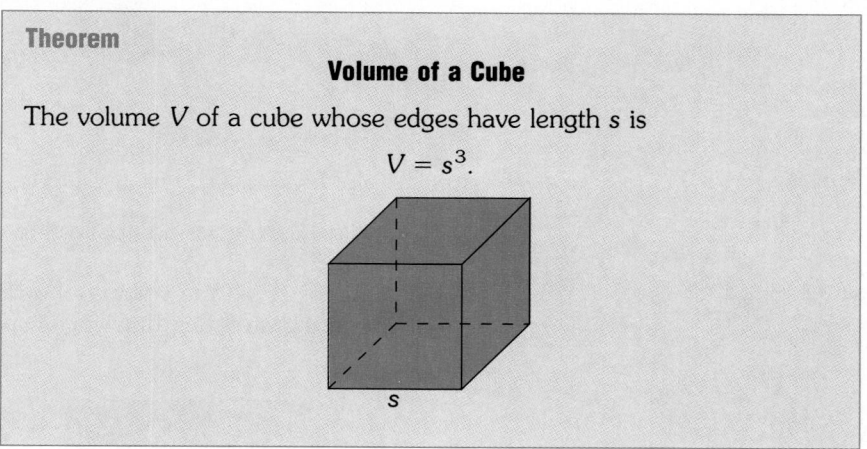

A useful interpretation of the volume of a right rectangular prism formula is that the volume is the product of the area of a base and the corresponding height. For example, the area of one base is $a \cdot b$ and the corresponding height is c. We could choose any face to serve as a base and measure the height perpendicularly from that base. Imagine a right prism as a deck of very thin cards which is transformed into an oblique prism (Figure 13.57).

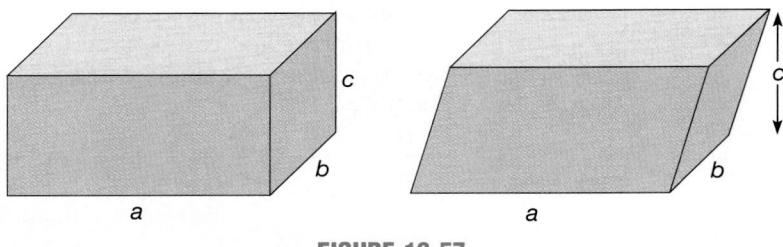

FIGURE 13.57

It is reasonable to assume that the oblique prism has the same volume as the original prism (thinking again of a deck of cards). Thus we can obtain the volume of the oblique prism by calculating the product of the area of a base and its corresponding height. The height is c, the distance between the planes containing its bases. This general result holds for all prisms.

Theorem

Volume of a Prism

The volume V of a prism whose base has area A and whose height is h is

$$V = Ah.$$

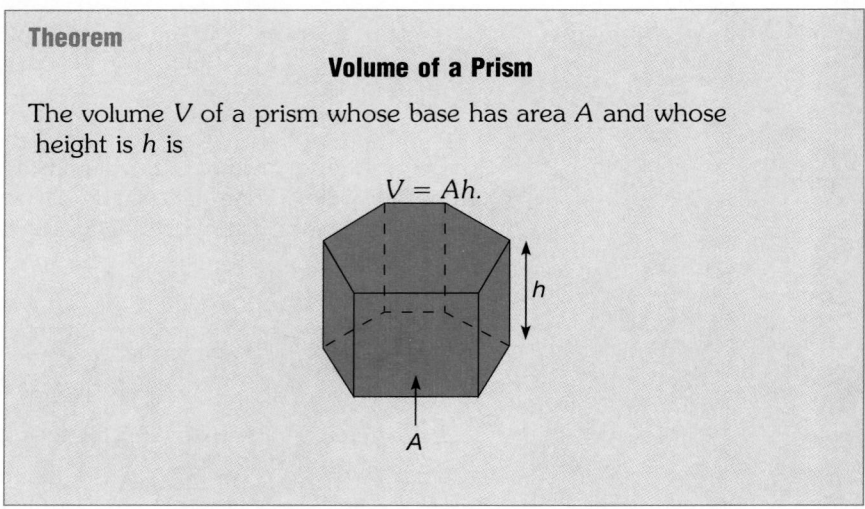

Example 13.16 gives an application of the volume of a prism formula.

EXAMPLE 13.16   Find the volume of a right triangular prism whose height is 4 and whose base is a right triangle with legs of lengths 5 and 12 (Figure 13.58).

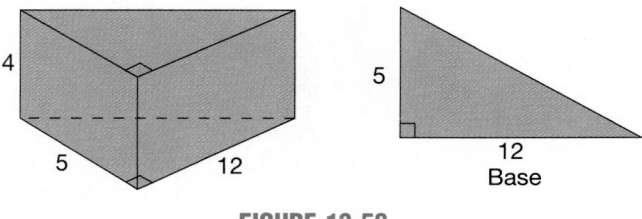

FIGURE 13.58

Solution
The base is a right triangle whose area is $(5 \times 12)/2 = 30$ square units. Hence $A = 30$ and $h = 4$, so the volume of the prism is $30 \times 4 = 120$ cubic units. ■

Cylinders

The volumes of a cylinder can be approximated using prisms with increasing numbers of sides in their bases (Figure 13.59). The volume of each prism is the product of the area of its base and its height. Hence we would expect the same to be true about a cylinder. This suggests the following volume formula (which can be proved using calculus).

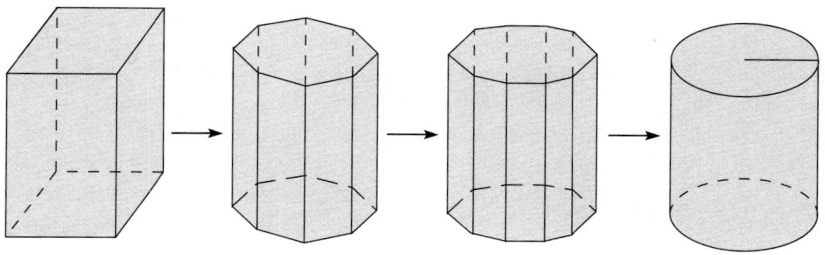

FIGURE 13.59

Theorem

Volume of a Cylinder

The volume V of a cylinder whose base has area A and whose height is h is

$$V = Ah.$$

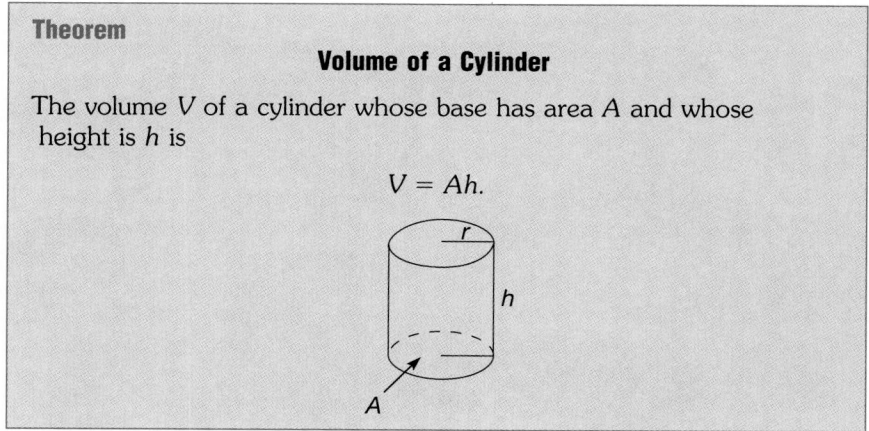

If the base of the cylinder is a circle of radius r, then $V = \pi r^2 h$.

Note that the volume of an arbitrary cylinder, such as those in Figure 13.60, is simply the product of the area of its base and its height.

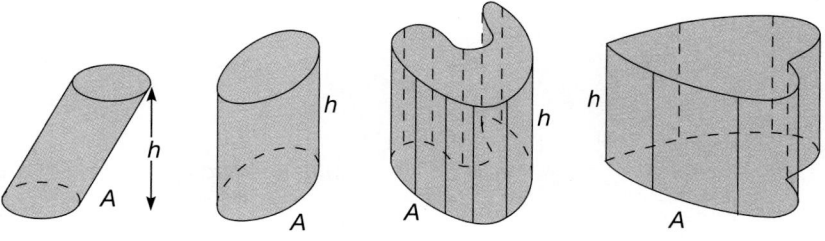

FIGURE 13.60

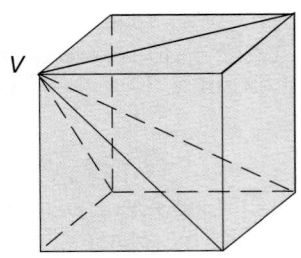

FIGURE 13.61

Pyramids

To determine the volume of a square pyramid we start with a cube and consider the four diagonals from a particular vertex to the other vertices (Figure 13.61). Taking the diagonals three at a time, we can identify three pyramids inside the cube (Figure 13.62). The pyramids are identical in size and shape and intersect only in faces or edges, so that each pyramid fills one-third of the cube. (Three copies of the pattern in Figure 13.63 can be folded into pyramids that can be arranged to form a cube.) Thus the volume of each pyramid is one-third of the volume of the cube. This result holds in general for pyramids with any base.

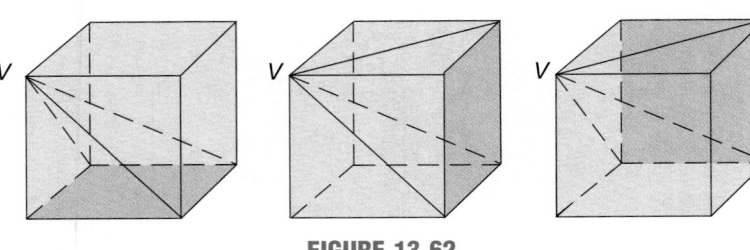

FIGURE 13.62

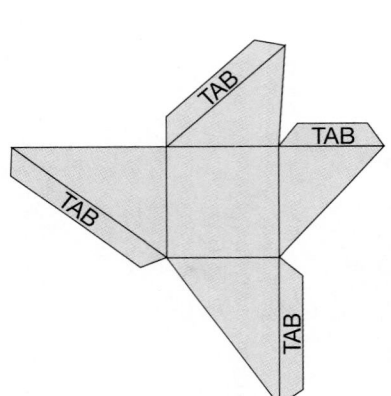

FIGURE 13.63

> **Theorem**
>
> ### Volume of a Pyramid
>
> The volume V of a pyramid whose base has area A and whose height is h is
>
> $$V = \frac{1}{3}Ah.$$
>
>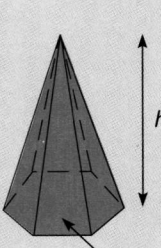

Cones

We can determine the volume of a cone in a similar manner by considering a sequence of pyramids with increasing numbers of sides in the bases (Figure 13.64). Since the volume of each pyramid is one-third of the volume of the smallest prism containing it, we would expect the volume of a cone to be one-third of the volume of the smallest cylinder containing it. This is, in fact, the case. That is, the volume of a cone is one-third of the product of the area of its base and its height. This holds for right and oblique cones.

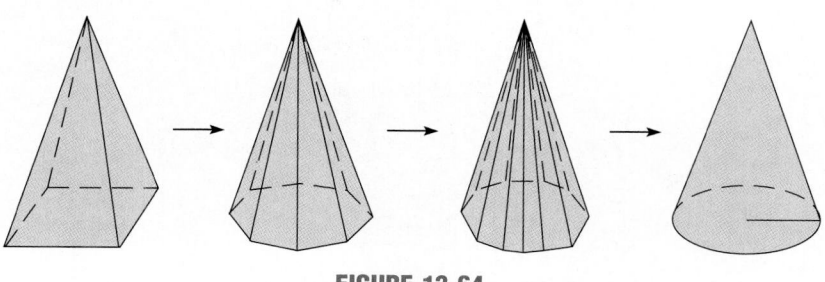

FIGURE 13.64

Theorem

Volume of a Cone

The volume V of a cone whose base has area A and whose height is h is

$$V = \frac{1}{3}Ah.$$

For a cone with a circular base of radius r, the volume of the cone is $\frac{1}{3}\pi r^2 h$.

Spheres

In Section 13.3 it was stated that Archimedes observed that the volume of a sphere is two-thirds the volume of the smallest cylinder containing the sphere. Figure 13.65 shows this situation. The volume of the cylinder is

$$V = (\pi r^2)2r = 2\pi r^3.$$

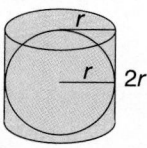

FIGURE 13.65

Hence the volume of the sphere is $\frac{2}{3}(2\pi r^3)$, or $\frac{4}{3}\pi r^3$. Thus we have derived a formula for the volume of a sphere (which confirms the result of Archimedes described in the Focus On).

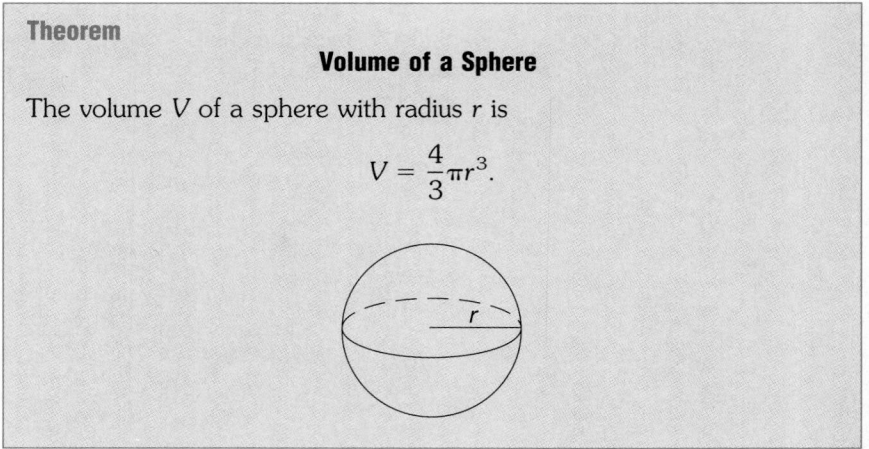

Theorem

Volume of a Sphere

The volume V of a sphere with radius r is

$$V = \frac{4}{3}\pi r^3.$$

As an aid to recall and distinguish between the formulas for the surface area and volume of a sphere, observe that the "r" in $4\pi r^2$ is *squared,* an area unit, whereas the "r" in $\frac{4}{3}\pi r^3$ is *cubed,* a volume unit.

Table 13.11 summarizes the volume and surface area formulas for right prisms, right circular cylinders, right regular pyramids, right circular cones, and spheres. The indicated dimensions are the area of the base, A; the height, h; the perimeter or circumference of the base, P or C; and the slant height, l. By observing similarities, one can minimize the amount of memorization.

TABLE 13.11

Geometric Shape	Surface Area	Volume
Right prism	$S = 2A + Ph$	$V = Ah$
Right circular cylinder	$S = 2A + Ch$	$V = Ah$
Right regular pyramid	$S = A + \frac{1}{2}Pl$	$V = \frac{1}{3}Ah$
Right circular cone	$S = A + \frac{1}{2}Cl$	$V = \frac{1}{3}Ah$
Sphere	$S = 4\pi r^2$	$V = \frac{4}{3}\pi r^3$

Cavalieri's Principle

The remainder of this section presents a more formal derivation of the volume and surface area of a sphere. First, to find the volume of a sphere, we use Cavalieri's principle, which compares solids where cross sections have equal areas.

Cavalieri's Principle

Suppose that two three-dimensional solids are contained between two parallel planes such that every plane parallel to the two given planes cuts cross sections of the solids with equal areas. Then the volumes of the solids are equal.

Figure 13.66 shows an illustration of Cavalieri's principle applied to cylinders. Notice that a plane cuts each cylinder, forming circular cross sections of area πr^2. Hence, by Cavalieri's principle, the cylinders have equal volume.

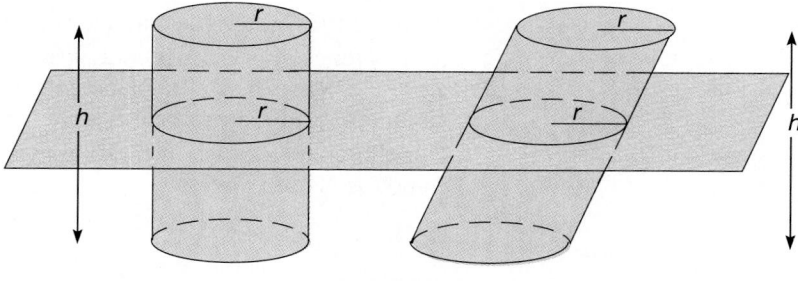

FIGURE 13.66

We can also apply Cavalieri's principle to the prisms in Figure 13.67. Cavalieri's principle explains why the volume of a prism or cylinder depends only on the base and height.

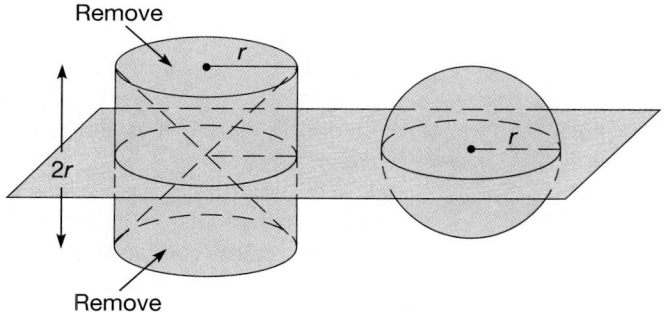

FIGURE 13.67

To determine the volume of a sphere, consider the solid shape obtained by starting with a cylinder of radius r and height $2r$, and removing two cones. We will call the resulting shape S (Figure 13.67). Imagine cutting shape S and the sphere with a plane that is a units above the center of the sphere. Figure 13.68 shows front and top views.

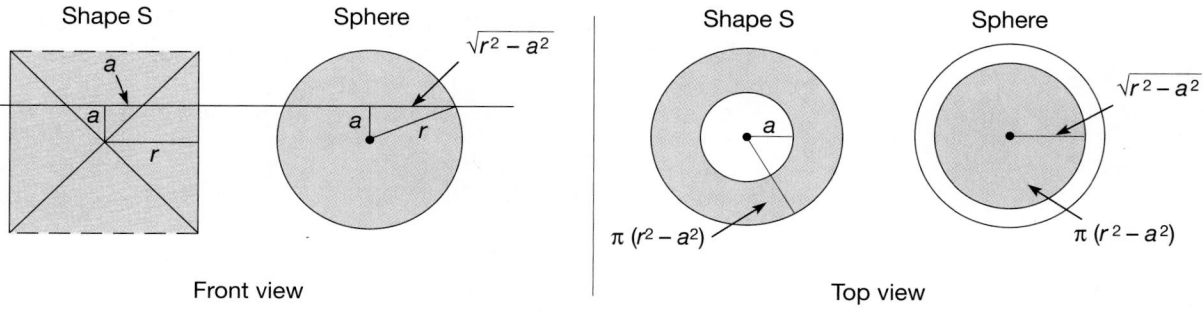

FIGURE 13.68

Using the top view, we show next that each cross-sectional area is $\pi(r^2 - a^2)$. First, for shape S, the cross section is a "washer" shape with outside radius r and inside radius a. Therefore, its area is $\pi r^2 - \pi a^2 = \pi(r^2 - a^2)$. Second, for the sphere, the cross section is a circle of radius $\sqrt{r^2 - a^2}$. (Refer to the right triangle in the front view and apply the Pythagorean theorem.) Hence the cross-sectional area of the sphere is $\pi(\sqrt{r^2 - a^2})^2$, or $\pi(r^2 - a^2)$ also. Thus the plane cuts equal areas, so that by Cavalieri's principle, the sphere and shape S have the *same* volume. The volume of shape S is the volume of the cylinder minus the volume of two cones that were removed. Therefore

$$\text{volume of shape } S = \pi r^2 \cdot (2r) - 2\left(\frac{1}{3}\pi r^2 \cdot r\right)$$

$$= 2\pi r^3 - \frac{2\pi}{3}r^3$$

$$= \frac{6\pi r^3}{3} - \frac{2\pi r^3}{3}$$

$$= \frac{4}{3}\pi r^3.$$

Since the sphere and shape S have the same volume, the volume of the sphere is $\frac{4}{3}\pi r^3$.

To determine the surface area of a sphere, we imagine the sphere comprised of many "pyramids" of base area A and height r, the radius of the sphere. In Figure 13.69, the "pyramid" has a base of area A and volume V. The ratio $\frac{A}{V}$ is

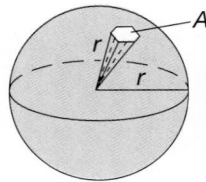

FIGURE 13.69

$$\frac{A}{V} = \frac{A}{\frac{1}{3}Ar} = \frac{3}{r}.$$

If we fill the sphere with a large number of such "pyramids," of arbitrarily small base area A, the ratio of $\frac{A}{V}$ should also give the ratio of the surface area of the sphere to the volume of the sphere. (The total volume of the "pyramids" is approximately the volume of the sphere, and the total area of the bases of the "pyramids" is approximately the surface area of the sphere.) Hence, for the sphere we expect

$$\frac{A}{V} = \frac{3}{r},$$

so

$$A = \frac{3}{r} \cdot V$$

$$= \frac{3}{r} \cdot \frac{4}{3}\pi r^3$$
$$= 4\pi r^2.$$

This is, in fact, the surface area of the sphere. Again, we would need calculus to verify the result rigorously.

Notice that the formulas obtained from Cavalieri's principle were the same as those obtained from Archimedes' observation.

MATHEMATICAL MORSEL

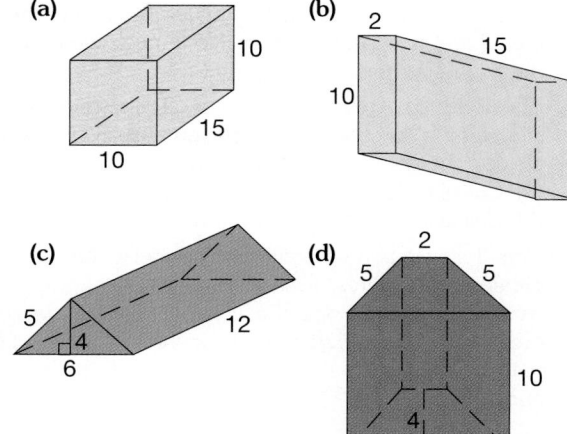

Quit snoring..and MOVE OVER!!

The sphere is one of the most commonly occurring shapes in nature. Raindrops, frog eggs, tomatoes, oranges, soap bubbles, the Earth, and the moon are a very few examples of spherelike shapes. The regular occurrence of the spherical shape is not coincidental. One explanation for the frequency of the sphere's appearance is that for a given surface area, the sphere encloses the greatest volume. In other words, a sphere requires the least amount of natural material to surround a given volume. This may help explain why animals curl up in a ball when it is cold outside.

EXERCISE/PROBLEM SET 13.4—PART A

Exercises

1. Find the volume of each prism.

(a)

(b)

(c)

(d)

2. Find the volume of each square pyramid and cone.

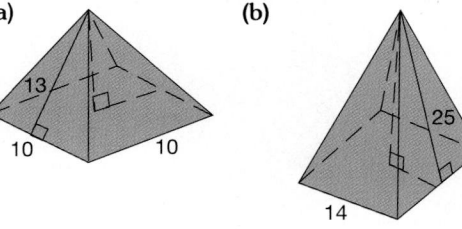

(a)

(b)

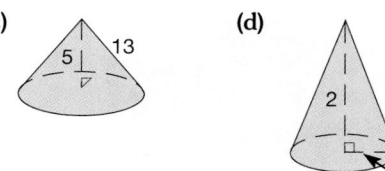

(c)

(d)

3. Find the volume of each can.
   (a) Coffee can   (b) Soup can
       $r = 7.6$ cm $r = 3.3$ cm
       $h = 16.3$ cm $h = 10$ cm
   (c) Juice can   (d) Shortening can
       $r = 5.3$ cm $r = 6.5$ cm
       $h = 17.7$ cm $h = 14.7$ cm

4. Find the volume of the following spheres (to the nearest whole cubic unit).
   (a) $r = 6$ (b) $r = 2.3$
   (c) $d = 24$ (d) $d = 6.7$

Problems

5. Following are shown base designs for stacks of unit cubes (see the problem sets in Section 12.1). For each one, determine the volume and total surface area (including the bottom) of the stack described.
   (a)

3	4	2
1	1	3

   (b)

	1	4
	2	

   (c)

3	3	3
1	2	3
1	2	3

6. Find the volume of each of the following solid figures, rounding to the nearest cubic inch.
   (a)

   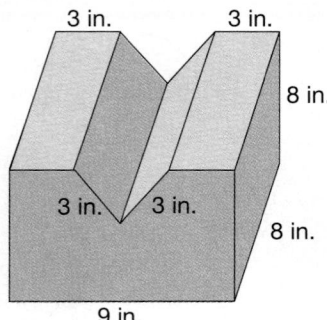

   3 in.   3 in.
                8 in.
   3 in.   3 in.
                8 in.
        9 in.

   (b)

   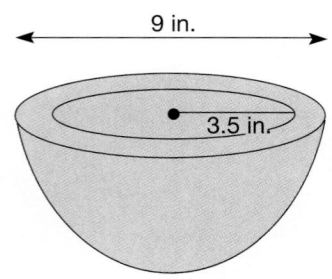

   9 in.
   3.5 in.

7. (a) How many square meters of tile are needed to tile the sides and bottom of the swimming pool illustrated?
   (b) How much water does the pool hold?

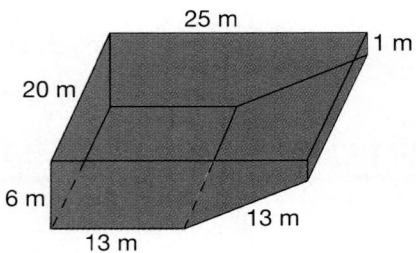

25 m
1 m
20 m
6 m
13 m
13 m

8. A standard tennis ball can is a cylinder that holds three tennis balls.
   (a) Which is greater, the circumference of the can or its height?
   (b) If the radius of a tennis ball is 3.5 cm, what percent of the can is occupied by air?

9. Find the volume of each right prism with the given features.
   (a) The bases are equilateral triangles with sides of length 8; height = 10.
   (b) The bases are trapezoids with bases of lengths 7 and 9 perpendicular to one side of length 6; height = 12.
   (c) The base is a right triangle with legs of length 5 and 12; height = 20.

10. The Great Wall of China is about 1500 miles long. The cross section of the wall is a trapezoid 25 feet high, 25 feet wide at the bottom, and 15 feet wide at the top. How many cubic yards of material make up the wall?

11. A cylindrical aquarium has a circular base with diameter 2 feet and height 3 feet. How much water does the aquarium hold, in cubic feet?

12. The Pyramid Arena in Memphis, Tennessee, has a square base that measures approximately 548 feet on a side. The arena is 321 feet high.
   (a) Calculate its volume.
   (b) Calculate its lateral surface area.

13. The following are patterns (or nets) for three-dimensional figures. Use the dimensions given to calculate for each one the volume and the surface area of the three-dimensional figure formed by the pattern. Round your answers to the nearest cm^3 or cm^2.

(a)

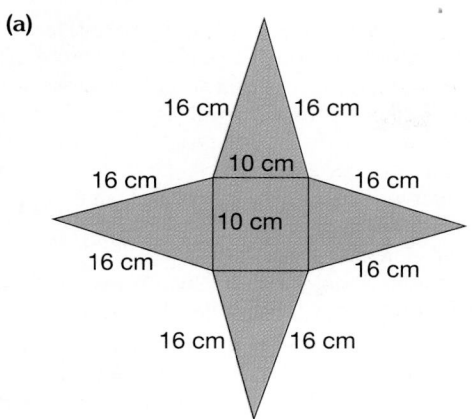

(b)

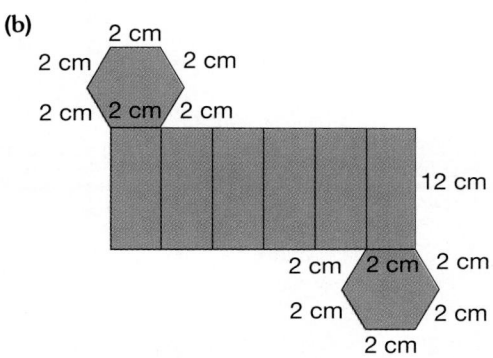

14. A scale model of a new engineering building is being built for display. A scale of 5 cm = 3 m is being used. The volume of the scale model is 396,000 cubic centimeters. What will be the volume of the finished structure in cubic meters?

15. Suppose that you want to have a concrete patio in the shape of a regular hexagon, 10 feet on each side.

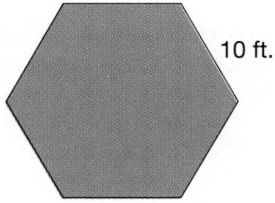

10 ft.

(a) What is the area of the top surface of the patio?
(b) If the patio is 4 inches thick, what volume of concrete will be needed?
(c) If concrete costs $45 per cubic yard, how much will the concrete for your patio cost, to the nearest cent?

16. Two designs for an oil storage tank are being considered: spherical and cylindrical. The two tanks would have the same capacity and would each have an inside diameter of 60 feet.
(a) What would be the height of the cylindrical tank?

(b) If one cubic foot holds 7.5 gallons of oil, what is the capacity of each tank in gallons?
(c) Which of the two designs has the smallest surface area and would thus require less material in its construction?

17. A sculpture made of iron has the shape of a right square prism topped by a sphere. The metal in each part of the sculpture is 2 mm thick. If the dimensions are as shown below and the density of iron is 7.87 g/cm^3, calculate the approximate weight of the sculpture in kilograms.

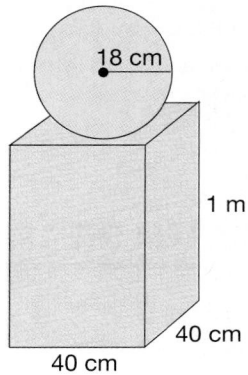

18 cm

1 m

40 cm

40 cm

18. The volume of an object with an irregular shape can be determined by measuring the volume of water it displaces.
(a) A rock placed in an aquarium measuring $2\frac{1}{2}$ feet long by 1 foot wide causes the water level to rise $\frac{1}{4}$ inch. What is the volume of the rock?
(b) With the rock in place, the water level in the aquarium is $\frac{1}{2}$ inch from the top. The owner wants to add to the aquarium 200 solid marbles, each with a diameter of 1.5 cm. Will the addition of these marbles cause the water in the aquarium to overflow?

19. Suppose that all the dimensions of a square prism are doubled.
(a) How would the volume change?
(b) How would the surface area change?

20. In designing a pool, it could be filled with three pipes each 9 centimeters in diameter, two pipes each 12 centimeters in diameter, or one pipe 16 centimeters in diameter. Which design will fill the pool the fastest?

21. (a) Find the volume of a cube with edges of length 2 meters.
(b) Find the length of the edges of a cube with volume twice that of the cube in part (a).

22. (a) How does the volume of a circular cylinder change if its radius is doubled?
(b) How does the volume of a circular cylinder change if its height is doubled?

23. The areas of the faces of a right rectangular prism are 24, 32, and 48 square centimeters. What is the volume of the prism?

24. A do-it-yourselfer wants to dig some holes for fence posts. He has the option of renting posthole diggers with diameter 6 inches or 8 inches. The amount of dirt removed by the larger posthole digger is what percent greater than the amount removed by the smaller?

25. A water tank is in the shape of an inverted circular cone with diameter 10 feet and height 15 feet. Another conical tank is to be built with height 15 feet but with one-half the capacity of the larger tank. Find the diameter of the smaller tank.

26. Lumber is measured in board feet. A **board foot** is the volume of a square piece of wood measuring 1 foot long, 1 foot wide, and 1 inch thick. A surfaced "two by four" actually measures $1\frac{1}{2}$ inches thick by $3\frac{1}{2}$ inches wide, a "two by six" measures $1\frac{1}{2}$ by $5\frac{1}{2}$, and so on ($\frac{1}{4}$ inch is planed off each rough surface). Plywood is sold in exact dimensions and is differentiated by thickness (e.g., $\frac{1}{2}$ inch, $\frac{5}{8}$ inch, etc.). Find the number of board feet in the following pieces of lumber.
(a) 6-foot long two by four
(b) 10-foot two by eight
(c) 4-foot by 8-foot sheet of $\frac{3}{4}$-inch plywood
(d) 4-foot by 6-foot sheet of $\frac{5}{8}$-inch plywood

27. An irrigation pump can pump 250 liters of water per minute. How many hours should the system work to water a rectangular field 75 m by 135 m to a depth of 3 cm?

EXERCISE/PROBLEM SET 13.4—PART B

Exercises

1. Find the volume of each prism.
(a)

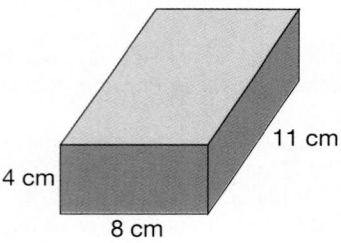

(b)

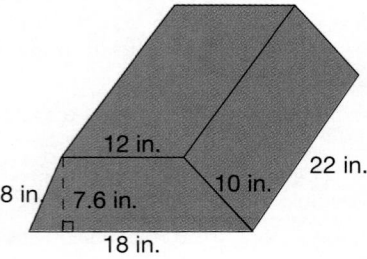

(c)

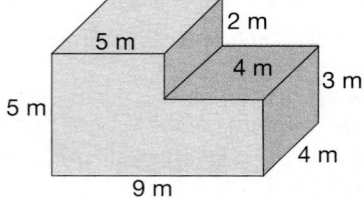

(d)

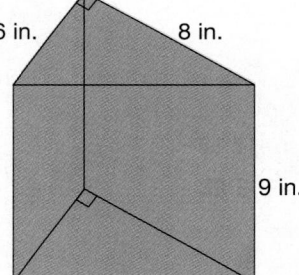

2. Find the volume of the following cylinders. Round your answers to the nearest cubic centimeter.
(a)

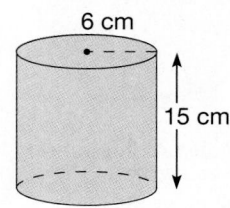

(b)

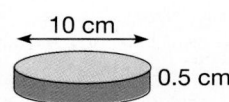

3. Find the volume of each pyramid.

(a)   **(b)**

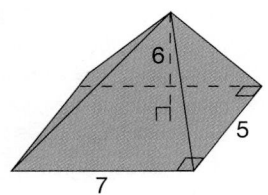

(c)

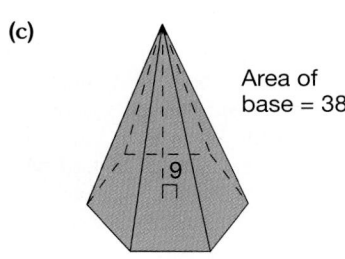

Area of
base = 38

4. Find the volume of each of the cones and rectangular pyramids in Exercise 4 of Exercise/Problem Set 13.3—Part B.

Problems

5. Find the volume of each solid figure in Exercise 7 of Exercise/Problem Set 13.3—Part B. Round your answers to the nearest cubic inch.

6. Following are base designs for stacks of unit cubes (see the problem sets in Section 12.1). For each one, determine the volume and surface area (including the bottom) of the stack described.

(a)

| 1 | 2 | 4 | 3 |

(b)

| 2 | 3 |
| 1 | 5 |

(c)

| 1 | 4 | 5 | 6 |
| 2 | 3 | | |

7. (a) Find the volume, to the nearest cubic centimeter, of a soft-drink can with a diameter of 5.6 centimeters and a height of 12 centimeters.

(b) If the can is filled with water, find the weight of the water in grams.

8. Given are three cardboard boxes.

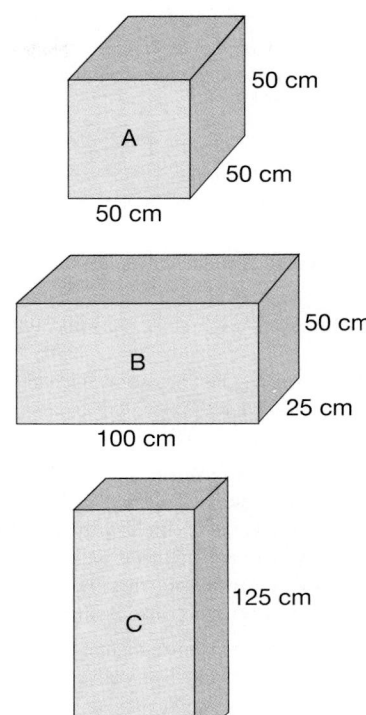

(a) Find the volume of each box.
(b) Find the surface area of each box.
(c) Do boxes with the same volume always have the same surface area?
(d) Which box used the least amount of cardboard?

9. The first three steps of a 10-step staircase are shown.

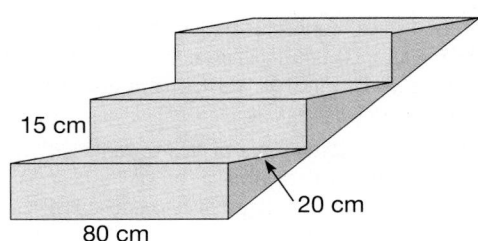

(a) Find the amount of concrete needed to make the exposed portion of the staircase.
(b) Find the amount of carpet needed to cover the fronts, tops, and sides of the concrete steps.

10. The Pyramid of Cheops has a square base 240 yards on a side. Its height is 160 yards.
   (a) What is its volume?
   (b) What is the surface area of the four exterior sides?

11. Arrange the volumes of the following figures from smallest to largest.

   1. A cube with edge length 1
   2. A sphere with diameter 1
   3. A right circular cone with diameter of base 1 and height $\frac{1}{2}$
   4. A right circular cylinder with diameter of base 1 and height 1

12. Find the volume of each right pyramid with the given features.
   (a) The base is a regular hexagon with sides of length 12; height = 14.
   (b) The base is a 10 by 18 rectangle; height = 12.

13. A vegetable garden measures 20 feet by 30 feet. The grower wants to cover the entire garden with a layer of mushroom compost 2 inches thick. She plans to haul the compost in a truck that will hold a maximum of 1 cubic yard. How many trips must she make with the truck to haul enough compost for the garden?

14. (a) A pipe 8 inches in diameter and 100 yards long is filled with water. Find the volume of the water in the pipe, in cubic yards.
   (b) A pipe 8 centimeters in diameter and 100 meters long is filled with water. Find the volume of the water in the pipe, in cubic meters.
   (c) Which is the easier computation, (a) or (b), or are they equivalent?

15. A soft-drink cup is in the shape of a right circular cone with capacity 250 milliliters. The radius of the circular base is 5 centimeters. How deep is the cup?

16. The circumference of a beach ball is 73 inches. How many cubic inches of air does the ball hold? Round your answer to the nearest cubic inch.

17. A 4-inch-thick concrete slab is being poured for a circular patio 10 feet in diameter. Concrete costs $50 per cubic yard. Find the cost of the concrete, to the nearest cent.

18. (a) If the ratio of the sides of two squares is $2:5$, what is the ratio of their areas?
   (b) If the ratio of the edges of two cubes is $2:5$, what is the ratio of their volumes?
   (c) If all the dimensions of a rectangular box are doubled, what happens to its volume?

19. It is estimated that the average diameter of peeled logs coming into your sawmill is 16 inches.
   (a) What is the thickness of the largest square timber that can be cut from the average log?
   (b) If the rest of the log is made into mulch, what percent of the original log is the square timber?

20. An aquarium measures 25 inches long by 14 inches wide by 12 inches high. How much does the water filling the aquarium weigh? (One cubic foot of water weighs 62.4 pounds.)

21. A right rectangular prism has a volume of 324 cubic units. Edge A measures twice that of edge B and nine times that of edge C. What are the dimensions of the prism?

22. While rummaging in his great aunt's attic, Bernard found a small figurine that he believed to be made out of silver. To test his guess, he looked up the density of silver in his chemistry book and found that it was 10.5 g/cm^3. He found that the figure weighed 149 g. To determine its volume he dropped it into a cylindrical glass of water. If the diameter of the glass was 6 cm and the figurine was pure silver, by how much should the water level in the glass rise?

23. Explain how Cavalieri's principle can be used to justify that the volume of an oblique prism or the volume of an oblique cylinder depends only on the base and height.

24. (a) You want to make the smallest possible cubical box to hold a sphere. If the radius of the sphere is r, what percent of the volume of the box will be air (to the nearest percent)?
   (b) For a child's toy, you want to design a cube that fits inside a sphere such that the vertices of the cube just touch the sphere. If the radius of the sphere is r, what percent of the volume of the sphere is occupied by the cube?

25. (a) How does the volume of a sphere change if its radius is doubled?
   (b) How does the surface area of a sphere change if its radius is doubled?

26. A rectangular piece of paper can be rolled into a cylinder in two different directions. If there is no overlapping, which cylinder has the greater volume, the one with the long side of the rectangle as its height, or the one with the short side of the rectangle as its height, or will the volumes be the same?

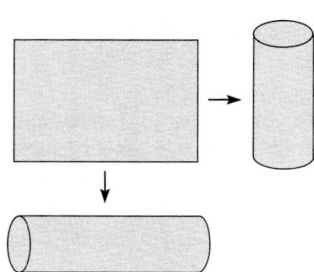

27. The following sphere, right circular cylinder, and right circular cone have the same volume. Find the height of the cylinder and the slant height of the cone.

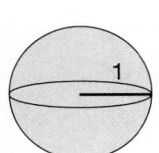 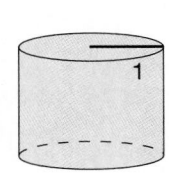 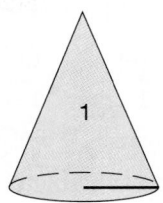

28. A baseball is composed of a spherical piece of cork with a 2-centimeter radius, which is then wrapped by string until a sphere with a diameter of 12 centimeters is obtained. If an arbitrary point is selected in the ball, what is the probability that the point is in the string?

29. A merchant had two unequal cubical boxes whose contents totaled exactly 6 cubic feet and whose dimensions were fractions. What were the dimensions of the two boxes?

30. Suppose that you have 10 separate unit cubes. Then the total volume is 10 cubic units and the total surface area is 60 square units. If you arrange the cubes as shown, the volume is still 10 cubic units, but now the surface area is only 36 square units (convince yourself this is true by counting faces). For each of the following problems, assume that all the cubes are stacked to form a single shape sharing complete faces (no loose cubes allowed).

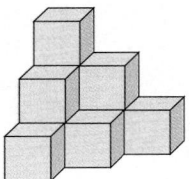

(a) How can you arrange 10 cubes to get a surface area of 34 square units? Draw a sketch.

(b) What is the greatest possible surface area you can get with 10 cubes? Sketch the arrangement.

(c) How can you arrange the 10 cubes to get the least possible surface area? What is this area?

(d) Answer the questions in parts (b) and (c) for 27 and 64 cubes.

(e) What arrangement has the greatest surface area for a given number of cubes?

(f) What arrangement seems to have the least surface area for a given number of cubes? (Consider cases with n^3 cubes for whole numbers n.)

(g) Biologists have found that an animal's surface area is an important factor in its regulation of body temperature. Why do you think desert animals such as snakes are long and thin? Why do furry animals curl up in a ball to hibernate?

31. If a tube of caulking lays a 40-foot cylindrical bead $\frac{1}{4}$ inch in diameter, how long will a $\frac{1}{8}$-inch bead be?

SOLUTION OF INITIAL PROBLEM

David was planning a motorcycle trip across Canada. He drew his route on a map and estimated the length of his route to be 115 centimeters. The scale on his map is 1 centimeter = 39 kilometers. His motorcycle's gasoline consumption is 75 miles per gallon of gasoline on the average. If gasoline costs $1.25 per gallon, how much should he plan to spend for gasoline? (What additional information does he need?)

Strategy: Use Dimensional Analysis

David set up the following ratios:

1 cm/39 km (map scale)

75 miles/1 gallon (gasoline consumption)

The length of his trip, then, is about

$$115 \text{ cm} \times \frac{39 \text{ km}}{1 \text{ cm}} = 115 \times 39 \text{ km} = 4485 \text{ km}.$$

If he knew how many kilometers are in 1 mile, he could convert the length of his trip to miles. (This is the additional information that he needs.) David looked this ratio up in an almanac and found 1 mile = 1.61 km (to two places). Thus the length of his trip is

$$4485 \text{ km} \times \frac{1 \text{ mile}}{1.61 \text{ km}} = \frac{4485}{1.61} \text{ miles}$$
$$= 2785.7 \text{ miles (to one decimal place).}$$

Hence David computed his gasoline expenses as follows:

$$2785.7 \text{ miles} \times \frac{1 \text{ gallon}}{75 \text{ miles}} \times \frac{1.25 \text{ dollars}}{\text{gallon}}$$
$$= \frac{2785.7 \times 1.25}{75} \text{ dollars} = \$46.43.$$

To use the strategy Use Dimensional Analysis, set up the ratios of units (such as km/cm) so that when the units are simplified (or canceled) as fractions, the resulting unit is the one that was sought.

Notice how the various units cancel to produce the end result in dollars. Summarizing, David converted distance (the length of his trip) to dollars (gasoline expense) via the product of ratios:

$$115 \text{ cm} \times \frac{39 \text{ km}}{1 \text{ cm}} \times \frac{1 \text{ mile}}{1.61 \text{ km}} \times \frac{1 \text{ gallon}}{75 \text{ miles}} \times \frac{1.25 \text{ dollars}}{1 \text{ gallon}} = \$46.43.$$

Additional Problems Where the Strategy "Use Dimensional Analysis" Is Useful

1. Bamboo can grow as much as 35.4 inches per day. If the bamboo continues to grow at this rate, about how many meters tall, to the nearest tenth of a meter, would it be at the end of a week? (Use 1 in. = 2.54 cm.)
2. A foreign car's gas tank holds 50 L of gasoline. What will it cost to fill the tank if regular gas is selling for $1.09 a gallon? (1 L = 1.057 qt.)
3. We see lightning before we hear thunder because light travels faster than sound. If sound travels at about 1000 km/hr through air at sea level at 15°C and light travels at 186,282 mi/sec, how many times faster is the speed of light than the speed of sound?

WRITING/DISCUSSING FOR UNDERSTANDING

1. Think of a nonstandard unit not mentioned in this chapter that is used in daily life to measure length. Describe situations in which this unit might be used. In what ways is the unit convenient to use, and in what ways could problems arise with its use?
2. Imagine yourself in the school cafeteria with a rectangular paper napkin. Describe attributes of the room or objects in it that could be measured using that nonstandard unit. What problems could arise from using a napkin as a unit?

3. Discuss the pros and cons of the United States converting to the metric system versus retaining the English system. Why do you think some are reluctant to change? How might you address their concerns?
4. Explain how the following NCTM Standards are reflected in this chapter.
   - Extend understanding of the process of measurement.
   - Estimate, make, and use measurements to describe and compare phenomena.
   - Select appropriate units and tools to measure to the degree of accuracy required in a particular situation.
   - Understand the structure and use of systems of measurement.
   - Extend their understanding of the concepts of perimeter, area, volume, angle measure, capacity, and weight and mass.
   - Develop formulas and procedures for determining measures to solve problems.

PROJECTS

1. Estimate the number of sixth-grade math textbooks currently in use in your state. Determine the approximate number of trees necessary to produce those books.
2. Suppose that one pair of shoes for each of the residents in your state were lined up toe to heel.
   (a) About how long would this line of shoes be in metric measure?
   (b) Estimate the number of hectares this arrangement of shoes might cover.
   (c) What would be the metric dimensions of the smallest cubical box that could contain the shoes?
   (d) Estimate the mass of this filled box in kilograms.

CHAPTER REVIEW

Major Ideas

1. The measurement process may involve informal measurement with "natural" measurement units, scientific measurement with standard units (e.g., English or metric units), or abstract (mathematical) measurement.
2. The metric system has all of the features of an ideal measurement system by design, while the English system does not.
3. Dimensional analysis simplifies conversion among types of units and is useful for solving applied problems involving units.
4. There is a sequence of interrelated formulas for the areas of many types of two-dimensional shapes.
5. The Pythagorean theorem can be applied to measure distance in two- and three-dimensional space.
6. There are interrelated formulas for the volumes and surface areas of three-dimensional shapes.

   Following is a list of key vocabulary, notation, and ideas for this chapter. Mentally review these items and, where appropriate, write down the meaning of each term. Then restudy the material that you are unsure of before proceeding to take the chapter test.

SECTION 13.1:   MEASUREMENT WITH NONSTANDARD AND STANDARD UNITS?

Vocabulary/Notation

Wholistic measurement **616**
Nonstandard units: "hand," "pace," "dash," "pinch," etc. **616**
Standard units **616**
English system of units for

> *Length:* inch (in.) **617**, foot (ft) **617**, yard (yd) **617**, mile (mi) **617**
>
> *Area:* square inch (in^2) **618**, square foot (ft^2) **618**, square yard (yd^2) **618**, acre **618**, square mile (mi^2) **618**
>
> *Volume:* cubic inch (in^3) **619**, cubic foot (ft^3) **619**, cubic yard (yd^3) **619**
>
> *Capacity:* teaspoon (tsp) **620**, tablespoon (tbs) **620**, liquid ounce (oz) **620**, cup (cp) **620**, pint (pt) **620**, quart (qt) **620**, gallon (gal) **620**, barrel (bar) **620**
>
> *Weight:* ounce **620**, pound **620**, ton **620**
>
> *Temperature:* degrees Fahrenheit (°F) **620**

Metric system of units for

> *Length:* meter (m) **621**, decimeter (dm) **621**, centimeter (cm) **621**, millimeter (mm) **621**, dekameter (dam) **621**, hectometer (hm) **621**, kilometer (km) **621**
>
> *Area:* square meter (m^2) **624**, square centimeter (cm^2) **624**, square millimeter (mm^2) **624**, are (a) **624**, hectare (ha) **624**, square kilometer (km^2) **624**
>
> *Volume:* liter (L) **626**, cubic decimeter (dm^3) **626**, cubic centimeter (cm^3) **626**, milliliter (mL) **626**, cubic meter (m^3) **626**, kiloliter (kL) **626**
>
> *Mass:* kilogram (kg) **627**, gram (g) **627**, metric ton (t) **627**
>
> *Temperature:* degrees Celsius (°C) **628**

Dimensional analysis **628**

Ideas

Measurement process **615**
Wholistic measurement of length **616**, area **616**, volume **616**, using nonstandard units, **616**
Scientific measurement of length, area, volume, weight, temperature, using standard units in the English system, **616–620**
Varying ratios among English units **617**
Properties of an ideal system of units **621**
Scientific measurement of length, area, volume, weight, temperature, using standard units in the metric system, **620–627**

SECTION 13.2: LENGTH AND AREA

Vocabulary/Notation

Ideas

SECTION 13.3: SURFACE AREA

Vocabulary/Notation

Ideas

SECTION 13.4:   VOLUME

Vocabulary/Notation

Ideas

PEOPLE IN MATHEMATICS

Andrew Gleason (1921–) says that he has always had a knack for solving problems. As a young man, he worked in cryptanalysis during World War II. The work involved problems in statistics and probability, and Andrew—despite having only a bachelor's degree—found that he understood the problems better than many experienced mathematicians. After the war, he made his mark in the mathematical world when he contributed to the solution of Hilbert's famous Fifth Problem. Today, Gleason is a longtime professor of mathematics at Harvard. "[As part of the School Mathematics Project] I worked with a group of kids who had just finished the first grade. One day I produced some squared paper and said, 'Here's how you multiply.' I drew a 3 × 4 rectangle and said, 'This is 3 times 4; we count the squares and get 12. So 3 × 4 is 12.' Then I did another, 4 × 5. Then I gave each kid some paper and said, 'You do some.' They were very soon doing two-digit problems."

Maria Agnesi (1718–1799) was famous for the highly regarded *Instituzioni Analitiche,* a 1020-page, two-volume presentation of algebra, analytic geometry, and calculus. Published in 1748, it brought order and clarity to the mathematics invented by Descartes, Newton, Leibniz and others in the seventeenth century. Maria was the eldest of 21 children in a wealthy Italian family. She was a gifted child, with an extraordinary talent for languages. Her parents encouraged her to excel, and she received the best schooling available. Maria began work on *Instituzióni Analitiche* at age 20, and finished it 10 years later, supervising its printing on presses installed in her home. After its publication, she was appointed honorary professor at the University of Bologna. But instead, Maria decided to dedicate her life to charity and religious devotion, and she spent the last 45 years of her life caring for the sick, aged, and indigent.

CHAPTER 13 TEST

Knowledge

1. True or false?
   (a) The prefix "milli" means "one thousand times."
   (b) The English system has all the properties of an ideal measurement system.
   (c) The formula for the volume of a circular cylinder is $V = \pi r^2 h$, where r is the radius of the base and h is the height.
   (d) The formula for the surface area of a sphere is $A = \frac{4}{3}\pi r^2$.
   (e) If, in a right triangle, the length of the hypotenuse is a and the lengths of the other two sides are b and c, then $a^2 + b^2 = c^2$.
   (f) The formula for converting degrees Celsius into degrees Fahrenheit is $F = \frac{9}{5}C + 32$.
   (g) One milliliter of water in its densest state has a mass of 1 kilogram.
   (h) The surface area of a right square pyramid whose base has sides of length s and whose triangular faces have height h is $2hs + s^2$.

Skill

2. If 1 inch is exactly 2.54 cm, how many kilometers are in a mile?

3. Seven cubic hectometers are equal to how many cubic decimeters?

4. What is the area of a circle whose circumference is 2?

5. What is the volume of a prism whose base is a rectangle with dimensions 7.2 cm by 3.4 cm and whose height is 5.9 cm?

6. Find the volume of a pyramid whose base is a pentagon with perimeter 17 cm and area 13 cm^2 and whose height is 12 cm.

Understanding

7. Show how one can use the formula for the area of a rectangle to derive the area of a parallelogram.

8. Explain why the interrelatedness attribute of an ideal system of measurement is useful in the metric system.

9. Describe one aspect of the metric system that should make it much easier to learn than the English system.

Problem Solving/Application

10. The cube shown has edges of length s.

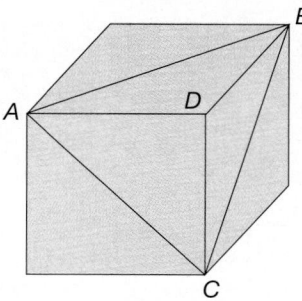

   (a) Find the area of $\triangle ABC$.
   (b) Find the volume of pyramid $ABCD$.

11. Sound travels 1100 feet per second in air. Assume that the earth is a sphere of diameter 7921 miles. How many hours would it take for a plane to fly around the equator at the speed of sound and at an altitude of 6 miles?

12. Find the surface area and volume of the following solids:
   (a) Four faces are rectangles; the other two are trapezoids with two right angles.

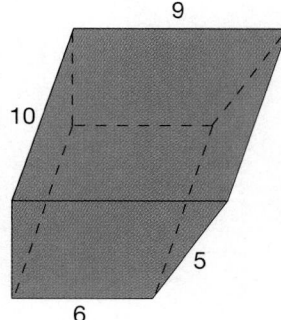

   (b) Right circular cylinder

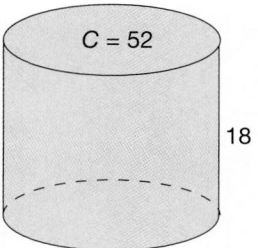

14

Geometry Using Triangle Congruence and Similarity

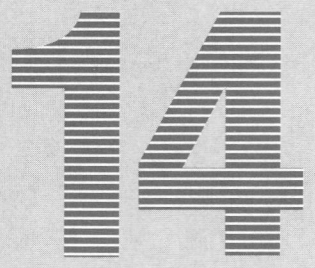

Euclid

Euclid: Father of Geometry

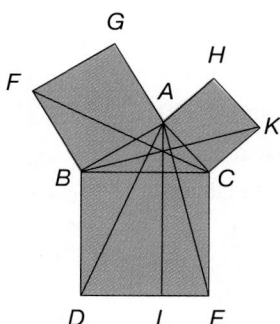

Euclid of Alexandria (circa 300 B.C.) has been called the "father of geometry." Euclid authored many works, but he is most famous for *The Elements,* which consisted of thirteen books, five of which are concerned with plane geometry, three with solid geometry, and the rest with geometric explanations of mathematics now studied in algebra.

After Plato (circa 400 B.C.) developed the method of forming a proof, and Aristotle (circa 350 B.C.) distinguished between axioms and postulates, Euclid organized geometry into a single logical system. Although many of the results of Euclidean geometry were already known, Euclid's unique contribution was the use of definitions, postulates, and axioms with statements to be proved, called propositions or theorems. The first such proposition was "Describe an equilateral triangle on a given finite straight line," which essentially showed how to construct an equilateral triangle with a given side length using only a compass and straightedge. Other famous theorems included in *The Elements* are the Pythagorean theorem, for which Euclid had his own original proof (see the figure), the Pons Asinorum theorem (the angles at the base of an isosceles triangle are congruent), and the proof of the infinitude of primes.

Modern geometers have revised Euclid's work to ensure more rigor. For example, Euclid defined a point as "that which has no parts," a line as "length without breadth," and a plane as "that which has only length and breadth."

In modern geometry, these terms are left as undefined because it is impossible to state precise definitions for all terms. Also, some of Euclid's theorems are now taken as postulates because the "proofs" that he offered had logical shortcomings. Nevertheless, most of the theorems and much of the development contained in a typical high school geometry course today are taken from Euclid's *Elements.*

Euclid founded the first school of mathematics in Alexandria, Greece. As one story goes, a student who had learned the first theorem asked Euclid, "But what shall I get by learning these things?" Euclid called his slave and said "Give him three pence, since he must make gain out of what he learns." As another story goes, a king asked Euclid if there were not an easier way to learn geometry than by studying *The Elements.* Euclid replied by saying, "There is no royal road to geometry."

STRATEGY 19: IDENTIFY SUBGOALS

Many complex problems can be broken down into "subgoals"—that is, intermediate results that lead to a final solution. Instead of seeking a solution to the entire problem directly, we can often obtain information that we can piece together to solve the problem. One way to employ the Identify Subgoals strategy is to think of other information that you wish the problem statement contained. For example, saying, "If I only knew such and such, I could solve it," suggests a subgoal, namely, the missing information.

Initial Problem

An eastbound bicycle enters a tunnel at the same time that a westbound bicycle enters the other end of the tunnel. The eastbound bicycle travels at 10 kilometers per hour, the westbound bicycle at 8 kilometers per hour. A fly is flying back and forth between the two bicycles at 15 kilometers per hour, leaving the eastbound bicycle as it enters the tunnel. The tunnel is 9 kilometers long. How far has the fly traveled in the tunnel when the bicycles meet?

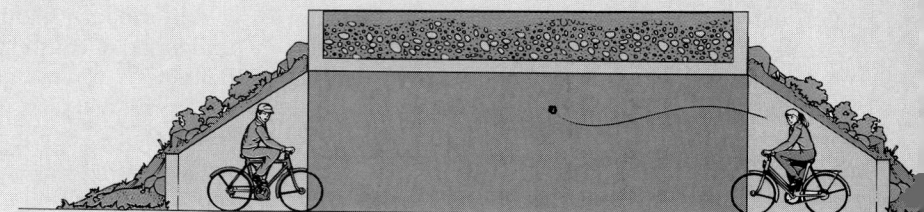

Clues

The Identify Subgoals strategy may be appropriate when:

- A problem can be broken down into a series of simpler problems.
- The statement of the problem is very long and complex.
- You can say, "If I only knew . . . , then I could solve the problem."
- There is a simple, intermediate step that would be useful.
- There is other information that you wished the problem contained.

A solution of the Initial Problem above appears on page 756.

INTRODUCTION

In Chapters 12 and 13 we studied a variety of two- and three-dimensional shapes and their properties. In this chapter we study congruence and similarity of triangles and applications of these ideas. Applications of congruence will include the construction of two-dimensional geometric shapes using specific instruments or tools. The classical construction instruments are an unmarked straightedge, a compass, and a writing implement, such as a pencil. From the time of Plato, the ancient Greeks studied geometric constructions. Applications of similarity will include indirect measurement and several other constructions.

14.1

CONGRUENCE OF TRIANGLES

Triangle Congruence

In an informal way, we say that two geometric figures are congruent if they can be superimposed so as to coincide. We will make this idea precise for specific figures.

Recall that if two line segments $\overline{AB}$ and $\overline{CD}$ have the same length, we say that they are congruent line segments. Similarly, if two angles $\angle PQR$ and $\angle STU$ have the same measure, we call them congruent angles. We indicate congruent segments and angles using marks as shown in Figure 14.1.

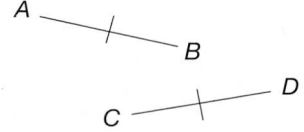

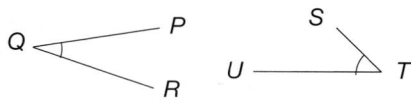

FIGURE 14.1

Suppose that we have two triangles, $\triangle ABC$ and $\triangle DEF$ and suppose that we pair up the vertices, $A \leftrightarrow D$, $B \leftrightarrow E$, $C \leftrightarrow F$ (Figure 14.2). This notation means that vertex A in $\triangle ABC$ is paired with vertex D in $\triangle DEF$, vertex B is paired with vertex E, and vertex C is paired with vertex F. Then we say that we have formed a **correspondence** between $\triangle ABC$ and $\triangle DEF$. Side

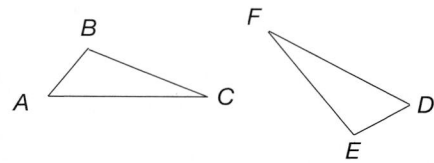

FIGURE 14.2

$\overline{AB}$ in $\triangle ABC$ corresponds to side $\overline{DE}$, side $\overline{BC}$ corresponds to side $\overline{EF}$, and side $\overline{AC}$ corresponds to side $\overline{DF}$. Similarly, $\angle ABC$, $\angle BAC$, and $\angle ACB$ correspond to $\angle DEF$, $\angle EDF$, and $\angle DFE$, respectively. We are especially interested in correspondences between triangles such that all corresponding sides and angles are congruent. If such a correspondence exists, the triangles are called congruent triangles (Figure 14.3).

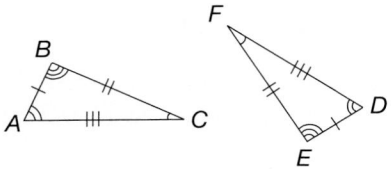

FIGURE 14.3

Definition

Congruent Triangles

Suppose that $\triangle ABC$ and $\triangle DEF$ are such that under the correspondence $A \leftrightarrow D$, $B \leftrightarrow E$, $C \leftrightarrow F$ all corresponding sides are congruent and all corresponding vertex angles are congruent. Then $\triangle ABC$ is **congruent** to $\triangle DEF$ and we write $\triangle ABC \cong \triangle DEF$.

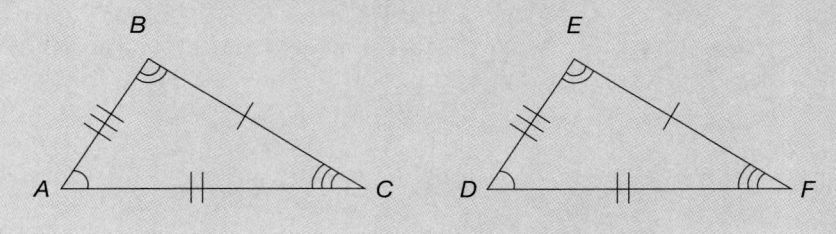

If two triangles are congruent, they have the same size and shape. However, they may be positioned differently in a plane or in space. Note that the symbol "$\cong$" stands for "is congruent to." Every triangle is congruent to itself under the correspondence that pairs each vertex with itself. To demonstrate that two triangles are congruent, we need to give the explicit correspondence between vertices and verify that corresponding sides and angles are congruent. Example 14.1 gives an illustration.

EXAMPLE 14.1   Show that the diagonal, $\overline{BD}$, of rectangle $ABCD$ on the square lattice in Figure 14.4 divides the rectangle into two congruent triangles $\triangle ABD$ and $\triangle CDB$.

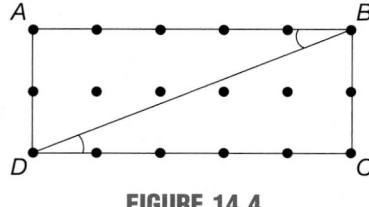

FIGURE 14.4

Solution

We observe that $AB = CD = 5$, $AD = CB = 2$, and $BD = DB$. Since $\overline{AB} \parallel \overline{DC}$, we have that $m(\angle ABD) = m(\angle CDB)$ by the alternate interior angle theorem. Similarly, since $\overline{AD} \parallel \overline{BC}$, we have $m(\angle BDA) = m(\angle DBC)$. Also, $m(\angle A) = m(\angle C) = 90°$ since $ABCD$ is a rectangle. Consequently, under the correspondence $A \leftrightarrow C$, $B \leftrightarrow D$, $D \leftrightarrow B$, all corresponding sides and corresponding angles are congruent. Thus $\triangle ABD \cong \triangle CDB$. ■

Example 14.1 shows that it is important for us to choose the correspondence between vertices in triangles *carefully*. For example, if we use the correspondence $A \leftrightarrow C$, $B \leftrightarrow B$, $D \leftrightarrow D$, it is *not* true that corresponding sides are congruent. For example, side $\overline{AB}$ corresponds to side $\overline{CB}$, yet $\overline{AB} \not\cong \overline{CB}$. Corresponding angles are not congruent under this correspondence either, since $\angle ABD$ is not congruent to $\angle CBD$.

There are simpler conditions that we can apply to verify the congruence of two triangles. Suppose that instead of having the three side lengths and three angle measures specified for a triangle, we are given only two of the side lengths and the measure of the angle formed by the two sides. Figure 14.5 shows an example. We can complete the triangle ($\triangle ABC$) in only one way, namely by connecting vertex B to vertex C. That is, the two given sides and the included angle determine a unique triangle. This observation is the basis of the side–angle–side congruence property.

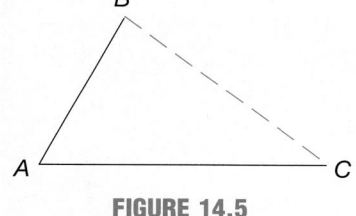

FIGURE 14.5

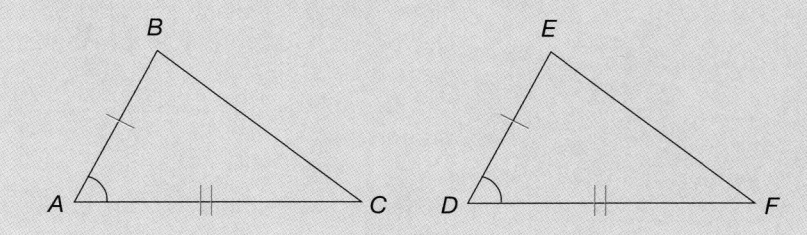

Side–Angle–Side (SAS) Congruence Property

If two sides and the included angle of a triangle are congruent, respectively, to two sides and the included angle of another triangle, then the triangles are congruent. Here, $\triangle ABC \cong \triangle DEF$.

The SAS congruence property tells us that it is sufficient to verify that two sides and an included angle of one triangle are congruent, respectively, to their corresponding parts of another triangle, to establish that the triangles are congruent. Example 14.2 gives an illustration.

EXAMPLE 14.2 In Figure 14.6, $\overline{AB} \cong \overline{AC}$ and $\angle BAP \cong \angle CAP$. Show that $\triangle BAP \cong \triangle CAP$.

Solution

Consider the correspondence $B \leftrightarrow C$, $A \leftrightarrow A$, $P \leftrightarrow P$. We have (i) $\overline{AP} \cong \overline{AP}$, (ii) $\angle BAP \cong \angle CAP$, and (iii) $\overline{AB} \cong \overline{AC}$. Hence, by (i), (ii), (iii), and the SAS congruence property, $\triangle BAP \cong \triangle CAP$. ■

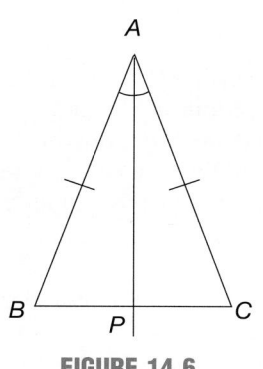

FIGURE 14.6

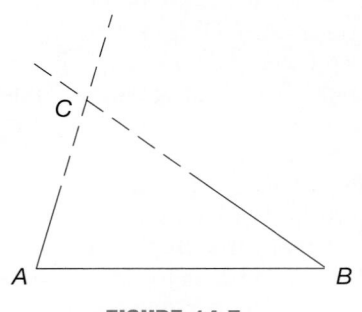

FIGURE 14.7

From the result of Example 14.2, we can conclude that $\angle ABP \cong \angle ACP$ in Figure 14.6 since these angles correspond in the congruent triangles. Thus the base angles of an isosceles triangle are congruent. In the problem set, we investigate the converse result, namely, that if two angles of a triangle are congruent, the triangle is isosceles.

A second congruence property for triangles involves two angles and their common side. Suppose that we are given two angles, the sum of whose measures is less than 180°. Also suppose that they share a common side. Figure 14.7 shows an example. The extensions of the noncommon sides of the angles intersect in a unique point C. That is, a unique triangle, $\triangle ABC$, is formed. This observation can be generalized as the angle–side–angle congruence property.

Angle–Side–Angle (ASA) Congruence Property

If two angles and the included side of a triangle are congruent, respectively, to two angles and the included side of another triangle, then the two triangles are congruent. Here, $\triangle ABC \cong \triangle DEF$.

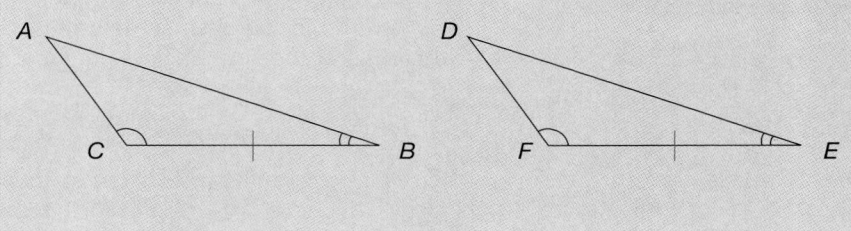

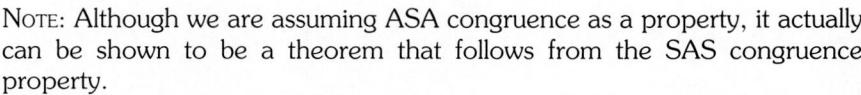

NOTE: Although we are assuming ASA congruence as a property, it actually can be shown to be a theorem that follows from the SAS congruence property.

Example 14.3 illustrates an application of the ASA congruence property.

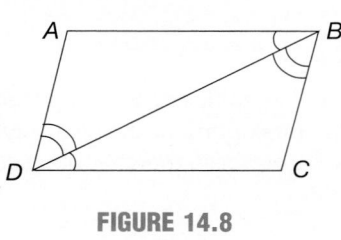

FIGURE 14.8

EXAMPLE 14.3   Show that the diagonal in Figure 14.8 divides a parallelogram into two congruent triangles.

Solution
Line $\overleftrightarrow{DB}$ is a transversal for lines $\overleftrightarrow{AB}$ and $\overleftrightarrow{DC}$. Since $\overleftrightarrow{AB} \parallel \overleftrightarrow{DC}$, we know (i) $\angle ABD \cong \angle CDB$ by the alternate interior angle property. Similarly, $\angle ADB$ and $\angle CBD$ are alternate interior angles formed by the transversal $\overleftrightarrow{BD}$ and parallel lines $\overleftrightarrow{AD}$ and $\overleftrightarrow{BC}$. Hence (ii) $\angle ADB \cong \angle CBD$. Certainly, (iii) $\overline{BD} \cong \overline{DB}$. Thus by (i), (ii), (iii), and the ASA congruence property, we have established that $\triangle ABD \cong \triangle CDB$. ■

Since $\triangle ABD \cong \triangle CDB$, the six corresponding parts of the two triangles are congruent. Thus the following theorem follows.

Theorem

Opposite Sides and Angles of a Parallelogram

Opposite sides of a parallelogram are congruent.
Opposite angles of a parallelogram are congruent.

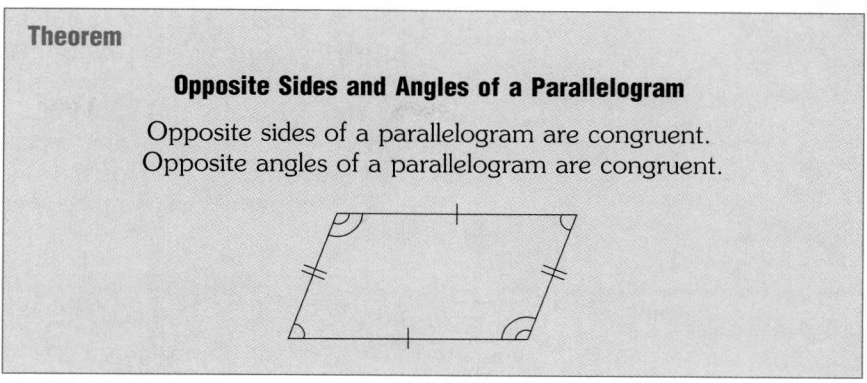

The complete verifications of these results about parallelograms are left for the problem set.

The third, and final congruence property for triangles that we will consider involves just the three sides. Suppose that we have three lengths, x, y, and z units long, where the sum of any two lengths exceeds the third, and we wish to form triangles with these as the lengths of the sides. If we lay out the longest side, we can pivot the shorter sides from the endpoints. Figure 14.9 illustrates this. Notice that in pivoting the shorter sides [Figure 14.9(c)], we are drawing parts of two circles of radii x and y units, respec-

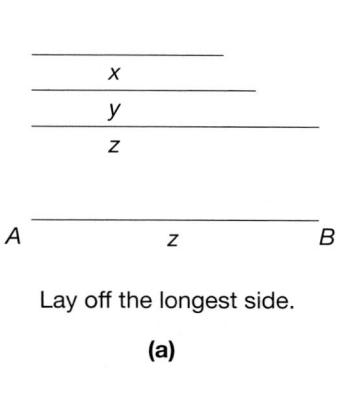

Lay off the longest side.

(a)

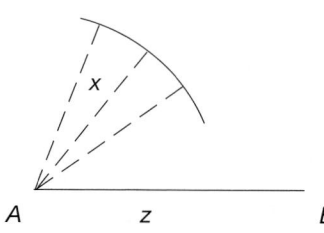

Pivot a shorter side from one endpoint.

(b)

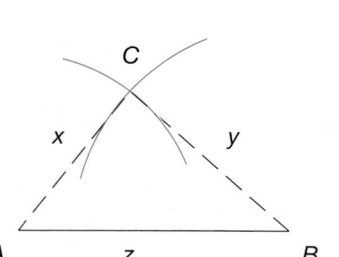

Pivot the third side from the other end.

(c)

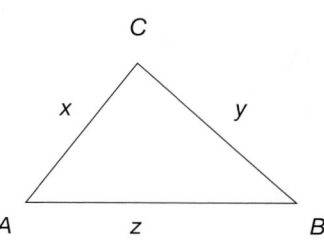

The two shorter sides can meet in only one point, C, above $\overline{AB}$.

(d)

FIGURE 14.9

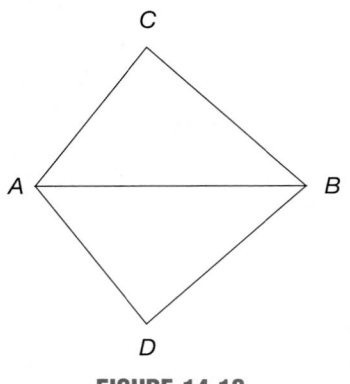

FIGURE 14.10

tively. The two circles intersect at point C above $\overline{AB}$ and form the unique triangle $\triangle ABC$. [NOTE: We could also have extended our circles below $\overline{AB}$ so that they would intersect in another point, say D (Figure 14.10).] Once points A and B have been located and the position of point C has been found (above $\overline{AB}$ here) *only one* such triangle, $\triangle ABC$, can be formed. This observation is the basis of the side–side–side congruence property. (NOTE: This property can also be proved from the SAS congruence property.)

Side–Side–Side (SSS) Congruence Property

If three sides of a triangle are congruent, respectively, to three sides of another triangle, then the two triangles are congruent. Here, $\triangle ABC \cong \triangle DEF$.

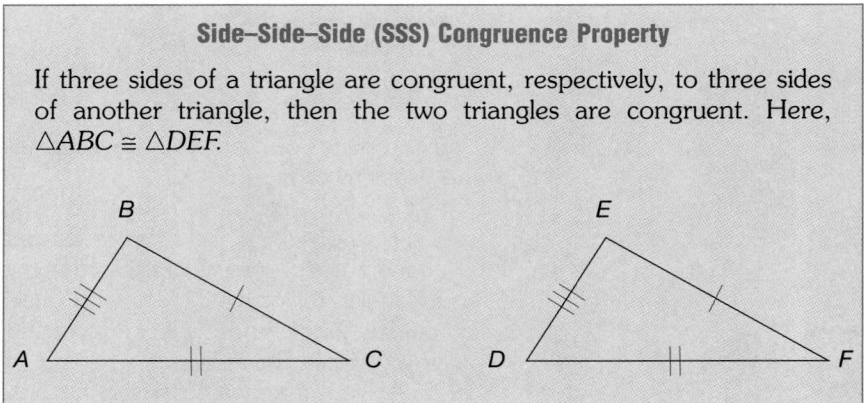

By the SSS congruence property it is sufficient to verify that corresponding sides in two triangles are congruent in order to establish that the triangles are congruent. The next example gives an application of the SSS congruence property.

EXAMPLE 14.4 Suppose that $ABCD$ is a kite with $\overline{AB} \cong \overline{AD}$ and $\overline{BC} \cong \overline{DC}$. Show that the diagonal $\overline{AC}$ divides the kite into two congruent triangles (Figure 14.11).

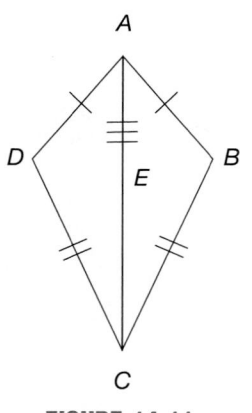

FIGURE 14.11

Solution
We know (i) $\overline{AB} \cong \overline{AD}$ and (ii) $\overline{BC} \cong \overline{DC}$. Also, (iii) $\overline{AC} \cong \overline{AC}$. Using the correspondence $A \leftrightarrow A$, $B \leftrightarrow D$, and $C \leftrightarrow C$, we have that all three pairs of corresponding sides of $\triangle ABC$ and $\triangle ADC$ are congruent. Thus $\triangle ABC \cong \triangle ADC$ by (i), (ii), (iii), and the SSS congruence property. ■

From the result of Example 14.4 we can make several observations about kites. In particular, $\angle BAC \cong \angle DAC$ since they are corresponding angles in the congruent triangles (Figure 14.11). That is, $\overleftrightarrow{AC}$ divides $\angle DAB$ into two congruent angles, and we say that line $\overleftrightarrow{AC}$ is the **angle bisector** of $\angle DAB$. Notice that $\overleftrightarrow{AC}$ is the angle bisector of $\angle BCD$, as well, since $\angle BCA \cong \angle DCA$. We also observe that $\angle ADC \cong \angle ABC$, since they are corresponding angles in the congruent triangles, namely $\triangle ADC$ and $\triangle ABC$. Thus two of the opposite angles in a kite are congruent.

We might wonder whether there are "angle–angle–angle," "angle–angle–side," or "side–side–angle" congruence properties. In the problem set, we will see that only one of these properties is a congruence property.

MATHEMATICAL MORSEL

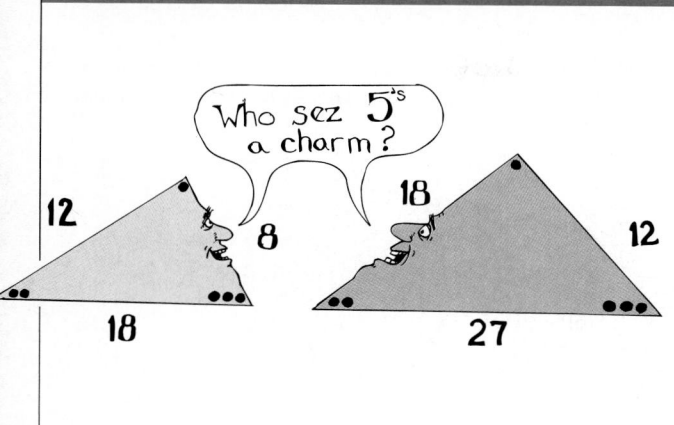

In his *Elements,* Euclid showed that in four cases, SAS, ASA, AAS, and SSS, if three corresponding parts of two triangles are congruent, all six parts are congruent in pairs. Interestingly, it is possible to have *five* (of the six) parts of one triangle congruent to *five* parts of a second triangle *without* the two triangles being congruent (i.e., the sixth parts are not congruent). Although it seems impossible, there are infinitely many such pairs of "5-con" triangles, as they have been named by a mathematics teacher. These 5-con triangles have three angles and two sides congruent. However, the congruent sides are not corresponding sides. Two such triangles are pictured.

EXERCISE/PROBLEM SET 14.1—PART A

Exercises

1. In a statement of congruence, the order in which the points are written indicates the correspondence between points.

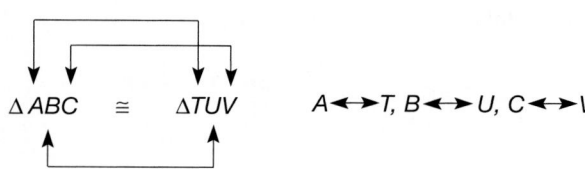

$\triangle ABC \quad \cong \quad \triangle TUV \qquad A \longleftrightarrow T, B \longleftrightarrow U, C \longleftrightarrow V$

In the following congruent triangles, give the correspondence.
 (a) $\triangle TEX \cong \triangle ARE$ **(b)** $\triangle PEN \cong \triangle CIL$
 (c) $\triangle ADE \cong \triangle EDA$

2. Given that $\triangle RST \cong \triangle JLK$, complete the following statements.
 (a) $\triangle TRS \cong \triangle$____   **(b)** $\triangle TSR \cong \triangle$____
 (c) $\triangle SRT \cong \triangle$____   **(d)** $\triangle JKL \cong \triangle$____

3. In the pairs of triangles given, congruent sides and angles are marked. Write an appropriate congruence statement about the triangles:
 (a)

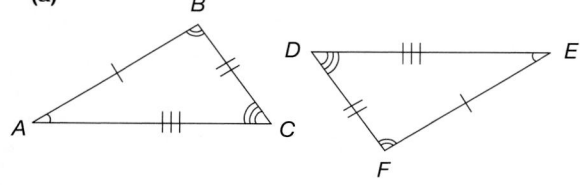

(b)

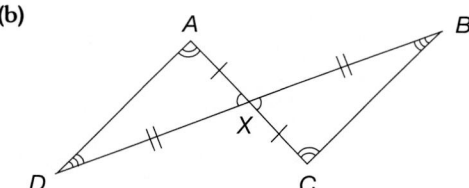

4. Given that $\triangle DEF \cong \triangle GIH$, complete the following statements.
 (a) $\overline{DE} \cong$ ____
 (b) $\overline{FE} \cong$ ____
 (c) $\overline{DF} \cong$ ____
 (d) $\angle D \cong$ ____
 (e) $\angle E \cong$ ____
 (f) $\angle F \cong$ ____

5. Use the definition of congruent triangles to show that the following pairs of triangles are congruent.

 (a)

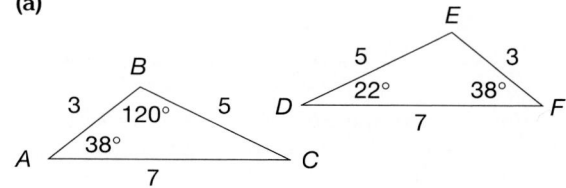

(b)

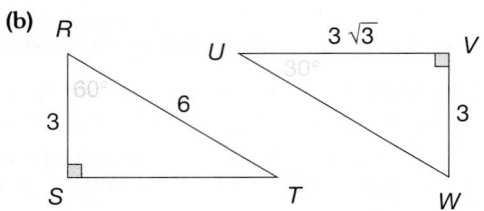

6. Given △MNO, answer the following questions.

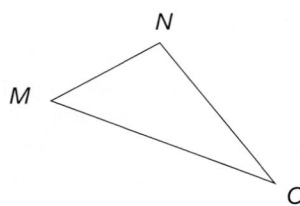

(a) ∠N is included by which sides?
(b) $\overline{MO}$ is the common side of which angles?
(c) What is the common side for ∠N and ∠O?
(d) What is the included angle for $\overline{NO}$ and $\overline{MO}$?

7. Could the SAS congruence property be used to show that the following pairs of triangles are congruent? If not, why not?

(a)

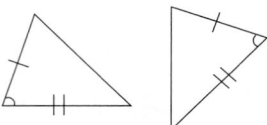

(b)

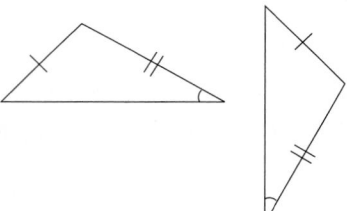

(c)

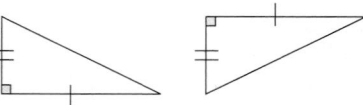

8. △ABC and △WXY are shown.

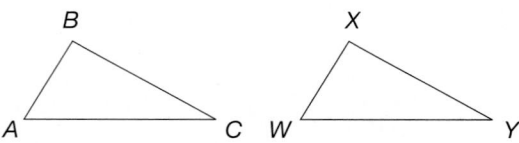

(a) To apply the SAS congruence property to prove △ABC ≅ △WXY, you could show $\overline{AB}$ ≅ ?, ∠B ≅ ?, and $\overline{BC}$ ≅ ?.

(b) Name two other sets of corresponding information that would allow you to apply the SAS congruence property.

9. Could the SSS congruence property be used to prove the following pairs of triangles congruent? Explain.

(a)

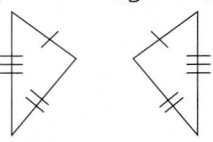

(b)

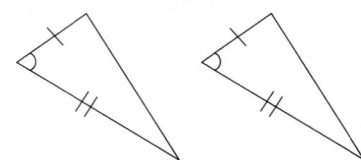

(c)

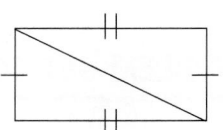

10. Are the following pairs of triangles congruent? Justify your answer.

(a)

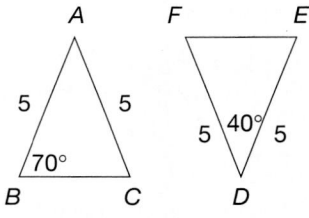

(b)

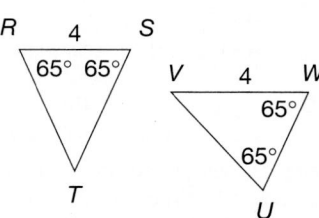

(c)

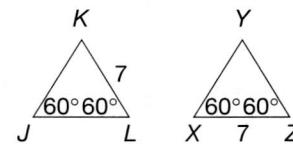

11. Consider △LMN and △RST. In order to use the SSS congruence property to prove that △LMN ≅ △RST, you must show that $\overline{LM}$ ≅ ?, $\overline{MN}$ ≅ ?, and $\overline{NL}$ ≅ ?.

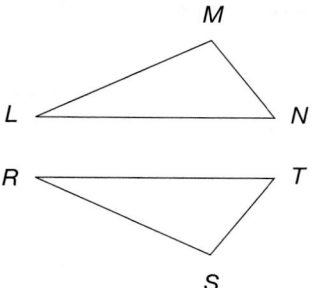

12. Verify that the following pairs of triangles are congruent. Give the justification of your answer.

(a)

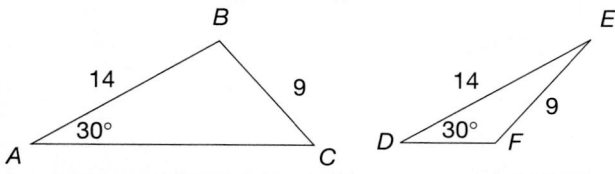

(b)

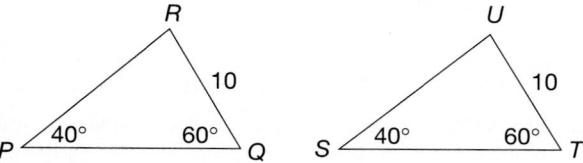

13. (a) Identify the pairs of corresponding parts of △ABC and △DEF that are congruent.

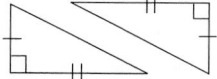

(b) Does △ABC appear to be congruent to △DEF?
(c) Do you think triangles can be shown congruent by an SSA property? Explain your answer.

14. (a) Identify the pairs of corresponding parts of △PQR and △STU that are congruent.

(b) Does △PQR appear to be congruent to △STU?
(c) Show that the triangles are congruent by ASA.

15. The parts of a *right* triangle are given special names, as indicated. Given below are pairs of congruent triangles and the corresponding congruent parts. Identify which congruence property of general triangles applies.

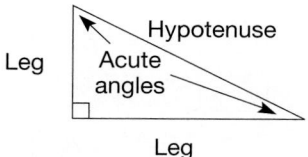

(a) Leg–leg

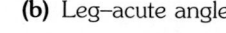

(b) Leg–acute angle

(c) Hypotenuse–acute angle

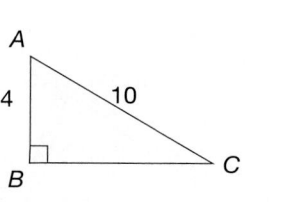

16. Shown are two right triangles.

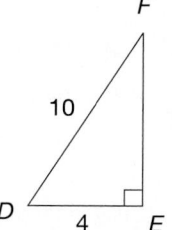

(a) Identify the pairs of corresponding congruent parts.
(b) Is there an SSA congruence property for general triangles that shows △ABC ≅ △DEF?
(c) By applying the Pythagorean theorem, what other pair of corresponding parts are congruent?
(d) Can we say that △ABC ≅ △DEF? Why? [NOTE: This demonstrates the hypotenuse–leg (HL) congruence property for right triangles.]

Problems

17. Two hikers, Ken and Betty, are standing on the edge of a river at point *A*, directly across from tree *T*. They mark off a certain distance to point *B*, where Betty remains. Ken travels that same distance to point *C*. Then he turns and walks directly away from the river to point *D*, where he can see Betty lined up with the tree.

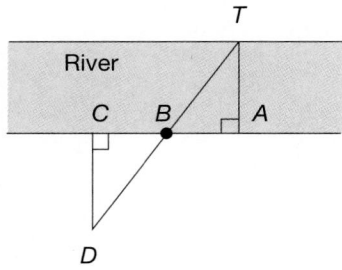

(a) Identify the corresponding pairs of sides and angles that are congruent.
(b) Is △*ABT* ≅ △*CBD*? Why or why not?
(c) How can they use the information they have to find the width of the river?

18. The pictured frameworks are straws that have been pinned together.

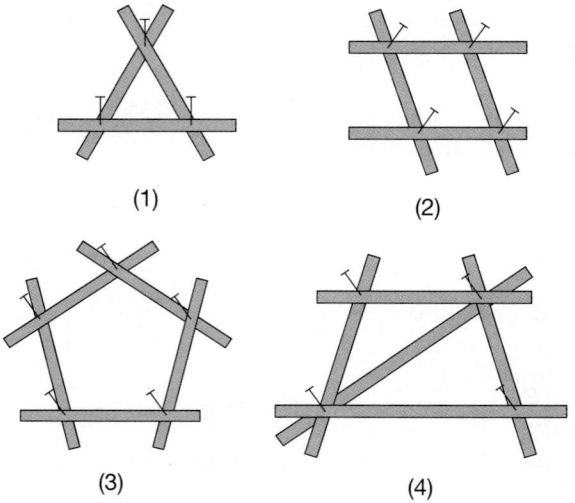

(1)   (2)

(3)   (4)

(a) Which of the frameworks are rigid (i.e., retain their shape when moved or when force is applied)?
(b) How does this explain why bridges and scaffolding are "triangulated"?

19. Are there any rigid quadrilaterals?

20. If possible, draw two noncongruent triangles that satisfy the following conditions. If not possible, explain why not.
(a) Three pairs of corresponding parts are congruent.
(b) Four pairs of corresponding parts are congruent.
(c) Five pairs of corresponding parts are congruent.
(d) Six pairs of corresponding parts are congruent.

21. Given are △*ABC* and △*JKL*. Congruent parts are indicated.

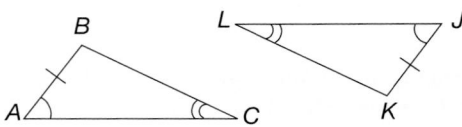

(a) Are ∠*B* and ∠*K* congruent? Justify your answer.
(b) Which congruence property can be used to show that △*ABC* ≅ △*JKL*?
(c) Does this justify another congruence property: angle–angle–side (AAS)?

22. Two quadrilaterals are given in which three sides and the two included angles of one are congruent, respectively, to three sides and the two included angles of the other. A proof that the two quadrilaterals are congruent verifies the SASAS congruence property for quadrilaterals.

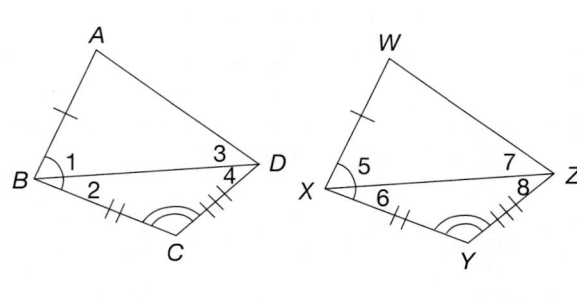

(a) Draw diagonals $\overline{BD}$ and $\overline{XZ}$. Which of the triangles formed are congruent? What is the reason?
(b) Show that ∠1 ≅ ∠5.
(c) Show that △*ABD* ≅ △*WXZ*. What additional corresponding parts of the quadrilateral are therefore congruent?
(d) Show that ∠*ADC* ≅ ∠*WZY*.
(e) Have all the corresponding parts of quadrilaterals *ABCD* and *WXYZ* been shown to be congruent?

23. Justify the following statement: If ∠*D* and ∠*E* are supplementary and congruent, they are right angles.

EXERCISE/PROBLEM SET 14.1—PART B

Exercises

1. The congruence $\triangle ABC \cong \triangle EFG$ can be rewritten as $\triangle ACB \cong \triangle EGF$. Rewrite this congruence in four other ways.

2. Each of the triangles below is congruent to $\triangle ABC$. Identify the correspondence and complete the statement $\triangle ABC \cong \triangle$ ____.

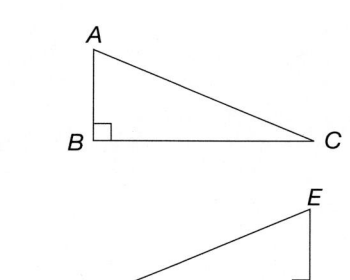

(a)

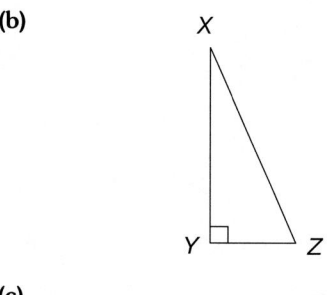

(b)

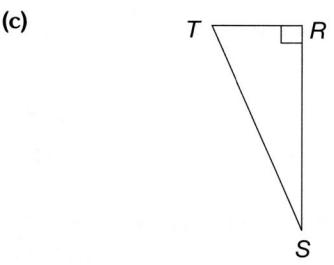

(c)

3. Using the triangles shown, answer the following questions.

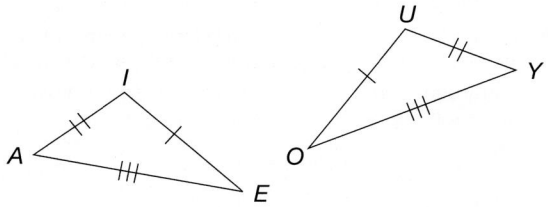

(a) Which side of $\triangle YOU$ corresponds to side $\overline{AE}$?
(b) Which angle of $\triangle AEI$ corresponds to $\angle U$?

(c) Are $\triangle AEI$ and $\triangle YOU$ congruent? Why or why not?
(d) If $m(\angle A)$ is 75°, then what is the measure of $\angle Y$?

4. (a) Write a congruence between the two triangles illustrated.

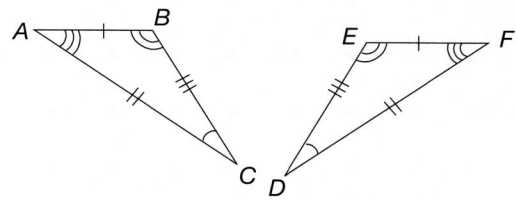

(b) Write six pairs of corresponding congruent parts of these triangles.

5. You are given $\triangle RST$ and $\triangle XYZ$ with $\angle S \cong \angle Y$.
   (a) To show $\triangle RST \cong \triangle XYZ$ by the SAS congruence property, what more would you need to know?
   (b) To show $\angle RST \cong \angle XYZ$ by the ASA congruence property, what more would you need to know? Give two different answers.

6. You are given $\triangle ABC$ and $\triangle GHI$ with $\overline{AB} \cong \overline{GH}$.
   (a) To show $\triangle ABC \cong \triangle GHI$ by the SSS congruence property, what more would you need to know?
   (b) To show $\triangle ABC \cong \triangle GHI$ by the SAS congruence property, what more would you need to know? Give two different answers.
   (c) To show $\triangle ABC \cong \triangle GHI$ by the ASA congruence property, what more would you need to know?

7. Identify the congruence property—SSS, SAS, or ASA—that could be used to show that the following pairs of triangles are congruent.
   (a)

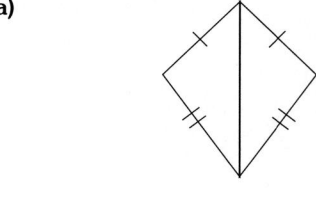

   (b)

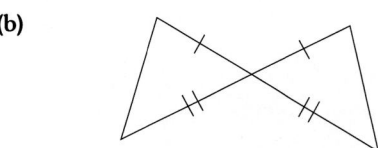

(c)

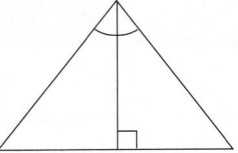

(d)

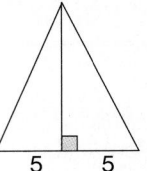

8. Verify that the following triangles are congruent.

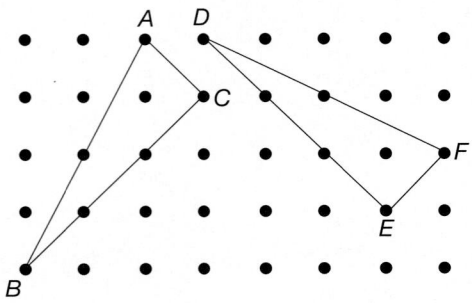

9. Are the following triangles congruent? Justify your answer.

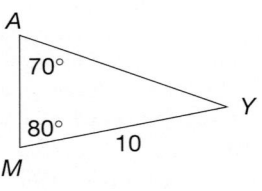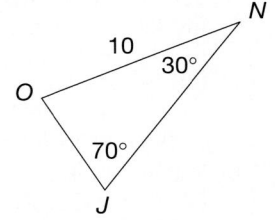

10. For each of the following, determine whether the pair of triangles is necessarily congruent. Justify your answers.

(a)

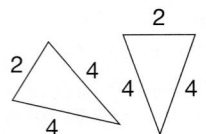

(b)

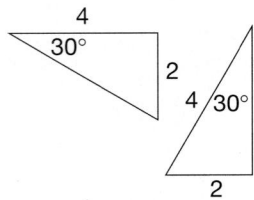

(c)

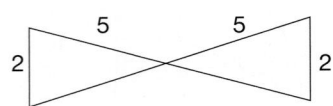

11. Could the ASA congruence property be used to show that the following pairs of triangles are congruent? If not, why not?

(a)

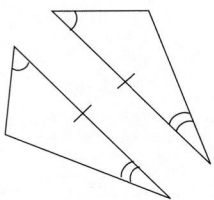

(b)

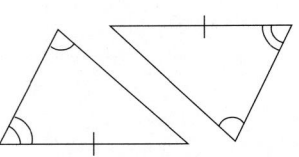

(c)

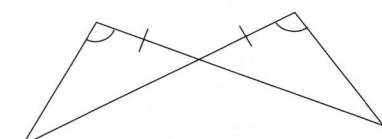

12. $\triangle LMN$ and $\triangle PQR$ are shown.

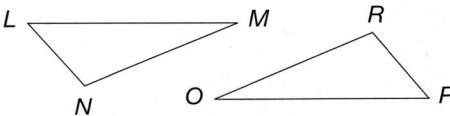

(a) To use the ASA congruence property to prove $\triangle LMN \cong \triangle PQR$, you could show that $\angle L \cong ?$, $\overline{LM} \cong ?$, and $\angle M \cong ?$.

(b) Name two other sets of corresponding information that would allow you to apply the ASA congruence property.

13. In each figure a pair of triangles is congruent. Name the pair of congruent triangles and tell why they are congruent. Be sure not to make any unwarranted assumptions about congruent parts.

(a)

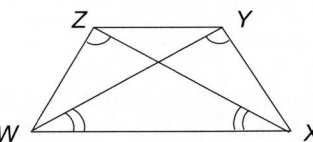

(b)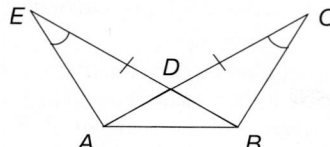

(c)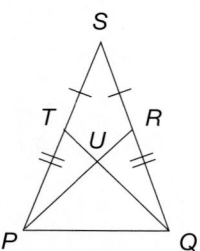

(d)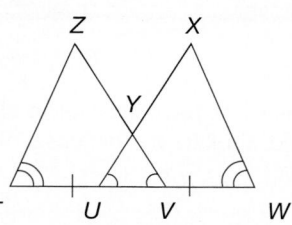

(e)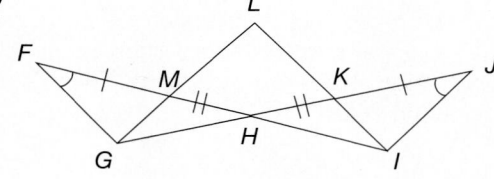

14. Verify that two congruent corresponding parts are not sufficient to guarantee that two triangles are congruent by drawing the following figures.
   (a) Draw $\triangle ABC$ and $\triangle XYZ$ with $AB = 5$ cm, $XY = 5$ cm, $AC = 4$ cm, $XZ = 4$ cm, but $m(\angle A) = 70°$, $m(\angle X) = 40°$. How do sides $\overline{BC}$ and $\overline{YZ}$ compare?
   (b) Draw $\triangle ABC$ and $\triangle XYZ$ with $AB = 8$ cm, $XY = 8$ cm, $AC = 6$ cm, $XZ = 6$ cm, but $BC = 10$ cm and $YZ = 8$ cm. How do $\angle A$ and $\angle X$ compare?

15. **(a)** Identify the pairs of corresponding parts of $\triangle ABC$ and $\triangle XYZ$ that are congruent.
   (b) Does $\triangle ABC$ appear to be congruent to $\triangle XYZ$?
   (c) Do you think triangles can be shown congruent by an AAA property? Explain your answer.

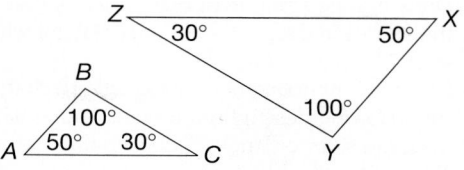

Problems

16. A saw blade is made by cutting six right triangles out of a regular hexagon as shown. If $\overline{XY}$ is cut the same at each tooth, why are the sharp points of the blade all congruent angles?

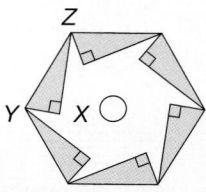

17. Given: $\overline{DC} \perp$ plane $\mathscr{P}$ at C
   $\overline{CA}$ and $\overline{CB}$ are in plane $\mathscr{P}$
   $\overline{AD} \cong \overline{BD}$

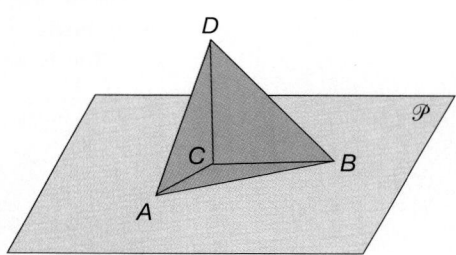

Prove the following statements.
   (a) $\angle DAB \cong \angle DBA$
   (b) $\triangle DCA \cong \triangle DCB$
   (c) $\angle CAB \cong \angle CBA$

18. Draw two noncongruent triangles that satisfy the following conditions.
   (a) Three pairs of parts are congruent.
   (b) Four pairs of parts are congruent.
   (c) Five pairs of parts are congruent.

19. Two quadrilaterals are congruent if any three angles and the included sides of one are congruent, respectively, to three angles and the included sides of the other (ASASA for congruent quadrilaterals). Use the picture shown to prove this statement.

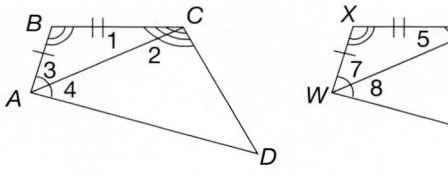

20. (a) Draw two noncongruent quadrilaterals that satisfy the following description: a quadrilateral with four sides of length 5 units.

(b) Draw two noncongruent quadrilaterals that satisfy the following description: a quadrilateral with two opposite sides of length 4 units and the other two sides of length 3 units.

(c) The SSS congruence property was sufficient to show that two triangles were congruent. Is a similar pattern (SSSS) sufficient to show that two quadrilaterals are congruent? Justify your answer.

21. Given parallelogram $ABCD$, prove the following properties using congruent triangles.

(a) $\overline{AB} \cong \overline{CD}$, $\overline{BC} \cong \overline{DA}$ (opposite sides are congruent).

(b) $\angle A \cong \angle C$, $\angle B \cong \angle D$ (opposite angles are congruent).

22. Justify the hypotenuse–leg congruence property for right triangles. In particular, right triangles $\triangle ABC$ and $\triangle XYZ$ are given with right angles at B and Y. Legs $\overline{AB}$ and $\overline{XY}$ are congruent and have length a. Hypotenuses $\overline{AC}$ and $\overline{XZ}$ are congruent with length c. Verify that $\triangle ABC \cong \triangle XYZ$.

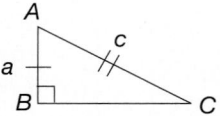 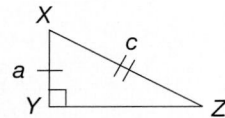

14.2

SIMILARITY OF TRIANGLES

Triangle Similarity

Informally, two geometric figures that have the same shape, but not *necessarily* the same size, are called similar. In the case of triangles we have the following definition.

Definition

Similar Triangles

Suppose that $\triangle ABC$ and $\triangle DEF$ are such that under the correspondence $A \leftrightarrow D$, $B \leftrightarrow E$, $C \leftrightarrow F$, all corresponding sides are proportional and all corresponding vertex angles are congruent. Then $\triangle ABC$ is **similar** to $\triangle DEF$ and we write $\triangle ABC \sim \triangle DEF$.

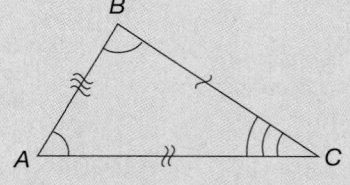 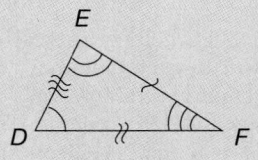

Saying that corresponding sides in $\triangle ABC$ and $\triangle DEF$ are proportional means that the ratios of corresponding sides are all equal. That is, if $\triangle ABC \sim \triangle DEF$, then $\dfrac{AB}{DE} = \dfrac{BC}{EF} = \dfrac{AC}{DF}$.

STUDENT PAGE SNAPSHOT

ACTIVITY
Congruence and Similarity

A. The drawing is by the artist M. C. Escher. Notice that if you cut out two salamanders and place one on top of the other, one would fit over the other exactly. The salamanders are congruent. **Congruent figures** have the same size and shape.

In the figures below, triangle ABC is congruent to triangle DEF.

Write: $\triangle ABC \cong \triangle DEF$.

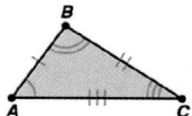 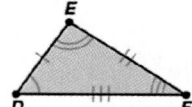

1. Trace $\triangle ABC$ and $\triangle DEF$. Use a ruler and a protractor to complete the following.
   a. $\overline{AB} = \blacksquare$ cm $\overline{DE} = \blacksquare$ cm
   b. $\overline{BC} = \blacksquare$ cm $\overline{EF} = \blacksquare$ cm
   c. $\overline{AC} = \blacksquare$ cm $\overline{DF} = \blacksquare$ cm
   d. $m\angle A = \blacksquare$ $m\angle D = \blacksquare$
   e. $m\angle B = \blacksquare$ $m\angle E = \blacksquare$
   f. $m\angle C = \blacksquare$ $m\angle F = \blacksquare$

In congruent figures the corresponding sides are congruent and the corresponding angles are congruent. In $\triangle ABC$ and $\triangle DEF$, $\overline{AB}$ corresponds to $\overline{DE}$. Write: $\overline{AB} \longleftrightarrow \overline{DE}$.

2. What are the other pairs of corresponding sides? of corresponding angles?

B. Look at the Escher drawing. Notice that the figures are the same shape but not necessarily the same size. **Similar figures** have the same shape but not necessarily the same size.

Triangle GHI is similar to triangle JKL.

Write: $\triangle GHI \sim \triangle JKL$.

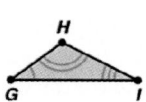 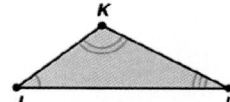

EXAMPLE 14.5 Suppose that $\triangle ABC \sim \triangle DEF$ with $AB = 5$, $BC = 8$, $AC = 11$, and $DF = 3$ (Figure 14.12). Find DE and EF.

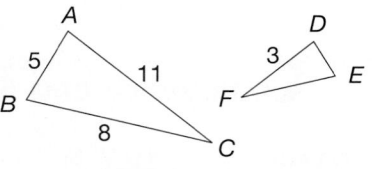

FIGURE 14.12

Solution

Since the triangles are similar under the correspondence $A \leftrightarrow D$, $B \leftrightarrow E$, $C \leftrightarrow F$, we know that $\dfrac{AB}{DE} = \dfrac{AC}{DF}$. Hence

$$\frac{5}{DE} = \frac{11}{3},$$

so that

$$DE = \frac{15}{11} = 1\frac{4}{11}.$$

Similarly, $\dfrac{BC}{EF} = \dfrac{AC}{DF}$, so that

$$\frac{8}{EF} = \frac{11}{3}.$$

Therefore,

$$EF = \frac{24}{11} = 2\frac{2}{11}. \qquad\blacksquare$$

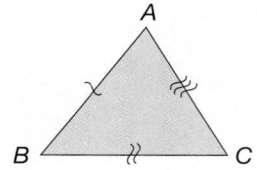

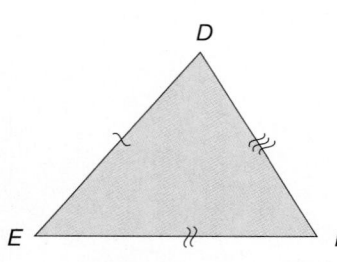

FIGURE 14.13

Suppose that $\triangle ABC \sim \triangle DEF$ (Figure 14.13). From the proportions, $\dfrac{AB}{DE} = \dfrac{BC}{EF} = \dfrac{AC}{DF}$, we see that there are several other proportions that we can form. For example, the proportion $\dfrac{AB}{BC} = \dfrac{DE}{EF}$ tells us that the ratio of the lengths of two sides of $\triangle ABC$, say $\dfrac{AB}{BC}$, is equal to the corresponding ratio from $\triangle DEF$, namely $\dfrac{DE}{EF}$.

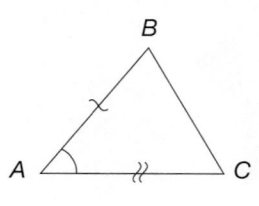

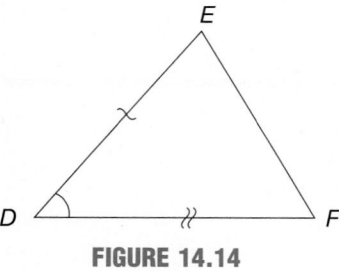

FIGURE 14.14

There are similarity properties for triangles analogous to the SAS, ASA, and SSS congruence properties for triangles. For example, suppose that $\triangle ABC$ and $\triangle DEF$ correspond so that $\dfrac{AB}{DE} = \dfrac{AC}{DF}$ and $\angle BAC \cong \angle EDF$; that is, two pairs of corresponding sides are proportional, and their included angles are congruent (Figure 14.14). Then $\triangle ABC \sim \triangle DEF$. Thus, we have an SAS similarity property for triangles, just as we have an SAS congruence property. We summarize the triangle similarity properties as follows.

Similarity Properties of Triangles

Two triangles, $\triangle ABC$ and $\triangle DEF$, are similar if and only if at least one of the following three statements is true.

1. Two pairs of corresponding sides are proportional and their included angles are congruent. (SAS similarity)

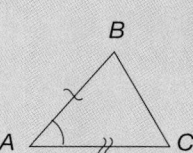 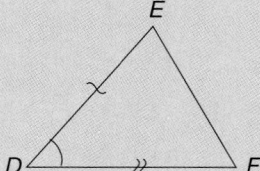

2. Two pairs of corresponding angles are congruent. (AA similarity)

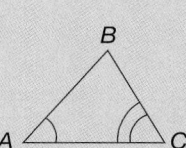 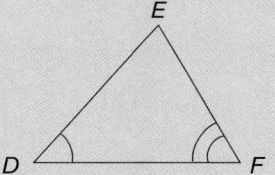

3. All three pairs of corresponding sides are proportional. (SSS similarity)

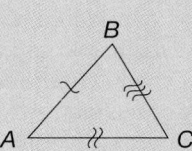 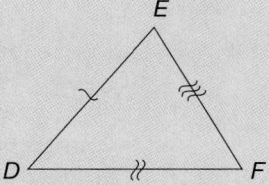

Notice that AA similarity is equivalent to AAA similarity since the measure of the third angle is known once the measures of two angles are known.

Indirect Measurement

Example 14.6 illustrates an application of the AA similarity property in **indirect measurement** [as opposed to direct measurement where a ruler (protractor) is placed on the segment (angle) to be measured].

EXAMPLE 14.6   A student who is 1.5 meters tall wishes to determine the height of a tree on the school grounds. The tree casts a shadow 37.5 m long at the same time that the student casts a shadow that is 2.5 m long (Figure 14.15). Assume that the tree and student are on level ground. How tall is the tree?

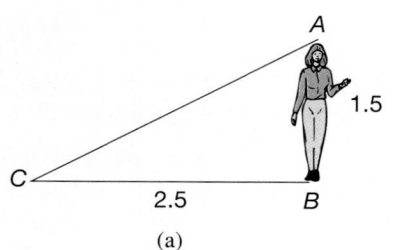

(a)

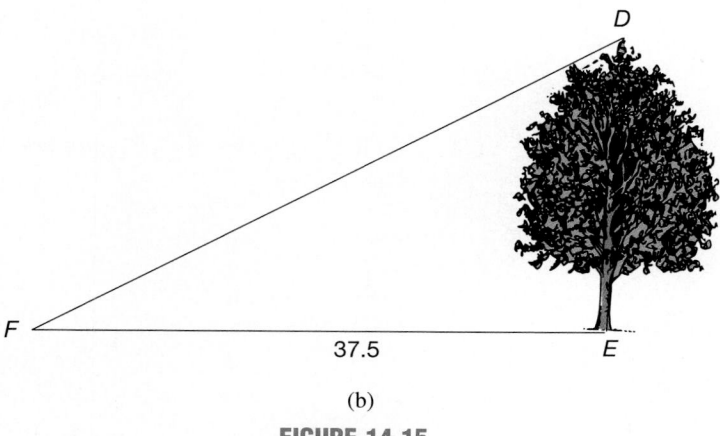

(b)

FIGURE 14.15

Solution

Let $\triangle ABC$ be a triangle formed by the line segment joining the top of the student's head and the ground, $\overline{AB}$, and the student's shadow, $\overline{BC}$. Notice that $\overline{AC}$ can be considered part of a light ray from the sun. Similarly, $\triangle DEF$ is formed by $\overline{DE}$, a line segment from the top of the tree to the ground, and the tree's shadow, $\overline{DF}$. Assume that the light ray containing $\overline{DF}$ is parallel to the ray containing $\overline{AC}$, so that $\angle ACB \cong \angle DFE$. (Use the corresponding angles property to verify this.) Then we have the pair of right triangles, $\triangle ABC$ and $\triangle DEF$.

We wish to find the distance DE. Using the AA similarity property, $\triangle ABC \sim \triangle DEF$. Hence $\dfrac{DE}{AB} = \dfrac{EF}{BC}$, so that $\dfrac{DE}{1.5} = \dfrac{37.5}{2.5}$, and

$$DE = \frac{1.5 \times 37.5}{2.5} = 22.5.$$

Thus the tree is 22.5 meters tall. ■

Fractals and Self-Similarity

In Section 9.3 we studied various types of functions and their graphs. These functions and others are used to model physical phenomena to solve problems. However, there are many instances, such as the shapes of waves and prices in the stock market, where behavior does not conform to "nice" functions. In 1982, Benoit Mandelbrot wrote the book *The Fractal Geometry of Nature* that popularized a form of geometry which attempts to study

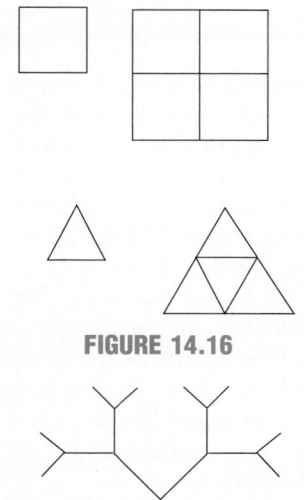

FIGURE 14.16

FIGURE 14.17

chaotic behaviors. The following discussion provides an introduction to the notion of self-similarity, which is part of this modern field of study.

The problem set in Chapter 1 contained several examples of reptiles, namely tiles that when arranged in the proper way produced new tiles of the same shape. Squares and equilateral triangles are simple examples of reptiles (Figure 14.16). Observe that as new shapes are constructed, they are similar to each of the previous shapes. Some trees also exhibit this idea. Figure 14.17 displays a part of a tree that begins with two branches and then grows two similar ones at the end of each new branch.

A more intricate pattern is shown in Figure 14.18. This construction begins with an equilateral triangle. Next, equilateral triangles are constructed on the middle thirds of the original triangle. The curve formed by repeating this process *indefinitely* is known as the **Koch curve**. Notice how each small triangle formed is similar to the preceding triangle. The Koch curve is said to be **self-similar** since the curve looks the same when magnified. In addition to being self-similar, the Koch curve has a finite area but an *infinite* perimeter!

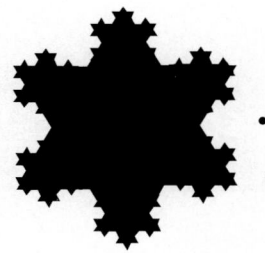

FIGURE 14.18

Another well-known shape that is self-similar is called the **Sierpinski triangle** or **Sierpinski gasket**. It is the shape that results from starting with an equilateral triangle and removing successively smaller ones from the centers of the newly formed triangles (Figure 14.19).

FIGURE 14.19

Shapes that occur in nature that exhibit self-similarity somewhat are broccoli, acorn and oak trees, and the shape of breaking waves. The study of fractal geometry and chaos theory are examples of two of the new fields of mathematics that have been popularized in the past 25 years, in large part due to the availability of high-speed computers.

MATHEMATICAL MORSEL

The Pythagorean theorem can be stated in words as follows: In a right triangle, the area of the square on the hypotenuse is equal to the sum of the areas of the squares on the two sides. Interestingly, this theorem also holds for shapes other than squares. For example, the area of the semicircle on the hypotenuse is equal to the sum of the areas of the semicircles on the two sides. The semicircles can be replaced by any regular polygons and the same relationship still holds. Even more surprising, this "Pythagorean" relationship holds for the areas of any three shapes constructed on the three sides of a right triangle, as long as the figures are similar.

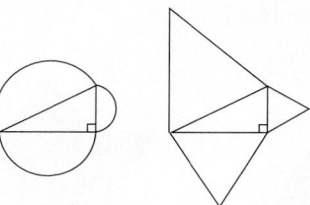

EXERCISE/PROBLEM SET 14.2—PART A

Exercises

1. Which of the following pairs of triangles are similar? If they are similar, explain why.

(a)

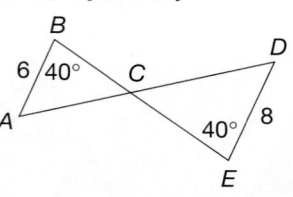

(b)

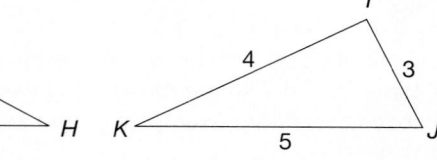

(c)

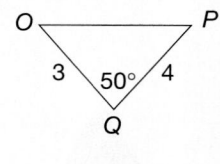

(d)

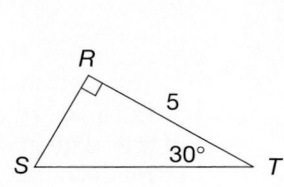
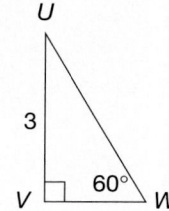

2. Given are pairs of similar triangles with some dimensions specified. Find the measures of the other sides.

(a)

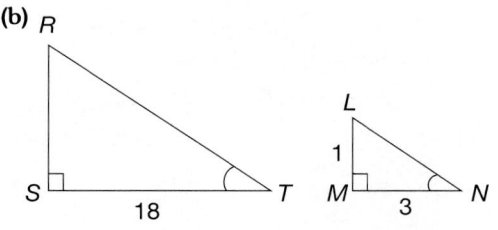

(b)

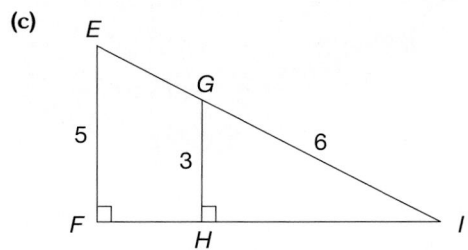

(c)

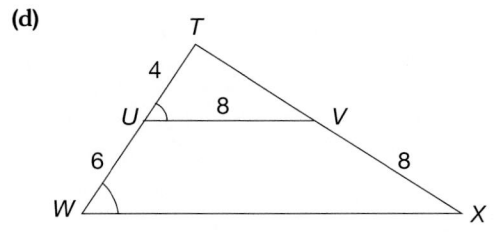

(d)

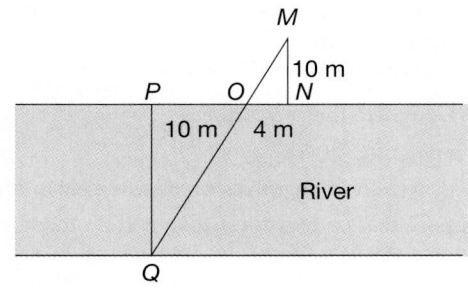

3. Using the measurements given, find the distance *PQ* across the river.

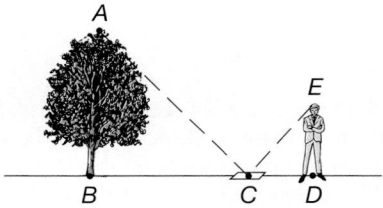

4. At a particular time, a tree casts a shadow 29 m long on horizontal ground. At the same time, a vertical pole 3 m high casts a shadow 4 m long. Calculate the height of the tree to the nearest meter.

5. True or false? Justify your reasoning.
  (a) If two triangles are similar, they are congruent.
  (b) If two triangles are congruent, they are similar.
  (c) All equilateral triangles are congruent.
  (d) All equilateral triangles are similar.

6. Another method of determining the height of an object uses a mirror placed on level ground. The person stands at an appropriate distance from the mirror so that he or she sees the top of the object when looking in the mirror.

  (a) Name two similar triangles in the diagram. Why are they similar?
  (b) Find the height of the tree if a person 1.5 meters tall sees the top of the tree when the mirror is 18 meters from the base of the tree and the person is standing 1 meter from the mirror.

Problems

7. A fashion doll popular with young girls for the last few decades is $11\frac{1}{2}$ inches tall and has a waist measurement of about 3 inches. Some concern has been expressed that this doll does not reflect realistic body proportions. Can you explain why? Suppose that a "life-size" model of the same proportions with height 5 ft 6 in. were constructed. What would its waist measurement be (to the nearest inch)?

8. Suppose that a film is being shown in class when a student sitting 5 feet in front of the projector puts his hand between the projector and the screen as shown.

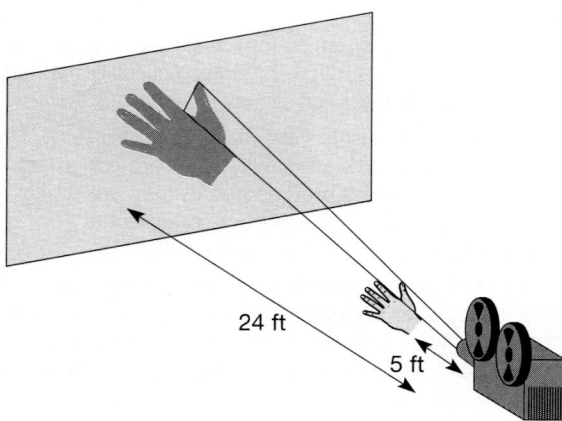

24 ft

5 ft

(a) If the projector is 24 feet from the screen and the student's thumb is 2 inches long, how long does his thumb appear to be on the screen?

(b) If the student were 10 feet in front of the projector, how would that change the image of the thumb on the screen?

9. Suppose that a tree growing on level ground must be cut down so that the approximate height of the tree needs to be calculated to determine where it should fall. A device that can be used to calculate the height is a right isosceles triangle cut from cardboard or wood. You must sight along the hypotenuse of the right triangle and walk forward or backward as necessary until the top of the tree is exactly in line with the hypotenuse. Also, the bottom side of the triangle must be in a horizontal line with the place where you are going to cut. The point at which you now stand is where the top of the tree will fall. Use similar triangles to explain why this method works.

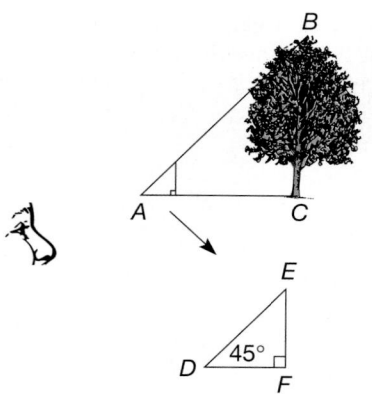

10. A new department store opens on a hot summer day. Kathy's job is to stand outside the main entrance and hand out a special supplement to incoming customers. The building is 30 feet tall and casts a shadow 8 feet wide in front of the store. If Kathy is 5 ft 6 in. tall, how far away from the building can she stand and still be in the shade?

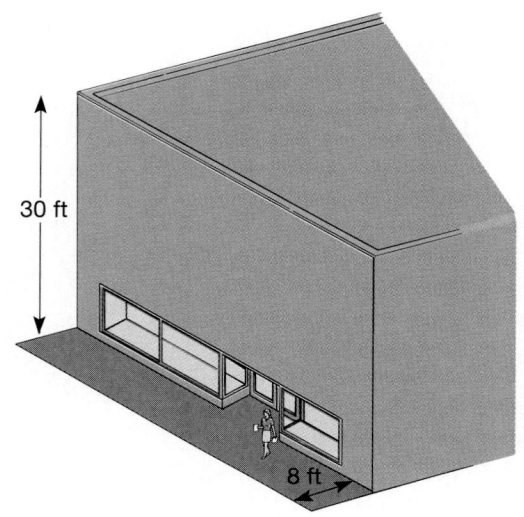

30 ft

8 ft

11. Suppose that parallel lines l_1, l_2, and l_3 are intersected by parallel transversals m and n.

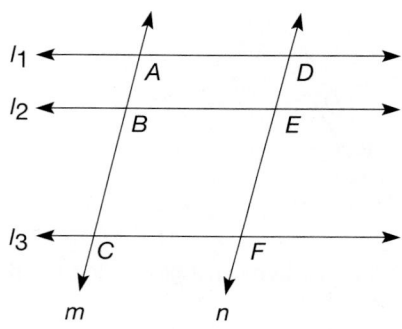

l_1

l_2

l_3

A D

B E

C F

m n

(a) Justify that quadrilaterals *ABED* and *BCFE* are parallelograms.

(b) Justify that $AB = DE$ and $BC = EF$.

(c) Complete the proportion $\dfrac{AB}{BC} = \dfrac{?}{?}$.

(d) Have parallel lines l_1, l_2, and l_3 intercepted proportional segments on transversals m and n?

12. Suppose that parallel lines l_1, l_2, and l_3 are intersected by transversals m and n which intersect at a point P. Let a, b, c, x, y, and z represent the lengths of the segments shown.

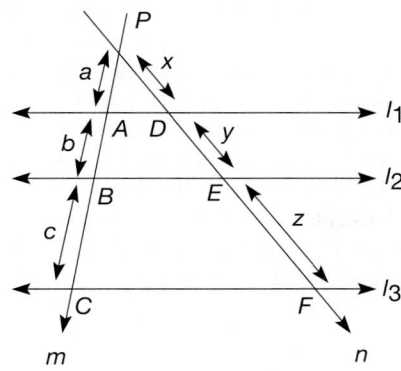

(a) Verify that $\triangle PAD \sim \triangle PBE \sim \triangle PCF$.
(b) Show that $ay = bx$.
(c) Show that $ay + az = bx + cx$.
(d) Show that $az = cx$.

(e) Combine parts (b) and (d) to show that $\dfrac{b}{c} = \dfrac{y}{z}$.

(f) Have parallel lines l_1, l_2, and l_3 intercepted proportional segments on transversals m and n?

13. The conclusions of Problems 11 and 12 can be summarized: Parallel lines intercept proportional segments on all transversals. Apply this result to complete the proportions below, when $l_1 \parallel l_2 \parallel l_3 \parallel l_4$.

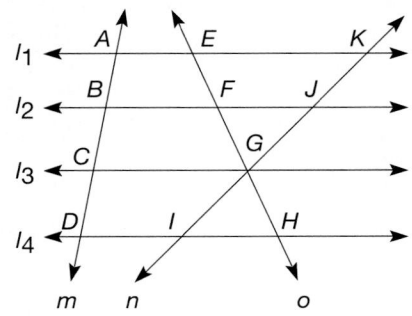

(a) $\dfrac{AB}{BC} = $ _____ $= $ _____

(b) $\dfrac{FG}{GH} = $ _____ $= $ _____

(c) $\dfrac{IJ}{JK} = $ _____ $= $ _____

14. Given $\triangle ABC$, where $\overline{DE} \parallel \overline{AB}$, find AB.

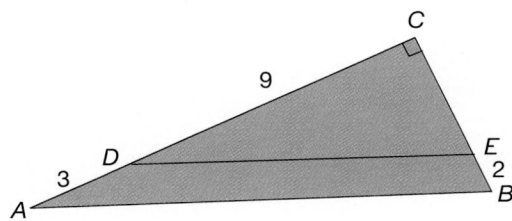

15. Some hikers wanted to measure the distance across a canyon. They sighted two boulders A and B on the opposite side. By measuring between C and D (points across from A and B), they found $AB = 60$ m. Find the distance across the canyon, BD, using the distances in the diagram. Assume that $\overleftrightarrow{AB} \parallel \overleftrightarrow{CD}$.

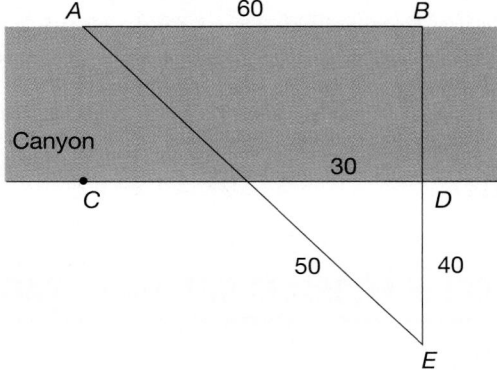

16. A paper cup is in the shape of a right circular cone with a diameter of 8 cm and a height of 12 cm.
(a) Suppose that the cup is filled with water to a depth of 8 cm. Calculate the volume of water in the cup. (HINT: Use similar triangles.) Round your answer to the nearest cubic centimeter.
(b) To what depth must the cup be filled in order to be half full of water? Round your answer to the nearest tenth of a centimeter.

17. Without measuring, find the lengths of segments $\overline{AP}$, $\overline{BP}$, $\overline{CP}$, and $\overline{DP}$ on the square lattice.

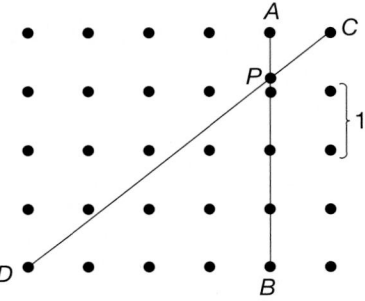

18. Two right triangles are similar, and the lengths of the sides of one triangle are twice the lengths of the corresponding sides of the other. Compare the areas of the triangles.

19. Explain how the figure shown can be used to find $\sqrt{a}$ for any given length a. (HINT: Prove that $x^2 = a$.)

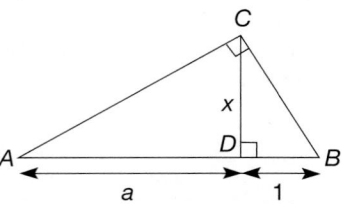

20. Assume that the original triangle in the construction of the Koch curve has sides of length 1.
  (a) What is the perimeter of the initial curve (the triangle)?
  (b) What is the perimeter of the second curve?

(c) What is the perimeter of the third curve?
(d) What is the perimeter of the nth curve?

21. Assume that the original triangle in the construction of the Koch curve has area 9.
  (a) What is the area of the second curve?
  (b) What is the area of the third curve?
  (c) What is the area of the fourth curve?
  (d) What is the area of the nth curve?

22. Prove the Pythagorean theorem using the following diagram and similar triangles.

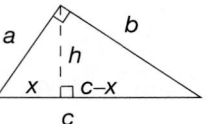

EXERCISE/PROBLEM SET 14.2—PART B

Exercises

1. Which of the following triangles is not similar to the other three triangles?

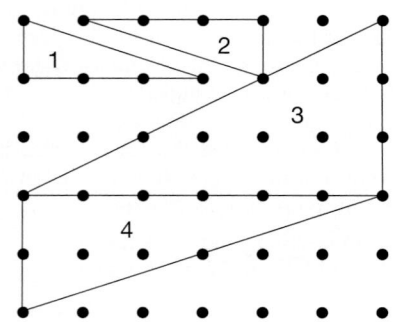

2. Given $\triangle ABC$ as shown, where $\overline{DE} \parallel \overline{AB}$, find AD.

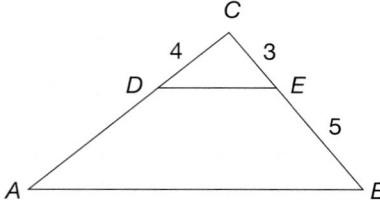

3. Given below are pairs of similar triangles with some dimensions specified. Find the measures of the other sides.

(a)

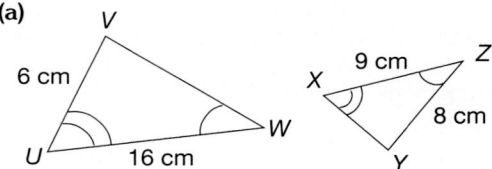

(b)

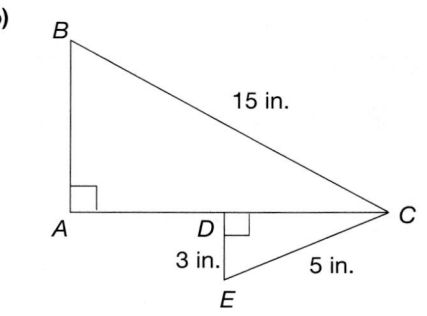

(c)

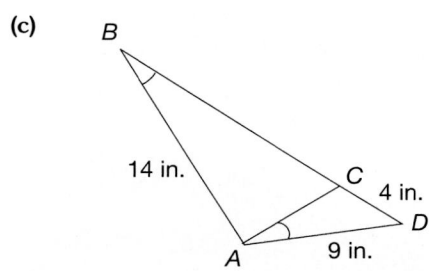

(d)

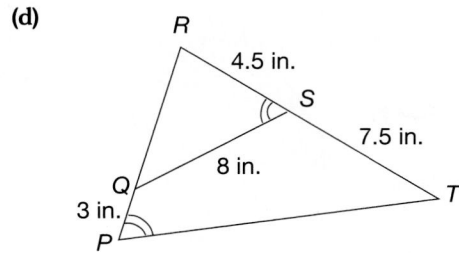

4. Tom and Carol are playing a shadow game. Tom is 6 feet tall and Carol is 5 feet tall. If Carol stands at the "shadow top" of Tom's head, their two combined shadows total 15 feet. How long is each shadow?

Problems

5. True or false? Justify your reasoning.
  (a) All isosceles triangles are congruent.
  (b) All isosceles triangles are similar.
  (c) All isosceles right triangles are congruent.
  (d) All isosceles right triangles are similar.

6. (a) A person 6 feet tall is in search of a tree 100 feet tall. If the person's shadow is 9 feet, what is the length of the shadow of the tree?
  (b) The person in part (a) walks 60 feet from the base of a tree and finds that the shadows of his head and the tree coincide. How tall is the tree?

7. Compute the ratios requested for the following pairs of figures.
  (a) Find the ratios of base:base, height:height, and area:area for this pair of similar triangles.

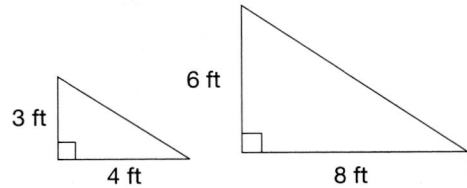

  (b) Find the ratios of base:base, height:height, and area:area for this pair of similar triangles.

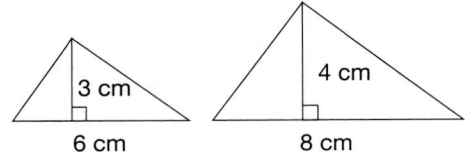

  (c) Find the ratios of length:length, width:width, and area:area for this pair of similar rectangles.

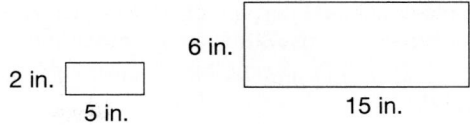

  (d) Do you see a pattern in the relationship between the ratios of the dimensions and the ratios of the areas? Test your conjecture by drawing several other pairs of similar geometric figures.

8. Is $\triangle ADC \sim \triangle CDB$? Explain.

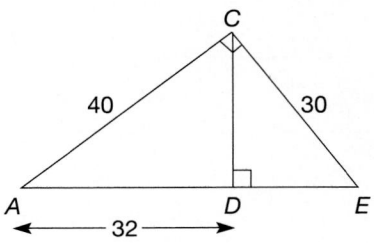

9. PQRS is a trapezoid.
  (a) Why is $\triangle PQT \sim \triangle RTS$?
  (b) Find a and b.

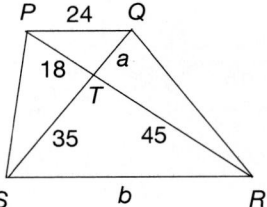

10. A boy and his friend wish to calculate the height of a flagpole. One boy holds a yardstick vertically at a point 40 feet from the base of the flagpole, as shown. The other boy backs away from the pole to a point where he sights the top of the pole over the top of the yardstick. If his position is 1 foot 9 inches from the yardstick and his eye level is 2 feet above the ground, find the height of the flagpole.

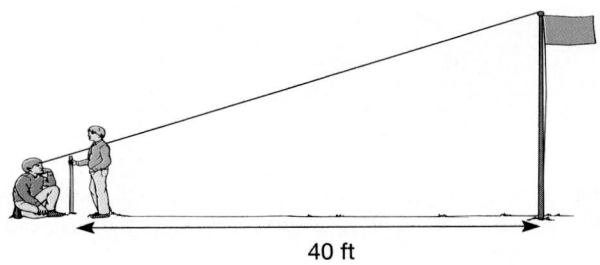

11. If parallel lines intercept congruent segments on a transversal m, what is true on any other transversal n?

12. Lines k, l, m, and n are parallel. Find a, b, c, and d.

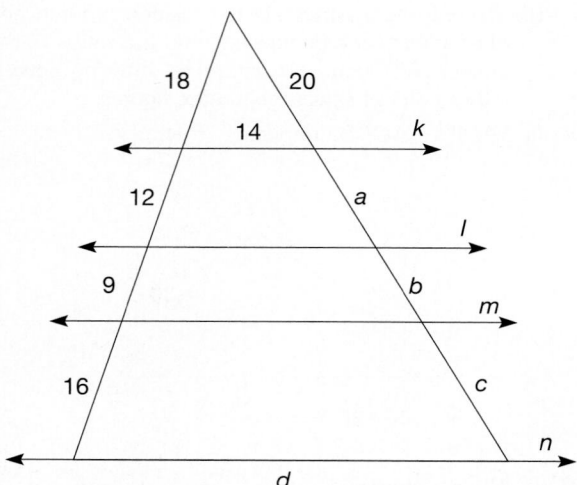

13. (a) Is $n \parallel \overleftrightarrow{AB}$? Explain.

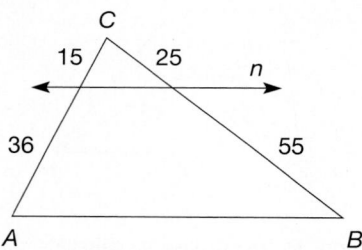

(b) Is $m \parallel \overleftrightarrow{CD}$? Explain.

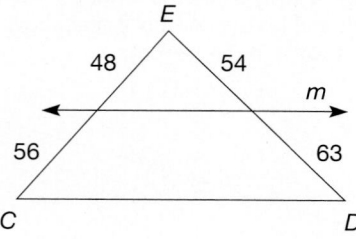

14. The Pythagorean theorem is often interpreted in terms of areas of squares as shown in the following figure.

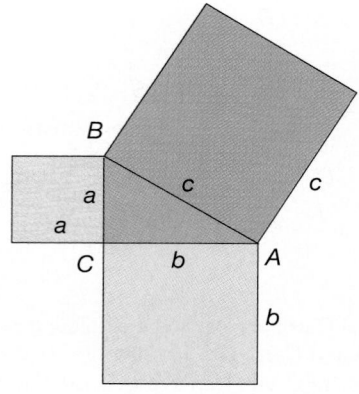

The equation $a^2 + b^2 = c^2$ means that the sum of the areas of the squares drawn on the legs of the right triangle equals the area of the square drawn on the hypotenuse. In fact, the theorem can be generalized to mean that if similar figures are drawn on each side of the right triangle, the sum of the areas of the two smaller figures equals the area of the larger figure. Verify that this is the case for each figure that follows.

(a)

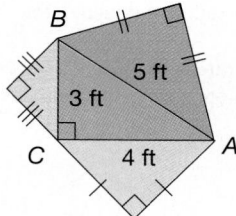

(b)

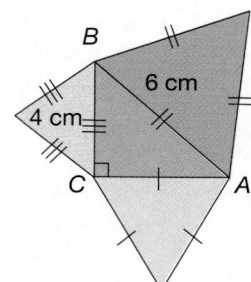

(c)

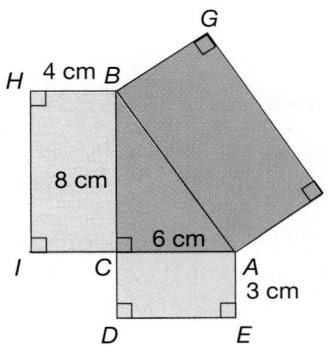

(d) (NOTE: Parallel sides are marked by arrowheads.)

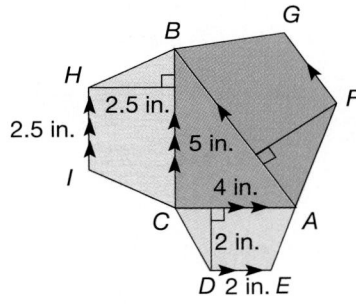

15. Given: $\overline{AB} \parallel \overline{CD}$, $BE = 1$, $CD = 5$, $CE = 3$, and $AD = 7$. Find AB, AE, and DE.

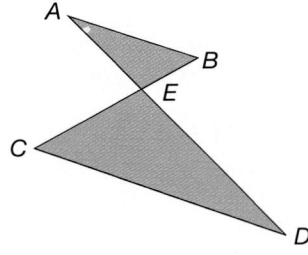

16. Some scouts want to measure the distance AB across a gorge. They estimated the distance AC to be 70 feet and AD to be 50 feet. how could they find the distance AB? Assume that C, B, and E are collinear, as are D, B, and F.

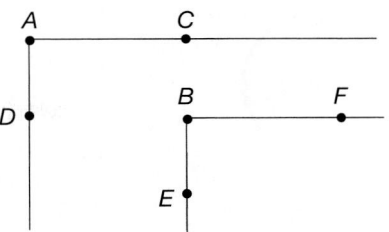

17. Prove: Two isosceles triangles, $\triangle ABC$ and $\triangle XYZ$, are similar if their nonbase angles, $\angle B$ and $\angle Y$, are congruent.

18. Prove that triangles are similar if their sides are respectively parallel to each other.

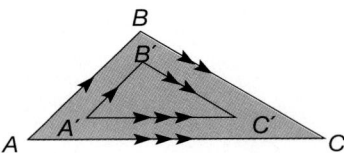

19. Assume that the original Sierpinski triangle has perimeter 3.
(a) What is the perimeter of the black portion of the second curve?
(b) What is the perimeter of the black portion of the third curve?
(c) What is the perimeter of the black portion of the fourth curve?
(d) What is the perimeter of the black portion of the nth curve?

20. Assume that the original Sierpinski triangle has area 1.
(a) What is the area of the black portion of the second curve?
(b) What is the area of the black portion of the third curve?
(c) What is the area of the black portion of the fourth curve?
(d) What is the area of the black portion of the nth curve?

14.3

BASIC EUCLIDEAN CONSTRUCTIONS

Geometric Constructions

In this section we study many of the classical compass and straightedge constructions. The following properties will be applied to constructions with a compass and straightedge.

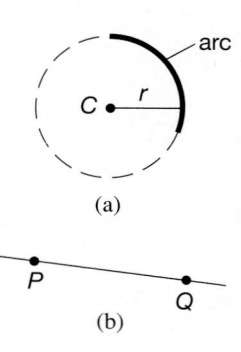

(a)

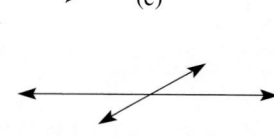

(b)

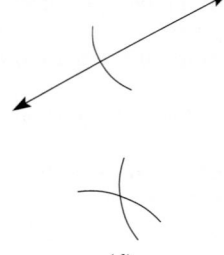

(c)

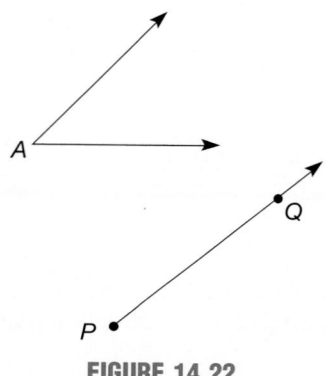

(d)

FIGURE 14.20

Compass and Straightedge Properties

1. For every positive number r and for every point C, we can construct a circle of radius r and center C. A connected portion of a circle is called an **arc** [Figure 14.20(a)].

2. Every pair of points P and Q can be connected by our straightedge to construct the line $\overleftrightarrow{PQ}$, the ray $\overrightarrow{PQ}$, and the segment $\overline{PQ}$ [Figure 14.20(b)].

3. A line l can be constructed if and only if we have located two points that are on l [Figure 14.20(c)]. Points are located only by the intersection of lines, rays, segments, or arcs [Figure 14.20(d)].

Construction 1.   Copy a line segment.

Given line segment $\overline{AB}$ [Figure 14.21(a)], line l, and point P [Figure 14.21(b)], locate point Q on l so that $\overline{PQ} \cong \overline{AB}$ [Figure 14.21(d)].

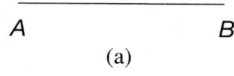

A B

(a)

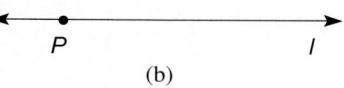

P l

(b)

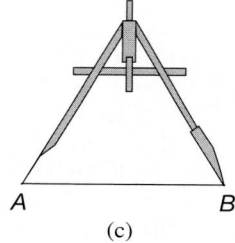

A B

(c)

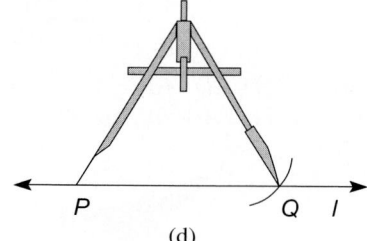

P Q l

(d)

FIGURE 14.21

Procedure (Figure 14.21)

1. Open the compass to length AB [Figure 14.21(c)].

2. With the point of the compass at P, mark off an arc of radius AB that intersects line l. Let Q be the point of intersection of the arc and line l [Figure 14.21(d)]. Then $\overline{PQ} \cong \overline{AB}$.

Justification (Figure 14.21)

On line $\overleftrightarrow{AB}$, the distance AB is a positive real number, say r. By the compass and straightedge property 1, we can construct an arc of a circle of radius r with center at P. The intersection of the arc of the circle and line l is the desired point Q.   ■

Construction 2.   Copy an angle.

Given an angle $\angle A$ and a ray $\overrightarrow{PQ}$, locate point S so that $\angle SPQ \cong \angle A$ (Figure 14.22).

FIGURE 14.22

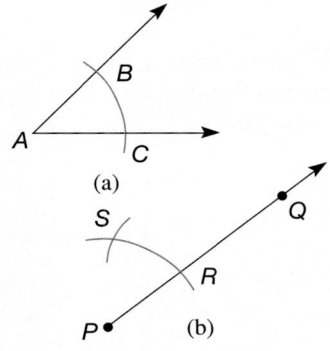

FIGURE 14.23

Procedure (Figure 14.23)

1. With the point of the compass at A, construct an arc that intersects each side of $\angle A$. Call the intersection points B and C [Figure 14.23(a)].
2. With the compass open to the radius AB, place the point at P and construct an arc of radius AB that intersects ray $\overrightarrow{PQ}$. Call the point of intersection point R [Figure 14.23(b)].
3. Place the point of the compass at C and open the compass to radius CB. Then, with the *same* compass opening, put the point of the compass at R and construct an arc of radius CB intersecting the first arc. Call the point of intersection of the two arcs point S [Figure 14.23(b)].
4. Construct ray $\overrightarrow{PS}$. Then $\angle BAC \cong \angle SPR$ (Figure 14.24).

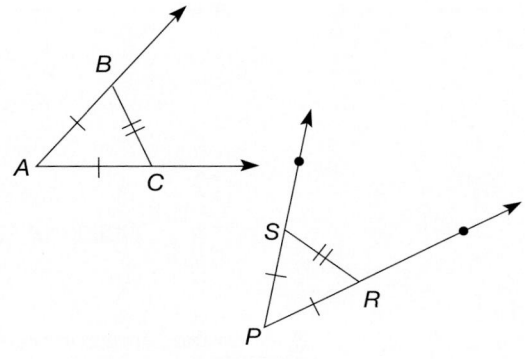

FIGURE 14.24

Justification (Figure 14.24)

Construct the line segments $\overline{BC}$ and $\overline{SR}$, and consider $\triangle BAC$ and $\triangle SPR$. From the construction procedure, we know that $\overline{AB} \cong \overline{AC} \cong \overline{PS} \cong \overline{PR}$ and that $\overline{BC} \cong \overline{SR}$. Consider the correspondence $A \leftrightarrow P$, $B \leftrightarrow S$, $C \leftrightarrow R$. Then $\triangle BAC \cong \triangle SPR$ by the SSS congruence property. Consequently, $\angle BAC \cong \angle SPR$, as desired. ■

Construction 3. Construct the perpendicular bisector of a line segment.

Given a line segment $\overline{AB}$, construct line l so that $l \perp \overline{AB}$ and l intersects $\overline{AB}$ at the midpoint of $\overline{AB}$ (Figure 14.25).

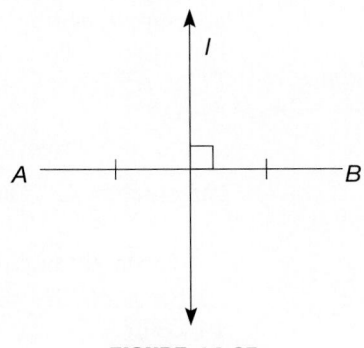

FIGURE 14.25

Procedure (Figure 14.26)

1. Place the compass point at A and open the compass to a radius r such that $r > \frac{1}{2}AB$; that is, r is more than one-half the distance AB. Construct arcs of radius r on each side of $\overline{AB}$ [Figure 14.26(a)].

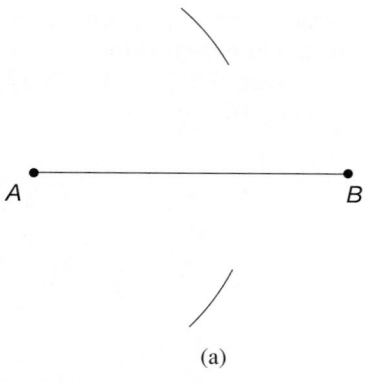

(a)

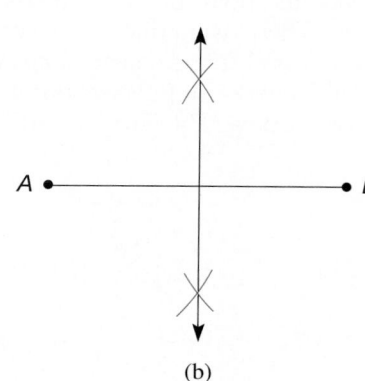

(b)

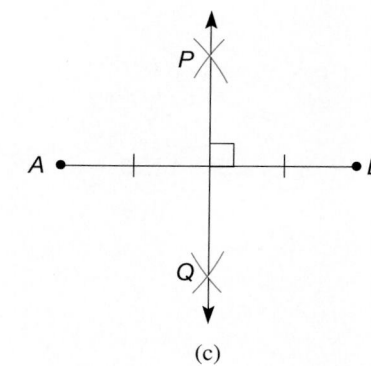

(c)

FIGURE 14.26

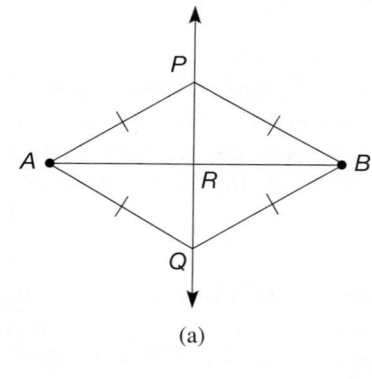

(a)

2. With the same compass opening, r, place the point of the compass at B and swing arcs of radius r on each side of $\overline{AB}$ [Figure 14.26(b)].
3. Let P be the intersection of the arcs on one side of $\overline{AB}$, and let Q be the intersection of the arcs on the other side of $\overline{AB}$. Construct line $\overleftrightarrow{PQ}$. Then line $\overleftrightarrow{PQ}$ is the perpendicular bisector of line segment $\overline{AB}$ [Figure 14.26(c)].

Justification (Figure 14.27)

We will give the major results and leave the details for the problem set. Construct segments $\overline{PA}$, $\overline{PB}$, $\overline{QA}$, and $\overline{QB}$. Let R be the intersection of PQ and $\overline{AB}$. By the construction procedure, $PA = PB = QA = QB$ [Figure 14.27(a)]. Also, $\overline{PQ} \cong \overline{PQ}$. Hence $\triangle APQ \cong \triangle BPQ$ by the SSS congruence property. Thus $\angle APQ \cong \angle BPQ$ [Figure 14.27(b)]. Consider $\triangle APR$ and $\triangle BPR$. They are congruent by the SAS congruence condition. Consequently, $AR = BR$, so $\overline{PQ}$ bisects $\overline{AB}$. We know that $\angle PRA$ and $\angle PRB$ are supplementary, so that all that remains is to show $\angle PRA \cong \angle PRB$. But this follows from the fact that $\triangle APR \cong \triangle BPR$. Therefore, $\overline{PQ} \perp \overline{AB}$. ■

(b)

FIGURE 14.27

Construction 4. Bisect an angle.

Given an angle $\angle ABC$ [Figure 14.28(a)], construct a line $\overleftrightarrow{BR}$ such that $\angle ABR \cong \angle CBR$; that is, $\overleftrightarrow{BR}$ is the **angle bisector** of $\angle ABC$ [Figure 14.28(b)].

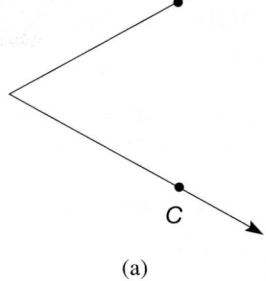
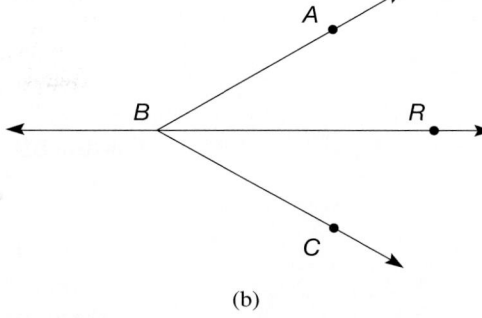

(a)   (b)

FIGURE 14.28

Procedure (Figure 14.29)

1. Place the point of the compass at B and construct an arc that intersects sides $\overrightarrow{BA}$ and $\overrightarrow{BC}$. Label the points of intersection P and Q, respectively [Figure 14.29(a)].

2. Place the point of the compass at P, and then at Q and construct intersecting arcs of the *same* radius. Label the intersection of the arcs R [Figure 14.29(b)].

3. Construct line $\overleftrightarrow{BR}$. Then line $\overleftrightarrow{BR}$ is the angle bisector of $\angle ABC$ [Figure 14.29(c)].

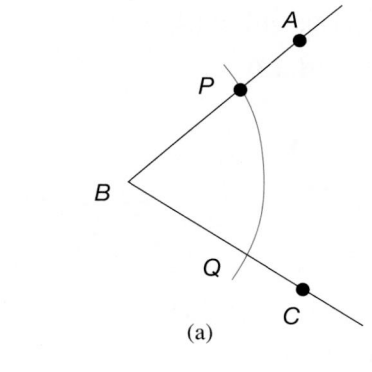
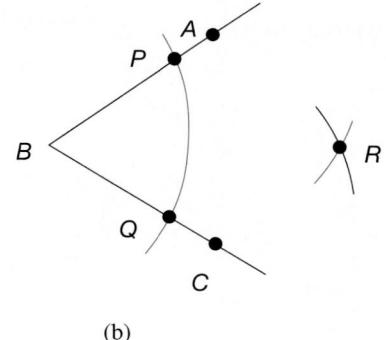

(a)   (b)

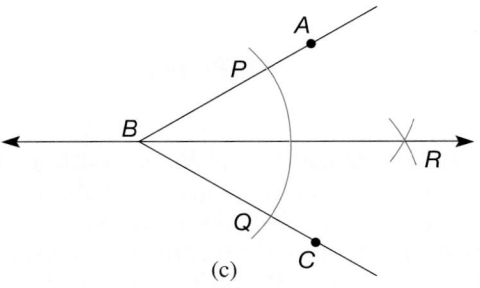
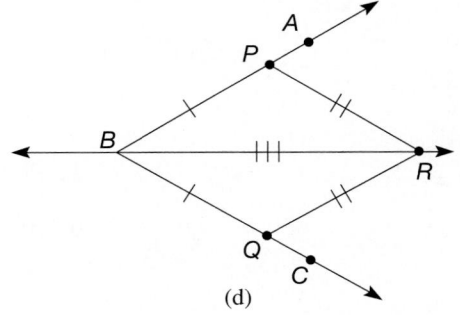

(c)   (d)

FIGURE 14.29

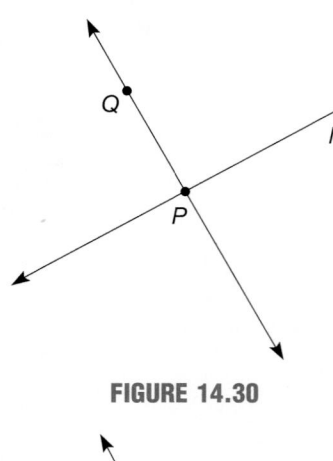

FIGURE 14.30

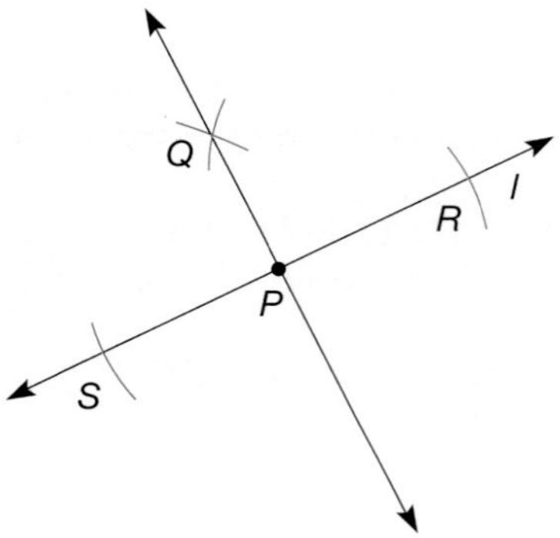

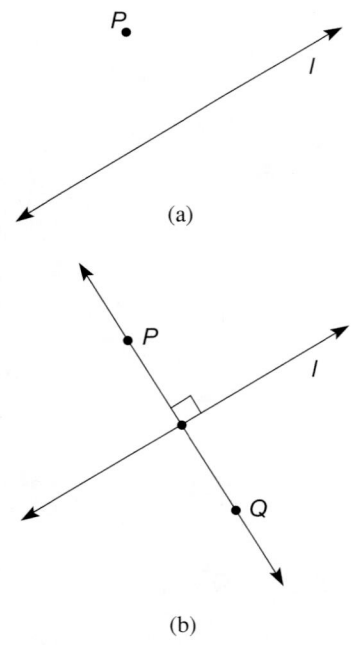

FIGURE 14.31

(a)

(b)

FIGURE 14.32

Justification [Figure 14.29(d)]
    By step 1, $\overline{PB} \cong \overline{QB}$, and by step 2, $\overline{RQ} \cong \overline{RP}$. Certainly $\overline{BR} \cong \overline{BR}$. Thus $\triangle PBR \cong \triangle QBR$ by the SSS congruence property, so that $\angle PBR \cong \angle QBR$, as desired.   ■

Construction 5.   Construct a line perpendicular to a given line through a specified point on the line.

    Given point P on l, construct $\overleftrightarrow{QP}$ such that $\overleftrightarrow{QP} \perp l$ (Figure 14.30).

    Procedure (Figure 14.31)
1. Place the point of the compass at P and construct arcs of a circle that intersect line l at points S and R.
2. Bisect the straight angle $\angle SPR$ using construction 4. Let point Q be the intersection of the arcs constructed in step 2 of construction 4.
3. The angle bisector, $\overleftrightarrow{QP}$, is perpendicular to line l.

    Justification (Figure 14.31)
    We know that $\angle SPR$ is a straight angle, since points S, P, and R are all on l. Hence $m(\angle SPR) = 180°$, so angle bisector $\overleftrightarrow{QP}$ divides $\angle SPR$ into two congruent angles, each measuring 90°. Thus $m(\angle QPR) = 90°$.   ■

Construction 6.   Construct a line perpendicular to a given line through a specified point not on the line.

    Given a line l and a point P, not on l [Figure 14.32(a)], construct a line $\overleftrightarrow{QP}$ such that $\overleftrightarrow{QP} \perp l$ [Figure 14.32(b)].

    Procedure (Figure 14.33)

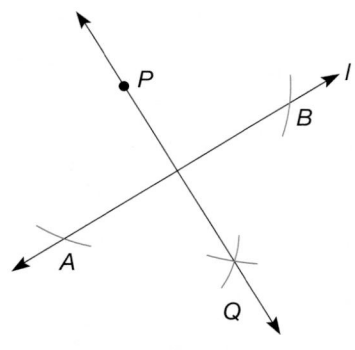

FIGURE 14.33

1. Place the point of the compass at P and construct an arc that intersects line l in two points. Label the points of intersection A and B.
2. With the *same* compass opening as in step 1, place the point of the compass at A, and then at B, to construct intersecting arcs on the side of l that does not contain P. Label the point of intersection of the arcs point Q.
3. Construct line $\overleftrightarrow{PQ}$. Then $\overleftrightarrow{PQ}$ contains P and is perpendicular to l.

Justification (Figure 14.34)

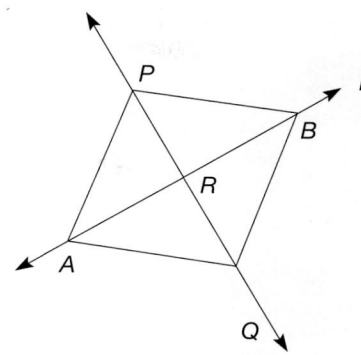

FIGURE 14.34

Let R be the intersection of $\overline{PQ}$ and $\overline{AB}$. Then the justification is exactly the same as for construction 3; that is, $\overline{PQ}$ is the perpendicular bisector of $\overline{AB}$, so that $\overleftrightarrow{PQ} \perp l$. (NOTE: The compass openings in step 2 can be different from those in step 1, as long as the arcs intersect *and* $AQ = BQ$.) ∎

Construction 7.   **Construct a line parallel to a given line through a specified point not on the line.**

Given a line l and a point P, not on l [Figure 14.35(a)], construct a line m such that $m \parallel l$ and P is on m [Figure 14.35(b)].

Procedure (Figure 14.36)

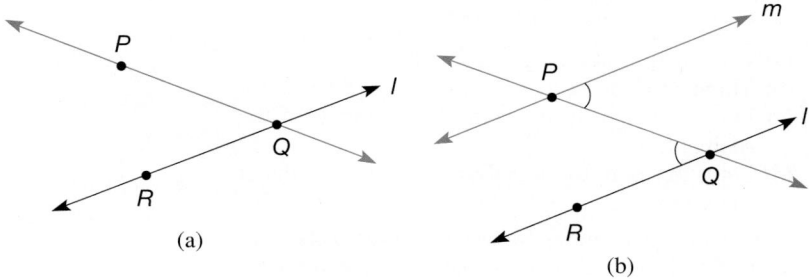

FIGURE 14.36

1. Let Q be any point on l and construct line $\overleftrightarrow{PQ}$.
2. Let R be another point on l [Figure 14.36(a)].
   Copy $\angle PQR$ using construction 2 so that the vertex is at P, one side is on line $\overleftrightarrow{QP}$, and the other is on line m [Figure 14.36(b)]. Then $m \parallel l$.

Justification [Figure 14.36(b)]
By construction 2, the pair of alternate interior angles at P and Q are congruent. Hence, by the alternate interior angles theorem, $m \parallel l$. ∎

MATHEMATICAL MORSEL

There are three famous problems of antiquity to be done using only a compass and straightedge.

1. Given a circle, construct a square of equal area.

2. Trisect any given angle; that is, construct an angle exactly one-third the measure of the given angle.

3. Construct a cube that has twice the volume of a given cube.

The ancients failed to solve these problems, not because their solutions were too difficult, but because the problems have *no* solutions! That is, mathematicians were able to prove that all three of the constructions above were impossible using *only* a compass and straightedge.

EXERCISE/PROBLEM SET 14.3—PART A

Exercises

1. Two segments are shown. Use construction 1 to construct segments that satisfy each of the following conditions.

$$\underline{\hspace{1.5cm}a\hspace{1.5cm}}$$
$$\underline{\hspace{2cm}b\hspace{2cm}}$$

(a) Congruent to the longer segment
(b) Three times as long as the shorter segment
(c) Equal in length to the sum of the lengths of the segments
(d) Equal in length to the difference of the lengths of the segments

2. Segments *a*, *b*, *c*, and *d* are as given. If possible, construct a triangle with sides specified. If not possible, explain why not.

$$\underline{\hspace{1cm}a\hspace{1cm}}$$
$$\underline{\hspace{1.3cm}b\hspace{1.3cm}}$$
$$\underline{\hspace{1.6cm}c\hspace{1.6cm}}$$
$$\underline{\hspace{2.3cm}d\hspace{2.3cm}}$$

(a) Sides *a*, *b*, and *c*
(b) Sides *a*, *b*, and *d*
(c) All sides the same length as *b*
(d) Two sides the same length as *c* and one side the same length as *a*

3. Given are an angle and a ray. Copy the angle such that the ray is one side of the copied angle.

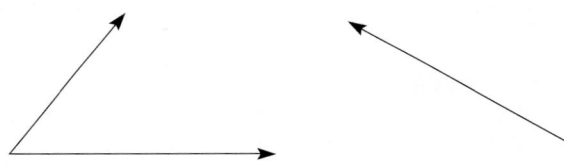

4. Construct the perpendicular bisector for each of the following segments.

(a) _____   **(b)**

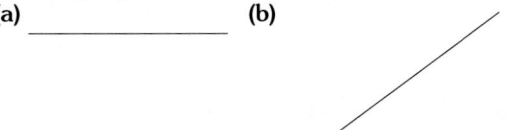

5. Construct the angle bisector for each of the following angles.

(a)

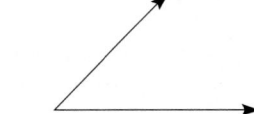

(b)

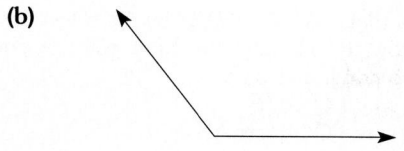

6. Construct a line perpendicular to the given line through point *P*.

(a)

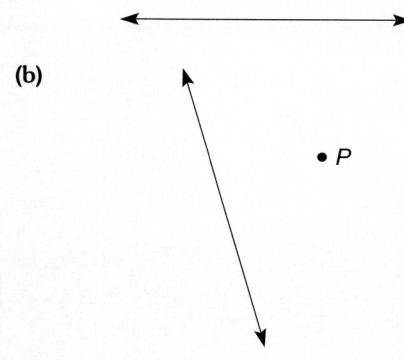

P

(b)

•*P*

7. Construct a line through point *P* parallel to the given line.

(a)   •*P*

(b)

• *P*

8. Using only compass and straightedge, construct angles with the following measures.
(a) 45°   **(b)** 60°   **(c)** 30°

9. Use your compass and straightedge and the following unit segment to construct the figures described.

_____ *u* _____

(a) Construct a right triangle with legs 3 units and 4 units in length. How long *should* the hypotenuse of your right triangle be? Use your compass to mark off units along the hypotenuse to check your answer.

(b) Construct a right triangle with legs 5 units and 12 units in length. How long *should* the hypotenuse of your right triangle be? Use your compass to mark off units along the hypotenuse to check your answer.

(c) Construct a right triangle with a leg 8 units and hypotenuse 17 units in length. How long *should* the other leg be? Use your compass to mark off units along the leg to check your answer.

10. Use △*ABC* to perform the construction described below.

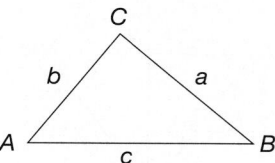

(a) Use your compass and straightedge to construct △*PQR* such that *PQ* = 3*c*, *PR* = 3*b*, and *QR* = 3*a*.

(b) How do the measures of ∠*A*, ∠*B* and ∠*C* compare to the measures of ∠*P*, ∠*Q*, and ∠*R*? (Use your protractor to check.)

(c) What can you conclude about the relationship between △*ABC* and △*PQR*? Justify your answer.

(d) Which of the three similarity properties of triangles does this construction verify?

11. A **median** of a triangle is a segment joining a vertex and the midpoint of the opposite side. Construct the three medians of the given triangle. Do they all meet at a single point?

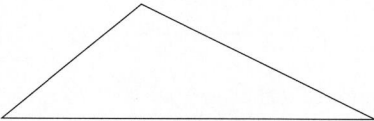

12. An **altitude** of a triangle is a segment from one vertex perpendicular to the line containing the opposite side. Construct the three altitudes of the given triangle. Do they all meet at a single point?

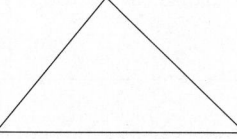

Problems

13. Both the medians and the angle bisectors of a triangle contain the vertices of the triangle. Under what circumstances will a median and an angle bisector coincide?

14. Both the perpendicular bisectors and medians of a triangle pass through the midpoints of the sides of the triangles. Under what circumstances will a perpendicular bisector and median coincide?

15. Complete the justification of construction 3, that is, that $\overleftrightarrow{PQ}$ is the perpendicular bisector of $\overline{AB}$.

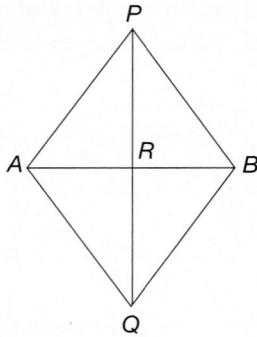

(a) To show that $\triangle APQ \cong \triangle BPQ$ by the SSS congruence property, identify the three pairs of corresponding congruent sides.

(b) To show that $\triangle APR \cong \triangle BPR$ by the SAS congruence property, identify the three pairs of corresponding congruent parts.

(c) Explain why $\overline{PQ} \perp \overline{AB}$.

(d) Explain why $\overline{PQ}$ bisects $\overline{AB}$.

16. Show the following result: If two angles of a triangle are congruent, the triangle is isosceles. (HINT: Bisect the third angle and apply AAS.)

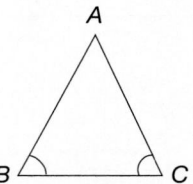

EXERCISE/PROBLEM SET 14.3—PART B

Exercises

1. Construct each of the following using a compass and straightedge.

(a) Perpendicular bisector of $\overline{PQ}$

(b) Bisector of $\angle R$

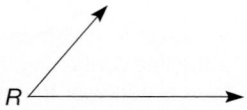

(c) Line perpendicular to l through P

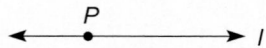

(d) Line perpendicular to l through P

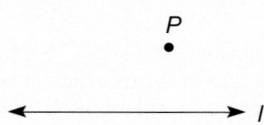

2. Draw an angle like the one shown, but with longer sides. Construct the following lines using a compass and straightedge.

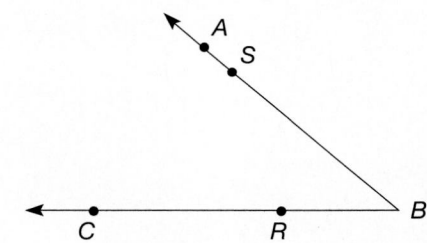

(a) The line perpendicular to $\overline{AB}$ at point S

(b) The line perpendicular to $\overline{BC}$ through point S

(c) The line parallel to $\overline{AB}$ through point R

(d) The line parallel to $\overline{BC}$ through point A

3. Given are two acute angles with measures a and b. Using compass and straightedge, construct the following.

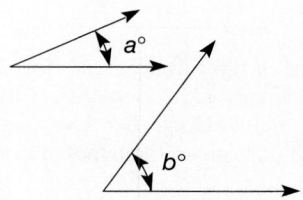

(a) An angle with measure $a + b$

(b) An angle with measure $2a$

(c) An angle with measure $b - a$

(d) An angle with measure $(a + b)/2$

4. Given are $\overline{AB}$, $\angle C$, and $\angle D$. Using construction techniques with compass and straightedge, construct the following.

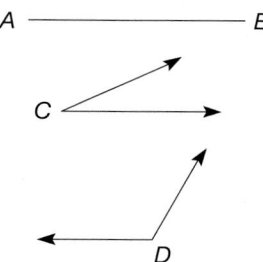

(a) A triangle with angles congruent to $\angle C$ and $\angle D$ and the included side congruent to $\overline{AB}$

(b) An isosceles triangle with two sides of length AB and the included angle congruent to $\angle D$

5. (a) Given below is a construction procedure for copying a triangle. Follow it to copy $\triangle RST$.

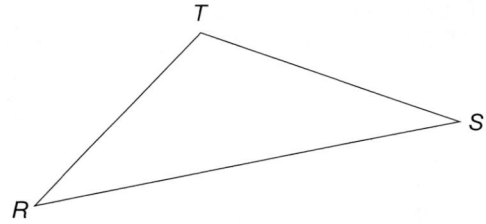

1. Draw a ray and copy segment $\overline{RS}$ of the triangle. Call the copy $\overline{DE}$.
2. Draw an arc with center D and radius RT.
3. Draw an arc with center E and radius ST. This arc should intersect the arc drawn in step 2. Call the intersection point F.
4. With a straightedge, connect points D and F and points E and F.

(b) Write a justification of the construction procedure.

6. Draw a figure similar to the one shown.

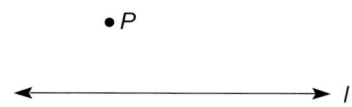

(a) Construct the line perpendicular to line l through point P. Call this line m.

(b) Construct a line through point P that is perpendicular to line m. Call this line k.

(c) What is the relationship between line k and line l? Explain why.

7. A method sometimes employed by drafters to bisect a line segment $\overline{AB}$ follows. Explain why this method works.

Angles of 45° are drawn at points A and B and the point of intersection of their sides, is labeled C. A perpendicular is drawn from point C to $\overline{AB}$. Point D bisects $\overline{AB}$.

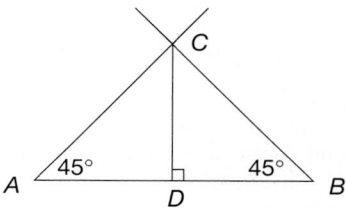

8. Use your compass and straightedge to construct each of the following, given the segments and angle shown below.

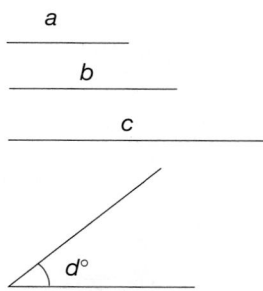

(a) A right triangle with legs a and b

(b) A right triangle with hypotenuse c and leg b

(c) A right triangle with angle d and leg b

(d) A right isosceles triangle with legs of length $\frac{1}{2}c$

9. Two neighbors at points A and B will share the cost of extending electric service from a road to their houses. A line will be laid that is equidistant from their two houses. How can they determine where the line should run?

● B

A ●

10. Use △ABC to perform the following construction: Use your compass and straightedge to construct △PQR such that ∠P ≅ ∠A and ∠Q ≅ ∠B.

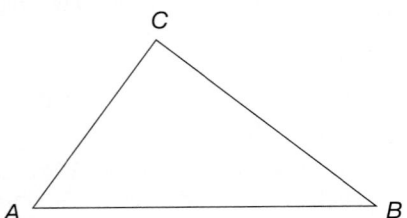

(a) What is the ratio of the lengths of corresponding sides of the triangles? That is, find $\dfrac{PQ}{AB}$, $\dfrac{PR}{AC}$, and $\dfrac{QR}{BC}$. (Use your ruler here.) How do the ratios compare?

(b) What can you conclude about the relationship between △ABC and △PQR? Justify your answer.

(c) Which of the three similarity properties of triangles does this construction verify?

11. Use △ABC and your compass and straightedge to perform the following construction: Construct △PQR where $PQ = 2c$, $PR = 2b$, and ∠P ≅ ∠A.

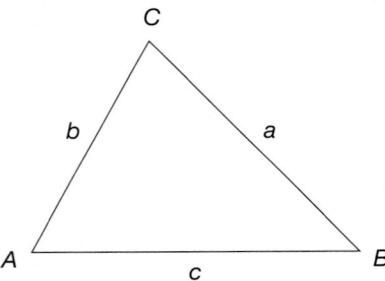

(a) How does the length of $\overline{RQ}$ compare to the length of $\overline{CB}$? (Use your compass to check your answer.) How do the measures of ∠B and ∠C compare to the measures of ∠Q and ∠R? (Use your compass or a protractor to compare the angles.)

(b) What can you conclude about the relationship between △ABC and △PQR? Justify your answer.

(c) Which of the three similarity properties of triangles does this construction verify?

Problems

12. Using AB as unit length, construct segments of the given length with compass and straightedge.

(a) $\sqrt{10}$ (b) $\sqrt{6}$ (c) $\sqrt{12}$ (d) $\sqrt{15}$

13. Both the perpendicular bisectors and altitudes of a triangle are perpendicular to the line containing the sides. Under what circumstances will a perpendicular bisector and altitude coincide?

14. A rectangle similar to rectangle $ABCD$ can be constructed as follows:

1. Draw diagonal $\overline{AC}$ in rectangle $ABCD$. Extend the diagonal through point C if you want a rectangle larger than $ABCD$.
2. Pick any point on $\overleftrightarrow{AC}$ and call it P.
3. Construct perpendiculars from point P to $\overleftrightarrow{AB}$ and to $\overleftrightarrow{AD}$.
4. Label the points of intersection Q and R. $ABCD \sim AQPR$. Explain why this is true.

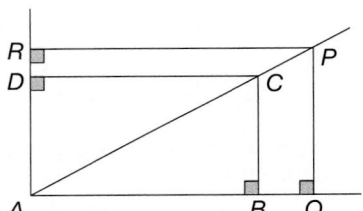

15. Prove the following result: If a point is equidistant from the endpoints of a segment, it is on the perpendicular bisector of the segment. (Hɪɴᴛ: Connect C with the midpoint D of segment $\overline{AB}$ and show that $\overline{CD}$ is perpendicular to $\overline{AB}$.)

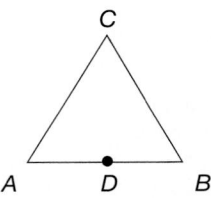

14.4

ADDITIONAL EUCLIDEAN CONSTRUCTIONS

Constructing Circumscribed and Inscribed Circles

There are several interesting constructions that we can perform that involve triangles and circles. In particular, every triangle can have a circle circumscribed around it, and every triangle can have a circle inscribed within it (Figure 14.37). The **circumscribed circle** contains the vertices of the polygon as points on the circle. The **inscribed circle** touches each side of the polygon in exactly one point.

In Figure 14.37, line $\overleftrightarrow{AB}$ is said to be **tangent** to the inscribed circle, since the line and circle intersect in exactly one point, and all other points of the circle lie entirely on one side of the line. Similarly, lines $\overleftrightarrow{BC}$ and $\overleftrightarrow{AC}$ are tangent to the inscribed circle.

In Figure 14.37, point P is the center of the circumscribed circle, so $PA = PB = PC$. Thus P is equidistant from the vertices of $\triangle ABC$. Point P is called the **circumcenter** of $\triangle ABC$. Point Q is the center of the inscribed circle and is called the **incenter** of $\triangle ABC$. The inscribed circle intersects each of the three sides of $\triangle ABC$ at R, S, and T. Notice that $QR = QS = QT$ since each length is the radius of the inscribed circle. To construct circumscribed and inscribed circles for a triangle, we need to construct the circumcenter and the incenter of the triangle. Example 14.7 provides the basis for constructing the circumcenter.

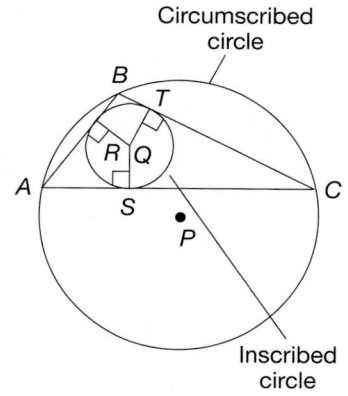

Circumscribed circle

Inscribed circle

FIGURE 14.37

EXAMPLE 14.7 Suppose that $\overline{AB}$ is a line segment with perpendicular bisector l. Show that point P is on l if and only if P is equidistant from A and B; that is, $AP = BP$ (Figure 14.38).

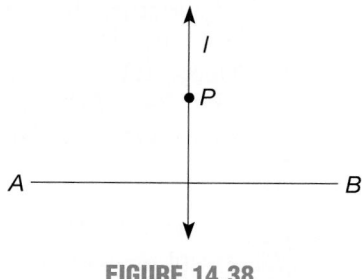

FIGURE 14.38

Solution

Suppose that P is on l, the perpendicular bisector of $\overline{AB}$. Let M be the midpoint of $\overline{AB}$ (Figure 14.39). Then $\triangle PMA \cong \triangle PMB$ by the SAS congruence property (verify this). Hence $PA = PB$, so P is equidistant from A and B. This shows that the points on the perpendicular bisector of $\overline{AB}$ are equidistant from A and B. To complete the argument, we would have to show that if a point is equidistant from A and B, then it must be on l. This is left for the problem set. ∎

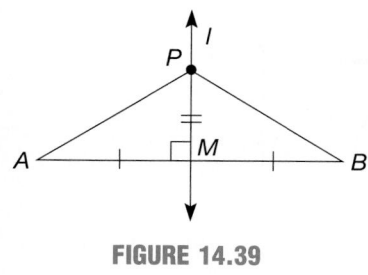

FIGURE 14.39

Example 14.7 shows that the circumcenter of a triangle must be a point on each of the perpendicular bisectors of the sides. Thus to find the circumcenter of a triangle, we find the perpendicular bisectors of the sides of the triangle. (Actually, any two of the perpendicular bisectors will suffice.)

Construction 8.   Construct the circumscribed circle of a triangle.

Procedure (Figure 14.40)
Given △ABC, construct point P which is equidistant from A, B, and C.

1. Using construction 3, construct line *l*, the perpendicular bisector of side $\overline{AC}$ [Figure 14.40(a)].

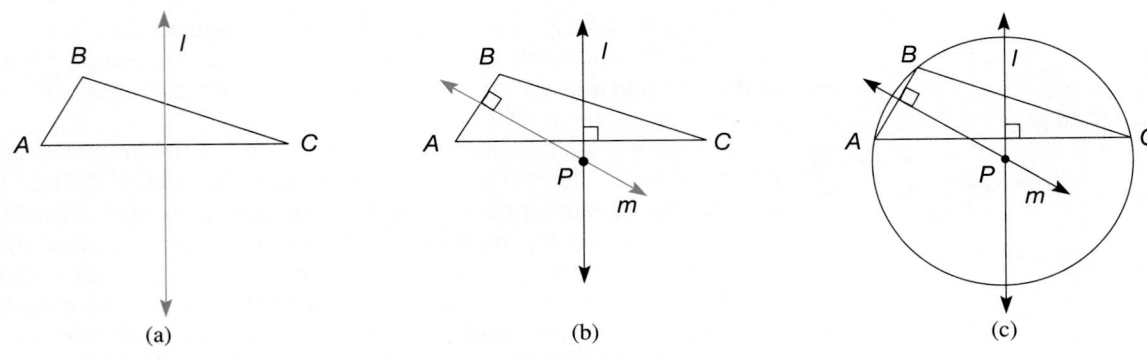

(a)   (b)   (c)

FIGURE 14.40

2. Similarly, construct line *m*, the perpendicular bisector of side $\overline{AB}$. The intersection of lines *l* and *m* is point *P*, the circumcenter of △ABC [Figure 14.40(b)]. The circle with center *P* and radius *PA* is the circumscribed circle of △ABC [Figure 14.40(c)].

Justification (Figure 14.40)
Since P is on line *l*, P is equidistant from A and C, by Example 14.7. Hence PA = PC. Also, P is on line *m*, so P is equidistant from A and B. Thus PA = PB. Combining results, we have PA = PB = PC. Thus the circle whose center is P and whose radius is PA will contain points A, B, and C. ■

In order to find the incenter of a triangle, we need to define what is meant by the distance from a point P to a line *l* [Figure 14.41(a)].

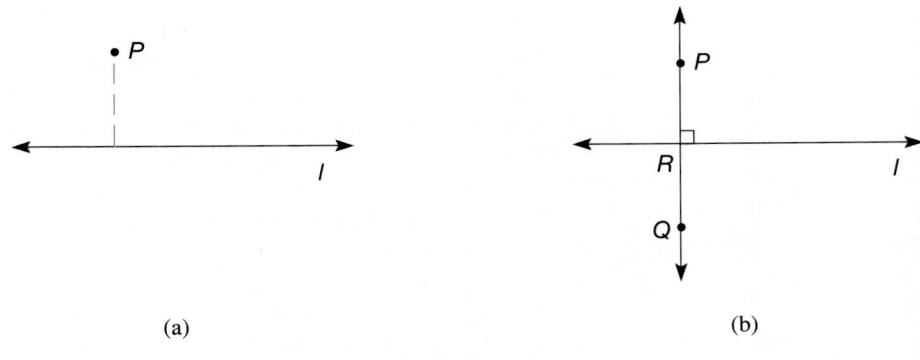

(a)   (b)

FIGURE 14.41

Suppose that $\overleftrightarrow{PQ}$ is the line through P that is perpendicular to l (construction 6). Let R be the intersection of line $\overleftrightarrow{PQ}$ and line l [Figure 14.41(b)]. Then we define the **distance from P to l** to be the distance PR. That is, we measure the distance from a point to a line by measuring along a line that is *perpendicular* to the given line, here l, through the given point, here P. Point R is the point on line l closest to point P.

To find the incenter of a triangle, we must locate a point that is equidistant from the sides of the triangle. Construction 9 shows us how to do this.

Construction 9. **Construct the inscribed circle of a triangle.**

Procedure (Figure 14.42)

1. Using construction 4, construct line l, the bisector of $\angle CAB$ [Figure 14.42(a)].

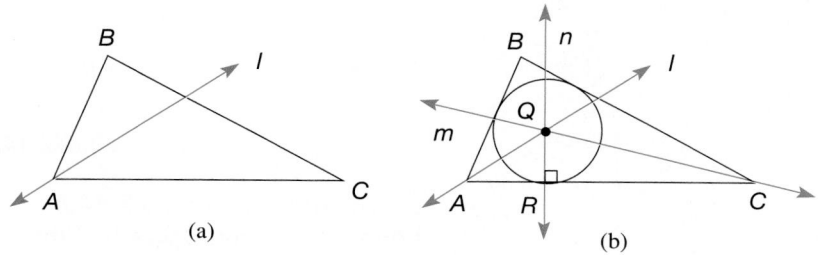

FIGURE 14.42

2. Similarly, construct line m, the bisector of $\angle BCA$. Let Q be the point of intersection of lines l and m. Then Q is the incenter of $\triangle ABC$ [Figure 14.42(b)]. To construct the inscribed circle, first construct the line n containing Q such that n is perpendicular to $\overline{AC}$. Let R be the intersection of line n and $\overline{AC}$. Then construct the circle, center at Q, whose radius is QR. This is the inscribed circle of $\triangle ABC$ [Figure 14.42(b)].

Justification

The justification for this construction is developed in the problem set. ∎

There are two other centers commonly associated with triangles, the orthocenter and the centroid. The **orthocenter** is the intersection of the altitudes and the **centroid** is the intersection of the medians of a triangle. The centroid has the property that it is the center of mass of a triangular region. That is, if a triangular shape is cut out of some material of uniform density, the triangle will balance at the centroid (Figure 14.43). These two centers are studied in the problem set.

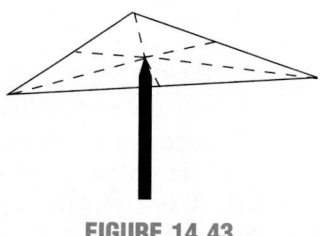

FIGURE 14.43

Constructing Regular Polygons

There are infinitely many values of n for which a regular n-gon can be constructed with compass and straightedge, *but* not for every n. In this subsection we will see how to construct several infinite families of regular n-gons. We will also learn a condition on the prime factorization of n that determines which regular n-gons can be constructed.

Construction 10.   Construct an equilateral triangle.

Procedure [Figure 14.44(a)]
1. Choose points A and B arbitrarily.
2. Place the compass point at A and open the compass to the distance AB.
3. With the compass point at A, construct arc 1 of radius AB. Do the same thing with the compass point at B to construct arc 2. Label the intersection of the arcs point C. Then $\triangle ABC$ is equilateral.

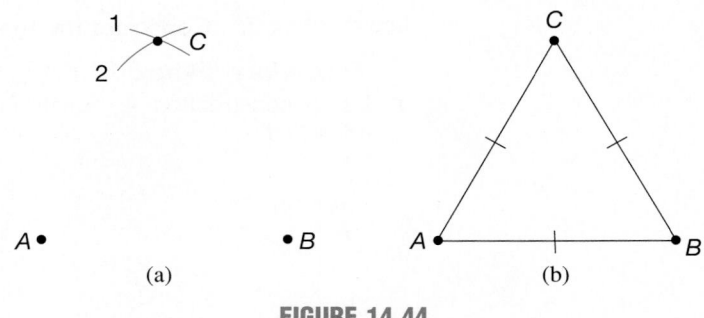

(a)   (b)

FIGURE 14.44

Justification [Figure 14.44(b)]
From steps 2 and 3, we find that $AB = AC = BC$. Hence $\triangle ABC$ is equilateral.   ■

We can use the construction of an equilateral triangle as the basis for constructing an infinite family of regular n-gons. For example, suppose that we find the circumscribed circle of an equilateral triangle [Figure 14.45(a)].

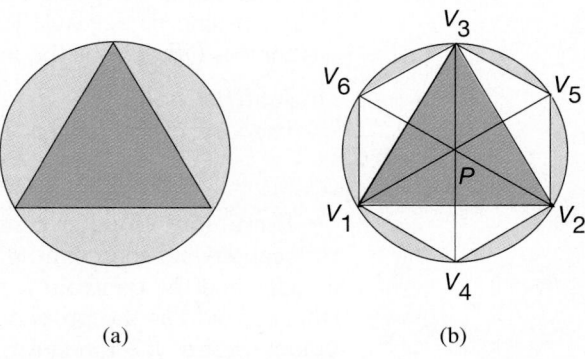

(a)   (b)

FIGURE 14.45

Let P be the circumcenter. Bisect the central angles, $\angle V_1PV_2$, $\angle V_2PV_3$, and $\angle V_3PV_1$, to locate points V_4, V_5, and V_6 on the circle [Figure 14.45(b)]. These six points are the vertices of a regular 6-gon (hexagon). Next bisect the central angles in the regular 6-gon, inscribed in a circle, to construct a regular 12-gon, then a 24-gon, and so on. Theoretically, then, we can construct an infinite family of regular n-gons, namely the family for $n = 3, 6, 12, 24, 48, \ldots, 3 \cdot 2^k, \ldots$ where k is any whole number.

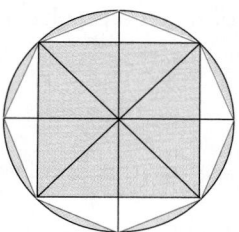

FIGURE 14.46

Since we know how to construct right angles, we can construct a square. Then if a square is inscribed in a circle, we can bisect the central angles to locate the vertices of a regular 8-gon, then a 16-gon, and so on (Figure 14.46). Thus we could theoretically construct a regular n-gon for $n = 2^k$, where k is any whole number greater than 1.

In general, once we have constructed a regular n-gon, we can construct an infinite family of regular polygons, namely those with $n \cdot 2^k$ sides, where k is any whole number. In the problem sets, we will investigate this family with $n = 5$. We will show that it is possible to construct a regular pentagon, and hence to construct regular n-gons for $n = 5, 10, 20, 40, 80, \ldots,$ $5 \cdot 2^k, \ldots,$ where k is a whole number.

A remarkable result about the construction of regular n-gons tells us precisely the values of n for which a regular n-gon can be constructed. In order to understand the result, we need a certain type of prime number, called a Fermat prime. A **Fermat prime** is a prime number of the form $F_k = 2^{(2^k)} + 1$, where k is a whole number.

For the first few whole-number values of k, we obtain the following results.

$$F_0 = 2^{(2^0)} + 1 = 2^1 + 1 = 3, \text{ a prime,}$$
$$F_1 = 2^{(2^1)} + 1 = 2^2 + 1 = 5, \text{ a prime,}$$
$$F_2 = 2^{(2^2)} + 1 = 2^4 + 1 = 17, \text{ a prime,}$$
$$F_3 = 2^{(2^3)} + 1 = 2^8 + 1 = 257, \text{ a prime,}$$
$$F_4 = 2^{(2^4)} + 1 = 2^{16} + 1 = 65,537, \text{ a prime,}$$
$$F_5 = 2^{(2^5)} + 1 = 2^{32} + 1 = (641) \cdot (6,700,417), \textit{ not a prime.}$$

Thus there are at least five Fermat primes, namely 3, 5, 17, 257, and 65,537, but not *every* number of the form $2^{(2^k)} + 1$ is a prime. (Also, not every prime is of the form $2^{(2^k)} + 1$. For example, 7 is a prime, but not a Fermat prime.) A result, due to the famous mathematician Gauss, gives the conditions that n must satisfy in order for a regular n-gon to be constructible.

Theorem

Gauss's Theorem for Constructible Regular *n*-gons

A regular n-gon can be constructed with straightedge and compass if and only if the only odd prime factors of n are distinct Fermat primes.

Gauss's theorem tells us that for constructible regular n-gons, the only odd primes that can occur in the factorization of n are Fermat primes with no Fermat prime factor repeated. The prime 2 can occur to any whole-number power. At this time, no Fermat primes larger than 65,537, F_4, are known, nor is it known whether any others *exist*. (As of 1990, it is known that F_6 through F_{21} are composite.) Example 14.8 illustrates several applications of Gauss's theorem.

EXAMPLE 14.8   For which of the following values of n can a regular n-gon be constructed?

(a) 40   **(b)** 45   **(c)** 60   **(d)** 64   **(e)** 21

Solution

(a) $n = 40 = 2^3 \cdot 5$. Since the only odd prime factor of 40 is 5, a Fermat prime, a regular 40-gon can be constructed.

(b) $n = 45 = 3^2 \cdot 5$. Since the (Fermat) prime 3 occurs more than once in the factorization of n, the odd prime factors are not *distinct* Fermat primes. Hence a regular 45-gon cannot be constructed.

(c) $n = 60 = 2^2 \cdot 3 \cdot 5$. The odd prime factors of n are the distinct Fermat primes 3 and 5. Therefore, a regular 60-gon can be constructed.

(d) $n = 64 = 2^6$. There are no odd factors to consider. Hence a regular 64-gon can be constructed.

(e) $n = 21 = 3 \cdot 7$. Since 7 is not a Fermat prime, a regular 21-gon cannot be constructed.   ■

The proof of Gauss's theorem is very difficult. The theorem is a remarkable result in the history of mathematics and helped make Gauss one of the most respected mathematicians of all time.

Constructing Segment Lengths

The use of similar triangles allows us to construct products and quotients of real-number lengths. Example 14.9 gives the construction for the product of two real numbers.

EXAMPLE 14.9   Suppose that a and b are positive real numbers representing the lengths of line segments (Figure 14.47) and we have a segment of length 1. Show how to construct a line segment whose length is $a \cdot b$.

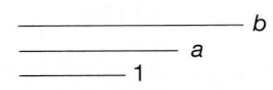

FIGURE 14.47

Solution

Let $\overline{PQ}$ be a line segment of length a [Figure 14.48(a)]. Let R be any point not on line $\overleftrightarrow{PQ}$ such that $PR = 1$ [Figure 14.48(b)]. Let S be a point on ray $\overrightarrow{PR}$ such that $PS = b$ [Figure 14.48(b)]. Construct segment $\overline{QR}$, and construct a line l through point S such that $l \parallel \overleftrightarrow{QR}$ [Figure 14.48(c)]. Let T be the intersection of lines l and $\overleftrightarrow{PQ}$. Then $\angle PQR \cong \angle PTS$ by the corresponding angles property. Since $\angle RPQ = \angle SPT$, we know that $\triangle PRQ \sim \triangle PST$

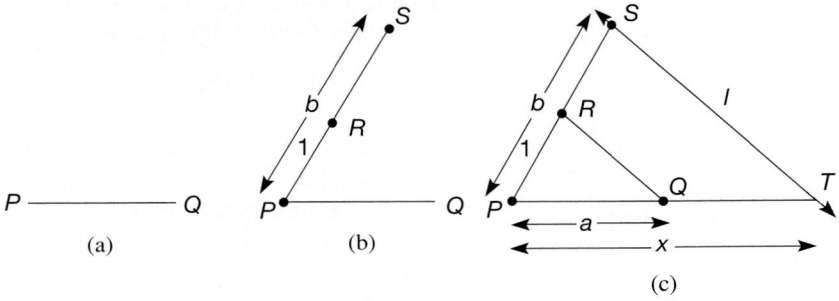

FIGURE 14.48

by the AA similarity property. Let $x = PT$. Then, using similar triangles,

$$\frac{a}{1} = \frac{x}{b},$$

so that $a \cdot b = x$. Thus we have constructed the product of the real numbers a and b. ∎

Other construction procedures with real-number lengths appear in the problem set.

MATHEMATICAL MORSEL

In writing his book on geometry, called *The Elements,* Euclid produced a new proof of the Pythagorean theorem. In 1907, when Elisha Loomis was preparing the manuscript for the book *The Pythagorean Proposition* (which eventually had over 370 *different* proofs of the Pythagorean theorem), he noted that there were two or three American textbooks on geometry in which Euclid's proof does not appear. He mused that the authors must have been seeking to show their originality or independence. However, he said, "The leaving out of Euclid's proof is like the play of Hamlet with Hamlet left out."

EXERCISE/PROBLEM SET 14.4—PART A

1. Copy the given triangle and construct the circle circumscribed about the triangle.

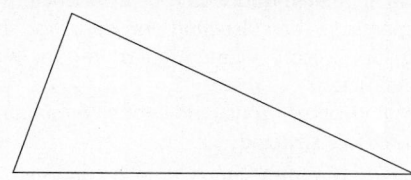

2. Copy the given triangle and construct the circle inscribed inside the triangle.

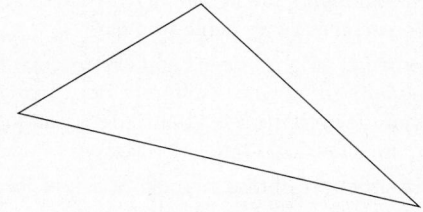

3. Construct an equilateral triangle with sides congruent to the given segment.

_____

4. Using only compass and straightedge, construct angles with the following measures.
(a) 15°   (b) 75°   (c) 105°

5. Construct a triangle with angles of 30°, 60°, and 90°. With your ruler, measure the lengths in centimeters of the hypotenuse and the shortest leg. Next, construct two more triangles of different sizes but with angles of 30°, 60°, and 90°. Again measure the lengths of the hypotenuse and the shortest leg. What is the relationship between the length of the hypotenuse and the length of the shorter leg in a 30°–60°–90° triangle?

6. (a) Follow steps 1 to 6 to inscribe a particular regular n-gon in a circle.

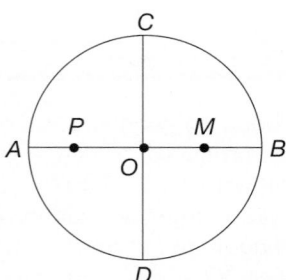

1. Draw a circle with center O.
2. In this circle, draw a diameter $\overline{AB}$.
3. Construct another diameter, $\overline{CD}$, that is perpendicular to $\overline{AB}$.
4. Bisect $\overline{OB}$. Let M be its midpoint.
5. Using M as the center and CM as the radius, draw an arc intersecting $\overline{AO}$. Call the intersection point P.
6. Mark off arcs of radius CP around the circle and connect consecutive points.

(b) What regular n-gon have you constructed?

7. (a) If you bisected the central angles of the regular n-gon constructed in the preceding problem and connected the consecutive points along the circle, what regular n-gon would be constructed?
(b) Repeating the bisecting process to this new regular n-gon, what regular n-gon would be constructed?
(c) List two other regular polygons of this family that can be constructed.

8. Which of the following regular n-gons can be constructed with compass and straightedge?
(a) 120-gon   (b) 85-gon   (c) 36-gon
(d) 80-gon   (e) 63-gon   (f) 75-gon
(g) 105-gon   (h) 255-gon   (i) 340-gon

9. The following construction procedure can be used to divide a segment into any given number of congruent segments. Draw a segment and follow the steps below.

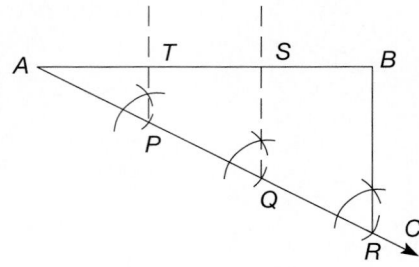

1. Construct any ray $\overrightarrow{AC}$ not collinear with $\overline{AB}$.
2. With any arbitrary compass setting, mark off three congruent segments on $\overrightarrow{AC}$ (here, $\overline{AP}$, $\overline{PQ}$, and $\overline{QR}$).
3. Construct $\overline{BR}$.
4. Construct lines parallel to $\overline{BR}$ through P and Q.

Into how many congruent pieces has $\overline{AB}$ been divided? (NOTE: To divide $\overline{AB}$ into k congruent segments, where k is a whole number, mark off k congruent segments on $\overline{AC}$ in step 2.)

10. We can simplify the procedure described in the preceding exercise by constructing only $\overline{SQ}$ parallel to $\overline{BR}$. Then use the compass opening as $\overline{SB}$ and mark off congruent segments along $\overline{AB}$.

A ——————————————— B

Use this technique to divide $\overline{AB}$ into six congruent pieces.

11. (a) Use the procedure in Exercise 10 to divide $\overline{AB}$ into four congruent pieces.

A ——————————————— B

(b) Find another procedure that can be used to divide $\overline{AB}$ into four congruent parts (using construction techniques from Section 14.3).

Problems

12. (a) Draw an acute triangle and find its circumcenter.
(b) Repeat part (a) with a different acute triangle.
(c) What do you notice about the location of the circumcenter of an acute triangle?

13. (a) Construct a right triangle and find its circumcenter.
(b) Repeat part (a) with a different right triangle.
(c) What do you notice about the location of the circumcenter of a right triangle?

14. (a) Construct an obtuse triangle and find its circumcenter.
(b) Repeat part (a) with a different obtuse triangle.
(c) What do you notice about the location of the circumcenter of an obtuse triangle?

15. A woman wants to divide a short strip of plastic into five congruent pieces but has no ruler available. If she has a pencil and a sheet of lined paper, how can she use them to mark off five congruent segments? (HINT: Refer to Problem 11 in Exercise/Problem Set 14.2—Part B.)

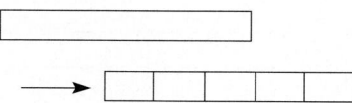

16. An interesting result called Aubel's theorem can be observed in the following construction.

1. Draw any quadrilateral $ABCD$.
2. Using compass and straightedge, construct a square on each side of quadrilateral $ABCD$.
3. Locate the midpoint of each square: M_1, M_2, M_3, M_4. Connect the midpoints of opposite squares with line segments.

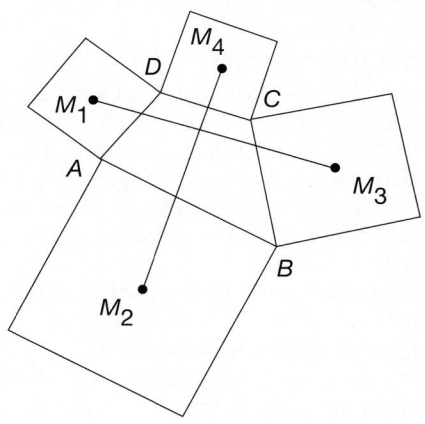

(a) Draw a convex quadrilateral and perform the steps described above. Use your ruler to measure the lengths of segments $\overline{M_1M_3}$ and $\overline{M_2M_4}$. Use your protractor to measure the angles formed where $\overline{M_1M_3}$ and $\overline{M_2M_4}$ intersect.
(b) Repeat the construction for two more quadrilaterals. Let one quadrilateral be convex, in which case the squares will overlap. Measure the segments and angles described in part (a).
(c) What conclusion can you draw?

17. In this section a construction was given to find the product of any two lengths. Use that construction to find the length $1/a$ for any given length a. The case $a > 1$ is shown in the following figure.

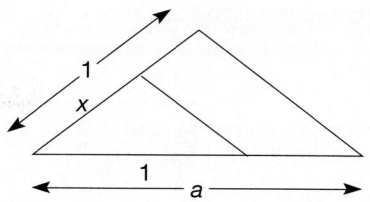

18. (a) If $\dfrac{a}{x} = \dfrac{x}{b}$, then x is called the **mean proportional** or **geometric mean** between a and b. One method of constructing the geometric mean is pictured. Assuming $a \geq b$, mark off AC, the length a, and find point B such that BC has length b, where B is between A and C. Then mark off BD, the length a, and draw two large arcs with centers A and D and radius a. If the arcs intersect at E, then $x = EB$. Following this method, construct the geometric mean between 1 and 2 where the length 1 is given. What length have you constructed?

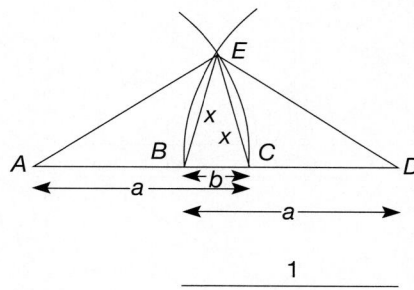

(b) Prove that the x in the diagram is, in fact, the geometric mean between the a and b given.

EXERCISE/PROBLEM SET 14.4—PART B

Exercises

1. Copy the given triangle and use a compass and straightedge to find the following.

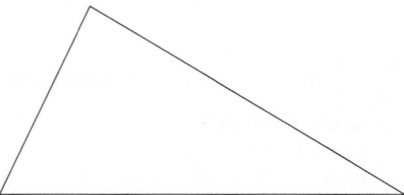

2. The three medians of a triangle are concurrent at a point called the **centroid**. This point is the center of gravity or balance point of a triangle. Construct the three medians of the following triangles and complete the statement below.

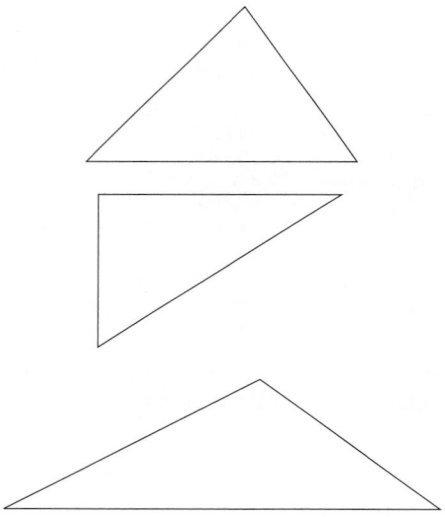

The centroid always lies _____ the triangle.

3. The lines containing the altitudes of a triangle meet at a single point, called the **orthocenter**. The position of the orthocenter is determined by the measures of the angles. Construct the three altitudes for each of the following triangles. Then complete the following statements.

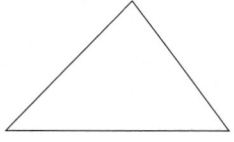

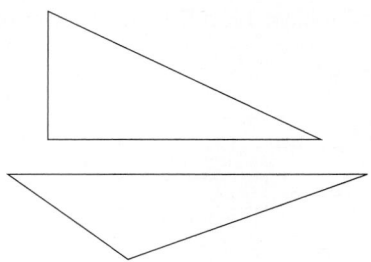

   (a) The orthocenter of an acute triangle lies _____ the triangle.
   (b) The orthocenter of a right triangle is the _____.
   (c) The orthocenter of an obtuse triangle lies _____ the triangle.

4. (a) Construct a circle using any compass setting. Without changing the compass setting, mark off arcs of the radius around the circle (each mark serving as center for next arc). Join consecutive marks to form a polygon. Is the polygon a regular polygon? If so, which one?
   (b) Prove your assertion in part (a).

5. Follow the steps below to construct a regular decagon. (A justification of this construction follows in Problem 17 of Exercise/Problem Set 14.5—Part B.)
   (a) Taking AB as a unit length, construct a segment $\overline{CD}$ of length $\sqrt{5}$. (HINT: Pythagorean theorem.)
   (b) Using $\overline{AB}$ and $\overline{CD}$, construct a segment $\overline{EF}$ of length $\sqrt{5} - 1$.
   (c) Bisect segment $\overline{EF}$ forming segment $\overline{EG}$. What is the length of $\overline{EG}$?
   (d) Construct a circle with radius AB.
   (e) With compass open a distance EG, make marks around the circle. Connecting adjacent points will yield a decagon.

A ———————————— B

6. List all regular polygons with fewer than 100 sides that can be constructed with compass and straightedge. (HINT: Apply Gauss's theorem.)

7. Explain how to construct angles with the following measures.
   (a) 135°
   (b) 75°
   (c) 72°
   (d) 108°

8. Given any rectangle *ABCD,* it is possible to construct a square with the same area as *ABCD* as follows.

1. Extend side $\overline{DC}$ through point C, and find P on $\overleftrightarrow{DC}$ such that $CB = CP$.

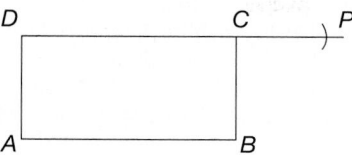

2. Find the midpoint M of $\overline{DP}$ and construct a circle with center M and radius DM.

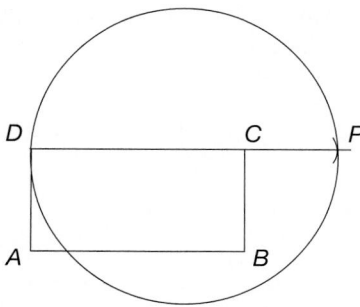

3. Extend side $\overline{BC}$ so that it intersects the circle at point Q. Construct a square with side $\overline{CQ}$.

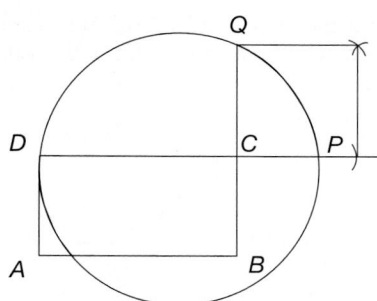

Follow the steps above to construct a square with the same area as rectangle $PQRS$. Then use your ruler to measure the sides of the rectangle and square in centimeters and verify that their areas are the same.

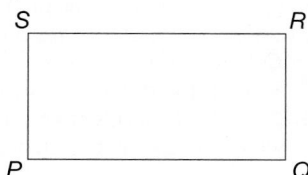

9. A golden rectangle, as described in Chapter 7, can be constructed using a compass and straightedge as follows.

1. Construct any square $ABCD$.
2. Bisect side $\overline{AB}$ and call the midpoint M.
3. Set the radius of your compass as MC. Using point M as the center of your arc, make an arc that intersects $\overleftrightarrow{AB}$ at P.
4. Construct $\overline{PQ} \parallel \overline{AD}$ and $\overline{DQ} \parallel \overline{AB}$.
5. Now $APQD$ is a golden rectangle.

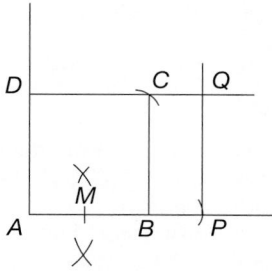

Construct a golden rectangle starting with a square that has sides of some length you choose. Using a ruler, measure the length and width of your rectangle in centimeters. Calculate the ratio of length:width for your rectangle. How does your ratio compare to the golden ratio?

10. Given the circle shown, find its center. (HINT: Pick any three points on the circle and form a triangle.)

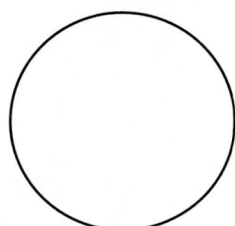

11. By constructing a variety of acute, right, and obtuse triangles and finding their incenters, determine if the incenter is always inside the triangle.

12. An interesting result attributed to Napolean Bonaparte can be observed in the following construction.

1. Draw any triangle $\triangle PQR$.
2. Using compass and straightedge, construct an equilateral triangle on each side of $\triangle PQR$.
3. Use your compass and straightedge to locate the centroid of each equilateral triangle: C_1, C_2, C_3.
4. Connect C_1, C_2 and C_3 to form a triangle.

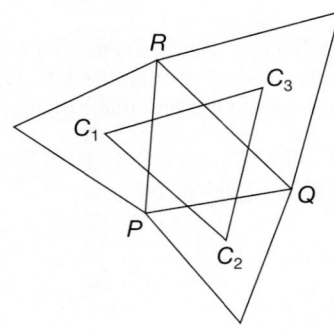

(a) Draw a triangle and perform the steps 1–4. What kind of triangle is $\triangle C_1 C_2 C_3$? Use your ruler and protractor to check.

(b) Repeat the construction for two different types of triangles $\triangle PQR$. What kind of triangle is $\triangle C_1 C_2 C_3$?

(c) Can you summarize your observations?

13. By Gauss's theorem we know that it is not possible to construct a regular heptagon (7-gon) using only straightedge and compass. It is possible, however, to make an angle measuring $\dfrac{180°}{7}$ or approximately 25.7° with toothpicks using a technique attributed to C. Johnson, *Mathematical Gazette*, No. 407, 1975. Seven congruent toothpicks can be arranged as shown below, where points A, B, C, and D are collinear.

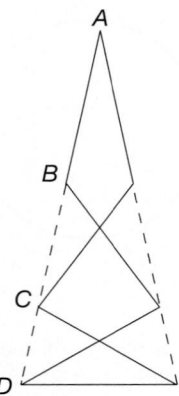

When the toothpicks are arranged in this way, the angle at A will measure $\dfrac{180°}{7}$.

(a) Arrange seven toothpicks as shown and then use your protractor to measure the angle at A.

(b) What is the measure of the central angle of a regular hexagon?

(c) If we were able to construct an angle of $\dfrac{180°}{7}$, how could we then construct a regular heptagon?

14. It has been shown that a regular n-gon can be constructed using a Mira if and only if n is of the form $2^r \cdot 3^s \cdot p_1 \cdots p_k$, where the $p_1, \ldots, p_k$ are primes of the form $2^u 3^v + 1$. Find the first 10 regular n-gons that can be constructed using a Mira.

Problems

15. To locate the incenter of a triangle, we need to locate a point that is equidistant from the sides of the triangle. Suppose that point A is equidistant from $\overrightarrow{YX}$ and $\overrightarrow{YZ}$. Show that $\overrightarrow{YA}$ is the angle bisector of $\angle XYZ$.

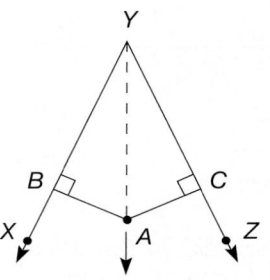

16. If line l is the bisector of $\angle BAC$ and point Q is on l, verify that Q is equidistant from the sides $\overline{AB}$ and $\overline{AC}$ of $\angle BAC$ by completing the following.

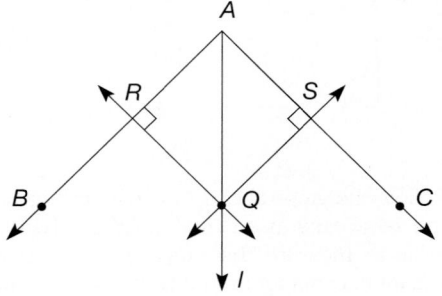

(a) Let line $\overleftrightarrow{QR}$ be perpendicular to $\overleftrightarrow{AB}$, where R is on $\overleftrightarrow{AB}$. What is the distance from Q to $\overleftrightarrow{AB}$?

(b) Let line $\overleftrightarrow{QS}$ be perpendicular to $\overleftrightarrow{AC}$, where S is on $\overleftrightarrow{AC}$. What is the distance from Q to $\overleftrightarrow{AC}$?

(c) Is $\triangle ARQ \cong \triangle ASQ$? Justify your answer.

(d) Explain why Q is therefore equidistant from $\overleftrightarrow{AB}$ and $\overleftrightarrow{AC}$.

17. Use the results of Problem 16 to justify construction 9, the procedure for constructing the incenter of a triangle.

14.5

GEOMETRIC PROBLEM SOLVING USING TRIANGLE CONGRUENCE AND SIMILARITY

In this section we apply triangle congruence and similarity properties to prove properties of geometric shapes. Many of these results were observed informally in Chapter 12. Our first example uses the SSS congruence property.

EXAMPLE 14.10 Show that the base angles of an isosceles trapezoid are congruent.

Solution
Suppose that $ABCD$ is an isosceles trapezoid with $\overline{AB} \parallel \overline{DC}$, $AD = BC$, and $AB < DC$ [Figure 14.49(a)]. Referring to Figure 14.49(b), let P be the point on $\overline{DC}$ such that $\overline{AP} \perp \overline{DC}$. Similarly, let Q be the point on $\overline{DC}$ such that $\overline{BQ} \perp \overline{DC}$. Then $AP = BQ$ since the parallel lines $\overleftrightarrow{AB}$ and $\overleftrightarrow{DC}$ are equidistant everywhere. Also, since $\triangle APD$ and $\triangle BQC$ are right triangles, we can use the Pythagorean theorem to show that $DP = CQ$ (verify). Hence $\triangle ADP \cong \triangle BCQ$ by the SSS congruence property. Consequently, $\angle ADP \cong \angle BCQ$, as desired.

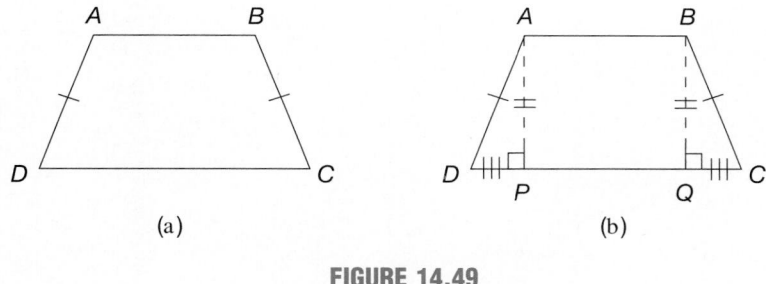

(a)   (b)

FIGURE 14.49

Our next result is an application of the SAS congruence property that establishes a property of the diagonals of a rectangle.

EXAMPLE 14.11 Show that the diagonals of a rectangle are congruent.

Solution
Suppose that $ABCD$ is a rectangle [Figure 14.50(a)]. Then $ABCD$ is a parallelogram (from Chapter 12). By a theorem in Section 14.1, the opposite sides of $ABCD$ are congruent [Figure 14.50(b)]. In particular, $\overline{AB} \cong \overline{DC}$. Consider $\triangle ABC$ and $\triangle DCB$; $\angle ABC \cong \angle DCB$ since they are both right angles. Also, $\overline{CB} \cong \overline{BC}$. Hence $\triangle ABC \cong \triangle DCB$ by the SAS congruence property. Consequently, $\overline{AC} \cong \overline{DB}$, as desired.

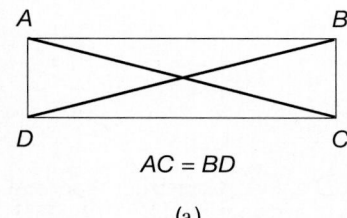

$AC = BD$

(a)

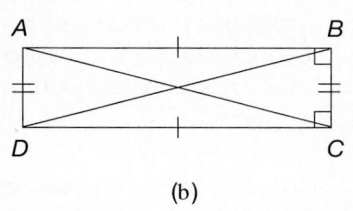

(b)

FIGURE 14.50

The next result is a form of a converse of the theorem in Example 14.11.

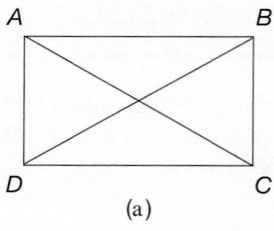

(a)

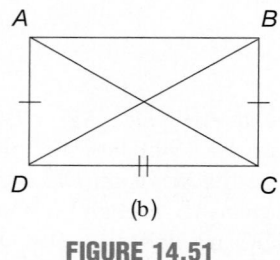

(b)

FIGURE 14.51

EXAMPLE 14.12 In parallelogram *ABCD,* if the diagonals are congruent, it is a rectangle.

Solution
Suppose that *ABCD* is a parallelogram with $\overline{AC} \cong \overline{BD}$ [Figure 14.51(a)]. Since *ABCD* is a parallelogram, $\overline{AD} \cong \overline{BC}$. Therefore, since $\overline{DC} \cong \overline{DC}$, $\triangle ADC \cong \triangle BCD$ by SSS [Figure 14-51(b)]. By corresponding parts, $\angle ADC \cong \angle BCD$. But $\angle ADC$ and $\angle BCD$ are also supplementary because $\overline{AD} \parallel \overline{BC}$. Consequently, $m\angle ADC = m\angle BCD = 90°$ and *ABCD* is a rectangle. ■

Next we verify that every rhombus is a parallelogram using the ASA congruence property and the alternate interior angles theorem.

EXAMPLE 14.13 Show that every rhombus is a parallelogram [Figure 14.52(a)].

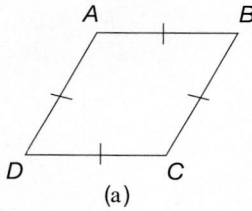

(a)

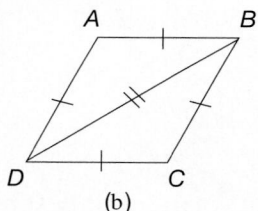

(b)

FIGURE 14.52

Solution
Let *ABCD* be a rhombus. Thus $\overline{AB} \cong \overline{BC} \cong \overline{CD} \cong \overline{DA}$. Construct diagonal $\overline{BD}$ and consider $\triangle ABD$ and $\triangle CDB$ [Figure 14.52(b)]. Since $\overline{BD} \cong \overline{DB}$, it follows that $\triangle ABD \cong \triangle CDB$ by the SSS congruence property. Hence $\angle ABD \cong \angle CDB$ since they are corresponding angles in the congruent triangles. By the alternate interior angles theorem, $\overline{AB} \parallel \overline{DC}$. Also $\angle ADB \cong \angle CBD$ so that $\overline{AD} \parallel \overline{BC}$. Therefore, *ABCD* is a parallelogram since the opposite sides are parallel. ■

Using several geometric constructions and the SSS congruence property, we can prove an important result about right triangles, namely the converse of the Pythagorean theorem.

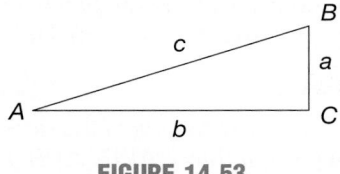

FIGURE 14.53

EXAMPLE 14.14 Suppose that the lengths of the sides of $\triangle ABC$ are a, b, and c with $a^2 + b^2 = c^2$ (Figure 14.53). Show that $\triangle ABC$ is a right triangle.

Solution
Construct a segment $\overline{DE}$ of length b using construction 1 [Figure 14.54(a)]. Next, using construction 5, construct line $\overleftrightarrow{EF}$ such that $\overleftrightarrow{EF} \perp \overline{DE}$ at point E [Figure 14.54(b)]. Next, locate point G on line $\overleftrightarrow{EF}$ so that $EG = a$, using construction 1 [Figure 14.54(c)]. Then $\triangle DEG$ is a right triangle. By the Pythagorean theorem, $DG^2 = DE^2 + EG^2 = a^2 + b^2$. Hence $DG^2 = c^2$ since $a^2 + b^2 = c^2$ by assumption. Thus $DG = c$ [Figure 14.54(d)]. But then $\triangle ACB \cong \triangle DEG$ by the SSS congruence property. Therefore, $\angle ACB \cong \angle DEG$, a right angle, so that $\triangle ACB$ is a right triangle. ∎

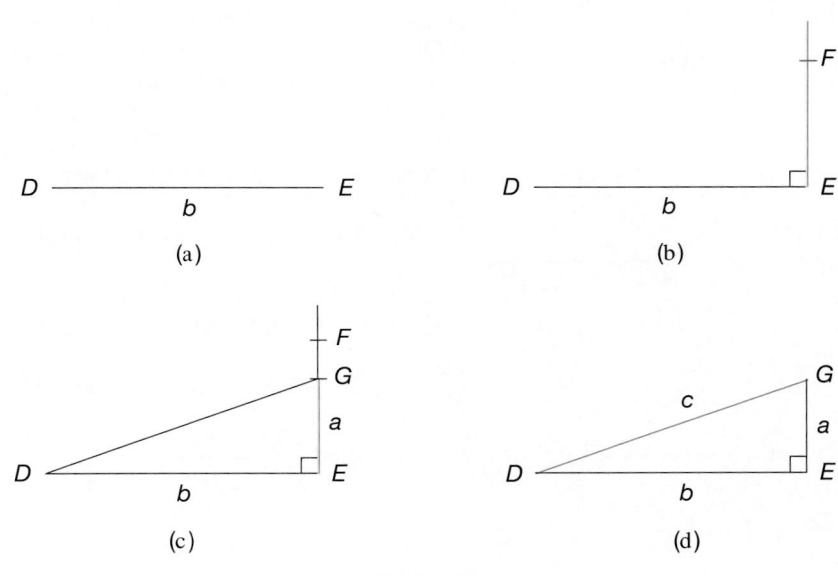

FIGURE 14.54

> **Theorem**
>
> ### Converse of the Pythagorean Theorem
>
> A triangle having sides of lengths a, b, and c, where $a^2 + b^2 = c^2$, is a right triangle.

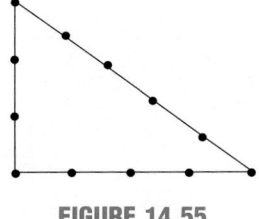

FIGURE 14.55

The converse of the Pythagorean theorem has an interesting application. When carpenters erect the walls of a house, usually they need to make the walls perpendicular to each other. A common way to do this is to use a 12-foot string loop with knots at 1-foot intervals (Figure 14.55). If this loop is stretched into a 3–4–5 triangle, the angle between the "3" and "4" sides must be a right angle by the converse of the Pythagorean theorem since $3^2 + 4^2 = 5^2$.

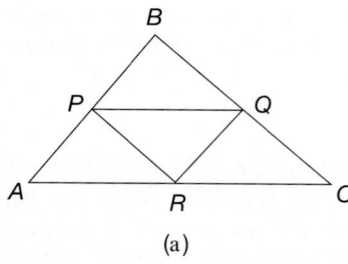

(a)

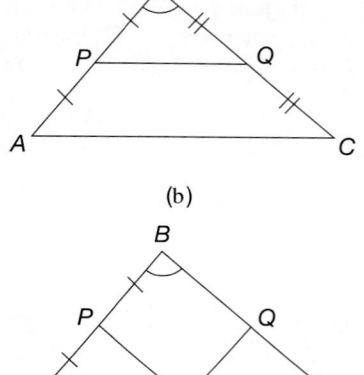

(b)

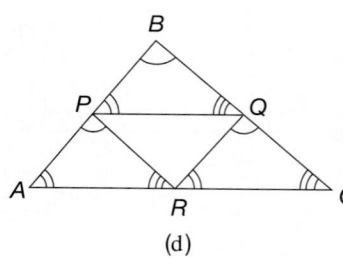

(c)

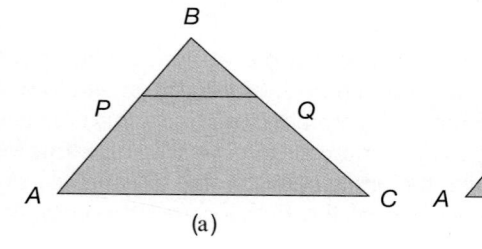

(d)

FIGURE 14.56

The next example presents an interesting result about the midpoints of the sides of a triangle using the SAS similarity property, the SSS similarity property, and the SAS congruence property.

EXAMPLE 14.15 Given $\triangle ABC$, where P, Q, R are the midpoints of the sides $\overline{AB}$, $\overline{BC}$, and $\overline{AC}$, respectively [Figure 14.56(a)], show that $\triangle APR$, $\triangle PBQ$, $\triangle RQC$, and $\triangle QRP$ are all congruent and that each triangle is similar to $\triangle ABC$.

Solution

Consider $\triangle ABC$ and $\triangle PBQ$ [Figure 14.56(b)]. We will first show that these triangles are similar using the SAS similarity property. Since P and Q are the midpoints of their respective sides, we know that $PB = \frac{1}{2}AB$ and that $BQ = \frac{1}{2}BC$. Certainly, $\angle ABC \cong \angle PBQ$, so that $\triangle ABC \sim \triangle PBQ$ by the SAS similarity property. Using a similar argument, we can show that $\triangle APR \sim \triangle ABC$ [Figure 14.56(c)] and that $\triangle RQC \sim \triangle ABC$ [Figure 14.56(d)]. Also, $\triangle QRP \sim \triangle ABC$ by the SSS similarity property (verify). Since $AP = PB$, $\triangle APR \cong \triangle PBQ$ by the ASA congruence property (verify). In similar fashion, we have $\triangle PBQ \cong \triangle RQC$. Combining our results, we can show that $\triangle RQC \cong \triangle QRP$ using the SSS congruence property. Thus we have that all four smaller triangles are congruent. ∎

We close this section with a result that is related to Example 14.15.

EXAMPLE 14.16 Refer to Figure 14.57(a). Suppose that $\triangle ABC$ is a triangle and points P and Q are on $\overline{AB}$ and $\overline{BC}$, respectively, such that $\dfrac{BP}{BA} = \dfrac{BQ}{BC}$; that is, P and Q divide $\overline{BA}$ and $\overline{BC}$ proportionally. Show that $\overline{PQ} \parallel \overline{AC}$ and $\dfrac{PQ}{AC} = \dfrac{BP}{BA}$.

Solution

Consider $\triangle BPQ$ [Figure 14.57(b)]. Since $\dfrac{BP}{BA} = \dfrac{BQ}{BC}$ and $\angle PBQ \cong \angle ABC$, we have that $\triangle ABC \sim \triangle PBQ$ by the SAS similarity property. Hence $\angle BPQ \cong \angle BAC$ since they are corresponding angles in the similar triangles [Figure 14.57(c)]. Thus $\overline{PQ} \parallel \overline{AC}$. Also, $\dfrac{PQ}{AC} = \dfrac{BP}{BA}$ since corresponding sides are proportional in the similar triangles (verify this). ∎

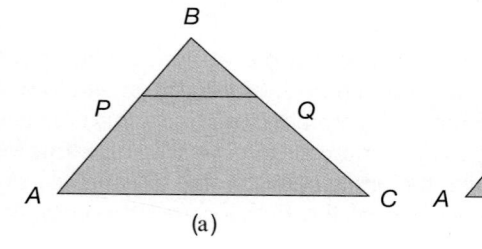

(a)

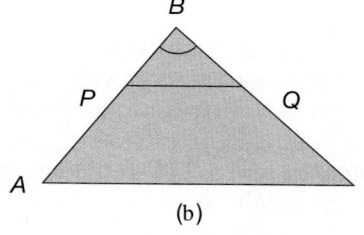

(b)

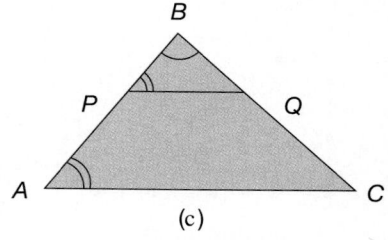

(c)

FIGURE 14.57

From Example 14.16 we see that a line segment that divides two sides of a triangle proportionally is parallel to the third side and proportional to it in the same ratio. In particular, if points P and Q in Example 14.16 were midpoints of the sides, then $\overline{PQ} \parallel \overline{AC}$ and $PQ = \frac{1}{2}AC$. The segment, such as $\overline{PQ}$, that joins the midpoints of two sides of a triangle is called a **midsegment** of the triangle.

Using the result of Example 14.16 regarding the midsegment of a triangle, we can deduce a surprising result about quadrilaterals. Suppose that $ABCD$ is any quadrilateral in the plane (Figure 14.58). Let P, Q, R, and S be the midpoints of the sides. We call $PQRS$ the **midquad** of $ABCD$ since it is a quadrilateral that is formed by joining midpoints of the sides of $ABCD$. By Example 14.16, $\overline{PQ} \parallel \overline{AC}$ and $\overline{SR} \parallel \overline{AC}$. Thus $\overline{PQ} \parallel \overline{SR}$. Similarly, $\overline{PS} \parallel \overline{QR}$. Therefore, $PQRS$ is a parallelogram.

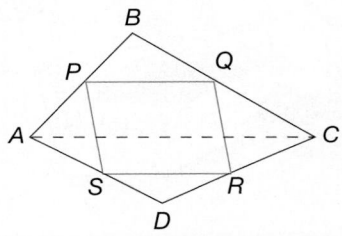

FIGURE 14.58

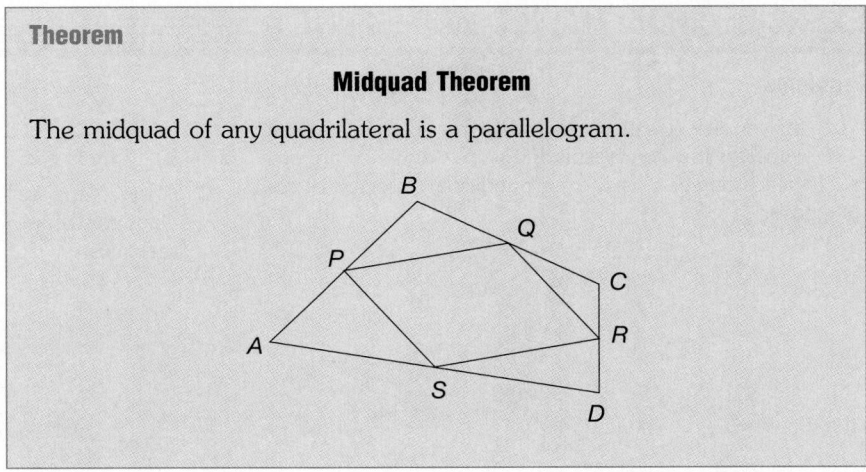

Theorem

Midquad Theorem

The midquad of any quadrilateral is a parallelogram.

The proof above shows that $PQRS$ is a parallelogram. But could it be a square? A rectangle? A rhombus? The problem set contains some problems that will lead you to decide precisely under what conditions these special quadrilaterals are possible.

Using congruence and similarity properties of triangles, we have been able to verify, in a deductive manner, many results that are visually plausible. That is, triangle congruence and similarity conditions permit us to verify conjectures about geometric shapes that we have formed through investigations of drawings, construction activities, or in other ways. Suggested activities for computer software to help students formulate and test geometric conjectures is contained in the Technology Section.

MATHEMATICAL MORSEL

Although the name of the Greek mathematician Pythagoras (circa 500 B.C.) is associated with the famous Pythagorean theorem, there is no doubt that this result was known prior to the time of Pythagoras. In fact, the discovery of a Babylonian method for finding the diagonal of a square, given the length of the side of the square, suggests that the theorem was known more than 1000 years before Pythagoras. Interestingly, it has been asserted that Pythagoras's greatest achievement was that he was the first European who insisted that postulates must be set down first when developing geometry, a contribution to mathematics often attributed to Euclid.

EXERCISE/PROBLEM SET 14.5—PART A

Problems

1. Answer the questions below to prove the following property: If a line bisects the vertex angle of an isosceles triangle, it is the perpendicular bisector of the base.

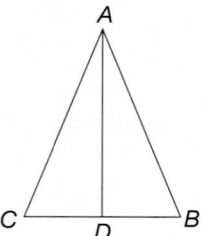

(a) You are given that $\triangle ABC$ is isosceles with base $\overline{BC}$ and that $\overline{AD}$ bisects $\angle CAB$. What pairs of angles or segments are congruent because of the given information?

(b) What other pair of corresponding angles of $\triangle ABD$ and $\triangle ACD$ are congruent? Why?

(c) What congruence property can be used to prove $\triangle ABD \cong \triangle ACD$?

(d) Why is $\angle ADC \cong \angle ADB$ and $\overline{DC} \cong \overline{DB}$?

(e) Why is $\overline{AD} \perp \overline{BC}$?

(f) Why is $\overline{AD}$ the perpendicular bisector of $\overline{BC}$?

2. Answer the following questions to prove that the diagonals of a rhombus bisect the vertex angles of the rhombus.

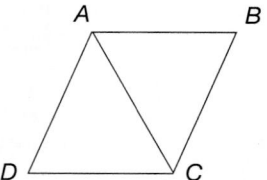

(a) Given the rhombus $ABCD$ and diagonal $\overline{AC}$, what pairs of corresponding sides of $\triangle ABC$ and $\triangle ADC$ are congruent?

(b) What other pair of corresponding sides are congruent? Why?

(c) What congruence property can be used to show that $\triangle ABC \cong \triangle ADC$?

(d) Why is $\angle BAC \cong \angle DAC$ and $\angle BCA \cong \angle DCA$?

(e) Why does $\overline{AC}$ bisect $\angle DAB$ and $\angle DCB$?

3. Given rhombus *ABCD* with diagonals meeting at point *E*, prove that the diagonals of a rhombus are perpendicular to each other. (HINT: Show that △*ABE* ≅ △*CBE* ≅ △*ADE*.)

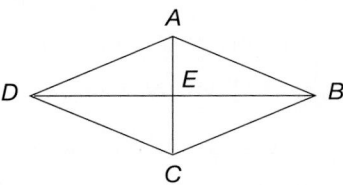

4. Prove: Consecutive angles of a parallelogram *ABCD* are supplementary.

5. A rectangle is sometimes defined as a parallelogram with at least one right angle. If parallelogram *PQRS* has a right angle at *P*, verify that *PQRS* has four right angles.

6. In quadrilateral *ABCD*, both pairs of opposite sides are congruent. Prove that *ABCD* is a parallelogram. (HINT: Draw a diagonal $\overline{BD}$.)

7. In quadrilateral *PQRS*, both pairs of opposite angles are congruent. Prove that *PQRS* is a parallelogram.

8. Prove that the diagonals of a parallelogram bisect each other.

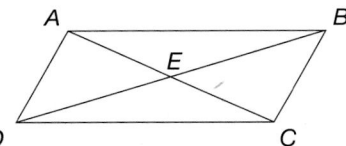

9. Quadrilateral *STUV* is a rhombus and ∠*S* is a right angle. Show that *STUV* is a square.

10. Quadrilateral *STUV* is a rhombus and diagonals $\overline{SU}$ and $\overline{TV}$ are congruent. Show that *STUV* is a square.

11. Construct a parallelogram with adjacent sides and one diagonal congruent to the given segments.

_____ a
one side

_____ b
second
side

_____ d
diagonal

12. Construct a rhombus with sides and one diagonal congruent to the given segment.

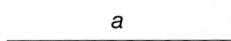
a

13. Construct an isosceles trapezoid with bases and legs congruent to the given segments.

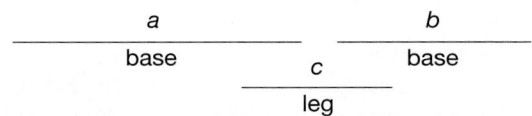

14. If $\overline{CD} \perp \overline{AB}$ in △*ABC* and *AC* is the geometric mean of *AD* and *AB*, prove that △*ABC* is a right triangle. (HINT: Show that △*ADC* ∼ △*ACB*.)

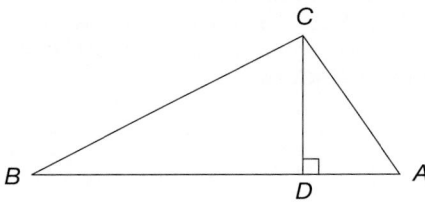

15. The midquad theorem in this section states that the midquad of any quadrilateral *PQRS* is a parallelogram.
   (a) Use the fact that each side of the midquad is parallel to and one-half the length of a diagonal of the quadrilateral to determine under what conditions the midquad $M_1M_2M_3M_4$ will be a rectangle.

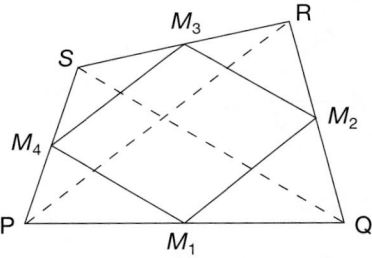

   (b) Under what conditions will the midquad $M_1M_2M_3M_4$ be a rhombus?
   (c) Under what conditions will the midquad $M_1M_2M_3M_4$ be a square?

16. Complete the following argument which uses similarity to prove the Pythagorean theorem. Let △*ABC* have ∠*C* as a right angle. Let $\overline{CD}$ be perpendicular to $\overline{AB}$.

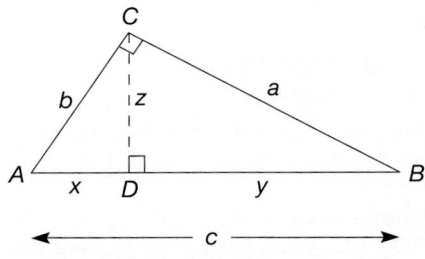

   (a) Then △*ADC* ∼ △*ACB*. Why?
   (b) Also △*BDC* ∼ △*BCA*. Why?

Thus $\dfrac{b}{x} = \dfrac{x + y}{b}$, or $b^2 = x^2 + xy$.

Also $\dfrac{a}{y} = \dfrac{x + y}{a}$, or $a^2 = xy + y^2$.

(c) Show that $a^2 + b^2 = c^2$.

17. Show that the SSS congruence property follows from the SAS congruence property. (HINT: Referring to the figure, assume the SAS congruence property and suppose that the respective sides of $\triangle ABC$ and $\triangle A'B'C'$ are congruent as marked. Assume that $\angle A$ is acute and then construct $\triangle ABD$ as illustrated so that $\angle BAD \cong \angle B'A'C'$ and $AD = A'C'$. Without using the SSS congruence property, show $\triangle BAD \cong \triangle B'A'C'$, $\triangle BAD \cong \triangle BAC$, etc.)

18. Show that the AA similarity property follows from the SAS similarity property. Referring to the figure, suppose that $\angle A \cong \angle A'$ and $\angle B \cong \angle B'$. Show that $\triangle ABC \sim \triangle A'B'C'$ *without* using the AA similarity property. (HINT: If $\dfrac{AC}{AB} = \dfrac{A'C'}{A'B'}$, then $\triangle ABC \sim \triangle A'B'C'$ by the SAS similarity property. If $\dfrac{AC}{AB} \neq \dfrac{A'C'}{A'B'}$, a D' can be found on $\overline{A'C'}$ such that $\dfrac{AC}{AB} = \dfrac{A'D'}{A'C'}$. Use the SAS similarity property to reach a contradiction.)

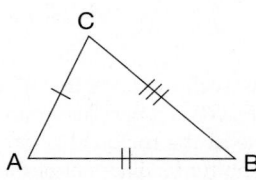

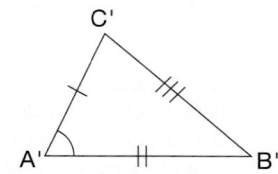

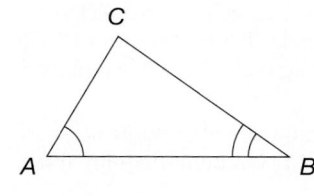

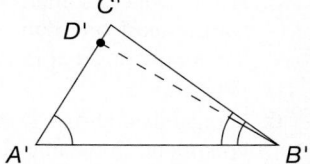

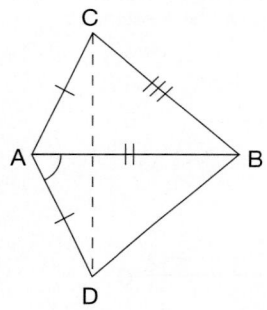

EXERCISE/PROBLEM SET 14.5—PART B

Problems

1. Given that $\triangle PQR$ is an equilateral triangle, show that it is also equiangular.

2. Another justification that the diagonal of a rhombus bisects the vertex angles follows from the questions below.
   (a) Since a rhombus is a parallelogram, $\overline{AB} \parallel \overline{CD}$ and $\overline{AD} \parallel \overline{BC}$. What pairs of angles are thereby congruent?
   (b) $\angle 1 \cong \angle 2$ and $\angle 3 \cong \angle 4$. Why?
   (c) Can we say $\angle 1 \cong \angle 4$ and $\angle 2 \cong \angle 3$? Why?

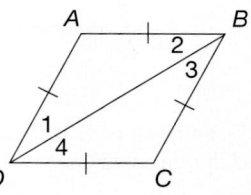

3. Given an isosceles trapezoid $ABCD$ with parallel bases $\overline{AB}$ and $\overline{DC}$, use congruent triangles to prove that diagonals $\overline{AC}$ and $\overline{BD}$ are congruent.

4. Prove: If a trapezoid is isosceles, its opposite angles are supplementary.

5. A rhombus is sometimes defined as a parallelogram with two adjacent congruent sides. If parallelogram *DEFG* has congruent sides $\overline{DE}$ and $\overline{EF}$, verify that it has four congruent sides (thus satisfying our definition of a rhombus).

6. Prove: If a pair of opposite sides of quadrilateral *ABCD* are parallel and congruent, the quadrilateral is a parallelogram. (HINT: Let $\overline{AB} \parallel \overline{DC}$, $\overline{AB} \cong \overline{DC}$; draw $\overline{BD}$.)

7. In quadrilateral *ABCD,* the diagonals bisect each other, meeting at point *E.* Prove that *ABCD* is a parallelogram.

8. Prove that *every* rectangle is a parallelogram.

9. Given parallelogram *LMNO* with perpendicular diagonals $\overline{LN}$ and $\overline{MO}$ meeting at point *P,* prove that *LMNO* is a rhombus.

10. Quadrilateral *HIJK* is a rectangle, and diagonals $\overline{HJ}$ and $\overline{IK}$, meeting at point *L,* are perpendicular. Prove that *HIJK* is a square.

11. Quadrilateral *HIJK* is a rectangle, and adjacent sides $\overline{HI}$ and $\overline{IJ}$ are congruent. Prove that *HIJK* is a square.

12. Construct a rectangle with a side and a diagonal congruent to the given segments.

_____   _____

     side   diagonal

13. Construct a square with diagonals congruent to the given segment.

_____

                d

14. (a) Prove: If diagonals of a quadrilateral are perpendicular bisectors of each other, the quadrilateral is a rhombus.
(b) Construct a rhombus with diagonals congruent to the two segments given.

_____

                a

_____

                b

15. Prove: Two isosceles triangles, $\triangle DEF$ and $\triangle RST,$ are similar if a base angle of one is congruent to a base angle of the other. (Let $\angle D$ and $\angle R$ be the congruent base angles and $\angle E$ and $\angle S$ be the nonbase angles.)

16. In $\triangle ABC$, $\overline{CD} \perp \overline{AB}$ and *CD* is the geometric mean of *AD* and *DB.* Prove that $\triangle ABC$ is a right triangle.

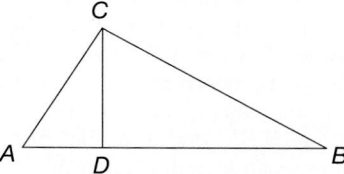

17. Refer to the figure. To inscribe a regular decagon in a circle of radius 1, it must be possible to construct the length *x.*

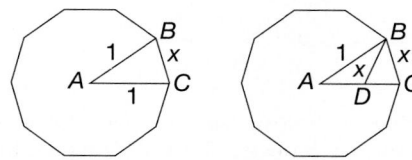

(a) What is $m(\angle BAC)$, $m(\angle ABC)$, and $m(\angle ACB)$?
(b) An arc of length *x* is constructed with center *B,* meeting $\overline{AC}$ at point *D.* What is $m(\angle BCD)$ and $m(\angle CBD)$?
(c) What is $m(\angle ABD)$? What special kind of triangle is $\triangle ABD$?
(d) What are the lengths of $\overline{AD}$ and $\overline{DC}$?
(e) Consider the following triangles copied from the drawing above. Label angle and side measures that are known. Are these triangles similar?

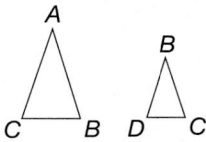

(f) Complete the proportions: $\dfrac{AC}{?} = \dfrac{BC}{?}$ or $\dfrac{1}{?} = \dfrac{x}{?}$
(g) Solve this proportion for *x.* [HINT: You may need to recall the quadratic formula. To solve the equation $ax^2 + bx + c = 0$,

$$\text{use } x = (-b + \sqrt{b^2 - 4ac})/2a.]$$

(h) Can we construct a segment of length *x?*

18. (a) Show that the diagonals of kite *ABCD* are perpendicular.
(HINT: Show that $\triangle AEB \cong \triangle AED$.)

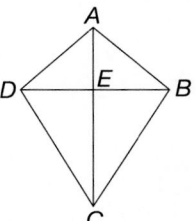

(b) Find a formula for the area of a kite in terms of the lengths of its diagonals.

19. Show that the ASA congruence property follows from the SAS congruence property. (HINT: Referring to the figure below, if $AC = A'C'$, then $\triangle ABC \cong \triangle A'B'C'$ by the SAS congruence property. If not, find a D' on $\overline{A'C'}$ such that $AC = A'D'$, show that $\triangle ABC \cong \triangle A'B'D'$, and use the SAS congruence property to reach a contradiction.)

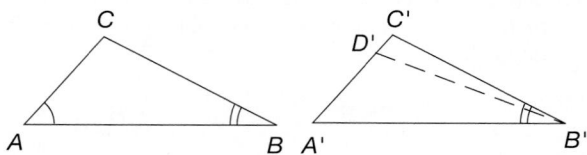

20. Show that the SSS similarity property follows from the SAS similarity property. (HINT: Referring to the figure, assume the SAS similarity property and suppose that the sides in $\triangle ABC$ and $\triangle A'B'C'$ are proportional, as marked. Assume that $\angle A$ is acute and construct $\triangle ABD$ as illustrated below so that $\angle BAD \cong \angle B'A'C'$ and $\dfrac{AD}{AB} = \dfrac{A'C'}{A'B'}$. Show that $\triangle BAD \sim \triangle B'A'C'$, $\triangle BAD \sim \triangle BAC$, and use the SAS congruence property.)

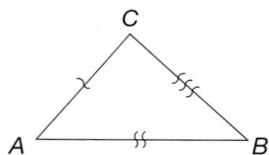

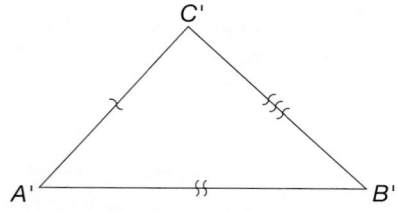

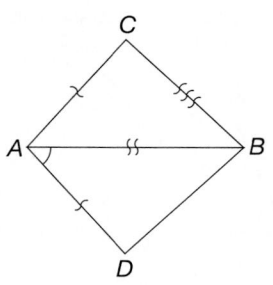

21. Euclid's proof of the Pythagorean theorem is as follows. Refer to the figure and justify each part.

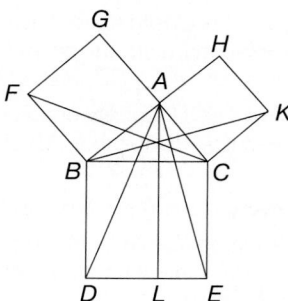

(a) Show that $\triangle ABD \cong \triangle FBC$ and $\triangle ACE \cong \triangle KCB$.

(b) Show that the area of $\triangle ABD$ plus the area of $\triangle ACE$ is one-half the area of square $BCED$.

(c) Show that the area of $\triangle FBC$ is one-half the area of square $ABFG$, and that the area of $\triangle KCB$ is one-half the area of square $ACKH$.

(d) Show that the area of square $ABFG$ plus the area of square $ACKH$ is the area of square $BCED$.

(e) How does this prove the Pythagorean theorem?

SOLUTION OF INITIAL PROBLEM

An eastbound bicycle enters a tunnel at the same time that a westbound bicycle enters the other end of the tunnel. The eastbound bicycle travels at 10 kilometers per hour, the westbound bicycle at 8 kilometers per hour. A fly is flying back and forth between the two bicycles at 15 kilometers per hour, leaving the eastbound bicycle as it enters the tunnel. The tunnel is 9 kilometers long. How far has the fly traveled in the tunnel when the bicycles meet?

Strategy: Identify Subgoals

We know the rate at which the fly is flying (15 km/h). If we can determine the time that the fly is traveling, we can determine the distance the fly travels, since distance = rate × time. Therefore, our subgoal is to find the time that the fly travels. But this is the length of time that it takes the two bicycles to meet.

Let t be the time in hours that it takes for the bicycles to meet. The eastbound bicycle travels $10 \cdot t$ kilometers and the westbound bicycle travels $8 \cdot t$ kilometers. This yields

$$10t + 8t = 9,$$

so that

$$18t = 9,$$

or

$$t = \frac{1}{2}.$$

Therefore, the time that it takes for the bicycles to meet is $\frac{1}{2}$ hour. (This reaches our subgoal.) Consequently, the fly travels for $\frac{1}{2}$ hour, so that the fly travels $15 \times \frac{1}{2} = 7\frac{1}{2}$ km.

Additional Problems Where the Strategy "Identify Subgoals" Is Useful

1. Find the smallest square that has a factor of 360.
2. The areas of the sides of a rectangular box are 24 cm^2, 32 cm^2, and 48 cm^2. What is the volume of the box?
3. Thirty-two percent of n is 128. Find n mentally.

WRITING/DISCUSSING FOR UNDERSTANDING

1. Describe how to construct all regular n-gons possible, using a compass and straightedge, for $n \leq 10$.
2. Identify and describe several pairs of congruent (or similar) triangles in your classroom or around your campus. Explain how you know that they are congruent (or similar).
3. Suppose that instead of compass and straightedge constructions, constructions using a protractor and straightedge were allowed. Would this change make constructions easier or more difficult to do? In particular, how would this affect the constructions of regular polygons?

PROJECTS

1. Choose an object whose height you cannot measure directly, such as a tree, building, or flagpole, and estimate its height. Then devise at least two methods using similar triangles to measure its height indirectly. Test

your method first by measuring the height of another object that you can measure directly. Then measure the height of the tree, building, and so on. Compare your result to your original estimate and describe the technique you used.

2. A transit and sonar are two ways to measure distances indirectly. Find out how these two methods work and find one other way to measure indirectly different from the methods in this chapter.

3. The book *The Pythagorean Proposition* contains over a hundred proofs of the Pythagorean theorem. If you can find a copy, peruse it and select two of your favorite proofs. Explain why you preferred those proofs.

4. Some very elegant designs can be created using only compass and straightedge. Make and color or paint some of your own. You may want to examine some geometry or art books to get ideas.

CHAPTER REVIEW

Major Ideas

1. Comparing combinations of sides and/or angles is sufficient to determine if two triangles are congruent or similar, using the SAS, ASA, and SSS congruence properties and the SAS, AA, and SSS similarity properties.

2. Basic geometric constructions with compass and straightedge can be justified using congruence and similarity properties of triangles.

3. The circumcenter, incenter, orthocenter, and centroid can be constructed using a compass and straightedge.

4. Infinitely many regular n-gons can be constructed, but only for certain values of n. Gauss's theorem determines precisely which regular polygons are constructible with compass and straightedge.

5. Congruence and similarity properties of triangles can be used to perform indirect measurements, and construct lengths representing real numbers.

6. The converse of the Pythagorean theorem can be used to determine if a triangle has a right angle.

Following is a list of key vocabulary, notation, and ideas for this chapter. Mentally review these items and, where appropriate, write down the meaning of each term. Then restudy the material that you are unsure of before proceeding to take the chapter test.

SECTION 14.1: CONGRUENCE OF TRIANGLES

Vocabulary/Notation

Congruent line segments, $\overline{AB} \cong \overline{DE}$ 697
Congruent angles, $\angle ABC \cong \angle DEF$ 697
Correspondence between $\triangle ABC$ and $\triangle DEF$, $A \leftrightarrow D, B \leftrightarrow E, C \leftrightarrow F$ 697
Congruent triangles, $\triangle ABC \cong \triangle DEF$ 698

Ideas

SAS congruence property 699
ASA congruence property 700
SSS congruence property 702

SECTION 14.2: SIMILARITY OF TRIANGLES

Vocabulary/Notation

Similar triangles, $\triangle ABC \sim \triangle DEF$ 710
Fractals 714
Self-similar 715

Ideas

SAS similarity property 713
AA similarity property 713
SSS similarity property 713
Applying similarity properties in indirect measurement 713
Self-similarity 715

SECTION 14.3: BASIC EUCLIDEAN CONSTRUCTIONS

Vocabulary/Notation

Arc 724
Angle bisector 726

Ideas

Compass and straightedge properties 724
Basic constructions with compass and straightedge:
    Copy a line segment 724
    Copy an angle 724
    Construct the perpendicular bisector of a line segment 725
    Bisect an angle 726
    Construct a line perpendicular to a given line through a point on the line 728
    Construct a line perpendicular to a given line through a point not on the line 728
    Construct a line parallel to a given line 729

SECTION 14.4: ADDITIONAL EUCLIDEAN CONSTRUCTIONS

Vocabulary/Notation

Circumscribed circle 735
Inscribed circle 735
Tangent line to a circle 735
Circumcenter 735
Incenter 735

Distance from a point to a line 737
Orthocenter 737
Centroid 737
Fermat prime 739

PEOPLE IN MATHEMATICS

Hypatia (370?–415) is the first woman mathematician to be mentioned in the history of mathematics. She was the daughter of the mathematician Theon of Alexandria, who is chiefly known for his editions of Euclid's *Elements*. At the university in Alexandria, she was a famous lecturer in philosophy and mathematics, but we do not know if she had an official teaching position. It is said that she followed the practice of philosophers of her time, dressing in a tattered cloak and holding public discussions in the center of the city. Hypatia became a victim of the prejudice of her time. Christians in Alexandria were hostile toward the university and the pagan Greek culture it represented. There were periodic outbreaks of violence, and during one of these incidents Hypatia was killed by a mob of Christian fanatics.

Benoit Mandelbrot (1924–) once said "Clouds are not spheres, mountains are not cones, coastlines are not circles and bark is not smooth, nor does lightning travel in a straight line." This is how he describes the inspiration for fractal geometry, a new field of mathematics that finds order in chaotic, irregular shapes and processes. Mandelbrot was largely responsible for developing the mathematics of fractal geometry, while at IBM's Watson Research Center. Before Mandelbrot, other mathematicians had considered the requisite mathematics, but they described it as "pathological," giving rise to "mathematical monstrosities." "The question I raised in 1967 is, 'How long is the coast of Britain?' and the correct answer is "It all depends." It depends on the size of the instrument used to measure length. As the measurement becomes increasingly refined, the measured length will increase. Thus, the coastline is of infinite length in some sense."

CHAPTER 14 TEST

Knowledge

1. True or false?
   (a) Two triangles are congruent if two sides and the included angle of one triangle are congruent, respectively, to two sides and the included angle of the other triangle.
   (b) Two triangles are similar if two sides of one triangle are proportional to two sides of the other triangle.
   (c) The opposite sides of a parallelogram are congruent.
   (d) The diagonals of a kite are perpendicular.
   (e) Every rhombus is a kite.
   (f) The diagonals of a parallelogram bisect each other.
   (g) The circumcenter of a triangle is the intersection of the altitudes.
   (h) The incenter of a triangle is equidistant from the vertices.

Skill

2. For which of the following values of n can a regular n-gon be constructed with compass and straightedge?
   (a) 36   (b) 85   (c) 144   (d) 4369

3. Construct a regular 12-gon with compass and straightedge.

4. Construct the circumcenter and incenter for the same equilateral triangle. What conclusion can you draw?

Understanding

5. Given segment $\overline{AB}$ below as the unit segment, construct a segment $\overline{AC}$ where the length of $\overline{AC}$ is $\sqrt{5}$. Then construct a square with area 5.

$$A \qquad\qquad B$$

6. Prove or disprove: If $\triangle ABC \cong \triangle CBA$, then $\triangle ABC$ is isosceles.

7. Prove or disprove: If $\triangle ABC \cong \triangle BCA$, then $\triangle ABC$ is equilateral.

Problem Solving/Application

8. Given: Trapezoid $ABCD$.

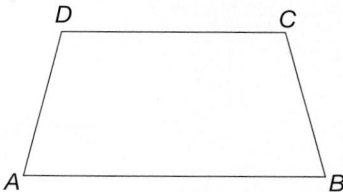

   (a) Prove: If $\angle A \cong \angle B$, then $\overline{AD} \cong \overline{BC}$.
   (b) Prove: If $\overline{AD} \cong \overline{BC}$, then $\angle A \cong \angle B$.

9. (a) According to Gauss's theorem, a regular 9-gon cannot be constructed with a compass and straightedge. Why?
   (b) What is the measure of a central angle in a regular 9-gon?
   (c) Suppose that one wanted to trisect a 60° angle (i.e., divide it into three congruent angles) with a compass and straightedge. What angle would be constructed?
   (d) What conclusion can you draw from parts (a), (b), and (c) regarding the possibility of trisecting a 60° angle?

10. In $\triangle ABC$, segment $\overline{PQ} \parallel \overline{BC}$ and $\angle AQP$ is a right angle.

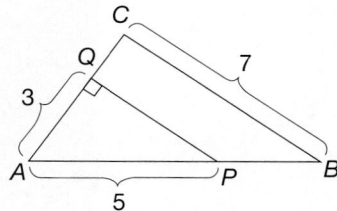

   (a) Find the length of $\overline{PQ}$.
   (b) Find the area of $\triangle ABC$.

Geometry Using Coordinates

René Descartes

René Descartes and Coordinate Geometry

The subjects of algebra and geometry had evolved on parallel tracks until René Descartes (1596–1650) developed a method of joining them. This important contribution made possible the development of the calculus. Because of this contribution, Descartes has been called the "father of modern mathematics." The coordinate system used in analytic geometry is called the Cartesian coordinate system in his honor.

Descartes' analytic geometry was designed to study the mathematical attributes of lines and curves by representing them via equations. These equations were obtained by picturing the curves in the plane.

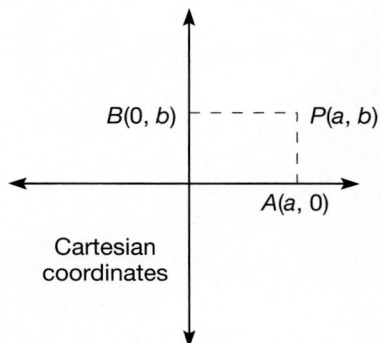

Cartesian coordinates

Each point, P, in the plane was labeled using pairs of numbers or "coordinates" determined by two perpendicular reference lines.

A second convenient way of representing curves in the plane is through the use of polar coordinates, where every point, P, of the plane can be located using a reference angle, θ, whose vertex is called the origin, and a distance, r, from the origin.

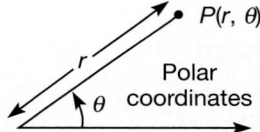

Polar coordinates

What is impressive about the coordinate approach, either Cartesian or polar, is that geometric problems can be represented using algebraic equations. Then algebra can be applied to these equations without regard to their geometric representations. Finally, the result of the algebra can be reinterpreted to produce a solution to the original geometric problem.

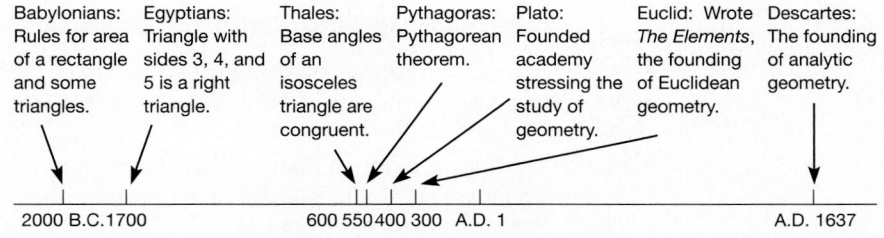

Babylonians: Rules for area of a rectangle and some triangles.

Egyptians: Triangle with sides 3, 4, and 5 is a right triangle.

Thales: Base angles of an isosceles triangle are congruent.

Pythagoras: Pythagorean theorem.

Plato: Founded academy stressing the study of geometry.

Euclid: Wrote *The Elements*, the founding of Euclidean geometry.

Descartes: The founding of analytic geometry.

2000 B.C. 1700   600 550 400 300   A.D. 1   A.D. 1637

STRATEGY 20: USE COORDINATES

In many two-dimensional geometry problems, we can use a "grid" of squares overlaid on the plane, called a coordinate system, to gain additional information. This numerical information can then be used to solve problems about two-dimensional figures. Coordinate systems also can be used in three-dimensional space and on curved surfaces such as a sphere (e.g., the Earth).

Initial Problem

A surveyor plotted a triangular building lot, drew the following diagram, and recorded the following data. What is the area of the lot, in square feet? (NOTE: East 207' means 207 feet east of stake S.)

Stake	Position Relative to S
U	East 207', North 35'
T	East 40', North 185'

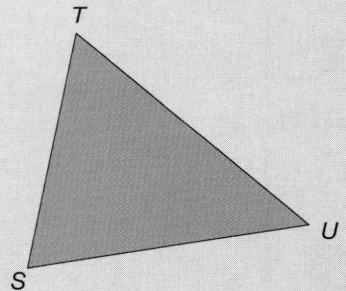

Clues

The Use Coordinates strategy may be appropriate when:

- A problem can be represented using two variables.
- A geometry problem cannot easily be solved by using traditional Euclidean methods.
- Finding representations of lines or conic sections.
- A problem involves slope, parallel lines, perpendicular lines, and so on.
- The location of a geometric shape with respect to other shapes is important.
- A problem involves maps.

A solution of the Initial Problem above appears on page 804.

INTRODUCTION

In this chapter we study geometry using the coordinate plane. Using a coordinate system on the plane, which was introduced in Section 9.3, we are able to derive many elegant geometrical results about lines, polygons, circles, and so on. In Section 15.1 we introduce the basic ideas needed to study geometry in the coordinate plane. Then in Section 15.2 we prove properties of geometric shapes using these concepts. Finally, Section 15.3 contains many interesting problems that can be solved using coordinate geometry.

15.1

DISTANCE AND SLOPE IN THE COORDINATE PLANE

Distance

The use of coordinates as developed in Section 9.3 allows us to analyze many properties of geometric figures. For example, we can find distances between points in the plane by using coordinates. Consider points $P(a, b)$ and $Q(c, d)$ (Figure 15.1). We can use point $R(c, b)$ to form a right triangle, $\triangle PQR$. Notice that the length of the horizontal segment $\overline{PR}$ is $c - a$ and that the length of the vertical segment $\overline{QR}$ is $d - b$. We wish to find the length of $\overline{PQ}$. By the Pythagorean theorem,

$$PQ^2 = PR^2 + QR^2,$$

so

$$PQ = \sqrt{PR^2 + QR^2}.$$

But

$$PR^2 = (c - a)^2 \quad \text{and} \quad QR^2 = (d - b)^2.$$

Hence $PQ = \sqrt{(c - a)^2 + (d - b)^2}$. This yields the following distance formula.

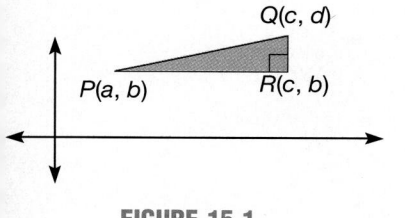

FIGURE 15.1

Theorem

Coordinate Distance Formula

If P is the point (a, b) and Q is the point (c, d), the distance from P to Q is

$$PQ = \sqrt{(c - a)^2 + (d - b)^2}.$$

STUDENT PAGE SNAPSHOT

ACTIVITY MATH *CONNECTION*: GEOMETRY

Finding Length

An airline navigator has plotted three airports and labelled them *A*, *B*, and *C* on a coordinate grid. How can the navigator find the distances between the airports?

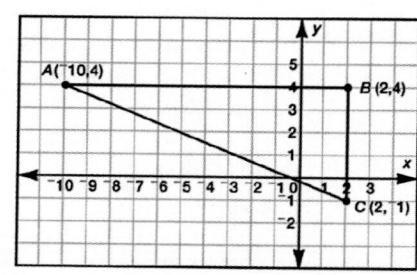

WORKING TOGETHER

1. Points *A* and *B* lie on a horizontal line. Count units to find the length of $\overline{AB}$.

2. Look at the *x*-coordinates of points *A* and *B*. How can you use them to find the length of $\overline{AB}$?

3. Points *B* and *C* lie on a vertical line. Count units to find the length of $\overline{BC}$.

4. Look at the *y*-coordinates of points *B* and *C*. How can you use them to find the length of $\overline{BC}$?

5. What method can you use to find the length of $\overline{AC}$?

To find the length of a horizontal or vertical line segment, the navigator subtracted the unlike coordinates of the endpoints and then found the absolute value.

	AB	**BC**
Unlike coordinates	⁻10, 2	4, ⁻1
Subtract	⁻10 − 2 = ⁻12	4 − (⁻1) = 5
Absolute value	|⁻12| = 12	|5| = 5

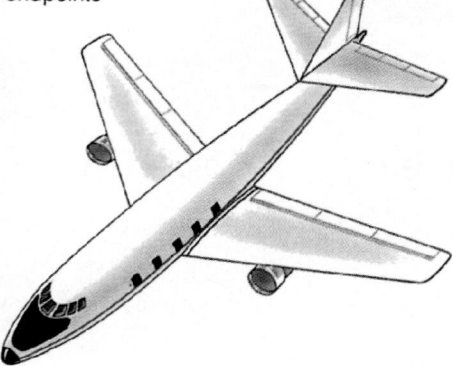

He then used the Pythagorean Theorem to find the length of the third line segment $\overline{AC}$.

$$AB^2 + BC^2 = AC^2$$
$$12^2 + 5^2 = AC^2$$
$$25 + 144 = AC^2$$
$$169 = AC^2$$
$$13 = AC$$

SHARING IDEAS

6. Why can the navigator use the Pythagorean Theorem to find the missing side?

7. Why can you not subtract coordinates to find the length of $\overline{AC}$?

8. How would you find the distance between two points—*Q* (3, 3) and *P* (⁻5, ⁻3)—that do not lie on a horizontal or a vertical line?

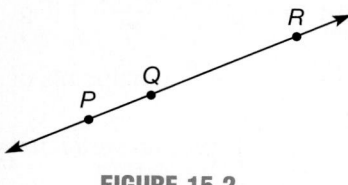

FIGURE 15.2

We have verified the coordinate distance formula in the case that $c \geq a$ and $d \geq b$. However, this formula holds for *all* pairs of points in the plane. For example, if $a \geq c$, we would use $(a - c)^2$ in the formula. But $(a - c)^2 = (c - a)^2$, so that the formula will yield the same result.

We can use the coordinate distance formula to determine if three points are collinear. Recall that points P, Q, and R are collinear with Q between P and R if and only if $PQ + QR = PR$; that is, the distance from P to R is the sum of the distances from P to Q and Q to R (Figure 15.2).

EXAMPLE 15.1   Use the coordinate distance formula to show that the points $P = (-8, -6)$, $Q = (0, 0)$, and $R = (12, 9)$ are collinear.

Solution

$$PQ = \sqrt{[0 - (-8)]^2 + [0 - (-6)]^2} = \sqrt{64 + 36} = 10$$
$$QR = \sqrt{(12 - 0)^2 + (9 - 0)^2} = 15$$
$$PR = \sqrt{[12 - (-8)]^2 + [9 - (-6)]^2} = 25$$

Thus $PQ + QR = 10 + 15 = 25 = PR$, so P, Q, and R are collinear.   ■

Example 15.1 is a special case of the following theorem.

Theorem

Collinearity Test

Points $P(a, b)$, $Q(c, d)$, and $R(e, f)$ are collinear with Q between P and R if and only if $PQ + QR = PR$, or equivalently,

$$\sqrt{(c - a)^2 + (d - b)^2} + \sqrt{(e - c)^2 + (f - d)^2}$$
$$= \sqrt{(e - a)^2 + (f - b)^2}.$$

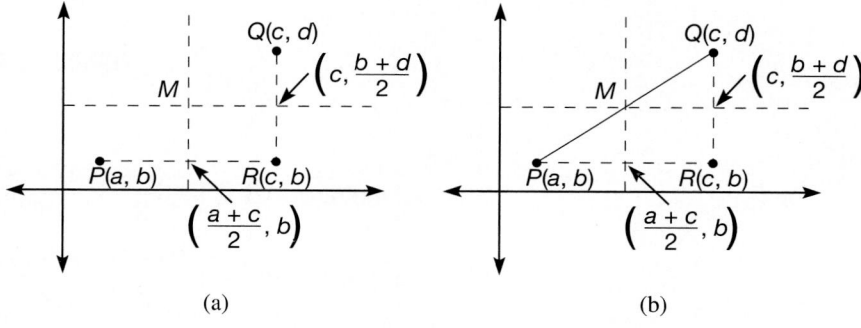

Next we determine the midpoint of a line segment (Figure 15.3).

(a)   (b)

FIGURE 15.3

\Consider $P(a, b)$ and $Q(c, d)$. Let M be the intersection of the vertical line through $\left(\dfrac{a + c}{2}, b\right)$ and the horizontal line through $\left(c, \dfrac{b + d}{2}\right)$ [Figure 15.3(a)]. Notice that $\left(\dfrac{a + c}{2}, b\right)$ and $\left(c, \dfrac{b + d}{2}\right)$ are the midpoints of $\overline{PR}$ and $\overline{QR}$, respectively. Hence $M = \left(\dfrac{a + c}{2}, \dfrac{b + d}{2}\right)$. We can verify that M is the midpoint of segment $\overline{PQ}$ by showing that $PM = MQ$ and that P, M, and Q are collinear [Figure 15.3(b)]. This is left for the problem set.

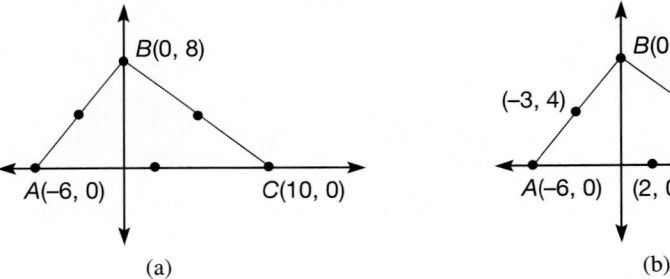

Theorem

Midpoint Formula

If P is the point (a, b) and Q is the point (c, d), the midpoint, M, of $\overline{PQ}$ is the point

$$\left(\frac{a + c}{2}, \frac{b + d}{2}\right).$$

EXAMPLE 15.2   Find the coordinates of the midpoints of the three sides of $\triangle ABC$, where $A = (-6, 0)$, $B = (0, 8)$, $C = (10, 0)$ [Figure 15.4(a)].

(a)

(b)

FIGURE 15.4

Solution

$$\text{midpoint of } \overline{AB} = \left(\frac{-6 + 0}{2}, \frac{0 + 8}{2}\right) = (-3, 4)$$

$$\text{midpoint of } \overline{BC} = \left(\frac{0 + 10}{2}, \frac{8 + 0}{2}\right) = (5, 4)$$

$$\text{midpoint of } \overline{AC} = \left(\frac{-6 + 10}{2}, \frac{0 + 0}{2}\right) = (2, 0) \text{ [Figure 15.4(b)]}$$

Slope

The slope of a line is a measure of its inclination from the horizontal.

Definition

Slope of a Line

Suppose that P is the point (a, b) and Q is the point (c, d).

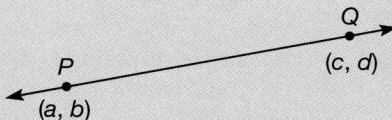

The **slope of line** $\overleftrightarrow{PQ}$ is the ratio $\dfrac{d - b}{c - a}$, provided $a \neq c$. If $a = c$, that is, $\overleftrightarrow{PQ}$ is vertical, then the slope of $\overleftrightarrow{PQ}$ is undefined.

Note that $\dfrac{d - b}{c - a} = \dfrac{b - d}{a - c}$, so that it does not matter which endpoint we use first in computing the slope of a line. However, we must be consistent in the numerator and denominator; that is, we subtract the coordinates of Q from the coordinates of P, or vice versa. The slope of a line is often defined informally as "rise over the run." The **slope of a line segment** is the slope of the line containing it.

EXAMPLE 15.3 Find the slope of the following lines: **(a)** line l containing $P(-8, -6)$ and $Q(10, 5)$, **(b)** line m containing $R(2, 1)$ and $S(20, 12)$, and **(c)** the line n containing $T(-3, 11)$ and $U(4, 11)$ (Figure 15.5).

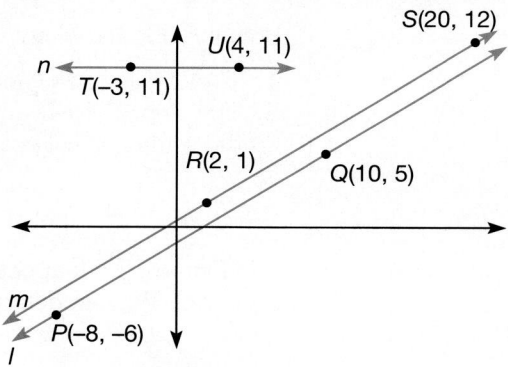

FIGURE 15.5

Solution
(a) Using the coordinates of P and Q, the slope of $l = \dfrac{5 - (-6)}{10 - (-8)} = \dfrac{11}{18}$.

(b) Using the coordinates of R and S, the slope of $m = \dfrac{12 - 1}{20 - 2} = \dfrac{11}{18}$.

Hence lines l and m have equal slopes.

(c) Using points T and U, the slope of line $n = \dfrac{11 - 11}{4 - (-3)} = 0$. Note that line n is horizontal.

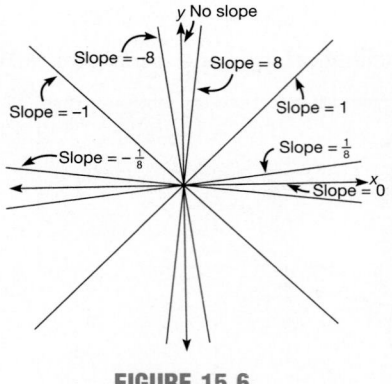

FIGURE 15.6

Figure 15.6 shows examples of lines with various slopes. A horizontal line, such as line n in Example 15.3, has slope 0. As the slope increases, the line "rises" to the right. A line that rises steeply from left to right has a large positive slope. A vertical line has no slope. On the other hand, a line that declines steeply from left to right has a *small* negative slope. For example, in Figure 15.6, the line with slope -8 is steeper than the line with slope -1. A line with a negative slope near zero, such as the line in Figure 15.6 having slope $-\frac{1}{8}$, declines gradually from left to right.

Using slopes, we can determine if several points are collinear. For example, if points P, Q, and R are collinear, then the slope of segment $\overline{PQ}$ is equal to the slope of segment $\overline{PR}$ (Figure 15.7). That is, if P, Q, and R are collinear, then $\dfrac{d - b}{c - a} = \dfrac{f - b}{e - a}$ provided that the slopes exist. If P, Q, and R are collinear and lie on a vertical line, then segments $\overline{PQ}$ and $\overline{PR}$ have no slope.

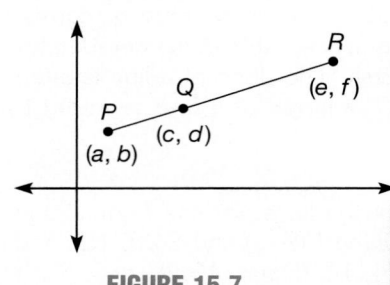

FIGURE 15.7

On the other hand, suppose that P, Q, and R are such that the slope of segment $\overline{PQ}$ is equal to the slope of segment $\overline{PR}$. It can be shown that the points P, Q, and R are collinear. The verification of this result involves similar triangles and is left for the problem set.

Theorem

Slope and Collinearity

Points P, Q, and R are collinear if and only if

1. The slopes of $\overline{PQ}$ and $\overline{QR}$ are equal, or
2. The slopes of $\overline{PQ}$ and $\overline{QR}$ are undefined (i.e., P, Q, and R are on the same vertical line).

In Figure 15.5 it appears that lines l and m, which have the same slope, are parallel. We can determine if two lines are parallel by computing their slopes.

Theorem

Slopes of Parallel Lines

Two lines in the coordinate plane are parallel if and only if

1. Their slopes are equal, or
2. Their slopes are undefined.

In Example 15.3, lines l and m each have slope $\frac{11}{18}$, and therefore are parallel by the slopes of parallel lines theorem. The verification of the slopes of parallel lines theorem is left for the problem set.

Just as we are able to determine if lines are parallel using their slopes, we can also identify perpendicular lines by means of their slopes. For example, consider line l in Figure 15.8(a). Since l contains $(0, 0)$ and (a, b), the

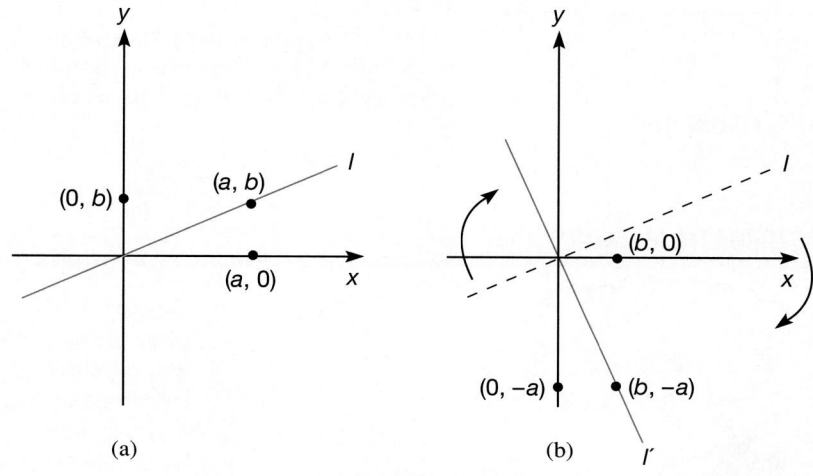

FIGURE 15.8

slope of l is $\dfrac{b - 0}{a - 0} = \dfrac{b}{a}$. If line l is rotated 90° clockwise around $(0, 0)$ to l', then l is perpendicular to l'. Also, point $(b, -a)$ is on l'. So the slope of l' is $\dfrac{-a - 0}{b - 0} = \dfrac{-a}{b}$. Therefore, the product of the slopes of the perpendicular lines l and l' is $\dfrac{b}{a} \times \dfrac{-a}{b} = -1$. Conversely, to show that *if* the product of the slopes of two lines is -1, *then* the lines are perpendicular, we can use a similar argument. This is left for the problem set. In summary, we have the following result.

Theorem

Slopes of Perpendicular Lines

Two lines in the coordinate plane are perpendicular if and only if

1. The product of their slopes is -1, or
2. One line is horizontal and the other is vertical.

Example 15.4 shows how slopes can be used to analyze the diagonals of a rhombus.

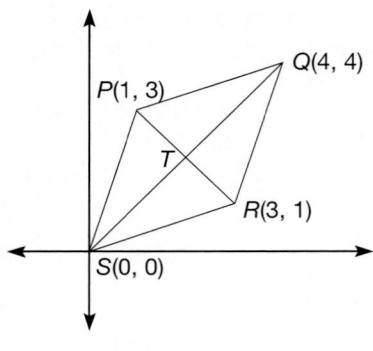

FIGURE 15.9

EXAMPLE 15.4   Show that the diagonals of *PQRS* in Figure 15.9 form right angles at their intersection.

Solution

The slope of diagonal $\overline{PR}$ is $\dfrac{2}{-2} = -1$, and the slope of diagonal $\overline{QS}$ is $\dfrac{4}{4} = 1$. Since the product of their slopes is -1, the diagonals form right angles at T by the slopes of perpendicular lines theorem. Each side of *PQRS* has length $\sqrt{10}$. Thus it is a rhombus. In fact, the result in Example 15.4 holds for *any* rhombus. This result is presented as a problem in Section 15.3. ∎

MATHEMATICAL MORSEL

Descartes was creative in many fields: philosophy, physics, cosmology, chemistry, physiology, and psychology. But he is best known for his contributions to mathematics. He was a frail child of a noble family. As one story goes, due to his frailty, Descartes had a habit of lying in bed, thinking for extended periods. One day, while watching a fly crawling on the ceiling, he set about trying to describe the path of the fly in mathematical language. Thus was born analytic geometry—the study of mathematical attributes of lines and curves.

EXERCISE/PROBLEM SET 15.1—PART A

Exercises

1. Find the slopes of the lines containing the following pairs of points.
   (a) (3, 2) and (5, 3)
   (b) (−2, 1) and (−5, −3)
   (c) (3, −5) and (−6, −5)
   (d) (4, −1) and (4, 2)

2. Use the ratio $\dfrac{d - b}{c - a}$ and the ratio $\dfrac{b - d}{a - c}$ to compute the slopes of the lines containing the following points. Do both ratios give the same result?
   (a) (−4, 5) and (6, −3)
   (b) (−2, −3) and (3, 2)

3. Classify the slopes of each line shown as positive, negative, zero, or undefined (no slope).

(a)

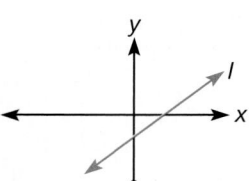

(b)

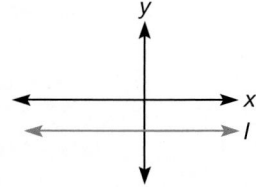

(c)

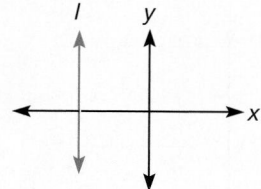

(d)

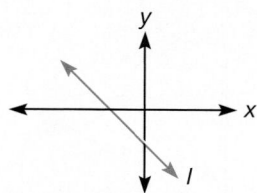

4. Use slopes to determine if $\overline{AB} \parallel \overline{PQ}$.
(a) $A(-1, 0)$, $B(4, 5)$, $P(3, 9)$, $Q(-2, 4)$
(b) $A(0, 4)$, $B(6, 8)$, $P(-4, -6)$, $Q(2, -2)$

5. Use slopes to determine if the given three points are collinear.
(a) $A(3, -2)$, $B(1, 2)$, and $C(-3, 10)$
(b) $A(0, 7)$, $B(2, 11)$, and $C(-2, 1)$

6. Find the distance between the following pairs of points.
(a) $(0, 0)$, $(3, -2)$
(b) $(-4, 2)$, $(-2, 3)$
(c) $(2, 3)$, $(-1, -5)$
(d) $(-3, 5)$, $(-3, -2)$

7. Determine if the following pairs of line segments are parallel.
(a) The segment from $(0, 2)$ to $(1, 3)$ and the segment from $(2, 0)$ to $(3, 2)$
(b) The segment from $(-5, 3)$ to $(-1, 2)$ and the segment from $(-3, 1)$ to $(0, 0)$
(c) The segment from $(-1, 1)$ to $(-1, 4)$ and the segment from $(1, 0)$ to $(1, 4)$
(d) The segment from $(-5, -3)$ to $(-3, -1)$ and the segment from $(-5, -4)$ to $(-2, -1)$

8. Determine if the quadrilaterals with the given vertices are parallelograms.
(a) $(1, 4)$, $(4, 4)$, $(5, 1)$, and $(2, 1)$
(b) $(1, -1)$, $(6, -1)$, $(6, -4)$, and $(1, -4)$
(c) $(1, -2)$, $(4, 2)$, $(6, 2)$, and $(3, -2)$
(d) $(-10, 5)$, $(-5, 10)$, $(10, -5)$, and $(5, -10)$

9. In each part, determine if the line segments joining the given points are perpendicular.
(a) $(3, 3)$, $(3, 9)$, and $(12, 9)$
(b) $(2, 8)$, $(7, 1)$, and $(14, 6)$
(c) $(-8, -3)$, $(8, 2)$, and $(6, 9)$
(d) $(-7, -2)$, $(-4, 4)$, and $(10, -3)$

10. Consider the following quadrilateral.

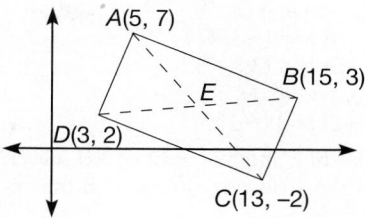

(a) Verify that $ABCD$ is a rectangle.
(b) What do you observe about the lengths BD and AC?
(c) What do you observe about $\overline{AE}$ and $\overline{CE}$? About $\overline{BE}$ and $\overline{DE}$?
(d) Are $\overline{AC}$ and $\overline{BD}$ perpendicular? Explain.
(e) Summarize the properties you have observed about rectangle $ABCD$.

11. Using only the 5×5 array of points, draw quadrilaterals having $\overline{AB}$ as a side.
(a) How many parallelograms are possible?
(b) How many rectangles?
(c) How many rhombuses?
(d) How many squares?

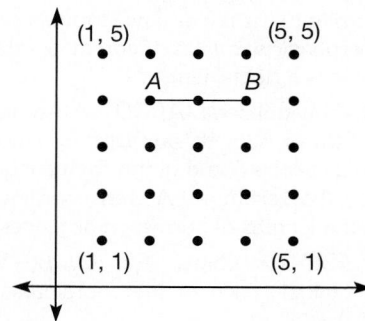

12. Use the distance formula to determine if points P, Q, and R are collinear.
(a) $P(-1, 4)$, $Q(-2, 3)$, and $R(-4, 1)$
(b) $P(-2, 1)$, $Q(3, 4)$, and $R(12, 10)$
(c) $P(-2, -3)$, $Q(2, -1)$, and $R(10, 3)$

13. Draw triangles that have vertices with the given coordinates. Describe the triangles as scalene, isosceles, equilateral, acute, right, or obtuse. Explain.
(a) $(0, 0)$, $(0, -5)$, $(5, -5)$
(b) $(-3, 1)$, $(1, 3)$, $(5, -5)$
(c) $(-2, -1)$, $(2, 2)$, $(6, -1)$
(d) $(-4, -2)$, $(-1, 3)$, $(4, -2)$

14. The endpoints of a segment are given. Find the coordinates of the midpoint of the segment.
  (a) (0, 2) and (−3, 2)
  (b) (−5, −1) and (3, 5)
  (c) (−2, 3) and (−3, 6)
  (d) (3, −5) and (3, −7)
  (e) (1, 5) and (3, 9)
  (f) (6, −2) and (−3, 5)

15. The point M is the midpoint of $\overline{AB}$. Given the coordinates of the following points, find the coordinates of the third point.
  (a) $A(−3, −1)$, $M(−1, 3)$
  (b) $B(−5, 3)$, $M(−7, 3)$
  (c) $A(1, −3)$, $M(4, 1)$
  (d) $M(0, 0)$, $B(−2, 5)$

16. Give the slope of a line perpendicular to $\overleftrightarrow{AB}$.
  (a) $A(1, 6)$, $B(2, 5)$
  (b) $A(0, 4)$, $B(−6, −5)$
  (c) $A(4, 2)$, $B(−5, 2)$
  (d) $A(−1, 5)$, $B(−1, 3)$

17. Given are the coordinates of the vertices of a triangle. Use the coordinate distance formula to determine if the triangle is a right triangle.
  (a) $A(−2, 5)$, $B(0, −1)$, $C(12, 3)$
  (b) $D(2, 3)$, $E(−2, −3)$, $F(−6, 1)$
  (c) $G(−3, −2)$, $H(5, −2)$, $I(1, 2)$

18. (a) Use the slopes of perpendicular lines theorem to determine if the triangles given in the preceding exercise are right triangles.
  (b) Is it easier to use the distance formula or the slopes of perpendicular lines theorem to show that a triangle is a right triangle?

19. Draw the quadrilateral $ABCD$ whose vertices are $A(3, 0)$, $B(6, 6)$, $C(6, 9)$, and $D(0, 6)$. Divide each of the coordinates by 3 and graph the new quadrilateral $A'B'C'D'$. For example, A' has coordinates $(1, 0)$. How do the lengths of corresponding sides compare?

20. Draw $\triangle ABC$ for points $A(2, 0)$, $B(−1, 2)$, and $C(0, 0)$. Multiply each of the coordinates by 2 and graph $\triangle A'B'C'$. For example, A' has coordinates $(4, 0)$.
  (a) How do the lengths of corresponding sides compare?
  (b) How do the areas of the two triangles compare?

Problems

21. In each of the following figures, a line segment $\overline{AB}$ is shown. Suppose that $\overline{AB}$ is revolved about the x-axis. Then a three-dimensional shape is generated. In each case, describe the shape (called a **surface of revolution**) that is generated and calculate its volume.

(a)

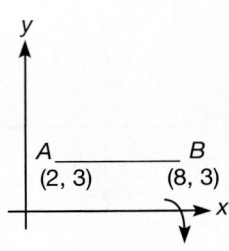

(b)

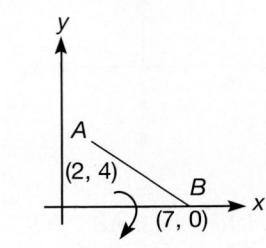

(c)

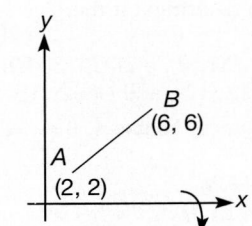

22. Cartesian coordinates may be generalized to three-dimensional space. A point in space is determined by giving its location relative to three axes as shown. Point P with coordinates (a, b, c) is plotted by going a along the x-axis, b along the y-direction, and c in the z-direction. Plot the following points in three-dimensional space.

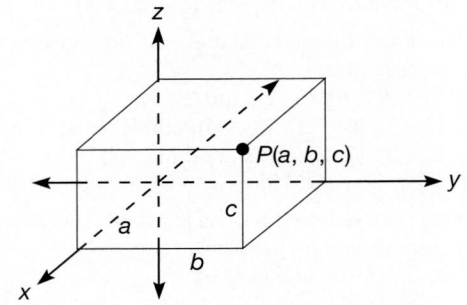

(a) $(2, 1, 3)$ **(b)** $(−2, 1, 0)$ **(c)** $(3, −1, −2)$

23. The three coordinate axes taken in pairs determine three coordinate planes:

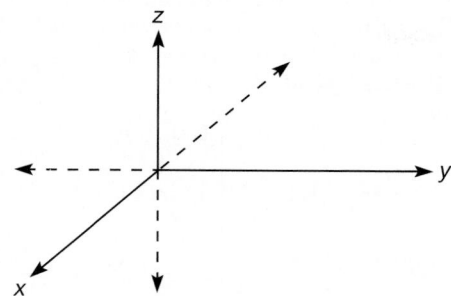

The (horizontal) xy-plane, where $z = 0$
The (vertical) yz-plane, where $x = 0$
The (vertical) xz-plane, where $y = 0$

These three planes divide space into eight portions, called **octants**. Looking above the xy-plane, the front right octant is octant 1. Octants 2, 3, and 4 are found by going counterclockwise through the other upper-level octants. The octant below octant 1 is octant 5, and 6 is below 2, 7 is below 3, and 8 is below 4. Given the points below, indicate in which octant each is found.
(a) (3, 2, 1)   **(b)** (−3, −2, 1)
(c) (−1, 2, −3)   **(d)** (−5, −3, −2)
(e) (6, −3, 5)   **(f)** (8, 4, −2)

24. In octant 1, the x-, y-, and z-coordinates are all positive. Characterize the coordinates in the remaining seven octants.

25. The coordinate distance formula can also be generalized to three-dimensional space. Let P have coordinates (a, b, c) and Q have coordinates (x, y, z). The faces of the prism are parallel to the coordinate planes.

(a) What are the coordinates of point R?

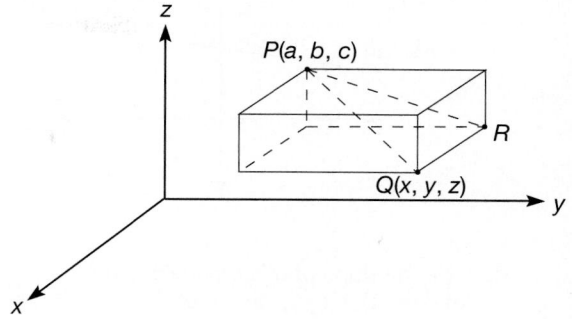

(b) What is the distance PR? (Hint: Pythagorean theorem.)
(c) What is the distance QR?
(d) What is the distance PQ? (Hint: Pythagorean theorem.)

26. In the development of the midpoint formula, points P and Q have coordinates (a, b) and (c, d), respectively, and M is the point $\left(\dfrac{a + c}{2}, \dfrac{b + d}{2} \right)$. Use the coordinate distance formula to verify that P, M, and Q are collinear and that $PM = MQ$.

27. Suppose that l is a line with an equation of the form $y = mx + b$. Show that if a point (x, y) in the plane satisfies the equation $y = mx + b$, then (x, y) is on line l. [Hint: Choose two points on l by giving x two values. Then show that the point $(x, mx + b)$ is collinear with the points you have chosen.]

28. Suppose that two different lines have equal slopes. Show that they are parallel. (Hint: Suppose that they intersect, and derive a contradiction.)

EXERCISE/PROBLEM SET 15.1—PART B

Exercises

1. Find the slope of each line containing the following pairs of points.
   (a) (−1, 2) and (6, −3)   **(b)** (6, 5) and (6, −2)

2. Given are the slopes of several lines. Indicate whether each line is horizontal, vertical, rises to the right, or rises to the left.
   (a) $\frac{3}{4}$ **(b)** No slope   **(c)** 0   **(d)** $-\frac{5}{6}$

3. Determine which pairs of segments are parallel.
   (a) The segment from (3, 5) to (8, 3) and the segment from (0, 8) to (8, 5)

(b) The segment from (−4, 5) to (4, 2) and the segment from (−3, −2) to (5, −5)
(c)

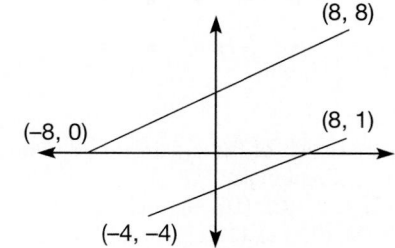

(d)

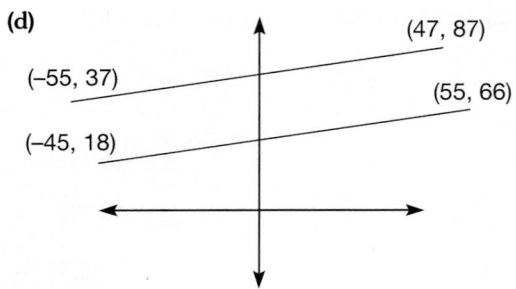

4. Give the slope of a line parallel to $\overleftrightarrow{PQ}$.
   (a) $P(6, 1)$, $Q(-6, 3)$ **(b)** $P(-5, -2)$, $Q(-4, 5)$
   (c) $P(2, -8)$, $Q(2, 9)$ **(d)** $P(-4, -2)$, $Q(-6, -3)$
5. Which, if any, of the triangles with the given vertices, is a right triangle?
   (a) $(4, 4)$, $(8, 16)$, and $(16, 12)$
   (b) $(3, -2)$, $(10, 11)$, and $(11, -11)$
   (c) $(8, -7)$, $(16, 8)$, and $(24, 3)$
6. Using only the 5×5 array of points, how many segments can be drawn making a right angle at an endpoint of the given segment?

(a)

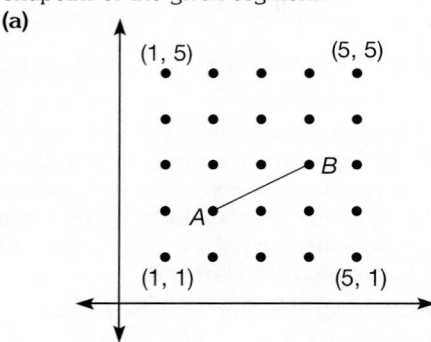

(b)

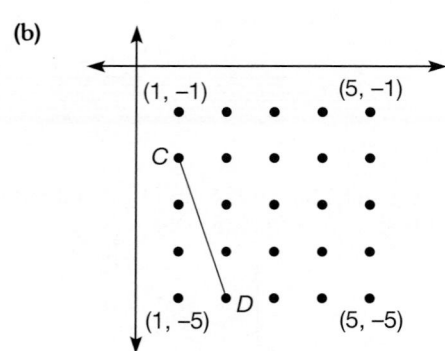

7. Determine which of the quadrilaterals, with the given vertices, is a rectangle.
   (a) $(0, 0)$, $(12, 12)$, $(16, 8)$, and $(4, -4)$
   (b) $(-3, 8)$, $(0, 12)$, $(12, 3)$, and $(9, -1)$
   (c) $(-10, -5)$, $(-6, 15)$, $(14, 11)$, and $(10, -9)$

8. Which of the following properties are true of the given kites? Explain.
   (a) The diagonals are congruent.
   (b) The diagonals are perpendicular to each other.
   (c) The diagonals bisect each other.
   (d) The kite has two right angles.
   (i)

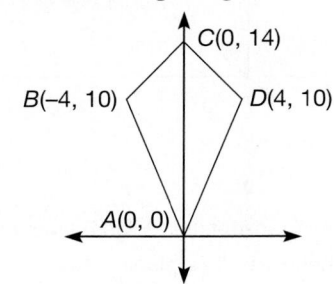

   (ii)

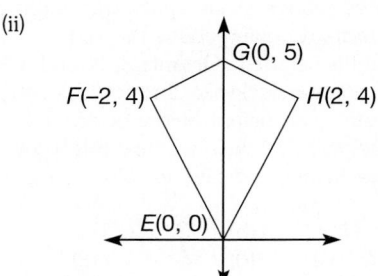

9. Which of the following properties are true of the given trapezoids? Explain.
   (a) The diagonals have the same length.
   (b) The diagonals are perpendicular to each other.
   (c) The diagonals bisect each other.
   (i)

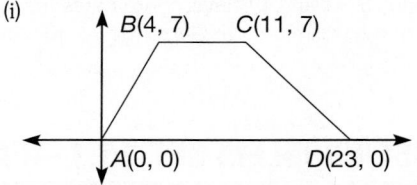

   (ii)

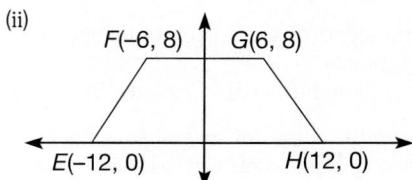

10. What general type of quadrilateral is $ABCD$, where $A = (0, 0)$, $B = (-4, 3)$, $C = (-1, 7)$, and $D = (6, 8)$? Describe it as completely as you can.
11. Find the distance between the following pairs of points.
    (a) $(1, 4)$ and $(-2, -3)$ **(b)** $(-5, 2)$ and $(1, -4)$

12. Which of the given points are collinear with $A(-2, -3)$ and $B(4, -1)$?
(a) $(1, -2)$ (b) $(7, 1)$ (c) $(12, 2)$ (d) $(-8, -5)$

13. The point M is the midpoint of $\overline{AB}$. Given the coordinates of the following points, find the coordinates of the third point.
(a) $A(-2, 4)$, $B(-1, 10)$
(b) $A(-1, -3)$, $B(5, 12)$
(c) $A(3, -5)$, $B(3, 7)$
(d) $A(2, 6)$, $M(4, -3)$
(e) $A(1, -3)$, $M(5, 2)$
(f) $M(-2, -5)$, $B(3, -4)$

14. Use slopes to show that $\overline{AB} \perp \overline{PQ}$.
(a) $A(0, 4)$, $B(-6, 3)$, $P(-2, -2)$, $Q(-3, 4)$
(b) $A(-2, -1)$, $B(2, 3)$, $P(4, 1)$, $Q(0, 5)$

15. (a) Draw quadrilateral $ABCD$ where $A(4, -2)$, $B(4, 2)$, $C(-2, 2)$, and $D(-2, -2)$.
(b) Multiply each coordinate by 3 and graph quadrilateral $A'B'C'D'$. For example, A' has coordinates $(12, -6)$.
(c) How do the perimeters of $ABCD$ and $A'B'C'D'$ compare?
(d) How do the areas of $ABCD$ and $A'B'C'D'$ compare?
(e) Repeat parts (b) to (d), but divide each coordinate by 2.

16. Find the coordinates of the midpoint of side $\overline{PQ}$ of $\triangle PQR$. Also find the length of the median to $\overline{PQ}$.
(a) $P(-4, -2)$, $Q(-2, 6)$, $R(6, 2)$
(b) $P(4, -1)$, $Q(-2, 5)$, $R(5, -2)$

17. The slope of a line represents how much the line "rises" (or falls if the slope is negative) as it "runs" to the right. For example, when the slope $\frac{3}{2}$ is expressed as a fraction, the 3 (numerator) is the amount the line rises as it runs 2 (denominator) to the right. Draw a similar diagram to represent the slopes of the following lines.

(a) $\frac{5}{3}$
(b) 4 (Hint: Express as $\frac{4}{1}$.)
(c) $-\frac{1}{2}$ (Hint: Put negative in numerator.)
(d) -3 (e) $\frac{6}{5}$ (f) $-\frac{3}{4}$

Problems

18. Three of the vertices of a parallelogram have coordinates $P(2, 3)$, $Q(5, 7)$, and $R(10, -5)$.
(a) Find the coordinates of the fourth vertex of the parallelogram. (Hint: There is more than one answer.)
(b) Determine the area of each parallelogram.

19. Describe the three-dimensional shape obtained when each of the following figures is revolved about the y-axis. Then calculate the surface area of the shape obtained.

(a)

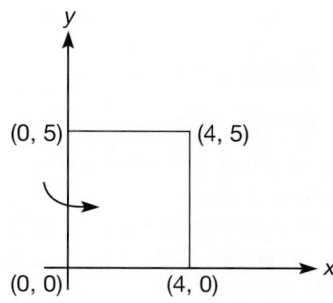

(b)

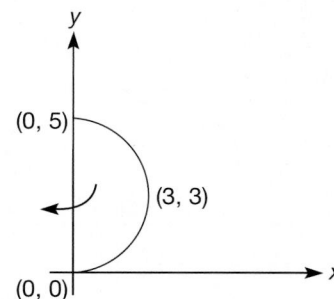

(c)

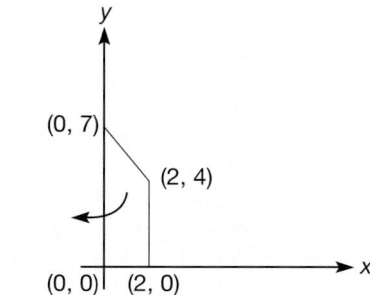

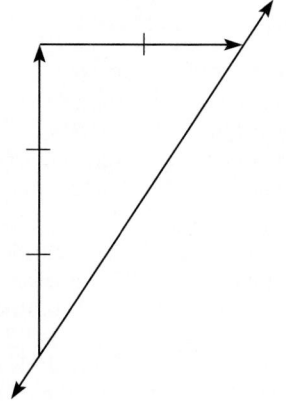

20. Let P, Q, R, and S be any points on line l as shown. By drawing horizontal and vertical segments, draw right triangles $\triangle PQO$ and $\triangle RST$. Follow the given steps to verify that the slope of line l is independent of the pairs of points selected.

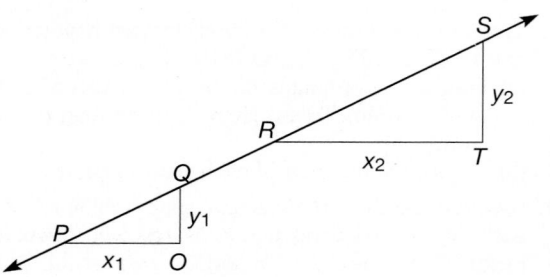

(a) Show that $\triangle PQO \sim \triangle RST$.

(b) Show that $\dfrac{y_1}{x_1} = \dfrac{y_2}{x_2}$.

(c) Is the slope of $\overline{PQ}$ equal to the slope of $\overline{RS}$? Explain.

21. Justify the following statement for the cases given. If two lines are parallel, their slopes are equal or neither has a slope.

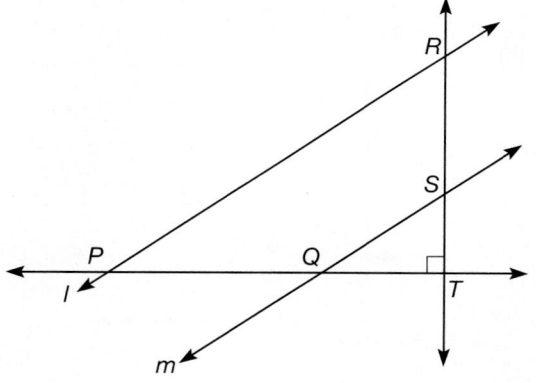

(a) Two vertical lines

(b) Two horizontal lines

(c) Two parallel lines l and m (nonvertical and non-horizontal)

(HINT: Draw a horizontal line and a vertical line as pictured.)

22. Prove the following statement: If the product of the slopes of l and m is -1, lines l and m are perpendicular. (HINT: Show that $\triangle OPQ$ is a right triangle.)

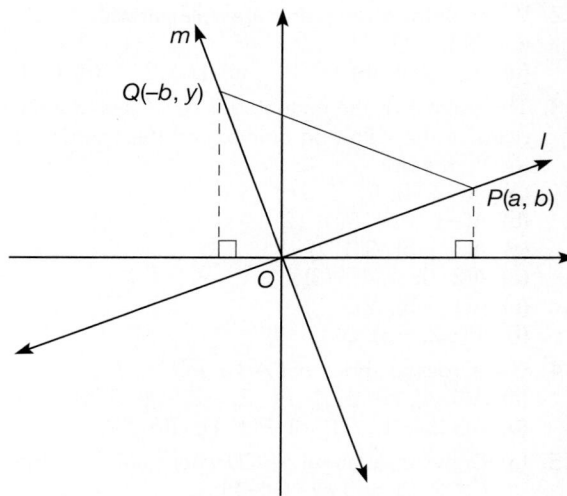

23. If the slope of $\overline{PQ}$ is equal to the slope of $\overline{PR}$, we can show that P, Q, and R are collinear. The following justification uses similar triangles and the triangle inequality.

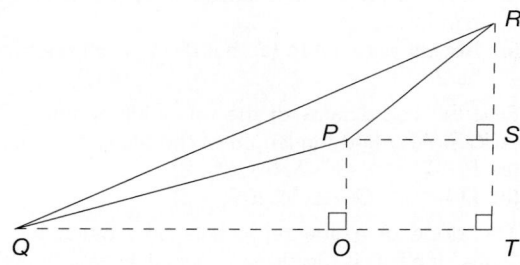

(a) Horizontal lines are drawn through points P and Q and vertical lines through P and R, intersecting at points O, S, and T as illustrated. If the slope of $\overline{PQ}$ and the slope of $\overline{PR}$ are equal, what two ratios of sides are equal?

(b) Show that $\triangle QOP \sim \triangle PSR$.

(c) Which sides are proportional?

(d) Verify that $\dfrac{QO + PS}{PS} = \dfrac{PO + RS}{RS}$.

(e) Show that $\triangle PSR \sim \triangle QTR$.

(f) Which sides are proportional?

(g) Verify that $QR = PR \cdot QT/PS$.

(h) Verify that $QP + PR = PR \cdot QT/PS$.

(i) Verify that points P, Q, and R are collinear.

24. Locations on the earth's surface are measured by two sets of circles. **Parallels of latitude** are circles at constant distances from the Equator used to identify locations North or South, called **latitude**. The latitude of the North Pole, for example, is 90° North, that of the Equator is 0°, and the South Pole's latitude is 90° South. Great circles through the North and South

Poles, called **meridians**, are used to identify locations East or West, called **longitude**. The half of the great circle through the poles and Greenwich, England, is called the **prime meridian**. Points on the prime meridian have longitude 0° East. Points east of Greenwich and less than halfway around the world from it have longitudes between 0 and 180° East. Points west of Greenwich and less than halfway around the world from it have longitudes between 0 and 180° West. Here are the latitudes and longitudes of several cities, to the nearest degree.

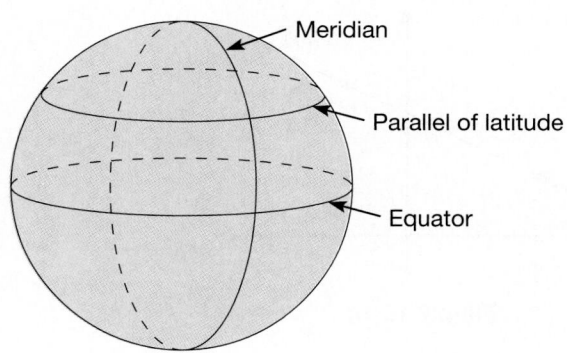

City	Latitude	Longitude
London	52°N	0°E
New York	41°N	74°W
Moscow	56°N	38°E
Nome, Alaska	64°N	165°W
Peking	40°N	116°E
Rio de Janeiro	23°S	43°W
Sydney	34°S	151°E

(a) Which cities are above the Equator? Which are below?

(b) Which city is farthest from the Equator?

(c) Are there points in the United States, excluding Alaska and Hawaii, with East longitudes? Explain.

(d) What is the latitude of all points south of the Equator and the same distance from the Equator as London?

(e) What is the longitude of a point exactly halfway around the world (north of the Equator) from New York?

(f) What are the latitude and longitude of a point diametrically opposite Sydney? That is, the point in question and Sydney are the endpoints of a diameter of the earth.

25. The **percent grade** of a highway is the amount that the highway rises (or falls) in a given horizontal distance. For example, a highway with a 4% grade rises 0.04 mile for every 1 mile of horizontal distance.

(a) How many feet does a highway with a 6% grade rise in 2.5 miles?

(b) How many feet would a highway with 6% grade rise in 90 miles if the grade remained constant?

(c) How is percent grade related to slope?

26. A freeway ramp connects a highway to an overpass 10 meters above the ground. The ramp, which starts 150 meters from the overpass, is 150.33 meters long and 9 meters wide. What is the percent grade of the ramp to three decimal places?

27. A pole is supported by two sets of guy wires fastened to the ground 15 meters from the pole. The shorter set of wires has slope $\frac{4}{3}$. The wires in the longer set are each 50 meters long.

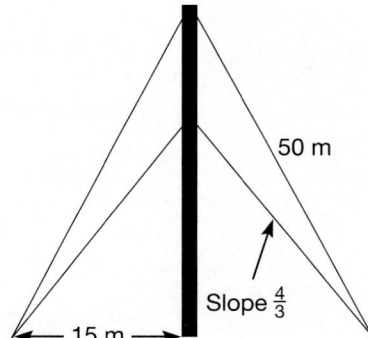

(a) How high above the ground is the shorter set of wires attached?

(b) What is the length of the shorter set of wires?

(c) How tall is the pole to the nearest centimeter?

(d) What is the slope of the longer set of wires to two decimal places?

28. Use the coordinate distance formula in three dimensions (Problem 23 in Part A) to find the distance between the following pairs of points.

(a) (1, 2, 3) and (2, 3, 1)

(b) (−1, 0, 5) and (6, 2, −1)

15.2

EQUATIONS AND COORDINATES

Equations of Lines

We can determine equations that are satisfied by the points on a particular line. For example, consider the line l containing points $(-4, 2)$ and $(2, 5)$ (Figure 15.10). Suppose that (x, y) is an arbitrary point on line l. We wish to find an equation in x and y that is satisfied by the coordinates of the point (x, y). We will use the slope of l to do this. Using the points

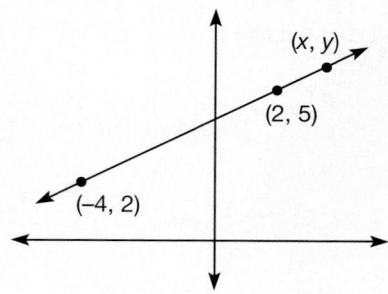

FIGURE 15.10

$(-4, 2)$ and $(2, 5)$, the slope of l is $\dfrac{5 - 2}{2 - (-4)} = \dfrac{1}{2}$. Using the points $(-4, 2)$ and (x, y), the slope of l is $\dfrac{y - 2}{x - (-4)} = \dfrac{y - 2}{x + 4}$. Since the slope of l is $\dfrac{1}{2}$ and $\dfrac{y - 2}{x + 4}$, we have

$$\frac{y - 2}{x + 4} = \frac{1}{2}.$$

Continuing,

$$y - 2 = \frac{1}{2}(x + 4),$$

$$y - 2 = \frac{1}{2}x + 2,$$

or finally,

$$y = \frac{1}{2}x + 4.$$

That is, we have shown that every point (x, y) on line l satisfies the equation $y = \frac{1}{2}x + 4$. [Note: We could also have used the points $(2, 5)$ and (x, y), and solved $\dfrac{y - 5}{x - 2} = \dfrac{1}{2}$ to obtain $y = \dfrac{1}{2}x + 4$.]

In our equation for line l, the "x" term is multiplied by the slope of l, namely $\frac{1}{2}$. Also, the constant term, 4, is the y-coordinate of the point at which l intersects the y-axis.

We can show that *every* line in the plane that is not vertical has an equation of the form $y = mx + b$, where m is the slope of the line and b, called the **y-intercept**, is the y-coordinate of the point at which the line intersects the y-axis (Figure 15.11). Generalizing from the preceding argument, suppose that l is a line containing the point $(0, b)$ such that the slope of l is m

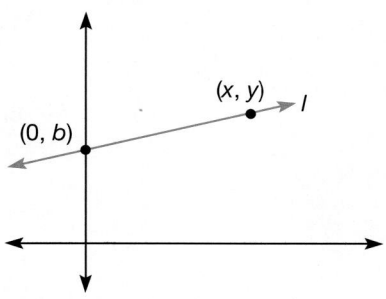

FIGURE 15.11

and that (x, y) is an arbitrary point on l (Figure 15.11). Then, since the slope of l is m, we have

$$\frac{y - b}{x - 0} = m,$$

so that

$$y - b = mx,$$
$$y = mx + b.$$

Thus every point (x, y) on l satisfies the equation $y = mx + b$.

It is also true that if (x, y) is a point in the plane such that $y = mx + b$, then (x, y) is on line l. The verification of this is left for the problem set. Thus the equation $y = mx + b$ describes all points (x, y) that are on line l.

If a line l is vertical and hence has no slope, it must intersect the horizontal axis at a point, say $(a, 0)$. Then all of the points on l will satisfy the equation $x = a$ (Figure 15.12). That is, the x-coordinate of each point on l is a, and the y-coordinate is an arbitrary real number.

We can summarize our results about equations of lines in the coordinate plane as follows:

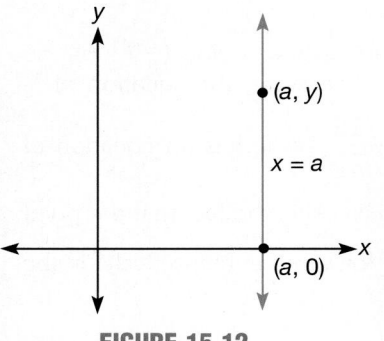

FIGURE 15.12

> **Theorem**
>
> ### Equation of a Line
>
> Every line in the plane has an equation of the form (1) $y = mx + b$ where m is the slope of the line and b is the y-intercept, or (2) $x = a$ if the slope of the line is undefined (i.e., the line is vertical).

The equation $y = mx + b$ is called the **slope-intercept equation of a line**, since m is the slope and b is the y-intercept of the line.

EXAMPLE 15.5   Find the equations for the lines l_1, l_2, l_3, and l_4 satisfying the following conditions (Figure 15.13).

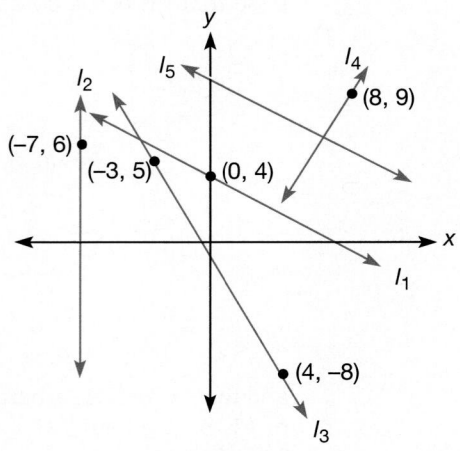

FIGURE 15.13

(a) l_1 has slope $\dfrac{-3}{5}$ and y-intercept 4.

(b) l_2 is a vertical line containing the point $(-7, 6)$.

(c) l_3 contains the points $(-3, 5)$ and $(4, -8)$.

(d) l_4 contains the point $(8, 9)$ and is perpendicular to the line l_5 whose equation is $y = \dfrac{-4}{7}x + 10$.

Solution

(a) By the equation of a line formula (1), the slope-intercept equation of l_1 is $y = \dfrac{-3}{5}x + 4$, since the slope of l_1 is $\dfrac{-3}{5}$ and the y-intercept is 4.

(b) The line l_2 is a vertical line containing the point $(-7, 6)$, so that l_2 also contains the point $(-7, 0)$. Therefore, the equation of l_2 is $x = -7$.

(c) The slope of l_3 is $\dfrac{5 - (-8)}{-3 - 4} = \dfrac{13}{-7} = \dfrac{-13}{7}$, so l_3 has an equation of the form $y = \dfrac{-13}{7}x + b$. We can find b by using the fact that the point $(-3, 5)$ is on l_3. We substitute -3 and 5 for x and y, respectively, in the equation of l_3, as follows:

$$5 = \frac{-13}{7}(-3) + b,$$

$$5 = \frac{39}{7} + b,$$

so

$$5 - \frac{39}{7} = b,$$

$$\frac{-4}{7} = b.$$

Therefore, the equation of l_3 is

$$y = \frac{-13}{7}x - \frac{4}{7}.$$

We could also have used the fact that $(4, -8)$ is on l_3 to find b.

(d) Since l_4 is perpendicular to the line $y = \dfrac{-4}{7}x + 10$, we know that the slope of l_4 is $\frac{7}{4}$, by the slopes of perpendicular lines theorem. Hence l_4 has an equation of the form $y = \frac{7}{4}x + b$. Since the point $(8, 9)$ is on l_4, we can substitute 8 for x and 9 for y in the equation $y = \frac{7}{4}x + b$. Thus we have

$$9 = \frac{7}{4} \cdot 8 + b,$$

$$9 = 14 + b,$$

$$-5 = b.$$

Consequently, the equation of l_4 is

$$y = \frac{7}{4}x - 5.$$ ■

Simultaneous Equations

Consider the equations $y = 4x + 2$ and $y = -3x + 5$. The first line has slope 4, and the second line has slope -3, so that the lines must intersect (Figure 15.14). We can find the point P where the two lines intersect by

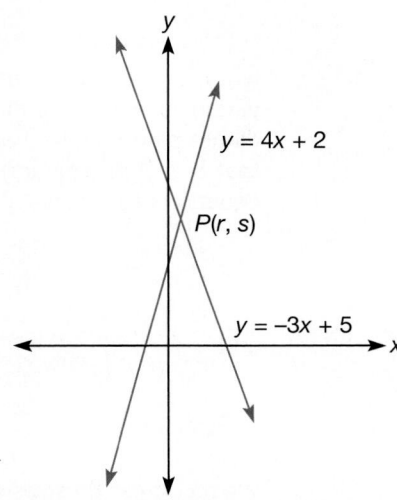

FIGURE 15.14

using the fact that P lies on *both* lines. That is, the coordinates of P must satisfy both equations. Hence if r and s are the coordinates of P, we must have $s = 4r + 2$ and $s = -3r + 5$, so that

$$4r + 2 = -3r + 5.$$

Therefore,

$$7r = 3 \quad \text{or} \quad r = \frac{3}{7}.$$

Thus the x-coordinate of P is $\frac{3}{7}$. Using the first of the two equations, we find

$$s = 4\left(\frac{3}{7}\right) + 2,$$

or

$$s = \frac{26}{7}.$$

Consequently, $P = (\frac{3}{7}, \frac{26}{7})$ is the point of intersection of the two lines. (We could have used either equation to find s, since r and s must satisfy both equations.) We say that the point $P = (\frac{3}{7}, \frac{26}{7})$ is a **simultaneous solution** of the equations, since it satisfies both of them. The equations whose simultaneous solution we seek are called **simultaneous equations** or a system of equations.

The algebraic process of solving simultaneous equations has an interesting geometric interpretation. When we solve a pair of simultaneous equations such as

$$(1)\ ax + by = c$$

and

$$(2)\ dx + ey = f,$$

where a, b, c, d, e, and f represent constant coefficients and x and y are variables, we are finding the point of intersection of two lines in the coordinate plane. Note that x and y appear to the first power only. In the case that $b \neq 0$ in equation (1), and $e \neq 0$ in equation (2), we can rewrite these equations as follows. (Verify this.)

$$(1)'\ y = -\frac{a}{b}x + \frac{c}{b}$$

and

$$(2)'\ y = -\frac{d}{e}x + \frac{f}{e}.$$

We recognize these as equations of *lines* in the plane. Suppose that line l has equation (1)$'$ as its equation and line m has equation (2)$'$ as its equation. Then there are three possible geometrical relationships between lines l and m.

(a) $l = m$ [Figure 15.15(a)].
(b) $l \parallel m$ and $l \neq m$ [Figure 15.15(b)].
(c) l intersects m in exactly one point (x, y) [Figure 15.15(c)].

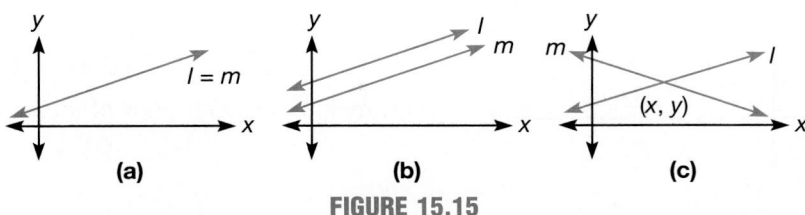

FIGURE 15.15

If $l = m$ as in case (a), then *all* the points (x, y) that satisfy the equation of l will also satisfy the equation of m. Thus, for this case, equations (1) and (2) will have infinitely many simultaneous solutions. For case (b) in which the lines l and m are different parallel lines, there will be no points in common for the two lines. Hence equations (1) and (2) will have no simultaneous solutions in this case. Finally, for case (c) in which the lines intersect in a unique point $P = (x, y)$, we will have only one simultaneous solution to the equations (1) and (2), namely, the x- and y-coordinates of point P.

Now let us consider this situation starting with the equations of the lines. If they have infinitely many solutions, the lines that they represent are coincident. If they have no solutions, their lines are different parallel lines. Finally, if they have a unique solution, their lines intersect in only one point. We can find conditions on the numbers a, b, c, d, e, and f in equations (1) and (2) in order to determine how many simultaneous solutions there are for the equations. This is left for the problem set.

Theorem

Solutions of Simultaneous Equations

Let a, b, c, d, e, and f be real-number constants and x and y be variables. Then the equations

$$ax + by = c$$

and

$$dx + ey = f$$

have 0, 1, or infinitely many solutions if and only if the lines they represent are parallel, intersect in exactly one point, or are coincident, respectively.

The following example illustrates the preceding geometrical interpretation of simultaneous equations.

EXAMPLE 15.6 Graph the following pairs of equations, and find their simultaneous solutions.

(a) $x + y = 7$
$-28 = -4x - 4y$

(b) $2x + y = 5$
$-12 + 3y = -6x$

(c) $x + y = 7$
$2x + y = 5$

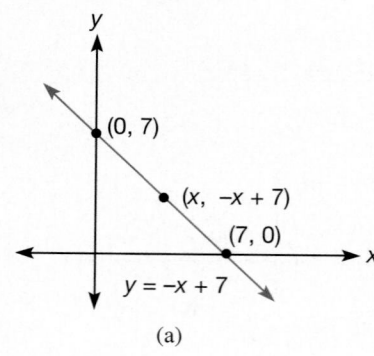

(a)

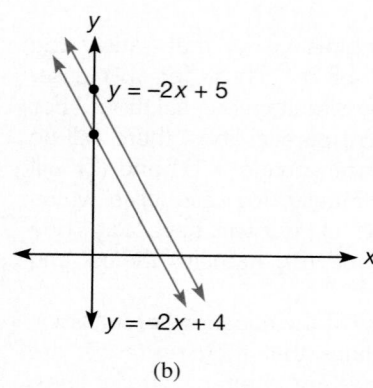

(b)

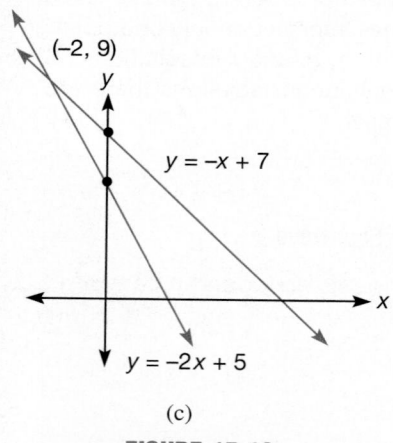

(c)

FIGURE 15.16

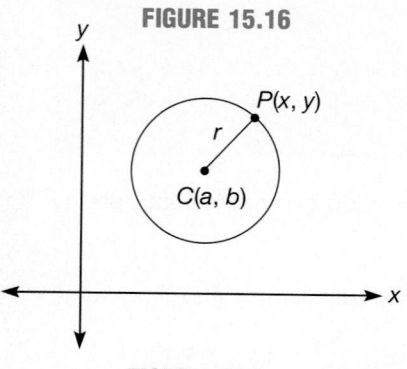

FIGURE 15.17

Solution

(a) We can rewrite the equations as follows:

$$(1) \; x + y = 7$$

and

$$(2) \; 4x + 4y = 28$$

or, multiplying both sides of the second equation by $\frac{1}{4}$,

$$(1)' \; x + y = 7$$

and

$$(2)' \; x + y = 7.$$

Hence the equations represent the *same* line, namely the line $y = -x + 7$ [Figure 15.16(a)]. Every point on this line is a simultaneous solution of the pair of equations.

(b) Rewrite the equations in slope-intercept form.

$$y = -2x + 5$$
$$y = -2x + 4.$$

Here, the equations represent lines with the same slope (i.e., parallel lines), but different y-intercepts. Therefore, the equations have no simultaneous solution [Figure 15.16(b)].

(c) Rewrite the equations in slope-intercept form.

$$y = -x + 7$$
$$y = -2x + 5.$$

Here the equations represent lines with different slopes, namely -1 and -2. The lines are intersecting lines [Figure 15.16(c)], so the equations will have a unique simultaneous solution. Equating the expressions for y, we obtain

$$-x + 7 = -2x + 5$$
$$x + 7 = 5$$
$$x = -2.$$

Substituting -2 for x in the first equation, we have $y = -(-2) + 7 = 9$. Thus the point $(-2, 9)$ is the only simultaneous solution of the two equations. [Check to see that $(-2, 9)$ is a simultaneous solution.] ■

Equations of Circles

Circles also have equations that can be determined using the distance formula. Recall that a circle is the set of points that are a fixed distance (i.e., the radius) from the center of the circle (Figure 15.17). Let the point $C = (a, b)$ be the center of the circle and r be the radius. Suppose that the point $P = (x, y)$ is on the circle. Then, by the definition of the circle, $PC = r$, so that $PC^2 = r^2$. But by the distance formula,

$$PC^2 = (x - a)^2 + (y - b)^2.$$

Therefore, $(x - a)^2 + (y - b)^2 = r^2$ is the equation of the circle.

> **Theorem**
>
> ### Equation of a Circle
>
> The circle with center (a, b) and radius r has the equation
> $$(x - a)^2 + (y - b)^2 = r^2.$$

EXAMPLE 15.7   Find the equation of the circle whose center is $(-5, 6)$ and whose radius is 3.

Solution
In the equation of a circle formula, $(a, b) = (-5, 6)$ and $r = 3$. Consequently, the equation of the circle is

$$[x - (-5)]^2 + (y - 6)^2 = 3^2$$

or

$$(x + 5)^2 + (y - 6)^2 = 9.$$

This circle is shown in Figure 15.18.

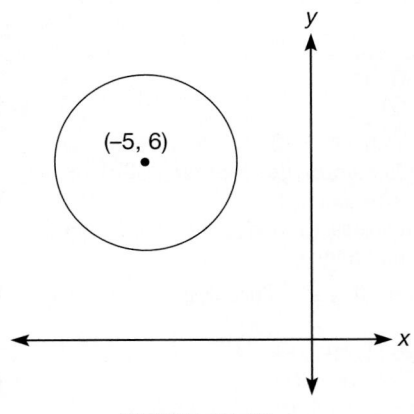

FIGURE 15.18

MATHEMATICAL MORSEL

Many words in mathematics have their origins in Hindu and Arabic words. The earliest Arabic arithmetic is that of al-Khowarizmi (circa A.D. 800). In referring to his book on Hindu numerals, a Latin translation begins "Spoken has Algoritmi." Thus we obtain the word "algorithm," which is a procedure for calculating. The mathematics book *Hisab-al-jabr-w'almugabalsh*, also written by al-Khowarizmi, became known as "al-jabr," our modern-day "algebra."

EXERCISE/PROBLEM SET 15.2—PART A

Exercises

1. Show that point P lies on the line with the given equation.
   (a) $y = 7x - 2$; $P(1, 5)$
   (b) $y = -\frac{2}{3}x + 5$; $P(-6, 9)$
   (c) $-2x = 6y + 3$; $P(7.5, -3)$
   (d) $3y = 4x + 2$; $P(4, 6)$

2. Write each equation in the form $y = mx + b$. Identify the slope and y-intercept.
   (a) $2y = 6x + 12$
   (b) $4y - 3x = 0$
   (c) $8y - 2 = 0$
   (d) $3x - 4y = 12$

3. Write the equation of the line, given its slope m and y-intercept b.
   (a) $m = 3$, $b = 7$
   (b) $m = -1$, $b = -3$
   (c) $m = \frac{2}{3}$, $b = 5$
   (d) $m = -3$, $b = -\frac{1}{4}$

4. Write the equation in slope-intercept form for $\overleftrightarrow{AB}$.
   (a) $A(6, 3)$, $B(0, 2)$
   (b) $A(-4, 8)$, $B(3, -6)$
   (c) $A(-5, 2)$, $B(-3, 1)$
   (d) $A(4, 7)$, $B(10, 7)$

5. Point P has coordinates $(-2, 3)$.
   (a) Give the coordinates of three other points on a horizontal line containing P.
   (b) Give the coordinates of two other points on a vertical line containing P.

6. Write the equation of each line that satisfies the following.
   (a) Vertical through $(1, 3)$
   (b) Vertical through $(-5, -2)$
   (c) Horizontal through $(-3, 6)$
   (d) Horizontal through $(3, -3)$

7. Write the equation of a line that passes through the given point and is parallel to the line whose equation is given.
   (a) $(5, -1)$; $y = 2x - 3$
   (b) $(1, -2)$; $y = -x - 2$
   (c) $(2, -5)$; $3x + 5y = 1$
   (d) $(-1, 0)$; $3x + 2y = 6$

8. Graph the line $3y = 4x + 3$, using the following steps:

   1. Rewrite the equation in the $y = mx + b$ form.
   2. What is its y-intercept? Plot the y-intercept.
   3. What is its slope? Use the slope to find another point on the line and then graph the line.

9. Graph the line described by each equation.
   (a) $y = 2x - 1$
   (b) $y = -3x + 2$
   (c) $y = \frac{1}{2}x + 1$
   (d) $x = -2$
   (e) $y = 3$
   (f) $2x = -6y$

10. Tell whether the line described by each equation slants up to the right, slants down to the right, is vertical, or is horizontal.
    (a) $y = 3x - 2$
    (b) $y = \frac{3}{4}x - 1$
    (c) $x = 2$
    (d) $y = x$
    (e) $y = -5$
    (f) $y = -\frac{4}{3}x$

11. (a) Graph the following lines on the same coordinate system.
       (i) $y = 2x + 3$
       (ii) $y = -3x + 3$
       (iii) $y = \frac{1}{2}x + 3$
    (b) What is the relationship between these lines?
    (c) Describe the lines of the form $y = cx + d$, where d is a fixed real number and c can be any real number.

12. The vertices of a triangle have coordinates $(0, 0)$, $(1, 5)$, and $(-4, 3)$. Find the equations of the lines containing the sides of the triangle.

13. Find the equation of the line containing the median $\overline{AD}$ of $\triangle ABC$ with vertices $A(3, 7)$, $B(1, 4)$, and $C(11, 2)$.

14. Find the equation of the line containing altitude $\overline{PT}$ of triangles PRS with vertices $P(3, 5)$, $R(-1, 1)$, and $S(7, -3)$.

15. One method of solving simultaneous linear equations is called the **graphical method**. The two lines are graphed and, if they intersect, the coordinates of the intersection point are determined. Graph the following pairs of lines to determine their simultaneous solutions, if any exist.
    (a) $y = 2x + 1$
        $y = \frac{1}{2}x + 4$
    (b) $x + 2y = 4$
        $x + 2y = -2$
    (c) $-2x + 3y = 9$
        $x + y = -2$
    (d) $-2x + 3y = 9$
        $4x - 6y = -18$

16. One algebraic method for solving a system of equations is called the **substitution method**. Solve the pair of equations

$$2x + y = 3$$
$$x - 2y = 5$$

using the following steps:

1. Express y in terms of x in the first equation.
2. Since the y value of the point of intersection satisfies both equations, we can substitute this new name for y in place of y in the second equation. Do this.
3. The resulting equation has only the variable x. Solve for x.
4. By substituting the x value into either original equation, the value of y is found. Solve for y.

17. Use the substitution method to find the solution of the following systems of linear equations.
    (a) $y = -2x + 3$
        $y = 3x - 5$
    (b) $2x - y = 6$
        $5x - y = 5$
    (c) $3x - 2y = 6$
        $x + 3y = 2$
    (d) $x + 4y = 9$
        $8x - y = 20$

18. (a) Do the following equations represent the same line, parallel lines, or intersecting lines?

    $$y = 3x - 5$$
    $$y = 3x + 2$$

    (b) When you apply the substitution method, what equation in x do you obtain?
    (c) In trying to solve for x, what equation results?
    (d) Is there any value of x that will make this equation true?
    (e) How does this compare with your conclusion in part (a)?

19. (a) Do the following equations represent the same line, parallel lines, or intersecting lines?

    $$2x - y = 6$$
    $$y = 2x - 6$$

    (b) When you apply the substitution method, what equation in x do you obtain?
    (c) In trying to solve for x, what equation results?
    (d) Is there any value of x that will make this equation true?
    (e) How does this compare with your conclusion in part (a)?

20. Another algebraic method of solving systems of equations is called the **elimination method** and involves eliminating one variable by adding or subtracting equivalent expressions. Consider the system

    $$2x + y = 7$$
    $$3x - y = 3$$

    1. Add the left-hand sides of the equations and the right-hand sides. Since the original terms were

equal, the resulting sums are also equal. Notice that the variable y is eliminated.
    2. Solve the equation you obtained in part 1.
    3. Substitute this value of the variable into one of the original equations to find the value of the other variable.

21. Sometimes another operation is necessary before adding the equations of a system in order to eliminate one variable.
    (a) What equation results when adding the given equations? Is one variable eliminated?

    $$2x - 3y = 6$$
    $$4x + 5y = 1$$

    (b) Now multiply the first equation by -2. Is one variable eliminated when the two equations are added?
    (c) What is the solution of the system of equations?

22. Solve the following systems of equations, using any method.
    (a) $y = 6x + 2$
        $y = 3x - 7$
    (b) $2x + y = -8$
        $x - y = -4$
    (c) $3x - y = 4$
        $6x + 3y = -12$
    (d) $3x + 5y = 9$
        $4x - 8y = 17$

23. Identify whether the following systems have a unique solution, no solution, or infinitely many solutions.
    (a) $y = 2x + 5$
        $y = 2x - 3$
    (b) $3x - 2 = y$
        $3x - y = 2$
    (c) $y = -x + 3$
        $y = 2x - 1$
    (d) $2x - 3y = 5$
        $3x - 2y = 5$
    (e) $4x - y = 6$
        $8x - 2y = 6$
    (f) $3x - y = 5$
        $-6x + 2y = -10$

24. Find five solutions to the system of equations in Example 15.6(a).

25. Show that point P lies on the circle with the given equation.
    (a) $P(3, 4)$; $x^2 + y^2 = 25$
    (b) $P(-3, 5)$; $x^2 + y^2 = 34$
    (c) $P(-3, 7)$; $(x + 1)^2 + (y - 2)^2 = 29$
    (d) $P(\sqrt{5}, -3)$; $x^2 + (y + 5)^2 = 9$

26. Identify the center and radius of each circle whose equation is given.
    (a) $(x - 3)^2 + (y - 2)^2 = 25$
    (b) $(x + 1)^2 + (y - 3)^2 = 49$

(c) $(x + 7)^2 + (y + 2)^2 = 36$

(d) $x^2 + (y - 5)^2 = 4$

27. Write the equation of a circle with center C and radius of length r.

(a) $C(0, 0)$; $r = 3$

(b) $C(1, 2)$; $r = 4$

(c) $C(-2, 3)$; $r = 2$

(d) $C(-3, -1)$; $r = \sqrt{10}$

28. Write the equation of the circle with center C that passes through point P.

(a) $C(3, -4)$, $P(2, -6)$

(b) $C(-2, 5)$, $P(-4, -3)$

29. Write the equation of the circle that has center P and passes through the origin.

(a) $P(-5, 12)$

(b) $P(-3, -5)$

30. Write the equation of the circle for which A and B are the endpoints of a diameter.

(a) $A(-2, -5)$, $B(4, 3)$

(b) $A(-2, -1)$, $B(6, -3)$

31. Find the equation of the circumscribed circle for the triangle whose vertices are $A(-1, 2)$, $B(-1, 8)$, and $C(-5, 4)$.

Problems

32. Another coordinate system in the plane, called **polar coordinates**, identifies a point with an angle θ and a real number r. For example, $(3, 60°)$ gives the coordinates of point P shown. The positive x-axis serves as the initial side of the angle. Angles may be measured positively (counterclockwise) or negatively (clockwise). Plot the following points and indicate which quadrant they are in or which axis they are on.

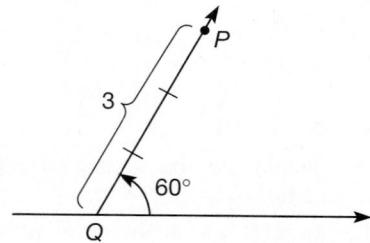

(a) $(5, 45°)$

(b) $(3, 125°)$

(c) $(1, -170°)$

(d) $(2, 240°)$

(e) $(1.5, 300°)$

(f) $(4, -270°)$

33. (a) Which of the following points, in the polar coordinate system, satisfy the equation $r = 3$?

$(3, 30°)$	$(3, 120°)$	$(3, 270°)$
$(3, 90°)$	$(6, 180°)$	$(3, 300°)$
$(5, 60°)$	$(3, 210°)$	$(2, 350°)$

(b) Plot the points that satisfy the equation in part (a). Sketch a curve that represents those points (and others that satisfy the equation). What curve do you get?

(c) Sketch the curve of the points that satisfy the equation $r = 5$.

34. Rectangle $ABCD$ is given. Point P is a point within the rectangle such that the distance from P to A is 3 units, from P to B is 4 units, and from P to C is 5 units. How far is P from D?

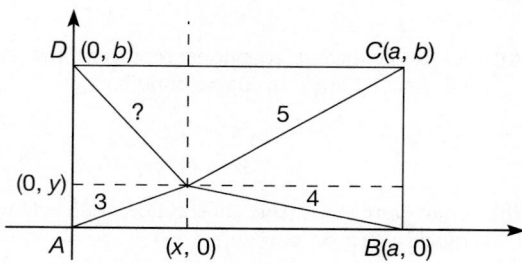

35. A catering company will cater a reception for $2.50 per person plus fixed costs of $100.

(a) Complete the chart below.

Number of People	30	50	75	100	n
Total Cost, y					

(b) Write a linear equation representing the relationship between number of people (x) and total costs (y).

(c) What is the slope of this line? What does it represent?

(d) What is the y-intercept of this line? What does it represent?

36. For the system of equations

$$ax + by = c$$
$$dx + ey = f,$$

find the conditions on a, b, c, d, e, and f, where b and e are nonzero, such that the equations have

(a) infinitely many solutions.

(b) no solution.

(c) a unique solution.

EXERCISE/PROBLEM SET 15.2—PART B

Exercises

1. For each of the following equations, find three points whose coordinates satisfy the equation.
   (a) $x - y = 4$ (b) $2x - 3y = 6$
   (c) $x = 3$ (d) $x + 4y = 0$

2. Identify the slope and the y-intercept for each line.
   (a) $y = -3x + 2$ (b) $y = \frac{3}{2}x - 5$
   (c) $2y = 5x - 6$ (d) $2x - 7y = 8$

3. Write the equation of each line, given its slope m and y-intercept b.
   (a) $m = -2$, $b = 5$ (b) $m = -\frac{7}{3}$, $b = -2$

4. Tell whether the line described by each equation slants up to the right, slants down to the right, is vertical, or is horizontal.
   (a) $y = 5x$ (b) $y = -\frac{1}{3}x - 1$
   (c) $y = -10$ (d) $x = -10$
   (e) $y + x = 0$ (f) $2y - 3x = 0$

5. (a) Graph the following lines on the same coordinate system.
      (i) $y = 2x$ (ii) $y = 2x + 3$ (iii) $y = 2x - 5$
   (b) What is the relationship among these lines?
   (c) Describe the lines of the form $y = cx + d$, where c is a fixed real number and d can be any real number.

6. Write the equation for $\overleftrightarrow{AB}$.
   (a) $A(5, 1)$, $B(0, -6)$ (b) $A(-5, 0)$, $B(1, -6)$
   (c) $A(-1, -3)$, $B(1, 5)$

7. Find the equation of the lines described below.
   (a) Slope -3 and y-intercept -5
   (b) Vertical line through $(-2, 3)$
   (c) Contains $(6, -1)$ and $(3, 2)$

8. Write the equation of the line that passes through the given point and is perpendicular to the line whose equation is given.
   (a) $(-2, 5)$; $y = -2x + 1$
   (b) $(6, 0)$; $y = \frac{2}{3}x - 1$
   (c) $(1, -3)$; $2x + 4y = 6$
   (d) $(-5, -4)$; $3x - 2y = 8$

9. Graph the line described by each equation.
   (a) $y = 2x + 5$ (b) $y = \frac{1}{3}x - 2$
   (c) $y = 3$ (d) $x = -4$

10. (a) Graph the following lines on the same coordinate system.
       (i) $x + y = 3$
       (ii) $x + y = -4$
       (iii) $x + y = 9$
    (b) What is the relationship among these lines?
    (c) Describe the lines of the form $x + y = c$, where c is any constant.

11. Find the equation of the perpendicular bisector of the segment whose endpoints are $(-3, -1)$ and $(6, 2)$.

12. Find the equations of the diagonals of the rectangle $PQRS$ with vertices $P(-2, -1)$, $Q(-2, 4)$, $R(8, 4)$, and $S(8, -1)$.

13. Find the equation of the perpendicular bisector of side $\overline{AB}$ of $\triangle ABC$, where $A = (0, 0)$, $B = (2, 5)$, and $C = (10, 5)$.

14. Find the coordinates of the circumcenter of $\triangle ABC$, where $A = (0, 0)$, $B = (0, 10)$, and $C = (8, 0)$.

15. Solve the following simultaneous equations using the graphical method. (See Exercise 15, Part A.)
    (a) $y = x$ (b) $y = 2x$
        $y = -x + 4$ $y = \frac{1}{2}x + 6$
    (c) $x + y = 5$ (d) $3y = 5x + 1$
        $y = -x - 5$ $-10x + 6y = 2$

16. Use the substitution method to find the solution of the following systems of linear equations, if a solution exists. If no solution exists, explain. (See Exercise 16, Part A.)
    (a) $y = 2x - 4$ (b) $4x + y = 8$
        $y = -5x + 17$ $5x + 3y = 3$
    (c) $x - 2y = 1$ (d) $x - y = 5$
        $x = 2y + 3$ $2x - 4y = 7$

17. Use the elimination method to solve the following systems of equations. (See Exercise 20, Part A.)
    (a) $5x + 3y = 17$
        $2x - 3y = -10$
    (b) $4x - 4y = -3$
        $7x + 2y = 6$

18. Solve the following systems of equations, using any method.
    (a) $y = 3x - 15$
        $y = -2x + 10$
    (b) $x + y = 5$
        $2x + y = 6$
    (c) $2x - 5y = 1$
        $x - 2y = 1$

19. Determine whether the following systems have a unique solution, no solution, or infinitely many solutions.
    (a) $2x - 3y = 6$
        $4x - 6y = -7$
    (b) $3x = 2y$
        $4x - y = 2$
    (c) $3y = 2x - 6$
        $4x - 6y = 12$

20. Identify the center and radius of each circle whose equation is given.
(a) $(x - 2)^2 + (y + 5)^2 = 64$
(b) $(x + 3)^2 + (y - 4)^2 = 20$

21. Write the equation of the circle given by each of the descriptions below.
(a) Center $(-1, -2)$ and radius $\sqrt{5}$
(b) Center $(2, -4)$ and passing through $(-2, 1)$
(c) Endpoints of a diameter at $(-1, 6)$ and $(3, -2)$

22. Find the equation of the circumscribed circle for the triangle whose vertices are $J(4, 5)$, $K(8, -3)$, and $L(-4, -3)$.

23. (a) Use the graphical method to predict solutions to the simultaneous equations

$$x^2 + y^2 = 1$$

$$y = \frac{x}{2} + 1$$

How many solutions do you expect?
(b) Use the substitution method to solve the simultaneous equations.

24. (a) Use the graphical method to predict solutions to the simultaneous equations

$$x^2 + y^2 = 1$$
$$x^2 + (y - 3)^2 = 1$$

How many solutions do you expect?
(b) Use the substitution method to solve the simultaneous equations.

25. Solve the following pairs of simultaneous equations.
(a) $x^2 + y^2 = 4$ (b) $x^2 + y^2 = 4$
$(x - 2)^2 + (y - 2)^2 = 4$ $y + x = 0$

Problems

26. (a) Sketch the graph of the equation $xy = 1$. Choose a variety of values for x. For example, use $x = -10, -5, -1, -0.5, -0.1, 0.1, 0.5, 1, 5, 10$, and other values. The graph is called a **hyperbola**.
(b) Why can't x or $y = 0$?
(c) What happens to the graph when x is near 0? Be sure to include cases when $x > 0$ and when $x < 0$.

27. (a) Sketch the graph of the equation $y = x^2$. Choose a variety of values for x. For example, use $x = -5, -2, -1, 0, 1, 2, 5$, and other values. The graph is called a **parabola**.
(b) Sketch a graph of the equation $y = -x^2$. How is its graph related to the graph in part (a)?

28. (a) Sketch the graph of the equation $\dfrac{x^2}{4} + \dfrac{y^2}{9} = 1$.
(HINT: Choose values of x between -2 and 2, and

note that each value of x produces two values of y.) The graph is called an **ellipse**.
(b) Sketch the graph of the equation $\dfrac{x^2}{9} + \dfrac{y^2}{4} = 1$.
Choose values of x between -3 and 3. How is the graph related to the graph in part (a)?

29. (a) Plot the point $A(5, 30°)$ using the polar coordinate system (see Problem 32 in Part A).
(b) Plot the point $B(5, 390°)$ using the polar coordinate system.
(c) Plot the point $C(-5, 210°)$ using the polar coordinate system. (HINT: At the origin, turn $210°$ and back up 5 units.)
(d) What do you observe about the points A, B, and C? Can a single point have different representations in the polar coordinate system?
(e) In the Cartesian coordinate system (with x- and y-coordinates), can a single point have different representations?

30. (a) Which points below, in the polar coordinate system, satisfy the equation $\theta = 75°$?

$(3, 75°)$	$(-2, 75°)$	$(-3, 75°)$	$(-1, 95°)$
$(5, 75°)$	$(4, 65°)$	$(0, 75)$	$(2, 75°)$

(b) Plot the points that satisfy the equation above. Sketch a curve that represents those points (and others that satisfy the equation). What curve do you get?
(c) Sketch the curve of the points that satisfy the equation $\theta = 135°$.

31. A cab company charges a fixed fee of $0.60 plus $0.50 per mile.
(a) Find the cost of traveling 10 miles; of traveling 25 miles.
(b) Write an expression for the cost, y, of a trip of x miles.

32. (a) A manufacturer can produce items at a cost of $0.65 per item with an operational overhead of $350. Let y represent the total production costs and x represent the number of items produced. Write an equation representing costs.
(b) The manufacturer sells the items for $1 per item. Let y represent the revenue and x represent the number of items sold. Write an equation representing revenue.
(c) How many items does the manufacturer need to sell to break even?

33. The junior class is planning a dance. The band will cost $400 and advertising costs will be $100. Food will be supplied at $2.00 per person.
(a) How many people need to attend the dance in order for the class to break even if tickets are sold at $7 each?

(b) How many people need to attend the dance in order for the class to break even if tickets are sold at $6 each?

(c) How many people need to attend the dance if the class wants to earn $400 profit and sells tickets for $6 each?

34. Find the area of a triangle formed by the x-axis, the y-axis, and the line $2x + 3y = 6$.

15.3

GEOMETRIC PROBLEM SOLVING USING COORDINATES

We can use coordinates to solve a variety of geometric problems. The following property of triangles provides an example.

EXAMPLE 15.8 Suppose that two medians of a triangle are congruent [Figure 15.19(a)]. Show that the triangle is isosceles. (Recall that a median is a line segment joining a vertex to the midpoint of the opposite side.)

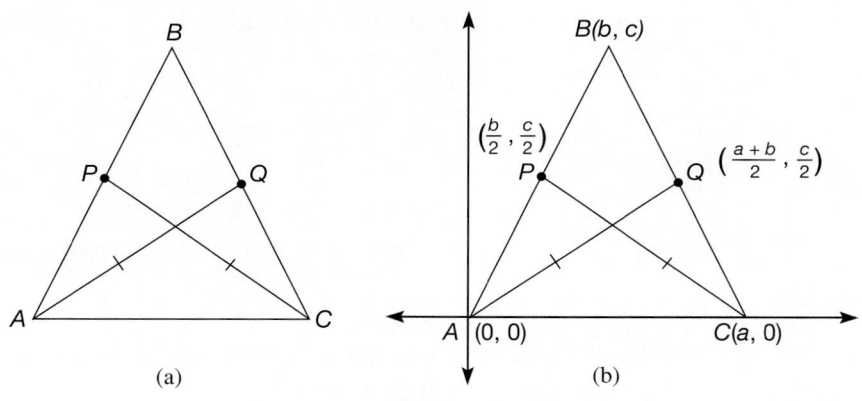

(a)   (b)

FIGURE 15.19

Solution

Choose a coordinate system so that $A = (0, 0)$, $C = (a, 0)$, and $B = (b, c)$ [Figure 15.19(b)]. Let P and Q be the midpoints of sides $\overline{AB}$ and $\overline{BC}$, respectively. Then $P = \left(\dfrac{b}{2}, \dfrac{c}{2}\right)$ and $Q = \left(\dfrac{a + b}{2}, \dfrac{c}{2}\right)$. We wish to show that $AB = BC$; that is, that $\sqrt{b^2 + c^2} = \sqrt{(b - a)^2 + c^2}$. Squaring both sides, we must show $b^2 + c^2 = b^2 - 2ab + a^2 + c^2$, or, simplifying, that $2ab = a^2$. We know that $AQ = CP$, so that

$$\left(\frac{a + b}{2}\right)^2 + \left(\frac{c}{2}\right)^2 = \left(\frac{b}{2} - a\right)^2 + \left(\frac{c}{2}\right)^2$$

$$= \left(\frac{b - 2a}{2}\right)^2 + \left(\frac{c}{2}\right)^2.$$

Expanding, we have

$$\frac{a^2 + 2ab + b^2}{4} + \frac{c^2}{4} = \frac{b^2 - 4ab + 4a^2}{4} + \frac{c^2}{4}$$
$$a^2 + 2ab + b^2 + c^2 = 4a^2 - 4ab + b^2 + c^2$$
$$6ab = 3a^2,$$

so that

$$2ab = a^2,$$

as desired. Thus $\overline{AB} \cong \overline{BC}$, so that $\triangle ABC$ is isosceles. ■

We can use coordinates to verify an interesting result about the three medians of any triangle.

Theorem

Centroid of a Triangle

The medians of $\triangle PQR$ are concurrent at a point G that divides each median in a ratio of $2:1$.

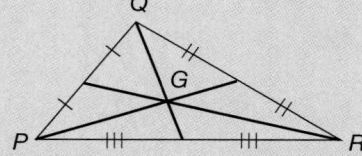

The point G is called the **centroid** of $\triangle PQR$.

Proof
Choose a coordinate system having $P(0, 0)$, $R(c, 0)$, and $Q(a, b)$ (Figure 15.20).

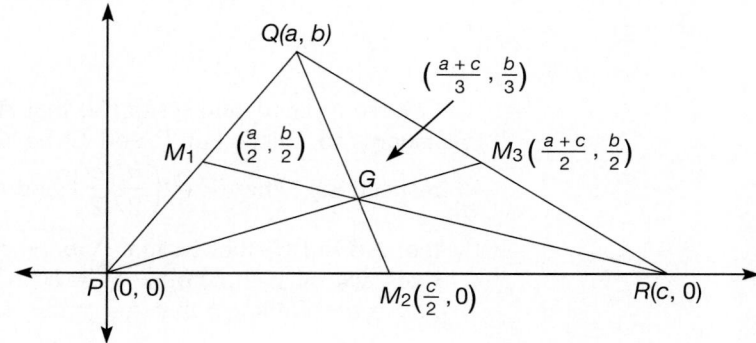

FIGURE 15.20

Let M_1, M_2, and M_3 be the midpoints of sides $\overline{PQ}$, $\overline{PR}$, and $\overline{QR}$.
Then $M_1 = \left(\frac{a}{2}, \frac{b}{2}\right)$, $M_2 = \left(\frac{c}{2}, 0\right)$, and $M_3 = \left(\frac{a+c}{2}, \frac{b}{2}\right)$.

Consider the point $G = \left(\dfrac{a+c}{3}, \dfrac{b}{3}\right)$. Using slopes, we will show that P, G, and M_3 are collinear.

$$\text{slope of } \overline{PG} = \frac{\dfrac{b}{3} - 0}{\dfrac{a+c}{3} - 0} = \frac{b}{a+c},$$

$$\text{slope of } \overline{PM_3} = \frac{\dfrac{b}{2} - 0}{\dfrac{a+c}{2} - 0} = \frac{b}{a+c}.$$

Therefore, P, G, and M_3 are collinear.

In a similar way, we can show that Q, G, and M_2 are collinear, as are R, G and M_1. This is left for the problem set. Hence point G is on all three medians, so that the medians intersect at G.

Finally, we will show that G divides the median $\overline{PM_3}$ in a ratio of $2:1$. The similar verification for the other two medians is left for the problem set.

$$PG = \sqrt{\left(\frac{a+c}{3}\right)^2 + \left(\frac{b}{3}\right)^2}$$

$$= \frac{\sqrt{(a+c)^2 + b^2}}{3}$$

$$GM_3 = \sqrt{\left(\frac{a+c}{2} - \frac{a+c}{3}\right)^2 + \left(\frac{b}{2} - \frac{b}{3}\right)^2}$$

$$= \sqrt{\left(\frac{a+c}{6}\right)^2 + \left(\frac{b}{6}\right)^2}$$

$$= \frac{\sqrt{(a+c)^2 + b^2}}{6}$$

$$= \frac{1}{2}PG.$$

Thus the ratio $PG:GM_3 = 2:1$.   ■

The next results shows how equations of lines can be used to verify properties of triangles. Other examples are in the problem set.

Theorem

Orthocenter of a Triangle

The altitudes of $\triangle PQR$ are concurrent at a point O called the **orthocenter** of the triangle.

Proof

Consider $\triangle PQR$ with altitudes l, m, and n from P, Q, and R, respectively [Figure 15.21(a)]. Choose a coordinate system having

$P(0, 0)$, $Q(a, b)$, and $R(c, 0)$ [Figure 15.21(b)]. Since $l \perp \overleftrightarrow{QR}$, the

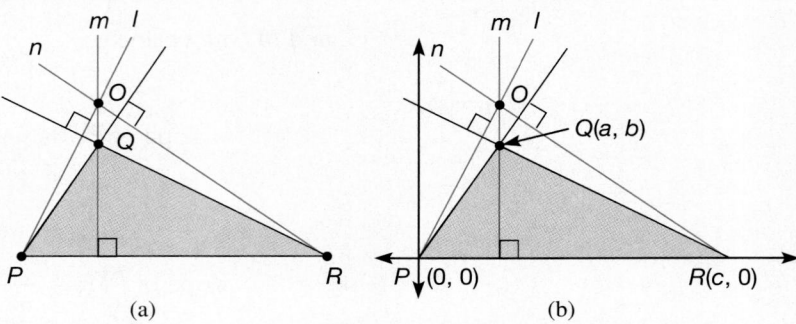

FIGURE 15.21

slope of l is $\dfrac{c - a}{b}$. (Verify.) Hence, the equation of l is $y = \dfrac{c - a}{b}x$, since l contains $(0, 0)$. The equation of m is $x = a$, since m is a vertical line through $Q(a, b)$. Thus l and m intersect at the point $O = \left(a, \dfrac{(c - a)a}{b} \right)$. (Verify.) To find the equation of n we first find its slope. Since $n \perp \overleftrightarrow{PQ}$, the slope of n is $\dfrac{-a}{b}$. (Verify.) Hence the equation of n is of the form $y = -\dfrac{a}{b}x + d$ for some d. Using the fact that $R = (c, 0)$ is on n, we have

$$0 = \frac{-a}{b}c + d, \quad so \quad d = \frac{ac}{b}.$$

Thus the equation of n is $y = \dfrac{-a}{b}x + \dfrac{ac}{b}$. To show that l, m, and n meet at one point, all we need to show is that the point $O = \left(a, \dfrac{(c - a)a}{b} \right)$ is on line n. Substituting a for x in the equation of n, we obtain

$$y = \frac{-a}{b}a + \frac{ac}{b}$$

$$= \frac{ac}{b} - \frac{aa}{b}$$

$$= \frac{(c - a)a}{b},$$

the y-coordinate of O! Hence the three altitudes, l, m, and n, intersect at point O. ∎

The next example illustrates a geometric construction in the coordinate plane using equations of lines and circles.

EXAMPLE 15.9 Find the equation of the circumscribed circle for the triangle whose vertices are $O = (0, 0)$, $P = (2, 4)$, and $Q = (6, 0)$ (Figure 15.22).

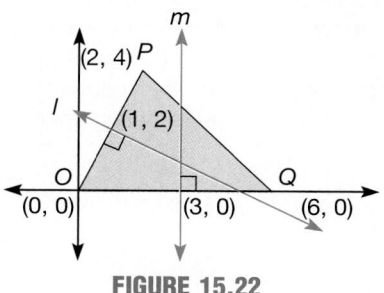

FIGURE 15.22

Solution

The circumscribed circle for a triangle contains all three vertices (see Chapter 14). First, we find the equations of lines l and m, the perpendicular bisectors of $\overline{OP}$ and $\overline{OQ}$. The intersection of lines l and m is the circumcenter of $\triangle OPQ$. To find the equation of line l, we need its slope. The slope of $\overline{OP}$ is $\dfrac{4 - 0}{2 - 0} = 2$, so that the slope of l is $-\frac{1}{2}$ by the slopes of perpendicular lines theorem. Hence the equation of line l is $y = -\frac{1}{2}x + b$, for some b. The midpoint of $\overline{OP}$ is $(1, 2)$, by the midpoint formula, so the point $(1, 2)$ satisfies the equation of line l. Thus $2 = (-\frac{1}{2})(1) + b$, so $b = \frac{5}{2}$. Therefore, the equation of line l is $y = -\frac{1}{2}x + \frac{5}{2}$.

Line m is vertical and contains $(3, 0)$, the midpoint of $\overline{OQ}$. Hence the equation of line m is $x = 3$. To find the circumcenter of $\triangle OPQ$, then, we need to find the point (x, y) satisfying the following simultaneous equations.

$$y = -\frac{1}{2}x + \frac{5}{2} \quad \text{and} \quad x = 3.$$

Using $x = 3$, we have

$$y = -\frac{1}{2}(3) + \frac{5}{2}, \quad \text{or} \quad y = 1.$$

Thus the point $C = (3, 1)$ is the circumcenter of $\triangle OPQ$.

To find the radius of the circumscribed circle, we use the distance formula. Since $(0, 0)$ is on the circle (we could use any vertex), the radius is $\sqrt{(3 - 0)^2 + (1 - 0)^2} = \sqrt{10}$. Thus, by the equation of a circle formula, the equation of the circumscribed circle is

$$(x - 3)^2 + (y - 1)^2 = 10.$$

As a check, verify that the vertices of the triangle, namely $(0, 0)$, $(6, 0)$, and $(2, 4)$ all satisfy this equation. Hence they are all on the circle. Figure 15.23 shows the circumscribed circle. ■

In this chapter we have restricted our attention to equations of circles and lines. However, using coordinates, it is possible to write equations for other sets of points in the plane and thus to investigate many other geometric problems, such as properties of curves other than lines and circles.

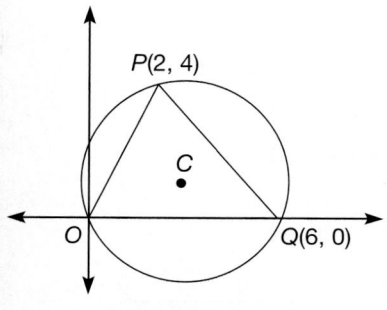

FIGURE 15.23

MATHEMATICAL MORSEL

Any three noncollinear points are contained on a circle. However, a remarkable result concerning nine points in a triangle, known as the nine-point circle theorem, states that the following nine points all lie on a *single* circle determined by $\triangle PQR$.

A, B, C: the midpoints of the sides.

D, E, F: the "feet" of the altitudes.

G, H, I: the midpoints of the segments joining the vertices (*P, Q, R*) to the orthocenter, *O*.

This circle is called the "Feuerbach circle" after a German mathematician, Karl Feuerbach, who proved several results about it.

EXERCISE/PROBLEM SET 15.3—PART A

Exercises

1. The coordinates of three vertices of a parallelogram are given. Find the coordinates of the fourth vertex. (There are three correct answers for each part.)
   (a) (0, 0), (0, 5), (3, 0)
   (b) (−2, −2), (2, 3), (5, 3)

2. The coordinates of three vertices of a square are given. Find the coordinates of the fourth vertex.
   (a) (−2, −1), (3, −1), (3, 4)
   (b) (−3, 0), (0, −2), (2, 1)

3. When using coordinate methods to verify results about polygons, it is often important how you choose the axes of the coordinate system. For example, it is often advantageous to put one vertex at the origin. Label the missing coordinates in the following pictures.
   (a) Square *ABCD*

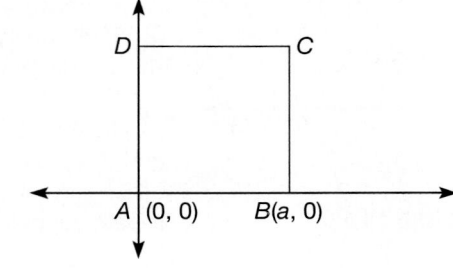

(b) Rectangle *EFGH*

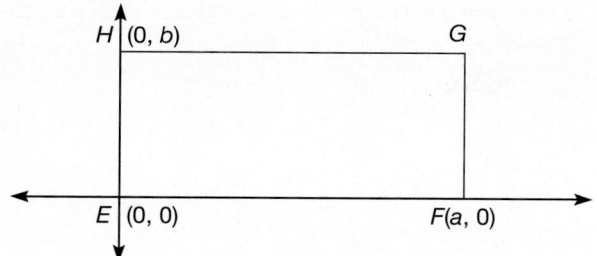

4. A square *TUVW* is placed in a coordinate system such that $\overleftrightarrow{TU}$ is the x-axis, $\overleftrightarrow{TW}$ is the y-axis, and *V* is in the first quadrant.
   (a) If the square has sides of length 5, find the coordinates of the vertices.
   (b) If the square has sides of length *s*, find the coordinates of the vertices.

5. Right triangle *QRS* is placed in a coordinate system as shown.

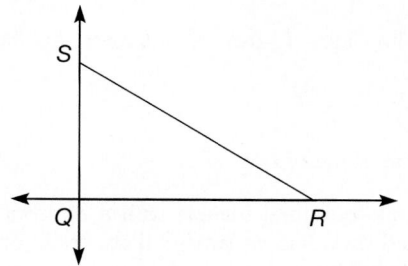

   (a) If $QR = 6$ and $QS = 4$, find the coordinates of the vertices of $\triangle QRS$.
   (b) If $QR = a$ and $QS = b$, find the coordinates of the vertices of $\triangle QRS$.

6. Given $R(5, -2)$, $S(3, 0)$, $T(-4, -1)$, and $U(-2, -3)$, show that *RSTU* is a parallelogram.

7. Given the coordinates of $A(4, 1)$, $B(0, 7)$, $C(3, 9)$, and $D(7, 3)$, show that *ABCD* is a rectangle.

Problems

8. Use coordinates to prove that the diagonals of a rectangle are congruent.

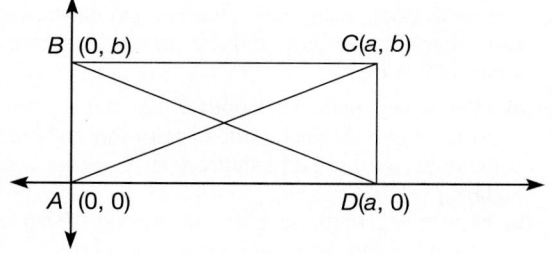

9. Given is $\triangle ABC$ with vertices $A(0, 0)$, $B(24, 0)$, and $C(18, 12)$.
   (a) Find the equation of the line containing the median from vertex *A*.
   (b) Find the equation of the line containing the median from vertex *B*.
   (c) Find the equation of the line containing the median from vertex *C*.
   (d) Find the intersection point of the lines in parts (a) and (b). Does this point lie on the line in part (c)?
   (e) What result about the medians is illustrated?

10. In Problem 9, let *M* be the centroid of the triangle (i.e., the point where the three medians are concurrent).
   (a) Find the length of the median from *A*, the length *AM*, and the ratio of *AM* to the length of the median from *A*.
   (b) Find the length of the median from *B*, the length *BM*, and the ratio of *BM* to the length of the median from *B*.
   (c) Find the length of the median from *C*, the length *CM*, and the ratio of *CM* to the length of the median from *C*.
   (d) Describe the location of the centroid.

11. Given is $\triangle ABC$ with vertices $A(0, 0)$, $B(a, b)$, and $C(c, 0)$ in the following figure. If $\triangle ABC$ is an isosceles triangle with $AB = BC$, show the following results.

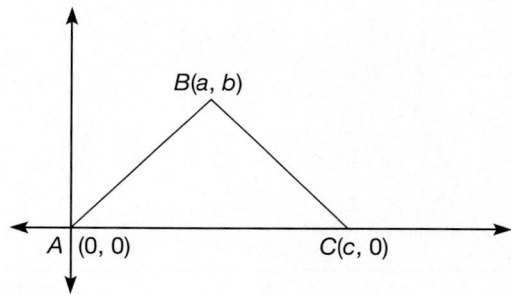

   (a) $c = 2a$
   (b) The median from *B* is perpendicular to $\overline{AC}$.

12. Given is $\triangle RST$ with vertices $R(0, 0)$, $S(8, 6)$, and $T(11, 0)$.
   (a) Find the equation of the line containing the altitude from vertex *R*.
   (b) Find the equation of the line containing the altitude from vertex *S*.
   (c) Find the equation of the line containing the altitude from vertex *T*.
   (d) Find the intersection point of the lines in parts (a) and (b). Does this point lie on the line in part (c)? What point is this?

13. Use coordinates to show that the diagonals of a parallelogram bisect each other.

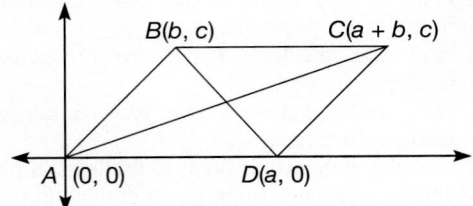

14. Given is $\triangle ABC$ with midpoints M and N of $\overline{AB}$ and $\overline{BC}$, respectively. Let A be $(0, 0)$, B be (a, b), and C be $(c, 0)$. Show the following relationships.
(a) $\overline{MN} \parallel \overline{AC}$
(b) $MN = \frac{1}{2}AC$

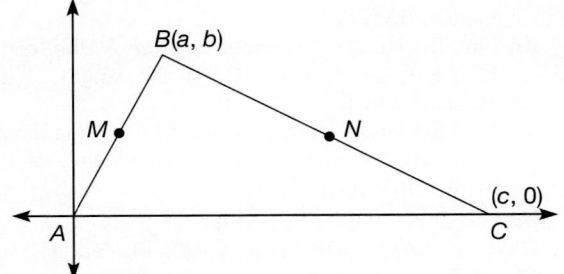

15. A quadrilateral $DEFG$ is shown on a coordinate system. Points M, N, O, and P are midpoints of the sides shown. Verify that $MNOP$ is a parallelogram.

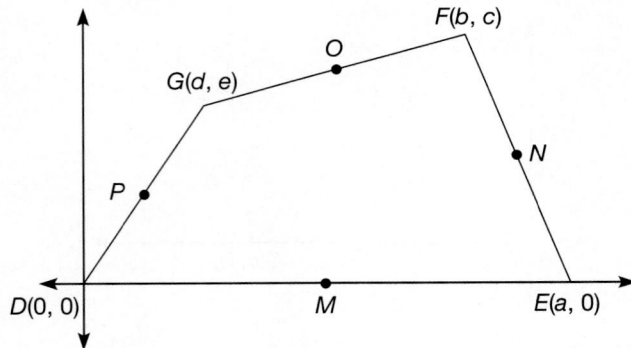

16. Use coordinates to verify that the diagonals of a square are perpendicular.

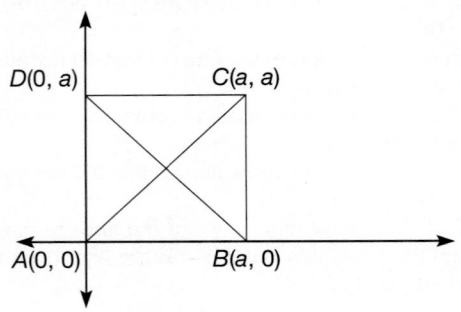

17. Use coordinates to verify that if a triangle is isosceles, the medians to the two congruent sides are congruent.

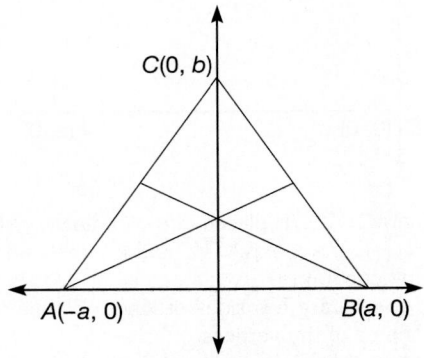

18. In the proof in this section concerning the orthocenter of a triangle, verify the following statements.

(a) The slope of l is $\dfrac{c - a}{b}$.

(b) The lines l and m intersect at the point
$$\left(a, \frac{(c - a)a}{b} \right).$$

(c) The slope of n is $\dfrac{-a}{b}$.

19. Can an equilateral triangle with a horizontal side be formed on a square lattice? If so, show one. If not, explain why not.

20. The other day, I was taking care of two girls whose parents are both mathematicians. The girls are both whizzes at math. When I asked their ages, one girl replied, "The sum of our ages is 18." The other stated, "The difference of our ages is 4." What are the girls' ages?

21. Seven cycle riders and nineteen cycle wheels go past. How many bicycles and how many tricycles passed by the house?

22. Mike and Joan invest $11,000 together. If Mike triples his money and Joan doubles hers, they will have $29,000. How much did each invest?

23. Marge went to the bookstore and paid $16.25 for a used math book, using only quarters and dimes. How many quarters and dimes did she have if she spent all of her 110 coins?

24. **(a)** How many paths of length 7 are there from A to C? (HINT: At each vertex, write the number of ways to get there directly from A. Look for a pattern.)
(b) How many of these paths go through B? (HINT: Apply the fundamental counting property.)

(c) What is the probability that the path will go through *B*?

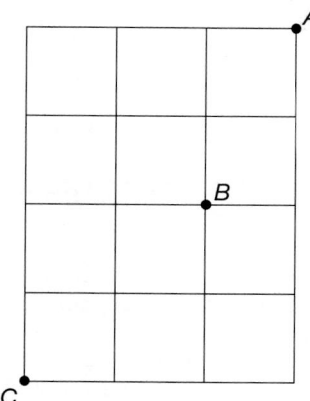

25. Suppose that you have a 5 × 5 square board and four checkers (or counters) that you can place anywhere on the board. Then you can use the four checkers to mark the corners of a square. For example,

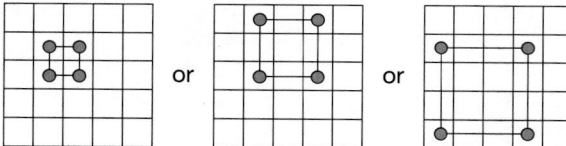

(a) How many different ways can you place the four checkers so that they form a square with horizontal and vertical sides?

(b) What if you also include "tilted squares," such as

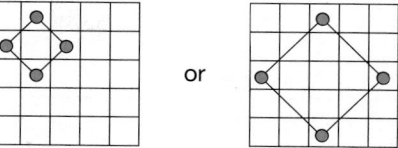

Now how many different squares can you form in all?

(c) Answer the questions above for a 6 × 6 square.

26. My son gave me a set of table mats he bought in Mexico. They were rectangular and were made of straw circles joined together in this way: All the circles on the edges of each mat were white and the inner circles black. I noted that there were 20 white circles and 15 black circles. Is it possible to make such a rectangular mat where the number of black circles is the same as the number of white circles?

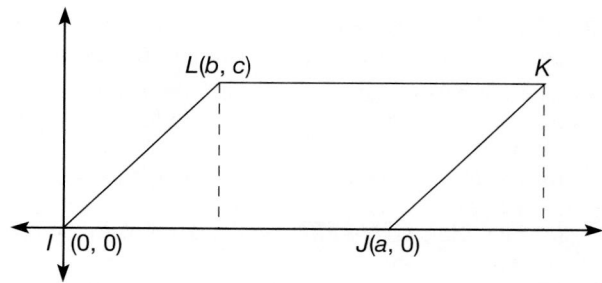

EXERCISE/PROBLEM SET 15.3—PART B

Exercises

1. The coordinates of three vertices of a rectangle are given. Find the coordinates of the fourth vertex.
(a) (4, −2), (4, 5), (−1, 2)
(b) (−2, 1), (0, −1), (3, 2)

2. Two vertices of a figure are (−4, 0) and (2, 0).
(a) Name the coordinates of the third vertex above the x-axis if the figure is an equilateral triangle. (HINT: One of the coordinates is irrational.)
(b) Name the coordinates of the other two vertices above the x-axis if the figure is a square.

3. Parallelogram *IJKL* is placed in a coordinate system such that *I* is at the origin and $\overline{IJ}$ is along the x-axis. The coordinates of *I*, *J*, and *L* are shown. Give the coordinates of point *K* in terms of *a*, *b* and *c*.

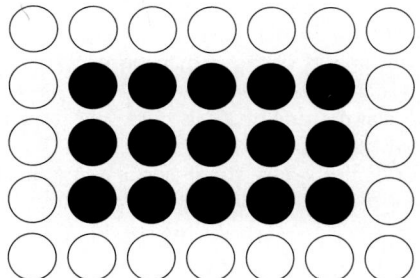

4. Rhombus *MNOP* is placed in a coordinate system such that *M* is at the origin and $\overline{MN}$ is along the x-axis. The coordinates for points *M*, *N*, and *P* are given.
(a) Find the coordinates of point *O* in terms of *a*, *b*, and *c*.

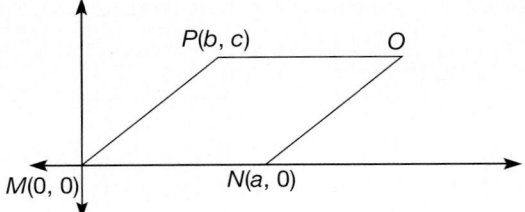

(b) What special relationship exists between a, b, and c because $MNOP$ is a rhombus?

5. The coordinate axes may be established in different ways. Suppose that rectangle $ABCD$ is a rectangle with $AB = 10$ and $AD = 8$. Find the coordinates of the vertices in each of the coordinate systems described.
(a) $\overleftrightarrow{AB}$ is the x-axis, and the y-axis is a line of symmetry.
(b) The x-axis is a horizontal line of symmetry (let $\overleftrightarrow{AB}$ also be horizontal) and the y-axis is a vertical line of symmetry.

6. Given is isosceles triangle XYZ with $XY = YZ$, $XZ = 8$, and the altitude from Y having length 5. Find the coordinates of the vertices in each of the coordinate systems described.
(a) X is at the origin, $\overleftrightarrow{XZ}$ is the x-axis, and Y is in the first quadrant.
(b) $\overleftrightarrow{XZ}$ is the x-axis, the y-axis is a line of symmetry, and the y-coordinate of Y is positive.

7. Given the points $A(-4, -1)$, $B(1, -1)$, $C(4, 3)$, and $D(-1, 3)$, show that $ABCD$ is a rhombus.

8. Draw quadrilaterals that have vertices with the given coordinates. Identify what special kind of quadrilateral each is, if appropriate.
(a) $(-6, -1)$, $(-4, 3)$, $(2, 3)$, $(4, -1)$
(b) $(2, 5)$, $(1, 8)$, $(-2, 3)$, $(-1, 0)$
(c) $(0, 5)$, $(-2, 0)$, $(0, -5)$, $(2, 0)$

9. Determine if the diagonals of $EFGH$ bisect each other, where $E(-1, -7)$, $F(-3, -5)$, $G(-2, 2)$, and $H(0, 0)$.

10. Given $P(-2, -8)$, $Q(3, -3)$, $R(1, -1)$, and $S(-4, -6)$, determine if the diagonals of $PQRS$ are congruent.

11. Given is $\triangle ABC$ with $A(-3, 6)$, $B(5, 8)$, and $C(3, 2)$.
(a) Let M be the midpoint of $\overline{AC}$. What are its coordinates?
(b) Let N be the midpoint of $\overline{BC}$. What are its coordinates?
(c) Find the slope of $\overline{MN}$ and the slope of $\overline{AB}$. What do you observe?
(d) Find the lengths of $\overline{MN}$ and $\overline{AB}$. What do you observe?

Problems

12. Given is an equilateral triangle on a coordinate system.

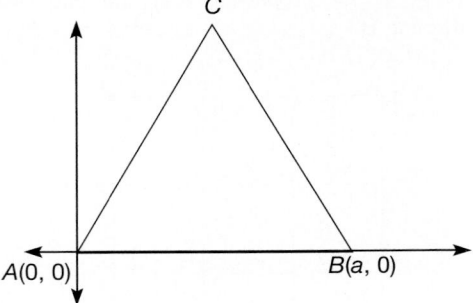

(a) Find the coordinates of point C.
(b) Find the perpendicular bisector of $\overline{AB}$, the median from point C, and the altitude from point C. Do these share points?
(c) Do the perpendicular bisector of $\overline{BC}$, the median, and the altitude from point A share points?
(d) Do the perpendicular bisector of $\overline{AC}$, the median, and the altitude from point B share points?
(e) What general conclusion about equilateral triangles have you shown?

13. Given is a trapezoid $ABCD$ with M the midpoint of side $\overline{AD}$ and N the midpoint of side $\overline{BC}$.

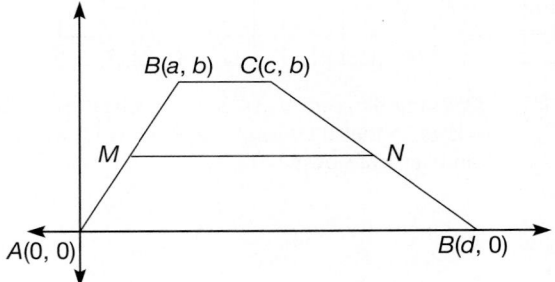

(a) Use coordinates to show that $MN = \frac{1}{2}(AB + CD)$ and $\overline{MN} \parallel \overline{AB}$.
(b) Use the information in part (a) to give a formula for the area of trapezoid $ABCD$.

14. Use coordinates to show that the midpoint of the hypotenuse of a right triangle is equidistant from all three vertices.

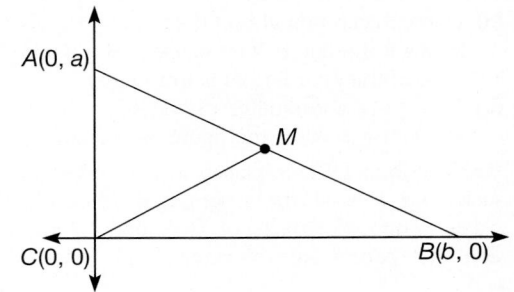

15. Rectangle $ABCD$ is given on a coordinate system as shown.
  (a) Find the coordinates of the midpoints M, N, O, and P.
  (b) Prove this proposition: If the midpoints of consecutive sides of a rectangle are connected, the quadrilateral formed is a rhombus.

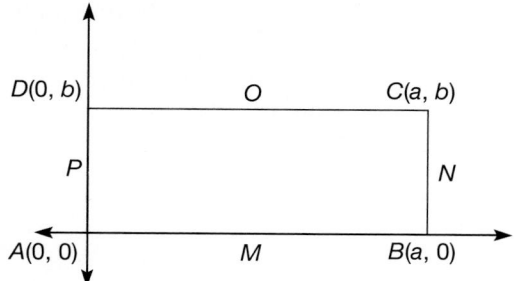

16. Use coordinates to show that the diagonals of an isosceles trapezoid are congruent.

17. Use coordinates to verify that the diagonals of a rhombus are perpendicular. (HINT: $a^2 = b^2 + c^2$.)

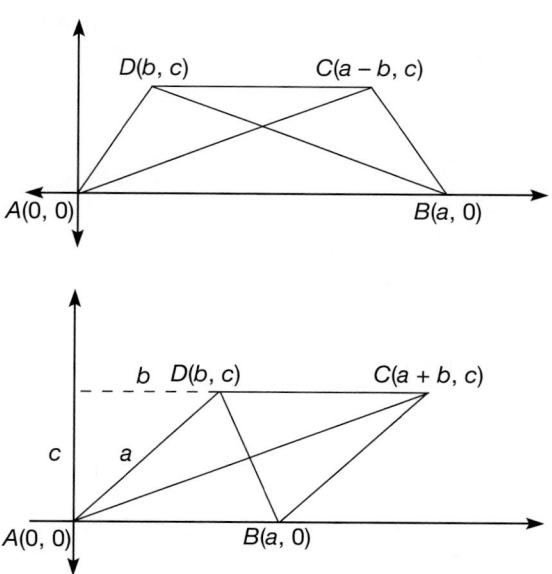

18. In the proof in this section concerning the centroid of a triangle, verify the following statements.
  (a) Points Q, G, and M_2 are collinear.
  (b) Points R, G, and M_1 are collinear.

19. In the proof in this section concerning the centroid of a triangle, verify the following statements.
  (a) The point G divides the median QM_2 in a ratio $2:1$.
  (b) The point G divides the median RM_1 in a ratio $2:1$.

20. Plot the following points and connect them to make a map of Oregon.

$A(-7, 5)$	$E(3, 4)$	$I(6, -2)$
$B(-5, 5)$	$F(6, 4)$	$J(6, -7)$
$C(-4, 3)$	$G(7, 3)$	$K(-8, -7)$
$D(0, 3)$	$H(5, -1)$	$L(-8, -3)$

Connect A to B to C, and so on back to A.
  (a) Make a map of Oregon in which all lengths are doubled from your original map.
  (b) Make a map of Oregon whose *area* is twice that of the original map. [This is not the same map as in part (a).]

21. (a) Given $ABCD$ is an arbitrary quadrilateral. Points M and N are the midpoints of the diagonals $\overline{AC}$ and $\overline{BD}$, respectively. Show that

$$AB^2 + BC^2 + CD^2 + DA^2 = BD^2 + AC^2 + 4(MN)^2.$$

  (b) What does the result in part (a) imply about a parallelogram?

22. Arrange the numbers 1, 2, 3, 4, 5, 6, 8, 9, 10, 11, 12, 13 around the cube shown so that the sum of the four edges that determine a face is always 28 and the sum of the three edges that lead into any vertex is 21.

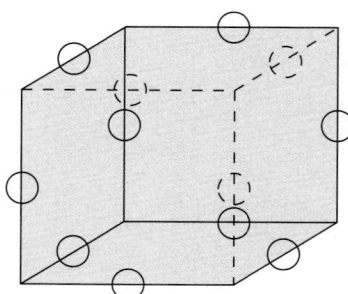

23. A quiz had some 3-point and some 4-point questions. A perfect score was 100 points. Find out how many questions were of each type if there were a total of 31 questions on the quiz.

24. A laboratory produces an alloy of gold, silver, and copper having a weight of 44 grams. If the gold weighs 3 grams more than the silver and the silver weighs 2 grams less than the copper, how much of each element is in the alloy?

25. The sum of two numbers is 148 and their difference is 16. What are the two numbers?

26. Six years ago, in a state park, the deer outnumbered the foxes by 80. Since then, the number of deer has doubled and the number of foxes has increased by 20. If there are now a total of 240 deer and foxes in the park, how many foxes were there 6 years ago?

SOLUTION OF INITIAL PROBLEM

A surveyor plotted a triangular building lot, drew the diagram in Figure 15.23, and recorded the data in the table. What is the area of the lot, in square feet?

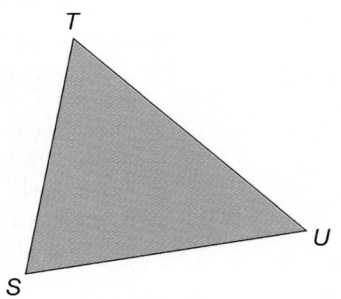

Stake	Position Relative to S
U	East 207′, North 35′
T	East 40′, North 185′

FIGURE 15.23

Strategy: Use Coordinates

First, place the triangle on a coordinate system and then surround it with a rectangle (Figure 15.24). Each triangle, A, B, and C, is a right triangle. We can compute the area of each triangle, then subtract their total areas from the area of the rectangle.

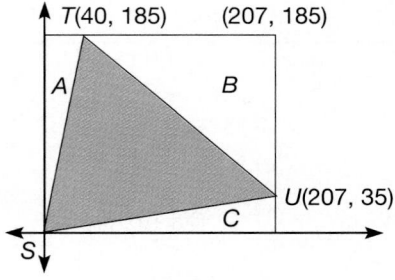

FIGURE 15.24

$$\text{Area of triangle } A = \frac{40 \times 185}{2} = 3700 \text{ ft}^2.$$

$$\text{Area of triangle } B = \frac{167 \times 150}{2} = 12{,}525 \text{ ft}^2.$$

$$\text{Area of triangle } C = \frac{207 \times 35}{2} = 3622.5 \text{ ft}^2.$$

$$\text{Area of rectangle } = 207 \times 185 = 38{,}295 \text{ ft}^2.$$

Hence the area of a surveyed triangle = 38,295 ft² − (3700 + 12,525 + 3622.5) ft² = 18,447.5 ft².

Additional Problems Where the Strategy "Use Coordinates" Is Useful

1. Prove that the diagonals of a kite are perpendicular. [HINT: Consider the kite with coordinates $(0,0)$, (a, b), $(-a, b)$, and $(0, c)$, where $c > b$.]
2. An explorer leaves base camp and travels 4 km north, 3 km west, and 2 km south. How far is he from the base camp?
3. Prove that $\overline{BC}$ is parallel to $\overline{DE}$, where D and E are the centers of the squares (Figure 15.25). (HINT: Use slopes.)

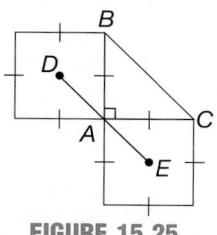

FIGURE 15.25

WRITING/DISCUSSING FOR UNDERSTANDING

1. A student claims that it does not make sense to say that a vertical line has "no slope." He says that it seems more reasonable to say that a horizontal line has no slope, since it is flat. How would you explain the distinction, in terms of slope, between horizontal and vertical lines so that it makes sense to this student?
2. Give a geometric interpretation of what happens when you solve a system of linear equations simultaneously. Be sure to include all possible solutions. How do the possibilities change when at least one of the equations is not linear?
3. Select two problems in Section 15.3, one whose proof is easier to do using coordinates (versus the triangle congruence proofs of Chapter 14) and a second that is easier to do using triangle congruence as opposed to coordinates. Based on these two examples, state which method you prefer and why.

PROJECTS

1. Matrices and determinants are two other ways to solve simultaneous equations. Show, by an example, how these two methods work.
2. Linear programming is a field of mathematics that involves intersecting lines. Prepare a brief report on linear programming. Be certain to mention important applications of linear programming.
3. Three types of graphs described in Exercise/Problem Set 15.2—Part B, the hyperbola, the ellipse, and the parabola, are examples of graphs called conic sections. Read more about the conic sections in your library, in a college algebra or geometry book. How are the graphs listed above related to a cone? What special properties do they possess?

4. Polar coordinates provide another way to locate points in the plane. Prepare a brief report on polar coordinates.

CHAPTER REVIEW

Major Ideas

1. A coordinate system for the plane provides a numerical approach to solving geometry problems.
2. Any two perpendicular lines can be used as the axes of a coordinate system.
3. The following attributes of a line segment can be computed using the coordinates of its endpoints: the length of the segment, the coordinates of its midpoint, and the slope of the segment.
4. The slopes of parallel lines are related, as are the slopes of perpendicular lines.
5. Lines and circles have equations that are satisfied by the coordinates of their points.
6. Simultaneous equations and their solutions can be interpreted geometrically.

Following is a list of key vocabulary, notation, and ideas for this chapter. Mentally review these items and, where appropriate, write down the meaning of each term. Then restudy the material that you are unsure of before proceeding to take the chapter test.

SECTION 15.1: DISTANCE AND SLOPE IN THE COORDINATE PLANE

Vocabulary/Notation

Slope of a line **769**
Slope of a line segment **769**

Ideas

Coordinate distance formula **765**
Collinearity test **767**
Midpoint formula **768**
Computing the slope of a line segment and the slope of a line **769**
Slope and collinearity **770**
Slopes of parallel lines theorem **770**
Slopes of perpendicular lines theorem **771**

SECTION 15.2: EQUATIONS AND COORDINATES

Vocabulary/Notation

y-intercept **781**
Slope-intercept equation of a line **781**
Simultaneous equations **783**

Ideas

SECTION 15.3:   GEOMETRIC PROBLEM SOLVING USING COORDINATES

Vocabulary/Notation

Ideas

PEOPLE IN MATHEMATICS

Shiing-Shen Chern (1911–) is noted for his pioneering work in differential geometry, a branch of mathematics that has been used to extend Einstein's theory of general relativity. Born and educated in China, Chern did advanced study in Germany and France during the 1930s. He returned to China to organize a mathematics institute in Shanghai. The largest part of his working life has been in the United States, at the Institute of Advanced Study, the University of Chicago, and the University of California at Berkeley. In 1982, the National Science Foundation created a center for advanced mathematical study at Berkeley, and Chern was chosen to become its first director. Its official name is the Mathematical Sciences Research Institute; the acronym MSRI is commonly pronounced "misery" by the researchers at the institute, perhaps in recognition of the frustrations they have experienced when attacking difficult problems.

H. S. M. Coxeter (1907–) is known for his researches and expositions of geometry. He is the author of 11 books, including *Introduction to Geometry*, *Pro- jective Geometry*, *Non-Euclidean Geometry*, *The Fifty-Nine Icosahedra*, and *Mathematical Recreations and Essays*. He contends that Russia, Germany, and Austria are the countries that do the best job of teaching geometry in the schools, because they still regard it as a subject worth studying. "In English-speaking countries, there was a long tradition of dull teaching of geometry. People thought that the only thing to do in geometry was to build a system of axioms and see how you would go from there. So children got bogged down in this formal stuff and didn't get a lively feel for the subject. That did a lot of harm."

CHAPTER 15 TEST

Knowledge

1. True or false?
   (a) A point $(a, 0)$ is on the x-axis.
   (b) The quadrants are labeled 1–4 clockwise beginning with the upper left quadrant.
   (c) The midpoint of the segment with endpoints $(a, 0)$ and $(b, 0)$ is $((a + b)/2, 0)$.
   (d) The y-intercept of a line is always positive.
   (e) A pair of simultaneous equations of the form $ax + by = c$ may have *exactly* 0, 1, or 2 simultaneous solutions.
   (f) The orthocenter of a triangle is the intersection of the altitudes.
   (g) The equation $x^2 + y^2 = r^2$ represents a circle whose center is the origin and whose radius is $\sqrt{r^2}$.
   (h) If two lines are perpendicular and neither line is vertical, the slope of each line is the multiplicative inverse of the slope of the other.

Skill

2. Find the length, midpoint, and slope of the line segment with endpoints $(1, 2)$ and $(5, 7)$.

3. Find the equations of the following lines.
   (a) The vertical line containing $(-1, 7)$
   (b) The horizontal line containing $(-1, 7)$
   (c) The line containing $(-1, 7)$ with slope 3
   (d) The line containing $(-1, 7)$ and perpendicular to the line $2x + 3y = 5$

4. Find the equation of the circle with center $(-3, 4)$ and radius 5.

5. Without finding the solutions, determine if the following pairs of equations have zero, one, or infinitely many simultaneous solutions.
   (a) $3x + 4y = 5$
   $\quad 6x + 8y = 11$
   (b) $3x - 2y = -9$
   $\quad x + y = -1$
   (c) $x - y = -1$
   $\quad y - x = 1$
   (d) $x + 5 = 0$
   $\quad 2x + 7y = 10$

Understanding

6. Determine how many simultaneous solutions the equations $x^2 + y^2 = r^2$ and $ax + by = c$ *may* have. Explain.

7. Explain why the following four equations could not contain the four sides of a rectangle, but *do* contain the four sides of a parallelogram.

$$2x - 4y = 7$$
$$2x - 4y = 13$$
$$3x + 5y = 8$$
$$3x + 5y = -2$$

Problem Solving/Application

8. Give the most complete description of the figure $ABCD$, where A, B, C, and D are the midpoints of the square determined by the points $(0, 0)$ $(a, 0)$, (a, a), and $(0, a)$, and where a is positive. Prove your assertion.

9. For the triangle pictured, prove the following relationships.

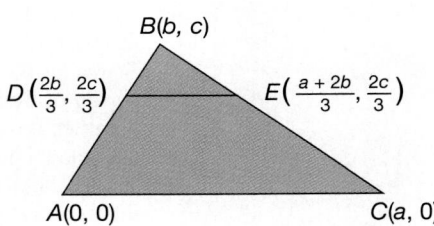

$B(b, c)$

$D\left(\frac{2b}{3}, \frac{2c}{3}\right)$ $E\left(\frac{a + 2b}{3}, \frac{2c}{3}\right)$

$A(0, 0)$ $C(a, 0)$

(a) $\overline{DE} \parallel \overline{AC}$ (b) $DE = \frac{1}{3}AC$
State the new theorem that you have proved.

Geometry Using Transformations

Circle Limit III

Shells and Starfish

The Geometrical Art of M. C. Escher

Maurits Escher was born in the Netherlands in 1898. Although his school experience was largely a negative one, he looked forward with enthusiasm to his two hours of art each week. His father urged him into architecture to take advantage of his artistic ability. However, that endeavor did not last long. It became apparent that Escher's talent lay more in the area of decorative arts than in architecture, so Escher began the formal study of art when he was in his twenties. His work includes sketches, woodcuts, mezzotints, lithographs, and watercolors.

Escher's links with mathematics and mathematical form are apparent. The following works illustrate various themes related to mathematics.

Approaches to Infinity:

Circle Limit III (1959) illustrates one of three Circle Limit designs based on a hyperbolic tessellation. Notice how the fish seem to swim to infinity. This work gave rise to a paper by H. S. M. Coxeter entitled "The Non-Euclidean Symmetry of Escher's Picture *Circle Limit III*."

Symmetries:

Shells and Starfish (1991) which was developed from a pattern of stars and diamond shapes on a square grid, possesses several rotation symmetries.

Metamorphosis:

Escher is perhaps most famous for his ever-changing pictures. *Fish* (1990) shows arched fish evolving, appearing, and disappearing across the drawing. Methods that lead to constructions such as these are discussed in this chapter.

FISH

STRATEGY 21: USE SYMMETRY

Several types of geometrical and numerical symmetry can occur in mathematical problems. Geometrical symmetry involves a correspondence between points that preserves shape and size. For example, the actions of sliding, turning, and flipping lead to types of symmetry. Numerical symmetry occurs, for example, when numerical values can be interchanged and yet the results are equivalent. As an illustration, suppose that 5 coins are tossed. Knowing that 3 heads and 2 tails can occur in 10 ways, we can determine the number of ways that 2 heads and 3 tails can occur. We simply replace each "head" by "tail," and vice versa, using the fact that each arrangement of n heads and m tails ($n + m = 5$) corresponds to exactly one arrangement of m heads and n tails. Hence there are also 10 ways that 2 heads and 3 tails can occur.

Initial Problem

Houses A and B are to be connected to a television cable line l, at a transformer point P. Where should P be located so that the sum of the distances, $AP + PB$, is as small as possible?

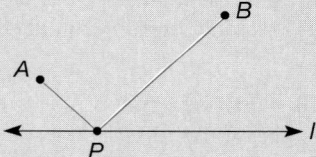

Clues

The Use Symmetry strategy may be appropriate when:

- Geometry problems involve transformations.
- Interchanging values does not change the representation of the problem.
- Symmetry limits the number of cases that need to be considered.
- Pictures or algebraic expressions are symmetric.

A solution of the Initial Problem above appears on page 872.

INTRODUCTION

In Chapter 12 we observed informally that many geometrical figures have symmetry properties, such as rotation or reflection symmetry. In this chapter we give a precise description of symmetry in the plane in terms of functions or mappings between points. Mappings of points in the plane will be called transformations. Using transformations, we give precise meanings to the ideas of congruence of figures and similarity of figures. Finally, by studying congruence and similarity via transformations, we can derive many important geometrical properties that can be used to solve geometry problems.

16.1

TRANSFORMATIONS

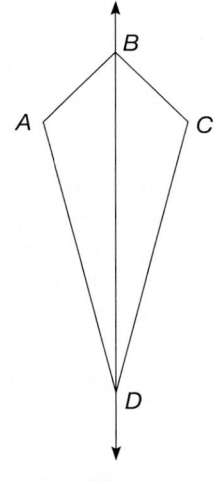

FIGURE 16.1

Isometries

In Chapter 12 we investigated symmetry properties of geometric figures by means of motions that make a figure coincide with itself. For example, the kite in Figure 16.1 has reflection symmetry since there is a line, $\overleftrightarrow{BD}$, over which the kite can be folded to make the two halves match.

Notice that when we fold the kite over $\overleftrightarrow{BD}$, we are actually forming a one-to-one correspondence between the points of the kite. For example, points A and C correspond to each other, points along segments $\overline{AB}$ and $\overline{CB}$ correspond, and points along segments $\overline{AD}$ and $\overline{CD}$ correspond. In this chapter we will investigate correspondences between points of the plane. A **transformation** is a one-to-one correspondence between points in the plane such that each point P is associated with a unique point P', called the **image** of P.

Transformations that preserve the size and shape of geometric figures are called **isometries** (*iso* means same and *metry* means measure) or **rigid motions**. In the remainder of this subsection, we'll study the various types of isometries.

Translations

Consider the following transformation that acts like a "slide."

EXAMPLE 16.1   Describe a transformation that will move △*ABC* of Figure 16.2 to coincide with △*A′B′C′*.

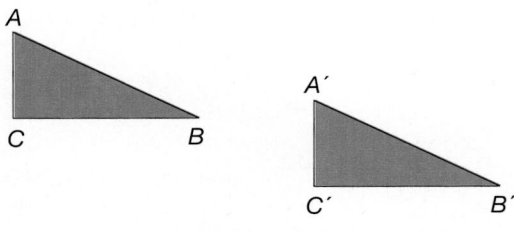

FIGURE 16.2

Solution
Slide the triangle so that A moves to A' (Figure 16.3).

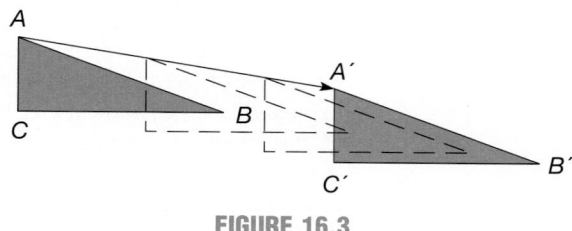

FIGURE 16.3

Since B' and C' are the same distance and direction from B and C, respectively, as A' is from A, point B' is the image of B and point C' is the image of C. Thus $\triangle ABC$ moves to $\triangle A'B'C'$. Trace $\triangle ABC$ and slide it according to the arrow from A to A' to verify this.   ■

The sliding motion of Example 16.1 can be described by specifying the distance and direction of the slide. The arrow from A to A' in Figure 16.3 conveys this information. A transformation that "slides" each point in the plane in the same direction and for the same distance is called a translation. For the transformations considered in this section, we will assume that we can obtain the image of a polygon by connecting the images of the vertices of the original polygon, as we did in Example 16.1.

To give a precise definition to a translation or "sliding" transformation, we need the concept of directed line segment. Informally, a line segment $\overline{AB}$ can be directed in two ways: (1) pointing from A to B or (2) pointing from B to A (Figure 16.4). We denote the **directed line segment** from A to B as $\overrightarrow{AB}$. Two directed line segments are called **equivalent** if they are parallel, have the same length, and point in the same direction.

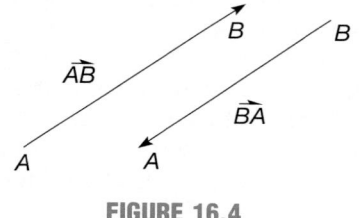

FIGURE 16.4

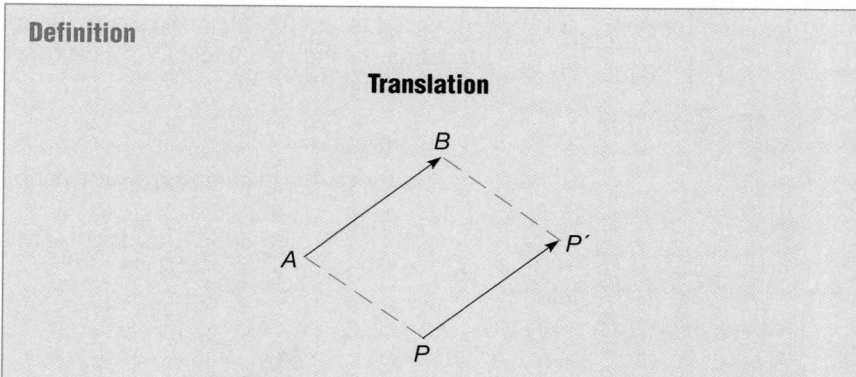

Definition
Translation

Suppose that A and B are points in the plane. The **translation** associated with directed line segment $\overrightarrow{AB}$, denoted T_{AB}, is the transformation that maps each point P to the point P' such that $\overrightarrow{PP'}$ is equivalent to $\overrightarrow{AB}$.

Directed segment $\overrightarrow{PP'}$ is equivalent to $\overrightarrow{AB}$ so that $\overrightarrow{PP'} \parallel \overrightarrow{AB}$ and $PP' = AB$. Thus quadrilateral $PP'BA$ is a parallelogram, since it has a pair of opposite sides that are parallel and congruent. We can imagine that P is "slid" by the translation T_{AB} in the direction from A to B, parallel to $\overleftrightarrow{AB}$, for a distance equal to $\overrightarrow{AB}$.

Rotations

An isometry that corresponds to turning the plane around a fixed point is described next.

EXAMPLE 16.2 Describe a transformation that will move $\triangle ABC$ of Figure 16.5 to coincide with $\triangle A'B'C'$.

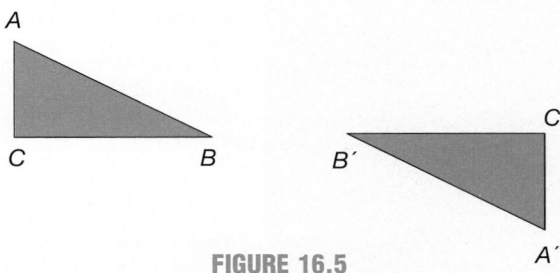

FIGURE 16.5

Solution

We can turn $\triangle ABC$ 180° around point P, the midpoint of segment $\overline{BB'}$, to coincide with $\triangle A'B'C'$ (Figure 16.6).

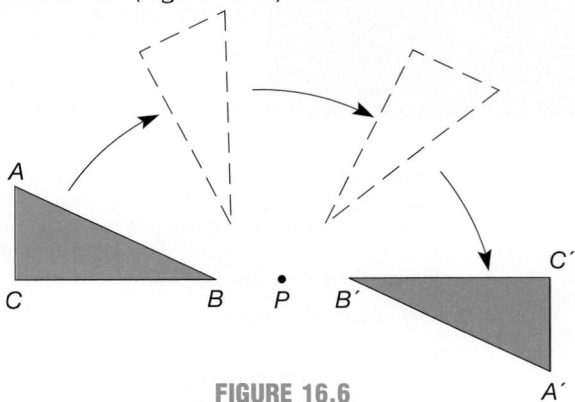

FIGURE 16.6

Trace $\triangle ABC$ and turn your tracing around point P to verify this. ■

A transformation that corresponds to a turning motion as in Example 16.2 is called a rotation. To define a rotation we need the concept of directed angle. Angle $\angle ABC$ is said to be a **directed angle** if it satisfies the following.

1. If $m(\angle ABC) = 0$, then the measure of the directed angle is 0°.
2. If $\angle ABC$ is a straight angle, then the measure of the directed angle is 180°.
3. See Figure 16.7.
   (a) Let ray $\overrightarrow{BA}$ be turned around point B through the smallest possible angle so that the image of ray $\overrightarrow{BA}$ coincides with ray $\overrightarrow{BC}$.
   (b) If the direction of the turn is *counterclockwise*, the measure of the directed angle is the *positive* number $m(\angle ABC)$. If the direction is *clockwise*, the measure is the *negative* number $-m(\angle ABC)$. We denote the directed angle $\angle ABC$ by $\measuredangle ABC$.

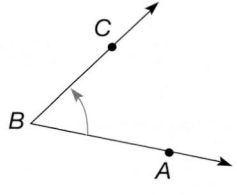

FIGURE 16.7

STUDENT PAGE SNAPSHOT

A<small>CTIVITY</small> Rotations

An astronomer is making drawings that show the movement of constellations through the sky over a period of four hours. How can she draw the image of each constellation after it has revolved about the North Star (*N*) to its new position?

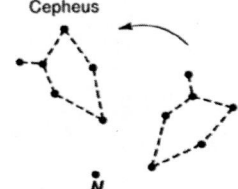

Cepheus

WORKING TOGETHER

When a figure moves to a new position by rotating through an angle about a point, as though it were attached to a wheel, the movement is a **rotation.** The new position is specified by the direction and the measure of the angle through which the figure moves. One complete rotation is 360°. *P'* is the rotated image of *P* through an angle of 60° counterclockwise about point *Q*.

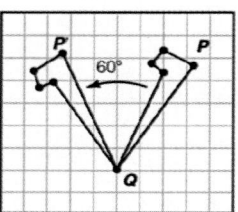

1. Using tracing paper copy the two images of the constellation Cepheus. Choose a vertex and its image and connect each with point *N*. What is the measure of the angle between the two segments drawn? How long are the segments? Repeat for each vertex. What can you conclude?

2. How would you draw the rotation image of a given figure?

3. Trace the diagram of the Big Dipper and point *N* on a sheet of graph paper. Then draw the rotation of the constellation through an angle of 85° counterclockwise about the point *N*.

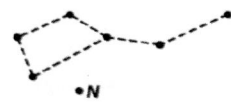

SHARING IDEAS

4. How did you draw the rotation of the Big Dipper? Compare your drawing with those of other students.

5. How is your rotated drawing of the Big Dipper different from a translation? from a reflection?

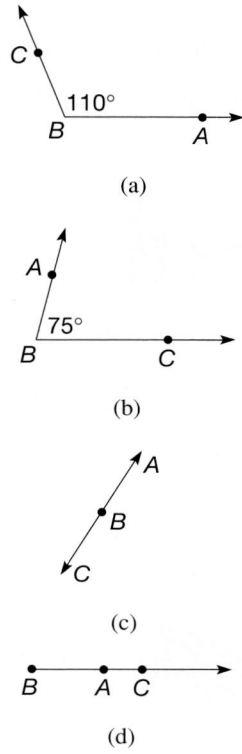

(a)

(b)

(c)

(d)

FIGURE 16.8

For directed angle $\measuredangle ABC$, ray $\overrightarrow{BA}$ is called the **initial side**, and ray $\overrightarrow{BC}$ is called the **terminal side**. In directed angle $\measuredangle ABC$, the initial side is given by the ray whose vertex is the vertex of the angle, here B, and which contains the point listed first in the name of the angle, here A. For example, in directed angle $\measuredangle CBA$ the initial side is $\overrightarrow{BC}$. Notice that the measure of directed angle $\measuredangle CBA$ is the *opposite* of the measure of directed angle $\measuredangle ABC$, since the initial side of directed angle $\measuredangle CBA$ is ray $\overrightarrow{BC}$, while the initial side of directed angle $\measuredangle ABC$ is $\overrightarrow{BA}$. Example 16.3 gives several examples of directed angles.

EXAMPLE 16.3 Find the measure of each of the directed angles $\measuredangle ABC$ in Figure 16.8.

Solution
(a) The measure of directed angle $\measuredangle ABC$ is $110°$, since initial side $\overrightarrow{BA}$ can be turned counterclockwise through $110°$ around point B to coincide with terminal side $\overrightarrow{BC}$.
(b) The measure of directed angle $\measuredangle ABC$ is $-75°$, since initial side $\overrightarrow{BA}$ can be turned clockwise through $75°$ to coincide with terminal side $\overrightarrow{BC}$.
(c) The measure of directed angle $\measuredangle ABC$ is $180°$, since $\angle ABC$ is a straight angle.
(d) The measure of directed angle $\measuredangle ABC$ is $0°$, since $m(\angle ABC) = 0°$. ■

We can now define a rotation. In Section 16.2 we prove that rotations are isometries.

Definition

Rotation

Suppose that O is a point in the plane and $\measuredangle ABC$ is a directed angle whose measure is a. The **rotation** with center O and angle with measure a, denoted $\boldsymbol{R_{O,a}}$, is the transformation that maps each point P other than O to the point P' such that:

1. the measure of directed angle $\measuredangle POP'$ is a, and
2. $OP' = OP$.

Point O is mapped to itself by $R_{O,a}$.

NOTE: If a is positive, $R_{O,a}$ is counterclockwise, and if a is negative, $R_{O,a}$ is clockwise. Intuitively, point P is "turned" by $R_{O,a}$ around the center, O, through a directed angle of measure a to point P'.

Reflections

Another isometry corresponds to flipping the plane over a fixed line.

EXAMPLE 16.4   Describe a transformation that will move $\triangle ABC$ of Figure 16.9 to coincide with $\triangle A'B'C'$.

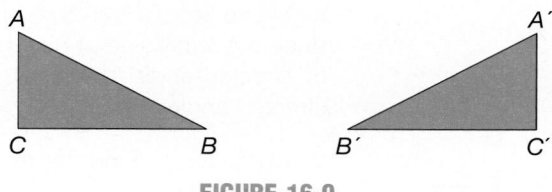

FIGURE 16.9

Solution

Flip $\triangle ABC$ over the perpendicular bisector of segment $\overline{AA'}$ (Figure 16.10).

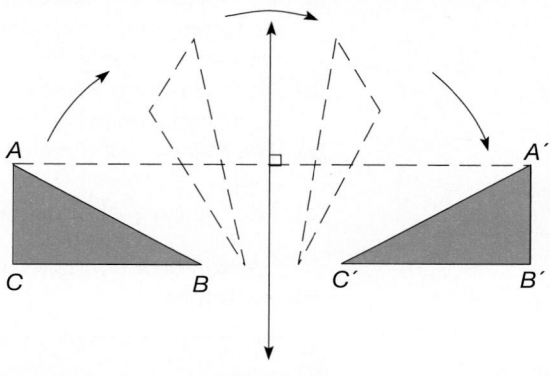

FIGURE 16.10

Then point A moves to point A', point B to B', and C to C'. Hence $\triangle ABC$ moves to $\triangle A'B'C'$. Trace Figure 16.9 and fold your tracing to verify this.   ■

A transformation that "flips" the plane over a fixed line is called a reflection.

Definition

Reflection

Suppose that l is a line in the plane. The **reflection** in line l, denoted M_l, is the transformation that maps points as follows:

1. Each point P not on line l is mapped to the point P' such that l is the perpendicular bisector of segment $\overline{PP'}$.
2. Each point Q on line l is mapped to itself.

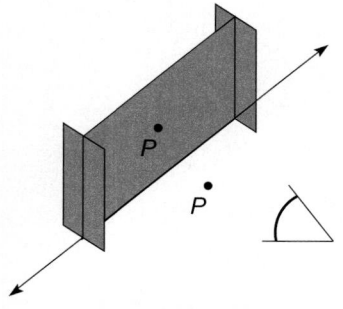

FIGURE 16.11

We denote the reflection in line $\overleftrightarrow{AB}$ by M_{AB}. (M is used for *mirror image*.) We can envision the effect of the reflection in line l by imagining a mirror in line l perpendicular to the plane. Then points on either side of l are mapped to the other side of l, and points on l remain fixed. A Mira can be used to find reflection images easily (Figure 16.11). We prove that reflections are isometries in the next section.

Glide Reflections

Next we define a transformation that is a combination of a translation and a reflection, called a glide reflection.

EXAMPLE 16.5   Is there a translation that will move $\triangle ABC$ of Figure 16.12 to coincide with $\triangle A'B'C'$? What about a rotation? Reflection?

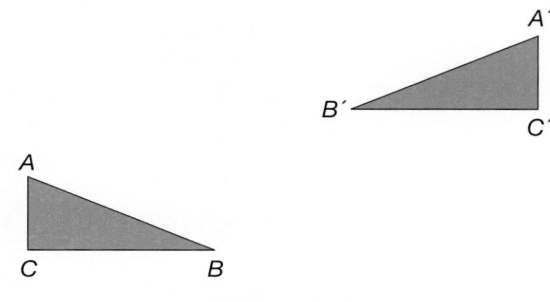

FIGURE 16.12

Solution
No single transformation that we have studied thus far will suffice. Use tracings to convince yourself. However, with a combination of a translation and a reflection, we can move $\triangle ABC$ to $\triangle A'B'C'$ (Figure 16.13). First, apply

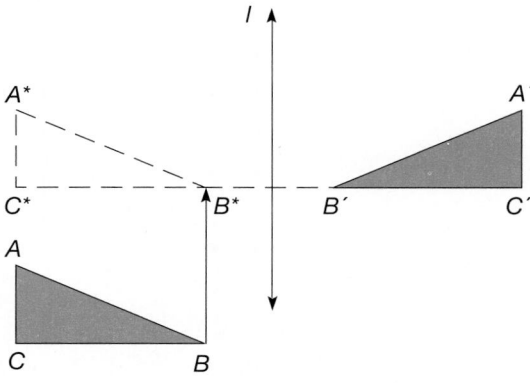

FIGURE 16.13

the translation T_{BB*} to move $\triangle ABC$ to $\triangle A*B*C*$, a triangle that can be reflected onto $\triangle A'B'C'$. Then reflect $\triangle A*B*C*$ in line l onto $\triangle A'B'C'$. Notice that directed line segment $\overrightarrow{BB*}$ is parallel to the reflection line l.   ∎

A transformation formed by combining a translation and a reflection over a line parallel to the directed line segment of the translation, as in Example 16.5, is called a glide reflection.

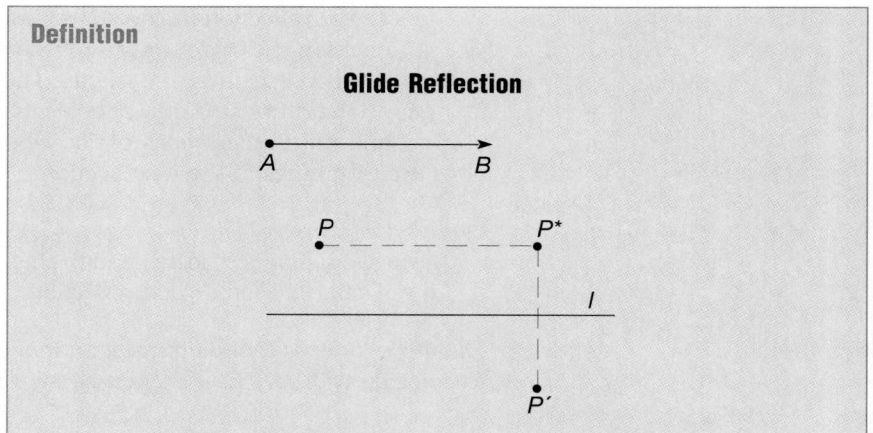

Definition

Glide Reflection

Suppose that A and B are different points in the plane and that line l is parallel to directed line segment $\overrightarrow{AB}$. The combination of the translation T_{AB} followed by the reflection M_l is called the **glide reflection** determined by $\overrightarrow{AB}$ and **glide axis** l. That is, P is first mapped to $P*$ by T_{AB}. Then $P*$ is mapped to P' by M_l. The combination of T_{AB} followed by M_l maps P to P'.

It can be shown that as long as $l \parallel \overrightarrow{AB}$, the glide reflection image can be found by translating first, then reflecting, or vice versa. Example 16.6 shows the effect of a glide reflection on a triangle.

EXAMPLE 16.6   In Figure 16.14(a), find the image of $\triangle PQR$ under the glide reflection T_{AB} followed by M_l.

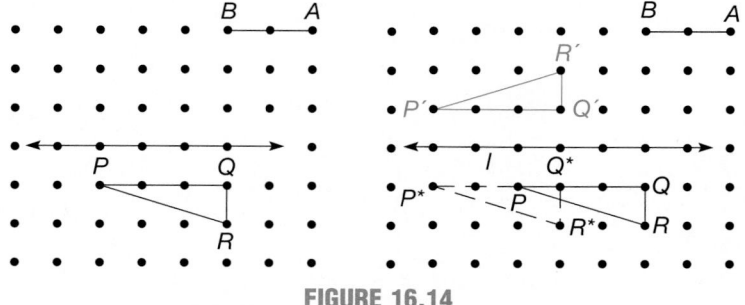

FIGURE 16.14

Solution
We observe that the translation T_{AB} maps each point two units to the left [Figure 16.14(b)]. That is, T_{AB} maps $\triangle PQR$ to $\triangle P*Q*R*$. The reflection M_l reflects $\triangle P*Q*R*$ across line l to $\triangle P'Q'R'$. Equivalently, we can reflect $\triangle PQR$ across line l, then slide its image to the left. In each case, the image of $\triangle PQR$ is $\triangle P'Q'R'$. Since glide reflections are combinations of two isometries, a translation and a reflection, they, too, are isometries.   ■

In Example 16.6 observe that $\triangle PQR$ was reflected across line l to $\triangle P'Q'R'$. Thus the "orientation" of $\triangle P'Q'R'$ is opposite that of $\triangle PQR$. In

Figure 16.15, $\triangle PQR$ is said to have **clockwise orientation** since tracing the triangle from P to Q to R is a clockwise tracing. Similarly, $\triangle P'Q'R'$ in Figure 16.15 has **counterclockwise orientation** since a tracing from P' to Q' to R' is counterclockwise.

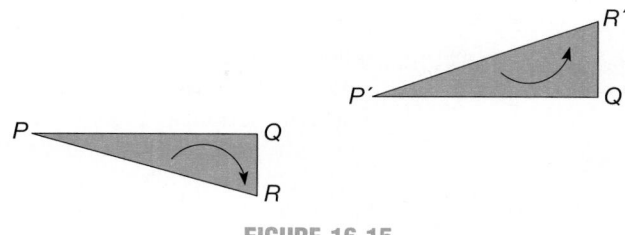

FIGURE 16.15

From the examples in this section, we can observe that translations and rotations preserve orientation, whereas reflections and glide reflections reverse orientation.

In elementary school, translations, rotations, reflections, and glide reflections are frequently called "slides," "turns," "flips," and "slide flips," respectively. Next, we will see how to apply these transformations to analyze symmetry patterns in the plane.

Symmetry

Consider a tessellation of the plane with parallelograms (Figure 16.16).

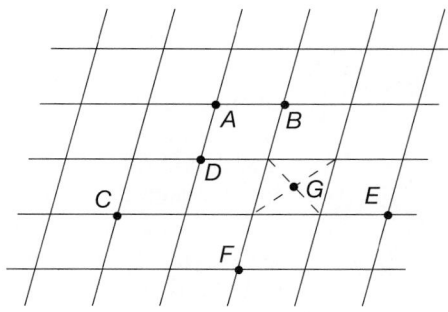

FIGURE 16.16

We can identify several translations that map the tessellation onto itself. For example, the translations T_{AB}, T_{CD}, and T_{EF} all map the tessellation onto itself. To see that T_{AB} maps the tessellation onto itself, make a tracing of the tessellation, place the tracing on top of the tessellation, and move the tracing according to the translation T_{AB}. The tracing will match up with the original tessellation. (Remember that the tessellation fills the plane.) A figure has **translation symmetry** if there is a translation that maps the figure onto itself. Every tessellation of the plane with parallelograms like the one in Figure 16.16 has translation symmetry.

For the tessellation in Figure 16.16, there are several rotations, through less than 360°, that map the tessellation onto itself. For example, the rotations $R_{A,180}$ and $R_{G,180}$ map the tessellation onto itself. Note that G is the

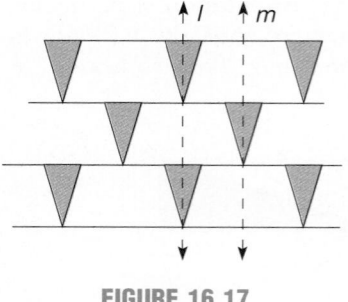

FIGURE 16.17

intersection of the diagonals of a parallelogram. (Use your tracing paper to see that these rotations map the tessellation onto itself.) A figure has **rotation symmetry** if there is a rotation through an angle greater than 0° and less than 360° that maps the figure onto itself.

In Figure 16.17, a tessellation with isosceles triangles and trapezoids is pictured. Again, imagine that the tessellation fills the plane. In Figure 16.17, reflection M_l maps the tessellation onto itself, as does M_m. A figure has **reflection symmetry** if there is a reflection that maps the figure onto itself. The tessellation in Figure 16.17 has translation symmetry and reflection symmetry, but not rotation symmetry.

Figure 16.18 illustrates part of a tessellation of the plane that has translation, rotation, and reflection symmetry.

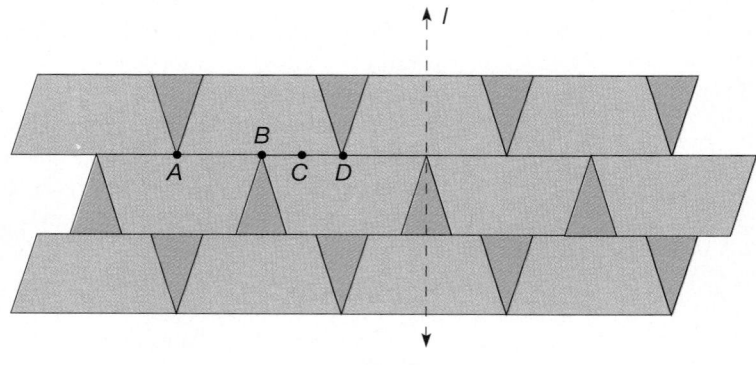

FIGURE 16.18

For example, $R_{C,180}$ is a rotation that maps the tessellation onto itself, where point C is the midpoint of segment $\overline{BD}$. (You can use a tracing of the tessellation to check this.) The translation T_{AD} can be used to show that the tessellation has translation symmetry, while the reflection M_l can be used to show reflection symmetry. This tessellation also has glide reflection symmetry. For example, consider the glide reflection formed by T_{AB} followed by M_{AB}. This glide reflection maps the tessellation onto itself. A figure has **glide reflection symmetry** if there is a glide reflection that maps the figure onto itself. (Notice that, in this case, neither the translation T_{AB}, nor the reflection M_{AB} alone, maps the tessellation to itself.)

Symmetrical figures appear in nature, art, and design. Interestingly, all symmetrical patterns in the plane can be analyzed using translations, rotations, reflections, and glide reflections.

Making Escher-Type Patterns

The artist M. C. Escher used tessellations and transformations to make intriguing patterns that fill the plane. Figure 16.19 shows how to produce such a pattern. Side $\overline{AB}$ of the square $ABCD$ [Figure 16.19(a)] is altered to form the outline of a cat's head [Figure 16.19(b)]. Then the curved side from A' to B' is translated so that A' is mapped to C' and B' is mapped to D'. Thus the curve connecting C' to D' is the same size and shape as the curve connecting A' to B'. All other points remain fixed [Figure 16.19(c)]. The resulting shape will tessellate the plane [Figure 16.19(c)]. Using translations, tessellations of the plane with parallelograms can be altered to make Escher-type patterns.

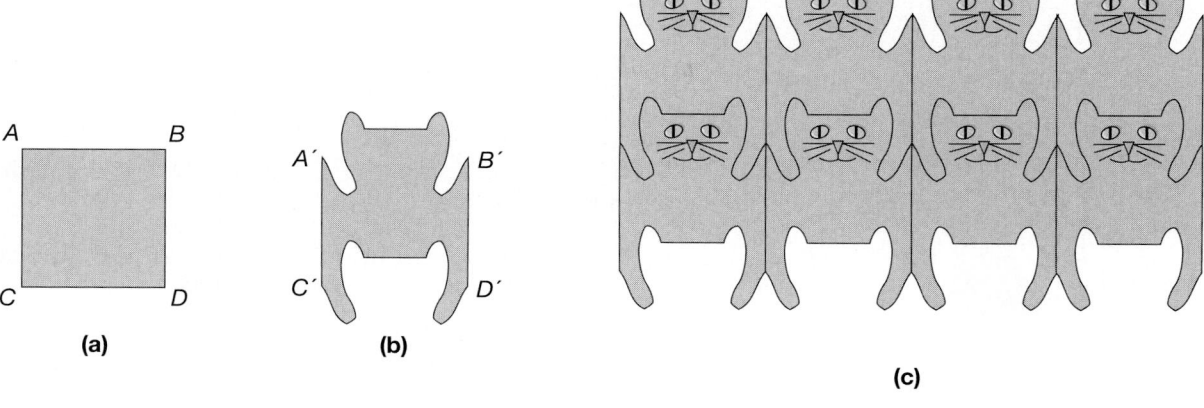

FIGURE 16.19

Rotations can also be used to make Escher-type drawings. Figure 16.20 shows a triangle that has been altered by rotation to produce an Escher-type pattern. Side $\overline{AC}$ of $\triangle ABC$ [Figure 16.20(a)] is altered arbitrarily, provided that points A and C are not moved [Figure 16.20(b)]. Then, using point C as the center of a rotation, altered side $\overline{AC}$ is rotated so that A is rotated to B [Figure 16.20(c)]. The result is an alteration of side $\overline{BC}$. The shape in Figure 16.20(c) will tessellate the plane as shown in Figure 16.20(d). Other techniques for making Escher-type patterns appear in the problem sets. Many Escher-type patterns are tessellations of the plane having a variety of types of symmetry. For example, the tessellation in Figure 16.19(c) has translation and reflection symmetry, while the tessellation in Figure 16.20(d) has translation and rotation symmetry.

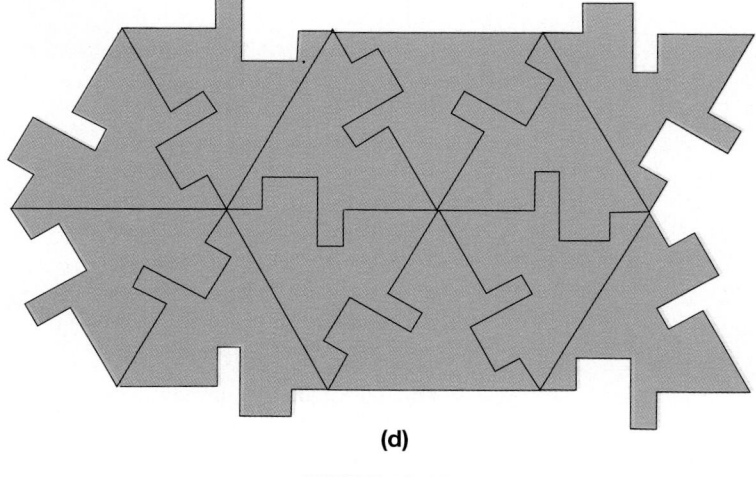

(d)

FIGURE 16.20

Similitudes

Thus far we have investigated transformations that preserve size and shape, namely isometries. Next we investigate transformations that preserve shape but not necessarily size.

Size Transformations

First we consider transformations that can change size.

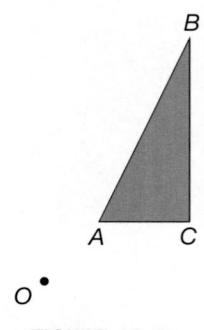

FIGURE 16.21

EXAMPLE 16.7   In Figure 16.21, find the image of $\triangle ABC$ under each of the following transformations.

(a) Each point P is mapped to the point P' on the ray $\overrightarrow{OP}$ such that $OP' = 2 \cdot OP$. That is, OP' is twice the distance OP.

(b) Each point P is mapped to the point P'' on the ray $\overrightarrow{OP}$ such that $OP'' = \frac{1}{2} \cdot OP$.

Solution

(a) To locate A', imagine ray $\overrightarrow{OA}$ [Figure 16.22(a)]. Then A' is the point on $\overrightarrow{OA}$ so that $OA' = 2 \cdot OA$. Locate B' and C' similarly. The image of $\triangle ABC$ is $\triangle A'B'C'$.

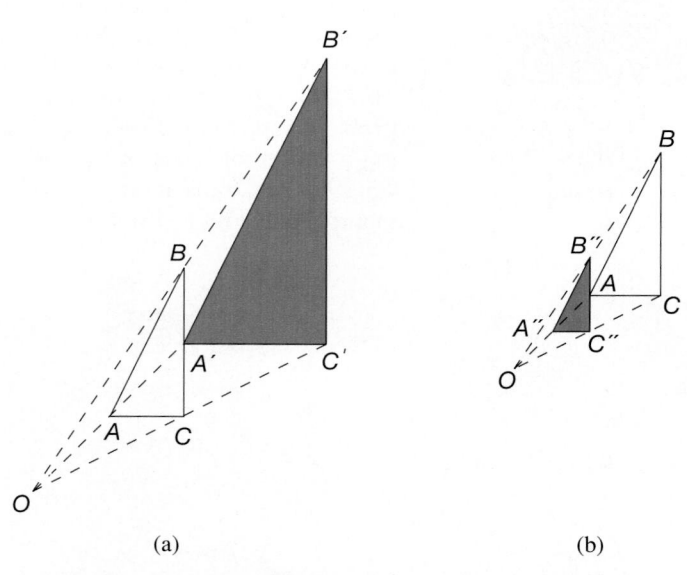

(a)   (b)

FIGURE 16.22

(b) To locate A'', imagine ray $\overrightarrow{OA}$ [Figure 16.22(b)]. Locate A'' on $\overrightarrow{OA}$ so that $OA'' = \frac{1}{2}OA$. Locate B'' and C'' similarly. The image of $\triangle ABC$ is $\triangle A''B''C''$. ∎

Transformations, such as those in Example 16.7 that uniformly stretch or shrink geometric shapes, are called size transformations.

Definition

Size Transformations

The **size transformation** $S_{O,k}$, with **center** O and **scale factor** k (where k is a positive real number), is the transformation that maps each point P to the point P' such that

1. P' is on ray $\overrightarrow{OP}$, and
$OP' = k \cdot OP$ where
   (a) **if** $k > 1$,
      then P is between O and P', or

   (b) if $k < 1$,
      then P' is between O and P.

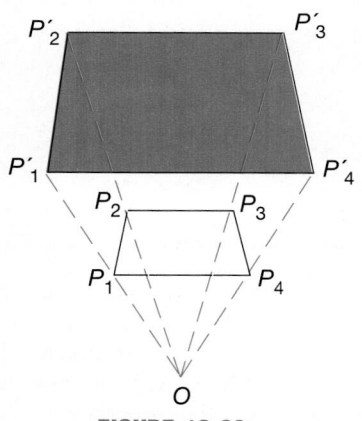

FIGURE 16.23

(NOTE: Size transformations are also called **magnifications**, **dilations**, and **dilitations**.)

Notice that points O, P, and P' are collinear. If $k > 1$, a size transformation enlarges shapes and if $k < 1$, a size transformation shrinks shapes. If $k = 1$, then $P' = P$ (i.e., each point is mapped to itself). Figure 16.23 illustrates the effect of a size transformation on a quadrilateral, with $k > 1$. A size transformation maps a polygon $\mathscr{P}$ to a polygon $\mathscr{P}'$ having the same shape, as illustrated in Figure 16.23. Also, we can show that a size transformation maps a triangle to a similar triangle.

Similitudes

Next we consider the combination of a size transformation followed by an isometry. Figure 16.24 illustrates this in a special case.

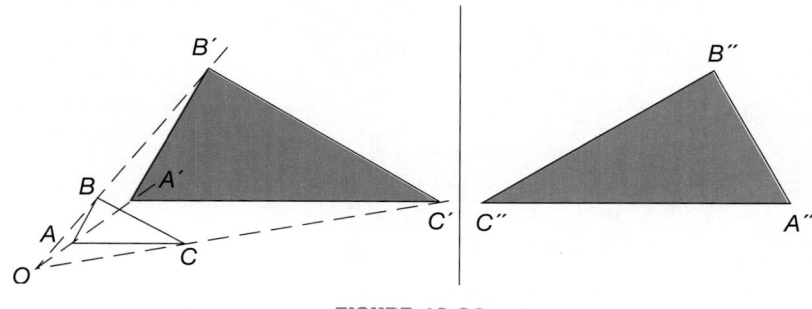

FIGURE 16.24

The size transformation $S_{O,k}$ maps $\triangle ABC$ to $\triangle A'B'C'$. By properties of size transformations, corresponding angles of $\triangle A'B'C'$ and $\triangle ABC$ are congruent, and corresponding sides of the two triangles are proportional. Thus, $\triangle A'B'C' \sim \triangle ABC$. The reflection, M_l maps $\triangle A'B'C'$ to $\triangle A''B''C''$. Since M_l is an isometry, we know that $\triangle A'B'C' \cong \triangle A''B''C''$. Therefore, corresponding angles of $\triangle A'B'C'$ and $\triangle A''B''C''$ are congruent, as are corresponding sides. Combining our results, we see that corresponding angles of $\triangle ABC$ and $\triangle A''B''C''$ are congruent and that corresponding sides are proportional. Hence $S_{O,k}$ followed by M_l maps $\triangle ABC$ to a triangle similar to it, namely $\triangle A''B''C''$.

Generalizing the discussion above, it can be shown that given similar triangles $\triangle ABC$ and $\triangle A''B''C''$, there exists a combination of a size transformation followed by an isometry that maps $\triangle ABC$ to $\triangle A''B''C''$.

Definition

Similitude

A **similitude** is a combination of a size transformation followed by an isometry.

In Figure 16.24 we also could have first flipped $\triangle ABC$ across l and then magnified it to $\triangle A''B''C''$. In general, it can be shown that any similitude also can be expressed as the combination of an isometry followed by a size transformation.

MATHEMATICAL MORSEL

Two symmetrical patterns are considered to be equivalent if they have exactly the same types of symmetry. As recently as 1891, it was finally proved that there are only 17 inequivalent symmetry patterns in the plane. However, the Moors, who lived in Spain from the eighth to the fifteenth centuries were aware of all 17 types of symmetry patterns. Examples of the patterns, such as the one shown here, were used to decorate the Moorish fortress, the Alhambra, in Granada.

EXERCISE/PROBLEM SET 16.1—PART A

Exercises

1. In each part, draw the image of the quadrilateral under the translation T_{AB}.

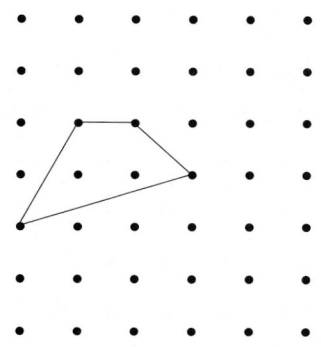

(a)

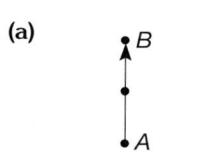

(b)

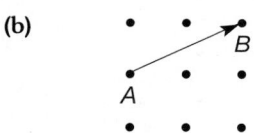

(c)

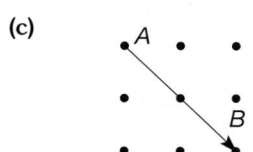

2. Draw $\overline{PQ}$ and $\overrightarrow{AB}$. With a sheet of tracing paper on top, trace segment $\overline{PQ}$ and point A. Slide the tracing paper (without turning) so that the traced point A moves to point B. Make impressions of points P and Q by pushing your pencil tip down. Label these impressions P' and Q'. Draw segment $\overline{P'Q'}$, the translation image of segment $\overline{PQ}$.

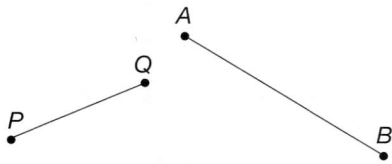

3. (a) On graph paper, draw three other directed line segments that describe T_{AB}. (HINT: The directed line segments must have the same length and direction.)

   (b) Draw three directed line segments that describe a translation which moves points down 3 units and right 4 units.

   (c) Draw two directed line segments that describe the translation which maps $\triangle RST$ to $\triangle R'S'T'$.

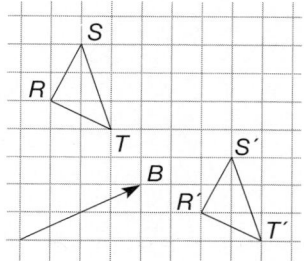

4. Find the coordinates of A' and B' that are the images of A and B under the following translations.

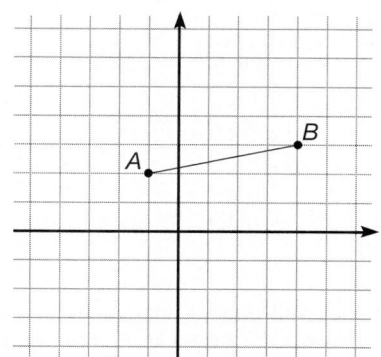

(a)

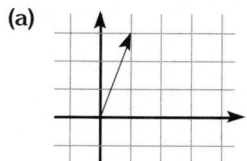

(b)

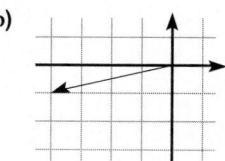

(c)

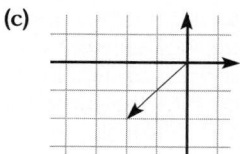

(d)

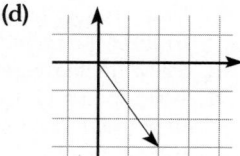

5. According to the definition of a translation, the quadrilateral $PP'BA$ is a parallelogram where P' is the image of P under T_{AB}. Use this to construct the image, P', with a compass and straightedge. (HINT: Construct the line parallel to $\overline{AB}$ through P.)

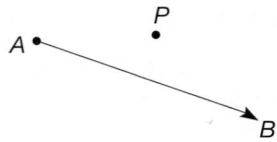

6. With compass and straightedge, construct the image of segment $\overline{AB}$ under translation T_{XY}.

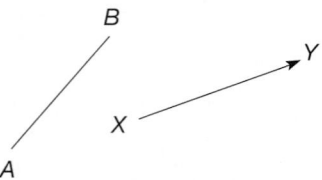

7. Find the measure of each of the following directed angles $\angle ABC$.

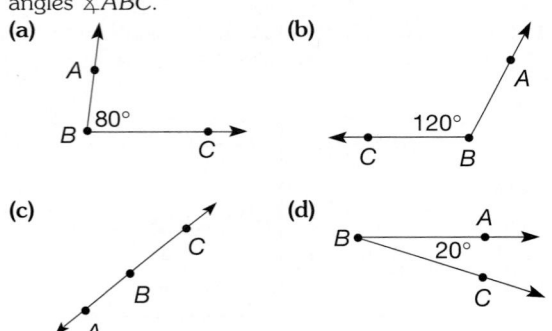

8. A protractor and tracing paper may be used to find rotation images. For example, find the image of point A under a rotation of $-50°$ about center O by following the steps below.

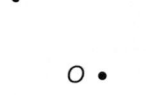

1. Draw ray $\overrightarrow{OA}$.
2. With ray $\overrightarrow{OA}$ as the initial side, use your protractor to draw a directed angle $\angle AOB$ of $-50°$.
3. Place tracing paper on top and trace point A.
4. Keep point O fixed and turn the tracing paper until point A is on ray $\overrightarrow{OB}$. Make an imprint with your pencil for A'.

9. Using a protractor and tracing paper, find the rotation image of point A about point O for the following directed angles.

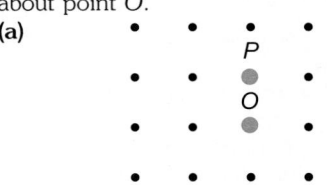

(a) 75°   (b) −90°   (c) −130°   (d) 180°

10. Find the 90° counterclockwise rotation of point P about point O.

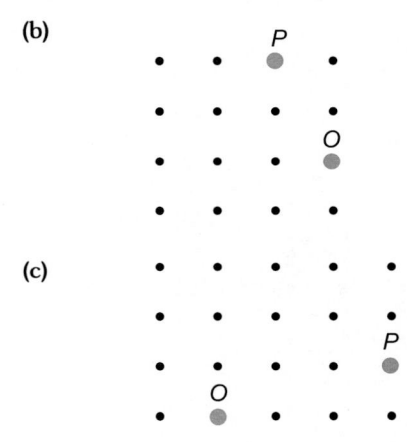

11. Find the rotation image of $\overline{AB}$ about point O for each of the following directed angles.

(a) −90°

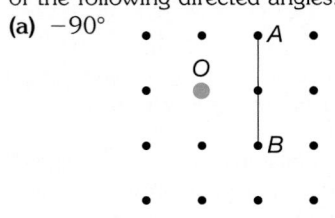

(b) 90°

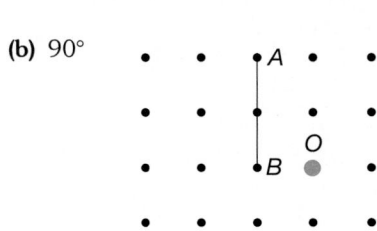

(c) 180°

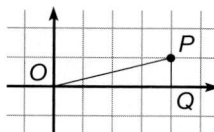

12. Give the coordinates of P', the point that is the image of P under $R_{O,90°}$. (HINT: Think of rotating $\triangle OPQ$.)

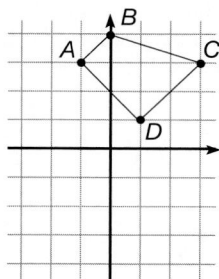

13. Give the coordinates of the images of the following points under $R_{O,90°}$.
   (a) (2, 3)   **(b)** (−1, 3)   **(c)** (−1, −4)
   (d) (−4, −2)   **(e)** (2, −4)   **(f)** (x, y)

14. Draw the image of quadrilateral $ABCD$ under $R_{O,180°}$. What are the coordinates of A', B', C', and D'?

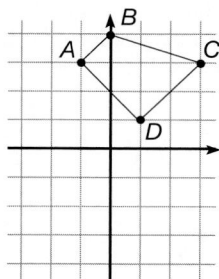

15. Give the coordinates of the images of the following points under $R_{O,180°}$.
   (a) (3, −1)   **(b)** (−6, −3)   **(c)** (−4, 2)
   (d) (x, y)

16. The rotation image of a point or figure may be found using a compass and straightedge. The procedure is similar to that with a protractor except that the directed angle is constructed rather than measured with a protractor. Also recall that $OA = OA'$. Construct the rotation image of A about point O for the following directed angles.

(a) −90°   **(b)** −45°   **(c)** 180°

17. The reflection image of point P can be found using tracing paper.

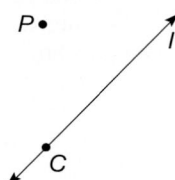

   1. Choose a point C on line l.
   2. Trace line l and points P and C on your tracing paper.
   3. Flip your tracing paper over, matching line l and point C.
   4. Make an impression for P'.

Using this procedure, find P'.

18. Find the reflection of point A in each of the given lines.

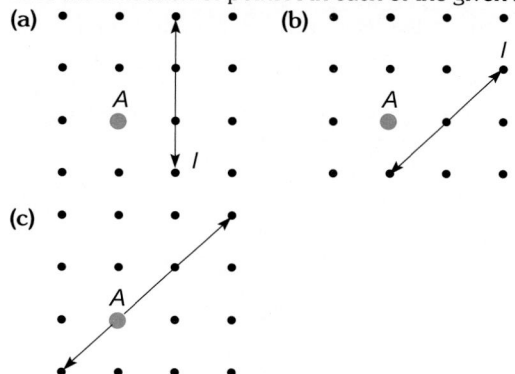

19. (a) Let M_x be the reflection in the x-axis. Graph the triangle with vertices $A(1, 2)$, $B(3, 5)$, and $C(6, 1)$ and its image under the reflection M_x.
   (b) What are the coordinates of the images of points A, B, and C under the reflection M_x?
   (c) If point P has coordinates (a, b), what are the coordinates of its image under M_x?

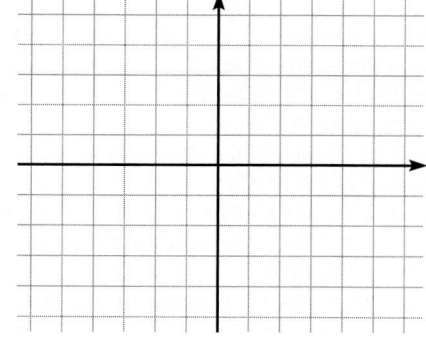

20. The reflection image of point A in line l can be constructed with compass and straightedge. Recall that line l is the perpendicular bisector of $\overline{AA'}$. If point P is the intersection of $\overline{AA'}$ and l, then $\overline{AA'} \perp l$ and $AP = PA'$. Using compass and straightedge, find A'.

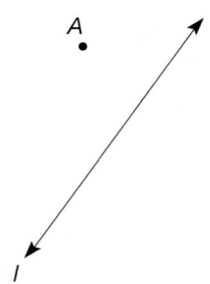

21. Given in the figure are $\overline{AB}$, $\overrightarrow{XY}$, and line l.

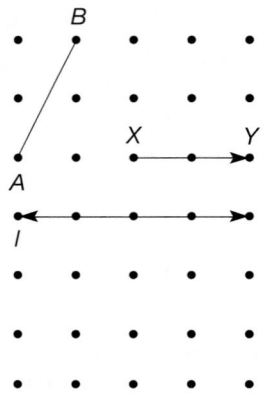

(a) Find the image of $\overline{AB}$ under the transformation T_{XY} followed by M_l.

(b) Find the image of $\overline{AB}$ under the transformation M_l followed by T_{XY}.

(c) What conclusion do you draw from parts (a) and (b) regarding the translation and reflection components of a glide reflection?

22. (a) Graph $\triangle ABC$ with $A(-2, 1)$, $B(0, 3)$, and $C(3, -2)$ and its image under this glide reflection: T_{PQ} followed by M_x.

(b) What are the coordinates of the images of points A, B, and C under this glide reflection: T_{PQ} followed by M_x?

(c) If point R has coordinates (a, b), what are the coordinates of its image under this glide reflection: T_{PQ} followed by M_x?

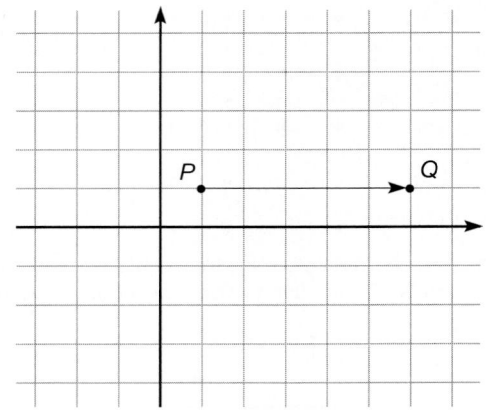

23. (a) Let M_y be the reflection in the y-axis. Graph $\triangle ABC$ with $A(-1, 3)$, $B(-3, 2)$, and $C(2, -3)$ and its image under this glide reflection: T_{RS} followed by M_y.

(b) What are the coordinates of the images of points A, B, and C under this glide reflection: T_{RS} followed by M_y?

(c) If point P has coordinates (a, b), what are the coordinates of its image under this glide reflection: T_{RS} followed by M_y?

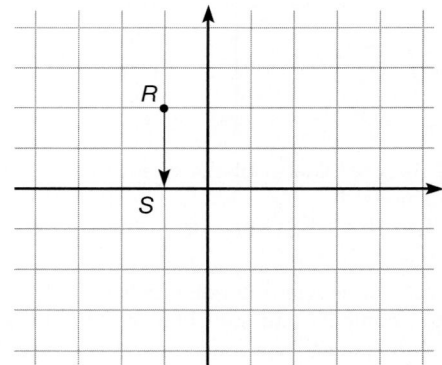

24. Which of the following triangles have the same orientation as the given triangle? Explain.

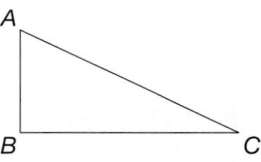

(a)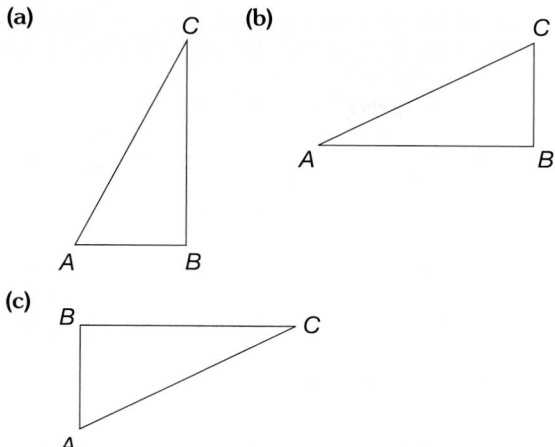

(b)

(c)

25. Use dot paper, a ruler, and a protractor, if necessary, to draw the image of quadrilateral *ABCD* under the transformation specified in each part.

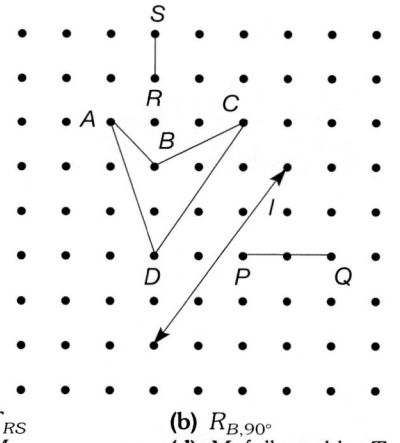

(a) T_{RS} **(b)** $R_{B,90°}$
(c) M_l **(d)** M_l followed by T_{PQ}

26. A portion of a tessellation is shown. If we trace the tessellation and slide it so that point *A* is on top of point *B*, the tessellation fits on top of itself. Find three other directions and mark points (such as *B*) that would be ending points for a translation beginning at *A*.

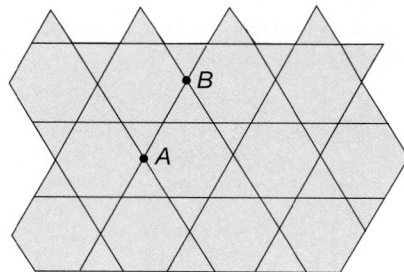

27. Point *A* in the tessellation portion shown is a center of rotational symmetry. Turning the tessellation about point *A*, through an angle of 60°, 120°, 180°, 240°, or 300° maps the tessellation onto itself. Find two other centers of rotational symmetry and give the possible angles for each point.

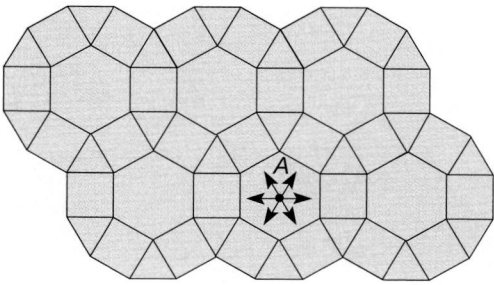

28. Line *l* is a line of reflection symmetry. Reflecting the tessellation in line *l* maps the tessellation onto itself. Find at least five other different lines of reflection symmetry.

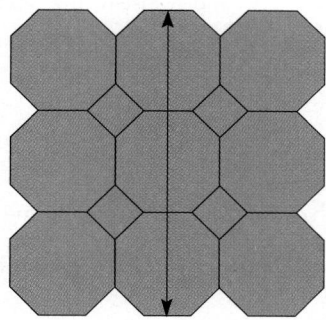

29. For each tessellation given below, find a reflection and translation, if possible, that combine to give a glide reflection symmetry.

(a)

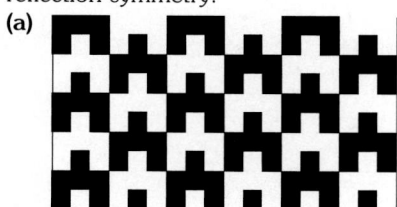

(b)

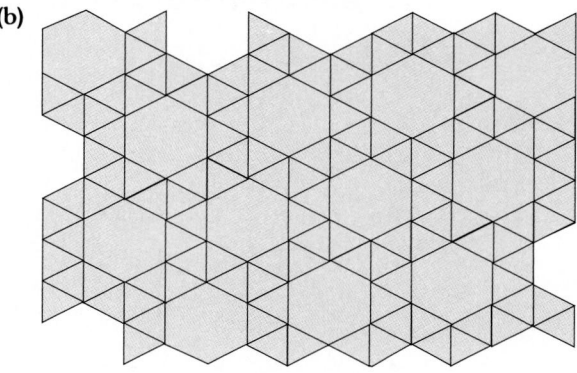

30. Trace a translation of the curve to the opposite side of the parallelogram. Verify that the resulting shape will tessellate the plane.

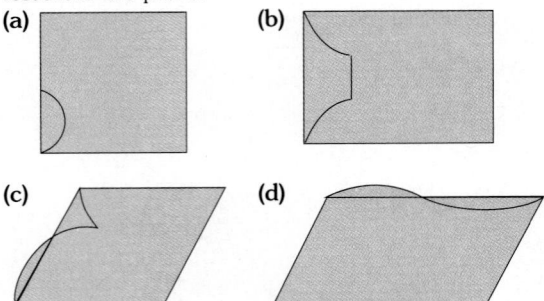

31. Both pairs of opposite sides of any parallelogram may be altered to form a tessellating shape. Begin with a parallelogram, here a rectangle.

1. Alter one side and translate the alteration to the opposite side.

2. Alter the other side and translate the alteration to the opposite side.
3. Verify that the resulting shape will tessellate the plane.

32. On the square lattice portions below, find $S_{O,2}(P)$.

(a)

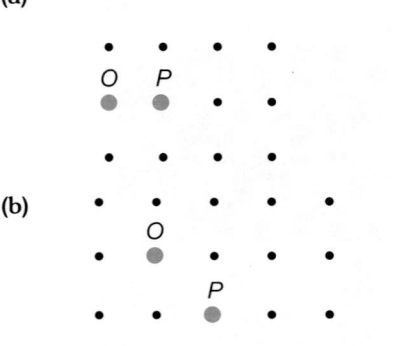

(b)

(c)

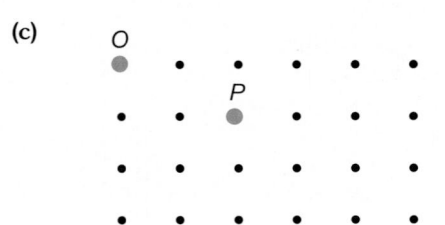

33. (a) Draw the image of the circle C_1 under $S_{O,2}$.
(b) Draw the image of the circle C_2 under $S_{P,1/2}$.

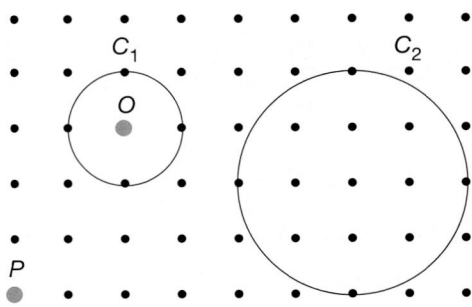

34. Use tracing paper and a ruler to draw the image of each figure under the given size transformation.
(a) $S_{P,3}$

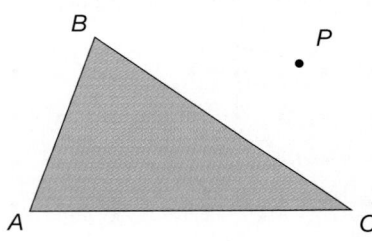

(b) $S_{P,2/3}$

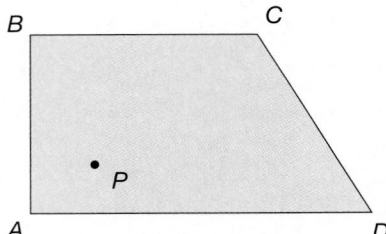

Problems

35. (a) Draw a line m whose image under T_{XY} passes through point A.
(b) Draw a second line n whose image under T_{XY} also passes through point A.

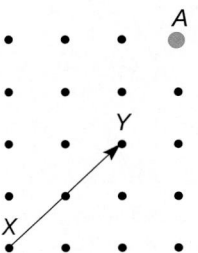

36. (a) Draw the image of each lattice point on line *l* under T_{AB}.
  (b) Does this suggest that the translation image of a line is a line?
  (c) What other relationship is there between the line and its translation image?

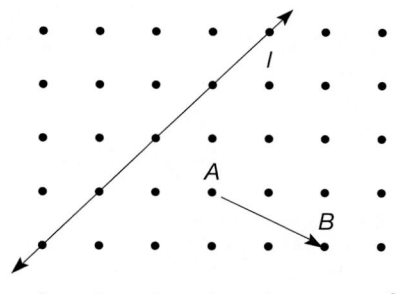

37. (a) Draw the image of each lattice point on line *l* under the rotation $R_{O,a}$. Does this suggest that the rotation image of a line is a line?

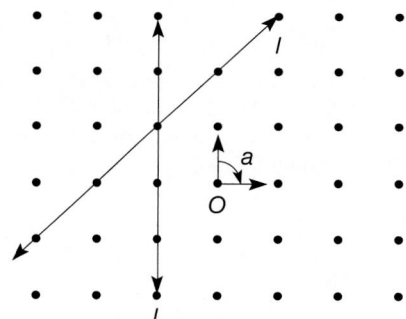

  (b) Draw the image of each lattice point on line *l* under the reflection M_l. Does this suggest that the reflection image of a line is a line?

38. Give an example of a transformation of each of the following types that maps *A* to *A'*.
  (a) Translation   **(b)** Rotation
  (c) Reflection   **(d)** Glide reflection

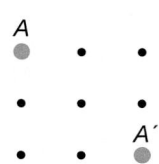

39. Give an example, if possible, of a transformation of each of the following types that maps $\overline{AB}$ to $\overline{A'B'}$.
  (a) Translation
  (b) Rotation
  (c) Reflection
  (d) Glide reflection

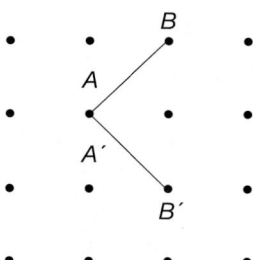

40. Several reflection transformations are described below. In each part draw figures and their images to find the reflection line. The notation $(x, y) \rightarrow (x, 2 - y)$ means that the point with coordinates (x, y) is mapped to the point with coordinates $(x, 2 - y)$.
  (a) $(x, y) \rightarrow (x, 2 - y)$
  (b) $(x, y) \rightarrow (x, 8 - y)$
  (c) $(x, y) \rightarrow (x, -4 - y)$

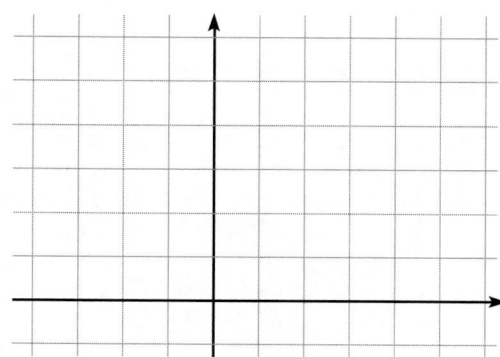

41. (a) Graph $\triangle ABC$, with $A(2, 1)$, $B(3, 4)$, and $C(6, 2)$, and its image under the reflection M_l, where *l* is the line $x = 1$.
  (b) What are the coordinates of the images of points *A*, *B*, and *C* under M_l?
  (c) If a point *P* has coordinates (x, y), what are the coordinates of its image under M_l?

EXERCISE/PROBLEM SET 16.1—PART B

Exercises

1. In each part, find the image of the given figure under the translation T_{AB}.

(a)

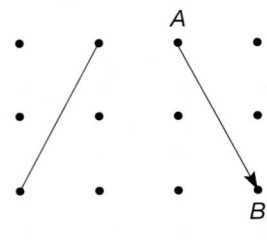

(b)

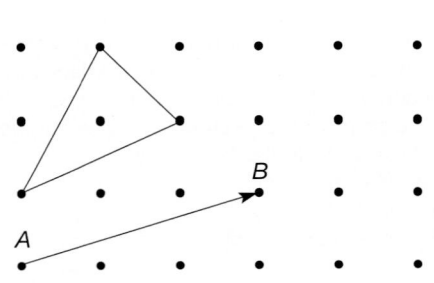

(c)

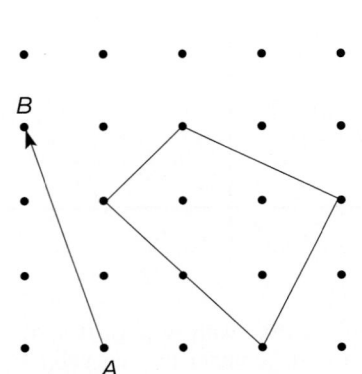

2. (a) Draw the image of line l under translation T_{XY}, (HINT: Find the images of points A and B.)

(b) Find a line q whose image under translation T_{XY} is line l.

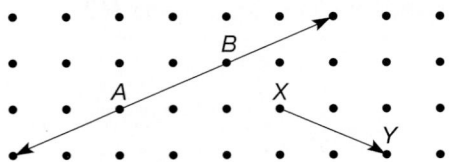

3. Draw $\triangle EFG$ and $\overrightarrow{XY}$. Draw the image of $\triangle EFG$ under translation T_{XY}.

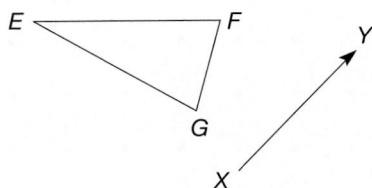

4. Given are the coordinates of a point P' that is the image of point P under T_{AB}. What are the coordinates of P in each case?

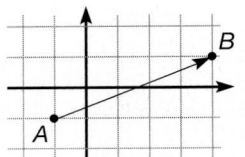

(a) $(6, 3)$ **(b)** $(-1, 2)$ **(c)** $(4, -1)$ **(d)** (x, y)

5. (a) Find the coordinates of the images of the vertices of quadrilateral $ABCD$ under T_{OX}.

(b) Given a point (x, y), what are the coordinates of its image under T_{OX}?

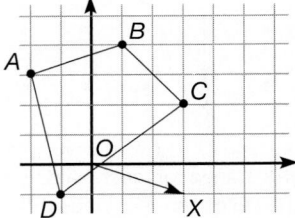

6. Find the coordinates of the point (x, y) under the following translations.

(a)

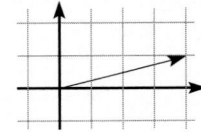

(b)

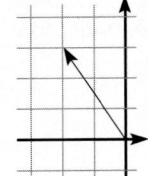

(c)

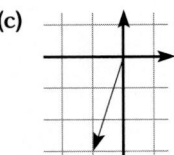

(d)

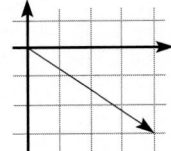

7. Using a compass and straightedge, construct the image of △ABC under the translation that maps R to S.

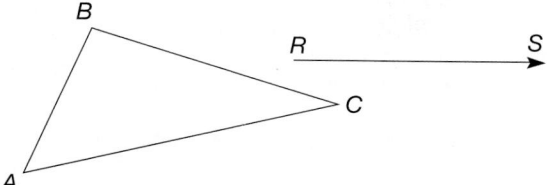

8. Given $\overline{AB}$ and point O, use a protractor and tracing paper to find the image of $\overline{AB}$ under $R_{O,a}$ for each of the following values of a.

(a) 60°   **(b)** −90°   **(c)** 180°

9. Use a protractor and ruler to find the 90° clockwise rotation of △ABC about point O.

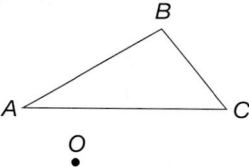

10. Find the 90° clockwise rotation about point O for each of the following segments.

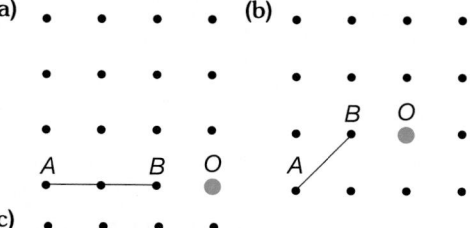

11. Find the 90° clockwise rotation about point O for each of the following quadrilaterals.

(a)

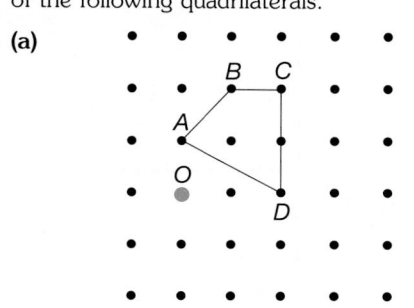

(b)

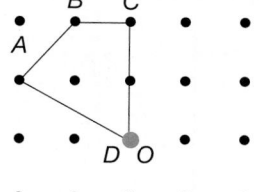

(c)

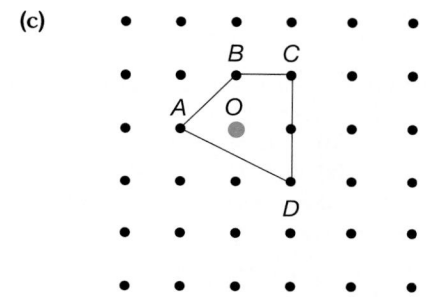

12. Find the line whose image under each of the following rotations is given.

(a) $R_{O,-90°}$

(b) $R_{O,90°}$

(c) $R_{O,180°}$

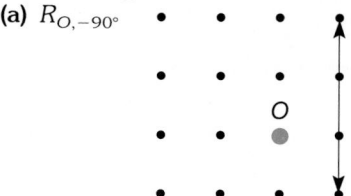

13. Draw the image of $\triangle ABC$ under $R_{O,-90°}$. What are the coordinates of A', B', and C'?

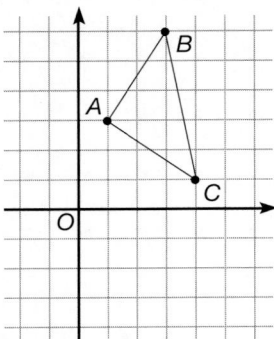

14. Give the coordinates of the images of the following points under $R_{O,-90°}$.
  (a) $(1, 5)$ **(b)** $(-1, 3)$ **(c)** $(-2, -4)$
  (d) $(-3, -1)$ **(e)** $(5, -2)$ **(f)** (x, y)

15. We could express the results of $R_{O,90°}$ applied to $(4, 2)$ in the following way:

$$(4, 2) \xrightarrow{R_{O,90°}} (-2, 4)$$

Complete the following statements.
  (a) $(x, y) \xrightarrow{R_{O,90°}} (?, ?)$

  (b) $(x, y) \xrightarrow{R_{O,-90°}} (?, ?)$

  (c) $(x, y) \xrightarrow{R_{O,180°}} (?, ?)$

16. Construct the 90° clockwise rotation of $\triangle ABC$ about point O.

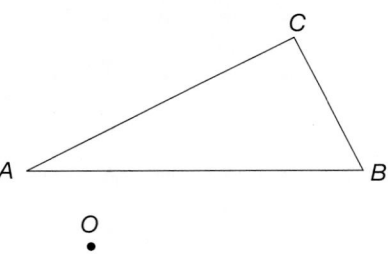

17. Using tracing paper, find the image of $\overline{AB}$ under M_l for the following segments.
  (a)   **(b)**

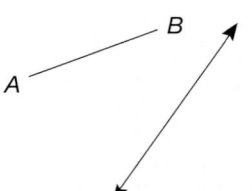
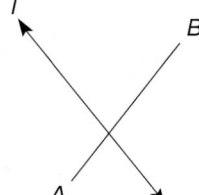

18. Find the reflection images of point P, segment $\overline{RS}$, and $\triangle ABC$ in line l.

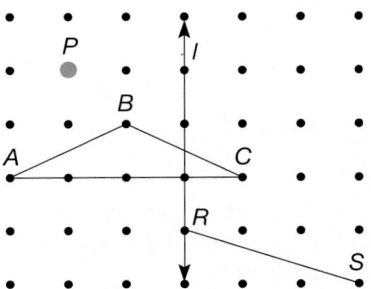

19. (a) Graph $\triangle ABC$ with $A(2, 1)$, $B(3, -5)$, and $C(6, 3)$ and its image under M_y, the reflection in the y-axis.
  (b) What are the coordinates of the points A, B, and C under M_y?
  (c) If point P has coordinates (a, b), what are the coordinates of its image under M_y?

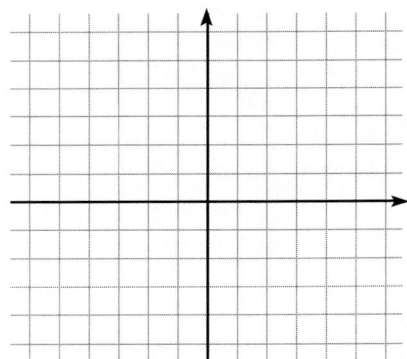

20. (a) Graph $\triangle ABC$, with $A(3, 1)$, $B(4, 3)$, and $C(5, -2)$, and its image under the reflection M_l, where l is the line $y = x$.
  (b) What are the coordinates of the images of points A, B, and C under M_l?
  (c) If a point P has coordinates (x, y), what are the coordinates of its image under M_l?

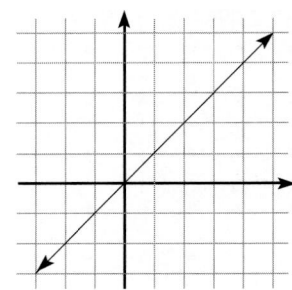

21. Using a compass and straightedge, construct the reflection of the following figures in line *l*.

(a)

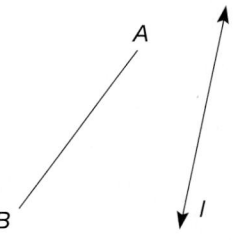

(b)

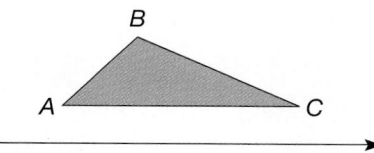

22. (a) Graph △ABC, with A(1, 1), B(3, 1), and C(4, 6), and its image under this glide reflection: T_{XY} followed by M_l where *l* is the line $y = x$.

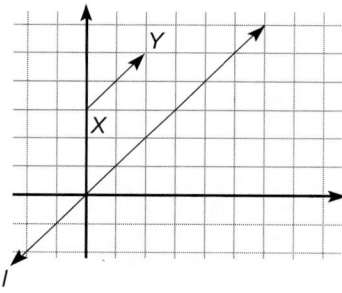

(b) What are the coordinates of the images of A, B, and C?

(c) If the point P has coordinates (x, y), what are the coordinates of its image under this glide reflection: T_{XY} followed by M_l?

23. Using a compass and straightedge, construct the glide reflection image of $\overline{AB}$ under the glide reflection: T_{XY} followed by M_l.

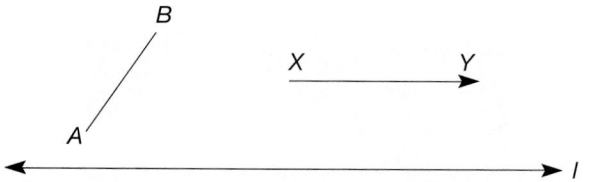

24. Which of the following polygons has the same orientation as the given polygon? Explain.

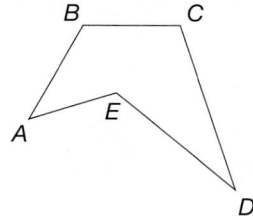

(a)

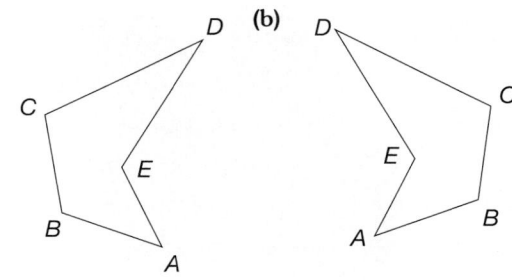

(b)

(c)

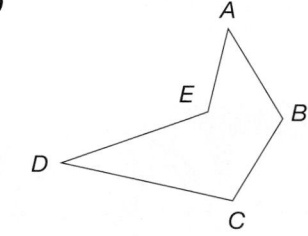

25. Use dot paper, a ruler, and a protractor, if necessary, to draw the image of quadrilateral *ABCD* under the transformation specified.

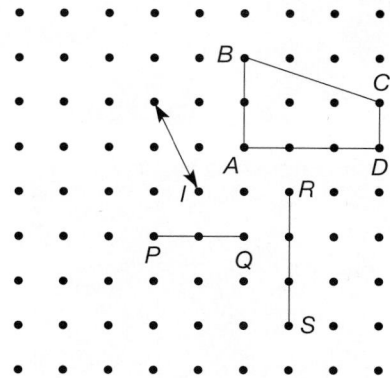

(a) T_{PQ} **(b)** $R_{Q,180°}$
(c) M_l **(d)** M_l followed by T_{RS}

26. For each tessellation, find at least four translations in different directions that map the tessellation onto itself. Indicate the starting and ending points of the translation.

(a)

(b)

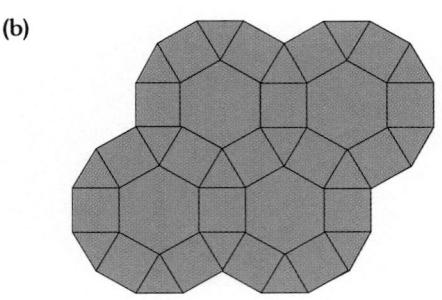

27. For each tessellation, find rotations that map the tessellation onto itself. Indicate the centers of rotation and possible angles (less than 360°) of each rotation.

(a)

(b)

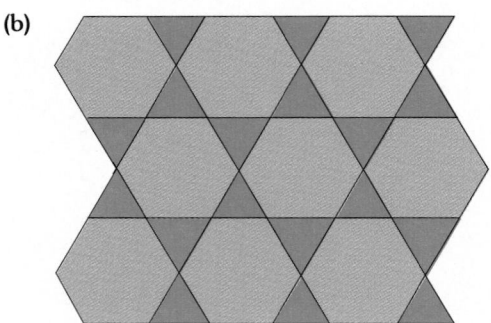

28. For each tessellation, find four lines of reflection symmetry.

(a)

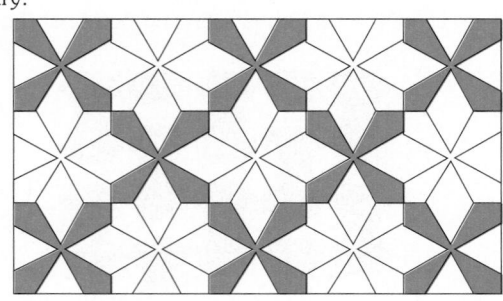

(b)

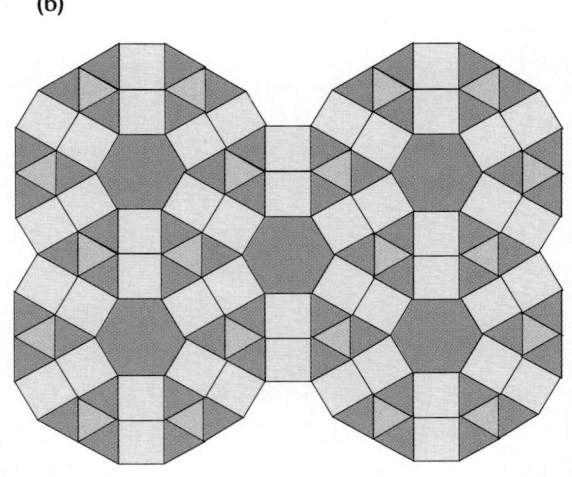

29. Identify the types of symmetry present in the following quilt patterns.

(a) Summer Stars

(b) Seesaw

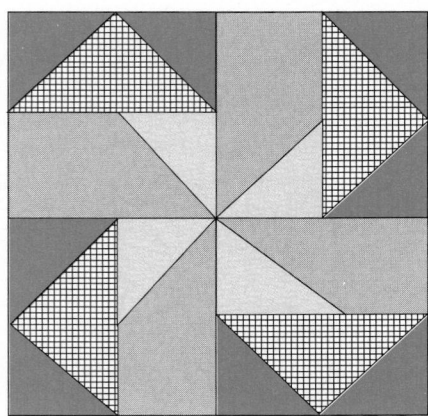

(c) Road to California

(d) Log Cabin

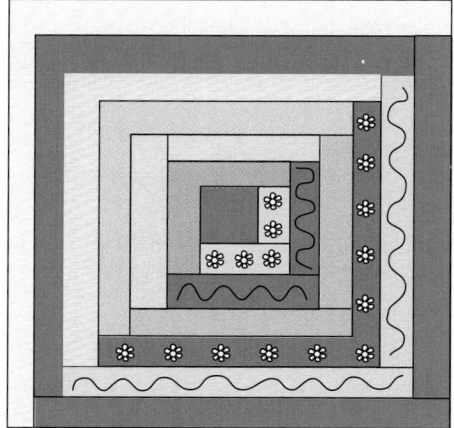

30. Trace the translation of the curves to the opposite sides to create a shape that tessellates. Use the grid to show that the shape will tessellate the plane.

(a)

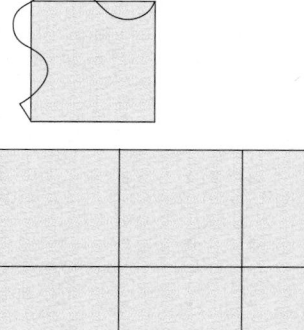

(b)

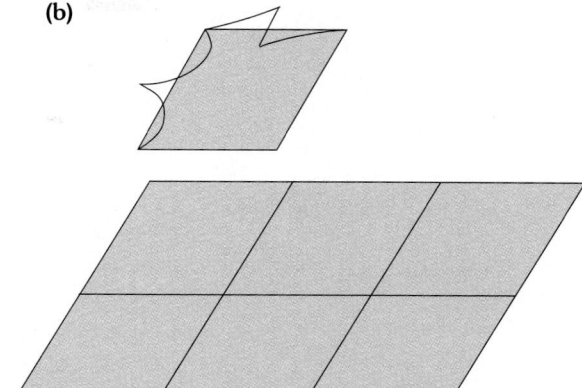

31. 1. Alter two adjacent sides of the given rectangle.
   2. Translate the alterations to the opposite sides of the rectangle.

   3. Use the grid to show that the new shape tessellates the plane.

32. 1. Alter sides $\overline{AB}$, $\overline{BC}$, and $\overline{CD}$.
   2. Translate the alterations to the opposite sides ($\overline{AB}$ to $\overline{ED}$, etc.).

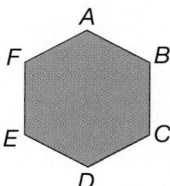

   3. Use the grid to verify that the shape will tessellate.

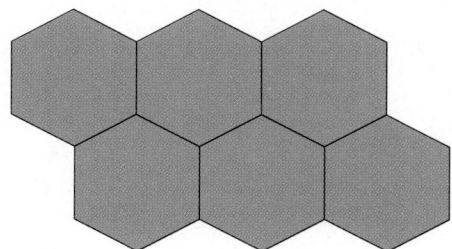

33. Find the image of $\overline{AB}$ under each of the transformations shown.

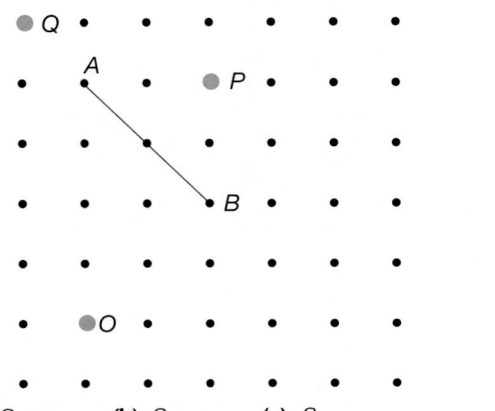

(a) $S_{O,1/2}$ **(b)** $S_{P,3/2}$ **(c)** $S_{Q,2}$

34. Use tracing paper and a ruler to draw the image of each figure under the given size transformation.

(a) $S_{P,1/2}$

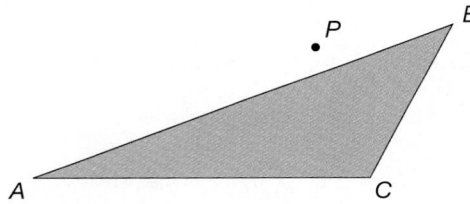

(b) $S_{P,3}$

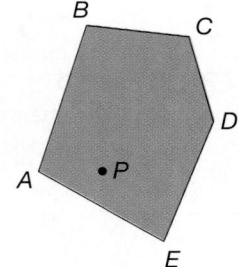

Problems

35. (a) Draw a line p whose translation image under T_{AB} is line p itself. (HINT: Each point of line p "slides" to a point on line p.)
(b) Draw two more lines with this property.

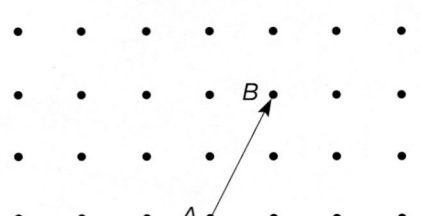

36. (a) Draw a line p such that the reflection image of p in line l is parallel to p. How many possible such lines p are there on this portion of a square lattice?
(b) Draw a line q that reflects onto itself under M_l.
(c) How many possible such lines q are there on this portion of a square lattice?

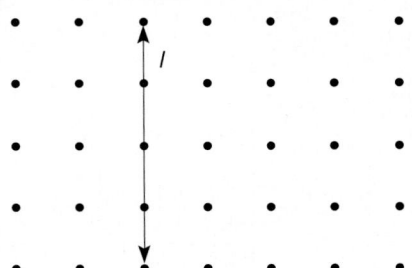

37. In the diagram, X' is the reflection image of point X in line l. Using only a straightedge, find the reflection image of P in line l. (HINT: When a set of collinear points is reflected in a line, its image is also a set of collinear points.)

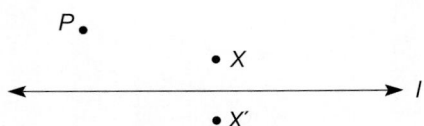

38. Describe a transformation of each of the following types (if possible) that maps $\overline{AB}$ to $\overline{A'B'}$.

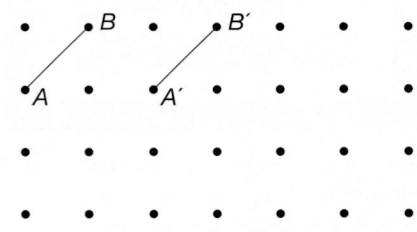

(a) Translation   **(b)** Rotation
(c) Reflection   **(d)** Glide reflection

39. Describe a transformation of each of the following types (if possible) that maps $\overline{AB}$ to $\overline{A'B'}$.

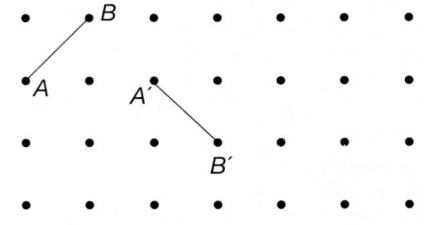

(a) Translation   **(b)** Rotation
(c) Reflection   **(d)** Glide reflection

40. For each transformation given below, plot $\triangle ABC$, with $A(2, 3)$, $B(-1, 4)$, and $C(-2, 1)$, and its image. Decide whether the transformation is a translation, rotation, reflection, glide reflection, or none of these. The notation $F(x, y)$ denotes the image of the point (x, y) under transformation F.

(a) $F(x, y) = (y, x)$

(b) $F(x, y) = (y, -x)$

(c) $F(x, y) = (x + 2, y - 3)$

(d) $F(x, y) = (2x, -y)$

(e) $F(x, y) = (-x + 4, -y + 2)$

(f) $F(x, y) = (-x, y + 2)$

41. In each part, a reflection is described. By drawing figures and their images, find the reflection line. The notation $M_l(x, y)$ denotes the image of the point (x, y) under M_l.

(a) $M_l(x, y) = (4 - x, y)$

(b) $M_l(x, y) = (10 - x, y)$

(c) $M_l(x, y) = (-2 - x, y)$

42. (a) Graph $\triangle ABC$ with $A(1, 4)$, $B(3, 5)$, and $C(5, 2)$, and its image under the reflection M_l where l is the line $y = 3$.

(b) What are the coordinates of the images of point A, B, and C under M_l?

(c) If P has coordinates (x, y), what are the coordinates of the image of P under M_l?

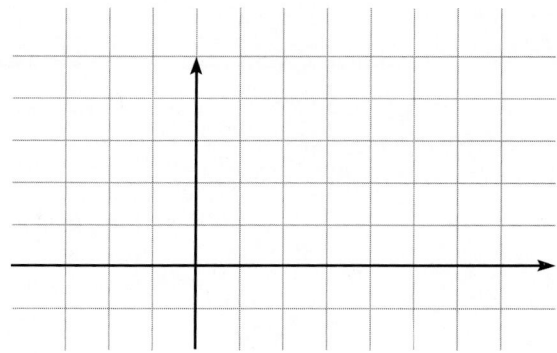

43. (a) Find the coordinates of the images of A, B, C, and D under the rotation $R_{O,90°}$.

(b) (Challenge) Generalize the rotation about any point (a, b) through the directed angle of $90°$; that is, give the coordinates of the rotation image of (x, y).

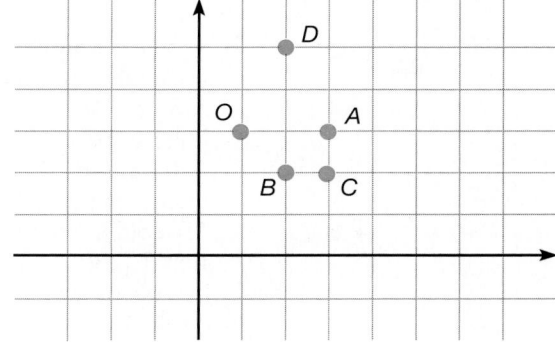

16.2

CONGRUENCE AND SIMILARITY USING TRANSFORMATIONS

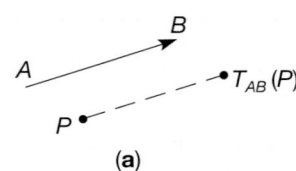

(a)

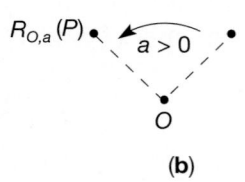

(b)

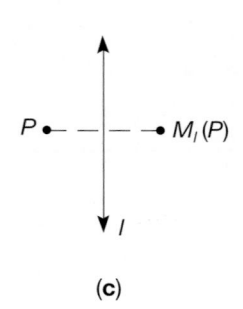

(c)

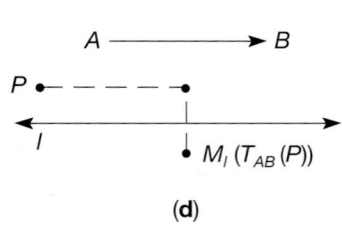

(d)

FIGURE 16.25

Congruence

In this section we study special properties of translations, rotations, reflections, and glide reflections. We apply some results on triangle congruence from Section 14.1 to verify some of these properties.

We will use the notation in Table 16.1 to denote images of points under transformations (Figure 16.25).

TABLE 16.1

Transformation	Image of Point P
Translation, T_{AB}	$T_{AB}(P)$ [Figure 16.25(a)]
Rotation, $R_{O,a}$	$R_{O,a}(P)$ [Figure 16.25(b)]
Reflection, M_l	$M_l(P)$ [Figure 16.25(c)]
Glide reflection T_{AB} followed by M_l	$M_l(T_{AB}(P))$ [Figure 16.25(d)]

For example, $T_{AB}(P)$ is read "T sub AB of P" or "the image of point P under the translation T_{AB}" [Figure 16.25(a)]. Similarly, $R_{O,a}(P)$ is read "R sub O,a of P" and denotes the image of point P under the rotation $R_{O,a}$ [Figure 16.25(b)]. The reflection image of point P in line l is denoted by $M_l(P)$ and read "M sub l of P" [Figure 16.25(c)]. Finally, the glide reflection image of point P, $M_l(T_{AB}(P))$, is read "M sub l of T sub AB of P" [Figure 16.25(d)]. Note that in the notation for the glide reflection, the transformation T_{AB} is applied first.

Next, we will investigate properties of the transformations listed in Table 16.1. In particular, we first will determine if they preserve distance; that is, if the distance between two points is the same as the distance between their images.

Suppose that we have a translation T_{AB} and that we consider the effect of T_{AB} on a line segment $\overline{PQ}$ (Figure 16.26). Let $P' = T_{AB}(P)$ and $Q' = T_{AB}(Q)$. According to the definition of a translation, $\overline{PP'} \parallel \overline{AB}$ and

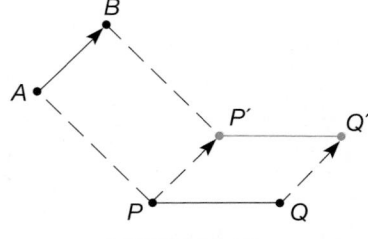

FIGURE 16.26

$PP' = AB$. Similarly, $\overline{QQ'} \parallel \overline{AB}$ and $QQ' = AB$. Combining our results, we see that $\overline{PP'} \parallel \overline{QQ'}$ and $PP' = QQ'$. (Check this.) Thus $PP'Q'Q$ is a parallelogram since opposite sides, $\overline{PP'}$ and $\overline{QQ'}$, are parallel and congruent. Consequently, $PQ = P'Q'$. We have verified that translations preserve distance, that is, that the distance $P'Q'$ is equal to the distance PQ. (Also, since

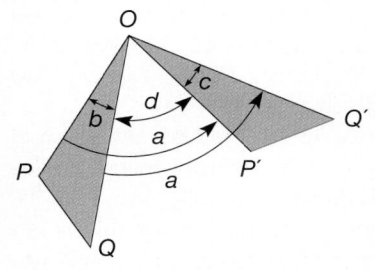

FIGURE 16.27

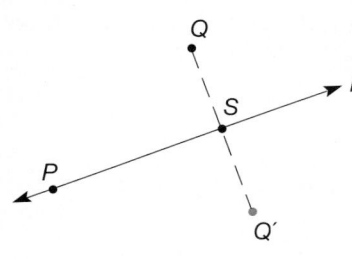

FIGURE 16.28

$\overline{PQ} \parallel \overline{P'Q'}$, we can deduce that a translation maps a line to a line parallel to the original line.)

Next, we show that rotations also preserve distance. Suppose that $R_{O,a}$ is a rotation with center O and angle with measure a. Consider the effect of $R_{O,a}$ on a line segment $\overline{PQ}$ (Figure 16.27). We wish to show that $PQ = P'Q'$. To do this, we will establish that $\triangle POQ \cong \triangle P'OQ'$ using the SAS congruence property. Since $OP = OP'$ and $OQ = OQ'$ by the definition of rotation $R_{O,a}$, all that remains is to show that $\angle POQ \cong \angle P'OQ'$. Let $b = m(\angle POQ)$, $c = m(\angle P'OQ')$, and $d = m(\angle QOP')$ (Figure 16.27). Here we are assuming that P rotates counterclockwise to P' and Q to Q'. (If it does not, a similar argument can be developed.) Then we have

$$b + d = a = d + c \quad \text{so that} \quad b + d = d + c.$$

Hence $b = c$, so that $m(\angle POQ) = m(\angle P'OQ')$. Thus $\triangle POQ \cong \triangle P'OQ'$, by the SAS congruence property. Consequently, we have that $\overline{PQ} \cong \overline{P'Q'}$, since they are corresponding sides in the congruent triangles. This shows that rotations preserve distance. Unlike translations, a rotation, in general, does not map a line to a line parallel to the original line. In fact, only rotations through multiples of 180° do.

Using triangle congruence, we can show that reflections also preserve distance. There are four cases to consider: (1) P and Q are on l; (2) only one of P or Q is on l; (3) P and Q are on the same side of l; and (4) P and Q are on opposite sides of l. In case 1, P and Q are fixed by M_l; that is, $M_l(P) = P' = P$, and $M_l(Q) = Q' = Q$, so that $P'Q' = PQ$. For case 2, suppose that P is on line l and Q is not on l (Figure 16.28). Let $Q' = M_l(Q)$ and let S be the intersection of segment $\overline{QQ'}$ and line l. Then $QS = Q'S$ and $\angle QSP$ is a right angle, by the definition of $M_l(Q)$. Hence $\triangle QSP \cong \triangle Q'SP$ by the SAS congruence condition. Consequently, $QP = Q'P'$, as desired. Cases 3 and 4 are somewhat more complicated and are left for the problem set.

In the case of a glide reflection, since both the translation and the reflection comprising the glide reflection preserve distance, the glide reflection must also preserve distance.

In the first section, a transformation that preserved size and shape was called an isometry. More formally, an **isometry** is a transformation that preserves distance (*iso* = equal, *metry* = measure). We have just shown that translations, rotations, reflections, and glide reflections are isometries. It can also be shown that isometries map lines to lines; that is, the image of a line l under an isometry is another line l'. Figure 16.29 illustrates this result for a translation, rotation, and reflection.

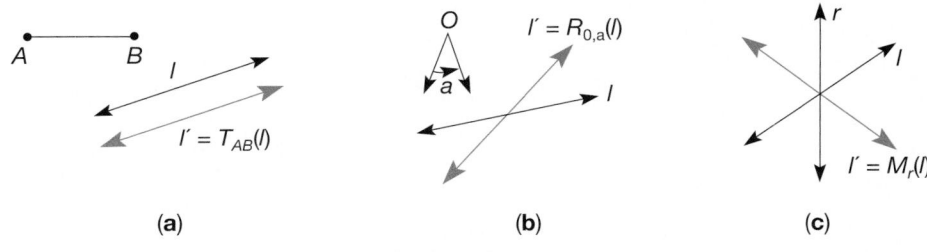

(a)   (b)   (c)

FIGURE 16.29

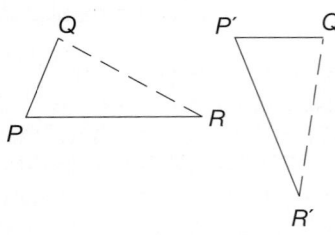

FIGURE 16.30

We can show that every isometry also preserves angle measure; that is, an isometry maps an angle to an angle that is congruent to the original angle (Figure 16.30). Consider $\angle PQR$ and its image, $\angle P'Q'R'$ under an isometry. Form $\triangle PQR$ and its image $\triangle P'Q'R'$ (Figure 16.30). We know that $PQ = P'Q'$, $QR = Q'R'$, and $PR = P'R'$. Thus $\triangle PQR \cong \triangle P'Q'R'$ by the SSS congruence property, so that $\angle PQR \cong \angle P'Q'R'$.

Because isometries preserve distance, we know that isometries map triangles to congruent triangles. Also, using the corresponding angles property, it can be shown that isometries preserve parallelism. That is, isometries map parallel lines to parallel lines. A verification of this is left for the problem set. We can summarize properties of isometries as follows.

Theorem

Properties of Isometries

1. Isometries map lines to lines, segments to segments, rays to rays, angles to angles, and polygons to polygons.
2. Isometries preserve angle measure.
3. Isometries map triangles to congruent triangles.
4. Isometries preserve parallelism.

We can analyze congruent triangles by means of isometries. Suppose, for example, that $\triangle ABC$ and $\triangle A'B'C'$ are congruent, have the same orientation, and the three pairs of corresponding sides are parallel as in Figure 16.31. Since the corresponding sides are parallel and congruent, it can be shown that the translation $T_{AA'}$, maps $\triangle ABC$ to $\triangle A'B'C'$.

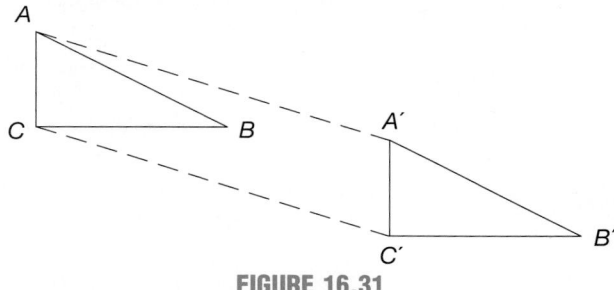

FIGURE 16.31

If $\triangle ABC$ and $\triangle A'B'C'$ are congruent, have the same orientation, and $\overline{AB} \nparallel \overline{A'B'}$, there is a rotation that maps $\triangle ABC$ to $\triangle A'B'C'$ (Figure 16.32).

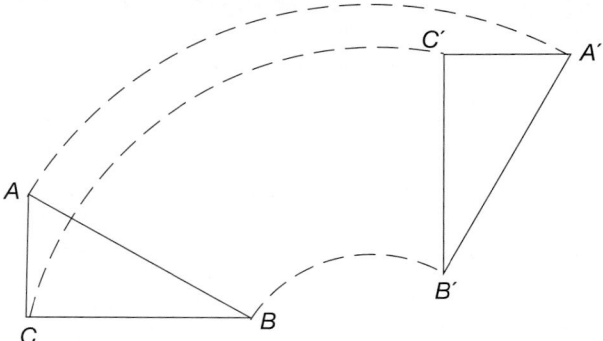

FIGURE 16.32

EXAMPLE 16.8   In Figure 16.33, $\triangle ABC \cong \triangle A'B'C'$. Find a rotation that maps $\triangle ABC$ to $\triangle A'B'C'$.

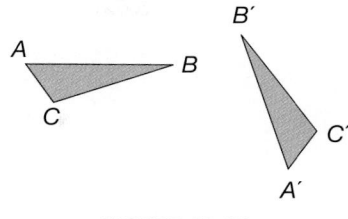

FIGURE 16.33

Solution
To find the center, O, of the rotation, we use the fact that O is equidistant from points A and A'. Hence O is on perpendicular bisector, l, of segment $\overline{AA'}$ (Figure 16.34).

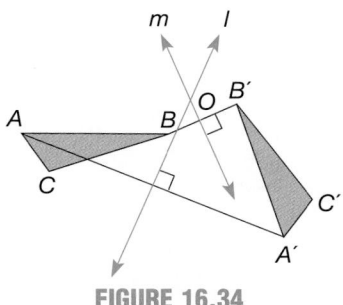

FIGURE 16.34

But O is also equidistant from B and B', so O is on m, the perpendicular bisector of $\overline{BB'}$. Hence $\{O\} = l \cap m$. The angle of the rotation is $\angle AOA'$ (Figure 16.35).

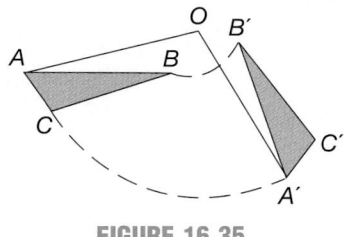

FIGURE 16.35   ■

Thus, if two congruent triangles have the same orientation, and a translation will not map one to the other, there is a rotation that will.

Next, suppose that $\triangle ABC$ and $\triangle A'B'C'$ are congruent and have opposite orientation. Further assume that there is a line l that is the perpendicular bisector of $\overline{AA'}$, $\overline{BB'}$, and $\overline{CC'}$ (Figure 16.36). Then, by the definition of a reflection, M_l maps $\triangle ABC$ to $\triangle A'B'C'$. If there is no reflection mapping $\triangle ABC$ to $\triangle A'B'C'$, then a glide reflection maps $\triangle ABC$ to $\triangle A'B'C'$. The next example shows how to find the glide axis of a glide reflection.

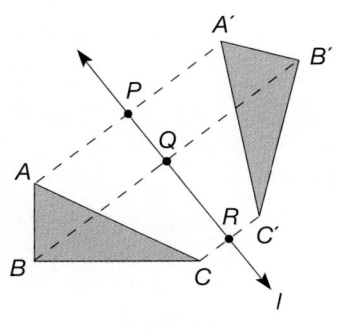

FIGURE 16.36

EXAMPLE 16.9   In Figure 16.37, $\triangle ABC \cong \triangle A'B'C'$. Find a glide reflection that maps $\triangle ABC$ to $\triangle A'B'C'$.

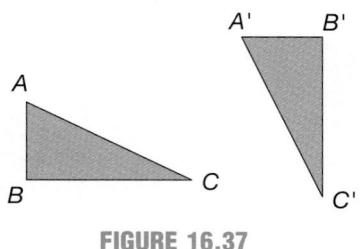

FIGURE 16.37

Solution
Since $\triangle ABC$ and $\triangle A'B'C'$ have opposite orientation, we know that either a reflection or glide reflection is needed. Since $\triangle A'B'C'$ does not appear to be a reflection image of $\triangle ABC$, we will find a glide reflection. Find the midpoints P, Q, and R of segments $\overline{AA'}$, $\overline{BB'}$, and $\overline{CC'}$, respectively (Figure 16.38).

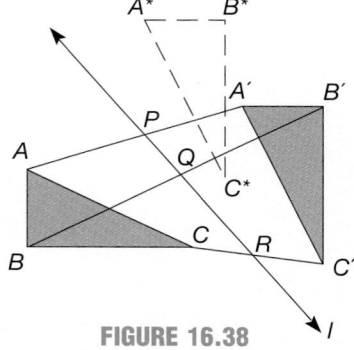
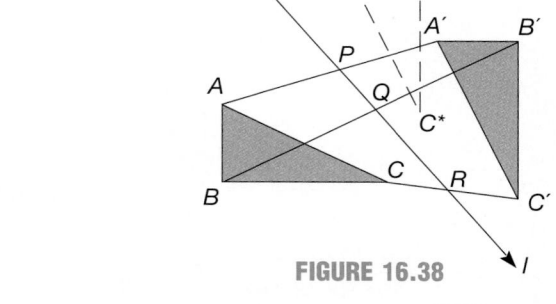

FIGURE 16.38

Then P, Q, and R are collinear and the line $\overleftrightarrow{PQ}$ is the glide axis of the glide reflection (Figure 16.39). (This result follows from Hjelmslev's theorem, which is too technical for us to prove here.) We reflect $\triangle ABC$ across line $\overleftrightarrow{PQ}$ to obtain $\triangle A*B*C*$. Then $\triangle A*B*C*$ is mapped to $\triangle A'B'C'$ by $T_{A*A'}$. Thus we see the effect of the glide reflection, M_{PQ} followed by $T_{A*A'}$, which maps $\triangle ABC$ to $\triangle A'B'C'$.   ■

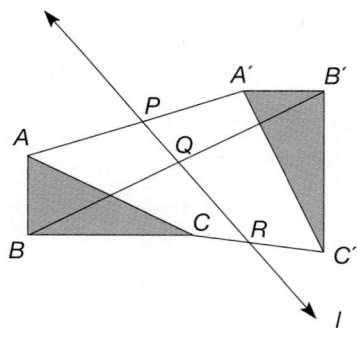

FIGURE 16.39

Thus, if two congruent triangles $\triangle ABC$ and $\triangle A'B'C'$ have opposite orientation, there exists either a reflection or a glide reflection that maps one to the other. We can summarize our results about triangle congruence and isometries as follows.

Theorem

Triangle Congruence and Isometries

$\triangle ABC \cong \triangle A'B'C'$ if and only if there is an isometry that maps $\triangle ABC$ to $\triangle A'B'C'$. If the triangles have the same orientation, the isometry is either a translation or a rotation. If the triangles have opposite orientation, the isometry is either a reflection or a glide reflection.

Based on our discussion above, it can be shown that there are only four types of isometries in the plane, namely translations, rotations, reflections, and glide reflections.

Isometries allow us to define congruence between general types of shapes (i.e., collections of points) in the plane.

Definition

Congruent Shapes

Two shapes, $\mathscr{S}$ and $\mathscr{S}'$, in the plane are **congruent** if and only if there is an isometry that maps $\mathscr{S}$ and $\mathscr{S}'$.

Figure 16.40 shows several pairs of congruent shapes. Can you identify the type of isometry, in each case, that maps shape $\mathscr{S}$ to shape $\mathscr{S}'$? In parts (a), (b), (c), and (d), respectively, of Figure 16.40, a translation, rotation, reflection, and glide reflection will map shape $\mathscr{S}$ to shape $\mathscr{S}'$.

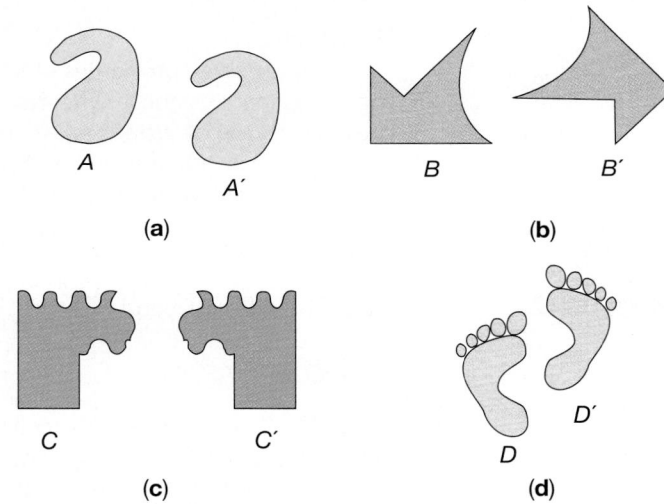

FIGURE 16.40

We can determine when two polygons are congruent by means of properties of their sides and angles. Suppose that there is a one-to-one correspondence between polygons $\mathscr{P}$ and $\mathscr{P}'$ such that all corresponding sides are congruent as are all corresponding angles. We can show that $\mathscr{P}$ is congruent to $\mathscr{P}'$. To demonstrate this, consider the polygons in Figure 16.41(a).

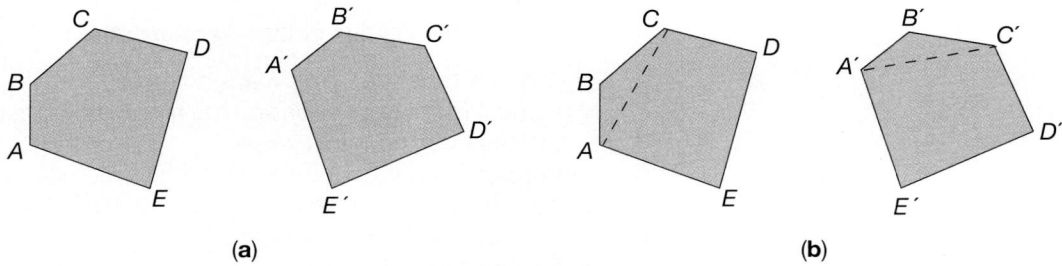

FIGURE 16.41

Suppose that the vertices correspond as indicated and that all pairs of corresponding sides and angles are congruent. Choose three vertices in $\mathscr{P}$, say A, B, and C, and their corresponding vertices A', B', and C' in $\mathscr{P}'$ [Figure 16.41(b)]. By the side–angle–side congruence condition, $\triangle ABC \cong \triangle A'B'C'$. Thus there is an isometry T that maps $\triangle ABC$ to $\triangle A'B'C'$. But then T preserves $\angle BCD$ and distance CD. Since $\mathscr{P}$ and $\mathscr{P}'$ have the same orientation, T must map segment $\overline{CD}$ to segment $\overline{C'D'}$. Similarly, T maps segment $\overline{DE}$ to segment $\overline{D'E'}$ and segment $\overline{EA}$ to segment $\overline{E'A'}$. From this we see that T maps polygon $\mathscr{P}$ to polygon $\mathscr{P}'$ so that the polygons are congruent.

Theorem

Congruent Polygons

Suppose that there is a one-to-one correspondence between polygons $\mathscr{P}$ and $\mathscr{P}'$ such that all pairs of corresponding sides and angles are congruent. Then $\mathscr{P} \cong \mathscr{P}'$.

Similarity

Next we study properties of size transformations and similitudes. Isometries preserve distance, whereas size transformations, hence similitudes, preserve *ratios* of distances. To see this, consider $\overline{PQ}$ and its image $\overline{P'Q'}$ under the size transformation $S_{O,k}$, where $k > 1$, and where O, P, and Q are not collinear (Figure 16.42). By definition, $OP' = k \cdot OP$, so $\dfrac{OP'}{OP} = k$, and $OQ' = k \cdot OQ$, so $\dfrac{OQ'}{OQ} = k$. Thus $\dfrac{OP'}{OP} = \dfrac{OQ'}{OQ}$. Since $\angle POQ = \angle P'OQ'$ and $\dfrac{OP'}{OP} = \dfrac{OQ'}{OQ}$, we can conclude that $\triangle POQ \sim \triangle P'OQ'$ by SAS similarity. By corresponding parts, $\dfrac{PQ}{P'Q'} = k$. In the case when O, P, and Q are not collinear the size transformation $S_{O,k}$ takes every segment $\overline{PQ}$ to a segment k times as long. This is also true in the case when O, P, and Q are collinear. Thus, in general, size transformations preserve ratios of distances.

Since size transformations preserve ratios of distances, the image of any triangle is similar to the original triangle by SSS similarity. Thus size transformations also preserve angle measure. A proof of this result and others in the following theorem are left for the problem set.

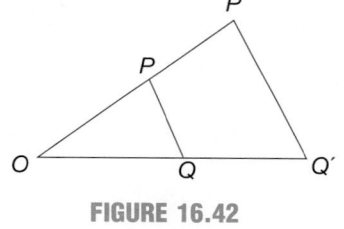

FIGURE 16.42

Theorem

Properties of Size Transformations

1. The size transformation $S_{O,k}$ maps a line segment $\overline{PQ}$ to a parallel line segment $\overline{P'Q'}$. In general, size transformations map lines to parallel lines and rays to parallel rays.
2. Size transformations preserve ratios of distances.
3. Size transformations preserve angle measure.
4. Size transformations preserve parallelism.
5. Size transformations preserve orientation.

The next example illustrates the use of size transformations to verify properties of polygons.

EXAMPLE 16.10 Let P be the point on side $\overline{AB}$ of $\triangle ABC$ such that $AB = 3 \cdot AP$ (Figure 16.43). Similarly, let Q be the point on $\overline{AC}$ such that $AC = 3 \cdot AQ$. Show that $\overline{PQ} \parallel \overline{BC}$ and $BC = 3 \cdot PQ$.

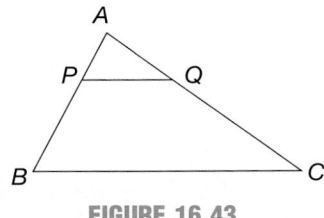

FIGURE 16.43

Solution
Consider $S_{A,3}$, that is, the size transformation with center A and scale factor 3. Then $S_{A,3}(P) = B$, and $S_{A,3}(Q) = C$. Hence, by the properties of size transformation $S_{A,3}$ maps segment $\overline{PQ}$ to segment $\overline{BC}$, and $\overline{PQ} \parallel \overline{BC}$, since size transformations map lines to parallel lines. Furthermore, the length of $\overline{BC}$ must be three times the length of segment $\overline{PQ}$, since size transformations preserve ratios of distances. ■

Recall that a similitude is a combination of a size transformation and an isometry. Thus the following properties of similitudes can be obtained by reasoning from the properties of size transformations and isometries. The verification of these properties are left for the problem set.

Theorem

Properties of Similitudes

1. Similitudes map lines to lines, segments to segments, rays to rays, angles to angles, and polygons to polygons.
2. Similitudes preserve ratios of distances.
3. Similitudes preserve angle measure.
4. Similitudes map triangles to similar triangles.
5. Similitudes preserve parallelism.

The next theorem and following example display the connection between the general notion of similarity and similar triangles.

Theorem

Triangle Similarity and Similitudes

$\triangle ABC \sim \triangle A'B'C'$ if and only if there is a similitude that maps $\triangle ABC$ to $\triangle A'B'C'$.

EXAMPLE 16.11   Suppose $\triangle ABC$ and $\triangle A'B'C'$ in Figure 16.44 are similar under the correspondence $A \leftrightarrow A'$, $B \leftrightarrow B'$, and $C \leftrightarrow C'$. Suppose also that $AC = 4$, $BC = 9$, $AB = 12$, and $A'C' = 7$.

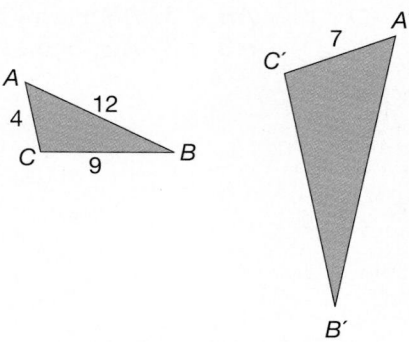

FIGURE 16.44

(a) Find $B'C'$ and $A'C'$.
(b) Find a similitude that maps $\triangle ABC$ to $\triangle A'B'C'$.

Solution
(a) Since corresponding sides are proportional, we must have $\dfrac{B'C'}{BC} = \dfrac{A'C'}{AC}$, or $\dfrac{B'C'}{9} = \dfrac{7}{4}$. Solving for $B'C'$, we find $B'C' = \dfrac{63}{4} = 15\dfrac{3}{4}$. Similarly, $\dfrac{A'C'}{AC} = \dfrac{A'B'}{AB}$, so that $\dfrac{A'B'}{12} = \dfrac{7}{4}$, from which we find $A'B' = 21$.

(b) Consider the size transformation $S_{A,7/4}$. Figure 16.45 shows the effect of $S_{A,7/4}$ on $\triangle ABC$. Note that B^* and C^* are the images of B and C,

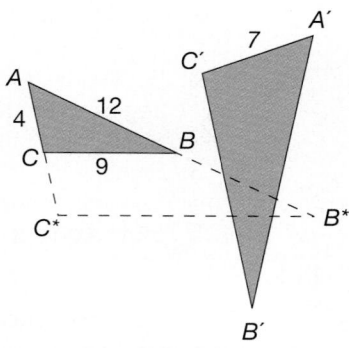

FIGURE 16.45

respectively, under this size transformation. Calculate that $AC^* = 7$, $AB^* = 21$, and $B^*C^* = 15\frac{3}{4}$. Hence $\triangle AB^*C^* \cong \triangle A'B'C'$ by the SSS congruence property. (In fact, any size transformation with scale factor $\frac{7}{4}$ will map $\triangle ABC$ to a triangle congruent to $\triangle A'B'C'$. For convenience, we chose point A as the center of the size transformation. However, we could have chosen any point as the center.)

Observe that $\triangle AB*C*$ and $\triangle A'B'C'$ have the same orientation. However, $\triangle A'B'C'$ is not a translation image of $\triangle AB*C*$. Therefore, there is a rotation that maps $\triangle AB*C*$ to $\triangle A'B'C'$. Thus $S_{A,7/4}$ followed by a rotation is a similitude that maps $\triangle ABC$ to $\triangle A'B'C'$ (Figure 16.46).

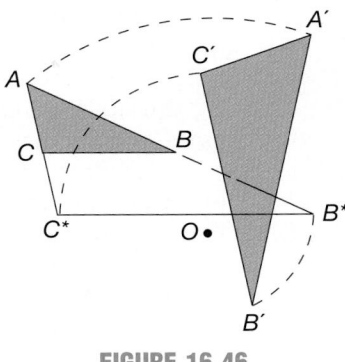

FIGURE 16.46   ■

We can define similarity of shapes in the plane via similitudes.

Definition

Similar Shapes

Two shapes, $\mathcal{S}$ and $\mathcal{S}'$, in the plane are **similar** if and only if there is a similitude that maps $\mathcal{S}$ to $\mathcal{S}'$.

Using the triangle similarity and similitudes theorem, we can show that two polygons are similar if there is a one-to-one correspondence between them such that all pairs of corresponding sides are proportional and all pairs of corresponding angles are congruent (Figure 16.47).

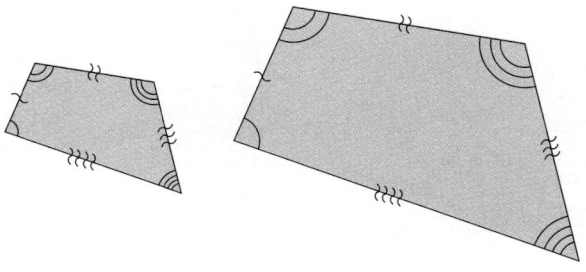

FIGURE 16.47

Theorem

Similar Polygons

Suppose that there is a one-to-one correspondence between polygons $\mathcal{P}$ and $\mathcal{P}'$ such that all pairs of corresponding sides are proportional and all pairs of corresponding angles are congruent. Then $\mathcal{P} \sim \mathcal{P}'$.

From the definition of similar shapes, we see that all congruent shapes are similar, since we can use the size transformation with scale factor 1 to serve as the similitude in mapping one congruent shape to the other. Hence all transformations that we have studied in this chapter—namely, isometries (translations, rotations, reflections, glide reflections), size transformations, and combinations of these transformations—are similitudes. Thus all the transformations that we have studied preserve shapes of figures. Finally, since there are only four types of isometries in the plane, it follows that every similitude is a combination of a size transformation and one of the four types of isometries: a translation, rotation, reflection, or glide reflection.

The approach to congruence and similarity of geometric shapes via isometries and similitudes is called **transformation geometry**. Transformation geometry provides additional problem-solving techniques in geometry that effectively complement approaches using triangle congruence and similarity and approaches using coordinates. We explore the use of transformations to solve geometry problems in the next section.

MATHEMATICAL MORSEL

One of the most famous problems in mathematics is the four-color problem. It states that at most four colors are required to color any two-dimensional map where no two neighboring countries have the same color. In 1976, Kenneth Appel and Wolfgang Haken of the University of Illinois solved this problem in a unique way. To check out the large number of cases, they wrote a program that took over 1200 hours to run on high-speed computers. Although there are mathematicians who prefer not to acknowledge this type of proof for fear that the computer may have erred, the problem is generally accepted as solved. For the purists, though, the famous Hungarian mathematician Paul Erdos is said to have mused that God has a thin little book that contains short, elegant proofs of all the significant theorems in mathematics. However, since the approach taken by Appel and Haken fills 460 pages in a journal, it may not be found in the thin little book.

EXERCISE/PROBLEM SET 16.2—PART A

Exercises

1. (a) What are the coordinates of points A and B?
(b) What are the coordinates of A' and B', where $A' = T_{OP}(A)$ and $B' = T_{OP}(B)$?
(c) Use the distance formula to verify that this translation has preserved distances (i.e., show that $AB = A'B'$).

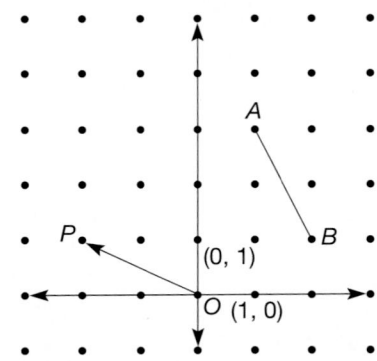

2. Consider $P(p, q)$, T_{OP}, $X(x, y)$, and $Y(x + p, y + q)$.

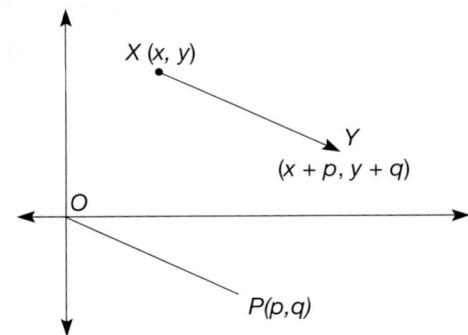

(a) Are the directed line segments $\overrightarrow{OP}$ and $\overrightarrow{XY}$ parallel?
(b) Do $\overrightarrow{OP}$ and $\overrightarrow{XY}$ have the same length? Explain.
(c) Is $Y = T_{OP}(X)$?

3. Consider $X(x, y)$ and $Y(-y, x)$.

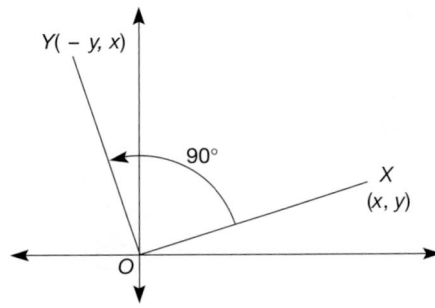

(a) Verify that $m(\angle XOY) = 90°$.
(b) Verify that $OX = OY$.
(c) Is $Y = R_{O,90°}(X)$? Why or why not?

4. Given that $R_{O,90°}(x, y) = (-y, x)$, find the coordinates of A' and B', where $A' = R_{O,90°}(A)$, $B' = R_{O,90°}(B)$, and A and B have coordinates $(5, 2)$ and $(3, -4)$, respectively. Verify that $R_{O,90°}$ preserves the distance AB.

5. (a) What are the coordinates of points A and B?
(b) What are the coordinates of A' and B', where $A' = M_y(A)$, $B' = M_y(B)$, where M_y is the reflection in the y-axis?
(c) Use the distance formula to verify that this reflection has preserved the distance AB (i.e., show that $AB = A'B'$).

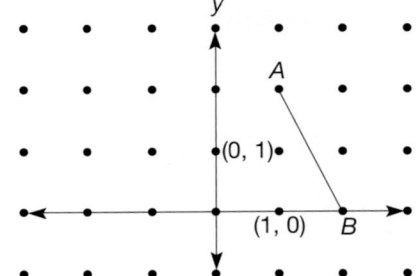

6. Let A be a point in the plane with coordinates (a, b).
(a) What are the coordinates of $A' = M_x(A)$, where M_x is the reflection in the x-axis?
(b) If points A and B have coordinates (a, b) and (c, d), respectively, verify that M_x preserves distances.

7. Consider $X(x, y)$, and $Y(y, x)$.

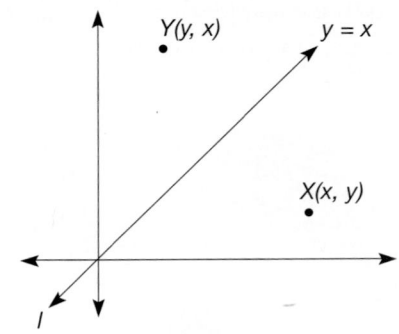

(a) Verify that the midpoint of $\overline{XY}$ lies on line l whose equation is $y = x$.
(b) Verify that $\overline{XY} \perp l$.
(c) Is $Y = M_l(X)$? Why or why not?

8. (a) What are the coordinates of points A and B?

(b) What are the coordinates of A' and B' where $A' = M_x(T_{PQ}(A))$ and $B' = M_x(T_{PQ}(B))$?

(c) Use the distance formula to verify that this glide reflection has preserved the distance AB (i.e., show that $AB = A'B'$).

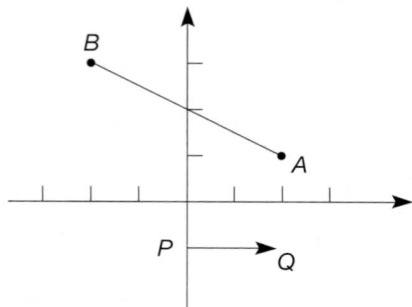

(b)

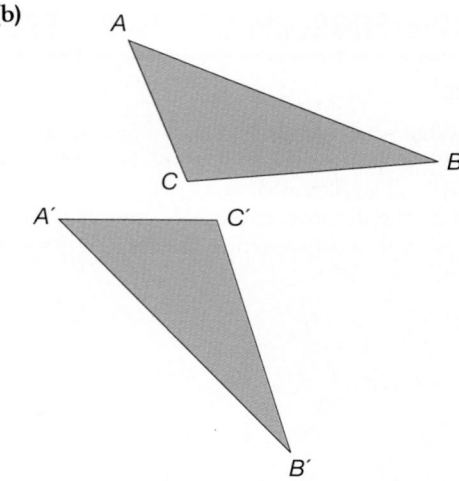

9. Consider the point X with coordinates (x, y) and the point Y with coordinates $(-x, -y)$.

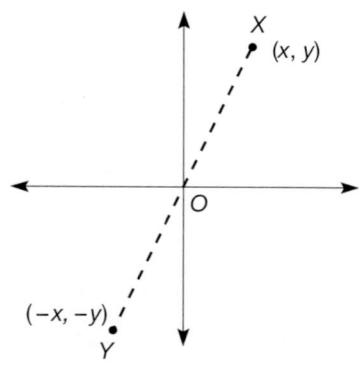

(a) Verify that $m(\angle XOY) = 180°$.

(b) Verify that $OX = OY$.

(c) Describe the transformation that maps X to Y.

10. In each case, is there a reflection that maps $\triangle ABC$ onto $\triangle A'B'C'$?

(a)

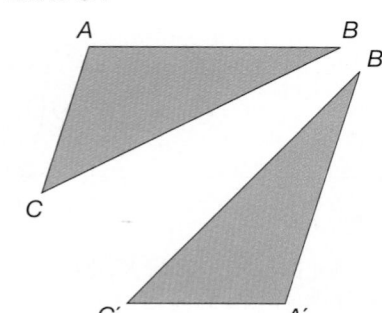

11. Determine the type of isometry that maps the shape on the left onto the shape on the right.

(a)

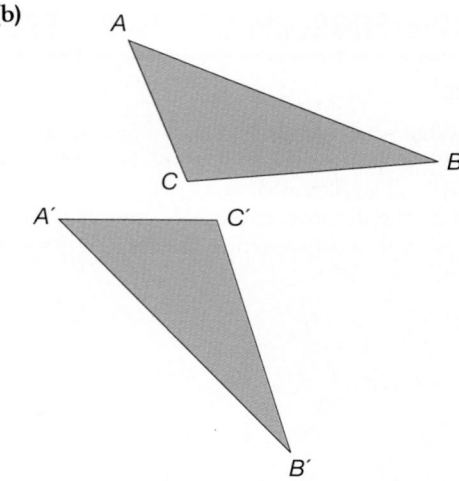

(b)

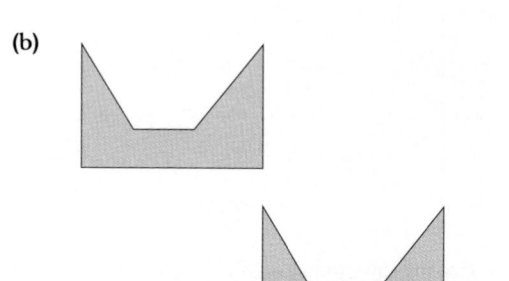

(c)

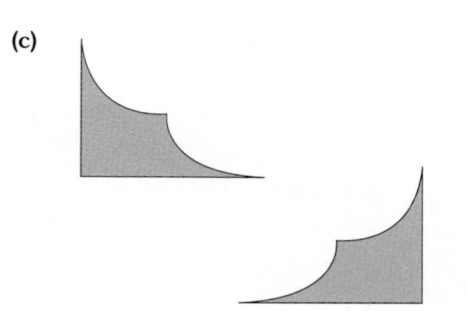

12. Find a translation, rotation, reflection, or glide reflection that maps $ABCD$ onto $A'B'C'D'$ in each case.

(a)

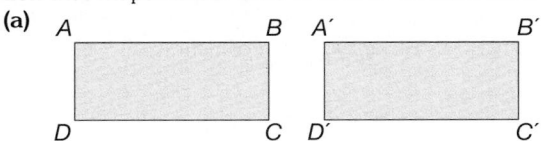

(b)

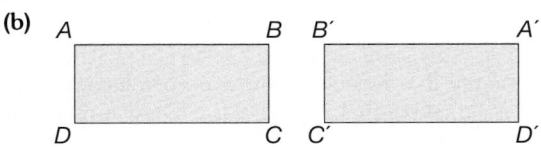

(c)

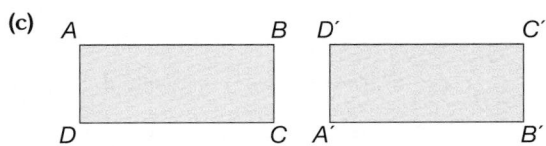

(d)

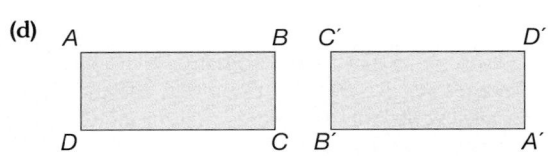

13. (a) Find the image of $\triangle ABC$ under the transformation $S_{P,2}$.

(b) Find the lengths of $\overline{AB}$ and $\overline{A'B'}$. What is the ratio $A'B'/AB$?

(c) Find the lengths of $\overline{BC}$ and $\overline{B'C'}$. What is the ratio $B'C'/BC$?

(d) Find the lengths of $\overline{AC}$ and $\overline{A'C'}$. What is the ratio $A'C'/AC$?

(e) In addition to their lengths, what other relationship exists between a segment and its image?

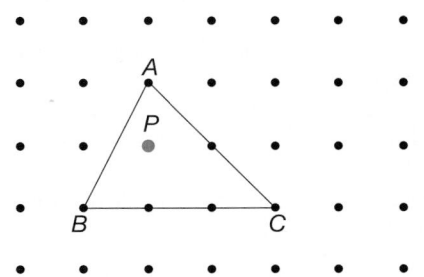

14. (a) Find the image of $\angle ABC$ under $S_{P,2}$.

(b) How do the measures of $\angle ABC$ and $\angle A'B'C'$ compare?

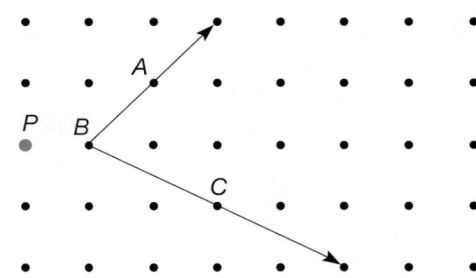

15. Is there a size transformation that maps $\triangle RST$ to $\triangle R'S'T'$? If so, find its center and scale factor. If not, explain why not.

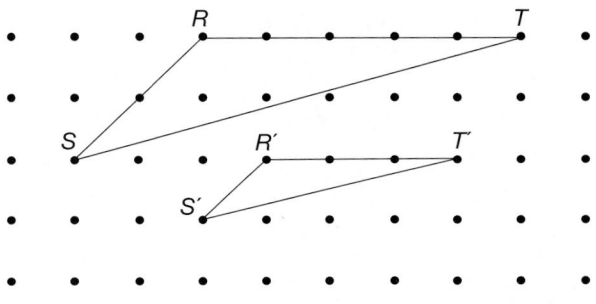

16. For each part, find a similitude that maps $\triangle ABC$ to $\triangle A'B'C'$. Describe each similitude as completely as you can.

(a)

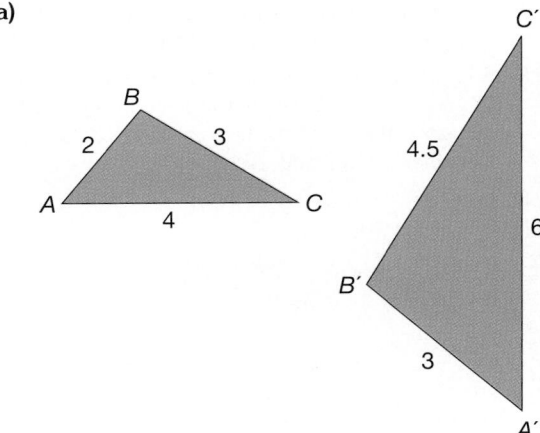

(b)

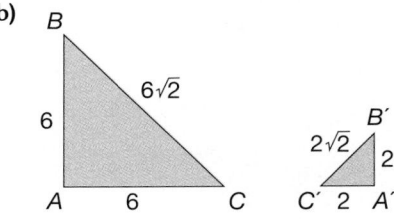

Problems

17. Let A, X, and B be points on line l with X between A and B and let A', X', and B' be the images of A, X, and B, respectively, under a translation T_{PQ}.

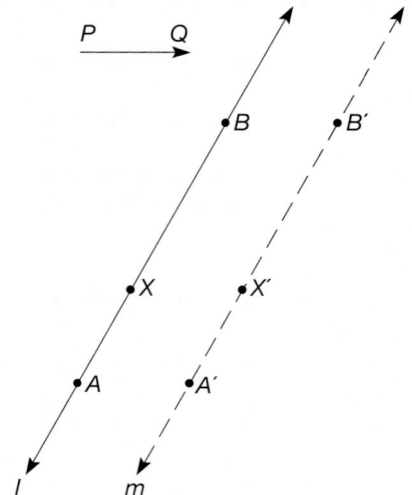

(a) Show that $BB'X'X$ and $BB'A'A$ are both parallelograms.

(b) Combine conclusions from part (a) and the uniqueness of line m through B' such that $l \parallel m$, to verify that A', X', and B' are collinear. This verifies that the translation image of a line is a set of collinear points. [NOTE: To show that $m = T_{PQ}(l)$ goes beyond the scope of this book.]

18. Suppose there is a translation that maps P to P', Q to Q', and R to R'. Verify that translations preserve angle measure; that is, show that $\angle PQR \cong \angle P'Q'R'$. (HINT: Consider $\triangle PQR$ and $\triangle P'Q'R'$.)

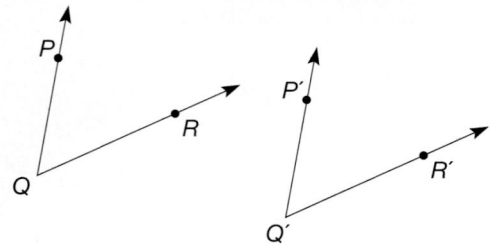

19. Given are parallel lines p and q. Suppose that a rotation maps p to p' and q and q'. Verify that $p' \parallel q'$ (i.e., that rotations preserve parallelism).

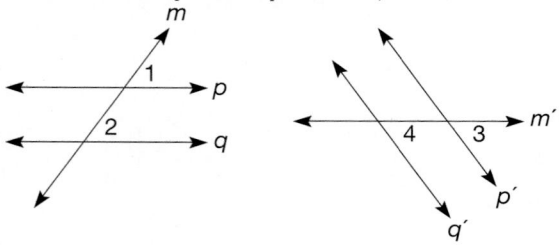

20. Suppose there is a reflection that maps A to A', B to B', and C to C'. Verify that reflections preserve collinearity; that is, if A, B, and C are collinear, show that A', B', and C' are collinear.

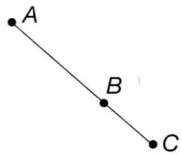

21. Verify that reflections preserve parallelism; that is, if $p \parallel q$, show that $p' \parallel q'$. (HINT: Draw a reflection line and the images p', q', and m'.)

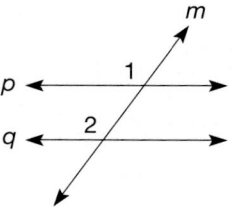

22. Given is $\triangle ABC$. An isometry is applied yielding images A', B', and C' of points A, B, and C, respectively. Verify that isometries map triangles to congruent triangles (i.e., show that $\triangle ABC \cong \triangle A'B'C'$).

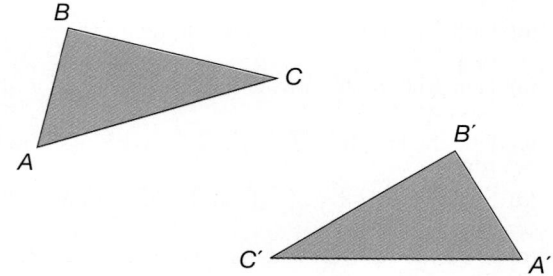

23. Given are points P and Q.

(a) How many translations are possible that map P to Q? Describe them.

(b) How many rotations are possible that map P to Q? Describe them.

(c) How many reflections map P to Q? Describe them.

(d) How many glide reflections map P to Q? Describe them.

24. (a) Find the center of the magnification that maps P to P' and Q to Q'.

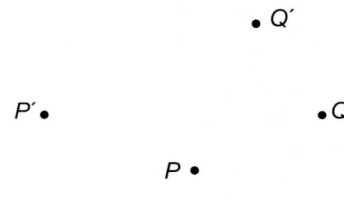

(b) Is the scale factor less than 1 or greater than 1?
(c) Repeat parts (a) and (b) for the following points.

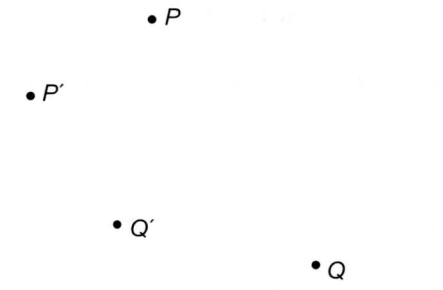

25. The size transformation $S_{P,k}$ maps Q to Q'. If P is on line l, describe how you would construct $S_{P,k}(R)$.

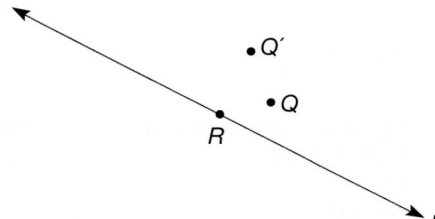

26. Given a size transformation that maps P to P' and Q to Q', describe how to construct the image of R under the same size transformation.

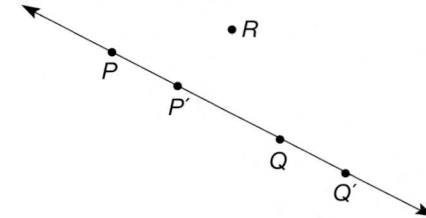

27. Suppose that P and Q are on the same side of line l, $P' = M_l(P)$ and $Q' = M_l(Q)$. Show that $P'Q' = PQ$.

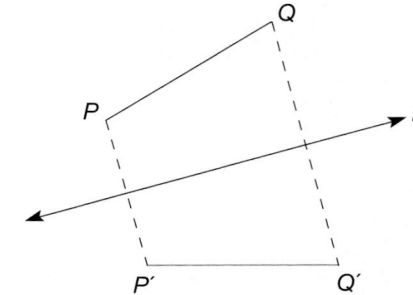

EXERCISE/PROBLEM SET 16.2—PART B

Exercises

1. (a) What are the coordinates of points A and B?
(b) Point P has coordinates $(4, 5)$. Let $A' = T_{OP}(A)$ and $B' = T_{OP}(B)$. What are the coordinates of A' and B'?
(c) Verify that T_{OP} has preserved the length of $\overline{AB}$.

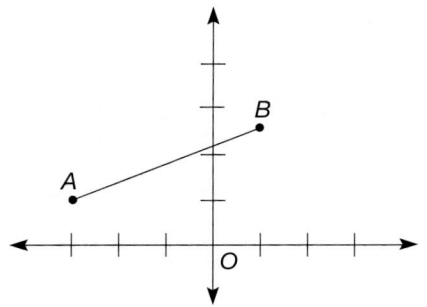

2. Given that $T_{OP}(x, y) = (x + p, y + q)$ and that points A and B have coordinates (a, b) and (c, d), respectively, answer the following.
(a) Find AB.

(b) What are the coordinates of A' and B' where $A' = T_{OP}(A)$ and $B' = T_{OP}(B)$?
(c) Find $A'B'$.
(d) Does this general translation preserve distances?

3. Consider $\triangle ABC$ pictured on the graph. The rotation $R_{O, -90°}$ takes a point with coordinates (x, y) to a point with coordinates $(y, -x)$.

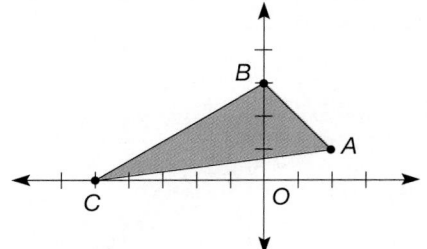

(a) Find the coordinates of A', B', and C' where $A' = R_{O, -90°}(A)$, $B' = R_{O, -90°}(B)$, and $C' = R_{O, -90°}(C)$.
(b) Is $\triangle ABC \cong \triangle A'B'C'$? Verify your answer.
(c) Is $\angle ABC \cong \angle A'B'C'$? Verify.

4. Given that $R_{O, 180°}(x, y) = (-x, -y)$, find the coordinates of A' and B' where $A' = R_{O, 180°}(A)$ and $B' = R_{O, 180°}(B)$ and A and B have coordinates $(-2, 3)$ and $(-3, -1)$, respectively. Verify that $R_{O, 180°}$ preserves the distance AB.

5. Described below are several rotations about the origin O. In each part, find the images of $P(1, 2)$ and $Q(4, -3)$, and verify that the rotation preserves distance.
   (a) $R_{O, 90°}(x, y) = (-y, x)$
   (b) $R_{O, -90°}(x, y) = (y, -x)$
   (c) $R_{O, 180°}(x, y) = (-x, -y)$

6. **(a)** What are the coordinates of points A and B?
   (b) What are the coordinates of A' and B' where $A' = M_x(A)$ and $B' = M_x(B)$?
   (c) Use the distance formula to verify that this reflection has preserved the distance AB (i.e., show that $AB = A'B'$).

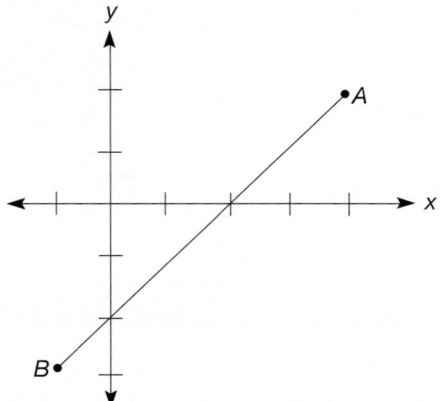

7. Let A be a point in the plane with coordinates (a, b).
   (a) What are the coordinates of $A' = M_y(A)$?
   (b) If points A and B have coordinates (a, b) and (c, d), respectively, verify that M_y preserves the distance AB.

8. Consider $\triangle ABC$ pictured on the following graph. The reflection M_l takes a point with coordinates (x, y) to a point with coordinates (y, x).

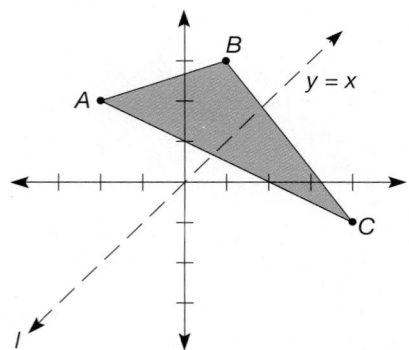

(a) Find the coordinates of A', B', and C', where $A' = M_l(A)$, $B' = M_l(B)$, and $C' = M_l(C)$.
(b) Is $\triangle ABC \cong \triangle A'B'C'$? Verify.
(c) Is $\angle ABC \cong \angle A'B'C'$? Verify.

9. **(a)** What are the coordinates of points A and B?
   (b) For $P(p, 0)$, what are the coordinates of A' and B', where $A = M_x(T_{OP}(A))$ and $B' = M_x(T_{OP}(B))$?
   (c) Verify that $M_x(T_{OP})$ preserves the distance AB.

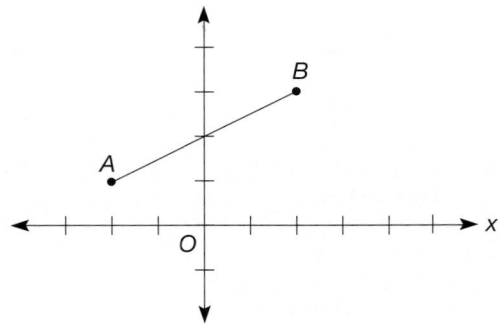

10. Described below are several glide reflections. Let points A and B have coordinates $(-2, 4)$ and $(5, -3)$, respectively. For each glide reflection, find the coordinates of A' and B'. Then verify that these glide reflections preserve the distance AB.
   (a) $M_l T_{OP}(x, y) = (x + 3, -y)$
   (b) $M_l T_{OP}(x, y) = (-x, y - 2)$
   (c) $M_l T_{OP}(x, y) = (y + 1, x + 1)$

11. Determine the type of isometry that maps the shape on the left onto the shape on the right.
   (a)

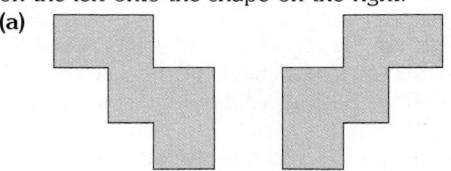

   (b)

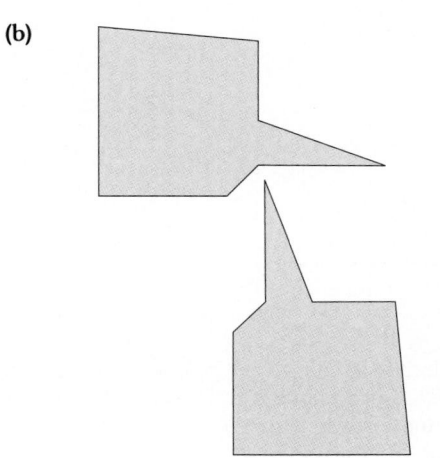

(c)

12. In each case, if there is a rotation that maps $\triangle ABC$ to $\triangle A'B'C'$, find its center.

(a)

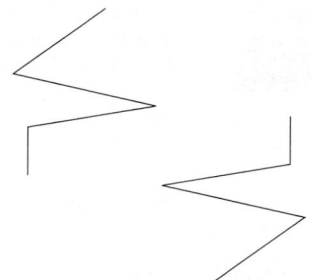

(b)

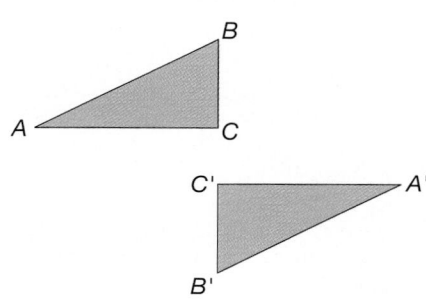

(c)

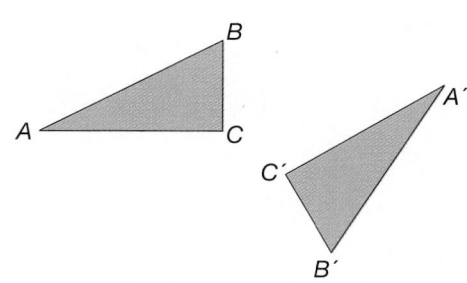

13. Find a translation, rotation, reflection, or glide reflection that maps $\triangle ABC$ to $\triangle A'B'C'$ in each case below.

(a)

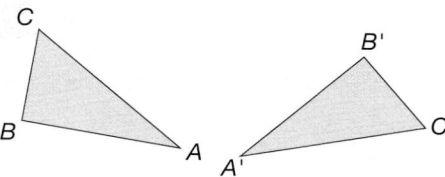

(b)

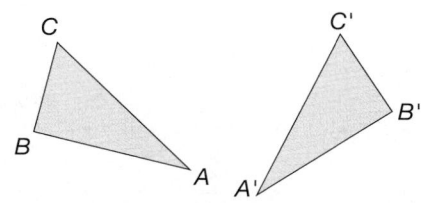

14. (a) Find the image of $\overline{AB}$ under the transformation $S_{P,3}$.
   (b) Verify that $PA' = 3PA$.
   (c) Verify that $PB' = 3PB$.
   (d) Find the length of $\overline{AB}$ and $\overline{A'B'}$. How do these lengths compare?

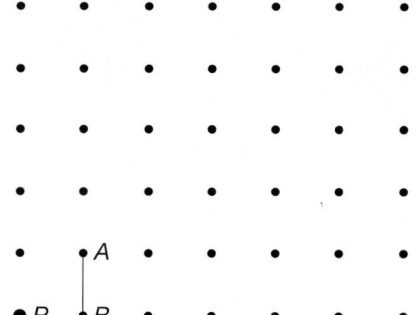

15. (a) Find the center P and a scale factor k such that the transformation $S_{P,k}$ maps the small figure to the large figure.
   (b) If $S_{P,h}$ maps the large figure onto the small figure, find the scale factor h.
   (c) How are k and h related?

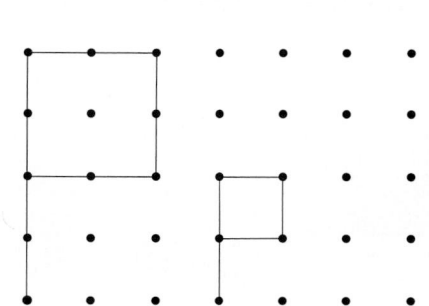

16. (a) Describe an isometry followed by a size transformation that maps circle A_1 to circle A_2.

(b) Are all circles similar? Explain why or why not.

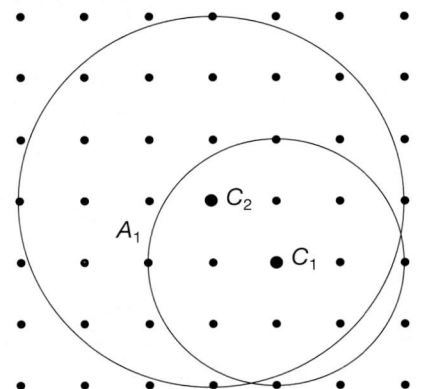

17. In each part, find a similitude that maps $\triangle ABC$ to $\triangle A'B'C'$. Describe each similitude as completely as possible.

(a)

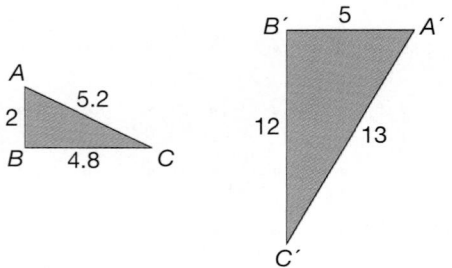

(b)

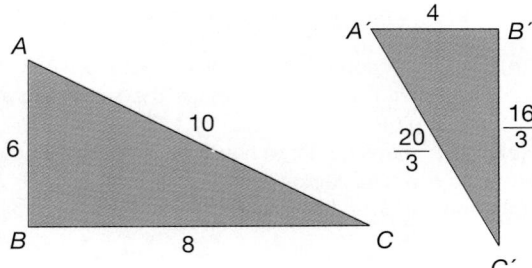

(c)

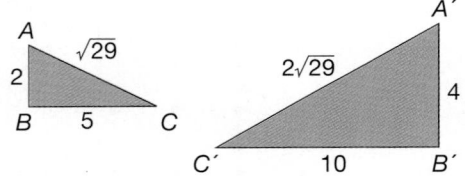

Problems

18. Suppose there exists a translation that maps line p to p' and line q to q'. Verify that translations preserve parallelism; that is, if $p \parallel q$, show that $p' \parallel q'$.

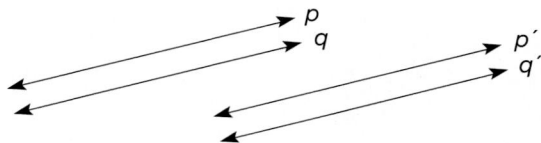

19. Let $R_{O,a}$ be a rotation that maps A to A', B to B', and C to C'. Verify that rotations preserve collinearity; that is, if A, B, and C are collinear, show that A', B', and C' are also collinear. (HINT: Show $A'B' + B'C' = A'C'$.)

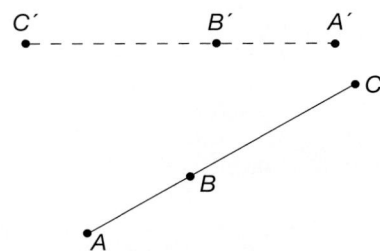

20. Let $R_{O,a}$ be a rotation that maps A to A', B to B', and C to C'. Verify that rotations preserve angle measure; that is, show that $\angle BAC \cong \angle B'A'C'$. (HINT: Consider $\triangle ABC$ and $\triangle A'B'C'$.)

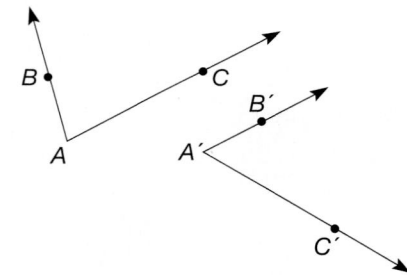

21. Let line l be chosen such that $B' = M_l(B)$. Let P be a point on l, and Q be the point where $\overline{BB'}$ intersects l. Show that $\angle BPQ \cong \angle B'PQ$.

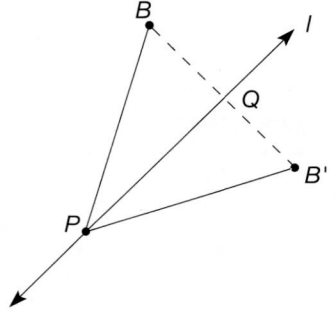

22. Given are two points A and B. A right triangle is drawn that has $\overline{AB}$ as its hypotenuse and point C at the vertex of the right angle. Line l is the perpendicular bisector of $\overline{AC}$.

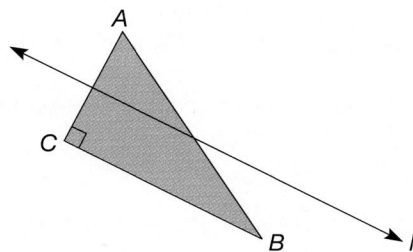

(a) Verify that $l \parallel \overline{CB}$.
(b) Verify that M_l followed by T_{CB} maps A to B.
(c) Find another directed line segment $\overrightarrow{NO}$ and line m such that M_m followed by T_{NO} maps A to B. (HINT: Draw another right triangle with AB as its hypotenuse.)
(d) At what point do line l and line m intersect? Will this be true for other glide axes?

23. Given are parallel lines p and q. Line p' is the image of line p under a certain isometry, and line q' is the image of line q under the same isometry. Verify that the isometry preserves parallelism (i.e., show that $p' \parallel q'$). (HINT: Use corresponding angles.)

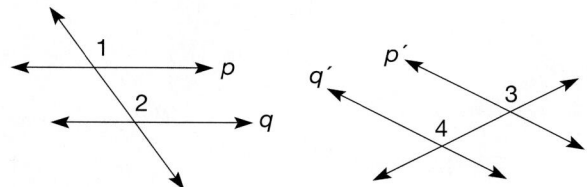

24. Construct the image of quadrilateral $ABCD$ under $S_{P,k}$, where $k = PA'/PA$. Describe your procedure.

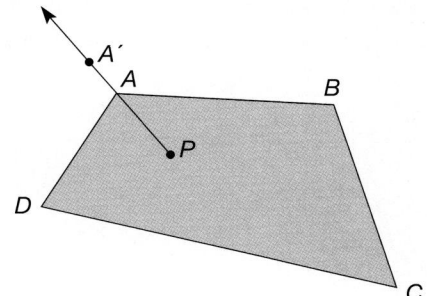

25. Given that A and B are on opposite sides of line l, $M_l(A) = A'$, and $M_l(B) = B'$, follow the steps to show that $AB = A'B'$.

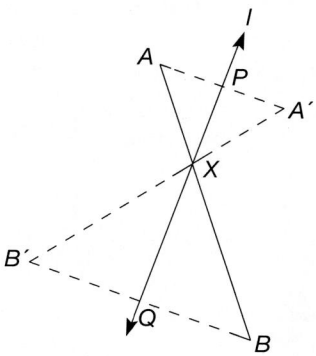

1. Let P be the intersection of l and AA', and Q be the intersection of l and BB'. Let X be the point where $\overline{AB}$ intersects line l. Let $X' = M_l(X)$. Where is X'?
2. Next, we wish to show that A', X', and B' are collinear. Give reasons why the following angles are congruent (one reason for each congruent symbol): $\angle BXQ \cong \angle AXP \cong \angle A'X'P \cong \angle B'X'Q$.
3. Let $a = m(\angle AXP)$ and $b = m(\angle A'XB)$. Use the fact that A, X, and B are collinear to show that $m(\angle AXP) + m(\angle PXA') + m(\angle A'XB) = a + a + b = 180°$. Determine the value for $m(\angle A'X'B')$ and justify your answer. Can we conclude that A', X', and B' are collinear?
4. Since X is on line l, we can conclude that $AX = A'X'$. Similarly, $BX = B'X'$. What is the reason for these conclusions?
5. Use what has been shown to verify $AB = A'B'$ and justify.

16.3

GEOMETRIC PROBLEM SOLVING USING TRANSFORMATIONS

The use of transformations provides an alternative approach to geometry and gives us additional problem-solving techniques. Our first example is a transformational proof of a familiar property of isosceles triangles.

EXAMPLE 16.12   Use isometries to show that the base angles of an isosceles triangle are congruent.

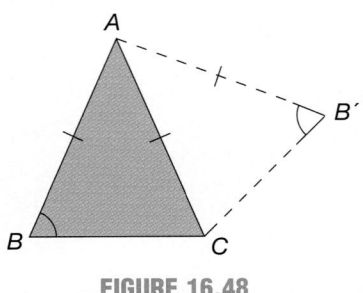

FIGURE 16.48

Solution
Let $\triangle ABC$ be isosceles with $\overline{AB} \cong \overline{AC}$ (Figure 16.48). Reflect $\triangle ABC$ in $\overleftrightarrow{AC}$, forming $\triangle AB'C$. As a result, we know that $\angle ABC \cong \angle AB'C$ and $\angle BAC \cong \angle B'AC$, since reflections preserve angle measure. Next, consider the rotation with center A and directed angle $\angle B'AC$. Since $\angle B'AC \cong \angle BAC$, and since $\overline{AB} \cong \overline{AC} \cong \overline{AB'}$, we know that this rotation maps $\triangle AB'C$ to $\triangle ACB$. Hence $\angle AB'C \cong \angle ACB$. Combining this with our observation above that $\angle AB'C \cong \angle ABC$, we have that $\angle ABC \cong \angle ACB$. ■

A particular type of rotation, called a half-turn, is especially useful in verifying properties of polygons. A **half-turn**, H_O, is a rotation through 180°, with any point, O, as the center. Figure 16.49 shows a half-turn

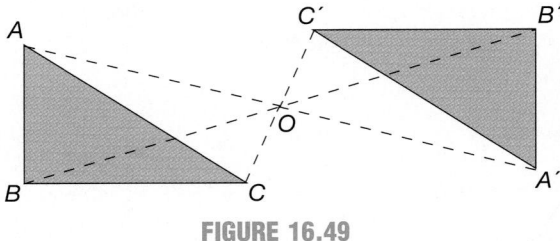

FIGURE 16.49

image of $\overline{ABC}$, with point O as the center. In Figure 16.49, $\overline{AB}$ is rotated by H_O to $\overline{A'B'}$, where it appears that $\overline{A'B'} \parallel \overline{AB}$. Next we verify that the half-turn image of a line is indeed parallel to the original line. In Figure 16.50, let l be a line and let O be the center of a half-turn. Notice that in

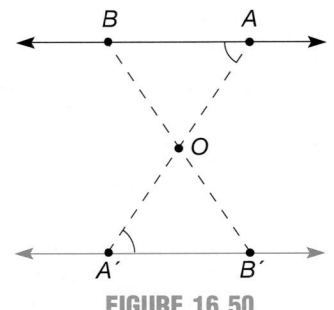

FIGURE 16.50

this case O is not on l. Since H_O is an isometry, it maps l to a line l'. Let A and B be points on l. Then A' and B', the images of A and B under the half-turn H_O, are on l'. Also, and most important, A, O, and A' are collinear, so that line $\overleftrightarrow{AA'}$ is a transversal for lines l and l' containing point O. Since H_O is an isometry, $\angle BAO \cong \angle B'A'O$. Thus, by the alternate interior angles theorem, $l \parallel l'$. In summary, we have shown that a half-turn, H_O, maps a line l to a line l' such that $l' \parallel l$. Figure 16.51 shows the two possible cases: namely, O is on l [Figure 16.51(a)] or O is not on l [Figure 16.51(b)]. If O is on l, the result follows immediately, since every line is parallel to itself.

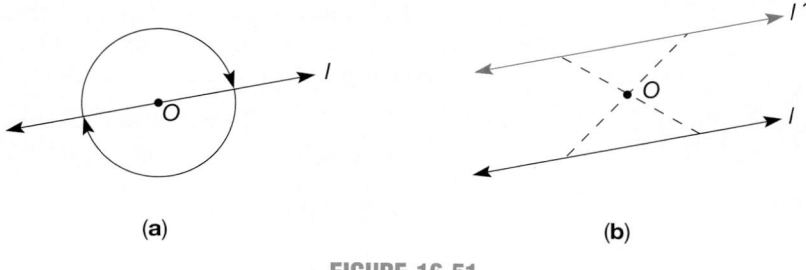

(a)   **(b)**

FIGURE 16.51

Example 16.13 illustrates the use of half-turns to verify a property of quadrilaterals.

EXAMPLE 16.13   Show that if the diagonals of a quadrilateral bisect each other, the quadrilateral is a parallelogram.

Solution
Suppose that $ABCD$ is a quadrilateral with diagonals $\overline{AC}$ and $\overline{BD}$ intersecting at point O, the midpoint of each diagonal (Figure 16.52). Consider the half-turn H_O. Then $H_O(A) = C$, $H_O(B) = D$, $H_O(C) = A$, and $H_O(D) = B$ (verify). Thus H_O maps side $\overline{AB}$ of quadrilateral $ABCD$ to side $\overline{CD}$ so that $\overline{AB} \parallel \overline{CD}$. Also, H_O maps $\overline{AD}$ to $\overline{CB}$ so that $\overline{AD} \parallel \overline{CB}$. Hence quadrilateral $ABCD$ is a parallelogram, since both pairs of its opposite sides are parallel. (NOTE: Since H_O is an isometry, this also shows that opposite sides of a parallelogram are congruent.)   ■

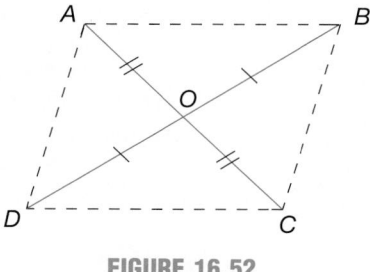

FIGURE 16.52

Transformations can also be used to solve certain applied problems. Consider the following pool table problem.

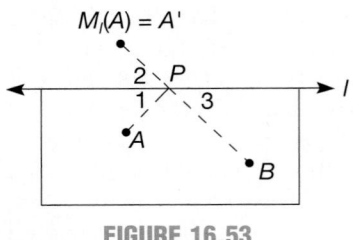

$M_l(A) = A'$

FIGURE 16.53

EXAMPLE 16.14   Cue ball A is to hit cushion l, then strike object ball B (Figure 16.53). Assuming that there is no "spin" on the cue ball, show how to find the desired point P on cushion l at which to aim the cue ball.

Solution
Reflect the cue ball, A, in line l. That is, find $M_l(A) = A'$ (Figure 16.53). Let P be the point at which the line $\overline{A'B}$ intersects cushion l. Then $\angle 1 \cong \angle 2$, since an angle is congruent to its reflection image, and $\angle 2 \cong \angle 3$, because they are vertical angles. Since the angle of incidence is congruent to the angle of reflection, we have that the cue ball should be aimed at point P. ∎

Examples of pool shot paths caroming or "banking" off several cushions appear in the problem set. Our next example concerns a minimal distance problem involving a translation.

EXAMPLE 16.15   Towns A and B are on opposite sides of a river (Figure 16.54). The towns are to be connected with a bridge, $\overline{CD}$, perpendicular to the river, so that the distance $AC + CD + DB$ is as small as possible. Where should the bridge be located?

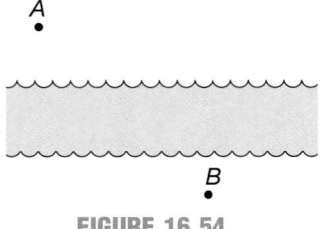

FIGURE 16.54

Solution
No matter where the bridge is located, distance CD, the width of the river, will be a constant in the sum $AC + CD + DB$ [Figure 16.55(a)]. Hence we wish to minimize the sum $AC + DB$. Let S be a translation in a direction from B toward the river and perpendicular to it, for a distance equal to the width of the river, d. Let $B' = S(B)$. Then the segment $\overline{AB'}$ is the shortest path from A to B'. Let point C be the intersection of $\overline{AB'}$ and line m, one side of the river [Figure 16.55(b)].

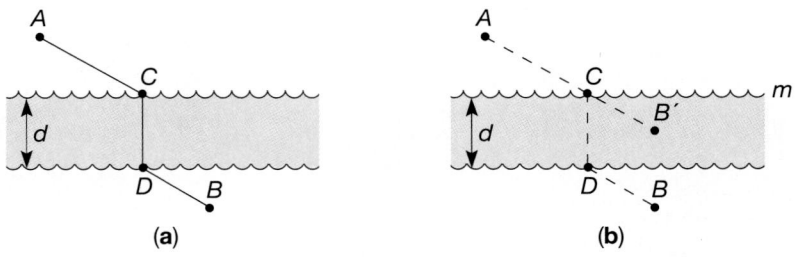

(a)   (b)

FIGURE 16.55

Let point D be the point opposite C on the other side of the river, where $\overline{CD} \perp m$. That is, $\overline{CD} \parallel \overline{B'B}$ and $CD = B'B$. Hence quadrilateral $BB'CD$ is a parallelogram since the opposite sides $\overline{CD}$ and $\overline{B'B}$ are congruent and parallel. Thus the sum $AC + CD + DB$ is as small as possible. ∎

We can verify the result of Example 14.16 using size transformations, as Example 16.16 illustrates.

EXAMPLE 16.16   Let $\triangle ABC$ be a triangle. Let points P and Q be on sides $\overline{AB}$ and $\overline{AC}$, respectively, such that $AB = k \cdot AP$ and $AC = k \cdot AQ$ (Figure 16.56). That is, $\overline{PQ}$ divides $\overline{AB}$ and $\overline{AC}$ proportionally. Show that $\overline{PQ} \parallel \overline{BC}$ and $BC = k \cdot PQ$.

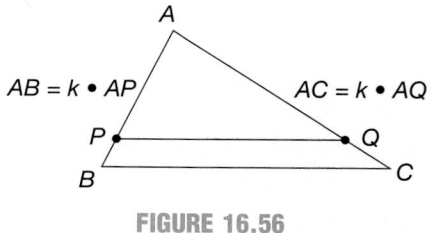

FIGURE 16.56

Solution

Consider the size transformation $S_{A,k}$. Then $S_{A,k}(P) = B$ since P is on $\overrightarrow{AB}$ and $AB = k \cdot AP$. Similarly, $S_{A,k}(Q) = C$. Hence the size transformation $S_{A,k}$ maps segment $\overline{PQ}$ to segment $\overline{BC}$. Thus, by properties of size transformations, $PQ \parallel BC$ and $BC = k \cdot PQ$. ■

Notice how quickly the result in Example 16.16 is established using a transformation approach.

MATHEMATICAL MORSEL

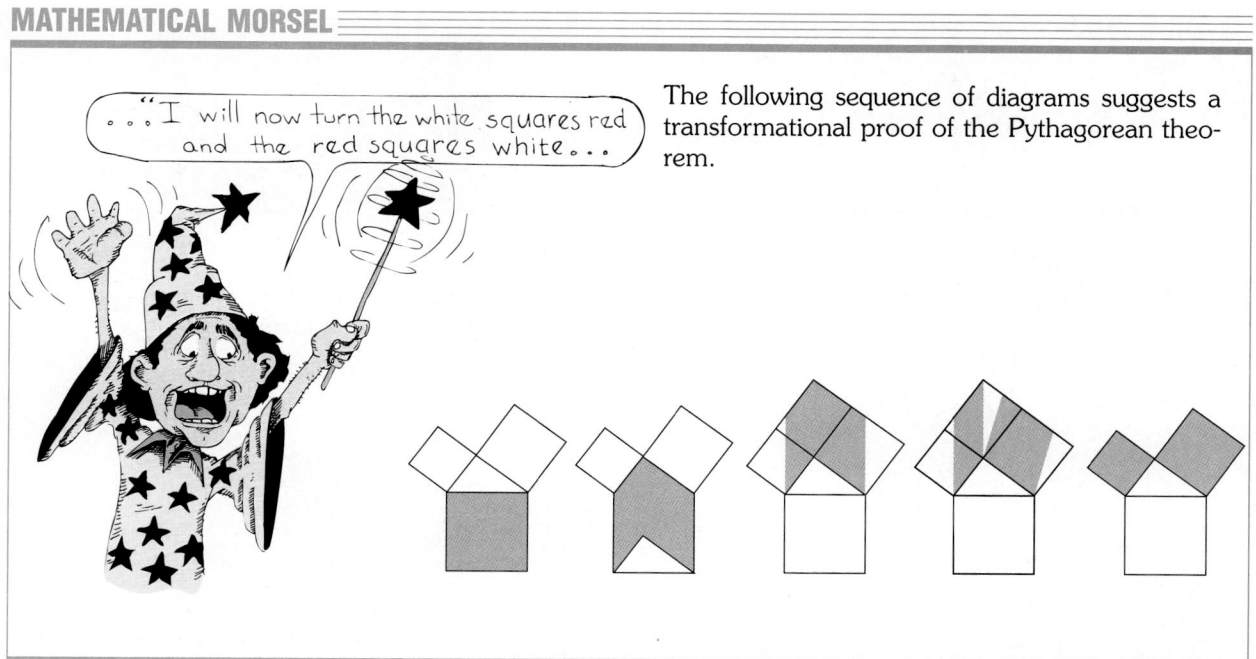

The following sequence of diagrams suggests a transformational proof of the Pythagorean theorem.

EXERCISE/PROBLEM SET 16.3—PART A

Exercises

1. *ABCD* is a square. Points *E, F, G, H* are the midpoints of the sides. List four reflections that map the square onto itself.

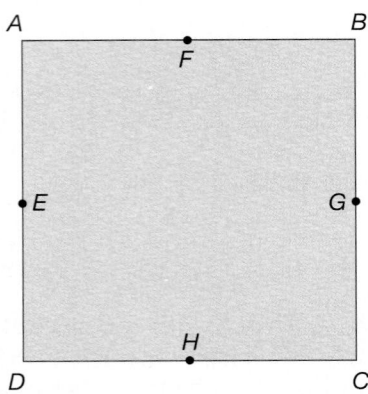

2. Figure *ABCD* is a kite. Point *E* is the intersection of the diagonals. Which of the following transformations can be used to show that △*ABC* ≅ △*ADC* using the transformation definition of congruence? Explain.

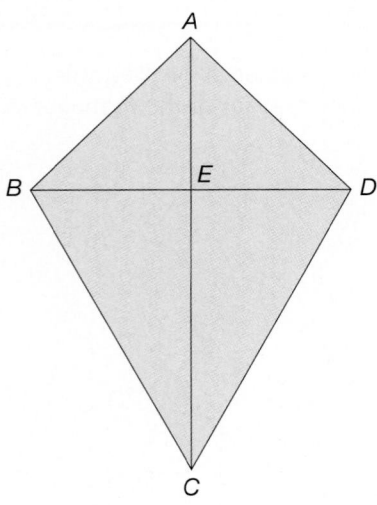

(a) H_E **(b)** T_{BE}
(c) $R_{E,90°}$ **(d)** M_{AC}

3. *ABCDEF* is a regular hexagon with center *O*.

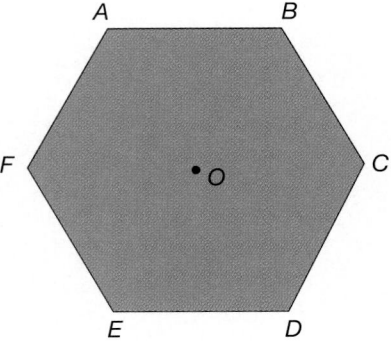

(a) List three reflections and three rotations that map the hexagon onto itself.
(b) How many isometries are there that map the hexagon onto itself?

4. *ABCD* is a rectangle. Points *E, F, G, H* are the midpoints of the sides. Find all the reflections and rotations that map *ABCD* onto itself.

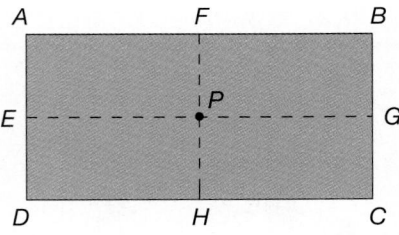

5. *ABCD* is an isosceles trapezoid. Are there two isometries that map *ABCD* onto itself? Explain.

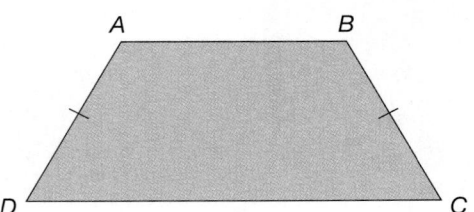

6. Euclid's proof of the Pythagorean theorem involves the following diagram. In the proof, Euclid states that $\triangle ABD \cong \triangle FBC$ and that $\triangle ACE \cong \triangle KCB$. Find two rotations that demonstrate these congruences.

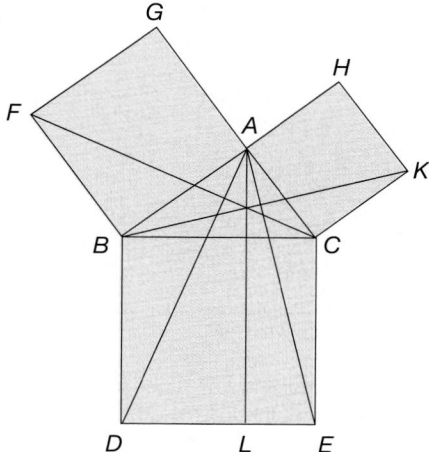

7. On the lattice shown, $ABCD$ is a parallelogram.

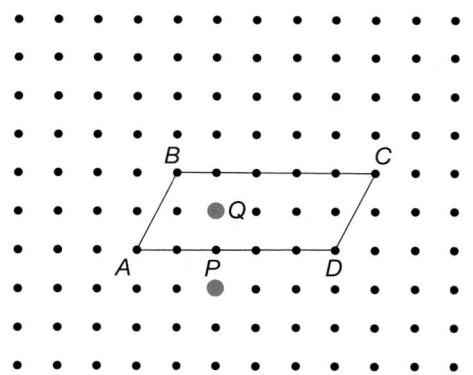

(a) Find the image of point P under the following sequence of half-turns: H_A, then H_B, then H_C, then H_D. That is, find $H_D(H_C(H_B(H_A(P))))$.

(b) Find $H_D(H_C(H_B(H_A(Q))))$.

(c) Write a conjecture based on your observations.

8. (a) Find $H_O(H_P(\triangle ABC))$ on the square lattice. Call the image $\triangle A'B'C'$. [HINT: Find $H_O(H_P(A))$, then $H_O(H_P(B))$, etc.]

(b) What type of isometry will map $\triangle ABC$ directly to $\triangle A'B'C'$? Be as precise as possible.

(c) Write a conjecture based on your observations.

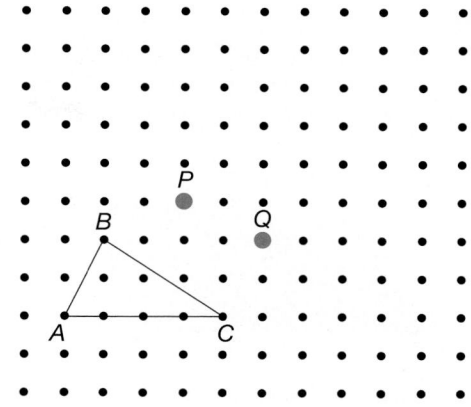

9. (a) Show how the combination of $R_{B,90°}$ followed by $S_{O,1/2}$ will map $\triangle ABC$ onto $\triangle A'B'C'$.

(b) Is $\triangle ABC \sim \triangle A'B'C'$? Explain.

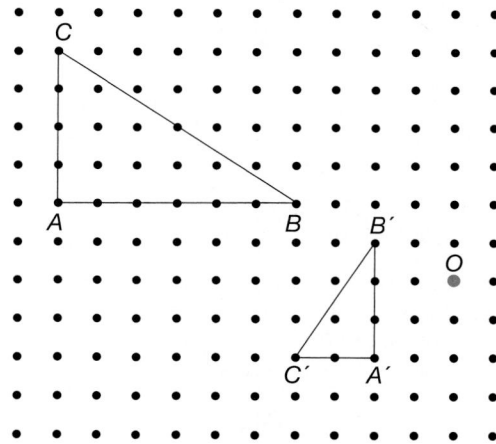

10. Find a combination of isometries that map $ABCD$ to $A'B'C'D'$, or explain why this is impossible.

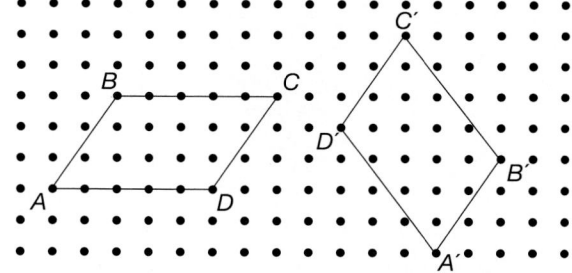

Problems

11. *ABCD* is a parallelogram. Show that the diagonal $\overline{AC}$ divides *ABCD* into two congruent triangles using the transformation definition of congruence. (Hint: Use a half-turn.)

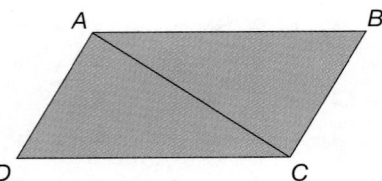

12. Use the results of Problem 11 to show that the following statements are true.
   (a) Opposite angles of a parallelogram are congruent.
   (b) Opposite sides of a parallelogram are congruent.

13. Suppose that point *B* is equidistant from points *A* and *C*. Show that *B* is on the perpendicular bisector of $\overline{AC}$. (Hint: Let *P* be a point on $\overline{AC}$ so that $\overline{BP}$ is the bisector of $\angle ABC$. Then use M_{BP}.)

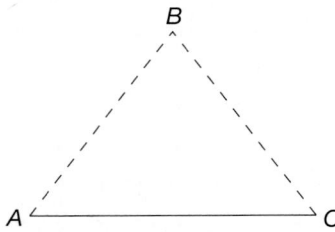

14. Let *ABCD* be a kite with $AB = AD$ and $BC = DC$. Explain how Problem 13 shows that the following statements are true.

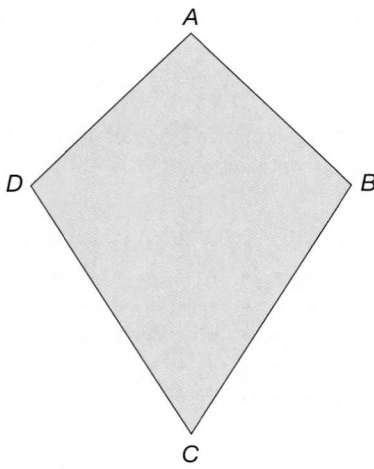

   (a) The diagonals of a kite are perpendicular.
   (b) A kite has reflection symmetry.

15. Suppose that $\triangle ABC$ is isosceles. Let *P* be the point on $\overline{BC}$ so that $\overrightarrow{AP}$ is the bisector of $\angle BAC$. Use M_{AP} to show that $\angle ABC \cong \angle ACB$.

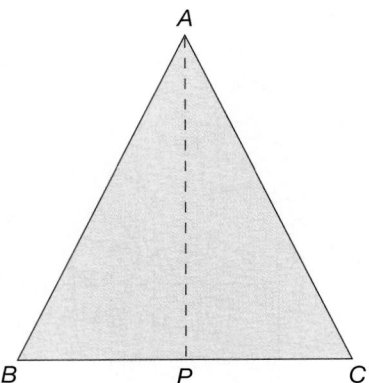

16. (a) Suppose that *r* and *s* are lines such that $r \parallel s$. Show that the combination of M_r followed by M_s is equivalent to a translation. [Hint: Let *A* be any point that is *x* units from *r*. Let $A' = M_r(A)$ be *y* units from *s*. Consider the distance from *A* to A'.]
   (b) How are the distance and direction of the translation related to lines *r* and *s*?

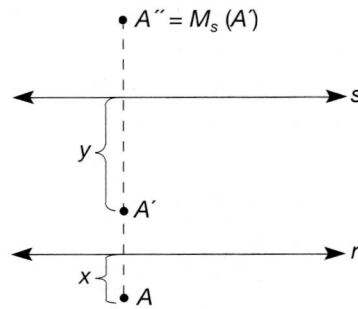

17. On the billiard table, ball *A* is to carom off two of the rails (sides) and strike ball *B*.

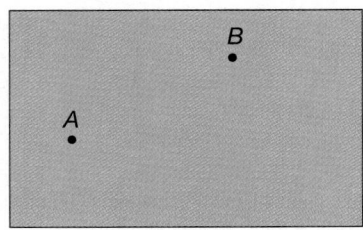

   (a) Draw the path for a successful shot.
   (b) Using a reflection and congruent triangles, give an argument justifying your drawing in part (a).

18. *ABCD* is a square with side length *a*, while *EFGH* is a square with side length *b*. Describe a similarity transformation that will map *ABCD* to *EFGH*.

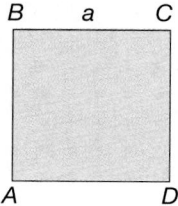
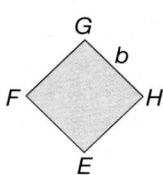

19. Points *A*, *B*, *C*, and *D* are midpoints of the edges of the cube. A plane through *A*, *B*, *C*, and *D* intersects the vertical edges at points *X* and *Y*. Show that the six points are the vertices of a regular hexagon.

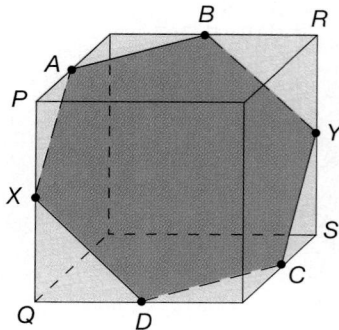

EXERCISE/PROBLEM SET 16.3—PART B

Exercises

1. Triangle *ABC* is equilateral. Point *G* is the circumcenter (also the incenter). Which of the following transformations will map △*ABC* onto itself?

(a) $R_{G,120°}$ (b) $R_{G,60°}$
(c) M_{AF} (d) $S_{C,1}$

2. For equilateral triangle *ABC* in Exercise 1, list three different rotations and three different reflections that map △*ABC* onto itself.

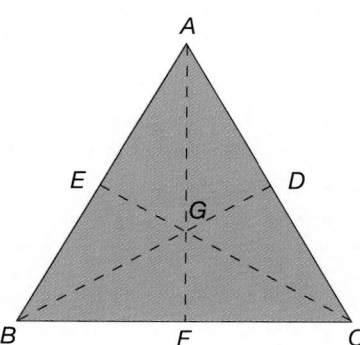

3. *ABCD* is a square. Point *P* is the intersection of the diagonals. Which of the following transformations map the square onto itself?
(a) $R_{P,90°}$ (b) H_P
(c) M_{AC} (d) M_{BD}

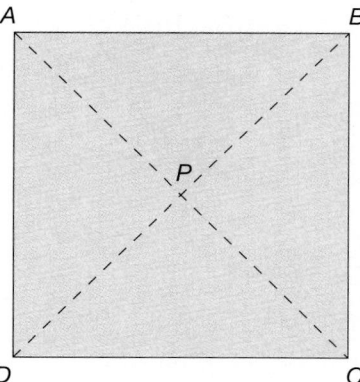

4. *ABCDE* is a regular pentagon with center *O*. Points *F*, *G*, *H*, *I*, *J* are the midpoints of the sides. List all the reflections and all the rotations that map the pentagon onto itself.

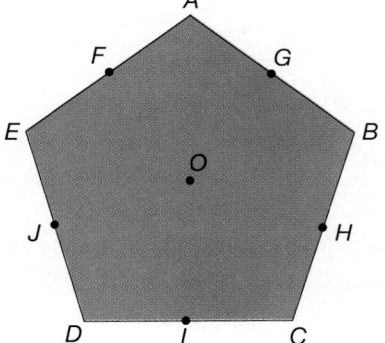

5. *ABCD* is a parallelogram. List all the isometries that map *ABCD* onto itself.

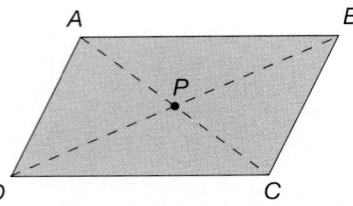

6. *ABCD* is a kite. List all the isometries that map *ABCD* onto itself.

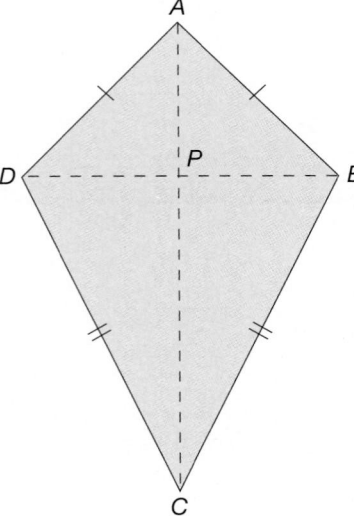

7. *ABCD* is a rhombus.

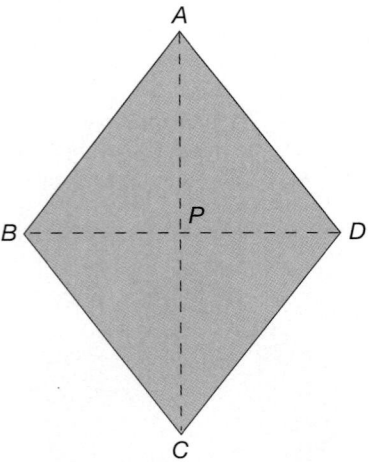

(a) List all the isometries that map *ABCD* onto itself.
(b) How is your solution related to Exercises 5 and 6?

8. (a) Using the triangle *ABC*, find the image of point *P* under the following sequence of half-turns:
$H_C(H_B(H_A(H_C(H_B(H_A(P))))))$.
(b) Apply the same sequence to point *Q*.
(c) Write a conjecture based on your observations.

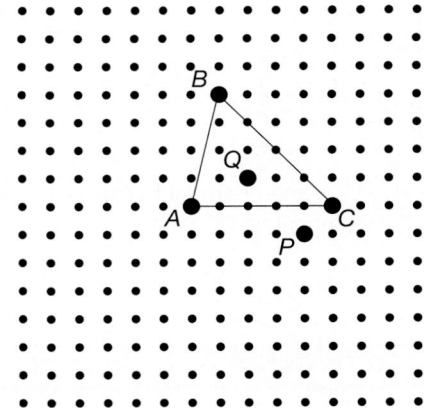

9. Show how the combination of M_r, followed by $S_{O,1/2}$ will map $\triangle ABC$ onto $\triangle A'B'C'$.

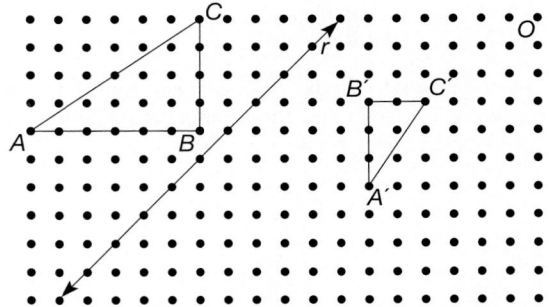

10. Find a combination of isometries that will map $\triangle ABC$ to $\triangle A'B'C'$, or explain why this is impossible.

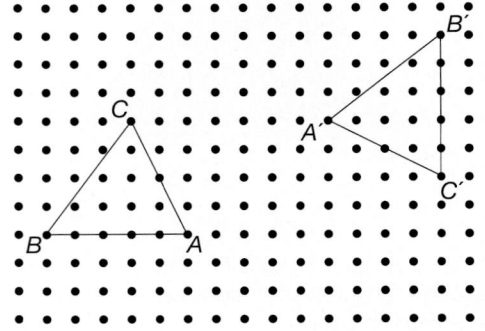

Problems

11. Points P, Q, and R are the midpoints of the sides of $\triangle ABC$.

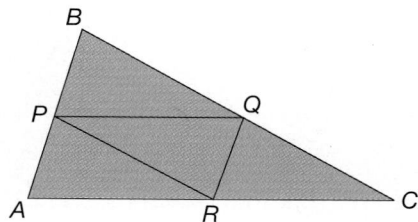

(a) Show $S_{A,2}(\triangle APR) = \triangle ABC$, $S_{B,2}(\triangle PBQ) = \triangle ABC$, and $S_{C,2}(\triangle QCR) = \triangle BCA$.

(b) How does part (a) show that $PBQR$ is a parallelogram?

12. Suppose that $ABCD$ is a parallelogram. Show that the diagonals $\overline{AC}$ and $\overline{BD}$ bisect each other. [HINT: Let P be the midpoint of $\overline{AC}$ and show that $H_P(B) = D$.]

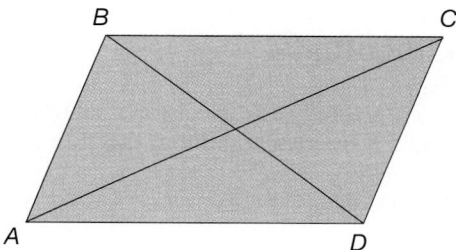

13. Suppose that $ABCD$ is a parallelogram and P is the intersection of the diagonals.

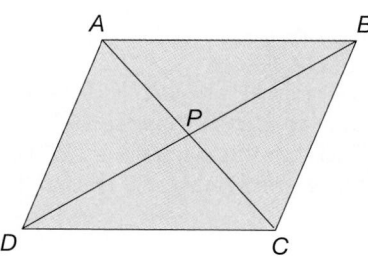

(a) Show that $H_P(A) = C$ and $H_P(B) = D$.

(b) How does part (a) show that a parallelogram has rotation symmetry?

14. Suppose that point B is on the perpendicular bisector l of $\overline{AC}$. Use M_l to show that $AB = BC$ (i.e., that B is equidistant from A and C).

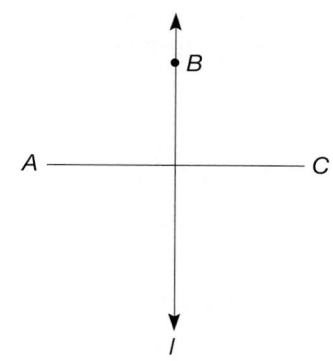

15. Suppose that lines r and s intersect at point P.

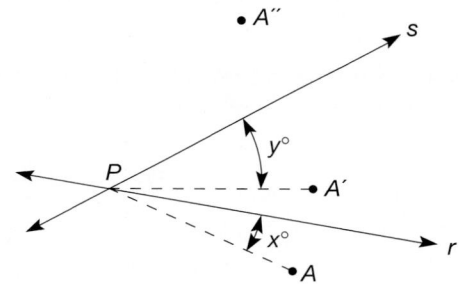

(a) Show that M_r followed by M_s is equivalent to a rotation.

(b) How are the center and angle of the rotation related to lines r and s?

[HINT: Let $A' = M_r(A)$ and suppose that the angle formed by $\overrightarrow{PA}$ and r measures x. Let $A'' = M_s(A')$ and suppose that the angle formed by $\overrightarrow{PA'}$ and s measures y.]

16. On the billiard table, ball A is to carom off three rails, then strike ball B.

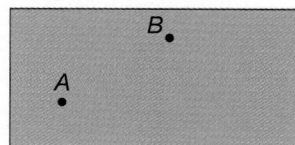

(a) Draw the path for a successful shot.

(b) Using three reflections, give an argument justifying your drawing in part (a).

17. Suppose that *ABCD* is a rhombus. Use reflections M_{AC} and M_{BD} to show that *ABCD* is a parallelogram.

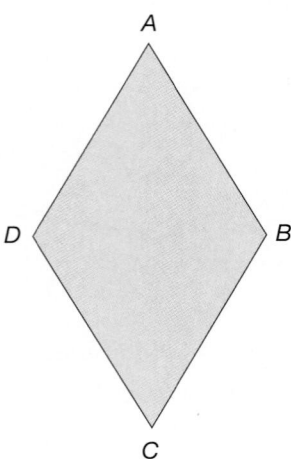

18. A **Reuleaux triangle** is a curved three-sided shape (see the figure). Each curved side is a part of a circle whose radius is the length of the side of the equilateral triangle. Find the area of a Reuleaux triangle if the length of the side of the triangle is 1.

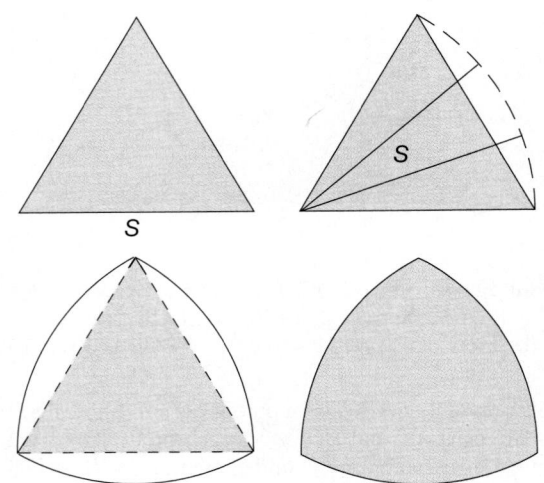

SOLUTION OF INITIAL PROBLEM

Houses *A* and *B* are to be connected to a television cable line *l*, at a transformer point *P*. Where should *P* be located so that the sum $AP + PB$ is as small as possible?

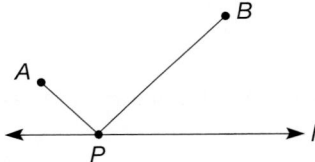

Strategy: Use Symmetry

Reflect point *B* across line *l* to point *B'*. Then $\triangle BPB'$ is isosceles, and line *l* is a line of reflection symmetry for $\triangle BPB'$. Hence $BP = B'P$, so the problem is equivalent to locating *P* so that the sum $AP + PB'$ is as small as possible. By the triangle inequality, we must have *A*, *P*, and *B'* collinear.

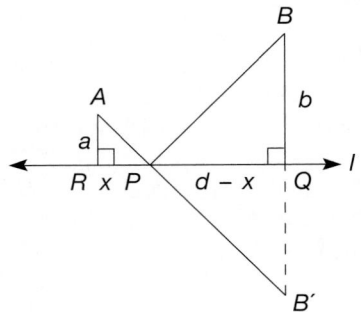

Let point Q be the intersection of $\overline{BB'}$ and l. Let R be the point on l such that $AR \perp l$. Since points A, P, and B' are collinear and $\triangle BPB'$ is isosceles, we have $\angle APR \cong \angle B'PQ \cong \angle BPQ$. But then, $\triangle APR \sim \triangle BPQ$ by the AA similarity property. Thus corresponding sides are proportional in these triangles. Let $RP = x$ and $RQ = d$, so that $PQ = d - x$. Then, by similar triangles,

$$\frac{x}{d-x} = \frac{a}{b}$$

so that

$$bx = ad - ax$$
$$ax + bx = ad$$
$$x(a + b) = ad$$
$$x = \frac{ad}{a+b}.$$

Hence locate point P along $\overline{RQ}$ so that $RP = \dfrac{ad}{a+b}$.

Additional Problems Where the Strategy "Use Symmetry" Is Useful

1. A 4×4 quilt of squares shown has reflective symmetry.

Explain how to find all such quilts having reflective symmetry that are made up of 12 light squares and 4 dark squares.

2. Find all three-digit numbers that can serve as house numbers when the numbers are installed upside-down or right-side up. Assume that the 1 and 8 are read the same both ways.

3. The 4th number in the 41st row of Pascal's triangle is 101,270. What is the 38th number of the 41st row?

WRITING/DISCUSSING FOR UNDERSTANDING

1. Describe how you determine the type of isometry that maps one of two congruent triangles onto the other.

2. Discuss the various outcomes when two isometries are performed, one followed by the other. For example, what are the possibilities when a reflection is followed by a reflection?

3. Taking a photograph is an application of a size transformation. Describe several other instances in society where size transformations are used.

PROJECTS

1. Review the subsection on Escher tessellations and prepare three or more of your designs based on his techniques.
2. Make a scrapbook of shapes having one or more of the symmetries discussed in this chapter.
3. Designs based on symmetries and patterns based on isometries and similitudes are found in many cultures. By finding pictures of pottery, weavings, and so on, of another culture, illustrate how they have used the geometry in this chapter.

CHAPTER REVIEW

Major Ideas

1. Transformations of the plane include the following types: translations, rotations, reflections, glide reflections, size transformations, and combinations thereof.
2. Isometries can be used to describe symmetry in the plane.
3. There are only four types of isometries in the plane.
4. Isometries describe congruence of figures.
5. Similitudes describe similarity of figures.
6. Transformations are effective in solving geometry problems.

Following is a list of key vocabulary, notation, and ideas for this chapter. Review these items by writing down the meaning of each term. Then check your answers and restudy the material that you are unsure of before proceeding to take the chapter test.

SECTION 16.1:   TRANSFORMATIONS

Vocabulary/Notation

Ideas

SECTION 16.2:   CONGRUENCE AND SIMILARITY USING TRANSFORMATIONS

Vocabulary/Notation

Ideas

SECTION 16.3:   GEOMETRIC PROBLEM SOLVING USING TRANSFORMATIONS

Vocabulary/Notation

Ideas

PEOPLE IN MATHEMATICS

Edward G. Begle (1914–1978) could be called the father of the "New Math." Influenced by the success of *Sputnik* in 1957, the U.S. government through its National Science Foundation, embarked on a systematic revision of the K–12 curriculum in the late 1950s. Although Begle was well on his way to becoming a first-rate research mathematician, he was asked to lead this effort, called the School Mathematics Study Group (SMSG), due to his unique talent for administration. He moved to Stanford, where he coordinated the SMSG for many years. In addition to this project, he initiated the National Longitudinal Study of Mathematical Abilities (NLSMA), which set a standard for subsequent such studies. Begle, whose respect for mathematics education grew as he worked with SMSG, stated that "Mathematics education is more complicated than you expected even though you expected it to be more complicated than you expected."

Jaime Escalante (1930–) began teaching at Garfield High in East Los Angeles as a seasoned mathematics teacher, having taught for 11 years in Bolivia. But he was not prepared for this rundown inner-city school, where gang violence abounded and neither parents nor students were interested in education. After the discouraging first day on the job, he vowed, "First I'm going to teach them responsibility, and I'm going to teach them respect, and then I'm going to quit." He succeeded, but stayed on to build, year after year, a team of mathematics students with the advanced calculus exam as their Olympic competition. He built their self-confidence and trained, coached, and prodded them as a coach might train athletes. Students would go to the advanced placement exam wearing their school jackets, yelling "Defense, Defense!" Today, Garfield High is, Escalante says "one of the best schools. I feel great when I see our kids going to the best colleges now." "My skills are really to motivate these kids, to make them learn, to give them 'ganas'—the desire to do something—to make them believe they can learn." The movie "Stand and Deliver" was about Mr. Escalante's successes as a teacher at Garfield.

CHAPTER 16 TEST

Knowledge

1. True or false?
  (a) A translation maps a line l to a line parallel to l.
  (b) If the direction of a turn is clockwise, the measure of the directed angle associated with the turn is positive.
  (c) A reflection reverses orientation.
  (d) A regular tessellation of square tiles has translation, rotation, reflection, and glide reflection symmetry.
  (e) An isometry preserves distance and angle measure.
  (f) An isometry preserves orientation.
  (g) A magnification preserves angle measure and ratios of length.
  (h) A similarity transformation is a magnification followed by an isometry.

Skill

2. Find the following points on the square lattice.
  (a) $T_{AB}(P)$
  (b) $R_{C,90°}(P)$
  (c) $M_{OC}(P)$
  (d) $T_{PB}(M_{OC}(P))$

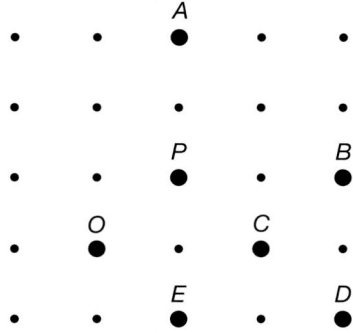

3. Determine which of the following types of symmetry apply to the tessellation shown here: translation, rotation, reflection, glide reflection (assume that the tessellation fills the plane).

4. Describe the following isometries as they relate to the triangles shown.

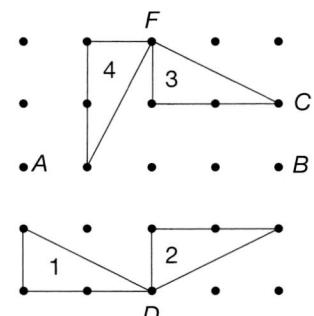

(a) The reflection that maps 3 to 2
(b) The rotation that maps 3 to 4
(c) The translation that maps 3 to 1

Understanding

5. Explain how to prove that the square $ABCD$ is similar to the square $EFGH$.

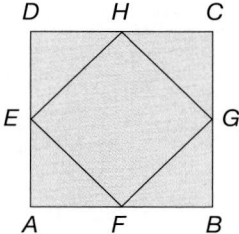

6. Explain why performing two glide reflections, one after the other, yields either a translation or a rotation.

7. Given that l, m, and n are perpendicular bisectors of sides $\overline{AB}$, $\overline{BC}$, and $\overline{AC}$, respectively, find the image of B after applying successively M_l followed by M_n followed by M_m.

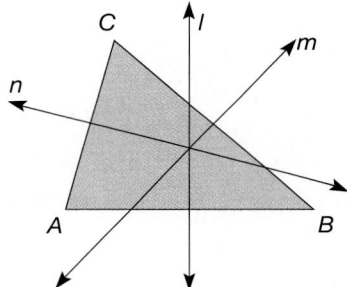

Problem Solving/Application

8. Find AB, AC, and CE for the figure shown.

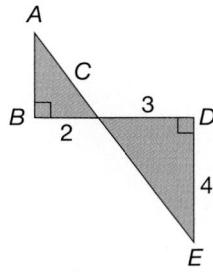

9. Given isosceles $\triangle ABC$, where M is the midpoint of AB, prove that $\overleftrightarrow{CM}$ is a symmetry line for $\triangle ABC$.

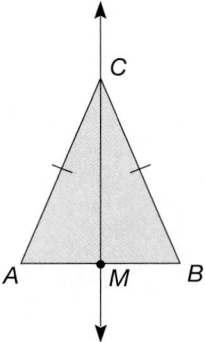

Technology Section

PROGRAMMING IN BASIC

The National Council of Teachers of Mathematics (NCTM) recommended in its 1980 *An Agenda for Action* that "mathematics programs take full advantage of the power of calculators and computers at all grade levels." Further, it is recommended that "teacher education programs for all levels of mathematics should include computer literacy, experience with computer programming, and the study of ways to make the most effective use of computers and calculators in instruction." The main goal of this section is to familiarize you with the use of a computer and to help you learn how to program using elementary commands of the programming language BASIC.

Although our use of computers is limited in this book, computers have wide application in schools. The following list provides a discussion of the ways that you can use computers with this book.

Computer Awareness. In this section you will learn about computers, their various components, and how to use them so that you feel comfortable when given the opportunity to work with one.

Programming. There are several reasons why learning how to program in BASIC will help you learn mathematics.

1. *To promote understanding of mathematical processes and procedures.* By writing programs, you will gain additional insight and understanding of many of the algorithms and other problem-solving techniques that are useful in mathematics.
2. *To generate data from which conclusions may be drawn.* A simple program can perform many computations in a short time. Thus a program could be used to generate a list of numbers from which patterns could be observed. The patterns may, in turn, help you better understand a concept or perform calculations more rapidly.
3. *To simulate experiments.* Computer programs can be used to simulate experiments that may take hours to do by hand.
4. *To solve problems.* A computer can solve problems involving a multitude of calculations that an individual person could not solve in a lifetime. Although the problems you solve in this book are not of that scope, there will be many examples and problems to show how advantageous computers can be.

Although computers are extremely helpful, there are many times when using mental methods with mathematics will be even faster than the fastest computer. Thus, because this book is a study of elementary mathematics, we use computers in combination with mathematics to enhance your ability to solve problems. In addition to our use of computers in this book, there are other ways that you can use them in the schools.

- To demonstrate new ideas to an entire class or to individual students through a tutorial or simulation.
- To provide drill and practice through innovative gaming programs.
- To collect and/or retrieve information from information banks, commonly called data bases.
- To administer and evaluate tests.
- To do word processing, graphics generation, and so on to create materials for your classes.
- To perform administrative tasks such as record keeping.

Most of us will work with a microcomputer, sometimes called a personal or desktop computer. Microcomputers fit conveniently on a desk, whereas their predecessors, mainframe computers, filled an entire room. As miniaturization advances, we may all use lap computers—that is, computers about the size of this textbook and weighing 3 to 4 pounds.

The four basic elements of a microcomputer system are (1) the input device (usually a keyboard), (2) the computer (where the information is processed), (3) the output device (usually a monitor or "screen"), and (4) the memory (either temporary or permanent) (Figure C.1). Two common devices found with a microcomputer system are (1) a printer (output), and (2) a disk drive, a storage device that is used for both input and output (Figure C.2).

FIGURE C.1

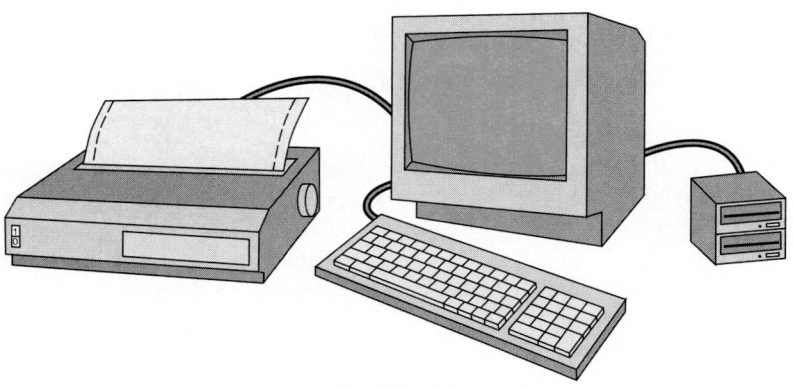

FIGURE C.2

Finally, there are a host of other input/output accessories that may be used with a computer. Among these are (1) a modem, an electronic device that allows your computer to send and receive information over a telephone line; (2) a graphics pad, an electronic "tablet" that you can write on and have the image appear on the monitor; (3) a "mouse," a little device that is hand-guided on the top of a desk to operate the computer instead of using certain parts of the keyboard; and (4) a joystick, game paddle, or other input device commonly used to play games. Virtually all computers can be purchased with "floppy" disk drives for storage. Computers also come with a hard disk drive, which is more expensive but much faster than floppy disk drives.

Elementary Commands

BASIC is one of the simplest computer languages. The word "BASIC" is an acronym for "Beginner's All-Purpose Symbolic Instruction Code." This language, written in 1964 at Dartmouth College by John Kemeny and Thomas Kurtz, allows us humans to give instructions to a computer. There are actually many versions of BASIC. In this book we use Applesoft BASIC, which is used with Apple computers.*

We begin our study of BASIC by first using it as a supercalculator. In BASIC a computer does operations using "algebraic logic." In other words, all operations are done working outward from the innermost parentheses, where exponentiation is done first, followed by multiplication and division, left to right, then addition and subtraction, left to right. If there is *ever* any doubt which operations should take precedence, insert parentheses for clarity and start with the innermost parentheses. The common mathematical symbols for operations and their computer counterparts are listed next.

Operation	Math Symbol	Computer Symbol	Mathematical Representation	Computer Representation
Addition	$+$	$+$	$a + b$	$a + b$
Subtraction	$-$	$-$	$a - b$	$a - b$
Multiplication	$\times$	$*$	$a \times b$	$a * b$
Division	$\div$	$/$	$a \div b$	a/b
Exponentiation		$\wedge$ or $\uparrow$	a^b	$a \wedge b$ or $a \uparrow b$

To perform calculations on a computer using BASIC, you need only type in the word **PRINT** followed by the calculation you wish to perform, followed by a press of the **RETURN** key (which we will denote by [R]).

EXAMPLE C.1   Calculate the following values using a computer. Also, check your answer mentally, by using a calculator, or both.
(a) $(5 + 2)17$ **(b)** $6^3 \div 8$
(c) $(7(13 - 4))^2$ **(d)** $(111^4 - 111^3) \div 55$

Solution
(a) PRINT (5 + 2) * 17 [R]   *Answer:* 119
(b) PRINT (6 $\wedge$ 3) / 8 [R]   *Answer:* 27
(c) PRINT (7 * (13 − 4)) $\wedge$ 2 [R]   *Answer:* 3969
(d) PRINT (111 $\wedge$ 4 − 111 $\wedge$ 3) / 55 [R]   *Answer:* 2,735,262   ■

In addition to performing mathematical operations, useful mathematical functions are available in most computer languages. Because we will use them later, we consider next three such functions.

---

*Apple is a registered trademark of Apple Computer, Inc.

SQR   The SQR function calculates the square root of a nonnegative number. (The square root of a number n is the nonnegative number r such that $r^2 = n$.) For example, PRINT SQR(4)[R] will yield 2, PRINT SQR(7)[R] will display 2.64575131 (the number of digits after the decimal point may vary depending on the version of BASIC), and so on. Square roots are discussed in detail in Chapter 9.

INT   The INT function assigns to any number, n, the greatest whole number less than or equal to n. For example, PRINT INT(3.172)[R] yields 3, PRINT INT(73.1)[R] yields 73, and so on. The INT function also works on negative numbers; negative numbers are studied beginning in Chapter 8.

RND   RND is a random number generator (technically, a pseudo-random-number generator, but this distinction is not important to us). The statement PRINT RND(1)[R] will yield an arbitrary number between 0 and 1. In general, a random number generator is a device that is used to produce a collection of numbers in a completely arbitrary (random) fashion. In addition to generating random numbers using a computer, lists of random numbers are found in various books. Random numbers may also be generated simply by writing numbers on slips of paper, depositing them in a box, shaking the box, and pulling out as many numbers as needed.

These three functions can be used alone or in combination with all operations.

EXAMPLE C.2 Calculate the following using a computer. Check the computer's output mentally or by using your calculator.
(a) `INT(SQR(17))`   **(b)** `SQR(11 + INT(3.27))`
(c) `7/2 - INT(7/2)`   **(d)** `INT(31 * SQR(43))`

Solution
(a) `PRINT INT(SQR(17))[R]`   *Answer:* 4
(b) `PRINT SQR(11 + INT(3.27))[R]`   *Answer:* 3.74165738
(c) `PRINT 7/2 - INT(7/2)[R]`   *Answer:* 0.5
(d) `PRINT INT(31 * SQR(43))[R]`   *Answer:* 203

When dealing with very large numbers, the numerals, both those you input and those that are displayed on the screen, may be expressed in scientific notation. Simply stated, a number is written in scientific notation if it is expressed as the product of a number between 1 and 10, and a power of 10. For example, the scientific notation for 35 is 3.5×10, for 10493 is 1.0493×10^4, and so on. In most computer languages, sufficiently large numbers are automatically expressed in scientific notation. If a 10-digit number is the most your computer will display, the 12-digit number 123456789012 will be expressed as $1.23456789E+11$, where $E+11$ represents 10^{11}.

The remainder of this section will be devoted to programming in BASIC. You will learn the elementary programming, system, and disk operating system commands needed to write and execute simple BASIC programs. Succinctly, **programming commands** allow you to write programs for the computer, **system commands** are instructions that are used to operate the computer itself, and **disk operating system (DOS) commands** are used to operate the disk drive storage device that accompanies most personal computers. A **program** is a sequence of instructions to be executed by a computer to solve a given problem. The following set of instructions is an example of a BASIC program and its output when it is executed. The program prints the squares of the whole numbers from 1 to 9.

EXAMPLE C.3

Program
```
10      REM FIRST PROGRAM
20      PRINT "FIRST PROGRAM"
30      FOR I = 1 TO 9          Program
40      PRINT I*I              Commands
50      NEXT I
60      END
RUN                 A System Command
FIRST PROGRAM
1
4
9
16                  Output—The result of
25                  running the program
36
49
64
81
```

Each of the numbered lines in Example C.3 displays an example of a BASIC programming command that will be introduced in this section. **RUN** is a system command that directs the computer to follow the instructions in the BASIC program. The computer does this by performing the instruction for each numbered line in increasing order of the line numbers, starting with the smallest line number first. Usually, line numbers in BASIC are selected in increments of 10 to allow for later insertions.

The next example is a program that finds the whole-number portion of the quotient of $576 \div 13$. (Note: The symbol [R] is *not* part of the program; it is displayed here and in the next few examples to remind you to press the RETURN key to enter the information.)

EXAMPLE C.4
```
10      PRINT INT(576/13) [R]
20      END [R]
RUN     [R]
44
```

If you also wanted to find the whole-number remainder of this division problem, you could insert the following line in your program.

```
15  PRINT (576 — 13 * INT(576/13)) [R]
```

The system command **LIST** will give a complete listing of the program, including all line numbers in numerical order.

EXAMPLE C.5
```
LIST [R]
10      PRINT INT(576/13)
15      PRINT (576 — 13 * INT(576/13))
20      END
```

Notice how line 15 is automatically inserted in the correct numerical order. Type RUN [R] to obtain the whole-number quotient and remainder. Your output should be

```
44
4
```

If you want to delete a line, type that line number and press [R]. To delete line 15, type

```
15   [R]
```

The listing of the program would now be the original program in Example C.4.

```
LIST [R]
10      PRINT INT(576/13)
20      END
```

Retyping a line is one way of making corrections in a program. However, as you learn more about your computer, you will learn more efficient editing techniques.

Up to now, we have been writing our programs in the computer's memory. This memory is not permanent. When the computer is turned off, the current program will be lost unless it is stored on a permanent storage device, such as a (floppy) disk. At the end of this section, you will learn commands to store programs permanently on a disk. For now we will write practice programs in the computer's memory. The computer's memory can be erased by typing the system command **NEW**. You should type NEW whenever you begin a new program.

EXAMPLE C.6
```
NEW     [R]
10      PRINT "PROGRAMMING IS FUN." [R]
20      END [R]
RUN     [R]
PROGRAMMING IS FUN.
```

Thus far we have introduced three system commands: RUN, LIST, and NEW. These are called system commands because they pertain to the operation of the computer system. Now we will study programming commands, that is, commands that are used to write programs in BASIC. We will discontinue writing [R] to represent RETURN, but remember that you must press the return key whenever you want to enter something into the computer. The programming commands that we cover in the rest of this section are PRINT, END, LET, and INPUT. Other BASIC commands—GOTO, IF-THEN, and FOR-NEXT—will be introduced in the next section.

The PRINT command was used earlier to obtain the results of calculations. The **PRINT** command in line 10 of Example C.6 is used to tell the computer to print the message within quotes, often called a **string** (either alphabetic or numeric characters or a combination of them). The PRINT statement can also be used for both printing messages within quotes and for printing the value of an expression.

EXAMPLE C.7

```
NEW
10       PRINT "THE AVERAGE OF 16 AND 6 IS ";
         (16 + 6)/2; "."
20       END
RUN
THE AVERAGE OF 16 AND 6 IS 11.
```

In Example C.7, line 10 prints the message within the quotes followed by the value of the expression. The semicolon separates the two outputs. You will discover in the exercises that semicolons and commas used in PRINT statements can be used to change the arrangement of the program's output on the screen.

Now insert the following for line 5.

```
5   REM AVERAGE PROGRAM
```

REM means remark. A REM statement describes and often clarifies what is happening in a program or any portion of a program. REM statements are ignored by the computer, but they make it easier for us to read and understand programs. Now LIST the current program.

```
LIST
5        REM AVERAGE PROGRAM
10       PRINT "THE AVERAGE OF 16 AND 6 IS ";
         (16 + 6)/2; "."
20       END
```

The command **END** should be put at the end of every program (even though it is not always necessary).

The command **LET** is used to assign a value to a variable. The statement "LET X = 6" assigns the value on the right-hand side of the equal sign to the variable name on the left-hand side. In BASIC there are usually two types of variables: numeric (numbers) and string (letters and/or numerals). We will start by working with **numeric variables**, that is, variables that accept number values.

EXAMPLE C.8

```
NEW
10       REM LET DEMO
20       LET X = 14
30       LET Y = 3
40       PRINT X ∧ Y
50       END
RUN
2744
```

When the program in Example C.8 is RUN, X is assigned the value 14 and Y the value 3. Due to line 40, the value of X^Y is displayed on the screen. Actually, in Applesoft BASIC you can omit the word LET if you wish. For example, if you change line 30 in Example C.8 to 30 Y = 3 and then type RUN, you should get the same output, namely 2744.

The following example illustrates the use of a **string variable**, a variable that represents a string of letters and/or numerals, called **alphanumeric variables**. (String variables are not used for numerical computations.) A string variable is distinguished by the $ to the right of it. The beginning and the end of the string are designated by enclosing the string in quotation marks.

EXAMPLE C.9

```
NEW
10      REM STRING VARIABLE DEMO
20      LET N$ = "KATHY"
30      PRINT N$
40      END
RUN
KATHY
```

In BASIC, variables can be named in several ways, as listed next.

1. A single letter (e.g., A, B, C, . . . , Z) for numeric or a single letter followed by a dollar sign (e.g., A$, B$, C$, . . . , Z$) for alphanumeric.
2. A single letter followed by a digit (e.g., A1, A2, M9, Z1) for numeric or A1$, . . . , A9$ for alphanumeric.

NOTE: The first character of any variable *must* be a letter, and *string variables must end in a $.*

Most versions of BASIC use two letters, such as PQ or RR, for variables. Also, some microcomputers use both uppercase and lowercase letters, and capital letters may be required for variables.

The programs we have written thus far have not allowed the user to insert values for the variables as the program is executed. The **INPUT** command is used for this purpose.

EXAMPLE C.10

```
NEW
10      REM INPUT DEMO
20      INPUT A, B
30      LET C = (A + B)/2
40      PRINT "THE AVERAGE OF";A;" AND ";B;" IS ";
        C; "."
50      END
RUN
?2, 4
THE AVERAGE OF 2 AND 4 IS 3.
RUN
?12
??10
THE AVERAGE OF 12 AND 10 IS 11.
```

When the program in Example C.10 is run, line 10 causes the computer to print a question mark, ?, which is a request for input. The computer then waits for the user to type the input followed by [R]. The user must type in a quantity or quantities of the desired variable type. If several quantities are called for, they can be entered on a single line separated by commas or on successive lines (e.g., 12, 10 [R] or 12 [R] 10 [R]). An error message will result if alphabetic characters are input for numeric variables. To avoid a possible ambiguity, it is helpful if the input command is preceded by a PRINT statement that requests the appropriate input. The insertion of the following lines helps to specify the type of input required.

```
12        PRINT "THIS PROGRAM FINDS THE AVERAGE OF
          TWO NUMBERS."
15        PRINT "ENTER TWO NUMBERS SEPARATED BY A
          COMMA."
```

Now LIST.

```
LIST
10        REM INPUT DEMO
12        PRINT "THIS PROGRAM FINDS THE AVERAGE OF
          TWO NUMBERS."
15        PRINT "ENTER TWO NUMBERS SEPARATED BY A
          COMMA."
20        INPUT A,B
30        LET C = (A + B)/2
40        PRINT "THE AVERAGE OF ";A; "AND"; B; "IS";C;
          "."
50        END
RUN
THIS PROGRAM FINDS THE AVERAGE OF TWO NUMBERS.
ENTER TWO NUMBERS SEPARATED BY A COMMA.
?2,13
THE AVERAGE OF 2 AND 13 IS 7.5.
```

We can also input string variables, as the next example illustrates.

EXAMPLE C.11

```
NEW
10        REM INPUT STRINGS
20        PRINT "ENTER YOUR NAME."
30        INPUT N$
40        PRINT "HELLO ";N$
50        END
RUN
ENTER YOUR NAME.
KATHY
HELLO KATHY
```

Branching and Looping Commands

If we want the computer to do something depending on a particular condition, we need the IF-THEN command. The program statement "100 IF X = 5 THEN GOTO 20" means if the value of the variable X is 5, then go to line 20 and proceed; otherwise, go to the next line. The use of IF-THEN is called **conditional branching** since the decision to branch to the next line in the program is determined by the IF condition. The result of executing an **IF-THEN** statement is determined as follows: If the IF condition is true, do the action written after the word THEN. If the IF condition is false, ignore the action written after the word THEN and go to the next program line.

EXAMPLE C.12

```
NEW
10      REM IF-THEN DEMO
20      PRINT "ENTER A NUMBER TO TEST TO SEE IF IT
        HAS A FACTOR OF 7."
30      INPUT A
40      IF A/7 = INT(A/7) THEN GOTO 70
50      PRINT A;" DOES NOT HAVE A FACTOR OF 7."
60      GOTO 80
70      PRINT A;" HAS A FACTOR OF 7."
80      END
```

The **GOTO** statement as shown in line 60 of Example C.12 provides **unconditional branching** to a specific line number (i.e., when using GOTO there is no conditional test as in the IF-THEN command). The program allows the input of a number at line 30. If 7 divides that number, the IF portion of line 40 is satisfied and the program branches to line 70. Otherwise, the program goes to line 50.

In Example C.12 an equality was used in the test in the IF portion in line 40. Inequalities may also be used. The various symbols that may be used are

$=$	equal to	$> =$	greater than or equal to
$>$	greater than	$< =$	less than or equal to
$<$	less than	$< >$	not equal to

Some programs using the GOTO statement may run indefinitely, as the next example illustrates.

EXAMPLE C.13

```
NEW
10      REM GOTO DEMO
20      PRINT "STOP THIS RUNAWAY MACHINE!"
30      GOTO 20
40      END
RUN
STOP THIS RUNAWAY MACHINE!
STOP THIS RUNAWAY MACHINE!
STOP THIS RUNAWAY MACHINE!
.
.
.
```

To stop this program, press "Control C" by holding down the control key *at the same time* that you press the "C" key. This action will interrupt the program.

The following program prints the cubes of the whole numbers from 1 to 10.

EXAMPLE C.14

```
NEW
10      REM INCREMENTING DEMO
20      LET X = 1
30      PRINT X ∧ 3
40      LET X = X + 1
50      IF X < = 10 THEN GOTO 30
60      END
```

When the program in Example C.14 is run, the statement "LET X = 1" starts the value of the variable X at 1. Line 30 prints the value of X^3. Line 40, "Let X = X + 1," adds 1 to the value of X and reassigns this new value to X. Since X is 2 initially at line 50, the condition of line 50 is true, so the computer branches to line 30. Line 50 tests to see if the value of X is less than or equal to 10. This computer program goes through the loop 10 times, each time increasing the value of X by 1.

Now let's insert lines in the program in Example C.14 that will generate the sum of the cubes of the whole numbers from 1 to 10 in addition to the list of the cubes.

```
15      LET S = 0
35      LET S = S + X ∧ 3
60      PRINT "THE SUM OF THE CUBES OF THE NUMBERS
        FROM 1 TO 10 IS ";S;"."
70      END
```

Line 15 sets the initial value of S, the sum, at 0. Line 35 reassigns S to the value of S plus X^3. Line 60 prints the final sum. Here is a LIST and a RUN of the program.

```
LIST
10      REM INCREMENTING DEMO
15      LET S = 0
20      LET X = 1
30      PRINT X ∧ 3
35      LET S = S + X ∧ 3
40      LET X = X + 1
50      IF X < = 10 THEN GOTO 30
60      PRINT "THE SUM OF THE CUBES OF THE NUMBERS
        FROM 1 TO 10 IS ";S;"."
70      END
RUN
1
8
27
64
125
216
343
512
729
1000
THE SUM OF THE CUBES OF THE NUMBERS FROM 1 TO
10 IS 3025.
```

The **FOR-NEXT** loop provides another way to repeat a sequence of BASIC statements. The program in Example C.14 is rewritten in Example C.15 using a FOR-NEXT loop.

EXAMPLE C.15

```
NEW
10      REM FOR-NEXT DEMO
20      LET S = 0
30      FOR X = 1 TO 10 STEP 1
40      PRINT X ∧ 3
50      LET S = S + X ∧ 3
60      NEXT X
70      PRINT "THE SUM OF THE CUBES OF THE NUMBERS
        FROM 1 TO 10 IS ";S;"."
80      END
```

When this program is run, X is assigned the value 1 in line 30. It retains this value as it passes through the body of the loop until it reaches line 60, where it is assigned the value 1 plus 1, or 2, from the STEP 1. Then it runs through the loop again. This procedure of increasing the value of X by 1 (the STEP value) and going through the loop is repeated until X exceeds 10, at which time the program proceeds to line 70. ∎

Notice that the program in Example C.15 is shorter than the one in Example C.14. In this case a combination of the IF-THEN and GOTO commands were essentially replaced by a FOR-NEXT loop.

The FOR-NEXT loop in Example C.15 increased X by 1 each time because of the statement STEP 1. However, a variable can be increased (**incremented**) by any positive number or decreased (**decremented**) by any negative number, as the following two examples illustrate. (Negative numbers are studied in Chapter 8.)

EXAMPLE C.16   Find all the sums of consecutive odd whole numbers, starting at 1 and going up to n, where $1 \leq n \leq 41$. (That is, find 1, 1 + 3, 1 + 3 + 5, and so on, up to 1 + 3 + 5 + · · · + 41.) You should see an interesting pattern.

Solution

```
NEW
10      REM THIS PROGRAM FINDS THE SUMS OF CON-
        SECUTIVE ODD NUMBERS STARTING WITH ONE.
20      LET S = 0
30      FOR N = 1 TO 41 STEP 2
40      S = S + N
50      PRINT N,S
60      NEXT N
70      END
```

In Example C.16 the initial value of N is 1 in line 30. Then, because of the "STEP 2" in line 30, the value of N increases by 2 each time. Thus the values for N are 1, 3, 5, 7, . . . , 41, or all odd numbers from 1 to 41.

The following diagram illustrates how the FOR-NEXT statement functions.

$$\text{Loop} \begin{cases} \rightarrow \text{FOR I} = \begin{bmatrix} \text{starting} \\ \text{number} \end{bmatrix} \text{TO} \begin{bmatrix} \text{finishing} \\ \text{number} \end{bmatrix} \text{STEP} \begin{bmatrix} \text{increment or} \\ \text{decrement} \end{bmatrix} \\ \text{Body of Loop} \\ \text{NEXT I} \end{cases}$$

The variable I is assigned the value of the starting number in the FOR statement. Then the body of the loop is run. In the NEXT statement, I is assigned the new value as determined by the STEP command. If the finishing number has not been reached, the loop is repeated using the next value of I. When the finishing number has been passed by, the program proceeds to the line following NEXT I.

The program in Example C.17 illustrates the use of FOR-NEXT to decrease the count from 10 down to 1.

EXAMPLE C.17

```
NEW
10      REM DECREMENT DEMO
20      FOR I=10 TO 1 STEP −1
30      PRINT I;" ";
40      NEXT I
50      PRINT
60      PRINT "BLAST OFF!"
70      END
RUN
10 9 8 7 6 5 4 3 2 1
BLAST OFF!
```

Example C.17 also contains some clever uses of the PRINT statement. The use of the statement PRINT by itself, if not followed by a comma or semicolon, causes the printout to skip one line; this use occurs in line 50. The semicolon or comma used in the PRINT statement in line 30 actually stops the line feed; that is, the computer will continue to print on the same line. Thus, in line 30, the values of the variable, I, are printed, each followed by a space and all on the same line.

Disk Operating System Commands

As mentioned earlier, you may wish to store a program permanently. To do this, you need to learn the DOS, or **Disk Operating System**, commands. A program can be saved by using the DOS command **SAVE**, followed by the program name (whatever name you choose). To save your current program, type SAVE BLASTOFF. After you press RETURN, you will notice that the disk drive will be activated. After the disk drive has stopped, you can check to make sure that your program has been stored on the disk by typing **CATALOG** [R] and checking to see if your program name (i.e., BLASTOFF) is listed.

While looking at the catalog, you may see some other programs on the disk that you would like to RUN. To do so, type

```
RUN  PROGRAM NAME [R]
```

For example, to run the program BLASTOFF, type

```
RUN  BLASTOFF [R]
```

(NOTE: You must type the program name *exactly* the way it appears in the catalog, spaces included.) Instead of running a program, you may wish to **LOAD** a program for editing purposes. In this case, type

```
LOAD  BLASTOFF [R]
```

or, in general, type

```
LOAD  PROGRAM NAME [R]
```

Finally, new diskettes must be initialized before they can be used. Turn on the computer with an operational diskette, that is, one that *is* initialized, in the disk drive. Then, after the disk drive has stopped, remove that diskette, insert a new diskette, and type INIT HELLO [R]. After the disk drive stops in about 30 seconds, the new diskette will be ready to be used.

Programming and System Commands Summary

Command	Definition	Example
Programming		
PRINT	Prints a message that is within quotes, the value of a variable or an expression, or both	50 PRINT "HELLO" 60 PRINT A,B 70 PRINT "AVERAGE" ;A
END	Usually, the final statement executed in program	60 END
REM	Allows for a description of part or all of a program to be placed within a program	10 REM CALCULATE AVERAGE
LET	Assigns a value to a variable	10 LET A\$ = "YES" 20 LET X = 6 30 LET X = 2 * 7 + 14 40 LET X = X + 5
INPUT	Allows the user to enter values of the variables as the program is RUN	10 INPUT N\$ 20 INPUT A,B,C
IF-THEN	Allows conditional branching; IF the condition is *true*, do the action written after the word THEN; otherwise, go to the next line.	90 IF X = 5 THEN GOTO 50 100 IF Y < X THEN PRINT "Y IS LESS THAN X"
GOTO	Allows unconditional branching	110 GOTO 20
FOR-NEXT	Provides a way to repeat a sequence of statements a specific number of times	10 FOR I = 1 TO 10 50 NEXT I

System

RUN	Directs the computer to execute the program	RUN RUN AVERAGE
LIST	Directs the computer to list the program	LIST
NEW	Erases the program currently in the memory of the computer	NEW

DOS

SAVE	Directs the computer to store the program on a storage device	SAVE AVERAGE
LOAD	Directs the computer to load a program from a storage device into the computer's memory	LOAD AVERAGE
CATALOG	Directs the computer to list the contents of the disk (or other storage device)	CATALOG

RUN used in conjunction with the name of a program in storage is actually a combination of the DOS command LOAD and the system command RUN.

EXERCISE/PROBLEM SET C.1

Problems 1 to 12 involve the use of elementary commands.

1. Calculate the following as a computer would.

(a) $3 + 4 * 5$

(b) $3 * 2 \wedge 3$

(c) $6 \wedge 2 / 9$

(d) $12/(3 * 2)$

(e) $2 * (7 - 1)$

(f) $5 + 2 \wedge 3 - 4$

(g) $(3 * (7 - 2)) \wedge 2$

(h) $3 * (7 - 2) \wedge 2$

(i) $27/3 * 5 - 2$

2. Without typing in the following programs, determine what the output will be.

(a)
```
10  LET A=8
20  LET B=2
30  PRINT A/B
40  END
```

(b)
```
10  LET A=6
20  LET B=2
30  PRINT "A/B = ";A-3
40  END
```

3. The BASIC statement "50 LET A = A + 1" does not mean that A is equal to A + 1. That we know is impossible. What it does mean is that A + 1 is evaluated and this value is assigned to the variable A. Without entering the following programs, determine their output.

(a)
```
10  LET A=4
20  LET A=A+1
30  PRINT A
40  END
```

(b)
```
10  LET S=0
20  LET X=6
30  LET S=S+X
40  PRINT S
50  END
```

(c)
```
10  LET M=6
20  LET X=50
30  LET M=M*X
40  PRINT M
50  END
```

(d)
```
10  LET R=5
20  LET R=R*R
30  LET R=R+R
40  PRINT R
50  END
```

4. Applesoft BASIC assigns a value of zero to all numerical variables at the beginning of program execution. This *initial* value is used until the variable is assigned another value by the program. Determine the output for each of the following programs.

(a)
```
10  LET A=B
20  LET A=A+B
30  PRINT 7*A
40  END
```

(b)
```
10  LET A=A+1
20  LET B=2*A∧3
30  PRINT A+B
40  END
```

(c)
```
10  LET A=3
20  LET B=A∧B
30  LET A=B∧A
40  PRINT A+B
50  END
```

(d)
```
10  LET A=5
20  LET B=2
30  LET A=B∧A
40  LET B=A∧B
50  PRINT A-B
60  END
```

5. (a) To clear the computer's memory, you should type _____. Do this. Enter the following program.

```
10   REM FUN DESIGN
20   PRINT "   X   "
30   PRINT "  XXX  "
40   PRINT "XXXXX"
50   PRINT "  XXX  "
60   PRINT "   X   "
70   END
```

(b) To have the computer do this program, you need to type _____. Do this.

(c) To have the computer print out the program in its memory, type _____. Do this.

(d) To delete line 40 you could type _____. Do this and run the resulting program.

6. In Applesoft BASIC, the function RND(X) behaves differently depending on the value of X:

1. If $X > 0$, RND(X) gives you a "random" number from 0 up to, but not including, 1.
2. If $X = 0$, RND(X) gives you the last random number generated by the computer.
3. If $X < 0$, RND(X) returns to the beginning of a specific sequence of random numbers.

We are primarily interested in using positive X values. And since RND(1) and RND(5) give us the same results, we will use RND(1) in general. To randomly generate 1 or 2 for an experiment (perhaps 1 = head and 2 = tail), we could use the statement

```
LET A=INT(2*RND(1))+1
```

Identify the possible outcomes of the following intermediate steps.

(a) RND(1)   **(b)** 2*RND(1)
(c) INT(2*RND(1))   **(d)** A

7. In general, if you would like to generate random numbers between a specific LOW and HIGH, inclusive, use the following statement:

```
LET N=INT(COEFF*RND(1))+LOW
```

where COEFF = HIGH − LOW + 1. Write an expression that will generate a random number between the following values.

(a) 10 and 100   **(b)** 50 and 250

8. Find a number to replace the ? to produce the given output in the following programs.

(a)
```
10   LET A=6
20   LET B=?
30   PRINT A+B
40   END
```
The output is 17.

(b)
```
10   LET A=?
20   LET B=2
30   PRINT A∧B
40   END
```
The output is 16.

(c)
```
10   LET A=?
20   LET A=A∧3
30   PRINT A∧3
40   END
```
The output is 512.

(d)
```
10   LET A=?
20   LET B=2*A
30   LET C=B∧2+2*B+1
40   PRINT C
50   END
```
The output is 49.

(e)
```
10   LET A=7
20   LET B=?
30   LET C=A∧B
40   PRINT C
50   END
```
The output is 343.

Problems 9 to 19 involve the use of branching and looping commands.

9. Write programs using FOR. . .NEXT. . .STEP statements that will output the following sequences of numbers.

(a) 1, 2, 3, . . . , 100   **(b)** 2, 4, 6, . . . , 60
(c) 1, 3, 5, . . . , 25   **(d)** 2, 5, 8, . . . , 62
(e) 100, 90, 80, . . . , 10

10. Determine the output for each of the following programs.

(a)
```
10   FOR X=1 TO 10
20   PRINT X∧2
30   NEXT X
40   END
```

(b)
```
10   FOR X=1 TO 5
20   PRINT INT(SQR(X))
30   NEXT X
40   END
```

(c)
```
10   FOR X=2 TO 10 STEP 2
20   PRINT X−1
30   NEXT X
40   END
```

(d)
```
10   FOR X=2 TO 100 STEP 2
20   IF SQR(X)=INT(SQR(X)) THEN
     PRINT X
30   NEXT X
40   END
```

(e)
```
10   FOR X=12 TO 1 STEP −1
20   IF 12/X=INT(12/X) THEN PRINT X
30   NEXT X
40   END
```

(f)
```
10   LET A=20
20   FOR X=2 TO A STEP 4
30   PRINT X*A
40   NEXT X
50   END
```

11. Describe the output of the following program.
```
10   FOR X = 1 TO 10
20   PRINT INT(10*RND(1))+1
30   NEXT X
40   END
```

12. In each of the program fragments given, indicate the computer's output for the given values of the variable.
(a) With A = 2 and B = 4,
```
100   IF (B<>2*A) THEN GOTO 120
110   PRINT "B IS TWICE A"
120   PRINT A,B
```

[NOTE: Here we enclosed the condition in parentheses so that an A would not precede THEN. The computer would misread it as AT (a reserved word) and give you an error message.]

(b) With X = 2, Y = 3, Z = 4,
```
100   IF Y−X<=Z THEN Z=Y−X
110   LET W=2*Z+1
120   PRINT W
```

(c) With A$ = "YES,"
```
100   IF A$<>"YES" THEN GOTO 10
110   PRINT "GOODBYE"
```

(NOTE: Two strings are equal if they agree character by character.)

13. In using the IF statement to make decisions you may have several different situations. It might be that if the condition is true, you want to perform a simple command and then proceed with the program. In this case it is handy to use the form

IF condition THEN command

Example: Any amount is input. If the amount is positive, a 5% tax is computed and printed out. Then the program proceeds to input the next number. (To end the program given, you would have to use CONTROL-C.)
```
10   INPUT "AMOUNT?";A
20   IF A>0 THEN PRINT
     "TAX IS ";.05*A
30   GOTO 10
40   END
```

Write a statement or statements that will accomplish the following.

(a) Three numbers X, Y, and Z have been input and the average computed and stored in A. You want to test how many of the numbers are above the average. If the first number is above the average, you want to increase the counter N, then proceed to check the other two similarly.
(b) Two numbers, A and B, will be input. If the first is larger, you want to print the message FIRST LARGER. Then you want to find and print their average.

14. Another situation may involve doing several commands if a condition is met, but take no action if it fails. In this case it is most efficient to write the condition so that it is reversed and the series of commands can follow. For example,
```
10   FOR X=1 TO 20
20   IF X/5=INT(X/5) THEN GOTO 40
30   GOTO 60
40   PRINT "5 DIVIDES ";X
50   PRINT "THE OTHER FACTOR IS ";X/5
60   NEXT X
```

would be more efficient as
```
10   FOR X=1 TO 20
20   IF X/5 < > INT(X/5) THEN GOTO 50
30   PRINT "5 DIVIDES ";X
40   PRINT "THE OTHER FACTOR IS ";X/5
50   NEXT X
```

Write a program to perform the specified task using the "efficient" format.
(a) The cost of renting a car is $100 plus 20 cents a mile for all miles driven above 100 miles. The mileage M is input. Print out the cost and the mileage driven above 100 miles (if any).
(b) The wholesale cost C of an item is input. If it is above $100, a 30% markup (0.30 times C) is to be added to the cost and printed out. If the cost is below $100, the price is not marked up. Print out the cost.

15. On many occasions, you will have instructions to follow, both if the condition is true and if it is false. In this case the condition can be written either way, with the computer branching to another line to follow instructions for the true case. Write a program to perform each task specified.
(a) A number X is input. If X is negative, print NEGATIVE; otherwise, print NONNEGATIVE.
(b) Two numbers X and Y are input. If the first is larger, print LARGER; otherwise, print NOT LARGER.
(c) A positive whole number N is input. Determine the first whole number (and print out) whose cube is greater than N.

16. Often when a program is written to handle data, we want to be able to run it with a varying number of data. One way is to set some value that would be impossible to have in the set of data and put in a test statement right after the input statement. Write such a statement for these circumstances.

    (a) If the input value A is zero, the computer is to transfer to the END statement on line 70.

    (b) If the input value P is −999, the computer is to jump to commands on line 150.

17. At the end of a program, it is convenient to allow the user to choose to repeat the program or not. Write a program fragment (beginning at line 100) that asks whether the user wishes to rerun the program. The user is to input Y for YES or N for NO. To repeat the program, it must return to line 20. Otherwise, the program is to print GOODBYE and end.

18. Determine what can replace each blank to produce the correct output in the following programs.

    (a)
```
10    FOR X=1 TO 5
20    _____
30    NEXT X
40    END
```
The output is 1, 4, 9, 16, 25.

    (b)
```
10    FOR X=3 TO 9 STEP 2
20    _____
30    NEXT X
40    END
```
The output is 14, 28, 42, 56.

    (c)
```
10    LET A=_____
20    FOR X=1 TO A
30    PRINT 4*X+1
40    NEXT X
50    END
```
The output is 5, 9, 13, 17.

    (d)
```
10    FOR X=__ TO __ STEP __
20    PRINT X∧3+7
30    NEXT X
40    END
```
The output is 132, 350, 736.

19. Determine what the following program does to any three-digit number you input.

```
10    PRINT "INPUT ANY THREE-DIGIT
      NUMBER."
20    INPUT N
30    A=INT(N/100)
40    B=N−10*INT(N/10)
50    IF A<>B THEN GOTO 70
60    PRINT N;" IS SPECIAL! WHY?"
70    PRINT "INPUT ANOTHER NUMBER OR
      CONTROL-C."
80    END
```

Following is a chapter-by-chapter collection of programs and problems. The prefix "B" refers to BASIC programs.

Chapter 1 (Introduction to Problem Solving)

Computer Program B1.1

```
10    REM THIS PROGRAM WILL DISPLAY
      THE FIRST N FIBONACCI NUMBERS.
20    HOME
30    PRINT "THIS PROGRAM WILL DISPLAY
      THE FIRST N FIBONACCI NUMBERS."
40    PRINT
50    INPUT "HOW MANY NUMBERS DO YOU
      WANT?";N
60    A = 1
70    PRINT A
80    B = 1
90    PRINT B
100   FOR X = 2 TO N
110   A = A + B
120   B = A − B
130   PRINT A
140   NEXT X
150   END
```

B1.1. Modify Computer Program B1.1 to find the quotients of successive pairs of numbers in the Fibonacci sequence, dividing one term by the following term.

B1.2. Write a program that will list the first 10 products resulting from the following pattern.

$$3 \times 3367 =$$
$$6 \times 3367 =$$
$$9 \times 3367 =$$

B1.3. Write a program that will count from 1 to 50 and list, as an ordered pair, the number and the cumulative sum up to each number.

B1.4. Modify your program in Problem B1.3 to list sums of every consecutive pair of the cumulative sums beginning with the first pair. What do you notice?

B1.5. Write a program that will display the first n even numbers and the first n odd numbers.

B1.6. Write a program that will find the sums of n consecutive odd numbers: 1 (one), 1 + 3 (two), 1 + 3 + 5 (three), and so on, for any n.

B1.7. **(a)** Write a program that will display the first 20 terms of an arithmetic sequence for any inputs a and d.

    (b) Write a program that will display the first 20 terms of a geometric sequence for any inputs a and r.

B1.8. **(a)** Write a program that will display the first 10 terms of an arithmetic sequence when an arbitrary term, the position of the term, and the difference are input.

(b) Write a program that will display the first 10 terms of a geometric sequence when an arbitrary term, the position of the term, and the ratio are input.

Chapter 2 (Sets, Whole Numbers, and Numeration)

Computer Program B2.1

```
10    REM THIS PROGRAM CONVERTS A
      NUMERAL IN BINARY FORM TO ITS
      DECIMAL EQUIVALENT.
20    HOME
30    PRINT "INPUT A BINARY NUMERAL WITH
      NO MORE THAN 20 DIGITS.": INPUT
      N:N1 = N
40    FOR X = 19 TO 0 STEP -1
50    P = 10∧X
60    M = INT ((N/P) + .01)
70    IF M = 1 THEN E = 2∧X: A = A +
      E:N = N - P
80    NEXT X
90    PRINT "THE DECIMAL FORM OF YOUR
      NUMBER IS ";A;"."
100   END
```

Computer Program B2.2

```
10    REM THIS PROGRAM CONVERTS A
      NUMBER LESS THAN 127 WRITTEN IN
      DECIMAL FORM TO ITS BINARY
      EQUIVALENT.
20    HOME
30    PRINT "INPUT A DECIMAL NUMBER LESS
      THAN 127.":INPUT N
40    FOR X = 0 TO 7
50    Y = N - 2*INT(N/2)
60    B = Y*10∧X + B
70    N = INT(N/2)
80    NEXT X
90    PRINT "YOUR DECIMAL NUMBER
      WRITTEN IN BASE 2 IS ";B;"."
100   END
```

B2.1. Modify Computer Program B2.2 to convert from base 10 to base 3.

B2.2. Modify Computer Program B2.2 to convert from base 10 to any base less than 10.

B2.3. Modify Computer Program B2.1 to convert from base 2 to base m where $10 > m$.

B2.4. Write a program that identifies the tens digit of any whole number which is input.

B2.5. Modify your program in Problem B2.4 to identify any specified digit of any whole number which is input.

Chapter 3 (Whole Numbers: Operations and Properties)

B3.1. Write a program that calculates the sum, difference, and product of any two whole numbers.

B3.2. Write a program that finds the quotient and remainder in a whole-number division problem.

Chapter 4 (Whole-Number Computation: Mental, Electronic, and Written)

B4.1. Write a program that randomly generates two three-digit numbers, asks you to estimate the sum, and then gives you the difference between your estimate and the exact sum.

B4.2. Modify your program in Problem B4.1 so that you can input any pair of numbers, estimate their product, and have the program give you the difference between your estimate and the exact product.

B4.3. Write a program that can help you find which numbers can be written as the difference of two consecutive squares. (HINT: Formulate a conjecture for $a^2 - b^2$ where $a > b$, for $a = 1$ to 20.)

Chapter 5 (Number Theory)

Computer Program B5.1

```
10    REM THIS PROGRAM FINDS THE PRIME
      FACTORIZATION OF ANY NUMBER
      GREATER THAN 1.
20    HOME
30    PRINT "ENTER ANY NUMBER GREATER
      THAN 1 TO FIND ITS PRIME
      FACTORIZATION."
40    INPUT N
50    PRINT N;"=";
60    LET X = 2
70    IF N/X < > INT (N/X) THEN X = 1:
      GOTO 130
80    PRINT X;
90    LET N = N/X
100   IF N = 1 THEN GOTO 200
110   PRINT "*";
120   GOTO 70
130   LET X = X + 2
140   IF N/X < > INT (N/X) THEN GOTO 130
150   PRINT X;
160   LET N = N/X
170   IF N = 1 THEN GOTO 200
180   PRINT "*";
190   GOTO 140
200   END
```

Computer Program B5.2

```
10    REM THIS PROGRAM FINDS THE GCF OF
      TWO COUNTING NUMBERS.
20    HOME
30    PRINT "THIS PROGRAM FINDS THE GCF
      OF ANY TWO COUNTING NUMBERS UP TO
      SEVEN DIGITS IN LENGTH."
40    PRINT "ENTER THE FIRST
      NUMBER.": INPUT M
50    PRINT "ENTER THE SECOND
      NUMBER.": INPUT N
60    R = M — INT (M/N)*N
70    IF R > .9 THEN M = N:N = R:GOTO
      60
80    PRINT
90    PRINT "THE GCF IS ";N; "."
100   END
```

B5.1. Modify Computer Program B5.2 to find both the GCF and the LCM of two numbers.

B5.2. Use your program in Problem B5.1 to find GCF(2205, 4725, 18375) and LCM(42534, 16983, 509490).

B5.3. Write a program that lists all the factors of a number as well as the number of these factors.

B5.4. Write a program that will display all the perfect numbers up to 500.

Chapter 6 (Fractions)

B6.1. Using Computer Program B5.2, write a program to express a fraction in its simplest form.

B6.2. Write a program that tests two fractions for equality.

B6.3. Modify your program in Problem B6.2 to determine the smaller of two unequal fractions.

B6.4. Modify your program in Problem B6.3 to find a fraction between two unequal fractions.

B6.5. Write a program to find the sum, difference, product, and quotient of two fractions.

B6.6. Modify your programs in Problems B6.3 and B6.4 to express your answers in simplest form.

B6.7. Write a program to find all fractions of the form $(A*10 + B)/(B*10 + C) = A/C$ where A, B, and C can be digits 1 through 9. For example, $\dfrac{1\!\!\!/6}{\!\!\!/64} = \dfrac{1}{4}$.

Chapter 7 (Decimals, Ratio, Proportion, and Percent)

Computer Program B7.1

```
10    REM THIS PROGRAM FINDS A FRACTION
      FROM A REPEATING DECIMAL
      REPRESENTATION WHERE THE REPETEND
      BEGINS IN THE TENTHS PLACE
20    HOME
30    PRINT "THIS PROGRAM FINDS THE
      FRACTION REPRESENTATION FROM ITS
      REPEATING DECIMAL FORM WHERE THE
      REPETEND BEGINS IN THE TENTHS
      PLACE."
40    PRINT
50    PRINT "INPUT ONE SET OF THE
      REPETEND.": INPUT R
60    PRINT
70    PRINT "INPUT THE NUMBER OF PLACES
      IN THE REPETEND.":INPUT P
80    PRINT
90    D = 10∧P—1
100   PRINT "THE FRACTION IS "R"/"D;
      "."
110   END
```

B7.1. Modify Computer Program B7.1 to write the fraction in simplest form.

B7.2. Modify your program in Problem B7.1 to find the fraction representation for a decimal whose repetend may begin after the tenths digit.

B7.3. Write a program to determine the fourth number in a proportion given three of the numbers.

B7.4. Using INT, write a program that will find the whole-number part and the decimal part of any (positive) decimal input (e.g., if 3.17 is input, then 3 and 0.17 are output).

B7.5. Write a program that will calculate the principal amount that results for any given initial amount, number of years, and interest rate, compounded annually.

B7.6. Modify your program in Problem B7.5 to take into account any compounding period as small as weekly.

B7.7. Write a program that will calculate how much of a lump sum one has to set aside at some annual rate (without compounding) to reach a certain goal amount in 10 years.

B7.8. Modify your program in Problem B7.7 to reflect quarterly compounding.

Chapter 9 (Rational Numbers and Real Numbers, with an Introduction to Algebra)

Computer Program B9.1

```
10    REM THIS PROGRAM SOLVES LINEAR
      EQUATIONS OF THE FORM AX + B =
      CX + D.
20    HOME
30    PRINT "TO SOLVE AN EQUATION OF THE
      FORM AX + B = CX + D ENTER A,
      THEN B, THEN C, THEN D."
40    INPUT A:INPUT B:INPUT C:INPUT D
50    IF A = C AND B = D THEN PRINT "THE
      EQUATION IS TRUE FOR ALL VALUES
      OF X."
60    IF A = C AND B < > D THEN PRINT
      "THERE IS NO SOLUTION."
70    IF A < > C THEN PRINT "THE VALUE
      OF X IS ";(D-B)/(A-C);"."
80    END
```

B9.1. Modify your program in Problem B6.1 to find the simplest form of any *rational number*.

B9.2. Modify your program in Problem B6.4 for *rational numbers*.

B9.3. Modify your program in Problem B6.5 for *rational numbers*.

B9.4. Modify your programs in Problems B9.2 and B9.3 to express answers in simplest form. (HINT: Problem B9.1.)

B9.5. Modify Computer Program B9.1 to solve inequalities.

Chapter 10 (Statistics)

Computer Program B10.1

```
10    REM THIS PROGRAM FINDS THE MEAN
      AND STANDARD DEVIATION OF A LIST
      OF NUMBERS.
20    REM VARIABLE INITIALIZATION
30    LET Y = 0
40    LET Z = 0
50    REM ENTER VALUES
60    PRINT "HOW MANY NUMBERS DO YOU
      HAVE?"
70    INPUT N
80    PRINT "ENTER YOUR NUMBERS, ONE AT
      A TIME, AFTER THE QUESTION MARK."
90    REM LOOP FOR ENTERING AND SUMMING
      NUMBERS
100   FOR I = 1 TO N
110   INPUT X
120   LET Y = Y + X ∧ 2
```

```
130   LET Z = Z + X
140   NEXT I
150   REM CALCULATION OF MEAN AND
      STANDARD DEVIATION
160   LET M = Z / N
170   LET S = SQR ((Y / N) − M ∧ 2)
180   PRINT "THE MEAN IS ";M;"."
190   PRINT "THE STANDARD DEVIATION IS
      ";S;"."
200   END
```

B10.1. Modify Computer Program B10.1 to find the unbiased standard deviation.

B10.2. Modify Computer Program B10.1 to find the *z*-scores for each number with respect to the standard deviation.

Chapter 11 (Probability)

Computer Program B11.1

```
10    REM TOY CARS ARE DISTRIBUTED
      UNIFORMLY IN CEREAL BOXES. THIS
      PROGRAM DETERMINES THE PROBABILITY
      OF OBTAINING ALL SIX TYPES OF CARS
      IN 10 BOXES OF CEREAL.
20    REM VARIABLE INITIALIZATION
30    LET S = 0
40    REM LOOP TO COMPUTE 1000 TRIALS
50    FOR X = 1 TO 1000
60    REM VARIABLE INITIALIZATION
70    LET A = 0: LET B = 0: LET C = 0:
      LET D = 0: LET E = 0: LET F = 0
80    REM LOOP THROUGH 10 BOXES OF
      CEREAL
90    FOR Y = 1 TO 10
100   REM RANDOM INTEGER FROM 1 TO 6
110   LET R = 1 + INT (6 * RND (1))
120   IF R = 1 THEN LET A = 1
130   IF R = 2 THEN LET B = 1
140   IF R = 3 THEN LET C = 1
150   IF R = 4 THEN LET D = 1
160   IF R = 5 THEN LET E = 1
170   IF R = 6 THEN LET F = 1
180   NEXT Y
190   REM DETERMINE IF ALL 6 TYPES OF
      CARS WERE FOUND.
200   IF A * B * C * D * E * F <> 0
      THEN LET S = S + 1
210   NEXT X
220   PRINT "THE PROBABILITY OF
      OBTAINING ALL SIX TYPES OF CARS IN 10
      BOXES IS ";S / 1000;"."
230   END
```

Computer Program B11.2

```
10   REM THIS PROGRAM FINDS THE
     PROBABILITY OF FINDING A PHONY
     PENNY IN 25 ROLLS WHERE THE SECOND
     PENNY FROM EACH END OF EVERY ROLL
     IS CHECKED.
20   REM VARIABLE INITIALIZATION
30   LET T = 0
40   REM LOOP THROUGH 100 TRIALS
50   FOR X = 1 TO 100
60   REM LOOP CHECKING THE 25 ROLLS
70   FOR Y = 1 TO 25
80   REM RANDOM INTEGER FROM 1 TO 50
90   LET A = INT (RND (1) * 50) + 1
100  IF A = 49 THEN GOTO 140
110  IF A = 2 THEN GOTO 140
120  NEXT Y
130  GOTO 150
140  LET T = T + 1
150  NEXT X
160  PRINT "THE PROBABILITY OF FINDING
     A PHONY PENNY IN 25 ROLLS IS ";
     T / 100;"."
170  END
```

B11.1. Modify Computer Program B11.1 to simulate a similar experiment except where you can input the number of boxes and the number of cars.

B11.2. Write a program to simulate families of five children to determine the probability of having at least four children of the same sex. Run your program of 1000 trials and compare your result with the theoretical probability.

B11.3. Modify Problem B11.2 to allow for a variable number of children and variable outcomes. (For example, run a simulation to find the probability of having an equal number of boys and girls in a family with 10 children.) Compare your results with theoretical probabilities.

B11.4. Write a program to simulate tossing a pair of dice 1000 times where your output displays each of the possible sums with their respective probabilities. Compare your results with the theoretical probabilities.

B11.5. Modify Computer Program B11.2 to simulate a similar experiment except where you can specify various places to look for the phony penny. Then compare the probabilities for various places to see if you notice a trend.

B11.6. Write a program to draw a card randomly from a 52-card deck consisting of 4 suits and 13 cards in each suit.

Chapter 13 (Measurement)

B13.1. Write a program that calculates the perimeter and area of a rectangle given its length and width.

B13.2. Write a program that calculates the perimeter and area of a trapezoid given the lengths of its four sides and its height.

B13.3. Write a program to find the area of a triangle given the lengths of its sides. (HINT: Use Hero's formula.)

B13.4. Write a program to find the surface area and volume of a right rectangular prism given its length, width, and height.

B13.5. Determine which dimensions you need and then write a program to find the surface area and volume of a right square prism.

B13.6. Determine which dimensions you need and then write a program to find the surface area and volume of a right circular cylinder and a right circular cone having the same base and height.

Chapter 14 (Geometry Using Triangle Congruence and Similarity)

B14.1. Write a program that checks to see if two triangles are similar using SAS similarity.

B14.2. Write a program that checks to see if two triangles are similar using SSS similarity.

Chapter 15 (Geometry Using Coordinates)

Computer Program B15.1

```
10    REM THIS PROGRAM SOLVES
      SIMULTANEOUS PAIRS OF LINEAR
      EQUATIONS.
20    REM ENTER DATA
30    PRINT "ENTER THE VALUES OF A, B,
      AND C IN THE FIRST EQUATION,
      AX + BY = C."
40    INPUT A,B,C
50    IF ABS (A) + ABS (B) < > 0 THEN
      GOTO 80
60    PRINT "EITHER A OR B MUST BE
      NONZERO. ENTER A, B, AND C AGAIN."
70    GOTO 40
80    PRINT "ENTER THE VALUES OF D, E,
      AND F IN THE SECOND EQUATION,
      DX + EY = F."
90    INPUT D,E,F
100   IF ABS (D) + ABS (E) < > 0 THEN
      GOTO 130
110   PRINT "EITHER D OR E MUST BE
      NONZERO. ENTER D, E, AND F AGAIN."
120   GOTO 90
130   REM DETERMINE TYPES OF SOLUTIONS
```

```
140  IF A * E < > B * D THEN GOTO 210
150  IF C * E < > B * F THEN GOTO 190
160  REM PRINT OUT RESULTS
170  PRINT "THE LINES COINCIDE. EVERY
     POINT OF THE FORM (Y = "; — A /
     B;"X + ";C / B;") IS A SOLUTION."
180  GOTO 220
190  PRINT "THE LINES ARE PARALLEL AND
     DISTINCT. THERE IS NO SOLUTION."
200  GOTO 220
210  PRINT "THE SOLUTION IS (";(B *
     F — C * E ) / (D * B — A * E);
     ",";(C * D — A * F) / (B * D —
     A * E);")."
220  END
```

B15.1. Write a program to find the slope, length, and midpoint of a line segment given the endpoints of the segment.

B15.2. Write a program to determine if three given points are collinear.

B15.3. Write a program using Hero's formula to find the area of a triangle given the coordinates of its vertices.

B15.4. Modify your program in Problem B15.3 to find the area of a convex quadrilateral given the coordinates of its vertices. (HINT: Draw a diagonal.)

C.2

PROGRAMMING IN LOGO: TURTLE GEOMETRY

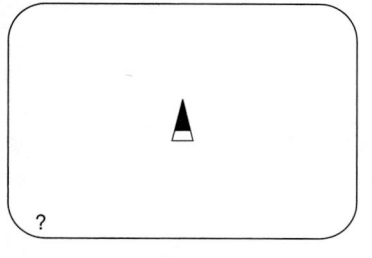

FIGURE C.3

Logo is a computer language that allows us to draw a variety of geometric shapes and patterns. In Logo's "turtle graphics" a small triangle, called the **turtle**, appears on the screen. We can direct the turtle to move about the screen and to show its path. To start Logo, insert a Logo language disk into the disk drive and turn on the computer. A message, such as "Welcome to Logo," will appear on the screen, followed by a question mark. The question mark indicates that the computer is waiting for a Logo command. Type **DRAW** to enter the "draw" mode (Figure C.3). The turtle appears in the center of the screen.

In draw mode we can direct the turtle using certain graphics commands, such as the following:

Graphics Command	Abbreviation	Effect
FORWARD	FD	Sends turtle forward a given number of turtle steps
BACK	BK	Sends turtle backward a given number of turtle steps
RIGHT	RT	Turns turtle to right a given number of degrees
LEFT	LT	Turns turtle to left a given number of degrees
PENUP	PU	Lifts turtle's pen
PENDOWN	PD	Lowers turtle's pen

(NOTE: All commands in this section are in Terrapin® Logo.* There is a summary of commands at the end of this section, including the Apple Logo versions.)

---

*Terrapin is a registered trademark of Terrapin, Inc.

Figure C.4 shows the effects of a sequence of Logo commands on the turtle.

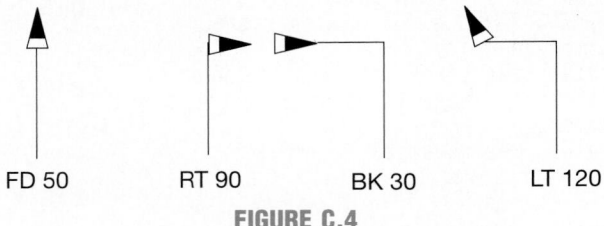

FIGURE C.4

Example C.18 gives a simple Logo routine.

EXAMPLE C.18   Write Logo commands to draw a square with side length 50 turtle steps.

Solution

```
FD    50
RT    90
FD    50
RT    90
FD    50
RT    90
FD    50
RT    90
```

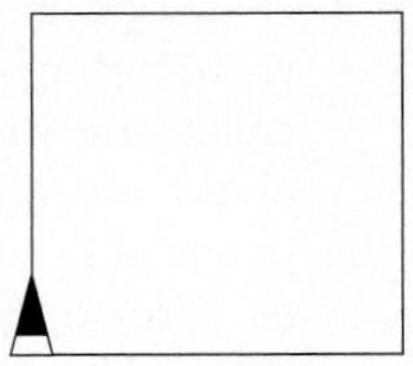

FIGURE C.5

Figure C.5 shows the screen after the commands have been executed. The turtle starts and ends in the lower left corner.   ■

In Example C.18, the first command, FD 50, sends the turtle ahead 50 turtle steps. (Note the space between FD and 50.) The second command, RT 90, turns the turtle 90° to the right. The third command, FD 50, sends the turtle ahead 50 turtle steps in its new orientation. The fourth command, RT 90, turns the turtle 90° to the right of its current orientation, and so on. Notice that the FORWARD (FD) command sends the turtle in the direction that it is pointing and not necessarily toward the top of the screen. Also, the RIGHT (RT) command turns the turtle the given number of degrees to the right of its current heading and not necessarily toward your right as you face the screen.

The commands BACK (BK) and LEFT (LT) move the turtle backward or to the left, respectively, relative to its current position and heading. Example C.19 illustrates the use of BACK and LEFT.

EXAMPLE C.19 Write Logo commands to draw perpendicular line segments.

Solution

```
FD   80
BK  160
FD   80
LT   90
FD   80
BK  160
FD   80
RT   90
```

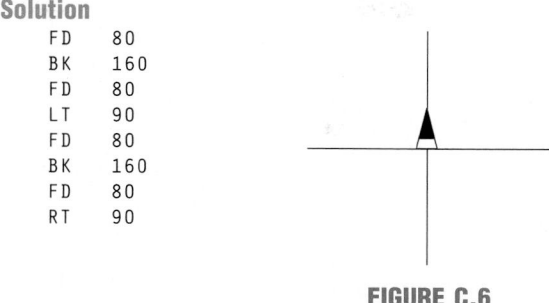

FIGURE C.6

Figure C.6 shows the screen after the commands have been executed. ■

Notice in Example C.19 that the last two commands, FD 80 and RT 90, are merely used to return the turtle to its initial or "home" position on the screen. The command HOME does this directly. That is, **HOME** sends the turtle to its original position in the center of the screen, pointing toward the top.

In Examples C.18 and C.19, distances and angles are measured using whole numbers. We can assign other real-number quantities in Logo by using decimals or arithmetic operations (+, −, *, /). For example, FD 47.9 sends the turtle ahead 47.9 turtle steps, while RT 135/4 turns the turtle to the right 33.75°. The commands SQRT and INTEGER also are useful in assigning numerical values. The command **SQRT** computes the square root of a nonnegative quantity. For example, FD SQRT 300 sends the turtle ahead $\sqrt{300}$, or about 17.3, turtle steps. The command **INTEGER** computes the integer part of a quantity. For example, FD INTEGER 17.6 sends the turtle ahead 17 turtle steps. The command FD − 17 sends the turtle *backward* 17 turtle steps. (Note that INTEGER simply truncates real numbers by eliminating their decimal parts.)

The following are helpful editing commands.

Editing Command	Effect
ESC or DELETE	Erases preceding character
← or →	Moves cursor left or right
DRAW	Clears the graphics screen and returns turtle to home position

There are other editing commands, which we will see later.

We can move the turtle without showing its path using the PENUP (PU) command. To resume showing the turtle's path, use PENDOWN (PD). Example C.20 shows an illustration.

EXAMPLE C.20   Write Logo commands to draw a dashed line segment.

Solution

```
FD    5
PU
FD    5
PD
FD    5
PU
FD    5
PD
FD    5
PU
FD    5
PD
FD    5
```

FIGURE C.7

Figure C.7 shows the screen after the commands have been executed. ∎

If a sequence of Logo commands is to be repeated, we can simplify the list of commands by using the **REPEAT** command. For example, we can shorten the list of commands in Example C.18, which draws a square in the following way.

```
REPEAT 4[FD 50 RT 90]
```

Here the sequence of commands inside the brackets is repeated four times. The REPEAT command requires a whole number indicating the number of repetitions (here four), followed by a sequence of commands in brackets. (Commands inside the brackets are separated by spaces.) The bracketed commands are repeated as many times as indicated.

The list of commands in Example C.20, which draws a dashed line, can be shortened considerably in the following way.

```
REPEAT 3[FD 5 PU FD 5 PD]
FD 5
```

The REPEAT command is useful in drawing regular polygons. Suppose that we wish to draw a regular pentagon with sides of length 40 (Figure C.8). An exterior angle of a regular pentagon measures 72°. Since the turtle turns through the *exterior angle* of the pentagon, we will repeatedly send it forward 40 steps and then turn it right 72°. We wish to do this five times; thus we will use the REPEAT command as follows:

```
REPEAT 5[FD 40 RT 72]
```

Figure C.9 shows the screen after the REPEAT command is executed. In the exercise/problem set, you will have the opportunity to draw other regular polygons.

Defining Logo Procedures

We can create Logo procedures that the computer can remember by entering the "edit" mode. A procedure is a list of Logo commands that has been given a specific name. A procedure is created in the following way:

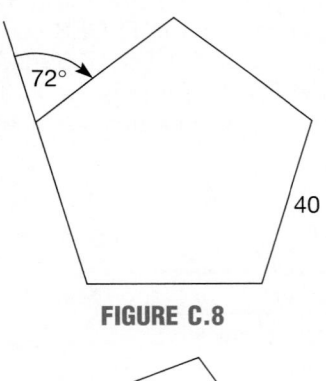

72°

40

FIGURE C.8

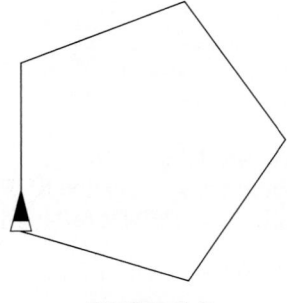

FIGURE C.9

First, type **TO** and the name of the procedure you wish to define. Next, type the list of commands comprising the procedure. Then type **END** followed by **CONTROL-C**. (Hold the "control" key down and press the C key.) For example, to define a procedure for drawing a regular pentagon *with horizontal base* (Figure C.8), type the following lines.

```
TO PENTAGON
LT 18
REPEAT 5[FD 40 RT 72]
RT 18
END
CTRL-C
```

We will use the abbreviation CTRL for the CONTROL key. The first line enters edit mode and names the procedure PENTAGON. The next lines followed by END make up the procedure. (END is the last line in every procedure.) The CTRL-C command directs the computer to remember the procedure, using the name PENTAGON. That is, the procedure becomes part of the computer's "workspace" of known Logo commands. The procedure thus can be executed, as a Logo command, simply by typing its name in draw mode. Example C.21 illustrates the use of a Logo procedure.

EXAMPLE C.21   Use a procedure to draw part of a tessellation with squares.

Solution
First define the procedure SQUARE as follows:

```
TO SQUARE
REPEAT 4[FD 50 RT 90]
END
CTRL-C
```

Then enter

```
PU
LT 90
FD 100
RT 90
PD
REPEAT 4[SQUARE RT 90 FD 50 LT 90]
PU
LT 90
FD 175
RT 90
BK 50
PD
REPEAT 3[SQUARE RT 90 FD 50 LT 90]
```

Figure C.10 shows the screen after the commands have been executed. ■

Once a procedure is defined, it can be used as part of another procedure. If you wish to stop while you are creating a procedure, type **CTRL-G**. This cancels the procedure and leaves you in edit mode. You can also use CTRL-G to stop a procedure while it is running in draw mode. If you are in edit mode and wish to return to draw mode, type DRAW. The following are additional editing commands.

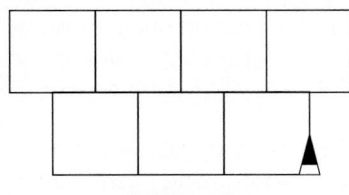

FIGURE C.10

Editing Command	Effect
CTRL-A	Moves cursor to start of current line
CTRL-E	Moves cursor to end of current line
CTRL-N	Moves cursor to next line
CTRL-P	Moves cursor to previous line
CTRL-X	Erases to end of current line
DRAW CLEARSCREEN	Clears graphics screen and enters draw mode
EDIT	Enters edit mode
TO (Procedure)	Enters edit mode and begins definition of indicated procedure
END	Ends definition of a procedure
EDIT (Procedure)	Enters edit mode and calls indicated procedure from workspace; procedure can now be edited and redefined

In addition, the following control characters are useful in managing the screen.

Control Character	Effect
CTRL-F	Shows full graphics screen
CTRL-T	Shows full text screen
CTRL-S	Shows split graphics/text screen

Using Variable Inputs

Thus far we have used fixed distances and angles in procedures. For example, in the procedure SQUARE from Example C.21 we specified the side length as 50. However, we could allow the side length to be a variable quantity whose value is input when the procedure is executed. The following procedure, SQUARE.2, draws a square of arbitrary side length.

```
TO SQUARE.2 :N
REPEAT 4[FD :N RT 90]
END
```

In the procedure SQUARE.2, the variable called ":N" is the side length. In Logo, any alphanumeric string preceded by a colon can be used to name a variable. To execute SQUARE.2, first define SQUARE.2 in edit mode, then enter draw mode. Next, type SQUARE.2, a space, and the value that you wish to assign to the variable :N. For example, to draw a square of side length 100, type SQUARE.2 100. You may use decimal numbers or arithmetic operations $(+, -, *, /)$, with parentheses if necessary, to input the value of :N. For example, typing SQUARE.2 14/3 will draw a square of side length $14 \div 3$.

Example C.22 gives a procedure for drawing arbitrary parallelograms. Notice that there are three variables to be input, namely, one of the vertex angles and the lengths of two of the sides.

EXAMPLE C.22   Write a procedure to draw an arbitrary parallelogram.

Solution

```
TO PARALLELOGRAM :ANGLE :SIDE1 :SIDE2
RT 90 — :ANGLE
REPEAT 2[FD :SIDE1 RT :ANGLE FD :SIDE2 RT
180 — :ANGLE]
END
```

Figure C.11 shows several examples of parallelograms drawn by PARALLELOGRAM.   ■

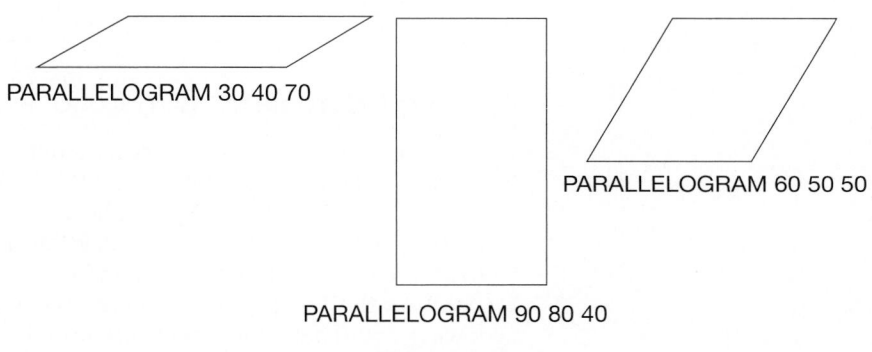

PARALLELOGRAM 30 40 70

PARALLELOGRAM 60 50 50

PARALLELOGRAM 90 80 40

FIGURE C.11

Note that the name of the procedure in Example C.22 is simply PARALLELOGRAM. The variables involved in a procedure are listed in the first line but are not part of the name.

Creating Logo Files

Logo procedures can be saved on an initialized disk using the filing command **SAVE**. (For information on initializing a disk, see Section C.1.) The SAVE command saves all of the procedures currently in the computer's workspace as a file. Thus, be sure that the workspace contains only the procedures that you wish to save together as a file. For example, suppose that you want to save the procedures PARALLELOGRAM and SQUARE.2 as a file called QUADS. To do so, define both of these procedures (in edit mode) in the workspace, then return to draw mode. Next, insert a formatted disk in the disk drive and type SAVE "QUADS. (Note the quote mark to the left of the file name.) The computer will create a file called QUADS on your disk. To read the file QUADS from the disk into the workspace, enter draw mode and type READ "QUADS (with quote mark). The following are helpful filing commands for creating files and managing the workspace and disk.

Filing/Managing Command	Effect
PRINTOUT TITLES (POTS)	Lists all procedures currently in the workspace
EDIT (Procedure)	Lists the indicated procedure currently in the workspace, in edit mode
ERASE (Procedure)	Erases the indicated procedure from the workspace
ERASE ALL	Erases all procedures from the workspace
SAVE "(Filename)	Saves all current procedures in the workspace as a file under the given name
READ "(Filename)	Reads the indicated file from the disk into the workspace
ERASEFILE "(Filename)	Erases the indicated file from the disk
CATALOG	Lists the names of all files currently on the disk

Using Coordinates with Logo

The Logo screen is actually a modified coordinate plane with the turtle's home position being the point (0, 0). The horizontal line through the "home" position is the x-axis. The vertical line through the home position is the y-axis. The plane is modified by the "wraparound" feature, that is, the turtle can go off the screen and reappear at the opposite edge. Hence a point on the turtle graphics screen has many sets of coordinates. The following coordinate commands are useful in changing the turtle's position.

Coordinate Command	Effect
SETX (n)	Slides the turtle horizontally to the point with x-coordinate n
SETY (n)	Slides the turtle vertically to the point with y-coordinate n
SETXY (n m)	Slides the turtle to the point (n, m)

(NOTE: The turtle's heading does not change when using SETX, SETY, or SETXY. The command **SETHEADING (SETH)** can be used to turn the turtle to a specific heading in degrees. For example, SETH 0 turns the turtle to the top of the screen, while SETH 180 turns the turtle to the bottom of the screen, as on a navigational compass.)

The following table illustrates the use of SETX, SETY, and SETXY.

Position Before			Position After	
X	Y	Command	X	Y
20	80	SETX 50	50	80
20	80	SETY 60	20	60
20	80	SETXY −30 40	−30	40

We can use the value of a variable to assign a coordinate value. For example, the command SETX :N sets the turtle's x-coordinate equal to the current value of the variable :N. Example C.23 illustrates the use of coordinates in drawing a reflection image.

EXAMPLE C.23   Draw the triangle with coordinates (10, 0), (50, 0), and (50, 90). Then draw its reflection image over the *y*-axis.

Solution

```
PU
SETXY 10  0
PD
SETXY 50  0
SETXY 50 90
SETXY 10  0
PU
SETXY −10  0
PD
SETXY −50  0
SETXY −50 90
SETXY −10  0
```

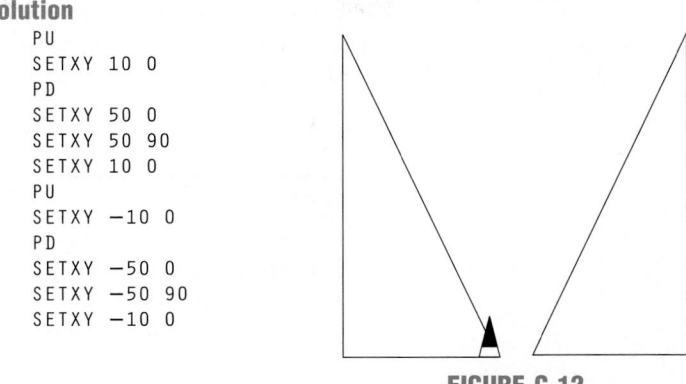

FIGURE C.12

Figure C.12 shows the screen after the commands have been executed. ■

Example C.24 illustrates the use of SETXY in drawing size transformation images.

EXAMPLE C.24   Draw the triangle whose vertices have coordinates (5, 5), (20, 5), and (20, 10). Then double each coordinate to show a size transformation image.

Solution

```
PU
SETXY 5 5
PD
SETXY 20  5
SETXY 20 10
SETXY 5 5
PU
SETXY 10 10
PD
SETXY 40 10
SETXY 40 20
SETXY 10 10
```

Figure C.13 shows the screen after the commands are executed. Notice that the larger triangle is the image of the smaller triangle under a size transformation with scale factor 2 and center (0, 0). ■

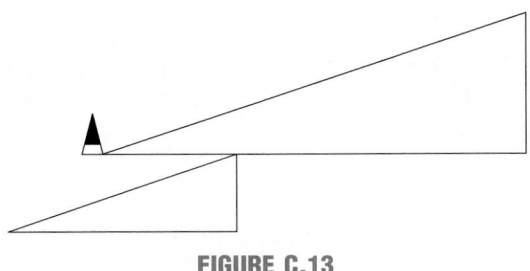

FIGURE C.13

The computer will tell you the turtle's current coordinates by means of the commands **XCOR** and **YCOR**. These commands are useful in conjunction with the command MAKE. The **MAKE** command allows us to assign a value to a variable within a procedure. For example, the command MAKE "X 10 assigns the variable :X the value 10. (Note the quotes but no colon in the MAKE command.) The following table shows several variations of the MAKE command.

Command	Effect
MAKE "N 5	Assigns :N the value 5
MAKE "N :N + 1	Adds 1 to the current value of :N
MAKE "X XCOR	Assigns :X the value of the turtle's current x-coordinate

Example C.25 gives a use of the MAKE command to draw a triangle starting anywhere on the screen using the SAS congruence condition.

EXAMPLE C.25   Draw a triangle given the lengths of two sides and the measure of the included angle.

Solution

```
TO SAS.TRIANGLE :SIDE1 :ANGLE :SIDE2
MAKE "X XCOR
MAKE "Y YCOR
FD :SIDE1
RT 180 - :ANGLE
FD :SIDE2
SETXY :X :Y
END
```

Figure C.14 shows the screen after the procedure has been executed. Notice that the two MAKE commands assign the coordinates of the turtle's initial position to variables called :X and :Y. Next, the turtle draws the first side, then the angle, then the second side. Finally, the turtle returns to its initial position by means of the SETXY command. This draws the third side of the triangle. ■

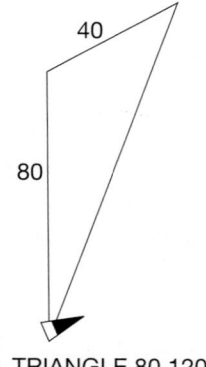

SAS. TRIANGLE 80 120 40
FIGURE C.14

There are many other features of Logo that you may find interesting. Additionally, many books of Logo activities are available for teachers to use in reinforcing geometry concepts.

Logo Command Summary

Commands are the same in three versions of Logo (Terrapin Logo, Apple Logo, PC Logo) unless noted otherwise below.

Terrapin Logo	Apple Logo	PC Logo	Effect
Graphics			
FORWARD (FD)			Sends turtle forward
BACK (BK)			Sends turtle backward
RIGHT (RT)			Turns turtle right
LEFT (LT)			Turns turtle left
PENUP (PU)			Lifts turtle's pen
PENDOWN (PD)			Lowers turtle's pen
DRAW	CLEARSCREEN (CS)	DRAW or CS	Clears screen, homes turtle
CLEARSCREEN (CS)	CLEAN	CLEAN	Clears screen, doesn't affect turtle
HOME			Homes turtle
SETX n			Slides turtle horizontally to n
SETY m			Slides turtle vertically to m
SETXY n m	SETPOS [n m]	SETXY [n m] or SETXY LIST n m	Slides turtle to (n, m)
SETHEADING (SETH) n			Sets turtle's heading to n degrees
XCOR			Gives turtle's x-coordinate
YCOR			Gives turtle's y-coordinate
Editing (*in the editor*)			
ESC or DELETE	Backspace or DELETE	Backspace	Erases previous character
Left (Right) arrow			Moves cursor left (right) one character
CTRL-A			Moves cursor to start of current line
CTRL-E			Moves cursor to end of current line
CTRL-N			Moves cursor to next line
CTRL-P	CTRL-Y	CTRL-P	Moves cursor to previous line
CTRL-X		CTRL-K	Erases to end of current line
EDIT			Enters edit mode
TO *Procedure*			Begins definition of *Procedure*
END			Ends definition of procedure
CTRL-C		Key F2 or key F3	Defines procedures in workspace, exits edit mode
CTRL-G		CTRL-BREAK	Cancels procedure
EDIT *Procedure*	EDIT "*Procedure*	EDIT *Procedure*	Enters edit mode and calls *Procedure* from the workspace

Terrapin Logo	Apple Logo	PC Logo	Effect
Control			
REPEAT n [List]			Executes list of commands n times
CTRL-F	CTRL-L	FS or key F4	Shows full graphics screen
CTRL-G		CTRL-G or CTRL-BREAK	Stops procedure execution
CTRL-S		SS or key F2	Shows split graphics/text screen
Filing/Managing			
POTS			Lists titles of procedures in workspace
ERASE *Procedure*	ERASE "*Procedure*	ERASE *Procedure*	Erases *Procedure* from workspace
ERASE ALL	ERALL	ERASE ALL	Erases all procedures from workspace
SAVE "*Filename*			Saves procedures in workspace as disk file under the name *Filename*
READ "*Filename*	LOAD "*Filename*	LOAD "Filename	Reads *Filename* from disk
ERASEFILE "*Filename*			Erases *Filename* from disk
CATALOG		CATALOG or DIR	Lists names of files on disk
Naming			
MAKE "V *value*			Assigns variable :V the given *value*
Numeric			
+, −, *, /			Addition, subtraction, multiplication, division
SQRT *quantity*			Computes square root of *quantity*
INTEGER *quantity*	INT *quantity*	INT *quantity*	Computes integer part of *quantity*

EXERCISE/PROBLEM SET C.2

1. Correct the following commands.

  (a) `FD50`

  (b) `RI 90`

  (c) `DRAW SQUARE`

  (d) `PU 40`

  (e) `SET X 20`

  (f) `SETXY 10,20`

  (g) `FD N`

  (h) `MAKE X=10`

2. (a) Predict the output of this routine.

```
FD    50
RT    90
FD    50
LT    90
FD    50
RT    90
FD    50
LT    90
FD    50
```

(b) Run the routine to check your prediction.

3. Write a routine to draw an angle of 72° and its angle bisector.

4. Write a routine to draw the perpendicular bisector of a line segment of length 100.

5. Write routines to draw each of the following figures.

(a)

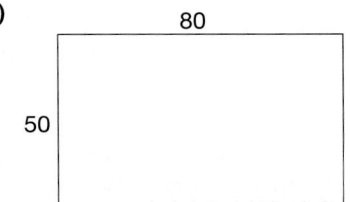

(b)

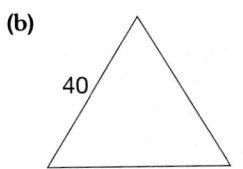

(c)

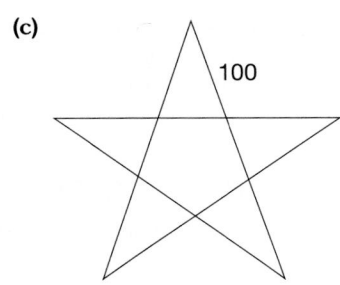

(d)

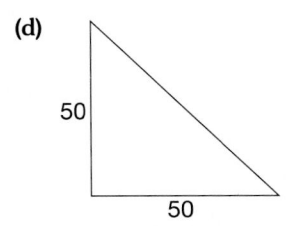

6. Write a procedure to draw parallel line segments that are inclined 50° to the horizontal.

7. Predict the output of the following routine. Then run the routine to check your prediction.

```
REPEAT 90[FD 1 RT1]
```

8. Write a procedure to draw a polygon approximating a circle.

9. Refer to Example C.22.
   (a) Give inputs to make the procedure PARALLELO-GRAM draw a square.
   (b) Give inputs to make PARALLELOGRAM draw a nonsquare rhombus.
   (c) What general types of quadrilaterals can be drawn using PARALLELOGRAM?

10. Consider the following procedure.

```
FD      100
RT      90
FD      100
RT      _____
FD      _____
```

Fill in the blanks so that a triangle with two sides of length 100 is drawn.

11. Write a procedure to draw an arbitrary square and its diagonals.

12. **(a)** Draw a rectangle with sides of lengths 40 and 70, including a diagonal.
   (b) Write a procedure to draw an arbitrary rectangle and both of its diagonals.

13. **(a)** Write a procedure to draw the quadrilateral whose vertices have coordinates $(0, 0)$, (x, y), $(-x, y)$, $(0, z)$. Run your procedure using various values of x, y, and z.
   (b) What type of quadrilateral does the turtle draw, in general?
   (c) What relationship must hold among x, y, and z in order for the quadrilateral to be a rhombus?
   (d) What relationship must hold among x, y, and z in order for the quadrilateral to be a square?

14. **(a)** Write a procedure called AXES that draws the co-ordinate axes. Make each line segment 200 turtle steps long.
   (b) Write a procedure called TRI that draws the triangle whose vertices have coordinates $(20, 5)$, $(50, 5)$, and $(50, 70)$. Run AXES, then TRI, without clearing the screen.

15. Write procedures to show the effects of the following transformations on the triangle drawn by TRI in Problem 14. Put AXES first in your procedure. Describe each transformation as completely as you can.
   (a) $(x, y) \rightarrow (x, -y)$ [This means that the point (x, y) is mapped to the point $(x, -y)$.]
   (b) $(x, y) \rightarrow (-x, -y)$
   [NOTE: SETXY requires parentheses around negative coordinates, e.g., SETXY (-20) (-5).]

16. Write procedures to show the effects of the following transformations on the triangle drawn by TRI in Problem 14. Describe each transformation as completely as you can.
   (a) $(x, y) \rightarrow (x - 100, y)$
   (b) $(x, y) \rightarrow (x - 100, -y)$

Following is a chapter-by-chapter collection of programs and problems. The prefix "L" refers to Logo programs.

Chapter 12 (Geometric Shapes)

Computer Program L12.1 (Draws a regular 7-gon)

```
REPEAT 7[FD 50 RT 360/7]
```

L12.1. Modify Computer Program L12.1 to draw a regular 10-gon with sides of length 20.

L12.2. Write a procedure called REG.POLY with variable input that draws an arbitrary regular n-gon for any value of n.

L12.3. Write a procedure called RIGHT.TRI with variable inputs that draws an arbitrary right triangle, given legs of length A and B.

Chapter 13 (Measurement)

Computer Program L13.1 (Draws a rectangle overlaid with squares)

```
HT
REPEAT    2[FD 40 RT 90 FD 70 RT 90]
REPEAT    4[FD 10 RT 90 FD 70 BK 70 LT 90]
HOME
RT        90
REPEAT    7[FD 10 LT 90 FD 40 BK 40 RT 90]
HOME
SETH      0
```

L13.1. **(a)** Modify Computer Program L13.1 into a procedure called RECTANGLE with variable inputs that draws a rectangle with sides of length A and B, overlaid with a grid of squares, each square having sides of length 10.
   (b) What is the area of each square in the grid, in square turtle steps?
   (c) Let 1 dekastep $= 10$ turtle steps. What is the area of the rectangle drawn in Computer Program L13.1, in square dekasteps?

Chapter 14 (Geometry Using Triangle Congruence and Similarity)

Computer Program L14.1 (Draws an angle of arbitrary measure and its bisector)

```
TO ANGLE.BISECT :ANGLE
  HT
  RT        90
  FD        100
  BK        100
  LT        :ANGLE
  FD        100
  BK        100
  RT        :ANGLE/2
```

```
  FD        120
  BK        120
  PU
  HOME
  PD
END
```

L14.1. Use Computer Program L14.1 to draw perpendicular line segments.

L14.2 **(a)** Write a procedure called SAS.TRI with variable inputs that draws an arbitrary triangle, given the lengths of two sides and the measure of the included angle.
   (b) What conditions on the inputs make the turtle draw the following types of triangles?
   (i) Right   (ii) Isosceles
   (iii) Obtuse   (iv) Right isosceles
   (v) Right scalene   (vi) Equilateral

L14.3. Write a procedure called MAGNIFY.TRI with variable inputs that draws a triangle using SAS.TRI, then enlarges each side by a constant multiple K.

Chapter 15 (Geometry Using Coordinates)

Computer Program L15.1 (Draws the coordinate axes)

```
TO AXES
  SETX      100
  SETX      (-100)
  HOME
  SETY      100
  SETY      (-100)
  HOME
END
```

L15.1. Write a procedure called TRI.COORDS with variable inputs that draws the coordinate axes and the triangle ABC whose vertices are the points $A(0, 0)$, $B(X1, Y1)$, and $C(X2, Y2)$.

L15.2. Modify the procedure TRI.COORDS to also draw the line segment connecting the midpoints of $\overline{AB}$ and $\overline{AC}$.

L15.3. Write a program that draws the coordinate axes and the triangle with vertices $(0, 0)$, $(20, 90)$, and $(100, 30)$ and all the medians.

L15.4. Write a procedure called MEDIANS with variable inputs that draws a triangle with one vertex $(0, 0)$, the other two arbitrary, and all the medians.

Chapter 16 (Geometry Using Transformations)

Computer Program L16.1 (Draws an arbitrary triangle, given the coordinates of the vertices as inputs)

```
TO TRI.PLOT :X1 :Y1 :X2 :Y2 :X3 :Y3
  PU
  SETXY :X1 :Y1
  PD
  SETXY :X2 :Y2
  SETXY :X3 :Y3
  SETXY :X1 :Y1
  PU
  HOME
  PD
END
```

L16.1. Write a procedure called X.REF with variable inputs that draws the triangle ABC where $A = (X1, Y1)$, $B = (X2, Y2)$, $C = (X3, Y3)$, and the reflection image of triangle ABC in the x-axis.

C.3

COMPUTER EXPLORATION SOFTWARE FOR GEOMETRY

BASIC and Logo are examples of programming languages. There are other, more user-friendly software graphics packages that can be used to explore various properties and relationships in geometry. For example, to learn more about the medians of an arbitrary triangle, one could use such a package to (1) draw a triangle, (2) find the midpoints of each side by referring to their endpoints and selecting a midpoint command, and (3) drawing each median by selecting its appropriate endpoints and using a command to draw the segment with these endpoints. In Figure C.15, $\triangle ABC$ has sides with midpoints D, E, F and medians $\overline{AD}$, $\overline{BE}$, and $\overline{CF}$.

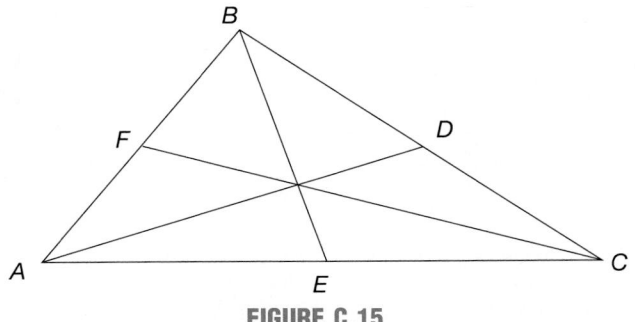

FIGURE C.15

Using the software, one can explore various relationships, for example, comparing the areas of the many triangles that are formed.

The power of this type of software is that it allows the user to make and check various conjectures. Once a conjecture has been formalized, the techniques learned in Chapters 14, 15, and 16 may be used to verify that the conjectures are true.

A list of computer exploration software for geometry with the types of computers that are required follows. After this list is a collection of problems involving geometric relationships that can be explored/discovered using these software packages.

Euclid's Toolbox. Addison-Wesley Publishing Company, Reading, MA 01867 (1-800-447-2226) **(MS-DOS)**

The Geometric Super Supposer. Sunburst Communications, 101 Castleton Street, Pleasantville, NY 10570-3498 (1-800-628-8897) **(Apple II)**

Geometer's Sketch Pad. Key Curriculum Press, 2512 Martin Luther King Jr. Way, Berkeley, CA 94704 (1-800-338-7638) **(Macintosh)**

EXERCISE/PROBLEM SET C.3

Make conjectures for the following exercises using exploration software. Then test your conjectures using a variety of shapes.

1. Ray $\overrightarrow{BD}$ is the bisector of $\angle ABC$. Points E and F are on $\overrightarrow{BC}$ and $\overrightarrow{AB}$, respectively, such that $\overline{DE} \perp \overleftrightarrow{BC}$ and $\overline{DF} \perp \overleftrightarrow{BA}$.

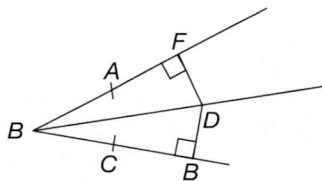

(a) Compare the distance DE with the distance DF.
(b) Write a conjecture based on your observations.

2. In $\triangle ABC$, $\overline{AD}$, $\overline{BE}$, and $\overline{CF}$ are the medians.

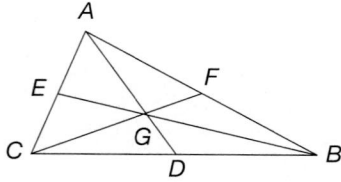

(a) Measure to demonstrate that $\overline{AD}$, $\overline{BE}$, and $\overline{CF}$ are concurrent; that is, they meet at a single point, G. (Hint: Label the point of intersection of $\overline{AD}$ and $\overline{BE}$, likewise for $\overline{BE}$ and $\overline{CF}$. Then measure the distance between the two intersection points.)
(b) How does the area of $\triangle ABE$ compare with the area of $\triangle ABD$?
(c) How does the area of $\triangle GCD$ compare with the area of $\triangle GCE$?
(d) Compare the areas of other triangles within $\triangle ABC$. Write a conjecture based on your observations.

3. Let G be the intersection of the medians in $\triangle ABC$; that is, G is the centroid of $\triangle ABC$.

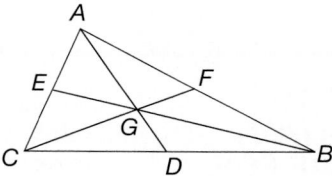

(a) Compute the ratios $AG:GD$, $BG:GE$, and $CG:GF$.
(b) Write a conjecture based on your observations in part (a).
(c) Measure the distance from G to side $\overline{BC}$. Compare this distance with the height from A to $\overline{BC}$.
(d) Repeat part (c) using side $\overline{AB}$ and the height from C, as well as side $\overline{AC}$ and the height from B.
(e) Write a conjecture based on your observations in part (d).

4. In $\triangle ABC$, point D is the midpoint of side $\overline{BC}$.

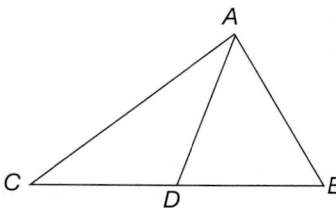

(a) Compare the areas of $\triangle ACD$ and $\triangle ADB$.
(b) Find a procedure for dividing $\triangle ABC$ into four triangles of equal area.
(c) Find a procedure for dividing $\triangle ABC$ into five triangles of equal area.
(d) Write a conjecture based on your observations.

5. In △*ABC*, rays $\overrightarrow{AD}$, $\overrightarrow{BE}$, and $\overrightarrow{CF}$ are the bisectors of the vertex angles.

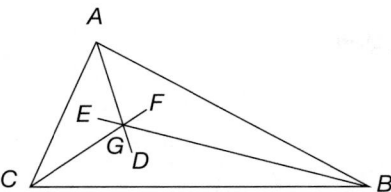

(a) Measure to demonstrate that the angle bisectors are concurrent. Let *G* be the point of intersection of the angle bisectors; that is, *G* is the incenter of △*ABC*.

(b) Compare *G* with the centers of the inscribed and circumscribed circles of △*ABC*.

(c) Write a conjecture based on your observations.

6. In △*ABC*, lines $\overleftrightarrow{DE}$, $\overleftrightarrow{FG}$, and $\overleftrightarrow{HI}$ are the perpendicular bisectors of the sides.

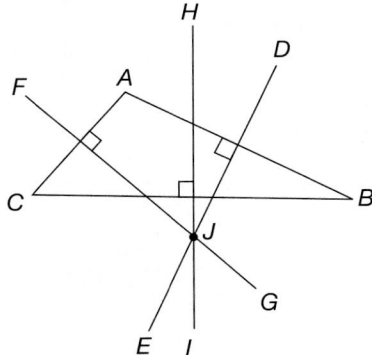

(a) Measure to demonstrate that the perpendicular bisectors are concurrent. Let *J* be the point of intersection of the perpendicular bisectors; that is, *J* is the circumcenter of △*ABC*.

(b) Compare the distances *JA*, *JB*, and *JC*.

(c) Write a conjecture based on your observations.

7. In △*ABC*, segments $\overline{AD}$, $\overline{BE}$, and $\overline{CF}$ are the altitudes.

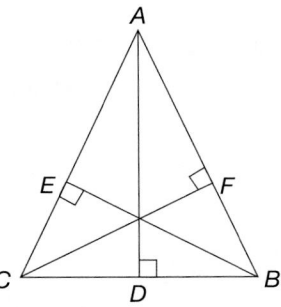

(a) Measure to demonstrate that the altitudes are concurrent. (They meet at the orthocenter of △*ABC*.)

(b) Compare the products $AD \cdot BC$, $BE \cdot AC$, and $CF \cdot AB$.

(c) How do the products in part (b) compare with the area of △*ABC*?

(d) Write a conjecture based on your observations.

8. *ABCD* is a parallelogram. Diagonals $\overline{AC}$ and $\overline{BD}$ intersect at point *E*.

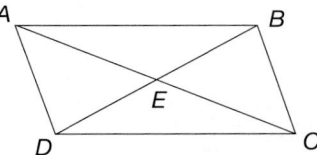

(a) Compare △*AEB* and △*CED*. Are they congruent? Compare △*AED* and △*CEB* also.

(b) Write a conjecture about corresponding pairs of triangles formed by diagonals of a parallelogram.

9. *ABCD* is a kite. Diagonals $\overline{AC}$ and $\overline{BD}$ intersect at point *E*.

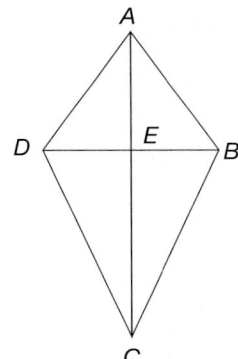

(a) Test to find pairs of congruent triangles.

(b) Write a conjecture based on your observations.

10. *ABCD* is a kite. Diagonals $\overline{AC}$ and $\overline{BD}$ intersect at point *E*.

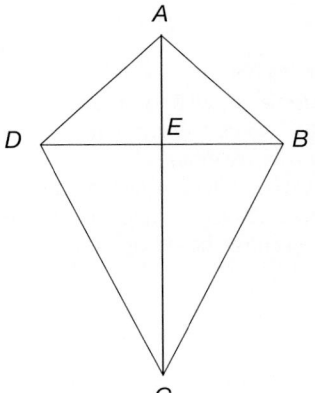

(a) Find the measure of ∠*AEB*.

(b) Write a conjecture based on your observations in part (a).

(c) Compare the area of *ABCD* with the product $AC \cdot BD$.

(d) Write a conjecture based on your observations.

11. *ABCD* is a rectangle. Diagonals $\overline{AC}$ and $\overline{DB}$ intersect at point *E*.

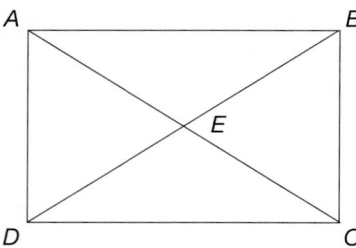

  (a) Compare the lengths *AC* and *DB*.
  (b) Write a conjecture based on your observations.
  (c) Compare △*ADC* and △*BCD*. Are they congruent?
  (d) Compare △*ADC*, △*DAB*, and △*CBA* also.
  (e) Write a conjecture based on your observations.

12. *ABCD* is rhombus. Diagonals $\overline{AC}$ and $\overline{BD}$ intersect at point *E*.

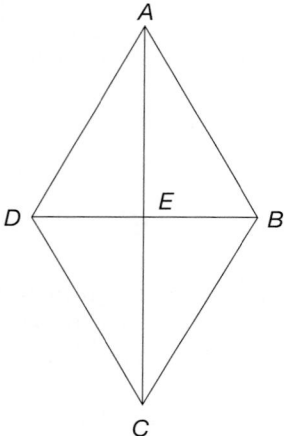

  (a) Measure to determine if *ABCD* is a parallelogram; for example, show that opposite sides are parallel.
  (b) Refer to Exercise 8 and write a conjecture based on your observations.
  (c) Explain why *ABCD* is also a kite.
  (d) Refer to Exercises 9 and 10 also, and write several conjectures based on your observations.

13. *ABCD* is a rectangle. Points *E*, *F*, *G*, and *H* are the midpoints of the sides.

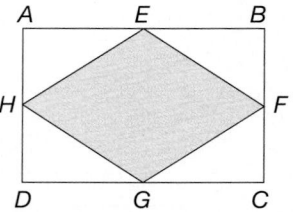

  (a) What special type of quadrilateral, if any, is *EFGH*? Compare the area of *ABCD* with the area of *EFGH*.
  (b) Repeat with *ABCD* a rhombus.
  (c) Repeat with *ABCD* a square.
  (d) Write several conjectures based on your observations.

14. *ABCD* is a square. Points *E* and *F*, *G* and *H*, *I* and *J*, and *K* and *L* trisect their respective sides.
  (a) What special type of quadrilateral, if any, is *EGIK*?
  (b) Compare the area of *ABCD* with the area of *EGIK*.
  (c) Write a conjecture based on your observations.

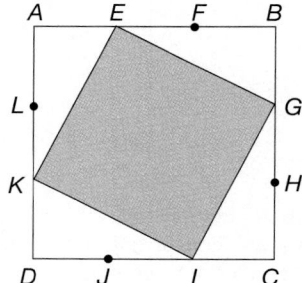

15. Repeat Problem 14 with *ABCD* a parallelogram that is not a rhombus or rectangle.

16. Repeat Problem 14 with *ABCD* a kite that is not a rhombus.

17. Repeat Problem 14 with *ABCD* a trapezoid.

18. Repeat Problem 14 with an arbitrary quadrilateral.

C.4

GRAPHICS CALCULATOR

Mem cleared

FIGURE C.16

Introduction

Graphics calculators provide a relatively new environment to help students learn and do mathematics. Although graphics calculators began to be used at the college and upper high school levels, they will probably begin to be used at the junior high school level, especially as prices drop.

The goal of this section is to show how a graphics calculator can be used to solve problems associated with graphing and the concept of function as represented in this book. We will use keystrokes of the TI-81 graphics calculator for our illustrations. Modest adjustments in keystroking will have to be made when using the TI-82, a recently introduced extended version of the TI-81, and other graphics calculators (Figure C.15).

Getting Started

Unless you have stored something in your calculator that you want to retain, you may wish to start new work with "a clean slate." (Warning: Do the following step only if you are certain there is nothing in your calculator that you want to save, since *everything* will be deleted from the calculator's memory.) This is accomplished by turning your calculator on by pressing ⎡ON⎤ and then pressing ⎡2nd⎤ <Reset> 2. Figure C.16 shows the message that should appear on your display after it is reset. Now your calculator is set as it was when it was new. Use the ⎡2nd⎤ key with the ⎡▲⎤ or ⎡▼⎤ key to adjust the contrast of your display if necessary.

Often you will be working in various "menus." You can always get to the blank display called the "home screen" by pressing ⎡2nd⎤ <QUIT>. Also, pressing the ⎡CLEAR⎤ key clears any display as well as moves to the home screen from a graph.

Evaluating Functions

In Section 2.3 values of functions are listed in tabular form. To use the calculator to graph or evaluate functions for given values, the function must be defined in the ⎡Y =⎤ list. Press ⎡Y =⎤ [Figure C.17(a)]. The blinking cursor after the Y1 awaits your entry. To enter the function $f(x) = 3x^2$, press 3 ⎡X|T⎤ ⎡x^2⎤ ⎡ENTER⎤ [Figure C.17(b)].

To evaluate the function $f(x) = 3x^2$ for $x = 5$, return to the home screen by pressing ⎡2nd⎤ <QUIT>. Next store 5 as a value for x by pressing 5 ⎡STO ▶⎤ ⎡X|T⎤ ⎡ENTER⎤. Then press ⎡2nd⎤ <Y-VARS> ⎡ENTER⎤ to access the function Y1 and press ⎡ENTER⎤ to evaluate the function [Figure C.17(c)]. The display shows that 5 has been assigned to X and that the function Y1 has value 75 ($= 3 \cdot 5^2$).

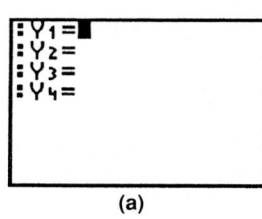

(a)

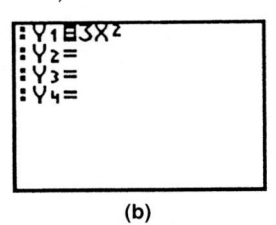

(b)

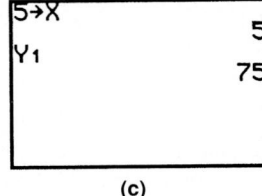

(c)

FIGURE C.17

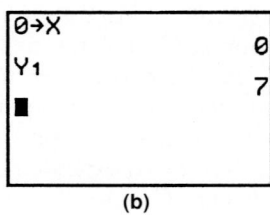

(a)

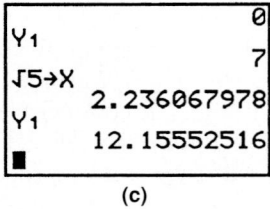

(b)

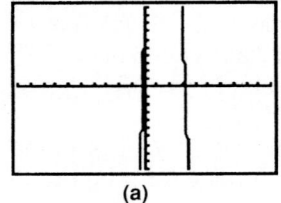

(c)

FIGURE C.18

EXAMPLE C.26 Evaluate the function $f(x) = x^3 + (0.2)x^2 - \pi x + 7$ for $x = 0$ and $x = \sqrt{5}$.

Solution

By substituting mentally, $f(0) = 7$. To find $f(\sqrt{5})$ we first enter the function as follows:

$\boxed{Y=}$ $\boxed{X|T}$ $\boxed{\wedge}$ 3 $\boxed{+}$ .2 $\boxed{X|T}$ $\boxed{x^2}$ $\boxed{-}$ $\boxed{2nd}$ $<\pi>$ $\boxed{X|T}$ $\boxed{+}$ 7 $\boxed{ENTER}$

[Figure C.18(a)].

Next we go to the home screen to enter the value 0 for x to find $f(0)$ (as a check) and $\sqrt{5}$ for x to find $f(\sqrt{5})$.

(i) First store 0 in x: $\boxed{2nd}$ $<QUIT>$ $\boxed{CLEAR}$ 0 $\boxed{STO \blacktriangleright}$ $\boxed{X|T}$ $\boxed{ENTER}$. Next evaluate $f(0)$: $\boxed{2nd}$ $<Y\text{-VARS}>$ $\boxed{ENTER}$ $\boxed{ENTER}$. This shows that for $x = 0$, Y1, or f(0), is 7 [Figure C.18(b)].

(ii) Evaluate $f(\sqrt{5})$ by first storing $\sqrt{5}$ as x and then finding Y1 for $x = \sqrt{5}$: $\boxed{2nd}$ $<QUIT>$ $\boxed{CLEAR}$ $\sqrt{5}$ $\boxed{STO \blacktriangleright}$ $\boxed{X|T}$ $\boxed{ENTER}$ $\boxed{2nd}$ $<Y\text{-VARS}>$ $\boxed{ENTER}$ $\boxed{ENTER}$ [Figure C.18(c)]. (Shortcut: When x is the variable, pressing $\boxed{STO \blacktriangleright}$ $\boxed{STO \blacktriangleright}$ is equivalent to pressing $\boxed{STO \blacktriangleright}$ $\boxed{X|T}$ $\boxed{ENTER}$.)

Graphing Functions

To graph a function, (i) the function must be entered in the calculator using $\boxed{Y=}$ and (ii) an appropriate scale for the calculator's display must be determined using $\boxed{RANGE}$. This second step is crucial! As an illustration, we graph the function $f(x) = -16x^2 + 50x + 5$. (NOTE: The negative sign preceding the 16 *must* be entered using the negative key, $\boxed{(-)}$, on the TI-81. The $\boxed{-}$ key, without the parentheses, is used as minus for subtraction, but *not* for a negative.) The graph is obtained by (i) entering the function $f(x)$ using $\boxed{Y=}$, and (ii) pressing $\boxed{ZOOM}$ 6 to show the graph on the standard viewing rectangle [Figure C.19(a)].

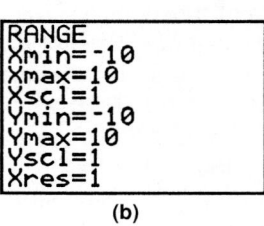

(a)

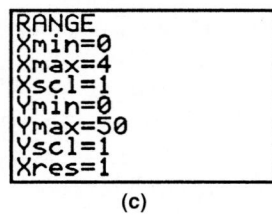

(b)

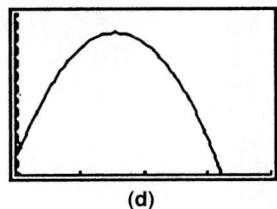

(c)

(d)

FIGURE C.19

The graph appears to be two lines that are almost vertical. However, if we change the $\boxed{RANGE}$ from the standard setting obtained when the calculator is reset [Figure C.19(b)] using different parameters as shown in Figure C.19(c), a different portion of the graph appears [Figure C.19(d)]. Appropriate parameters for the viewing rectangle are often dictated by the problem being solved. These parameters may be estimated by mentally substituting numbers into the function to determine reasonable scales for the x- and y-axes. However, there may be situations that take several changes in the range before arriving at an acceptable form of the graph. Sometimes the $\boxed{ZOOM}$ key is used to bring graphs into "focus."

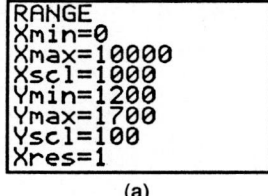

(a)

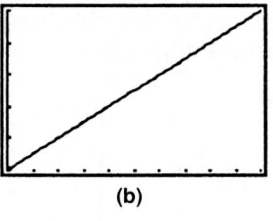

(b)

FIGURE C.20

EXAMPLE C.27 Graph the function $f(x) = 1200 + (0.05)x$ (which appears in Example 9.16).

Solution
From the context of the problem it is reasonable to assume that the salesperson's sales could vary from 0 up to at least \$10,000. Thus x can be set to vary from 0 to 10,000 (with increments of 1000). Consequently, $f(x)$ should vary from $f(0) = 1200 + (0.05)0 = 1200$ to $f(10,000) = 1200 + (0.05)10,000 = 1700$ (with increments of 100). Thus we set the $\boxed{\text{RANGE}}$ to reflect these parameters [Figure C.20(a)]. Next we enter $f(x)$ in $\boxed{\text{Y} =}$ and press $\boxed{\text{GRAPH}}$ [Figure C.20(b)]. Although not labeled on the calculator's display, the scale marks on the x-axis begin at 0 and end at 10,000, and the marks on the y-axis begin at 1200 and end at 1700. ∎

If a function is given by a formula such as $f(x) = -16x^2 + 50x + 5$, various values of $f(x)$ can be found by substituting for x in the formula for $f(x)$. On the other hand, if a value is given for $f(x)$, finding the corresponding value for x was not an easy task in the past. Some more advanced calculators and sophisticated computer software can now be used to find a value for x in many cases. Also a graphics calculator can be used to find good estimates of such values, as shown next.

EXAMPLE C.28 Find a value for x where the function $h(x) = -3(x + 5)^2 + 7$ attains its maximum value.

Solution
Figure C.21(a) shows the graph of the function h on a standard display. To determine where the function assumes its maximum, press $\boxed{\text{TRACE}}$. Notice that the $\boxed{\text{TRACE}}$ feature begins where the value of x is as close to zero as possible. The display shows values for x and y. Pressing the $\boxed{\blacktriangleleft}$ key several times brings the flashing square cursor to the lower right-hand part of the curve [Figure C.21(b)]. Using the $\boxed{\blacktriangleleft}$ key, move the cursor to the topmost point of the graph to see that when $x = -4.947368$, the value of y is 6.9916898. This is the best estimate the calculator can make here due to the limitation of the resolution of the current display. The *exact* maximum value for the function $h(x) = -3(x + 5)^2 + 7$ is 7 when $x = -5$. [To see this, observe that $-3(x + 5)^2$ is never positive, so its greatest value would be when $-3(x + 5)^2 = 0$ or when $x = -5$.] ∎

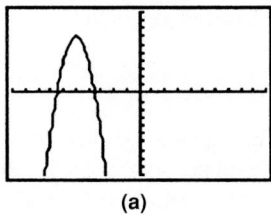

(a)

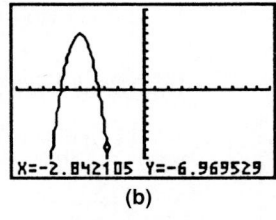

(b)

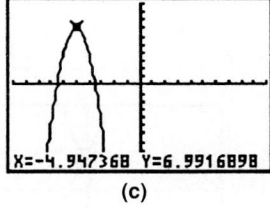

(c)

FIGURE C.21

The technique shown in Example C.28 is a powerful tool for solving problems. In particular, using $\boxed{\text{TRACE}}$ can be used to solve problems such as Problem 16 in Exercise/Problem Set 9.3—Part A.

The next example shows the graphs of two other functions studied in Section 9.3.

EXAMPLE C.29   Graph the following functions:
(a) $f(x) = 2^x$ **(b)** $g(x) = x(20 - 2x)^2$.

Solution

(a) Observe that for $x < 0$, 2^x is greater than zero. Also, for $x > 0$, 2^x increases rapidly as x increases. Figure C.22(a) shows this function graphed on a standard display. We can improve this graph by changing the range to Ymin $= -5$ and Ymax $= 20$ [Figure C.22(b)].

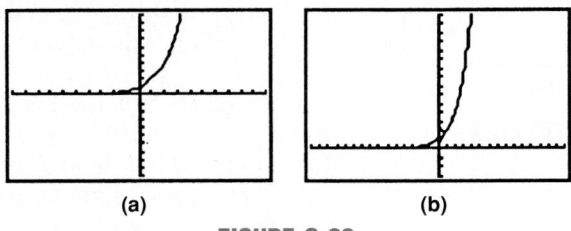

(a)   (b)

FIGURE C.22

(b) Next we graph $g(x) = x(20 - 2x)^2$ on a standard display [Figure C.23(a)].

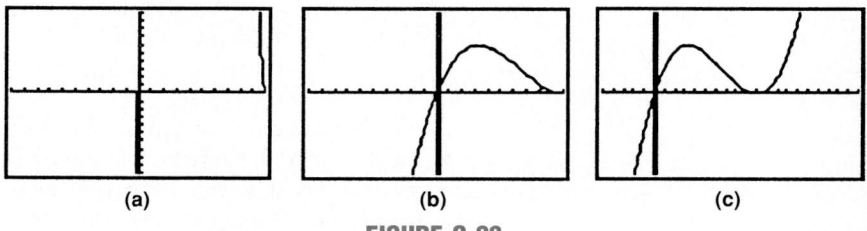

(a)   (b)   (c)

FIGURE C.23

This graph is not very informative. Since $g(0) = 0$, $g(1) = 18^2 = 324$, and $g(-1) = -22^2 = -484$, the range needs to be set to allow for numbers on the y-axis that are greater than 324 and less than -484. Figure C.23(b) shows the graph for Ymin $= -1000$ and Ymax $= 1000$. Although this scaling provides more information about the shape of the graph for the vertical scale, setting Xmin $= -5$ and Xmax $= 20$ gives an even clearer picture [Figure C.23(c)]. This example illustrates once more how adjusting the display's range for x and y to find an appropriate viewing rectangle is critical.   ◼

Solving Simultaneous Equations Graphically

In Section 15.2 the pair of simultaneous equations (i) $y = 4x + 2$ and (ii) $y = -3x + 5$ is solved algebraically. Now we solve them using a graphics calculator by entering the two functions :Y1 $= 4x + 2$ and :Y2 $= -3x + 5$ and then graphing them in the same viewing rectangle [Figure C.24]. Their simultaneous solution is the point where the two lines intersect. By using $\boxed{\text{TRACE}}$ on this display, it is difficult to see when the cursor is at the point of intersection. The $\boxed{\text{ZOOM}}$ key can be used to clarify this

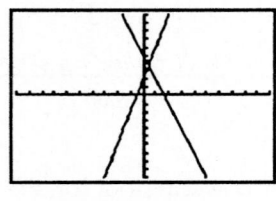

FIGURE C.24

situation. Here we will zoom in on a small box surrounding the point of intersection so that the trace key can be used effectively. The following steps show how to use the $\boxed{\text{ZOOM}}$ [BOX] function.

1. Press $\boxed{\text{ZOOM}}$ 1 [Figure C.25(a)].

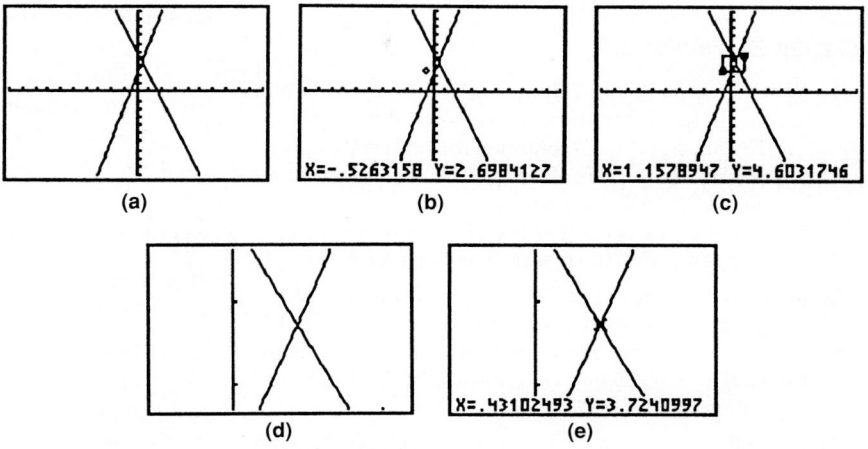

FIGURE C.25

2. Use the arrow keys to move the blinking cursor to one corner of a small rectangular box that will surround the point and press $\boxed{\text{ENTER}}$. Figure C.25(b) shows the lower left-hand corner of one such box.
3. Move the cursor to the diagonally opposite corner of the rectangular box. Figure C.25(c) shows a box formed in this manner.
4. Press $\boxed{\text{ENTER}}$ Figure C.25(d) shows how the interior of the box in Figure C.25(c) is expanded to the entire display.
5. Use the $\boxed{\text{TRACE}}$ key to estimate the coordinates of the intersection point [Figure C.25(e)].

Figure C.25(e) estimates that $x = 0.4302493$ and $y = 3.7240997$.

The exact coordinates are $x = \frac{3}{7} \approx .429$ and $y = 3\frac{5}{7} \approx 3.714$. A closer estimate may be obtained by applying $\boxed{\text{ZOOM}}$ [BOX] and $\boxed{\text{TRACE}}$ to the graph in Figure C.25(d) once again.

The purpose of this section has been to provide you with an introduction to a graphics calculator. These calculators are very sophisticated, yet relatively easy to use. Hopefully, your curiosity will lead you to discover how such a calculator can be used to solve many other types of problems in this book. The techniques illustrated in this section should be applied to solving exercises and problems throughout this book, especially in Sections 2.3, 9.3, and 15.2.

EXERCISE/PROBLEM SET C.4

The following exercises and problems, which can be solved using a graphics calculator, are correlated to sections in the book.

Chapter 2—Section 2.3

1. (a) Find the 101st, 202nd, 303rd, . . . , 909th terms for the arithmetic sequence that begins 1, 18, 35, 52, . . . by entering the appropriate function in $\boxed{Y=}$ and evaluating it for each of the numbers 101, 202, and so on.
   (b) Think of a way to find the other nine terms mentally, after the 101st term has been found.

2. (a) Find the 7th, 11th, 15th, and 17th terms of the geometric sequence that begins 7, 24.5, 85.75, ... Show as many digits as your display allows.
   (b) Find a second way to find the four terms in (a) without using the $\boxed{\text{Y-VARS}}$ key.

3. Evaluate the following functions. List all the digits on your display.
   (a) $f(x) = x^7 + 3x^6 - 1$ for $x = 2.7$
   (b) $g(x) = 3.71^{x-2}$ for $x = 9.1$
   (c) $h(x) = (x + 3)^2(x - 2)(x + 1)^3$ for $x = 1.9$
   (d) $k(x) = \dfrac{x^2 + 2x + 3}{2x - 7}$ for $x = \pi$

Chapter 9—Section 9.3

4. Graph the following functions on the standard viewing rectangle.
   (a) $f(x) = 3x^2 + 2x - 1$ (b) $h(x) = x^3 + 5x + \pi$
   (c) $k(x) = 5x^{0.2}$ (d) $m(x) = x^2 + x^3 + 2^x$

5. A **zero of a function** is a value at which the function takes on the value zero. Graphically, this is a point where the y-coordinate is zero, or where the graph crosses the x-axis. Using the $\boxed{\text{TRACE}}$ key, estimate the zeros of the following functions.   NOTE: Use $\boxed{\text{ZOOM}}$ [Box] feature here at least once.
   (a) $f(x) = x^3 + 2x^2 + 3x - 1$
   (b) $f(x) = 3^{0.5x} - 7$

6. The graph of the function $f(x) = x^2$ is a parabola.
   (a) Graph $f(x) = x^2$ on a standard viewing rectangle.
      NOTE: Since this graph is symmetric with respect to the y-axis, the y-axis is its axis of symmetry.
   (b) Graph $f(x) = (x + 3)^2$ on the standard viewing rectangle. Which point on the x-axis does its axis of symmetry contain?
   (c) Graph $f(x) = (x - 7)^2$ on the standard viewing rectangle. Which point on the x-axis does its axis of symmetry contain?

(d) State a generalization regarding the axis of symmetry of a parabola of the form $f(x) = (x + a)^2$.

7. (a) Graph $h(x) = \sqrt{x}$ on the standard viewing rectangle.
   (b) What is the domain of this function? The range?
   (c) Enter $g(x) = -\sqrt{x}$ as a *second* function (namely, enter $-\sqrt{x}$ as Y2 in the $\boxed{Y=}$ menu). Press $\boxed{\text{ZOOM}}$ 6 to graph $h(x)$ and $g(x)$ simultaneously on the standard viewing rectangle. Does this graph have an axis of symmetry? If so, describe it.
   (d) Is the graph in part (c) the graph of a function? Explain.

Chapter 10—Section 10.1

8. A histogram or a bar graph may be drawn on a T1-81 using the STAT feature as follows:

   1. Press $\boxed{\text{2nd}}$ <STAT> $\boxed{\blacktriangleright}$ $\boxed{\blacktriangleright}$ <Edit>. Then input your data followed by its frequency where x1 represents a piece of data and y1 its frequency.
   2. Use the $\boxed{\text{RANGE}}$ to enter values for x1 that will include the smallest value and greatest values for x and the smallest and greatest for their frequency.
   3. Graph the histogram using $\boxed{\text{2nd}}$ <STAT> ($\blacktriangleright$) <HIST> $\boxed{\text{ENTER}}$. For example, to create a graph for the data 9, 9, 9, 11, 17, 17, 17, 17, we enter x1 as 9, y1 as 3, x2 as 11, y2 as 1, x3 as 17, and y3 as 4. For the range, x varies from 0 to 18 and y for 0 to 4. The graph appears next.

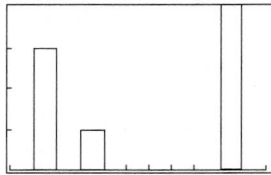

   (a) Graph the histogram for the following data: 1, 1, 1, 1, 2, 2, 3, 3, 3, 4, 4, 4, 4, 5, 5, 5, 5, 5, 5.
   (b) Prepare a histogram for Class 1 in Table 10.5 using intervals 0–9, 10–19, 20–29, 30–39, and 40–49 for the horizontal axis as in Figure 10.2.

Chapter 15—Section 15.2

9. Solve the following pairs of equations graphically using the $\boxed{\text{TRACE}}$ feature. Use the $\boxed{\text{ZOOM}}$ [Box] feature at least once when finding your estimate.
   (a) $\sqrt{2}\,x + \pi y = 7$ (b) $y = x^2 + 3$
      $-5x - \sqrt{3}\,y = 1$ $3x = 2y - 7$

10. Determine the possible number of simultaneous solutions for a pair of equations representing (i) a line and (ii) a parabola. Then find pairs of equations for each case you cited. Check by graphing.

Topic 1: Elementary Logic

Logic allows us to determine the validity of arguments, in and out of mathematics. The validity of an argument depends on its logical form and not on the particular meaning of the terms it contains. For example, the argument, "All Xs are Ys; all Ys are Zs; therefore all Xs are Zs" is valid no matter what X, Y, and Z are. In this topic section we will study how logic can be used to represent arguments symbolically and to analyze arguments using tables and diagrams.

Statements

Often, ideas in mathematics can be made clearer through the use of variables and diagrams. For example, the equation $2m + 2n = 2(m + n)$, where the variables m and n are whole numbers, can be used to show that the sum of any two arbitrary even numbers, $2m$ and $2n$ here, is the even number $2(m + n)$. Figure T1.1 shows that $(x + y)^2 = x^2 + 2xy + y^2$, where each term in the expanded product is the area of the rectangular region so designated.

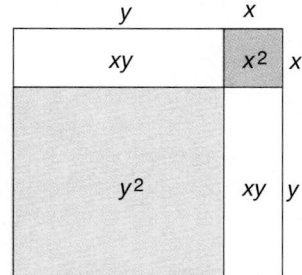

FIGURE T1.1

In a similar fashion, symbols and diagrams can be used to clarify logic. Statements are the building blocks on which logic is built. A **statement** is a declarative sentence that is true or false but not both. Examples of statements are:

1. Alaska is geographically the largest state of the United States.   (True)
2. Texas is the largest state of the United States in population.   (False)
3. $2 + 3 = 5$.   (True)
4. $3 < 0$.   (False)

The following are not statements.

1. Oregon is the best state.   (Subjective)
2. Help!   (An exclamation)
3. Where were you?   (A question)
4. The rain in Spain.   (Not a sentence)
5. This sentence is false.   (Neither true nor false!)

Statements are usually represented symbolically by lowercase letters (e.g., p, q, r, and s).

New statements can be created from existing statements in several ways. For example, if p represents the statement "The sun is shining," then the **negation** of p, written $\sim p$ and read "not p," is the statement "The sun is not shining." When a statement is true, its negation is false and when a statement is false, its negation is true; that is, a statement and its negation have opposite truth values. This relationship between a statement and its negation is summarized using a **truth table**:

p	$\sim p$
T	F
F	T

This table shows that when the statement p is T, then $\sim p$ is F and when p is F, $\sim p$ is T.

Logical Connectives

Two or more statements can be joined, or connected, to form **compound statements**. The four commonly used **logical connectives** "and," "or," "if-then," and "if and only if" are studied next.

And

If p is the statement "It is raining" and q is the statement "The sun is shining," then the **conjunction** of p and q is the statement "It is raining and the sun is shining" or, symbolically, "$p \wedge q$." The conjunction of two statements p and q is true exactly when both p and q are true. This is displayed in the next truth table.

p	q	$p \wedge q$
T	T	T
T	F	F
F	T	F
F	F	F

Notice that the two statements p and q each have two possible truth values, T and F. Hence there are four possible combinations of T and F to consider.

Or

The **disjunction** of statements p and q is the statement "p or q," symbolically, "$p \vee q$." In practice, there are two common uses of "or": the exclusive "or" and the inclusive "or." The statement "I will go or I will not go" is an example of the use of the **exclusive "or,"** since either "I will go" is true or "I will not go" is true, but both cannot be true at the same time. The **inclusive "or"** (called "and/or" in everyday language) allows for the situation in which both parts are true. For example, the statement "It will rain or the sun will shine" uses the inclusive "or"; it is true if (1) it rains, (2) the sun shines, or (3) it rains and the sun shines. That is, the inclusive "or" in $p \vee q$

allows for both p and q to be true. In mathematics, we agree to use the inclusive "or" whose truth values are summarized in the next truth table.

p	q	$p \lor q$
T	T	T
T	F	T
F	T	T
F	F	F

EXAMPLE T1.1   Determine if the following statements are true or false, where p represents "Rain is wet" and q represents "Black is white."
(a) $\sim p$ **(b)** $p \land q$ **(c)** $(\sim p) \lor q$
(d) $p \land (\sim q)$ **(e)** $\sim(p \land q)$ **(f)** $\sim[p \lor (\sim q)]$

Solution
(a) p is T, so $\sim p$ is F.
(b) p is T and q is F, so $p \land q$ is F.
(c) $\sim p$ is F and q is F, so $(\sim p) \lor q$ is F.
(d) p is T and $\sim q$ is T, so $p \land (\sim q)$ is T.
(e) p is T and q is F, so $p \land q$ is F and $\sim(p \land q)$ is T.
(f) p is T and $\sim q$ is T, so $p \lor (\sim q)$ is T and $\sim[p \lor (\sim q)]$ is F.   ■

If-Then
   One of the most important compound statements is the implication. The statement "If p, then q," denoted by "$p \to q$," is called an **implication** or **conditional** statement; p is called the **hypothesis** and q is called the **conclusion**. To determine the truth table for $p \to q$, consider the following conditional promise given to a math class: "If you average at least 90% on all tests, then you will earn an A." Let p represent "Your score is at least 90% on all tests" and q represent "You earn an A." Then there are four possibilities:

Average at Least 90%	Earn an A	Promise Kept
Yes	Yes	Yes
Yes	No	No
No	Yes	Yes
No	No	Yes

Notice that the only way the promise can be broken is in line 2. In lines 3 and 4, the promise is not broken since an average of at least 90% was not attained. (In these cases, a student may still earn an A—it does not affect the promise either way.) This example suggests the following truth table for the conditional.

p	q	$p \to q$
T	T	T
T	F	F
F	T	T
F	F	T

One can observe that the truth values for $p \wedge q$ and $q \wedge p$ are always the same. Also, the truth tables for $p \vee q$ and $q \vee p$ are identical. However, it is not the case that the truth tables of $p \rightarrow q$ and $q \rightarrow p$ are identical. Consider this example: Let p be "You live in New York City" and q be "You live in New York State." Then $p \rightarrow q$ is true, whereas "$q \rightarrow p$" is not true since you may live in Albany, for example. The conditional $q \rightarrow p$ is called the converse of $p \rightarrow q$. As the example shows, a conditional may be true, whereas its converse may be false. On the other hand, a conditional and its converse may both be true. There are two other variants of a conditional that occur in mathematics, the contrapositive and the inverse.

Given conditional: $p \rightarrow q$

The **converse** of $p \rightarrow q$ is $q \rightarrow p$.

The **inverse** of $p \rightarrow q$ is $(\sim p) \rightarrow (\sim q)$.

The **contrapositive** of $p \rightarrow q$ is $(\sim q) \rightarrow (\sim p)$.

The following truth table displays the various truth values for these four conditionals.

p	q	$\sim p$	$\sim q$	Conditional $p \rightarrow q$	Contrapositive $\sim q \rightarrow \sim p$	Converse $q \rightarrow p$	Inverse $\sim p \rightarrow \sim q$
T	T	F	F	T	T	T	T
T	F	F	T	F	F	T	T
F	T	T	F	T	T	F	F
F	F	T	T	T	T	T	T

Notice that the columns of truth values under the conditional $p \rightarrow q$ and its contrapositive are the same. When this is the case, we say that the two statements are logically equivalent. In general, two statements are **logically equivalent** when they have the same truth tables. Similarly, the converse of $p \rightarrow q$ and the inverse of $p \rightarrow q$ have the same truth table, hence they, too, are logically equivalent. In mathematics, replacing a conditional with a logically equivalent conditional often facilitates the solution of a problem.

EXAMPLE T1.2   Prove that if x^2 is odd, then x is odd.

Solution
Rather than trying to prove that the given conditional is true, consider its logically equivalent contrapositive: If x is not odd (i.e., x is even), then x^2 is not odd (i.e., x^2 is even). Even numbers are of the form $2m$, where m is a whole number. Thus the square of $2m$, $(2m)^2 = 4m^2 = 2(2m^2)$, is also an even number since it is of the form $2n$, where $n = 2m^2$. Thus if x is even, then x^2 is even. Therefore, the contrapositive of this conditional, our original problem, is also true.   ∎

If and Only If

The connective "p if and only if q," called a **biconditional** and written $p \leftrightarrow q$, is the conjunction of $p \rightarrow q$ and its converse $q \rightarrow p$. That is, $p \leftrightarrow q$ is logically equivalent to $(p \rightarrow q) \wedge (q \rightarrow p)$. The truth table of $p \leftrightarrow q$ follows.

p	q	$p \rightarrow q$	$q \rightarrow p$	$(p \rightarrow q) \wedge (q \rightarrow p)$	$p \leftrightarrow q$
T	T	T	T	T	T
T	F	F	T	F	F
F	T	T	F	F	F
F	F	T	T	T	T

Notice that the biconditional $p \leftrightarrow q$ is true when p and q have the same truth values and false otherwise.

Often in mathematics the words "necessary" and "sufficient" are used to describe conditionals and biconditionals. For example, the statement "Water is necessary for the formation of ice" means "If there is ice, then there is water." Similarly, the statement "A rectangle with two adjacent sides the same length is a sufficient condition to determine a square" means "If a rectangle has two adjacent sides the same length, then it is a square." Symbolically we have the following:

$p \rightarrow q$ means q **is necessary for** p

$p \rightarrow q$ means p **is sufficient for** q

$p \leftrightarrow q$ means p **is necessary and sufficient for** q

Arguments

Deductive or **direct reasoning** is a process of reaching a conclusion from one (or more) statements, called the hypothesis (or hypotheses). This somewhat informal definition can be rephrased using the language and symbolism in the preceding section. An **argument** is a set of statements where one of the statements is called the conclusion and the rest comprise the hypothesis. A **valid argument** is an argument in which the conclusion must be true whenever the hypothesis is true. In the case of a valid argument we say that the conclusion *follows from* the hypothesis. For example, consider the following argument: "If it is snowing, then it is cold. It is snowing. Therefore, it is cold." In this argument, when the two statements in the hypothesis, namely "If it is snowing, then it is cold" and "It is snowing" are both true, then one can conclude that "It is cold." That is, this argument is valid since the conclusion follows from the hypothesis.

An argument is said to be an **invalid argument** if its conclusion can be false when its hypothesis is true. An example of an invalid argument is the following: "If it is raining, then the streets are wet. The streets are wet. Therefore, it is raining." For convenience, we will represent this argument symbolically as $[(p \rightarrow q) \wedge q] \rightarrow p$. This is an invalid argument, since the streets could be wet from a variety of causes (e.g., a street cleaner, an open fire hydrant, etc.) without having had any rain. In this example, $p \rightarrow q$ is true and q may be true, while p is false. The next truth table also shows that this argument is invalid, since it is possible to have the hypothesis $[(p \rightarrow q) \wedge q]$ true with the conclusion p false.

p	q	$p \rightarrow q$	$(p \rightarrow q) \wedge q$
T	T	T	T
T	F	F	F
F	T	T	**T**
F	F	T	F

The argument with hypothesis $[(p \rightarrow q) \wedge \sim p]$ and conclusion $\sim q$ is another example of a common invalid argument form, since when p is F and q is T, $[(p \rightarrow q) \wedge \sim p]$ is T and $\sim q$ is F.

There are three important valid argument forms that are used repeatedly in logic. These are discussed next.

1. Modus Ponens: $[(p \rightarrow q) \wedge p] \rightarrow q$

In words modus ponens, which is also called the **law of detachment**, says that whenever a conditional statement and its hypothesis are true, the conclusion is also true. That is, the conclusion can be "detached" from the conditional. An example of the use of this law follows.

If a number ends in zero, then it is a multiple of 10.

Forty is a number that ends in zero.

Therefore, 40 is a multiple of 10.

(NOTE: Strictly speaking, the sentence "a number ends in zero" is an "open" sentence since no particular number is specified; hence the sentence is neither true nor false as given. The sentence "Forty is a number that ends in zero" is a true statement. Since the use of open sentences is prevalent throughout mathematics, we will permit such "open" sentences in conditional statements without pursuing an in-depth study of such sentences.)

The following truth table verifies that the law of detachment is a valid argument form.

p	q	$p \rightarrow q$	$(p \rightarrow q) \wedge p$
T	**T**	T	**T**
T	F	F	F
F	T	T	F
F	F	T	F

Notice that in line 1 in the preceding truth table, when the hypothesis $(p \rightarrow q) \wedge p$ is true, the conclusion, q, is also true. This law of detachment is used in *everyday* language and thought.

Diagrams can also be used to determine the validity of arguments. Consider the following argument.

All mathematicians are logical.

Pólya is a mathematician.

Therefore, Pólya is logical.

This argument can be pictured using an **Euler diagram** (Figure T1.2). The "mathematician" circle within the "logical people" circle represents the statement "All mathematicians are logical." The point labeled "Pólya" in the

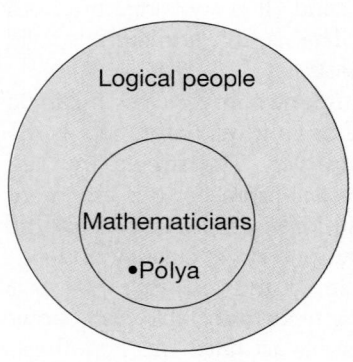

FIGURE T1.2

"mathematician" circle represents "Pólya is a mathematician." Since the "Pólya" point is within the "logical people" circle, we conclude that "Pólya is logical."

The second common valid argument form follows.

2. **Hypothetical Syllogism:** $[(p \to q) \land (q \to r)] \to (p \to r)$

   The following argument is an application of this law:

   If a number is a multiple of eight, then it is a multiple of four.

   If a number is a multiple of four, then it is a multiple of two.

   Therefore, if a number is a multiple of eight, it is a multiple of two.

Hypothetical syllogism, also called the **chain rule**, can be verified using an Euler diagram (Figure T1.3). The circle within the "multiples of 4" circle represents the "multiples of 8" circle. Then the "multiples of 4" circle is within the "multiples of 2" circle. Thus, from the diagram, it must follow that "If a number is a multiple of 8, then it is a multiple of 2" since all the multiples of 8 are within the "multiples of 2" circle.

The following truth table also proves the validity of hypothetical syllogism.

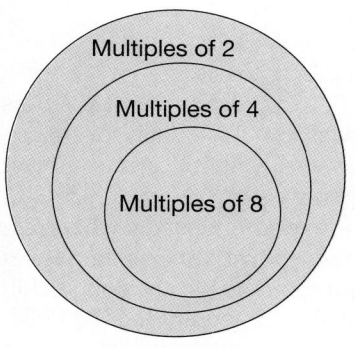

FIGURE T1.3

p	q	r	$p \to q$	$q \to r$	$p \to r$	$(p \to q) \land (q \to r)$
T	T	T	T	T	**T**	**T**
T	T	F	T	F	F	F
T	F	T	F	T	T	F
T	F	F	F	T	F	F
F	T	T	T	T	**T**	**T**
F	T	F	T	F	T	F
F	F	T	T	T	**T**	**T**
F	F	F	T	T	**T**	**T**

Observe that in rows 1 and 5 the hypothesis $(p \to q) \land (q \to r)$ is true. In both of these cases, the conclusion, $p \to r$, is also true; thus the argument is valid.

The final valid argument we study here is used often in mathematical reasoning.

3. **Modus Tollens:** $[(p \to q) \land \sim q] \to \sim p$

   Consider the following argument.

   If a number is a power of 3, then it ends in a 9, 7, 1, or 3.

   The number 3124 does not end in a 9, 7, 1, or 3.

   Therefore, 3124 is not a power of 3.

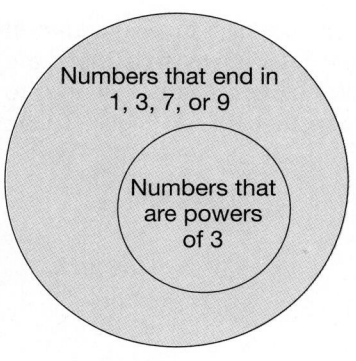

FIGURE T1.4

This argument is an application of modus tollens. Figure T1.4 illustrates this argument. All points outside the larger circle represent numbers not ending in 1, 3, 7, or 9. Clearly, any point outside the larger circle must be outside the smaller circle. Thus, since 3124 is outside the "powers of 3" circle, it is not a power of 3. In words, modus tollens says that whenever a conditional is true and its conclusion is false, the hypothesis is also false.

The next truth table provides a verification of the validity of this argument form.

p	q	$p \to q$	$(p \to q) \wedge \sim q$	$\sim p$
T	T	T	F	F
T	F	F	F	F
F	T	T	F	T
F	F	T	**T**	**T**

Notice that row 4 is the only instance when the hypothesis $(p \to q) \wedge \sim q$ is true. In this case, the conclusion of $[(p \to q) \wedge (\sim q)] \to \sim p$, namely $\sim p$, is also true. Hence the argument is valid. Notice how the validity of modus tollens also can be shown using modus ponens with a contrapositive: $[(p \to q) \wedge \sim q] \leftrightarrow [(\sim q \to \sim p) \wedge \sim q]$ and $[(\sim q \to \sim p) \wedge \sim q] \to \sim p$.

All three of these valid argument forms are used repeatedly when reasoning, especially in mathematics. The first two should seem quite natural since we are schooled in them informally from the time we are young children. For example, a parent might say to a child: "If you are a good child, then you will receive presents." Needless to say, every little child who wants presents learns to be good. This, of course, is an application of the law of detachment.

Similarly, consider the following statements:

If you are a good child, then you will get a new bicycle.

If you get a new bicycle, then you will have fun.

The conclusion children arrive at is "If I am good, then I will have fun," an application of the law of syllogism.

The three argument forms we have been studying can also be applied to statements that are modified by "quantifiers," that is, words such as "all," "some," "every," or their equivalents. Here, again, Euler diagrams can be used to determine the validity or invalidity of various arguments. Consider the following argument.

All logicians are mathematicians.

Some philosophers are not mathematicians.

Therefore, some philosophers are not logicians.

The first line of this argument is represented by the Euler diagram in Figure T1.5. However, since the second line guarantees that there are "some" philosophers outside the "mathematician" circle, a dot is used to represent at least one philosopher who is *not* a mathematician (Figure T1.6).

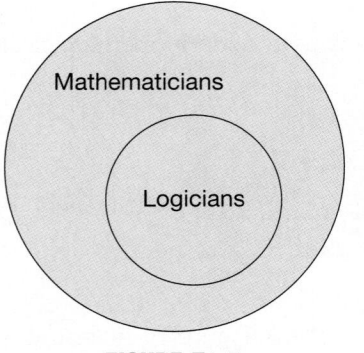

FIGURE T1.5

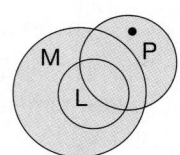

FIGURE T1.6

Observe that, due to the dot, there is always a philosopher who is not a logician; hence the argument is valid. (Note that the word "some" means "at least one.")

Next consider the argument:

All rock stars have green hair.

No presidents of banks are rock stars.

Therefore, no presidents of banks have green hair.

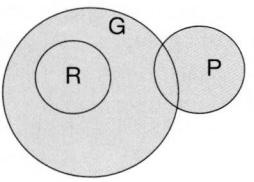

FIGURE T1.7

An Euler diagram that represents this argument is shown in Figure T1.7, where G represents all people with green hair, R represents all rock stars, and P represents all bank presidents. Note that Figure T1.7 allows for presidents of banks to have green hair, since the circles G and P may have an element in common. Thus the argument, as stated, is invalid since the hypothesis can be true while the conclusion is false. The validity or invalidity of the arguments given in the problem set can be determined in this way using Euler diagrams. Be sure to consider *all* possible relationships among the sets before drawing any conclusions.

EXERCISE/PROBLEM SET T1—PART A

Exercises

1. Determine which of the following are statements.
   (a) What's your name?
   (b) The rain in Spain falls mainly in the plain.
   (c) Happy New Year!
   (d) Five is an odd number.

2. Write the following in symbolic form using p, q, r, $\sim$, $\wedge$, $\vee$, $\rightarrow$, $\leftrightarrow$, where p, q, and r represent the following statements:

   p: The sun is shining.
   q: It is raining.
   r: The grass is green.

   (a) If it is raining, then the sun is not shining.
   (b) It is raining and the grass is green.
   (c) The grass is green if and only if it is raining and the sun is shining.
   (d) Either the sun is shining or it is raining.

3. If p is T, q is F, and r is T, find the truth values for the following:
   (a) $p \wedge \sim q$
   (b) $\sim(p \vee q)$
   (c) $(\sim p) \rightarrow r$
   (d) $(\sim p \wedge r) \leftrightarrow q$
   (e) $(\sim q \wedge p) \vee r$
   (f) $p \vee (q \leftrightarrow r)$
   (g) $(r \wedge \sim p) \vee (r \wedge \sim q)$
   (h) $(p \wedge q) \rightarrow (q \vee \sim r)$

4. Write the converse, inverse, and contrapositive for each of the following statements.
   (a) If I teach third grade, then I am an elementary school teacher.
   (b) If a number has a factor of 4, then it has a factor of 2.

5. Construct one truth table that contains truth values for all of the following statements and determine which are logically equivalent.
   (a) $(\sim p) \vee (\sim q)$
   (b) $(\sim p) \vee q$
   (c) $(\sim p) \wedge (\sim q)$
   (d) $p \rightarrow q$
   (e) $\sim(p \wedge q)$
   (f) $\sim(p \vee q)$

Problems

6. Determine the validity of the following arguments.
   (a) All professors are handsome.
       Some professors are tall.
       Therefore, some handsome people are tall.
   (b) If I can't go to the movie, then I'll go to the park.
       I can go to the movie.
       Therefore, I will not go to the park.
   (c) If you score at least 90%, then you'll earn an A.
       If you earn an A, then your parents will be proud.
       You have proud parents.
       Therefore, you scored at least 90%.

(d) Some arps are bomps.
All bomps are cirts.
Therefore, some arps are cirts.

(e) All equilateral triangles are equiangular.
All equiangular triangles are isoceles.
Therefore, all isosceles triangles are equilateral.

(f) If you work hard, then you will succeed.
You do not work hard.
Therefore, you will not succeed.

(g) Some girls are teachers.
All teachers are college graduates.
Therefore, all girls are college graduates.

(h) If it doesn't rain, then the street won't be wet.
The street is wet.
Therefore, it rained.

7. Determine a valid conclusion that follows from each of the following statements and explain your reasoning.
(a) If you study hard, then you will be popular. You will study hard.
(b) If Scott is quick, then he is a basketball star. Scott is not a basketball star.
(c) All friends are respectful.
All respectful people are trustworthy.
(d) Every square is a rectangle.
Some parallelograms are rhombuses.
Every rectangle is a parallelogram.

8. Which of the laws (modus ponens, hypothetical syllogism, or modus tollens) is being used in each of the following arguments?

(a) If Joe is a professor, then he is learned. If you are learned, then you went to college. Joe is a professor, so he went to college.
(b) All women are smart. Helen of Troy was a woman. So Helen of Troy was smart.
(c) If you have children, then you are an adult. Bob is not an adult, so he has no children.
(d) If today is Tuesday, then tomorrow is Wednesday. Tomorrow is Saturday, so today is not Tuesday.
(e) If I am broke, I will ride the bus. When I ride the bus, I am always late. I'm broke, so I am going to be late.

9. Decide the truth value of each proposition.
(a) Alexander Hamilton was once president of the United States.
(b) The world is flat.
(c) If dogs are cats, then the sky is blue.
(d) If Tuesday follows Monday, then the sun is hot.
(e) If Christmas day is December 25, then Texas is the largest state in the United States.

10. Draw an Euler diagram to represent the following argument and decide if it is valid.

All timid creatures (T) are bunnies (B).

All timid creatures are furry (F).

Some cows (C) are furry.

Therefore, all cows are timid creatures.

EXERCISE/PROBLEM SET T1—PART B

Exercises

1. Let r, s, and t be the following statements:

r: Roses are red.

s: The sky is blue.

t: Turtles are green.

Translate the following statements into English.
(a) $r \wedge s$ (b) $r \wedge (s \vee t)$
(c) $s \to (r \wedge t)$ (d) $(\sim t \wedge t) \to \sim r$

2. Fill in the headings of the following table using p, q, $\wedge$, $\vee$, $\sim$, and $\to$.

p	q				
T	T	T	F	T	T
T	F	F	T	F	T
F	T	T	T	F	F
F	F	T	T	F	T

3. Suppose that $p \to q$ is known to be false. Give the truth values for the following:

(a) $p \vee q$
(b) $p \wedge q$
(c) $q \to p$
(d) $\sim q \to p$

4. Prove that the conditional $p \to q$ is logically equivalent to $\sim p \vee q$.

5. State the hypothesis (or hypotheses) and conclusion for each of the following arguments.
(a) All football players are introverts. Tony is a football player, so Tony is an introvert.
(b) Bob is taller than Jim, and Jim is taller than Sue. So Bob is taller than Sue.
(c) All penguins are elegant swimmers. No elegant swimmers fly, so penguins don't fly.

6. Use a truth table to determine which of the following are always true.
   (a) $(p \to q) \to (q \to p)$ **(b)** $\sim p \to p$
   (c) $[p \land (p \to q)] \to q$ **(d)** $(p \lor q) \to (p \land q)$
   (e) $(p \land q) \to p$

7. Using each pair of statements, determine whether (i) p is necessary for q; (ii) p is sufficient for q; (iii) p is necessary and sufficient for q.

   (a) p: Bob has some water. q: Bob has some ice, composed of water.

   (b) p: It is snowing. q: It is cold.

   (c) p: It is December. q: 31 days from today it is January.

Problems

8. If possible, determine the truth value of each statement. Assume that a and b are true, p and q are false, and x and y have unknown truth values. If a value can't be determined, write "unknown."
   (a) $p \to (a \lor b)$ **(b)** $b \to (p \lor a)$
   (c) $x \to p$ **(d)** $a \lor p$
   (e) $b \land q$ **(f)** $b \to x$
   (g) $a \land (b \lor x)$ **(h)** $(y \lor x) \to a$
   (i) $(y \land b) \to p$ **(j)** $(a \lor x) \to (b \land q)$
   (k) $x \to a$ **(l)** $x \lor p$
   (m) $\sim x \to x$ **(n)** $x \lor (\sim x)$
   (o) $\sim(y \land (\sim y))$

9. Rewrite each argument in symbolic form, then check the validity of the argument.
   (a) If today is Wednesday (w), then yesterday was Tuesday (t). Yesterday was Tuesday, so today is Wednesday.

(b) The plane is late (l) if it snows (s). It is not snowing. Therefore, the plane is not late.
(c) If I do not study (s), then I will eat (e). I will not eat if I am worried (w). Hence, if I am worried, I will study.
(d) Meg is married (m) and Sarah is single (s). If Bob has a job (j), then Meg is married. Hence Bob has a job.

10. Use the following Euler diagram to determine which of the following statements are true. (Assume that there is at least one person in every region within the circles.)

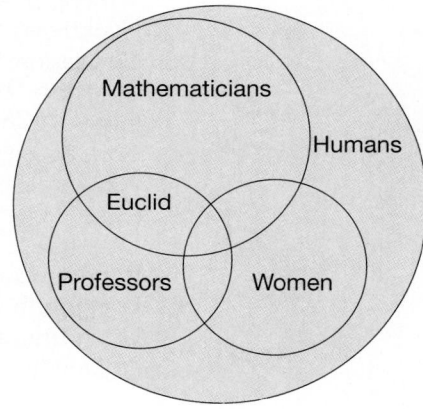

   (a) All women are mathematicians.
   (b) Euclid was a woman.
   (c) All mathematicians are men.
   (d) All professors are humans.
   (e) Some professors are mathematicians.
   (f) Euclid was a mathematician and human.

TOPIC REVIEW

Major Ideas

1. Logic is used to determine if arguments are valid or invalid.

2. Statements and arguments can be represented symbolically and pictorially.

3. Valid arguments can be identified using truth tables and diagrams.

   Following is a list of key vocabulary, notation, and ideas for this topic. Mentally review these items and, where appropriate, write down the meaning of each term. Then restudy the material that you are unsure of before proceeding to take the topic test.

Vocabulary/Notation

Ideas

ELEMENTARY LOGIC TEST

Knowledge

1. True or false?
 (a) The disjunction of p and q is true whenever p is true and q is false.
 (b) If $p \rightarrow q$ is true, then $\sim p \rightarrow \sim q$ is true.
 (c) In the implication $q \rightarrow p$, the hypothesis is p.
 (d) $[(p \rightarrow q) \wedge (q \rightarrow r)] \rightarrow (p \rightarrow r)$ is the modus tollens.
 (e) "I am older than 20 or younger than 30" is an example of an exclusive "or."
 (f) A statement is a sentence that is true or false, but not both.
 (g) The converse of $p \rightarrow q$ is $\sim p \rightarrow \sim q$.
 (h) $p \rightarrow q$ means p is necessary for q.

Skill

2. Find the converse, inverse, and contrapositive of each.
 (a) $p \rightarrow \sim q$ **(b)** $\sim p \rightarrow q$ **(c)** $\sim q \rightarrow \sim p$

3. Decide the truth value of each statement.
 (a) $4 + 7 = 11$ and $1 + 5 = 6$.
 (b) $2 + 5 = 7 \leftrightarrow 4 + 2 = 8$.
 (c) $3 \cdot 5 = 12$ or $2 \cdot 6 = 11$.
 (d) If $2 + 3 = 5$, then $1 + 2 = 4$.
 (e) If $3 + 4 = 6$, then $8 \cdot 4 = 31$.
 (f) If 7 is even, then 8 is even.

4. Use Euler diagrams to check the validity of each argument.
 (a) Some men are teachers. Sam Jones is a teacher. Therefore, Sam Jones is a man.
 (b) Gold is heavy. Nothing but gold will satisfy Amy. Hence nothing that is light will satisfy Amy.
 (c) No cats are dogs. All poodles are dogs. So some poodles are not cats.
 (d) Some cows eat hay. All horses eat hay. Only cows and horses eat hay. Frank eats hay, so Frank is a horse.

(e) All chimpanzees are monkeys. All monkeys are animals. Some animals have two legs. So some chimpanzees have two legs.

5. Complete the following truth table.

p	q	p ∧ q	p ∨ q	p → q	~p	~q	~q ↔ p	~q → ~p
T				T				
	T	F						
F			F					T
			T	F				

Understanding

6. Using an Euler diagram, display an invalid argument. Explain.

7. Is it ever the case that the conjunction, disjunction, and implication of two statements are all true at the same time? All false? If so, what are the truth values of each statement? If not, explain why not.

Problem Solving/Application

8. In a certain land, every resident either always lies or always tells the truth. You happen to run into two residents, Bob and Sam. Bob says, "If I am a truth teller, then Sam is a truth teller" Is Bob a truth teller? What about Sam?

9. The binary connective ↕ is defined by the following truth table:

p	q	p ↕ q
T	T	F
T	F	T
F	T	T
F	F	T

Compose a statement using only the connective ↕ that is logically equivalent to
(a) ~p   **(b)** p ∧ q   **(c)** p ∨ q

Topic 2: Relations

Relationships between objects or numbers can be analyzed using ideas from set theory. For example, on the set {1, 2, 3, 4}, we can express the relationship "a is a divisor of b" by listing all the ordered pairs (a, b) for which the relationship is true, namely {(1, 1), (1, 2), (1, 3), (1, 4), (2, 2), (2, 4), (3, 3), (4, 4)}. In this topic section we study properties of relations.

Relations are used in mathematics to represent a relationship between two numbers or objects. For example, when we say, "3 is less than 7," "2 is a factor of 6," and "Triangle ABC is similar to triangle DEF," we are expressing relationships between pairs of numbers in the first two cases and triangles in the last case. More generally, the concept of relation can be applied to arbitrary sets. A set of ordered pairs can be used to show that certain pairs of objects are related. For example, the set {(Hawaii, 50), (Alaska, 49), (New Mexico, 48)} lists the newest three states of the United States and their number of statehood. This relation can be verbally described as "_____ was state number _____ to join the United States"; for example, "Alaska was state number 49 to join the United States."

A diagrammatic way of denoting relationships is through the use of **arrow diagrams**. For example, in Figure T2.1, each arrow can be read "_____ was the vice-president under _____" where the arrow points to the President.

When a relation can be described on a single set, an arrow diagram can be used on that set in two ways. For example, the relation "is a factor of" on the set {2, 4, 6, 8} is represented in two equivalent ways in Figure T2.2, using one set in part (a) and two copies of a set in part (b). The advantage of using two sets in an arrow diagram is that relations between *two different* sets can be pictured, as in the case of the newest states (Figure T2.3).

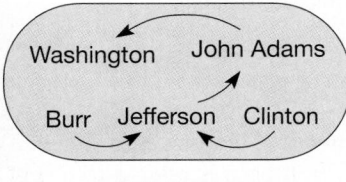

FIGURE T2.1

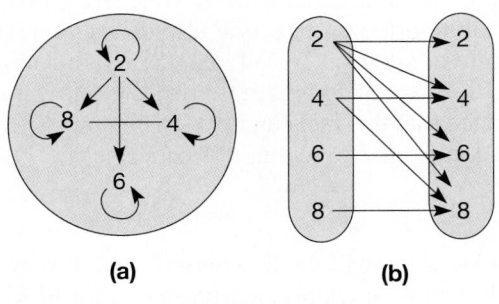

(a)　　　　**(b)**

FIGURE T2.2

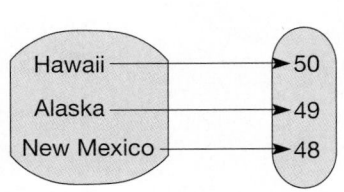

FIGURE T2.3

Formally, a **relation** R from set A to set B is a subset of $A \times B$, the Cartesian product of A and B. If $A = B$, we say that R is a relation on A. In our example about the states, set A consists of the three newest states and B consists of the numbers 48, 49, and 50. In the example above, "is a factor of," the sets A and B were the same, namely, the set {2, 4, 6, 8}. This last relation is represented by the following set of ordered pairs:

$$R = \{(2, 2), (2, 4), (2, 6), (2, 8), (4, 4), (4, 8), (6, 6), (8, 8)\}$$

Notice that R is a subset of {2, 4, 6, 8} $\times$ {2, 4, 6, 8}.

In the case of a relation R on a set A, that is, where $R \subseteq A \times A$, there are three useful properties that a relation may have.

Reflexive Property

A relation R on a set A is said to be **reflexive** if $(a, a) \in R$ for all $a \in A$. We say that R is reflexive if *every* element in A is related to itself. For example, the relation "is a factor of" on the set $A = \{2, 4, 6, 8\}$ is reflexive since every number in A is a factor of itself. In general, in an arrow diagram, a relation is reflexive if every element in A has an arrow pointing to itself (Figure T2.4).

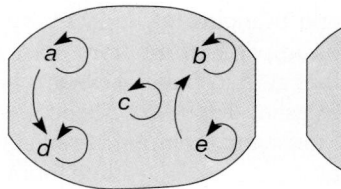 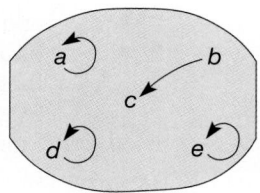

(a) Reflexive relation.   **(b)** Not reflexive (since neither b nor c is related to itself).

FIGURE T2.4

Symmetric Property

A relation R on a set A is said to be **symmetric** if whenever $(a, b) \in R$, then $(b, a) \in R$ also; in words, if a is related to b, then b is related to a. Let R be the relation "is the opposite of" on the set $A = \{1, -1, 2, -2\}$. Then $R = \{(1, -1), (-1, 1), (2, -2), (-2, 2)\}$; that is, R has all possible ordered pairs (a, b) from $A \times A$ if a is the opposite of b. The arrow diagram of this relation is shown in Figure T2.5.

Notice that for a relation to be symmetric, whenever an arrow points in one direction, it must point in the opposite direction also. Thus the relation "is the opposite of" is symmetric on the set $\{1, -1, 2, -2\}$. The relation "is a factor of" on the set {2, 4, 6, 8} is *not* symmetric, since 2 is a factor of 4, but 4 is not a factor of 2. Notice that this fact can be seen in Figure T2.2(a), since there is an arrow pointing from 2 to 4, but not conversely.

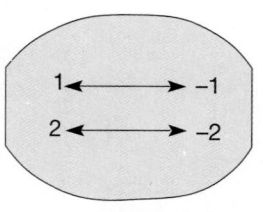

FIGURE T2.5

Transitive Property

A relation R on a set A is **transitive** if whenever $(a, b) \in R$ and $(b, c) \in R$, then $(a, c) \in R$. In words, a relation is transitive if for all a, b, c in A, if a is related to b and b is related to c, then a is related to c. Consider the relation "is a factor of" on the set {2, 4, 6, 8, 12}. Notice that 2 is a factor of 4 and 4 is a factor of 8 *and* 2 is a factor of 8. Also, 2 is a factor of 4 and 4 is a factor of 12 *and* 2 is a factor of 12. The last case to consider, involving 2, 6, and 12, is also true. Thus "is a factor of" is a transitive relation on the set {2, 4, 6, 8, 12}. In an arrow diagram, a relation is transitive if whenever there is an "*a* to *b*" arrow and a "*b* to *c*" arrow, there is also an "*a* to *c*" arrow (Figure T2.6).

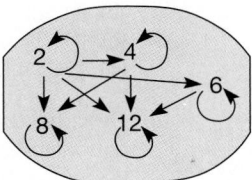 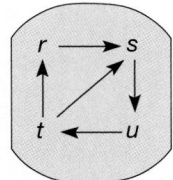

(a) Transitive relation

(b) Not a transitive relation, since $(r, s) \in R$ and $(s, u) \in R$, but $(r, u) \notin R$ (there is no arrow from r to u).

FIGURE T2.6

Now consider the relation "has the same ones digit as" on the set of numbers {1, 2, 3, . . . , 40}. Clearly, every number has the same ones digit as itself; thus this relation is reflexive; it is also symmetric and transitive. Any relation on a set that is reflexive, symmetric, and transitive is called an **equivalence relation**. Thus the relation "has the same ones digit as" is an equivalence relation on the set {1, 2, 3, . . . , 40}. There are many equivalence relations in mathematics. Some common ones are "is equal to" on any set of numbers and "is congruent to" and "is similar to" on sets of geometric shapes.

An important attribute of an equivalence relation R on a set A is that the relation imparts a subdivision, or partitioning, of the set A into a collection of nonempty, pairwise disjoint subsets (i.e., the intersection of any two subsets is $\varnothing$). For example, if the numbers that are related to each other in the preceding paragraph are collected together into sets, the relation R on the set {1, 2, 3, . . . , 40} is represented by the following set of nonempty, pairwise disjoint subsets:

$$\Big\{ \{1, 11, 21, 31\}, \{2, 12, 22, 32\}, . . . , \{10, 20, 30, 40\} \Big\}$$

That is, all of the elements having the same ones digit are grouped together.

Formally, a **partition** of a set A is a collection of nonempty, pairwise disjoint subsets of A whose union is A. It can be shown that *every equivalence relation on a set A gives rise to a unique partition of A and*, conversely, that *every partition of A yields a corresponding equivalence relation.* The partition associated with the relation "has the same shape as" on a set of shapes is shown in Figure T2.7. Notice how all the squares are grouped together, since they have the "same shape."

FIGURE T2.7

EXERCISE/PROBLEM SET T2—PART A

Exercises

1. Express the following relations in arrow diagram form in their ordered pair representation.

(a)

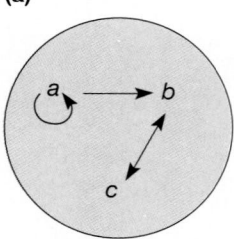

(b)

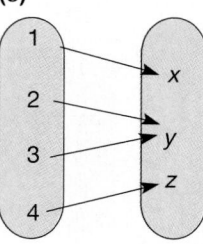

(c)

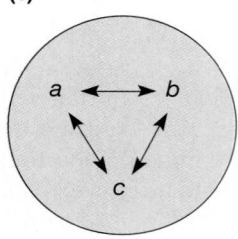

2. Determine if the relations represented by the following diagrams are reflexive, symmetric, or transitive. Which of them are equivalence relations?

(a)

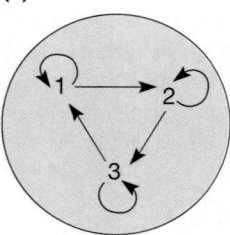

(b)

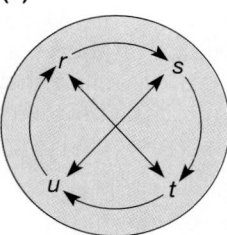

(c)

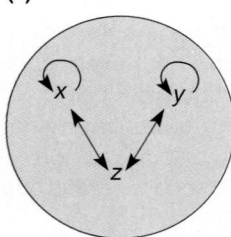

(d)

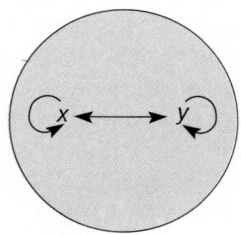

3. Determine if the relations represented by the following sets of ordered pairs are reflexive, symmetric, or transitive. Which of them are equivalence relations?

   (a) {(1, 1), (2, 1), (2, 2), (3, 1), (3, 2), (3, 3)}
   (b) {(1, 2), (1, 3), (2, 3), (2, 1), (3, 2), (3, 1)}
   (c) {(1, 1), (1, 3), (2, 2), (3, 2), (1, 2)}
   (d) {(1, 1), (2, 2), (3, 3)}

4. Describe the partitions associated with the following equivalence relations.

   (a) "Has the same surname as" on the collection of all people
   (b) "Has the same tens digit as" on the set collection {1, 2, 3, 4, . . .}
   (c) "Has the primary residence in the same state as" on the set of all people in the United States

5. Determine which of the reflexive, symmetric, and transitive properties are satisfied by the following relations. Which relations are equivalence relations?

   (a) "Less than" on the set {1, 2, 3, 4, . . .}
   (b) "Has the same shape as" on the set of all triangles
   (c) "Is a factor of" on the set {1, 2, 3, 4, . . .}
   (d) "Has the same number of factors as" on the set {1, 2, 3, 4, . . .}

6. Fractions are numbers of the form $\frac{a}{b}$, where a and b are whole numbers and $b \neq 0$. Fraction equality is defined as $\frac{a}{b} = \frac{c}{d}$ if and only if $ad = bc$. Determine whether fraction equality is an equivalence relation. If it is, describe the equivalence class that contains $\frac{1}{2}$.

EXERCISE/PROBLEM SET T2—PART B

Exercises

1. List all ordered pairs of each of the following relations on the sets listed. Which, if any, is an equivalence relation?
   (a) Domain: {1, 2, 3, 4, 5, 6}
       Relation: "Has the same number of factors as"
   (b) Domain: {2, 4, 6, 8, 10, 12}
       Relation: "Is a multiple of"
   (c) Domain: {1, 2, 3, 4, 5, 6, 7, 8}
       Relation: "Has more factors than"

2. Name the relations suggested by the following ordered pairs [e.g., (Hawaii, 50) has the name "is state number"].
   (a) (Lincoln, 16)
       (Madison, 4)
       (Reagan, 40)
       (McKinley, 25)
   (b) (Atlanta, GA)
       (Dover, DE)
       (Austin, TX)
       (Harrisburg, PA)
   (c) (George III, England)
       (Philip, Spain)
       (Louis XIV, France)
       (Alexander, Macedonia)
   (d) (21, 441)
       (12, 144)
       (38, 1444)
       (53, 2809)

3. Make an arrow diagram for each relation.
   (a)

   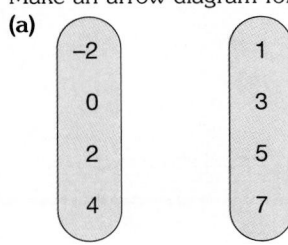

   Description: "is greater than"
   (b)

   Aaron, 23   20
   Sam, 17   25
   Judy, 29   27
   Amy, 14   11
   Sarah, 30

   Description: "is younger than"

(c)

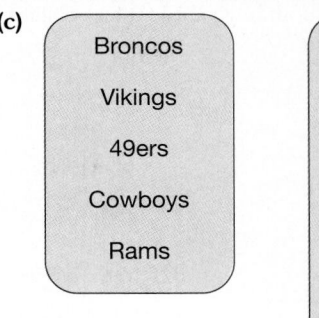

Description: "is an NFL team representing"

(d)

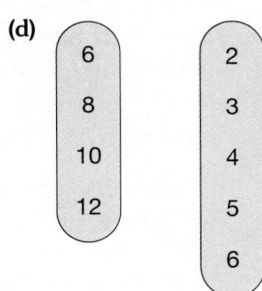

Description: "has a factor of"

4. Determine which of the reflexive, symmetric, or transitive properties hold for these relations:
   (a) {(1, 2), (1, 3), (1, 4), (2, 3), (2, 4), (3, 4)}
   (b) {(1, 2), (2, 3), (1, 4), (2, 4), (4, 2), (2, 1), (4, 1), (3, 2)}

5. Determine if the relations represented by the following arrow diagrams are reflexive, symmetric, or transitive. Which are equivalence relations?
   (a)   (b)

   (c)   (d)

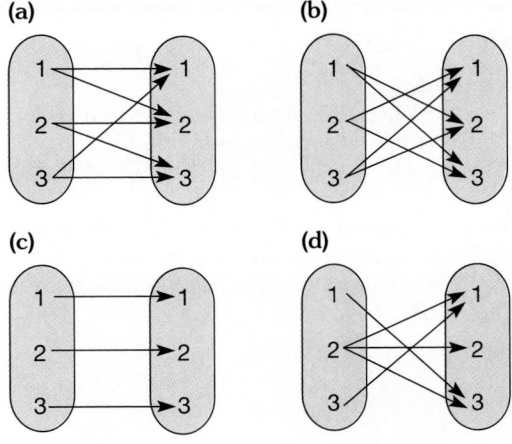

6. Equations are equivalent if they have the same solution set. For example, $3x - 2 = 7$ and $2x + 4 = 10$ are equivalent since they both have {3} as their solution set.

Explain the connection between the notion of equivalent equations and equivalence classes.

TOPIC REVIEW

Major Ideas

1. Relations can be used to describe relationships between objects.
2. Equivalence relations are particularly useful in mathematics.

Following is a list of key vocabulary, notation, and ideas for this topic. Mentally review these items and, where appropriate, write down the meaning of each term. Then restudy the material that you are unsure of before proceeding to take the topic test.

Vocabulary/Notation

Arrow diagram **939**
Relation **940**
Reflexive property **940**
Symmetric property **940**

Transitive property **940**
Equivalence relation **941**
Partition **941**

Ideas

Relations as subsets of the Cartesian product of sets **940**
Equivalence relations and partitions **941**

RELATIONS TEST

Knowledge

1. True or false?
  (a) "If a is related to b, then b is related to a" is an example of the reflexive property.
  (b) The ordered pair (6, 24) satisfies the relation "is a factor of."
  (c) Every equivalence relation satisfies the reflexive, symmetric, and converse properties.
  (d) A relation R from set A to set B is always a subset of $A \times B$.

Skill

2. Express the following relations using ordered pairs, and determine which satisfy the symmetric property.
  (a)   **(b)**

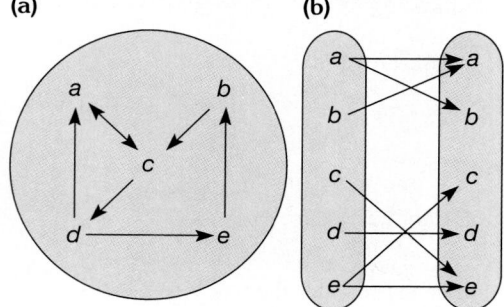

(c)

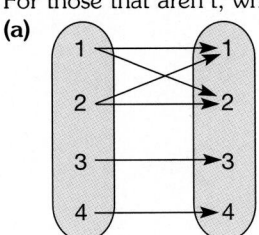

3. Which, if any, of the following are equivalence relations? For those that aren't, which properties fail?

(a)

(b)

(c) {(1, 1), (1, 2), (2, 1), (2, 2), (2, 3), (3, 2), (3, 3)}

Understanding

4. Using the relations on the set $S = \{1, 2, 3, 4, 5, 6, 7, 8, 9, 10, 11, 12\}$, determine all ordered pairs (a, b) that satisfy the equations. Which of the relations are reflexive, symmetric, or transitive?

(a) $a + b = 11$ **(b)** $a - b = 4$

(c) $a \cdot b = 12$ **(d)** $a/b = 2$

5. If the relation {(1, 2), (2, 1), (3, 4), (2, 4), (4, 2), (4, 3)} on the set {1, 2, 3, 4} is to be altered to have the properties listed, what other ordered pairs, if any, are needed?

(a) Reflexive   **(b)** Symmetric

(c) Transitive   **(d)** Reflexive and transitive

Problem Solving/Application

6. Your approximate ideal exercise heart rate is determined as follows: Subtract your age from 220 and multiply this by 0.75. Find a formula that expresses this exercise heart rate as related to one's age.

Topic 3: Advanced Counting Techniques: Permutations and Combinations

The fundamental counting property in Chapter 11 can be used to count the number of ways that several events can occur in succession. It states that if an event A can occur in r ways and an event B can occur in s ways, then the two events can occur in succession in $r \times s$ ways. This property can be generalized to more than two events. For example, suppose that at a restaurant you have your choice of three appetizers, four soups, five main courses, and two desserts. Altogether, you have $3 \times 4 \times 5 \times 2$ or 120 complete meal choices. In this topic we will apply the fundamental counting property to develop counting techniques for complicated arrangements of objects.

Permutations

An ordered arrangement of objects is called a **permutation**. For example, for the three letters C, A, and T, there are six different three-letter permutations or "words" that we can make: ACT, ATC, CAT, CTA, TAC, and TCA. If we add a fourth letter to our list, say S, then there are exactly 24 different four-letter permutations, which are listed as follows:

ACST	CAST	SACT	TACS
ACTS	CATS	SATC	TASC
ASCT	CSAT	SCAT	TCAS
ASTC	CSTA	SCTA	TCSA
ATCS	CTAS	STAC	TSAC
ATSC	CTSA	STCA	TSCA

We used a systematic list to write down all the permutations by alphabetizing them in columns. Even so, this procedure is cumbersome and would get out of hand with more and more objects to consider. We need a general principle for counting permutations of several objects.

Let's go back to the case of three letters and imagine a three-letter permutation as a "word" that fills three blanks _ _ _. We can count the number of permutations of the letters A, C, and T by counting the number of choices we have in filling each blank and applying the fundamental counting property. For example, in filling the first blank, we have 3 choices, since any of the three letters can be used: $\underset{3}{\_}$ _ _. Then, in filling the second blank we have 2 choices *for each of the first three choices,* since either of the two remaining letters can be used: $\underset{3\ 2}{\_\ \_}$ _. Finally, to fill the third blank we have the one remaining letter: $\underset{3\ 2\ 1}{\_\ \_\ \_}$. Hence, by the fundamental counting property, there are $3 \times 2 \times 1$ or 6 ways to fill all three blanks. This agrees with our list of the six permutations of A, C, and T.

We can apply this same technique to the problem of counting the four-letter permutations of A, C, S, and T. Again, imagine filling four blanks using each of the four letters. We have 4 choices for the first letter, 3 for the second, 2 for the third, and 1 for the fourth: $\underset{4\ 3\ 2\ 1}{\_\ \_\ \_\ \_}$. Hence, by the fundamental counting property, we have $4 \times 3 \times 2 \times 1$ or 24 permutations, just as we found in our list.

Our observations above lead to the following generalization: Suppose that we have n objects from which to form permutations. There are n choices for the first object, $n - 1$ choices for the second object, $n - 2$ for the third, and so on, down to 1 choice for the last object. Hence, by the fundamental counting property, there are $n \times (n - 1) \times (n - 2) \times \cdots \times 3 \times 2 \times 1$ permutations of the n objects. For every whole number n, $n > 0$, the product $n \times (n - 1) \times (n - 2) \times \cdots \times 3 \times 2 \times 1$ is called **n factorial** and is written using an exclamation point as **$n!$**. (Zero factorial is defined to be 1.)

EXAMPLE T3.1   Evaluate the following expressions involving factorials.

(a) 5!   **(b)** 10!   **(c)** $\dfrac{10!}{7!}$

Solution
(a) $5! = 5 \times 4 \times 3 \times 2 \times 1 = 120$
(b) $10! = 10 \times 9 \times 8 \times 7 \times 6 \times 5 \times 4 \times 3 \times 2 \times 1 = 3,628,800$
(c) $\dfrac{10!}{7!} = \dfrac{10 \times 9 \times 8 \times 7 \times 6 \times 5 \times 4 \times 3 \times 2 \times 1}{7 \times 6 \times 5 \times 4 \times 3 \times 2 \times 1}$
$= 10 \times 9 \times 8 = 720$

[NOTE: The fraction in (c) was simplified first to make the calculation easier.]■

Many calculators have a factorial key, such as $\boxed{n!}$ or $\boxed{x!}$. Entering a whole number and then pressing this key yields the factorial in the display.

Using factorials, we can count the number of permutations of n distinct objects.

Theorem   The number of permutations of n distinct objects, taken all together, is $n!$

EXAMPLE T3.2

(a) Miss Murphy wants to seat 12 of her students in a row for a class picture. How many different seating arrangements are there?

(b) Seven of Miss Murphy's students are girls and 5 are boys. In how many different ways can she seat the 7 girls together on the left, then the 5 boys together on the right?

Solution

(a) There are $12! = 479,001,600$ different permutations, or seating arrangements, of the 12 students.

(b) There are $7! = 5040$ permutations of the girls and $5! = 120$ permutations of the boys. Hence, by the fundamental counting property, there are $5040 \times 120 = 604,800$ arrangements with the girls seated on the left. ■

We will now consider permutations of a set of objects taken from a larger set. For example, suppose that in a certain lottery game, four different digits are chosen from the digits zero through nine to form a four-digit number. How many different numbers can be made? There are 10 choices for the first digit, 9 for the second, 8 for the third, and 7 for the fourth. By the fundamental counting property, then, there are $10 \times 9 \times 8 \times 7$ or 5040 different possible winning numbers. Notice that the number of permutations of 4 digits chosen from 10 digits is $10 \times 9 \times 8 \times 7 = 10!/6! = 10!/(10 - 4)!$.

We can generalize the observation above to permutations of r objects from n objects—in the example about 4-digit numbers, $n = 10$ and $r = 4$. Let $_nP_r$ denote the number of permutations of r objects chosen from n objects.

Theorem   The number of permutations of r objects chosen from n objects, where $0 \leq r \leq n$, is

$$_nP_r = \frac{n!}{(n - r)!}.$$

To justify this result, imagine making a sequence of r of the objects. We have n choices for the first object, $n - 1$ choices for the second object, $n - 2$ choices for the third object, and so on down to $n - r + 1$ choices for the last object. Thus we have

$$_nP_r = n \times (n - 1) \times (n - 2) \times \cdots \times (n - r + 1)$$
$$= \frac{n!}{(n - r)!} \text{ total permutations.}$$

Many calculators have a special key for calculating nPr. To use this key, press the value of n, then the $\boxed{nPr}$ key, then the value of r, then $\boxed{=}$. The value of nPr will be displayed. If such a key is not available, the following keystrokes may be used: n $\boxed{x!}$ $\boxed{\div}$ $\boxed{(}$ n $\boxed{-}$ r $\boxed{)}$ $\boxed{x!}$ $\boxed{=}$.

EXAMPLE T3.3 Using the digits 1, 3, 5, 7, and 9, with no repetitions of digits, how many
(a) one-digit numbers can be made?
(b) two-digit numbers can be made?
(c) three-digit numbers can be made?
(d) four-digit numbers can be made?
(e) five-digit numbers can be made?

Solution
Each number corresponds to a permutation of the digits. In each case, $n = 5$.
(a) With $r = 1$, there are $5!/(5 - 1)! = 5$ different one-digit numbers.
(b) With $r = 2$, there are $5!/(5 - 2)! = 5!/3! = 20$ different two-digit numbers.
(c) With $r = 3$, there are $5!/(5 - 3)! = 60$ different three-digit numbers.
(d) With $r = 4$, there are $5!/(5 - 4)! = 120$ different four-digit numbers.
(e) With $r = 5$, there are $5!/(5 - 5)! = 5!/0! = 120$ different five-digit numbers. Recall that $0!$ is defined as 1. ■

Combinations

A collection of objects, *in no particular order*, is called a **combination**. Using the language of sets, we find that a combination is a subset of a given set of objects. For example, suppose that in a group of five students, Barry, Harry, Larry, Mary, and Teri, three students are to be selected to make a team. Each of the possible three-member teams is a combination. How many such combinations are there? We can answer this question by using our knowledge of permutations and the fundamental counting property.

Suppose that C is the number of possible combinations of three students chosen from the group of five. Each of the three-member teams can be arranged into 3! permutations. Thus we can form all of the *permutations* of three students by first selecting the three-member *combinations* (in C ways), and then arranging each combination into 3! permutations (Figure T3.1).

All Possible 3-Person Permutations		Corresponding Combinations
BHL, BLH, HBL, HLB, LBH, LHB	↔	{B, H, L}
BHM, BMH, HBM, HMB, MBH, MHB	↔	{B, H, M}
BHT, BTH, HBT, HTB, TBH, THB	↔	{B, H, T}
⋮		⋮
LMT, LTM, MLT, MTL, TLM, TML	↔	{L, M, T}
Total number of permutations	=	Total number of combinations times 6 (= 3!), since there are 6 arrangements for each combination.

FIGURE T3.1

Thus, by the fundamental counting property, the total number of permutations of three students chosen from five is $C \times 3!$. But we know that the number of such permutations is $5!/(5 - 3)!$. Therefore, we can solve for C as follows:

$$C \times 3! = \frac{5!}{(5 - 3)!}$$

$$C = \frac{5!}{(5 - 3)!3!} = 10.$$

In general, let $_nC_r$ denote the number of combinations of r objects chosen from a set of n objects. Then the total number of permutations of the r objects chosen from n, namely $n!/(n - r)!$, is equal to $_nC_r \times r!$, since each of the $_nC_r$ combinations yields $r!$ permutations. Thus we have the following result.

> **Theorem** The number of combinations of r objects chosen from n objects, where $0 \le r \le n$, is
>
> $$_nC_r = \frac{n!}{(n - r)! \times r!}.$$

(NOTE: Occasionally, $_nC_r$ is denoted $\binom{n}{r}$ and read "n choose r.")

Many calculators have a key for calculating $_nC_r$. It is used like the $\boxed{nPr}$ key; press the value of n, then $\boxed{nCr}$, then the value of r, followed by $\boxed{=}$. The value of $_nC_r$ will be displayed.

EXAMPLE T3.4
(a) Evaluate $_6C_2$, $_{10}C_4$, $_{10}C_6$, and $_{10}C_{10}$.
(b) How many five-member committees can be chosen from a group of 30 people?
(c) How many different 12-person juries can be chosen from a pool of 20 jurors?

Solution

(a) $\quad _6C_2 = \frac{6!}{4! \times 2!} = \frac{6 \times 5 \times 4 \times 3 \times 2 \times 1}{4 \times 3 \times 2 \times 1 \times 2 \times 1} = 15.$

$_{10}C_4 = \frac{10!}{6! \times 4!} = \frac{10 \times 9 \times 8 \times 7 \times 6!}{6! \times 4 \times 3 \times 2 \times 1} = 210.$

$_{10}C_6 = \frac{10!}{4! \times 6!} = 210$ from the previous calculation.

$_{10}C_{10} = \frac{10!}{0! \times 10!} = 1.$

(b) The number of committees is $_{30}C_5 = \dfrac{30!}{25! \times 5!}$

$= 142{,}506.$

(c) The number of juries is $_{20}C_{12} = \dfrac{20!}{8! \times 12!}$

$= 125{,}970.$ ∎

Pascal's Triangle and Combinations

Recall Pascal's triangle, the first six rows of which appear in Figure T3.2.

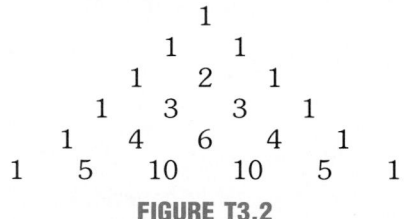

FIGURE T3.2

It can be shown that the entries are simply values of $_nC_r$. For example, in the row beginning 1, 4, 6, the entries are the values of $_nC_r$ for $n = 4$, and $r = 0, 1, 2, 3,$ and 4. In general, in the row beginning 1, n, the entries are the values of $_nC_r$, where $r = 0, 1, 2, 3, \ldots, n$.

EXAMPLE T3.5   A fair coin is tossed 5 times. Find the number of ways that two heads and three tails can appear.

Solution
An outcome can be represented as a five-letter sequence of H's and T's representing heads and tails. For example, THHTT represents a successful outcome. To count the successful outcomes, we imagine filling a sequence of five blanks, _ _ _ _ _, with two H's and three T's. There are $_5C_2 = 10$ ways of selecting two of the five blanks for the H's, so that there are 10 ways that two heads and three tails can appear. (Notice that once two blanks have been selected for heads, the remaining three blanks will be filled with tails.) Verify that this agrees with the method using Pascal's triangle.   ■

The final example shows the power of using combinations rather than generating Pascal's triangle.

EXAMPLE T3.6   On a 30-item true/false test, in how many ways can 27 or more answers be correct?

Solution
We can represent an outcome as a 30-letter sequence of C's and I's, for correct and incorrect. To count the number of ways that exactly 27 answers are correct, we count the number of ways that 27 of the 30 positions can have a C in them. There are $_{30}C_{27} = 4060$ such ways. Similarly, there are $_{30}C_{28} = 435$ ways that 28 answers are correct, $_{30}C_{29} = 30$ ways that 29 are correct, and $_{30}C_{30} = 1$ way that all 30 are correct. Thus there are $4060 + 435 + 30 + 1 = 4526$ ways to get 27 or more answers correct. (Using Pascal's triangle to solve this problem would involve generating 30 of its rows—a tedious procedure!)   ■

EXERCISE/PROBLEM SET T3—PART A

Exercises

1. Compute each of the following. Look for simplifications first.

   (a) $\dfrac{10!}{8!}$ (b) $\dfrac{12!}{8!\,4!}$ (c) $_9P_6$ (d) $_6C_2$

2. Certain automobile license plates consist of a sequence of three letters followed by three digits.
   (a) If there are no repetitions of letters permitted, how many possible license plates are there?
   (b) If no letters and no digits are repeated, how many possible license plates are there?

3. A combination lock has 40 numbers on it.
   (a) How many different three-number combinations can be made?
   (b) How many different combinations are there if the numbers must all be different?
   (c) How many different combinations are there if the second number must be different from the first and third?
   (d) Why is the name "combination" lock inconsistent with the mathematical meaning of combination?

4. (a) How many different five-member teams can be made from a group of 12 people?
   (b) How many different five-card poker hands can be dealt from a standard deck of 52 cards?

5. (a) Verify that the entries in Pascal's triangle in the 1, 4, 6, 4, 1 row are true values of $_4C_r$ for $r = 0, 1, 2, 3, 4$.
   (b) Verify that $_5C_3 = {}_4C_2 + {}_4C_3$.
   (c) Show that, in general, $_{n+1}C_r = {}_nC_{r-1} + {}_nC_r$.
   (d) Explain how the result in part (c) shows that the entries in the "1, n, . . ." row of Pascal's triangle are the values of $_nC_r$ for $r = 0, 1, 2, \ldots, n$.

6. Ten coins are tossed. Find the probability that the following number of heads appear.
   (a) 9   (b) 7   (c) 5   (d) 3   (e) 1

Problems

7. In a popular lottery game, five numbers are to be picked randomly from 1 to 36, with no repetitions.
   (a) How many ways can these five winning "numbers" be picked without regard to order?
   (b) Answer the same question for picking six numbers.

8. Suppose that there are 10 first-class seats on an airplane. How many ways can the following numbers of first-class passengers be seated?

   (a) 10   (b) 9   (c) 8   (d) 5
   (e) r, where $0 \le r \le 10$

9. Ten chips, numbered 1 through 10, are in a hat. All of the chips are drawn out in succession.
   (a) In how many different sequences can the chips be drawn?
   (b) How many of the sequences have chip 5 first?
   (c) How many of the sequences have an odd-numbered chip first?
   (d) How many of the sequences have an odd-numbered chip first and an even-numbered chip last?

10. How many five-letter "words" can be formed from the letters P-I-A-N-O if all the letters are different and the following restrictions exist.
    (a) There are no other restrictions.
    (b) The first letter is P.
    (c) The first letter is a consonant.
    (d) The first letter is a consonant and the last letter is a vowel (a, e, i, o, or u).

11. (a) Show that $_{20}C_5 = {}_{20}C_{15}$ without computing $_{20}C_5$ or $_{20}C_{15}$.
    (b) Show that, in general, $_nC_r = {}_nC_{n-r}$.
    (c) Given that $_{50}C_7 = 99{,}884{,}400$, find $_{50}C_{43}$.

12. (Refer to the Initial Problem in Chapter 1.) The digits 1 through 9 are to be arranged in the array so that the sum in each row is 17.

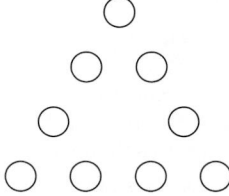

    (a) How many possible arrangements are there?
    (b) How many total arrangements are there with 1, 2, and 3 in the corners?
    (c) Start with 1 at the top, 2 in the lower left corner, and 3 in the lower right corner. Note that the two digits in the 1–2 row must sum to 14. How many two-digit sums of 14 are there using 4, 5, 6, 7, 8, and 9?
    (d) How many total solutions are there using 1, 2, and 3 as in part (c) and 5 and 9 in the 1–2 row?
    (e) How many solutions are there for the puzzle, counting all possible arrangements?

The following probability problems involve the use of combinations and permutations.

13. (a) Four students are to be chosen at random from a group of 15. How many ways can this be done?

(b) If Glenn is one of the students, what is the probability that he is one of the three chosen? (Assume that all students are equally likely to be chosen.)

(c) What is the probability that Glenn and Mickey are chosen?

14. Five cards are dealt at random from a standard deck. Find the probability that the hand contains the following cards.

(a) 4 aces

(b) 3 kings and 2 queens

(c) 5 diamonds

(d) An ace, king, queen, jack, and ten

15. In a group of 20 people, 3 have been exposed to virus X and 17 have not. Five people are chosen at random and tested for exposure to virus X.

(a) In how many ways can the 5 people be chosen?

(b) What is the probability that *exactly* one of the people in the group has been exposed to the virus?

(c) What is the probability that 1 or 2 people in the group have been exposed to the virus?

EXERCISE/PROBLEM SET T3—PART B

Exercises

1. Compute the following:

(a) $_{20}P_{15}$ **(b)** $\dfrac{23!}{13!\,10!}$ **(c)** $_{10}C_3$

(d) $\dfrac{(n+1)!}{(n-2)!}$

2. Which is greater?

(a) $_6P_2$ or $_6C_2$ **(b)** $_{12}P_2$ or $_6C_2$

(c) $_{12}C_2$ or $_{12}P_2$ **(d)** $_{12}C_9$ or $_{12}P_2$

3. Solve for n.

(a) $_nP_2 = 72$ **(b)** $_nC_2 = 66$

4. In how many ways can 8 chairs be arranged in a line?

5. If no repetitions are allowed, using the digits 0, 1, 2, 3, 4, 5, 6, 7, 8, 9:

(a) How many 2-digit numbers can be formed?

(b) How many of these are odd?

(c) How many of these are even?

(d) How many are divisble by 3?

(e) How many are less than 40?

6. A student must answer 7 out of 10 questions on a test.

(a) How many ways does she have to do this?

(b) How many if she must answer the first two?

Problems

7. If a student must take 6 tests, T1, T2, T3, T4, T5, T6, in how many ways can the student take the tests if:

(a) T2 must be taken immediately after T1?

(b) T1 and T2 can't be taken immediately after one another?

8. How many ways can the offices of president, vice-president, treasurer, secretary, parlimentarian, and representative be filled from a class of 30 students?

9. Using the word $MI_1S_1S_2I_2S_3S_4I_3P_1P_2I_4$, where each repeated letter is distinguishable, how many ways can the letters be arranged?

10. In any arrangement (list) of the 26 letters of the English alphabet, which has 21 consonants and 5 vowels, must there be some place where there are at least 3 consonants in a row? 4? 5?

11. If there are 10 chips in a box, 4 red, 3 blue, 2 white, and 1 black, and two chips are drawn, what is the probability that

(a) the chips are the same color?

(b) exactly one is red?

(c) at least one is red?

(d) neither is red?

12. In how many ways can be numbers 1, 2, 3, 4, 5, 6, 7 be arranged so that

(a) 1 and 7 are adjacent?

(b) 1 and 7 are not adjacent?

(c) 1 and 7 are exactly three spaces apart?

13. There are 12 books on a shelf: 5 volumes of an encyclopedia, 4 of an almanac, and 3 of a dictionary. How many arrangements are there? How many arrangements are there with each set of titles together?

14. If a team of 4 players must be made from 8 boys and 6 girls, how many teams can be made if

(a) there are no restrictions?

(b) there must be 2 boys and 2 girls?

(c) they must all be boys?

(d) they must all be girls?

TOPIC REVIEW

Major Ideas

1. Permutations and combinations can be used in complex counting problems, for example, in probability.

Following is a list of key vocabulary, notation, and ideas for this topic. Mentally review these items and, where appropriate, write down the meaning of each term. Then restudy the material that you are unsure of before proceeding to take the topic test.

Vocabulary/Notation

Permutation **947**
Factorial, $n!$ **948**
The number of permutations of r objects chosen from n objects, nPr **949**
Combination **950**
The number of combinations of r objects chosen from n objects, nCr **951**

Ideas

Counting permutations **948**
Counting combinations **950**
Relating Pascal's triangle and combinations **952**

ADVANCED COUNTING TECHNIQUES TEST

Knowledge

1. True or false?
  (a) An ordered arrangement of objects is a combination.
  (b) The number of permutations of r objects chosen from n objects, where $0 \leq r < n$, is $\dfrac{n!}{(n-r)!\,r!}$.
  (c) Since combinations take order into account, there are more combinations than permutations of n objects.
  (d) $_{n+1}P_r = {}_nP_{r-1} + {}_nP_r$.
  (e) The "words" (i) abcd and (ii) bcad are the same combination of the letters a, b, c, d.
  (f) $_nC_r = {}_nC_{n-r}$.
  (g) The number of combinations of n distinct objects, taken all together, is $n!$.
  (h) The entries in Pascal's triangle are the values of $_nC_r$.

Skill

2. Calculate:
  (a) $7!$ **(b)** $\dfrac{15!}{9!\,6!}$ **(c)** $_6P_3$ **(d)** $_{12}C_4$

Understanding

3. Out of 12 friends, you want to invite 7 over to watch a football game.
  (a) How many ways can this be done?
  (b) How many, if two of your friends won't come if the other one is there?

4. In how many ways can the questions on a 10-item test be arranged in different orders?

5. How many different teams of 2 men and 4 women can be formed from 9 men and 5 women? How many ways can this team be seated in a line?

Problem Solving/Application

6. There are 5 roads between Alpha, Kansas and Beta, Missouri. Also, there are 8 roads between Beta, Missouri and Omega, Nebraska, and 2 from Alpha to Omega not through Beta.

    (a) How many ways can you get from Alpha to Omega by passing through Beta?

    (b) How many ways in a round-trip, passing through Beta only once?

7. A senate committee of 4 is to be chosen from 7 Democrats, 8 Republicans, and 2 Independents.
    (a) How many ways can the committee be chosen?
    (b) How many, if it can't be all one party?
    (c) How many, if there must be the same number of Republicans and Democrats?

8. (a) Complete $_nC_0 + {}_nC_1 + {}_nC_2 + \cdots + {}_nC_n$ for $n = 3, 4, 5$.

    (b) What would the sum be for 6, 10, 20, n? (Find a formula.)

    (c) How is this sum related to Pascal's triangle?

Topic 4: Clock Arithmetic: A Mathematical System

Mathematical systems that were studied in Chapters 1 through 8 consisted of the infinite sets of whole numbers, fractions, and integers, together with their usual operations and properties. However, there are also mathematical systems involving finite sets.

Clock Arithmetic

The hours of a 12-clock are represented by the finite set {1, 2, 3, 4, 5, 6, 7, 8, 9, 10, 11, 12}. The problem "If it is 7 o'clock, what time will it be in 8 hours?" can be represented as the addition problem $7 \oplus 8$ (we use a circle around the "plus" sign here to distinguish this clock addition from the usual addition). Since 8 hours after 7 o'clock is 3 o'clock, we write $7 \oplus 8 = 3$. Notice that $7 \oplus 8$ can also be found simply by adding 7 and 8, then subtracting 12, the clock number, from the sum, 15. Instead of continuing to study 12-clock arithmetic, we will simplify our discussion about clock arithmetic by considering the 5-clock next (Figure T4.1).

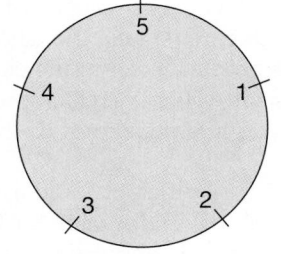

FIGURE T4.1

$\oplus$	0	1	2	3	4
0	0	1	2	3	4
1	1	2	3	4	0
2	2	3	4	0	1
3	3	4	0	1	2
4	4	0	1	2	3

FIGURE T4.2

In the 5-clock, the sum of two numbers is found by adding the two numbers as whole numbers, except that when this sum is greater than 5, 5 is subtracted. Thus, in the 5-clock, $1 \oplus 2 = 3$, $3 \oplus 4 = 2$ (i.e., $3 + 4 - 5$), and $3 \oplus 3 = 1$. Since $1 \oplus 5 = 1$, $2 \oplus 5 = 2$, $3 \oplus 5 = 3$, $4 \oplus 5 = 4$, and $5 \oplus 5 = 5$, the clock number 5 acts like the additive identity. Because of this, it is common to replace the clock number with a zero. Henceforth, 0 will be used to designate the clock number. Addition in the 5-clock is summarized in the table in Figure T4.2.

It can be shown that 5-clock addition is a commutative, associative, and closed binary operation. Also, 0 is the additive identity, since $a \oplus 0 = a$ for all numbers a in the 5-clock. Finally, every 5-clock number has an opposite or additive inverse: $1 \oplus 4 = 0$ (the identity), so 4 and 1 are opposites of each other; $2 \oplus 3 = 0$, so 2 and 3 are opposites of each other; and $0 \oplus 0 = 0$, so 0 is its own opposite.

Subtraction in the 5-clock can be defined in three equivalent ways. First, similar to the take-away approach for whole numbers, a number can be subtracted by counting backward. For example, $2 \ominus 4 = 3$ on the 5-clock, since counting backward 4 from 2 yields 1, 0, 4, 3. One can also use the missing-addend approach, namely $2 \ominus 4 = x$ if and only if $2 = 4 \oplus x$. Since $4 \oplus 3 = 2$, it follows that $x = 3$. Finally, $2 \ominus 4$ can be found by the adding the opposite method; that is, $2 \ominus 4 = 2 \oplus 1 = 3$, since 1 is the opposite of 4.

EXAMPLE T4.1   Calculate in the indicated clock arithmetic.
(a) $6 \oplus 8$ (12-clock)   **(b)** $4 \oplus 4$ (5-clock)
(c) $7 \oplus 4$ (9-clock)   **(d)** $8 \ominus 2$ (12-clock)
(e) $1 \ominus 4$ (5-clock)   **(f)** $2 \ominus 5$ (7-clock)

Solution
(a) In the 12-clock, $6 \oplus 8 = 6 + 8 - 12 = 2$.
(b) In the 5-clock, $4 \oplus 4 = 4 + 4 - 5 = 3$.
(c) In the 9-clock, $7 \oplus 4 = 7 + 4 - 9 = 2$.
(d) In the 12-clock, $8 \ominus 2 = 6$ since $8 = 2 \oplus 6$.
(e) In the 5-clock, $1 \ominus 4 = 1 + 1 = 2$ by adding the opposite.
(f) In the 7-clock, $2 \ominus 5 = 2 + 2 = 4$. ◼

$\otimes$	0	1	2	3	4
0	0	0	0	0	0
1	0	1	2	3	4
2	0	2	4	1	3
3	0	3	1	4	2
4	0	4	3	2	1

FIGURE T4.3

Multiplication in clock arithmetic is viewed as repeated addition. In the 5-clock, $3 \otimes 4 = 4 \oplus 4 \oplus 4 = 2$. The 5-clock multiplication table is shown in Figure T4.3.

As with addition, there is a shortcut method for finding products. For example, to find $3 \otimes 4$ in the 5-clock, first multiply 3 and 4 as whole numbers. This result, 12, exceeds 5, the number of the clock. In the 5-clock, imagine counting 12 starting with 1, namely, 1, 2, 3, 4, 5, 1, 2, 3, 4, 5, 1, 2. Here you must go around the circle twice ($2 \times 5 = 10$) plus two more clock numbers. Thus $3 \otimes 4 = 2$. Also, notice that 2 is the remainder when 12 is divided by 5. In general, to multiply in any clock, first take the whole-number product of the two clock numbers. If this product exceeds the clock number, divide by the clock number—the remainder will be the clock product. Thus $7 \otimes 9$ in the 12-clock is 3 since 63 leaves a remainder of 3 when divided by 12.

As with clock addition, clock multiplication is a commutative and associative closed binary operation. Also, $1 \otimes n = n \otimes 1 = n$, for all n, so 1 is the multiplicative identity. Since $1 \otimes 1 = 1$, $2 \otimes 3 = 1$, and $4 \otimes 4 = 1$, every nonzero element of the 5-clock has a reciprocal or multiplicative inverse. Notice that $0 \otimes n = 0$ for all n, since 0 is the additive identity (zero); this is consistent with all of our previous number systems, namely zero times any clock number is zero.

Division in the 5-clock can be viewed using either of the following two equivalent approaches: (1) missing factor or (2) multiplying by the reciprocal of the divisor. For example, using (1), $2 \oslash 3 = n$ if and only if $2 = 3 \otimes n$. Since $3 \otimes 4 = 2$, it follows that $n = 4$. Alternatively, using (2), $2 \div 3 = 2 \otimes 2 = 4$, since 2 is the reciprocal of 3 in the 5-clock.

Although every nonzero number in the 5-clock has a reciprocal, this property does not hold in every clock. For example, consider the multiplication table for the 6-clock (Figure T4.4). Notice that the number 1 does not appear in the "2" row. This means that there is no number n in the 6-clock such that $2 \otimes n = 1$. Also consider 2 in the 12-clock and the vari-

$\otimes$	0	1	2	3	4	5
0	0	0	0	0	0	0
1	0	1	2	3	4	5
2	0	2	4	0	2	4
3	0	3	0	3	0	3
4	0	4	2	0	4	2
5	0	5	4	3	2	1

FIGURE T4.4

ous multiples of 2. Observe that they are always even; hence 1 is never a multiple of 2. Thus 2 has no reciprocal in the 12-clock. This lack of reciprocals applies to *every* n-clock, where n is a composite number. For example, in the 9-clock, the number 3 (as well as 6) does not have a reciprocal. Thus, in composite number clocks, some divisions are impossible.

EXAMPLE T4.2 Calculate in the indicated clock arithmetic (if possible).
(a) $5 \otimes 7$ (12-clock)   **(b)** $4 \otimes 2$ (5-clock)
(c) $6 \otimes 5$ (8-clock)   **(d)** $1 \oslash 3$ (5-clock)
(e) $2 \oslash 5$ (7-clock)   **(f)** $2 \oslash 6$ (12-clock)

Solution
(a) $5 \otimes 7 = 11$ in the 12-clock since $5 \times 7 = 35$, and 35 divided by 12 has a remainder of 11.
(b) $4 \otimes 2 = 3$ in the 5-clock since $4 \times 2 = 8$, and 8 divided by 5 has a remainder of 3.
(c) $6 \otimes 5 = 6$ in the 8-clock since 30 divided by 8 has a remainder of 6.
(d) $1 \oslash 3 = 1 \otimes 2 = 2$ in the 5-clock since 2 is the reciprocal of 3.
(e) $2 \oslash 5 = 2 \otimes 3 = 6$ in the 7-clock since 3 is the reciprocal of 5.
(f) $2 \oslash 6$ in the 12-clock is not possible because 6 has no reciprocal. ■

Other aspects of various clock arithmetics that can be studied such as ordering, fractions, and equations are covered in the problem set.

Congruence Modulo m

Clock arithmetics are examples of finite mathematical systems. Interestingly, some of the ideas found in clock arithmetics can be extended to the (infinite) set of integers. In clock arithmetic, the clock number is the additive identity (or the zero). Thus a natural association of the integers with the 5-clock, say, can be obtained by wrapping the integer number line around the 5-clock, where 0 corresponds to 5 on the 5-clock, 1 with 1 on the clock, -1 with 4 on the clock, and so on (Figure T4.5).

In this way, there are infinitely many integers associated with each clock number. For example, in the 5-clock in Figure T4.5, the set of integers associated with 1 is $\{. \ . \ . \ , -14, -9, -4, 1, 6, 11, . \ . \ . \}$. It is interesting to note that the difference of any two of the integers in this set is a multiple of 5. In general, this fact is expressed symbolically as follows:

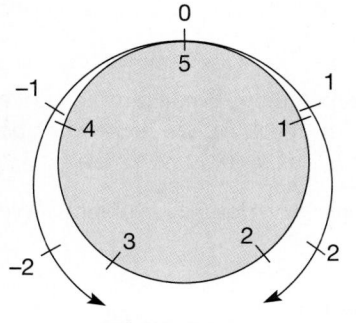

FIGURE T4.5

Definition
Congruence mod m
Let a, b, and m be integers, $m \geq 2$. Then $a \equiv b \bmod m$ if and only if $m \mid (a - b)$.

In this definition, we need to use an extended definition of divides to the system of integers. We say that $a \mid b$, for integers a ($\neq 0$) and b, if there is an integer x such that $ax = b$. The expression $a \equiv b \bmod m$ is read **a is congruent to b mod m**. The term "mod m" is an abbreviation for "modulo m."

EXAMPLE T4.3   Using the definition, determine which are true. Justify your conclusion.

(a) $13 \equiv 7 \bmod 2$ **(b)** $5 \equiv 11 \bmod 6$
(c) $-5 \equiv 15 \bmod 6$ **(d)** $-7 \equiv -22 \bmod 5$

Solution
(a) $13 \equiv 7 \bmod 2$ is true since $13 - 7 = 6$ and $2 \mid 6$.
(b) $5 \equiv 11 \bmod 6$ is true since $5 - 11 = -6$ and $6 \mid -6$.
(c) $-5 \equiv 14 \bmod 6$ is false since $-5 - 14 = -19$ and $6 \nmid -19$.
(d) $-7 \equiv -22 \bmod 5$ is true since $-7 - (-22) = 15$ and $5 \mid 15$.   ■

If the "mod m" is omitted from the congruence relation $a \equiv b \bmod m$, the resulting expression, $a \equiv b$, looks much like the equation $a = b$. In fact, congruences and equations have many similarities, as can be seen in the following seven results. (For simplicity, we will omit the "mod m" henceforth unless a particular m needs to be specified. As before, $m \geq 2$.)

1. $a \equiv a$ for all clock numbers a.
   This is true for any m since $a - a = 0$ and $m \mid 0$.
2. If $a \equiv b$, then $b \equiv a$.
   This is true since if $m \mid (a - b)$, then $m \mid -(a - b)$ or $m \mid (b - a)$.
3. If $a \equiv b$ and $b \equiv c$, then $a \equiv c$.
   The justification of this is left for the problem set.
4. If $a \equiv b$, then $a + c \equiv b + c$.
   If $m \mid (a - b)$, then $m \mid (a - b + c - c)$, or $m \mid [(a + c) - (b + c)]$; that is, $a + c \equiv b + c$.
5. If $a \equiv b$, then $ac \equiv bc$.
   The justification of this is left for the problem set.
6. If $a \equiv b$ and $c \equiv d$, then $ac \equiv bd$.
   Results 5 and 3 can be used to justify this as follows: If $a \equiv b$, then $ac \equiv bc$ by result 5. Also, if $c \equiv d$, then $bc \equiv bd$ by result 5. Since $ac \equiv bc$ and $bc \equiv bd$, we have $ac \equiv bd$ by result 3.
7. If $a \equiv b$ and n is a whole number, then $a^n \equiv b^n$.
   This can be justified by using result 6 repeatedly. For example, since $a \equiv b$ and $a \equiv b$ (using $a \equiv c$ and $b \equiv d$ in result 6), we have $aa \equiv bb$ or $a^2 \equiv b^2$. Continuing, we obtain $a^3 \equiv b^3$, $a^4 \equiv b^4$, and so on.

Congruence mod m can be used to solve a variety of problems. We close this section with one such problem.

EXAMPLE T4.4   What are the last two digits of 3^{30}?

Solution
The number 3^{30} is a large number, and its standard form will not fit on calculator displays. However, suppose that we could find a smaller number, say n, that did fit on a calculator display so that n and 3^{30} have the same last two digits. If n and 3^{30} have the same last two digits, then $3^{30} - n$ has zeros in its last two digits, and vice versa. Thus we have that $100 \mid (3^{30} - n)$, or $3^{30} \equiv n \bmod 100$. We now proceed to find such an n. Since 3^{30} can be

written as $(3^6)^5$, let's first consider $3^6 = 729$. Because the last two digits of 729 are 29, we can write $3^6 \equiv 29 \bmod 100$. Then, from 7 above, $(3^6)^5 \equiv 29^5 \bmod 100$. Since $29^5 = 20{,}511{,}149$ and $20{,}511{,}149 \equiv 49 \bmod 100$, by 3 above we can conclude that $(3^6)^5 \equiv 49 \bmod 100$. Thus, 3^{30} ends in 49. ■

EXERCISE/PROBLEM SET T4—PART A

Exercises

1. Calculate in the clock arithmetics indicated.
    (a) $8 \oplus 11$ (12-clock)
    (b) $1 \ominus 5$ (7-clock)
    (c) $3 \otimes 4$ (6-clock)
    (d) $3 \ominus 2$ (5-clock)
    (e) $7 \oplus 6$ (10-clock)
    (f) $5 \ominus 7$ (9-clock)
    (g) $4 \otimes 7$ (11-clock)
    (h) $2 \oplus 9$ (13-clock)

2. Find the opposite and reciprocal (if it exists) for each of the following.
    (a) 3 (7-clock)   (b) 5 (12-clock)
    (c) 7 (8-clock)   (d) 4 (8-clock)

3. In clock arithmetics, a^n means $a \times a \times \cdots \times a$ (n factors of a). Calculate in the clocks indicated.
    (a) 7^3 (8-clock)   (b) 4^5 (5-clock)
    (c) 2^6 (7-clock)   (d) 9^4 (12-clock)

4. Determine if these congruences are true or false.
    (a) $14 \equiv 3 \bmod 3$
    (b) $-3 \equiv 7 \bmod 4$
    (c) $43 \equiv -13 \bmod 14$
    (d) $7 \equiv -13 \bmod 2$
    (e) $23 \equiv -19 \bmod 7$
    (f) $-11 \equiv -7 \bmod 8$

5. Explain how to use the 5-clock addition table to find $1 \ominus 4$ in the 5-clock.

6. Using the 5-clock table, explain why 5-clock addition is commutative.

7. In the 5-clock, $\frac{1}{3}$ is defined to be $1 \oslash 3$, which equals $1 \otimes 2 = 2$. Using this definition of a clock fraction, calculate $\frac{1}{3} \oplus \frac{1}{2}$. Then add $\frac{1}{3}$ and $\frac{1}{2}$ as you would fractions, except do it in 5-clock arithmetic. Are your answers the same in both cases? Try adding, subtracting, multiplying, and dividing $\frac{3}{4}$ and $\frac{2}{3}$ in 5-clock in this way.

Problems

8. Suppose that "less than" is defined in the 5-clock as follows: $a < b$ if and only if $a \oplus c = b$ for some nonzero number c. Then $1 < 3$ since $1 \oplus 2 = 3$. However, $3 < 1$ also since $3 \oplus 3 = 1$. Thus, although this definition is consistent with our usual definition, it produces a result very different from what happens in the system of whole numbers. For each of the following, find an example that is inconsistent with what one would expect to find for whole numbers.
    (a) If $a < b$, then $a \oplus c < b \oplus c$.
    (b) If $a < b$ and $c \neq 0$, then $ac < bc$.

9. Find all possible replacements for x to make the following true.
    (a) $3 \otimes x = 2$ in the 7-clock
    (b) $2 \otimes x = 0$ in the 12-clock
    (c) $5 \otimes x = 0$ in the 10-clock
    (d) $4 \otimes x = 5$ in the 8-clock

10. Prove: If $a + c \equiv b + c$, then $a \equiv b$.

11. Prove: If $a \equiv b$ and $b \equiv c$, then $a \equiv c$.

12. Find the last two digits of 3^{48} and 3^{49}.

13. Find the last three digits of 4^{101}.

EXERCISE/PROBLEM SET T4—PART B

Exercises

1. Calculate in the clock arithmetics indicated.
   (a) $3 \otimes (4 \oplus 5)$ and $(3 \otimes 4) \oplus (3 \otimes 5)$ in the 7-clock
   (b) $2 \otimes (3 \oplus 6)$ and $(2 \otimes 3) \oplus (2 \otimes 6)$ in the 12-clock
   (c) $5 \otimes (7 \ominus 3)$ and $(5 \otimes 7) \ominus (5 \otimes 3)$ in the 9-clock
   (d) $4 \otimes (3 \ominus 5)$ and $(4 \otimes 3) \ominus (4 \otimes 5)$ in the 6-clock
   (e) What do parts (a) to (d) suggest?

2. Calculate as indicated [i.e., in $2^4 \otimes 3^4$, calculate 2^4, then 3^4, then multiply your results, and in $(2 \otimes 3)^4$, calculate $2 \otimes 3$, then find the fourth power of your product].
   (a) $3^2 \otimes 5^2$ and $(3 \otimes 5)^2$ in the 7-clock
   (b) $2^3 \otimes 3^3$ and $(2 \otimes 3)^3$ in the 6-clock
   (c) $5^4 \otimes 6^4$ and $(5 \otimes 6)^4$ in the 10-clock
   (d) What do parts (a) to (c) suggest?

3. Make a 7-clock multiplication table and use it to find the reciprocals of 1, 2, 3, 4, 5, and 6.

4. Find the following in the 6-clock.
   (a) -2 (b) -5 (c) $(-2) \otimes (-5)$ (d) $2 \otimes 5$
   (e) -3 (f) -4 (g) $(-3) \otimes (-4)$ (h) $3 \otimes 4$
   What general result similar to one in the integers is suggested by (c), (d), (g), and (h)?

5. In each part, describe all integers n, where $-20 \leq n \leq 20$, which make these congruences true.
   (a) $n \equiv 3 \bmod 5$ (b) $4 \equiv n \bmod 7$
   (c) $12 \equiv 4 \bmod n$ (d) $7 \equiv 7 \bmod n$

6. Show, by using an example in the 12-clock, that the product of two nonzero numbers may be zero.

7. List all of the numbers that do not have reciprocals in the clock given.
   (a) 8-clock   (b) 10-clock   (c) 12-clock
   Based on your findings, predict the numbers in the 36-clock that don't have reciprocals. Check your prediction.

Problems

8. Find reciprocals of the following:
   (a) 7 in the 8-clock   (b) 4 in the 5-clock
   (c) 11 in the 12-clock   (d) 9 in the 10-clock
   (e) What general idea is suggested by parts (a) to (d)?

9. State a definition of "square root" for clock arithmetic that is consistent with our usual definition. Then find all square roots of the following if they exist.
   (a) 4 in the 5-clock   (b) 1 in the 8-clock
   (c) 3 in the 6-clock   (d) 7 in the 12-clock
   (e) What do you notice that is different or similar about square roots in clock arithmetics?

10. The system of rational numbers was divided into the three disjoint sets: (i) negatives, (ii) zero, and (iii) positives. The set of positives was closed under both addition and multiplication. Show that it is impossible to find two disjoint nonempty sets to serve as positives and negatives in the 5-clock. (HINT: Let 1 be positive and another number be negative, say $-1 = 4$. Then show that if the set of positive 5-clock numbers is closed under addition, this situation is impossible. Observe that this holds in all clock arithmetics.)

11. Explain why multiplication is closed in any clock.

12. Prove: If $a \equiv b$, then $ac \equiv bc$.

13. Prove or disprove: If $ac \equiv bc \bmod 6$ and $c \not\equiv 0 \bmod 6$, then $a \equiv b \bmod 6$.

14. Suppose that you want to know the remainder when 3^{100} is divided by 7. If r is the remainder and q is the quotient, then $3^{100} = 7q + r$ or $3^{100} - r = 7q$. Thus $7 \mid (3^{100} - r)$ or $3^{100} \equiv r \bmod 7$. (Recall that for the remainder r, we have $0 \leq r < 7$.) Now $3^5 = 243 \equiv 5 \bmod 7$. So $(3^5)^2 \equiv 5^2 \bmod 7$ or $3^{10} \equiv 25 \equiv 4 \bmod 7$. Thus $3^{100} = (3^{10})^{10} \equiv 4^{10} \bmod 7$. But $4^{10} = 16^5 \equiv 2^5 \equiv 4 \bmod 7$. Thus the remainder is 4. Find the remainder when 7^{101} is divided by 8. (HINT: $7^{101} = 7^{100} \cdot 7$.)

TOPIC REVIEW

Major Ideas

1. Clock arithmetic illustrates mathematical systems involving finite sets.
2. Congruences modulo m have properties similar to equations and can be used to solve problems involving integers.

Following is a list of key vocabulary, notation, and ideas for this topic. Mentally review these items and, where appropriate, write down the meaning of each term. Then restudy the material that you are unsure of before proceeding to take the topic test.

Vocabulary/Notation

Clock arithmetic **957**
  Addition, $a \oplus b$ **957**
  Subtraction, $a \ominus b$ **957**
  Multiplication, $a \otimes b$ **958**
  Division, $a \oslash b$ **959**
Congruence modulo m, $a \equiv b \bmod m$ **959**

Ideas

Properties of addition in clock arithmetic **957**
Three approaches to subtraction in clock arithmetic **958**
Properties of multiplication in clock arithmetic **958**
Two approaches to division in clock arithmetic **958**
Solving problems using congruence modulo m **960**

CLOCK ARITHMETIC TEST

Knowledge

1. True or false?
  (a) The 12-clock is comprised of the numbers 0, 1, 2, 3, 4, 5, 6, 7, 8, 9, 10, 11, 12.
  (b) Addition in the 5-clock is associative.
  (c) The number 1 is the additive identity in the 7-clock.
  (d) The number 4 is its own multiplicative inverse in the 5-clock.
  (e) Now every clock has an additive inverse for each of its elements.
  (f) Every number is congruent to itself mod m.
  (g) If $a \equiv b \bmod 7$, then either $a - b = 7$ or $b - a = 7$.
  (h) If $a \equiv b$ and $c \equiv b$, then $a \equiv c$.

Skill

2. Calculate.
  (a) $5 \oplus 9$ in the 11-clock
  (b) $8 \otimes 8$ in the 9-clock
  (c) $3 \ominus 7$ in the 10-clock
  (d) $4 \oslash 9$ in the 13-clock
  (e) 2^4 in the 5-clock
  (f) $(2 \ominus 5)^3 \otimes 6$ in the 7-clock

3. Show how to do the following calculations easily mentally by applying the commutative, associative, identity, inverse, or distributive properties.
  (a) $3 \oplus (9 \oplus 7)$ in the 10-clock
  (b) $(8 \otimes 3) \otimes 4$ in the 11-clock
  (c) $(5 \otimes 4) \oplus (5 \otimes 11)$ in the 15-clock
  (d) $(6 \otimes 3) \oplus (3 \otimes 4) \oplus (3 \otimes 3)$ in the 13-clock

4. Find the opposite and the reciprocal (if they exist) of the following numbers in the indicated clocks. Explain.
   (a) 4 in the 7-clock   (b) 4 in the 8-clock
   (c) 0 in the 5-clock   (d) 5 in the 12-clock

5. In each part, describe the set of all numbers n that make the congruence true.
   (a) $n \equiv 4 \bmod 9$ where $-15 \le n \le 15$
   (b) $15 \equiv 3 \bmod n$ where $1 < n < 20$
   (c) $8 \equiv n \bmod 7$

Understanding

6. Using a clock as a model, explain why 4 does not have a reciprocal in the 12-clock.

7. Explain (a) why 0 cannot be used for m and (b) why 1 is not used for m in the definition of $a \equiv b \bmod m$.

8. Explain why $a \equiv a \bmod m$.

Problem Solving/Application

9. If January 1 of a non-leap year falls on a Monday, show how congruence mod 7 can be used to determine the day of the week for January 1 of the next year.

Connections to School Mathematics

In March 1989, the National Council of Teachers of Mathematics (NCTM) published the *Curriculum and Evaluations Standards for School Mathematics*, which is commonly referred to as *The Standards*. This book set standards for teachers, school districts, states, and publishers that could "be used as criteria against which their programs could be judged" for the 1990s. These recommendations were welcomed by the mathematics education community, and much of the reform movement in the 1990s can be traced to this document. The following pages contain brief summary statements of the Standards for Grades K–4 and 5–8. Then these standards are keyed to pages from the Macmillan/McGraw-Hill's *Math in Action* school mathematics series to illustrate how many of these recommendations are being implemented in classrooms. This is a first step in learning about *The Standards*. In the early 1990s, the NCTM produced series of booklets called the *Addenda Series*, which expanded on many of the original standards. In addition, the NCTM's journal for elementary teachers, *The Arithmetic Teacher*, continues to publish articles that expand on *The Standards*.

In March 1991, the NCTM published the *Professional Standards for Teaching Mathematics*. This book is designed to help teachers learn to teach in the spirit of *The Standards* and consistent with the latest research findings.

The materials described above, as well as information regarding membership in the NCTM, may be obtained by writing to NCTM, 1906 Association Drive, Reston, VA 22091 or by calling 1-800-235-7566.

CURRICULUM STANDARDS FOR GRADES K–4

Standard 1: Mathematics As Problem Solving

In grades K–4, the study of mathematics should emphasize problem solving so that students can
- use problem solving approaches to investigate and understand mathematical content;
- formulate problems from everyday and mathematical situations;
- develop and apply strategies to solve a wide variety of problems;
- verify and interpret results with respect to the original problem;
- acquire confidence in using mathematics meaningfully.

Standard 2: Mathematics As Communication

In grades K–4, the study of mathematics should include numerous opportunities for communication so that students can
- relate physical materials, pictures, and diagrams to mathematical ideas;
- reflect on and clarify their thinking about mathematical ideas and situations;
- relate their everyday language to mathematical language and symbols;
- realize that representing, discussing, reading, writing, and listening to mathematics are a vital part of learning and using mathematics.

Standard 3: Mathematics As Reasoning

In grades K–4, the study of mathematics should emphasize reasoning so that students can
- draw logical conclusions about mathematics;
- use models, known facts, properties, and relationships to explain their thinking;
- justify their answers and solution processes;
- use patterns and relationships to analyze mathematical situations;
- believe that mathematics makes sense.

Standard 4: Mathematical Connections

In grades K–4, the study of mathematics should include opportunities to make connections so that students can
- link conceptual and procedural knowledge;
- relate various representations of concepts or procedures to one another;
- recognize relationships among different topics in mathematics;
- use mathematics in other curriculum areas; use mathematics in their daily lives.

Standard 5: Estimation

In grades K–4, the curriculum should include estimation so students can
- explore estimation strategies;
- recognize when an estimate is appropriate;
- determine the reasonableness of results;
- apply estimation in working with quantities, measurement, computation, and problem solving.

Standard 6: Number Sense and Numeration

In grades K–4, the mathematics curriculum should include whole number concepts and skills so that students can
- construct number meanings through real-world experiences and the use of physical materials;
- understand our numeration system by relating counting, grouping, and place-value concepts;
- develop number sense;
- interpret the multiple uses of numbers encountered in the real world.

Standard 7: Concepts of Whole-Number Operations

In grades K–4, the mathematics curriculum should include concepts of addition, subtraction, multiplication, and division of whole numbers so that students can
- develop meaning for the operations by modeling and discussing a rich variety of problem situations;
- relate the mathematical language and symbolism of operations to problem situations and informal language;
- recognize that a wide variety of problem structures can be represented by a single operation;
- develop operation sense.

Standard 8: Whole-Number Computation

In grades K–4, the mathematics curriculum should develop whole-number computation so that students can
- model, explain, and develop reasonable proficiency with basic facts and algorithms;
- use a variety of mental computation and estimation techniques;
- use calculators in appropriate computational situations;
- select and use computation techniques appropriate to specific problems and determine whether the results are reasonable.

Standard 9: Geometry and Spatial Sense

In grades K–4, the mathematics curriculum should include two- and three-dimensional geometry so that students can
- describe, model, draw, and classify shapes;
- investigate and predict the results of combining, subdividing, and changing shapes;
- develop spatial sense;
- relate geometric ideas to number and measurement ideas;
- recognize and appreciate geometry in their world.

Standard 10: Measurement

In grades K–4, the mathematics curriculum should include measurement so that students can
- understand the attributes of length, capacity, weight, area, volume, time, temperature, and angle;
- develop the process of measuring and concepts related to units of measurement;
- make and use estimates of measurement;
- make and use measurements in problem and everyday situations.

Standard 11: Statistics and Probability

In grades K–4, the mathematics curriculum should include experiences with data analysis and probability so that students can
- collect, organize, and describe data;
- construct, read, and interpret displays of data;
- formulate and solve problems that involve collecting and analyzing data;
- explore concepts of chance.

Standard 12: Fractions and Decimals

In grades K–4, the mathematics curriculum should include fractions and decimals so that students can
- develop concepts of fractions, mixed numbers, and decimals;
- develop number sense for fractions and decimals;
- use models to relate fractions to decimals and to find equivalent fractions;
- use models to explore operations on fractions and decimals;
- apply fractions and decimals to problem situations.

Standard 13: Patterns and Relationships

In grades K–4, the mathematics curriculum should include the study of patterns and relationships so that students can
- recognize, describe, extend, and create a wide variety of patterns;
- represent and describe mathematical relationships;
- explore the use of variables and open sentences to express relationships.

CURRICULUM STANDARDS FOR GRADES 5–8

Standard 1: Mathematics As Problem Solving

In grades 5–8, the mathematics curriculum should include numerous and varied experiences with problem solving as a method of inquiry and application so that students can
- use problem-solving approaches to investigate and understand mathematical content;
- formulate problems from situations within and outside mathematics;
- develop and apply a variety of strategies to solve problems, with emphasis on multistep and nonroutine problems;
- verify and interpret results with respect to the original problem situation;
- generalize solutions and strategies to new problem situations;
- acquire confidence in using mathematics meaningfully.

Standard 2: Mathematics As Communication

In grades 5–8, the study of mathematics should include opportunities to communicate so that students can
- model situations using oral, written, concrete, pictorial, graphical, and algebraic methods;
- reflect on and clarify their own thinking about mathematical ideas and situations;
- develop common understandings of mathematical ideas, including the role of definitions;
- use the skills of reading, listening, and viewing to interpret and evaluate mathematical ideas;
- discuss mathematical ideas and make conjectures and convincing arguments;
- appreciate the value of mathematical notation and its role in the development of mathematical ideas.

Standard 3: Mathematics As Reasoning

In grades 5–8, reasoning shall permeate the mathematics curriculum so that students can
- recognize and apply deductive and inductive reasoning;
- understand and apply reasoning processes, with special attention to spatial reasoning and reasoning with proportions and graphs;
- make and evaluate mathematical conjectures and arguments;
- validate their own thinking;
- appreciate the pervasive use and power of reasoning as a part of mathematics.

Standard 4: Mathematical Connections

In grades 5–8, the mathematics curriculum should include the investigation of mathematical connections so that students can
- see mathematics as an integrated whole;
- explore problems and describe results using graphical, numerical, physical, algebraic, and verbal mathematical models or representations;

- use a mathematical idea to further their understanding of other mathematical ideas;
- apply mathematical thinking and modeling to solve problems that arise in other disciplines, such as art, music, psychology, science, and business;
- value the role of mathematics in our culture and society.

Standard 5: Number and Number Relationships

In grades 5–8, the mathematics curriculum should include the continued development of number and number relationships so that students can
- understand, represent, and use numbers in a variety of equivalent forms (integer, fraction, decimal, percent, exponential, and scientific notation) in real-world and mathematical problem situations;
- develop number sense for whole numbers, fractions, decimals, integers, and rational numbers;
- understand and apply ratios, proportions, and percents in a wide variety of situations;
- investigate relationships among fractions, decimals, and percents;
- represent numerical relationships in one- and two-dimensional graphs.

Standard 6: Number Systems and Number Theory

In grades 5–8, the mathematics curriculum should include the study of number systems and number theory so that students can
- understand and appreciate the need for numbers beyond the whole numbers;
- develop and use order relations for whole numbers, fractions, decimals, integers, and rational numbers;
- extend their understanding of whole-number operations to fractions, decimals, integers, and rational numbers;
- understand how the basic arithmetic operations are related to one another;
- develop and apply number theory concepts (e.g., primes, factors, and multiples) in real-world and mathematical problem situations.

Standard 7: Computation and Estimation

In grades 5–8, the mathematics curriculum should develop the concepts underlying computation and estimation in various contexts so that students can
- compute with whole numbers, fractions, decimals, integers, and rational numbers;
- develop, analyze, and explain procedures for computation and techniques for estimation;

- develop, analyze, and explain methods for solving proportions;
- select and use an appropriate method for computing from among mental arithmetic, paper-and-pencil, calculator, and computer methods;
- use computation, estimation, and proportions to solve problems;
- use estimation to check the reasonableness of results.

Standard 8: Patterns and Functions

In grades 5–8, the mathematics curriculum should include explorations of patterns and functions so that students can
- describe, extend, analyze, and create a wide variety of patterns;
- describe and represent relationships with tables, graphs, and rules;
- analyze functional relationships to explain how a change in one quantity results in a change in another;
- use patterns and functions to represent and solve problems.

Standard 9: Algebra

In grades 5–8, the mathematics curriculum should include explorations of algebraic concepts and processes so that students can
- understand the concepts of variable, expression, and equation;
- represent situations and number patterns with tables, graphs, verbal rules, and equations and explore the interrelationships of these representations;
- analyze tables and graphs to identify properties and relationships;
- develop confidence in solving linear equations using concrete, informal, and formal methods;
- investigate inequalities and nonlinear equations informally;
- apply algebraic methods to solve a variety of real-world and mathematical problems.

Standard 10: Statistics

In grades 5–8, the mathematics curriculum should include exploration of statistics in real-world situations so students can
- systematically collect, organize and describe data;
- construct, read, and interpret tables, charts, and graphs;
- make inferences and convincing arguments that are based on data analysis;
- evaluate arguments that are based on data analysis;
- develop an appreciation for statistical methods as powerful means for decision making.

Standard 11: Probability

In grades 5–8, the mathematics curriculum should include explorations of probability in real-world situations so that students can
- model situations by devising and carrying out experiments or simulations to determine probabilities;
- model situations by constructing a sample space to determine probabilities;
- appreciate the power of using a probability model by comparing experimental results with mathematical expectations;
- make predictions that are based on experimental or theoretical probabilities;
- develop an appreciation for the pervasive use of probability in the real world.

Standard 12: Geometry

In grades 5–8, the mathematics curriculum should include the study of the geometry of one, two, and three dimensions in a variety of situations so that students can
- identify, describe, compare, and classify geometric figures;
- visualize and represent geometric figures with special attention to developing spatial sense;
- explore transformations of geometric figures;
- represent and solve problems using geometric models;
- understand and apply geometric properties and relationships;
- develop an appreciation of geometry as a means of describing the physical world.

Standard 13: Measurement

In grades 5–8, the mathematics curriculum should include extensive concrete experiences using measurement so that students can
- extend their understanding of the process of measurement;
- estimate, make, and use measurements to describe and compare phenomena;
- select appropriate units and tools to measure to the degree of accuracy required in a particular situation;
- understand the structure and use of systems of measurement;
- extend their understanding of the concepts of perimeter, area, volume, angle measure, capacity, and weight and mass;
- develop the concepts of rates and other derived and indirect measurements;
- develop formulas and procedures for determining measures to solve problems.

SUMMARY OF CHANGES IN CONTENT AND EMPHASIS IN K–4 MATHEMATICS

Increased Attention

Number
- Number sense.
- Place-value concepts.
- Meaning of fractions and decimals.
- Estimation of quantities.

Operations and Computation
- Meaning of operations.
- Operation sense.
- Mental computation.
- Estimation and the reasonableness of answers.
- Selection of an appropriate computational method.
- Use of calculators for complex computation.
- Thinking strategies for basic facts.

Geometry and Measurement
- Properties of geometric figures.
- Geometric relationships.
- Spatial sense.
- Process of measuring.
- Concepts related to units of measurement.
- Actual measuring.
- Estimation of measurements.
- Use of measurement and geometry ideas throughout the curriculum.

Probability and Statistics
- Collection and organization of data.
- Exploration of chance.

Patterns and Relationships
- Pattern recognition and description.
- Use of variables to express relationships.

Problem Solving
- Word problems with a variety of structures.
- Use of everyday problems.
- Applications.
- Study of patterns and relationships.
- Problem-solving strategies.

Instructional Practices
- Use of manipulative materials.
- Cooperative work.
- Discussion of mathematics.
- Questioning.
- Justification of thinking.
- Writing about mathematics.
- Problem-solving approach to instruction.
- Content integration.
- Use of calculators and computers.

Decreased Attention

Number
- Early attention to reading, writing, and ordering numbers symbolically.

Operations and Computation
- Complex paper-and-pencil computations.
- Isolated treatment of paper-and-pencil computations.
- Addition and subtraction without renaming.
- Isolated treatment of division facts.
- Long division.
- Long division without remainders.
- Paper-and-pencil fraction computation.
- Use of rounding to estimate.

Geometry and Measurement
- Primary focus on naming geometric figures.
- Memorization of equivalencies between units of measurement.

Problem Solving
- Use of clue words to determine which operation to use.

Instructional Practices
- Rote practice.
- Rote memorization of rules.
- One answer and one method.
- Use of worksheets.
- Written practice.
- Teaching by telling.

SUMMARY OF CHANGES IN CONTENT AND EMPHASIS IN 5–8 MATHEMATICS

Increased Attention	*Decreased Attention*

Problem Solving
- Pursuing open-ended problems and extended problem-solving projects.
- Investigating and formulating questions from problem situations.
- Representing situations verbally, numerically, graphically, geometrically, or symbolically.

Communication
- Discussing, writing, reading, and listening to mathematical ideas.

Reasoning
- Reasoning in spatial contexts.
- Reasoning with proportions.
- Reasoning from graphs.
- Reasoning inductively and deductively.

Connections
- Connecting mathematics to other subjects and to the world outside the classroom.
- Connecting topics within mathematics.
- Applying mathematics.

Number/Operations/Computation
- Developing number sense.
- Developing operation sense.
- Creating algorithms and procedures.
- Using estimation both in solving problems and in checking the reasonableness of results.
- Exploring relationships among representations of, and operations on, whole numbers, fractions, decimals, integers, and rational numbers.
- Developing an understanding of ratio, proportion, and percent.

Patterns and Functions
- Identifying and using functional relationships.
- Developing and using tables, graphs, and rules to describe situations.
- Interpreting among different mathematical representations.

Algebra
- Developing an understanding of variables, expressions, and equations.
- Using a variety of methods to solve linear equations and informally investigate inequalities and nonlinear equations.

Statistics
- Using statistical methods to describe, analyze, evaluate, and make decisions.

Problem Solving
- Practicing routine, one-step problems.
- Practicing problems categorized by types (e.g., coin problems; age problems)

Communication
- Doing fill-in-the-blank worksheets.
- Answering questions that require only yes, no, or a number as responses.

Reasoning
- Relying on outside authority (teacher or an answer key).

Connections
- Learning isolated topics.
- Developing skills out of context.

Number/Operations/Computation
- Memorizing rules and algorithms.
- Practicing tedious paper-and-pencil computations.
- Finding exact forms of answers.
- Memorizing procedures, such as cross-multiplication, without understanding.
- Practicing rounding numbers out of context.

Patterns and Functions
- Topics seldom in the current curriculum.

Algebra
- Manipulating symbols.
- Memorizing procedures and drilling on equation solving.

Statistics
- Memorizing formulas.

Probability

- Creating experimental and theoretical models of situations involving probabilities.

Geometry

- Developing an understanding of geometric objects and relationships.
- Using geometry in solving problems.

Measurement

- Estimating and using measurement to solve problems.

Instructional Practices

- Actively involving students individually and in groups in exploring, conjecturing, analyzing, and applying mathematics in both a mathematical and a real-world context.
- Using appropriate technology for computation and exploration.
- Using concrete materials.
- Being a facilitator of learning.
- Assessing learning as an integral part of instruction.

Probability

- Memorizing formulas.

Geometry

- Memorizing geometric vocabulary.
- Memorizing facts and relationships.

Measurement

- Memorizing and manipulating formulas.
- Converting within and between measurement systems.

Instructional Practices

- Teaching computations out of context.
- Drilling on paper-and-pencil algorithms.
- Teaching topics in isolation.
- Stressing memorization.
- Being the dispenser of knowledge.
- Testing for the sole purpose of assigning grades.

The next two tables list where standards are illustrated in the following 16 pages.

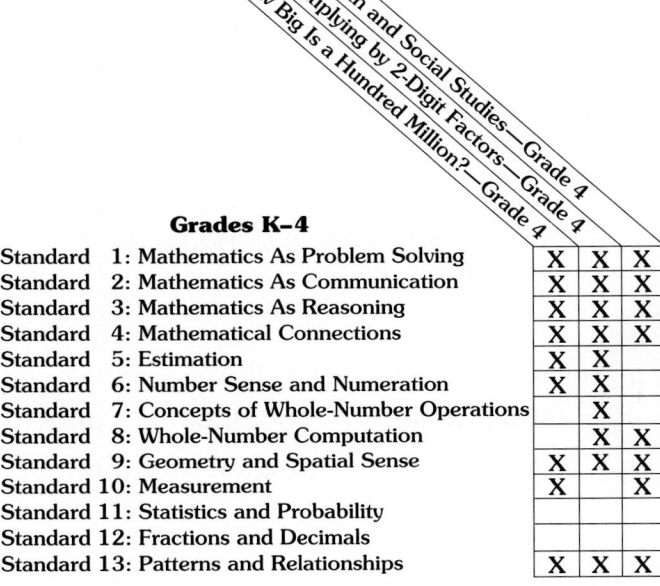

Grades K–4

Standard	How Big Is a Hundred Million?—Grade 4	Multiplying by 2-Digit Factors—Grade 4	Math and Social Studies—Grade 4
Standard 1: Mathematics As Problem Solving	X	X	X
Standard 2: Mathematics As Communication	X	X	X
Standard 3: Mathematics As Reasoning	X	X	X
Standard 4: Mathematical Connections	X	X	X
Standard 5: Estimation	X	X	
Standard 6: Number Sense and Numeration	X	X	
Standard 7: Concepts of Whole-Number Operations		X	
Standard 8: Whole-Number Computation		X	X
Standard 9: Geometry and Spatial Sense	X	X	X
Standard 10: Measurement	X		X
Standard 11: Statistics and Probability			
Standard 12: Fractions and Decimals			
Standard 13: Patterns and Relationships	X	X	X

Grades 5–8

Standard	Math and Art—Grade 5	Buying a New or Used Item—Grade 5	The Maya Calandar—Grade 5	Area of Irregular Figures—Grade 6	Probability and Prediction—Grade 6	Percent of a Number—Grade 6	Misleading Statistics—Grade 7	Building the Best Box—Grade 8
Standard 1: Mathematics As Problem Solving	X	X	X	X	X	X	X	X
Standard 2: Mathematics As Communication	X	X	X	X	X	X	X	X
Standard 3: Mathematics As Reasoning	X	X	X	X	X	X	X	X
Standard 4: Mathematical Connections	X	X	X	X	X	X	X	X
Standard 5: Number and Number Relationships	X	X	X		X	X	X	X
Standard 6: Number Systems and Number Theory			X		X	X	X	
Standard 7: Computation and Estimation			X	X	X	X	X	X
Standard 8: Patterns and Functions	X		X					X
Standard 9: Algebra						X		
Standard 10: Statistics							X	
Standard 11: Probability					X			
Standard 12: Geometry	X							X
Standard 13: Measurement			X	X		X	X	X

ACTIVITY

How Big Is a Hundred Million?

How tall would a stack of 100,000,000 sheets of paper be? Would it be as tall as your school? as tall as a mountain?

You can use what you know about numbers to estimate the height of the stack.

WORKING TOGETHER

Make a stack of 100 sheets of paper.

1. What object in your classroom is about this tall?

2. How many stacks of 100 do you need to make a stack of 1,000?

3. How would you estimate the height of a stack of 1,000 sheets of paper? What object in your classroom is about this tall?

4. How could you estimate the height of a stack of 10,000 sheets of paper? of 100,000 sheets? of 1,000,000 sheets?

5. How do your estimates compare with your height? with the height of your classroom? with the height of your school?

6. Estimate the height of 100,000,000 sheets of paper. Tell how you made the estimate. Can you think of something this tall?

SHARING IDEAS

7. How did you use place value to help you estimate?

8. Compare your method for estimating the heights of the stacks with those of others. How were the methods the same? How were they different?

ON YOUR OWN

Choose at least one activity. You may wish to try more than one.

9. About how many pages are in all the books in your school or neighborhood library? How did you find this number?

10. Estimate how long it would take you to count to 100,000,000. How did you make this estimate?

11. About how many steps do you take to get to school? 100? 1,000? 1,000,000? Tell how you estimated this number.

12. Look in newspapers and magazines for large numbers. Write about how you think these large numbers were counted.

ACTIVITY

Multiplying by 2-Digit Factors

Mrs. Mack is donating a large quilt to a charity auction. The quilt is made of colored squares sewn together. It is shaped like a rectangle that is 36 squares long and 24 squares wide. How many squares are in the quilt?

Estimate. Then draw a diagram to solve the problem.

WORKING TOGETHER

Step 1 On graph paper draw a rectangle that is 36 squares long and 24 squares wide.

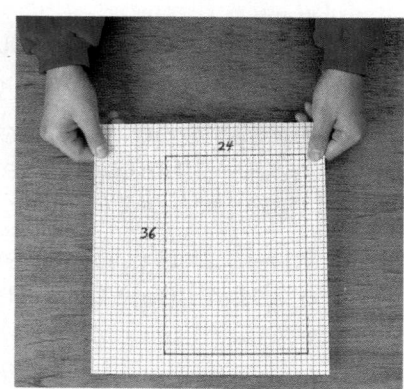

Step 2 Separate the rectangle into 4 sections like this:

Section A: 6 squares long by 4 squares wide

Section B: 6 squares long by 20 squares wide

Section C: 30 squares long by 4 squares wide

Section D: 30 squares long by 20 squares wide

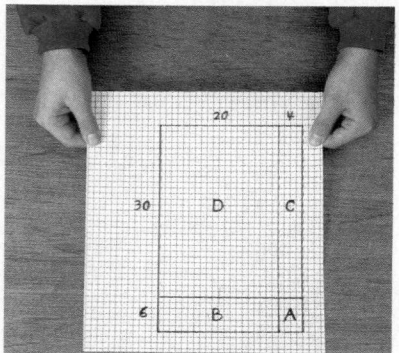

How many squares are in each section?

1. A   **2.** B   **3.** C   **4.** D

5. How many squares are there in the diagram?

6. How many squares are there in the quilt?

SHARING IDEAS

7. How did you find the number of squares in each section?

8. Write a multiplication sentence to show how to find the number of squares in each section.

9. How did separating the entire rectangle into smaller rectangular sections make it easier to find the total number of squares?

ON YOUR OWN

Draw a diagram to solve. Write multiplication sentences to show the number of squares in each section.

10. David and his mother are working on a quilt that is 21 squares long and 23 squares wide. How many squares are in their quilt?

11. Mrs. Henderson's quilt won an award at the quilting bee. Her quilt is 42 squares long and 56 squares wide. How many squares are in her quilt?

12. *Write a problem* that involves multiplying two 2-digit numbers. Solve your problem. Ask others to solve it.

CURRICULUM CONNECTION

Math and Social Studies

People from many different cultures have built pyramids as monuments or temples. One of the most famous pyramids still standing is the Great Pyramid of Khufu in Giza, Egypt. This monument to the pharaoh, or ruler, Khufu, was built from 2,300,000 blocks of stone. When it was built, it was 146 meters tall. Each of its four sides is 230 meters long.

What is the perimeter of the Great Pyramid?

Think: Perimeter is the distance around an object. Each of the four sides of the pyramid is 230 meters long.

$$230 + 230 + 230 + 230 = 920$$

The perimeter of the Great Pyramid is 920 meters.

ACTIVITIES

1. The Pyramid of Quetzalcoatl in Cholula, Mexico, stands 64 meters tall, and each of its four sides is 350 meters long. What is its perimeter? How does its perimeter compare to the Great Pyramid's perimeter? Find out why it was built.

2. Find out about other pyramids. Who built them and why? What were they built of? When and where were they built? Have any pyramids been built recently?

CURRICULUM CONNECTION

Math and Art

The Hopi of northern Arizona make beautifully designed coiled baskets. Most Hopi baskets have colorful patterns. Sometimes the patterns are repeated irregularly around the basket. Other times the patterns may show *symmetry*. A figure has symmetry if it can be folded so that one part matches the other part exactly. The fold line of such a figure is a *line of symmetry*. Figures that do not have symmetry are *asymmetrical* as opposed to symmetrical.

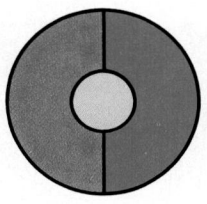

Symmetrical   Asymmetrical

What if you want to use the design labeled *asymmetrical* as part of a symmetrical design? How could you use the asymmetrical figure in a symmetrical pattern?

Think: You need to position the design so that when it is folded in the middle, the two pieces match exactly. Although the figure itself is asymmetrical, you can repeat it to make a symmetrical design by turning the asymmetrical figure over as shown on the left.

ACTIVITIES

1. Design a basket. You may use graph paper and different color markers. Show your understanding of symmetry by making one part of your design symmetrical and another part asymmetrical. Label each.

2. The Navajo people of New Mexico have designed beautiful rugs as well as jewelry and other crafts. Research Navajo crafts for examples of rugs that have symmetrical and asymmetrical designs. Prepare an oral report for your class.

DECISION MAKING

COOPERATIVE LEARNING

Problem Solving: Buying a New or Used Item

SITUATION

Julie wants to buy a bicycle. She plans to use the bicycle to ride to school each day and to ride for fun.

PROBLEM

Should Julie buy a new or a used bicycle?

DATA

For Sale: Girl's 10-speed bike, yellow, excellent cond., 6 mo. old, $68. Call 333-4256

BICYCLE BILL'S NEW AND USED BICYCLES

$105

$185

$250

10-speed bicycle
All frame sizes and styles
Red, blue, white
1-year warranty

12-speed bicycle
All frame sizes and styles
Blue, black, silver
2-year warranty

18-speed all-terrain bicycle
All frame sizes and styles. Red, blue
2-year warranty

All used bicycles guaranteed for 30 days.

Used Girls' Bicycles

26" red all-terrain fair condition 12-speed 5 years old .... $ 82
20" green 10-speed good condition 10 years old .... $ 59
28" pink 10-speed excellent condition 2 years old $115

Used Boys' Bicycles

For Sale: Girl's 10-speed bike, orange, 24", good cond., 4-yr. old, $35. Call days: 852-6721

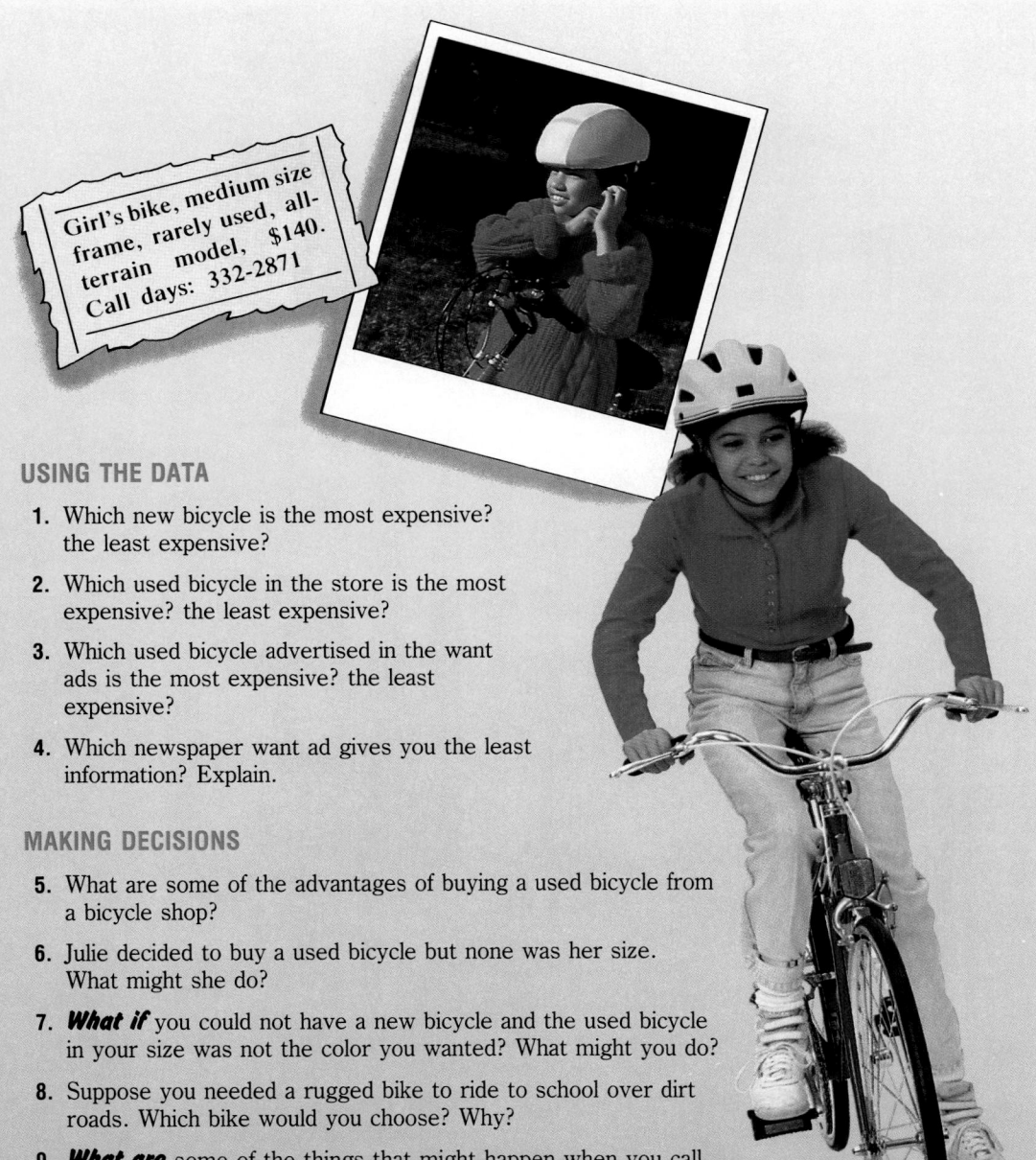

Girl's bike, medium size frame, rarely used, all-terrain model, $140. Call days: 332-2871

USING THE DATA

1. Which new bicycle is the most expensive? the least expensive?

2. Which used bicycle in the store is the most expensive? the least expensive?

3. Which used bicycle advertised in the want ads is the most expensive? the least expensive?

4. Which newspaper want ad gives you the least information? Explain.

MAKING DECISIONS

5. What are some of the advantages of buying a used bicycle from a bicycle shop?

6. Julie decided to buy a used bicycle but none was her size. What might she do?

7. *What if* you could not have a new bicycle and the used bicycle in your size was not the color you wanted? What might you do?

8. Suppose you needed a rugged bike to ride to school over dirt roads. Which bike would you choose? Why?

9. *What are* some of the things that might happen when you call about a used bike listed in the want ads?

10. *Write a list* of other things you should think about when deciding whether to buy a new or used bicycle.

11. *What if* you are going to buy a bicycle? Would you choose a new or a used bicycle? Why?

THE MAYA CALENDAR

The Maya calendar was based on a number of different cycles. One cycle is the *vague year*, made up of eighteen 20-day periods plus 5 days, for a total of 365 days. It is called "vague" because the earth actually takes about $365\frac{1}{4}$ days to make one revolution around the sun. Over a long period of time, the extra $\frac{1}{4}$ day throws off the cycle. Eventually the seasons occur in a different part of the cycle.

Another cycle in the Maya calendar is called the *ritual almanac*. This cycle contained 260 days. For the most part it was used to keep track of rituals and ceremonies. With this cycle, a new year might begin in the summer months in some years and in the winter months in other years.

Every 18,980 days the cycles of the vague year and the ritual almanac coincided. At that time, great festivals and celebrations were held.

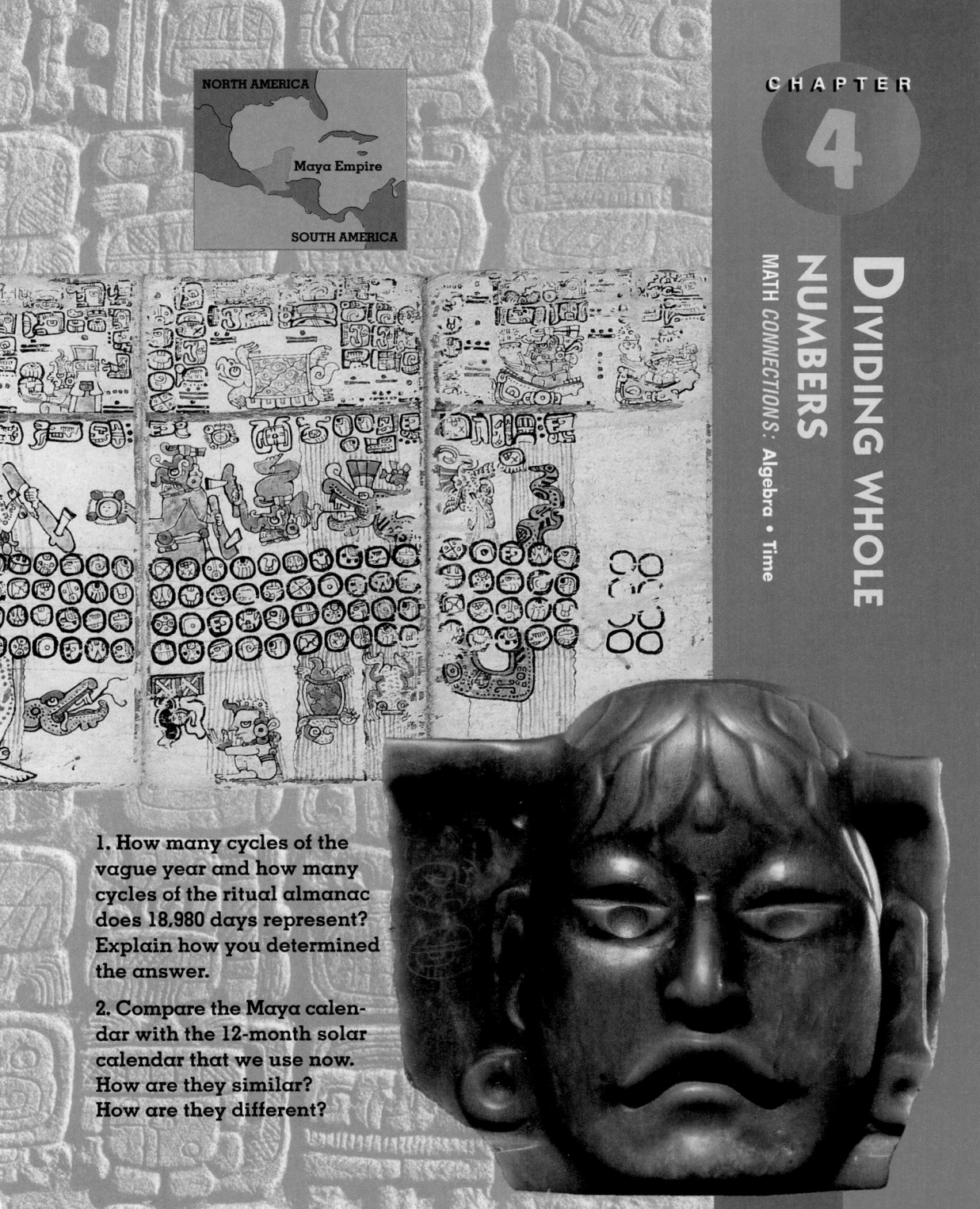

1. How many cycles of the
vague year and how many
cycles of the ritual almanac
does 18,980 days represent?
Explain how you determined
the answer.

2. Compare the Maya calendar with the 12-month solar
calendar that we use now.
How are they similar?
How are they different?

ACTIVITY
Areas of Irregular Figures

A camera in a high-altitude balloon took a photo of a lake as a part of a mapmaking research project. To measure the area of the lake, a mapmaker put a grid on top of the photo. The sides of each square stand for 1 mi. About what is the area of the lake in square miles?

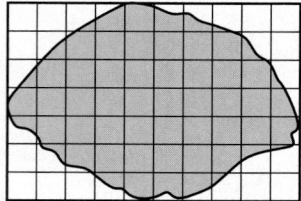

WORKING TOGETHER

1. Trace and shade the lake on a piece of grid paper. Make sure you shade it so you can see the lines on the grid paper.

2. Using the lines of your grid paper, draw the biggest figure you can that lies completely within your lake. Count the squares.

3. Using the lines of your grid paper, enclose your lake in the smallest figure you can. Count the squares between the two figures you drew.

4. How can you use the information in Problems 2 and 3 to approximate the area of the lake?

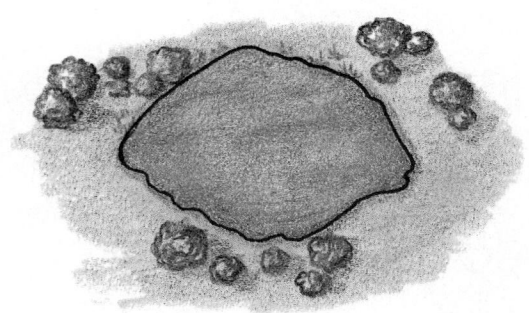

Here is how Natasha found the area. She counted 29 squares inside the lake. To that number she added one-half of 30, the number of squares between the two figures. So her estimate of the area of the lake is

$$29 + \left(\frac{1}{2} \times 30\right) = 29 + 15 = 44 \text{ square miles.}$$

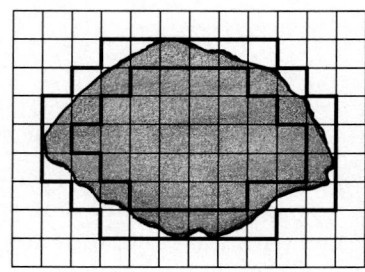

SHARING IDEAS

5. This estimation method uses one-half the number of squares between the two figures. Why do you think this number is used?

6. Find the area of the face of a quarter by tracing it on grid paper and then estimating. Then use the formula on page 440 to find the area. How does your estimate compare with the formula answer?

ACTIVITY Probability and Prediction

Without looking you reach in and pick a cube from the bag at the right. You record its color and replace the cube. You shake the bag, pick another cube, and record its color. In 20 draws how many times would you expect to pick a blue cube? a red cube? a green cube?

WORKING TOGETHER

1. Use your centimeter cubes to model the experiment above. Predict how many times you will pick each color in 20 draws. Then actually try it. Record your results.

2. **What if** you were to pick a cube 40 times? What results would you predict for each color? Try it. Are the actual results closer to the prediction this time?

3. Look at your results for 20 picks. What is the ratio of blue cubes picked to the total number of picks? What ratio do you get for red? for green?

4. Answer Problem 3 for 40 picks. Compare the ratios for 40 picks to those for 20 picks. What can you conclude?

These are Eli's results for the experiment. He concluded that the ratios would be about the same no matter how many picks there were.

blue: 20 picks, $\frac{11}{20}$ 40 picks, $\frac{22}{40}$

green: 20 picks, $\frac{3}{20}$ 40 picks, $\frac{7}{40}$

red: 20 picks, $\frac{6}{20}$ 40 picks, $\frac{11}{40}$

SHARING IDEAS

5. In simplest form, what is the probability of picking a blue cube from the bag?

6. Look at Eli's results for 20 picks. Multiply the probability of picking blue by 20. How does this compare to the actual number of times Eli picked blue?

7. Look at Eli's results for 40 picks. Multiply the probability of picking green and of picking red by 40. How do your numbers compare with the actual number of times Eli picked these colors?

8. How can you use the probability of an event to predict the number of favorable outcomes?

MATH *CONNECTION:* ALGEBRA

Percent of a Number: Using Algebraic Equations and Proportions

A. A seventh-grade class is having a Trivia Olympics Night. The students need to prepare 175 questions, of which 20% will be about sports. How many questions will be about sports?

You can use an equation to find the percent of a number.

Let n = the number of questions about sports.

n = 20% of 175

Solve: n = 20% of 175

You can solve the equation in either of two ways.

Using a fraction equivalent	Using a decimal equivalent
20% of 175 = n	20% of 175 = n
$\frac{1}{5} \times 175 = n$	$0.2 \times 175 = n$
$\frac{175}{5} = n$	$35 = n$
$35 = n$	

There will be 35 questions about sports.

1. Is 35 a reasonable answer? Why?

B. You can also use a proportion to find the percent of a number.
Find 20% of 175.

Write a proportion.

Let n = the number you are looking for.

Think: 20% = $\frac{20}{100}$

$$\overset{\frown{\text{part}}}{\underset{\smile{\text{whole}}}{\frac{20}{100} = \frac{n}{175}}}$$

Solve the proportion using cross products.

$100 \times n = 20 \times 175$

$100n = 3{,}500$

$n = 35$

Misleading Statistics

A. Look at the bars on the graph. It appears that females live more than three times as long as males in each country.

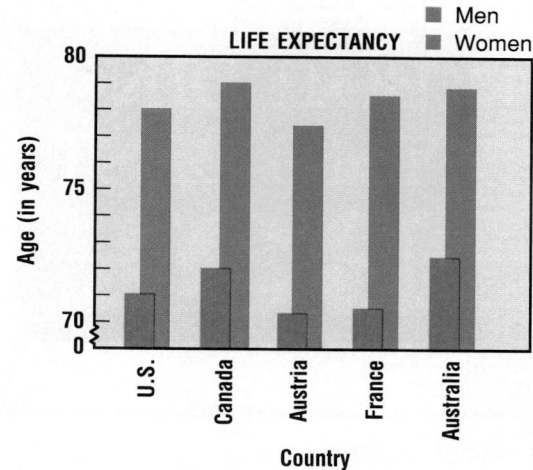

Use the scale on the graph to find the difference in life expectancies in each country:

United States: 78 − 71 = 7 years
Canada: 78.9 − 71.9 = 7 years
Austria: 77.2 − 70.1 = 7.1 years
France: 78.4 − 70.4 = 8 years
Australia: 78.7 − 72.6 = 6.1 years

In each country females live only about 7 years more than males, not nearly three times as long.

1. Why is the graph misleading?

2. How could you change the graph to give a clearer representation of the situation?

B. When you look at the graph, it appears that whole milk contains three to four times as much fat. But, using the scale on the graph, you find that there are 8 grams of fat in whole milk and 5 grams in 2% milk.

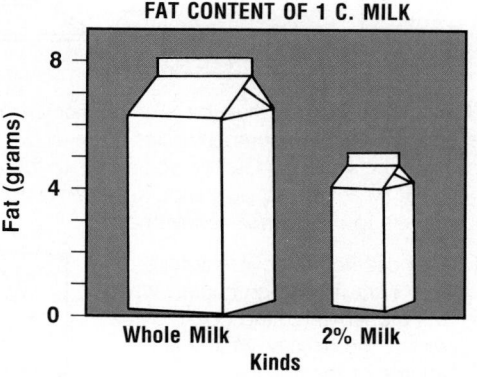

Think: $\frac{8}{5}$, or about $1\frac{1}{2}$

There is about $1\frac{1}{2}$ times as much fat in whole milk as in 2% milk.

3. How could you show this data in a more informative way?

TRY OUT

4. From the graph, about how many times as long as a $1 bill does a $20 bill appear to last?

5. About how many times as long as a $1 bill does a $20 actually last?

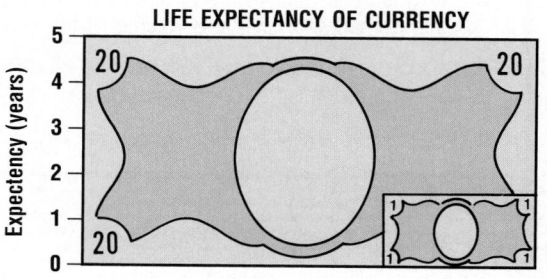

BUILDING THE BEST BOX

Measuring

A. Suppose you are the senior designer for Premium Packages. The company warehouse is overstocked with square pieces of cardboard 20 cm by 20 cm. By cutting and removing equal-size squares from the corners of the cardboard and then folding up the sides, your machines can produce open boxes.

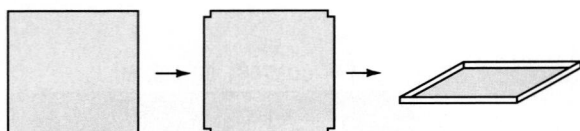

The height of the box must be a whole number of centimeters, and the company sales manager wants a box with the greatest possible volume. Your job is to figure out what size squares should be removed from the corners to meet these requirements.

1. Suppose you remove a square of side 1 cm from each corner. What will the length of the box be? the width? the height? What will the volume of the box be?

2. Suppose you remove a square of side 2 cm from each corner. What will the volume of the box be?

3. Do you think the volume will increase or decrease as you remove larger and larger squares? Why?

4. What is the largest square you can remove? Why?

To organize your information, you make a table like the one below.

Dimensions of Squares Removed	Dimension of Open Box	Volume
1 cm × 1 cm		
2 cm × 2 cm		

5. Complete the table.

6. What are the dimensions of the box with the greatest volume?

B. Suppose now that you can remove squares with dimensions other than whole centimeters. What size squares should you remove to build the box with greatest volume?

7. Between what two whole-number lengths do you think the side of this new square will be? Why?

8. Experiment with different-size squares (use tenths of centimeters). Try to find a strategy for the way you work. Can you find a greater volume than before?

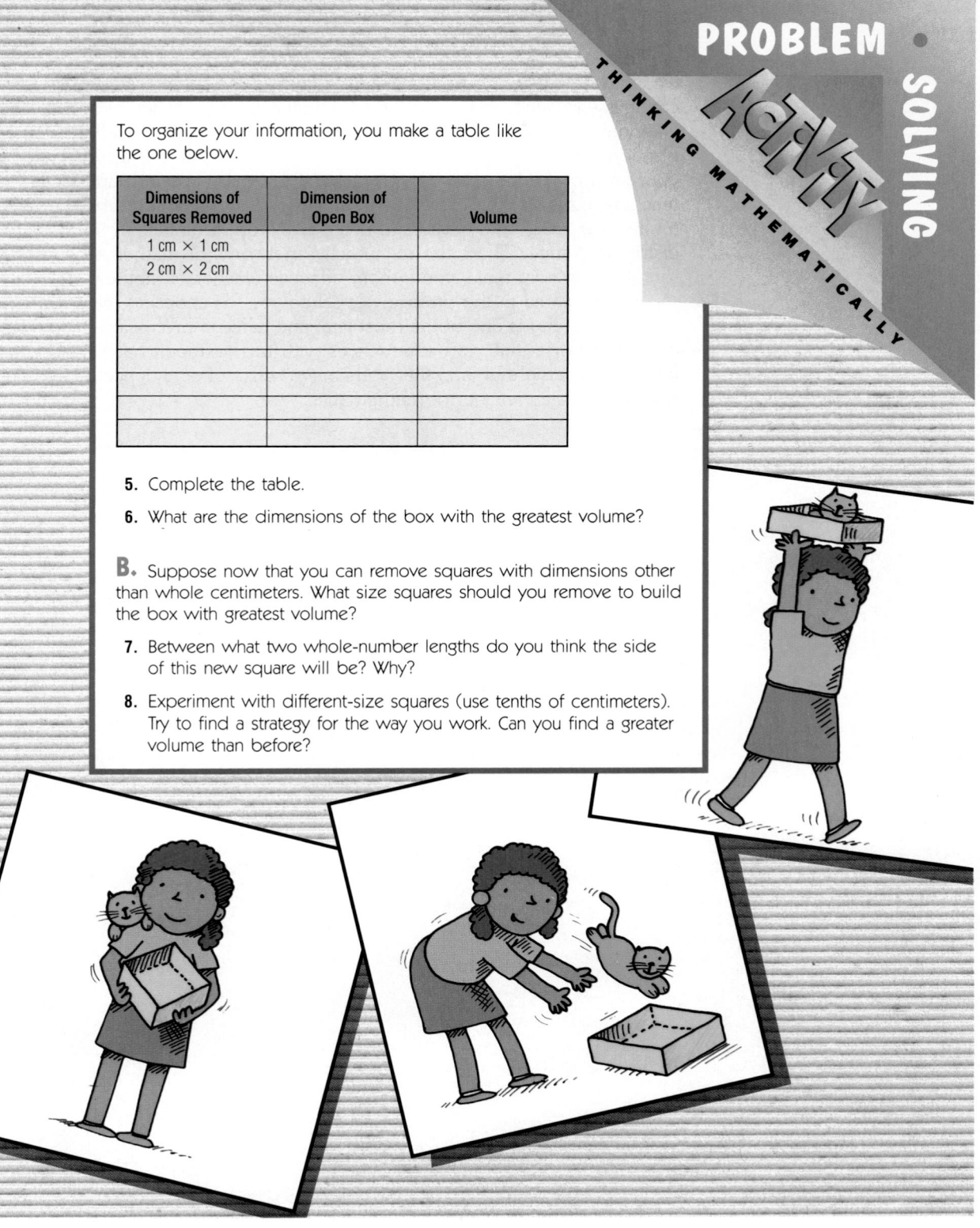

In your career as a teacher, you will see many changes in education that we cannot predict. There are some things that you can do to keep up with changes and trends in teaching. First, join teacher organizations such as the National Council of Teachers of Mathematics and your state's affiliate organization. In so doing, you will receive one or more journals appropriate to your level of mathematics teaching. Such journals contain many ideas for teachers, class activities, references, and information about inservice opportunities. Second, take advantage of inservice opportunities in your school district and state. There are many active networks of mathematics educators that can help make you a more effective teacher of mathematics.

As we stated in the preface, we salute you for choosing teaching as a career. Teaching is one of the most vital and fulfilling professions in our society. We hope that your experiences with this textbook have been challenging and insightful, and that you have a sense of confidence about your preparation as a teacher of mathematics.

Answers to Exercise/Problem Sets–Part A and Tests, Chapter Tests, Technology Section, and Topics Section

SECTION 1.1—PART A

1. 8.
2. 36 ft × 78 ft.
3. 88.
4. $9 = 4 + 5$. If n is odd, then both $n - 1$ and $n + 1$ are even and $n = \dfrac{n - 1}{2} + \dfrac{n + 1}{2}$.
5. $6 \div 6 + 6 + 6 = 13$
6.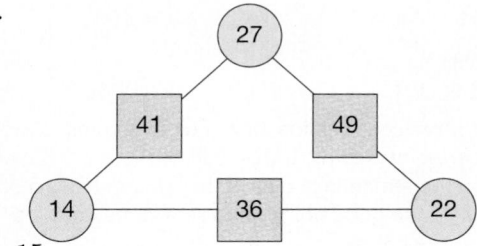
7. 15.
8. Pour as much as possible from two of the 3-liter pails into the 5-liter pail; one liter will be left in the 3-liter pail.
9.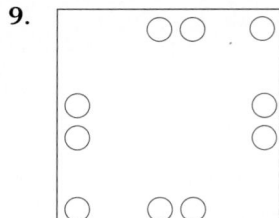
10. No; $0 + 1 + 2 + 3 + 4 + 5 + 6 + 7 + 8 + 9 = 45$, which is too large.
11. For example, beginning at corner: 8, 2, 6, 7, 3, 4, 9, 5, 1.

12. Row 1: 9, 3, 4; row 2: 8, 2, 5; row 3: 7, 6, 1.
13. $3 \cdot 5 \cdot 7 \cdot 9 \cdot 11 \cdot 13 \cdot 15 \cdot 17 = 34{,}459{,}425$.
14. 52.
15. Bill.
16. **(a)** 1839. **(b)** 47.
17. For example, row 1: 3, 5; row 2: 7, 1, 8, 2; row 3: 4, 6.
18.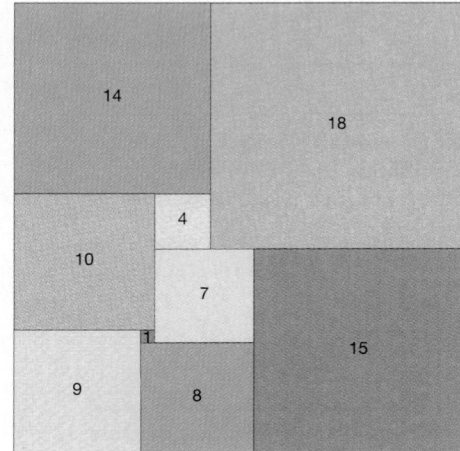
19. 21 years old.
20. 35 or 64.
21. U = 9, S = 3, R = 8, A = 2, P = 1, E = 0, C = 7.
22. At least 90 cents per hour.
23. 14 moves.

A1

24. Start both timers. When the 5-minute timer expires, start it again. When the 8-minute timer expires, start it again; the 5-minute timer will have 2 minutes left on it. When the 5-minute timer expires, start measuring, since the 8-minute timer will have 6 minutes left.

25. 3.

26. Top pair: 8, 5; second pair from the top: 4, 1; third pair from the top: 6, 3; bottom pair: 2, 7. There are other correct answers.

27. $\dfrac{4(n + 10) + 200}{4} - n = (n + 10) + 50 - n = n + 60 - n = 60.$

28. For example, $98 - 7 + 6 + 5 - 4 + 3 - 2 + 1 = 100$, and $9 - 8 + 76 + 6 - 5 + 4 - 3 + 21 = 100$.

29. 130 drops 160 off on the top floor and returns. 210 takes the elevator to the top while 130 stays behind. 160 returns and comes up to the top with 130.

30. 1 and 12, 9 and 10.

SECTION 1.2—PART A

1. **(a)** 9, 16, 25.   **(b)** 9.   **(c)** 13.
  (d) 23. $(1 + 3 + 5 + \cdots + (2n - 1) = n^2).$

2. **(a)** 32.   **(b)** $\dfrac{1}{27}$.   **(c)** 21.   **(d)** 1287.

3. **(a)**

D	D	D
	D	D
	□	

(b)

○		◹
		→

4. **(a)** $5556^2 - 4445^2 = 11,111,111.$
  (b) $55555556^2 - 44444445^2 = 1,111,111,111,111,111.$

5.

60	6	10
30	6	5
2	1	2

6. **(a)**

Triangular Number	Number of Dots in Shape
1	1
2	3
3	6
4	10
5	15
6	21

(b)

(c) 55 dots.
(d) Yes, the 13th number.
(e) No, the 16th number has 136 and the 17th number has 153.
(f) $\dfrac{n(n + 1)}{2}.$
(g) $\dfrac{100(101)}{2} = 5050.$

7. **(a)** $3 + 6 = 9.$
  (b) $10 + 15 = 25.$
  (c) $45 + 55 = 100$, $190 + 210 = 400$, $(n - 1)$st $+$ nth.
  (d) 36 is the 8th triangular number and is the 6th square number.
  (e) Some possible answers:
  $4 - 1 = 3$ $64 - 36 = 28$
  $49 - 4 = 45$ $64 - 9 = 55$
  $64 - 49 = 15$ $169 - 64 = 105$

8. 18 pages.

9. $1993 \times (1 + 2 + 3 + 4 + \cdots + 1994).$

10. Do a three-coin version first. For five coins, start by comparing two coins. If they balance, use a three-coin test on the remaining coins. If they do not balance, add in one of the good coins and use a three-coin test.

11. $10,737,418.23 if paid the second way.

12. For n triangles, perimeter $= n + 2.$

13. 34, 36, 44, 54, 76, 146.

14. **(a)** 50, 500, etc.   **(b)** 25, 250, etc.
  (c) 4, 40, 400, etc.   **(d)** 75, 750, etc.

15. 119 0s are necessary.
  11 9s are necessary.

16. **(a)** In the 4, 6, 12, 14, . . . column.
  (b) In the 2, 8, 10, 16, . . . column.
  (c) In the 3, 7, 11, 15, . . . column.
  (d) In the 5, 13, . . . column.

17. 13.

18. $100^3 = 1,000,000.$

19. 34, 55, 89, 144, 233, 377;
  $144 \cdot 233 = 33,552.$

20. 987.

21. (a) Sums are 1, 1, 2, 3, 5, 8, 13. Each sum is a Fibonacci number.
   (b) Next three sums: 21, 34, 55.

22. (a) Sum is 20.
   (b) Sum of numbers inside the circle is always twice the number directly below the circle.

23. Pilot should fly when there is no wind.

24. (a)

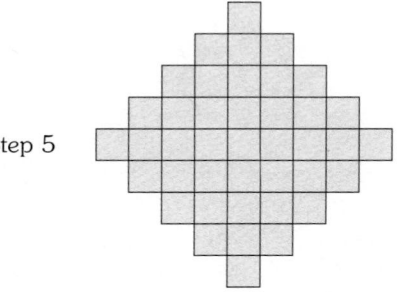

Step 5

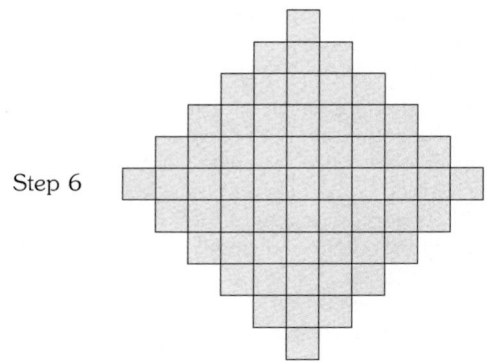

Step 6

(b)

Step	Number of Squares
1	1
2	5
3	13
4	25
5	41
6	61

(c) 85.

(d) 10th, 181; 20th, 761; 50th, 4901.

25. 23.

26. (a) 18.   **(b)** 66.

Chapter 1 Test

1. Exercises are routine applications of known procedures, whereas problems require the solver to take an original mental step.

2. Understand the problem; make a plan; carry out the plan; look back.

3. Guess and test; use a variable; look for a pattern; make a list; solve a simpler problem; draw a picture.

4. 4×4: 1, 2, 3, 4; 2: 3, 4, 1, 2; 3: 4, 3, 2, 1; 4: 2, 1, 4, 3. The 2×2 is impossible. 3×3: 1, 2, 3; 3, 2, 1; 2, 1, 3.

5. 6.

6. 30.

7. Head and tail are 4 inches long and the body is 22 inches long.

8. 256.

SECTION 2.1—PART A

1. (a) {6, 7, 8}.   **(b)** {2, 4, 6, 8, 10, 12, 14}.
   (c) {2, 4, 6, . . . , 150}.   **(d)** {9, 10, 11, . . .}.
   (e) {1, 3, . . . , 99}.   **(f)** { }.

2. (a) T.   **(b)** F.   **(c)** T.   **(d)** F.   **(e)** T.
   (f) T.   **(g)** F.   **(h)** T.   **(i)** F.   **(j)** T.

3. $\varnothing$, {a}, {b}, {c}, {a, b}, {a, c}, {b, c}, {a, b, c}.

4. $\varnothing$, {$\triangle$}, {$\bigcirc$}

5.
$x \leftarrow a$ $x \quad a$ $x \quad a$ $x \quad a$
$y \quad b$ $y \quad b$ $y \quad b$ $y \quad b$
$z \quad c$ $z \leftarrow c$ $z \quad c$ $z \quad c$.

6. (a)

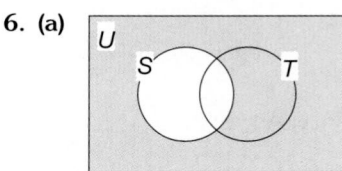

(b)

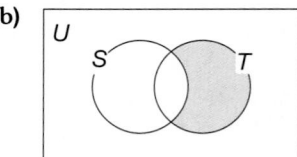

(c)

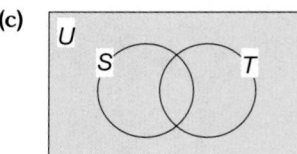

7. (a)

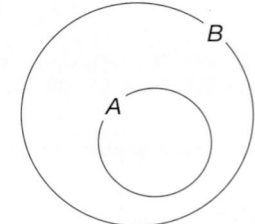

(b)

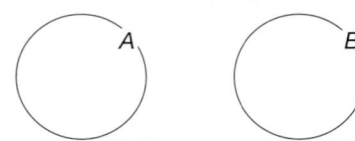

(c)

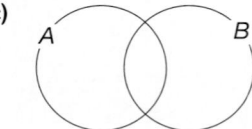

8. (a) {b, c}.   **(b)** {b, c, e}.   **(c)** {a}.

9.
(a) Women *or* Americans who have won Nobel prizes.
(b) Nobel prize winners who are American women.
(c) American winners of Nobel prize in chemistry.

10. (a) {0, 1, 2, 3, 4, 5, 6, 8, 10}.
(b) {0, 2, 4, 6, 8, 10}.   **(c)** {0, 2, 4}.
(d) {0, 4, 8}.   **(e)** {2, 6, 10}.
(f) {1, 2, 3, 5, 6, 10}.

11. (a) {January, June, July, August}.
(b) {January}.
(c) ∅.
(d) {January, June, July}.
(e) {March, April, May, September, October, November}.
(f) {January}.

12. (a) Yes; compare Figures 2.4 and 2.5.
(b) Not necessarily; if $x \in X - Y$, then $x \in X \cup Y$, but $x \notin X \cap Y$.

13. (a)

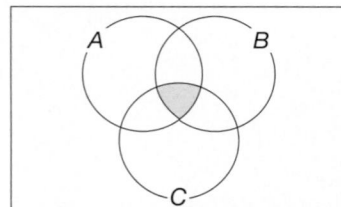

(b)

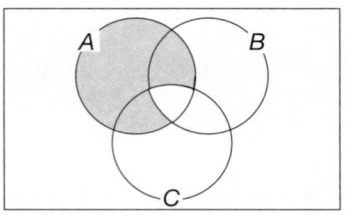

(c)

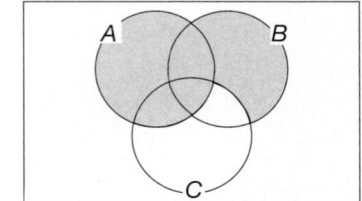

14. (a) $(B \cap C) - A$.   **(b)** $C - (A \cup B)$.
(c) $(A \cup (B \cap C)) - (A \cap B \cap C)$.
NOTE: There are many other correct answers.

15. (a) Yes.
(b) {3, 6, 9, 12, 15, 18, 21, 24, . . .}.
(c) {6, 12, 18, 24, . . .}.
(d) $A \cup B = A$, $A \cap B = B$.

16. (a) Region inside circle or triangle.
(b) Region inside both circle and rectangle.
(c) Region inside rectangle combined with region inside both circle and triangle.
(d) Region inside any of the three figures.
(e) Small corner of rectangle that is also inside triangle and circle.
(f) Same as part (e).

17. (a) $\overline{A \cup B} = \overline{A} \cap \overline{B} = \{6\}$. Yes, the sets are the same.
(b) $\overline{A \cup B}$ and $\overline{A} \cap \overline{B}$ are both represented by

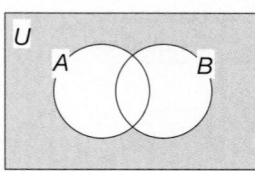

Yes, the diagrams are the same.

18. (a) {(a, b), (a, c)}.   **(b)** {(5, a), (5, b), (5, c)}.
(c) {(a 1), (a, 2), (a, 3), (b, 1), (b, 2), (b, 3)}.
(d) {(2, 1), (2, 4), (3, 1), (3, 4)}.
(e) {(a, 5), (b, 5), (c, 5)}.
(f) {(1, a), (2, a), (3, a), (1, b), (2, b), (3, b)}.

19. (a) 8.   **(b)** 12.

20. (a) 2.   **(b)** 4.   **(c)** Not possible.
(d) 25.   **(e)** 0.   **(f)** Not possible.

21. (a) $A = \{a\}$, $B = \{2, 4, 6\}$.   **(b)** $A = B = \{a, b\}$.

22. (a) T.   (b) F.   (c) F.   (d) F.   (e) F.
23. (a) 2.   (b) 99.   (c) 201.
24. (a) Three elements; eight elements.
(b) y elements; $x + y$ elements.
25. 24.
26. (a) 1.   (b) 2.   (c) 4.   (d) 8.   (e) 32.
(f) $2 \cdot 2 \cdot 2 \cdot \cdots \cdot 2$ (2 appears n times).
27. (a) Possible.   (b) Not possible.
28. (a) When $D \subseteq E$.
(b) When $E = \{\ \}$ or when $E \subseteq D$.
(c) When $E = D$.
29. The Cartesian product of the set of skirts with the set of blouses will determine how many outfits can be formed; 56 in this case.
30. 31 matches.
31. (a) 7.   (b) 19.   (c) 49.
32. Twenty-five were butchers, bakers, *and* candlestick makers.
33. Yes. Use lines perpendicular to the base.
34. Yes.

SECTION 2.2—PART A

1. 314−781−9804, identification; 13905, identification; 6, cardinal; 7814, identification; 28, ordinal; $10, cardinal; 20, ordinal.
2. (a) Attribute common to all sets that match the set $\{a, b, c, d, e, f, g\}$.
(b) Attribute common to all sets that match $\{a\}$.
(c) Impossible.
(d) How many elements are in the empty set?
3. Put in one-to-one correspondence with the set $\{1, 2, 3, 4, 5, 6\}$.
4. 8; 5.
5. 9 is greater than 4; counting chant: 4 comes before 9; whole-number line: 4 is to the left of 9; set method: a set of 4 elements can be matched to a proper subset of a set with 9 elements.
6. If $A = \{a, b, c, d, e\}$, then $n(A) = 5$. If $B \subset A$, then $n(B) = 0, 1, 2, 3,$ or 4 since if B is a proper subset of A, A must contain at least one element that is not in B. So the numbers smaller than 5 are 0, 1, 2, 3, and 4.
7. (a)

(b)

(c)

(d)

8. (a) LXXVI.   (b) XLIX.   (c) CXCII.
(d) MDCCXLI.
9. (a)
(b)
(c)
(d)

10. (a)
(b)
(c)
(d)

11. (a) 12.   (b) 4270.   (c) 3614.   (d) 1991.
(e) 976.   (f) 3245.   (g) 42.   (h) 404.
(i) 3010.   (j) 14.   (k) 52.   (l) 333.
12. (a)

(b) CXXXI.
(c)

13. **(a)** Egyptian.
    (b) Mayan.
    (c) No. For example, to represent 10 requires 2 symbols in the Mayan system, but only one in either the Egyptian or Babylonian systems.

14. **(a)** (i) 42, (ii) 625, (iii) 3533, (iv) 89,801.
    (b) (i) πε, (ii) ψμδ, (iii) βρυγ, (iv) καφλδ.
    (c) No.

15. IV and VI, IX and XI, and so on; the Egyptian system was not positional, so there should not be a problem with reversals.

16. **(a)** (i) 30, (ii) 24, (iii) 47, (iv) 57.
    (b) Add the digits of the addends (or subtrahend and minuend).

17. MCMXCII. It was introduced in the fall of 1992.

SECTION 2.3—PART A

1. **(a)** $7(10) + 0(1)$.
   (b) $3(100) + 0(10) + 0(1)$.
   (c) $7(100) + 4(10) + 6(1)$.
   (d) $9(100) + 8(10) + 4(1)$.
   (e) $6(10^7) + 6(10^3) + 6(10)$.
   (f) $8(10^5) + 4(10^4) + 1(1)$.

2. **(a)** 1207.   **(b)** 500,300.   **(c)** 8,070,605.
   (d) 2,000,033,040.   **(e)** 60,900,000.

3. **(a)** Two billion.   **(b)** Eighty-seven trillion.
   (c) Fifty-two trillion, six hundred seventy-two billion, four-hundred five million, one hundred twenty-three thousand, one hundred thirty-nine.
   (d) Ninety-eight quadrillion.

4. Any three of the following: digits 0, 1, 2, 3, 4, 5, 6, 7, 8, 9; grouping by tens; place value; additive; multiplicative.

5. **(a)** For example, loop all columns having three x's. Then, group these loops in sets of three. Finally, draw one loop around three of these groups.
   (b) 1121_{three}.

6. 3223_{four}.

7. 1, 2, 1, 3.

8. **(a)**

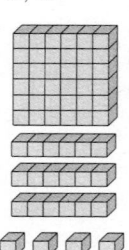

(b)

(c)

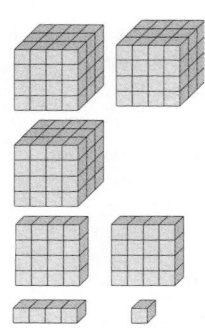

9. **(a)**

10	1
• •	• • • •

(b)

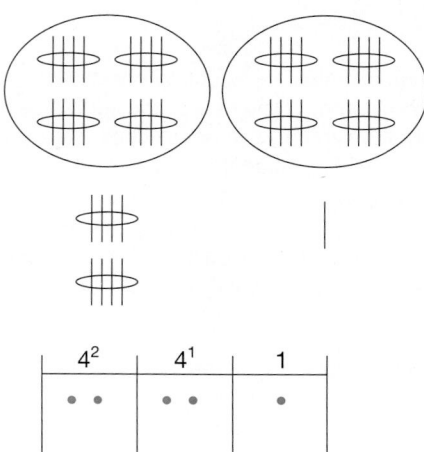

4^2	4^1	1
• •	• •	•

(c)

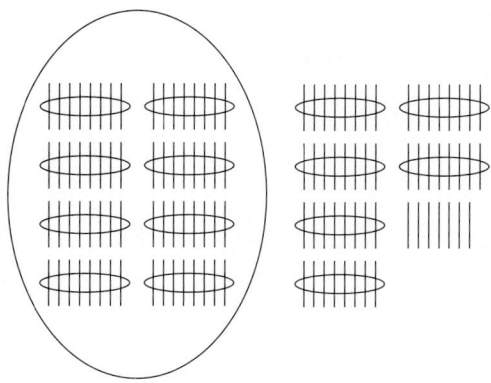

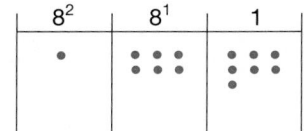

10. (a) 222_{five}.   **(b)** 333_{five}; 32143_{five}.

11. (a) $15_{seven} = 1(7) + 5(1)$.
   (b) $123_{seven} = 1(7^2) + 2(7) + 3(1)$.
   (c) $5046_{seven} = 5(7^3) + 0(7^2) + 4(7) + 6(1)$.

12. (a) In base five, 1, 2, 3, 4, 10, 11, 12, 13, 14, 20, 21, 22, 23, 24, 30, 31, 32, 33, 34, 40, 41, 42, 43, 44, 100.
   (b) In base two, 1, 10, 11, 100, 101, 110, 111, 1000, 1001, 1010, 1011, 1100, 1101, 1110, 1111, 10000.
   (c) In base three, 1, 2, 10, 11, 12, 20, 21, 22, 100, 101, 102, 110, 111, 112, 120, 121, 122, 200, 201, 202, 210, 211, 212, 220, 221, 222, 1000.
   (d) 255, 300, 301, 302 (in base six).
   (e) 310_{four}.   **(f)** 1000_{nine}.

13. (a) 613_{eight}.   **(b)** 23230_{four}.   **(c)** 110110_{two}.

14. (a) 194.   **(b)** 328.   **(c)** 723.   **(d)** 129.
   (e) 1451.   **(f)** 20,590.

15. (a) 202_{six}; 62_{twelve}.   **(b)** 332_{six}; $T8_{twelve}$.
   (c) 550_{six}; 156_{twelve}.   **(d)** 15142_{six}; $14E2_{twelve}$.

16. (a) 7_{nine}.   **(b)** 32_{nine}.   **(c)** 255_{nine}.

17. 23.

18. Improper digit symbols for the given bases. Can't have an 8 in base eight or a 4 in base three.

19. 1024 pages.

20. 57.

21. (a) If final answer is *abcdef*, then the first two digits (*ab*) give the month of birth, the second two (*cd*) give the date of birth, and the last two (*ef*) give the year of birth.
   (b) If birthday is *ab/cd/ef*, then the result will be $100,000a + 10,000b + 1,000c + 100d + 10e + f$. For example, begin by calculating $4(10a + b) + 13$.

22. (a) Seven.   **(b)** Forty-seven.   **(c)** Twelve.
   (d) $x > 5$, $x = 3y - 5$.

23. (a) It must be 0, 2, 4, 6, or 8.
   (b) It must be 0 or 2.
   (c) It must be a 0.
   (d) It may be any digit in base 5.

24. Convert the number to base 2. Since the largest possible telephone number, 999-9999, is between $2^{23} = 8388608$ and $2^{24} = 16777216$, the base two numeral will have at most 24 digits. Ask, in order, if each digit is 1. This takes 24 questions. Then convert back to base ten.

SECTION 2.4—PART A

1. (a) Not a function since *b* is paired with two different numbers.
   (b) Function.
   (c) Function.
   (d) Not a function since 3 is paired with two different numbers.

2. (a) (0, 0), (2, 10), (4, 116). Range: {0, 10, 116}.
   (b) (1, 3), (2, 4), (9, 11) Range: {3, 4, 11}.
   (c) (1, 2), $\left(2, \frac{9}{4}\right)$, $\left(3, \frac{64}{27}\right)$. Range: $\left\{1, \frac{9}{4}, \frac{64}{27}\right\}$.

3. (a) Yes.   **(b)** Yes.
   (c) No since the number 1 is paired with two different numbers.
   (d) Yes.
   (e) No, since the letter *b* is paired with both *b* and *c* (and the letter *d* is paired with both *e* and *f*).

4. (a) 100.   **(b)** 81.
   (c) 3.   **(d)** 2.

5. (a) Function.   **(b)** Function.
   (b) Not a function since some college graduates have more than one degree.
   (c) Function.

6. (a) {(0, 0), (1, 0), (4, 60)}, $\begin{matrix} 0 \to 0 \\ 1 \nearrow 0, \\ 4 \to 60 \end{matrix}$

x	$f(x)$
0	0
1	0
4	60

(b) $f(x) = \sqrt{x}$ for $x \in \{1, 4, 9\}$, $\begin{matrix} 1 \to 1 \\ 4 \to 2, \\ 9 \to 3 \end{matrix}$

x	$f(x)$
1	1
4	2
9	3

(c) $f(x) = 2x$ for $x \in \{1, 2, 10\}$, {(1, 2), (2, 4), (10, 20)}

x	$f(x)$
1	2
2	4
10	20

(d) $f(x) = 11x$ for $x \in \{5, 6, 7\}$,
{(5, 55), (6, 66), (7, 77)}, $\begin{matrix} 5 \to 55 \\ 6 \to 66. \\ 7 \to 77 \end{matrix}$

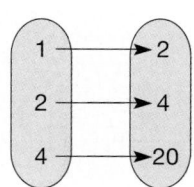

7. (a) 29, 18, 17.   **(b)** 7, 10, 4.
(c) $\dfrac{7}{9}, \dfrac{6}{9}, \dfrac{5}{6}$.   **(d)** 5, 3, 4.

8. (a) Arithmetic, 5, 1002.
(b) Geometric, 2, 14×2^{199}.
(c) Arithmetic, 10, 1994.
(d) Neither.

9. 228.

10. (a) 0.44.   **(b)** 0.56.   **(c)** 0.67.   **(d)** 4.61.

11. (a) 32; 212; 122; −40.   **(b)** 0; 100; 40; −40.
(c) Yes; −40.

12. 3677.

13. (a) $C(x) = 85 + 35x$.

(b) $C(18) = 715$.
The total amount spent by a member after 18 months is $715.

(c) After 27 months.

14. (a) $r = \dfrac{1}{2}$.

(b) 2400, 1200, 600, 300, 150, 75.

15. (a)

n	$T(n)$
1	4
2	12
3	20
4	28
5	36
6	44
7	52
8	60

(b) Arithmetic sequence with $a = 4$ and $d = 8$.

(c) $T(n) = 4 + (n - 1)8$ or $T(n) = 8n - 4$.

(d) $T(20) = 156$; $T(150) = 1196$.

(e) Domain: {1, 2, 3, 4, . . .}.
Range: {4, 12, 20, 28, . . .}.

16. (a)

n	$T(n)$
1	3
2	9
3	18
4	30
5	45
6	63
7	84
8	108

(b) No.

(c) $T(n) = \dfrac{3n(n + 1)}{2}$.

(d) $T(15) = 360$.
$T(100) = 15, 150$.

(e) Domain: {1, 2, 3, 4, . . .}.
Range: {3, 9, 18, 30, . . .}.

17. (a)

n = Number of Years	Annual Interest Earned	Value of Account
0	0	100
1	5	105
2	5	110
3	5	115
4	5	120
5	5	125
6	5	130
7	5	135
8	5	140
9	5	145
10	5	150

(b) Arithmetic sequence with $a = 100$ and $d = 5$. $A(n) = 100 + 5n$.

18. (a)

n = Number of Years	Annual Interest Earned	Value of Account
0	0	100
1	5	105
2	5.25	110.25
3	5.51	115.76
4	5.79	121.55
5	6.08	127.63
6	6.38	134.01
7	6.70	140.71
8	7.04	147.75
9	7.39	155.13
10	7.76	162.89

(b) Geometric sequence with $a = 100$ and $r = 1.05$. $A(n) = 100(1.05)^n$.

(c) $12.89.

19. $h(1) = 48$, $h(2) = 64$, $h(3) = 48$; 4 seconds.

PROBLEMS WHERE THE STRATEGY "DRAW A DIAGRAM" IS USEFUL

1. Draw a tree diagram. There are $3 \cdot 2 \cdot 2 = 12$ combinations.

2. Draw a diagram tracing out the taxi's path: 5 blocks north and 2 blocks east.

3. Draw a diagram showing the four cities: 15,000 arrive at Canton.

CHAPTER 2 TEST

1. (a) F.   **(b)** T.   **(c)** T.   **(d)** T.   **(e)** F.
(f) F.   **(g)** T.   **(h)** F.   **(i)** F.   **(j)** F.

2. (a) $\{a, b, c, d, e\}$.   **(b)** $\{ \ \}$ or $\varnothing$.   **(c)** $\{b, c\}$.
(d) $\{(a, e), (a, f), (a, g), (b, e), (b, f), (b, g), (c, e), (c, f), (c, g)\}$.
(e) $\{d\}$.   **(f)** $\{e\}$.

3. (a) 32.   **(b)** 944.   **(c)** 381.   **(d)** 96.
(e) 21.   **(f)** 142.

4. (a) $7 \times 100 + 5 \times 10 + 9$.
(b) $7 \times 1000 + 2$.
(c) $1 \times 2^6 + 1 \times 2^3 + 1$.

5. IV ≠ VI; thus position is important, but there is no place value as in 31 ≠ 13, where the first 3 means "3 tens" and the second three means "3 ones."

6. (a) True for all A and B.
(b) True for all A and B.
(c) True whenever $A = B$.
(d) True whenever $A = B$ or where A or B is empty.

7. (b, a), (b, c), (d, a), (d, c).

8. 2, 6, 10, 14, . . . is an arithmetic sequence and 2, 6, 18, 54, . . . is geometric.

9. 97.

10. $a = 6$, $b = 8$.

SECTION 3.1—PART A

1.

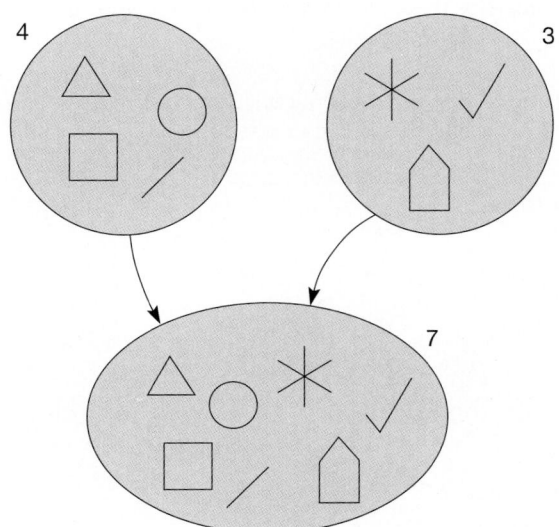

2. (a) (i) 5,   (ii) 5,   (iii) 5.   **(b)** Cases (i) and (ii).

3.

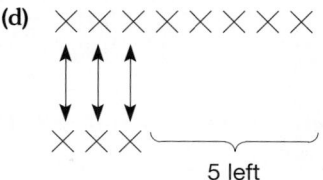

0   1   2   3   4   5   6   7   (8)

4. (a) Closed.   **(b)** Closed.
(c) Not closed, $1 + 2 = 3$.
(d) Not closed, $1 + 2 = 3$.
(e) Closed.   **(f)** Closed.
(g) Not closed, $1 + 1 = 2$.
(h) Not closed, $1 + 1 = 2$.
(i) Closed.
(j) Not closed, $1 + 16 = 17$.

5. (a) Closure.   **(b)** Commutativity.
(c) Associativity and commutativity.
(d) Identity.
(e) Commutativity.
(f) Associativity and commutativity.

6. (a) $6 + (0 + 3)$.
(b) $(0 + 6) + 3$ or $3 + (6 + 0)$.   **(c)** $6 + 3$.

7. Associative property and commutative property for whole-number addition.

8. (a) $0 + 0 = 0$, $0 + 1 = 1$, $1 + 0 = 1$, $1 + 1 = 10_{two}$.
(b) (i), (ii), and (iv) are true.
(c) No; they follow from the commutative and associative properties.

9. (a) $8 - 3$ is 8 "take away" 3 or 5; $8 - 3 = c$ if and only if $8 = 3 + c$ or $c = 5$.
(b)

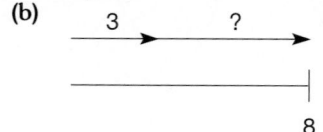

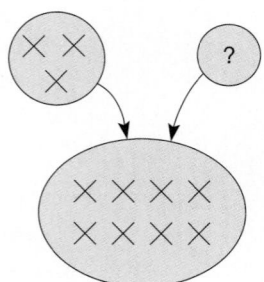

(c)

(d)

10. (a) Yes.   **(b)** Yes.
(c) No.   **(d)** Yes.
(e) No.   **(f)** No.

11. (a) No; that is, $3 - 5$ is not a whole number.
(b) No; that is, $3 - 5 \neq 5 - 3$.
(c) No; that is, $(6 - 3) - 1 \neq 6 - (3 - 1)$.
(d) No, $5 - 0 = 5$ but $0 - 5 \neq 5$.

12. (a) $z \leq y$, $y - z \leq x$.
(b) $y \leq x$, $z \leq x - y$.

13. (a) Take-away model, since \$120 has been removed from the original amount of \$200.

$$200 - 120 = x$$

(b) Comparison approach, since 2 different sets of tomato plants are being compared.

$$24 - 18 = x$$

(c) Missing-addend model, since we need to know what additional amount will make savings equal \$1795.

$$1240 + x = 1795.$$

14. (a) In base six, $1 + 5 = 10$,
$2 + 4 = 10$, $2 + 5 = 11$,
$3 + 3 = 10$, $3 + 4 = 11$,
$3 + 5 = 12$, $4 + 4 = 12$,
$4 + 5 = 13$, $5 + 5 = 14$.
(b) (i) $5_{six} + ? = 13_{six}$; 4_{six},
(ii) $4_{six} + ? = 5_{six}$; 1_{six},
(iii) $4_{six} + ? = 12_{six}$; 4_{six},
(iv) $2_{six} + ? = 10_{six}$; 4_{six},
(v) $3_{six} + ? = 12_{six}$; 5_{six},
(vi) $3_{six} + ? = 11_{six}$; 4_{six}.

15. (a) $3_{\text{six}} + 2_{\text{six}} = 5_{\text{six}}$,
$5_{\text{six}} - 3_{\text{six}} = 2_{\text{six}}$,
$5_{\text{six}} - 2_{\text{six}} = 3_{\text{six}}$.
(b) $5_{\text{six}} + 2_{\text{six}} = 11_{\text{six}}$,
$2_{\text{six}} + 5_{\text{six}} = 11_{\text{six}}$,
$11_{\text{six}} - 2_{\text{six}} = 5_{\text{six}}$.

16. The rest of the counting numbers.

17. $123 - 45 - 67 + 89 = 100$.

18.

25	11	12	22
14	20	19	17
18	16	15	21
13	23	24	10

19. Sums of numbers on all six sides are the same as are sums on the "half-diagonals," lines from center to edge.

20. (a) (i) 363, (ii) 4884, (iii) 55.
(b) 69, 78, 79, or 89.

21. 4, 8, 12, 16, 20.

22. In the sum $n(A) + n(B)$, elements in $A \cap B$ are counted twice. Hence subtract $n(A \cap B)$ from $n(A) + n(B)$.

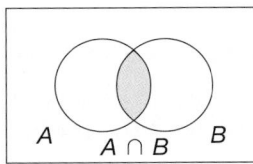

23. Yes. Consider a pan balance where $a + c$ chips on one pan balance $b + c$ chips on the other pan. Remove c chips from each pan and observe that they still balance.

SECTION 3.2—PART A

1. (a)

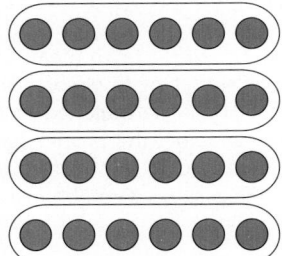

(b)

0 6 12 18 24

(c)
× × × × × ×
× × × × × ×
× × × × × ×
× × × × ×

2. Stack them $3 \times 5 \times 2$.

3. $n(A) \cdot n(\varnothing) = n(\varnothing)$, so $a \cdot 0 = 0$.

4. (a) No. **(b)** Yes. **(c)** No. **(d)** Yes.
(e) Yes. **(f)** Yes. **(g)** Yes. **(h)** Yes.
(i) Yes. **(j)** Yes.

5. (a) Commutative. **(b)** Commutative.
(c) Distributive over addition. **(d)** Identity.
(e) Distributive over subtraction. **(f)** Associative.
(g) Multiplication by 0.
(h) Distributive over addition.

6. (a) $4 \cdot 60 + 4 \cdot 37$. **(b)** $21 \cdot 6 + 35 \cdot 6$.
(c) $3 \cdot 29 + 3 \cdot 30 + 3 \cdot 6$. **(d)** $5x - 5 \cdot 2y$.
(e) $37 \cdot 60 - 37 \cdot 22$. **(f)** $a \cdot 7 - ab + az$.

7. (a) $(6 \times 100) - (6 \times 1) = 594$.
(b) $(5 \times 50) - (5 \times 1) = 245$.
(c) $(7 \times 20) - (7 \times 1) = 133$.
(d) $(6 \times 50) - (6 \times 3) = 282$.

8. (a) 42. **(b)** 91. **(c)** 140.
(d) In each case the answer is $7n$ because of the distributive property:

$$2n + 5n = (2 + 5)n = 7n.$$

9. (a) $45(11) = 45(10 + 1)$.
(b) $39(102) = 39(100 + 2)$.
(c) $23(21) = 23(20 + 1)$.
(d) $97(101) = 97(100 + 1)$.

10. Push 1; multiplicative identity.

11. Use missing factor definition of division.

12. (a) $48 = 8 \times 6$. **(b)** $51 = 3 \cdot x$.
(c) $x = 5 \cdot 13$. **(d)** $24 = 12 \cdot x$.
(e) $x = 27 \cdot 3$. **(f)** $a = b \cdot x$.

13. (a) 0. **(b)** 2. **(c)** 12. **(d)** 8. **(e)** 32.
(f) 13.

14. (a) Cartesian product, since the set of possibilities is {small, medium, large} × {cola, diet cola, lemon-lime, root beer, orange}.

$$x = 3 \cdot 5$$

(b) Rectangular array approach, since students form a moving array of 72 rows and 4 columns.

$$n = 72 \cdot 4$$

(c) Repeated addition, since the bill could be found by adding 70¢ + 70¢ + 70¢ + · · · + 70¢ where the sum has 25 terms.

$$c = 25 \cdot 70$$

15. (a) (In base 5)

×	0	1	2	3	4
0	0	0	0	0	0
1	0	1	2	3	4
2	0	2	4	11	13
3	0	3	11	14	22
4	0	4	13	22	31

(b) (i) $3 \times 2 = 11$, $11 \div 3 = 2$, $11 \div 2 = 3$,
(ii) $3 \times 4 = 22$, $4 \times 3 = 22$, $22 \div 4 = 3$,
(iii) $2 \times 4 = 13$, $4 \times 2 = 13$, $13 \div 4 = 2$.

16. (a) $3 \div 2 \neq$ whole number.
(b) $4 \div 2 \neq 2 \div 4$.
(c) $(12 \div 3) \div 2 \neq 12 \div (3 \div 2)$.
(d) $5 \div 1 = 5$ but $1 \div 5 \neq 5$.
(e) $12 \div (4 + 2) \neq 12 \div 4 + 12 \div 2$.

17. Yes.

18. (a) Row 1: 4, 3, 8; row 2: 9, 5, 1; row 3: 2, 7, 6.
(b) Row 1: 2^4, 2^3, 2^8; row 2: 2^9, 2^5, 2^1; row 3: 2^2, 2^7, 2^6.

19. $31 + 33 + 35 + 37 + 39 + 41 = 216$; $43 + 45 + 47 + 49 + 51 + 53 + 55 = 343$; $57 + 59 + 61 + 63 + 65 + 67 + 69 + 71 = 512$.

20. 9, 5, 4, 6, 3, 2, 1, 7, 8.

21. $\dfrac{2(n + 10) + 100}{2} - n = 60.$

22. 1st place: Pounce   Michelle
2nd place: Hippy   Kevin
2nd place: Hoppy   Jason
3rd place: Bounce   Wendy

23. 3 cups of tea, 2 cakes, and 7 people.

24. $5 \times 6 \times 7 \times 8 \times 9 = 15{,}120$.

25. 3^{29}.

26. Put three on each pan. If they balance, the lighter one of the other two will be found in the next weighing. If three of the coins are lighter, then weigh one of this three against another of this three. If they balance, the third coin is the lighter one. If they do not balance, choose the lighter one.

27. Yes, providing $c \neq 0$.

SECTION 3.3—PART A

1. (a) 19.   **(b)** 9.   **(c)** 16.

2. $2 < 10$, $8 < 10$, $10 > 2$, $10 > 8$.

3. (a) Yes.
(b) Yes.

4. (a) 3^4.   **(b)** $2^4 \cdot 3^2$.   **(c)** $6^3 \cdot 7^2$.   **(d)** $x^2 y^4$.
(e) $a^2 b^2$ or $(ab)^2$.   **(f)** $5^3 6^3$ or $(5 \cdot 6)^3$.

5. (a) $3 \cdot x \cdot x \cdot y \cdot y \cdot y \cdot y \cdot y \cdot z$.
(b) $7 \cdot 5 \cdot 5 \cdot 5$.
(c) $7 \cdot 5 \cdot 7 \cdot 5 \cdot 7 \cdot 5$.

6. (a) 5^7.   **(b)** 3^{10}.   **(c)** 10^7.   **(d)** 2^8.
(e) 5^4.   **(f)** 6^7.

7. $3^2 \cdot 3^4$ is an abbreviated form of $(3 \cdot 3)(3 \cdot 3 \cdot 3 \cdot 3)$ so there is a total of 6 factors of 3, which can be written as 3^6. The student's answer means a product of six 9s.

8. In general, $(a + b)^n \neq a^n + b^n$. For example, $(1 + 2)^2 = 3^2 = 9$, but $1^2 + 2^2 = 1 + 4 = 5$.

9. (a) 117,649.   **(b)** 1.   **(c)** 80.
(d) 8,000.   **(e)** 307.   **(f)** 324.

10. (a) $x = 6$.   **(b)** $x = 5$.
(c) x can be any whole number.

11. (a) $6^{10} = (2 \cdot 3)^{10} = 2^{10} \cdot 3^{10} < 3^{10} \cdot 3^{10} = 3^{20}$.
(b) $9^9 = (3^2)^9 = 3^{18} < 3^{20}$.
(c) $12^{10} = (4 \cdot 3)^{10} = 4^{10} \cdot 3^{10} > 3^{10} \cdot 3^{10} = 3^{20}$.

12. (a) 200¢ or $2.00.
(b) 6400¢ or $64.00.
(c) Price = $25 \cdot 2^n$.

13. When $a = n(A)$ and $b = n(B)$, $a < b$ means A can be matched to a proper subset of B. Also, $b < c$ when $c = n(C)$ means that B can be matched to a proper subset of C. In that matching, the proper subset of B that matches A is matched to a proper subset of a proper subset of C. Thus since A can be matched to a proper subset of C, $a < c$.

14. (a) $17 + 18 + 19 + \cdots + 25 = 4^3 + 5^3$;
$26 + 27 + 28 + \cdots + 36 = 5^3 + 6^3$.
(b) $9^3 + 10^3 = 82 + 83 + \cdots + 100$.
(c) $12^3 + 13^3 = 145 + \cdots + 169$.
(d) $n^3 + (n + 1)^3 = (n^2 + 1) + (n^2 + 2) + \cdots + (n + 1)^2$.

15. $4(2^4) = 64$.

16. (a) The only one-digit squares are 1, 4, and 9. The only combination of these that is a perfect square is 49.
(b) 169, 361.
(c) 1936, 2500, 3600, 4900, 6400, 8100, 9025.
(d) 1225, 1444, 4225.
(e) 1681.
(f) 4900, 9409.

17. The second one.

18. Using variables, this problem is equivalent to showing that $10a + b$ divides evenly into $(10a)^2 - b^2$, or that $x + y$ divides into $x^2 - y^2$. But $x^2 - y^2 = (x + y)(x - y)$. Thus $x + y$ divides into $x^2 - y^2$ exactly $x - y$ times.

19. (a) If $a < b$, then $a + n = b$ for some nonzero n. Then $(a + c) + n = b + c$, or $a + c < b + c$.
(b) If $a < b$, then $a - c < b - c$ for all c, where $c \le a$, $c \le b$. *Proof:* If $a < b$, then $a + n = b$ for some nonzero n. Hence $(a - c) + n = b - c$, or $a - c < b - c$.

PROBLEMS WHERE THE STRATEGY "USE DIRECT REASONING" IS USEFUL

1. Since the first and last digits are the same, their sum is even. Since the sum of the three digits is odd, the middle digit must be odd.

2. Michael, Clyde, Jose, Andre, Ralph.

3. The following triples represent the amount in the 8-, 3-, and 5-liter jugs, respectively after various pourings: (8, 0, 0), (5, 3, 0), (5, 0, 3), (2, 3, 3), (2, 1, 5), (7, 1, 0), (7, 1, 0), (4, 3, 1), (4, 0, 4).

CHAPTER 3 TEST

1. (a) F.   **(b)** T.   **(c)** T.   **(d)** F.   **(e)** F.
(f) F.   **(g)** F.   **(h)** T.   **(i)** F.   **(j)** T.

2. (a) $30 + 10 + 9 + 2$.   **(b)** $40 + 80 + 7 + 7$.
(c) $(5 \cdot 2)73$.   **(d)** $10 \times 33 + 2 \times 33$.

3. 64 R 1.

4. (a) 3^{19}.   **(b)** 5^{24}.   **(c)** 7^{15}.   **(d)** 2^2.
(e) 14^{15}.   **(f)** 36^{12}.

5. (a) $13(97 + 3)$; distributivity.
(b) $(194 + 6) + 86$; associativity and commutativity.
(c) $23(7 + 3)$; commutativity and distributivity.
(d) $(25 \cdot 8)123$; commutativity and associativity.

6. *B*.

7. (a) $(7^3)^4 = (7 \cdot 7 \cdot 7)^4 = (7 \cdot 7 \cdot 7)(7 \cdot 7 \cdot 7)(7 \cdot 7 \cdot 7)(7 \cdot 7 \cdot 7) = 7^{12}$.
(b) $(7^3)^4 = 7^3 \cdot 7^3 \cdot 7^3 \cdot 7^3 = 7^{3+3+3+3} = 7^{12}$.

8. $\{2, 3, 4, 5, \ldots\}$.

9. One number is even and one number is odd.

SECTION 4.1—PART A

1. (a) 105.   **(b)** 4700.   **(c)** 1300.   **(d)** 120.

2. (a) $43 - 17 = 46 - 20 = 26$.
(b) $62 - 39 = 63 - 40 = 23$.
(c) $132 - 96 = 136 - 100 = 36$.
(d) $250 - 167 = 283 - 200 = 83$.

3. (a) 579.   **(b)** 903.   **(c)** 215.   **(d)** 333.

4. (a) $198 + 387 = 200 + 385 = 585$.
(b) $84 \times 5 = 42 \times 10 = 420$.
(c) $99 \times 53 = 5300 - 53 = 5247$.
(d) $4125 \div 25 = 4125 \times \frac{4}{100} = 165$.

5. (a) $16 \times 21 = 8 \times 42 = 4 \times 84 = 2 \times 168 = 336$.
(b) $4 \times 72 = 2 \times 144 = 288$.
(c) $8 \times 123 = 4 \times 246 = 2 \times 492 = 984$.
(d) $16 \times 211 = 8 \times 422 = 4 \times 844 = 2 \times 1688 = 3376$.

6. (a) 290,000,000,000.   **(b)** 14,700,000,000.
(c) 91,000,000,000.   **(d)** 84×10^{14}.
(e) 140×10^{15}.   **(f)** 102×10^{15}.

7. (a) (i) 4000 to 6000, (ii) 4000, (iii) 4900, (iv) about 5000.
(b) (i) 1000 to 5000, (ii) 1000, (iii) 2400, (iv) about 2700.
(c) (i) 7000 to 11,000, (ii) 7000, (iii) 8100, (iv) about 8400.

8. (a) 600 to 1200.   **(b)** 20,000 to 60,000.
(c) 3200 to 4000.

9. (a) $63 \times 97 \approx 63 \times 100 = 6300$.
(b) $51 \times 212 \approx 50 \times 200 = 10,000$.
(c) $3112 \div 62 \approx 3000 \div 60 = 50$.
(d) $103 \times 87 \approx 100 \times 87 = 8700$.
(e) $62 \times 58 \approx 60 \times 60 = 3600$.
(f) $4254 \div 68 \approx 4200 \div 70 = 60$.

10. (a) 370.   **(b)** 700.   **(c)** 1130.   **(d)** 460.
(e) 3000.

11. (a) $4 \times 350 = 1400$.   **(b)** 60^3.
(c) 500^4.   **(d)** $5 \times 800 = 4000$.

12. (a) $32 + 20 = 52$, $52 + 9 = 61$, $61 + 50 = 111$, $111 + 6 = 117$.
(b) $54 + 20 = 74$, $74 + 8 = 82$, $82 + 6 = 142$, $142 + 7 = 149$.
(c) $19 + 60 = 79$, $79 + 6 = 85$, $85 + 40 = 125$, $125 + 9 = 134$.
(d) $62 + 80 = 142$, $142 + 4 = 146$, $146 + 20 = 166$, $166 + 7 = 173$, $173 + 80 = 253$, $253 + 1 = 254$.

13. Underestimate so that fewer than the designated amount of pollutants will be discharged.

14. There are many acceptable ways to estimate; four are illustrated for each case.
(a) $31 \times 23 \approx 31 \times 20 = 620$
$31 \times 23 \approx 30 \times 23 = 690$
$31 \times 23 \approx 32 \times 25 = 800$
$31 \times 23 \approx 30 \times 20 = 600$.
(b) $35 \times 46 \approx 35 \times 50 = 1750$
$35 \times 46 \approx 30 \times 46 = 1380$
$35 \times 46 \approx 40 \times 40 = 1600$
$35 \times 46 \approx 35 \times 40 = 1400$.
(c) $48 \times 27 \approx 48 \times 25 = 1200$
$48 \times 27 \approx 50 \times 27 = 1350$
$48 \times 27 \approx 50 \times 30 = 1500$
$48 \times 27 \approx 50 \times 25 = 1250$.
(d) $76 \times 12 \approx 76 \times 10 = 760$
$76 \times 12 \approx 80 \times 12 = 960$
$76 \times 12 \approx 80 \times 10 = 800$
$76 \times 12 \approx 70 \times 15 = 1050$.

15. There are many acceptable estimates. One reasonable one is listed for each part.
(a) 42 and 56.   **(b)** 12 and 20.
(c) 1 and 4.   **(d)** 81 and 256.

16. (a) $52 - 35$: $52 - 30 = 22$, $22 - 5 = 17$.
(b) $173 - 96$: $173 - 90 = 83$, $83 - 6 = 77$.
(c) $241 - 159$: $241 - 100 = 141$, $141 - 50 = 91$, $91 - 9 = 82$.
(d) $83 - 55$: $83 - 50 = 33$, $33 - 5 = 28$.

17. (a) $84 \div 14 = 42 \div 7 = 6$.
(b) $234 \div 26 = 117 \div 13 = 9$.
(c) $120 \div 15 = 240 \div 30 = 8$.
(d) $168 \div 14 = 84 \div 7 = 12$.

18. (a) $37(13 + 98) = 37(111) = 4107$ and $37 \times 13 + 37 \times 98 = 4107$.
(b) $132 + (276 + 498) = 132 + (274 + 500) = 406 + 500 = 906$
$(132 + 276) + 498 = 408 + 498 = 400 + 506 = 906$.
(c) $57 \cdot (93 \cdot 81) = 57 \cdot 7533 = 429,381$
$(57 \cdot 93) \cdot 81 = 5301 \cdot 81 = 429,381$.
(d) $49 \cdot 59 + 59 \cdot 87 = 2891 + 5133 = 8024$
$59(49 + 87) = 59 \cdot 136 = 8024$.

19. (a) $17 \times 817 \times 100 = 1,388,900$.
(b) $10 \times 98 \times 673 = 659,540$.
(c) $50 \times 4 \times 674 \times 889 = 119,837,200$.
(d) $8 \times 125 \times 783 \times 79 = 61,857,000$.

20. (a) $374\ \boxed{+}\ \boxed{=}\ \boxed{=}\ \boxed{=}\ \boxed{=}\ \boxed{=}\ \boxed{2244}$,
$374\ \boxed{\times}\ 6\ \boxed{=}\ \boxed{2244}$.
(b) $149\ \boxed{+}\ \boxed{=}\ \boxed{=}\ \boxed{=}\ \boxed{596}$,
$149\ \boxed{\times}4\ \boxed{=}\ \boxed{596}$.
(c) $564\ \boxed{+}\ \boxed{=}\ \boxed{=}\ \boxed{=}\ \boxed{=}\ \boxed{=}\ \boxed{=}\ \boxed{=}\ \boxed{=}\ \boxed{=}\ \boxed{=}$
$\boxed{6204}$, $564\ \boxed{\times}\ 11\ \boxed{=}\ \boxed{6204}$.
(d) $12321\ \boxed{+}\ \boxed{=}\ \boxed{=}\ \boxed{=}\ \boxed{=}\ \boxed{=}\ \boxed{=}\ \boxed{=}\ \boxed{=}$
$\boxed{110889}$, $12321\ \boxed{\times}\ 9\ \boxed{=}\ \boxed{110889}$.

21. (a) $374\ \boxed{-}\ 83\ \boxed{=}\ \boxed{=}\ \boxed{=}\ \boxed{=}\ \boxed{42}$
(b) $491\ \boxed{-}\ 97\ \boxed{=}\ \boxed{=}\ \boxed{=}\ \boxed{=}\ \boxed{=}\ \boxed{6}$.
(c) $1293\ \boxed{-}\ 317\ \boxed{=}\ \boxed{=}\ \boxed{=}\ \boxed{=}\ \boxed{25}$.
(d) $24984\ \boxed{-}\ 8976\ \boxed{=}\ \boxed{=}\ \boxed{7032}$

22. (a) 4^5.   **(b)** 3^7.   **(c)** 4^7.   **(d)** 3^6.
23. (a) 12, 7.   **(b)** 31, 16.   **(c)** 6, 111.
(d) 119, 828.
24. $10^2 + 100^2 = 10,100$; $588^2 + 2353^2 = 5882353$.
25. Yes, yes, no.
26. (a) Yes.   **(b)** Yes.   **(c)** Yes.
27. Yes, yes, no.
28. (a) 1357×90.   **(b)** 6666×66.
(c) $78 \times 93 \times 456$.   **(d)** $123 \times 45 \times 67$.
29. To find a range for $742 - 281$, find $700 - 200 = 500$ and $700 - 300 = 400$. The answer is between 400 and 500.
30. 177,777,768,888,889.
31. 5643, 6237.
32. (a) 4225, 5625, 9025.
(b) $(10a + 5)^2 = 100a^2 + 100a + 25 = 100a(a + 1) + 25$.
33. Yes.
34. The first factor probably ends in 9 rather than 8.
35. (a) $50^2 - 4^2 = 2484$.
(b) $81 \times 79 = 80^2 - 1 = 6399$.
(c) $122 \times 118 = 120^2 - 2^2 = 14,396$.
(d) $1210 \times 1190 = 1200^2 - 10^2 = 1,439,900$.
36. True, Express the product as $(898,000 + 423) \times (112,000 + 303)$. Use distributivity twice, then add.
37. $(439 \times 6352) \times 1000 + 268 \times 6352 = 3,009,864,336$.
38. (a) $76 \times (54 + 97)$.   **(b)** $(4 \times 13)^2$.
(c) $13 + (59^2 \times 47)$.   **(d)** $(79 - 43) \div 2 + 17^2$.

39. (a) $57 \times 53 = 3021$.
   (b) $(10a + b)(10a + 10 - b) = 100a^2 + 100a + 10b - b^2 = 100a(a + 1) + b(10 - b)$.
   (c) Problem 32 is the special case when $b = 5$.

40. (i) Identify the digit in the place to which you are rounding.
   (ii) If the digit in the place to its right is a 5, 6, 7, 8, or 9, add one to the digit to which you are rounding. Otherwise, leave the digit as it is.
   (iii) Put zeros in all the places to the right of the digit to which you are rounding.

SECTION 4.2—PART A

1. (a)

(b)

$= 47$

$= 142$

2. Expanded form; commutative and associative properties of addition; distributive property of multiplication over addition; single-digit addition facts; place value.

3. (a) 986.   **(b)** 747.   **(c)** 2822.

4. (a) 994.   **(b)** 1693.

5. (a) 751.   **(b)** 1332.   **(c)** 1641.

6. (a) Simple; requires more writing.
   (b) Simple; requires more writing and crossing out numbers.
   (c) Simple; requires more space; requires drawing lattice.
   (d) Fewer symbols; more complicated due to the carry.

7. (a) BB BBB SSSSSSS   **(b)** BB BB SS SS.
   (c) BBB SSSS = BB SSSSSSSSS S SSSS.

8. 8, 12, 13, 12.

9. (a) 477.   **(b)** 776.   **(c)** 1818.

10. (a) 358, 47,365, 1,814,736.
   (b) Complement of $B = 999 - B$, so $A + (999 - B) = A + 1000 - B - 1 = 1000 + (A - B) - 1$; so to get $A - B$ cross off the 1 in the 1000s place and add 1 to $A + (999 - B)$.

11. Left-hand sum; compare sum of each column, from left to right.

12. The sum is 5074 both ways!

13.

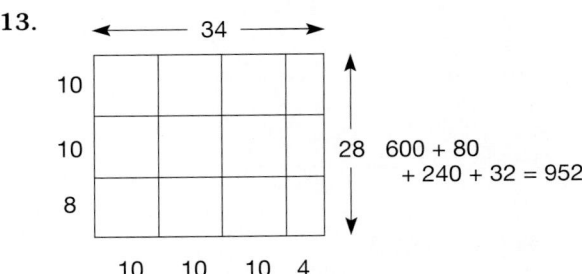

14. Expanded form; distributivity; expanded form; associativity for ×; place value; place value; addition.

15. 8000; low; high.

16. (a) 1426.   **(b)** 765.   **(c)** 11,376.
   (d) 552,832.

17. (a) 3525.   **(b)** 153,244.   **(c)** 684,288.

18. (a) 56.   **(b)** 42.   **(c)** 60.

19. Subtract 6 seven times to reach 0.

20. (a) 9, R = 2.   **(b)** 11, R = 1.   **(c)** 12, R = 3.

21. (a) (i) 15 R 74,   (ii) 499 R 70,   (iii) 3336 R 223.
   (b) Yes. The product of the divisor and the decimal part of the remainder equals the remainder, within the accuracy of the calculator.

22. Larry is not carrying properly; Curly carries the wrong digit; Moe forgets to carry.

23. One answer is $359 + 127 = 486$.

24. (a) For example, $863 + 742 = 1605$.
   (b) For example, $347 + 268 = 615$.

25. $1 + 2 + 34 + 56 + 7 = 100$; also, $1 + 23 + 4 + 5 + 67 = 100$.

26. (a) $990 + 077 + 000 + 033 + 011$.
   (b) (i) $990 + 007 + 000 + 003 + 111$
      (ii) $900 + 070 + 000 + 030 + 111$
      (iii) $000 + 700 + 000 + 300 + 111$.

27. (a) Equal.   **(b)** Differ by 2.   **(c)** Yes.
   (d) Difference of products is 10 times the vertical 10s-place difference.

28. (a)

(b) $1 + 2 + 3 + 4 = \frac{1}{2}(4 \times 5)$.
(c) $\frac{1}{2}(50 \times 51) = 1275$; $\frac{1}{2}(75 \times 76) = 2850$.

29. $888 + 777 + 444 = 2109$; $888 + 666 + 555 = 2109$.

30. Bob: 184; Jennifer: 120; Suzie: 206; Tom: 2081.

31.
$$
\begin{array}{r}
5314 \times 79 \\
\hline
28 \\
736 \\
2109 \\
3527 \\
45 \\
\hline
419806
\end{array}
$$

SECTION 4.3—PART A

1. (a) 11_{three}.   **(b)** 18_{twelve}.   **(c)** 15_{eight}.
(d) 13_{twelve}.

2. (a) 3_{four}.   **(b)** 11_{four}.   **(c)** 100_{four}.
(d) 120_{four}.   **(e)** 331_{four}.   **(f)** 1303_{four}.
(g) 12013_{four}.   **(h)** 13332_{four}.

3. (a) 154_{nine}.   **(b)** $1TT_{\text{twelve}}$.

4. (a) 4_{six}.   **(b)** 456_{seven}.   **(c)** 2322_{four}.

5. (a) 2_{four}.   **(b)** 2_{four}.   **(c)** 20_{four}.
(d) 13_{four}.   **(e)** 31_{four}.   **(f)** 103_{four}.

6. $10201_{\text{three}} - 2122_{\text{three}} = 10201_{\text{three}} + 100_{\text{three}} - 10000_{\text{three}} + 1_{\text{three}} = 1002_{\text{three}}$; the sums, in columns, of a number and its complement must be all twos.

7. (a) 122_{four}.   **(b)** 234_{five}.   **(c)** 132_{four}.
(d) 302_{six}.   **(e)** 1463_{eight}.   **(f)** 101011111_{two}.
(g) 969_{twelve}.   **(h)** 65601_{seven}.   **(i)** 20101_{five}.

8.
$$
3_{\text{five}} \overline{\left) 4023_{\text{five}} \right.}
$$
$$
\begin{array}{r}
3000 \\
\hline
1023_{\text{five}} \\
300 \\
\hline
223_{\text{five}} \\
220 \\
\hline
3_{\text{five}}
\end{array}
\qquad
\begin{array}{l}
1000_{\text{five}} \\
\\
100_{\text{five}} \\
\\
40_{\text{five}} \\
1_{\text{five}} \\
\hline
1141_{\text{five}}
\end{array}
$$
$Q = 1141_{\text{five}}$
$R = 0$

9. Six.

10. Steve has $2, Tricia has $23, Bill has $40, Jane has $50.

11. 39,037,066,084.

12. 125.

PROBLEMS WHERE THE STRATEGY "USE INDIRECT REASONING" IS USEFUL

1. Assume that x *can* be even. Then $x^2 + 2x + 1$ is odd. Therefore, x cannot be even.

2. Suppose that n is odd. Then n^4 is odd; therefore, n cannot be odd.

3. Assume that both x and y are odd. Then $x = 2m + 1$ and $y = 2n + 1$ for whole numbers m and n. Thus $x^2 = 4m^2 + 4m + 1$ and $y^2 = 4n^2 + 4n + 1$, or $x^2 + y^2 = 4(m^2 + n^2 + m + n) + 2$, which has a factor of 2 but not 4. Therefore, it cannot be a square since it only has one factor of 2.

CHAPTER 4 TEST

1. (a) F.   **(b)** F.   **(c)** F.   **(d)** F.

2. (a) One possibility is   **(b)** One possibility is
$$
\begin{array}{r}
376 \\
+594 \\
\hline
10 \\
160 \\
800 \\
\hline
970
\end{array}
\qquad
\begin{array}{r}
56 \\
\times\ 73 \\
\hline
18 \\
150 \\
420 \\
3500 \\
\hline
4088
\end{array}
$$

3. (a)

(b)

4. (a) $54 + 93 + 16 + 47 = 54 + 16 + 93 + 47 = 70 + 140 = 210$.
(b) $9225 - 2000 = 7225$.
(c) $3497 - 1362 = 2135$.
(d) $25 \times 52 = \frac{100}{4} \times 52 = 100 \times \frac{52}{4} = 1300$.

5. 234 R 8.

6. (a) (i) 2500, (ii) 2500 to 2900, (iii) 2660, (iv) 2600.
(b) (i) 350,000,   (ii) 350,000   to   480,000,
(iii) 420,000, (iv) 420,000.

7. $32 \times 21 = (30 + 2)(20 + 1) = (30 + 2)20 + (30 + 2)1 = 30 \cdot 20 + 2 \cdot 20 + 30 \cdot 1 + 2 \cdot 1 = 600 + 40 + 30 + 2 = 672$.

8. Since we are finding 321×20, not simply 321×2.

9. Commutativity and associativity.

10. H = 2, E = 5, S = 6.

11. $a = 7, b = 5, c = 9$; 62,015.

SECTION 5.1—PART A

1. 2, 3, 5, 7, 11, 13, 17, 19, 23, 29, 31, 37, 41, 43, 47, 53, 59, 61, 67, 71, 73, 79, 83, 89, 97.

2.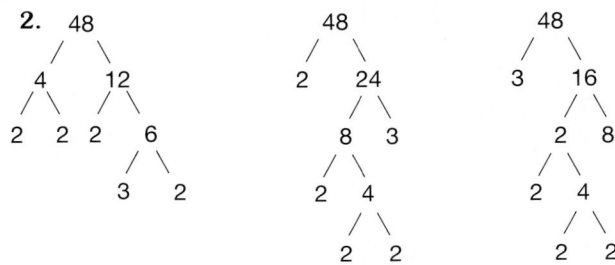

3. (a) $2^2 \times 3^2$. (b) 2×3^3. (c) $2 \times 3 \times 17$.
   (d) $2^3 \times 5^3$.

4. (a) $2^3 \times 3^3$. (b) $2^2 \times 3 \times 5 \times 7^2$.
   (c) $3 \times 5^2 \times 11$.
   (d) $2 \times 3^2 \times 7 \times 11^2 \times 13$.

5. (a) $2^2 \times 3^2$. (b) 1, 2, 3, 4, 6, 9, 12, 18, 36.
   (c) $4 = 2^2$, $6 = 2 \times 3$, $9 = 3^2$, $12 = 2^2 \times 3$, $18 = 2 \times 3^2$.
   (d) The divisors of 36 have the same prime factors as 36, and they appear at most as many times as they appear in the prime factorization of 36.
   (e) It has at most two 13s and five 29s and has no other prime factors.

6. (a), (c), (e), (g), and (h).

7. (a) F. (b) F; $3 \nmid 1$. (c) T; $4 \mid 00$. (d) T
   (e) T; $8 \mid 608$ and $3 \mid (3 + 2 + 5 + 6 + 8)$.
   (f) F; $9 \nmid 16 = 1 + 3 + 7 + 5$. (g) T.
   (h) T.

8. 1, 3, and 7.

9. 1, 2, 4, 8.

10. (a) $8 \mid 152$ since $8 \times 19 = 152$.
    (b) $x = 15,394$ by long division.
    (c) Yes. $15,394 \times 8 = 123,152$.

11. (a) 4 only. (b) 3, 4. (c) 3, 4, 9. (d) 3, 9.

12. (a) T. (b) T. (c) F. (d) F.

13. (a) and (c).

14. For 5, $5 \mid 10(a \cdot 10 + b)$ or $5 \mid (a \cdot 10^2 + b \cdot 10)$; therefore, if $5 \mid c$, then $5 \mid (a \cdot 10^2 + b \cdot 10 + c)$.

15. (a), (b), (d), and (e).

16. (a) Yes. (b) No.
    (c) Composite numbers greater than 4.

17. 333,333,331 has a factor of 17.

18. $p(0) = 17$, $p(1) = 19$, $p(2) = 23$, $p(3) = 29$; $p(16) = 16^2 + 16 + 17 = 16(17) + 17$ is not prime.

19. (a) They are all primes.
    (b) The diagonal is made up of the numbers from the formula $n^2 + n + 41$.

20. The numbers with an even number of ones have 11 as a factor. Also, numbers that have a multiple-of-three number of ones (e.g., 111) have 3 as a factor. That leaves the numbers with 5, 7, 11, 13, and 17 ones for you to factor.

21. Only 7 (= 5 + 2). For the rest, since one of the two primes would have to be even, two is the only candidate, but the other summand would then be a multiple of 5.

22. $5 = 1 + 4$, $17 = 1 + 16$, $29 = 4 + 25$, $37 = 1 + 36$, $41 = 16 + 25$, $53 = 4 + 49$, $61 = 25 + 36$, $73 = 9 + 64$, $89 = 25 + 64$, $97 = 16 + 81$.

23. There are no other pairs, since every even number besides 2 is composite.

24. 3 and 5, 17 and 19, 41 and 43, 59 and 61, 71 and 73, 101 and 103, 107 and 109, 137 and 139, 149 and 151, 179 and 181, 191 and 193, 197 and 199.

25. (b) Let n be a odd whole number greater than 6. Take prime p (not 2) less than n. $n - p$ is an even number which is a sum of primes a and b. Then $n = a + b + p$.

26. Yes.

27. 34,227 and 36,070.

28. (a) 6. (b) 3.

29. 2520.

30. $2^2 \times 3 \times 5 = 60$.

31. 3; Proof: $n + (n + 1) + (n + 2) = 3n + 3 = 3(n + 1)$.

32. Use a variable; the numbers a, b, $a + b$, $a + 2b$, $2a + 3b$, $3a + 5b$, $5a + 8b$, $8a + 13b$, $13a + 21b$, $21a + 34b$ have a sum of $55a + 88b$, which is $11(5a + 8b)$, or 11 times the seventh number.

33. (a) Use distributivity.
    (b) $1001! + 2, 1001! + 3, \dots, 1001! + 1001$.

34. $3.52 is not a multiple of 3.

35. 504. Since the number is a multiple of 7, 8, and 9, the only three-digit multiple is $7 \cdot 8 \cdot 9$.

36. 61.

37. 7 and 11.

38. (a) Apply the test for divisibility by 11 to any four-digit palindrome.
(b) A similar proof applies to *every* palindrome with an even number of digits.

39. 151 and 251.

40. 7 | 2443 (349 times), 7 | 443,002 (63,286 times). If 7 | $(1000a + b)$, then show 7 | $(1000b + a)$. 7 | $(1000a + b)$ means $7n = 1000a + b$. Since 7 | 1001, 7 | [$(1001a + 1001b) - (1000a + b)$], or 7 | $(a + 1000b)$.

41. $289 = 17^2$.

42. 11 | [$a(1001) + b(99) + c(11) - a + b - c + d$] if and only if 11 | $(-a + b - c + d)$. Therefore, we only need to check the $-a + b - c + d$ part.

43. $11 \times 1,010,101,010 = 1,111,111,111$
$13 \times 8,547,008,547 = 111,111,111,111$
$17 \times 65,359,477,124,183 =$
$1,111,111,111,111,111$.

44. (a) $n = 1$.   **(b)** $n = 6$.   **(c)** $n = 10$.

SECTION 5.2—PART A

1. (a) 6.   **(b)** 9.   **(c)** 12.   **(d)** 16.
(e) 60.   **(f)** 2016.

2. (a) Multiples, generally; exceptions are 0 (a multiple of 18 but not a divisor) and 18 (both a multiple and divisor).
(b) LCM(12, 18) ($\neq 0$).
(c) LCM(a, b), unless $a = b$, in which case GCF $(a, b) =$ LCM(a, b).

3. (a) 2.   **(b)** 6.   **(c)** 6.   **(d)** 18.   **(e)** 1.
(f) 17.

4. (a) 6.   **(b)** 121.   **(c)** 3.   **(d)** 2.

5. (a) 6.   **(b)** 1.   **(c)** 5.   **(d)** 14.   **(e)** 13.
(f) 29.

6. (a) 24.   **(b)** 20.   **(c)** 63.   **(d)** 30.
(e) 40.   **(f)** 72.

7. (a) $2^3 \cdot 3^2 \cdot 5 \cdot 7$.   **(b)** $2^2 \cdot 3^2 \cdot 5 \cdot 7 \cdot 11$.
(c) $2^4 \cdot 3 \cdot 5 \cdot 7$.

8. (a) $a = 2 \times 3^3$.   **(b)** $a = 2^2 \times 7^3 \times 11^2$.

9. (a) 6.   **(b)** 13.   **(c)** 8.   **(d)** 37.

10. (a) All except 6, 12, 18, 20, 24.
(b) 12, 18, 20, 24.
(c) 6.

11. (c).

12. (a).

13. (a) 1.   **(b)** $2^1 = 2$.   **(c)** $2^2 = 4$.
(d) $2^1 \times 3^1 = 6$.   **(e)** $2^4 = 16$.
(f) $2^2 \times 3 = 12$.   **(g)** $2^6 = 64$.
(h) $2^3 \times 3 = 24$.

14. (a) 2, 3, 5, 7, 11, 13; primes.
(b) 4, 9, 25, 49, 121, 169; primes squared.
(c) 6, 10, 14, 15, 21, 22; the product of two primes, or 8, 27, 81 or any prime to the third power.
(d) 2^4, 3^4, 5^4, 7^4, 11^4, 13^4; a prime to the fourth power.

15. 6, 28, 496, 8128.

16. 5, 7, 11, 13, 17, 19, 23.

17. 1, 4, 9, 16, 25, . . .; all lockers numbered with a perfect square number.

18. 16 candy bars.

19. Chickens, $2; ducks, $4; and geese, $5.

20. None, since each has only one factor of 5.

21. 773.

22. (a) 11, 101, 1111.   **(b)** 1111.

23. 41, 7, 11, 73, 67, 17, 13.

24. 31.

25. $343 = 7 \cdot 49$. Let $a + b = 7$. Then 7 | $(10a + 10b)$. But 7 | 91, so 7 | $91a$. Then 7 | $(10a + 10b + 91a)$ or 7 | $(100a + 10b + a)$.

26. GCF(54, 27) = 27, LCM(54, 27) = LCM(54, 18) = LCM(18, 27) = 54.

PROBLEMS WHERE THE STRATEGY "USE PROPERTIES OF NUMBERS" IS USEFUL

1. Mary is 71 unless she married and had children very young.

2. Four folding machines and three stamp machines since the LCM of 45 and 60 is 180.

3. Let p and q be any two primes. Then $p^6 q^{12}$ will have $7 \cdot 13 = 91$ factors.

CHAPTER 5 TEST

1. (a) F.   **(b)** T.   **(c)** T.   **(d)** F.   **(e)** T.
(f) T.   **(g)** T.   **(h)** F.   **(i)** F.   **(j)** T.

2. (a) $2^3 \cdot 5 \cdot 3$.   **(b)** $2^4 \cdot 5^2 \cdot 3^3$.
(c) $3^2 \cdot 7 \cdot 13$.

3. (a) 2, 4, 8, 11.   **(b)** 2, 3, 5, 6, 10.
(c) 2, 3, 4, 5, 6, 8, 9, 10.

4. (a) 24.   **(b)** 16.   **(c)** 27.

5. (a) $2^3 \cdot 3$; $2^4 \cdot 3^2 \cdot 5$.   **(b)** 7; $2 \cdot 3 \cdot 5 \cdot 7^2$.
(c) $2^3 \cdot 3^4 \cdot 5^3$; $2^7 \cdot 3^5 \cdot 5^7$.   **(d)** $41, 128, 207$.

6. All the crossed-out numbers greater than 1 are composite.

7. No, because if two numbers are equal, they must have the same prime factorization.

8. $x + (x + 1) + (x + 2) + (x + 3) = 4x + 6 = 2(2x + 3)$.

9. $2^3 \cdot 3^2 \cdot 5 \cdot 7 = 2520$.

10. If two other prime numbers differ by 3, one is odd and one is even. The even one must have a factor of 2.

11. (a) $2^3 \cdot 5$.   **(b)** $2^3 \cdot 3^3 \cdot 5$.

SECTION 6.1—PART A

1. (a)

(b)

(c)

2. (a)

(b)

(c)

(d)

3. Yes. The parts have equal areas.

4. (a) $\frac{1}{10}$.   **(b)** $\frac{1}{4}$.   **(c)** $\frac{1}{3}$.   **(d)** $\frac{1}{3}$.

5.

6. (a) $\frac{4}{1}, \frac{8}{2}, \frac{12}{3}, \frac{16}{4}, \frac{20}{5}, \frac{24}{6}$.
(b) $\frac{8}{18}, \frac{12}{27}, \frac{16}{36}, \frac{20}{45}, \frac{24}{54}$.

7. (a), (b), and (d).

8. (b) and (d).

9. (a) $\frac{3}{4}$.   **(b)** $\frac{7}{8}$.   **(c)** $\frac{9}{13}$.   **(d)** $\frac{11}{5}$ **(e)** $\frac{21}{17}$.
(f) $\frac{14}{3}$.   **(g)** $\frac{5}{7}$.   **(h)** $\frac{29}{2}$.

10. (a) $5\frac{15}{32}$.   **(b)** $2\frac{185}{216}$.   **(c)** $5\frac{28}{111}$.   **(d)** $62\frac{1}{3}$.

11. (a) Not equal.   **(b)** Not equal.   **(c)** Equal.
(d) Equal.

12. $\frac{4}{27}$.

13. (a) (i) $\frac{11}{17} < \frac{12}{17} < \frac{13}{17}$, (ii) $\frac{1}{7} < \frac{1}{6} < \frac{1}{5}$, (iii) $\frac{7}{13} < \frac{14}{25} < \frac{4}{7}$,
(iv) $\frac{2}{9} < \frac{3}{11} < \frac{5}{18} < \frac{7}{23}$.
(b) Increasing numerators, decreasing denominators.

14. (a) $\frac{17}{23} < \frac{51}{68}$.   **(b)** $\frac{50}{687} < \frac{43}{567}$.   **(c)** $\frac{597}{2511} < \frac{214}{897}$.
(d) $\frac{531}{16,134} < \frac{93}{2811} < \frac{3}{87}$.

15. (a) $\frac{51}{92}, \frac{55}{100}$.   **(b)** $\frac{1}{4}, \frac{25}{100}$.   **(c)** $\frac{110}{141}, \frac{78}{100}$.

16. (a) $\frac{3}{7} = \frac{24}{56}, \frac{3}{8} = \frac{21}{56}$, so $\frac{23}{56}$ works.
(b) $\dfrac{35}{2 \cdot 17 \cdot 18}$ or $\dfrac{171}{10 \cdot 18 \cdot 17}$, and so on.
(c) $\frac{89}{99}$.
(d) $\dfrac{10(ad) \pm 1}{10(bd)}$, $+ 1$ if $ad < bc$ and -1 if $ad > bc$.

17. (a) The fractions are decreasing.
(b) The fraction may be more than 1.

18. Texas had the higher rate.

19. (a) $25/100$.   **(c)** $20/100$.   **(d)** $12/100$.
(e) $125/1000$.   **(f)** $6875/10,000$.
(h) $225/1000$.   **(j)** $2/10$.   **(l)** $57 \cdot 5^6/10^6$.
(m) $45/100$.   **(n)** $75 \cdot 5^7/10^7$.
(p) $4/10$.
When the fraction is in simplest form, the prime factorization of the denominator must have only 2s and/or 5s.

20. (a) $x = y$.   **(b)** $y = z$.

21. (a) 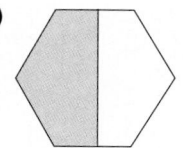 **(b)**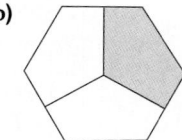

(c) 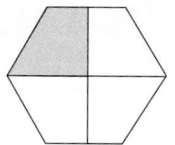 **(d)**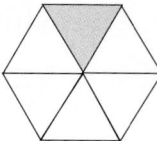

(e) 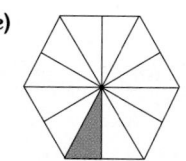 **(f)**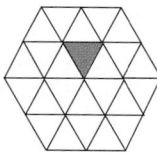

22. Yes, since $\dfrac{288 \cdots 86}{588 \cdots 83} = \dfrac{26 \cdot 11 \cdots 1}{53 \cdot 11 \cdots 1} = \dfrac{26}{53}$.

23. (a) False. **(b)** False. **(c)** True. **(d)** True.

24. $\frac{1}{8}$.

SECTION 6.2—PART A

1. (a)

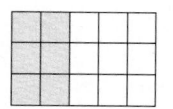   +   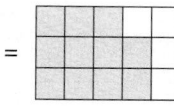   =

$\dfrac{2}{5}$ $\dfrac{1}{3}$ $\dfrac{11}{15}$

(b)

$\dfrac{2}{5}$ + $\dfrac{1}{3}$

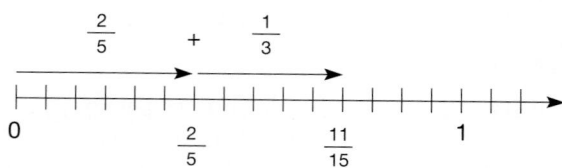

2. (a) 3/4. **(b)** 3/4. **(c)** 16/21.
(d) 167/144. **(e)** 460/663. **(f)** 277/242.
(g) 617/1000. **(h)** 99/100.
(i) 15,059/100,000.

3. One way would be to use an area model for fraction addition.

4. (a) $\frac{23}{6}$. **(b)** $\frac{23}{8}$. **(c)** $\frac{26}{5}$. **(d)** $\frac{64}{9}$.

5. (a)

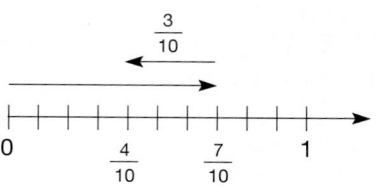

(b)

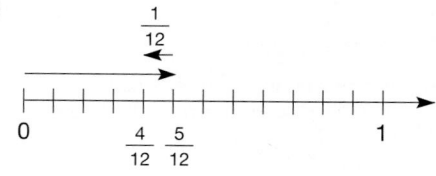

(c)

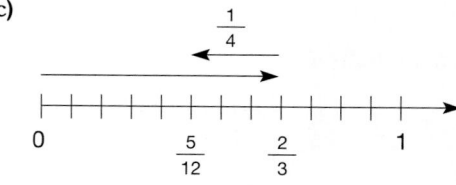

6. (a) 4/11. **(b)** 13/63. **(c)** Not defined.
(d) 1/20. **(e)** 23/54. **(f)** 154/663.
(g) 11/1000. **(h)** 153/1,000,000.
(i) 141/1,675,069.

7. (a) $3\frac{11}{12}$; $1\frac{5}{12}$. **(b)** $13\frac{8}{21}$; $2\frac{1}{21}$. **(c)** $38\frac{1}{12}$; $6\frac{1}{4}$.

8. (a) $1\frac{1}{9}$ **(b)** $2\frac{5}{6}$ **(c)** $10\frac{1}{5}$

9. (a) $8\frac{3}{7} - 3 = 5\frac{3}{7}$ **(b)** $9\frac{4}{8} - 3 = 6\frac{1}{2}$.
(c) $11\frac{5}{7} - 7 = 4\frac{5}{7}$ **(d)** $8\frac{2}{6} - 4 = 4\frac{1}{3}$.

10. (a) (i) 13 to 15, (ii) 14.
(b) (i) 13 to 15, (ii) $14\frac{1}{2}$.
(c) (i) 15 to 18, (ii) 16.

11. (a) $10 + 3\frac{1}{2} = 13\frac{1}{2}$. **(b)** $9\frac{1}{2} + 5\frac{1}{2} = 15$.
(c) $7 + 5 + 2\frac{1}{2} = 14\frac{1}{2}$.

12. (a) $\frac{3}{7} + \frac{2}{7} = \frac{5}{7}$. **(b)** $\frac{1}{3} + \frac{1}{6} = \frac{1}{2}$. **(c)** $\frac{2}{5} + \frac{9}{40} = \frac{5}{8}$.

13. (a) $1 \_ 9 \rfloor 20$. **(b)** $13 \rfloor 45$.
(c) $1 \_ 29 \rfloor 30$. **(d)** $13 \rfloor 35$.

14. (a) $\frac{59}{56} = 1\frac{3}{56}$. **(b)** $\frac{554}{675}$. **(c)** $\frac{1}{35}$. **(d)** $\frac{73}{156}$.

15. (a) $\dfrac{a}{b} < \dfrac{c}{d}$ means for some nonzero $\dfrac{m}{n}$, $\dfrac{a}{b} + \dfrac{m}{n} = \dfrac{c}{d}$ and $\dfrac{c}{d} < \dfrac{e}{f}$ means for some nonzero $\dfrac{p}{q}$, $\dfrac{c}{d} + \dfrac{p}{q} = \dfrac{e}{f}$. Replacing $\dfrac{c}{d}$ in the second equation yields $\left(\dfrac{a}{b} + \dfrac{m}{n}\right) + \dfrac{p}{q} = \dfrac{e}{f}$, or $\dfrac{a}{b} + \left(\dfrac{m}{n} + \dfrac{p}{q}\right) = \dfrac{e}{f}$, where $\dfrac{m}{n} + \dfrac{p}{q}$ is a nonzero fraction, so $\dfrac{a}{b} < \dfrac{e}{f}$, by the alternative definition.

(b) $\dfrac{a}{b} < \dfrac{c}{d}$ means for some nonzero $\dfrac{m}{n}$,

$\dfrac{a}{b} + \dfrac{m}{n} = \dfrac{c}{d}$, so $\dfrac{c}{d} + \dfrac{e}{f} = \left(\dfrac{a}{b} + \dfrac{m}{n}\right) = \dfrac{e}{f} = $

$\left(\dfrac{a}{b} + \dfrac{e}{f}\right) + \dfrac{m}{n}$. Thus $\dfrac{a}{b} + \dfrac{e}{f} < \dfrac{c}{d} + \dfrac{e}{f}$, by the

alternative definition.

(c) As in parts (a) and (b), show that $\dfrac{a}{b} \cdot \dfrac{e}{f} +$

$\dfrac{m}{n} \cdot \dfrac{e}{f} = \dfrac{c}{d} \cdot \dfrac{e}{f}$, thus $\dfrac{a}{b} \cdot \dfrac{e}{f} < \dfrac{c}{d} \cdot \dfrac{e}{f}$.

16. $1 - \dfrac{1}{2^{100}} = \dfrac{2^{100} - 1}{2^{100}}$.

17. $\frac{5}{12}$.

18. Let $t =$ years of lifetime, $t = 72$ years.

19. (a) $\frac{3}{6}$.   **(b)** 18.   **(c)** 56.   **(d)** $\frac{18}{56}$.
   (e) No, $\frac{3}{10} \oplus \frac{1}{2} = \frac{4}{12} = \frac{1}{3} \neq \frac{9}{28}$.

20. (a) 1.   **(b)** 1.
   (c) Yes; only for perfect numbers.

21. When borrowing 1, he does not think of it as $\frac{5}{5}$. Have him use blocks (i.e., base 5 pieces could be used with long = 1).

22. The sum is 1.

23. (a) $\frac{1}{5} = \frac{1}{6} + \frac{1}{30}$.   **(b)** $\frac{1}{7} = \frac{1}{8} + \frac{1}{56}$.
   (c) $\frac{1}{17} = \frac{1}{18} + \frac{1}{306}$.

24. Yes. $\dfrac{1 + 3 + 5 + 7 + 9}{11 + 13 + 15 + 17 + 19}$,

$\dfrac{1 + 3 + 5 + 7 + 9 + 11}{13 + 15 + 17 + 19 + 21 + 23}$. In general, the numerator is $1 + 3 + \cdots + (2n - 1) = n^2$ and the denominator is $[1 + 3 + \cdots + (2m - 1)] - [1 + 3 + \cdots + (2n - 1)]$, where $m = 2n$. This difference is $m^2 - n^2 = 4n^2 - n^2 = 3n^2$. Thus the fraction is always $n^2/3n^2 = \frac{1}{3}$.

25. 28 matches.

SECTION 6.3—PART A

1. (a)

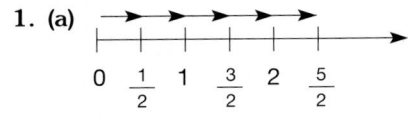

(b)

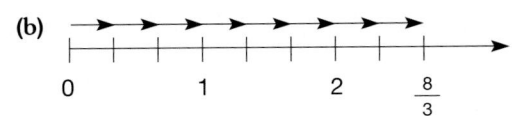

2. (a)

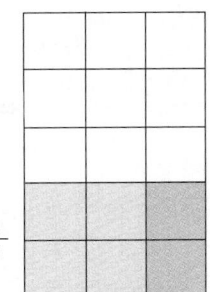

$\frac{2}{5}$

—

(b)

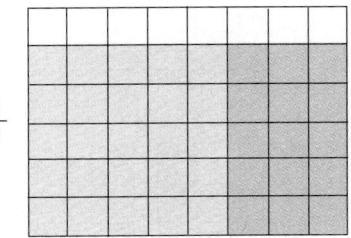

$\frac{5}{6}$

$\frac{3}{8}$

(c)

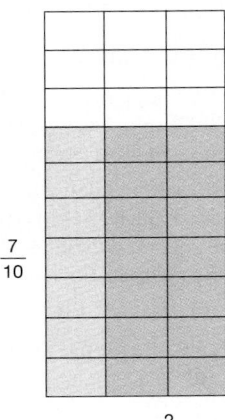

$\frac{7}{10}$

$\frac{2}{3}$

3. (a) $\dfrac{3}{5} \times \dfrac{3}{4} = \dfrac{9}{20}$.

   (b) $\dfrac{4}{7} \times \dfrac{1}{6} = \dfrac{4}{42}$.

4. (a) $\frac{21}{11}$.   **(b)** $\frac{1}{3}$.   **(c)** $\frac{9}{121}$.   **(d)** $\frac{1}{108}$.

5. (a) $<$.   **(b)** $\frac{4}{3} > \frac{2}{3}$.   **(c)** Order is reversed.

6. (a) 5.   **(b)** $\frac{4}{3}$.   **(c)** $\frac{33}{39}$ or $\frac{11}{13}$.

7. (a) $\frac{5}{4}$.   **(b)** 1.   **(c)** $\frac{13}{7}$.   **(d)** $\frac{1}{2}$.

8. (a) $\frac{3}{14}$.   **(b)** $\frac{1}{5}$.   **(c)** $\frac{2}{5}$.   **(d)** $\frac{15}{26}$.
   (e) $\frac{8}{3}$.   **(f)** $\frac{5}{42}$.   **(g)** $\frac{2}{9}$.   **(h)** $\frac{5}{8}$.
   (i) $\frac{5}{18}$.   **(j)** $\frac{17}{24}$.

9. (a) $11\frac{5}{9}$.   **(b)** $\frac{341}{32} = 10\frac{21}{32}$.   **(c)** 9.
(d) $\frac{250}{63} = 3\frac{61}{63}$.   **(e)** $\frac{15}{4} = 3\frac{3}{4}$.   **(f)** 6.

10. (a) $21 \times \frac{3}{7} = 9$.   **(b)** $35 \times \frac{3}{7} = 15$.   **(c)** $1\frac{1}{9}$.
(d) $3 \times 54 + \frac{5}{9} \times 54 = 162 + 30 = 192$.

11. (a) $4 \div \frac{1}{3} = 12$.

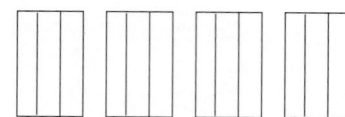

(b) $2\frac{1}{2} \div \frac{1}{4} = 10$.

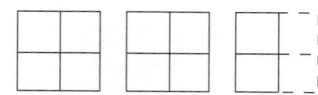

(c) $3 \div \frac{3}{4} = 4$.

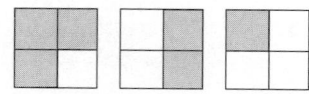

12. (a) $30 \times 5 = 150$.   **(b)** $56 \div 8 = 7$.
(c) $72 \div 9 = 8$.   **(d)** $31 \times 6 = 186$.

13. (a) $3 \times 6 = 18$.   **(b)** $4 \times 8 = 32$.
(c) $5^3 = 125$.

14. (a) $\frac{98}{117}$.   **(b)** $\frac{4}{9}$.   **(c)** 1.   **(d)** $\frac{88}{217}$.

15. (a) Associativity for fraction addition.
(b) Distributivity for multiplication over addition.
(c) Associativity for fraction multiplication.

16. Definition of addition for fractions; definition of multiplication for fractions; distributivity for multiplication over addition for whole numbers; definition of addition for fractions; definition of multiplication for fractions.

17. (a) No.   **(b)** No.   **(c)** Yes.   **(d)** No.

18. (a) Yes.   **(b)** No, negative fractions not defined yet.   **(c)** Yes.   **(d)** Yes.

19. (a) $14 \,\lrcorner\, 15$.   **(b)** $2 \,\lrcorner 4 \,\lrcorner\, 5$.
(c) $3 \,\lrcorner\, 4$.   **(d)** 18.

20. (a) $\frac{15}{31}$.   **(b)** $\frac{56}{67}$.   **(c)** $\frac{231}{102}$ or $\frac{77}{34}$.

21. 32 loads.

22. Approximately 10,700,000 barrels per day.

23. 432.

24. (a) $12\frac{4}{5}$ gallons, or nearly 13 gallons.
(b) About $5\frac{1}{2}$ gallons more.

25. 45 minutes.

26. 60.

27. 8:00.

28. (a) $2\frac{1}{2}$ cups.   **(b)** $\frac{5}{8}$ cup.   **(c)** $\frac{25}{12}$ or $2\frac{1}{12}$ cups.

29. Gale, 9 games; Ruth, 5 games; Sandy, 10 games.

30. (a) \$54,150.   **(b)** After 8 years.

31. 1.

32. (a) $\dfrac{11}{16 \times 5}$.   **(b)** Yes.   **(c)** $4\frac{11}{8} \div 2 = 2\frac{11}{16}$; $10\frac{9}{16} \div 2 = 5\frac{9}{32}$.

33. Sam: $\frac{18}{12} = 1\frac{1}{2}$, addition (getting common denominator); Sandy: $\frac{20}{9} = 2\frac{2}{9}$, division (using reciprocal).

34. For example,
(a) $\frac{3}{5} \times \frac{8}{9}$.   **(b)** $\frac{5}{8} \div \frac{3}{6}$.   **(c)** $\frac{3}{5} \times \frac{8}{4}$.   **(d)** $\frac{8}{3} \div \frac{5}{6}$.

35. 60.

36. 10.

PROBLEMS WHERE THE STRATEGY "SOLVE AN EQUIVALENT PROBLEM" IS USEFUL

1. Solve by finding how many numbers are in $\{7, 14, 21, \ldots, 392\}$, or in $\{1, 2, 3, \ldots, 56\}$.

2. Rewrite 2^{30} as 8^{10} and 3^{20} as 9^{10}. Since $8 < 9$, we have $8^{10} < 9^{10}$.

3. First find eight such fractions between 0 and 1, namely $\frac{1}{9}, \frac{2}{9}, \frac{3}{9}, \ldots, \frac{8}{9}$. Then divide each of these fractions by 3: $\frac{1}{27}, \frac{2}{27}, \frac{3}{27}, \ldots, \frac{8}{27}$.

CHAPTER 6 TEST

1. (a) T.   **(b)** F.   **(c)** F.   **(d)** T.   **(e)** T.
(f) F.   **(g)** T.   **(h)** F.

2. (a) $\frac{2}{3}$.   **(b)** $\frac{17}{18}$.   **(c)** $\frac{2}{5}$.   **(d)** $\frac{41}{189}$.

3. (a) $\frac{38}{11}$.   **(b)** $5\frac{11}{16}$.   **(c)** $\frac{37}{7}$.   **(d)** $11\frac{2}{11}$.

4. (a) $\frac{3}{4}$.   **(b)** $\frac{7}{3}$.   **(c)** $\frac{16}{92}$.

5. (a) $\frac{31}{36}$.   **(b)** $\frac{11}{75}$.   **(c)** $\frac{3}{4}$.   **(d)** $\frac{64}{49}$.

6. (a) $\frac{5}{2} \cdot (\frac{3}{4} \cdot \frac{2}{5}) = (\frac{5}{2} \cdot \frac{2}{5}) \cdot \frac{3}{4} = \frac{3}{4}$.
(b) $\frac{4}{7} \cdot \frac{3}{5} + \frac{4}{5} \cdot \frac{3}{5} = (\frac{4}{7} + \frac{4}{5})\frac{3}{5} = \frac{48}{35} \cdot \frac{3}{5} = \frac{144}{175}$.
(c) $(\frac{13}{17} + \frac{5}{11}) + \frac{4}{17} = (\frac{13}{17} + \frac{4}{17}) + \frac{5}{11} = 1\frac{5}{11}$.
(d) $\frac{3}{8} \cdot \frac{5}{7} - \frac{4}{8} \cdot \frac{3}{7} = \frac{3}{8}(\frac{5}{7} - \frac{4}{7}) = \frac{3}{8} \cdot \frac{17}{63} = \frac{51}{504} = \frac{17}{168}$.

7. The fraction $\frac{6}{12}$ represents 6 of 12 equivalent parts (or 6 eggs), whereas $\frac{12}{24}$ represents 12 of 24 equivalent parts (or 12 halves of eggs). NOTE: This works best when the eggs are hard-boiled.

8. $\dfrac{a}{b} < \dfrac{c}{d}$ if and only if $\dfrac{ad}{bd} < \dfrac{bc}{bd}$ if and only if $ad < bc$.

9. NOTE: For simplicity we will express our fractions using a common denominator. $\dfrac{a}{c}\left(\dfrac{b}{c} - \dfrac{d}{c}\right) = \dfrac{a}{c}\left(\dfrac{b-d}{c}\right) = \dfrac{a(b-d)}{c^2} = \dfrac{ab - ad}{c^2} = \dfrac{ab}{c^2} - \dfrac{ad}{c^2} = \dfrac{a}{c} \cdot \dfrac{b}{c} - \dfrac{a}{c} \cdot \dfrac{d}{c}$.

10. $\dfrac{n}{n+1} < \dfrac{n+1}{n+2}$ if and only if $n(n+2) < (n+1)^2$. However, since $n^2 + 2n < n^2 + 2n + 1$, the latter inequality is always true when $n \geq 0$.

11. 90.

12. $240,000.

SECTION 7.1—PART A

1. **(a)** $\dfrac{64}{1000}$. **(b)** $\dfrac{13,578}{10,000}$ or $1\dfrac{3578}{10,000}$. **(c)** $\dfrac{51}{100,000}$.

2. **(a)** $3(100) + 5(10) + 1 + 2(1/10) + 6(1/100)$.

   (b) $7(1000) + 6(100) + 5(10) + 4 + 3(1/10) + 2(1/100) + 1/1000$.

   (c) $6(10) + 2 + 3(1/10) + 5(1/100) + 4(1/1000) + 7(1/10,000) + 5(1/100,000)$.

3. **(a)** Thirteen thousandths.
   (b) Eighty-two ten thousandths.
   (c) Ninety-two ten billionths.
   (d) Sixty-eight million, four hundred eight-five thousand, five hundred thirty-two.
   (e) Seven million, five hundred eighty-nine thousand, six hundred thirty-two and twelve thousand, three hundred forty-five hundred thousandths.
   (f) Eight hundred fifty-nine and eighty thousand, five hundred nine millionths.
   (g) Twenty-three million, one hundred eight-seven thousand, two hundred thirteen and twenty million, thirty thousand, four billionths.
   (h) One hundred eleven billion, one million, two thousand, three and ten billion, two hundred thousand, three ten trillionths.

4. There should be no "and." The word "and" is reserved for indicating the location of the decimal point.

5. (b), (c), (d), and (e).

6. **(a)** 0.085, 0.58, 0.85.
   (b) 780.9999, 781.345, 781.354.
   (c) 4.09, 4.099, 4.9, 4.99.
   (d) 8.0019929, 8.010019, 8.01002.
   (e) 0.5, 0.5005, 0.505, 0.55.

7. **(a)** $\dfrac{5}{9} < \dfrac{19}{34}$.   **(b)** $\dfrac{18}{25} < \dfrac{38}{52}$.

8. **(a)** $18.47 - 10 = 8.47$, equal additions.
   (b) $1.3 \times 70 = 91$, commutativity and distributivity.
   (c) $7 + 5.8 = 12.8$, commutativity and associativity.
   (d) $17 \times 2 = 34$, associativity and commutativity.
   (e) 0.05124, powers of ten.
   (f) 39.07, left to right.
   (g) $72 + 4 = 76$, distributivity.
   (h) 15,000, powers of ten.

9. **(a)** 5.9×10^1.   **(b)** 4.326×10^3.
   (c) 9.7×10^4.   **(d)** 1.0×10^6.
   (e) 6.402×10^7.   **(f)** 7.1×10^{10}.

10. **(a)** 6,750,000.   **(b)** 12.5.
    (c) 0.00019514.   **(d)** 0.000044.
    (e) 1.5×10^7.   **(f)** 2.96×10^{28}.
    (g) 1.5×10^3.   **(h)** 2.96×10^4.

11. **(a)** 4.16×10^{16} m.
    (b) 3.5×10^9 m.

12. **(a)** $\frac{1}{4} \times 44 = 11$.   **(b)** $\frac{3}{4} \times 80 = 60$.
    (c) $35 \times \frac{2}{5} = 14$.   **(d)** $\frac{1}{5} \times 65 = 13$.
    (e) $65 \times \frac{4}{5} = 52$.   **(f)** $380 \times \frac{1}{20} = 19$.

13. **(a)** 16 to 19; $5 + 6 + 7 = 18$.
    (b) 420 to 560; $75 \times 6 = 450$.
    (c) 10.
    (d) 40.

14. **(a)** $48 \div 3 = 16$.   **(b)** $\frac{1}{4} \times 88 = 22$.
    (c) $125 \times \frac{1}{5} = 25$.   **(d)** $56,000 \times \frac{1}{4} = 14,000$.
    (e) $15,000 \div 750 = 20$.   **(f)** $\frac{3}{5} \times 500 = 300$.

15. **(a)** 97.3.   **(b)** 350.   **(c)** 350.   **(d)** 0.018.
    (e) 0.0183.   **(f)** 0.5.   **(g)** 0.50.

16. One possible answer is

26.2	20.96	47.16
52.4	31.44	10.48
15.72	41.92	36.68

17. $7.93.

18. $31,250.

19. 8, 10, 12, 14, 16.

SECTION 7.2—PART A

1. **(a)** (i) 47.771, (ii) 0.586, (iii) 485.84.
   (b) Same as in (a).

2. **(a)** (i) 0.17782, (ii) 14.29666, (iii) 154.2, (iv) 4.7.
   (b) Same as in part (a).

3. 4.6025.

4. $1.5561 \div 0.273 = 5.7$ and $1.5561 \div 5.7 = 0.273$.

5. **(a)** 3.658×10^6.   **(b)** 5.893×10^9.

6. **(a)** 5.2×10^2.   **(b)** 8.1×10^3.

7. **(b)** (i) 1.0066×10^{15}, (ii) 1.28×10^{14}, (iii) 3.468×10^{40}, (iv) 9.5×10^{14}, (v) 4.6656×10^{55}.

8. **(a)** 1.438×10^8 m.
   (b) About 1.2×10^8 m.

9. (a) $0.\overline{7}$.   **(b)** $0.47\overline{12}$.   **(c)** $0.\overline{18}$.   **(d)** $0.35\overline{0}$.
(e) $0.\overline{14}$.   **(f)** $0.453\overline{1596}$.

10. (a) 0.31743174317431.   **(b)** 0.31741741741741.
(c) 0.31747474747474.   **(d)** 0.31744444444444.
(e) 0.31740000000000.   **(f)** 0.11591231159123.

11. (a) $\frac{16}{99}$.   **(b)** $\frac{43}{111}$.   **(c)** $\frac{359}{495}$.
(d) $\frac{335}{1111}$.   **(e)** $\frac{469}{900}$.   **(f)** $\frac{46}{24975}$.

12. (a) $1\frac{1}{8}$.   **(b)** $7\frac{3}{4}$.   **(c)** $\frac{3}{16}$.

13. (a) 0.1_{two}.   **(b)** 0.0001_{two}.
(c) $0.\overline{01}_{two}$.   **(d)** $0.\overline{0011}_{two}$.

14. Approximately 1600 light-years.

15. Nonterminating; denominator is not divisible by only 2 or 5 after simplification.

16. (a) $\frac{1}{8}$.   **(b)** $\frac{1}{16}$.   **(c)** $1/5^8$.   **(d)** $1/2^{17}$.

17. (a) $\frac{3}{9}=\frac{1}{3}$.   **(b)** $\frac{5}{9}$.   **(c)** $\frac{7}{9}$.   **(d)** $2\frac{8}{9}$.   **(e)** 6.

18. (a) $\frac{3}{99}=\frac{1}{33}$.   **(b)** $\frac{5}{99}$.   **(c)** $\frac{7}{99}$.   **(d)** $\frac{37}{99}$.
(e) $\frac{64}{99}$.   **(f)** $5\frac{97}{99}$.

19. (a) $\frac{3}{999}=\frac{1}{333}$.   **(b)** $\frac{5}{999}$.   **(c)** $\frac{7}{999}$.   **(d)** $\frac{19}{999}$.
(e) $\frac{827}{999}$.   **(f)** $3\frac{217}{999}$.

20. (i) $\frac{23}{99}$, **(ii)** $\frac{10}{999}$, **(iii)** $\frac{769}{999}$, **(iv)** $\frac{9}{9}=1$, **(v)** $\frac{57}{99}=\frac{19}{33}$, **(vi)** $\frac{1827}{9999}=\frac{203}{1111}$.

21. (a) $1/99999=0.\overline{00001}$.
(b) $x/99999$ where $1\le x\le 99998$, where digits in x are not all the same.

22. (a) 2.   **(b)** 6.   **(c)** 0.   **(d)** 7.

23. Disregarding the first two digits to the right of the decimal point in the decimal expansion of $\frac{1}{71}$, they are the same.

24. $0.94376=364\div 365\times 363\div 365$ and so on.

SECTION 7.3—PART A

1. (a) $5:6$. **(b)** $\frac{5}{11}$. **(c)** Cannot be determined. **(d)** 15.

2. Each is an ordered pair of numbers. For example, part (a) measures efficiency of an engine.

3. (a) $\frac{1}{4}$.   **(b)** $\frac{2}{5}$.   **(c)** $\frac{5}{1}$ or 5.

4. 3.8, yes.

5. (a) 30.   **(b)** 585.   **(c)** 20.   **(d)** 18.
(e) 8.   **(f)** 30.

6. (a) 0.64.   **(b)** 8.4.   **(c)** 0.93.
(d) 1.71.   **(e)** 2.17.   **(f)** 0.01.

7. (a) $24:2=48:4=96:8=192:16$.
(b) $13.50:1=27:2=81:6$.
(c) $300:12=100:4=200:8$.
(d) $20:15=4:3=16:12$.
(e) $32:8=16:4=48:12$.

8. (a) 62.5 mph.   **(b)** 88 kph.

9. 249 cartons.

10. (a) 17 cents for 15 ounces.
(b) 29 ounces for 13 cents.
(c) 73 ounces for 96 cents.

11. 40 ounces.

12. $16\frac{1}{2}$ days.

13. 15.

14. 1024 ounces.

15. About $30\frac{2}{3}$ years.

16. 4.8 pounds.

17. 24,530 miles.

18. About 1613 feet.

19. About 29″.

20. (a) 30.   **(b)** About $314.29.   **(c)** $550.

21. 10; 9.

22. (a) 2.48 AU.
(b) 93,000,000 miles or 9.3×10^7 miles.
(c) 2.31×10^8 miles.

23. (a) Approx. 416,666,667.
(b) Approx. 6,944,444.
(c) Approx. 115,741.
(d) About 12 noon.
(e) About 22.5 seconds before midnight.
(f) Less than $\frac{1}{10}$ of a second before midnight (0.0864 second before midnight).

24. 120 miles away.

25. $17.50.

26. 119¢ (50, 25, 10, 10, 10, 10, 1, 1, 1, 1). 219¢ if a silver dollar is used.

27. Yes; the first player always wins by going to a number with ones digit one.

28. Start both timers at the same time. Start cooking the object when the 7-minute timer runs out—there will be 4 minutes left on the 11-minute timer. When the 11-minute timer runs out, turn it over to complete the 15 minutes.

29. $\frac{8}{7}\times 11=12\frac{4}{7}$ seconds.

30. 1, 2, 4, 8, 16, 32, 2816 cents.

31. 4, 7, 28, $3n-2$.

SECTION 7.4—PART A

1. (a) 0.37.   **(b)** 0.527.   **(c)** 0.7921.   **(d)** 3.02.
(e) 0.003.   **(f)** 0.00065.

2. (a) 530%.   **(b)** 72%.   **(c)** 19.2%.
(d) 2500%.   **(e)** 7.5%.   **(f)** 0.38%.

3. (a) $\frac{18}{25}$. (b) $\frac{653}{1000}$. (c) $5\frac{21}{50}$. (d) $\frac{3}{10,000}$.

4. (a) 75%. (b) $166\frac{2}{3}$%. (c) 80%. (d) 15%.
   (e) 28%. (f) 87.5%.

5. (a) (i) 5, (ii) 6.87, (iii) 0.458, (iv) 3290.
   (b) (i) 12, (ii) 0.93, (iii) 600, (iv) 3.128.
   (c) (i) 13.5, (ii) 7560, (iii) 1.08, (iv) 0.0099.

6. (a) $1.65. (b) $2.25. (c) $5.25. (d) $3.60.

7. (a) 32. (b) 37. (c) 183. (d) 70.
   (e) 122. (f) 270.

8. (a) 252. (b) 144. (c) 231. (d) 195.
   (e) 40. (f) 80.

9. (a) 56. (b) 76. (c) 68. (d) 37.5.
   (e) 150. (f) $133\frac{1}{3}$.

10. (a) 40% × 70 = 28. (b) 60% × 30 = 18.
   (c) 125% × 60 = $\frac{5}{4}$ × 60 = 75.
   (d) 50% × 2 = 1. (e) 20% × 70 = 14.
   (f) 10% × 300 = 30. (g) 1% × 60 = 0.6.
   (h) 400% × 180 = 4 × 180 = 720.

11. (a) $\frac{42}{75} = \frac{x}{100}$. (b) $\frac{x}{964} = \frac{17}{100}$.
   (c) $\frac{156.6}{x} = \frac{37}{100}$. (d) $\frac{8\frac{3}{4}}{12\frac{1}{3}} = \frac{x}{100}$.
   (e) $\frac{12\frac{1}{3}}{x} = \frac{225}{100}$.

12. (a) 33.6. (b) 2.7. (c) 82.4.
   (d) 48.7%. (e) 55.5%. (f) 123.5.
   (g) 33.3%. (h) 213.3. (i) 0.5.
   (j) 0.1.

13. (a) 56.7. (b) 115.5. (c) 375.6.

14. (a) 350. (b) 2850. (c) 15,680. (d) 4400.

15. (a) 22. (b) 0.6. (c) 70. (d) 650.

16. 8.5%.

17. 1946 students.

18. (a) $5120.76. (b) About $53.05 more.

19. $(100)(1.0004839)^{15} = 100.73$, about 73 cents.

20. 5.7%; 94.3%.

21. (a) About $1.18 × 10^{11}$. (b) 82.4%.

22. (a) 69.5 quadrillion BTU.
   (b) Nuclear   8.2%
       Crude oil   24.9%
       Natural gas   28.1%
       Renewables   8.8%
       Coal   30.1%
       Percentages don't add up to 100% due to rounding.

23. The discount is 13% or the sales price should be $97.75.

24. $5000.

25. (a) 250. (b) 480. (c) 15.

26. $4875.

27. (a) About 16.3%. (b) About 34.8%.
   (c) $3.64 × 10^{14}$ square meters.
   (d) 0.44% or about $\frac{11}{25}$ of 1%.

28. No; 3 grams is 4% of 75 grams, but 7 grams is 15% of $46.\overline{6}$ grams, giving different U.S. RDA of protein.

29. 31.68 inches.

30. The result is the same.

31. 32%.

32. 119 to 136.

33. If the competition had x outputs, then $x + 0.4x = 6$, or $1.4x = 6$. There is no whole number for x; therefore, the competition couldn't have had x outputs.

34. 10% + 5% = 15% off, whereas 10% off, then 5% off is equivalent to finding 90% × 95% = 85.5%, or 14.5% off. Conclusion: Add the percents.

35. An increase of about 4.9%.

36. The player who is faced with 3 petals loses. Reasoning backward, so is the one faced with 6 since whatever she takes, the opponent can force her to 3. The same for 9. Thus the first player will lose. The key to this game is to leave the opponent on a multiple of 3.

37. Let P be the price. Option (i) is $P × 80\% × 106\%$, whereas (ii) is $P × 106\% × 80\%$. By commutativity, they are equal.

38. $14,751.06.

39. $59,000.

40. $9052.13.

41. $\frac{4.5}{111.2} = 4.05\%$.

42. $50,000. If you make a table, you can see that you will keep more of your money up to $50,000, namely 50% of $50,000, or $25,000. However, at $51,000 you only keep 49% of $51,000, or $24,990 and it goes down from there until you keep $0 at $100,000! Observe that there is symmetry around $50,000.

PROBLEMS WHERE THE STRATEGY "WORK BACKWARD" IS USEFUL

1. Working backward, we have 87 − 59 + 18 = 46. So they must have gone 46 floors the first time.

2. If she ended up with 473 cards, she brought 473 − 9 + 2 − 4 − 2 + 7 − 5 + 3 = 465.

3. Working backward, {[(13.4 + 6)3 ÷ 2] − 9} ÷ 6 = 13 is the original number.

CHAPTER 7 TEST

1. (a) F. (b) T. (c) T. (d) F. (e) F.
   (f) T. (g) T. (h) T.

2. (a) 17.519. (b) 6.339. (c) 83.293.
   (d) 500.

3. (a) $\frac{103}{1000} < \frac{400}{1000}$ and $0.1 < 0.4$; therefore, $0.103 < 0.4$.
   (b) $\frac{997}{10,000} < \frac{1000}{10,000}$ and $0.09 < 0.10$; therefore, $0.0997 < 0.1$.

4. (a) $0.\overline{285714}$. (b) 0.625. (c) $0.1458\overline{3}$.
   (d) $0.\overline{4}$.

5. (a) Terminating. (b) Nonterminating.
   (c) Terminating.

6. (a) $\frac{4}{11}$. (b) $\frac{11}{30}$. (c) $\frac{909}{2500}$.

7. (a) 0.52, $\frac{52}{100}$. (b) 125%, $\frac{125}{100}$. (c) 0.68, 68%.

8. 18.

9. 123,456,789 has prime factors other than 2 or 5.

10. $37 \div 100 \times 58$ is 37% of 58.

11. 7.

12. $2520.

13. 522.

14. 9.6 inches.

SECTION 8.1—PART A

1. (a)

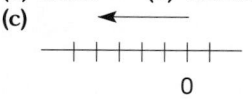

   (b)

   (c)

2.

3. (a) *RRR*. (b) *BBBB*.
   (c)

   (d)

4. (a) -3. (b) 4. (c) 0. (d) 168.
   (e) -56. (f) 1235.

5. (a)

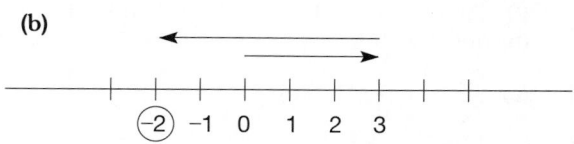

   or *BBBBBRRR = BB*; 2.

   (b)

   or *BBBRRRRR = RR*; -2.

   (c)

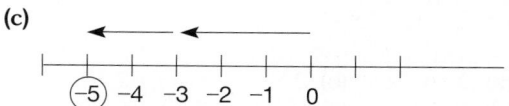

   or *RRR RR = -5*.

6. $64.

7. (a) $-14 + 6 = (-8 + (-6)) + 6 = -8 + (-6 + 6) = -8 + 0 = -8$.
   (b) $17 + (-3) = (14 + 3) + (-3) = 14 + (3 + (-3)) = 14 + 0 = 14$.
   (c) $-21 + 11 = (-10 + (-11)) + 11 = -10 + (-11 + 11) = -10 + 0 = -10$.

8. (a) BBB BBBB / RRRR $= -4$ (b) BBBB BBBBB / RRRRR $= 9$
   (c) RRR RRR / BBB $= 3$ (d) BBBB / RRRR $= 4$

9. (a) $7 - (-3) = n$ if and only if $7 = -3 + n$; therefore, $n = 10$.
   (b) $(-5) - (-8) = n$ if and only if $(-5) = -8 + n$; therefore, $n = 3$.
   (c) $-2 - 7 = n$ if and only if $-2 = 7 + n$; therefore, $n = -9$.

10. (a) $15 + (-6) = 9$.   **(b)** $-5 + (-7) = -12$.
(c) $5 + 2 = 7$.   **(d)** $-3 + 7 = 4$.

11. (a) -4.   **(b)** 12.   **(c)** 1.   **(d)** 1.   **(e)** -8.
(f) -6.

12. (a) 26.   **(b)** -5.   **(c)** 370.   **(d)** -128.

13. Top: 5; second: -1, 6; third: -2, 1.

14. (a) -5.   **(b)** 12.   **(c)** -78.   **(d)** 1.
(e) 9.   **(f)** 8.

15. (a) T.   **(b)** F.   **(c)** F.   **(d)** T.

16. (a) Five minus two.
(b) Negative six or opposite of six (both equivalent).
(c) Opposite of three.
(d) Opposite of negative five, for example.
(e) Ten minus the opposite of negative two, for example.
(f) Opposite of p.

17. (a) Negative.   **(b)** Positive.   **(c)** Neither.

18. (a) 5.   **(b)** 17.   **(c)** 2.   **(d)** -2.   **(e)** -2.
(f) 2.

19. Just closure holds.

20. If $a - b = c$, then $a + (-b) = c$. Then $a + (-b) + b = c + b$, or $a = b + c$.

21. (a) (i) When a and b have the same sign or when one or both are 0, (ii) when a and b have opposite signs, (iii) never, (iv) all integers will work.
(b) Only condition (iv).

22. (a) (i) $9 - 4$, (ii) $4 - 9$, (iii) $4 - 4$, (iv) $9 - ((4 - 4) - 4)$, (v) $(9 - 4) - 4$, (vi) $((9 - 4) - 4) - 4$.
(b) All integers.
(c) Any integer that is a multiple of 4.
(d) If GCF$(a, b) = 1$, then all integers; otherwise, just multiples of GCF.

23. Second: 2, -24; third: 4, -2, -22; bottom: -7.

24. As long as we have integers, this algorithm is coorect. Justification: $72 - 38 = (70 + 2) - (30 + 8) = (70 - 30) + (2 - 8) = 40 + (-6) = 34$.

SECTION 8.2—PART A

1. (a) $2 + 2 + 2 + 2 = 8$ or $4 \times 2 = 8$.

(b) $(-3) + (-3) + (-3) = -9$ or $3 \times (-3) = -9$.

(c) $(-1) + (-1) + (-1) + (-1) + (-1) + (-1) = -6$ or $6 \times (-1) = -6$.

2. (a) (i) $6 \times (-1) = -6$, $6 \times (-2) = -12$, $6 \times (-3) = -18$; (ii) $9 \times (-1) = -9$, $9 \times (-2) = -18$, $9 \times (-3) = -27$.

(b) Positive times negative equals negative.

3. (a) Put in 3 groups of 2 red chips, -6.
(b) Put in 3 groups of 4 red chips, -12.
(c) Put in 5 groups of 2 red chips, -10.

4. (a) Begin with at least 12 red and 12 black chips; remove 3 groups of 4 black chips, leaving -12.
(b) Begin with at least 8 red and 8 black chips; remove 2 groups of 4 red chips, leaving 8.
(c) Begin with at least 2 red and 2 black chips; remove 2 groups of 1 red chip, leaving 2.

5. Distributivity of multiplication over addition; additive inverse; multiplication by 0.

6. Distributivity of multiplication over addition; additive inverse; multiplication by 0.

7. (a) 16.   **(b)** -27.   **(c)** 16.   **(d)** 25.
(e) -243.   **(f)** 64.

8. Adding the opposite approach to subtraction; distributivity of multiplication over addition: $(-a)b = -(ab)$; adding opposite approach; distributivity of multiplication over subtraction.

9. (a) $24 = -4 \times n$.   **(b)** $-42 = -6 \times n$.
(c) $-48 = -12 \times n$.   **(d)** $-56 = 7 \times n$.

10. (a) 3.   **(b)** -86.   **(c)** -34.   **(d)** 907.

11. (a) -2592.   **(b)** 1938.   **(c)** 97,920.
(d) -47.   **(e)** -156.   **(f)** 1489.

12. Yes.

13. (a) $\frac{1}{100}$.   **(b)** $\frac{1}{64}$.   **(c)** $\frac{1}{64}$.   **(d)** $\frac{1}{125}$.

14. (a) $\frac{1}{4^2} \cdot 4^6 = 4^4$.   **(b)** $4^{-2+6} = 4^4$.

(c) $\frac{1}{5^6}$, 5^{-6}.   **(d)** Yes.

15. (a) $\frac{1/3^2}{3^5} = \frac{1}{3^7}$.   **(b)** $3^{-2-5} = 3^{-7} = \frac{1}{3^7}$.

(c) 6^{10}, 6^{10}.   **(d)** Yes.

16. (a) $\frac{1}{(3^2)^3} = \frac{1}{3^6}$.   **(b)** $3^{2(-3)} = 3^{-6} = \frac{1}{3^6}$.

(c) 5^6, 5^6.   **(d)** Yes.

17. (a) $3^3 = 27$.   **(b)** 6.   **(c)** $3^8 = 6561$.

18. (a) 4×10^{-4}.   **(b)** 1.6×10^{-6}.
(c) 4.95×10^{-10}.   **(d)** 8.071×10^{-20}.

19. (a) 7.22×10^{-25}.   **(b)** 8.28×10^{-26}.
(c) 2.5×10^{-10}.   **(d)** 4×10^{-37}.
(e) 8×10^{14}.   **(f)** 2.05×10^{-7}.

20. 0.0000000003 meters.

21. (a) -3 is left of 2.

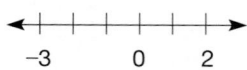

(b) -6 is left of -2.

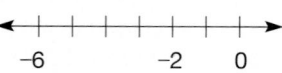

(c) -12 is left of -3.

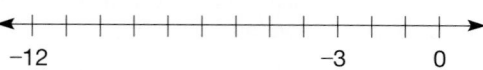

22. (a) $-5, -2, 0, 2, 5$.
(b) $-8, -6, -5, 3, 12$.
(c) $-11, -8, -5, -3, -2$.
(d) $-108, -72, -36, 23, 45$.

23. $43{,}200, -240, -180, 12, -5, 3$.

24. (a) -10 and -8.   **(b)** -8.   **(c)** No.

25. (a) ? $-$
(b) (i) ? $+$ (ii) $+\ -$ (iii) $+\ -$?
     $-$? $-\ +$ $-\ +$

26. 1.99×10^{-23} grams per atom of carbon.

27. (a) 1.11×10^{-2}.
(b) About 2.33×10^{8} seconds or 7.37 years.

28. (a) (i) When x is negative. (ii) when x is nonnegative (zero or positive), (iii) never, (iv) all integers.
(b) Only (iv).

29. This is correct, by $a(-1) = -a$.

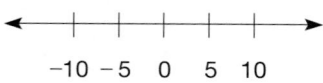

30. Put the amounts on a number line, where positive numbers represent assets and negative numbers represent liabilities. Clearly, $-10 < -5$.

31. First row: $-2, -9, 12$; second row: $-36, 6, -1$; third row: $3, -4, -18$.

32. $x < y$ means $y = x + p$ for some $p > 0$, $y^2 = (x + p)^2 = x^2 + 2xp + p^2$. Since $x > 0$ and $p > 0$, $2xp + p^2 > 0$. Therefore, $x^2 < y^2$.

33. 100 sheep, 0 cows, and 0 rabbits or 1 sheep, 19 cows, and 80 rabbits.

34. True. Every whole number can be expressed in the form $3n$, $3n + 1$, or $3n + 2$. If these three forms are squared, the squares will be of the form $3m$ or $3m + 1$.

35. Let the top row contain the numbers x, y, and z. Let the left-hand column contain a, b, and c. Each diagonal has a sum of $a + b + c + x + y + z$.

36. Assume $ab = 0$ and $b \neq 0$. Then $ab = 0 \cdot b$. Since $ac = bc$ and $c \neq 0$ implies that $a = b$, we can cancel the b's in $ab = 0 \cdot b$. Hence $a = 0$.

PROBLEMS WHERE THE STRATEGY "USE CASES" IS USEFUL

1. Case 1: odd + even + odd = even.
Case 2: even + odd + even = odd.
   Since only Case 1 has an even sum, two of the numbers must be odd.

2. $m^2 - n^2$ is positive when $m^2 > n^2$.
Case 1: $m > 0$, $n > 0$. Here m must be greater than n.
Case 2: $m > 0$, $n < 0$. Here $m > -n$.
Case 3: $m < 0$, $n > 0$. Here $-m > n$.
Case 4: $m < 0$, $n < 0$. Here $m < n$.

3. Case 1: If $n = 5m$, then $n^2 = 25m^2$, hence is a multiple of 5.
Case 2: If $n = 5m + 1$, then $n^2 = 25m^2 + 10m + 1$, which is one more than a multiple of 5.
Case 3: If $n = 5m + 2$, then $n^2 = 25m^2 + 20m + 4$, which is 4 more than (hence one less than) a multiple of 5.
Case 4: If $n = 5m + 3$, then $n^2 = 25m^2 + 30m + 9$, which is one less than a multiple of 5.
Case 5: If $n = 5m + 4$, then $n^2 = 25m^2 + 40m + 16$, which is one more than a multiple of 5.

CHAPTER 8 TEST

1. (a) T.   **(b)** F.   **(c)** F.   **(d)** T.   **(e)** F.
(f) F.   **(g)** F.   **(h)** T.

2. (a) -6 **(b)** 42.   **(c)** 48.   **(d)** -8.
(e) -30.   **(f)** 3.   **(g)** -52.   **(h)** -12.

3. (a) $3(-4 + 2) = 3(-2) = -6$,
     $3(-4) + 3(2) = -12 + 6 = -6$.
(b) $-3(-5 + (-2)) = -3(-7) = 21$,
     $(-3)(-5) + (-3)(-2) = 15 + 6 = 21$.

4. (a) 8.2×10^{12}.   **(b)** 6×10^{-6}.

5. (a) Associativity.
(b) Associativity and commutativity.
(c) Distributivity.
(d) Commutativity and distributivity.

6. (a) (i) $BBBBBBBBBBBBB\cancel{R}\cancel{R}\cancel{R}\cancel{R} = 13$,
     (ii) $8 - (-5) = 8 + 5 = 13$,
     (iii) $8 - (-5) = c$ if and only if $8 = c + (-5)$; $c = 13$.
(b) (i) $RR \rightarrow BBBBB\cancel{R}\cancel{R}\cancel{R}\cancel{R}\cancel{R}\cancel{R} = 5$,
     (ii) $(-2) - (-7) = -2 + 7 = 5$,
     (iii) $(-2) - (-7) = c$ if and only if $-2 = c + (-7)$; $c = 5$.

7. (a) Negative.   **(b)** Negative.   **(c)** Positive.
(d) Positive.

8. (a) 30, −30.   **(b)** 120, 60.   **(c)** −900, −3600.
(d) −1, −2.

9.

9	−12	3
−6	0	6
−3	12	−9

10.

−256	2	−64
8	32	128
−16	512	−4

SECTION 9.1—PART A

1. (a) $\dfrac{-2}{3}$ where $-2, 3$ are integers.

(b) $\dfrac{-31}{6}$ where $-31, 6$ are integers.

(c) $\dfrac{10}{1}$ where $10, 1$ are integers.

2. (a), (b), and (d).

3. (a) $\dfrac{-5}{7}$.   **(b)** $\dfrac{-3}{5}$.   **(c)** $\dfrac{2}{5}$.   **(d)** $\dfrac{-4}{5}$.

4. (a) $\dfrac{-1}{9}$.   **(b)** $\dfrac{-4}{3}$.   **(c)** $\dfrac{1}{4}$.

(d) 0.   **(e)** $\dfrac{1}{77}$.   **(f)** $\dfrac{-1}{8}$.

5. (a) 2.   **(b)** $\dfrac{-5}{3}$.   **(c)** $\dfrac{2}{7}$.   **(d)** $\dfrac{5}{16}$.

6. (a) $\dfrac{2}{3}$.   **(b)** 2.   **(c)** $\dfrac{5}{7}$.   **(d)** $\dfrac{-31}{36}$.

(e) $\dfrac{29}{24}$.   **(f)** $\dfrac{1}{30}$.

7. (a) $\dfrac{14}{27}$.   **(b)** $\dfrac{-35}{18}$.   **(c)** $\dfrac{5}{18}$.   **(d)** $\dfrac{1}{4}$.

(e) $\dfrac{1}{7}$.   **(f)** $\dfrac{-18}{55}$.

8. (a) $\dfrac{-11}{17}$.   **(b)** $\dfrac{-3}{14}$.   **(c)** $\dfrac{31}{21}$.   **(d)** $\dfrac{2}{7}$.

(e) $\dfrac{-3}{5}$.   **(f)** $\dfrac{11}{24}$.

9. (a) -3.   **(b)** $\dfrac{-2}{3}$.   **(c)** $\dfrac{7}{10}$.

10. (a) $\dfrac{2}{3}$.   **(b)** -1.   **(c)** $\dfrac{-3}{5}$.

11. (a) $\dfrac{-1}{3}$.   **(b)** $\dfrac{7}{6}$.   **(c)** $\dfrac{-5}{2}$.   **(d)** $\dfrac{-17}{11}$.

12. (a) $\dfrac{-9}{7}$.   **(b)** $\dfrac{4}{3}$.   **(c)** $\dfrac{7}{10}$.

13. (a) $\dfrac{4}{3}$.   **(b)** $\dfrac{-1}{6}$.   **(c)** $\dfrac{-9}{20}$.   **(d)** $\dfrac{-7}{5}$.

14. (a) $\dfrac{-5}{6}, \dfrac{-1}{6}, \dfrac{3}{6}$.   **(b)** $\dfrac{-9}{8}, \dfrac{-7}{8}, \dfrac{-5}{8}$.

(c) $\dfrac{-5}{6}, \dfrac{-2}{3}, \dfrac{-7}{12}$.

15. (a) $\dfrac{-2}{3} < \dfrac{-5}{8}$.   **(b)** $\dfrac{-17}{12} < \dfrac{-7}{5}$.

(c) $\dfrac{-7}{9} < \dfrac{-5}{7}$.

16. (a) $\dfrac{1}{21}$.   **(b)** $\dfrac{7}{12}$.   **(c)** $\dfrac{5}{6}$.

17. (a) $\dfrac{-9}{11} < \dfrac{-3}{11}$.   **(b)** $\dfrac{-1}{3} < \dfrac{2}{5}$.

(c) $\dfrac{-9}{10} < \dfrac{-5}{6}$.   **(d)** $\dfrac{-9}{8} < \dfrac{-10}{9}$.

18. (a) $x < \dfrac{-4}{3}$.   **(b)** $x < \dfrac{-1}{12}$.

(c) $x < \dfrac{-18}{35}$.   **(d)** $x > \dfrac{-13}{35}$.

19. (a) $x < \dfrac{3}{2}$.   **(b)** $x < \dfrac{-3}{4}$.

(c) $x < \dfrac{-5}{2}$.

20. (a) $x > \dfrac{5}{4}$.   **(b)** $x > -\dfrac{3}{2}$.

(c) $x > \dfrac{5}{2}$.   **(d)** $x < \dfrac{-56}{15}$.

21. (a) $x < \dfrac{1}{6}$.   **(b)** $x < \dfrac{1}{5}$.

(c) $x < \dfrac{-10}{9}$.   **(d)** $x > \dfrac{3}{2}$.

22. (a) Associative—addition.
(b) Commutative—multiplication.
(c) Distributive—multiplication over addition.
(d) Property of less than and addition.
(e) Property of less than and multiplication by a negative.

23. (a) $-90{,}687$.   **(b)** -77.   **(c)** $-16{,}261$.
(d) $-86{,}266{,}944$.

24. (a) $\dfrac{-164}{837}$. (b) $\dfrac{-19}{528}$. (c) $\dfrac{-455}{3456}$.

(d) $1\frac{329}{703}$.

25. (a) $\dfrac{-43}{88} < \dfrac{-37}{76}, \dfrac{-80}{164} = \dfrac{-20}{41}$.

(b) $\dfrac{-59}{97} < \dfrac{-68}{113}, \dfrac{-127}{210}$.

(c) $\dfrac{-113}{217} < \dfrac{-163}{314}, \dfrac{-276}{531} = \dfrac{-92}{177}$.

(d) $\dfrac{-545}{522} < \dfrac{-812}{779}, \dfrac{-1357}{1301}$.

26. $a/b = an/bn$ if and only if $a(bn) = b(an)$. The last equation is true due to associativity and commutativity of integer multiplication.

27. (a) $\dfrac{a}{b} \cdot \dfrac{c}{d} = \dfrac{ac}{bd}$ (definition of multiplication), ac and bd are integers (closure of integer multiplication); therefore, $\dfrac{ac}{bd}$ is a rational number. Similar types of arguments hold for parts (b) to (e).

28. (a) $a/b = c/d + e/f$.

(b) If $a/b - c/d = e/f$, then $a/b + (-c/d) = e/f$. Add c/d to both sides. Then $a/b = c/d + e/f$. Also, if $a/b = c/d + e/f$, add $-c/d$ to both sides. Then $a/b + (-c/d) = e/f$ or $a/b - c/d = e/f$.

(c) If $a/b - c/d = e/f$, then $a/b = c/d + e/f$. Adding $-c/d$ to both sides will yield $a/b + (-c/d) = e/f$. Hence, $a/b - c/d = a/b + (-c/d)$.

29. $\dfrac{a}{b}\left(\dfrac{c}{d} + \dfrac{e}{f}\right) = \dfrac{a}{b}\left(\dfrac{cf + de}{df}\right) = \dfrac{a(cf + de)}{bdf} =$

$\dfrac{acf + ade}{bdf} = \dfrac{acf}{bdf} + \dfrac{ade}{bdf} = \dfrac{ac}{bd} + \dfrac{ae}{bf} = \dfrac{a}{b} \cdot \dfrac{c}{d} =$

$\dfrac{a}{b} \cdot \dfrac{e}{f}$, using addition and multiplication of rational numbers and distributivity of integers.

30. If $a/b < c/d$, then $a/b + p/q = c/d$ for some positive p/q. Therefore, $a/b + p/q + e/f = c/d + e/f$, or $a/b + e/f + p/q = c/d + e/f$ for positive p/q. Thus $a/b + e/f < c/d + e/f$.

SECTION 9.2—PART A

1. (a) Irrational. (b) Rational. (c) Irrational.
(d) Rational.

2. (b) and (c).

3. No; if it did, π would be a rational number. This is an approximation to π, accurate to the hundredths place.

4. $0.56, 0.565565556\ldots, 0.565566555666\ldots,$
$0.\overline{56}, 0.\overline{566}, 0.56656665\ldots, 0.5\overline{66}.$

5. For example, $\sqrt{10}, \sqrt{11}, \sqrt{12}, 3.060060006\ldots,$

6. (a) Distributive of multiplication over addition.
(b) Yes; 8π. (c) No.

7. (a) $2 \times 3 = 6$. (b) $2 \times 5 = 10$.
(c) $3 \times 4 = 12$. (d) $3 \times 5 = 15$.
(e) $\sqrt{a} \times \sqrt{b} = \sqrt{a \times b}$.

8. (a) 19. (b) 27. (c) 56. (d) 71.

9. (a) 24, 2.4. (b) 37, 3.7. (c) 61, 0.61.
(d) 93, 0.93.

10. (a) $4\sqrt{3}$. (b) $4\sqrt{2}$. (c) $5\sqrt{2}$.

11. (a) 10. (b) 22. (c) $6\sqrt{3}$.

12. (a) $\sqrt{2}$. (b) $\sqrt{3}$.

13. (a) $\sqrt{34}$. (b) $\sqrt{20} = 2\sqrt{5}$.
(c) 6.

14. (a) 29; exact. (b) 28.106939; approx.
(c) 36.5; exact. (d) 25.804263; approx.

15. (a) $0.3 < 0.5477225$. (b) $0.5 < 0.7071067$.
(c) $0.7 < 0.83666$. (d) $0.98 < 0.9899494$.
Square root is larger than number.

16. (a) 5. (b) 2. (c) 243. (d) 81.
(e) 8. (f) $\frac{1}{125}$.

17. (a) 25. (b) 3.80 (rounded).
(c) 7,547,104 (rounded).
(d) 9,018,968 (rounded).

18. (a) -4. (b) 3. (c) Does not exist.
(d) 2.

19. (a) 5.2; exact. (b) 3.83247; approx.
(c) 9.1; exact. (d) 6.8; exact.

20. (a) -8. (b) 5. (c) $\dfrac{-5}{9}$. (d) $3\sqrt{2}$.

21. (a) 9. (b) 5. (c) 5. (d) $\dfrac{9}{8}$. (e) $\dfrac{-7}{6}$.
(f) 2π.

22. (a) 11. (b) 3. (c) -2. (d) -18.
(e) -7. (f) $\dfrac{26}{15}$.

23. (a) $x < 4$. (b) $x \le \dfrac{32}{21}$. (c) $x < 6\sqrt{5} + 3\sqrt{2}$.
(d) $x > -9\pi$.

24. (a) $x < \dfrac{-7}{2}$. (b) $x > \dfrac{10}{3}$. (c) $x \le 2$.
(d) $x > \dfrac{-45}{2}$. (e) $x > \dfrac{27}{8}$. (f) $x < -1$.

25. (a) $x > \dfrac{-11}{3}$.   **(b)** $x \le 4$.   **(c)** $x > \dfrac{9}{5}$.

(d) $x \le \dfrac{22}{27}$.

26. Let $\sqrt{3} = a/b$. Then $3 = a^2/b^2$ or $a^2 = 3b^2$. Count prime factors.

27. When you get to the step $a^2 = 9 \cdot b^2$, this can be written as $a^2 = 3^2 \cdot b^2$. Thus both sides have an even number of prime factors and no contradiction arises.

28. Assume not. Then $(a/b)^3 = 2$ for some rational a/b.

29. (a) By closure of real-number multiplication, $5\sqrt{3}$ is a real number, and thus a rational or an irrational number. Assume that it is rational, say m. $\sqrt{3} = m/5$. Since $m/5$ is rational and $\sqrt{3}$ is irrational, we have a contradiction. Therefore, $5\sqrt{3}$ must be irrational.

(b) Argue as in part (a); replace 5 with any nonzero rational and $\sqrt{3}$ with any irrational.

30. (a) $1 + \sqrt{3} = a/b$, so $\sqrt{3} = (a - b)/b$, which is a rational number, and this is a contradiction because $\sqrt{3}$ is an irrational number.

(b) Argue as in part (a); assume that the number is rational and solve for $\sqrt{3}$.

31. (a) Apply 34(b).   **(b)** Apply 35(b).
(c) Apply 35(b).

32. $\sqrt{a} + \sqrt{b} \ne \sqrt{a + b}$ except when $a = 0$ or $b = 0$. There is no consistent analogy between multiplication and addition.

33. $\sqrt{a} \cdot \sqrt{b} = \sqrt{ab}$ is true for all a and b, where $a \ge 0$ and $b \ge 0$.

34. $\{(3n, 4n, 5n) \mid n \text{ is a nonzero whole number}\}$ is an infinite set of Pythagorean triples.

35. If $u = 2$, $v = 1$, then $a = 4$, $b = 3$, $c = 5$. If $u = 3$, $v = 2$, then $a = 12$, $b = 5$, $c = 13$.

36. 3, 4, 5; 1, 2, 3; 2, 3, 4; -1, 0, 1.

37. 111,556 m².

38. Yes; 1 or -1.

39. Cut from the longer wire a piece that is $\frac{1}{3}$ the sum of the lengths of the original pieces.

SECTION 9.3—PART A

1. $A(3, 0)$; $B(2, 4)$; $C(-2, 1)$; $D(-5, -2)$; $E(0, -4)$; $F(5, -4)$.

2. (a)

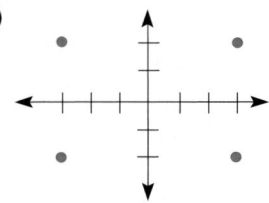

(b)

(c)

(d)

3.

4. (a) Domain = $\{x \mid -2 \le x \le 3\}$.
Range = $\{y \mid -1 \le y \le 3\}$.
(b) Not a function.
(c) Not a function.
(d) Domain = $\{-2, -1, 0, 1, 2, 3, 4\}$.
Range = $\{-1, 0, 1, 2\}$.
(e) Not a function.
(f) Domain is the set of all real numbers.
Range is the set of all positive real numbers.

5. (a) (i) 4,   (ii) 0,   (iii) 2.
(b) Domain = $\{x \mid -3 \le x \le 6\}$.
Range = $\{y \mid -4 \le y \le 4\}$.
(c) -5, 2.5, 4.5.

6. (a) $d(4) = 2.4$, $d(5.5) \approx 2.81$.

(b) Approximately 2.16.

(c) Domain is the set of all nonnegative real numbers. Range is the set of all nonnegative real numbers up to the farthest number of miles one can see.

(c)

x	g(x)
−2	−19.3
−1	−11.7
0	−4.5
1	2.7
2	9.9

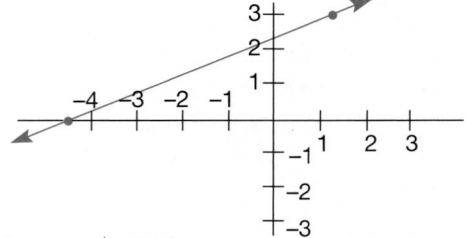

7. (a)

x	f(x)
−2	−1
−1	1
0	3
1	5
2	7

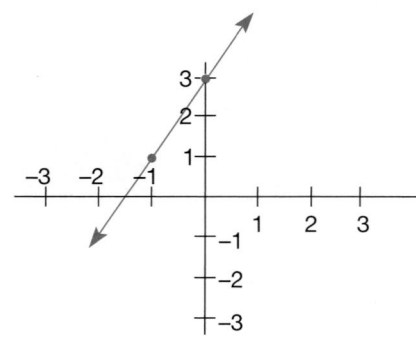

8. (a)

x	h(x)
−2	0
−1	1.5
0	0
1	−0.5
2	4

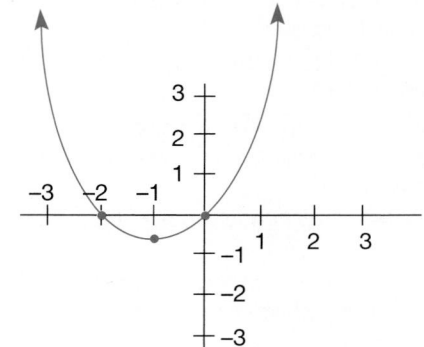

(b)

x	m(x)
−2	50
−1	45
0	40
1	35
2	30

(b)

x	r(x)
−2	$\frac{1}{9}$
−1	$\frac{1}{3}$
0	1
1	3
2	9

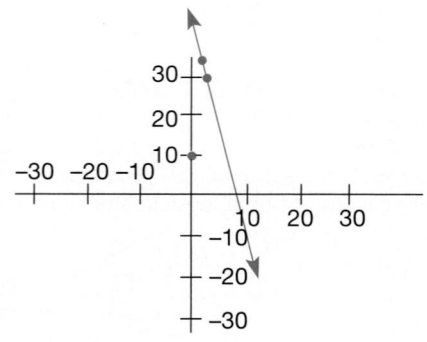

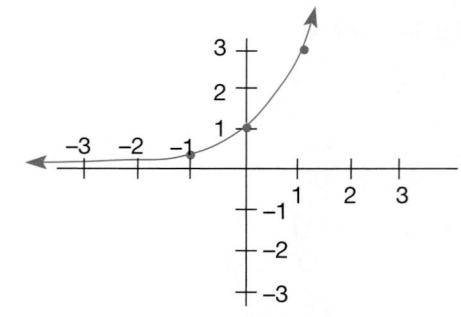

(c)

x	s(x)
−2	−6
−1	3
0	2
1	1
2	−6

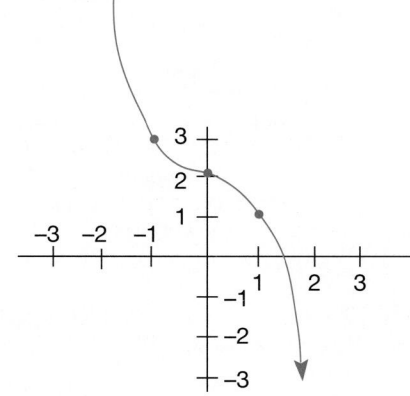

9. (a) (i) 2,   (ii) 7,   (iii) −5,   (iv) 0.

(b)

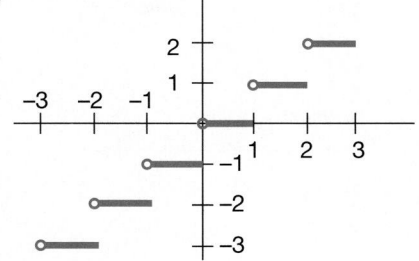

10. (a) (i)

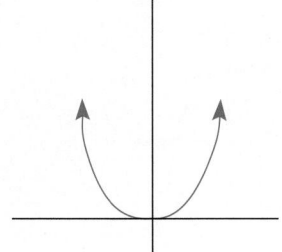

(ii)

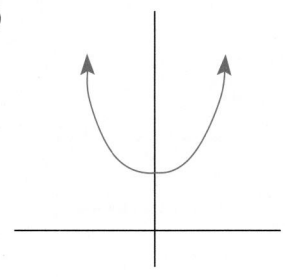

(iii)

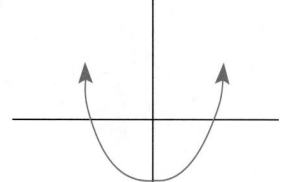

(iv)

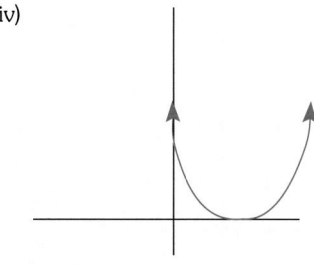

(v)

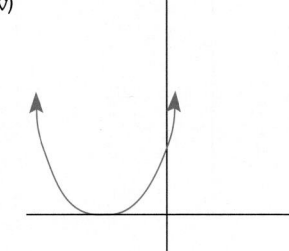

(b) (ii) shifts the graph of (i) two units up,   (iii) shifts the graph of (i) two units down,   (iv) shifts the graph of (i) two units to the right,   (v) shifts the graph of (i) two units to the left.

(c) The graph of $f(x) = x^2 + 4$ should be the same as the graph in (i) except it is shifted up 4 units. The graph of $f(x) = (x−3)^2 + 4$ should be the same as the graph in (i) except it is shifted up 3 units to the right.

11. (a)

(i)

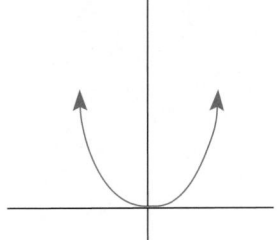

(ii)

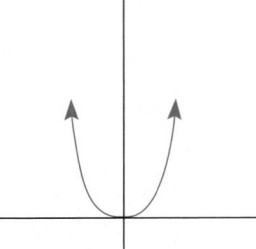

(iii)

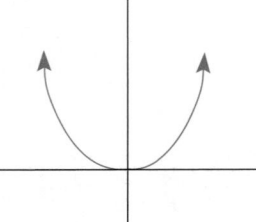

(iv)

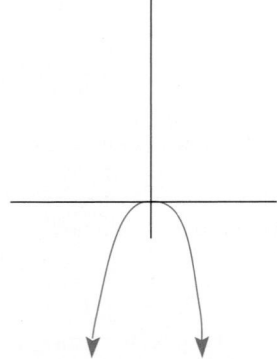

(b) Positive coefficients greater than one have the effect of narrowing the graph. Positive coefficients between 0 and 1 have the effect of broadening the graph. Multiplying by -1 has the effect of reflecting the graph in the x-axis. Thus the coefficient -3 would narrow the original graph and reflect it in the x-axis.

(c) The graph of $f(x) = -5x^2$ would narrow the graph in (i) and reflect it in the x-axis.

12. (a) (i) 29¢, (ii) $1.21, (iii) $1.67, (iv) $1.79.

(b) Domain is 0 oz through 16 oz.
Range = {29¢, 52¢, 75¢, 98¢, $1.21, $1.33, $1.44, $1.56, $1.67, $1.79}.

(c)

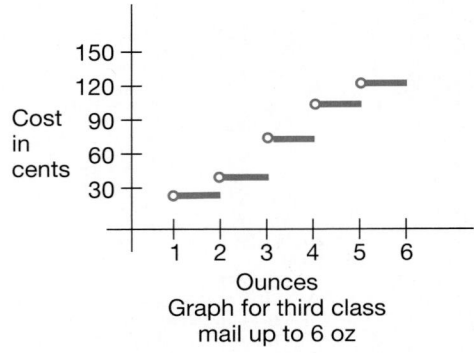

Graph for third class
mail up to 6 oz

(d) 20×29 cents = $5.80 for 20 pieces of first class
or $\frac{3}{4} \times 20 = 15$ oz is $1.79.

13. (a)

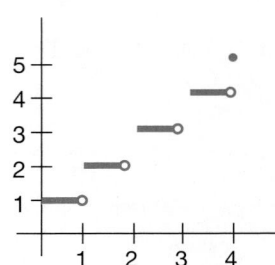

(b)

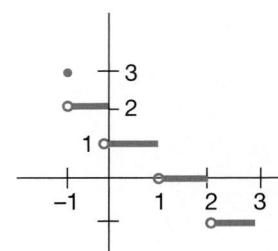

(c)

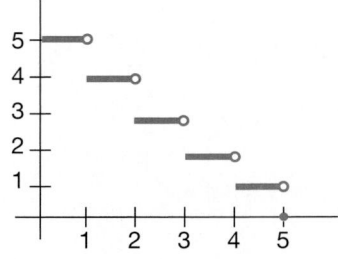

(d)

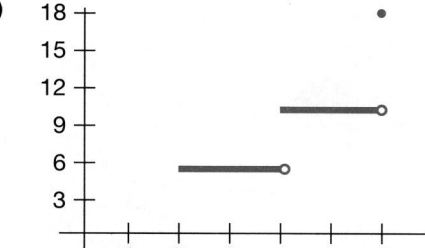

14. (a) (iv).   **(b)** (ii).   **(c)** (iii).

15. (a) The length of the shadow varies as time passes. Exponential.

(b) $L(5) = 150$, $L(8) = 1100$, $L(2.5) = 50$.

(c) 4.5, 6.

(d) It is too dark to cast a shadow.

16. (a)

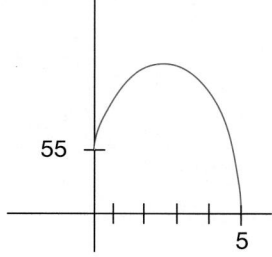

(b) Approximately 0.55 second and 3.8 seconds.

(c) In approximately 5.1 seconds.

(d) Approximately 131 feet.

17. (a)

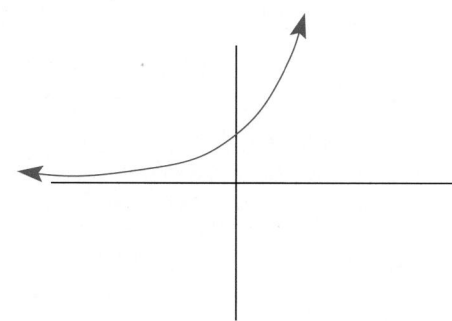

(b) 5.86.

(c) Approximately 34.5 years.

(d) Approximately 41 years.

18. (a).

19. $T(n) = \dfrac{n}{4} + 40$.

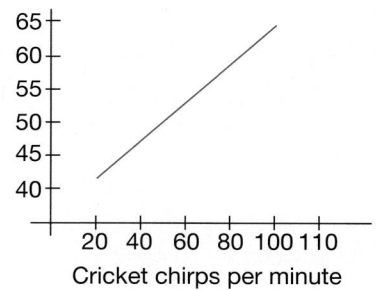

PROBLEMS WHERE THE STRATEGY "SOLVE AN EQUATION" IS USEFUL

1. $27,000.

2. 840.

3. 4.

CHAPTER 9 TEST

1. (a) F.   **(b)** T.   **(c)** F.   **(d)** F.   **(e)** T.
    (f) F.   **(g)** T.   **(h)** F.

2. (a) $\dfrac{-23}{21}$,   **(b)** $\dfrac{-6}{55}$.   **(c)** $\dfrac{-1}{28}$.

3. (a) Commutativity and associativity.
    (b) Commutativity, distributivity, and identity for multiplication.

4. (a) $\left\{ x \mid x > \dfrac{-12}{7} \right\}$.   **(b)** $\{\frac{177}{98}\}$.

5. (a) 729.   **(b)** 128.   **(c)** $\frac{1}{243}$.

6. (a)   **(b)**

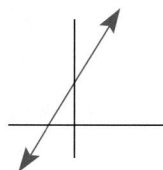   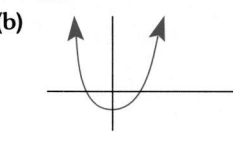

(c)

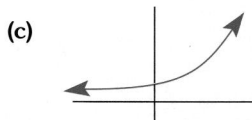

7. $\dfrac{-3}{7} = \dfrac{-3}{7} \cdot \dfrac{-1}{-1} = \dfrac{(-3)(-1)}{7(-1)} = \dfrac{3}{-7}$.

8. No. For example, $\dfrac{1}{-2} < \dfrac{-1}{3}$, however $3 \not< 2$.

9. $\dfrac{1}{5^{-7}} = \dfrac{1}{(1/5^7)} = 5^7$.

10. Suppose $\sqrt{8} = \dfrac{a}{b}$, where $\dfrac{a}{b}$ is a rational number. Then $8b^2 = a^2$. But this is impossible since $8b^2$ has an odd number of factors of 2, whereas a^2 has an even number.

11. 105.

12. Only when $x = 0$ or when $a = b$.

13. $t = 3$.

SECTION 10.1—PART A

1. (a) 58, 63, 65, 67, 69, 70, 72, 72, 72, 74, 74, 76, 76, 76, 76, 76, 78, 78, 80, 80, 80, 82, 85, 85, 86, 88, 92, 92, 94, 95, 98.   **(b)** 58, 98.   **(c)** 76.

(d)

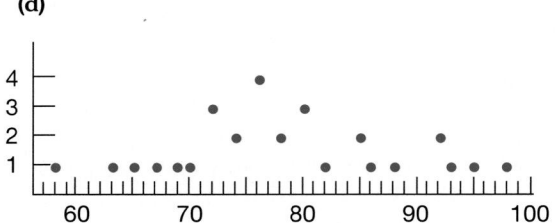

(e) 91–100 5
81–90 5
71–80 14
61–70 4
51–60 1

(f)

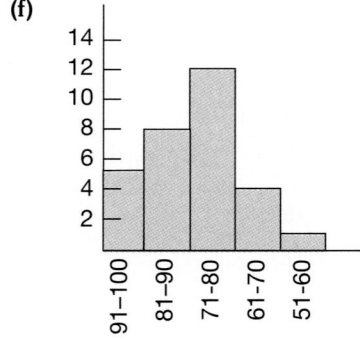

(g) 71–80.

2. (a)

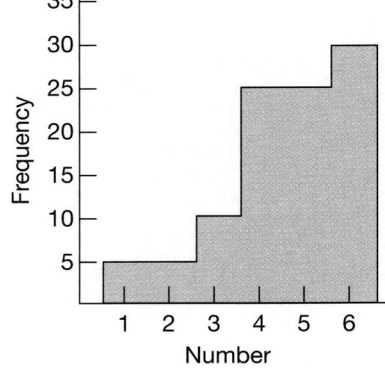

(b) No. If it were a fair die, each face would appear about the same number of times.

3. (a) $15,000,000.   **(b)** $5,000,000.
(c) $85,000,000.

4. (a) Each stick figure represents 5,000,000 students.
(b) 1900s, 1910s, 1920s, 1950s, 1960s.
(c) Bar or line graph.

5. (a) Portland.   **(b)** 4 months; 0 months.
(c) December (6.0 inches); July (0.5 inch).
(d) August (4.0 inches); January (2.7 inches).
(e) New York City (40.3 inches) (Portland's total = 37.6 inches).

6. (a)

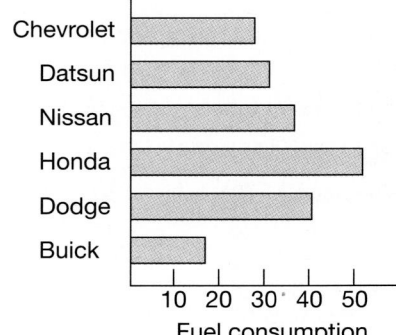

(b) Buick Riviera; Honda Civic Coupe.
(c) Nissan Pulsar; Buick Riviera.
(d) Chevrolet Cavalier, $3111.11; Datson 200SX, $3000; Nissan, $2400; Honda, $1647.06; Dodge, $2048.78; Buick, $5250.

7. (a) Taxes.   **(b)** 20.3%.   **(c)** 64°.
(d) Natural resources.
(e) Social assistance, transportation, health and rehabilitation, and natural resources.
(f) 23°, 26°.

8. Grants to local governments, $1,269,000,000; salaries and fringe benefits, $1,161,000,000; grants to organizations and individuals, $873,000,000; operating $621,000,000; other, $576,000,000.

9. (a)

=1,000,000,000 people

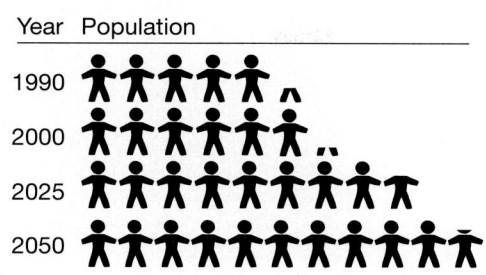

Year	Population
1990	
2000	
2025	
2050	

(b)

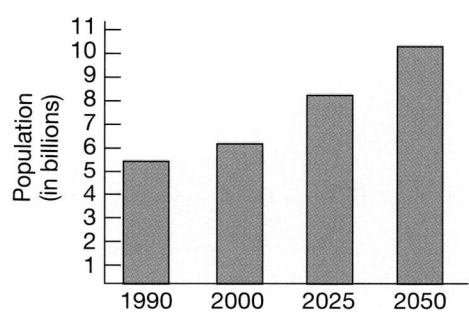

(c)

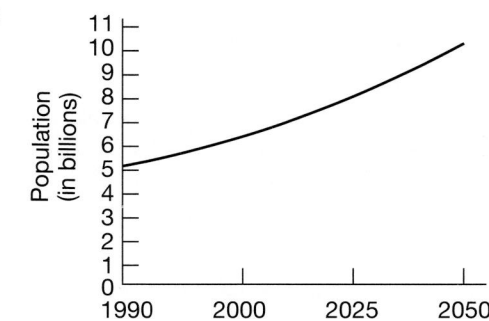

(d)

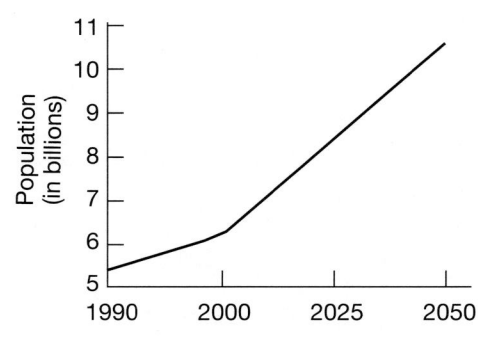

This graph, since it is steeper.

10. (a)

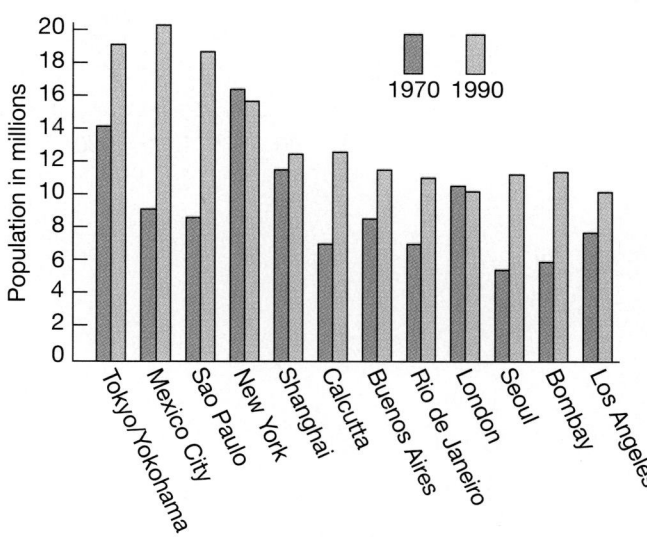

(b) São Paulo.

(c) New York.

11. (a)

15.	8 9
16.	1 3 4
17.	0 5
18.	1 2 5 5 5
19.	2 4
20.	2 3 6 9 9
21.	1 4 8
22.	0 0 1

(b)

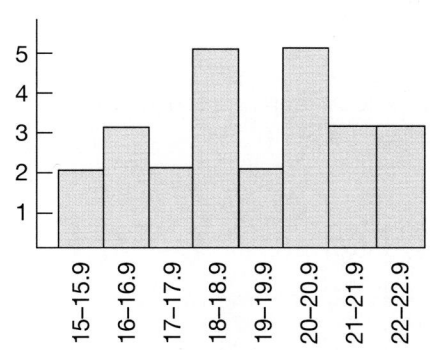

12. (a)

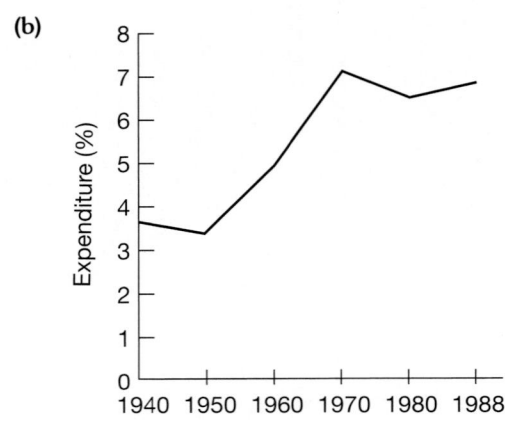

(b)

(c) The first. The second.

13. (a)

Class 2		Class 1
	5	7 8 9
8 7 6	6	0 2
9 7 7 5	7	2 5 6 6 9
7 7 5 5 4 3 2	8	0 0 1 6 6 6 7
5 2 2 2 0 0	9	3 3 3

(b) Class 2, since there are more high scores and fewer low scores.

14. (a) Double bar graph or pictograph for comparing two sets of data.

(b)

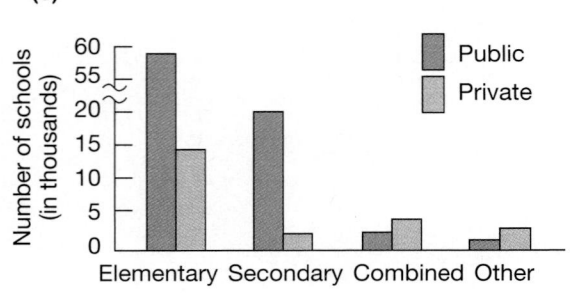

15. (a) Circle graph—compares parts of a whole.

(b)

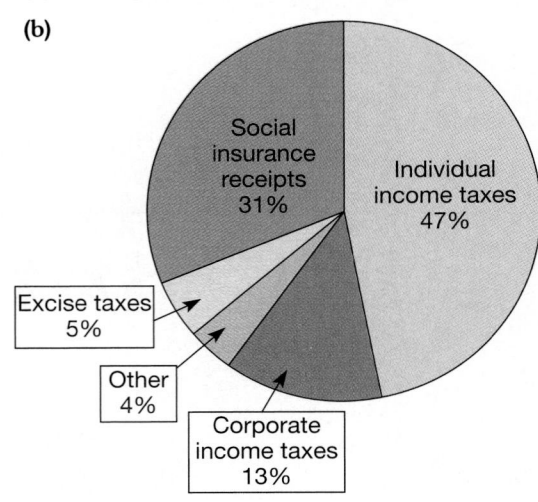

16. (a) Line graph or bar graph to show trends.

(b)

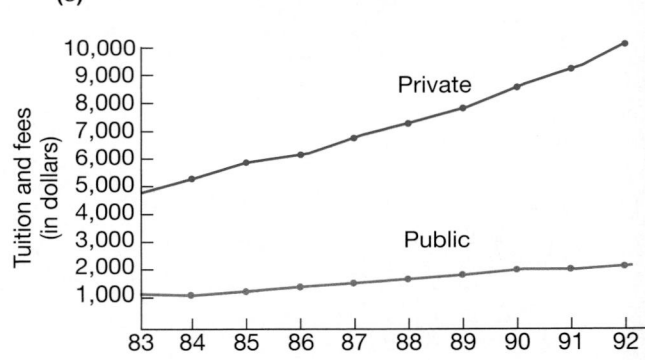

(c) Private—graph is generally steeper.

17. (a) Pictograph or bar graph.

(b)

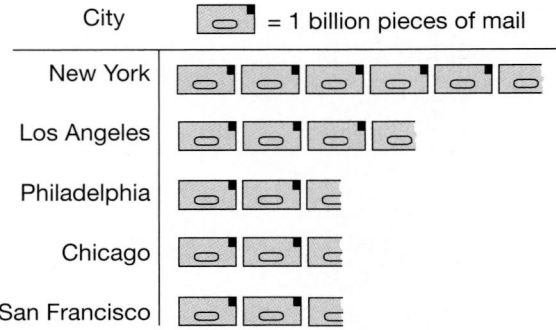

18. (a) Bar graph or line graph to show a trend.

(b)

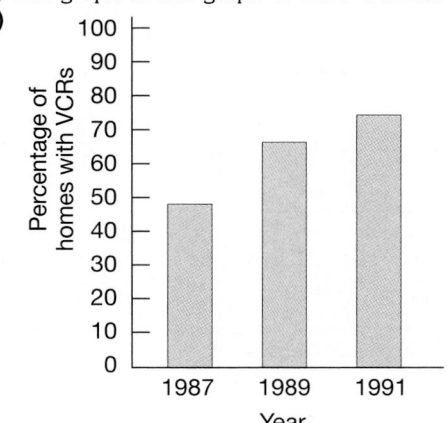

19. (a) Multiple bar graph or line graph to show a trend.

(b)

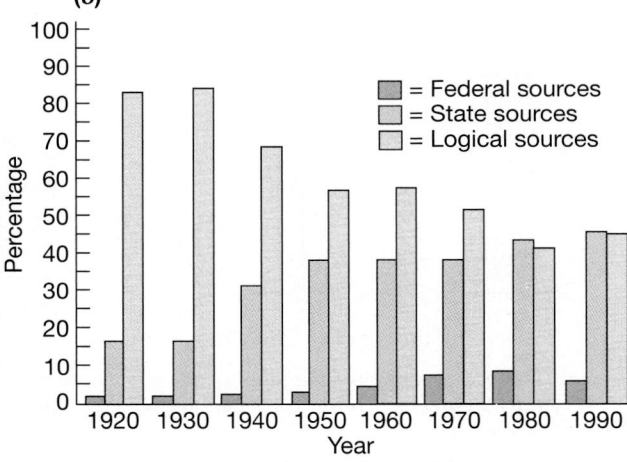

(c) Federal funds increased steadily until sometime during the 1980s, then decreased. State funds increased steadily. Local funds decreased steadily until the 1980s and provide less than half of school funds.

20. (a) Multiple bar graphs to compare data for two years.

(b)

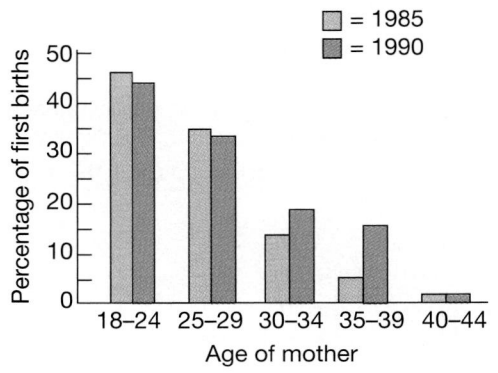

21. (a)

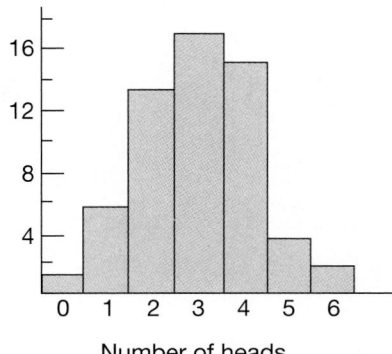

(b) 0, 2%; 1, 10%; 2, 23%; 3, 30%; 4, 25%; 5, 7%; 6, 3%.

(c) 10 times.

22. (a) HH, HT, TH, TT.   **(b)** 5.   **(c)** 10.

(d) 5.   **(e)**

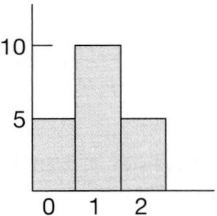

23. Suppose that $a^2 + b^2 + c^2 = d^2 + e^2 + f^2$. Show that $(10a + d)^2 + (10b + e)^2 + (10c + f)^2$ equals $(10d + a)^2 + (10e + b)^2 + (10f + c)^2$.

24. 4624, 6084, 6400, 8464.

SECTION 10.2—PART A

1. (a) $9.8\overline{3}$; 9.5; 9.

(b) $14.1\overline{6}$; 13.5; no mode.

(c) $0.48\overline{3}$; 1.9; no mode.

(d) $-4.\overline{2}$; 0; 0.

2. (a) 3.3; 3.5; 5.

(b) 6; 6; no mode.

(c) 26; 26; no mode.

(d) 11.55; 12; 10.

(e) 16.77; 16.65; 17.9 and 15.4.

(f) $-10/7$; 0; 5.

3. 47; 47; 47.

4. No student is average overall. On the math test, Doug is closest to the mean; on the reading test, Rob is closest.

5. Mode, since this represents the most frequently sold size.

6.

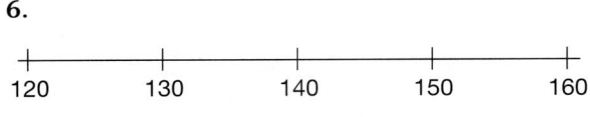

7. (a)

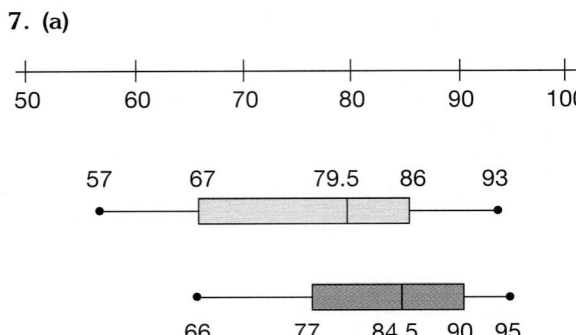

(b) Class 2; all five statistics are higher than their counterparts for Class 1.

8. (a) 0; 0.   **(b)** 2; $\sqrt{2}$.
(c) 6.67; 2.58 (to two places).
(d) 371.61; 19.28 (to two places).

9. (a) 2; $\sqrt{2}$.   **(b)** 18; $3\sqrt{2}$.   **(c)** 50; $5\sqrt{2}$.
(d) 72; $6\sqrt{2}$. If the variance is v and the standard deviation is s, and if all data are multiplied by r, the new variance is $r^2 v$ and the new standard deviation is $\sqrt{r^2} \cdot s$.

10. (a) 8; $\sqrt{8}$.   **(b)** 8; $\sqrt{8}$.   **(c)** 8; $\sqrt{8}$.
(d) 16; 4. Adding/subtracting a constant amount does not change the variance or standard deviation.

11. 35; 30; 30; 275; 16.58 (to two places).

12. -0.55, -1.76, 0.36, 1.71, -0.32, -0.1, 0.66.

13.

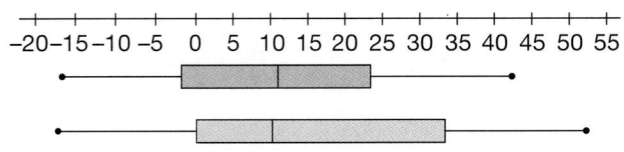

A trend toward greater growth west of the Mississippi.

14. (a)

4	93 75 75 52 42 26 14 07
5	86 73 63 48 36 34 21 21 12 12 11
6	60
7	55 14

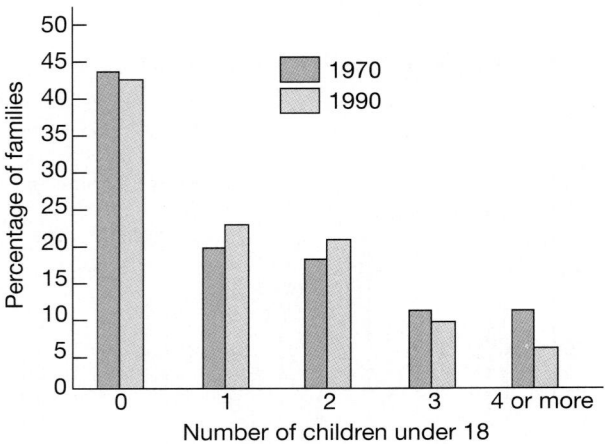

(b) Aaron's and Ruth's totals are both mild outliers.

15. (a) Line graphs on the same axes or multiple bar graphs.
(b) Multiple bar graphs:

(c) There was a greater percentage of childless families in 1988, while the trend among families with children was to have fewer.
(d) 1.2 and 0.9.

16. 293.

17. 76.81 to two places.

18. 1456.

19. (a) 50th percentile.
(b) 84th; 97.5th; 16th; 2.5th.
(c) 65; 55; 75; 95.

20. Test 1; her z-score (0.65) is slightly higher than on test 2 (0.63).

21. (a) The distribution with the smaller variance.
(b) The distribution with the larger mean.

22. (a) 1.14 (to two places.)   **(b)** 1.99 (to two places).
(c) 97.5%.

23. (a) 32.5.   **(b)** 30; no.

24. Impossible to qualify.

25. (a) 1, 6, 12, 8, 0.
(b) $4 \times 4 \times 4$; 8, 24, 24, 8, 0; $5 \times 5 \times 5$; 27, 54, 36, 8, 0.
(c) $n \times n \times n$: $(n-2)^3$, $6(n-2)^2$, $12(n-2)$, 8, 0.

PROBLEMS WHERE THE STRATEGY "LOOK FOR A FORMULA" IS USEFUL

1. The first allowance yields $7 + 21 + 35 + \cdots + 7(2 \cdot 30 - 1)$, which equals $7(1 + 3 + 5 + \cdots + 59)$. Since $1 + 3 + 5 + \cdots + (2n - 1) = n^2$ and 59 is $2 \cdot 30 - 1$, the total is $7 \cdot 30^2 = \$63.00$. The other way, the total is $30 \cdot 2 = \$60$. He should choose the first way.

2. Let x be its original height. Its height after several days would be given by $x\left(\dfrac{3}{2}\right)\left(\dfrac{4}{3}\right)\left(\dfrac{5}{4}\right) \cdots$. One can see that the product of these fractions lead to this formula:
$$\left(\frac{3}{2}\right)\left(\frac{4}{3}\right)\left(\frac{5}{4}\right) \cdots \left(\frac{n+1}{n}\right) = \frac{n+1}{2}.$$ Therefore, since $\dfrac{n+1}{2} > 100$ when $n + 1 > 200$, or when $n > 199$, it would take 199 days.

3. Pairing the first rays on the right with the remaining rays would produce 99 angles. Pairing the second ray on the right with the remaining ones would produce 98 angles. Continuing in this way we obtain $99 + 98 + 97 + \cdots + 1$ such angles. But this sum is $(99 \cdot 98)/2$ or 4950. Thus there are 4950 different angles formed.

CHAPTER 10 TEST

1. **(a)** F.   **(b)** F.   **(c)** F.   **(d)** F.   **(e)** T.
   (f) T.   **(g)** F.   **(h)** T.

2. $108°$.

3. Mean is 6; median is 6; mode is 3; range is 7.

4. 11, 14, 20, 23.

5. 5.55.

6. 0, 6, 6, 7, 8, 9. There are many other possibilities.

7. 3, 3. (Actually, any *single* number is a correct answer.)

8. 15.

9. 23.

10. Science, since its *z*-score is the highest.

SECTION 11.1—PART A

1. (c).

2. **(a)** {H, T}.   **(b)** {A, B, C, D, E, F}.
   (c) {1, 2, 3, 4}.   **(d)** {red, yellow, blue}.

3. **(a)** {HHHH, HHHT, HHTH, HTHH, THHH, HHTT, HTHT, THHT HTTH, THTH, TTHH, HTTT, THTT, TTHT, TTTH, TTTT}.
   (b) {HHHH, HHHT, HHTH, HTHH, HHTT, HTHT, HTTH, HTTT}.

(c) {HHHT, HHTH, HTHH, THHH}.
(d) Same as part (a).
(e) {HHTH, HHTT, THTH, THTT}.

4. **(a)** {1, 2, 3, 4, 5, 6, 7, 8, 9, 10, 11, 12}.
   (b) {2, 4, 6, 8, 10, 12}.
   (c) {1, 2, 3, 4, 5, 6, 7}.
   (d) {6, 12}.
   (e) $\varnothing$.

5. **(a)** {(H, 1), (H, 2), (H, 3), (H, 4), (T, 1), (T, 2), (T, 3), (T, 4)}.
   (b) {(H, P), (H, G), (H, Y), (T, P), (T, G), (T, Y)}.

6. **(a)** $\frac{12}{60} = \frac{1}{5}$.   **(b)** $\frac{28}{60} = \frac{7}{15}$.   **(c)** $\frac{31}{60}$.

7. **(a)** Point up is generally more likely.
   (b) $\frac{42}{60} = \frac{7}{10}$; $\frac{18}{60} = \frac{3}{10}$.   **(c)** 70; 30.

8. **(a)** $\frac{1}{6}$.   **(b)** $\frac{9}{36} = \frac{1}{4}$.   **(c)** $\frac{21}{36} = \frac{1}{4}$.   **(d)** 0.
   (e) 1.

9. **(a)** $\frac{1}{5}$.   **(b)** $\frac{2}{5}$.   **(c)** $\frac{3}{5}$.   **(d)** $\frac{2}{5}$.

10. **(a)** $\frac{3}{8}$.   **(b)** $\frac{1}{2}$ (or $\frac{3}{6}$).   **(c)** $\frac{5}{12}$.

11. **(a)** $\frac{1}{3}$.   **(b)** $\frac{2}{3}$.   **(c)** $\frac{2}{3}$.   **(d)** $\frac{1}{3}$.

12. **(a)** $\frac{3}{4}$.   **(b)** $\frac{4}{13}$.   **(c)** $\frac{11}{26}$.   **(d)** $\frac{4}{13}$.

13. **(a)** $\frac{7}{16}$.   **(b)** $\frac{12}{16} = \frac{3}{4}$.

14. **(a)** $\frac{1}{3}$.   **(b)** $\frac{1}{3}$.   **(c)** $\frac{1}{3}$.   **(d)** 1.
   (e) $\frac{1}{2}, \frac{1}{8}, \frac{3}{8}, 1$; yes.

15. **(a)** Getting a blue on the first spin or a yellow on one spin; $\frac{10}{16}$.
   (b) Getting a yellow on both spins; $\frac{1}{16}$.
   (c) Not getting a yellow on either spin; $\frac{9}{16}$.

16. **(a)** Probability that the student is a sophomore or is taking English.
   (b) Probability that the student is a sophomore taking English.
   (c) Probability that the student is not a sophomore.

17. **(a)** 6; $\frac{1}{2}$.   **(b)** 30; $\frac{7}{30}$.   **(c)** 20; $\frac{1}{20}$.

18. **(a)** 4, 5, 6, 5, 4, 3, 2, 1.
   (b) $\frac{5}{12}, \frac{1}{3}, \frac{1}{4}, \frac{11}{12}$.

19. **(a)** 100.   **(b)** 20.   **(c)** $\frac{20}{100} = \frac{1}{5}$.

20. $\frac{1}{16}$.

SECTION 11.2—PART A

1. **(a)** 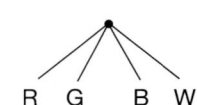   **(b)**

   (c) 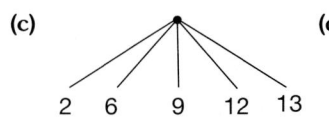   **(d)**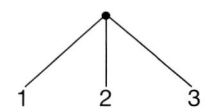

2. (a)

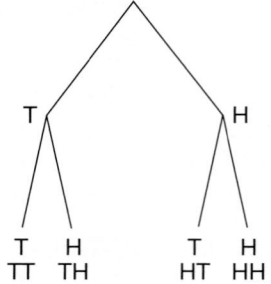

(b)

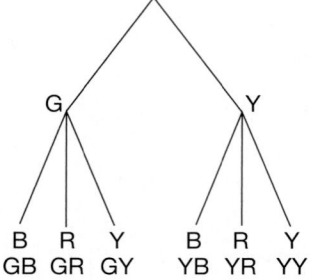

(c)

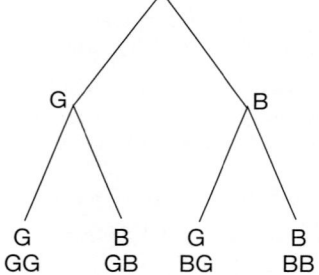

3. (a)

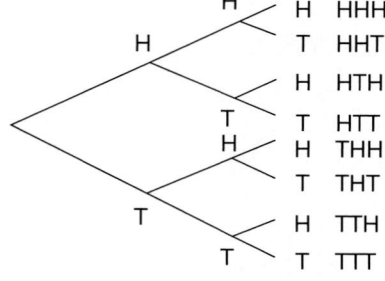

(b)

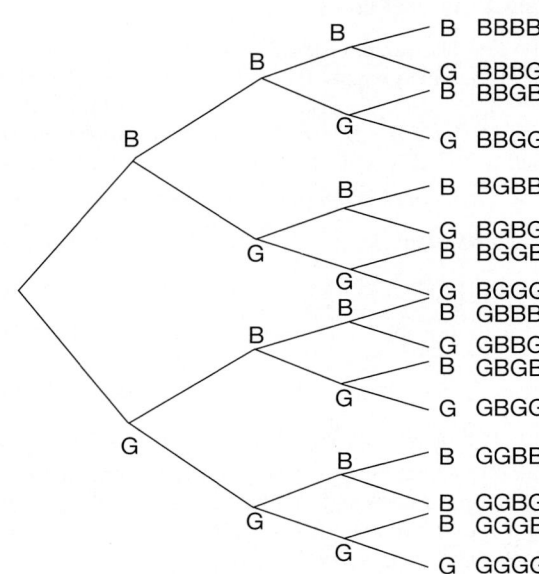

4. (a) – (d)

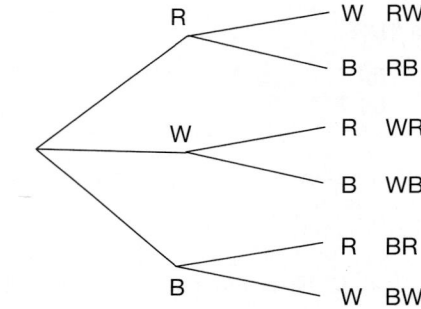

(e) 6 outcomes.

5.

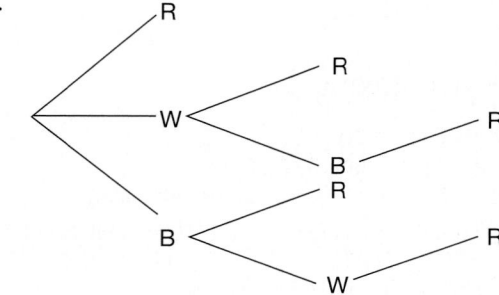

6. (a) 2.   **(b)** 6.   **(c)** 6.   **(d)** $2 \times 6 \times 6 = 72$.

7. (a)

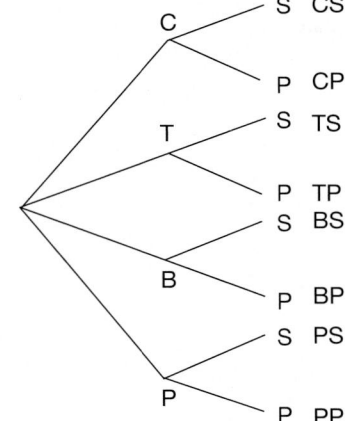

(b) 8.   **(c)** $4 \cdot 2 = 8$, yes.

8. (a) Number of ways of getting 0 heads (1), 1 head (4), 2 heads (6), 3 heads (4), or 4 heads (1).
(b) $\frac{4}{16} = \frac{1}{4}$.   **(c)** $\frac{15}{16}$.   **(d)** Against.

9. (a)

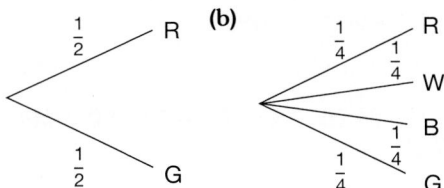

(c)

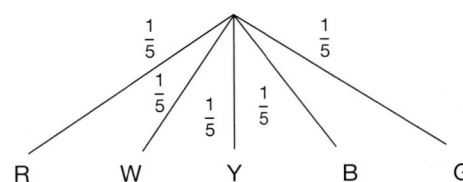

10. (a) $R - \frac{2}{5}, W - \frac{3}{5}$.   **(b)** $B - \frac{1}{3}, G - \frac{2}{3}$.

11. (a) $A - \frac{1}{3}, B - \frac{1}{3}, C - \frac{1}{3}$.
(b) $A - \frac{1}{3}, B - \frac{1}{6}, C - \frac{1}{2}$.
(c) $A - \frac{1}{4}, B - \frac{1}{4}, C - \frac{1}{2}$.

12. (a) $10 \times 10 = 100$.
(b) $9 \times 10 \times 10 = 900$.
(c) $10 \times 9 \times 8 \times 7 = 5040$.
(d) $9 \times 10 \times 10 \times 10 \times 10 = 90{,}000$.

13. (a) $8 \cdot 7 \cdot 6 = 336$.   **(b)** $3 \cdot 2 \cdot 1 = 6$.
(c) $\frac{6}{336} = \frac{1}{56}$.

14. (a)

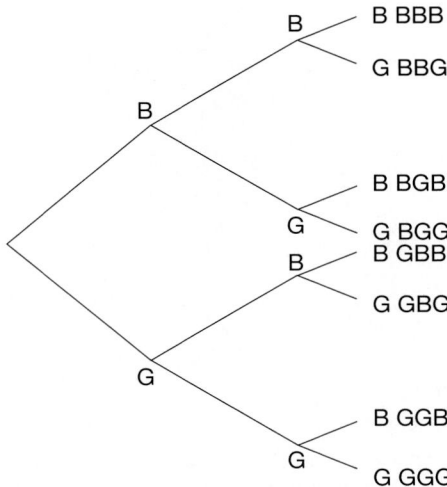

(b) 1; 3; 3; 1.
(c) They are the 1, 3, 3, 1 row.

15. (a) 1, 4, 6, 4, 1; $\frac{1}{16}, \frac{1}{4}, \frac{3}{8}, \frac{1}{4}, \frac{1}{16}$.
(b) 3 hits and 1 miss.

16. (a) Each branch has probability of $\frac{1}{2}$.
(b) $\frac{1}{2} \times \frac{1}{2} = \frac{1}{4}$ (top branch), $\frac{1}{2} \times \frac{1}{2} \times \frac{1}{2} = \frac{1}{8}$ (*BMM*).
(c) (i) $\frac{1}{8} + \frac{1}{8} = \frac{1}{4}$ (*MBB* and *BMB*),
(ii) $\frac{1}{4} + \frac{1}{8} + \frac{1}{8} = \frac{1}{2}$ (*BMM*, *MBM*, and *MM*),
(iii) $\frac{1}{8} + \frac{1}{8} + \frac{1}{8} + \frac{1}{8} = \frac{1}{2}$ (*BMB*, *BMM*, *MBB*, and *MBM*).

17. (a) $\frac{2}{5}$.   **(b)** $B = \frac{3}{5}, M = \frac{2}{5}$.   **(c)** $\frac{4}{25}$.   **(d)** $\frac{18}{125}$.
(e) $\frac{12}{25}$.   **(f)** $\frac{81}{125}$.

18. (a) $\frac{2}{3}$ for each branch; $\frac{8}{27}$.
(b) Both paths have probability $(\frac{2}{3})^3(\frac{1}{3}) = \frac{8}{81}$; $\frac{8}{81} + \frac{8}{81} + \frac{8}{81} = \frac{8}{27}$.
(c) *BBAAA*, *BABAA*, *BAABA*, *ABBAA*, *ABABA*, *AABBA*; $(\frac{2}{3})^3(\frac{1}{3})^2 = \frac{8}{243}$; $\frac{16}{81}$.
(d) $\frac{8}{27} + \frac{8}{27} + \frac{16}{81} = \frac{64}{81}$; $\frac{17}{81}$.

19. (a)

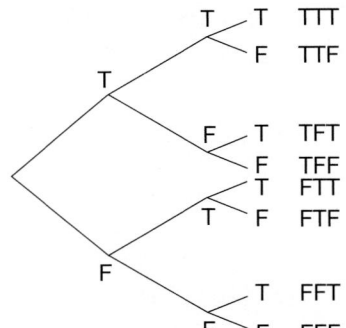

(b) 8.   **(c)** 1.   **(d)** $\frac{1}{8}$.

20. (a)

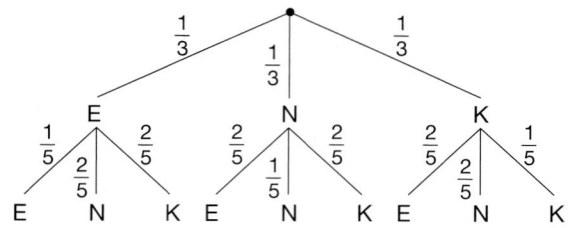

(b) {(E, E), (E, N), (E, K), (N, E), (N, N), (N, K), (K, E), (K, N), (K, K)}.

(c) {(E, E), (N, N), (K, K)}.

(d) $\frac{1}{5}$.   **(e)** $\frac{1}{15}$.

21. 4 socks.

22. $\frac{6}{7}$. This is the probability of having at least one male among three puppies given that one is a female.

23. $\frac{37}{55}$.

SECTION 11.3—PART A

1. (a) They each equal $1:1$, so are equivalent.
   (b) $60/40 = 1.5$ while $65/45 = 1.44$, so $60:40$ is more favorable.

2. (a) (i) $6:30$ or $1:5$, (ii) $33:3$ or $11:1$,
   (iii) $18:18$ or $1:1$.   **(b)** (i) $5:1$, (ii) $1:11$,
   (iii) $1:1$.

3. (a) $\frac{1}{6}$.   **(b)** $1:5$.   **(c)** $5:1$.

4. (a) $3:2$, $2:3$.   **(b)** $1:3$, $3:1$.   **(c)** $5:1$, $1:5$.

5. (a) $\frac{9}{10}$.   **(b)** $\frac{2}{7}$.   **(c)** $\frac{12}{17}$.

6. (a) $\frac{1}{9}$.   **(b)** $\frac{3}{8}$.   **(c)** $\frac{5}{11}$.

7. (a) $12.   **(b)** $4.50.   **(c)** $5.   **(d)** $3.

8. (a) $\frac{1}{6}$.   **(b)** $\frac{1}{3}$.   **(c)** 0.

9. (a) $\frac{2}{7}$.   **(b)** $\frac{5}{7}$.   **(c)** $\frac{4}{7}$.

10. (a) $\frac{8}{15}$.   **(b)** $\frac{6}{15} = \frac{2}{5}$.   **(c)** $\frac{1}{2}$.   **(d)** $\frac{3}{8}$.

11. (a) $\frac{3}{5}$.   **(b)** $\frac{11}{12}$.   **(c)** $\frac{31}{60}$.   **(d)** 1.   **(e)** $\frac{31}{55}$.
   (f) $\frac{31}{36}$.

12. (a) $\frac{13}{16}$.   **(b)** $\frac{13}{21}$.   **(c)** $\frac{15}{16}$.   **(d)** $\frac{5}{14}$.   **(e)** 1.
   (f) $\frac{1}{2}$.

13. 750.

14. 47,350 people.

15. (a) $2.50.   **(b)** $1.50.   **(c)** $3.50.

16. (a) $40.00.   **(b)** $25.   **(c)** Scholarship A.

17. Answers will vary; theoretical probability is $\frac{12}{32} = 0.375$.

18. Answers will vary.

19. Answers will vary; theoretical value is $0.6\overline{3}$.

20. (a) $\frac{22}{100} = \frac{11}{50}$.   **(b)** Answers will vary.

21. (a) Disagree to be correct.   **(b)** p^4.   **(c)** q^4.
   (d) $p^4 + q^4$.
   (e) For $1:1$—$\frac{1}{2}, \frac{1}{2}, \frac{1}{16}, \frac{1}{16}, \frac{1}{8} = 0.13$; for $2:1$—$\frac{2}{3}, \frac{1}{3}, \frac{16}{81}, \frac{1}{81}, \frac{17}{81} = 0.21$; for $3:1$—$\frac{3}{4}, \frac{1}{4}, \frac{81}{256}, \frac{1}{256}, \frac{82}{256} = 0.32$; for $3:2$—$\frac{3}{5}, \frac{2}{5}, \frac{81}{625}, \frac{16}{625}, \frac{97}{625} = 0.15$.
   (f) Prospects for series longer than 4 games is greater when teams are evenly matched.

22. (a) p^4q; $4p^4q$.   **(b)** $4pq^4$.   **(c)** $4p^4q + 4pq^4$.

23. (a) $10p^4q^2$.   **(b)** $10p^2q^4$.
   (c) $10p^4q^2 + 10p^2q^4$.

24. (a) $20p^4q^3$.   **(b)** $20p^3q^4$.
   (c) $20p^4q^3 + 20p^3q^4$.

25. (a) For $X = 4$, p^4, q^4, $p^4 + q^4$; for $X = 5$, $4p^4q$, $4pq^4$, $4p^4q + 4pq^4$; for $X = 6$, $10p^4q^2$, $10p^2q^4$, $10p^4q^2 + 10p^2q^4$; for $X = 7$, $20p^4q^3$, $20p^3q^4$, $20p^4q^3 + 20p^3q^4$.
   (b) 0.125, 0.25, 0.3125, 0.3125.
   (c) 5.8 games.

26. Roll a standard (six-face) die until each of the numbers from 1 through 5 appears. Ignore 6. Count the number of rolls needed. This is one trial. Repeat at least 100 times and average the number of rolls needed in all the trials. Your average should be around 11. Theoretical expected value $= 11.42$.

PROBLEMS WHERE THE STRATEGY "DO A SIMULATION" IS USEFUL

1. Sketch a hexagon, flip coins, and play the game several times to determine the experimental probability of winning.

2. Toss a die twice. If a 1 or a 2 turns up on the die, the man received his coat. Toss it again. If a 1 or a 2 turns up, the woman receives her coat. Repeat several times. Another simulation could be done using pieces of paper labeled 1 through 6.

3. Using your textbook, perform several trials of this situation to determine the experimental probability.

CHAPTER 11 TEST

1. (a) F.   **(b)** T.   **(c)** F.   **(d)** F.   **(e)** T.
   (f) F.   **(g)** F.   **(h)** F.

2. 144.

3. $\frac{47}{56}$.

4. $\frac{5}{12}$.

5. $\frac{5}{11}$.

6. $1 = P(A \cup \overline{A}) = P(A) + P(\overline{A})$; therefore, $P(\overline{A}) = 1 - P(A)$.

7. Both can be used to find the total number of outcomes in an event.

8.

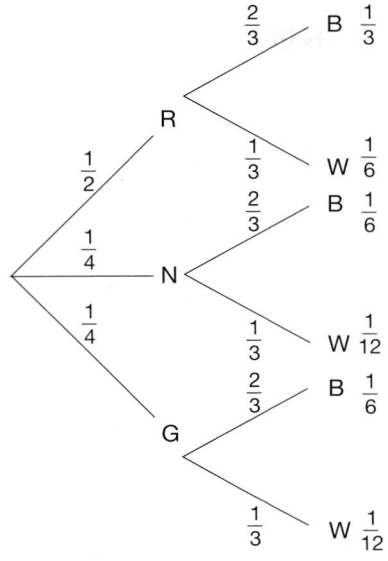

9. $\frac{537}{1024}$.

10.

Sums; n	2	3	4	5	6	7	8	9	10	11	12
Ways	1	2	3	4	5	6	5	4	3	2	1
$14 - n$	12	11	10	9	8	7	6	5	4	3	2

Note the symmetry in this table.

11. $\frac{1}{4}$.

SECTION 12.1—PART A

1. (a) Line D.   **(b)** Yes.

2. Same length in all three cases.

3. (a) 12 triangles.   **(b)** 20 parallelograms.

4. (a) 31.   **(b)** 18.

5. (a) b, d.   **(b)** a, c, e, f.   **(c)** a, e.   **(d)** d, f.

6.

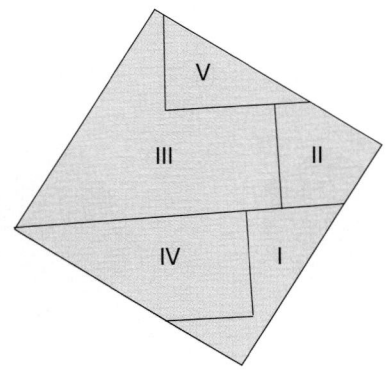

7. (a)

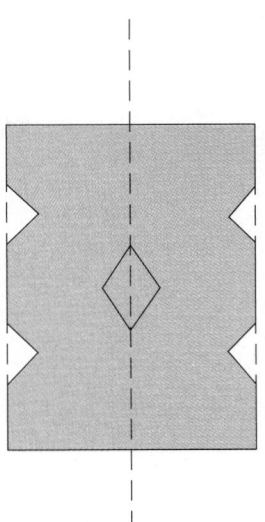

(b)

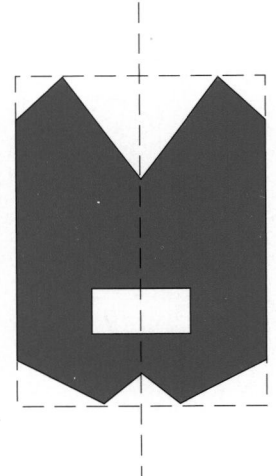

(c)

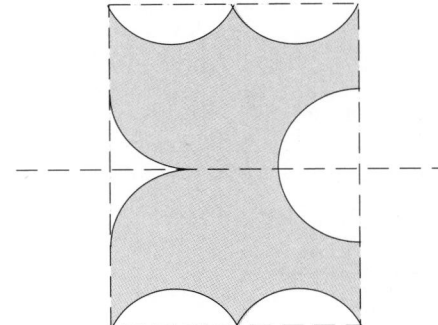

8. (a)

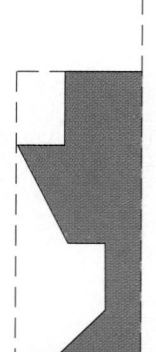

(b)

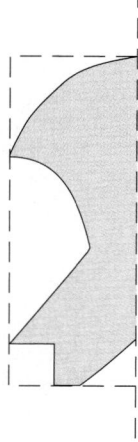

(c)

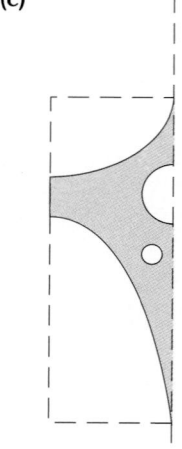

These figures show the fold line on the right. Figures could also be drawn with the fold line on the left.

9.

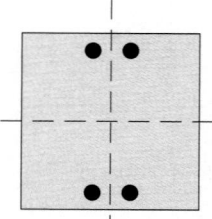

10. Several possibilities exist for each part.

(a)   **(b)**

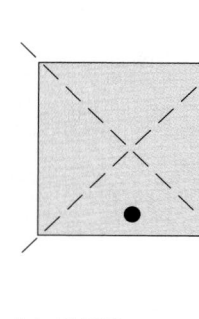

(c)   **(d)**

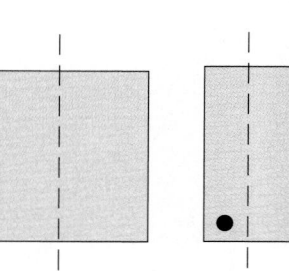

11. (a) FHQO.
  (b) ADPK, and so on.
  (c) KQHI, and so on.
  (d) ABL, FGH, OPQ.
  (e) MNO, MOS, COM.
  (f) MNOS.
  (g) COSM, CONM.
  (h) CLK, and so on.
  (i) CAL, ROP.
  (j) DEFO, MORK, KQHJ, and so on.
  (k) BCKL.

12. (a) (ii), draw a diagonal.
  (b) (i), rotate $\frac{1}{2}$ turn.
  (c) (i), reflect over vertical line.
  (d) (ii), rotate $\frac{1}{4}$ turn.

13. Both types of lines.

14. All but (c).

15. (a) 12.   **(b)** 4.   **(c)** 1.   **(d)** 1.

16. (a)   **(b)**

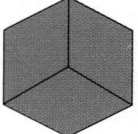
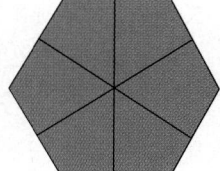

SECTION 12.2—PART A

1. (c).

2. Diagonals of a square have the same length, bisect each other, are perpendicular, and bisect the vertex angles.

3. **(a)** 5 lines.   **(b)** 6 lines.   **(c)** 7 lines.
     (d) 8 lines.   **(e)** n lines.

4. **(a)** Vertex, midpoint.
     (b) Vertex, vertex, midpoint, midpoint.

5. **(a)** 2.   **(b)** 1.   **(c)** 2.   **(d)** 0.

6. They all do; 180°.

7. **(a)** S, N.   **(b)** S.   **(c)** None.   **(d)** C, S, N.

8.

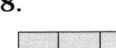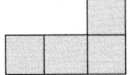

9.

10. **(a)** (i).
     (b) (iii), equilateral triangles inside isosceles.
     (c) (ii), intersection is "isosceles right triangles."
     (d) (i), equilateral triangles have 60° angles.

11. Flip the tracing over so that point A of the tracing is matched with point D, and point B of the tracing is matched with point C. Then diagonal $\overline{AC}$ of the tracing will coincide with diagonal $\overline{DB}$.

12. Rotate $\frac{1}{4}$, $\frac{1}{2}$, $\frac{3}{4}$, and 1 full turn around the center.

13. Rotate $\frac{1}{3}$, $\frac{2}{3}$, and 1 full turn around the center.

14. **(a)** Fold on diagonal $\overline{AC}$. Then $\angle ADC$ coincides with $\angle ABC$. $\angle A$ is not necessarily congruent to $\angle C$.
     (b) *Both* pairs of opposite angles are congruent, since a rhombus is a kite in two ways.

15. **(a)** Fold one diagonal along itself so that opposite vertices coincide. Then the other diagonal lies along the fold line.
     (b) Rotate $\frac{1}{2}$ turn around the center, E. Then $\overline{AE}$ in the tracing coincides with $\overline{CE}$, and $\overline{BE}$ in the tracing coincides with $\overline{DE}$.

16.

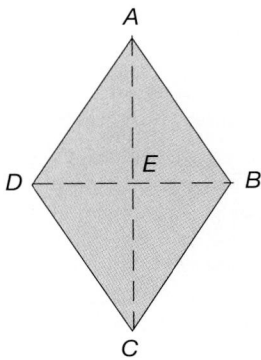

17. **(a)** 4 triangles: 2–9–9, 4–8–8, 6–7–7, 8–6–6.
     5 triangles: 2–11–11, 4–10–10, 6–9–9, 8–8–8, 10–7–7.
     (b) 4 triangles: 3–8–9, 4–7–9, 5–6–9, 5–7–8.
     7 triangles: 3–10–11, 4–9–11, 5–9–10, 5–8–11, 6–7–11, 6–8–10, 7–8–9.
     (c) None. 1 triangle: 8–8–8.

SECTION 12.3—PART A

1. **(a)** 10.   **(b)** 4.   **(c)** 6.

2. **(a)** 40.   **(b)** 24.   **(c)** 7.

3. **(a)** Obtuse.   **(b)** Right.   **(c)** Acute.

4. **(a)** 20.   **(b)** 6.   **(c)** 10.   **(d)** 2.   **(e)** 8.

5. **(a)** 30°.   **(b)** 20°.   **(c)** 60°.
     (d) Not possible.

6. **(a)** $m(\angle C) = 50°$, $\overline{AC} = 6.8$ cm.
     (b) $m(\angle C) = 109°$, $\overline{AC} = 5.8$ cm.

7. $m(\angle 1) = m(\angle 2) = m(\angle 3) = m(\angle 4) = 90°$. Any angle drawn from endpoints of a diameter of a circle and with its vertex on the circle will measure 90°.

8. $m(\angle AFB) = 60°$, $m(\angle CFD) = 35°$.

9. $m(\angle 1) = 54°$, $m(\angle 2) = 126°$.

10. $m(\angle 1) = 80°$ $m(\angle 11) = 80°$
$m(\angle 2) = 100°$ $m(\angle 12) = 100°$
$m(\angle 3) = 135°$ $m(\angle 13) = 125°$
$m(\angle 4) = 125°$ $m(\angle 14) = 55°$
$m(\angle 5) = 55°$ $m(\angle 15) = 100°$
$m(\angle 6) = 125°$ $m(\angle 16) = 80°$
$m(\angle 7) = 55°$ $m(\angle 17) = 100°$
$m(\angle 8) = 45°$ $m(\angle 18) = 80°$
$m(\angle 9) = 135°$ $m(\angle 19) = 125°$
$m(\angle 10) = 45°$ $m(\angle 20) = 55°$.

11. $m(\angle 1) = m(\angle 2)$, given; $m(\angle 2) = m(\angle 3)$, vertical angles have the same measure; $m(\angle 1) = m(\angle 3)$; $l \parallel m$, corresponding angles property.

12. (a) $m(\angle 1) = m(\angle 6)$, given; $m(\angle 1) = m(\angle 3)$, vertical angles have the same measure; $m(\angle 3) = m(\angle 6)$; $l \parallel m$, corresponding angles property.
   (b) $l \parallel m$, given; $m(\angle 1) = m(\angle 4)$, corresponding angles property; $m(\angle 4) = m(\angle 6)$, vertical angles have the same measure; $m(\angle 1) = m(\angle 6)$.
   (c) Two lines are parallel if and only if at least one pair of alternate exterior angles formed have the same measure.

13. $m(\angle A) = 72°$.

14. Since $\angle DAB$ is a right angle, $\overleftrightarrow{DA} \perp \overleftrightarrow{AB}$ and $\angle 1$ is a right angle also. However, since both are right angles, $\angle 1 \cong \angle ADC$ and $\overleftrightarrow{AB} \parallel \overleftrightarrow{DC}$ by the corresponding angles property. Similarly, show $\overline{AD} \parallel \overline{BC}$.

15. (a) (i)   (ii)   (iii)   (iv)

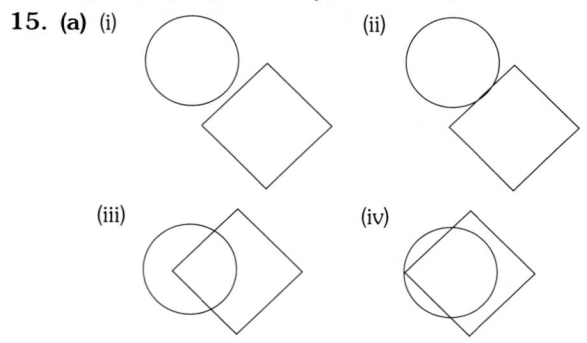

   (b) 8 points.

16. (a) (i)   (ii)   (iii)   (iv)

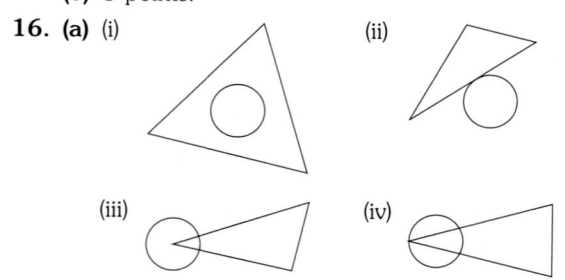

   (b) 6 points.

17. 3 lines → 7 regions
4 lines → 11 regions
5 lines → 16 regions
10 lines → 56 regions
n lines → $\dfrac{n(n+1)}{2} + 1$ regions.

SECTION 12.4—PART A

1. (a) 540°.   **(b)** 1080°.

2. (a) 105°.   **(b)** 108°.
   (c) 110°, 60°, 80°, 110°.

3. (a) 150°, 30°, 30°.   **(b)** 157.5°, 22.5°, 22.5°.
   (c) 144°, 36°, 36°.   **(d)** 162°, 18°, 18°.
   (e) 160°, 20°, 20°.   **(f)** 170°, 10°, 10°.

4. (a) 90°.   **(b)** 4°.   **(c)** 30°.   **(d)** $(180 - x)°$.

5. 25 sides.

6. (a) 40.   **(b)** 8.   **(c)** 36.   **(d)** 120.

7. (a) Less than 1.   **(b)** Less than 180°.
   (c) Always less than 180°.

8. (a)

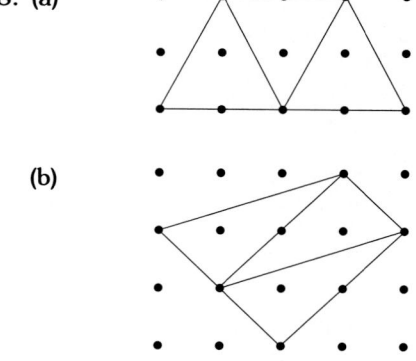

   (b)

     These patterns can be continued.

9. The triangle surrounded by the shaded regions is a right triangle. The two small squares include a total of four triangles—the same area covered by the larger square. Thus if two short sides of the triangle are a and b, the hypotenuse c, we have $a^2 + b^2 = c^2$.

10. (a) Yes.   **(b)** Have equal measure.   **(c)** Have same measure.   **(d)** Equals 180°, supplementary.

11. E and D are midpoints of $\overline{AB}$ and $\overline{AC}$, respectively. Lines $\overleftrightarrow{ED}$ and $\overleftrightarrow{BC}$ do not meet in tessellation, so are parallel. Since $ED = BF = FC$, $BC = 2ED$.

12. (a) Square vertex figure, triangular vertex figure.
(b) All.

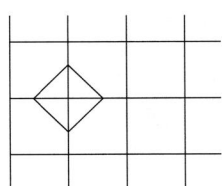
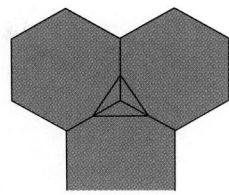

13. (a) Trapezoid, isosceles triangle.   **(b)** No.

14. (a)

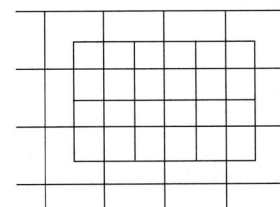
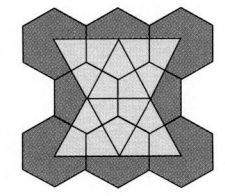

(b) (i) Hexagons, (ii) squares, (iii) triangles.

15. 3, 0, 0; 4, 1, 2; 5, 2, 5; 6, 3, 9; 7, 4, 14; 8, 5, 20; n, $n - 3$, $\dfrac{n(n - 3)}{2}$.

16. 190.

17. $a = 70°$, $b = 130°$, $c = 120°$, $d = 20°$, $e = 20°$, $f = 80°$, $g = 60°$, $h = 100°$.

18. 180°.

SECTION 12.5—PART A

1. (a) A cube in a corner or a cube outside on the outside corner of a cube.
(b) One of the corners.

2. (a) 54.   **(b)** 14.   **(c)** 34.

3. (a)

2	3
1	

, 2-3, 1-3.

(b)

1	3	2
1		

, 1-3-2, 1-3.

(c)

1	1
3	1
2	

, 3-1, 2-3-1.

4. (a) (ii).
(b) (i)

3	2	4	2
3	2	4	2

(ii)

3	3	3	3
1	2	3	3
1	2	2	3
1	1	1	3

(iii)

6	6	6	6	6	6
6	6	6	6	6	6
6	6	6	6	6	6
3	3	3	6	6	6
3	3	3	6	6	6
3	3	3	6	6	6

(c) (i) 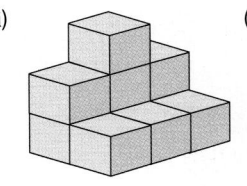   (ii)

(iii)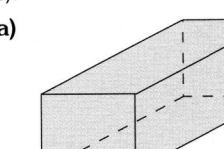

5. (a) (i) *ABC*, *DEF*, (ii) *ACFD*, *BCFE*, *ABED*, (iii) *DEF*, *ABED*, (iv) right triangular prism.
(b) (i) *MPTQ*, *NOSR*, (ii) *MNOP*, *OSTP*, *MNRQ*, *RSTQ*, (iii) *MNRQ*, *NOSR*, *RSTQ*, (iv) right trapezoidal prism.

6. (a) Square pyramid.   **(b)** Triangular pyramid.
(c) Octagonal pyramid.

7. (a) Cone.   **(b)** Hexagonal pyramid.   **(c)** Cube.
(d) Pentagonal prism.   **(e)** Cylinder.
(f) Sphere.

8. (a) Yes; 5.   **(b)** Yes; 4.   **(c)** No.   **(d)** Yes; 1.
(e) No.   **(f)** Yes; 2.

9. (c).

10. (a)

(b)

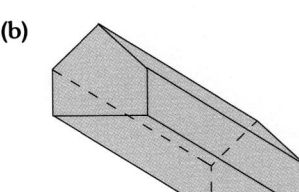

11. **(a)** Yes; *F*, *G*, *H*, *I*, *J*.   **(b)** No.   **(c)** 108°.

12. **(a)** Right square pyramid.
(b) Right hexagonal prism.
(c) Regular octahedron.
(d)

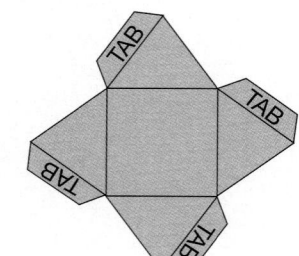

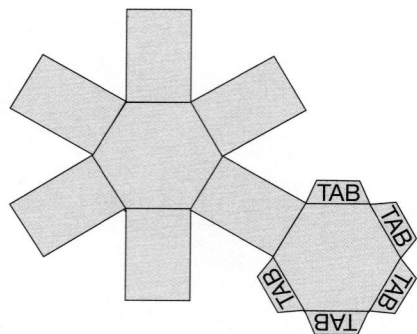

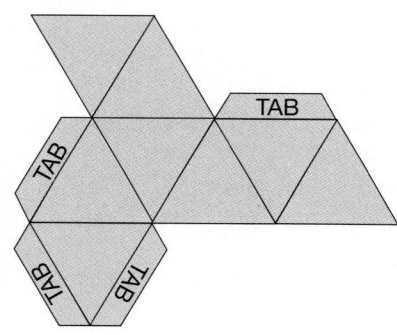

13. **(a)**

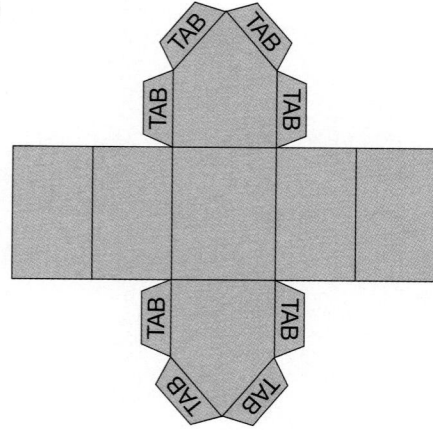

(b)

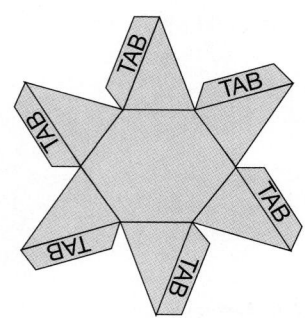

14. **(a)** No.   **(b)** No.   **(c)** Less than.

15. **(a)** No.   **(b)** Yes.   **(c)** Three.

16. **(a)** 3, 4, or 5 triangles.   **(b)** 3 squares.
(c) 3 pentagons.   **(d)** No.
(e) Tetrahedron, octahedron, icosahedron, cube, dodecahedron.

17. **(a)** 6.   **(b)** 12.   **(c)** Octahedron.

18. **(a)** 180°.   **(b)** 180°.   **(c)** 180°.
(d) $4 \times 180° = 720°$.

19. Cube: 8, 90°, 720°, octahedron: 6, 120°, 720°; dodecahedron: 20, 36°, 720°; icosahedron: 12, 60°, 720°.

20. **(a)** Triangle: 5, 6, 11, 9; quadrilateral: 6, 8, 14, 12; pentagon: 7, 10, 17, 15; hexagon: 8, 12, 20, 18; *n*-gon: $n + 2$, $2n$, $3n + 2$, $3n$.
(b) Yes.

21. **(a)** Rectangle.   **(b)** Circle.

22. **(a)** Rectangle.   **(b)** Pentagon.   **(c)** Kite.

23. 12 vertices, hexagonal prism.

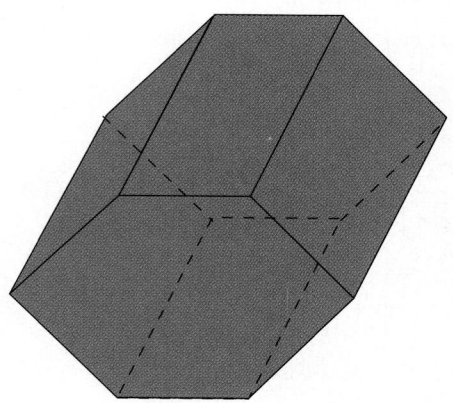

24. **(a)** (iii).   **(b)** (ii).

25. **(a)** 3.   **(b)** 6.   **(c)** 9.

26. 3.

27. **(a)** Order 3.   **(b)** 4.

28. **(a)** Order 2.   **(b)** 6.

29. A parallelogram.

30. (a) Yes.   (b) Prisms with bases that tessellate the plane (i.e., triangles, quadrilaterals, regular hexagons).   (c) Only the cube.

PROBLEMS WHERE THE STRATEGY "USE A MODEL" IS USEFUL

1. Trace, cut out, and fold these shapes as a check. Only (b) forms a closed box.

2. Try this arrangement with pennies. Six can be placed around one.

3. Try this with several tennis balls. The maximum number that can be stacked into a pyramid is $25 + 16 + 9 + 4 + 1 = 55$.

CHAPTER 12 TEST

1. (a) F.   (b) T.   (c) T.   (d) T.   (e) T.
   (f) T.   (g) T.   (h) T.   (i) F.   (j) F.
   (k) F.   (l) F.   (m) T.   (n) T.

2. Fold so that point A folds onto point C. Observe that $\overline{BD}$ lies along the fold line. Thus $\overline{AC} \perp \overline{BD}$.

3. 90° and 135°.

4. 144°.

5. 9; 12 (not including a 0° or 360° rotation).

6. 60°, 120°, 60°, 60°.

7. 7; 7; 12.

8. $m(\angle 3) + m(\angle 4) = 180°$. Proof: $180° = m(\angle 2) + m(\angle 4) = m(\angle 3) + m(\angle 4)$.

9. By 8, any two consecutive interior angles are supplementary. Thus if one angle measures 90°, they all must.

10. 64 vertices, 34 faces.

11. Since there are 7 triangles, the sum of all the angle measures is $7 \cdot 180° = 1260°$. If the measures of the central angles are subtracted, the result, $1260° - 360° = 900°$, yields the sum of the measures of all the vertex angles.

12. The measures of the vertex angles of regular 5-gons and regular 7-gons are 108° and $128\frac{4}{7}°$, respectively, and there is no combination of these that will total 360°. Thus it is impossible to tessellate the plane using only regular 5-gons and regular 7-gons.

SECTION 13.1—PART A

1. (a) Height, width (with ruler); weight (scale); how much weight it will hold (by experiment).
   (b) Diameter, height (with ruler); volume (pouring water into it); weight (scale).
   (c) Height, length (with ruler); surface area (cover with sheets of paper); weight (scale).
   (d) Height, length, width (with ruler); volume (pour water into it); surface area (cover it); weight (scale).

2. (a) Waist, hips, length from neck to waist or to hemline, bust or chest, length of arm.
   (b) Length and width of foot, height of arch.
   (c) Height, weight, heartbeat, blood pressure.
   (d) Height, strength, height of jump, number of situps in 1 minute.

3. (a) 63,360 inches.   (b) 8 furlongs.
   (c) 40 rods.   (d) 1760 yards.

4. (a) $437\frac{1}{2}$.   (b) 256.   (c) 7000.   (d) 32,000.

5. (a) 5.5.   (b) 9.   (c) 12.

6. The area of Connecticut is approximately 5000 square miles.

7. (a) 29.   (b) $4\frac{5}{6}$.   (c) $14\frac{1}{2}$.

8. (a) 100.   (b) 75.   (c) 3100.   (d) 3060.
   (e) 76.   (f) 0.0093.   (g) 2.3.   (h) 0.035.
   (i) 0.125.   (j) 0.764.

9. (a) A square meter can be covered with square millimeters, 1000 rows each having 1000 square millimeters. Thus $1000 \times 1000 = 1,000,000$ square millimeters covers a square meter or $1 \text{ mm}^2 = \dfrac{1}{1,000,000} = 0.000001 \text{ m}^2$.
   (b) A square with area 1 km² can be covered with square meters, 1000 rows of 1000 square meters. Thus $1000 \times 1000 = 1,000,000$ square meters.

10. (a) 100.   (b) 6.1.   (c) 0.000564.   (d) 8.21.
    (e) 382,000.   (f) 950.   (g) 6.54.
    (h) 0.00961.

11. (a) 1000 dm³.   (b) 3 places right.
    (c) 3 places left.

12. (a) 9.5.   (b) 7000.   (c) 0.94.   (d) 4750.
    (e) 0.057.   (f) 32,000.

13. (a) 10^6.   (b) 10^{-3}.   (c) 10^{-6}.   (d) 10^3.
    (e) 10^{-2}.   (f) 10^{-12}.

14. (a) 600.   (b) 1.3.   (c) 1.56.   (d) 300,000.
    (e) 136,000.   (f) 56.

15. (a) 10^9; gigameter.   (b) 10^3; kilometer.
    (c) 10^{-12}; picometer.   (d) 10^{-3}; millimeter.

16. (a) 28 mm.   (b) 148 cm.   (c) 27 cm.
    (d) 205 m.   (e) 72 m.   (f) 512 km.

17. (a) 900 mL.   (b) 15 mL.   (c) 473 mL.
(d) 10 L.   (e) 200 mL.   (f) 200 L.

18. (a) 177°C.   (b) 16°C.   (c) −18°C.
(d) 58°C.   (e) −88°C.

19. (a) 34.   (b) 18, 18.   (c) mL.   (d) kg.
(e) dm^3, kg.   (f) mL, g.

20. (a) 60 minutes/1 hour.   (b) 1 hour/3600 sec.
(c) 1 yard/36 inches.   (d) 1 day/24 hours.

21. (a) 57.6 oz.   (b) 4840 ft/min.   (c) 616 in./sec.
(d) $0.40/min.

22. (a) 4.   (b) 16.   (c) 1 cup.   (d) 2 quarts.

23. (a) 240.   (b) 480.   (c) 48.

24. (a) 15.24 cm.   (b) 91.44 m.   (c) 402.336 m.
(d) 0.621 mi.

25. (a) 750 mi/hr.   (b) 6,570,000 mi/yr.

26. 7.5 gallons.

27. 2.7×10^{13} cells.

28. (a) 8.94 kg/dm^3.   (b) 0.695 g/cm^3.
(c) 7.8 g/cm^3.

29. The length of a foot is based on a prototype and is not exactly reproducible. Converting linear measure, for example, uses ratios: 12 inches:1 foot; 3 feet: 1 yard; 1760 yards:1 mile; so measures are not easily convertible. Volumes of in^3, quarts, and pounds are not related directly.

30. (a) Approx. 5,874,600,000,000 miles.
(b) Approx. 446,460,000,000,000 miles.
(c) Approx. 43 minutes.

31. $\dfrac{100 \text{ mi}}{\text{hr}} \times \dfrac{5280 \text{ ft}}{1 \text{ mi}} \times \dfrac{1 \text{ hr}}{3600 \text{ sec}} = 146\frac{2}{3}$ ft/sec.
Therefore, the length of the second train is 5 sec $\times$ 146$\frac{2}{3}$ ft/sec = 733$\frac{1}{3}$ ft.

32. (a) 6,272,640 cubic inches, 3630 cubic feet.
(b) 225,060 pounds.   (c) 27,116 gallons.

33. (a) 1, 4, 6 are measured directly. 2 is 4 to 6, 3 is 1 to 4, 5 is 1 to 6, and 7 is 1 to 8.
(b) 4. There are several ways. One is 1, 4, 6, 7.
(c) 4. There are several ways. One is 1, 4, 6, 8.

34. (a) $300.   (b) $18.75/hr.   (c) 4.
(d) $108.80.

35. 3 km/hour.

SECTION 13.2—PART A

1. (a) 4.34.   (b) 1.91.   (c) 6.65.   (d) 4.22.

2. (a) 2.43 + 1.91 = 4.34, yes.
(b) 4.34 + 4.22 ≠ 6.65, no.
(c) 2.43 + 1.91 + 2.31 = 6.65, yes.

3. (a) $-2\sqrt{5}$.   (b) $\frac{17}{6}$.   (c) 7π.
(d) $\dfrac{-13}{6} = -2.1\overline{6}$.

4. (a) $q - p$.   (b) $\dfrac{q - p}{2}$.
(c) $p + \dfrac{q - p}{2} = \dfrac{p + q}{2}$.   (d) Yes.
(e) $\dfrac{-2.5 + 13.9}{2} = 5.7$.

5. (a) 9.8.   (b) 2.95.   (c) −10.9.   (d) −2.4.

6. (a) $q - p$.   (b) $\dfrac{2p + q}{3}$.   (c) $\dfrac{p + 2q}{3}$.
(d) $m = 2.9, n = 9.4$.

7. $PQ = p - q, QR = q - r, PR = p - r, PQ + QR = (p - q) + (q - r) = p + (-q) + q + (-r) = p + 0 + (-r) = p + (-r) = p - r = PR$.

8. (a) 17.7.   (b) −8.5.   (c) −10.2.   (d) 11.1.

9. (a) $a = 7.6, A = 115.52$.
(b) $b = 12, A = 81.6$.
(c) $b = 35.6, P = 99.4$.

10. No.

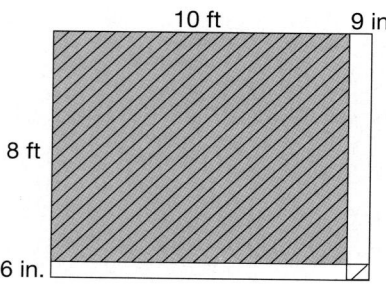

Shaded area would be carpeted. Unshaded would not.

11. They should buy 30 square yards (ramp needs about 29.1 square yards).

12. (a) 40.2; 68.88.   (b) 38.6; 59.15.
(c) 90; 418.86.

13. (a) 182.4; 1386.24.   (b) 49.1; 111.87.
(c) 195.6; 1292.94.

14. (a) $9.6\pi \approx 30.16$; $(4.8)^2\pi \approx 72.38$.
(b) $13.3\pi \approx 41.78$; $(6.65)^2\pi \approx 138.93$.
(c) $3\pi^2 \approx 29.61$; $(3\pi/2)^2\pi \approx 69.76$.

15. (a) $\overline{CD}$.   (b) $\frac{1}{2}\sqrt{20}\sqrt{5} = 5$.
(c) AC.   (d) $\frac{1}{2}\sqrt{10}\sqrt{10} = 5$.
(e) Yes.

16. 520 miles.

17. (a) 30 cm^2.   (b) 9.9 m^2.
(c) 8.2 km^2.   (d) 60 m^2.

18. (a) $\frac{1}{2}(6)(8) = 24$ square units.
(b) $\sqrt{12(6)(4)(2)} = 24$ square units.

19. (a) $b \cdot h$.   **(b)** $\frac{1}{2}(b + b) \cdot h = \frac{1}{2}(2b) \cdot h = b \cdot h$.
(c) Yes.

20. (a) (i) $8\sqrt{3}$, (ii) $2\sqrt{15}$, (iii) $6\sqrt{7}$, (iv) 16.
(b) Rhombus (iv).

21. (a) Approximately 6.54 cm^2.
(b) Approximately 43.8 m^2.
(c) Approximately 39.1 in^2.

22. (a) $\frac{3}{2}$.   **(b)** 6.   **(c)** 1:4.

23. (a) $\sqrt{10}$.   **(b)** $\sqrt{13}$.

24. (a) 15.   **(b)** 104.   **(c)** $\sqrt{34}$.   **(d)** 7.

25. 25 feet.

26. 24 by 48.

27. Yes.

28. Area of large square = sum of areas of smaller pieces:

$$c^2 = 4(\tfrac{1}{2}ab) + (b - a)^2$$
$$c^2 = 2ab + b^2 - 2ab + a^2$$
$$c^2 = a^2 + b^2.$$

29. (a) $\sqrt{l^2 + w^2}$.   **(b)** $\sqrt{l^2 + w^2 + h^2}$.
(c) $\sqrt{5600} \approx 74.8$ cm.

30. (b) and (c).

31. (a) 33.2, 41.5, 99.6.   **(b)** 301.2, 753, 18,900.3.
(c) 106.2, 177, 424.8.

32. (a) 24, 30.   **(b)** $18 + 6\sqrt{2}$, 27.

33. (a) $\frac{1}{2}r(FG)$.
(b) $\frac{1}{2}r(AB + BC + CD + DE + EF + FG + GH + HA)$
(c) $\frac{1}{2}$(apothem) (perimeter).

34. (a) $9\sqrt{3}$.   **(b)** 8.   **(c)** $150\sqrt{3}$.   **(d)** 320.
(e) 2500.   **(f)** 1000.

35. (a), (c), and (d).

36. (a) Subdivide. Areas are indicated. Total area = 13.

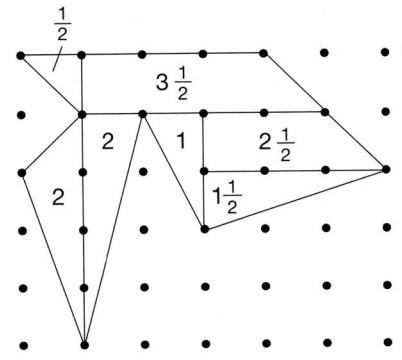

(b) (i) $\frac{14}{2} + 0 - 1 = 6$, (ii) $\frac{35}{2} + 68 - 1 = 84\frac{1}{2}$.

37. 3, 2, 1.

38. 5 and 8.

39. No; consider different cases.

40. Use the rope to form a 3–4–5 right triangle (3 + 4 + 5 = 12 units). The angle between side 3 and side 4 is a right angle.

41. (a) Obtuse.   **(b)** Right.   **(c)** Acute.
(d) Right.   **(e)** Acute.   **(f)** Obtuse.

42. (a) When $c < a + b$.
(b) When $c = \sqrt{a^2 + b^2}$.
(c) When $c < \sqrt{a^2 + b^2}$.
(d) When $\sqrt{a^2 + b^2} < c < a + b$.

43. 65.5 square units.

44. (a) 7.5°; when lines are parallel, alternate interior angles have the same measure.
(b) $\dfrac{500}{7.5} = \dfrac{x}{360}$, $x = 24,000$ miles.
(c) He was off by 901.55 miles.

45. 2.23 cm.

46. Area of region = π.

47. $32\pi - 64$.

48. (a) $\pi/4$ or 78.5%.   **(b)** $\pi/4$ or 78.5%.
(c) They both irrigate the same amount.
(d) It doesn't pay to use more sprinklers with a smaller radius. Check this in the $n \times n$ case.

49. $6 + 3\sqrt{3}$.

50. The polar route would be one-fourth of earth's circumference, or $\frac{1}{4}(2\pi \cdot 6380) = 10,022$ km. The east–west route travels along a circle centered at point F. $PF^2 + FC^2 = r^2$ and $PF = FC$, so $FP = \dfrac{r}{\sqrt{2}} = \dfrac{6380}{\sqrt{2}} \approx 4511$. This route is $\frac{1}{2}(2\pi \cdot 4511) = 14,173$. The polar route is shorter.

51. (a) The area of the smaller circle (100π) is larger than the area between the circles (96π).
(b) $\sqrt{200}$ or $10\sqrt{2}$.

52. They are the same.

53. (a) $P = 3, A = \dfrac{\sqrt{3}}{4}$.   **(b)** $P = \dfrac{9}{2} = 4, A = \dfrac{3\sqrt{3}}{16}$.
(c) $P = \dfrac{27}{4}, A = \dfrac{9\sqrt{3}}{64}$.   **(d)** $P = \dfrac{81}{8}, A = \dfrac{27\sqrt{3}}{256}$.
(e) $P = 3\left(\dfrac{3}{2}\right)^n, A = \dfrac{3^{n-1}\sqrt{3}}{4^n}$.

SECTION 13.3—PART A

1. (a) 800.   **(b)** 400.   **(c)** 216.   **(d)** 240.

2. (a) 360.   **(b)** 896.   **(c)** 300π.   **(d)** 6π.

3. (a) 1141 cm^2.   **(b)** 276 cm^2.
(c) 766 cm^2.   **(d)** 866 cm^2.

4. **(a)** 452.   **(b)** 66.   **(c)** 1810.   **(d)** 141.

5. **(a)** 43 cm². **(b)** 166 cm². **(c)** 1247 cm².

6. 5.

7. **(a)** SA $= 2 \times \frac{1}{2} \times 8 \times 4\sqrt{3} + 3 \times 8 \times 10 = 32\sqrt{3} + 240$.
   (b) SA $= 96 + 12(22 + 2\sqrt{10})$.
   (c) SA $= 60 + 30 \times 20 = 660$.

8. **(a)** $B = 6 \times \frac{1}{2} \times \frac{5}{2}\sqrt{3} \times 5 = \frac{75}{2}\sqrt{3}$.
   (b) $A = 2(\frac{75}{2}\sqrt{3}) + 6 \times 5 \times 10 = 75\sqrt{3} + 300$.

9. The new box will require 4 times as much cardboard as the old box.

10. **(a)** A $6 \times 6 \times 1$ prism of cubes.
    (b) A $9 \times 2 \times 2$ prism of cubes.
    (c) A $3 \times 4 \times 3$ prism of cubes.
      Surface area is 66 square units.
    (d) A $36 \times 1 \times 1$ prism of cubes.
      Surface area is 146 square units.

11. 10.044 m².

12. $12 \times 8 \times 6$.

13. **(a)** 1.088×10^{12} 6380 km.   **(b)** 5.12×10^8 km².
    (c) 26.5%.

14. Surface area is $\frac{1}{4}$ of the original.

15. SA $= 36 + 2\pi\left(\dfrac{3}{\pi}\right)^2 = 36 + \dfrac{18}{\pi}$.

16. 150π.

17. Each stripe covers $\frac{1}{3}$ of the surface area, so the red stripe covers about 2094 cm².

10. 1.47×10^8 yd³.

11. About 9.42 (exactly 3π).

12. **(a)** Approximately 32,100,000 ft³.
    (b) Approximately 462,000 ft².

13. **(a)** Volume $\approx$ 478 cm³; surface area $\approx$ 404 cm².
    (b) Volume $\approx$ 249 cm³; surface area $\approx$ 165 cm².

14. 85,536 m³.

15. **(a)** $150\sqrt{3}$ square feet.   **(b)** $50\sqrt{3}$ cubic feet.
    (c) $144.34.

16. **(a)** $h = 40$ feet.
    (b) Approximately 848,000 gallons.
    (c) The sphere has the smaller surface area.

17. 36.3 kg.

18. **(a)** 90 in³.   **(b)** No.

19. **(a)** 8 times.   **(b)** 4 times.

20. 12-cm pipes.

21. **(a)** 8 m³.   **(b)** $\sqrt[3]{16} = 2\sqrt[3]{2}$.

22. **(a)** 4 times.   **(b)** 2 times.

23. 192 cm³.

24. $100 \times \dfrac{64 - 36}{36}\% \approx 78\%$.

25. $\dfrac{10}{\sqrt{2}} \approx 7.07$ ft.

26. **(a)** 2.625.   **(b)** 9.375.   **(c)** 24.   **(d)** 15.

27. 20.25 hours.

SECTION 13.4—PART A

1. **(a)** 1500.   **(b)** 300.   **(c)** 144.   **(d)** 200.

2. **(a)** 400.   **(b)** 1568.   **(c)** 240π.   **(d)** 1.5π.

3. **(a)** 2958 cm³.   **(b)** 342 cm³.
   (c) 1562 cm³.   **(d)** 1951 cm³.

4. **(a)** 905.   **(b)** 51.   **(c)** 7238.   **(d)** 157.

5. **(a)** Volume $= 14$; surface area $= 62$.
   (b) Volume $= 7$; surface area $= 38$.
   (c) Volume $= 21$; surface area $= 54$.

6. **(a)** 540 in³.   **(b)** 101 in³.

7. **(a)** 900 m².   **(b)** 2400 m³.

8. **(a)** Circumference ($2\pi r$) is greater than height ($6r$).
   (b) $33\frac{1}{3}\%$ (one-third) of the can.

9. **(a)** $V = \frac{1}{2} \times 8 \times 4\sqrt{3} \times 10 = 160\sqrt{3}$.
   (b) $V = 48 \times 12 = 576$.
   (c) $V = \frac{1}{2} \times 5 \times 12 \times 20 = 600$.

ADDITIONAL PROBLEMS WHERE THE STRATEGY "USE DIMENSIONAL ANALYSIS" IS USEFUL

1. 6.3 m.

2. $14.40.

3. Light is 1,079,270 times faster than sound.

CHAPTER 13 TEST

1. **(a)** F.   **(b)** F.   **(c)** T.   **(d)** F.   **(e)** F.
   (f) T.   **(g)** F.   **(h)** T.

2. $1 \text{ mile} \cdot \dfrac{5280 \text{ feet}}{1 \text{ mile}} \cdot \dfrac{12 \text{ inches}}{1 \text{ foot}} \cdot \dfrac{2.54 \text{ cm}}{1 \text{ inch}} \cdot \dfrac{1 \text{ km}}{100,000 \text{ cm}} = 1.609$ km.

3. 7,000,000,000 dm³; from hm³ to dm³ is a move right of three steps on the metric converter and each step involves moving the decimal point three places.

4. Area is $1/\pi$ or approximately 0.318 cubic unit.

5. Volume $= (7.2)(3.4)(5.9) \text{ cm}^3 = 144.432 \text{ cm}^3$.

6. Volume $= \dfrac{(13)(12)}{3} = 52 \text{ cm}^3$.

7. Cutting off one piece with a cut perpendicular between two bases and reassembling gives us a rectangle. The two sides of the rectangle correspond to the base and height of the parallelogram and thus the formula follows.

8. It aids in comparing and converting measurements of volume, capacity, and mass; for example, 1 cm^3 of volume equals 1 mL and, if water, weighs 1 g.

9. The convertibility of the metric system makes it easier to learn because the prefixes have the same meaning for all measurements, and converting between measurements involves factors of 10 and thus just movement of the decimal point.

10. (a) Area $= \sqrt{3}s^2/2$ square units; $\triangle ABC$ is an equilateral triangle with sides of length $s\sqrt{2}$ and height $\sqrt{6}s/2$.
    (b) Use $\triangle ADC$ as a base. Its area is $s^2/2$ and the height BD from this base is s, so the volume equals $s^3/6$.

11. The circumference flown is 7933π miles; 7933π miles $\cdot \dfrac{5280 \text{ feet}}{1 \text{ mile}} \cdot \dfrac{1 \text{ second}}{1100 \text{ feet}} \cdot \dfrac{1 \text{ hour}}{3600 \text{ seconds}} \approx 33$ hours.

12. (a) Surface area $= 300$ square units; volume $= 300$ cubic units.
    (b) Surface area $= 936 + 1352/\pi \approx 1366$ square units; volume $= 12{,}168/\pi \approx 3873$ cubic units.

SECTION 14.1—PART A

1. (a) $T \leftrightarrow A, E \leftrightarrow R, X \leftrightarrow E$.
   (b) $P \leftrightarrow C, E \leftrightarrow I, N \leftrightarrow L$.
   (c) $A \leftrightarrow E, D \leftrightarrow D, E \leftrightarrow A$.

2. (a) KJL.   (b) KLJ.   (c) LJK.   (d) RTS.

3. (a) $\triangle ABC \cong \triangle EFD$ or equivalent statement.
   (b) $\triangle AXD \cong \triangle CXB$ or equivalent.

4. (a) $\overline{GI}$.   (b) $\overline{HI}$.   (c) $\overline{GH}$.   (d) $\angle G$.
   (e) $\angle I$.   (f) $\angle H$.

5. (a) $m(\angle A) = m(\angle F) = 38°, m(\angle B) = m(\angle E) = 120°,$ $m(\angle C) = m(\angle D) = 22°, AB = FE = 3, BC = ED = 5, CA = DF = 7$; thus $\triangle ABC \cong \triangle FED$.
   (b) $m(\angle R) = m(\angle W) = 60°, m(\angle S) = m(\angle V) = 90°,$ $m(\angle T) = m(\angle U) = 30°, RS = WV = 3, ST = VU = 3\sqrt{3}, TR = UW = 6$; thus $\triangle RST \cong \triangle WVU$.

6. (a) $\overline{MN}$ and $\overline{ON}$.   (b) $\angle M$ and $\angle O$.   (c) $\overline{NO}$.
   (d) $\angle O$.

7. (a) Yes.
   (b) No, congruent angles are not included angles.
   (c) Yes.

8. (a) $\overline{WX}; \angle X; \overline{XY}$.
   (b) $\overline{BC} \cong \overline{XY}, \angle C \cong \angle Y, \overline{CA} \cong \overline{YW}; \overline{CA} \cong \overline{YW},$ $\angle A \cong \angle W, \overline{AB} \cong \overline{WX}$.

9. (a) Yes.   (b) No.   (c) Yes.

10. (a) Yes; $m(\angle C) = 70°, m(\angle A) = 40°, m(\angle E) = m(\angle F) = 70°$, so $\triangle ABC \cong \triangle DEF$ by SAS or ASA.
    (b) No; $m(\angle T) = 50°, VU = 4, m(\angle V) = 50°$, but there is no correspondence of the sides.
    (c) Yes; by SAS, ASA, or SSS since the two triangles are equilateral.

11. $\overline{RS}; \overline{ST}; \overline{TR}$.

12. (a) Use SSS or SAS.   (b) Use SSS.

13. (a) $\angle A \cong \angle D, \overline{AB} \cong \overline{DE}, \overline{BC} \cong \overline{EF}$.
    (b) No.
    (c) No; this example is a counterexample.

14. (a) $\angle P \cong \angle S, \angle Q \cong \angle T, \overline{QR} \cong \overline{TU}$, and $m(\angle R) = m(\angle U) = 80°$, so $\angle R \cong \angle U$.
    (b) Yes.
    (c) $m(\angle R) = 80° = m(\angle U)$, so we can use $\angle R, \overline{RQ}, \angle Q$ and $\angle U, \overline{UT}$, and $\angle T$.

15. (a) SAS.   (b) ASA.   (c) AAS.

16. (a) $\overline{AB} \cong \overline{DE}$ (leg), $\angle B \cong \angle E, \overline{AC} \cong \overline{DF}$ (hypotenuse).
    (b) No.
    (c) $BC = EF = \sqrt{84}$, so $\overline{BC} \cong \overline{EF}$.
    (d) Yes; SAS.

17. (a) $\overline{AB} \cong \overline{CB}$ (they measured it off), $\angle TAB$ and $\angle DCB$ are both right angles (directly across and directly away from), $\angle TBA \cong \angle DBC$ (vertical angles).
    (b) Yes; ASA.
    (c) $\overline{DC} \cong \overline{TA}$, so they can measure $\overline{DC}$ and that equals the width of the river.

18. (a) 1 and 4.
    (b) Since triangles are rigid figures, any scaffolding based on triangles will not collapse.

19. No.

20. (a) For example, have 3 pairs of angles congruent.
    (b) Not possible. Consider possible cases:
        (1) 3 sides, 1 angle, apply SSS;
        (2) 2 sides, 2 angles (third angle would also have to be), apply ASA;
        (3) 1 side, 3 angles, apply ASA.
    (c) Not possible, $\cong$ by either SSS or ASA.
    (d) Not possible, $\cong$ by definition.

21. (a) Yes; $m(\angle B) = 180 - [m(\angle A) + m(\angle C)]$ and $m(\angle K) = 180 - [m(\angle J) + m(\angle L)]$, so using congruences indicated $m(\angle B) = m(\angle K)$.

(b) ASA.   **(c)** Yes.

22. (a) $\triangle BCD \cong \triangle XYZ$, by SAS congruence property.

(b) $\angle ABC \cong \angle WXY$ (given), $\angle 2 \cong \angle 6$ [corresponding parts of congruent triangles in part (a)], thus $m(\angle ABC) - m(\angle 2) = m(\angle WXY) - m(\angle 6)$ or $m(\angle 1) = m(\angle 5)$, so $\angle 1 \cong \angle 5$.

(c) $\overline{AB} \cong \overline{WX}$ (given), $\angle 1 \cong \angle 5$ [part (b)], $\overline{BD} \cong \overline{XZ}$ [corresponding parts of congruent triangles in part (a)], so $\triangle ABD \cong \triangle WXZ$ by SAS congruence property; $\angle A \cong \angle W$, $\overline{AD} \cong \overline{WZ}$.

(d) $\angle 3 \cong \angle 7$ [corresponding parts of congruent triangles in part (c)], $\angle 4 \cong \angle 8$ [corresponding parts of congruent triangles in part (a)], so $m(\angle 3) + m(\angle 4) = m(\angle 7) + m(\angle 8)$ and $m(\angle ADC) = m(\angle WZY)$.

(e) Yes, and the quadrilaterals are thus congruent.

23. $m(\angle D) + m(\angle E) = 180$ (supplementary), $m(\angle D) = m(\angle E)$ (congruent), $m(\angle D) + m(\angle D) = 180$ (substitution), $2m(\angle D) = 180$, so $m(\angle D) = 90$ and $m(\angle E) = 90$.

SECTION 14.2—PART A

1. (a) $\triangle ABC \sim \triangle DEC$, by AA similarity.
(b) $\triangle FGH \sim \triangle IJK$, by SSS similarity.
(c) $\triangle LMN \sim \triangle OPQ$, by SAS similarity.
(d) $\triangle RST \sim \triangle VWU$, by AA similarity.

2. (a) $EF = 10$, $DF = 14$.
(b) $RS = 6$, $RT = 6\sqrt{10}$, $LN = \sqrt{10}$.
(c) $EI = 10$, $HI = 3\sqrt{3}$, $FI = 5\sqrt{3}$.
(d) $TV = \frac{16}{3}$, $WX = 20$.

3. 25 meters.

4. 22 meters.

5. (a) F; triangle may have sides with different lengths.
(b) T; by AA.
(c) F; see part (a).
(d) T; by AA.

6. (a) $\triangle ABC \sim \triangle EDC$, by AA similarity. We assume that both the tree and the person are perpendicular to the ground, and that the angle of incidence $\angle ECD$, is congruent to the angle of reflection, $\angle ACB$.
(b) 27 meters.

7. 17 inches; not a realistic waist measurement for an average woman.

8. (a) 9.6 in.
(b) Image would be half as long (i.e., the thumb would be 4.8 inches long).

9. $\triangle ABC \approx \triangle DEF$, so $\triangle ABC$ is also a right isosceles triangle. Therefore, the height $\overline{BC}$ is the same length as the leg $\overline{AC}$.

10. 6.53 feet.

11. (a) $\overline{AB} \parallel \overline{DE}$ and $\overline{AD} \parallel \overline{BE}$ from given information, and therefore $ABED$ is a parallelogram by definition. Similarly, $\overline{BC} \parallel \overline{EF}$, $\overline{BE} \parallel \overline{CF}$, and $BCFE$ is a parallelogram.
(b) Opposite sides of parallelogram are congruent.
(c) DE/EF.   **(d)** Yes.

12. (a) $\angle P \cong \angle P \cong \angle P$, $\angle PAD \cong \angle PBE \cong \angle PCF$ (corresponding angles property), so that $\triangle PAD \sim \triangle PBE \sim \triangle PCF$ by AA similarity property.
(b) $a/(a + b) = x/(x + y)$, so $a(x + y) = x(a + b)$, $ax + ay = xa + xb$, or $ay = bx$.
(c) $a/(a + b + c) = x/(x + y + z)$, so $a(x + y + z) = x(a + b + c)$, $ax + ay + az = ax + bx + cx$, or $ay + az = bx + cx$.
(d) Combining parts (b) and (c) yields $bx + az = bx + cx$ or $az = cx$.
(e) $bx/cx = ay/az$ or $b/c = y/z$.   **(f)** Yes.

13. (a) $EF/FG = KJ/JG$.   **(b)** $BC/CD = JG/GI$.
(c) $DB/BA = HF/FE$.

14. $\dfrac{9}{3} = \dfrac{CE}{2}$, so $CE = 6$. Thus $8^2 + 12^2 = AB^2$, so $AB = \sqrt{208} = 4\sqrt{13}$.

15. $\dfrac{40}{30} = \dfrac{40 + BD}{60}$, so $BD = 40$.

16. (a) 60 cm^3.   **(b)** 9.5 cm.

17. $AP = \frac{4}{5}$; $BP = \frac{16}{5}$; $CP = \sqrt{41}/5$; $DP = 4\sqrt{41}/5$.

18. The area of the larger triangle will be four times the area of the smaller triangle.

19. $\triangle ADC \sim \triangle CDB$; therefore, $\dfrac{a}{x} = \dfrac{x}{1}$, or $a = x^2$.

20. (a) 3.   **(b)** 4.   **(c)** $5\frac{1}{3}$.
(d) $3\left[1 + \dfrac{1}{3} + 4\left(\dfrac{1}{3^2}\right) + \cdots + 4^{n-2}\left(\dfrac{1}{3^{n-1}}\right)\right]$.

21. (a) 12.   **(b)** $13\frac{1}{3}$.   **(c)** $13\frac{25}{27}$.
(d) $3\left[3 + 1 + 4\left(\dfrac{1}{3^2}\right) + \cdots + 4^{n-2}\left(\dfrac{1}{3^{2n+4}}\right)\right]$.

22. The three triangles are similar by AA similarity. Therefore, $\dfrac{a}{x} = \dfrac{c}{a}$, or (i) $a^2 = cx$ and $\dfrac{b}{c - x} = \dfrac{c}{b}$, or (ii) $b^2 = c^2 - cx$. Substituting a^2 for cx in (ii) we have $b^2 = c^2 - a^2$, or $a^2 + b^2 = c^2$.

SECTION 14.3—PART A

1. (a) _____)

   (b) _____)_____)_____)

   (c) _____)_____)

   (d) _____)_____)

   $b - a$

2. (a), (c), and (d) are possible; (b) is not possible (does not satisfy triangle inequality).

3. Follow the steps of construction 2.

4. Follow the steps of construction 3.

5. Follow the steps of construction 4.

6. Follow the steps of constructions 5 and 6.

7. Follow the steps of construction 7.

8. (a) Bisect a 90° angle.
   (b) Construct equilateral triangle.
   (c) Bisect angle in part (b).

9. (a) 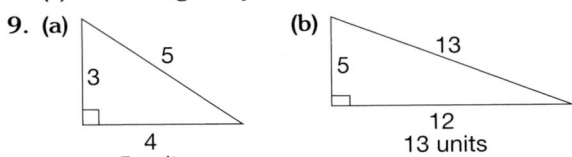 (b)

   (c)

   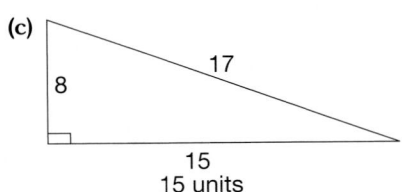

10. (b) $\angle A \cong \angle P$, $\angle B \cong \angle Q$, $\angle C \cong \angle R$.
    (c) $\triangle ABC \sim \triangle PQR$, since angles are congruent and all sides are proportional.
    (d) SSS similarity.

11. Yes.

12. Yes.

13. They do in an equilateral triangle. In *every* isosceles triangle the median to the base and the angle bisector of the vertex angle coincide.

14. They do in an equilateral triangle. In *every* isosceles triangle the perpendicular bisector of the base and median to the base coincide.

15. (a) $\overline{PA} \cong \overline{PB}$, $\overline{QA} \cong \overline{QB}$ (by construction), $\overline{PQ} \cong \overline{PQ}$.
    (b) $\overline{PA} \cong \overline{PB}$, $\angle APR \cong \angle BPR$ [corresponding angles of congruent triangles in part (a)], $\overline{PR} \cong \overline{PR}$.

    (c) $\angle PRA$ and $\angle PRB$ are supplementary by definition since A, R, and B are collinear, $\angle PRA \cong \angle PRB$ since they are corresponding angles of congruent triangles in part (b). Since these angles are supplementary and congruent, they are right angles.
    (d) $\overline{AR} \cong \overline{BR}$ since they are corresponding sides of congruent triangles in part (a). And, by definition, $\overline{PQ}$ bisects $\overline{AB}$.

16. Bisect $\angle A$ and call the intersection of the angle bisector with $\overline{BC}$ point D. Then $\angle B \cong \angle C$ (given), $\angle BAD \cong \angle CAD$ (angle bisector), and $\overline{AD} \cong \overline{AD}$. Therefore, $\triangle BAD \cong \triangle CAD$ and corresponding sides $\overline{AB}$ and $\overline{AC}$ are congruent. By definition $\triangle ABC$ is isosceles.

SECTION 14.4—PART A

1. Follow the steps of construction 8.

2. Follow the steps of construction 9.

3. Follow the steps of construction 10.

4. (a) Bisect a 90° angle.
   (b) Construct equilateral triangle.
   (c) Bisect angle in part (b).

5. (c) The hypotenuse is twice as long as the shortest leg.

6. (b) Regular pentagon.

7. (a) Regular decagon.
   (b) Regular 20-gon.
   (c) 40, 80, any of form $5 \cdot 2^k$.

8. (a), (b), (d), (h), and (i).

9. The resulting segments $\overline{AT}$, $\overline{TS}$, and $\overline{SB}$ are congruent, thus dividing $\overline{AB}$ into three congruent parts.

10.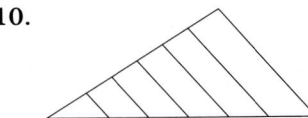

11. (a) Use the same procedure except mark off four congruent segments on $\overline{AC}$.
    (b) Use construction 3 to find midpoint M of $\overline{AB}$. Then repeat construction 3 to bisect $\overline{AM}$ and $\overline{MB}$.

12. (c) It lies inside the triangle.

13. (c) It is the midpoint of the hypotenuse.

14. (c) It is outside the triangle.

15. Lay the piece diagonally across the ruled paper so that the edge of the piece acts as a transversal. If the piece crosses six parallel lines, portions of the ruler between them will be congruent.

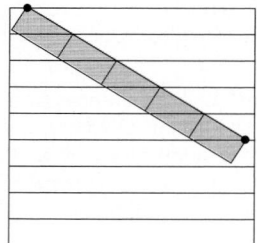

16. (c) $M_1M_3 = M_2M_4$ and $\overline{M_1M_3} \perp \overline{M_2M_4}$ (Aubel's theorem).

17. Case 1: $a > 1$.

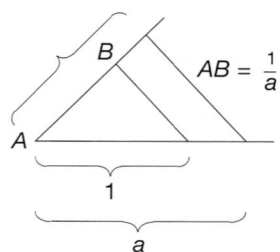

$AB = \dfrac{1}{a}$

Case 2: $a < 1$.

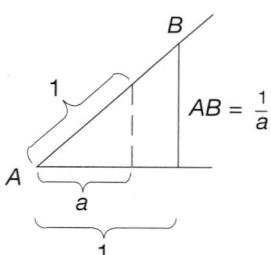

$AB = \dfrac{1}{a}$

Case 3: If $a = 1$, then $\dfrac{1}{a} = 1$.

18. (a) $\sqrt{2}$.

(b) $\triangle AEC$ and $\triangle EBC$ are both isosceles triangles sharing base angle $\angle ECB$ and are therefore similar by AA similarity property. Corresponding sides are thus proportional, so $AE/EB = EC/BC$ or $a/x = x/b$.

SECTION 14.5—PART A

1. (a) $\overline{AC} \cong \overline{AB}$, $\angle CAD \cong \angle BAD$.
(b) $\angle C \cong \angle B$, opposite congruent sides.
(c) ASA.
(d) Corresponding parts of congruent triangles are congruent.
(e) $\angle ADC$ and $\angle ADB$ are right angles since they are congruent and supplementary.
(f) $\overline{AD} \perp \overline{BC}$ and $\overline{AD}$ bisects $\overline{BC}$ (divides it into 2 congruent pieces).

2. (a) For example, $\overline{AB} \cong \overline{AD}$, $\overline{BC} \cong \overline{DC}$.
(b) $\overline{AC} \cong \overline{AC}$ (congruent to itself).
(c) SSS.
(d) Corresponding parts of congruent triangles are congruent.
(e) By definition of angle bisector.

3. $\overline{AB} \cong \overline{CB}$ (rhombus), $\angle ABE \cong \angle CBE$ (vertex angle bisected by diagonal), $\overline{BE} \cong \overline{BE}$ (common side), $\triangle ABE \cong \triangle CBE$ (SAS), so $\angle AEB \cong \angle CEB$ (corresponding parts). Thus $\overline{AC}$ is perpendicular to $\overline{BD}$, since $\angle AEB$ and $\angle CEB$ are congruent and supplementary.

4. $\overline{AB} \parallel \overline{DC}$ by definition of a parallelogram, $\angle A$ and $\angle D$ are supplementary since they are interior angles on the same side of a transversal. Similarly, since $\overline{AD} \parallel \overline{BC}$, $\angle A$ and $\angle B$ are supplementary.

5. Since $\overline{PQ} \parallel \overline{SR}$ and $\overline{PS} \parallel \overline{QR}$ and interior angles on the same side of the transversal are supplementary, $\angle Q$ and $\angle S$ must also be right angles ($90° + 90° = 180°$). Further, since opposite angles of a parallelogram are congruent, $\angle R$ must also be a right angle.

6. $\overline{AB} \cong \overline{DC}$, $\overline{BC} \cong \overline{AD}$ (given) and $\overline{BD} \cong \overline{DB}$ so $\triangle ABD \cong \triangle CDB$ (SSS congruence property). Thus $\angle ABD \cong \angle CDB$ (corresponding parts of congruent triangles), so $\overline{AB} \parallel \overline{DC}$ (alternate interior angles theorem). Similarly, $\angle CBD \cong \angle ADB$ (corresponding parts of congruent triangles), so $\overline{BC} \parallel \overline{AD}$ (alternate interior angles theorem).

7. $m(\angle P) = m(\angle R) = m(\angle Q) = m(\angle S)$ (opposite angles are congruent); $m(\angle P) + m(\angle Q) + m(\angle R) + m(\angle S) = 360°$ (vertex angles of quadrilateral total 360°); $m(\angle P) + m(\angle Q) + m(\angle P) + m(\angle Q) = 360°$, so $m(\angle P) + m(\angle Q) = 180°$; thus $\angle P$ and $\angle Q$ are supplementary and $\overline{PS} \parallel \overline{QR}$ (interior angles on same side of transversal are supplementary). Similarly, $m(\angle P) + m(\angle S) + m(\angle P) + m(\angle S) = 360°$, $m(\angle P) + m(\angle S) = 180°$, P and S are supplementary, and $\overline{PQ} \parallel \overline{SR}$. Since both pairs of opposite sides are parallel, $PQRS$ is a parallelogram.

8. Since $\overline{AB} \parallel \overline{CD}$, we have $\angle EBA \cong \angle EDC$ and $\angle EAB \cong \angle ECD$. Also, $AB = CD$. Therefore, $\triangle EAB \cong \triangle ECD$ (ASA congruence property). By corresponding parts, $\overline{AE} \cong \overline{CE}$ and $\overline{BE} \cong \overline{DE}$.

9. Since $STUV$ is a rhombus, it has 4 congruent sides. We need to show that it has 4 right angles. Since a rhombus is a parallelogram, opposite angles $\angle S$ and $\angle U$ are congruent (right angles) and adjacent angles are supplementary; $\angle V$ and $\angle T$ are thus right angles.

10. $\overline{SV} \cong \overline{TU}$ (all sides are congruent), $\overline{ST} \cong \overline{TS}$, and $\overline{TV} \cong \overline{SU}$ (diagonals congruent), so $\triangle STV \cong \triangle TSU$ (SSS congruence property). Thus supplementary angles $\angle TSV$ and $\angle STU$ (adjacent angles of parallelogram are supplementary) are also congruent (corresponding parts of congruent triangles). Therefore, $\angle TSV$ and $\angle STU$ are both right angles. Similarly, $\angle SVU$ and $\angle TUV$ are right angles.

11. Using the SSS congruence property, construct $\triangle ABC$, where $AB = a$, $BC = b$, and $AC = d$. Using $\overline{AC}$ as one side, similarly construct $\triangle CDA$, where $CD = a$ and $DA = b$. $ABCD$ will be the desired parallelogram.

12. Construct an equilateral $\triangle ABC$. Using $\overline{AC}$ as one side, construct equilateral $\triangle CDA$. $ABCD$ is the desired rhombus.

13. Construct $\overline{AB}$ the length of the longer base. Construct a segment whose length is $a - b$ and bisect this segment. Mark off an arc centered at A with length $(a - b)/2$, intersecting $\overline{AB}$ at R and an arc centered at B with the same length, intersecting $\overline{AB}$ at S. At R and S construct segments perpendicular to $\overline{AB}$. With compass set at length c mark off an arc centered at B intersecting perpendicular from S at point C. Similarly, draw an arc from A intersecting the perpendicular from R at point D. $ABCD$ is the desired isosceles trapezoid.

14. $AD/AC = AC/AB$ (AC is geometric mean) and $\angle A \cong \angle A$, so $\triangle ADC \sim \triangle ACB$ (SAS similarity property). Therefore, $\triangle ADC \cong \angle ACB$ and since $\angle ACD$ is a right angle, so is $\angle ACB$. Thus $\triangle ABC$ is a right triangle.

15. (a) $M_1M_2M_3M_4$ will be a rectangle when the diagonals $\overline{PR}$ and $\overline{QS}$ are perpendicular.
(b) $M_1M_2M_3M_4$ will be a rhombus when the diagonals $\overline{PR}$ and $\overline{QS}$ are congruent.
(c) $M_1M_2M_3M_4$ will be a square when the diagonals $\overline{PR}$ and $\overline{QS}$ are both perpendicular and congruent.

16. (a) AA similarity property.
(b) AA similarity property.
(c) $a^2 + b^2 = x^2 + xy + xy + y^2 = x^2 + 2xy + y^2 = (x + y)^2 + c^2$.

17. $\triangle BAD \cong \triangle B'A'C'$ by SAS. Therefore, $BD = B'C' = BC$. Since $\triangle ACD$ and $\triangle BDC$ are both isosceles, their base angles are congruent. By addition, $\angle ACB \cong \angle ADB$. Thus $\triangle BAD \cong \triangle BAC$ by SAS. Therefore, $\triangle B'A'C' \cong \triangle BAC$ since they are both congruent to $\triangle BAD$.

ADDITIONAL PROBLEMS WHERE THE STRATEGY "IDENTIFY SUBGOALS" IS USEFUL

1. Factoring 360 into its prime factorization, we have $360 = 2^3 \cdot 3^2 \cdot 5$. To find the smallest square having $2^3 \cdot 3^2 \cdot 5$ as a factor, we need to find the smallest number with the same prime factors but with *even* exponents. Thus $2^4 \cdot 3^2 \cdot 5^2 = 3600$ is the smallest such number.

2. Subgoal: Find the lengths of the sides. Volume is 192 cm^2.

3. If 32% of n is 128, then 16% of n is 64, or 8% of n is 32, or 1% of n is ____. Therefore, $n = 400$.

CHAPTER 14 TEST

1. (a) T.   (b) F.   (c) T.   (d) T.   (e) T.
(f) T.   (g) F.   (h) F.

2. (b) and (d).

3. Construct an equilateral triangle and circumscribe a circle about it. Then bisect the central angles twice.

4. The circumcenter and incenter for an equilateral triangle are the same point.

5. Construct a right triangle with sides of length 1 and 2. The hypotenuse will have length $\sqrt{5}$. Construct a square with sides of length $\sqrt{5}$.

6. From $\triangle ABC \cong \triangle CBA$, we have $\angle A \cong \angle C$. Sides opposite congruent angles are congruent and thus $\triangle ABC$ is isosceles.

7. From $\triangle ABC \cong \triangle BCA$, we have $\angle A \cong \angle B$ and $\angle B \cong \angle C$. Thus $\angle A \cong \angle B \cong \angle C$ and $\triangle ABC$ is equilateral.

8. (a) Let P and Q be points on $\overline{AB}$ such that $\overline{DP} \perp \overline{AB}$ and $\overline{CQ} \perp \overline{AB}$. Since parallel lines are everywhere equidistant, $\overline{DP} \cong \overline{CQ}$. Also, $\angle APD \cong \angle BQC$ since they are both right angles and $\angle A \cong \angle B$ (given). Thus $\angle ADP \cong \angle BCQ$. Hence $\triangle APD \cong \triangle BQC$ by the ASA congruence property and $\overline{AD} \cong \overline{BC}$.
(b) As in part (a) draw $\overline{DP}$ and $\overline{CQ}$. Then show that $\overline{AP} \cong \overline{BQ}$ by the Pythagorean theorem. Thus $\triangle APD \cong \triangle BQC$ by the SSS congruence property and $\angle A \cong \angle B$.

9. (a) Because the prime factorization of 9 includes two 3s.
(b) 40°.
(c) 20°.
(d) It is impossible.

10. (a) 4.   (b) $\frac{147}{8}$.

SECTION 15.1—PART A

1. (a) $\frac{1}{2}$.   **(b)** $\frac{4}{3}$.   **(c)** 0.   **(d)** No slope.

2. (a) $\dfrac{-3-5}{6-(-4)} = \dfrac{-8}{10} = \dfrac{-4}{5}$ and $\dfrac{5-(-3)}{-4-6} = \dfrac{8}{-10} = \dfrac{-4}{5}$; yes.

   (b) $\dfrac{2-(-3)}{3-(-2)} = \dfrac{-3-2}{-2-3} = 1$; yes.

3. (a) Positive.   **(b)** Zero.   **(c)** No slope.
   (d) Negative.

4. (a) Slopes of $\overline{AB}$ and $\overline{PQ}$ equal 1.
   (b) Slopes equal $\frac{2}{3}$.

5. (a) Yes.   **(b)** No.

6. (a) $\sqrt{13}$.   **(b)** $\sqrt{5}$.   **(c)** $\sqrt{73}$.   **(d)** 7.

7. (a) $\dfrac{3-2}{1-0} = 1$, $\dfrac{2-0}{3-2} = 2$, not parallel.

   (b) $\dfrac{2-3}{-1-(-5)} = \dfrac{-1}{4}$, $\dfrac{1-0}{-3-0} = \dfrac{1}{-3} = \dfrac{-1}{3}$, not parallel.

   (d) Parallel, as both are vertical (slopes are undefined).

   (d) $\dfrac{-1-(-3)}{-3-(-5)} = \dfrac{2}{2} = 1$, $\dfrac{-1-(-4)}{-2-(-5)} = 1$, parallel.

8. (a) Top and bottom are both horizontal, $\dfrac{4-1}{1-2} = -3$, $\dfrac{4-1}{4-5} = -3$; parallelogram.

   (b) Top, bottom are both horizontal, sides are vertical; parallelogram.

   (c) Top, bottom are horizontal, $\dfrac{2-(-2)}{4-1} = \dfrac{4}{3}$, $\dfrac{2-(-2)}{6-3} = \dfrac{4}{3}$, parallelogram.

   (d) $\dfrac{10-(-5)}{-5-10} = \dfrac{15}{-15} = -1$, $\dfrac{5-(-10)}{-10-5} = \dfrac{15}{-15} = -1$, parallel; $\dfrac{10-5}{-5-(-10)} = 1$, $\dfrac{-5-(-10)}{10-5} = \dfrac{5}{5} = 1$, parallelogram.

9. (a) One side horizontal, one vertical.
   (b) $\dfrac{8-1}{2-7} = \dfrac{7}{-5}$, $\dfrac{6-1}{14-7} = \dfrac{5}{7}$, perpendicular.
   (c) $\dfrac{9-2}{6-8} = \dfrac{7}{-2}$, $\dfrac{2-(-3)}{8-(-8)} = \dfrac{5}{16}$, not perpendicular.
   (d) $\dfrac{4-(-2)}{-4-(-7)} = \dfrac{6}{3} = 2$, $\dfrac{4-(-3)}{-4-10} = \dfrac{7}{-14} = -\dfrac{1}{2}$, perpendicular.

10. (a) $\overline{AD}$ and $\overline{BC}$ have slope $\frac{5}{2}$; $\overline{AB}$ and $\overline{CD}$ have slope $-\frac{2}{5}$, so $\overline{AB} \perp \overline{AD}$, $\overline{AB} \perp \overline{BC}$, $\overline{BC} \perp \overline{CD}$, and $\overline{AD} \perp \overline{CD}$.

   (b) $AC = \sqrt{(5-13)^2+[7-(-2)]^2} = \sqrt{145}$; $BD = \sqrt{(15-3)^2+(3-2)^2} = \sqrt{145}$; so $AC = BD$.
   (c) All are equal.
   (d) No, the slope of $\overline{AC} = -\frac{9}{8}$, the slope of $\overline{BD} = \frac{1}{12}$.
   (e) Diagonals are congruent and bisect each other, but are not necessarily perpendicular.

11. (a) 12.   **(b)** 4.   **(c)** 1.   **(d)** 1.

12. (a) $\sqrt{2} + 2\sqrt{2} = 3\sqrt{2}$; yes.
   (b) $\sqrt{34} + \sqrt{117} \neq \sqrt{277}$; no.
   (c) $2\sqrt{5} + 4\sqrt{5} = 6\sqrt{5}$; yes.

13. (a) Isosceles right.   **(b)** Scalene right.
   (c) Obtuse isosceles.   **(d)** Scalene acute.

14. (a) $\left(\dfrac{-3}{2}, 2\right)$.   **(b)** $(-1, 2)$.   **(c)** $\left(\dfrac{-5}{2}, \dfrac{9}{2}\right)$.
   (d) $(3, -6)$.   **(e)** $(2, 7)$.   **(f)** $\left(\dfrac{3}{2}, \dfrac{3}{2}\right)$.

15. (a) $(1, 7)$.   **(b)** $(-9, 3)$.   **(c)** $(7, 5)$.
   (d) $(2, -5)$.

16. (a) 1.   **(b)** $\dfrac{-2}{3}$.   **(c)** No slope.   **(d)** 0.

17. (a) $AB = \sqrt{40}$, $BC = \sqrt{160}$, $AC = \sqrt{200}$. Since $AC^2 = AB^2 + BC^2$, $\triangle ABC$ is a right triangle.
   (b) $DE = \sqrt{52}$, $EF = \sqrt{32}$, $DF = \sqrt{68}$. Since $DF^2 \neq DE^2 + EF^2$, $\triangle DEF$ is not a right triangle.
   (c) $GH = 8$, $HI = \sqrt{32} = GI$. Since $GH^2 = HI^2 + GI^2$, $\triangle GHI$ is a right triangle.

18. (a) Show that two legs are perpendicular by finding their slopes.
   (b) It is probably easier to use slopes.

19. Sides of $A'B'C'D'$ are $\frac{1}{3}$ the length of the corresponding sides of $ABCD$.

20. (a) $A'B' = 2AB$.
   (b) Area of $\triangle A'B'C'$ is four times the area of $\triangle ABC$.

21. (a) Right circular cylinder with radius 3 and height 6. Volume $= 54\pi$ cubic units.
   (b) Right circular cone with radius 4 and height 5. Volume $= \dfrac{80\pi}{3}$ cubic units.
   (c) Part of a right circular cone with height 4 and bases having radii 2 and 6. Volume $= \dfrac{208\pi}{3}$ cubic units.

22. (a)

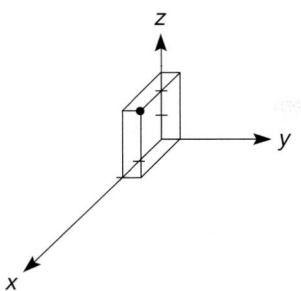

(b)

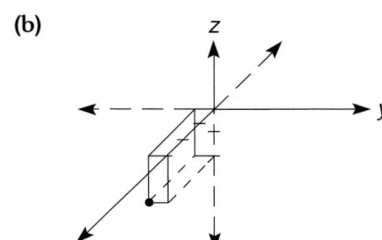

(c)

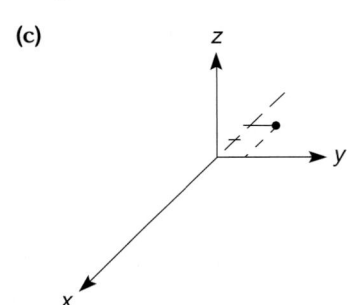

23. (a) 1.   **(b)** 3.   **(c)** 6.   **(d)** 7.   **(e)** 4.
(f) 5.

24. $2(-, +, +)$, $3(-, -, +)$, $4(+, -, +)$, $5(+, +, -)$,
$6(-, +, -)$, $7(-, -, -)$, $8(+, -, -)$.

25. (a) (a, y, z).   **(b)** $\sqrt{(y - b)^2 + (z - c)^2}$.
(c) $PQ = \sqrt{QR^2 + PR^2} =$
$\sqrt{(x - a)^2 + (y - b)^2 + (z - c)^2}$.

26. $PM + MQ = \sqrt{\left(\dfrac{c - a}{2}\right)^2 + \left(\dfrac{d - b}{2}\right)^2} +$

$\sqrt{\left(\dfrac{c - a}{2}\right)^2 + \left(\dfrac{d - b}{2}\right)^2} =$

$2\sqrt{\dfrac{(c - a)^2 + (d - b)^2}{4}} = \sqrt{(c - a)^2 + (d - b)^2}$ and

$PQ = \sqrt{(c - a)^2 + (d - b)^2}$; since $PM + MQ = PQ$,
P, M, and Q are collinear. Also,

$PM^2 = \left(\dfrac{a + c}{2} - a\right)^2 + \left(\dfrac{b + d}{2} - b\right)^2$

$= \left(\dfrac{a + c}{2} - \dfrac{2a}{2}\right)^2 + \left(\dfrac{b + d}{2} - \dfrac{2b}{2}\right)^2$

$= \left(\dfrac{c - a}{2}\right)^2 + \left(\dfrac{d - b}{2}\right)^2$

$MQ^2 = \left(c - \dfrac{a + c}{2}\right)^2 + \left(d - \dfrac{b + d}{2}\right)^2$

$= \left(\dfrac{c - a}{2}\right)^2 + \left(\dfrac{d - b}{2}\right)^2 = PM^2.$

Hence $PM = MQ$.

27. Assume that (x, y) does not lie on line l. The slope from
(x, y) to the point $(0, b)$ is $(y - b)/(x - 0)$. Since (x, y)
satisfies the equation $y = mx + b$, $(y - b)/x = m$.
Thus there are two lines through $(0, b)$ with a slope
equal to m [the line l and the line through (x, y)]. This
contradicts a property of points and lines (Chapter 13).
Therefore, the assumption is false and (x, y) must lie
on line l.

28. Suppose the lines intersect at P. Let Q be a point on
the first line, and R be on the second line such that
$Q \neq P \neq R$. Then the slope of $\overline{PQ}$ = slope of $\overline{PR}$ so
that P, Q, and R are collinear. But then the lines coin-
cide, a contradiction. Hence the lines are parallel.

SECTION 15.2—PART A

1. (a) $5 = 7(1) - 2 = 5$.
(b) $9 = -\frac{2}{3}(-6) + 5 = 4 + 5 = 9$.
(c) $-2(7.5) = 6(-3) + 3$, $-15 = -18 + 3 = -15$.
(d) $3(6) = 4(4) + 2$, $18 = 16 + 2 = 18$.
2. (a) $y = 3x + 6$; 3; 6.   **(b)** $y = \frac{3}{4}x$; $\frac{3}{4}$; 0.
(c) $y = \frac{1}{4}$; 0; $\frac{1}{4}$.   **(d)** $y = \frac{3}{4}x - 3$; $\frac{3}{4}$; -3.
3. (a) $y = 3x + 7$.   **(b)** $y = -x - 3$.
(c) $y = \frac{2}{3}x + 5$.   **(d)** $y = -3x - \frac{1}{4}$.
4. (a) $y = \frac{1}{6}x + 2$.   **(b)** $y = -2x$.
(c) $y = -\frac{1}{2}x - \frac{1}{2}$.   **(d)** $y = 7$.
5. (a) Any point of form $(x, 3)$ for any x.
(b) Any point of form $(-2, y)$ for any y.
6. (a) $x = 1$.   **(b)** $x = -5$.   **(c)** $y = 6$.
(d) $y = -3$.
7. (a) $y = 2x - 11$.   **(b)** $y = -x - 1$.
(c) $y = -\frac{3}{5}x - \frac{19}{5}$.   **(d)** $y = -\frac{3}{2}x - \frac{3}{2}$.
8. 1. $y = \frac{4}{3}x + 1$.   2. 1.   3. $\frac{4}{3}$.

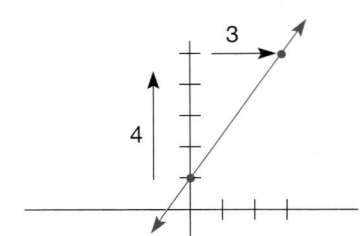

9. (a) 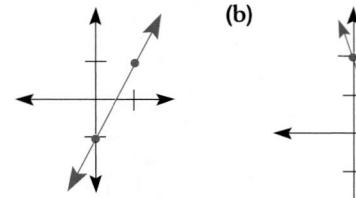 **(b)**

(c) 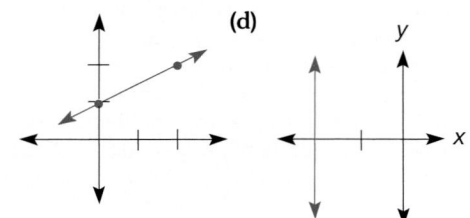 **(d)**

(e) 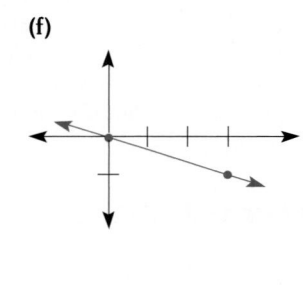 **(f)**

10. (a) Up.   **(b)** Up.   **(c)** Vertical.   **(d)** Up.
(e) Horizontal.   **(f)** Down.

11. (b) They all pass through $(0, 3)$.
(c) A family of lines passing through $(0, d)$.

12. $y = 5x$, $y = -\frac{3}{4}x$, $y = \frac{2}{5}x + \frac{23}{5}$.

13. Point D is $(6, 3)$; equation of median is $y = -\frac{4}{3}x + 11$.

14. $y = 2x - 1$.

15. (a) $(2, 5)$.   **(b)** No solution.   **(c)** $(-3, 1)$.

(d) Infinitely many solutions of the form $(x, \frac{2}{3}x + 3)$.

16. 1. $y = -2x + 3$.   2. $x - 2(-2x + 3) = 5$.
3. $x = \frac{11}{5}$.   4. $y = -\frac{7}{5}$.

17. (a) $(\frac{8}{5}, -\frac{1}{5})$.   **(b)** $(-\frac{1}{3}, -\frac{20}{3})$.   **(c)** $(2, 0)$.
(d) $(\frac{89}{33}, \frac{52}{33})$.

18. (a) Parallel, hence no solution.
(b) $3x - 5 = 3x + 2$.
(c) $-5 = 2$.
(d) No.
(e) There will be no solution; this agrees with the conclusion of part (a).

19. (a) Same line, hence infinite number of solutions.
(b) $2x - (2x - 6) = 6$.
(c) $6 = 6$.
(d) It is a true equation, so any value of x will satisfy.
(e) Any x value may be picked with its corresponding
y value, so there are infinitely many solutions; this
agrees with part (a).

20. 1. $5x = 10$.   2. $x = 2$.   3. $y = 3$.

21. (a) $6x + 2y = 7$; no.
(b) Yes, result is $11y = -11$.   **(c)** $(\frac{3}{2}, -1)$.

22. (a) $(-3, -16)$.   **(b)** $(-4, 0)$.   **(c)** $(0, -4)$.
(d) $(\frac{157}{44}, -\frac{15}{44})$.

23. (a) No solution.   **(b)** Infinitely many.
(c) Unique solution.   **(d)** Unique solution.
(e) No solution.   **(f)** Infinitely many.

24. Among the infinitely many solutions are $(0,7)$, $(1, 6)$,
$(2, 5)$, $(3, 4)$, $(4, 3)$.

25. (a) $3^2 + 4^2 = 9 + 16 = 25$.
(b) $(-3)^2 + 5^2 = 9 + 25 = 34$.
(c) $(-3 + 1)^2 + (7 - 2)^2 = 4 + 25 = 29$.
(d) $(\sqrt{5})^2 + (-3 + 5)^2 = 5 + 4 = 9$.

26. (a) $(3, 2)$; $r = 5$.   **(b)** $(-1, 3)$; $r = 7$.
(c) $(-7, -2)$; $r = 6$.   **(d)** $(0, 5)$; $r = 2$.

27. (a) $x^2 + y^2 = 9$.
(b) $(x - 1)^2 + (y - 2)^2 = 16$.
(c) $(x + 2)^2 + (y - 3)^2 = 4$.
(d) $(x + 3)^2 + (y + 1)^2 = 10$.

28. (a) $(x - 3)^2 + (y + 4)^2 = 5$.
(b) $(x + 2)^2 + (y - 5)^2 = 68$.

29. (a) $(x + 5)^2 + (y - 12)^2 = 169$.
(b) $(x + 3)^2 + (y + 5)^2 = 34$.

30. (a) $(x - 1)^2 + (y + 1)^2 = 25$.
(b) $(x - 2)^2 + (y + 2)^2 = 17$.

31. $(x + 2)^2 + (y - 5)^2 = 10$.

32. (a) 1.   **(b)** 2.   **(c)** 3.   **(d)** 3.   **(e)** 4.
(f) y-axis.

33. (a) $(3, 30°)$, $(3, 90°)$, $(3, 120°)$, $(3, 210°)$, $(3, 270°)$,
$(3, 300°)$.
(b) Circle with center at origin, radius of 3.
(c) Circle centered at the origin with radius of 5.

34. AP: $x^2 + y^2 = 9$ ①

  BP: $(a - x)^2 + y^2 = 16$ ②

  CP: $(a - x^2) + (b - y)^2 = 25$ ③

  DP: Want to find $x^2 + (b - y)^2 = DP^2$

    ③ − ② $(b - y)^2 - y^2 = 9$

    +   ① $\underline{x^2 + y^2 = 9}$

      $(b - y)^2 + x^2 = 18$, so $DP = \sqrt{18}$.

35. (a) $175, $225, $287.50, $350, 2.5n + 100.
(b) $y = 2.5x + 100$.
(c) 2.5; cost per person.
(d) 100; the fixed costs.

36. (a) $ae = bd$ and $ce = bf$.
(b) $ae = bd$ and $ce \neq bf$.
(c) $ae \neq bd$.

SECTION 15.3—PART A

1. (a) $(3, 5)$, $(-3, 5)$, or $(3, -5)$.
(b) $(1, -2)$, $(-5, -2)$, or $(9, 8)$.
2. (a) $(-2, 4)$.   **(b)** $(-1, 3)$.
3. (a) $C(a, a)$, $D(0, a)$.   **(b)** $G(a, b)$.
4. (a) $T(0, 0)$, $U(5, 0)$, $V(5, 5)$, $W(0, 5)$.
(b) $T(0, 0)$, $U(S, 0)$, $V(S, S)$, $W(0, S)$.
5. (a) $Q(0, 0)$, $R(6, 0)$, $S(0, 4)$.
(b) $Q(0, 0)$, $R(a, 0)$, $S(0, b)$.

6. Slope of $\overline{RS} = \dfrac{-2 - 0}{5 - 3} = -1$; slope of $\overline{TU} = \dfrac{-1 + 3}{-4 + 2} = -1$; $\overline{RS} \parallel \overline{TU}$; slope of $\overline{ST} = \dfrac{0 + 1}{3 + 4} = \dfrac{1}{7}$; slope of $\overline{RU} = \dfrac{-2 + 3}{5 + 2} = \dfrac{1}{7}$; $\overline{ST} \parallel \overline{RU}$. Since both pairs of opposite sides are parallel, $RSTU$ is a parallelogram.

7. Slope of $\overline{AB} = -\dfrac{3}{2}$ and slope of $\overline{CD} = -\dfrac{3}{2}$, so $\overline{AB} \parallel \overline{CD}$. Slope of $\overline{BC} = \dfrac{2}{3}$ and slope of $\overline{AD} = \dfrac{2}{3}$, so $\overline{BC} \parallel \overline{AD}$. Since $(-\dfrac{3}{2})(\dfrac{2}{3}) = -1$, $\overline{AB} \perp \overline{BC}$. Thus $ABCD$ is a parallelogram (opposite sides parallel) with a right angle, and thus a rectangle.

8. $AC = \sqrt{a^2 + b^2}$; $BD = \sqrt{(0 - a)^2 + (b - 0)^2} = \sqrt{a^2 + b^2}$.

9. (a) $y = \dfrac{2}{7}x$.   **(b)** $y = -\dfrac{2}{5}x + \dfrac{48}{5}$.
(c) $y = 2x - 24$.   **(d)** $(14, 4)$; yes.
(e) The medians are concurrent (meet at a single point).

10. (a) $3\sqrt{53}$; $2\sqrt{53}$; $\dfrac{2}{3}$.   **(b)** $3\sqrt{29}$; $2\sqrt{29}$; $\dfrac{2}{3}$.
(c) $6\sqrt{5}$; $4\sqrt{5}$; $\dfrac{2}{3}$.
(d) On any median, $\dfrac{2}{3}$ of the distance from the vertex point.

11. (a) If $AB = BC$, then $\sqrt{a^2 + b^2} = \sqrt{(a - c)^2 + b^2}$ or $a^2 = (a - c)^2$, $a^2 = a^2 - 2ac + c^2$, $c^2 = 2ac$, and then $c = 2a$.
(b) The midpoint of $\overline{AC}$ has coordinates $(a, 0)$ and thus the median from B is vertical and thereby perpendicular to horizontal $\overline{AC}$.

12. (a) $y = \dfrac{1}{2}x$.   **(b)** $x = 8$.   **(c)** $y = -\dfrac{4}{3}x + \dfrac{44}{3}$.
(d) $(8, 4)$, yes, orthocenter.

13. The midpoint of $\overline{AC}$ is $\left(\dfrac{a + b}{2}, \dfrac{c}{2}\right)$. The midpoint of $\overline{BD}$ is $\left(\dfrac{b + a}{2}, \dfrac{c}{2}\right)$. The diagonals meet at the midpoint of each, thus bisecting each other.

14. $M = \left(\dfrac{a}{2}, \dfrac{b}{2}\right)$ and $N = \left(\dfrac{a + c}{2}, \dfrac{b}{2}\right)$.
(a) The slope of $\overline{MN} = 0$, as does the slope of $\overline{AC}$, so $\overline{MN} \parallel \overline{AC}$.
(b) $MN = \sqrt{\left(\dfrac{a}{2} - \dfrac{a + c}{2}\right)^2 + \left(\dfrac{b}{2} - \dfrac{b}{2}\right)^2} = \sqrt{\left(-\dfrac{c}{2}\right)^2} = \dfrac{c}{2}$ and $AC = \sqrt{c^2} = c$, so $MN = \dfrac{1}{2}AC$.

15. Slope of $\overline{MN}$ = slope of $\overline{OP} = \dfrac{c}{b}$, so $\overline{MN} \parallel \overline{OP}$. Slope of $\overline{MP}$ = slope of $\overline{ON} = \dfrac{e}{d - a}$, so $\overline{MP} \parallel \overline{ON}$. Therefore $DEFG$ is a parallelogram.

16. Slope of $\overline{AC} = \dfrac{a - 0}{a - 0} = 1$; slope of $\overline{BD} = \dfrac{a - 0}{0 - a} = -1$; since $1(-1) = -1$, $\overline{AC} \perp \overline{BC}$.

17. $AN = \sqrt{\left(-a - \dfrac{a}{2}\right)^2 + \left(-\dfrac{b}{2}\right)^2} = \sqrt{\left(\dfrac{3a}{2}\right)^2 + \left(\dfrac{b}{2}\right)^2}$;
$BM = \sqrt{\left(a + \dfrac{a}{2}\right)^2 + \left(-\dfrac{b}{2}\right)^2} = \sqrt{\left(\dfrac{3a}{2}\right)^2 + \left(\dfrac{b}{2}\right)^2}$.

18. (a) The slope of $\overline{QR}$ is $\dfrac{b}{a - c}$, so the slope of l (perpendicular to $\overline{QR}$) is $-\left(\dfrac{a - c}{b}\right)$ or $\dfrac{c - a}{b}$.
(b) Since the point has an x-coordinate of a, it is on line m. Substituting into $y = \dfrac{c - a}{b}x$ yields $\dfrac{(c - a)a}{b} = \left(\dfrac{c - a}{b}\right)a$, which is satisfied, so the point lies on line l also.
(c) The slope of $\overline{PQ}$ is $\dfrac{b}{a}$, so the slope of n (perpendicular to $\overline{PQ}$) is $\dfrac{-a}{b}$.

19. Impossible. The length of the horizontal side is $2a$. The height is b, a whole number. Also, $\sqrt{a^2 + b^2} = 2a$, so $a^2 + b^2 = 4a^2$, $b^2 = 3a^2$, $\dfrac{b}{a} = \sqrt{3}$, which is irrational.

20. 7 and 11.

21. 5 tricycles and 2 bicycles.

22. Mike, $7000; Joan, $4000.

23. 75 dimes and 35 quarters.

24. (a) 35.   (b) 18.   (c) $\frac{18}{35}$.

25. (a) 30.
    (b) 30 [from part (a)] + 18 = 48.
    (c) 55 + 50 = 105.

26. Yes, a 5×12 mat or a 6×8 mat.

ADDITIONAL PROBLEMS WHERE THE STRATEGY "USE COORDINATES" IS USEFUL

1. One of the diagonals of the kite is on the y-axis and the other is on the x-axis. Thus they are perpendicular.

2. On a coordinate map, starting at $(0, 0)$, where north is up, he goes to $(0, 4)$, then to $(-3, 4)$, then to $(-3, 2)$. Thus his distance from base camp is $\sqrt{3^2 + 2^2} = \sqrt{13}$ km.

3. Place the figure on a coordinate system with A at the origin, $B = (0, 2m)$, and $C = (2m, 0)$. Then $E = (m, -m)$ and $D = (-m, m)$. The slope of $\overline{BC} = -1$, as does the slope of $\overline{DE}$. Thus they are parallel.

CHAPTER 15 TEST

1. (a) T.   (b) F.   (c) T.   (d) F.   (e) F.
    (f) T.   (g) T.   (h) F.

2. Length is $\sqrt{41}$; midpoint is $(3, 4.5)$; slope is $\frac{5}{4}$.

3. (a) $x = -1$.   (b) $y = 7$.   (c) $y = 3x + 10$.
    (d) $2y - 3x = 17$.

4. $(x + 3)^2 + (y - 4)^2 = 5^2$, or $x^2 + 6x + y^2 - 8y = 0$.

5. (a) 0.   (b) 1.   (c) Infinitely many.   (d) 1.

6. 0, 1, or 2 since a circle and a line may meet in 0, 1, or 2 points.

7. The first pair of lines is parallel, the last pair is parallel, but no two of the lines are perpendicular.

8. $ABCD$ is a square since it is a parallelogram whose diagonals are perpendicular and congruent (verify).

9. (a) The slopes of $\overline{DE}$ and $\overline{AC}$ are both zero.
    (b) $\dfrac{a + 2b}{3} - \dfrac{2b}{3} = \dfrac{a}{3}$. Therefore, $DE = \frac{1}{3}AC$. In $\triangle ABC$, if $DB = \frac{1}{3}AB$ and $EB = \frac{1}{3}CB$, then $DE = \frac{1}{3}AC$ and $\overline{DE} \parallel \overline{AC}$.

SECTION 16.1—PART A

1. (a) 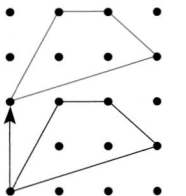   (b)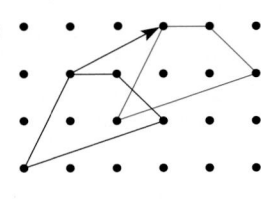

    (c)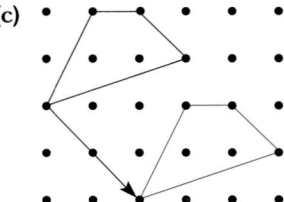

2.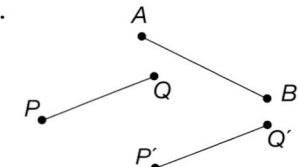

3. (a) Any directed line segment that goes right 4, up 2.
    (b)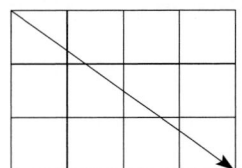
    (c) Down 4, right 5.

4. (a) $A'(0, 5)$, $B'(5, 6)$.   (b) $A'(-5, 1)$, $B'(0, 2)$.
    (c) $A'(-3, 0)$, $B'(2, 1)$.   (d) $A'(1, -1)$, $B'(6, 0)$.

5. Construct a line through P parallel to $\overline{AB}$. Then with a compass, mark off $\overline{PP'}$ having the length of $\overline{AB}$. NOTE: P' should be to the right and above B.

6. Follow the procedure of Problem 6 to find the image of A and the image of B.

7. (a) $-80°$.   (b) $120°$.   (c) $180°$.   (d) $-20°$.

8.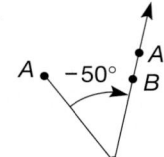

9. (a)

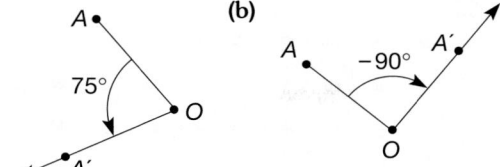

(b)

(c)

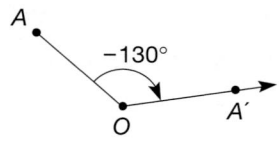

(d)

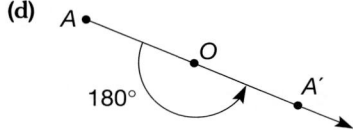

10. (a)

(b)

(c)

11. (a)   **(b)**

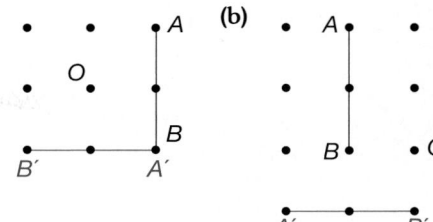

(c)

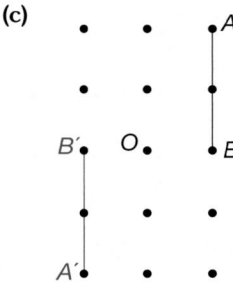

12. $(-1, 4)$.

13. (a) $(-3, 2)$.   **(b)** $(-3, -1)$.   **(c)** $(4, -1)$.
(d) $(2, -4)$.   **(e)** $(4, 2)$.   **(f)** $(-y, x)$.

14. $A'(1, -3)$; $B'(0, -4)$; $C'(-3, -3)$; $D'(-1, -1)$.

15. (a) $(-3, 1)$.   **(b)** $(6, 3)$.   **(c)** $(4, -2)$.
(d) $(-x, -y)$.

16. (a)

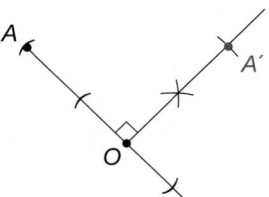

(b)

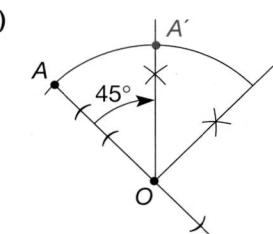

(c)

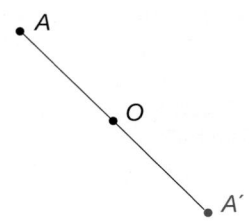

17.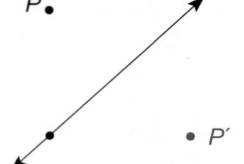

25. (a)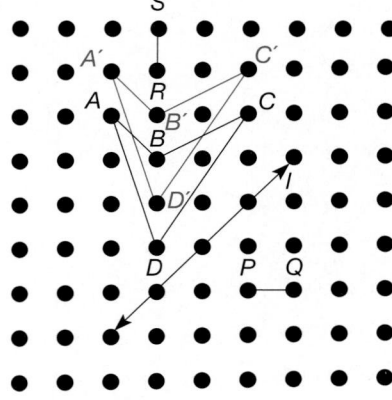

18. (a) **(b)**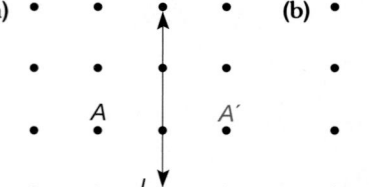

(c)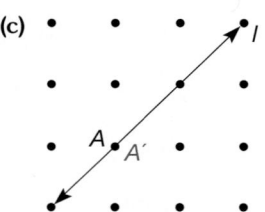

19. (b) $(1, -2)$, $(3, -5)$, $(6, -1)$.   **(c)** $(a, -b)$.

(b)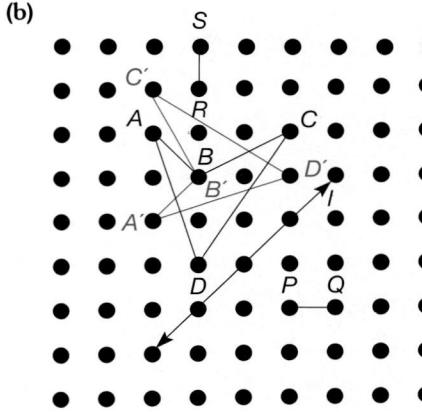

20. Construct a line through A perpendicular to l (to point P on l), extend beyond l, and mark off A' such that $PA' = AP$.

21. (a), (b)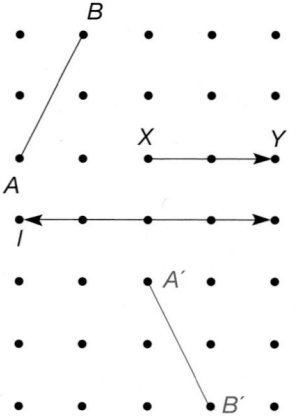

(c) They are interchangeable.

22. (b) $(3, -1)$, $(5, -3)$, $(8, 2)$.   **(c)** $(a + 5, -b)$.

23. (b) $(1, 1)$, $(3, 0)$, $(-2, -5)$.   **(c)** $(-a, b - 2)$.

24. (a) Same; A to B to C is clockwise in each case.
(b) Opposite.   **(c)** Opposite.

(c)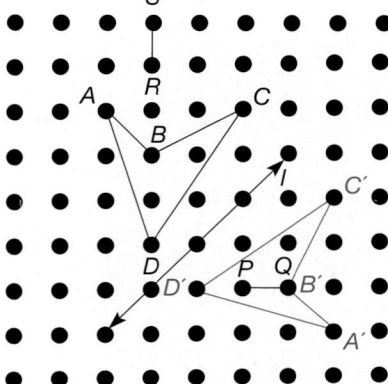

(d)

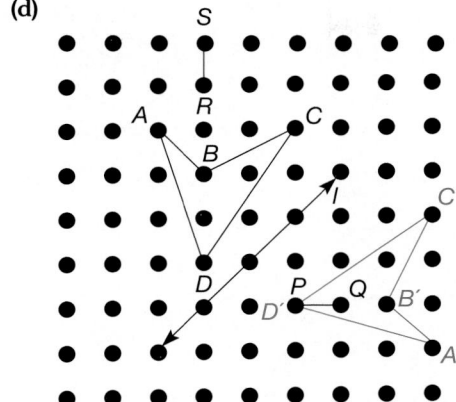

26.

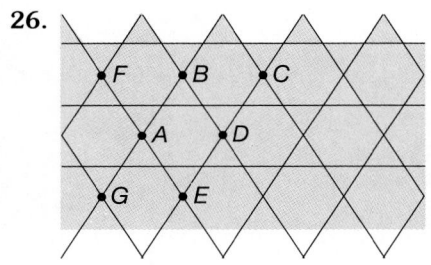

27.

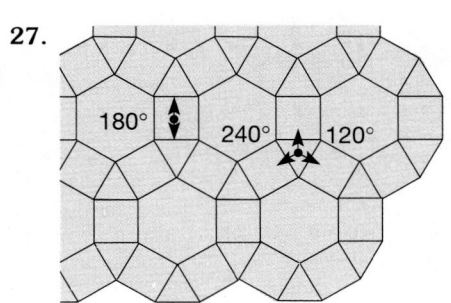

28.

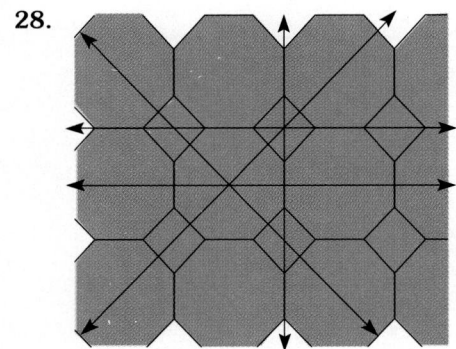

29. (a)

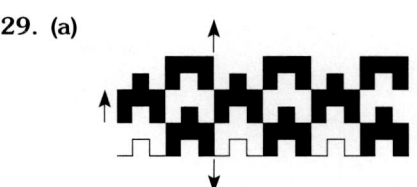

(b) None.

30. (a)

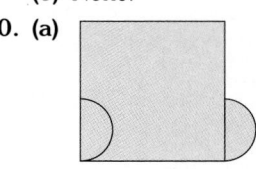

(b)

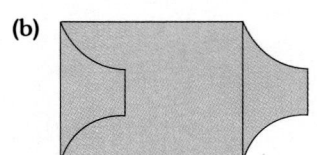

(c)

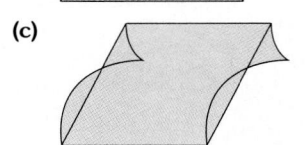

(d)

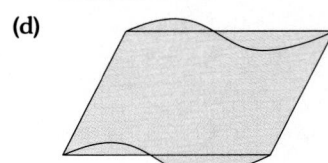

31. (a)

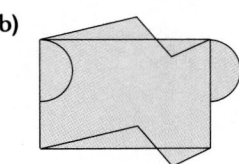

(b)

(c)

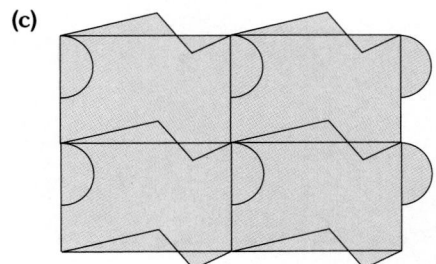

32. (a)

(b)

(c)

33. (a)

(b)

34. (a)

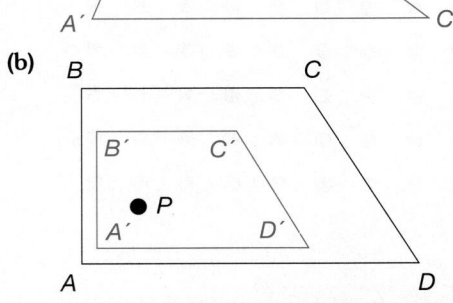

(b)

35. (a), (b). All such lines must contain the first point to the left of Y.

36. (a)

(b) Yes.   **(c)** They are parallel.

37. (a) Yes.   **(b)** Yes.

38. (a) $T_{AA'}$.

(b) $R_{0, -90}$ is one possibility.

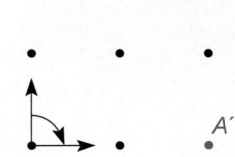

(c) M_l.

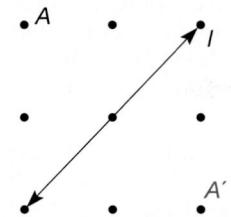

(d) T_{XY} followed by M_l is one possibility.

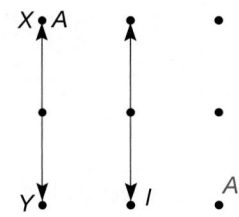

39. (a) Not possible.
(b)

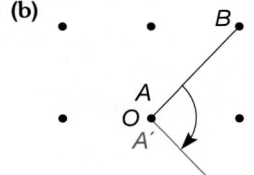

(c)

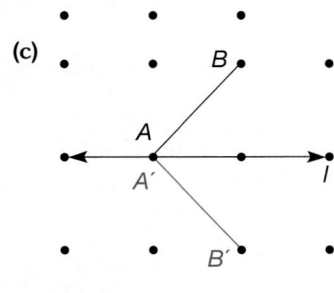

(d) Not possible.

40. (a) $y = 1$.   **(b)** $y = 4$.   **(c)** $y = -2$.

41. (b) $(0, 1)$; $(-1, 4)$; $(-4, 2)$.   **(c)** $(2 - x, y)$.

SECTION 16.2—PART A

1. (a) $(1, 3)$; $(2, 1)$.   **(b)** $(-1, 4)$; $(0, 2)$.
(c) $AB = \sqrt{(1-2)^2 + (3-1)^2} = \sqrt{5}$; $A'B' = \sqrt{(-1-0)^2 + (4-2)^2} = \sqrt{5}$.

2. (a) Yes, both have slope $\frac{q}{p}$.
(b) Yes, both have length $\sqrt{p^2 + q^2}$.
(c) Yes, by definition.

3. (a) $\overline{OX} \perp \overline{OY}$ since (slope of $\overline{OX}$)(slope of $\overline{OY}$) = $\left(\frac{y}{x}\right) \cdot \left(\frac{x}{-y}\right) = -1$.
(b) $OX = \sqrt{x^2 + y^2}$, $OY = \sqrt{(-y)^2 + x^2} = \sqrt{y^2 + x^2}$.
(c) Yes, by definition.

4. $A' = (-2, 5)$, $B' = (4, 3)$; $AB = \sqrt{2^2 + 6^2} = 2\sqrt{10}$ and $A'B' = \sqrt{(-6)^2 + 2^2} = 2\sqrt{10}$, so $AB = A'B'$.

5. (a) $(1, 2)$ and $(2, 0)$.   **(b)** $(-1, 2)$ and $(-2, 0)$.
(c) $AB = \sqrt{(1-2)^2 + (2-0)^2} = \sqrt{5}$; $A'B' = \sqrt{(-1+2)^2 + (2-0)^2} = \sqrt{5}$.

6. (a) $(x, -y)$.
(b) $AB = \sqrt{(a-c)^2 + (b-d)^2}$; $A' = (a, -b)$, $B' = (c, -d)$, and $A'B' = \sqrt{(a-c)^2 + (-b+d)^2} = \sqrt{(a-c)^2 + (b-d)^2}$.

7. (a) The midpoint of $\overline{XY} = \left(\frac{x+y}{2}, \frac{y+x}{2}\right)$. Since its $x-$ and $y-$ coordinates are equal, it lies on line l.
(b) The slope of $\overline{XY} = \frac{x-y}{y-x} = -1$ and the slope of line l is 1. Since $(-1)(1) = -1$, $\overline{XY} \perp l$.
(c) Yes, line l is the perpendicular bisector of $\overline{XY}$.

8. (a) $(2, 1)$; $(-2, 3)$.   **(b)** $(4, -1)$; $(0, -3)$.
(c) $AB = \sqrt{(2+2)^2 + (1-3)^2} = 2\sqrt{5}$; $A'B' = \sqrt{(4-0)^2 + (-1+3)^2} = 2\sqrt{5}$.

9. (a) X, O, and Y are collinear since slope of $\overline{OX} =$ slope of $\overline{OY} = \frac{y}{x}$ and share point O. Therefore, $\angle XOY$ is a straight angle.
(b) $OX = OY = \sqrt{x^2 + y^2}$.
(c) The half-turn $R_{O, 180°}$.

10. (a) Yes.   **(b)** No.

11. (a) Reflection.   **(b)** Translation.
(c) Glide reflection.

12. (a) Translation.   **(b)** Reflection.
(c) Glide reflection.   **(d)** Rotation.

13. (a)

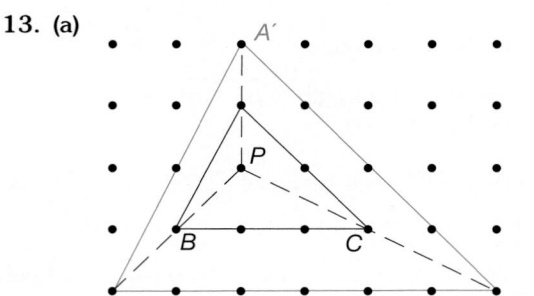

(b) $\sqrt{5}$, $2\sqrt{5}$; 2.   **(c)** 3, 6; 2.
(d) $2\sqrt{2}$, $4\sqrt{2}$; 2.   **(e)** They are parallel.

14. (a)

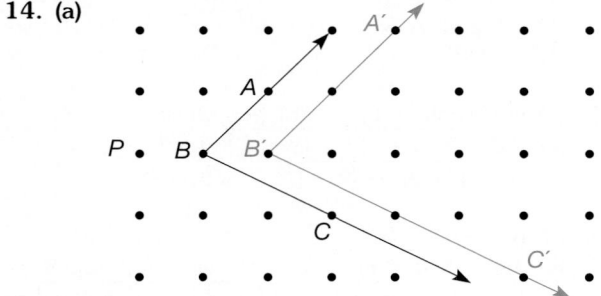

(a) They are equal.

15. No; the lines $\overleftrightarrow{SS'}$, $\overleftrightarrow{RR'}$, and $\overleftrightarrow{TT'}$ do not meet at a common point. (If it were a size transformation, they would meet at the center). Also, $RS/R'S' = 2$ but $RT/R'T' = \frac{5}{3} \neq 2$, so the ratios of sides are not equal.

16. (a) A size transformation of scale factor $\frac{3}{2}$ followed by a rotation.
(b) A size transformation of scale factor $\frac{1}{3}$ followed by a glide reflection.

17. (a) Since $\overrightarrow{PQ}$, $\overrightarrow{BB'}$, $\overrightarrow{XX'}$, and $\overrightarrow{AA'}$ are equivalent directed line segments by the definition of T_{PQ}, $\overline{PQ} \parallel \overline{BB'} \parallel \overline{XX'} \parallel \overline{AA'}$ and $\overline{PQ} \cong \overline{BR'} \cong \overline{XX'} \cong \overline{AA'}$. In each case, one pair of opposite sides are congruent and parallel, so $BB'X'X$ and $BB'A'A$ are both parallelograms.
(b) $\overleftrightarrow{B'X'} \parallel \overleftrightarrow{BA}$ and $\overleftrightarrow{B'A'} \parallel \overleftrightarrow{BA}$ since they contain opposite sides of parallelograms. However, since through B' there can only be one line parallel to $\overleftrightarrow{BA}$, $\overleftrightarrow{B'X'}$ and $\overleftrightarrow{B'A'}$ must be the same line. Therefore, A', X', and B' are collinear.

18. Since translations preserve distances, $PQ = P'Q'$, $QR = Q'R'$, and $RP = R'P'$. Thus $\triangle PQR \cong \triangle P'Q'R'$. Therefore, $\angle PQR \cong \angle P'Q'R'$, since they are corresponding parts of congruent triangles.

19. $p \parallel q$ implies that $\angle 1 \cong \angle 2$. Since rotations preserve angle measures, $\angle 1 \cong \angle 3$ and $\angle 2 \cong \angle 4$. Thus $\angle 3 \cong \angle 4$ and $p' \parallel q'$ by the corresponding angles property.

20. Since reflections preserve distances, $AB = A'B'$, $BC = B'C'$, and $AC = A'C'$. Since A, B, and C are collinear, $AB + BC = AC$. Therefore, $A'B' + B'C' = AB + BC = AC = A'C'$ and A', B', and C' are collinear.

21. $p \parallel q$ implies that $\angle 1 \cong \angle 2$. Since reflections preserve angle measures, $\angle 1 \cong \angle 1'$ and $\angle 2 \cong 2'$, where $\angle 1'$ and $\angle 2'$ are the images, respectively, of $\angle 1$ and $\angle 2$. Thus $\angle 2' \cong \angle 1'$ and $p' \parallel q'$ by the corresponding angles property.

22. Since isometries map segments to segments and preserve distances, $\overline{AB} \cong \overline{A'B'}$, $\overline{BC} \cong \overline{B'C'}$, and $\overline{CA} \cong \overline{C'A'}$. Thus, by the SSS congruence property, $\triangle ABC \cong \triangle A'B'C'$.

23. (a) One, just S_{PQ}.
(b) Infinitely many; the center C may be any point on the perpendicular bisector of $\overline{PQ}$ and $\angle PCG$ is the rotation angle.
(c) One; the reflection line is the perpendicular bisector of $\overline{PQ}$.
(d) Infinitely many; reflect P to S in any line through the midpoint of $\overline{PQ}$, then translate T_{SQ}.

24. (a) The point where $\overleftrightarrow{PP'}$ and $\overleftrightarrow{QQ'}$ intersect.
(b) Greater than 1.
(c) Where $\overleftrightarrow{PP'}$ and $\overleftrightarrow{QQ'}$ intersect, less than 1.

25. Construct line through Q' parallel to $\overline{QR}$. The intersection of that line and l is R'.

26. Construct line through P' parallel to $\overline{PR}$ and also the line through Q' parallel to $\overline{QR}$. These two lines will intersect at the point R'.

27. Let point R be the intersection of line l and segment $\overline{PP'}$, and let S be the intersection of l and $\overline{QQ'}$. Then $R' = R$ and $\triangle QRS \cong \triangle Q'RS$ as in case 2. Hence $RQ = RQ'$ and $\angle QRS \cong \angle Q'RS$. Thus $\angle PRQ \cong \angle P'RQ'$. We can see this by subtracting $m(\angle QRS)$ from 90°, which is the measure of $\angle PRS$, and subtracting $m(\angle Q'RS)$ from 90°, which is the measure of $\angle P'RS$. Thus $\triangle PRQ \cong \triangle P'RQ'$ by the SAS congruence property. Consequently, $\overline{PQ} \cong \overline{P'Q'}$, since these sides correspond in $\triangle PRQ$ and $\triangle P'RQ'$. Thus $PQ = P'Q'$, as desired.

SECTION 16.3—PART A

1. M_{AC}, M_{BD}, M_{EG}, M_{FH}.

2. (d), since $A \rightarrow A$, $B \rightarrow D$, $C \rightarrow C$, $D \rightarrow B$.

3. (a) M_{AD}, M_{BE}, M_{CF}.
(b) Any three of $R_{O,60°}$; $R_{O,120°}$; H_O; $R_{O,240°}$; $R_{O,300°}$; or $R_{O,360°}$.

4. M_{EG}, M_{FH}, H_P, $R_{P,360°}$.

5. Yes. Let E and F be the midpoints of sides $\overline{AB}$ and $\overline{CD}$. Then M_{EF} and $R_{A,360°}$ will work.

6. Use $R_{B,90°}$ to map $\triangle ABD$ to $\triangle FBC$. Use $R_{C,-90°}$ to map $\triangle ACE$ to $\triangle KCB$.

7. (a) $H_D(H_C(H_B(H_A(P)))) = P$.
   (b) $H_D(H_C(H_B(H_A(Q)))) = Q$.
   (c) This combination of four half-turns around the vertices of a parallelogram maps each point to itself.

8. (a)

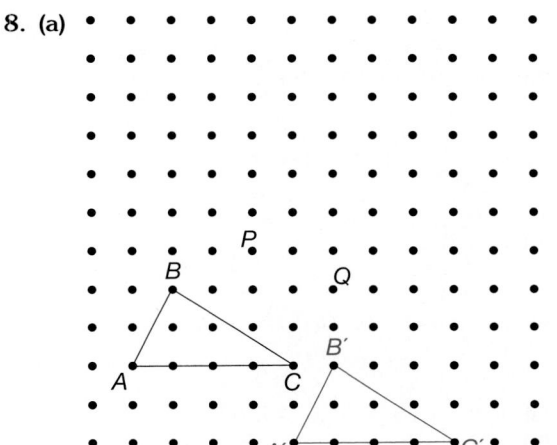

   (b) Translation from P toward Q, twice the distance PQ.
   (c) The combination of the half-turns, H_P followed by H_Q, is equivalent to the translation T_{PQ} applied twice.

9. (b) Yes; $R_{B,90°}$ followed by $S_{O,1/2}$ is a similarity transformation.

10. Impossible. Even though corresponding sides have the same length, corresponding diagonals do not. Yet, isometries preserve distance.

11. Let M be the midpoint of $\overline{AC}$. Hence $H_M(A) = C$, $H_M(C = A$. We know that $H_M(B)$ is on $\overleftrightarrow{CD}$, since $H_M(\overleftrightarrow{AB}) \parallel \overleftrightarrow{AB}$ and C is on $H_M(\overleftrightarrow{AB})$. Similarly, $H_M(B)$ is on $\overleftrightarrow{AD}$, so that $H_M(B)$ is on $\overleftrightarrow{CD} \cap \overleftrightarrow{AD}$. That is, $H_M(B) = D$. Hence $H_M(\triangle ABC) = \triangle CDA$ so that $\triangle ABC \cong \triangle CDA$.

12. (a) $H_M(\angle ADC) = \angle CBA$, so that $\angle ADC \cong \angle CBA$. Similarly, $\angle BAD \cong \angle DCB$.
   (b) $H_M(\overline{AB}) = \overline{DC}$, so $\overline{AB} \cong \overline{DC}$, and so on.

13. Let $l = \overleftrightarrow{BP}$. Then $M_l(A)$ is on $\overline{BC}$, but since $AB = BC$, we must have $M_l(A) = C$. Thus $M_l(\triangle ABP) = \triangle CBP$, so $\triangle ABP \cong \triangle CBP$. Hence $\angle BPA \cong \angle BPC$, but since these angles are supplementary, each is a right angle. Since $AR = CR$, $\overleftrightarrow{BR}$ is the perpendicular bisector of $\overline{AC}$.

14. (a) From Problem 13, points A and C are on the perpendicular bisector of $\overline{BD}$, so $\overline{AC} \perp \overline{BD}$.
   (b) Since $\overline{AC}$ is the perpendicular bisector of $\overline{BD}$, $M_{AC}(B) = D$, $M_{AC}(D) = B$, $M_{AC}(A) = A$, and $M_{AC}(C) = C$. Hence $M_{AC}(ABCD) = (ADCB)$, so the kite has reflection symmetry.

15. Let $l = \overleftrightarrow{AP}$. Then $M_l(B)$ is on $\overrightarrow{AC}$ since $\angle BAP \cong \angle CAP$. But since $AB = AC$, we must have $M_l(B) = C$. Thus $M_l(C) = B$, so that $M_l(\triangle ABP) = \triangle ACP$. Hence $\angle ABP \cong \angle ACP$.

16. (a) $AA' = 2x$ and $A'A'' = 2y$, so that $AA'' = 2(x + y)$. Also, A, A', and A'' are collinear since $\overline{AA'} \perp r$, $r \parallel s$, and $\overline{A'A''} \perp s$. Hence M_r followed by M_s is equivalent to the translation $T_{AA''}$. Since A was arbitrary, M_r followed by M_s is $T_{AA''}$.
   (b) The direction of the translation is perpendicular to r and s, from r toward s, and the distance is twice the distance between r and s.

17. (a) (Any two intersecting rails can be used.) Let $B' = M_l(B)$, and $B'' = M_m(B')$. Let $P = \overleftrightarrow{AB''} \cap l$. Shoot ball A toward point P.
   (b) Let $Q = \overline{PB'} \cap l$. Then use an argument like in Example 16.14.

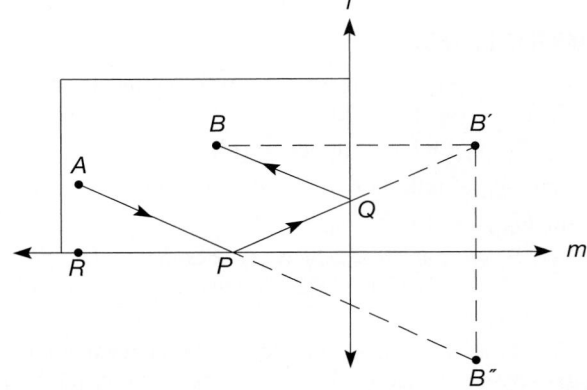

18. Consider $M_{A,b/a}$. This size transformation will map $ABCD$ to a square $A'B'C'D'$ congruent to $EFGH$. Then, from Section 16.2, we know that there is an isometry J that maps $A'B'C'D'$ to $EFGH$. Hence the combination of $S_{A,b/a}$ and J is the desired similarity transformation.

19. To show that X is the midpoint of edge $\overline{PQ}$, suppose that X is closer to P. Turn the cube upside down to see that Y, the image of X, must be closer to S. Look at the original cube in a mirror parallel to the face containing R, S, and C. Then we see the same configuration with point Y playing the role of X and S playing the role of Q. Hence X is closer to Q! This is impossible. Thus X and Y are midpoints. The equilateral hexagon $ABYCDX$ has six rotation symmetries, so it must be regular.

ADDITIONAL PROBLEMS WHERE THE STRATEGY "USE SYMMETRY" IS USEFUL

1. Place any two squares on a 4 × 4 square grid. Reflect those two squares across a diagonal and across a vertical line through the center as shown. If two more squares are produced in either of these cases, that pattern will have reflective symmetry with four dark squares.

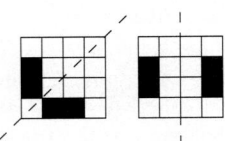

2. There are three digits that read the same upside down: 0, 1, and 8. Since house numbers do not begin with zero, there are 2 · 3 · 3 = 18 different such house numbers.

3. Pascal's triangle has reflective symmetry along a vertical line through its middle. In the 41st row, the 1st and 41st numbers are equal, as are the 2nd and 40th, the 3rd and 39th, and the 4th and 38th. Thus the 38th number is 101,270.

CHAPTER 16 TEST

1. **(a)** T.   **(b)** F.   **(c)** T.   **(d)** T.   **(e)** T.
   (f) F.   **(g)** T.   **(h)** T.

2. **(a)** D.   **(b)** E.   **(c)** E.   **(d)** D.

3. Translation, reflection, and glide reflection.

4. **(a)** M_{AB}.   **(b)** $R_{F,-90}$.   **(c)** S_{CD}.

5. Let P be the intersection of $\overline{EG}$ and $\overline{FH}$. Then $R_{P,45} M_{P,\sqrt{2}}(EFGH) = ABCD$; thus $ABCD$ is similar to $EFGH$.

6. The result of two glide reflections yields an isometry that preserves orientation. Therefore, the isometry must be a translation or a rotation.

7. B.

8. $AB = \frac{8}{3}$; $AC = \frac{10}{3}$; $CE = 5$.

9. $\triangle AMC \cong \triangle BMC$ by SSS. Therefore, $\angle AMC \cong \angle BMC$, or $m(\angle AMC) = m(\angle BMC) = 90°$. Thus, if $M_{CM}(A) = B$ and $M_{CM}(C) = C$, then $M_{CM}(\triangle ABC) = \triangle BAC$. This means that $\overleftrightarrow{CM}$ is a symmetry line for $\triangle ABC$.

SECTION C.1

1. **(a)** 23.   **(b)** 24.   **(c)** 4.   **(d)** 2.
   (e) 12.   **(f)** 9.   **(g)** 225.   **(h)** 75.   **(i)** 43.

2. **(a)** 4.   **(b)** $A/B = 3$.

3. **(a)** 5.   **(b)** 6.   **(c)** 300.   **(d)** 50.

4. **(a)** 0.   **(b)** 3.   **(c)** 2.   **(d)** −992.

5. **(a)** NEW   **(b)** RUN   **(c)** LIST   **(d)** 40

6. **(a)** $0 \le x < 1$.   **(b)** $0 \le x < 2$.   **(c)** 0 or 1.
   (d) 1 or 2.

7. **(a)** LET N=INT(91*RND(1))+10
   (b) LET N=INT(201*RND(1))+50

8. **(a)** 11.   **(b)** 4.   **(c)** 2.   **(d)** 3.   **(e)** 3.

9. **(a)**
```
FOR X=1 TO 100
PRINT X
NEXT X
```
   (b)
```
FOR X=2 TO 60 STEP 2
PRINT X
NEXT X
```
   (c)
```
FOR X=1 TO 25 STEP 2
PRINT X
NEXT X
```
   (d)
```
FOR X=2 TO 62 STEP 3
PRINT X
NEXT X
```
   (e)
```
FOR X=100 TO 10 STEP −10
PRINT X
NEXT X
```

10. **(a)** 1, 4, 9, 16, 25, 36, 49, 64, 81, 100.
    (b) 1, 1, 1, 2, 2.   **(c)** 1, 3, 5, 7, 9.
    (d) 4, 16, 36, 64, 100.   **(e)** 12, 6, 4, 3, 2, 1.
    (f) 40, 120, 200, 280, 360.

11. Prints out 10 random whole numbers between 1 and 10.

12. **(a)** B IS TWICE A   **(b)** 3   **(c)** GOODBYE
         2   4

13. **(a)**
```
IF X>A THEN N=N+1
IF Y>A THEN N=N+1
IF Z>A THEN N=N+1
PRINT "ABOVE AVERAGE";N
```
    (b)
```
IF A>B THEN PRINT "FIRST LARGER"
PRINT "THE AVERAGE IS ";(A+B)/2
```

14. **(a)**
```
10   INPUT M
20   LET C=100
30   IF M<=100 THEN GOTO 70
40   LET D=M−100
50   PRINT "EXTRA MILEAGE";D
60   LET C=C+0.2*D
70   PRINT "COST IS ";C
80   END
```
    (b)
```
10   INPUT C
20   IF C<=100 THEN GOTO 60
30   LET M=0.3*C
40   PRINT "MARKUP IS ";M
50   LET C=C+M
60   PRINT "COST NOW IS ";C
70   END
```

15. (a)
```
10   INPUT X
20   IF X < 0 THEN GOTO 50
30   PRINT "NONNEGATIVE"
40   GOTO 60
50   PRINT "NEGATIVE"
60   END
```

(b)
```
10   INPUT N
20   X = 1
30   IF X∧3 > N THEN GOTO 60
40   X = X + 1
50   GOTO 30
60   PRINT X
70   END
```

(c)
```
10   INPUT X, Y
20   IF X>Y THEN GOTO 50
30   PRINT "NOT LARGER"
40   GOTO 60
50   PRINT "LARGER"
60   END
```

16. (a) `IF A = 0 THEN GOTO 70`
(b) `IF P = −999 THEN GOTO 150`

17.
```
100   PRINT "DO YOU WISH TO REPEAT THIS PRO-
      GRAM?"
110   PRINT "ENTER Y FOR YES, N FOR NO"
120   INPUT A$
130   IF A$="Y" THEN GOTO 20
140   PRINT "GOODBYE"
150   END
```

18. (a) `PRINT X∧2`   **(b)** `PRINT 7*(X−1)`
(c) 4   **(d)** 5, 9, 2

19. The special numbers are the ones where the first and last digits are equal—the palindromes.

SECTION C.2

1. (a) `FD 50`   **(b)** `RT 90`   **(c)** `DRAW`   **(d)** `PU`
(e) `SETX 20`   **(f)** `SETXY 10 20`
(g) `FD :N`   **(h)** `MAKE "X 10`

2. Stair steps.

3.
```
FD 100
RT 108
FD 100
BK 100
RT 36
FD 100
BK 50
```

4.
```
RT 90
FD 100
BK 50
LT 90
FD 50
BK 100
```

5. (a) `REPEAT 2[FD 50 RT 90 FD 80 RT 90]`
(b)
```
RT 30
REPEAT 3[FD 40 RT 120]
LT 30
```
(c)
```
FD 50
RT 135
FD 50*SQRT(2)
RT 135
FD 50
```
(d)
```
RT 18
REPEAT 5[FD 100 RT 144]
LT 18
```

6. For example,
```
RT 40
FD 50
BK 100
FD 50
PU
LT 40
FD 60
PD
RT 40
FD 50
BK 100
```

7. "Curve" resembling a quarter of a circle.

8. `REPEAT 360[FD 1 RT 1]`

9. (a) Let `:ANGLE = 90` and `:SIDE1 = :SIDE2`
(b) Let `:SIDE1 = :SIDE2`
(c) Parallelogram, rectangle, rhombus, square.

10. `RT 135    FD 100*SQRT(2)`

11.
```
TO SQUARE.DIAGS :SIDE
   FD :SIDE
   RT 90
   FD :SIDE
   HOME
   RT 90
   FD :SIDE
   LT 90
   FD :SIDE
   BK :SIDE
   LT 45
   FD :SIDE*SQRT(2)
END
```

12. (a)
```
FD 40
RT 90
FD 70
HOME
RT 90
FD 70
LT 90
FD 40
```

(b)
```
TO RECT.DIAGS :SIDE1 :SIDE 2
FD :SIDE1
MAKE "X XCOR
MAKE "Y YCOR
RT 90
FD :SIDE2
HOME
RT 90
FD :SIDE2
LT 90
FD :SIDE1
BK :SIDE1
SETXY :X :Y
END
```

13. (a)
```
TO QUAD :X :Y :Z
SETXY :X :Y
SETXY 0 :Z
SETXY (-:X) :Y
HOME
END
```

(b) Kite.   **(c)** $z = 2y$.

(d) $x = \pm y$ and $z = 2y$.

14. (a)
```
TO AXES
PU
HOME
PD
FD 100
BK 200
HOME
RT 90
FD 100
BK 200
HOME
```

(b)
```
TO TRI
PU
SETXY 20 5
PD
SETXY 50 5
SETXY 50 70
SETXY 20 5
END
```

15. (a)
```
TO TRANS.15A
AXES
TRI
PU
SETXY 20 (-5)
PD
SETXY 50 (-5)
SETXY 50 (-70)
SETXY 20 (-5)
END
```
Reflection over x-axis.

(b)
```
TO TRANS.15B
AXES
TRI
PU
SETXY (-20) (-5)
PD
SETXY (-50) (-5)
SETXY (-50) (-70)
SETXY (-20) (-5)
END
```
Half-turn around (0, 0).

16. (a)
```
TO TRANS.A
AXES
TRI
PU
SETXY (-80) 5
PD
SETXY (-50) 5
SETXY (-50) 70
SETXY (-80) 5
END
```
Translation 100 steps to the left.

(b)
```
TO TRANS.B
AXES
TRI
PU
SETXY (-80) (-5)
PD
SETXY (-50) (-5)
SETXY (-50) (-70)
SETXY (-80) (-5)
END
```
Glide reflection: translation is 100 steps to left, reflection is over x-axis.

SECTION C.3

Conjectures may vary from those given here.

1. (a) $DE = DF$.
  (b) Points on the angle bisector are equidistant from the sides of the angle.

2. (a) Let $G = \overline{AD} \cap \overline{BE}$ and let $H = \overline{BE} \cap \overline{CF}$. Measure to show $GH = 0$.
  (b) The areas are equal.
  (c) The areas are equal.
  (d) The medians of a triangle meet to form six smaller triangles of equal area.

3. (a) Each ratio is $2:1$.
  (b) The centroid of a triangle divides each median in a ratio of $2:1$.
  (c) The distance from the centroid of a triangle to a side is one-third of the corresponding height.

4. (a) The areas are equal.

(b) Subdivide $\overline{BC}$ into four congruent line segments with points called D, E, and F. Then $\overline{AD}$, $\overline{AE}$, and $\overline{AF}$ divide $\triangle ABC$ into four triangles of equal area.

(c) Subdivide $\overline{BC}$ into five congruent line segments. Connect their endpoints to A.

(d) A triangle can be subdivided into n triangles of equal area by subdividing one of the sides into n congruent line segments and connecting their endpoints to the opposite vertex.

5. (a) Let $G = \overline{AD} \cap \overline{BE}$ and $H = \overline{BE} \cap \overline{CF}$. Measure to show that $GH = 0$.

(b) G is the center of the inscribed circle.

(c) The angle bisectors of a triangle meet at the center of the inscribed circle.

6. (a) Let $J = \overline{DE} \cap \overline{FG}$ and $K = \overline{FG} \cap \overline{HI}$. Measure to show that $JK = 0$.

(b) $JA = JB = JC$.

(c) The perpendicular bisectors of the sides of a triangle meet at the center of the circumscribed circle.

7. (a) Let $\overline{AD} \cap \overline{BE} = G$ and $\overline{BE} \cap \overline{CF} = H$. Measure to show that $GH = 0$.

(b) The products are equal.

(c) Each product is twice the area of the triangle.

(d) The area of a triangle is one-half the product of a base and its corresponding height.

8. (a) Yes; $\triangle AED \cong \triangle CEB$.

(b) The diagonals of a parallelogram meet to form two pairs of congruent triangles, all having the same area.

9. (a) $\triangle ADE \cong \triangle ABE$, $\triangle CDE \cong \triangle CBE$, $\triangle ADC \cong \triangle ABC$.

(b) The diagonals of a kite form several pairs of congruent triangles.

10. (a) $\angle AEB = 90°$.

(b) The diagonals of a kite meet to form two pairs of congruent triangles.

(c) $AC \cdot BD$ is twice the area of $ABCD$.

(d) The area of a kite is one-half the product of the lengths of its diagonals.

11. (a) $AC = DB$.

(b) The diagonals of a rectangle are congruent.

(c) Yes.

(d) $\triangle ACD \cong \triangle DAB \cong \triangle CBA$.

(e) The sides and diagonals of a rectangle form four congruent triangles.

12. (a) $m(\angle DAC) = m(\angle ACB)$, so $\overline{AD} \parallel \overline{BC}$. Also, $m(\angle BAC) = m(\angle DCA)$, so $\overline{AB} \parallel \overline{DC}$.

(b) All four small triangles are congruent.

(c) $AD = AB$ and $CD = CB$, so $ABCD$ is a kite by definition.

(d) Each diagonal of a rhombus divides the rhombus into two congruent isosceles triangles. The diagonals of a rhombus are perpendicular. The area of a rhombus is one-half the product of the lengths of its diagonals.

13. (a) Rhombus; the area of $ABCD$ is twice the area of $EFGH$.

(b) Rectangle; same as part (a).

(c) Square; same as part (a).

(d) The midpoints of the sides of a rhombus/rectangle/square $ABCD$ are the vertices of a rectangle/rhombus/square whose area is one-half the area of $ABCD$.

14. (a) A square.

(b) The area of $ABCD$ is 1.8 times the area of $EGIK$.

(c) Alternate trisection points of the sides of a square are the vertices of a square whose area is $\frac{5}{9}$ the area of the original square.

15. (a) A parallelogram.

(b) Same as Problem 14(b).

(c) Same as Problem 14(c) except for parallelogram instead of square.

16. (a) Not a special type.

(b) Same as Problem 14(b).

(c) Same as Problem 14(c) except that the trisection points are simply the vertices of a quadrilateral.

17. Same as Problem 16.

18. Same as Problem 16.

SECTION C.4

1. (a) $f(101) = 1701$, $f(202) = 5135$, $f(303) = 5135$, $f(404) = 6852$, $f(505) = 8569$, $f(606) = 10286$, $f(707) = 12003$, $f(808) = 13720$, $f(909) = 15437$.

(b) Observe that difference for the sequence is $d = 17$ and thus each number we are evaluating is $101 \times 17 = 1717$ greater than the preceding one.

2. (a) $f(7) = 12867.85938$, $f(11) = 1939083.147$, $f(15) = 289768158.6$, $f(17) = 3549659942$.

(b) Raise the ratio $r = 3.5$ to the appropriate power and multiply by 7.

3. (a) 2207.296787.   **(b)** 11029.47291.

(c) -58.557989.   **(d)** -26.71930403.

4. (a)

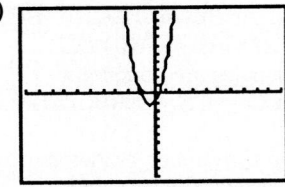

(b)

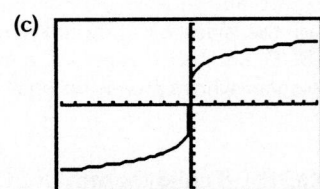

(c)

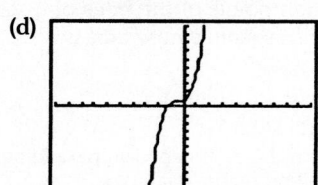

(d)

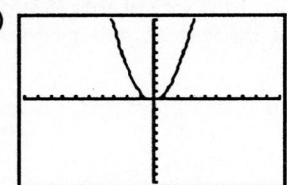

5. (a) Approximately 0.28 and -1.16.
(b) Approximately 3.5.

6. (a)

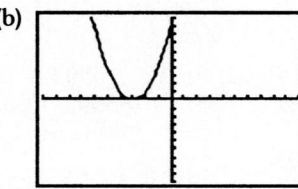

(b)

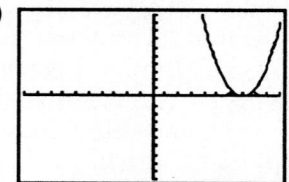

$(-3, 0)$

(c)

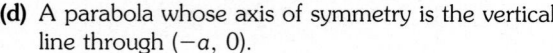

$(7, 0)$

(d) A parabola whose axis of symmetry is the vertical line through $(-a, 0)$.

7. (a)

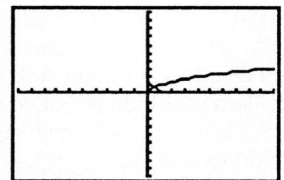

(b) The domain and range are each the set of all real numbers greater than zero.

(c)

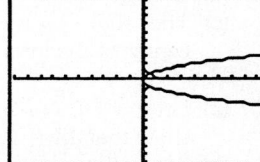

(d) The graph in part (c) is not the graph of a function since it fails the vertical line test (it has two values of y for 1, for example).

8. (a) The graph is given with its range.

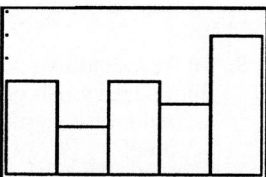

(b) The graph is given with its range.

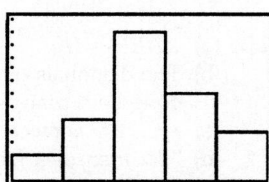

9. (a) $x \approx -1.16$, $y \approx 2.75$.
(b) $x \approx 0.31$, $y \approx 3$ and $x \approx 1.75$, $y \approx 6.1$.

10. There may be (i) zero (no intersections on the graph), (ii) one (one point of intersection on the graph), or (iii) two (two points of intersection on the graph) simultaneous solutions. An example for each of these situations is shown next. However, other correct examples are possible.

(i) Zero: $y = x^2 - 1$
$y = -2$

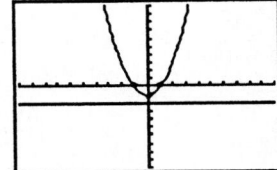

(ii) One: $y = x^2 - 1$
$y = -1$

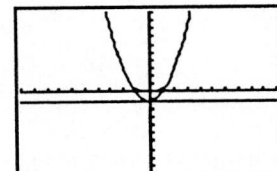

(iii) Two: $y = x^2 - 1$
$y = 1$.

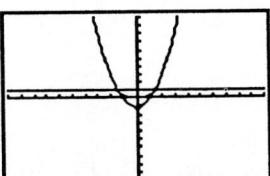

SECTION T1—PART A

1. (b) and (d).

2. (a) $q \to \sim p$.   (b) $q \wedge r$.   (c) $r \leftrightarrow (q \wedge p)$.
(d) $p \vee q$.

3. (a) T.   (b) F.   (c) T.   (d) T.   (e) T.
(f) T.   (g) T.   (h) T.

4. (a) If I am an elementary school teacher, then I teach third grade. If I do not teach third grade, then I am not an elementary school teacher. If I am not an elementary school teacher, then I do not teach third grade.

(b) If a number has a factor of 4, then it has a factor of 2. If a number does not have a factor of 2, then it does not have a factor of 4. If a number does not have a factor of 4, then it does not have a factor of 2.

5.

p	q	$\sim p$	$\sim q$	$(\sim p) \vee (\sim q)$	$(\sim p) \vee q$	$(\sim p) \wedge (\sim q)$	$p \to q$	$\sim (p \wedge q)$	$\sim (p \vee q)$
T	T	F	F	F	T	F	T	F	F
T	F	F	T	T	F	F	F	T	F
F	T	T	F	T	T	F	T	T	F
F	F	T	T	T	T	T	T	T	T

6. (a) Valid.   (b) Invalid.   (c) Invalid.
(d) Valid.   (e) Invalid.   (f) Invalid.
(g) Invalid.   (h) Valid.

7. (a) You will be popular.   (b) Scott is not quick.
(c) All friends are trustworthy.
(d) Every square is a parallelogram.

8. (a) Syllogism.   (b) Syllogism and detachment.
(c) Contraposition.   (d) Contraposition.
(e) Syllogism.

9. (a) T.   (b) T.   (c) T.   (d) T.   (e) F.

10. Invalid.

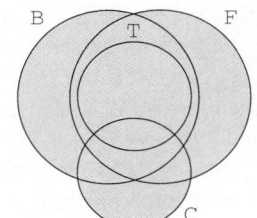

ELEMENTARY LOGIC TEST

1. (a) T.   (b) F.   (c) F.   (d) F.   (e) F.
(f) T.   (g) F.   (h) T.

2. (a) $\sim q \to p$, $\sim p \to q$, $q \to \sim p$.
(b) $q \to \sim p$, $p \to \sim q$, $\sim q \to p$.
(c) $\sim p \to \sim q$, $q \to p$, $p \to q$.

3. (a) T.   (b) F.   (c) F.   (d) F.   (e) T.
(f) T.

4. (a) I.   (b) V.   (c) V.   (d) I.   (e) I.

5.

p	q	$p \wedge q$	$p \vee q$	$p \to q$	$\sim p$	$\sim q$	$\sim q \leftrightarrow p$	$\sim q \to \sim p$
T	T	T	T	T	F	F	F	T
F	T	F	T	T	T	F	T	T
F	F	F	F	T	T	T	F	T
T	F	F	T	F	F	T	T	F

6. For example: Some Bs are As. All Cs are Bs. Therefore, all Cs are As.

7. All are true when both the hypothesis and conclusion are true. The only time an implication is false, the disjunction is true. Therefore, they are not all false at the same time.

8. Both Bob and Sam are truth tellers.

9. (a) $p \uparrow p$.   **(b)** $(p \uparrow q) \uparrow (p \uparrow q)$.
(c) $(p \uparrow p) \uparrow (q \uparrow q)$.

SECTION T2—PART A

1. (a) $\{(a, a), (a, b), (b, c), (c, b)\}$.
(b) $\{(1, x), (2, y), (3, y), (4, z)\}$.
(c) $\{(r, s), (s, t), (t, u), (u, r), (r, t), (t, r), (s, u), (u, s)\}$.

2. (a) Symmetric, transitive.
(b) Reflexive.
(c) None.
(d) Reflexive, symmetric, and transitive, thus an equivalence relation.

3. (a) R, T.   **(b)** S.   **(c)** Transitive.
(d) R, S, T, equivalence relation.

4. (a) Each person is contained in a subset having all people with the same surname.
(b) The partition has 10 subsets. The numbers in each subset have the same tens digit.
(c) All residents in the United States are in disjoint subsets where residents of the same state are together.

5. (a) Transitive only.
(b) All three, therefore an equivalence relation.
(c) Reflexive and transitive only.
(d) All three, thus an equivalence relation.

6. Fraction equality is an equivalence relation. The equivalence class containing $\frac{1}{2}$ is $\{\frac{1}{2}, \frac{2}{4}, \frac{3}{6}, \frac{4}{8}, \frac{5}{10}, \ldots\}$.

RELATIONS TEST

1. (a) F.   **(b)** T.   **(c)** F.   **(d)** T.
2. (a) $\{(a, b), (a, c), (b, a), (b, c), (c, a), (c, d), (d, a), (d, e), (e, b)\}$.
(b) $\{(a, a), (a, b), (b, a), (c, e), (d, d), (e, c)\}$, symmetric.
(c) $\{(1, 2), (2, 1), (-2, 3), (-1, -1), (-3, -2), (-2, -3), (3, -2)\}$, symmetric.

3. (a) Yes.   **(b)** Neither symmetric nor transitive.
(c) Not transitive.

4. (a) $\{(1, 10), (2, 9), (3, 8), (4, 7), (5, 6), (6, 5), (7, 4), (8, 3), (9, 2), (10, 1)\}$, symmetric.
(b) $\{(12, 8), (11, 7), (10, 6), (9, 5), (8, 4), (7, 3), (6, 2), (5, 1)\}$.
(c) $\{(1, 12), (12, 1), (2, 6), (6, 2), (3, 4), (4, 3)\}$, symmetric.
(d) $\{(12, 6), (10, 5), (8, 4), (6, 3), (4, 2), (2, 1)\}$.

5. (a) $\{(1, 1), (2, 2), (3, 3), (4, 4)\}$.   **(b)** None.
(c) $\{(1, 1), (2, 2), (3, 3), (4, 4), (1, 4), (4, 1), (3, 2), (2, 3)\}$.
(d) Same as part (c).

6. $f(x) = 0.75(220 - x)$.

SECTION T3—PART A

1. (a) 90.   **(b)** 495.   **(c)** 60,480.   **(d)** 15.

2. (a) 15,600,000.   **(b)** 11,232,000.

3. (a) 64,000.   **(b)** 59,280.   **(c)** 60,840.
(d) The order of the numbers is important.

4. (a) $_{12}C_5 = 792$.   **(b)** $_{52}C_5 = 2,598,960$.

5. (a) $_4C_0 = \dfrac{4!}{(4-0)!0!} = 1$; $_4C_1 = \dfrac{4!}{(4-1)!1!} = 4$, and so on.
(b) $_5C_3 = \dfrac{5!}{3!\,2!} = 10$, $_4C_2 = \dfrac{4!}{2!\,2!} = 6$, $_4C_3 = \dfrac{4!}{3!\,1!} = 4$, and $10 = 6 + 4$.
(c) $_nC_{r-1} + {}_nC_r = \dfrac{n!}{(r-1)!(n-r+1)!} + \dfrac{n!}{r!(n-r)!} = \dfrac{n!\,r}{r!(n-r+1)!} + \dfrac{n!\,(n-r+1)}{r!(n-r+1)!} = \dfrac{(n+1)!}{r!(n+1-r)!} = {}_{n+1}C_r$.
(d) Each "inside" entry is equal to the sum of the nearest two entries above it.

6. (a) $\dfrac{_{10}C_9}{2^{10}}$.   **(b)** $\dfrac{_{10}C_7}{2^{10}}$.   **(c)** $\dfrac{_{10}C_5}{2^{10}}$.   **(d)** $\dfrac{_{10}C_3}{2^{10}}$.
(e) $\dfrac{_{10}C_1}{2^{10}}$.

7. (a) 376,992.   **(b)** 1,947,792.

8. (a) $10!$.   **(b)** $10!$.   **(c)** $_{10}C_8 \cdot 8!$.
(d) $_{10}C_5 \cdot 5!$.   **(e)** $_{10}C_r \cdot r!$.

9. (a) $10!$.   **(b)** $9!$.   **(c)** $5 \cdot 9!$.   **(d)** $25 \cdot 8!$.

10. (a) $5!$.   **(b)** $4!$.   **(c)** $2 \cdot 4!$.   **(d)** $2 \cdot 3 \cdot 3!$.

11. (a) $\dfrac{20!}{15!\,5!} = \dfrac{20!}{5!\,15!}$.   **(b)** $\dfrac{n!}{(n-r)!\,r!} = \dfrac{n!}{r!\,(n-r)!}$.
(c) 99,884,400.

12. (a) $9!$.   **(b)** $6!$.   **(c)** 2.   **(d)** 8.   **(e)** 96.

13. (a) $_{15}C_4 = 1365$.   **(b)** $\dfrac{364}{1365}$.   **(c)** $\dfrac{78}{1365}$.

14. (a) $\dfrac{48}{_{52}C_5}$.   **(b)** $\dfrac{24}{_{52}C_5}$.   **(c)** $\dfrac{_{13}C_5}{_{52}C_5}$.   **(d)** $\dfrac{4^5}{_{52}C_5}$.

15. (a) $_{20}C_5$.   **(b)** $\dfrac{3 \cdot {}_{17}C_4}{_{20}C_5} = 0.46$.
(c) $\dfrac{_3C_1 \cdot {}_{17}C_4 + {}_3C_2 \cdot {}_{17}C_3}{_{20}C_5} = 0.134$.

ADVANCED COUNTING TECHNIQUES TEST

1. **(a)** F.   **(b)** F.   **(c)** F.   **(d)** F.   **(e)** T.
   (f) T.   **(g)** F.   **(h)** T.
2. **(a)** 5040.   **(b)** 5005.   **(c)** 120.   **(d)** 495.
3. **(a)** $_{12}C_7 = 792$.   **(b)** $2 \cdot {}_{10}C_6 = 420$.
4. $_{10}P_{10} = 10! = 3,628,800$.
5. $_9C_2 \cdot {}_5C_4 = 36 \cdot 5 = 180$. Any team of 6 players can be seated in $_6P_6 = 6! = 720$ ways in a line.
6. **(a)** $5 \cdot 8 = 40$.   **(b)** $5 \cdot 8 \cdot 2 = 80$.
7. **(a)** $_{17}C_4 = 2380$.   **(b)** $_{17}C_4 - {}_7C_4 - {}_8C_4 = 2275$.
   (c) $_7C_1 \cdot {}_8C_1 \cdot {}_2C_2 + {}_7C_2 \cdot {}_8C_2$.
8. **(a)** 8 for $n = 3$, 16 for $n = 4$, 32 for $n = 5$.
   (b) 64, 1024, $2^{20} = 1,048,576$, 2^n.
   (c) It is the sum of the entries in row n.

SECTION T4—PART A

1. **(a)** 7.   **(b)** 3.   **(c)** 0.   **(d)** 4.   **(e)** 3.
   (f) 7.   **(g)** 6.   **(h)** 6.
2. **(a)** 4, 5.   **(b)** 7, 5.   **(c)** 1, 7.
   (d) 4, does not exist.
3. **(a)** 7.   **(b)** 4.   **(c)** 1.   **(d)** 9.
4. **(a)** F.   **(b)** F.   **(c)** T.   **(d)** T.   **(e)** T.
   (f) T.
5. $1 - 4 = n$ if and only if $1 = 4 + n$. Look for a "1" in the "4" row; the number heading the column the "1" is in represents n, namely 2.
6. The table is symmetric across the upper left/lower right diagonal through 2, 4, 1, 3, 5.
7. $\frac{1}{3} \oplus \frac{1}{2} = 2 \oplus 3 = 5$, $\frac{1}{3} \oplus \frac{1}{2} = \frac{2}{1} \oplus \frac{3}{1} = 5$. (NOTE: Normally $\frac{1}{3} = \frac{2}{6}$, but $6 = 1$ in the 5-clock.) Yes. For example, $\frac{3}{4} \oplus \frac{2}{3} = 2 \oplus 4 = 1$. On the other hand, $\frac{3}{4} \oplus \frac{2}{3} = \frac{17}{12}$, and $\frac{17}{12} = \frac{2}{2} = 1$ in 5-clock arithmetic.
8. **(a)** If $1 < 2$, then $1 + 3 < 2 + 3$. But $4 \not< 0$ in the rationals.
   (b) If $2 < 3$ and $2 \neq 0$, then $2 \cdot 2 < 2 \cdot 3$. But $4 \not< 1$ in the rationals.

9. **(a)** $\{3\}$.   **(b)** $\{0, 6\}$.   **(c)** $\{0, 2, 4, 6, 8\}$.
   (d) $\{ \ \}$.
10. If $a + c \equiv b + c$, then $a + c + (-c) \equiv b + c + (-c)$, or $a \equiv b$.
11. If $a \equiv b$ and $b \equiv c$, then $m \mid (a - b)$ and $m \mid (b - c)$. Therefore, $m \mid [(a - b) + (b - c)]$ or $m \mid (a - c)$. Thus $a \equiv c$.
12. 61, 83.
13. 504.

CLOCK ARITHMETIC TEST

1. **(a)** F.   **(b)** T.   **(c)** F.   **(d)** T.   **(e)** F.
   (f) T.   **(g)** F.   **(h)** T.
2. **(a)** 3.   **(b)** 1.   **(c)** 6.   **(d)** 12.   **(e)** 1.
   (f) 6.
3. **(a)** $3 \oplus (9 \oplus 7) = 10 \oplus 9 = 9$.
   (b) $(8 \otimes 3) \otimes 4 = 8 \otimes 1 = 8$.
   (c) $(5 \otimes 4) \oplus (5 \otimes 11) = 5 \otimes 0 = 0$.
   (d) $(6 \otimes 3) \oplus (3 \otimes 4) \oplus (3 \otimes 3) = 3 \otimes 0 = 0$.
4. **(a)** 3, 2.   **(b)** 4; the reciprocal doesn't exist since all multiples of 4 are either 4 or 8 in the 8-clock.   **(c)** 0; the reciprocal doesn't exist since all multiples of 0 are 0 in the 5-clock.   **(d)** 7, 5.
5. **(a)** $\{-14, -5, 4, 13\}$.   **(b)** $\{2, 3, 4, 6, 12\}$.
   (c) $\{7k + 1; k$ is any integer$\}$.
6. All multiples of 4 land on 4, 8, or 12, never on 1.
7. **(a)** 0 cannot be a divisor.   **(b)** 1 divides everything, thus all numbers would be congruent.
8. Because m divides $a - a$.
9. There are 365 days in a non-leap year and $365 \equiv 1$ mod 7. Thus January 1 will fall one day later, or on a Tuesday.

Index

S

GEOMETRY FORMULAS FOR PERIMETER, CIRCUMFERENCE, AREA, VOLUME, AND SURFACE AREA

Rectangle
$P = 2a + 2b$
$A = ab$

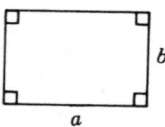

Square
$P = 4s$
$A = s^2$

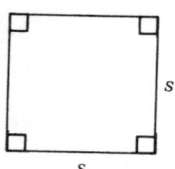

Triangle
$P = a + b + c$
$A = \frac{1}{2} bh$

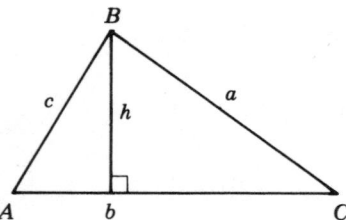

Parallelogram
$P = 2a + 2b$
$A = bh$

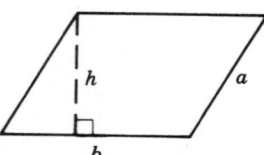

Trapezoid
$P = a + b + c + d$
$A = \frac{1}{2}(a + b)h$

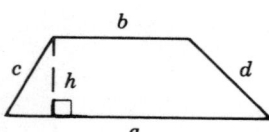

Regular n-gon
$P = ns$
$A = \frac{1}{2} rP$

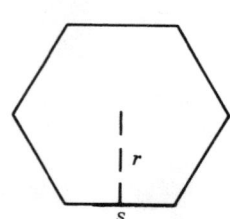

Circle
$C = 2\pi r$
$A = \pi r^2$

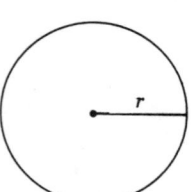

Right Rectangular Prism
$V = abc$
$S = 2(ab + ac + bc)$

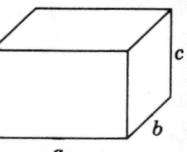

Cube
$V = s^3$
$S = 6s^2$

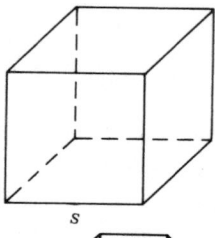

Right Prism
$V = Ah$
$S = 2A + Ph$

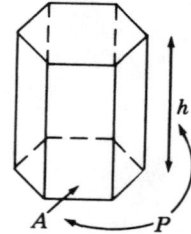

Right Regular Pyramid
$V = \frac{1}{3} Ah$
$S = A + \frac{1}{2} Pl$

Right Circular Cylinder
$V = Ah$
$\quad = (\pi r^2)h$
$S = 2A + Ch$
$\quad = 2(\pi r^2) + (2\pi r)h$

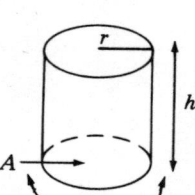
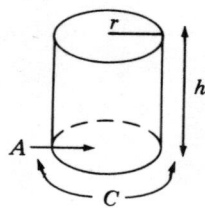

Right Circular Cone
$V = \frac{1}{3} Ah$
$\quad = \frac{1}{3}(\pi r^2)h$
$S = A + \frac{1}{2} Cl$
$\quad = \pi r^2 + \pi r\sqrt{h^2 + r^2}$

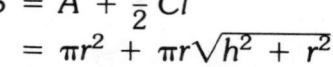
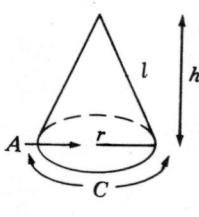

Sphere
$V = \frac{4}{3} \pi r^3$
$S = 4\pi r^2$

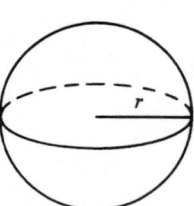